WRITERSMARKET.COM

Instant access
to thousands of editors and agents

Sure, you already know **Poet's Market** is the essential tool for selling your poetry. Now, to complement your trusty "poet's bible," you can subscribe to WritersMarket.com! **It's $10 off the regular price!**

As a purchaser of **2005 Poet's Market**, get a $10 discount off the regular $29.99 subscription price for WritersMarket.com. Simply enter coupon code **WM5MB** on the subscription page at www.WritersMarket.com.

www.WritersMarket.com
The Ultimate Research Tool for Writers

Tear out your handy bookmark
for fast reference to symbols and abbreviations used in this book

---

2005 POET'S MARKET
KEYS TO SYMBOLS

N this market is newly established and appearing for the first time in *Poet's Market*

this market did not appear in the previous edition of *Poet's Market*

this market is located in Canada

$ this market pays a monetary amount

this market welcomes submissions from beginning poets

this market prefers submissions from skilled, experienced poets; will consider work from beginning poets

this market prefers submissions from poets with a high degree of skill and experience

this market has a specialized focus

this market is currently closed to *all* submissions

• indicates market information of special note

ms, mss manuscript(s)

b&w black & white (art/photo)

SASE self-addressed, stamped

D1122137

(For words and expressions relating specifically to poetry and submissions, see the Glossaries in the back of this book)

—TEAR ALONG PERFORATION—

2005 POET'S MARKET
KEYS TO SYMBOLS

N this market is newly established and appearing for the first time in *Poet's Market*

★ this market did not appear in the previous edition of *Poet's Market*

✦ this market is located in Canada

$ this market pays a monetary amount

○ this market welcomes submissions from beginning poets

◐ this market prefers submissions from skilled, experienced poets; will consider work from beginning poets

◑ this market prefers submissions from poets with a high degree of skill and experience

◎ this market has a specialized focus

⊘ this market is currently closed to *all* submissions

• indicates market information of special note

ms, mss manuscript(s)

b&w black & white (art/photo)

SASE self-addressed, stamped envelope

IRC International Reply Coupon (replaces return postage when mailing to countries other than your own)

(For words and expressions relating specifically to poetry and submissions, see the Glossaries in the back of this book)

— TEAR ALONG PERFORATION —

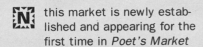

WRITERSMARKET.COM

Here's what you'll find at WritersMarket.com:

✹ **More than 5,600 listings** — At WritersMarket.com, you'll find thousands of listings that couldn't fit in the book! It's the most comprehensive database of verified markets available.

✹ **Easy-to-use searchable database** — Looking for a specific magazine or book publisher? Just type in the title or keyword for broad category results.

✹ **Listings updated daily** — It doesn't look good to address your query letter to the wrong editor or agent. . .and with WritersMarket.com, that will never happen. You'll be on top of all the industry developments. . .as soon as they happen!

✹ **Personalized for you** — Stay on top of your publishing contacts with Submission Tracker; Store your best-bet markets in Favorites Folders; and get updates to your publishing areas of interest, every time you log in.

Subscribe today and save $10!

WRITERSMARKET.COM

SEARCH WRITER'S MARKET

Your Writer's Market
Favorites Folders

Search Markets
Agent Q&A
Market Watch
Spotlight Market
Recent WM Changes
Submission Tracker

Encyclopedia
Web Resources
Free Newsletter
Expert Advice

Writersdigest.com
Writing Workshops

FAQs
Contact Us
Customer Help
Home

Choose a type of publication to narrow your search or use the form below to search all of WritersMarket.com.

BOOK PUBLISHERS
Large corporations to literary houses, industry-related publishers and more.

LITERARY AGENTS
Writers' business representatives, selling book outlines or manuscripts and negotiating deals.

CONSUMER MAGAZINES
Magazines for the general public or a specific niche.

TRADE MAGAZINES
Publications fostering professionals in a particular occupation or industry.

SCREENWRITING MARKETS
Scripts for TV, movies and business or educational purposes.

PLAYWRITING MARKETS
Stage plays and drama publishers.

CONTESTS & AWARDS
Competitions and awards for all types of writing.

GREETING CARDS & GIFT IDEAS
Includes greeting cards as well as gift items such as postcards and calendars.

SYNDICATES
Newspaper, magazine or radio syndicates distributing columns, articles, cartoons or other written material.

NEWSPAPERS
Local, regional and national newspapers.

ONLINE CONSUMER PUBLICATIONS
Online Publications for the general public or a specific niche of consumers.

ONLINE TRADE PUBLICATIONS
Online Publications intended only for professionals in a particular occupation or industry.

Search by Market Name:
Search by Market Location: All
Search by Area Code:
Search by Website URL:

updated DAILY

Tear out your handy bookmark
for fast reference to symbols and abbreviations used in this book

2005 Poet's Market

Nancy Breen, Editor

Erika Kruse, Assistant Editor

WRITER'S DIGEST BOOKS

CINCINNATI, OH

CORRECTION

In the 2004 edition of *Poet's Market*, an Insider Report titled "Roaming the Southwest" was published. We have since been notified by the article's subject, renowned poet and editor Ray Gonzalez, that the article was not based on an interview with him by the author of the article. *Poet's Market* deeply regrets this error, and extends our apologies to Mr. Gonzalez and to our readers.

Many thanks to the following for special assistance with this edition of *Poet's Market:* Shannon Bodenstein, Madelyn Eastlund, Kevin McHugh, Michael Schweer, and Michael Dylan Welch.

Editorial Director, Writer's Digest Books: Barbara Kuroff
Managing Editor, Writer's Digest Books: Alice Pope

Writer's Market website: www.writersmarket.com
Writer's Digest Books website: www.writersdigest.com

International Standard Serial Number 0883-5470
International Standard Book Number 1-58297-275-3

Cover design by Nick and Diane Gliebe, Design Matters

Interior design by Clare Finney

Attention Booksellers: This is an annual directory of F+W Publications. Return deadline for this edition is December 31, 2005.

Contents

From the Editor

This volume of *Poet's Market* marks the 20th edition since founder and original editor, Judson Jerome, created this resource in 1985. I remember my pleasure at spotting that first *Poet's Market* on the bookstore shelf.

In a mood of nostalgia, I recently pulled out that inaugural edition, curious to see what that editor addressed and how concerns might have differed then. I was surprised to find much of the same advice we offer in this edition: the same cautions about becoming familiar with markets, about learning to write well before pursuing publication, about preparing manuscripts and communicating with editors in a professional manner.

I spotted a quote from Mr. Jerome that speaks to 2005 poets as well. (Those who knew Judson Jerome often called him "Jud," but I never had the opportunity to meet him—I still think of him as the authoritative poetry columnist in *Writer's Digest*, a mentor-in-print from my teen years on.) In his introductory "Writing and Publishing Poetry" in the 1986 edition, Mr. Jerome says, ". . . most of us yearn for the satisfaction of seeing our work in print, even when we recognize that few will read and appreciate it."

Nineteen editions later, that remark still rings true. We all want to be published; and, even with the recent upswing in poetry's popularity and the increased exposure of Internet publication, most of us probably will not reach a wide audience with our work. However, that doesn't (at least, shouldn't) prevent us from devoting ourselves as seriously to our craft as if millions eagerly awaited our every line.

In this 2005 edition of *Poet's Market*, we provide articles and Insider Reports to assist you in that devotion to good writing. Poets/instructors **John Bensko**, **Kathy Fagan**, and **Tim Seibles** offer perspectives on the poetry workshop experience. **Michael Dylan Welch** discusses (and illuminates) the writing of haiku. Poets **Jared Carter** and **Marie Jordan** comment on unique aspects of their work. Poet/editor/writer **Amy Ratto** examines the revision process, and **Dr. James Barnes** shares his experience as screener for the T. S. Eliot Prize. Finally, **Nikki Giovanni** looks back over her career of 30-plus years and talks about changes—in her work, her viewpoint, and the world in general.

And, of course, we've assembled a wealth of listings, from journals and chapbook publishers to contests and writers' conferences. Because, in this 20th edition of *Poet's Market*, we're still working to fulfill Judson Jerome's vision for that first edition—to make the path to publication easier for poets everywhere.

Nancy Breen

Nancy Breen
poetsmarket@fwpubs.com

Getting Started

(and Using This Book)

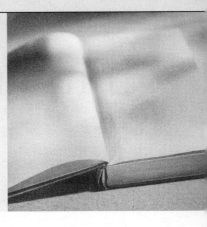

Delving into the pages of *Poet's Market* indicates a commitment—you've decided to take that big step and begin submitting your poems for publication. Good for you! How do you *really* begin, though? Here are eight quick tips to help make sense of the marketing/submission process. Follow these suggestions, study the markets in this book carefully, and give proper attention to the preparation of your manuscript. And remember, you're already pursuing your dream of seeing your poems in print.

1. Read. And read. Then read some more. You'll never develop your skills if you don't immerse yourself in poetry of all kinds. It's essential to study the masters; however, from a marketing standpoint, it's equally vital to read what your contemporaries are writing and publishing. Read journals and magazines, chapbooks and collections, anthologies for a variety of voices; scope out the many poetry sites on the Internet. Develop an eye for quality, then use that eye to assess your own work. Don't rush to publish until you know you're writing the best poetry you're capable of producing.

2. Know what you like to write—and what you write best. Ideally you should be experimenting with all kinds of poetic forms, from free verse to villanelles. However, there's sure to be a certain style with which you feel most comfortable, that conveys your true "voice." Whether you favor more formal, traditional verse or avant-garde poetry that breaks all the rules, you should identify which markets publish work similar to yours. Those are the magazines and presses you should target to give your submissions the best chance of being read favorably—and accepted! (See the Subject Index beginning on page 522 to see how some magazines and presses specify their needs.)

3. Learn the "biz." Poetry may not be a high-paying writing market, but there's still a right way to go about the "business" of submitting and publishing poems. Learn all you can by reading writing-related books and magazines. Read the articles and interviews in this book for plenty of helpful advice. Surf the Internet for a wealth of sites filled with writing advice, market news, and informative links. (See Additional Resources on page 475 for some leads.)

4. Research those markets. Start by studying the listings in *Poet's Market*. Each gathers the names, addresses, editorial preferences, and other pertinent information in one place. (The Publishers of Poetry section begins on page 38, with the Contests & Awards section following on page 392. Also, the indexes at the back of this book provide insights to what a publication or publisher might be looking for.)

You should be reading a variety of published poetry (see #1 above). That's the best way to gauge the kinds of poetry a market publishes. However, you need to go a step further. Study several issues of a magazine/journal or several of a press's books to get a feel for the

Submission Tracker

Poem Title	Publication/ Contest	Editor/Contact	Date Sent	Date Returned	Date Accepted	Date Published	Pay Received	Comments

ICONS FOR
EASY
REFERENCE

INDICATES
LEVEL OF
OPENNESS

EDITOR'S
COMMENT

COMMON
ABBREVIATIONS

2005 POET'S MARKET KEYS TO SYMBOLS

N this market is newly established and appearing for the first time in *Poet's Market*

this market did not appear in the previous edition of *Poet's Market*

this market is located in Canada

this market is located outside the US and Canada

$ this market pays a monetary amount

this market welcomes submissions from beginning poets

this market prefers submissions from skilled, experienced poets; will consider work from beginning poets

this market prefers submissions from poets with a high degree of skill and experience

this market has a specialized focus

this market is currently closed to *all* submissions

• indicates market information of special note

ms, mss manuscript(s)

b&w black & white (art/photo)

SASE self-addressed, stamped envelope

IRC International Reply Coupon (replaces return postage when mailing to countries other than your own)

(For words and expressions relating specifically to poetry and submissions, see the Glossaries in the back of this book)

style and content of each. If the market has a Web address (when available, websites are included in the contact information for each listing in this book), log on and take a look. Check out the site for poetry samples, reviews and other content, and especially guidelines! If a market isn't online, send for guidelines and sample copies. Guidelines give you the lowdown on what an editor expects of submissions, the kind of "insider information" that's too valuable to ignore.

5. Start slowly. As tempting as it may be to send your work straight to *The New Yorker* or *Poetry*, try to adopt a more modest approach if you're just starting out. Most listings in this book show symbols that reflect the level of writing a magazine or publisher would prefer to receive. The (◯) symbol indicates a market that welcomes submissions from beginning or unpublished poets. As you gain confidence and experience (and increased skill in your writing), move on to markets coded with the (◑) symbol. Later, when you've built a publication history, submit to the more prestigious magazines and presses (the ● markets). Although it may tax your patience, slow and steady progress is a proven route to success.

6. Be professional. Professionalism is not something you should "work up to." Make it show in your first submission, from the way you prepare your manuscript to the attitude you project in your communications with editors.

Follow guidelines. Submit a polished manuscript. (See Frequently Asked Questions on page 7 for details on manuscript formatting and preparation.) Choose poems carefully with the editor's needs in mind. *Always* include a SASE (self-addressed stamped envelope) with any submission or inquiry. Such practices show respect for the editor, the publication, and the process; and they reflect *your* self-respect and the fact that you take your work seriously. Editors love that; and even if your work is rejected, you've made a good first impression that could help your chances with your next submission.

7. Keep track of your submissions. First, do *not* send out the only copies of your work. There are no guarantees your submission won't get lost in the mail, misplaced in a busy editorial office, or vanish into a black hole if the market winds up closing down. Create a special file folder for poems you're submitting. Even if you use a word processing program and store your manuscripts on disk, keep a hard copy file as well.

Second, establish a tracking system so you always know which poems are where. This can be extremely simple: index cards, a chart made up on the computer, or even a simple notebook used as a log. (You can photocopy an enlarged version of the Submission Tracker on page 3 or use it as a model to design your own.) Note the titles of the poems submitted (or the title of the manuscript, if submitting a collection); the name of the publication, press, or contest; date sent; and date returned *or* date accepted. Additional information you may want to log includes the name of the editor/contact, date the accepted piece is published, the pay received, rights acquired by the publication or press, and any pertinent comments.

Without a tracking system, you risk forgetting where and when pieces were submitted. This is even more problematic if you simultaneously send the same poems to different magazines. And if you learn of an acceptance at one magazine, you must notify the others that the poem you sent them is no longer available. You run a bigger chance of overlooking someone without an organized approach. This causes hard feelings among editors you may have inconvenienced, hurting your chances with these markets in the future.

Besides, a tracking system gives you a sense of accomplishment, even if your acceptances are infrequent at first. After all, look at all those poems you've sent out! You're really working at it, and that's something to be proud of.

8. Learn from rejection. No one enjoys rejection, but every writer faces it. The best way to turn a negative into a positive is to learn as much as you can from your rejections. Don't let them get you down. A rejection slip isn't a permission slip to doubt yourself, condemn your poetry, or give up.

Look over the rejection. Did the editor provide any comments about your work or reasons why your poems were rejected? Probably he or she didn't. Editors are extremely busy and don't necessarily have time to comment on rejections. If that's the case, move on to the next magazine or publisher you've targeted and send your work out again.

If, however, the editor *has* commented on your work, pay attention. It counts for something that the editor took the time and trouble to say anything, however brief, good, or bad. And consider any remark or suggestion with an open mind. You don't have to agree, but you shouldn't automatically disregard it, either. Tell your ego to sit down and be quiet, then use the editor's comments to review your work from a new perspective. You might be surprised how much you'll learn from a single scribbled word in the margin; or how encouraged you'll feel from a simple ''Try again!'' written on the rejection slip.

Keep these eight tips in mind as you prepare your poetry manuscript, and keep *Poet's Market* at hand to help you along. Believe in yourself and don't give up! As the wealth of listings in this book show, there are many opportunities for beginning poets to become published poets.

GUIDE TO LISTING FEATURES

On page 6 is an example of the market listings you'll find in the Publishers of Poetry section. Note the callouts that identify various format features of the listing. A key to the symbols used at the beginning of all listings is located on page 4 and on the inside back cover of this book.

ICONS FOR EASY
REFERENCE

WHERE TO SUBMIT

POETS RECENTLY
PUBLISHED

SPECIAL COMMENT

E-MAIL/WEBSITE
INFORMATION

$ ⊘ MAÑOA: A PACIFIC JOURNAL OF INTERNATIONAL WRITING
1733 Donaghho Rd., Honolulu HI 96822. Fax: (808)956-3083. E-mail: mjournal-l@hawaii.edu. Website: http://manoajournal.hawaii.edu. Established 1989. **Poetry Editor:** Frank Stewart.
• Poetry published in *Mañoa* has also appeared in volumes of *The Best American Poetry*.
Magazine Needs: *Mañoa* appears twice/year. "We are a general interest literary magazine and consider work in many forms and styles, regardless of the authors' publishing history. However, we are not for the beginning writer. It is best to look at a sample copy of the journal before submitting." Has published poetry by Arthur Sze, Ai, Linda Gregg, Jane Hirshfield, and Ha Jin. *Mañoa* is 240 pages, 7x10, offset-printed, flat-spined. Receives about 1,000 poems/year, accepts 2%. Press run is over 2,500 for several hundred subscribers. Subscription: $22/year. Sample: $10.
How to Submit: Query by mail or e-mail. Submit 3-5 poems at a time. Seldom comments on rejected poems. Guidelines available on website. Responds in 6 weeks. Always sends prepublication galleys. Pays "competitive" amount plus 2 contributor's copies. Reviews current books and chapbooks of poetry. Send materials for review consideration to reviews editor.
Advice: "We are not a regional journal, but each issue features a particular part of Asia or the Pacific; these features, which include poetry, are assembled by guest editors. The rest of each issue features work by poets from the U.S. and elsewhere."

TYPES OF POETRY
CONSIDERED

ADDITIONAL INFORMATION

DESCRIPTION OF
PUBLICATION

SUBMISSION DETAILS

Frequently Asked Questions

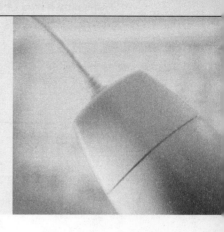

A t *Poet's Market*, we hear certain essential questions on a regular basis. The following FAQ section ("frequently asked questions") provides the expert knowledge you need to submit your poetry like a pro.

Important Note: Most basic questions such as "How many poems should I send?", "How long should I wait for a reply?", and "Are simultaneous submissions okay?" can be answered by simply reading the listings in the Publishers of Poetry section. See the introduction to that section for an explanation of the information contained in the listings. Also, see the Glossary of Listing Terms on page 485.

Important

Is it okay to submit handwritten poems?

Usually, no. Now and then a publisher or editor makes an exception and accepts handwritten manuscripts. However, check the preferences stated in each listing. If no mention is made of handwritten submissions, assume your poetry should be typed or computer-printed.

How should I format my poems for submission to magazines and journals?

If you're submitting poems by regular mail (also referred to as *land mail*, *postal mail*, or *snail mail*), follow this format (also see sample on page 8):

Poems should be typed or computer-printed on white 8½×11 paper of at least 20 lb. weight. Left, right, and bottom margins should be at least one inch. Starting ½ inch from the top of the page, type your name, address, telephone number, and e-mail address (if you have one), and number of lines in the poem in the *upper right* corner, individual lines, single spaced. Space down about six lines and type the poem title, either centered or flush left. The title may appear in all caps or in upper and lower case. Space down another two lines (at least) and begin to type your poem. Poems are usually single spaced, although some magazines may request double-spaced submissions. (Be alert to each market's preferences.) Double space between stanzas. Type one poem to a page. For poems longer than one page, type your name in the *upper left* corner; on the next line type a key word from the title of your poem, the page number, and indicate whether the stanza begins or is continued on the new page (i.e., ECHOES AT FLATROCK, Page 2, continue stanza *or* begin new stanza).

If you're submitting poems by e-mail (also see sample on page 9):

First, make sure the publication accepts e-mail submissions. This information, when available, is included in all *Poet's Market* listings. In most cases, include poems within the body of your e-mail, *not* as attachments. This is the preference of many editors accepting e-mail submissions because of the danger of viruses, the possibility of software incompatibility, and other concerns. Editors who consider e-mail attachments taboo may even delete the message without ever opening the attachment.

Articles & Information

Mailed submission format

DO leave ¹/₂" margin on top, at least 1" on sides and bottom.

DO list contact information and number of lines in upper right corner.

DO space down about 6 lines.

DO type title in all caps or upper/lower case. Center it or type flush with left margin.

DON'T type a by-line but **DO** space down at least 2 lines.

DO double-space between stanzas.

DO type poems single-spaced unless guidelines specify double spacing.

For multi-page poems, **DO** show your name, key word(s) from title, page number, and "continue stanza" or "new stanza."

DO space down at least 3 lines before resuming poem.

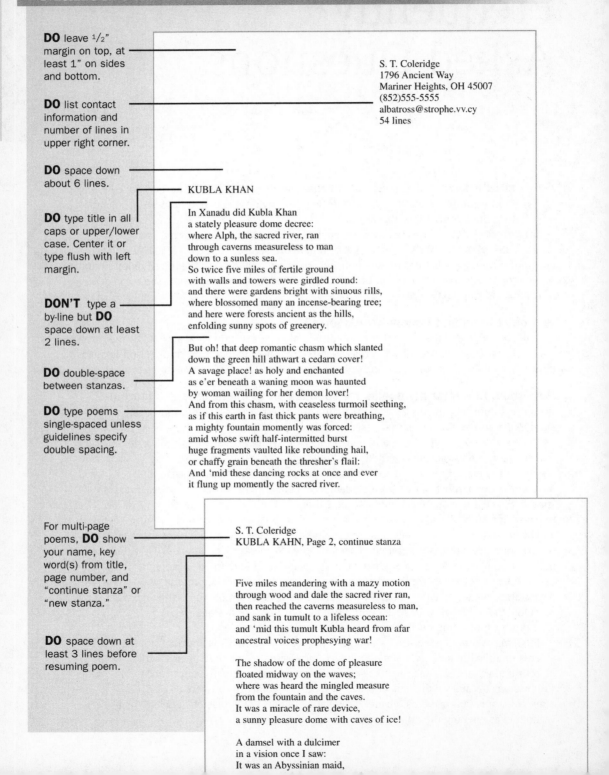

S. T. Coleridge
1796 Ancient Way
Mariner Heights, OH 45007
(852)555-5555
albatross@strophe.vv.cy
54 lines

KUBLA KHAN

In Xanadu did Kubla Khan
a stately pleasure dome decree:
where Alph, the sacred river, ran
through caverns measureless to man
down to a sunless sea.
So twice five miles of fertile ground
with walls and towers were girdled round:
and there were gardens bright with sinuous rills,
where blossomed many an incense-bearing tree;
and here were forests ancient as the hills,
enfolding sunny spots of greenery.

But oh! that deep romantic chasm which slanted
down the green hill athwart a cedarn cover!
A savage place! as holy and enchanted
as e'er beneath a waning moon was haunted
by woman wailing for her demon lover!
And from this chasm, with ceaseless turmoil seething,
as if this earth in fast thick pants were breathing,
a mighty fountain momently was forced:
amid whose swift half-intermitted burst
huge fragments vaulted like rebounding hail,
or chaffy grain beneath the thresher's flail:
And 'mid these dancing rocks at once and ever
it flung up momently the sacred river.

S. T. Coleridge
KUBLA KAHN, Page 2, continue stanza

Five miles meandering with a mazy motion
through wood and dale the sacred river ran,
then reached the caverns measureless to man,
and sank in tumult to a lifeless ocean:
and 'mid this tumult Kubla heard from afar
ancestral voices prophesying war!

The shadow of the dome of pleasure
floated midway on the waves;
where was heard the mingled measure
from the fountain and the caves.
It was a miracle of rare device,
a sunny pleasure dome with caves of ice!

A damsel with a dulcimer
in a vision once I saw:
It was an Abyssinian maid,

E-mail submission format

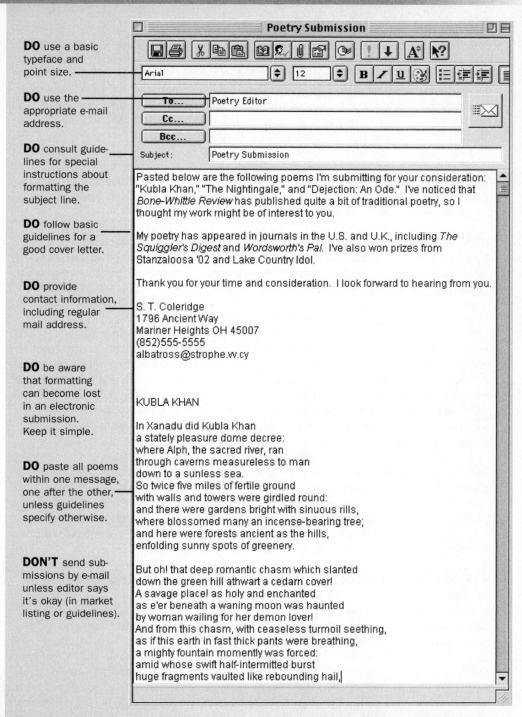

DO use a basic typeface and point size.

DO use the appropriate e-mail address.

DO consult guidelines for special instructions about formatting the subject line.

DO follow basic guidelines for a good cover letter.

DO provide contact information, including regular mail address.

DO be aware that formatting can become lost in an electronic submission. Keep it simple.

DO paste all poems within one message, one after the other, unless guidelines specify otherwise.

DON'T send submissions by e-mail unless editor says it's okay (in market listing or guidelines).

Poetry Submission

Arial   12   **B** *I* <u>U</u>

To...   Poetry Editor
Cc...
Bcc...
Subject: Poetry Submission

Pasted below are the following poems I'm submitting for your consideration: "Kubla Khan," "The Nightingale," and "Dejection: An Ode." I've noticed that *Bone-Whittle Review* has published quite a bit of traditional poetry, so I thought my work might be of interest to you.

My poetry has appeared in journals in the U.S. and U.K., including *The Squiggler's Digest* and *Wordsworth's Pal.* I've also won prizes from Stanzaloosa '02 and Lake Country Idol.

Thank you for your time and consideration. I look forward to hearing from you.

S. T. Coleridge
1796 Ancient Way
Mariner Heights OH 45007
(852)555-5555
albatross@strophe.w.cy

KUBLA KHAN

In Xanadu did Kubla Khan
a stately pleasure dome decree:
where Alph, the sacred river, ran
through caverns measureless to man
down to a sunless sea.
So twice five miles of fertile ground
with walls and towers were girdled round:
and there were gardens bright with sinuous rills,
where blossomed many an incense-bearing tree;
and here were forests ancient as the hills,
enfolding sunny spots of greenery.

But oh! that deep romantic chasm which slanted
down the green hill athwart a cedarn cover!
A savage place! as holy and enchanted
as e'er beneath a waning moon was haunted
by woman wailing for her demon lover!
And from this chasm, with ceaseless turmoil seething,
as if this earth in fast thick pants were breathing,
a mighty fountain momently was forced:
amid whose swift half-intermitted burst
huge fragments vaulted like rebounding hail,

Of course, other editors do accept, and even prefer e-mail submissions as attachments. This information should be clearly stated in the market listing. If it's not, you're probably safer submitting your poems in the body of the e-mail. (All the more reason to pay close attention to details given in the listings.)

Note, too, the number of poems the editor recommends including in the e-mail submission. If no quantity is given specifically for e-mails, go with the number of poems an editor recommends submitting in general. Identify your submission with a notation in the subject line. Some editors simply want the words "Poetry Submission" while others want poem titles. Check the market listing for preferences. **Note:** Because of spam, filters, and other concerns, some editors are strict about what must be printed in the subject line and how. If you're uncertain about any aspect of e-mail submission formats, double-check the website (if available) for information or contact the publication for directions.

If you're submitting poems by disk:

Submit poems by disk *only* when the publication indicates this is acceptable. Even then, if no formatting preferences are given, contact the publisher for specifics before sending the disk. Make sure your disk is virus-free. Always include a hardcopy (i.e., printed copy) of your submission with the disk.

What is a chapbook? How is it different from a regular poetry book?

A chapbook is a booklet averaging 24-50 pages in length (some may be shorter), usually digest sized ($5^1/2 \times 8^1/2$, although chapbooks can come in all sizes, even published within the pages of a magazine). Typically, a chapbook is saddle-stapled with a soft cover (card or special paper); however, chapbooks can also be produced with a plain paper cover the same weight as the pages, especially if the booklet is photocopied.

A chapbook is a much smaller collection of poetry than a full-length book (which runs anywhere from 50 pages to well over 100 pages, longer for "best of" collections and retrospectives). There are probably more poetry chapbooks being published than full-length books, and that's an important point to consider. Don't think of the chapbook as a poor relation to the full-length collection. While it's true a chapbook won't attract big reviews, qualify for major prizes, or find national distribution through large bookstores, it's a terrific way for a poet to build an audience (and reputation) in increments, while developing the kind of publishing history that may attract the attention of a book publisher one day.

Although some presses consider chapbook-length submissions, many choose manuscripts through competitions. Check each publisher's listing for requirements, send for guidelines or visit the website (absolutely vital if a competition is involved), and check out some sample chapbooks the press has already produced (these are usually available from the publisher). Chapbook publishers are usually just as choosy as book publishers about the quality of work they accept. Submit your best work in a professional manner. (See the Chapbook Publishers Index on page 491 for markets that consider chapbook manuscripts.)

How do I format a collection of poems to submit to a book/chapbook publisher?

Before you send a manuscript to a book/chapbook publisher, request guidelines (or consult the publisher's website, if one is available). Requirements vary regarding formatting, query letters and samples, length, and other considerations. Usually you will be using $8^1/2 \times 11$ 20 lb. paper; left, right, and bottom margins of at least one inch; your name and title of your collection in the top left corner of every page; one poem to a page (although poems certainly may run longer than one page); and pages numbered consecutively. Individual publisher requirements may include a title page, table of contents, credits page (indicating where previously published poems originally appeared), and biographical note.

If you're submitting your poetry book or chapbook manuscript to a competition, you *must* read and follow the guidelines. Failure to do so could disqualify your manuscript. Guidelines for a competition may call for a special title page, a minimum and maximum number of pages, the absence of the poet's name anywhere in the manuscript, and even a special entry form to accompany the submission.

What is a cover letter? Do I have to send one? What should it say?

A cover letter is your introduction to the editor, telling him a little about yourself and your work. Most editors indicate their cover letter preferences in their listings in the Publishers of Poetry section. If an editor states that a cover letter is "required," absolutely send one! It's also better to send one if a cover letter is "preferred." Experts disagree on the necessity and appropriateness of cover letters, so use your own judgment when preferences aren't clear in the listing.

A cover letter should be professional but also allow you to present your work in a personal manner. (See the fictional cover letter on page 12 as an example.) Keep your letter brief, no more than one page. Address your letter to the correct contact person. (Use "Poetry Editor" if no contact name appears in the listing.) Include your name, address, phone number, and e-mail address (if available). If a biographical note is requested, include 2-3 lines about your job, interests, why you write poetry, etc. Avoid praising yourself or your poems in your letter (your submission should speak for itself). Include titles (or first lines) of the poems you're submitting. List a few of your most recent publishing credits, but no more than five. (If you haven't published any poems yet, you may skip this. However, be aware that some editors are interested in and make an effort to publish new writers.) Show your familiarity with the magazine to which you're submitting—comment on a poem you saw printed there, tell the editor why you chose to submit to her magazine, mention poets the magazine has published. Use a business-style format for a professional appearance, and proofread carefully; typos, misspellings, and other errors make a poor first impression. Remember that editors are people, too. Respect, professionalism, and kindness go a long way in poet/editor relationships.

What is a SASE? An IRC (with SAE)?

A SASE is a self-addressed stamped envelope. Don't let your submission leave home without it! You should also include a SASE if you send an inquiry to an editor. If your submission is too large for an envelope (for instance, a bulky book-length collection of poems), use a box and include a self-addressed mailing label with adequate return postage paper clipped to it.

An IRC is an International Reply Coupon, enclosed with a self-addressed envelope for manuscripts submitted to foreign markets. Each coupon is equivalent in value to the minimum postage rate for an unregistered airmail letter. IRCs may be exchanged for postage stamps at post offices in all foreign countries that are members of the Universal Postal Union (UPU). When you provide the adequate number of IRCs and a self-addressed envelope (SAE), you give a foreign editor financial means to return your submission (U.S. postage stamps cannot be used to send mail *to* the United States from outside the country). Purchase price is $1.75 per coupon. Call your local post office to check for availability (sometimes only larger post offices sell them).

Important note about IRCs: Foreign editors sometimes find the IRCs have been stamped incorrectly by the U.S. post office when purchased. This voids the IRCs and makes it impossible for the foreign editor to exchange the coupons for return postage for your manuscript. When buying IRCs, make sure yours have been stamped correctly before you leave the counter. (Each IRC should be stamped on the bottom *left* side of the coupon, not the right.) More information about International Reply Coupons, including an image of a correctly stamped IRC, is available on the USPS website (www.usps.com).

Important

Preparing Your Cover Letter

DO type on one side of 8 ½ x 11 20-pound paper.

DO proofread carefully.

DO use a standard 12-point typeface (like Times New Roman).

DO list the poems you're submitting for consideration.

DO mention something about the magazine and about yourself.

DO be brief!

Perry Lineskanner
1954 Eastern Blvd.
Pentameter, OH 45007
(852) 555-5555
soneteer@trochee.vv.cy

April 24, 2005

Spack Saddlestaple, Editor
The Squiggler's Digest
Double-Toe Press
P.O. Box 54X
Submission Junction, AZ 85009

Dear Mr. Saddlestaple:

Enclosed are three poems for your consideration for *The Squiggler's Digest*: "Josh's Complaint," "Sydney in July," and "Pheasant Hills."

Although I'm a long-time reader of *The Squiggler's Digest*, this is my first submission to your publication. However, my poetry has appeared in other magazines, including *The Bone-Whittle Review*, *Bumper-Car Reverie*, and *Stock Still*. I've won several awards through the annual Buckey Versefest! contests, and my chapbook manuscript was a finalist in the competition sponsored by Hollow Banana Press. While I devote a great deal of time to poetry (both reading and writing), I'm employed as a website editor — which inspires more poetry than you might imagine.

Thank you for the opportunity to submit my work. Your time and attention are much appreciated, and I look forward to hearing from you.

Sincerely,

Perry Lineskanner

Note: The names used in this letter are intended to be fictional; any resemblance to real people, publications, or presses is purely coincidental.

To save trouble and money, poets sometimes send disposable manuscripts to foreign markets and inform the editor to discard the manuscript after it's been read. Some enclose an IRC and SAE for reply only; others establish a deadline after which they will withdraw the manuscript from consideration and market it elsewhere.

How much postage does my submission need?

As much as it takes; you do *not* want your manuscript to arrive postage due! Purchase a postage scale or take your manuscript to the post office for weighing. Remember, you'll need postage on two envelopes: the one containing your submission and SASE, and the return envelope itself. Submissions without SASEs usually will not be returned (and possibly may not even be read).

First Class Postage is 37 cents for the first ounce, 23 cents for each additional ounce up to 13 ounces. So, if your submission weighs in at five ounces, you'll need to apply $1.29 in postage. Note that three pages of poetry, a cover letter, and a SASE can be mailed for one First-Class stamp using a #10 (business-size) envelope; the SASE should be either a #10 envelope folded in thirds or a #9 envelope. Larger envelopes may require different rates, so check with your post office.

Mail over 13 ounces is sent Priority Mail automatically. Priority Mail Flat Rate, using the envelope provided by the Postal Service, costs $3.85 regardless of weight or destination. If sending a bulky manuscript (a full-length book manuscript, for instance), check with the post office for rates.

For complete U.S. Postal Service information, including rates and increases, a postage calculator, and the option to buy stamps online with a credit card, see their website at www.usps.gov. Canadian Postal Service information is available at www.canadapost.ca.

What does it mean when an editor says "no previously published" poems? Does this include poems that have appeared in anthologies?

If your poem appears *anywhere* in print for a public audience, it's considered "previously" published. That includes magazines, anthologies, websites and online magazines, and even programs (say for a church service, wedding, etc.). See the following explanation of rights, especially *second serial (reprint) rights* and *all rights* for additional concerns about previously published material.

What rights should I offer for my poems? What do these different rights mean?

Usually editors indicate in their listings what rights they acquire. Most journals and magazines license *first rights* (a.k.a. *first serial rights*), which means the poet offers the right to publish the poem for the first time in any periodical. All other rights to the material remain with the poet. (Note that some editors state that rights to poems "revert to authors upon publication" when first rights are acquired.) When poems are excerpted from a book prior to publication and printed in a magazine/journal, this is also called *first serial rights*. The addition of *North American* indicates the editor is the first to publish a poem in a U.S. or Canadian periodical. The poem can still be submitted to editors outside of North America or to those who acquire reprint rights.

When a magazine/journal licenses *one-time rights* to a poem (also known as *simultaneous rights*), the editor has *nonexclusive* rights to publish the poem once. The poet can submit that same poem to other publications at the same time (usually markets that don't have overlapping audiences).

Editors/publishers open to submissions of work already published elsewhere seek *second serial (reprint) rights*. The poet is obliged to inform them where and when the poem previously appeared so they can give proper credit to the original publication. In essence, chap-

Postage information

First-Class Mail Rates

First ounce	$0.37
Each addit'l ounce	$0.23

First-Class Mail Rates

Weight not over (ounces)	Rate	Weight not over (ounces)	Rate
1	$0.37	8	1.98
2	0.60	9	2.21
3	0.83	10	2.44
4	1.06	11	2.67
5	1.29	12	2.90
6	1.52	13	3.13
7	1.75		

Source: Website of the United States Postal Service (www.usps.com)

U.S. and Canadian Postal Codes

AL	Alabama	MN	Minnesota	VA	Virginia
AK	Alaska	MS	Mississippi	WA	Washington
AZ	Arizona	MO	Missouri	WV	West Virginia
AR	Arkansas	MT	Montana	WI	Wisconsin
CA	California	NE	Nebraska	WY	Wyoming
CO	Colorado	NV	Nevada		
CT	Connecticut	NH	New Hampsire	**Canada**	
DE	Delaware	NJ	New Jersey	AB	Alberta
DC	District of	NM	New Mexico	BC	British Columbia
	Columbia	NY	New York	MB	Manitoba
FL	Florida	NC	North Carolina	NB	New Brunswick
GA	Georgia	ND	North Dakota	NL	Newfoundland &
GU	Guam	OH	Ohio		Labrador
HI	Hawaii	OK	Oklahoma	NS	Nova Scotia
ID	Idaho	OR	Oregon	NT	Northwest
IL	Illinois	PA	Pennsylvania		Territories
IN	Indiana	PR	Puerto Rico	NU	Nunavut
IA	Iowa	RI	Rhode Island	ON	Ontario
KS	Kansas	SC	South Carolina	PE	Prince Edward
KY	Kentucky	SD	South Dakota		Island
LA	Louisiana	TN	Tennessee	QC	Quebec
ME	Maine	TX	Texas	SK	Saskatchewan
MD	Maryland	UT	Utah	YT	Yukon
MA	Massachusetts	VT	Vermont		
MI	Michigan	VI	Virgin Islands		

Articles & Information

book or book collections license reprint rights, listing the magazines in which poems previously appeared somewhere in the book (usually on the copyright page or separate credits page).

If a publisher or editor requires you to relinquish *all rights*, be aware that you are giving up ownership of that poem or group of poems. You cannot resubmit the work elsewhere, nor can you include it in a poetry collection without permission or negotiating for reprint rights to be returned to you. Before you agree to this type of arrangement, ask the editor first if he or she is willing to acquire first rights instead of all rights. If you receive a refusal, simply write a letter withdrawing your work from consideration. Some editors will reassign rights to a writer after a given amount of time, such as one year.

With the growth in Internet publishing opportunities, *electronic rights* have become very important. These cover a broad range of electronic media, including online magazines, CD recordings of poetry readings, and CD-ROM editions of magazines. When submitting to an electronic market of any kind, find out what rights the market acquires upfront (many online magazines also stipulate the right to archive poetry they've published so it's continually available on their websites).

What is a copyright? Should I have my poems copyrighted before I submit them for publication?

Copyright is a proprietary right that gives you the power to control your work's reproduction, distribution, and public display or performance, as well as its adaptation to other forms. In other words, you have legal right to the exclusive publication, sale, or distribution of your poetry. What's more, your "original works of authorship" are protected as soon as they are "fixed in a tangible form of expression," or written down. Since March 1989, copyright notices are no longer required to secure protection, so it's not necessary to include them on your poetry manuscript. Also, in many editors' minds, copyright notices signal the work of amateurs distrustful and paranoid about having work stolen.

If you still want to indicate copyright, use the (c) symbol or the word *copyright*, your name, and the year. Furthermore, if you wish you can register your copyright with the Copyright Office for a $30 fee. (Since paying $30 per poem is costly and impractical, you may prefer to copyright a group of poems for that single fee.) Further information is available from the U.S. Copyright Office, Library of Congress, 101 Independence Ave., Washington DC 20559-6000. You can also call the Copyright Public Information Office at (202)707-3000 between 8:30 a.m. and 5:00 p.m. weekdays (EST). Copyright forms can be ordered from (202)707-9100 or downloaded from www.copyright.gov/ (this Library of Congress website includes advice on filling out forms, general copyright information, and links to copyright-related websites).

Special note regarding Copyright Office mail delivery: The "effective date of registration" for copyright applications is usually the day the Copyright Office actually receives all elements of the application (application form, fee, and copies of work being registered). Because of security concerns, all USPS and private-carrier mail is being screened off-site prior to arrival at the Copyright Office. This can add 3-5 days to delivery time and could, therefore, impact the effective date of registration.

Roundtable: Workshops

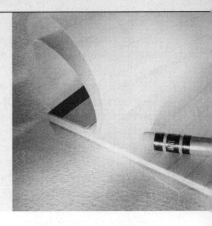

by Will Allison

For the poet who's been working in isolation, a workshop can be invaluable, providing feedback from other poets and offering membership in a community of (as Kathy Fagan puts it) fellow "word addicts." But first, a poet must decide if he or she is ready to take the plunge; and, if so, must then figure out how best to use the feedback received. In the following interview, three poet/teachers discuss their approaches to workshops and offer suggestions on how to make the most of the workshop experience.

John Bensko teaches poetry and fiction in the MFA Program at the University of Memphis. His first book, *Green Soldiers*, won the Yale Series of Younger Poets Award. More recent books of poetry are *The Waterman's Children* (University of Massachusetts Press) and *The Iron City* (University of Illinois Press). His collection of stories, *Sea Dogs*, was published by Graywolf Press in 2004.

Kathy Fagan is the author of the National Poetry Series selection *The Raft* (Dutton, 1985), the Vassar Miller Prize-winner *MOVING & ST RAGE* (University of North Texas, 1999), and *The Charm* (Zoo, 2002). She is currently professor of English and director of the creative writing program at The Ohio State University, where she also co-edits *The Journal*.

Tim Seibles is the author of *Hammerlock*, *Body Moves*, and *Hurdy-Gurdy*. His newest collection, *Buffalo Head Solo*, was published by the Cleveland State University Poetry Center in summer 2004. He has led workshops for Cave Canem, a retreat for African American writers, and for the Hurston-Wright Foundation. He lives in Norfolk, Virginia, where he teaches at Old Dominion University.

How are your workshops typically structured?

John Bensko: We take poems home and write comments to prepare for oral critiques in class. Students must discuss both strengths and weaknesses. I encourage them to explore their responses and explain the underlying reasons. I never let the poet comment or defend until everyone, including me (who usually goes last), has their say. We also discuss outside reading—poems and essays on poetry. I lecture some, but it's usually woven into the workshop as issues arise.

Kathy Fagan: I teach workshops at three levels: beginning undergrad, advanced undergrad, and grad level, specifically for MFA students. At the beginning level, I teach basic

WILL ALLISON (willalliso@aol.com) lives in Indianapolis with his wife and daughter. His short stories have appeared in *Zoetrope: All Story*, *Kenyon Review*, *Atlanta Magazine*, *Shenandoah*, *American Short Fiction*, and other magazines.

skills—prosody, poetic terms, metaphor, imagery, etc.—and our goal is to jettison our preconceived notions of poetry (as song lyric, self-expression, sentiment, or doggerel, say) and try something structured, image-laden, and linguistically and psychologically dense and/or suggestive. I give students exercises throughout the quarter, from sestina writing assignments to persona writing assignments, in order to level the playing field, and we go from there. My personal goal in this course is to return students to a kind of innocence with language. I want to get them to quit manipulating language in the ways of the marketplace—in clichéd ways, in other words—and let language surprise them again, delight them, amuse them, and move them profoundly. It's about refreshing their verbal abilities, I guess.

Tim Seibles: Generally speaking, in my workshop, the person whose work is being discussed is not allowed to join the fray until his or her classmates have finished their examination of the poem. This keeps him or her from arguing with readers about what works and what doesn't, what communicates well and what remains confusing. I also instruct the students not to address their comments to the author, to actually pretend he or she is not in the room. This gives the writer the extremely rare opportunity to "overhear" what people honestly think about what they've written. (I've found that when students address the author directly, they will try to "be friendly" and/or pad their criticism with fluff.)

How does a poet know if he or she is ready for a workshop? And under what circumstances would you advise a poet *not* to take a workshop?

John Bensko: If you've read a fair amount of poetry and can put words on paper, you're ready. Don't take a workshop if you merely want to be praised; are not willing to listen to others and try to understand them; are defensive or prone to take everything personally; carry dangerous weapons.

Kathy Fagan: A poet is ready for a workshop if he or she is hungry to learn, eager to read and discuss the work of model poets, open to other points of view, ready for the responsibilities of membership in a literary community, and willing to accept criticism and work hard on revisions. If a poet thinks of himself or herself as published and, therefore, finished—a poet-made as opposed to a poet-in-the-making—I'd suggest he or she not take a workshop. Likewise, if a poet doesn't read other poets, I'd suggest he or she quit writing poetry altogether.

Tim Seibles: I believe a poet is ready for a workshop as soon as he or she develops the hunger to know *what readers really think* about his or her work. Occasionally, I have encountered people who only want to join a workshop so they can get more praise and affirmation than their girlfriend/boyfriend, mom/dad can give them. If that is the case, I recommend they continue to work on their own until they are ready and willing to take honest criticism about their poems.

For the new poet, what's the greatest benefit of participating in a workshop?

John Bensko: I tell my entering students this class won't be like others. Here, you'll see into other people's inner lives and learn to see into your own in ways that are ultimately more important than anything you learn about the craft of poetry. With luck, you'll learn to step outside yourself and see your own writing as others see it, which is vital to becoming a better writer.

Kathy Fagan: Meeting a small gang of certifiable word-addicts like oneself.

Tim Seibles: New poets often suffer from the delusion that, because they feel so much about their work, everyone must feel so much about their work. A workshop gives them an opportunity to come to grips with the real difficulty of making inner feelings and perceptions apparent to others. Also, in many cases, a workshop gives the new poet his or her first chance to be a part of a community of people who value words and the fires words can start. Such relief from isolation is a necessary part of sustaining one's self as a writer in a culture that too often prizes distraction over crucial speech.

How can a student know when to embrace workshop criticism and when to reject it?

John Bensko: Never reject it. Try to understand it for what it is, realizing who it comes from and what their biases are. This is true of both positive and negative responses. Some readers are more careful and thoughtful and feeling than others. Some are better read and have a better sense of how original, or unoriginal, your poem is. Learn who to trust, and never jump to conclusions. Often an inarticulate person will offer wonderful insights if you'll take time to understand, while an articulate person may make you believe complete falsehoods about your work. Let a little time go by. Many times, you'll reject negative criticism only to realize later that, well, yes, they hit upon a weakness even though they didn't explain it well. I know a student has really gotten it when they come back with a revision that takes my suggestions and pushes them to their imaginative fulfillment.

Be cautious of positive comments. Few things are more deadly than everyone congratulating each other. Usually, major breakthroughs come when a wall of frustration builds up and the writer has to find a way beyond it.

Kathy Fagan: This is a complicated question. My first impulse is to say that students shouldn't be concerned about making this distinction at first, especially if the student is young or inexperienced or new to workshop. In my experience, almost any constructive feedback is valuable—if not for the poem at hand, then perhaps for poems to follow. If not for the poems to follow, then for developing a sense of audience and of what our critics' own strengths and weaknesses are as writers and readers. Of course, there is such a thing as criticism that arises out of envy, ignorance, bias, and that kind of nonsense, but I've found all but the bias to be rare in poetry workshops I've taught; and we can't avoid our own biases, so we've got to learn to detect them and admit to them in workshop settings. If a student regularly receives unhelpful remarks from the same reader, I suggest he/she focus instead on the readers who are making helpful remarks, which I define for myself as observations and insights that help me to become a better poet, not necessarily those that consist primarily of unqualified praise. I think I was lucky as a student to find one or two good readers per workshop for my poems, if that, but learning is not just about finding sympathetic readers; it's about having others challenge your assumptions, thereby helping you to intelligently formulate your own informed aesthetic.

Tim Seibles: There is no clear way to know which criticism one should take and which one should reject. I advise my students to approach all such comments with curiosity rather than defensiveness, so that when someone does, in fact, offer a pertinent critique, they'll be prepared to use it. I also tell them there's no harm in trying on various suggestions. The ones that seem to add to your work, take seriously; the ones that don't, you must brush aside. (Also, one can use only the critical suggestions one can understand and apply. Even good suggestions must be brushed aside by the author if he or she can't really grasp how they improve his or her work.) I trust that the truly committed writer will keep working long enough to understand and use the most relevant suggestions he or she is given.

As a workshop leader, what do you do to keep egos from getting bruised—or overinflated?

John Bensko: In a written statement at the beginning, I explain how difficult the workshop experience can be and how important it is to focus on the work and not on personalities. I follow this with a genial sharing of my own frequent experiences at getting crushed. Individual conferences can help students sort out their emotions. The overinflated problem is rarer and usually corrects itself by the next poem or two, the real world being what it is.

Kathy Fagan: For one thing, I hope I make it clear from the beginning that what we do mostly as writers is fail; that failure is to be expected; that even the greatest poets who ever lived wrote only a small number of memorable poems. I focus on apprenticeship to the craft, by requiring students to write exercises, to keep reading journals, and to present the work of "model" poets to the class. Most of my teaching involves a kind of matchmaking; once I identify a student's sensibility, I refer her or him to published poets whom I know to have similar psychological, aesthetic, and structural concerns or approaches. I also stress challenging ourselves as writers. The students catch on pretty quickly to my emphasis on the unfamiliar. I ask them to resist complacency and insist students challenge themselves to try new things. At the upper levels, I ask the students who have been writing sonnets to try something experimental, and I ask the students who have been doing free-verse autobiographical narratives to try a rhymed persona poem, for example. I also hope that humor, my own and the cultivation of others', alleviates some of the ego that can get out of hand in a poetry classroom.

Tim Seibles: Because most every poet is emotionally attached to his or her writing, it is difficult to keep the balance between giving honest criticism and giving a crushing blow to someone's ego. I try to be reasonably consistent in giving both encouragement and tough suggestions when leading workshop discussions. When leading more advanced workshops in which the participants have experience taking criticism, I am less worried about the tenderness of their feelings. Most often, I find more advanced students already have some confidence about what they do and, consequently, really want to know more about where their work is weak. Regarding the gifted students, I do praise their bright moments, but usually there is still plenty they need help with, so I don't worry too much about anyone getting a "big head" in my class.

Do you believe such a thing as the "workshop poem" exists?

John Bensko: The surrealist workshop poem, confessional workshop poem, postmodern workshop poem, LANGUAGE workshop poem, trying-not-to-be-a-workshop-poem workshop poem—perhaps all poetry teachers believe they are doing the "new" thing and freeing their students from this onerous creature. Fact is, great original works of the imagination are few and far between, so the taint of the workshop is to be expected. Trying too hard to avoid it can cause further ills. Supposedly experimental poems are often more boring than an obviously derivative poem about a dead grandmother, which may at least have emotional honesty. The danger is that people play it safe by being imitative, or else they learn a more seductive way of playing it safe: being "experimental" and not writing clearly, so nobody knows what they're doing and, therefore, they can't be criticized without the critic risking exposure as an ignoramus.

At its best, a workshop trains people not to be afraid to develop their imaginations genuinely and deeply, so that even if there's a hint of workshop about a poem, the imagination connects with the reader.

Kathy Fagan: The so-called workshop poem is an anti-academic construct formulated to bash MFA and other creative writing programs, but it's not a reality. There are plenty of things in academia to criticize—as there are in government, organized religion, big business, and other bureaucratic institutions—but young writers in poetry workshops around the country probably isn't one of them. And honestly, in all my years as a teacher, and before that a student, I have never seen such a thing as a workshop poem.

Tim Seibles: If the "workshop poem" exists, it is the poem that is overly cautious and risks little—in terms of form, tone, subject matter, etc. It is the poem desperate for approval, the poem written with the workshop "looking over the poet's shoulder," so the author isn't really focused on what he or she needs to say, but on what will win favor in the workshop.

Is it possible to get "workshopped out"?

John Bensko: After years of workshops, I still love to see how people think and feel and write and read. Some people, though, become dependent on the workshop. Like a convenient crutch, it causes them to lean too much on others' opinions. The quality of a workshop depends on who's in it. Being around people with first-rate imaginations never loses its value.

Kathy Fagan: The workshop experience doesn't lose its value, per se, but students can get burned out, yes. After all, writing poetry is a solitary activity. The workshop is not writing poetry; it's a community of apprentice poets led by a master poet, all of whom are engaged in a discussion of the process of writing, how to improve one's work, and other subject matter important to poets. At least, that is the way a university workshop operates. A student who has absorbed all he or she can from the instructor and the other students, it's possible that she or he could "burn out" on the workshop experience. Perhaps it's time to be one's own best critic, or it's essential for the poet to devote all the free time he/she has to writing itself.

There are other factors involved in burnout, too. Sometimes a person needs stimulation outside the classroom: needs to go to an art museum, or go hiking, or get a job, or care for a child or an ailing loved one. People do things in their lives, value things in their lives besides poetry, as they should, and sometimes those things can appear to be in conflict with workshop goals. At those times when workshop can't be a priority, a student might feel the need to take a break.

Tim Seibles: I believe it is possible to get "workshopped out" in basically three ways: 1) A person has taken workshops for so long that he or she doesn't write unless it's *for the workshop*; 2) a person is so used to getting advice from the "over-mind" of the workshop, he/she simply does not trust his/her own thoughts and insights and must have each poem "approved" by peers; or 3) the residual cacophony of workshop opinions has become so loud it drowns out a person's own way of imagining a poem. Any one of these kinds of burnout will eventually result in putting down the pencil once and for all.

What's the most important ingredient for a successful workshop?

John Bensko: People who read actively; listen to and engage with others; are supportive but also willing to give constructive criticism; are willing to dig into the depths of their emotional life; observe carefully; love language; want to learn; want to develop their imaginations; and realize that writing requires constant work. A workshop leader must combine these qualities with those of confidence and humility.

Kathy Fagan: An open mind.

Tim Seibles: All successful workshops have in common an atmosphere of mutual respect and a generally established love for poems and what they can do. With both of these things in place, the writers relax and grow more thirsty for honest readings of their work, because it's clear the critiques are not "attacks" but carefully considered offerings for the poem's betterment.

Haiku

10 Strategies

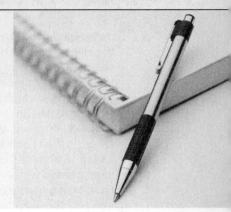

by Michael Dylan Welch

n his poem "Japan," former U.S. poet laureate Billy Collins revels in the experience of reading a haiku, "the one about the one-ton temple bell / with the moth sleeping on its surface." He repeats the poem to himself over and over in various parts of the house, even bending down to the dog, whispering the poem "into each of his long white ears." When Collins says the poem to himself in the mirror, he explains that he becomes the heavy bell and that "the moth is life with its papery wings." He nears the end of his 35-line poem by saying that, "later, when I say it to you in the dark, / you are the bell, / and I am the tongue of the bell, ringing you." We flow along with the poet's thoughts, going where the haiku takes him. We, too, see the image, the contrast, and may ponder what it means for us.

All good haiku have this open and expansive quality, a capability for resonance that engages the reader. Billy Collins reads Buson's *tsurigane ni tomarite nemuru kochô kana* in translation and is able to dwell in the poem for a day, to meditate upon it, to let it enlarge for him. "It feels," he tells us, "like eating / the same small, perfect grape / again and again." Because of its brevity, haiku can only say so much. Yet it really does say so much. It does this by relying on implication, on what is not said. No wonder haiku has been called an "unfinished" poem. The reader must finish it, bringing his or her own experience into the picture. The poem itself makes the most of this expectation by focusing on the universal in the particular, and the particular in the universal. A haiku makes us aware of what we already know, but may not know that we know.

But how does haiku do this? And how can understanding the strategies of writing haiku aid you in improving your poetry? No matter what sorts of poetry you prefer, haiku techniques can help you write better poetry. Here are ten tips for improving your poetry with haiku.

1. Focus on concrete images

Good haiku are concrete and objective. They are not about abstractions such as beauty or ugliness, which are interpretations of the mind, but about things themselves that may only happen to be beautiful or ugly, qualities that may even be irrelevant. Haiku have things in them like glossy pebbles that are smooth to the thumb. They do not present subjective

MICHAEL DYLAN WELCH is editor and publisher of *Tundra* and of Press Here haiku and tanka books. He is also vice president of the Haiku Society of America, president of the Tanka Society of America, and director of the "Poets in the Park" annual poetry conference. His own poetry, including haiku and tanka, has been published in hundreds of journals and anthologies in ten languages. He lives with his wife and son in Sammamish, Washington, and works as an editor for the world's largest corporate website.

interpretations such as how you feel about these things. Haiku have real toads in them. If you don't like the toads, you are free to jump if you want—without the poet having to tell you how to react. By including such clear images in your writing, as haiku does, you can bring stories and experience to life. By describing things, rather than your reaction to things, you trust these objects to have their own emotional impact. And by choosing certain objects to name or describe, you can begin to shape or direct the emotional response you desire.

T.S. Eliot talked about this as the "objective correlative," which he defined in a 1919 essay ("Hamlet and His Problems"): "The only way of expressing emotion in the form of art is by finding an 'objective correlative'; in other words, a set of objects, a situation, a chain of events which shall be the formula of that *particular* emotion; such that when the external facts, which must terminate in sensory experience, are given, the emotion is immediately evoked." Haiku poets rely on objective correlatives all the time, even if they never think about them. Did Buson ponder how we feel about the weight of a temple bell, or the delicateness of a moth or butterfly on its dull or shiny surface? That doesn't matter. What matters is how these images make us feel, and how we react to them. Buson, like many other masters of haiku in both Japanese and English, has the grace to let the image be itself, and trusts us to react to it however we will.

In an essay titled "Images," from *Twentieth Century Pleasures* (Ecco Press), Robert Hass writes, "Images are not quite ideas, they are stiller than that, with less implication outside themselves. And they are not myth, they do not have that explanatory power; they are nearer to pure story. Nor are they always metaphors; they do not say this is that, they say this is." He adds later, "It simply presents and by presenting asserts the adequacy and completeness of our experience of the physical world." That's exactly what a haiku does. It says, simply, *this is*, and trusts the image to work in asserting the adequacy, and even joy, of pure existence.

2. Come to your senses

The image, of course, need not be purely visual. As Eliot notes, the objects or situation or events we describe terminate in a sensory experience. This is what haiku focuses on as the "image"—sensory experience. Whatever we see, hear, touch, taste, or smell is ripe as haiku fodder. What we imagine, think, conclude, or feel emotionally quickly begins to interrupt and be inappropriate; we want to produce these results, not start with them. This is an extension of that old writing adage, "show, don't tell."

Just as sensory impressions make an immediate connection with readers in haiku, so can they get under our skin in other poetry. It is through the senses that the world enters our bodies, how the future becomes our past, how we experience life. Our five senses tell us we are alive, and make real what we know and feel around us.

Lee Gurga, in his book *Haiku: A Poet's Guide* (Modern Haiku Press), reminds readers that haiku "focus on perception rather than invention, so writing them trains poets to become aware of all their senses." Poetry, because it is a language of the body, can communicate strongly through the senses. As a result, sharpening sensory awareness, as commonly happens with haiku, is a worthwhile goal for any poet.

3. Control objectivity and subjectivity

Haiku focus on objective images in the here and now. But what is objective? What is subjective? The best haiku tend to be objective, partly because the objective description (of the thing, the noun) works well to bring about emotional response when we trust the image to do so. As William J. Higginson explains in *The Haiku Handbook* (Kodansha), "words that are too concerned with how *I* respond prevent *you* from responding freely to the object or event that caused my response." Thus, it's helpful for us to draw back, to be aware of when "we" (the self, the ego) intrude too much in our poetic descriptions. It's a sort of poetic graciousness, where the poet is a good host for the reader's emotional reactions, enabling them to flower where they will.

4. Distinguish between description and inference

One thing we can do in our poetry is to realize where we are being subjective, where we are being objective, and why. A related skill is to learn the difference between description and inference. Scientists, who typically seek objective proof, are cautioned against inference in drawing certain conclusions, for inference can be subjective. Description, as is common in haiku, dwells on actual observation—the concrete and objective. Description may *imply* certain things, but implication is not the same as inference. The poet, if writing about his or her own inferences, runs the risk of deflating his or her poems by not allowing the reader to draw conclusions. The poet may imply something. The reader may infer. Inference dwells on logic rather than direct observation. The haiku may present the premises of a syllogism, but never the conclusion. The reader provides the conclusion, and this sort of collaboration is what a good haiku seeks.

Thus, the poet can add energy and strength to his or her writing by converging on what is actually observed rather than what he or she infers. If you smell a rose scent, you can infer that a rose is nearby, but if you want to describe this, the subtlety of describing just the scent is typically more powerful than just naming the rose. And then you let the reader figure out, just as you do, that a rose is around the corner. A rose may always be a rose, but saying only that you smell the rose may make it more immediate and profound than naming it. By being aware of what you really do perceive, as opposed to infer, you can tap into the perceptions you have and rely on those in your poetry so that the reader, too, may make the same leaping inferences that you do.

5. Seek immediacy and accessibility

A good haiku often captures or produces a moment of epiphany: a moment of realization, understanding, or suchness. One way haiku crystallizes epiphanies is by being immediate and accessible, avoiding artifice. The poem happens now, in the present tense, and focuses on the common and the simple. Yet somehow the ordinary becomes extraordinary, because the effect of the poem is transcendent. And yet it begins with something as immediate and everyday as a nail clipping getting lost in the carpet.

Whether haiku can mean something larger or not is a matter of debate. Roland Barthes, in *The Empire of Signs* (Hill and Wang), said that haiku signifies only itself, the thing as it is. This may be true, and there is certainly value in seeing and respecting the thing itself. Ultimately, by focusing on the objects of existence, haiku engages the possibility of representational and numinous transcendence. This may be why haiku are often described as having an "aha" moment. Life is full of penetrating moments, and haiku notices them and seeks to freeze the instant, not coldly or lifelessly, but with the profound immediacy of a lightning flash.

There's a place for the erudite and challenging in poetry, but if something is too obscure or difficult, it can alienate. Jack Kerouac said that haiku should be as simple as porridge. What he meant is that it dwells in the ordinary, the everyday; in other words, the immediate and accessible. A haiku using a common Anglo-Saxon word rather than a Latinate one, such as "dog" rather than "canine," becomes more primal, more universal. This is how the ordinary has strength, and part of how haiku celebrating the ordinary—using ordinary rather than elaborate language—somehow becomes extraordinary.

6. Control formal devices

As Ezra Pound once wrote, "I believe in an 'absolute rhythm' . . .in poetry which corresponds to the emotion or shade of emotion to be expressed." In longer poetry, sometimes such a rhythm might be metrical, but in a poem as short as a haiku, metrical form and other devices quickly overpower the poem. This is why haiku never have titles, almost never rhyme, and tend to minimize or eliminate alliteration, metaphor, simile, and other poetic tricks. Some of these devices point to the poem or the maker's cleverness rather than to a sensory perception or an intuitive physical experience. A longer poem has room for a wider range of devices than haiku, of course, but it's worth noting the limitations of these devices, and how they can be signs of themselves rather than signs for something else.

7. Find the right form

It's a common belief that the defining characteristic of haiku is form. Haiku, however, is better understood as a *genre* of poetry, of which form (and not necessarily a particular form) is only one aspect. Writing in the *Kodansha Encyclopedia of Japan*, Japanese scholar Shigehisa Kuriyama asserts that "The 5-7-5 pattern by itself does not make a haiku." The 5-7-5 arrangement applies to traditional (meaning not all) haiku in Japanese, but such a set syllabic form does not apply to Western languages for various reasons, the chief of them being that Japanese sound symbols are not equal to syllables. Copying merely the number without understanding what is being counted is like saying 100 yen is equal to 100 dollars. Many haiku scholars, translators, linguists, and poets have frequently written about this. Schoolteacher pronouncements die hard, though; and, thus, it may come as a surprise that it's not a set syllabic form that matters most in haiku, but seasonal reference and a two-part juxtapositional structure.

But what is one to do with haiku if it is not 5-7-5? The three-line arrangement common in English is a Western contrivance, for haiku in Japanese is written in a single vertical line. The three lines do give the haiku a sense of being a poem, but how long should the lines be? What most leading haiku poets writing in English have done, as readily seen in anthologies such as Cor van den Heuvel's *The Haiku Anthology* (W. W. Norton), is to let form arise from what needs to be said—an *organic* form. Though she does not address haiku, Denise Levertov's essays on this topic are worth a read for some of this theory. As Roland Barthes has written, "The brevity of the haiku is not formal; the haiku is not a rich thought reduced to a brief form, but a brief event which immediately finds its proper form." Thus, one does not compress into the fewest words possible, but the fewest words *necessary*.

In Japanese, the prescribed syllabic form comes very naturally, and the malleability of the grammar allows greater flexibility in word order than English, making it easier to achieve the 5-7-5 arrangement. English has capacities that Japanese does not, but a poet's slavish adherence to syllabic form in haiku, in English, immediately makes the reader aware of the *form* ahead of the intuition. But why write like that when you want to mean something, or convey a keen perception, rather than merely fill a bucket? Regardless of the form, its scaffolding should be nearly invisible. To return again to Barthes, "the work of reading which is attached to [haiku] is to suspend language, not to provoke it."

What poets can learn from haiku in this regard is an awareness of the effect of form on the poem. Finding the right form, whether metrical or organic, or deliberately violating a form, can set the poem's tone the way a string quartet can transport diners in an upscale restaurant.

8. Follow seasonal rhythms

As just mentioned, one of the two key characteristics of haiku is seasonal reference. Haiku center on season words, known as *kigo* in Japanese, that not only anchor the poem in time but allusively embrace other poems that employ the same season word. The seasons in Japan are highly pronounced; thus, it is no wonder that Japanese poetry celebrates seasonal change. As we know from Ecclesiastes, everything has its season, and across the world we intuitively interpret seasons as metaphors for life's passages. As poets, if we can be more aware of seasonal archetypes and the subtle seasonal changes around us, and tap into them, our poetry can become more connected to nature and to the earth we live on—the ultimate environmental poem. With seasonal connections, our poetry can also be more entwined with the primal human progression from birth to death.

The seasonal reference can be subtle, however, and need not stoop to the cheapest seasonal trick of naming the season. The Japanese have categorized the multitudes of seasonal phenomena in haiku almanacs known as *saijiki*. An example of such a book in English is William J. Higginson's *Haiku World* (Kodansha), where we can learn that "cicada" is a late-summer season word, and that "pothole" is classified as late winter. The reasons for such classifications have to do with Japanese seasonal traditions and when a given phenomenon reaches its typical zenith, reasons that are challenged by problems of latitude and altitude. Despite the hazards of classification, haiku poets recognize these archetypes and use them to gain greater evocativeness than the haiku's three brief lines would otherwise possess.

furuike ya	old pond . . .
kawazu tobikomu	a frog leaps in
mizu no oto	water's sound

(The translation of Bashô's "old pond" is from William J. Higginson with Penny Harter, *The Haiku Handbook: How to Write, Share, and Teach Haiku*, copyright © 1985, published by Kodansha International, by permission of the translator.)

Bashô's famous frog poem, here in Higginson's translation, is not just a poem about the frog's splash (written in 1686, when predominately the frog was celebrated for its croaking), but an archetypal evocation of spring and change. As a spring season word, the frog and its vitality contrast with the veneration and possible stagnation of the old pond. The new focus on the frog's jump and the sound it makes in water, rather than the sound of its singing, provides a freshness of image that matches the vitality of spring. The seasonal awareness thus enlarges the poem, much as the moth on the temple bell in Buson's poem contrasts the fragility of spring and youth with the winter-like permanence of the ageless bell.

Haiku translator R. H. Blyth has described haiku as "a hand beckoning, a door half-opened, a mirror wiped clean. It is a way of returning to nature, to our moon nature, our cherry blossom nature, our falling leaf nature." The moon is autumn, the blossom spring, the leaf autumn. It is this seasonal essence and everything it implies that haiku reveres and relies on, and these evocations can extend to longer poetry.

9. Trust juxtaposition

The other key characteristic of haiku is its two-part juxtapositional structure. In Japanese haiku, a *kireji*, or cutting word, separates the poem's two parts (one of the parts, in English, is spread over two lines). This juxtapositional structure is not only grammatical, in that one line is a separate fragment, distinct from the rest of the poem, but often imagistically juxtaposed as well.

thunderclap . . .
the frayed shoestring
snaps

("Thunderclap" from *To Hear the Rain: Selected Haiku of Peggy Lyles*, published by Brooks Books, Decatur, IL; 2002)

In this haiku by Peggy Willis Lyles, what does the thunder, redolent of summer, have to do with the snapping of a shoestring? That's the technique of juxtaposition at work, like the montage and cutting techniques of modern film, where the juxtaposition of images implies a progression or emotion. Something is not stated, and does not need to be, because the reader can figure it out. Does the thunder's suddenness cause the person tying her shoe to be startled, thus jerking the shoelace with enough force to snap it? Or does the juxtaposition suggest that the unexpectedness and quickness of a thunderclap is akin to the sudden snapping of a shoestring? Probably both. Haiku translator Harold G. Henderson, in *Haiku in English* (Tuttle), talks of this as "internal comparison," where one thing may be compared with another, sometimes obliquely, without the relationship being explained. Thus, the objective in haiku is not merely to juxtapose, but to create an effect with that juxtaposition. The two parts of the haiku create a gap that the poet trusts the reader to leap across, much like the instantaneous process of getting a pun. This is leaping poetry of the smallest size but largest order, and the same techniques of juxtaposition and internal comparison can be used in longer poetry.

10. Discover more about haiku

Every rule or suggestion can prove the value of its opposite, so certainly poets have a variety of ways to approach poetry. The techniques presented here are common to haiku published in such journals as Lee Gurga's *Modern Haiku*, the Haiku Society of America's *Frogpond*, and my own publication, *Tundra: The Journal of the Short Poem*. These techniques may be more readily apparent in haiku than they are in longer genres; thus, understanding how they work in haiku may help some poets extend them to their longer poetry. These techniques are also common in the related Japanese poetic genres of tanka (the lyrical five-line precursor to haiku), senryu (a more humorous or satirical version of haiku), haibun (elliptical prose interspersed with haiku), haiga (paintings combining haiku and calligraphy), and renku (formal linked verse).

More than just applying these techniques to your longer poetry, though, how about writing haiku? Roland Barthes once wrote that "The haiku has this rather fantasmagorical property: that we always suppose we ourselves can write such things easily." He is right, but why not explore haiku to see why it is not as easy as it seems? There is much to discover.

Bad Habits

And How to Break Them

by Nancy Breen

In the "Advice" section of the listing for *Harp-Strings Poetry Journal*, editor Madelyn Eastlund says, "Some things I've noticed in the past year or two are the number of submissions with no SASE, submissions stuffed into very small envelopes, failure to put the poet's name on each poem submitted; and, evidently, attention not paid to what the magazine lists as 'needs,' because we get haiku, tanka, and other short verse. We also get 8-12 poems submitted with a note that 'this is from my book'; or worse, we get entire [book-length] manuscripts, especially by e-mail, and must return them because we are not a press."

Such comments from editors aren't unusual, in the listings or elsewhere. Beginning poets, especially, often start off in the worst possible way by ignoring basic procedures for submitting poetry. A lot of these poets may not be reading market listings and guidelines in the first place, so it's hard to reach them and gently advise them to change their ways. However, many poets at all experience levels *do* consult market listings; and some of these poets persist in believing they are the exception to the rules, with work that transcends such pedestrian concerns as editorial guidelines.

Even those of us who are more seasoned and submit our poetry with the best of intentions probably violate the guidelines now and then. Unfortunately, such lapses can handicap our chances of having work accepted. The following are the most common examples editors cite of poets behaving badly. Recognize any habits you need to correct?

Not reading publications before submitting

It's surprising how often poets send work blindly to an editor with no regard to needs or preferences. Granted, researching a publication can be a challenge, especially when the market is a smaller journal not carried by bookstores or the local library. While we heartily endorse purchasing a sample copy (by mail, if necessary), we acknowledge it's not economically feasible to buy a copy of *every* journal on your list of target markets (especially when poets get no financial reward for an acceptance and actually lose money on the cost of supplies and postage).

Still, there are ways to familiarize yourself with a publication. For one thing, read the market listing thoroughly. Editors take great pains to explain what they do or don't like and how they want work submitted (more on this later); plus, many generously offer special comments under "Advice" in the listings to further assist potential contributors.

NANCY BREEN is editor of *Poet's Market*. Her chapbook, *Rites and Observances*, was published in 2004 by Finishing Line Press.

If guidelines are available, send for them (postage is minimal for this). Better yet, many magazines offer their guidelines by e-mail or online. Publication websites often present much valuable information, including sample poems, magazine covers, and names of poets that can give you a thorough background on the tastes and style of the editor and the journal.

If you're wise enough to read an actual copy of the magazine, evaluate more than the poetry. Review any seemingly peripheral material: the letter from the editor, the contributors' notes, even ads. You can learn as much about the magazine from these items as from the poetry the editor chooses to publish.

Submitting inappropriate work

Once you know the journal, pay attention to what the editor wants to publish, then use your head. Don't rationalize that a magazine publishing mostly free verse might jump at the chance to consider your long epic in heroic couplets. Don't convince yourself that your experimental style will be a good fit for the traditional journal filled with rhyming poetry. Editors know what they want. Don't be arrogant, and don't go into denial about whether a certain journal and your poetry are made for each other. It's counterproductive and ultimately wastes postage (not to mention your time and the editor's).

There's a buzz phrase that seems to appear in every other market listing: "no greeting card verse." It's effective shorthand for a style of poetry the editor does not want to see under any circumstances. If you don't know what "greeting card verse" means, find out. Go read some greeting cards, the rhyming, sentimental ones in particular. Listen to how they sound, think about their purpose and how much (or how little) they're meant to say. If your poetry has a similar sound and doesn't delve any deeper than a greeting card sentiment, make a special effort to avoid the "no greeting card verse" editors at all costs! (It's interesting to note that greeting card editors have their own problems with poets who believe their work would make wonderful greeting cards. *Poetry and greeting card verse are two completely different things!* Obviously, some poets behave badly no matter what the area of publishing.)

Submitting an unreasonable number of poems

If an editor recommends sending 3-5 poems (a typical range), don't send six. Don't send a dozen poems and tell the editor to pick the five he/she wants to consider. If the editor doesn't specify a number (or the listing says "no limit"), don't take that as an invitation to mail off 20 or 30 poems. The editors and staff of literary magazines are busy enough as it is. They won't react with eager anticipation to your brick-heavy envelope or to the massive electronic file you e-mailed. In fact, they may decide they don't have time to cope with your submission.

Never send off a collection of poetry, whether book- or chapbook-length, if you haven't researched the press and studied their guidelines. Many small presses now read collections of poetry only through competitions, and they have strict rules to follow. Other presses may not publish collections at all, or do so in a limited capacity or by invitation only. Others may publish a magazine or journal and nothing more. Also note: Magazines and journals rarely consider long collections of poetry. Do your homework, save yourself the expense, and stop riling editors.

One more thing: Don't go to the other extreme and send only *one* poem, unless an editor makes it clear that that's okay. One poem doesn't give an editor much of a perspective on your work, plus there are many reasons why a given poem isn't accepted that have nothing to do with quality. You do yourself and the editor a disservice by submitting a single poem for consideration.

Ignoring recommended formatting for submissions

If an editor wants submissions by postal mail only, don't send by e-mail. If an editor accepts e-mail submissions but doesn't want attachments, copy your poems into the body of the message, or follow whatever special instructions the editor may provide. An editor usually has reasons for accepting submissions by certain methods. Follow your own rules at your peril. (For instance, an editor who states "no attachments" may automatically delete from the Inbox any e-mails with attachments—and without reading a word of the poetry submitted. Don't expect an apology for this if you ignore the guidelines.)

If an editor makes a point of describing a preferred manuscript format, follow it. Some formatting elements can be assumed unless the editor states otherwise. For instance, *always* use 8½×11 white paper; no colored paper or eye-catching graphics. Always use a standard typeface in a standard point size. With computer-generated submissions especially, some poets like to go crazy with creative type flourishes. Please resist the temptation. That goes for poem titles as well. Make everything clean, crisp, and easy to read. Visual enhancements aren't going to persuade an editor your poem is better than it is.

Always put your name and address on every page of your submission. Number pages if individual poems extend beyond one page. Publishing gets messy, manuscripts get jumbled, pages go astray. An unidentified manuscript page may wind up a discarded page because the editor doesn't know which submission it belongs to. You're *supposed* to put your name on every page. Why make life more difficult by omitting this step?

For most magazine submissions, use a #10 business envelope. A #10 allows the right number of poems, plus cover letter and SASE, to fit comfortably without folding the pages awkwardly or stuffing the envelope to bursting. For your return envelope, you can fold a #10 or use a #9. Either is acceptable. Don't use leftover envelopes from your Christmas cards or label over reply envelopes from junk mail. You'll mark yourself as an amateur (an inconsiderate one at that) and drive the editor crazy.

And while we're on the subject of envelopes . . .

Omitting a SASE (self-addressed stamped envelope)

We hear comments at *Poet's Market* about how regularly editors state, "Include a SASE with your submission." It's obvious, say the critics, it's standard procedure. Why hammer the point home in listing after listing?

Why? Because too many poets aren't listening (as Madelyn Eastlund points out at the beginning of this article). Here's a simple rule: Unless the editor gives alternate instructions, include a SASE, whether submitting poems or writing with an inquiry. It's polite, it's professional. Several times over the past year, poets contacted me because editors hadn't returned their work. "You included a SASE?" I asked. "Well, I think I did," one said. "Oh, was I supposed to?" replied another. (The most maddening answer: "Included a *what*?")

Editors won't take special time and trouble (not to mention expense) to return submissions to poets who don't bother to include a SASE. Maybe your submission will be read, maybe it won't—but it probably will not be returned, so don't get mad at the editors when this happens.

Sometimes an editor will forego the SASE if you include a note saying he/she can recycle the manuscript after considering it. Often competitions automatically recycle manuscripts and state so in their guidelines. However, don't assume this is standard operating procedure unless an editor specifically mentions it. And understand you probably won't hear anything more about your submission if it's rejected.

Writing bad cover letters (or omitting them completely)

When I started submitting poems to magazines back in the 1970s, few editors expected cover letters. Now cover letters have become an established part of the submission process. While there are editors who remain indifferent about the necessity of a cover letter, others consider it rude to be sent a submission without any other communication from the poet.

To be safe, send a cover letter. Think of it as a polite introduction to the editor. Keep it short and direct. (See page 11 in Frequently Asked Questions for more tips on cover letters and an example.) Be aware of some important Don'ts:

- **Don't** list all the magazines where your work has appeared; limit yourself to five magazine titles, although some editors believe even this is unnecessary. The work you're submitting has to stand on its own.
- **Don't** tell the editor what a good poet you are. Also don't tell him/her how good someone else thinks you are (whether that someone is your mother or a former U.S. Poet Laureate). Bragging in general creates a bad impression—just the opposite of what you should be aiming for.
- **Don't** tell the editor how to edit, lay out, or print your poem. First, you're projecting the assumption the editor is going to want your poem before it's even been read. Second, you're usurping the editor's control over the magazine. Neither is good for poet/editor relations.
- **Don't** point out the poem is copyrighted in your name. All poems are automatically copyrighted in the poet's name as soon as they're ''fixed'' (i.e., written down), and editors know this. Don't plaster the copyright symbol all over your poems or make saber-rattling statements about rights, protection under the law, and what will happen to anyone who attempts to plagiarize your poetry. Doing so suggests you think the editor might try to steal your work. That's just not nice.

And that brings us to our last point . . .

Not playing well with editors

There *are* bad editors out there. We all know that. However, as someone who communicates with plenty of editors each year while putting together *Poet's Market*, I can state with reasonable confidence that the number of bad editors is miniscule. (I define ''bad'' editors as truly dishonest individuals who rip people off, prey on poets' desires to be published, or treat poets and their work with flagrant disregard.)

Most editors are hard-working poetry lovers dedicated to publishing their magazines, journals, books, and chapbooks. They honestly want to find and promote good poetry. They aspire to turn submissions around as quickly as possible and to treat all poets with respect. They don't want to steal your work. They aren't paid for their labor and probably are lucky if they don't have to dip into their own pockets just to keep their magazines going.

Among these editors you may discover, now and then, the disorganized editor and the overwhelmed editor. These are the ones who cause heartache (and heartburn) by closing up shop without returning manuscripts or failing to honor paid requests for subscriptions and sample copies. More often than not, their transgressions are rooted in chaos and irresponsibility, not malicious intent. Frustrating as such editors are, they're not out to get you.

That's why poets should finesse their communications regarding a problem, especially in initial letters and e-mail. For instance, #1 on the Poets' Complaint List is slow response time. If an editor states a five-week response time in a listing, some poets fly into a fury if they don't have their work returned by week six. Understand that no editor can predict fully all the challenges that may arise in a magazine's production cycle.

For instance, college-oriented journals often are student-staffed and may change editors with each academic year. Funds for the journal may be cut unexpectedly by administration belt-tightening, or a grant could be cancelled. The editorial office may be moved to another part of the university. An exam schedule could impact a publishing schedule. All of these things cause problems and delays.

Then again, a literary journal may be a one-person home-based operation. The editor may get sick or have illness in the family. His or her regular job may suddenly demand lots of overtime. There may be divorce or death to cope with. A computer could crash. Or the editor may need to scramble for money before the magazine can go to the printer. Emergencies happen and they take their toll on deadlines. The last thing the editor wants is to inconvenience poets and readers, but sometimes life gets in the way.

That's not to say poets shouldn't feel exasperated when they're inconvenienced or ill treated. None of us likes to see our creations vanish or pay good money for something we're never going to receive. However, exasperated is one thing; outraged is another. Too often poets go on the offensive with editors and make matters worse.

It's important to remember that editors and their magazines/presses aren't service-oriented businesses, like the phone company. Getting huffy with an editor as if arguing with the cable provider about an overcharge is inappropriate. Attitude isn't going to get you anywhere; in fact, it could create additional obstacles. (And, let's face it, attitude isn't going to move a truly "bad" editor, either.) Keep your cool and stay professional. If your interactions with the offending editor remain unsatisfactory (no reply to polite inquiries about a manuscript, for example), take appropriate action (see below). Don't act like a crank. At best, no one will take you seriously. At worst, you'll create a negative impression you probably don't deserve.

What if editors behave badly?

An editor is rude: If it's a matter of bad attitude, take it with a grain of salt. Maybe he or she is having a difficult day. If there's abusive language and excessive profanity involved, let us know about it. (See the complaint procedure on the following page.)

An editor harshly criticizes your poem: If an editor takes time to comment on your poetry, even if feedback seems overly critical, consider the suggestions with an open mind. Try to find something valid and useful in the comments. If, after you've given the matter fair consideration, you think the editor was out of line, forget about it and move on. Don't rush to defend your poetry, and don't wave your bruised ego in the editor's face. Allow that the editor has a right to his/her opinion—as do you.

An editor is slow to respond to a submission: As I said earlier, there can be many reasons why an editor's response takes longer than the time frame stated in the market listing or guidelines. Allow a few more weeks to pass beyond the deadline, then write a polite inquiry to the editor about the status of your manuscript. (Include a SASE if sending by postal mail.) Understand that an editor may not be able to read your letter right away if deadlines are pressing or if he/she is embroiled in a personal crisis. It's hard, but try to be patient. However, if you haven't received a reply to your inquiry after a month or so . . .

An editor won't return your manuscript: Decide whether you want to invest any more time in this journal or publisher. If you conclude you've been patient long enough, write a firm but professional letter to the editor withdrawing your manuscript from consideration. Request that the manuscript be returned; but know, too, that the "bad" editor probably won't bother to send it back or reply in any way. Keep a copy of your withdrawal letter for your files, make a new copy of your manuscript, and look for a better market.

Also, contact *Poet's Market* by letter or e-mail with details of your experience. We always look into problems with editors, although we don't withdraw a listing on the basis of a single complaint unless we find further evidence (negative comments in an online writers' forum, for example). We do, though, keep complaints on file and watch for patterns regarding any specific market.

An editor takes your money: If you sent a check for a subscription or sample copy you haven't yet received, review your bank statement to see if the check has been cashed. If it has, send the editor a query mentioning he/she has cashed your check but you haven't yet received the material you were expecting. Give the editor the benefit of the doubt: an upcoming issue of a magazine may be running late, your subscription may have been overlooked by mistake, or your copy was lost in transit or sent in error to the wrong address.

If your check has *not* been cashed, query the editor to see if your order was ever received. It may have been lost (in the mail or on the editor's desk), the editor may be holding several checks to cash at one time, or the editor may be waiting to cash checks until a tardy issue is finally published.

In either case, if you get an unsatisfactory response from the editor (or no response at all), wait a few weeks and try again. If the matter still has not been resolved, let us know about it. We're especially interested in publishers who take money from poets but don't deliver the goods. Be sure to send us all the details of the transaction plus copies of any correspondence (yours and the editor's). We can't pursue your situation in any legal way, but we can ban an unscrupulous publisher from *Poet's Market* and keep the information as a resource if we get later complaints.

Should you continue trying to get your money back from such editors? That's your decision. If your loss is under ten dollars (for a subscription or sample copy, say), it might cost you less in the long run to let the matter go. Your time and aggravation are worth something. And the fee for a ''stop payment'' order on a check can be hefty, possibly more than the amount you sent the editor to begin with. Yes, it's infuriating to be cheated, but sometimes fighting on principle costs more than it's worth.

If your monetary loss is significant (for instance, you ponied up a couple hundred dollars in a subsidy publishing agreement), consider contacting your state attorney general's office for advice about small claims court, filing a complaint, and other actions you can take.

Complaint Procedure

Important

If you feel you have not been treated fairly by a market listed in *Poet's Market*, we advise you to take the following steps:

- First, try to contact the market. Sometimes one phone call or letter can quickly clear up the matter. Document all your communications with the market.

- When you contact us with a complaint, provide the details of your submission, the date of your first contact with the market, and the nature of your subsequent communication.

- We will file a record of your complaint and further investigate the market.

- The number and severity of complaints will be considered when deciding whether or not to delete a market from the next edition of *Poet's Market*.

Are You Being Taken?

There are many publishing opportunities for poets, from traditional magazines and journals to contests, websites, and anthologies. Along with that good news comes with this warning: There are also many opportunities for poets to be taken. How do you know whether an opportunity is legitimate? Listed below are some of the most common situations that cost poets disappointment, frustration—and cash. Watch out for them when you're submitting your work, and *don't* let your vanity be your guide.

Anthologies

Has this happened to you? You see an ad in a perfectly respectable publication announcing a poetry contest with big cash prizes. You enter, and later you receive a glowing letter congratulating you on your exceptional poem, which the contest sponsor wants to include in his deluxe hardbound anthology of the best poetry submitted to the contest. The anthology costs only $55 (or whatever, could be more). You don't have to buy it—they'll still publish your poem—but wouldn't you be proud to own one? And wouldn't it be nice to buy additional copies to give to family and friends? And for an extra charge you can include a biographical note. And so on . . .

Of course, when the anthology arrives, you may be disappointed. The quality of the poetry isn't what you were expecting, with several poems crammed unattractively onto a page. It turns out everyone who entered the contest was invited to be published; you basically paid cash to see your poem appear in a phone book-like volume with no literary merit at all.

Are you being taken? Depends on how you look at it. If you bought into the flattery heaped on you and believed you were being published in an exclusive, high quality publication, no doubt you feel duped. On the other hand, if all you were after was seeing your poem in print, even knowing you'd have to pay for the privilege, then you got what you wanted. (Unless you've deceived yourself into believing you've truly won an honor and now have a worthy publishing credit; you don't).

You'll really feel taken if you fall for additional spiels, like having your poem printed on coffee mugs and t-shirts (you can do this much cheaper yourself through quick-print shops) or spending large sums on awards banquets and conferences. Also, find out what rights the contest sponsor acquires before you submit a single line of poetry. You may be relinquishing all rights to your poem simply by mailing it in or submitting it through a website. The poem may no longer belong to you; if so, the publisher can do whatever he wishes with it. Don't let your vanity propel you into a situation you'll always regret.

Reading and contest fees

Suppose you notice a promising market for your poetry, but the editor requires a set fee simply to consider your work. You see a contest that interests you, but you have to pay the sponsor fee just to enter. Are you being taken?

In the case of reading fees, keep these points in mind: Is the market so exceptional that you feel it's worth risking the cost of the reading fee to have your work considered? What makes it so much better than markets that do *not* charge fees? Has the market been around awhile, with an established publishing schedule? What are you paid if your work is accepted? Are reasonably priced samples available so you can judge the production values and quality of the writing?

Reading fees don't necessarily signal a suspicious market. In fact, they're increasingly popular as editors struggle with the costs of publishing books and magazines, including the man-hours required to read loads of (often bad) submissions. However, fees represent an additional financial burden on poets, who often don't receive any monetary reward for their poems to begin with. It's really up to individual poets to decide whether paying a fee is beneficial to their publishing efforts. Think long and hard about fee-charging markets that are new and untried, don't pay poets for their work (at the very least a print publication should offer a contributor's copy), charge high prices for sample copies, or set fees that seem unreasonable ($1/poem is an average fee).

Entry fees for contests are less worrisome. Usually, these funds are used to establish prizes, pay judges, and cover the expenses of running and promoting the contest (including publishing a "prize" issue of a magazine). Other kinds of contests charge entry fees, from Irish dancing competitions to bake-offs at a county fair. Why not poetry contests?

That's not to say you shouldn't be cautious. Watch out for contests that charge higher-than-average fees, especially if the fees are out of proportion to the amount of prize money being given. (Look through the Contests & Awards section beginning on page 392 to get a sense of what most competitions charge; you'll also find contests in listings throughout the Publishers of Poetry section, page 38.) Try to find out how long the contest has been around, and verify whether prizes have been awarded each year. In the case of book and chapbook contests, send for a sample copy to confirm that the publisher puts out a quality product. Beware any contest that tells you you've won something, then demands payment for an anthology, trophy, or other item. (It's okay if a group offers an anthology for a modest price without providing winners with free copies. Most state poetry societies have to do this; but they also present cash awards in each category of the contest, and their entry fees are low.)

Subsidy Publishers

Poetry books are a hard sell to the book-buying public. Few of the big publishers handle them, and those that do feature the "name" poets (major prize winners and contemporary masters with breathtaking reputations). Even the small presses publish only so many books per year—far less than the number of poets writing.

No wonder poets feel desperate enough to turn to subsidy publishers (also called "vanity publishers"). These operations charge a sum to print a given number of copies of a poetry book. They promise promotion and distribution; the poet receives a certain percentage of the print run, along with a promise of royalties after the printing costs are met.

Are you being taken? The situation sounds okay, but the whole picture is painted rosier than it really is. Often the sum the publisher charges is inflated, and the finished books may be of dubious quality. Bookstores won't stock subsidy-published books (especially poetry), and promotion efforts often consist of sending review copies far and wide, even though such volumes are rarely reviewed. In some particularly tricky situations, the poet may not even own rights to his or her own work any more. Regardless, the poet is left with a stack of unsold books (it's not unusual for the publisher to offer the balance of the print run to the poet for a certain price). What appeared to be a dream realized turns out to be a dead end.

Before shelling out huge sums to a subsidy publisher for more books than you'll ever need, consider self-publishing. Literary history is starred with great poets who published their own works (Walt Whitman is one of the most well known). Talk to some local printers about the kind of book you have in mind, see what's involved, and get some price quotes. If the cost is too high for your budget, consider doing a more modest publication through a quick-print shop. Chapbooks (about 24 pages) are an ideal length and can be produced attractively, softbound and saddle-stapled, for a reasonable cost. (You can even lay out and typeset the whole chapbook on your computer.) You'll have something beautiful to share with family and friends, to sign and sell at readings, and you might be able to persuade a supportive local bookstore to put a few copies on its shelves. Best of all, you'll still own and control your work; and if you turn a profit, every cent goes to you.

Obviously, poets who don't stay on their toes may find themselves preyed upon. And a questionable publishing opportunity doesn't have to be an out-and-out rip-off for you to feel cheated. In every situation, you have a choice *not* to participate. Exercise that choice, or at least develop a healthy sense of skepticism before you fling yourself and your poetry at the first smooth talker who compliments your work. Poets get burned because they're much too impatient to see their work in print. Calm your ego, slow down, and devote that time, energy, and money toward reading other poets and improving your own writing. You'll find that getting published will eventually take care of itself.

Helpful Websites

For More Info

The following websites include specific information about questionable poetry publishers and awards. For more websites important to poets, see Additional Resources on page 475.

- Answers to frequently asked questions about poetry awards from the Academy of American Poets: *www.poets.org/awards/faq.cfm*

- Poets will find warnings and other valuable publishing information on the Preditors & Editors website: *www.anotherealm.com/prededitors/*

- Writer Beware tracks contests, publishers, and literary agents: *www.sfwa.org/beware*

- Online "Scam Kit" from The Writer's Center: *www.writer.org/resources/scamkit.htm*

Self-Promotion

A Chance to Share

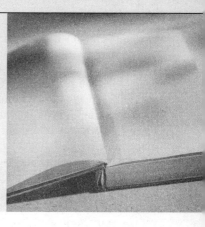

These days, all writers have to become involved in promoting themselves and their work. This is especially true for poets. Does the idea of "putting yourself out there" make you uncomfortable? Think of self-promotion as a means of sharing poetry as well as promoting it. Here are a few suggestions to get you started:

Meet the public.

Do poetry readings and book signings. Get in touch with bookstores and coffeehouses: call, send postcards (see below) or press releases, let them know you're available. Find out when and where open mic readings are scheduled. Sign up, read your poems. If you've published a book or chapbook, be creative about handselling your collection. It's hard to break into the big chain bookstores, but the small, independent stores may be happy to stock your publication (especially if you're a local author) and arrange a book signing.

Widen your scope: Would the local historical society be interested in an appearance? Is there a community group who might enjoy having you read and sign books as part of their meeting program? Would a friend be willing to sponsor a "poetry night" house party with you as the featured reader?

Do postcards.

Think specially designed postcards, not the plain ones you buy at the post office. You can create postcards on your computer, or paste up a master design from typewritten copy and clip art. If you design the postcards on your computer, you can print them out yourself as well. (Special perforated postcard stock for home printers is available in various sizes at your local office supply store.) Or you can take your master design to a quick print shop and have the postcards printed there. (If you're printing a lot of postcards, this might be the less expensive option.)

Postcards can be informational (i.e., used to announce a reading or new publication). They can also be used to share your poetry. Simply type one of your poems on one side of the card, using an attractive, readable font. Leave the other side blank; or, if the poem is from a book or chapbook you want to promote, indicate the title of the collection and include ordering information. Keep all text and design elements on the far left side of the postcard back so they don't interfere with the addressee portion of the card.

Postcard mailings get results, but remember that postcards don't have to be mailed to be effective. Don't be shy about giving out postcards at readings, especially your poem postcards. Offer to sign them. Your audience will enjoy having a personalized souvenir of your reading, and they may decide later to order your book or chapbook.

Use your poem postcards for personal communications, too. Turn a simple note into a chance to enhance someone's day with poetry.

Step into the media spotlight.

It doesn't have to be a *big* spotlight. Your community newspaper probably prints "news-maker" tidbits like award and publication announcements, and it may even be interested in doing a feature on a "local poet." (Regional magazines are another possibility.) Newspapers usually have calendar sections where you can list a reading or bookstore appearance. (Be sure to provide all the necessary details.) TV and radio stations may also broadcast arts and entertainments calendars, and locally produced programs may be very happy to schedule a poet for an interview segment or to promote a reading. You never know until you ask. (Be polite, never pushy.)

Create a website.

It's helpful to have a URL to list on press releases, business cards, and postcards. A website is a shortcut for anyone who wants to know more about you, from biographical information to samples of your poetry. Your website can be as complicated or as simple as you wish. There are plenty of books and software programs available to help, even if you're a first-timer with few computer skills. There's also lots of free information on the Web, from tutorials to HTML guides. Enter the words "basic web development" or "beginner web development" in your favorite search engine to call up all the resources you'll need. (Also, the word processing software on your computer may provide how-tos and automatic formatting for web page development.)

Whether you try these approaches or come up with some new, creative techniques of your own, don't hesitate to promote yourself and your work. Every reading, book signing, interview, and website is an opportunity to attract new readers to poetry.

Important Market Listing Information

Important

- Listings are based on questionnaires completed by editors and on subsequent verified copy. Listings are not advertisements *nor* are markets necessarily endorsed by the editors of this book.

- Information in the listings comes directly from the publishers and is as accurate as possible. However, publications and editors come and go, and poetry needs fluctuate between the publication date of this directory and the date of purchase.

- If you are a poetry publisher and would like to be considered for a listing in the next edition, send a SASE (or SAE and IRC) with your request for a questionnaire to *Poet's Market*—QR, 4700 East Galbraith Road, Cincinnati OH 45236 or e-mail us at poetsmarket@fwpubs.com. Questionnaires and questionnaire requests received after February 15, 2005, will be held for the 2007 edition.

- *Poet's Market* reserves the right to exclude any listing that does not meet its requirements.

Publishers of Poetry

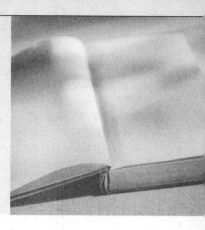

I n today's literary world, poetry is published in a variety of ways: in magazines; in literary and academic journals; in books and chapbooks produced by both large and small presses; in anthologies assembled by poetry societies and other groups; on CDs and tapes that feature poets reading their own work; and on the Internet in sites ranging from individual web pages to sophisticated digital publications.

In *Poet's Market*, we strive to gather as much information about these markets as possible. Each listing in the Publishers of Poetry section gives an overview of the various activities for a single operation as described by the editors/publishers who replied to our queries. These include magazines/journals, books/chapbooks, contests, workshops, readings, organizations, and whatever else each editor/publisher thinks will be of interest to our readers. For those publishers with projects at different addresses, or who requested their activities be broken out into other sections of the book, we've cross-referenced the listings so the overview will be complete.

HOW LISTINGS ARE FORMATTED

To organize all this information within each listing, we follow a basic format:

Symbols. Each listing begins with symbols that reflect various aspects of that operation: (🆕) this market is newly established and new to *Poet's Market*; (⭐) this market did not appear in the 2004 edition; (🍁) this market is located in Canada or (🌐) outside the U.S. and Canada; (**$**) this market pays a monetary amount (as opposed to contributor's copies); (🔾) this market welcomes submissions from beginning poets; (🔼) this market prefers submissions from skilled, experienced poets, will consider work from beginning poets; (🔽) this market prefers submissions from poets with a high degree of skill and experience; (🎯) this market has a specialized focus (listed in parentheses after title); and (🚫) this market is currently closed to *all* submissions. (Keys to these symbols are listed on the inside back cover of this book and on page 4).

Contact Information. Next you'll find all the information you need to contact the market, as provided by each editor/publisher: names (in bold) of all operations associated with the market (with areas of specialization noted in parentheses where appropriate); regular mail address; telephone number; fax number; e-mail address; website address; year the market was established; the name of the person to contact (with that person's title in bold); and membership in small press/publishing organizations (when provided).

Magazine Needs: This is an important section to study as you research potential markets. Here you'll find the editor's or publisher's overview of the operation and stated preferences (often in his or her own words), plus a list of recently published poets; production information about the market (size of publication, printing/binding methods, art/graphics); statistics regarding the number of submissions the market receives vs. the number accepted; and distribution and price information.

How to Submit: Another important section. This one gets down to specifics—how many poems to send; minimum/maximum number of lines; preferences regarding previously published poems and simultaneous submissions, as well as electronic submissions; payment, rights, and response times; and a lot more.

Book/Chapbook Needs and How to Submit: Same as the information for magazines with added information tailored to book/chapbook publishers.

Contest/Award Offerings: Information about prizes and competitions associated with the market.

Also Offers: Check this section for conferences/workshops, readings and other activities, or organizations sponsored by or affiliated with the market.

Advice: Offers direct quotes from editors and publishers about everything from pet peeves to tips on writing to views on the state of poetry today.

GETTING STARTED, FINDING MARKETS

If you don't have a publisher in mind, just begin reading through the listings, possibly making notes as you go (don't hesitate to write in the margins, underline, use highlighters; it also helps to flag markets that interest you with Post-it Notes). Browsing the listings is an effective way to familiarize yourself with the information presented and the publishing opportunities available.

If you have a specific market in mind, however, begin with the General Index. This is where *all* listings are alphabetized (i.e., all the markets included within a single listing). For instance, what if you want to check out Frith Press? If you turn to the ''F'' listings in the Publishers of Poetry section, you won't find this publisher. The information appears as part of the *Ekphrasis* listing (along with the *Ekphrasis* prize). In the General Index, though, Frith Press is listed individually along with the page number for *Ekphrasis* so you can go straight to the source for the information you need. (Sound confusing? Try it, it works.)

The General Index also lists markets from the 2004 edition that don't appear in this book, along with a two-letter code explaining the absence (see the introduction to the General Index on page 537 for an explanation of these codes). In addition, markets that have changed names since the 2004 edition are listed in the General Index, cross-referenced to the new titles.

REFINE YOUR SEARCH

In addition to the General Index, we provide several more specific indexes to help you refine your marketing plan for your poems. The editors/publishers themselves have indicated how and where they want their listings indexed, and not every listing appears in one of these specific indexes. Therefore, use them only to supplement your other research efforts:

Chapbook Publishers Index provides a breakdown of markets that publish chapbooks.

Book Publishers Index indicates markets looking for book-length collections of poetry.

Openness to Submissions Index breaks out markets according to the symbols (⬜ ◓ ◒ ◉) that appear at the beginning of each listing, signposts indicating the level of writing a market prefers to see. (For an explanation of these symbols, see page 4, or the inside back cover of this book.)

Geographical Index sorts markets by state and by countries outside the U.S. Some markets are more open to poets from their region, so use this index when you're pinpointing local opportunities.

Subject Index groups markets into categories according to areas of interest. These include all specialized markets (appearing with the ◉ symbol) as well as broader categories such as online markets, poetry for children, markets that consider translations, and others. Save time when looking for a specific type of market by checking this index first.

THE NEXT STEP

Once you know how to interpret the listings in this section and identify markets for your work, the next step is to start submitting your poems. See Getting Started (and Using This Book) on page 2 and Frequently Asked Questions on page 7 for advice, guidelines about preparing your manuscript, and proper submission procedures.

ADDITIONAL INFORMATION

The Publishers of Poetry section includes five Insider Reports: **Jared Carter** discusses how regional poetry illuminates universal themes; **Amy Ratto** offers advice on the revision process; **Marie Jordan** comments on the magic and power of poetry; **Nikki Giovanni** looks back on her 30-year career as writer and poet and the changes she's experienced; and **Paul Raymond Martin** reveals his ''secrets'' to good poetry writing.

This section also includes the covers of ten literary magazines that reflect the range of print publications being produced today. Such images tell a lot about a publication's style and content, as do the accompanying comments by editors regarding why the cover images were selected. (When evaluating a potential market for your work, consider everything that makes up the product—the poets being published, style and quality of content, guidelines, editorial comments, cover art, and even ads.)

And remember, the opportunities in the Publishers of Poetry section are only part of the picture. Study the sections that follow (Contests & Awards, Conferences & Workshops, Organizations, and Publications & Websites of Interest) for additional market leads, competitions, and educational and informational sources of special interest to poets.

Publishers of Poetry

☻ A SMALL GARLIC PRESS (ASGP); AGNIESZKA'S DOWRY (AgD)

5445 Sheridan #3003, Chicago IL 60640. E-mail: marek@enteract.com and ketzle@ketzle.net (send submissions to both e-mail addresses simultaneously). Website: http://asgp.org. Established 1995. **Co-Editors:** Marek Lugowski and katrina grace craig.

Magazine Needs *Agnieszka's Dowry (AgD)* is "a magazine published both in print and as a permanent Internet installation of poems and graphics, letters to Agnieszka. The print version consists of professionally crafted chapbooks. The online version comprises fast-loading pages employing an intuitive if uncanny navigation in an interesting space, all conducive to fast and comfortable reading. No restrictions on form or type. We use contextual and juxtapositional tie-ins with other material in making choices, so visiting the online *AgD* or reading a chapbook of an *AgD* issue is required of anyone making a submission." Single copy: $2 plus $2 shipping, if ordered from website by an individual. Make checks payable to A Small Garlic Press.

How to Submit Submit 5-10 poems at a time, by e-mail to Katja and Marek simultaneously. "Please inform us of the status of publishing rights." E-mail submissions only, plain text ("unless you are in prison—prisoners may make submissions by regular mail and we will waive the requirements that they read a print issue"). Sometimes comments on rejected poems. Guidelines and annotated catalog available on website only. Responds online or by SASE usually in 2 months. Pays one contributor's copy. Acquires one-time rights where applicable.

Book/Chapbook Needs & How to Submit A Small Garlic Press (ASGP) publishes up to 3 chapbooks of poetry/year. Query with a full online ms, ASCII (plain text) only.

☻ ◎ THE AARDVARK ADVENTURER; THE ARMCHAIR AESTHETE; PICKLE GAS PRESS (Specialized: humor)

31 Rolling Meadows Way, Penfield NY 14526. (585)388-6968. E-mail: bypaul@netacc.net. Established 1996. **Editor:** Paul Agosto.

Magazine Needs *The Aardvark Adventurer* is "a quarterly family-fun newsletter-style zine of humor, thought, and verse. Very short stories (less than 500 words) are sometimes included." Prefers "light, humorous verse; any style; any 'family acceptable' subject matter; length limit 32 lines. Nothing obscene, overly forboding, no graphic gore or violence." Has published poetry by Paul Humphrey, Ray Gallucci, Max Gutmann, and Theone DiRocco. *The Aardvark Adventurer* is 6-12 pages, $8\frac{1}{2} \times 14$, photocopied, corner-stapled, with many playful b&w graphics. Receives about 500 poems/year, accepts about 40%. Press run is 150 for 100 subscribers. Single copy: $2; subscription: $5. Sample: $2. Make checks payable to Paul Agosto. "Subscription not required, but subscribers given preference."

Magazine Needs Also publishes *The Armchair Aesthete*, a quarterly digest-sized zine of "fiction and poetry of thoughtful, well-crafted concise works. Interested in more fiction submissions than poetry though." Line length for poetry is 30 maximum. *The Armchair Aesthete* is 40-60 pages, digest-sized, quality desktop-published, photocopied, card cover, includes ads for other publications and writers' available chapbooks. Each issue usually contains 10-15 poems and 9-14 stories. Receives about 300 poems/year, accepts about 25-30%. Subscription: $10/year. Sample postpaid: $3. Make checks payable to Paul Agosto.

How to Submit For both publications, accepts previously published poems and simultaneous submissions, if indicated. Accepts e-mail submissions (pasted into body of message). Cover letter preferred. Time between acceptance and publication is up to 9 months. Seldom comments on rejected poems. *The Aardvark Adventurer* occasionally publishes theme issues, but *The Armchair Aesthete* does not. Guidelines for both magazines available by SASE. Responds in 2 months. Pays one contributor's copy. Acquire one-time rights. The staff of *The Aardvark Adventurer* reviews books and chapbooks of poetry in 100 words. The staff of *The Armchair Aesthete* occasionally reviews chapbooks. Send materials for review consideration.

Advice *"The Aardvark Adventurer* is a perfect opportunity for the aspiring poet, a newsletter-style publication with a very playful format."

☑ ABBEY; ABBEY CHEAPOCHAPBOOKS

5360 Fallriver Row Court, Columbia MD 21044. E-mail: greisman@aol.com. Established 1970. **Editor:** David Greisman.

Magazine Needs & How to Submit *Abbey,* "a more-or-less quarterly informalzine looking for poetry that does for the mind what the first sip of Molson Ale does for the palate. No pornography or politics." Has published poetry and artwork by Richard Peabody, Robin Merrill, Patricia Rourke, Ruth Moon Kempher, D.E. Steward, Carol Hamilton, Harry Calhoun, Wayne Hogan, and Edmund Conti. With the exception of landmark issues like 2004's *Abbey* #100, a 100-plus-page extravaganza, the usual *Abbey* is 20-26 pages, magazine-sized, photocopied, and held together with one low-alloy metal staple in the top left corner. Publishes about 150 of 1,000 poems received/year. Press run is 200. Subscription: $2. Sample: 50¢. Responds in one month "except during baseball season." Pays 1-2 contributor's copies.

Book/Chapbook Needs & How to Submit *Abbey Cheapochapbooks* come out once or twice every 5 years, averaging 10-15 pages. For chapbook consideration, query with 4-6 samples, bio, and list of publications. Responds in 2 months "including baseball season." Pays 25-50 author's copies.

Advice The editor says he is "definitely seeing poetry from two schools—the nit'n'grit school and the textured/reflective school. I much prefer the latter."

⊞ ☑ ◎ ABIKO ANNUAL WITH JAMES JOYCE FW STUDIES (Specialized: translations)

8-1-7 Namiki, Abiko-shi, Chiba-ken 270-1165 Japan. Phone/fax: 011-81-471-84-5873. E-mail: hce@j com.home.ne.jp. Website: http://members.jcom.home.ne.jp/hce. Established 1988. **Contact:** Dr. Tatsuo Hamada.

Magazine Needs *Abiko* is a literary-style annual journal "heavily influenced by James Joyce's *Finnegan's Wake.* We publish all kinds, with an emphasis like Yeats's quote: 'Truth seen in passion is the substance of poetry!' We prefer poetry like Eliot's or Donne's. We include originals and translations from Japanese and other languages." Has published poetry by Eileen Malone, James Fairhall, and Danetta Loretta Saft. *Abiko Annual* is about 350 pages, 14.8cm × 21cm, perfect-bound, with coated paper cover. Press run is 300 for 50 subscribers of which 10 are libraries. Sample: $25.

How to Submit Submission guidelines available on website. Send materials for review consideration.

Advice "Please remember U.S. postage does not work in Japan with SAEs! Send 2 IRCs."

⊞ ☑ ACUMEN MAGAZINE; EMBER PRESS

6 The Mount, Higher Furzeham, Brixham, South Devon TQ5 8QY England. Website: www.acumen-poetry.co.uk. Press established 1971. *Acumen* established 1984. **Poetry Editor:** Patricia Oxley.

Magazine Needs *Acumen* appears 3 times/year (in January, May, and September) and is a "general literary magazine with emphasis on good poetry." Wants "well-crafted, high-quality, imaginative poems showing a sense of form. No experimental verse of an obscene type." Has published poetry by Ruth Padel, William Oxley, Hugo Williams, Peter Porter, Danielle Hope, and Leah Fritz. *Acumen* is 100 pages, A5, perfect-bound. "We aim to publish 120 poems out of 12,000 received." Press run is 650 for 400 subscribers of which 20 are libraries. Subscription: $45 surface/$50 air. Sample copy: $15.

How to Submit Submit 5-6 poems at a time. Accepts simultaneous submissions, if not submitted to UK magazines; no previously published poems. Responds in one month. Pays "by negotiation" and one contributor's copy. Staff reviews books of poetry in up to 300 words (single book format) or 600 words (multi-book format). Send materials for review consideration to Glyn Pursglove, 25

St. Albans Rd., Brynmill, Swansea, West Glamorgan SA2 0BP Wales. "If a reply is required, please send IRCs. One IRC for a decision, 3 IRCs if work is to be returned."
Advice "Read *Acumen* carefully to see what kind of poetry we publish. Also read widely in many poetry magazines, and don't forget the poets of the past—they can still teach us a great deal."

⊘ ADASTRA PRESS

16 Reservation Rd., Easthampton MA 01027-2536. Established 1980. **Publisher:** Gary Metras.
Book/Chapbook Needs "Adastra is primarily a chapbook publisher using antique equipment and methods, i.e., hand-set type, letterpress printing, hand-sewn bindings. Any titles longer than chapbook length are by special arrangement and are from poets who have previously published a successful chapbook or two with Adastra. Editions are generally released with a flat-spine paper wrapper, and some titles have been bound in cloth. Editions are limited, ranging from 200- to 400-copy print runs. Some of the longer titles have gone into reprint and these are photo-offset and perfect-bound. Letterpress chapbooks by themselves are not reprinted as single titles. Once they go out of print, they are gone. Instead, I have released *The Adastra Reader, Collected Chapbooks, 1979-1986* (1987), and am assembling *The Adastra Reader II, Collected Chapbooks, 1987-1992*. These anthologies collect the first 12 chapbooks and the second 12, respectively, and I am now planning the third series. I am biased against poems that rhyme and/or are religious in theme. Sequences and longish poems are always nice to present in a chapbook format. There are no guidelines other than these. Competition is keen. Less than .5% of submissions are accepted." Published chapbooks include *Digger's Blues* by Jim Daniels, *Behind Our Memories* by Michael Hettich, and *Three* by Stephen Philbrick. Publishes 2-4 chapbooks/year. Sample hand-crafted chapbook: $6 postpaid.
How to Submit "I am overcommitted and will not read new submissions this or next year."

◪ ADEPT PRESS; SMALL BRUSHES

P.O. Box 391, Long Valley NJ 07853-0391. Established 1999. **Editor:** Jan Epps Turner.
Magazine Needs Published quarterly, *Small Brushes* "looks for poetry of literary quality, including humor and nostalgia. We value unity, coherence, emphasis, accessibility, and want to see poetry expressed without the use of vulgarity. Striving for universality and ageless connections of the human spirit, we avoid issues of a narrow religious, social, or political character and overly sentimental or personal poems. We rarely use a poem over 42 lines." Has published poetry by John P. Kristofco, Christy Berlowitz, Kurt Krumpholz, Laverne Frith, Tom Walsh, and David Napolin. *Small Brushes* is 28 pages, digest-sized, desktop-published, photocopied and saddle-stapled, with heavyweight textured paper cover. Receives over 1,000 poems/year, accepts about 16%. Publishes about 40 poems/issue. Press run is 100 for contributors, subscriptions, and shelf sales. Single copy: $3; subscription: $10/year (4 issues). Make checks payable to Adept Press. "Subscriptions are for a few loyal readers and a way for contributors to get extra copies at a savings by specifying the issues or any 4 copies they want. Otherwise, we neither require nor expect contributors to subscribe. Subscription purchase does not affect our choice of poetry, so please do not send a check with first submissions. Samples (old issues), with our guidelines enclosed, can be obtained by sending a self-addressed catalog envelope (6×9) with 83¢ postage attached."
How to Submit Submit 3-4 poems at a time. No previously published poems or simultaneous submissions. Cover letter requested. "Please include a brief bio in your cover letter, and place your name and address at the top of each manuscript page. Send SASE if you want any manuscript returned (standard envelope and first-class postage only)." Time between acceptance and publication is up to one year. Responds in up to 3 months. Pays one contributor's copy. Rights remain with authors and artists.

✪ ◪ $ ◎ ADRIFT (Specialized: Irish nationality)

46 E. First St., #3D, New York NY 10003. Established 1980. **Editor:** Thomas McGonigle.
Magazine Needs *Adrift* appears twice/year. "The orientation of the magazine is Irish, Irish-Ameri-

Publishers of Poetry

can. I expect the reader-writer knows and goes beyond Yeats, Kavanagh, Joyce, O'Brien." Open to all kinds of submissions, but does not want to see "junk." Has published poetry by James Liddy, Thomas McCarthy, Francis Stuart, and Gilbert Sorrentino. *Adrift* is 32 pages, magazine-sized, offset-printed on heavy stock, saddle-stapled, with matte card cover. Circulation is 1,000 for 200 subscribers, of which 50 are libraries. Single copy: $4; subscription: $8. Sample: $5. Make checks payable to T. McGonigle.

How to Submit Accepts simultaneous submissions. Pays varying rates, plus one contributor's copy. Reviews books of poetry. Send materials for review consideration.

☐ ADVOCATE, PKA's PUBLICATION

1881 Little West Kill Rd., Prattsville NY 12468. (518)299-3103. Established 1987.

Magazine Needs *Advocate* is a bimonthly advertiser-supported tabloid (12,000 copies distributed free) using "original, previously unpublished works, such as feature stories, essays, 'think' pieces, letters to the editor, profiles, humor, fiction, poetry, puzzles, cartoons, or line drawings." Wants "nearly any kind of poetry, any length, but not religious or pornographic. Poetry ought to speak to people and not be so oblique as to have meaning only to the poet. If I had to be there to understand the poem, don't send it. Now looking for horse-related poems, stories, drawings, and photos." Accepts about 25% of poems received. Sample: $4.

How to Submit No previously published poems or simultaneous submissions. Time between acceptance and publication is up to 6 months. "Occasionally" comments on rejected poems. Responds in 2 months. Pays 2 contributor's copies. Acquires first rights only.

Advice "All submissions and correspondence must be accompanied by a SASE with sufficient postage."

✪ ☑ ◎ AETHLON: THE JOURNAL OF SPORT LITERATURE (Specialized: sports/recreation)

Sports Literature Association, East Tennessee State University, Box 70270, Johnson City TN 37614. (423)439-5189. E-mail: sla@etsu.edu. Website: www.etsu.edu/english/aethlon.htm. Established 1983. **Contact:** Poetry Editor.

Magazine Needs *Aethlon* publishes a variety of sport-related literature, including scholarly articles, fiction, poetry, and reviews; 2 issues annually in fall and spring. Subject matter must be literary with sport theme; no restrictions regarding form, length, style, or purpose. Does not want "doggerel, cliché-ridden, or oversentimental" poems. Has published poetry by Joseph Bathanti, David Allen Evans, John Grey, John B. Lee, Barbara Smith, and Matthew J. Spireng. *Aethlon* is 200 pages, digest-sized, offset-printed, flat-spined, with illustrations and some ads. Publishes 12-15 poems/issue. Circulation is 1,000 for 750 subscribers of which 250 are libraries. Subscription included with membership ($50 for individuals; $75 institutional) in the Sports Literature Association. Sample: $20.

How to Submit "Only typed manuscripts with SASE considered." No simultaneous submissions. No e-mail submissions. Responds in up to 2 months. Backlog is up to one year. Pays one contributor's copy.

Also Offers ListServ: h-arete@h-net.msu.edu.

$☑ AGNI

Boston University, 236 Bay State Rd., Boston MA 02215. (617)353-7135. Fax: (617)353-7134. E-mail: agni@bu.edu. Website: www.bu.edu/agni. Established 1972. **Editors:** Sven Birkerts and Eric Grunwald.

• Work published in *AGNI* has been regularly included in *The Best American Poetry* and *Pushcart Prize* anthologies.

Magazine Needs *AGNI* is a biannual journal of poetry, fiction, and essays "by both emerging and established writers. We publish quite a bit of poetry in forms as well as 'language' poetry, but we don't begin to try and place parameters on the 'kind of work' that *AGNI* selects.'' Wants readable, intelligent poetry—mostly lyric free verse (with some narrative and dramatic)—that somehow communicates tension or risk. Has published poetry by Adrienne Rich, Seamus Heaney, Maxine Scates, Rosanna Warren, Chinua Achebe, and Ha Jin. *AGNI* is typeset, offset-printed, and perfect-bound. Publishes about 40 poems/issue. Circulation is 3,000 for subscription, mail order, and bookstore sales. Subscription: $17. Sample: $10, $12 for 30th Anniversary Poetry Anthology.

How to Submit ''Our reading period runs from September 1st until May 31st. Please submit no more than 5 poems at a time. No fancy fonts, gimmicks. Send SASE, no preformatted reply cards. No work accepted via e-mail. Brief, sincere cover letters.'' Accepts simultaneous submissions; no previously published poems. Pays $10/page, $150 maximum, plus 2 contributor's copies and a one-year subscription. Acquires first serial rights.

☐ THE AGUILAR EXPRESSION

1329 Gilmore Ave., Donora PA 15033. (724)379-8019. E-mail: xyz0@access995.com. Established 1986. **Editor/Publisher:** Xavier F. Aguilar.

Magazine Needs *The Aguilar Expression* appears annually in October. ''In publishing poetry, I try to exhibit the unique reality that we too often take for granted and acquaint as mediocre. We encourage poetics that deal with *now*, which our readers can relate to.'' Has published poetry by Martin Kich and Gail Ghai. *The Aguilar Expression* is 4-20 pages, photocopied on $8\frac{1}{2} \times 11$ sheets. Receives about 20-30 poems/month, accepts about 5-10. Circulation is 300. Sample: $8. Make checks payable to Xavier Aguilar.

How to Submit ''We insist that all writers send a SASE for writer's guidelines before submitting.'' Submit up to 3 poems at a time in a clear, camera-ready copy, 30-line limit, any topic/style. Does not accept e-mail submissions. Cover letter, including writing background, and SASE for contact purposes, required with submissions. Reads mss in January, February, and March. Manuscripts received in any other months will be discarded unopened. ''Send copies; manuscripts will not be returned.'' Responds in 2 months. Pays 2 contributor's copies.

☑ AHSAHTA PRESS; SAWTOOTH POETRY PRIZE

MFA Program in Creative Writing, Boise State University, 1910 University Dr., Boise ID 83725. (208)426-2195. Fax: (208)426-4373. E-mail: ahsahta@boisestate.edu. Website: http://ahsahtapress .boisestate.edu. Director: Janet Holmes. **Contact:** Editor.

Book/Chapbook Needs Ahsahta Press has been publishing contemporary poetry of the American West since 1976. ''It has since expanded its scope to publish poets nationwide, seeking out and publishing the best new poetry from a wide range of aesthetics—poetry that is technically accomplished, distinctive in style, and thematically fresh.'' Has published *Spell*, by Dan Beachy-Quick; *Leave the Room to Itself*, by Graham Foust; *Forbidden City*, by Peggy Hamilton; *Dear, Read*, by Lisa Fishman; *Welkin*, by Aaron McCollough, as well as work by Wyn Cooper, Craig Cotter, Sandra Alcosser, and Cynthia Hogue.

How to Submit Submit only during their March 1 through May 31 reading period. Send complete ms and letter-sized SASE for reply. Accepts multiple and simultaneous submissions. Responds in up to 3 months. Forthcoming, new, and backlist titles available from website. Most backlist titles: $9.95; most current titles: $14.95.

Contest/Award Offerings Sawtooth Poetry Prize publishes a book-length collection of poetry judged by a nationally recognized poet (2004 judge was Claudia Rankine).

Also Offers Publishes a letterpress broadside series drawn from Ahsahta Press authors. Query first.

Advice ''Ahsahta seeks distinctive, non-imitative, unpredictable, and innovatively crafted work. Please check out our website for examples of what we publish.''

⚒ $⬛ ◎ AIM MAGAZINE (Specialized: social issues, ethnic, political)

P.O. Box 1174, Maywood IL 60153. (773)874-6184. Fax: (206)543-2746. E-mail: apiladoone@aol.c om. Website: www.aimmagazine.org. Established 1974. **Poetry Editor:** Ruth Apilado.

Magazine Needs *Aim* appears quarterly, "dedicated to racial harmony and peace." Uses 3-4 poems ("poetry with social significance mainly"—average 32 lines) in each issue. Accepts poetry written by high school students. Has published poetry by J. Douglas Studer, Wayne Dowdy, Ned Pendergast, and Maria DeGuzman. *Aim* is magazine-sized with glossy cover. Receives about 30 submissions/year, accepts about half. Circulation is 10,000 for 3,000 subscribers of which many are the libraries of K-12 schools, colleges, and universities. Single copy: $7.50; subscription: $20. Sample: $5.

How to Submit Accepts simultaneous submissions. A list of upcoming themes is available for SASE. Responds in 6 weeks. Pays $3/poem and one contributor's copy. Does not send an acceptance notice: "We simply send payment and magazine copy."

Advice "Read the work of published poets."

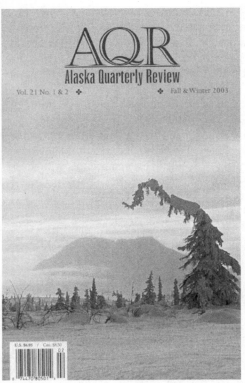

This cover photograph "elegantly and simply captures the beauty of extreme cold and Alaska's arctic light," says editor Ronald Spatz. Photo © 2003 by Anne Raup.

⬛ ALASKA QUARTERLY REVIEW

University of Alaska Anchorage, 3211 Providence Dr., Anchorage AK 99508. Phone/fax: (907)786-6916. E-mail: ayaqr@uaa.alaska.edu. Website: www.uaa.alaska.edu/aqr. Established 1981. **Executive Editor:** Ronald Spatz.

● Poetry published in *Alaska Quarterly Review* has been selected for inclusion in *The Best American Poetry*, *Pushcart Prize*, and *Beacon's Best* anthologies.

Magazine Needs *Alaska Quarterly Review* "is a journal devoted to contemporary literary art. We publish both traditional and experimental fiction, poetry, literary nonfiction, and short plays." Has published poetry by Kim Addonizio, Tom Lux, Pattiann Rogers, John Balaban, Albert Goldbarth, Jane Hirshfeld, Billy Collins, and Dorianne Laux. Wants all styles and forms of poetry "with the most emphasis perhaps on voice and content that displays 'risk,' or intriguing ideas or situations." Publishes 2 double-issues/year, each using between 40-125 pages of poetry. *Alaska Quarterly Review* is 224-300 pages, digest-sized, professionally printed, perfect-bound, with card cover with color or b&w photo. Receives up to 5,000 submissions/year, accepts 40-90. Circulation is 3,500 for 500 subscribers of which 32 are libraries. Subscription: $10. Sample: $6.

How to Submit Does not accept fax or e-mail submissions. Manuscripts are *not* read from May 15 through August 15. Responds in up to 4 months, sometimes longer during peak periods in late winter. Pay depends on funding. Acquires first North American serial rights. Guest poetry editors have included Stuart Dybek, Jane Hirshfield, Stuart Dischell, Maxine Kumin, Pattiann Rogers, Dorianne Laux, Peggy Shumacher, Nancy Eimers, Michael Ryan, and Billy Collins.

◐ ◎ ALBATROSS; THE ANABIOSIS PRESS (Specialized: nature)

2 South New St., Bradford MA 01835. (978)469-7085. E-mail: rsmyth@mva.net. Website: http://members.mva.net/rsmyth/anabiosis. **Editor:** Richard Smyth.

Magazine Needs *Albatross* appears "as soon as we have accepted enough quality poems to publish an issue—about one a year. We consider the albatross to be a metaphor for an environment that must survive. This is not to say that we publish only environmental or nature poetry, but that we are biased toward such subject matter. We publish mostly free verse, 200 lines/poem maximum, and we prefer a narrative style, but again, this is not necessary. We do not want trite rhyming poetry which doesn't convey a deeply felt experience in a mature expression with words." Also publishes interviews with established writers. Has published poetry by Ryan G. Van Cleave, Luis Cuauhtemoc Berriozabal, Cara Chamberlain, Richard Alan Bunch, and Peggy Landsman. *Albatross* is 28 pages, digest-sized, laser-typeset, with linen cover, and some b&w drawings. Subscription: $5/2 issues. Sample: $3.

How to Submit Submit 3-5 poems at a time. "Poems should be typed single-spaced, with name, address, and phone number in upper left corner." No simultaneous submissions. Accepts e-mail submissions if included in body of message. Name and address must accompany e-mail submissions. Cover letter not required; "We do, however, need bio notes and SASE for return or response." Guidelines available for SASE or on website. Responds in up to one month, has 3-month backlog. Pays one contributor's copy. Acquires all rights. Returns rights provided that "previous publication in *Albatross* is mentioned in all subsequent reprintings."

Contest/Award Offerings Holds a chapbook contest. Submit 16-20 pages of poetry, any theme, any style. **Deadline:** June 30 of each year. Include name, address, and phone number on the title page. **Reading fee:** $10 (check payable to Anabiosis Press). Winner receives $100 and at least 50 copies of his/her published chapbook. All entering receive a free copy of the winning chapbook.

Advice "We expect a poet to read as much contemporary poetry as possible. We want to be moved. When you read our poetry, we hope that it moves you in the same way that it moves us. We try to publish the kind of poetry that you would want to read again and again."

$ ◐ ◎ ALIVE NOW (Specialized: spirituality; themes)

1908 Grand Ave., P.O. Box 340004, Nashville TN 37203-0004. E-mail: AliveNow@upperroom.org. Website: www.alivenow.org or www.upperroom.org. **Contact:** Melissa Tidwell.

Magazine Needs *Alive Now* is a bimonthly devotional magazine that invites readers to enter an ever-deepening relationship with God. "*Alive Now* seeks to nourish people who are hungry for a sacred way of living. Submissions should invite readers to see God in the midst of daily life by exploring how contemporary issues impact their faith lives. Each word must be vivid and dynamic and contribute to the whole. We make selections based on a list of upcoming themes. Manuscripts which do not fit a theme will be returned." Considers avant-garde and free verse. *Alive Now* is 64 pages with photographs and art. Accepts 20 poems/year. Circulation is 70,000. Subscription: $14.95 for one year (6 issues); $23.95 for 2 years (12 issues). Additional subscription information, including foreign rates, available on website.

How to Submit Submit 5 poems at a time. Line length for poetry is 10 minimum, 45 maximum. Submissions should be typed, double-spaced, on 8½ × 11 paper; include SASE. "If you are submitting material for more than one theme, send a SASE for each theme represented. On each page you submit, include your name, address, social security number, and the theme for which the piece is being sent." **All poems must relate to themes.** List of upcoming themes and guidelines available for SASE or on website. "We will notify contributors of manuscript status when we make final decisions for a theme, 3 months before the issue date. We place manuscripts on hold for specific issues; authors are free to reques their manuscripts be returned to them at any time." Pays $35 and up on acceptance. Purchases newspaper, periodical, and electronic rights; may purchase one-time use.

Advice "*Alive Now* is ecumenical, including both lay persons and church professionals. Our readers are primarily adults, from young adults to older adults, and include persons of many cultures and ethnic backgrounds."

☐ ◎ THE ALLEGHENY REVIEW (Specialized: undergraduate students); THE ALLEGHENY REVIEW AWARD IN POETRY

Box 32, Allegheny College, Meadville PA 16335. E-mail: review@allegheny.edu. Website: http://review.allegheny.edu. Established 1983. **Faculty Advisor:** Christopher Bakken.

Magazine Needs "Each year *The Allegheny Review* compiles and publishes a review of the nation's best undergraduate literature. It is entirely composed of and by college undergraduates." *The Allegheny Review* is digest-sized, flat-spined, professionally printed, with glossy card cover with b&w photo. Single copy: $4. Sample: $4 and 11×18 SASE.

How to Submit Submit 5 poems. No fax or e-mail submissions. "Each poem should have author's name and address clearly indicated. Only submissions accompanied by a SASE should expect a response from the editors." Submissions should be accompanied by cover letter "stating which college the poet is attending, year of graduation, and a very brief bio." Current deadlines available by e-mail or on website. Responds in early March.

Contest/Award Offerings "Submissions for *The Allegheny Review* Award in Poetry are read in the fall semester of each year. All submissions accompanied by an entry fee receive a one-year subscription to the journal and are considered for publication. In March, a nationally-recognized poet awards $250 to the contest winner." Guidelines available by e-mail or on website.

Advice "Familiarize yourself with any journal to which you submit your work for publication, and send only your very best work. While *The Allegheny Review* has no particular stylistic preferences, you will have a better sense of the kind of writing we tend to publish if you do. And when you submit, please take enough pride in your work to do so professionally. Handwritten or poorly typed and proofed submissions definitely convey an impression—a negative one."

$☑ ALLIGATOR JUNIPER

Prescott College, 301 Grove Ave., Prescott AZ 86301. (928)350-2012. E-mail: aj@prescott.edu. Website: www.prescott.edu/highlights/alligator_juniper.html. Established 1995. **Contact:** Poetry Editor.

Magazine Needs *Alligator Juniper* is a contest publication appearing annually in May. "We publish work based only on artistic merit." Has published poetry by Elton Glaser and Fatima Lim-Wilson. *Alligator Juniper* is 200 pages with b&w photography. Receives about 1,200-1,500 poems/year, accepts about 6-20. Press run is 1,500 for 600 subscribers; 200 distributed free to other reputable journals, MFA programs, and writers' colonies. Subscription: $12/2 years (2 issues). Sample: $7.50. "We publish one issue per year and it's always a contest, requiring a $10 fee which allows us to pay a $500 first prize in each category—fiction, poetry, creative nonfiction, and photography. All entrants receive a copy of the next issue."

How to Submit Submit up to 5 poems at a time with reading fee. Include SASE for response only; mss are not returned. "All entrants receive a personal letter from one of our staff regarding the status of their submissions." Accepts simultaneous submissions; no previously published poems. No e-mail or fax submissions. Cover letter is required. **Postmark Deadline:** October 1. "We read and select what we will publish from all the work submitted so far that calendar year." **Reading fee:** $10/entry (5 poems or 5 pages of poetry). Time between acceptance and publication is 3-5 months. "Finalists are selected in-house and passed on to a different guest judge each year." Occasionally publishes theme issues. Guidelines available for SASE, by e-mail, or on website. Responds in 5 months. Each year, one winner receives $500 plus 4 contributor's copies; all other poets whose work is selected for publication receive payment in contributor's copies only.

◙ THE ALSOP REVIEW

122 Broad Creek Rd., Laurel DE 19956. E-mail: alsop@alsopreview.com. Website: www.alsoprevie
w.com/. Established 1998. **Editor/Founder:** Jaimes Alsop.

Magazine Needs *The Alsop Review* "aims to merge the print and Web world, to bring established
print writers to the Web, and highlight those writers whose reputations are still word-of-mouth."
Wants "well-crafted verse with a strong voice. No pornography, overtly religious work, greeting
card verse, or sloppy writing." Has published poetry by Lola Haskins, Dorianne Laux, A.E. Stallings,
and Kim Addonizio. Receives about 1,000 poems/year, accepts about 2%.

How to Submit Submit 3-5 poems at a time. Accepts simultaneous submissions; no previously
published poems. Cover letter preferred. "Submissions may only be sent via e-mail in body of
message." Time between acceptance and publication is one month. Seldom comments on rejected
poems. Guidelines available by e-mail or on website. Responds in one month. Acquires first rights.

Also Offers *The Alsop Review* "sponsors annual poetry and fiction contests, and runs the most
popular workshop on the Web (The Gazebo)."

⊠ ◙ AMARYLLIS

P.O. Box 6330, Montgomery AL 36106-0330. Fax: (334)244-3740. E-mail: nanderso@mail.aum.edu.
Established 1985. **Editors:** Nancy Anderson, Lynn Jinks, Donald Nobles.

Magazine Needs *Amaryllis* appears annually in December, "more often depending on submissions." A national magazine publishing high-quality poetry, fiction, essays, and reviews, *Amaryllis*
is open to all forms and styles, including experimental forms, with no restriction on subject. Does
not want trite verse or inspirational work. *Amaryllis* is 75-150 pages, digest-sized, professionally
offset-printed, perfect-bound, with heavy matte cardstock cover with line illustration. Accepts about
5% of poems submitted. Press run is 500. Single copy: $5. Sample: $3. Make checks payable to
Amaryllis.

How to Submit Submit 7 poems at a time. Any length poetry will be considered. No previously
published poems or simultaneous submissions. No fax, e-mail, or disk submissions. Cover letter
is required. "Please submit in triplicate and include SASE for response." Reads submissions year
round. Time between acceptance and publication varies. Poems are circulated to an editorial board.
"All submissions are discussed by 3 editors; works are reviewed in a roundtable discussion."
Seldom comments on rejected poems. Guidelines available in magazine, for SASE, by fax, or by e-
mail. Responds in 2 months. Sometimes sends prepublication galleys. Pays 5 contributor's copies.
Acquires one-time rights. Reviews books of poetry in 1,000 words, single and multi-book format.

◙ ◎ AMAZE: THE CINQUAIN JOURNAL (Specialized: American cinquain)

10529 Olive St., Temple City CA 91780. E-mail: cinquains@hotmail.com. Website: www.amaze-
cinquain.com. Established 2002. **Editor:** Deborah P. Kolodji. **Webmaster:** Lisa Janice Cohen.

Magazine Needs *Amaze: The Cinquain Journal* is a biannual literary journal (in both print and
online webzine format) devoted to the cinquain poetry form. "The webzine is published on a
continuous flow basis, as we accept submissions for the current issue. The print version is published
2 months after submissions close for the webzine." Wants American cinquains as invented by
Adelaide Crapsey (5 lines with a 2-4-6-8-2 syllable pattern) and cinquain variations (mirror cinquains, crown cinquains, cinquain sequences, etc.). Does not want any poetry not based upon the
American cinquain, nor "grammar-lesson" cinquains based upon parts of speech. Nothing hateful,
racist, or sexually explicit. Has published poetry by an'ya, Ann K. Schwader, Michael McClintock,
naia, and Denis Garrison. The print version of *Amaze* is 40-50 pages, digest-sized, photocopied,
saddle-stapled, with card stock cover with photograph/artwork. Receives about 1,500 poems/year,
accepts about 200. Publishes about 100 poems/issue. Press run is 100-200 for 25 subscribers. Single
copy: $6 US, $7.50 non-US; subscription: $12 US, $15 non-US. Make checks payable to Deborah P.
Kolodji, or pay online through PayPal.

How to Submit Submit 1-10 poems at a time. Line length for poetry is 5. Accepts previously published poems; no simultaneous submissions. Accepts e-mail submissions; no fax or disk submissioins. E-mail submissions preferred, with poems in the body of the e-mail. Do not send attachments. Include SASE with postal submissions. Reads submissions "on a continuous flow." Time between acceptance and publication is 3 weeks for webzine, up to 8 months for print journal. "Poems are evaluated on quality, form, and content." Often comments on rejected poems. Guidelines available for SASE or on website. Responds in up to 6 weeks. Acquires one-time rights.

⊕ ☑ AMBIT

17 Priory Gardens, Highgate, London N6 5QY England. Phone: 020 8340 3566. Website: www.ambit magazine.co.uk. **Editor:** Martin Bax. **Poetry Editors:** Martin Bax, Carol Ann Duffy, and Henry Graham.

Magazine Needs *Ambit* is a 96-page quarterly of avant-garde, contemporary, and experimental work. Subscription: £25 UK, £27/€48 rest of Europe, £29/$56 overseas (individuals); £36 UK, £38/€ 64 rest of Europe, £40/$73 overseas (institutions). Sample: £6.50 UK, £7/€15 rest of Europe, £8/ $18 overseas.

How to Submit Submit up to 6 poems at a time, typed double-spaced. No previously published poems or simultaneous submissions. Guidelines available in magazine or on website. Pay is "variable plus 2 contributor's copies. SAE vital for reply." Staff reviews books of poetry. Send materials for review consideration to review editor.

Advice "Read a copy of the magazine before submitting!"

☑ AMERICA; FOLEY POETRY CONTEST (Specialized: religious, Catholic; social; political)

106 W. 56th St., New York NY 10019. (212)581-4640. Fax: (212)399-3596. Website: www.americam agazine.org. Established 1909. **Poetry Editor:** Paul Mariani.

 • "Because of a large backlog, we are only accepting poems submitted for the Foley Poetry Contest." (see below)

Magazine Needs *America* is a weekly journal of opinion published by the Jesuits of North America. Primarily publishes articles on religious, social, political, and cultural themes. *America* is 36 pages, magazine-sized, professionally printed on thin stock, with thin paper cover. Circulation is 39,000. Subscription: $48. Sample: $2.75.

Contest/Award Offerings The Foley Poetry Contest offers annual award of $1,000 and 2 contributor's copies for the winning poem. Submissions must be unpublished and may not be entered in other contests. Submit one poem/person, not to exceed 30 lines of verse, in any form. "Name, address, telephone number, and e-mail address (where there is one) should be appended to the bottom of the page. Poems will not be returned, and e-mailed poems are not accepted." Guidelines available in magazine, for SASE, or on website. **Postmark deadline:** was January 1-April 16 for 2004. 2003 competition received 1,366 entries. 2003 winner was Susanna Childress (for "To Things Cursory"). Winner will be announced in the mid-June issue of *America* and on the website.

☑ AMERICAN LITERARY REVIEW

University of North Texas, P.O. Box 311307, Denton TX 76203-1307. (940)565-2755. E-mail: americ anliteraryreview@yahoo.com. Website: www.engl.unt.edu/alr. **Editor:** John Tait. **Poetry Editors:** Bruce Bond and Corey Marks.

Magazine Needs *American Literary Review* is a biannual publishing all forms and modes of poetry and fiction. "We are especially interested in originality, substance, imaginative power, and lyric intensity." Has published poetry by Matthew Rohrer, Dara Wier, Pattiann Rogers, Donald Revell, Laura Kasischke, and David Biespiell. *American Literary Review* is about 120 pages, digest-sized, attractively printed, perfect-bound, with color card cover with photo. Subscription: $10/year, $18/ 2 years. Sample: $6 (US), $8 (ROW).

How to Submit Submit up to 5 typewritten poems at a time. No fax or e-mail submissions. Cover letter with author's name, address, phone number, and poem titles required. Guidelines available for SASE or on website. Responds in up to 4 months. Pays 2 contributor's copies.

Contest/Award Offerings Sponsors poetry and fiction contest in alternating years. Most recent poetry contest was in 2004. Send SASE for details.

⚞ ⚟ THE AMERICAN POETRY JOURNAL; THE AMERICAN POET PRIZE

P.O. Box 640746, San Jose CA 95164-0746. Website: www.americanpoetryjournal.com. Established 2004. **Editor:** J.P. Dancing Bear.

Magazine Needs *The American Poetry Journal*, published biannually, "seeks to publish work using poetic device, favoring image, metaphor, and good sound. We like alliteration, extended metaphors, image, movement, and poems that can pass the 'so what' test. *The American Poetry Journal* has in mind the reader who delights in discovering what a poem can do to the tongue and what the poem paints on the cave of the mind." Wants poems "that exhibit strong, fresh imagery, metaphor, and good sound." Does not want "narratives about family, simplistic verse, annoying word hodge-podges." Has published poetry by C.J. Sage, S.D. Lishan, Jason Gray, Hailey Leithhauser, and Barbara Crooker. *The American Poetry Journal* is 60 pages, digest-sized. Accepts about 1% of poems submitted. Publishes about 30-40 poems/issue. Single copy: $6; subscription: $10. Make checks payable to J.P. Dancing Bear.

How to Submit Submit 3-5 poems at a time. Accepts simultaneous submissions; no previously published poems. No e-mail or disk submissions. Cover letter is preferred. Reads submissions all year. Time between acceptance and publication is 6 months. "Poems are read first for clarity and technique, then read aloud for sound quality." Seldom comments on rejected poems. Guidelines available in magazine, for SASE, or on website. Responds in 6 weeks. Pays one contributor's copy. Acquires first rights.

Contest/Award Offerings "We offer The American Poet Prize, awarding $300 and publication. All entries will be considered for publication and receive a year's subscription. Send 3 original, unpublished poems without identifiers on the page, a cover letter with poem titles, author's name, contact information, optional stamped postcard for delivery confirmation, and SASE." **Entry fee:** $10. Make checks payable to J.P. Dancing Bear. **Deadline:** was June 30 for 2004.

Advice "Read an issue before submitting."

◎ AMERICAN RESEARCH PRESS (Specialized: paradoxism)

P.O. Box 141, Rehoboth NM 87322. E-mail: M_L_Perez@yahoo.com. Website: www.gallup.unm. edu/ ~ smarandache/ebooksliterature.htm. Established 1990. **Publisher:** Minh Perez.

Book/Chapbook Needs American Research Press publishes 2-3 poetry paperbacks/year. Wants experimental poetry dealing with paradoxism. No classical poetry. See website for poetry samples. Has published poetry by Al. Florin Tene, Anatol Ciocanu, Nina Josu, and Al Bantos.

How to Submit Submit 3-4 poems at a time. No previously published poems or simultaneous submissions. Cover letter preferred. Submit seasonal poems one month in advance. Time between acceptance and publication is one year. Seldom comments on rejected poems. Responds to queries in one month. Pays 100 author's copies. Order sample books by sending SASE.

Also Offers Free e-books available on website.

$◙ THE AMERICAN SCHOLAR

1606 New Hampshire Ave., NW, Washington DC 20009. (202)265-3808. Established 1932. Website: www.pbk.org/pubs/amscholar.htm. **Associate Editor:** Sandra Costich. **Poetry Editor:** Robert Farnsworth.

• Poetry published here has been included in the *Pushcart Prize* anthology.

Magazine Needs *American Scholar* is an academic quarterly which uses about 5 poems/issue. "The usual length of our poems is 34 lines." The magazine has published poetry by John Updike, Philip Levine, and Rita Dove. What little poetry is used in this high-prestige magazine is accomplished, intelligent, and open (in terms of style and form). Study before submitting. Sample: $9; subscription: $25/year, $48/2 years, $69/3 years. Make checks payable to The American Scholar, P.O. Box 354, Mt. Morris IL 61054.

How to Submit Submit up to 4 poems at a time; "no more for a careful reading. Poems should be typed, on one side of the paper, and each sheet should bear the name and address of the author and the name of the poem." Guidelines available for SASE. Always sends prepublication galleys. Pays $50/poem and 3 contributor's copies. Acquires first rights only.

AMERICAN TANKA (Specialized: form/style, tanka)

P.O. Box 120-024, Staten Island NY 10312. E-mail: info@americantanka.com. Website: www.americantanka.com. Established 1996. **Contact:** Editor.

Magazine Needs *American Tanka* appears annually each spring and is devoted to single English-language tanka. Wants "concise and vivid language, good crafting, and echo of the original Japanese form." Does not want anything that is not tanka. Has published poetry by Sanford Goldstein, Marianne Bluger, Michael McClintock, Michael Dylan Welch, Jane Reichhold, and George Swede. *American Tanka* is 95-120 pages, digest-sized, perfect-bound, with glossy cover. Single copy: $12; subscription: $20.

How to Submit Submit up to 5 poems at a time; "submit only once per reading period." No previously published poems or simultaneous submissions. Accepts submissions by e-mail (pasted into body of message) and through online submission form. Reads manuscripts from September 15 to February 15. Guidelines available for SASE, by e-mail, or on website. Responds in up to 2 months. Acquires first North American serial rights.

Advice "Become familiar with the tanka form by reading both translations and English-language tanka. In your own tanka, be natural and concrete and vivid. Avoid clichés, overcrowded imagery, or attempting to imitate Japanese poems."

AMERICAN TOLKIEN SOCIETY; MINAS TIRITH EVENING-STAR; W.W. PUBLICATIONS (Specialized: fantasy, Tolkien)

P.O. Box 7871, Flint MI 48507-0871. E-mail: americantolkiensociety@yahoo.com. Established 1967. **Editor:** Amalie A. Helms.

Magazine Needs & How to Submit Journals and chapbooks use poetry of fantasy about Middle-Earth and Tolkien. Has published poetry by Thomas M. Egan, Anne Etkin, Nancy Pope, and Martha Benedict. *Minas Tirith Evening-Star* is digest-sized, offset from typescript, with cartoon-like b&w graphics. Press run is 400 for 350 subscribers of which 10% are libraries. Single copy: $3.50; subscription: $12.50. Sample: $3. Make checks payable to American Tolkien Society. No simultaneous submissions; previously published poems "maybe." Accepts submissions by postal mail, e-mail (pasted into body of message/attachment), and on disk. Cover letter preferred. "We do not return phone calls unless collect." Editor sometimes comments on rejected poems. Occasionally publishes theme issues. Guidelines available for SASE or by e-mail. Responds in 2 weeks. Sometimes sends prepublication galleys. Pays one contributor's copy. Reviews related books of poetry; length depends on the volume, "a sentence to several pages." Send materials for review consideration.

Book/Chapbook Needs & How to Submit Under the imprint of W.W. Publications, publishes collections of poetry 50-100 pages. For book or chapbook consideration, submit sample poems. Publishes 2 chapbooks/year.

Also Offers Membership in the American Tolkien Society is open to all, regardless of country of residence, and entitles one to receive the quarterly journal. Dues are $12.50 per annum to addresses in US, $12.50 in Canada, and $15 elsewhere. Sometimes sponsors contests.

Advice "Adhere to the guidelines and show talent."

$⬚ ◎ ANCIENT PATHS (Specialized: religious, Christian)

P.O. Box 7505, Fairfax Station VA 22039. E-mail: SSBurris@msn.com. Website: www.LitertureClassics.com/ancientpaths/. Established 1998. **Editor:** Skylar H. Burris.

Magazine Needs *Ancient Paths* is published annually in September "to provide a forum for quality Christian literature. It contains poetry, short stories, art, and chapbook reviews." Wants "traditional rhymed/metrical forms and free verse; subtle Christian themes. I seek poetry that makes the reader both think and feel. No 'preachy' poetry, inconsistent meter, or obtrusive rhyme; no stream of conscious or avant-garde work; no esoteric academic poetry." Has published poetry by Giovanni Malito, Ida Fasel, Diane Glancy, Walt McDonald, and Donna Farley. *Ancient Paths* is 48 pages, digest-sized, photocopied, perfect-bound, with cardstock cover, b&w art. Receives about 400 poems/year, accepts about 10%. Press run is 175 for about 55 paid subscribers, 30 individual copy sales; 80 distributed free to churches, libraries, and authors. Subscription: $5/year (1 issue); $9.50/2 years (2 issues). Sample: $2 back issue, $5 current issue. Make checks payable to Skylar Burris.

How to Submit Submit up to 5 poems at a time, single-spaced. Line length for poetry is 60 maximum. Accepts previously published poems and simultaneous submissions. Accepts e-mail submissions, but regular mail submissions preferred. "E-mail submissions should be pasted directly into the message, single spaced, one poem per message, using a small or normal font size, with name and address at the top of each submission. Use subject heading: ANCIENT PATHS SUBMISSION, followed by your title." Cover letter not required. "Name, address, and line count on first page. Note if the poem is previously published and what rights (if any) were purchased." Time between acceptance and publication is up to one year. Often comments on rejected poems. Guidelines available for SASE or on website. Responds in "3-4 weeks if rejected, longer if being seriously considered." Pays $1/poem and one contributor's copy. Acquires one-time or reprint rights. Reviews other magazines and chapbooks in 100 words. Contact Skylar H. Burris.

Advice "Read the great religious poets: John Donne, George Herbert, T.S. Eliot, Lord Tennyson. Remember not to preach. This is a literary magazine, not a pulpit. This does not mean you do not communicate morals or celebrate God. It means you are not overbearing or simplistic when you do so."

⬚ ANHINGA PRESS; ANHINGA PRIZE

P.O. Box 10595, Tallahassee FL 32302-0595. (850)521-9920. Fax: (850)442-6323. E-mail: info@anhinga.org. Website: www.anhinga.org. Established 1972. **Poetry Editor:** Rick Campbell.

Book/Chapbook Needs The press publishes "books and anthologies of poetry. We want to see contemporary poetry which respects language. We're inclined toward poetry that is not obscure, that can be understood by any literate audience." Has published *The Secret History of Water* by Silvia Curbelo as well as works by Naomi Shibab Nye, Robert Dana, Lola Haskins, and Ruth L. Schwartz (the 2000 Anhinga Prize winner).

How to Submit Considers simultaneous submissions. Accepts submissions on disk and by postal mail; no e-mail submissions. Include SASE with all submissions.

Contest/Award Offerings The annual Anhinga Prize awards $2,000 and publication to a book-length poetry ms. Send SASE for rules. Submissions accepted February 15 to May 1. **Entry fee:** $20. Past judges include William Stafford, Louis Simpson, Henry Taylor, Hayden Carruth, Marvin Bell, Donald Hall, and Joy Harjo. "Everything we do is on our website."

Advice "Write good poetry. Read contemporary poetry. Not necessarily in that order."

☑ ANTHOLOGY; ANTHOLOGY, INC.

P.O. Box 4411, Mesa AZ 85211-4411. E-mail: info@anthology.org. Website: www.anthology.org. Executive Editor: Sharon Skinner. **Poetry Editor:** Trish Justrish.

Magazine Needs *Anthology* appears quarterly and intends to be "the best poetry, prose, and art magazine." Wants "poetry with clear conceit. Evocative as opposed to provocative. We do not dictate form or style, but creative uses are always enjoyed. Graphic horror and pornography are not encouraged." Has published poetry by Terry Thomas, Lyn Lifshin, Gary Every, Buddy Wakefield, and Brad Buchanan. *Anthology* is 32 pages, magazine-sized, saddle-stapled, with b&w drawings and clip art inside. Press run is 1,000 for 150 subscribers of which 10 are libraries; 50-75 distributed free to local coffeehouses, beauty parlors, doctors' offices, etc. Single copy: $4.95; subscription: $18 (4 issues). Make checks payable to *Anthology*.

How to Submit Submit up to 5 poems at a time with SASE. Line length for poetry is 100 maximum. No previously published poems or simultaneous submissions. "Do not send handwritten work or unusual fonts." Include name and address on each page of submission. Time between acceptance and publication is up to 8 months. Guidelines available for SASE or on website. Responds in 3 months. Pays one contributor's copy. Acquires one-time rights.

Contest/Award Offerings Sponsors annual contest with cash and other prizes for both poetry and short stories. **Entry fee:** $1/poem required. Send SASE for guidelines.

Advice "Send what you write, not what you think an editor wants to hear. And always remember that a rejection is seldom personal, it is just one step closer to a yes."

☑ ☑ THE ANTIGONISH REVIEW

P.O. Box 5000, Antigonish NS B2G 2W5 Canada. (902)867-3962. Fax: (902)867-5563. E-mail: TAR@stfx.ca. Website: www.antigonishreview.com. Established 1970. **Co-Editors:** Allan Quigley and Jeanette Lynes. **Poetry Editor:** Peter Sanger.

Magazine Needs *The Antigonish Review* appears quarterly and "tries to produce the kind of literary and visual mosaic that the modern sensibility requires or would respond to." Wants poetry not over "80 lines, i.e., 2 pages; subject matter can be anything; the style is traditional, modern, or post-modern limited by typographic resources. Purpose is not an issue." No "erotica, scatalogical verse, excessive propaganda toward a certain subject." Has published poetry by Andy Wainwright, W.J. Keith, Michael Hulse, Jean McNeil, M. Travis Lane, and Douglas Lochhead. *The Antigonish Review* is 144 pages, digest-sized, flat-spined with glossy card cover, offset-printing, using "in-house graphics and cover art, no ads." Receives 2,500 submissions/year; accepts about 10%. Press run is 1,000 for 950 subscribers. Subscription: $24. Sample: $5.

How to Submit Submit 5-10 poems at a time. No simultaneous submissions or previously published poems. Include SASE (or SAE and IRCs if outside Canada). "We cannot use U.S. postage." Accepts fax submissions. No e-mail submissions. Time between acceptance and publication is up to 8 months. Editor sometimes comments on rejected poems. Guidelines available for SASE, by e-mail, or on website. Responds in up to 6 months. Pays 2 contributor's copies. Acquires first North American serial rights.

☑ $☑ ARC: CANADA'S NATIONAL POETRY MAGAZINE; THE CONFEDERATION POETS PRIZE; POEM OF THE YEAR CONTEST

P.O. Box 7219, Ottawa ON K1L 8E4 Canada. E-mail: arc.poetry@cyberus.ca. Website: www.cyberus.ca/~arc.poetry. Established 1978. **Managing Editor:** Anita Lahey.

  • *Arc* received both gold and silver National Magazine Awards in 2001.

Magazine Needs *Arc* is a biannual of poetry, poetry-related articles, interviews, and book reviews. "Our tastes are eclectic. Our focus is Canadian, but we also publish writers from elsewhere." Has published poetry by Evelyn Lau, Michael Crummey, Erin Mouré, Patricia Young, and Joelene Heathcote. *Arc* is 120 pages, perfect-bound, with varnished 4-color cover, artwork, and ads. Receives about

750 submissions/year, accepts about 40-50 poems. Press run is 1,500 for 1,000 subscribers. Single copy/sample copy: $12.50 Canadian/Canada; $18 Canadian/US; $20 Canadian/overseas. Subscription (4 issues): $40 Canadian/Canada; $52 Canadian/US; $66 Canadian/overseas.

How to Submit Submit 5-8 poems, single-spaced, with name and address on each page. No previously published poems or simultaneous submissions. Cover letter required. Guidelines available for SAE and IRC or on website; upcoming themes on website and in magazine. Responds in up to 6 months. Pays $30 Canadian/page plus 2 contributor's copies. Acquires first Canadian serial rights.

Contest/Award Offerings The Confederation Poets Prize is an annual award of $100 for the best poem published in *Arc* that year. *Arc* also sponsors a "Poem of the Year Contest." 1st Prize: $1,000; 2nd Prize: $750; 3rd Prize: $500. **Deadline:** June 30. Other awards include the Lampman Award for Poetry, Critic's Desk Award, and the Diana Brebner Prize for Poetry.

⊕ ∅ ARC PUBLICATIONS

Nanholme Mill, Shaw Wood Rd., Todmorden, Lancashire OL14 6DA United Kingdom. Phone: (01706)812338. Website: www.arcpublications.co.uk. Established 1969. **Partners:** Tony Ward, Angela Jarman, and Rosemary Jones.

- "At present we are not accepting submissions."

ARCTOS PRESS; HOBEAR PUBLICATIONS

P.O. Box 401, Sausalito CA 94966-0401. (415)331-2503. E-mail: runes@aol.com. Website: http://members.aol.com/RUNES. Established 1997. **Editor:** CB Follett.

Book/Chapbook Needs Arctos Press, under the imprint HoBear Publications, publishes 1-2 paperbacks/year. "We publish quality, perfect-bound books and anthologies of poetry, usually theme-oriented, in runs of 1,000." Has published *GRRRRR, A Collection of Poems About BEARS* (anthology); *Prism*, poems by David St. John; *Fire Is Favorable to the Dreamer*, poems by Susan Terris; and others.

How to Submit "We do not accept unsolicited manuscripts unless a current call has been posted in *Poets & Writers* and/or elsewhere, at which time up to 5 poems related to the theme should be sent." Accepts previously published poems (if author holds the rights) and simultaneous submissions ("if we are kept informed"). Accepts submissions by postal mail only. Guidelines and upcoming themes available on website and for SASE. Pays one contributor's copy; discounts available on additional copies.

Also Offers *Runes, A Review of Poetry* (see separate listing in this section).

∅ ARIES: A JOURNAL OF CREATIVE EXPRESSION

Dept. of Languages and Literature, Texas Wesleyan University, 1201 Wesleyan St., Fort Worth TX 76105-1536. (817)531-4907. Fax: (817)531-6503. E-mail: aries_journal@yahoo.com (inquiries only; no submissions). Website: www.ariesjournal.com. Established 1985. **General Editor:** Stacia Dunn Neeley.

Magazine Needs *Aries* appears annually in August, publishing quality poetry, b&w art, fiction, essays, and one-act plays. Wants poetry in all forms up to 50 lines. "Special needs: original Spanish language poetry and translation thereof (send *both* versions)." Does not want erotica. Has published poetry by Virgil Suárez, Richard Robbins, Susan Smith Nash, Gerald Zipper, and Lynn Veach Sadler. *Aries* is 60 pages, digest-sized, offset-printed, perfect-bound, with heavy cardstock cover and b&w art (1500 dpi scans). Receives about 600 poems/year, accepts about 10%. Press run is 300 for 100 subscribers of which 3 are libraries, 125 shelf sales. Single copy: $6; subscription: $6. Make checks payable to *Aries* General Editor, Stacia Neeley.

How to Submit Submit up to 5 poems. Line length for poetry is 3 minimum, 50 maximum. Accepts simultaneous submissions; no previously published poems. No fax, e-mail, or disk submissions. Cover letter is required. "Blind submissions only: cover letter with titles; no identifying marks on submissions." Accepts submissions September 1 through January 31 only. Time between acceptance and publication is 3 months. "Three editors read every submission blindly. Personal response to *every* submission accompanied by a SASE or functioning e-mail address." Always comments on rejected poems. Guidelines available in magazine, for SASE, by e-mail, or on website. Responds in up to 6 months (notification of acceptance in April). Offers 50% off first contributor's copy. Acquires first rights.

Advice "Write in the voice that speaks from your unique position in the world. Our editors tend to choose works where 'there's something at stake.' "

✒ ⊚ ARJUNA LIBRARY PRESS; JOURNAL OF REGIONAL CRITICISM (Specialized: surrealism, science fiction/fantasy, spirituality, symbols)

1025 Garner St. D, Space 18, Colorado Springs CO 80905-1774. Library established 1963; press established 1979. **Editor-in-Chief:** Count Prof. Joseph A. Uphoff, Jr.

Magazine Needs "The Arjuna Library Press is avant-garde, designed to endure the transient quarters and marginal funding of the literary phenomenon (as a tradition) while presenting a context for the development of current mathematical ideas in regard to theories of art, literature, and performance; photocopy printing allows for very limited editions and irregular format. Quality is maintained as an artistic materialist practice." Publishes "surrealist prose poetry, visual poetry, dreamlike, short and long works; no obscene, profane (will criticize but not publish), unpolished work." Has published work by B.Z. Niditch, Dr. Shari O'Brien, David Lawrence, Holly Day, John Grey, and Woodrow G. Moore, II. *Journal of Regional Criticism* is published on loose photocopied pages of collage, writing, and criticism, appearing frequently in a varied format. Press run is one copy each. Reviews books of poetry "occasionally." Send materials for review consideration. "Upon request will treat material as submitted for reprint, one-time rights."

Book/Chapbook Needs & How to Submit Arjuna Library Press publishes 6-12 chapbooks/year, averaging 50 pages each. Sample: $2.50. Currently accepting one or two short poems, with a cover letter and SASE, to be considered for publication. Accepts submissions by post only. Guidelines available for SASE.

Advice "Trying to win awards by satisfying requirements is craft, the effort of an artisan. This is a good way to learn and is like copying the work of the old masters such as painters do. If a poet has a personal goal, instead, and practices without overbearing reference or influence, as the work improves or succeeds the awards will be automatic. They will be offered and need not be sought after."

⊡ ⊚ ARKANSAS REVIEW: A JOURNAL OF DELTA STUDIES (Specialized: regional)

P.O. Box 1890, State University AR 72467-1890. (870)972-3043. Fax: (870)972-3045. E-mail: tswillia @astate.edu. Website: www.clt.astate.edu/arkreview. Established 1968 (as *Kansas Quarterly*). **General Editor & Creative Materials Editor:** Tom Williams.

Magazine Needs Appearing 3 times/year, the *Arkansas Review* is "a regional studies journal devoted to the 7-state Mississippi River Delta. Interdisciplinary in scope, we publish academic articles, relevant creative material, interviews, and reviews. Material must respond to or evoke the experiences and landscapes of the 7-state Mississippi River Delta (St. Louis to New Orleans)." Has published poetry by Walt McDonald, Gordon Osing, and Colleen McElroy. *Arkansas Review* is 92 pages, magazine-sized, photo offset-printed, saddle-stapled, with 4-color cover, photos, drawings, and paintings. Receives about 500 poems/year, accepts about 5%. Press run is 600 for 400 subscribers of which 300 are libraries, 20 shelf sales; 50 distributed free to contributors. Subscription: $20. Sample: $7.50. Make checks payable to ASU Foundation.

How to Submit No limit on number of poems submitted at a time. No previously published poems or simultaneous submissions. Accepts submissions by postal mail, e-mail (pasted into body of message/as attachment), and on disk. Cover letter with SASE preferred. Time between acceptance and publication is about 6 months. Poems are circulated to an editorial board. "The Creative Materials Editor makes the final decision based—in part—on recommendations from other readers." Often comments on rejected poems. Occasionally publishes theme issues. Guidelines available for SASE or by e-mail. Responds in 4 months. Pays 5 contributor's copies. Acquires first rights. Staff reviews books and chapbooks of poetry in 500 words, single and multi-book format. Send materials for review consideration to Tom Williams. ("Inquire in advance.")

☑ ARSENIC LOBSTER

% Brandon Follett, 11855 Ginger Creek Dr., Boise ID 83713. Established 2000. **Contact:** Brandon Follett, editor.

Magazine Needs *Arsenic Lobster*, which appears biannually in April and October, "prints succulent poems for toxic people. Honed lyricism, stripped narrative." Wants "surgical steel punk, arterial ink, ecstatic gremlins, and hysterical saints. Be charlie-horse hearted and heavily quirked." Does not want "marmalade, hyacinths, or the art of gardening. No cicadas, wheelbarrows, or fond reflections on the old county fair. Nothing about Tai Chi. Nothing written with a cat on your lap." Has published poetry by Daniel Stewart, John Oliver Simon, Cecilia Woloch, Margaret Aho, Rebecca Loudon, Rob Cook, and J.P. Dancingbear. *Arsenic Lobster* is 35 pages, digest-sized, saddle-stapled, with illustrated card stock cover. Publishes about 30 poems/issue. Press run is 300. Single copy $5; subscription: $10/year. Make checks payable to Brandon Follett.

How to Submit Submit 4-7 poems at a time. Accepts previously published poems and simultaneous submissions. ("Please inform us.") No fax, e-mail, or disk submissions. "Free verse poems and biographical cover letters (not credit lists) preferred; SASE a must." Reads submissions all year. Time between acceptance and publication is 6 months. Guidelines available for SASE. Responds in one month. Pays one contributor's copy. Acquires first/one-time rights. Reviews chapbooks and other magazines/journals. Send materials for review consideration.

☑ ART TIMES: COMMENTARY AND RESOURCE FOR THE FINE & PERFORMING ARTS

P.O. Box 730, Mt. Marion NY 12456. Phone/fax: (845)246-6944. E-mail: poetry@arttimesjournal.com. Website: www.arttimesjournal.com. Established 1984. **Poetry Editor:** Raymond J. Steiner.

Magazine Needs *Art Times* is a monthly tabloid newspaper devoted to the fine and performing arts. Focuses on cultural and creative articles and essays, but also publishes some poetry and fiction. Wants "poetry that strives to express genuine observation in unique language; poems no longer than 20 lines each." *Art Times* is 20-26 pages, newsprint, with reproductions of artwork, some photos; advertisement-supported. Receives 300-500 poems/month, accepts about 40-50/year. Circulation is 27,000, of which 5,000 are subscriptions; most distribution is free through galleries, theatres, etc., in the Northeast Corridor of the US. Subscription: $15/year. Sample: $1 with 9×12 SAE and 3 first-class stamps.

How to Submit Submit 4-5 typed poems at a time, up to 20 lines each. "All topics; all forms." Include SASE with all submissions. No e-mail submissions. Has an 18-month backlog. Guidelines available for SASE. Responds in 6 months. Pays 6 contributor's copies plus one-year subscription.

⚏ $☑ ARTFUL DODGE

Dept. of English, College of Wooster, Wooster OH 44691. E-mail: dbourne@wooster.edu. Website: www.wooster.edu/artfuldodge/. Established 1979. **Poetry Editor:** Philip Brady.

Magazine Needs *Artful Dodge* is an annual literary magazine that "takes a strong interest in poets who are continually testing what they can get away with successfully in regard to subject, perspective, language, etc., but who also show mastery of current American poetic techniques—its varied textures and its achievement in the illumination of the particular. What all this boils down to is that we require high craftsmanship as well as a vision that goes beyond one's own storm windows, grandmothers, or sexual fantasies—to paraphrase Hayden Carruth. Poems can be on any subject, of any length, from any perspective, in any voice, but we don't want anything that does not connect with both the human and the aesthetic. Thus, we don't want cute, rococo surrealism, someone's warmed-up, left-over notion of an avant-garde that existed 10-100 years ago, or any last bastions of rhymed verse in the civilized world. On the other hand, we are interested in poems that utilize stylistic persuasions both old and new to good effect. We are not afraid of poems which try to deal with large social, political, historical, and even philosophical questions—especially if the poem emerges from one's own life experience and is not the result of armchair pontificating. We often offer encouragement to writers whose work we find promising, but *Artful Dodge* is more a journal for the already emerging writer than for the beginner looking for an easy place to publish. We also have a sustained commitment to translation, especially from Polish and other East European literatures, and we feel the interchange between the American and foreign works on our pages is of great interest to our readers. We also feature interviews with outstanding literary figures." Has published poetry by Gregory Orr, Julia Kasdorf, Denise Duhamel, Tess Gallagher, and William Heyen. *Artful Dodge* is digest-sized, perfect-bound, professionally printed, with glossy cover, art, and ads. There are about 60-80 pages of poetry in each issue. Receives at least 2,000 poems/year, accepts about 60. Press run is 1,000 for 100 subscribers of which 30 are libraries. Sample: $7 for current issue, $5 for others.

How to Submit "Simultaneous submissions are fine, if we are informed of acceptance elsewhere. Please limit submissions to 6 poems. Long poems may be of any length, but send only one at a time. We encourage translations, but we ask for original text and statement from translator that he/she has copyright clearance and permission of author." Responds in up to one year. Pays 2 contributor's copies, plus, currently, $5/page honorarium because of grants from the Ohio Arts Council. Send materials for review consideration; however, "there is no guarantee we can review them!"

$☑ ARTS & LETTERS JOURNAL OF CONTEMPORARY CULTURE

Campus Box 89, Georgia College & State University, Milledgeville GA 31061. (478)445-1289. E-mail: al@gcsu.edu. Website: http://al.gcsu.edu. Established 1999. **Editor:** Martin Lammon. **Poetry Editor:** Susan Atefat-Peckham.

- Work published in *Arts & Letters Journal* has received two Pushcart Prizes.

Magazine Needs *Arts & Letters Journal of Contemporary Culture* is a biannual journal devoted to contemporary arts and literature, featuring ongoing series such as The World Poets, Translation Series, and The Mentors Interview Series. Wants work that is of the highest literary and artistic quality. Does not want genre fiction, light verse. Has published poetry by Margaret Gibson, Marilyn Nelson, Stuart Lishan, R.T. Smith, Laurie Lamon, and Miller Williams. *Arts & Letters Journal of Contemporary Culture* is 180 pages, offset-printed, perfect-bound, with glossy cover with varied artwork, and internal b&w photographs and color prints; includes ads. Receives about 4,000 poems/year, accepts about .5%. Publishes about 10 poems/issue. Press run is 1,500 for 1,000 subscribers of which 12 are libraries. Single copy: $8 plus $1 postage for current issue; subscription: $15 for 2 issues (one year). Sample: $5 plus $1 postage for back issue. Make checks payable to Georgia College & State University.

How to Submit Submit 5 poems at a time. No previously published poems. "Simutaneous submissions are accepted if we are notified immediately of publication elsewhere." No fax, e-mail, or disk submissions. Cover letter is preferred. Include SASE. Reads submissions September 1 through April 1. Poems are circulated to an editorial board. "Poems are screened, discussed by group of readers, then if approved, submitted to Poetry Editor for final approval." Seldom comments on rejected poems. Guidelines available in magazine, for SASE, by e-mail, or on website. Responds in 2 weeks. Always sends prepublication galleys. Pays $10/published page, $50 minimum, plus 2 contributor's copies. Acquires one-time rights. Reviews books of poetry in 2,000 words, multi-book format. Query first to Martin Lammon.

Also Offers Annual Arts & Letters Prize for Poets ($1,000, publication, and visit to campus for awards program) and annual Arts & Letters Workshops (May of each year, one-week residential workshops in several genres, including poetry).

◨ ◲ ASCENT: ASPIRATIONS FOR ARTISTS MAGAZINE

1560 Arbutus Dr., Nanoose Bay BC V9P 9C8 Canada. (250)468-7313. E-mail: ascentaspirations@sha w.ca. Website: www.bcsupernet.com/users/ascent. Established 1997. **Editor:** David Fraser.

Magazine Needs *Ascent: Aspirations for Artists Magazine* appears quarterly and is "a quality electronic publication specializing in poetry, short fiction, essays, and visual art. *Ascent* is dedicated to encouraging aspiring poets and fiction writers. We accept all forms of poetry on any theme. Poetry needs to be unique and to touch the reader emotionally with relevant human, social, and philosophical imagery." Does not want poetry "that focuses on mainstream overtly religious verse." Has published poetry by Janet Buck and Taylor Graham. *Ascent* is 40 pages, published online with photographs and paintings. Receives about 200 poems/year, accepts about 20%. Publishes about 10 poems/issue.

How to Submit Submit 1-5 poems at a time. Accepts previously published poems and simultaneous submissions. Accepts e-mail submissions (prefers electronic submissions within the body of the e-mail or as attachment in Word); no disk submissions. Reads submissions all year on a quarterly basis. Time between acceptance and publication is 3 months. Editor makes decisions on all poems. Seldom comments on rejected poems. Occasionally publishes theme issues. List of upcoming themes available on website. Responds in 3 months. Acquires one-time rights.

Advice "Write with passion for your material. In terms of editing, always proofread to the point where what you submit is the best it possibly can be. Never be discouraged if your work is not accepted; it may be just not the right fit for the current publication."

◲ ASHEVILLE POETRY REVIEW

P.O. Box 7086, Asheville NC 28802. (828)649-0217. E-mail: editor@ashevillereview.com. Website: www.ashevillereview.com. Established 1994. **Founder/Managing Editor:** Keith Flynn.

Magazine Needs *Asheville Poetry Review* appears "every 200 days. We publish the best regional, national, and international poems we can find. We publish translations, interviews, essays, historical perspectives, and book reviews as well." Wants "quality work with well-crafted ideas married to a dynamic style. Any subject matter is fit to be considered so long as the language is vivid with a clear sense of rhythm." Has published poetry by Robert Bly, Yevgeny Yevtushenko, Eavan Boland, and Fred Chappell. *Asheville Poetry Review* is 160-180 pages, digest-sized, perfect-bound, laminated, with full-color cover, b&w art inside. Receives about 3,500 poems/year, accepts about 5-10%. Press run is 1,000. Subscription: $22.50/2 years, $43.50/4 years. Sample: $13. "We prefer poets purchase a sample copy prior to submitting."

How to Submit Submit 3-5 poems at a time. Accepts simultaneous submissions; no previously published poems. No submissions by e-mail. Cover letter required. Include comprehensive bio, recent publishing credits, and SASE. Submission deadlines: January 15 and July 15. Time between acceptance and publication is up to one year. Poems are circulated to an editorial board. Seldom comments on rejected poems. Occasionally publishes theme issues. Guidelines and upcoming themes available for SASE. Responds in up to 7 months. Pays one contributor's copy. Rights revert back to author upon publication. Reviews books and chapbooks of poetry. Send materials for review consideration.

◲ ATLANTA REVIEW; ATLANTA REVIEW POETRY 2005

P.O. Box 8248, Atlanta GA 31106. E-mail: dan@atlantareview.com. Website: www.atlantareview.c om. Established 1994. **Editor:** Dan Veach.

● Work published in this review has been included in the *Pushcart Prize* anthologies.

Magazine Needs *Atlanta Review* is a semiannual primarily devoted to poetry, but also features fiction, interviews, essays, and fine art. Wants "quality poetry of genuine human appeal." Has published poetry by Seamus Heaney, Billy Collins, Derek Walcott, Maxine Kumin, and Thomas Lux. *Atlanta Review* is 128 pages, digest-sized, professionally printed on acid-free paper, flat-spined, with glossy color cover and b&w artwork. Receives about 10,000 poems/year, accepts about 1%. Press run is 2,500 for 1,000 subscribers of which 50 are libraries, 1,000 shelf sales. Single copy: $6; subscription: $10. Sample: $5.

How to Submit No previously published poems. No e-mail submissions unless outside North America. Issue deadlines are June 1 and December 1. Time between acceptance and publication is 6 months. Seldom comments on rejected poems. Guidelines available for SASE. Responds in 2 weeks. Pays 2 contributor's copies plus author's discounts. Acquires first North American serial rights.

Contest/Award Offerings *Atlanta Review* also sponsors POETRY 2005, an annual international poetry competition. Prizes: $1,000; 5 $100 awards; 20 International Publication Awards; 30 International Merit Awards. Winners announced in leading literary publications. All entries considered for publication in *Atlanta Review*. **Entry fee:** $5 for the first poem, $3 for each additional. No entry form or guidelines necessary. **Postmark deadline:** May 13, 2005.

Advice "Subscribers for 2005 will receive a 320-page 10th anniversary anthology at no extra cost."

$☑ THE ATLANTIC MONTHLY

Dept. PM, 77 North Washington St., Boston MA 02114. Website: www.theatlantic.com. Established 1857. **Poetry Editor:** Peter Davison. **Assistant Poetry Editor:** David Barber.

Magazine Needs *The Atlantic Monthly* publishes some of the most distinguished poetry in American literature, including work by Maxine Kumin, Stanley Plumly, Rodney Jones, Linda Gregerson, Philip Levine, Ellen Bryant Voigt, and W.S. Merwin. Has a circulation of 500,000, of which 5,800 are libraries. Receives some 60,000 poems/year, accepts about 30-35, has an "accepted" backlog of under one year. Sample: $4.95.

How to Submit Submit 3-5 poems with SASE. No simultaneous submissions. No fax or e-mail submissions. Responds in 3 weeks. Always sends prepublication galleys. Pays about $4/line. Acquires first North American serial rights only.

Advice Wants "to see poetry of the highest order; we do *not* want to see workshop rejects. Watch out for workshop uniformity. Beware of the present tense. Be yourself."

☑ THE AUROREAN: A POETIC QUARTERLY; THE UNROREAN; ENCIRCLE PUBLICATIONS

P.O. Box 219, Sagamore Beach MA 02562. (508)833-0805. E-mail: Cafpoet37@aol.com (cannot review submissions or reply to mss by e-mail). Press established 1992; magazine established 1995. **Editor:** Cynthia Brackett-Vincent.

Magazine Needs *The Aurorean* has been published continuously every March, June, September, and December since December 1995. Wants poetry "that is inspirational (not overly religious), meditational, or reflective of the Northeast. Seasonal focus. Need short (up to 6 lines) poems, haiku, and well-done humor. We use mostly free verse, only occasional rhyme. We welcome the beginner and the well published. No ranting, swearing for shock value alone. Nothing hateful." Will publish poetry by children "if it works." Has published poetry by Harris Gardner, Benita Glickman, John P. Kristofco, and Susan Landon. *The Aurorean* is digest-sized, professionally printed, perfect-bound, and seasonally designed each issue. Publishes 36 pages of poetry (one of haiku), and 5 pages of contributors' bios. Press run is 550. Single copy: $6 US, $7 international; subscription: $21 US, $25 international (for 4 issues). Make checks payable to *The Aurorean*.

How to Submit Line length for poetry is 40 maximum. Accepts previously published and simultaneous submissions if notified at time of submission ("if they are simultaneous, be aware that none can be withdrawn once we have gone to press"). Cover letter is required. "Fold cover letter separately and fold poems together. Poems folded individually are a nightmare for editors, and we are unable to review them. Include SASE with sufficient postage for return/reply. All manuscripts are acknowledged with a postcard or by e-mail upon receipt. Notice of acceptance and proofs are always sent; poets will be asked to return a 50-word bio upon acceptance. (We cannot edit a long bio and will not use information from a cover letter for a bio.) Poets may specifically send a 50-word bio with their submission if they choose." Pay 3 contributor's copies/accepted poem.

Contest/Award Offerings A) Features a "Poet-of-the-Quarter" (a body of work that best captures the season of that issue); awards publication of up to 3 poems with a 100-word bio, 10 copies of magazine, and a one-year subscription. B) "Also, in each issue, an independent judge picks 'Best Poem'; winner receives $20. C) Anyone may send entries for 'Poetic-Quote-of-the-Season.' Send 4 lines maximum from a not-too-obscure poet. Source MUST be cited to verify quote, which cannot be acknowledged or returned. Winner receives 2 free issues. D) Editor recommends one chapbook per issue (small blurb and ordering information; we do not publish reviews). For chapbook to be considered, it must be published within the last 6 months. Cannot be acknowledged or returned."

Also Offers *The Unrorean*, a broadsheet, appears twice/year, publishing poems too long, experimental, or dark for the magazine. "Still, nothing hateful." Broadsheet is 11×17, laser-printed, 2-4 pages. Sample: $2 postpaid. Include SASE for return/reply. No proofs, acknowledgements, or bios; open submission dates. Pays one contributor's copy/poem. "Poets may submit for the magazine or broadsheet individually. Work sent to the magazine now will also be considered for the broadsheet, unless otherwise requested in cover letter."

Advice "Be familiar with your markets. Keep writing. Try to support the markets that support poets. *Poet's Market* is your best friend."

$⬛ AUSABLE PRESS

1026 Hurricane Rd., Keene NY 12942-9719. E-mail: editor@ausablepress.com. Website: www.ausablepress.com. Established 1999. **Editor:** Chase Twichell. Member: CLMP.

Book/Chapbook Needs & How to Submit Ausable Press wants poetry "that investigates and expresses human consciousness in language that goes where prose cannot." Interested in work by new poets. Does not want children's poetry or poetry for children, light verse, inspirational poetry, illustrated poetry, or journal entries. Has published poetry by William Matthews, C.K. Williams, Steve Orlen, Julianne Buchsbaum, Khaled Mattawa, Patrick Donnelly, Karen Whalley, Eric Pankey, Adrian Blevins, and James Richardson. Publishes 4-6 paperback or hardback titles/year. Number of pages varies, offset-printed, paper and cloth editions. Guidelines available for SASE or on website. Accepts unsolicited mss in June only. **Charges reading fee of $20.** Responds to queries in one week; to mss in up to 4 months. Pays royalties of 10%, advance of $1,000, and 20 author's copies (out of a press run of 1,000).

Advice "This is not a contest. Ausable Press is under no obligation to publish any of the manuscripts submitted. Response time can be as long as 3-4 months, so please be patient."

◎ AVOCET, A JOURNAL OF NATURE POEMS (Specialized: nature, spirituality)

P.O. Box 8041, Calabasas CA 91372-8041. Website: www.csun.edu/~pjs44945/avocet.html. First issue published fall 1997. **Editor:** Patricia Swenson.

Magazine Needs *Avocet* is a quarterly poetry journal "devoted to poets seeking to understand the beauty of nature and its interconnectedness with humanity." Wants "poetry that shows man's interconnectedness with nature; discovering the Divine in nature." Does not want "poems that have rhyme or metrical schemes, cliché, abstraction, or sexual overtones." Has published poetry by Donna J. Waidtlow, Fred Boltz, Joan Goodwin, Peter Leverich, Sharron Kollmeyer, and Judy Snow. *Avocet* is 30 pages, 4¼×5½, professionally printed, saddle-stapled, with card cover and some illustrations. Single copy: $5; subscription: $20. Make checks payable to Patricia Swenson.

How to Submit Submit up to 5 poems at a time. Accepts previously published poems if acknowledged; no simultaneous submissions. Cover letter and SASE required. Time between acceptance and publication is up to 6 months. Responds in up to 3 months. Pays one contributor's copy.

◎ THE AWAKENINGS REVIEW (Specialized: people living with mental illness)

University of Chicago, Center for Psychiatric Rehabilitation, 7230 Arbor Dr., Tinley Park IL 60477. (708)614-4770. Fax: (708)614-4780. E-mail: rklundin@uchicago.edu. Website: www.ucpsychrehab .org. Established 1999. **Editor:** Robert Lundin.

Magazine Needs *The Awakenings Review* appears biannually to publish works by people living with mental illness: consumers, survivors, family members, ex-patients. Wants "meaningful work, good use of the language. Need not be about mental illness." Has published poetry Joan Rizzo, Wanda Washko, Ben Beyerlein, and Trish Evers. *The Awakenings Review* is 150 pages, digest-sized, perfect-bound, b&w, glossy cover, with some art/graphics. Receives about 800 poems/year, accepts about 20%. Publishes about 80 poems/issue. Press run is 1,000 for 100 subscribers of which 2 are libraries, 600 shelf sales; 300 are distributed free to contributors, friends. Single copy $15; subscription: $30. Sample: $10. Make checks payable to *Awakenings Review*.

How to Submit Submit 5 poems at a time. No previously published poems or simultaneous submissions. Does not accept e-mail submissions. Cover letter is preferred. Include SASE and short bio. Submit seasonal poems 6 months in advance. Time between acceptance and publication is 8 months. Poems are read by a board of editors. Often comments on rejected poems. Poet "must live with mental illness: consumer, survivor, family member, ex-patient." Occasionally publishes theme issues. Guidelines available in magazine, for SASE, or by e-mail. Responds in one month. Always sends prepublication galleys. Pays 4 contributor's copies. Acquires first rights. Send materials for review consideration.

Advice "Include a cover letter with your publishing experience. We value knowing your relationship to mental illness: consumer, survivor, family member, friend, professional."

◪ AXE FACTORY REVIEW; CYNIC PRESS

P.O. Box 40691, Philadelphia PA 19107. E-mail: cynicpress@yahoo.com. *Axe Factory* established 1986. Cynic Press established 1996. **Editor/Publisher:** Joseph Farley.

Magazine Needs *Axe Factory* is published 1-4 times/year to "spread the disease known as literature. The content is mostly poetry and essays. We now use short stories, too." Wants "eclectic work. Will look at anything but suggest potential contributors purchase a copy of the magazine first to see what we're like. No greeting card verse. If children wish to submit poetry, parents should read the magazine to see if they want their children in it, as much material is adult in nature." Has published *River Architecture: poems from here & there* by Louis McKee, and poetry by Taylor Graham, A.D. Winans, Normal, and John Sweet. *Axe Factory* is 20-40 pages, magazine-sized, saddle-stapled, neatly printed with light card cover. Press run is 200. Single copy: $9 (current issue); subscription: $24 for 4 issues. Sample: $8 (back issue). Make checks payable to Cynic Press or Joseph Farley.

How to Submit Submit up to 10 poems. Accepts previously published poems "sometimes, but let me know up front" and simultaneous submissions. Cover letter preferred, "but not a form letter, tell me about yourself." Often comments on rejected poems. Pays 1-2 contributor's copies. " 'Featured poet' receives more." Reserves right to anthologize poems under Cynic Press; all other rights returned. Several anthologies planned; upcoming themes available for SASE, by e-mail, and in publication. Reviews books of poetry in 10-1,000 words. Send materials for review consideration.

Book/Chapbook Needs & How to Submit Cynic Press occasionally publishes chapbooks. Published *Yellow Flower Girl* by Xu Juan, *Under the Dogwoods* by Joseph Banford, *Ceiling of Mirrors* by Shane Allison, and *13 Ways of Looking at Godzilla* by Michael Hafer. **Reading fee:** $20. No guarantee of publication. All checks to Cynic Press. Contest information available by e-mail.

Advice "Writing is a form of mental illness, spread by books, teachers, and the desire to communicate."

⊠ ☑ THE BALTIMORE REVIEW

P.O. Box 36418, Towson MD 21286. E-mail: susan@susanmuaddidarraj.com. Website: www.baltimorereview.org. Established 1996. **Editor:** Susan Muaddi Darraj. Founding Editor: Barbara Diehl.

Magazine Needs *The Baltimore Review*, "an eclectic collection of writing from Baltimore and beyond," appears twice/year (winter and summer) and showcases creative nonfiction, short fiction, and poetry. "We invite submissions from writers in the Baltimore region, as well as nationally and internationally." No restrictions on length or form, but they do not want to see "sentimental-mushy, loud, or very abstract poetry; corny humor; poorly crafted or preachy poetry." *The Baltimore Review* is 128 pages, 6×9, offset-lithograph-printed, perfect-bound, with 10 pt. CS1 cover, includes front and back cover photos. Publishes 20-30 poems/issue. Subscription: $15/year, $26/2 years. Sample: $10.95 (includes $2 p&h). Make checks payable to *The Baltimore Review*.

How to Submit Submit 1-4 poems at a time. No previously published poems. Accepts simultaneous submissions, "but notify us immediately if your work is accepted elsewhere." No fax or e-mail submissions. Cover letter is preferred. SASE required for response. Reads submissions year round. Time between acceptance and publication is up to 6 months. "Poems are circulated to at least 2 reviewers." Sometimes comments on rejected poems. Guidelines available on website. Responds in up to 4 months. Pays 2 contributor's copies, reduced rate for additional copies.

Contest/Award Offerings Sponsors an annual poetry contest: 1st Prize: $300 plus publication in *The Baltimore Review*; 2nd Prize: $150; 3rd Prize: $50. "Submit 1-4 poems, no more than 5 pages total. All forms and styles accepted, including prose poems." **Entry fee:** $12 (includes copy of issue in which 1st Prize winner is published) or $20 (includes one-year subscription). See website for complete details.

⊠ ☑ BANYAN REVIEW

P.O. Box 921, Smithville TX 78957. (512)626-0159. E-mail: editor@banyanreview.com. Website: www.banyanreview.com. Established 2003. **Editor:** Shelley Renee-Ruiz.

Magazine Needs *Banyan Review* is a biannual online journal publishing poetry, fiction, nonfiction, and book reviews. Wants "literary fiction, well-crafted poetry, and nonfiction." Does not want "poetry that has been published elsewhere." Has published poetry by Leo Love, T.K. Kenyon, Karen Harryman, Birute Serota, Margot McCall, and Radames Ortiz. Receives about 300 poems/year. Publishes about 20 poems/issue.

How to Submit Submit 3-5 poems at a time. Accepts simultaneous submissions; no previously published poems. Accepts e-mail submissions (pasted into body of message); no disk submissions. Reads submissions year round. Submit seasonal poems 2 months in advance. Time between acceptance and publication is 2-3 months. "Submissions are reviewed by the editor and, occasionally, a guest editor." Seldom comments on rejected poems. Occasionally publishes theme issues. List of upcoming themes and guidelines available on website. Responds in up to 3 months. Sometimes sends prepublication galleys. No payment. Acquires first rights. Reviews books and chapbooks of poetry and other magazines/journals in 200-500 words. Send materials for review consideration to Shelley Renee-Ruiz.

Advice "Please read the journal before submitting work."

⊠ ◻ BARBARIC YAWP; BONEWORLD PUBLISHING

3700 County Rt. 24, Russell NY 13684. (315)347-2609. Established 1996. **Editors:** John and Nancy Berbrich.

Magazine Needs *Barbaric Yawp* appears quarterly, "publishing the best fiction, poetry, and essays available"; encourages beginning writers. "We are not preachers of any particular poetic or literary

Publishers of Poetry

school. We publish any type of quality material appropriate for our intelligent and wide-awake audience; all types considered, blank, free, found, concrete, traditional rhymed and metered forms. We do not want any pornography, gratuitous violence, or any whining, pissing, or moaning." Has published poetry by Errol Miller, Mark Spitzer, and Jeff Grimshaw. *Barbaric Yawp* is a 60-page booklet, stapled with 67 lb. cover, line drawings. Receives 1,000 poems/year, accepts about 5%. Press run is 120 for 40 subscribers of which 4 are libraries. Single copy: $4; subscription: $15/year (4 issues). Sample: $3. Make checks payable to John Berbrich.

How to Submit Submit up to 5 poems at a time, no more than 50 lines each, and include SASE. All types considered. Accepts previously published poems and simultaneous submissions. Accepts submissions by postal mail only. One-page cover letter preferred; include a short publication history (if available) and a brief bio. No deadlines; reads year round. Time between acceptance and publication is up to 6 months. Often comments on rejected poems. Guidelines available for SASE. Responds in up to 2 months. Pays one contributor's copy. Acquires one-time rights.

Advice "Don't get discouraged. Read much, write much, submit much. Get used to rejection. Get tough. Believe in yourself and others as well."

☑ BARDSONG, THE JOURNAL FOR CELEBRATING THE CELTIC SPIRIT; "CELTIC VOICE" WRITING CONTEST (Specialized: Celtic-themed)

P.O. Box 775396, Steamboat Springs CO 80477-5396. Fax: (970)879-2657. E-mail: agilpin@bardson gpress.com. Website: www.bardsongpress.com. Established 1997. **Editor:** Ann Gilpin. Member: SPAN, PMA, CIPA.

Magazine Needs *Bardsong* is a Celtic-themed literary magazine appearing semi-annually. "Our quest is to encourage and celebrate Celtic heritage and culture through poetry, short stories, essays, creative nonfiction, reviews, interviews, and artwork. We are looking for work that reflects the ageless culture, history, symbolism, mythology, and spirituality that belongs to Celtic heritage. Any style or format is welcome. If it is not Celtic themed, don't submit it." *Bardsong* is laser-printed, saddle-stitched. Sample: $6.50. Make checks payable to Bardsong Press.

How to Submit Submit up to 3 poems at a time (2 pages/poem maximum). Accepts simultaneous submissions ("notify us if the piece is published elsewhere before acceptance with us"). Accepts e-mail submissions (at submissions@bardsongpress.com); no fax submissions. Cover letter preferred. Include brief bio and publication credits. No book-length poetry collections. Guidelines available for SASE or on website. Responds in 4 months. Pays 2 contributor's copies/contribution.

Contest/Award Offerings Annual "Celtic Voice" Writing Contest. **Entry fee:** $10. Small cash award and copies of magazine in which poem is published. Guidelines available for SASE, by e-mail, or on website. **Deadline:** September 30.

Advice "Please follow the publisher's guidelines; professionalism counts."

$☑ BARNWOOD PRESS; BARNWOOD

P.O. Box 146, Selma IN 47383. (765)288-0149. Fax: (765)285-3765. E-mail: tkoontz@bsu.edu. Website: www.barnwoodpress.org. Established 1975. **Editor:** Tom Koontz.

Magazine Needs *Barnwood* appears online "to serve poets and readers by publishing excellent poems." Does not want "expressions of prejudice such as racism, sexism." Has published poetry by Bly, Goedicke, Friman, and Stafford. Receives about 1,500 poems/year, accepts about 2%.

How to Submit Submit 1-3 poems at a time. Accepts simultaneous submissions; no previously published poems. Accepts submissions by postal mail only. "SASE or no response." Reads submissions September 1 through May 31 only. Time between acceptance and publication is one day. Seldom comments on rejected poems. Responds in one month. Pays $25/poem. Acquires one-time rights.

Book/Chapbook Needs & How to Submit Barnwood Press publishes one paperback and one chapbook of poetry/year. Has recently published *Blessing* by Daviv Watts and *Whatever You Can Carry* by Stephen Herz. Chapbooks are usually 12-32 pages, offset-printed, saddle-stapled, with paper cover and cover art; size varies. Query first with a few sample poems and cover letter with brief bio and publication credits. Responds to queries and mss in one month. Payment varies. Order sample books or chapbooks from website.

Advice "Emphasize imagination, passion, engagement, artistry."

BARROW STREET; BARROW STREET PRESS

P.O. Box 1831, New York NY 10156. E-mail: info@barrowstreet.org. Website: www.barrowstreet.org. Established 1998. **Editors:** Patricia Carlin, Peter Covino, Lois Hirshkowitz, Melissa Hotchkiss.

- Poetry published in *Barrow Street* has been selected for inclusion in *The Best American Poetry 2001*, *2002*, and *2003*.

Magazine Needs "*Barrow Street*, a poetry journal appearing twice yearly, is dedicated to publishing new and established poets." Wants "poetry of the highest quality; open to all styles and forms." Has published poetry by Kim Addonizio, Lyn Hejinian, Brian Henry, Jane Hirshfield, Phillis Levin, and Molly Peacock. *Barrow Street* is 96-120 pages, digest-sized, professionally printed and perfect-bound with glossy cardstock cover with color or b&w photography. Receives about 3,000 poems/year, accepts about 3%. Press run is 1,000. Subscription: $15/year, $28/2 years, $42/3 years. Sample: $8.

How to Submit Submit up to 5 poems at a time. Accepts simultaneous submissions (when notified); no previously published poems. Cover letter with brief bio preferred. Reads submissions year round. Poems are circulated to an editorial board. Seldom comments on rejected poems. Publishes theme issues occasionally. Guidelines available for SASE or on website. Responds in up to 6 months. Always sends prepublication galleys. Pays 2 contributor's copies. Acquires first rights.

Contest/Award Offerings Barrow Street Press was established in 2002. Recently published *Selah* by Joshua Corey. Submit ms to Barrow Street Press Book Contest. Publication of ms in book form and $1,000 awarded to "best previously unpublished manuscript of poetry in English." Manuscript should be single-spaced on white $8\frac{1}{2} \times 11$ paper. Photocopies acceptable. Include 2 title pages and an acknowledgments page listing any poems previously published in journals or anthologies. Author's name, address, and daytime phone number should appear on first title page only. Include SASE for notification. **Entry fee:** $25. Make checks payable to Barrow Street. Deadline in 2004 was June 30. See website for current guidelines.

Advice "Submit your strongest work."

BATHTUB GIN; PATHWISE PRESS

P.O. Box 2392, Bloomington IN 47402. E-mail: charter@bluemarble.net. Website: http://home.bluemarble.net/~charter/btgin.htm. Established 1997. **Editor:** Christopher Harter.

Magazine Needs *Bathtub Gin*, a biannual appearing in April and October, is "an eclectic aesthetic . . . we want to keep you guessing what is on the next page." Wants poetry that "takes a chance with language or paints a vivid picture with its imagery . . . has the kick of bathtub gin, which can be experimental or a sonnet. No trite rhymes . . . Bukowski wannabes (let the man rest) . . . confessionals (nobody cares about your family but you)." Has published poetry by Kell Robertson, Mark Terrill, Carmen Germain, and Lindsay Wilson. *Bathtub Gin* is about 60 pages, digest-sized, laser-printed, saddle stapled, with 80 lb. coverstock cover, includes photography, collages, line drawings. "We feature a 'News' section where people can list their books, presses, events, etc." Receives about 1,200 poems/year, accepts about 5%. Press run is 250 for 50 subscribers, 60 shelf sales; 10 distributed free to reviewers, other editors, and libraries. Subscription: $8. Sample: $5; foreign orders add $2; back issues: $3.50. Make checks payable to Christopher Harter.

How to Submit Submit 4-6 poems at a time. Include SASE. Accepts previously published poems and simultaneous submissions. Accepts submissions by postal mail and by e-mail (pasted into body of message). "Three- to five-line bio required if you are accepted for publication . . . if none [provided], we make one up." Cover letter required. Reads submissions June 1 through September 15 only, but accepts contributions for 2 issues. Time between acceptance and publication is up to 8 months. Often comments on rejected poems. Guidelines available in magazine, for SASE, by e-mail, or on website. Responds in up to 2 months. Pays one contributor's copy. "We also sell extra copies to contributors at a discount, which they can give away or sell at full price."

Book/Chapbook Needs & How to Submit Pathwise Press's goal is to publish chapbooks, broadsides, and "whatever else tickles us." Has published *Bone White and Raven Black* by John Gohmann, *You Write Your Life Like Fiction* by Gordon Annand, *The United Colors of Death* by Mark Terrill, and *Living Room, Earth* by Carmen Germain. For publishing guidelines, send SASE or visit website.

Advice "Submission etiquette goes a long way. Always include a cover letter. I receive too many submissions with no cover letter to explain what the poems are for (*Bathtub Gin* or a chapbook or what?). Make sure the poems are neat and without typos; if you don't care about your submission, why should I?"

✅ BAY AREA POETS COALITION (BAPC); POETALK
P.O. Box 11435, Berkeley CA 94712-2435. E-mail: poetalk@aol.com. Established 1974. **Editor:** Maggie Morley. **Associate Editor:** John Rowe.

Magazine Needs *Poetalk*, the quarterly poetry journal of the BAPC, publishes about 65 poets in each issue. "BAPC has 150 members, 30 subscribers, but *Poetalk* is open to all. No particular genre. Rhyme must be well done." Has published poetry by John McKernan, Taylor Graham, Barry Ballard, Carol Hamilton, Simon Perchik, and Michael Casey. *Poetalk* is 36 pages, digest-sized, photocopied, saddle-stapled, with heavy card cover. Circulation is 300 + for members, subscribers, and contributors. Subscription: $8/year. Sample: SASE with 83¢ postage. Also publishes an annual anthhology (26th edition: 120 pages, out in Summer 2005), giving one page to each member of BAPC (minimum 6 months). BAPC Membership: $15/year, includes subscription to *Poetalk*, copy of anthology, and other privileges; extra outside US.

How to Submit Submit up to 4 poems at a time, no more than twice/year. Short poems (under 35 lines) are preferred; longer poems of outstanding quality accepted. Cover letter and SASE required. "Manuscripts should be clearly typed, single-spaced, and include author's name and mailing address on every page. Include e-mail address if you have one." Accepts previously published poems and simultaneous submissions, but must be noted. Responds in up to 4 months. Pays one contributor's copy. All rights revert to authors upon publication.

Contest/Award Offerings Sponsors yearly contest. Guidelines available in early September for SASE or by e-mail.

Also Offers BAPC holds monthly readings (in Berkeley, CA).

Advice "If you don't want suggested revisions, you need to say so clearly in your cover letter or indicate on each poem submitted."

✅ ◎ BAY WINDOWS (Specialized: gay/lesbian)
631 Tremont St., Boston MA 02118. E-mail: rKikel@baywindows.com. Website: http://BayWindows.com. Established 1983. **Poetry Editor:** Rudy Kikel.

Magazine Needs *Bay Windows* is a weekly gay and lesbian newspaper published for the New England community, regularly using "short poems of interest to lesbians and gay men. Poetry that is 'experiential' seems to have a good chance with us, but we don't want poetry that just 'tells it like it is.' Our readership doesn't read poetry all the time. A primary consideration is giving pleasure. We'll overlook the poem's (and the poet's) tendency not to be informed by the latest poetic theory, if it does this: pleases. Pleases, in particular, by articulating common gay or lesbian experience, and by doing that with some attention to form. I've found that a lot of our choices were made because of a strong image strand. Humor is always welcome—and hard to provide with craft.

Obliquity, obscurity? Probably not for us. We won't presume on our audience.'' Has published poetry by Judson Evans, Wyn Davison, Hugh Coyle, Kathleen Jacobsen, Maggie Morley, and Dennis Rhodes. ''We will be trying to run 8 poems each month.'' Receives about 300 submissions/year, accepts about 10%, has a 3-month backlog. Press run is 24,000 for a circulation of 60,000. Single copy: 50¢; subscription: $40. Sample: $3.

How to Submit Submit 3-5 poems at a time, ''up to 30 lines are ideal; include short biographical blurb and SASE. No submissions via e-mail, but poets may request info via e-mail.'' Editor ''often'' comments on rejected poems. Responds in up to 6 months. Pays one contributor's copy ''unless you ask for more.'' Acquires first rights. Reviews books of poetry in about 750 words—''Both single and omnibus reviews (the latter are longer).''

◨ ◎ BEAR CREEK HAIKU (Specialized: haiku/senryu; poems under 11 lines)

P.O. Box 3787, Boulder CO 80307. Established 1991. **Editor:** Ayaz Daryl Nielsen.

Magazine Needs *Bear Creek Haiku* appears irregularly in an extra-small format, publishing poems of 11 lines or less. Wants especially haiku/senryu plus poetry of any form and style no longer than 11 lines. Has published poetry by Pat Waters, Jeff Havens, Don Wentworth, Laurel Starkey, Kelly Jean White, and Ed Markowski. *Bear Creek Haiku* is 12 pages, photocopied on legal-sized colored paper that is cut in thirds, stacked 3-high, folded in the middle, and stapled (finished size is $2\frac{1}{2} \times 7$ inches). Includes sumi ink artwork by Laurel A. Starkey. Receives about 1,000 poems/year, accepts about 15%. Publishes about 11-15 poems/issue. Press run is 50-70, distributed free to poets, a homeless person who occasionally sells copies at a traffic interchange for spare coins, plus 2 subscribers. Single copy: free for SASE; subscription: $5/year. Make checks payable to Daryl Nielsen.

How to Submit Submit 5-20 poems at a time. Line length for poetry is 1 minimum, 11 maximum. Accepts previously published poems and simultaneous submissions. No fax, e-mail, or disk submissions. ''Name and address on each page, with several haiku on each page. Keep your mailing expenses to 2 first-class stamps, one of which is on the SASE.'' Reads submissions year round. Submit seasonal poems anytime. Time between acceptance and publication varies, averages 2 months. ''If a poem is remotely close, we'll ask poet about revision—and then publish the original and revised poem together. Appreciate poetic interaction, albeit usually brief.'' Often comments on rejected poems. Responds in one month. Pays 2 contributor's copies. Acquires first rights.

Also Offers ''Continuing yearly, we will publish an anthology including all poets published the prior year, with one copy going to each poet the first quarter of following year. Will contact potential victims about chapbooks.''

Advice ''We appreciate receiving your own personal favorites, be they simultaneously submitted or published elsewhere or never before seen. Write, create your poems—the heart, spirit, shadow, ancestors, an occasional editor, etc. will benefit deeply.''

$◎ THE BEAR DELUXE (Specialized: nature/ecology)

P.O. Box 10342, Portland OR 97296-0342. (503)242-1047. E-mail: bear@orlo.org. Website: www.orl o.org. Established 1993. **Editor:** Tom Webb. **Contact:** Poetry Editor.

- Note: *The Bear Deluxe* is published by Orlo, a nonprofit organization exploring environmental issues through the creative arts.

Magazine Needs *The Bear Deluxe* is a semiannual that ''provides a fresh voice amid often strident and polarized environmental discourse. Street-level, non-dogmatic, and solution-oriented, *The Bear Deluxe* presents lively creative discussion to a diverse readership.'' Wants poetry with ''innovative environmental perspectives, not much longer than 50 lines. No rants.'' Has published poetry by Judith Barrington, Robert Michael Pyle, Mary Winters, Stephen Babcock, Carl Hanni, and Derek Sheffield. *Bear Deluxe* is 60 pages, 11×14, newsprint with brown Kraft paper cover, saddle-stapled, with lots of original graphics and b&w photos. Receives about 1,200 poems/year, accepts about 20-30. Press run is 20,000 for 750 subscribers of which 20 are libraries, 18,000 distributed free on the streets of the Western US and beyond. Subscription: $16. Sample: $3. Make checks payable to Orlo.

How to Submit Submit 3-5 poems at a time, up to 50 lines each. Accepts previously published poems and simultaneous submissions, "so long as noted." Accepts e-mail submissions, "in body of message. We can't respond to e-mail submissions but do look at them." Poems are reviewed by a committee of 7-9 people. Publishes one theme issue/year. List of upcoming themes and guidelines available for SASE. Responds in 6 months. Pays $10/poem, 5 contributor's copies (more if willing to distribute), and subscription. Acquires first or one-time rights.

$ ⃞ ◎ BEAR STAR PRESS; DOROTHY BRUNSMAN POETRY PRIZE (Specialized: regional)

185 Hollow Oak Dr., Cohasset CA 95973. (530)891-0360. E-mail: bspencer@bearstarpress.com. Website: www.bearstarpress.com Established 1996. **Publisher/Editor:** Beth Spencer.

Book/Chapbook Needs Bear Star Press accepts work by poets from Western and Pacific states ("Those in West of Central time zone"). "Bear Star is committed to publishing the best poetry it can attract. Each year it sponsors a contest open to poets from Western and Pacific states, although other eligibility requirements change depending on the composition of our list up to that point. From time to time we add to our list other poets from our target area whose work we admire." Wants "well-crafted poems. No restrictions as to form, subject matter, style, or purpose." Has published *Poems in Which* by Joseph Di Prisco, *The Archival Birds* by Melissa Kwaswy, *The Bandsaw Riots* by Arlitia Jones, *Closet Drama* by Kandie St. Germain, and *The Book of Common Betrayals* by Lynne Knight. Publishes 1-2 paperbacks/year and occasionally chapbooks. Books are usually 35-75 pages, professionally printed, and perfect-bound; size varies. Chapbooks are usually $7; full-length collections, $12.

How to Submit "Poets should enter our annual book competition. Other books are occasionally solicited by publisher, sometimes from among contestants who didn't win." Accepts previously published poems and simultaneous submissions. "Prefer single-spaced manuscripts in plain font such as Times New Roman. SASE required for results. Manuscripts not returned but are recycled." Generally reads submissions September through November. Guidelines available for SASE or on website. **Contest entry fee:** $16. Time between acceptance and publication is up to 9 months. Poems are circulated to an editorial board. "I occasionally hire a judge. More recently I have taken on the judging with help from poets whose taste I trust." Seldom comments on rejected poems. Responds to queries regarding competitions in 1-2 weeks. Contest winner notified February 1 or before. Contest pays $1,000 and 25 author's copies (out of a press run of up to 750).

Advice "Send your best work, consider its arrangement. A 'Wow' poem early on keeps me reading."

⃞N ⃞ BECOMING: THE UNDERGROUND JOURNAL

P.O. Box 201468, San Antonio TX 78220. E-mail: BecomingJournal@yahoo.com. Website: www.BecomingJournal.org. Established 2003. **Editor:** Nicole Provencher.

Magazine Needs *Becoming: The Underground Journal* appears 2 times/year (winter & summer) and features poetry, short fiction, photos, visual art, and reviews. Wants poetry "that is not found in the more mainstream and commercial markets; not limited to specific style or genre, as long as the words, images, thoughts, and concepts contained are well crafted. As the title denotes, this magazine will serve as an alternative to the mainstream art, that while readily available, barely skims the top of the true potential of the art community." Has published poetry by Duane Locke, Simon Perchik, David Krump, Michael Ladd, Stephen Mead, and Christopher Barnes. *Becoming* is 32 pages, digest-sized, professionally-printed, side-stapled, with cardstock cover with artwork, includes all types of visual art plus ads (if sponsored). Receives about 1,000 poems/year, accepts about 16%. Publishes about 20 poems/issue. Press run is 500 for 20 subscribers of which 3 are libraries, 150 shelf sales; 100 are distributed free to publishers and galleries. Single copy: $6.50;

subscription: $13/year (2 issues). Sample: $5. Make checks payable to Nicole Provencher.

How to Submit Submit 5-7 poems at a time. Line length for poetry is one page maximum (no minimum). Accepts simultaneous submissions when noted; no previously published poems. Accepts e-mail submissions (pasted into body of message); no disk submissions. Cover letter is required. "Cover letter should accompany submissions regardless of submission method, and should include name, address, telephone number, and e-mail, as well as short bio, resume, or artist statement. Include contact information in top right-hand corner of each page when submitting via U.S. mail; attachments sent via e-mail should include submitter's name and title of work as the title of the attachment." Submission deadlines are March 15 and September 15; if deadline has passed, submissions will be held for next issue. Submit seasonal poems 2 months in advance. Time between acceptance and publication is up to 6 months. "Poems are selected and discussed by editor and selection of guest co-editors. All final decisions are made by editor." Often comments on rejected poems ("when merited, when poem is close to selection, or if requested"). Those who wish to submit work are strongly encouraged to visit website or view sample issue. "Purchase for submission is not required, although support is greatly appreciated." Occasionally publishes theme issues. List of upcoming themes available on website. Guidelines available in magazine, for SASE, by e-mail, or on website. Responds in up to 4 months. Sometimes sends prepublication galleys. Pays one contributor's copy; additional copies available to contributors at discount. Acquires one-time rights; also retains right to publish work on website, and for educational and advertising purposes. Reviews books of poetry and other magazines/journals in 200 words. "For review requests for book, art, or spoken word recordings, please address materials to *Becoming Journal*, Attn: Review Editor. A cover letter with resume or artist statement must be included with all review requests. For additional submission information, please query: BecomingJournal@yahoo.com."

Also Offers Online supplement at www.BecomingJournal.org.

Advice "In order to improve both the poet and the poetry, you must read both moderns and classics as well as bad and good verse. Learn from your own biases and preferences for style, and never be afraid to improve your art from the compliments and criticism you receive. Editing and strengthening your poetry through these elements will help with more than publication, as it will improve the message your poetry reveals. Speaking this message is the true aim of any superior poet."

☐ ◎ BELHUE PRESS (Specialized: gay)

2501 Palisade Ave., Suite A1, Riverdale, Bronx NY 10463. E-mail: belhuepress@earthlink.net. Website: www.perrybrass.com. Established 1990. **Editor:** Tom Laine.

Book/Chapbook Needs A small press specializing in gay male poetry, publishing 3 paperbacks/year—no chapbooks. "We are especially interested in books that get out of the stock poetry market." Wants "hard-edged, well-crafted, fun and often sexy poetry. No mushy, self pitying, confessional, boring, indulgent, teary, or unrequited love poems—yuck! Poets must be willing to promote book through readings, mailers, etc." "We have a $10 sample and guideline fee. Please send this before submitting any poetry. We have had to initiate this due to a deluge of bad, amateur, irrelevant submissions. After fee, we will give constructive criticism when necessary."

How to Submit Query first with 6 pages of poetry and cover letter. Accepts previously published poems and simultaneous submissions. Time between acceptance and publication is one year. Often comments on rejected poems. Will request criticism fees "if necessary." Responds "fast" to queries and submitted mss. No payment information provided.

Advice "The only things we find offensive are stupid, dashed off, 'fortune cookie' poems that show no depth or awareness of poetry. We like poetry that, like good journalism, tells a story."

◪ BELLINGHAM REVIEW; THE 49TH PARALLEL POETRY AWARD

M.S. 9053, Western Washington University, Bellingham WA 98225. E-mail: bhreview@cc.wwu.edu. Website: www.wwu.edu/~bhreview/. Established 1975. **Editor:** Brenda Miller. **Contact:** Poetry Editor.

Magazine Needs *Bellingham Review* appears twice/year. "We want well-crafted poetry but are open to all styles," no specifics as to form. Has published poetry by David Shields, Tess Gallagher, Gary Soto, Jane Hirshfield, Albert Goldbarth, R.T. Smith, and Rebecca McClanahan. *Bellingham Review* has 30-40 pages of poetry, is digest-sized, perfect-bound, with art and matte cover. Circulation is 1,500. Subscription: $14/year, $27/2 years, $41/3 years. Sample: $7. Make checks payable to The Western Foundation/*Bellingham Review*.

How to Submit Submit 1-3 poems at a time with SASE. Accepts simultaneous submissions with notification. No fax or e-mail submissions. General submissions must be postmarked October 1 through February 15 only. Guidelines available for SASE or on website. Responds in 2 months. Pays one contributor's copy, a year's subscription, plus monetary payment (if funding allows). Acquires first North American serial rights.

Contest/Award Offerings The 49th Parallel Poetry Award offers $1,000 annually for 1st Prize, plus publication in and a year's subscription to the *Bellingham Review*. Runners-up and finalists may be considered for publication. Submissions must be unpublished and not accepted for publication elsewhere; work under consideration elsewhere must be withdrawn from the competition if accepted for publication. Submit up to 3 poems. "Poems within a series will each be treated as a separate entry." For each entry, include a 3×5 index card stating the title of the work, the category (poetry), the author's name, phone number, address, and e-mail. "Make sure writing is legible on this card. Author's name must not appear anywhere on the manuscript." Include SASE for announcement of winners. Manuscripts will not be returned. No fax or e-mail submissions. Guidelines available for SASE or on website. **Entry fee:** $15 for first entry (up to 3 poems); $10 each additional poem. Make checks payable to The Western Foundation/*Bellingham Review*. "Everyone entering the competition will receive a complimentary 2-issue subscription to the *Bellingham Review*." **Postmark deadline:** between December 1 and March 15. 2003 winner was Simone Muench for "Window." 2003 contest judge was Robert Wrigley. Winners will be announced in summer.

◨ BELLOWING ARK; BELLOWING ARK PRESS

P.O. Box 55564, Shoreline WA 98155. (206)440-0791. E-mail: bellowingark@bellowingark.org. Website: www.bellowingark.org. Established 1984. **Editor:** Robert R. Ward.

Magazine Needs *Bellowing Ark* is a bimonthly literary tabloid that "publishes only poetry which demonstrates in some way the proposition that existence has meaning or, to put it another way, that life is worth living. We have no strictures as to length, form, or style; only that the work we publish is, to our judgment, life-affirming." Does not want "academic poetry, in any of its manifold forms." Has published poetry by James Hobbs, Len Blanchard, Paula Milligan, Esther Cameron, Margaret Hodge, and Jacqueline Hill. *Bellowing Ark* is 32 pages, tabloid-sized, printed on electro-bright stock with b&w photos and line drawings. Circulation is 1,000, of which 275 are subscriptions and 500 are sold on newsstands. Subscription: $18/year. Sample: $4.

How to Submit Submit 3-6 poems at a time. "Absolutely *no* simultaneous submissions." Accepts submissions by postal mail and on disk only. Guidelines available for SASE or on website. Responds to submissions in up to 3 months and publishes within the next 2 issues. Occasionally will criticize a ms if it seems to "display potential to become the kind of work we want." Sometimes sends prepublication galleys. Pays 2 contributor's copies. Reviews books of poetry. Send materials for review consideration.

Book/Chapbook Needs & How to Submit Bellowing Ark Press publishes collections of poetry by *invitation only*.

◨ ◎ BELL'S LETTERS POET (Specialized: subscribers)

P.O. Box 2187, Gulfport MS 39505-2187. E-mail: jimbelpoet@aol.com. Established 1956. **Publisher/Editor:** Jim Bell.

Magazine Needs *Bell's Letters Poet* is a quarterly which you must buy ($5.50/issue, $22 subscription) to be included. "Many say they stop everything the day it arrives," and judging by the many letters from readers, that seems to be the case. Though there is no payment for poetry accepted, many patrons send cash awards to the poets whose work they especially like. Poems are "four to 20 lines in good taste." Wants "clean writing; no vulgarity, no artsy vulgarity." Has published poetry by Dawn Zapletal, Virginia Ditomas, Dolores Malaschak, and Patrick Flavin. *Bell's Letters Poet* is about 60 pages, digest-sized, photocopied on plain bond paper (including cover), and saddle-stapled. Sample: $5. "Send a poem (20 lines or under, in good taste) with your sample order and we will publish in our next issue."

How to Submit Submit 4 poems at a time. No simultaneous submissions. Accepts previously published poems "if cleared by author with prior publisher." Accepts submissions by postal mail only. Accepted poems by subscribers are published immediately in the next issue. Guidelines available in magazine or for SASE. Deadline for poetry submissions is 2 months prior to publication. Reviews books of poetry by subscribers. "The Ratings" is a competition in each issue. Readers are asked to vote on their favorite poems, and the "Top 40" are announced in the next issue, along with awards sent to the poets by patrons. *Bell's Letters Poet* also features a telephone and e-mail exchange among poets, a birth-date listing, and a profile of its poets.

Advice "Tired of seeing no bylines this year? Subscription guarantees a byline in each issue."

◪ BELOIT POETRY JOURNAL; CHAD WALSH POETRY PRIZE

P.O. Box 151, Farmington ME 04938. (207)778-0020. E-mail: sharkey@maine.edu (for information only). Website: www.bpj.org. Established 1950. **Editors:** John Rosenwald and Lee Sharkey.

● Poetry published in the *Beloit Poetry Journal* has been included in *The Best American Poetry* and *Pushcart Prize* anthologies.

Magazine Needs *Beloit Poetry Journal* is a well-known, long-standing quarterly of quality poetry and reviews. "For over years of continuous publication, we have been distinguished for the extraordinary range of our poetry and our discovery of strong new poets. We publish the best poems we receive, without bias as to length, school, subject, or form. To diversify our offerings, we occassionally publish chapbooks, most recently *Poets Under Twenty-Five*. These are almost never the work of a single poet." Wants "visions broader than the merely personal; fresh music; language that makes us laugh and weep, recoil, resist—and pay attention. We tend to prefer poems that make the reader share an experience rather than just read about it; these we keep for up to 4 months, circulating them among our readers, and continuing to winnow. At the quarterly meetings of the Editorial Board, we read aloud all the surviving poems and put together an issue of the best we have." Has published poetry by Lucille Clifton, Bei Dao, Albert Goldbarth, Patricia Goedicke, Janet Holmes, Glori Simmons, and Peter Streckfus. *Beloit Poetry Journal* is about 48 pages, digest-sized, saddle-stapled, and attractively printed with tasteful art on the card cover. Circulation is 1,250 for 725 subscribers of which 225 are libraries. Subscription: individuals $18/year, institutions $23/year. Sample (including guidelines): $5. Guidelines without sample available for SASE.

How to Submit Submit any time, without query, any legible form; no bios necessary. No previously published poems or simultaneous submissions. "Any length of manuscript, but most poets send what will go in a business envelope for one stamp. Don't send your life's work." No e-mail submissions. Pays 3 contributor's copies. Acquires first serial rights. Editor for Reviews and Excanges reviews books by and about poets in an average of 500 words, usually single book format. Send materials for review consideration to Marion Stocking, 24 Berry Cove Rd., Lamoine ME 04605.

Contest/Award Offerings The journal awards the Chad Walsh Poetry Prize ($3,000 in 2003) to a poem or group of poems published in the calendar year. "Every poem published in 2005 will be considered for the 2005 prize."

Advice "We are always watching for fresh insights, live forms, and language."

$⊘ ◎ BIBLE ADVOCATE (Specialized: religious, Christian)

P.O. Box 33677, Denver CO 80233. E-mail: bibleadvocate@cog7.org. Website: www.cog7.org/BA. Established 1863. **Associate Editor:** Sherri Langton.

Magazine Needs *Bible Advocate*, published 10 times/year, features "Christian content—to advocate the Bible and represent the church." Wants "free verse, some traditional; 5-20 lines, with Christian/ Bible themes." Does not want "avant garde poetry." *Bible Advocate* is 24 pages, magazine-sized with most poetry set up with 4-color art. Receives about 30-50 poems/year, accepts about 10-20. Press run varies for 13,500 subscribers with all distributed free.

How to Submit Submit no more than 5 poems at a time, 5-20 lines each. Accepts previously published poems (with notification) and simultaneous submissions. Accepts e-mail submissions with text included in body of message; no attachments. "No fax or handwritten submissions, please." Cover letter preferred. Time between acceptance and publication is up to one year. "I read them first and reject those that won't work for us. I send good ones to editor for approval." Seldom comments on rejected poems. Publishes theme issues. Guidelines and upcoming themes available for SASE and on website. Responds in 2 months. Pays $20 and 2 contributor's copies. Acquires first, reprint, electronic, and one-time rights.

Advice "Avoid trite or forced rhyming. Be aware of the magazine's doctrinal views (send for doctrinal beliefs booklet)."

◎ ⊘ BIBLIOPHILOS (Specialized: bilingual/foreign language, ethnic/nationality, nature/ecology, social issues)

200 Security Building, Fairmont WV 26554. Established 1981. **Editor:** Gerald J. Bobango; for CA, OR, WA submissions, send to Susanne Olson, P.O. Box 39843, Griffith Station, Los Angeles CA 90039.

Magazine Needs "*Bibliophilos* is an academic journal, for the literati, illuminati, amantes artium, and those who love animals; scholastically oriented, for the liberal arts. Topics include fiction and nonfiction, literature and criticism, history, art, music, theology, philosophy, natural history, educational theory, contemporary issues and politics, sociology, and economics. Published in English, French, German, and Romanian." Wants "traditional forms, formalism, structure, rhyme; also blank verse. Aim for concrete visual imagery, either in words or on the page. No inspirational verse, or anything that Ann Landers or Erma Bombeck would publish." Accepts poetry written by children, ages 10 and up. Has published poetry by Raymond HV Gallucci, Cornelia Snider Yarrington, Francine L. Trevens, Daniel Green, and Patricia Fain Hutson. *Bibliophilos* is 72 pages, digest-sized, laser photography printed and saddle-stapled with light card cover, includes clip art, ads. Receives about 200 poems/year, accepts about 30%. Press run is 300 for 200 subscribers. Subscription: $18/year, $35/2 years. Sample: $5.25. Make checks payable to *The Bibliophile*. West Virginia residents please add 6% sales tax.

How to Submit Closed to unsolicited submissions. Query first with SASE and $5.25 for sample and guidelines. Then, if invited, submit 3-5 poems at a time. Accepts previously published poems and simultaneous submissions. Cover letter with brief bio preferred. Time between acceptance and publication is up to one year. Often comments on rejected poems. Guidelines available for SASE. Responds in 2 weeks. Pays 2 contributor's copies. Acquires first North American serial rights. Staff reviews books and chapbooks of poetry in 750-1,000 words, single book format. Send materials for review consideration.

Contest/Award Offerings Sponsors poetry contest. 1st Prize: $25 plus publication. Send SASE for rules.

Advice "Do not send impressionistic, 'Why did he/she leave me, I can't live without him/her' poems about 'relationships,' which have no meaning beyond the author's psyche. Send poetry lamenting the loss of millions of acres of farmland to miserable Wal-Marts, or the lives lost by industrial rape and pollution."

$ ▣ ◎ BIRCH BROOK PRESS (Specialized: anthologies, nature, sports/recreation, translations, popular culture)

P.O. Box 81, Delhi NY 13753. (212)353-3326 (messages only). E-mail: birchbrkpr@catskill.net (no submissions). Website: www.birchbrookpress.info. Established 1982. **Contact:** Poetry Editor. Member: American Academy of Poets, Small Press Center, American Typefounders Fellowship.

Book/Chapbook Needs Birch Brook "is a letterpress book printer/typesetter/designer that uses monies from these activities to publish several titles of its own each year with cultural and literary interest." Specializes in literary work, flyfishing, baseball, outdoors, anthologies, translations of classics, books about books. Has published *The Moonlit Door* by Frank Fagan, *Shadwell Hills* by Rebecca Lilly, *Contemporary Martyrdom* by John Popielaski, *Longing for Laura* by A.M. Juster, *Beowulf* by Bertha Rogers, and *Walking the Perimeters of the Plate Glass Window Factory* by Jared Smith. Publishes 4 paperbacks and/or hardbacks per year. The press specializes "mostly in anthologies with specific subject matter." Books are "handset letterpress editions printed in our own shop."

How to Submit Query first with sample poems or send entire ms. No e-mail submissions. Accepts submissions by postal mail *only*. "Must include SASE with submissions." Occasionally comments on rejected poems. Authors may obtain sample books by sending SASE for free catalog. Guidelines also available for SASE. Pays from $5-25 for publication in anthology.

Advice "Send your best work, and see other Birch Brook Press books."

✪ ▣ ◎ BIRMINGHAM POETRY REVIEW (Specialized: translations)

English Dept., HB205, 1530 Third Ave. S., University of Alabama at Birmingham, Birmingham AL 35294. (205)934-4250. Website: www.uab.edu/english/bpr. Established 1988. **Co-Editors:** Robert Collins and Adam Vines.

Magazine Needs *Birmingham Poetry Review* appears twice/year in July and January, publishing poetry of "any style, form, length, or subject. We are biased toward exploring the cutting edge of contemporary poetry. Style is secondary to the energy, the fire the poem possesses. We don't want poetry with cliché-bound, worn-out language." Has published poetry by Andrew Glaze, Charles Harper Webb, Allison Joseph, Richard Hague, and Walt McDonald. *Birmingham Poetry Review* is 50 pages, digest-sized, offset-printed, with b&w cover. Press run is 700 for 300 subscribers. Subscription: $5/year. Sample: $2.50.

How to Submit Submit 3-5 poems, "no more. No cover letters. We are impressed by good writing; we are unimpressed by publication credits." SASE required. No simultaneous or multiple submissions; previously published poems only if they are translations. Editor sometimes comments on rejected poems. Guidelines available for SASE. Responds in 6 months. Pays 2 contributor's copies and one-year subscription.

Contest/Award Offerings *Birmingham Poetry Review* Dean's Award: $500 annually for the best poem or group of poems published in *Birmingham Poetry Review*. No reading fees or special submission requirements. All poems submitted to *Birmingham Poetry Review* and accepted for publication are eligible.

Advice "Advice to beginners: Read as much good contemporary poetry, national and international, as you can get your hands on. Then be persistent in finding your own voice."

▣ THE BITTER OLEANDER; FRANCES LOCKE MEMORIAL AWARD

4983 Tall Oaks Dr., Fayetteville NY 13066-9776. (315)637-3047. Fax: (315)637-5056. E-mail: bones4 4@ix.netcom.com. Website: www.bitteroleander.com. Established 1974. **Editor/Publisher:** Paul B. Roth.

● Poetry published in *The Bitter Oleander* has been included in *The Best American Poetry*.

Magazine Needs *The Bitter Oleander* appears biannually in April and October, publishing "imaginative poetry; poetry in translation; serious language." Wants "highly imaginative poetry whose language is serious. We prefer short poems of no more than 30 lines. Highly interested in translations. Has published poetry by Christine Boyka Kluge, Robert Bly, Alan Britt, Duane Locke, Silvia Scheibli, Anthony Seidman, and Charles Wright. *The Bitter Oleander* is 128 pages, digest-sized, offset-printed, perfect-bound with glossy 4-color cover, cover art, ads. Receives about 10,000 poems/year, accepts about 1%. Press run is 1,500; 1,000 shelf sales. Single copy: $8; subscription: $15. Make checks payable to Bitter Oleander Press.

How to Submit Submit up to 5 poems at a time with name and address on each page. No previously published poems or simultaneous submissions. No e-mail submissions unless outside US. Cover letter preferred. Does not read mss during July. Time between acceptance and publication is 6 months. Guidelines available for SASE or on website. "All poems are read by the editor only, and all decisions are made by this editor." Often comments on rejected poems. Responds within one month. Pays one contributor's copy.

Contest/Award Offerings Sponsors the Frances Locke Memorial Award, awarding $1,000 and publication. Submit any number of poems. **Entry fee:** $10/5 poems, $2 each additional poem. **Postmark deadline:** March 15 through June 15.

Advice "We simply want poetry that is imaginative and serious in its performance of language. So much flat-line poetry is written today that anyone reading one magazine or another cannot tell the difference."

⬛ ◨ BLACK TIE PRESS

P.O. Box 570084, Houston TX 77257-0084. E-mail: petergravis@earthlink.net. Website: http://home.earthlink.net/~blacktiepress/. Established 1986. **Publisher and Editor:** Peter Gravis.

Book/Chapbook Needs "Black Tie Press is committed to publishing innovative, distinctive, and engaging writing. We publish books; we are not a magazine or literary journal. We are not like the major Eastern presses, university presses, or other small presses in poetic disposition. To get a feel for our publishing attitude, we urge you to buy one or more of our publications before submitting. Prefer the exotic, the surreal, the sensual—work that provokes, shocks . . . work that continues to resonate long after being read. Surprise us." Does not want "rhyme or fixed forms, unless remarkably well done. No nature, animal, religious, or pet themes." Has published poetry by Steve Wilson, Guy Beining, Laura Ryder, Donald Rawley, Harry Burrus, and Jenny Kelly. Sample: $8.

How to Submit "We have work we want to publish; hence, unsolicited material is not encouraged. However, we will read and consider material from committed, serious writers as time permits. Query with 4 sample poems. Again, unsolicited material is not encouraged. No reply without SASE." Cover letter with bio preferred. Responds in 6 weeks. Always sends prepublication galleys. Author receives percent of press run.

Advice "Too many writers are only interested in getting published and not interested in reading or supporting good writing. Black Tie hesitates to endorse a writer who does not, in turn, promote and patronize (by actual purchases) small press publications. Once Black Tie publishes a writer, we intend to remain with that artist."

$◨ BLACK WARRIOR REVIEW

P.O. Box 862936, Tuscaloosa AL 35486-0027. (205)348-4518. E-mail: bwr@ua.edu. Website: http://webdelsol.com/bwr. Established 1974. **Editor:** Dan Kaplan. **Poetry Editor:** Braden Phillips-Welborn.

• Poetry published in *Black Warrior Review* has been included in volumes of *The Best American Poetry* and *Pushcart Prize* anthologies.

Magazine Needs *Black Warrior Review* is a biannual review appearing in March and October. Has published poetry by W.S. Merwin, Anne Carson, Mark Doty, Jane Miller, Medbh McGuckian, C.D. Wright, and Tomaz Salamun. *Black Warrior Review* is 180 pages, digest-sized. Press run is 2,000.

Subscription: $14/year, $25/2 years, $30/3 years. Sample: $8. Make checks payable to the University of Alabama.

How to Submit Submit 3-6 poems at a time. Accepts simultaneous submissions if noted. No electronic submissions. Responds in up to 5 months. Pays up to $50 and one-year subscription. Acquires first rights. Reviews books of poetry in single or multi-book format. Send materials for review consideration.

Advice "Subscribe or purchase a sample copy to see what we're after. For 30 years, we've published new voices alongside Pulitzer Prize winners. Freshness and attention to craft, rather than credits, impress us most."

THE BLIND MAN'S RAINBOW; THE BLIND PRESS BI-ANNUAL POETRY CONTEST; THE BLIND PRESS

P.O. Box 18219, Denver CO 80218-0219. Fax: (303)830-7366. E-mail: editor@bmrpoetry.com. Website: www.bmrpoetry.com. Established 1993. **Editor:** Melody Sherosky. **Assistant Editor:** Nate Condron.

Magazine Needs *The Blind Man's Rainbow* is a quarterly publication "whose focus is to create a diverse collection of quality poetry and art." Wants "all forms of poetry (Beat, rhyme, free verse, haiku, etc.), though excessively long poems are less likely to be accepted. All subject matter accepted." *The Blind Man's Rainbow* is 24-30 pages, magazine-sized, photocopied and side-stapled, paper cover with art, line drawings inside. Receives about 500 submissions/month. Subscription: $14 US, $18 foreign. Sample: $4 US, $5 foreign. Make checks payable to The Blind Man's Rainbow or Melody Sherosky.

How to Submit Submit 2-10 poems at a time with name and address on each poem. Include SASE. Accepts previously published poems and simultaneous submissions, "but it is nice to let us know." Accepts submissions on disk and by post only; no e-mail. Cover letter preferred. "Submissions returned only if requested and with adequate postage." Time between acceptance and publication is up to one year. Often comments on rejected poems. Guidelines available for SASE, by e-mail, or on website. Responds in up to 6 months. Pays one contributor's copy. Acquires one-time rights.

Contest/Award Offerings The Blind Press Bi-annual Poetry Contest. Attention: Melody Sherosky, Editor. **Deadlines:** May 15 and November 15. **Entry fee:** $4 for first poem, $2 each additional poem. No more than 10 poems/person. There is no line limit. "Poetry must follow our regular poetry guidelines. Submissions must be accompanied by a short bio. Contest submissions will not be returned. Three cash prizes will be awarded as a percentage payout of the entry fees received. Winners will be announced in the magazine and on website. Winning poems and poet bios will be featured in the issue following the contest deadline (July and January, respectively). Winning poets will be notified before publication of the issue featuring their poems. We accept inquiries by mail, fax, or e-mail."

Also Offers Additional services offered include designing and distributing advertising and promotional materials for artists and writers. "We design, produce, and distribute chapbooks, postcards, bookmarks, and flyers. Interested parties should contact us with project ideas for a price quote."

BLUE LIGHT PRESS; THE BLUE LIGHT POETRY PRIZE AND CHAPBOOK CONTEST

P.O. Box 642, Fairfield IA 52556. (641)472-7882. E-mail: bluelightpress@aol.com. Established 1988. **Chief Editor:** Diane Frank.

Book/Chapbook Needs Publishes 2 paperbacks, 3 chapbooks/year. "We like poems that are imagistic, emotionally honest, and uplifting, where the writer pushes through the imagery to a deeper level of insight and understanding. No rhymed poetry." Has published poetry by Xue Di, Laurie Kuntz, Viktor Tichy, Tom Centolella, Michaelangelo Tata, Christopher Buckley, and Diane Averill. Xue Di's *Forgive* is 32 pages, digest-sized, professionally printed with Chinese calligraphy and elegant matte card cover. Cost is $8 plus $2 p&h. Also published 3 anthologies of visionary poets.

How to Submit Does not accept e-mail submissions. Guidelines available for SASE or by e-mail. Has an editorial board. "We work in person with local poets, have an ongoing poetry workshop, give classes, and will edit/critique poems by mail—$30 for 4 poems. We also have an online poetry workshop. Send an e-mail for guidelines."

Contest/Award Offerings Sponsors the Blue Light Poetry Prize and Chapbook Contest. "The winner will be published by Blue Light Press, receive a $100 honorarium and 50 copies of his or her book, which can be sold for $8 each, for a total of $500." Submit ms of 10-24 pages, typed or printed with a laser or inkjet printer. Include SASE. No ms will be returned without a SASE. **Entry fee:** $10. Make checks payable to Blue Light Press. Send SASE for more information.

Advice "Read some of the books we publish, especially one of the anthologies. We like to publish poets with a unique and expanded vision and gorgeous or unusual language. Stay in the poem longer and see what emerges in your vision and language."

◢ BLUE MESA REVIEW

Dept. of English, Humanities Bldg. #217, University of New Mexico, Albuquerque NM 87131-1106. (505)277-6155. Fax: (505)277-5573. E-mail: bluemesa@unm.edu. Website: www.unm.edu/~blue mesa. Established 1989 by Rudolfo Anaya. **Editor:** Julie Shigekuni. **Poetry Editor:** Amy Beeder.

Magazine Needs *Blue Mesa Review* is an annual review of poetry, short fiction, creative essays, and book reviews. Wants "all kinds of free, organic verse; poems of place encouraged. Limits: 4 poems or 6 pages of poetry; one story; one essay. We accept theoretical essays as well as fiction, poetry, and nonfiction." Has published poetry by Virgil Suárez, David Axelrod, Paula Gunn Allen, and Brian Swann. *Blue Mesa Review* is about 250 pages, digest-sized, professionally printed and flat-spined with glossy cover, photos, and graphics. Receives about 1,000 poems/year, accepts about 10% or less. Press run is 1,000 for 600 shelf sales. Sample: $12.

How to Submit "Please submit 2 copies of everything with your name, address, and telephone number on each page. Fax numbers and e-mail addresses are also appreciated." No previously published poems or simultaneous submissions. No fax or e-mail submissions. Cover letter required. Accepts mss from July 1 through October 1 only. Poems are then passed among readers and voted on. Guidelines available on website. Responds to mss by mid-December to mid-January. Pays 2 contributor's copies.

◢ BLUE MONK POEMS & STORIES; BLUE MONK PRESS

P.O. Box 53103, New Orleans LA 70153-3103. (504)495-2102. E-mail: editors@bluemonkpress.com (inquiries) or submissions@bluemonkpress.com (submissions). Website: www.bluemonkpress.c om. Established 1999. **Editors:** Joseph Kees and Brian Kees.

Magazine Needs *Blue Monk Poems & Stories* is a biannual journal of poems, stories, and art. "We are open to any subject matter, style, or purpose. For the most part, we do not like rhyming poetry." Has published poetry by Christopher Cunningham, Hosho McCreesh, Errol Miller, Gordon Massman, T. Kilgore Splake, and Lyn Lifshin. *Blue Monk* is 100 pages, digest-sized (also appears online), typeset, flat-spined, with quality card stock cover with art, includes photos, paintings, mixed media reproductions, and 3 pages of ads. Receives about 1,000 poems/year, accepts about 10%. Publishes about 40 poems/issue. Press run is 1,000 for 50 subscribers of which 2 are libraries, 600 shelf sales; 200 are distributed free to artists/contributors/reviewers. Single copy: $5; subscription: $8.50. Sample: $4. Make checks payable to Blue Monk Press.

How to Submit Submit 3-6 poems at a time. Accepts simultaneous submissions; no previously published poems. Accepts e-mail and disk submissions. Include SASE and very short bio. "We don't care where you went to school." Reads submissions all year. Time between acceptance and publication is 6 months. Poems are circulated to an editorial board. Seldom comments on rejected poems. Guidelines available in magazine, for SASE, or on website. Responds in 2 months. Pays 2 contributor's copies. Acquires first North American serial rights and anthology rights. Reviews books and chapbooks of poetry and other magazines/journals in 500-1,000 words, single book format. Send materials for review consideration to Brian Kees/Joseph Kees at Blue Monk Press.

Book/Chapbook Needs & How to Submit Blue Monk Press publishes work "that is a collage of awful hangovers, parasitic louses, sleepless nights, empty beer cans, neurosis, and brutality." Publishes 2 stab-books/year. Stab-books are usually 50-70 pages, typeset, with Japanese stab-binding, quality card stock cover, and art/graphics. Responds to queries in 3 months; to mss in 6 months. Pays royalties of 15-20%. Order sample stab-books by sending $5 to Blue Monk Press.

☑ THE BLUE MOUSE; SWAN DUCKLING PRESS

P.O. Box 586, Cypress CA 90630. E-mail: swduckling@aol.com. Established 1998. **Editor:** Mark Bruce. **Poetry Editor:** René Diedrich.

Magazine Needs *The Blue Mouse* appears quarterly. Wants "poetry based on personal experience. Short poems in which common experience is related in an uncommon way." Does not want "abstract, philosophical musings, literary rehashes, Gramma's oven poetry, doggerel, cowboy poetry, smut, Bukowski imitators." Has published poetry by Katya Giritsky, Lyn Lyfshin, Michael Kramer, Rachel Rose, and B.Z. Niditch. *The Blue Mouse* is 32 pages, copied, stapled, with blue cover, no artwork. Receives about 200 poems/year, accepts about 40. Publishes about 15 poems/issue. Press run is 350 for 20 subscribers; 320 are distributed free to coffeehouses and poetry readings. Single copy: $1.50; subscription: $6. Make checks payable to Swan Duckling Press.

How to Submit Submit 4 poems at a time. Line length for poetry is 2 minimum, 35 maximum. No previously published poems or simultaneous submissions. Accepts e-mail submissions; no disk submissions. Cover letter is preferred. "Remember SASE. One poem per page, typed or typeset." Time between acceptance and publication is 6 months. "We only have 2 editors. If we like it, it goes in. Be prepared to edit." Often comments on rejected poems "if the poems are close but missing something." Guidelines available for SASE or by e-mail. Responds in 6 months. Pays 2 contributor's copies. "Poet keeps copyrights."

Contest/Award Offerings Swan Duckling Press publishes 4 chapbooks/year. Manuscripts are selected through annual competition. **Deadline:** Competition opens in July, ends October 31. **Entry fee:** $15, includes subscription to *Mouse* and copy of winning chapbook. Chapbook mss may include previously published poems. "Other than contest, chapbooks are published by invitation *only*."

Advice "Don't think we're related to that cartoon mouse down the road. Our mouse is gaining respect because we choose good, compelling poems. Don't send mediocre stuff."

☑ BLUE UNICORN, A TRIQUARTERLY OF POETRY; BLUE UNICORN POETRY CONTEST

22 Avon Rd., Kensington CA 94707. (510)526-8439. E-mail: staff@blueunicorn.org. Website: www. blueunicorn.org. Established 1977. **Poetry Editors:** Ruth G. Iodice, John Hart, and Fred Ostrander.

Magazine Needs *Blue Unicorn* appears in October, February, and June. Wants "well-crafted poetry of all kinds, in form or free verse, as well as expert translations on any subject matter. We shun the trite or inane, the soft-centered, the contrived poem. Shorter poems have more chance with us because of limited space." Has published poetry by James Applewhite, Kim Cushman, Patrick Worth Gray, Joan LaBombard, James Schevill, and Gail White. *Blue Unicorn* is "distinguished by its fastidious editing, both with regard to contents and format." *Blue Unicorn* is 56 pages, narrow digest-sized, finely-printed, saddle-stapled, with some art. Features 40-50 poems in each issue, all styles, with the focus on excellence and accessibility. Receives over 35,000 submissions/year, accepts about 200, has a one-year backlog. Single copy: $7, foreign add $3; subscription: $18/3 issues, foreign add $6.

How to Submit Submit 3-5 typed poems on $8\frac{1}{2} \times 11$ paper. No simultaneous submissions or previously published poems. No e-mail submissions. "Cover letter OK, but will not affect our selection." Guidelines available for SASE or on website. Responds in 3 months (generally within 6 weeks), sometimes with personal comment. Pays one contributor's copy.

Contest/Award Offerings Sponsors an annual contest with small entry fee, prizes of $150, $75, $50, and sometimes special awards; distinguished poets as judges; publication of 3 top poems and 6 honorable mentions in the magazine. **Entry fee:** $6 for first poem, $3 for others. Write for current guidelines. Criticism occasionally offered.

Advice "We would advise beginning poets to read and study poetry—both poets of the past and of the present; concentrate on technique; and discipline yourself by learning forms before trying to do without them. When your poem is crafted and ready for publication, study your markets and then send whatever of your work seems to be compatible with the magazine you are submitting to."

◎ BLUELINE (Specialized: regional)

Dept. PM, English Dept., Potsdam College, Potsdam NY 13676. Fax: (315)267-2043. E-mail: blueline @potsdam.edu. Established 1979. **Editor-in-Chief:** Rick Henry. Member: CLMP.

Magazine Needs Appearing in May, *Blueline* "is an annual literary magazine dedicated to prose and poetry about the Adirondacks and other regions similar in geography and spirit." Wants "clear, concrete poetry that goes beyond mere description. We prefer a realistic to a romantic view. We do not want to see sentimental or extremely experimental poetry." Usually uses poems of 75 lines or fewer, though "occasionally we publish longer poems" on "nature in general, Adirondack Mountains in particular. Form may vary, can be traditional or contemporary." Has published poetry by L.M. Rosenberg, John Unterecker, Lloyd Van Brunt, Laurence Josephs, Maurice Kenny, and Nancy L. Nielsen. *Blueline* is 200 pages, digest-sized, with 90 pages of poetry in each issue. Press run is 600. Sample copies: $7 for back issues.

How to Submit Submit 3 poems at a time. Include short bio. No simultaneous submissions. Submit September 1 through November 30 only. Poems are circulated to an editorial board. Occasionally comments on rejected poems. Guidelines available for SASE or by e-mail. Responds in up to 3 months. Pays one copy. Acquires first North American serial rights. Reviews books of poetry in 500-750 words, single or multi-book format.

Advice "We are interested in both beginning and established poets whose poems evoke universal themes in nature and show human interaction with the natural world. We look for thoughtful craftsmanship rather than stylistic trickery."

$◙ BOA EDITIONS, LTD.; A. POULIN, JR. POETRY PRIZE

260 East Ave., Rochester NY 14604. (585)546-3410. Website: www.boaeditions.org. Established 1976. **Poetry Editor:** Thom Ward.

Book/Chapbook Needs & How to Submit Has published some of the major American poets, such as W.D. Snodgrass, John Logan, Isabella Gardner, Richard Wilbur, and Lucille Clifton. Also publishes introductions by major poets of those less well-known. For example, Gerald Stern wrote the foreword for Li-Young Lee's *Rose*. Guidelines available for SASE or on website. Pays advance plus 10 author's copies.

Contest/Award Offerings A. Poulin, Jr. Poetry Prize for first-book mss. **Deadline:** August-December annually. Guidelines available on website in May.

◙ BOGG PUBLICATIONS; BOGG

422 N. Cleveland St., Arlington VA 22201-1424. Established 1968. **Poetry Editors:** John Elsberg (USA), Wilga Rose (Australia: 13 Urara Rd., Avalon Beach, NSW 2107 Australia), and Sheila Martindale (Canada: P.O. Box 23148, 380 Wellington St., London, Ontario NGA 5N9 Canada).

Magazine Needs Appearing twice/year, *Bogg* is "a journal of contemporary writing with an Anglo-American slant. Its contents combines innovative American work with a range of writing from England and the Commonwealth. It includes poetry (to include haiku and tanka, prose poems, and experimental/visual poems), very short experimental or satirical fiction, interviews, essays on the small press scenes both in America and in England /the Commonwealth, reviews, review essays, and line art. We also publish occasional free-for-postage pamphlets.'' The magazine uses a great deal of poetry in each issue (with several featured poets)—''poetry in all styles, with a healthy leavening of shorts (under 10 lines). Seeks original voices.'' Accepts all styles, all subject matter. ''Some have even found the magazine's sense of play offensive. Overt religious and political poems have to have strong poetical merits—statement alone is not sufficient.'' *Bogg* started in England and in 1975 began including a supplement of American work; it now is published in the US and mixes US, Canadian, Australian, and UK work with reviews of small press publications from all of those areas. Has published work by Hugh Fox, Ann Menebraker, John M. Bennett, Marcia Arrieta, Kathy Ernst, and Steve Sneyd. *Bogg* is 56 pages, typeset, saddle-stapled, in a digest-sized format ''that leaves enough white space to let each poem stand and breathe alone.'' There are about 45 pages of poetry/issue. Receives over 10,000 American poems/year, accepts about 100-150. Press run is 850 for 400 subscribers of which 20 are libraries. Single copy: $6; subscription: $15 for 3 issues. Sample: $4.

How to Submit Submit 6 poems at a time. No simultaneous submissions. No fax or e-mail submissions. Cover letters preferred. ''They can help us get a 'feel' for the writer's intentions/slant.'' SASE required or material discarded (''no exceptions.'') Prefers typewritten manuscripts, with author's name and address on each sheet. ''We will reprint previously published material, but with a credit line to a previous publisher.'' Guidelines available for SASE. Responds in one week. Pays 2 contributor's copies. Acquires one-time rights. Reviews books and chapbooks of poetry in 250 words, single book format. Send materials to relevant editor (by region) for review consideration.

Book/Chapbook Needs & How to Submit Their occasional pamphlets and chapbooks are by *invitation only*, the author receiving 25% of the print run. Obtain free chapbook samples by sending digest-sized SASE. ''At least 2 ounces worth of postage.''

Advice ''Become familiar with a magazine before submitting to it. Long lists of previous credits irritate me. Short notes about how the writer has heard about *Bogg* or what he or she finds interesting or annoying in the magazine I read with some interest.''

◪ BOMBAY GIN

Naropa University, 2130 Arapahoe Ave., Boulder CO 80302. (303)546-3540. Fax: (303)546-5297. E-mail: bgin@naropa.edu. Website: www.naropa.edu/gin.html. Established 1974. **Contact:** Samantha Wall.

Magazine Needs ''*Bombay Gin*, appearing in June, is the annual literary magazine of the Jack Kerouac School of Disembodied Poetics at Naropa University. Produced and edited by MFA students, *Bombay Gin* publishes established writers alongside those who have been previously unpublished. It has a special interest in works that push conventional literary boundaries. Submission of poetry, prose, visual art, translation, and works involving hybrid forms and cross-genre exploration are encouraged.'' Recent issues have included works by Lisa Jarnot, Anne Waldman, Wang Ping, Thalia Field, Anselm Hollo, and Alice Notley. *Bombay Gin* is 124 pages, digest-sized, professionally printed, perfect-bound with color card cover, includes art and photos. Receives about 300 poems/year, accepts about 5%. Press run is 500 for 400 shelf sales; 100 distributed free to contributors. Single copy: $12.

How to Submit ''Submit up to 3 pages of poetry (12 pt. Times New Roman). Translations are also accepted. Guidelines are the same as for original work. Translators are responsible for obtaining any necessary permissions. Art may be submitted as slides, negatives, or prints.'' No previously published poems or simultaneous submissions. Accepts disk submissions (PC format). Cover letter preferred. Reply with SASE only. **Deadline:** December 1. Submissions are read December 15 through March 15. Guidelines available for SASE or on website. Notification of acceptance/rejection: April 15. Pays 2 contributor's copies. Acquires one-time rights.

✍ ◎ BORDERLANDS: TEXAS POETRY REVIEW (Specialized: regional, bilingual); WRITERS' LEAGE OF TEXAS

P.O. Box 33096, Austin TX 78764. E-mail: borderlands_tpr@hotmail.com. Website: www.borderlands.org. Established 1992. **Contact:** Editor.

Magazine Needs *Borderlands* appears twice/year publishing "high-quality, outward-looking poetry by new and established poets, as well as brief reviews of poetry books and critical essays. Cosmopolitan in content, but particularly welcomes Texas and Southwest writers." Wants "outward-looking poems that exhibit social, political, geographical, historical, feminist, or spiritual awareness coupled with concise artistry. We also seek poems in two languages (one of which must be English), where the poet has written both versions. Please, no introspective work about the speaker's psyche, childhood, or intimate relationships." Has published poetry by Walter McDonald, Naomi Shihab Nye, Mario Susko, Wendy Barker, Larry D. Thomas, and Reza Shirazi. *Borderlands* is 100-150 pages, digest-sized, offset, perfect-bound, with 4-color cover, art by local artists. Receives about 2,000 poems/year, accepts about 120. Press run is 1,000. Subscription: $18/year, $34/2 years. Sample: $12.

How to Submit Submit 5 typed poems at a time. No previously published poems or simultaneous submissions. No e-mail submissions. Include SASE (or SAE and IRCs) with sufficient postage to return poems. Seldom comments on rejected poems. Guidelines available for SASE and on website. Responds in 6 months. Pays one copy. Acquires first rights. Reviews books of poetry in one page. Also uses 3- to 6-page essays on single poets and longer essays (3,500-word maximum) on contemporary poetry in some larger context (query first). Address poetry submissions to "Editors, *Borderlands*."

Also Offers The Writers' League of Texas is a state-wide group open to the general public. Established in 1981, the purpose of the Writers' League of Texas is "to provide a forum for information, support, and sharing among writers; to help members improve and market their skills; and to promote the interests of writers and the writing community." Currently has 1,600 members. Annual membership dues are $45. Send SASE for more information to: The Writers' League of Texas, 1501 W. 5th St., Suite E-2, Austin TX 78703.

▦ ✍ BORDERLINES; ANGLO-WELSH POETRY SOCIETY

Nant Y Brithyll, Llangynyw, Powys SY21 OJS United Kingdom. Established 1977. **Editor:** Kevin Bamford.

Magazine Needs *Borderlines* is published biannually in June and December to encourage reading and writing of poetry. "We try to be open-minded and look at anything. We do not normally publish very long poems. Most poems fit on one page. No poems about poems; unshaped recitals of thoughts and/or feelings." Has published poetry by Peter Abbs, Mike Jenkins, and Vuyelwa Carlin. *Borderlines* is 40-48 pages, digest-sized, neatly printed and saddle-stapled with light card cover, art on cover only. Receives about 600 poems/year, accepts about 16%. Press run is 200 for 100 subscribers of which 8 are libraries. Single copy: £2.50 UK, £3.50 other EU countries, £4.50 non-EU countries; subscription: £5 UK, £7 other EU countries, £9 non-EU countries (payment in sterling only). Make checks payable to Anglo-Welsh Poetry Society.

How to Submit Accepts submissions by postal mail only. Cover letter preferred. "Please write name and address on each poem sheet." Time between acceptance and publication is up to 6 months. Seldom comments on rejected poems. Guidelines available for SASE (or SAE and IRC). Responds in 6 weeks. Sometimes sends prepublication galleys. Pays one contributor's copy.

Also Offers "The Anglo-Welsh Poetry Society is a group of people interested in the reading, writing, and promotion of poetry, particularly in the Marches—the Anglo-Welsh border country. It is based in the border counties of Shropshire and Montgomeryshire, though there are members all over the country. A core group of members meets on the first Tuesday of the month at the Loggerheads pub in Shrewsbury. Other meetings such as readings, workshops, and poetry parties are arranged at intervals over the course of the year. A monthly newsletter gives information of interest to members on events, publications, competitions, and other news of the poetry world.'' Membership fee for AWPS is £10/year.

◙ BORN MAGAZINE

P.O. Box 1313, Portland OR 97207-1313. E-mail: editor@bornmagazine.org. Website: www.bornma gazine.org. Established 1996. **Editor:** Anmarie Trimble. **Contributing Editors:** Jennifer Grotz, Bruce Smith, Tenaya Darlington.

Magazine Needs *Born Magazine* appears quarterly as ''an experimental online revue that marries literary arts and interactive media. We publish 6-8 multimedia 'interpretations' of poetry and prose in each issue, created by interactive artists in collaboration with poets and writers.'' Wants poems suited to ''interpretation into a visual or interactive form. Due to the unusual, collaborative nature of our publication, we represent a variety of styles and forms of poetry.'' Has published poetry by Edward Hirsch, Michele Glazer, Crystal Williams, Major Jackson, Joyelle McSweeney, and Bruce Beasley. Publishes about 6-8 poems/online issue.

How to Submit Submit 2-5 poems at a time. Accepts previously published poems; no simultaneous submissions. Accepts e-mail submissions. ''Prefer electronic submissions as Word documents or .txt files. Also accept hard copies; electronic format on disk or via e-mail will be required upon acceptance.'' Reads submissions year round. Submit seasonal poems 4 months in advance. Time between acceptance and publication is 1-3 months. ''Poems must be accepted by the editor and one contributing editor. Selected works are forwarded to our art department, which chooses an artist partner to work with the writer. Artist and writer collaborate on a concept, to be realized by the artist.'' Never comments on rejected poems. Guidelines available on website. Responds in 3 weeks to e-mail queries. Always sends prepublication galleys. No pay. ''We can offer only the experience of participating in a collaborative community, as well as a broad audience. (We average 32,000 readers to our site per month.)'' Acquires one-time rights.

Advice ''We accept new and previously published work. *Born*'s mission is to nurture creativity and co-development of new literary art forms on the Web.''

$◙ BOSTON REVIEW; BOSTON REVIEW POETRY CONTEST

E53-407, MIT, 30 Wadsworth St., Cambridge MA 02139-4307. (617)258-0805. Fax: (617)252-1549. E-mail: review@mit.edu. Website: www.bostonreview.net. Established 1975. **Poetry Editors:** Mary Jo Bang and Timothy Donnelly.

• Poetry published in this review has been included in volumes of *The Best American Poetry*.

Magazine Needs *Boston Review* is a bimonthly tabloid-format magazine of arts, culture, and politics. ''We are open to both traditional and experimental forms. What we value most is originality and a strong sense of voice.'' Has published poetry by Gilbert Sorrentino, Heather McHugh, Richard Howard, Allen Grossman, Cole Swenson, Tan Lin, and Claudia Rankine. Receives about 3,000 submissions/year, accepts about 30 poems/year. Circulation is 20,000 nationally including sub-scriptions and newsstand sales. Single copy: $3.50; subscription: $17. Sample: $4.50.

How to Submit Submit 3-5 poems at a time. Submissions and inquiries are accepted via postal mail only. Cover letter with brief bio encouraged. Has a 6- to 12-month backlog. Responds in 3 months. Pays $40/poem plus 5 contributor's copies. Acquires first serial rights. Reviews books of poetry. Only using *solicited* reviews. Send materials for review consideration.

Contest/Award Offerings Sponsors an annual poetry contest. Awards publication and $1,000. Sub-mit up to 5 unpublished poems, no more than 10 pages total, with postcard to acknowledge receipt. **Deadline:** June 1. **Entry fee:** $15. Guidelines available for SASE or on website.

$◪ BOULEVARD

PMB 325, 6614 Clayton Rd., Richmond Heights MO 63117. (314)862-2643. E-mail: ballyman@hotm ail.com. Website: www.boulevardmagazine.com. Established 1985. **Editor:** Richard Burgin.

- Poetry published in *Boulevard* has been frequently included in *The Best American Poetry* and *Pushcart Prize* anthologies.

Magazine Needs *Boulevard* appears 3 times/year. "*Boulevard* strives to publish only the finest in fiction, poetry, and nonfiction (essays and interviews; we do not accept book reviews). While we frequently publish writers with previous credits, we are very interested in publishing less experienced or unpublished writers with exceptional promise. We've published everything from John Ashbery to Donald Hall to a wide variety of styles from new or lesser known poets. We're eclectic. We are interested in original, moving poetry written from the head as well as the heart. It can be about any topic. Do not want to see poetry that is uninspired, formulaic, self-conscious, unoriginal, insipid." No light verse. Has published poetry by Albert Goldbarth, Molly Peacock, Bob Hicok, Alice Friman, Dick Allen, and Tom Disch. *Boulevard* is 175-250 pages, digest-sized, professionally printed, flat-spined, with glossy card cover. Press run is 3,500 for 1,200 subscribers of which 200 are libraries. Subscription: $12/3 issues, $20/6 issues, $25/9 issues. Sample: $7 plus 5 first-class stamps and SASE. Make checks payable to Opojaz, Inc.

How to Submit Submit up to 5 poems at a time. Line length for poetry is 200 maximum. No previously published poems. "*Boulevard* does allow, even encourages, simultaneous submissions, but we want to be notified of this fact." Does not accept fax or e-mail submissions. All submissions must include SASE. Author's name and address must appear on each submission, with author's first and last name on each page. Cover letters encouraged but not required. Reads submissions October 1 through April 30 only. Editor sometimes comments on rejected poems. Guidelines available for SASE, by e-mail, or on website. Responds in less than 2 months. Pays $25-300/poem (sometimes more), depending on length, plus one contributor's copy. Acquires first-time publication and anthology rights.

Advice "Write what you really want to, the best way you know how, instead of trying to write what you think editors want."

☑ BRANCHES; UCCELLI PRESS; BEST OF BRANCHES

P.O. Box 85394, Seattle WA 98145-1394. E-mail: editor@branchesquarterly.com (inquiries); submit @branchesquarterly.com (submissions). Website: www.branchesquarterly.com. Established 2001. **Editor:** Toni La Ree Bennett.

Magazine Needs *Branches* is a quarterly online journal "dedicated to publishing the best of known and unknown artists and authors, presenting, when possible, verbal and visual art together in a way that expands their individual meanings." Wants poetry that is "educated but not pretentious. Seeking an eclectic, sophisticated mix of poetry, short prose, art, photos, fiction, essays, and translations. No rhyming unless specific form. No greeting card verse, or openly sectarian religious verse (spirituality okay)." Has published poetry by John Amen, Janet Buck, A.E. Stallings, Richard Jordan, Corrine de Winter, and John Sweet. *Branches* is published online, equivalent to about 30 pages in print. *Best of Branches* is an annual print version. Receives about 2,000 poems/year, accepts about 5%. Publishes about 25 poems/issue.

How to Submit Submit 3-5 poems at a time. Accepts simultaneous submissions; no previously published poems "unless by invitation." Accepts fax and e-mail (pasted into body of message) submissions; no disk submissions. Cover letter is strongly encouraged; include poem titles in cover letter. "Preferred method of submission is to e-mail work in body of message to submit@branchesq uarterly.com. Send art/photos as jpeg attachments. Submitters must be willing to have their work appear with other verbal or visual art of editor's choosing." Reads submissions continually; see website for issue deadlines. Submit seasonal poems 3 months in advance. Time between acceptance and publication is up to 3 months. Seldom comments on rejected poems. Guidelines available on website. Responds in up to 6 months. Always sends prepublication galleys (online only). Pays one contributor's copy of *Best of Branches* annual print version to those who will be published in it. Acquires first rights and retains right to archive online unless otherwise negotiated.

Advice *"Branches* is a place where 'the undefined and exact combine' (Verlaine). Artists live in a privileged, neglected place in our society. We are expected to make concrete the fluid, to tell the future, to work without recompense, and walk around naked. I'm looking for solid craftsmanship and an honest attempt to articulate the undefined."

✦ ◎ BREAKTHROUGH, INC.; THE BREAKTHROUGH INTERCESSOR (Specialized: intercessory prayer)

P.O. Box 121, Lincoln VA 20160. (540)338-4131. Fax: (540)338-1934. E-mail: breakthrough@interc essors.org. Website: www.intercessors.org. Established 1980. **Editor:** Andrea Doudera. Managing Editor: Trudi Schwarting.

Magazine Needs & How to Submit Published quarterly, *The Breakthrough Intercessor* is focused toward "encouraging people in prayer and faith; preparing and equipping those who pray." Accepts poetry very rarely due to space limitations. Has published poetry by Norman Vincent Peale. *The Breakthrough Intercessor* is 44 pages, magazine-sized, professionally-printed, saddle-stapled with self cover, includes art/graphics. Press run is 8,000. Subscription: $15. Make checks payable to Breakthrough, Inc. Accepts previously published poems. Accepts fax, e-mail (pasted into body of message), and disk submissions. Time between acceptance and publication varies. Poems are circulated to an editorial board.

◪ THE BRIAR CLIFF REVIEW

Briar Cliff College, 3303 Rebecca St., Sioux City IA 51104-2340. E-mail: emmons@briarcliff.edu. Website: www.briarcliff.edu/bcreview/. Established 1989. **Managing Editor:** Tricia Currans-Sheehan. **Poetry Editor:** Jeanne Emmons. Member: CLMP; American Humanities Index.

 • *The Briar Cliff Review* has received the Columbia Scholastic Association Gold Crown and the Associated Collegiate Press Pacemaker Award.

Magazine Needs *The Briar Cliff Review*, appearing in April, is an attractive annual "eclectic literary and cultural magazine focusing on (but not limited to) Siouxland writers and subjects." Wants "quality poetry with strong imagery; especially interested in regional, Midwestern content with tight, direct, well-wrought language. No allegorical emotional landscapes." Has published poetry by Gaylord Brewster, Vivian Shipley, and Michael Carey. *The Briar Cliff Review* is 88 pages, magazine-sized, professionally printed on 80 lb. dull text paper, perfect-bound, with 4-color cover on dull stock, b&w and color photos inside. Receives about 600 poems/year, accepts about 24. Press run is 1,000. Sample: $15.

How to Submit Submissions should be typewritten or letter quality, with author's name and address on the first page, with name on following pages. Accepts simultaneous submissions, but expects prompt notification of acceptance elsewhere; no previously published poems. No fax or e-mail submissions. Cover letter with short bio required. "No manuscripts returned without SASE." Reads submissions August 1 through November 1 only. Time between acceptance and publication is up to 6 months. Seldom comments on rejected poems. Responds in 6 months. Pays 2 contributor's copies. Acquires first serial rights.

Contest/Award Offerings *The Briar Cliff Review* also sponsors a contest. Awards $500 and publication. Send 3 poems for consideration. **Entry fee:** $15. **Deadline:** November 1.

ℕ ◪ BRICK & MORTAR REVIEW; BRICK & MORTAR REVIEW'S BIANNUAL POETRY CONTEST

1463 E. Republican St. #116, Seattle WA 98112. E-mail: email@bmreview.com. Website: www.bmr eview.com. Established 2003. **Senior Editor:** Jack Stull.

Magazine Needs *Brick & Mortar Review* appears quarterly. Wants poetry "that is grounded in concrete language, i.e., that evokes images. Avoid the use of empty, fluffy language such as beautiful, freedom, amazed, spectacular, love, etc. Of course, these words can be used in the right context, but sparingly. Also, avoid over-rhyming. We don't mind an occasional rhyme if it's natural, but we don't want poetry that is forced into rhyme schemes (unless it is exceptional)." *Brick & Mortar Review* is published online only.

How to Submit Submit 3 or more poems, up to 10 at a time. Accepts simultaneous submissions; no previously published poems. Accepts e-mail submissions (pasted into body of message); no disk submissions. Cover letter is preferred. "For regular mail, include a SASE or indicate that you would like an e-mail response. For e-mail submissions, we respond by e-mail. On your cover page, please include a brief bio (a few sentences about yourself), and make sure your name is on every page you submit." Reads submissions year round. Time between acceptance and publication can be months. "The editors independently review the submissions and then meet to discuss and vote." Seldom comments on rejected poems. Guidelines available on website. Responds in 2 months. No payment. Acquires one-time rights.

Contest/Award Offerings Offers biannual award of 1st Prize: $1,000; 2nd Prize: $250; 3rd Prize: $100; plus 3 Honorable Mentions. All winning poetry is published on the website. Pays winners from other countries by International Money Order. Submissions may be entered in other contests (with notification of acceptance elsewhere). Submit 3 or more poems of any length. "If submitting by e-mail, make sure it's clear where each poem begins and ends; also write 'contest' in the subject box (see website for more details on submitting electronically). If submitting by ground mail, please type 'contest' on your cover page. Both e-mail and ground mail submissions should include a brief bio (2-3 sentences about yourself)." Guidelines available on website. **Entry fee:** $5/poem. "We accept U.S. dollars and International Money Orders, but credit cards online are the best way for foreign entries." **Deadline:** "We accept entries year round. Awards are given at the beginning of winter and summer." Judges are the editors. Winners will be announced on the website and possibly other places, such as *Poets & Writers*. "Avoid the overuse of empty language. This means we want poetry that evokes images, that shows rather than tells. An occasional rhyme is okay, but we're not interested in poetry that conforms to rhyme schemes."

🅰 ◎ BRICKHOUSE BOOKS, INC.; NEW POETS SERIES, INC./CHESTNUT HILLS PRESS; STONEWALL SERIES (Specialized, Stonewall only: gay/lesbian/bisexual)

541 Piccadilly Rd., Baltimore MD 21204. (410)704-2869 or 828-0724. Fax: (410)704-3999. E-mail: charriss@towson.edu. Website: www.towson.edu/~ harriss/!bhbwebs.ite/bhb.htm. Established 1970. **Editor/Director:** Clarinda Harriss.

• New Poets Series, Chestnut Hills Press, and Stonewall are imprints of BrickHouse Books.

Book/Chapbook Needs BrickHouse and The New Poets Series, Inc. bring out first books by promising new poets. Poets who have previously had book-length mss published are not eligible. Prior publication in journals and anthologies is strongly encouraged. Wants "excellent, fresh, nontrendy, literate, intelligent poems. Any form (including traditional), any style." BrickHouse Books and New Poets Series pay 20 author's copies (out of a press run of 1,000), the sales proceeds going back into the corporation to finance the next volume. "BrickHouse has been successful in its effort to provide writers with a national distribution; in fact, The New Poets Series was named an Outstanding Small Press by the prestigious Pushcart Awards Committee, which judges some 5,000 small press publications annually." Chestnut Hills Press publishes author-subsidized books—"High-quality work only, however. Chestnut Hills Press has achieved a reputation for prestigious books, printing only the top 10% of manuscripts Chestnut Hills Press and New Poets Series receive." Chestnut Hills Press authors receive proceeds from sale of their books. The Stonewall series publishes work with a gay, lesbian, or bisexual perspective. New Poets Series/Chestnut Hills Press has published books by Chester Wickwire, Ted McCrorie, Sharon White, Mariquita McManus, and Jeff Mann. BrickHouse publishes 64- to 112-page works. Chapbooks: $8. Full-length books: $10.

How to Submit "Do not query by phone or fax; e-mail or postal mail queries only. Send a 50- to 55-page manuscript, $10 reading fee, and cover letter giving publication credits and bio. Indicate if manuscript is to be considered for BrickHouse, New Poets Series, Chestnut Hills Press, or Stone-wall." Accepts simultaneous submissions. No e-mail submissions. "Cover letters should be very brief, businesslike, and include an accurate list of published work." Editor sometimes comments briefly on rejected poems. Responds in up to one year. Manuscripts "are circulated to an editorial board of professional, publishing poets. BrickHouse is backlogged, but the best 10% of the manuscripts it receives are automatically eligible for Chestnut Hills Press consideration," a subsidy arrangement. Send $5 and a 7×10 SASE for a sample volume.

⊠ BRIGHT HILL PRESS; BRIGHT HILL PRESS POETRY BOOK AWARD; BRIGHT HILL PRESS POETRY CHAPBOOK AWARD; WORD THURSDAYS READING SERIES; WORD THURSDAYS LITERARY WORKSHOPS; RADIO BY WRITERS; SHARE THE WORDS HIGH-SCHOOL POETRY COMPETITION; WORD AND IMAGE GALLERY
P.O. Box 193, 94 Church St., Treadwell NY 13846-0193. (607)829-5055. Fax: (607)829-5056. E-mail: wordthur@stny.rr.com. Website: www.brighthillpress.org. Established 1992. **Editor-in-Chief/Founding Director:** Bertha Rogers. Member: Council of Literary Magazines and Presses, NYC.

Book/Chapbook Needs Bright Hill Press publishes 2-3 paperbacks and one chapbook annually chosen through competition. **Considers mss submitted through competition only.** (See below.) Also publishes anthology. No beginners; no unpublished poets/writers. Has published poetry by Barbara Hurd, Barry Ballard, Claudia M. Reder, Beth Copeland Vargo, Richard Deutch, Matthew J. Spireng, Lisa Harris, and Judith Neeld.

Contest/Award Offerings 1) **Bright Hill Press Poetry Book Award** offers annual award of $1,000 and publication for a poetry ms of 48-64 pages. Prize includes 25 author's copies. Pays winners from other countries by certified check or International Money Order. Submissions may be entered in other contests. Submit ms of 48-64 pages, paginated (includes bio, contents, acknowledgments, 2 title pages—one with name, address, and phone number, one with title of manuscript only) and secured with bulldog clip. Include SASE for results only; mss not returned. Guidelines available for SASE or by e-mail. **Entry fee:** $20. Does not accept entry fees in foreign currencies; U.S. International Money Order only. **Postmark deadline:** November 30. Competition receives over 300 entries/year. Past winners include Lisa Rhoades (2002), Barbara Hurd (2001), and Richard Deutch (2000). Winners will be announced in summer of the year following the contest. Copies of winning books available for $12 plus $3.05 postage from BHP Sample Books at the address above. "Publish your poems in literary magazines before trying to get a whole manuscript published. Publishing individual poems is the best way to hone your complete manuscript." 2) **Bright Hill Press Poetry Chapbook Award** offers annual award of $250 and publication for a poetry ms of 16-24 pages. Prize includes 25 author's copies. Pays winners from other countries by certified check or International Money Order. Submissions may be entered in other contests. Submit ms of 16-24 pages, paginated (includes bio, contents, acknowledgments, 2 title pages—one with name, address, and phone number, one with title of manuscript only) and secured with bulldog clip. Include SASE for results only; mss not returned. Guidelines available for SASE or by e-mail. **Entry fee:** $10. Does not accept entry fees in foreign currencies; U.S. International Money Order only. **Postmark deadline:** July 31. Competition receives over 300 entries/year. Past winners include Shelby Stephenson (2002), Barry Ballard (2001), and Matthew J. Spireng (2000). Winners will be announced in summer of the year following the contest. Copies of winning chapbook available for $6 plus $2.50 postage from BHP Sample Books at the address above.

Also Offers Words Thursdays (reading series); Radio by Writers (a Catskills radio series heard on WJFF, the Sullivan Co. NPR affiliate); Share the Words High-School Annual Oral Poetry Competition; Word and Image gallery at the Bright Hill Center; Speaking the Words Tour and Festival; and the Word Thursdays Literary Workshops for Kids and Adults. See website for further information.

(Also administers the New York State Literary Map and the New York State Council on the Arts Literary Curators website at www.nyslittree.org.)

Advice "Read poetry; read fiction. Send your poetry/fiction out for publication; when it comes back, revise it and send it out again."

☑ ◎ BRILLIANT CORNERS: A JOURNAL OF JAZZ & LITERATURE (Specialized: jazz-related literature)

Lycoming College, Williamsport PA 17701. (570)321-4279. Fax: (570)321-4090. E-mail: bc@lycoming.edu. Website: www.lycoming.edu/BrilliantCorners. Established 1996. **Editor:** Sascha Feinstein.

Magazine Needs *Brilliant Corners*, a biannual, publishes jazz-related poetry, fiction, and nonfiction. "We are open to length and form, but want work that is both passionate and well crafted—work worthy of our recent contributors. No sloppy hipster jargon or improvisatory nonsense." Has published poetry by Amiri Baraka, Jayne Cortez, Yusef Komunyakaa, Philip Levine, Colleen McElroy, and Al Young. *Brilliant Corners* is 100 pages, digest-sized, commercially printed and perfect-bound with color card cover with original artwork, includes ads. Accepts about 5% of work received. Press run is 800 for 200 subscribers. Subscription: $12. Sample: $7.

How to Submit Submit 3-5 poems at a time. Previously published poems "very rarely, and only by well established poets"; no simultaneous submissions. No e-mail or fax submissions. Cover letter preferred. Reads submissions September 1 through May 15 only. Seldom comments on rejected poems. Responds in 2 months. Pays 2 contributor's copies. Acquires first North American serial rights. Staff reviews books of poetry. Send materials for review consideration.

✪ ⊘ BROODING HERON PRESS

101 Bookmonger Rd., Waldron Island WA 98297. Established 1984. **Editor:** Sam Green.

Book/Chapbook Needs Brooding Heron Press publishes up to 3 chapbooks/year. "No restrictions other than excellence." Does not want "prose masquerading as poetry or poems written for form's sake." Has published books by Denise Levertov, James Laughlin, John Haines, David Lee, Donald Hall, and Gary Snyder.

How to Submit "We're too backlogged to look at anything new until 2006." Accepts previously published poems; no simultaneous submissions. Cover letter required. Time between acceptance and publication varies. Never comments on rejected poems. Responds within 6 weeks. "We print 300 books per title, bound in paper and cloth. Payment is 10% of the press run. Author retains copyright." This press has received many awards for fine printing. Write for catalog to order samples.

$◎ BROOKS BOOKS PRESS; MAYFLY (Specialized: haiku)

3720 N. Woodridge Dr., Decatur IL 62526. (217)877-2966. E-mail: brooksbooks@q-com.com. Website: www.family-net.net/~brooksbooks. Established 1976. **Editors:** Randy and Shirley Brooks.

• Their books have received National Haiku Society of America Merit Awards.

Magazine Needs Appearing in winter and summer, *Mayfly* publishes haiku exclusively. Wants "well-crafted haiku, with sensual images honed like a carved jewel, to evoke an immediate emotional response as well as a long-lasting, often spiritual, resonance in the imagination of the reader." Has published haiku by George Swede, Peggy Lyles, Lee Gurga, and Masajo Suzuki. *Mayfly* is 16 pages, 3½×5, professionally printed on high-quality stock, saddle-stapled, one haiku/page. Publishes 32 of an estimated 1,800 submissions. Subscription: $8. Sample: $4

How to Submit Submit no more than 5 haiku/issue. No previously published haiku or simultaneous submissions. Accepts e-mail submissions "except from the USA." Submission deadlines are May 15 and November 15. Guidelines available for SASE. Pays $10/haiku; no copies.

Book/Chapbook Needs & How to Submit Brooks Books, formerly High/Coo Press, publishes English-language haiku books, chapbooks, magazines, and bibliographies. "Our goal is to feature the individual haiku as literary event, and to celebrate excellence in the art through collections by the best contemporary writers practicing the art of haiku.'' Has published *Almost Unseen: Selected Haiku of George Swede*; dual-language books of haiku by contemporary Japanese writers; chapbooks; and haiga web collections. Brooks Books considers mss "by invitation only."

Advice "Publishing poetry is a joyous work of love. We publish to share those moments of insight contained in evocative haiku. We aren't in it for fame, gain, or name. We publish to serve an enthusiastic readership."

◔ BRYANT LITERARY REVIEW

Faculty Suite F, Bryant College, Smithfield RI 02917. Website: http://web.bryant.edu/~blr. Established 2000. **Editor:** Tom Chandler. Member: CLMP.

Magazine Needs *Bryant Literary Review* appears annually in May and publishes poetry, fiction, photography, and art. "Our only standard is quality." Has published poetry by Michael S. Harper, Mary Crow, Denise Duhamel, and Baron Wormster. *Bryant Literary Review* is 125 pages, digest-sized, offset-printed, perfect-bound, with 4-color cover with art or photo. Receives about 3,000 poems/year, accepts about 1%. Publishes about 25 poems/issue. Press run is 2,500. Single copy: $8; subscription: $8.

How to Submit Submit 3-5 poems at a time. Cover letter is required. "Include SASE; please submit only *once* each reading period." Reads submissions September 1 through December 31. Time between acceptance and publication is 5 months. Seldom comments on rejected poems. Guidelines available in magazine or on website. Responds in 3 months. Pays 2 contributor's copies. Acquires one-time rights.

Advice "No abstract expressionist poems, please. We prefer accessible work of depth and quality."

$◔ ◎ BUGLE: JOURNAL OF ELK COUNTRY AND THE HUNT (Specialized: elk conservation, nature/ecology)

Rocky Mountain Elk Foundation, P.O. Box 8249, Missoula MT 59807-8249. (406)523-4538. Fax: (406)543-7710. E-mail: bugle@rmef.org. Website: www.elkfoundation.org. Established 1984. **Assistant Editor:** Paul Queneau.

Magazine Needs *Bugle* is the bimonthly publication of the nonprofit Rocky Mountain Elk Foundation, whose mission is to ensure the future of elk, other wildlife, and their habitat. "The goal of *Bugle* is to advance this mission by presenting original, critical thinking about wildlife conservation, elk ecology, and hunting." Wants "high-quality poems that explore the realm of elk, the 'why' of hunting, or celebrate the hunting experience as a whole. Prefer one page. Free verse preferred. No 'Hallmark' poetry." Has published poetry by Mike Fritch, John Whinery, and Ted Florea. *Bugle* is 130 pages, magazine-sized, professionally printed on coated stock and saddle-stapled with full-color glossy cover with photo or illustration, includes photos, illustrations, ads. Receives about 50 poems/year, accepts about 10%. Press run is 132,000. Subscription: $30 membership fee. Sample: $5.95. Make checks payable to Rocky Mountain Elk Foundation.

How to Submit "Poets may submit as many poems as they'd like at a time." Accepts simultaneous submissions. Accepts e-mail (prefer attached file in Word), fax, and disk submissions. Cover letter preferred. Time between acceptance and publication varies. "Poems are screened by assistant editor first; those accepted then passed to editorial staff for review and comment; final decision based on their comments. We will evaluate your poem based on content, quality, and our needs for the coming year." Rarely comments on rejected poems. Publishes special sections. Guidelines available for SASE, by fax, by e-mail, or on website. Responds in 3 months. "The Rocky Mountain Elk Foundation is a nonprofit conservation organization committed to putting membership dollars into protecting elk habitat. So we appreciate, and still receive, donated work. However, if you would like to be paid for your work, our rate is $100/poem, paid on acceptance. Should your poem appear in *Bugle*, you will receive 3 complimentary copies of the issue." Acquires first North American serial rights. Staff reviews other magazines.

Advice "Although poetry has appeared periodically in *Bugle* over the years, it has never been a high priority for us, nor have we solicited it. A lack of high-quality work and poetry appropriate for the focus of the magazine has kept us from making it a regular feature. However, we've decided to attempt to give verse a permanent home in the magazine . . . Reading a few issues of *Bugle* prior to submitting will give you a better sense of the style and content of the magazine."

✦ ◙ BULK HEAD; BRIDGE BURNER'S PUBLISHING

P.O. Box 5255, Mankato MN 56002-5255. E-mail: editor@bulkhead.org. Website: www.bulkhead.org. Established 2000. **Editor:** Curtis Meyer.

Magazine Needs *Bulk Head* appears quarterly, publishing quality poetry, fiction, and nonfiction. "We like angst. We like anything experimental. Shorter poems. No religious stuff (unless angry). Nothing rhyming. No song lyrics." Has published poetry by Paul Dilsaver, Janet Buck, Greg Kosmicki, Leslie Bentley, Matt Mason, and Duane Locke. *Bulk Head* is published online only with b&w photos. Receives about 120 poems/year, accepts about 30%. Publishes about 10-20 poems/issue. Single copy: free online; subscription: free online.

How to Submit Submit 3 poems at a time. Line length for poetry is 2-4 minimum, 50 maximum. No previously published poems or simultaneous submissions. Accepts e-mail submissions only. Cover letter is required. "Include a short bio." Reads submissions up to the date of publication. Time between acceptance and publication is up to 3 months. "For now, this is a one-man operation." Seldom comments on rejected poems. Guidelines available on website. Responds in up to 3 months. Acquires first rights, one-time rights. Reviews books and chapbooks of poetry and other magazines/journals. Send materials for review consideration.

Book/Chapbook Needs & How to Submit Bridge Burner's Publishing presents work of "genius, anger, unpublished greatness." Publishes 1-2 paperbacks, 1-2 chapbooks/year. Books/chapbooks are usually 16-80 pages. Query first, with a few sample poems and a cover letter with brief bio and publication credits. "We will consider polished collections for chapbooks." Responds to queries in 2 weeks; to mss in 2 months. Order sample books/chapbooks by sending $15 to Bridge Burner's.

Contest/Award Offerings Annual Bulk Head Poetry Contest. **Entry fee:** $1. Check website for details. "We've decided to publish a print edition of *Bulk Head* starting later this year. Details will be on the website."

Advice "We are open to anything, but we prefer writing stripped of all romance and glamour. We especially like constructive angst. Don't shoot up your office or school! Write a poem instead."

Ⓝ ◙ THE BURNSIDE REVIEW

P.O. Box 1782, Portland OR 97207. E-mail: burnsidereview@yahoo.com. Established 2004. **Editor:** Sid Miller. **Co-Editor:** Bill Bogart.

Magazine Needs The editors of *The Burnside Review* hope "to showcase not only the number of great poets in the Northwest, but throughout the country. Translations also welcome. We want poems that find the beauty in the ugly, that break our hearts, that show everything that is human, that can find the natural in the urban and the urban in the natural. Open to all forms, we like the narrative, but would love to see a movement toward the lyrical. Think O'Hara, Neruda, Soto, Jon Anderson." Wants mix of longer and short poems. Does not want "anything usual, love poems, anything political or that rhymes. If you can't say it with the words and the language, then you surely can't with line breaks and fonts." *The Burnside Review* is 40-50 pages, digest-sized, professionally-printed, saddle-stapled, with glossy card cover with photograph, includes art/graphics. Accepts about 50-60 poems/year. Publishes about 25-30 poems/issue. Press run is 250 for 50 subscribers, 50 shelf sales. Single copy: $5; subscription: $8. Make checks payable to Sid Miller.

How to Submit Submit 3-5 poems at a time. Accepts simultaneous submissions; no previously published poems. No e-mail or fax submissions. Cover letter is required. "Include brief bio and SASE. Please include your name and e-mail address on every poem." Reads submissions year round. Submit seasonal poems 3-6 months in advance. Time between acceptance and publication is up to 6 months. "We both read all poems; if there's a consensus, you're in." Often comments on rejected poems. Guidelines available for SASE or by e-mail. Responds in one month. Pays one contributor's copy. Acquires first rights. Review books and chapbooks of poetry in 500 words or less, single book format. Send materials for review consideration to the editor.

⦿ BUTTON MAGAZINE

P.O. Box 26, Lunenburg MA 01462. E-mail: Aiolia@worldnet.att.net. Website: http://moonsigns.n et. Established 1993. **Editor:** Sally Cragin. **Contact:** Maude Piper.

Magazine Needs *Button* "is New England's tiniest magazine of fiction, poetry, and gracious living." Wants "poetry about the quiet surprises in life, not sentimental, and true moments carefully preserved. Brevity counts." Has published poetry by William Corbett, Amanda Powell, Brendan Galvin, Jean Monahan, Mary Campbell, Diana Der-Hovanessian, Kevin McGrath, and Ed Conti. *Button*, published annually, is 30 pages, $4\frac{1}{4} \times 5\frac{1}{2}$, saddle-stapled, with card stock offset cover with illustrations that incorporate one or more buttons. Press run is 1,200 for more than 500 subscribers; 750 shelf sales. Subscription: $5/4 issues, $25/lifetime. Sample: $2 and a first-class stamp.

How to Submit Submit no more than 2 poems at a time. No previously published poems. "Do not submit more than twice in one year." Cover letter required. Time between acceptance and publication is up to 6 months. Poems are circulated to an editorial board. Often comments on rejected poems. Guidelines available by e-mail. Responds in 4 months. Pays honorarium, subscription, and at least 5 contributor's copies. Acquires first North American serial rights.

Advice "Read excellent work always, particularly just before you begin to write. Having the rhythms of Dickinson, Gunn, and Eliot coursing though your frontal cortex can only be a boon. Also, you know that word 'I'? Try to write a version of your poem without that one letter."

$⦿ ⦿ BYLINE MAGAZINE; BYLINE LITERARY AWARDS (Specialized: writing)

P.O. Box 5240, Edmond OK 73083-5240. (405)348-5591. E-mail: MPreston@bylinemag.com. Website: www.bylinemag.com. Established 1981. **Editor:** Marcia Preston. **Poetry Editor:** Sandra Soli.

Magazine Needs *ByLine* is a magazine for the encouragement of writers and poets, using 8-10 poems/issue about writers or writing. Has published poetry by Judith Tate O'Brien, Katharyn Howd Machan, and Harvey Stanbrough. *ByLine* is magazine-sized, professionally printed, with illustrations, cartoons, and ads. Has more than 3,000 subscriptions and receives about 2,500 poetry submissions/year, of which about 100 are used. Subscription: $24. Sample: $5.

How to Submit Submit up to 3 poems at a time, no reprints. No e-mail or fax submissions, please. Guidelines available for SASE or on website. Responds within 6 weeks. Pays $10/poem. Acquires first North American serial rights.

Contest/Award Offerings Sponsors up to 20 poetry contests, including a chapbook competition open to anyone. Send #10 SASE for details. Also sponsors the *ByLine* Short Fiction and Poetry Awards, open only to subscribers. Prize: $250. Send SASE for guidelines.

Advice "We are happy to work with new writers, but please read a few samples to get an idea of our style. We would like to see more serious poetry about the creative experience (as it concerns writing)."

⦿ CALIFORNIA QUARTERLY; CALIFORNIA STATE POETRY SOCIETY

P.O. Box 7126, Orange CA 92863-7126. (949)854-8024. E-mail: jipalley@aol.com. Established 1972. **Editors:** Julian Palley and Kate Ozbirn.

Magazine Needs *California Quarterly* is the official publication of the California State Poetry Society (an affiliate of the National Federation of State Poetry Societies) and is designed "to encourage the writing and dissemination of poetry." Wants poetry on any subject, 60 lines maximum. "No geographical limitations. Quality is all that matters." Has published poetry by Michael L. Johnson, Lyn Lifshin, and Joanna C. Scott. *California Quarterly* is 64 pages, digest-sized, offset-printed, perfect-bound, with heavy paper cover with art. Receives 3,000-4,000 poems/year, accepts about 5%. Press run is 500 for 300 subscribers of which 24 are libraries, 20-30 shelf sales. Membership in CSPS is $25/year and includes a subscription to *California Quarterly*. Sample (including guidelines): $6.

How to Submit Submit up to 6 "relatively brief" poems at a time, with name and address on each sheet. Include SASE. No previously published poems. Accepts submissions by postal mail only; no e-mail submissions. Seldom comments on rejected poems. Guidelines available for SASE. Responds in up to 8 months. Pays one contributor's copy. Acquires first rights. Rights revert to poet after publication.

Contest/Award Offerings CSPS also sponsors an annual poetry contest. Awards vary. All entries considered for *California Quarterly*. For inquiries about the contest, write, with SASE, to Maura Harvey, Annual Contest Chair, P.O. Box 2672, Del Mar CA 92014.

Advice "Since our editor changes with each issue, we encourage poets to resubmit."

☐ ◎ CALYX, A JOURNAL OF ART & LITERATURE BY WOMEN (Specialized: women, lesbian, multicultural); CALYX BOOKS

P.O. Box B, Corvallis OR 97339-0539. (541)753-9384. Fax: (541)753-0515. E-mail: calyx@proaxis.com. Established 1976. **Senior Editor:** Beverly McFarland. **Managing Editor:** Micki Reaman.

Magazine Needs *Calyx* is a journal edited by a collective editorial board. Publishes poetry, prose, art, book reviews, essays, and interviews by and about women. Wants "excellently crafted poetry that also has excellent content." Has published poetry by Maurya Simon, Diane Averill, Carole Boston Weatherford, and Eleanor Wilner. *Calyx* appears 3 times every 18 months and is 6×8, handsomely printed on heavy paper, flat-spined, with glossy color cover, 128-144 pages, of which 50-60 are poetry. Poems tend to be lyric free verse that makes strong use of image and symbol melding unobtrusively with voice and theme. Single copy: $9.50. Sample: $11.50.

How to Submit Send up to 6 poems with SASE and short bio. "We accept copies in good condition and clearly readable. We focus on new writing, but occasionally publish a previously published piece." Accepts simultaneous submissions, "if kept up-to-date on publication." No fax or e-mail submissions. *Calyx* is open to submissions October 1 through December 31 only. Manuscripts received when not open to reading will be returned unread. Guidelines available for SASE or by e-mail. Responds in 9 months. Pays one contributor's copy/poem and subscription. Send materials for review consideration.

Book/Chapbook Needs & How to Submit Calyx Books publishes one book of poetry/year. All work published is by women. Has published *Black Candle* by Chitra Divakaruni. However, Calyx Books is closed for ms submissions until further notice.

Advice "Read the publication and be familiar with what we have published."

✪ ✧ $◨ ◎ CANADIAN WRITER'S JOURNAL (Specialized: writing)

White Mountain Publications, Box 1178, New Liskeard ON P0J 1P0 Canada. (705)647-5424. Fax: (705)647-8366. E-mail: cwj@cwj.ca. Website: www.cwj.ca. **Editor:** Deborah Ranchuk.

Magazine Needs *Canadian Writer's Journal* is a digest-sized bimonthly, publishing mainly short "how-to" articles of interest to writers at all levels. Uses a few "short poems or portions thereof as part of 'how-to' articles relating to the writing of poetry, and occasional short poems with tie-in to the writing theme. We try for 90% Canadian content but prefer good material over country of origin, or how well you're known." Subscription: $35/year, $67.50/2 years, add 7% gst in Canada. Sample: $8.

How to Submit Submit up to 5 poems ("poems should be titled"). Include SASE ("U.S. postage accepted; do not affix to envelope"). No previously published poems. Accepts fax and e-mail ("Include in body of message, not as attachment. Write 'Submission' in the subject line.") submissions. Hard copy and SASE (or SAE and IRC) required if accepted. Responds in 3 months. Token payment. Pays $2-7.50 and one contributor's copy/poem.

⬛ $☑ THE CAPILANO REVIEW

2055 Purcell Way, North Vancouver BC V7J 3H5 Canada. (604)984-1712. E-mail: tcr@capcollege.bc .ca. Website: www.capcollege.bc.ca/about/publications/capilano-review/tcr/index.html. Established 1972. **Editor:** Sharon Thesen.

Magazine Needs *The Capilano Review* is a literary and visual arts review appearing 3 times/year. Wants "avant-garde, experimental, previously unpublished poetry of sustained intelligence and imagination. We are interested in poetry that is new in concept and in execution." Has published poetry by bill bissett, Phyllis Webb, and Michael Ondaatje. *The Capilano Review* comes in a handsome digest-sized format, 115 pages, flat-spined, finely printed on semi-glossy stock with a glossy full-color card cover. Circulation is 1,000. Sample: $9 prepaid.

How to Submit Submit 5-6 poems, minimum, with cover letter and SAE and IRC (no US postage). No simultaneous submissions. No e-mail or disk submissions. Responds in up to 5 months. Pays $50-200, subscription, plus 2 contributor's copies. Acquires first North American serial rights.

Advice "*The Capilano Review* receives several manuscripts each week; unfortunately the majority of them are simply inappropriate for the magazine. The best advice we can offer is to read the magazine before you submit."

$☐ ◎ CAPPER'S; BRAVE HEARTS (Specialized: inspirational, humor, themes)

1503 SW 42nd St., Topeka KS 66609-1265. (785)274-4300. Fax: (785)274-4305. Website: www.cappers.com or www.braveheartsmagazine.com. Established 1879. **Editor:** Ann Crahan.

Magazine Needs & How to Submit *Capper's* is a biweekly tabloid (newsprint) going to 240,000 mail subscribers, mostly small-town and rural families. Wants short poems (4-16 lines preferred, lines of one-column width) "relating to everyday situations, nature, inspirational, humorous. Most poems used in *Capper's* are upbeat in tone and offer the reader a bit of humor, joy, enthusiasm, or encouragement." Has published poetry by Elizabeth Searle Lamb, Robert Brimm, Margaret Wiedyke, Helena K. Stefanski, Sheryl L. Nelms, and Claire Puneky. Publishes 6-8 poems in each issue. Not available on newsstand. Send $1.95 for sample. Submit 5-6 poems at a time, 14-16 lines. No simultaneous submissions. No e-mail or fax submissions. Returns mss with SASE. Publishes seasonal theme issues. Upcoming themes available for SASE. Responds in 3 months. Pays $10-15/poem. Additional payment of $5 if poem is used on website. Acquires one-time rights.

Magazine Needs & How to Submit *Brave Hearts* is an inspirational magazine appearing quarterly in February, May, August, and November. Features themes and humorous poems. "Poems should be short (16 lines or less)." Does not accept poetry by children. Sample: $4.95. Accepts submissions by postal mail only. Guidelines and themes available for SASE. Pays on acceptance and one contributor's copy.

Advice "Poems chosen are upbeat, sometimes humorous, always easily understood. Short poems of this type fit our format best."

☐ ◎ THE CARIBBEAN WRITER (Specialized: regional, Caribbean)

University of the Virgin Islands, RR 02, P.O. Box 10,000, Kingshill, St. Croix, USVI 00850. (340)692-4152. Fax: (340)692-4026. E-mail: qmars@uvi.edu. Website: www.TheCaribbeanWriter.com. Established 1987. **Editor:** Marvin E. William. **Contact:** Ms. Quilin Mars.

• Poetry published in *The Caribbean Writer* was included in the 2002 *Pushcart Prize* anthology.

Magazine Needs *The Caribbean Writer* is a literary anthology, appearing in July, with a Caribbean focus. The Caribbean must be central to the literary work, or the work must reflect a Caribbean heritage, experience, or perspective. Has published poetry by Virgil Suárez, Thomas Reiter, Kamau Brathwaite, and Opal Palmer Adisa. *The Caribbean Writer* magazine is over 300 pages, digest-sized, handsomely printed on heavy stock, perfect-bound, with glossy card cover, uses advertising and b&w art by Caribbean artists. Press run is 1,200. Single copy: $12 plus $4 postage; subscription: $20. Sample: $7 plus $4 postage. (Note: postage to and from the Virgin Islands is the same as within the US.)

How to Submit Submit up to 5 poems. Accepts simultaneous submissions; no previously published poems. Accepts e-mail (as attachment), disk, and postal submissions; no fax submissions. Blind submissions only: name, address, phone number, e-mail address, and title of ms should appear in cover letter along with brief bio. Title only on ms. Deadline is September 30 of each year. Guidelines available in magazine, for SASE, by e-mail, or on website. Pays 2 contributor's copies. Acquires first North American serial rights. Reviews books of poetry and fiction in 1,000 words. Send materials for review consideration.

Contest/Award Offerings All submissions are eligible for the Daily News Prize ($300) for the best poem or poems, The Marguerite Cobb McKay Prize to a Virgin Island author ($200), the David Hough Literary Prize to a Caribbean author ($500), the Canute A. Brodhurst Prize for Fiction ($400), and the Charlotte and Isidor Paiewonsky Prize ($200) for first-time publication.

☑ THE CAROLINA QUARTERLY; THE CHARLES B. WOOD AWARD

CB #3520 Greenlaw Hall, University of North Carolina, Chapel Hill NC 27599-3520. (919)962-0244. E-mail: cquarter@unc.edu. Website: www.unc.edu/depts/cqonline. Established 1948. **Contact:** Poetry Editor.

Magazine Needs *Carolina Quarterly* appears 3 times/year publishing fiction, poetry, reviews, non-fiction, and graphic art. No specifications regarding form, length, subject matter, or style of poetry. Considers translations of work originally written in languages other than English. Has published poetry by Denise Levertov, Richard Wilbur, Robert Morgan, Ha Jin, and Charles Wright. *The Carolina Quarterly* is about 90 pages, digest-sized, professionally-printed and perfect-bound, with one-color matte card cover, a few graphics and ads. Receives about 6,000 poems/year, accepts about 1%. Press run is 900 for 200 library subscriptions and various shelf sales. Subscription: $12 (individuals), $15 (institutions). Sample: $5.

How to Submit Submit 1-6 poems at a time. No previously published poems or simultaneous submissions. No e-mail submissions. SASE required. Poems are circulated to an editorial board. "Manuscripts that make it to the meeting of the full poetry staff are discussed by all. Poems are accepted by majority consensus." Seldom comments on rejected poems. Responds in 4 months. "Poets are welcome to write or phone about their submission's status, but please wait about 4 months before doing so." Pays 2 contributor's copies. Acquires first rights. Reviews books of poetry. Send materials for review consideration (attn: Editor).

Contest/Award Offerings The Charles B. Wood Award for Distinguished Writing is given to the author of the best poem or short story published in each volume of *The Carolina Quarterly*. Only those writers *without* major publications are considered, and the winner receives $500.

☑ ◎ CAROLINA WREN PRESS (Specialized: women, ethnic, gay/lesbian, social issues)

120 Morris St., Durham NC 27701. (919)560-2738. Fax: (919)560-2759. E-mail: carolina@carolinaw renpress.org. Website: www.carolinawrenpress.org. Established 1976. **Contact:** David Kellogg.

Book/Chapbook Needs Publishes one book/year "usually through our chapbook series. Primarily women and minorities, though men and majorities also welcome." Has published poetry by George Elliott Clarke, Andrea Selch, Evie Shockley, and Erica Hunt.

How to Submit "We read manuscripts all the time, but your best bet is to submit as part of our biannual poetry contest. See website for current guidelines."

☑ ◎ **CATAMOUNT PRESS; COTYLEDON (Specialized: short free verse poems of 10 lines or less, haiku, tanka)**

2519 Roland Rd. SW, Huntsville AL 35805-4147. Established 1992. **Editor:** Georgette Perry.

Magazine Needs *Cotyledon*, established in 1997 and published 4 times/year, is a miniature magazine. Wants poems up to 10 lines. Nature and the environment are favorite subjects, but a variety of subject matter is needed. Has published poetry by Kevin Hull, Taylor Graham, Paul Sohar, Jerrey Bauer, Don Winter, and Lonnie Hull Dupont. *Cotyledon* is 16 pages, $3^1/2 \times 4^1/4$, photocopied, saddle-stapled, with bond cover and b&w art. Sample: $1 or 3 unattached first-class stamps.

How to Submit Submit 3-6 poems at a time with cover letter and SASE. Accepts previously published poems if identified as such. Send 3 unattached first-class stamps for a sample, guidelines, and news of press offerings and plans. Responds in 2 months. Pays at least 2 contributor's copies.

Book/Chapbook Needs & How to Submit ''Catamount Press publishes very few chapbooks, so please do not submit a manuscript. Get acquainted with us first by submitting to *Cotyledon*, or by querying.''

Advice ''Look over a copy and submit a few poems. If you don't hit in several tries, *Cotyledon* may not be the place for you. Selecting poems *is* subjective, and the editor has a vision of where he/she wants to go. Let's both be laid back.''

⬧ ☑ **CAVEAT LECTOR**

400 Hyde St., Apt. 606, San Francisco CA 94109-7445. Phone/fax: (415)928-7431. E-mail: editors@caveat-lector.org. Website: http://caveat-lector.org. Established 1989. **Editors:** Christopher Bernard, Ho Lin, and Adam Sass.

Magazine Needs Appearing 2 times/year, ''*Caveat Lector* is devoted to the arts and to cultural and philosophical commentary. We publish visual art and music as well as literary and theoretical texts. We are looking for accomplished poems, something that resonates in the mind long after the reader has laid the poem aside. We want work that has authenticity of emotion and high craft; whether raw or polished, that rings true—if humorous, actually funny, or at least witty. Classical to experimental. 500-line limit.'' Has published poetry by Deanne Bayer, Simon Perchik, Alfred Robinson, and E.S. Hilbert. *Caveat Lector* is 36-64 pages, $11 \times 4^1/4$, photocopied and saddle-stapled with color matte-gloss cover. Receives 200-600 poems/year, accepts about 1%. Press run is 300 for 20 subscribers, 200 shelf sales. Single copy: $3.50; subscription: $15/4 issues. Sample: $3.

How to Submit Submit up to 6 short poems (up to 50 lines each), 3 medium-length poems (51-100 lines), or one long poem (up to 500 lines) at a time ''on any subject, in any style, as long as the work is authentic in feeling and appropriately crafted.'' Place name, address, and (optional) telephone number on each page. Include SASE, cover letter, and brief bio (30 words or less). Accepts simultaneous submissions, ''but please inform us.'' Reads submissions from January to June. Time between acceptance and publication is one year. Sometimes comments on rejected poems. Guidelines available for SASE. Responds in one month. Pays 2 contributor's copies. Acquires first publication rights.

Advice ''The two rules of writing are: 1. Rewrite it again. 2. Rewrite it again. The writing level of most of our submissions is pleasingly high. A rejection by us is not always a criticism of the work, and we try to provide comments to our more promising submitters.''

☑ **CEDAR HILL PUBLICATIONS; CEDAR HILL REVIEW**

E-mail: cedarhill_bks@hotmail.com. Established 1996. **Poetry Editor:** Maggie Jaffe.

- ''Except for *Roque Dalton ReLoaded*, an anthology dedicated to the Salvadoran poet, we're suspending publication of the magazine but will still consider books of poetry.''

Book/Chapbook Needs & How to Submit Favors contemporary themes and engaged poetry. Has published poetry by Jimmy Santiago Baca, Lucille Lang Day, Sharon Doubiago, Yvette Hatrak, Richard Hoffman, Carol Lem, Michael McIrvin, Deborah Small, and Marilyn Zuckerman. Submit

10 poems and publication credits, September through May, to Maggie Jaffe, 3730 Arnold Ave., San Diego CA 92104-3444. Books are usually 64-80 pages, digest-sized, professionally printed, and perfect-bound.

☑ CENTER: A JOURNAL OF THE LITERARY ARTS

Center for the Literary Arts, 202 Tate Hall, University of Missouri, Columbia MO 65211-1500. (573)882-4971. E-mail: cla@missouri.edu. Website: www.missouri.edu/~center. Established 2000. **Contact:** Poetry Editor.

Magazine Needs *Center: A Journal for the Literary Arts* appears annually in April. Wants well-crafted verse of any kind. Also interested in seeing sequences, part or whole. Has published poetry by Annie Finch, Eric Pankey, Maura Stanton, Floyd Skloot, Simon Perchik, and Barbara Lefcowitz. *Center: A Journal* is 100+ pages, digest-sized, perfect-bound, with 4-color card cover, 3 ads for literary journals. Receives about 1,000 poems/year, accepts about 30. Publishes about 20-35 poems/issue. Press run is 500 for 100 subscribers. Single copy: $6 (current issue). Sample: $3 (back issue). Make checks payable to *Center: A Journal*.

How to Submit Submit 3-6 poems at a time. Simultaneous submissions OK with notification; no previously published poems. Accepts e-mail submissions from international poets only. Cover letter is preferred. Reads submissions July 1 through November 30. "Submissions received outside of the reading period will be returned unread." Time between acceptance and publication is up to 5 months. "An editorial board of experienced writers in our creative writing program reviews all submission as they arrive." Seldom comments on rejected poems. Guidelines available for SASE or on website. Responds in up to 4 months. Acquires first North American serial rights; rights revert to poets upon publication.

☑ CHAFFIN JOURNAL

Dept. of English, Case Annex 467, Eastern Kentucky University, Richmond KY 40475-3102. (859)622-3080. Established 1998. **Editor:** Robert W. Witt.

Magazine Needs *The Chaffin Journal* appears annually in December. Publishes quality short fiction and poetry by new and established writers/poets. Wants any form, subject matter, or style. Does not want "poor quality." Has published poetry by Taylor Graham, Diane Glancy, Judith Montgomery, Simon Perchik, Philip St. Clair, and Virgil Suárez. *The Chaffin Journal* is 120 pages, digest-sized, offset-printed, perfect-bound, with plain cover with title only. Receives about 500 poems/year, accepts about 10%. Publishes about 40-50 poems/issue. Press run is 300 for 65 subscribers of which 4 are libraries, 180 shelf sales; 40-50 are distributed free to contributors. Single copy: $6; subscription: $6 annually. Make checks payable to *The Chaffin Journal*.

How to Submit Submit 5 poems at a time. Accepts simultaneous submissions; no previously published poems. No fax, e-mail, or disk submissions. Cover letter is preferred. "Submit typed pages with only one poem per page. Enclose SASE." Reads submissions June 1 through October 1. Time between acceptance and publication is 6 months. Poems are reviewed by the general editor and 2 poetry editors. Never comments on rejected poems. Guidelines available in magazine. Responds in 3 months. Pays one contributor's copy. Acquires one-time rights.

Advice "Submit quality work during our reading period; include cover letter and SASE."

☑ ☐ ◎ CHALLENGER INTERNATIONAL; ISLAND SCHOLASTIC PRESS (Specialized: teen/young adult)

(250)991-5567. E-mail: lukivdan@hotmail.com. Website: http://challengerinternational.20m.com/index.html. Established 1978. **Editor:** Dan Lukiv.

Magazine Needs *Challenger international*, a literary annual, contains poetry, short fiction, novel excerpts, and black pen drawings. Open to "any type of work, especially by teenagers (*Ci*'s mandate: to encourage young writers, and to publish their work alongside established writers), provid-

ing it is not pornographic, profane, or overly abstract.'' *Ci* has published poetry from Canada, the continental US, Hawaii, Switzerland, Russia, Malta, Italy, Slovenia, Ireland, Korea, and Columbia. *Ci* is about 20 pages, magazine-sized, photocopied and side-stapled. Press run is 50. *Ci* is distributed free to McNaughton Centre Secondary Alternate School students.
How to Submit Accepts previously published poems and simultaneous submissions. Cover letter required with list of credits, if any. Accepts submissions by e-mail only. ''Sometimes we edit to save the poet rejection.'' Responds in 4 months. Pays one contributor's copy.
Book/Chapbook Needs & How to Submit Island Scholastic Press publishes chapbooks of work by authors featured in *Ci*. Pays 3 author's copies. Copyright remains with author. Distribution of free copies through McNaughton Centre.
Advice ''We like imagistic poetry that makes sense.''

CHAPMAN (Specialized: ethnic/nationality); CHAPMAN PUBLISHING
4 Broughton Place, Edinburgh EH1 3RX Scotland. Phone: (0131)557-2207. Fax: (0131)556-9565. E-mail: chapman-pub@blueyonder.co.uk. Website: www.chapman-pub.co.uk. Established 1970. **Editor:** Joy Hendry. **Assistant Editor:** Edmund O'Connor.
Magazine Needs *Chapman*, published 3 times/year, ''is controversial, influential, outspoken, and intelligent. Established in 1970, it has become a dynamic force in Scottish culture covering theatre, politics, language, and the arts. Our highly-respected forum for poetry, fiction, criticism, review, and debate makes it essential reading for anyone interested in contemporary Scotland. *Chapman* publishes the best in Scottish writing—new work by well-known Scottish writers in the context of lucid critical discussion. It also, increasingly, publishes international writing. With our strong commitment to the future, we energetically promote new writers, new ideas, and new approaches.'' Also interested in receiving poetry dealing with women's issues and feminism. Has published poetry and fiction by Alasdair Gray, Liz Lochhead, Sorley MacLean, T.S. Law, Edwin Morgan, Willa Muir, Tom Scott, and Una Flett. *Chapman* is 144 pages, digest-sized, perfect-bound, professionally printed in small type on matte stock with glossy card cover, art in 2 colors. Press run is 2,000 for 900 subscribers of which 200 are libraries. Receives ''thousands'' of poetry submissions/year, accepts about 200, has a 4- to 6-month backlog. Single copy: £6; subscription: £18. Sample: £4 (overseas).
How to Submit Submit 4-10 poems at a time, one poem/page. ''We do not usually publish single poems.'' No simultaneous submissions. Cover letter required. ''Submissions must be accompanied by a SASE/IRC. Please send sufficient postage to cover the return of your manuscript. Do not send foreign stamps.'' Responds ''as soon as possible.'' Always sends prepublication galleys. Pays contributor's copies. Staff reviews books of poetry. Send materials for review consideration.
Book/Chapbook Needs Chapman Publishing is currently not accepting submissions.
Advice ''Poets should not try to court approval by writing poems especially to suit what they perceive as the nature of the magazine. They usually get it wrong and write badly.''

$ CHAPULTEPEC PRESS
4222 Chambers, Cincinnati OH 45223. (513)681-1976. E-mail: chapultepecpress@hotmail.com. Website: www.TokyoRoseRecords.com. Established 2001. **Contact:** David Garza.
Book/Chapbook Needs & How to Submit Chapultepec Press publishes books of poetry/literature, essays, social/political issues, art, music, film, history, popular science; library/archive issues and bilingual works. Wants ''poetry/literature that works as a unit, that is caustic, fun, open-ended, worldly, mature, relevant, stirring, evocative. Bilingual. No poetry/literature collections without a purpose, that are mere collections. Also looking for broadsides/posters/illuminations.'' Publishes 3-5 books/year. Books are usually 1-100 pages, with art/graphics. Query first with a few sample poems, or a complete ms, and cover letter with brief bio and publication credits. Responds to

queries and mss in up to 2 months. Pays advance of $5-15 and 3-5 author's copies. Order sample books by sending $3 to David Garza.

Advice "Write as if your life depends on it . . . because it does."

$⊘ THE CHARITON REVIEW

English Dept., Brigham Young University, Provo UT 84602. (801)422-1503. Established 1975. **Editor:** Jim Barnes.

Magazine Needs *The Chariton Review* began in 1975 as a twice yearly literary magazine and in 1978 added the activities of the press (now defunct). The poetry published in the magazine is "open and closed forms—traditional, experimental, mainstream. We do not consider verse, only poetry in its highest sense, whatever that may be. The sentimental and the inspirational are not poetry for us. Also, no more 'relativism': short stories and poetry centered around relatives." Has published poetry by Michael Spence, Kim Bridgford, Sam Maio, Andrea Budy, Charles Edward Eaton, Wayne Dodd, and J'laine Robnolt. *The Chariton Review* is over 100 pages, digest-sized, flat-spined, professionally printed, with glossy cover with photographs. Receives 8,000-10,000 submissions/year, accepts about 35-50, with never more than a 6-month backlog. Press run is about 600 for 400 subscribers of which 100 are libraries. Subscription: $9/year, $15/2 years. Sample: $5.

How to Submit Submit 5-7 poems at a time, single-spaced typescript. No simultaneous submissions. Do *not* write for guidelines. Responds quickly; accepted poems often appear within a few issues of notification. Always sends prepublication galleys. Pays $5/printed page. Acquires first North American serial rights. **Contributors are expected to subscribe or buy copies.** Send materials for review consideration.

▨ ⊕ ⊘ CHASE PARK

% David Harrison Horton, Foreign Affairs Dept., Nanjing University of Economics, 128 Tie Lu Bei Jie, Nanjing 210003 China. E-mail: twentymule@yahoo.com. Website: www.geocities.com/twentymule/index.html. Established 2000. **Editor:** David Harrison Horton.

• *"Chase Park* **is currently on an extended hiatus and not reading manuscripts at this time. Please check** *Poets & Writers* **or our website for status updates."**

$⊘ THE CHATTAHOOCHEE REVIEW

Georgia Perimeter College, 2101 Womack Rd., Dunwoody GA 30338. (770)551-3019. Website: www.chattahoochee-review.org. Established 1980. **Editor-in-Chief:** Lawrence Hetrick.

Magazine Needs *The Chattahoochee Review* is a quarterly of poetry, short fiction, essays, reviews, and interviews, published by Georgia Perimeter College. "We publish a number of Southern writers, but *Chattahoochee Review* is not by design a regional magazine. All themes, forms, and styles are considered as long as they impact the whole person: heart, mind, intuition, and imagination." Has published poetry by A.E. Stalling, Carolyne Wright, Coleman Barks, Ron Rash, and Fred Chappell. *Chattahoochee Review* is 140 pages, digest-sized, professionally printed on cream stock with reproductions of artwork, flat-spined, with one-color card cover. Recent issues feature a wide range of forms and styles augmenting prose selections. Press run is 1,250, of which 300 are complimentary copies sent to editors and "miscellaneous VIPs." Subscription: $16/year. Sample: $6.

How to Submit Writers should send one copy of each poem and a cover letter with bio material. No simultaneous submissions. Time between acceptance and publication is up to 4 months. Publishes theme issues. Guidelines and a list of upcoming themes available for SASE. Responds to queries in 2 weeks; to mss in 3 months. Pays $50/poem and 2 contributor's copies. Acquires first rights. Staff reviews books of poetry and short fiction in 1,500 words, single or multi-book format. Send materials for review consideration.

N ☑ CHAUTAUQUA LITERARY JOURNAL; CHAUTAUQUA LITERARY JOURNAL ANNUAL CONTEST

P.O. Box 613, Chautauqua NY 14722. E-mail: CLJEditor@aol.com. Established 2003. **Editor:** Richard Foerster.

Magazine Needs *Chautauqua Literary Journal* is an annual magazine of poetry, short fiction, creative nonfiction, and book reviews, published in June. "We welcome poems that exhibit the writer's craft and attention to language, employ striking images and metaphors, engage the mind as well as the emotions, and reveal insights into the larger world of human concerns. The editor invites traditional as well as experimental work." Does not want "hackneyed inspirational versifying, poems typed in all capitals or on pastel paper." Has published poetry by Betty Adcock, Ellen Bass, William Heyen, Colette Inez, Margaret Gibson, and Gabriel Welsch. *Chautauqua Literary Journal* is 196 pages, digest-sized, offset-printed, with notch adhesive binding and glossy 10 pt. CS1 stock with original artwork, includes ads. Receives about 2,000 poems/year, accepts about 50. Publishes 50 poems/issue. Press run is 2,000 for 1,200 subscribers, 500 shelf sales; 300 are distributed free to contributors and VIPs. Single copy: $12.95; subscription: $10. Make checks payable to The Writers' Center at Chautauqua, Inc.

How to Submit Submit a maximum of 4 poems at a time. Accepts simultaneous submissions (if notified); no previously published poems. No e-mail or disk submissions. Cover letter is preferred. "Prefer single-spaced manuscripts in 12 pt. font. Cover letters should be brief and mention recent publications (if any). SASE is mandatory." Reads submissions year round. Time between acceptance and publication is up to one year. "The editor is the sole arbiter, but we do have advisory editors who periodically make recommendations." Sometimes comments on rejected poems. Guidelines available for SASE or by e-mail. Responds in 3 months or less. Always sends prepublication galleys. Pays 2 contributor's copies. Acquires first rights plus one-time non-exclusive rights to reprint accepted work in an anniversary issue. Reviews books and chapbooks of poetry in 750-1,000 words, single and multi-book format. Send materials for review consideration to *Chautauqua Literary Journal*/Reviews, P.O. Box 2039, York Beach ME 03910.

Contest/Award Offerings Annual contest awards two $1,500 prizes (payable upon publication), one for best poem or group of poems, one for best prose work. Winners selected in anonymous competitions by the magazine's editor and advisory staff. Winning entries are published in *Chautauqua Literary Journal*, and all work entered is considered for publication. Submit up to 6 poems or a maximum of 500 lines. Each entry will be judged for overall artistic excellence; the poems do not have to be related by theme. Only original, previously unpublished work is eligible. See guidelines (available for SASE) for formatting instructions. **Entry fee:** $15 U.S./entry. Make checks payable to The Writers' Center at Chautauqua, Inc. Each entrant will receive a copy of *Chautauqua Literary Journal* that contains the prize-winning entries. **Postmark deadline:** September 30. Winners will be announced in early January. **Mail to:** *Chautauqua Literary Journal* Annual Contests, P.O. Box 2039, York Beach ME 03910 (do not mail entries to Chautauqua, NY address).

Also Offers The Writers' Center at Chautauqua (see separate listing in the Conferences & Workshops section).

Advice "Poets who are not avid readers of contemporary poetry will most likely not be writing anything of interest to us."

✪ $☑ CHELSEA; CHELSEA AWARD FOR POETRY

P.O. Box 773, Cooper Station, New York NY 10276-0773. Established 1958. **Editor:** Alfredo de Palchi. **Associate Editor:** Andrea Lockett.

- Work published in *Chelsea* has been included in *The Best American Poetry*, in the *Beacon's Best* anthologies, and in *Pushcart Prizes*.

Magazine Needs *Chelsea* is a long-established, high-quality literary biannual, appearing in June and December, that aims to promote intercultural communication. "We look for intelligence and sophisticated technique in both experimental and traditional forms. We are also interested in translations of contemporary poets. Although our tastes are eclectic, we lean toward the cosmopolitan avant-garde. We would like to see more poetry by writers of color. Do not want to see 'inspirational' verse, pornography, or poems that rhyme merely for the sake of rhyme." *Chelsea* is 192-240 pages, digest-sized, perfect-bound, offset-printed, with full-color art on card cover, occasional photos, ads. Press run is 2,100 for 900 subscribers. Subscription: $13 domestic, $16 foreign. Sample: $6.

How to Submit Submissions of 5-8 pages of poetry are ideal; long poems should not exceed 10 pages. Must be typed double-spaced; include brief bio. No previously published poems or simultaneous submissions. Reads submissions from September to June. Guidelines available for SASE. Responds within up to 5 months. Always sends prepublication galleys. Pays $15/page and 2 contributor's copies. Acquires first North American serial rights and one-time non-exclusive reprint rights.

Contest/Award Offerings The *Chelsea* Award for Poetry offers annual award of $1,000 and publication in *Chelsea* for the best group of poems selected by the editors in anonymous competition. All work entered is considered for publication. Submissions must be unpublished; may not be under consideration elsewhere or scheduled for book publication within 8 months of the competition deadline. Submit 4-6 poems, the entire entry not to exceed 500 lines. Poems do not need to be related thematically. Manuscripts must be typed (single-spaced for poetry). Poet's name should not appear on the ms itself; include a single, separate cover sheet with title(s), poet's name, address, and telephone number, plus e-mail address. No entries or inquiries by phone, fax, or e-mail. Manuscripts cannot be returned; include SASE for competition results. Guidelines available for SASE. **Entry fee:** $10 (includes subscription to *Chelsea*). **Cannot accept fees by personal check; only money order or bank check will be accepted.** Make fee payable to Chelsea Associates, Inc. **Postmark deadline:** December 15. Winners will be announced about 2 months after the deadline.

Advice "Read first what kind of poetry is published in *Chelsea*. Beginners should realize editors of little magazines are always overworked and that it is necessary haste and not a lack of concern or compassion that makes rejections seem coldly impersonal."

☐ CHILDREN, CHURCHES AND DADDIES; SCARS PUBLICATIONS
829 Brian Court, Gurnee IL 60031. E-mail: ccandd96@scars.tv. Website: http://scars.tv (*cc&d mag* button). Established 1993. **Editor/Publisher:** Janet Kuypers.

Magazine Needs *Children, Churches and Daddies (The Unreligious, Non-Family-Oriented Literary Magazine)* is published "monthly and contains poetry, prose, art, and essays. We specialize in electronic issues and collection books. We accept poetry of almost any genre, but we're not keen on rhyme for rhyme's sake, and we're not keen on religious poems (look at our current issue for a better idea of what we're like). We are okay with gay/lesbian/bisexual, nature/rural/ecology, political/social issues, women/feminism. We do accept longer works, but within 2 pages for an individual poem is appreciated. We don't go for racist, sexist (therefore we're not into pornography, either), or homophobic stuff." Has published poetry by Rochelle Holt, Angeline Hawkes-Craig, Cheryl Townsend, Kurt Nimmo, Pete McKinley, and Janine Canan. Print versions of *Children, Churches and Daddies* have ranged from 30 to 100 pages, have been both digest-sized and standard-sized, photocopied, saddle-stapled, with art and ads. Receives hundreds of poems/year, accepts about 40%. Press run "depends." Sample: $6. Make checks payable to Janet Kuypers.

How to Submit Accepts submissions by e-mail (pasted into body of message or as attachment) or on disk only. When submitting via e-mail in body of message, explain in preceding paragraph that it is a submission; for disk submissions, mail floppy disk with ASCII text, or Macintosh disk. Accepts previously published poems and simultaneous submissions. Comments on rejected poems if asked. Guidelines available for SASE, by e-mail, or on website. Responds in 2 weeks.

Also Offers Scars Publications sometimes sponsors a book contest. Write or e-mail (Editor@scars.tv) for information. "The website is a more comprehensive view of what *Children, Churches and*

Publishers of Poetry

Daddies does. All the information is there.'' Also able to publish chapbooks. Write for more information.

✷ CHIRON REVIEW; CHIRON BOOKS; KINDRED SPIRIT PRESS

702 N. Prairie, St. John KS 67576-1516. (620)786-4955. E-mail: chironreview@hotmail.com. Website: www.geocities.com/SoHo/Nook/1748/. Established 1982 as *The Kindred Spirit*. **Editor:** Michael Hathaway.

Magazine Needs *Chiron Review* is a quarterly tabloid using photographs of featured writers. No taboos. Has published poetry by Sam Pierstorff, Linda Rocheleau, Will Inman, Ian Young, and Shane Allison. Each issue ''contains dozens of poems.'' Press run is about 1,000. Subscription: $15 US, $30 overseas. Sample: $5 US, $10 overseas or institutions.

How to Submit Submit 3-6 poems at a time, ''typed or printed legibly, not folded separately.'' No simultaneous submissions or previously published poems. No e-mail submissions; accepts submissions by postal mail only. Very seldom publishes theme issues. Guidelines and upcoming themes available for SASE or on website. Responds in 2 months. Pays one contributor's copy with a discount on additional copies. Acquires first-time rights. Reviews books of poetry in 500-700 words. Send materials for review consideration.

Book/Chapbook Needs & How to Submit For book publication, query. Publishes 1-3 chapbooks/year, flat-spined, professionally printed. Pays 25% of press run of 100-200 copies.

Also Offers Personal Publishing Program is offered under the Kindred Spirit Press imprint. ''Through special arrangements with a highly specialized printer, we can offer extremely short run publishing at unbelievably low prices.'' Information available for SASE.

$✷ ◎ THE CHRISTIAN CENTURY (Specialized: Christian, social issues)

Dept. PM, 104 S. Michigan Ave., Suite 700, Chicago IL 60603. (312)263-7510. Fax: (312)263-7540. Website: www.ChristianCentury.com. Established 1884. Named *The Christian Century* 1900, estab. again 1908, joined by *New Christian* 1970. **Poetry Editor:** Jill Peláez Baumgaertner.

Magazine Needs This ''ecumenical weekly'' is a liberal, sophisticated journal of news, articles of opinion, and reviews from a generally Christian point-of-view, using approximately one poem/issue, not necessarily on religious themes but in keeping with the literate tone of the magazine. Wants ''poems that are not statements but experiences, that do not talk about the world but show it. We want to publish poems that are grounded in images and that reveal an awareness of the sounds of language and the forms of poetry even when the poems are written in free verse.'' Does not want ''pietistic or sentimental doggerel.'' Has published poetry by Jeanne Murray Walker, Ida Fasel, Kathleen Norris, Luci Shaw, J. Barrie Shepherd, and Wendell Berry. *Christian Century* is about 30 pages, magazine-sized, saddle-stapled, printed on quality newsprint, includes b&w art, cartoons, and ads. Sample: $3.

How to Submit Submit poems of up to 20 lines, typed double-spaced, one poem/page. Include your name, address, and phone number on each page. ''Prefer shorter poems.'' No simultaneous submissions. Submissions without SASE or SAE and IRCs will not be returned. Pays usually $20/poem plus one contributor's copy and discount on additional copies. Acquires all rights. Inquire about reprint permission. Reviews books of poetry in 300-400 words, single book format; 400-500 words, multi-book format.

✷ ◎ CHRISTIAN GUIDE (Specialized: Christian)

P.O. Box 14622, Knoxville TN 37914. E-mail: Godpoems@aol.com. Established 1989. **Poetry Editor:** J. Brian Long.

Magazine Needs *The Christian Guide* is a regional, quarterly publication featuring articles, announcements, advertisements, photographs, and poetry. ''We seek positive, accessible poetry that concerns itself with the interaction between God and the nature of (and surrounding) mankind in micro- or macrocosm. All poems themed to the gentler tenets of the devotion reciprocated between Heaven and Earth are welcomed, but only the most well-crafted will be accepted.'' Does not want forced, trite rhyme. Has published poetry by Jill Alexander Essbaum, C.E. Chaffin, Teresa White, Dennis Greene, Charles Semones, and Leo Yankevich. *The Christian Guide* has a varied number of pages, is magazine-sized with full-color cover with photographs and/or artwork, includes b&w and full-color ads. Publishes about 1-3 poems/issue. Press run is 25,000. Single copy or subscription: free for SASE.

How to Submit Submit 1-5 poems at a time. Maximum length for poetry is 200 words. Accepts previously published poems and simultaneous submissions. Accepts e-mail submissions (pasted into body of message); no fax or disk submissions. Cover letter is required. ''Include brief bio, list of publishing credits, and a SASE.'' Reads submissions year round. Submit seasonal poems 6 months in advance. Seldom comments on rejected poems. Occasionally publishes theme issues. List of upcoming themes and guidelines available for SASE or by e-mail. Responds in 3 months. Pays 2 contributor's copies. Acquires one-time rights.

Advice ''Subtlety. Subtlety. Subtlety. We are seeking poems that inspire awe, but do so by speaking to (and through) the reader with that 'small, still voice.' ''

⚡ $⊘ THE CHRISTIAN SCIENCE MONITOR

The Home Forum Page, One Norway St., Boston MA 02115. Website: www.csmonitor.com. Established 1908. **Poetry Editor:** Sara Steindorf.

Magazine Needs *Christian Science Monitor* is an international daily newspaper. Poetry used regularly in The Home Forum section. Wants ''finely crafted poems that explore and celebrate daily life; that provide a respite from daily news and from the bleakness that appears in so much contemporary verse.'' Does not want ''work that presents people in helpless or hopeless states; poetry about death, aging, or illness; or dark, violent, sensual poems. No poems that are overtly religious or falsely sweet.'' Considers free verse and fixed forms. Publishes 2 poems/week. Has published work by Diana Der-Hovanessian, Marilyn Krysl, and Michael Glaser.

How to Submit Submit up to 5 poems at a time, typed. ''For us, 20 lines is a long poem.'' No previously published poems or simultaneous submissions. E-mails not encouraged; no attachments. Include all contact information on ms (name and address on each page); SASE must be included. Responds in one month. Pays $25 (haiku) to $45.

⊘ ◎ CHRISTIANITY AND LITERATURE (Specialized: religious, spirituality/ inspirational)

Dept. of Humanities, Pepperdine University, 24255 Pacific Coast Highway, Malibu CA 90263. **Poetry Editor:** Maire Mullins.

Magazine Needs *Christianity and Literature* is a quarterly scholarly journal publishing about 6-8 poems/issue. Press run is 1,350 for 1,125 subscribers of which 525 are libraries, 600 individuals. Single copy: $7; subscription: $25/year, $45/2 years. Make checks payable to CCL.

How to Submit Submit 1-6 poems at a time. No previously published poems or simultaneous submissions. Accepts submissions by surface mail only. Cover letter is required. Submissions must be accompanied by SASE. Time between acceptance and publication is 3-4 months. ''Poems are chosen by our poetry editor.'' Responds within one month. Pays 2 contributor's copies ''and a dozen offprints to poets whose work we publish.'' Rights revert to poets upon written request. Reviews poetry collections in each issue (no chapbooks).

Advice ''We look for poems that are clear and surprising. They should have a compelling sense of voice, formal sophistication (though not necessarily rhyme and meter), and the ability to reveal the spiritual through concrete images. We cannot return submissions that are not accompanied by SASE.''

$ ☑ ◎ CHRYSALIS READER (Specialized: spirituality; themes)

Rt. 1 Box 4510, Dillwyn VA 23936-9616. Fax: (434)983-1074. E-mail: chrysalis@hovac.com. Established 1985. **Editor:** Carol S. Lawson. **Poetry Editor:** Robert F. Lawson.

Magazine Needs *Chrysalis Reader* is published by the Swedenborg Foundation as a "contribution to the search for spiritual wisdom." Appearing annually in September, it is a "book series that challenges inquiring minds through the use of literate and scholarly fiction, essays, and poetry. Nothing overly religious or sophomoric. Poetry that surprises, that pushes the language, gets our attention." Has published work by Robert Bly, Linda Pastan, Wesley McNair, Wyn Cooper, William Kloefkorn, and Virgil Suárez. *Chrysalis Reader* is 208 pages, 7 × 10, professionally printed on archival paper, perfect-bound, with coated coverstock, illustrations, and photos. Receives about 1,000 submissions/year, accepts about 12 poems. Press run is 3,500. Sample: $10.

How to Submit Submit no more than 5 poems at one time with SASE. No previously published poems; accepts simultaneous submissions "if notified immediately when work is accepted elsewhere." Reads submissions year round. Time between acceptance and publication is typically 18 months. Upcoming themes include "Relationships" (2005), "Passages" (2006), and "Other Worlds" (2007). Guidelines and upcoming themes also available for SASE. Responds in 3 months. Always sends prepublication galleys.

Charlene Wakefield's hot air balloons, as well as the artistic process of broken china mosaic, embodies the spirit of serendipity addressed in the *Chances Are* issue. Cover design by Caroline Kline.

Pays $25 and 3 contributor's copies. Acquires first-time rights. "We expect to be credited for reprints after permission is given."

Advice "Purchase a back issue or request your favorite bookstore to order a reading copy so that you can better gauge what to submit."

✳ ☑ CIDER PRESS REVIEW

777 Braddock Lane, Halifax PA 17032. E-mail: editor@ciderpressreview.com. Website: http://cider pressreview.com. Established 1997. **Co-Editors:** Caron Andregg and Robert Wynne.

Magazine Needs *Cider Press Review* appears annually and features "the best new work from contemporary poets." Wants "thoughtful, well-crafted poems with vivid language and strong images. We prefer poems that have something to say. We would like to see more well-written humor. No didactic, inspirational, greeting-card verse; therapy or religious doggerel." Has published poetry by Jackson Wheeler, Janet Holmes, W.D. Snodgrass, Thomas Lux, Linda Pastan, and Gary Young. *Cider Press Review* is 120 pages, digest-sized, offset-printed, perfect-bound, with 2-color coated card cover. Receives about 1,500 poems/year, accepts about 5%. Press run is 750. Subscription: $22/2 issues. Sample: $10.

How to Submit Submit up to 5 poems at a time. Accepts simultaneous submissions; no previously published poems. Accepts submissions by postal mail only; "Authors outside North America may send *queries* by e-mail. Poets whose work is accepted will be expected to provide a copy of the poem on disk or via e-mail. Do not send unsolicited disk or e-mail submissions." Cover letter with short bio preferred. ''Please include a SASE.'' Reads submissions from April to August only. Time between acceptance and publication is up to 10 months. Poems are circulated to an editorial board. Guidelines available for SASE. Responds in up to 6 months. Pays one contributor's copy. Acquires first North American serial rights.

⊠ $🖉 THE CINCINNATI REVIEW

P.O. Box 210069, Cincinnati OH 45221-0069. (513)556-3954. E-mail: editors@cincinnatireview.com. Website: www.cincinnatireview.com. Established 2003. **Poetry Editor:** James Cummins.

Magazine Needs *The Cincinnati Review* is a biannual journal ''devoted to publishing the best new poetry and literary fiction, as well as book reviews, essays, and interviews. Open to any schools, styles, forms, as long as the poem is well made and sophisticated in its language use and subject matter.'' *The Cincinnati Review* is 180-200 pages, digest-sized, perfect-bound, with matte paperback cover with full-color art, includes 8-page full-color insert and ads. Publishes about 50 poems/issue. Press run is 1,500. Single copy: $7; subscription: $12.

How to Submit Submit up to 10 pages of poetry at a time. Accepts simultaneous submissions with notification; no previously published poems. No e-mail or disk submissions. Cover letter is preferred. SASE required. Reads submissions September 1 through June 30. Time between acceptance and publication is 6 months. ''First-round reading by small, trained staff. Final decisions made by genre editors.'' Seldom comments on rejected poems. Guidelines available for SASE or on website. Responds in one month. Always sends prepublication galleys. Pays $30/page and 2 contributor's copies. Acquires first North American serial rights. Reviews books of poetry in 1,500 words, single book format.

Advice ''Be honest with yourself, if nobody else. Try to keep in clear view your motivation in general as a writer, as well as the *raison d'etre* of the particular piece you're working on.''

✪ ◯ THE CIRCLE MAGAZINE; HIGHWIRE PRESS

173 Grandview Rd., Wernersville PA 19565. (610)678-6650. Fax: (610)678-6550. E-mail: circlemag@aol.com. Website: www.circlemagazine.com. Established 1998. **Editor:** Penny Talbert.

Magazine Needs *The Circle Magazine* is a quarterly literary magazine ''where culture and subculture meet. Read the poetry we currently publish'' for style and content. Does not want anything religious or predictable. Has published poetry by Ace Boggess, Virgil Suarez, and Janet Buck. *The Circle Magazine* is 48-52 pages, digest-sized, offset-printed, saddle-stapled, with 2-color gloss cover. Receives about 4,000 poems/year, accepts about 1%. Publishes about 10 poems/issue. Press run varies. Single copy: $4; subscription: $15.

How to Submit Submit 3-5 poems at a time. Line length for poetry is 4 minimum, 50 maximum. Accepts previously published poems and simultaneous submissions. Accepts e-mail submissions (pasted into body of message); no fax or disk submissions. Cover letter is preferred. Include name, address, and e-mail with all submissions. Reads submissions year round. Time between acceptance and publication is 3-5 months. Poems are circulated to an editorial board. Seldom comments on rejected poems. Guidelines available on website. Responds in up to 4 months. Pays one contributor's copy. Acquires one-time rights. Reviews books and chapbooks of poetry.

Book/Chapbook Needs & How to Submit Highwire Press publishes poetry chapbooks and nonfiction. Publishes 1-2 chapbooks/year. Manuscripts selected through open submission. Chapbooks are 40-52 pages, offset-printed, perfect-bound, gloss cover. Query first, with a few sample poems and a cover letter with brief bio and publication credits. Chapbook mss may include previously published poems. ''We normally solicit poets we're interested in publishing.'' Responds to queries in up to 2 months; to mss in up to 8 months. **Approximately 50% of books/chapbooks are author-subsidy published.**

Also Offers Annual poetry contest.

✚ ◐ ◎ THE CLAREMONT REVIEW (Specialized: teens/young adults)

4980 Wesley Rd., Victoria BC V8Y 1Y9 Canada. (250)658-5221 ext. 253. Fax: (250)658-5387. Website: www.theClaremontReview.com. Established 1991. **Contact:** Janice McCachen.

Magazine Needs *The Claremont Review* is a biannual review that publishes poetry and fiction written by those ages 13 to 19. Each Fall issue also includes an interview with a prominent Canadian writer. Wants "vital, modern poetry with a strong voice and living language. We prefer works that reveal something of the human condition. No clichéd language nor copies of 18th- and 19th-century work." Has published poetry by Claire Battershill, Danielle Hubbard, and Jennifer Slade. *The Claremont Review* is 110 pages, digest-sized, professionally printed, perfect-bound, with an attractive color cover. Receives 600-800 poems/year, accepts about 120. Press run is 700 for 200 subscribers of which 50 are libraries, 250 shelf sales. Subscription: $15/year, $25/2 years. Sample: $8.

How to Submit Submit poems typed one to a page with author's name at the top of each. Accepts simultaneous submissions; no previously published poems. Cover letter with brief bio required. Reads submissions September through June only. Always comments on rejected poems. Guidelines available on website. Responds in up to 6 weeks (excluding July and August). Pays one contributor's copy, and funds when grants allow it. Acquires first North American serial rights.

Advice "Read excerpts on the website, and content of back issues."

◑ ◎ CLARK STREET REVIEW (Specialized: form/style, narrative and prose poetry)

P.O. Box 1377, Berthoud CO 80513. E-mail: clarkreview@earthlink.net. Established 1998. **Editor:** Ray Foreman.

Magazine Needs Appearing 8 times/year, *Clark Street Review* publishes narrative poetry and short shorts—"to give writers and poets cause to keep writing by publishing their best work." Wants "narrative poetry under 100 lines that reaches readers who are mostly published poets and writers. Subjects are open. No obscure or formalist work." Has published poetry by Louis McKee, Mariann Ritzer, Alan Catlin, Al De Genova, and Laurel Speer. *Clark Street Review* is 20 pages, digest-sized, photocopied, and saddle-stapled with paper cover. Receives about 1,000 poems/year, accepts about 10%. Press run is 200 for 150 subscribers. Subscription: $10 for 10 issues postpaid for writers. Single copy: $2. Make checks payable to R. Foreman.

How to Submit Submit 1-5 poems at a time. Line length for poetry is 20 minimum, 75 maximum. Accepts previously published poems and simultaneous submissions. "Disposable sharp copies. Maximum width—65 characters. Include SASE for reply. No cover letter." Time between acceptance and publication is 4 months. "Editor reads everything with a critical eye of 30 years of experience in writing and publishing small press work." Often comments on rejected poems. Guidelines available for SASE or by e-mail. Responds in 3 weeks. Acquires one-time rights.

Advice "*Clark Street Review* is geared to the more experienced poet and writer deeply involved in the writer's life. There are tips and quotes throughout each issue writers appreciate. As always, the work we print speaks for the writer and the magazine. We encourage communication between our poets by listing their e-mail addresses. Publishing excellence and giving writers a reason to write is our only aim. Well-crafted, interesting, and accessible human narrative poems will see ink in *CSR*."

✚ ◐ ◎ CLEVELAND STATE UNIVERSITY POETRY CENTER; CSU POETRY SERIES; CLEVELAND POETS SERIES (Specialized: regional/Ohio); CLEVELAND STATE UNIVERSITY POETRY CENTER PRIZES

Cleveland State University Poetry Center, 2121 Euclid Ave., Cleveland OH 44115-2214. (216)687-3986 or toll-free: (888)278-6473. Fax: (216)687-6943. E-mail: poetrycenter@csuohio.edu. Website: www.csuohio.edu/poetrycenter. The Poetry Center was established in 1962; first publications in 1971. **Coordinator:** Rita Grabowski.

Book/Chapbook Needs The Poetry Center publishes the CSU Poetry Series for poets in general

Publishers of Poetry

Jared Carter

The universality of the local

Photo by Minnick Editorial

Reading one of Jared Carter's books can be likened to having a conversation with a local historian in a small-town diner. You hear a wealth of particulars mixed with myths and news about the neighbors, all leavened with a bit of gossipy humor. "I seek out people like that," Carter remarks, "in places where everyone else has forgotten why a particular feature of the town or the community has remained. With luck you find a few people who remember hearing about it from their parents or their grandparents."

Most of Carter's poems, particularly the narratives, are set in a place called Mississinewa County. Carter introduced this fictional Indiana landscape in his first full-length collection, *Work, for the Night Is Coming*, which won the Walt Whitman Award in 1980. Mississinewa County was described as being "east of Spoon River, west of Winesburg, and slightly north of Raintree County." This nod to Edgar Lee Masters and Sherwood Anderson is more than literary namedropping.

Carter admires those writers along with many other "regional" artists such as Faulkner, Flannery O'Connor, Sarah Orne Jewett, and Ted Kooser—writers who chose to remain close to their subject matter. Like them, Carter has worked to find the secret of making his landscape universal without sacrificing its local character. His language, while simple and accessible, loses nothing in its elegance.

William Stafford, with whom Carter was acquainted during his younger years, once wrote, "All events and experiences / are local somewhere." The admiration and respect Carter has garnered from readers and critics vindicates his pride in maintaining his regional connections. Dana Gioia, a poet, critic, and current head of the National Endowment for the Arts, has pointed out that Carter "is the rare poet who is rooted in a certain place, which of course is Indiana, yet he deals with it in such a way that it is of universal interest."

Carter's ties to Indiana are strong. He was born in Elwood, in north-central Indiana, in 1939. His father and grandfather were general contractors, and the family had been in the area for generations. Raised and educated locally, Carter attended Yale on scholarship. A stint in the Army Signal Corps fortuitously landed him in France in the early 1960s. But gradually the Midwestern landscape drew him back, and Carter has lived in Indianapolis since the late 1960s.

There is an elegiac tone in many of Carter's poems. The traditions of rural Midwestern life are rapidly fading from memory. Many young persons have moved to the sprawling urban centers and the subdivisions that fill the fields where corn and soybeans once grew. Wal-Marts and outlet malls have replaced the hub of small-town main streets. Those towns within commuting distance now serve as bedroom communities artificially sustained by their connection with a city rather than the land as it existed in generations past.

Carter's elegies are hardly sentimental or nostalgic; rather, they are clear-eyed and tough. He knows Midwestern life, and he admires its traditions of sturdy self-reliance and strong community ties. But he also knows the potential for hardship and tragedy to be found in that same world. In "The Gleaning," a poem in his second book, *After the Rain*, Carter describes a threshing-machine accident that kills a farm worker. A childhood friend, now the local barber, comes to the farm to prepare the dead man's body for the funeral:

> . . . As he works up a lather
> and brushes it onto his cheeks,
> he tells him the latest joke. He strops
> the razor, tests it against his thumb,
> and scolds him for not being more careful.

While the world of strops, straight razors, and threshing machines, a world where corpses are viewed in the parlor, is not part of most readers' memories or experience, the sense of community connection and loss transcends its historical backdrop:

> And as though his friend had fallen asleep
> and it were time now for him to stand up
> and stretch his arms and look at his face . . .
> the barber trims the lamp, and leans down,
> and says, for the last time, his name.

In Patrick Kavanagh's sonnet, "Epic," in which the poet has just witnessed a boundary dispute between farmers, the ghost of Homer whispers in the poet's mind, *"I made the Iliad from such a local row. Gods make their own importance."* Kavanagh (or Homer, for that matter) would have no trouble recognizing the "heroes" of "The Madhouse," a narrative poem from *Work, for the Night Is Coming*, in which the town's former football stars and poolroom denizens challenge a Ku Klux Klan march in the 1920s. It has the feel of a story recounted many times, the edges worn smooth by time and re-telling:

> Then I was not born. My father,
> who saw it, was still in high school;
> and there are others who remember
> the poolroom on the avenue.

The poolroom becomes the Heorot Hall of *Beowulf* fame, where handsome young warriors bide their time. Mythmaking knows no time or place as the anonymous author of the Anglo-Saxon epic opens his story:

> So. The Spear-Danes in days gone by
> and the kings who ruled them had courage and greatness.
> We have heard of those princes' heroic campaigns.

The princes of "The Madhouse," too, have achieved immortality in Carter's lines:

> *That*
> *was years ago. They're all dead now,*
> *Swede and the Baxter boys, and*
> *Handsome Richard O'Reilly . . .*

Modern encroachments such as rural electrification and the building of flood-control reservoirs continue to change Mississinewa County. In Carter's poems there is an urge to commemorate and to preserve, before the traditional world slips away entirely beneath the waters. "Monument City" and "The Purpose of Poetry" examine the consequences of damming the Mississinewa River.

In the first poem, a narrator visits a favorite aunt whose house will soon disappear beneath the floodwaters. The retired schoolmarm has asked the local undertaker to photograph the house and grounds so that something might be preserved for posterity (multitasking is an essential part of rural life, though Mississinewa residents would be unfamiliar with the term). Carter, with photographic clarity, shows the essence of this woman's life and its intricate web of relationships. However, not all lives can be preserved. In "The Purpose of Poetry," an aging farmer, knowing that his farm will soon be inundated, shoots his two dogs and then turns the gun on himself.

For Carter, even seemingly inanimate objects, such as geodes—commonplace crystalline formations sometimes found along rivers and streams—present cause for both celebration and lamentation:

> *They are useless, there is nothing*
> *To be done with them, no reason, only*
>
> *The finding . . .*

"Geodes" elevates these "useless" clumps of stone and crystal, turning them into a metaphor for the fleeting impermanence of human existence:

> *I want to know only that things gather themselves*
> *With great patience, that they do this forever.*

In 1999, Carter's *Les Barricades Mystérieuses: Thirty-Two Villanelles* was published by Cleveland State University Poetry Center (which now publishes all three of his collections). It continues the Mississinewa County saga, if not as overtly as Carter's earlier work. It offers a strictly formal perspective, and the exclusive use of the repetitive villanelle is new. Also, the book is more contemplative than narrative in its approach to the history it contains. But, in general, Carter eschews terms and labels such as "formal" or "free verse." His aim is to write honest, evocative poetry.

For all his traditional ways, does he live in a log cabin and write on sheets of foolscap with a quill pen? Not at all. He acquired a word processor in the early 1980s, almost as soon as they were made available. And today he's online 24/7 with his own website, a collection of poems and photographs that can be accessed at www.jaredcarter.com.

Carter is grateful for all the help he has received. He can look back on a career that includes a Guggenheim, two NEA grants, and the Indiana Governor's Arts Award. "Poets don't require much, in material terms, to get their work done," he says, "but their psychic needs can be considerable. I've been fortunate. I'm part of a community, and I'm in touch with persons who believe in poetry, art, and craftsmanship. It wasn't always that way.

There were long years of apprenticeship. But I benefited from the encouragement of others, and I persevered.''

And we are all so much richer that he did.

—*Barney F. McClelland*

Barney F. McClelland has published numerous short stories, articles, and poems on both sides of the Atlantic in such publications as *Acorn* (Dublin Writers Group), *Oxford Magazine* (Miami University Press), and *The New Formalist*. His poetry chapbooks have been published by An Cailleach Press, KOTA Press, and Seaweed Sideshow Circus. He currently works as a freelance writer and editor in Cincinnati, Ohio.

and the Cleveland Poets Series for Ohio poets. ''Open to many kinds of form, length, subject matter, style, and purpose. Should be well-crafted, clearly of professional quality, ultimately serious (even when humorous). No light verse, devotional verse, or verse in which rhyme and meter seem to be of major importance.'' Recent CSU Poetry Series publications include *The Job of Being Everbody* by Douglas Goetsch, *Double Exposure* by Sarah Kennedy, *Guide to Native Beasts* by Mary Quade, and The Saint of Letting Small Fish Go by Eliot Khalil Wilson. Publications in the Cleveland Poets Series include *One of Everything* by Diane Gilliam Fisher.

Contest/Award Offerings Books are chosen for publication from the entries to the 2 contest categories: First Book and Open Competition, the latter for poets who have published a collection of a least 48 pages with a press run of at least 500. **Entry fee:** $20. **Postmark deadline:** February 1. Winners receive $1,000, 50 author's copies, and publication. The Cleveland Poets Series (for Ohio poets) offers 80 copies of a press run of 800. To submit for all series, send mss between November 1 and February 1 only. Responds to all submissions for the year by the end of summer. Accepts simultaneous submissions (if notified of acceptance elsewhere). No e-mail submissions. Manuscripts should be ''clear and contain a minimum of 40 pages of poetry and a table of contents, pages numbered.'' Manuscript should include 2 cover sheets—the first including ms title, poet's name, address, phone number, and e-mail; the second including ms title only. Poet's name should appear on first cover sheet and nowhere else on ms. Do not send acknowledgments, cover letters, or bio. Manuscripts cannot be returned. Guidelines available for SASE, by e-mail, by fax, or on website.

🌐 ◎ CLÓ IAR-CHONNACHTA (Specialized: bilingual/foreign language, Irish)

Indreabhán, Co. Galway, Ireland. Phone: +353-91-593307. Fax: +353-91-593362. E-mail: cic@iol. ie. Website: www.cic.ie. Established 1985. **Contact:** Deirdre O'Toole.

Book/Chapbook Needs Publishes books of Irish-language and bilingual poetry. Has published collections of poetry by Cathal Ó Searcaigh, Nuala Ní Dhomhnaill, Gabriel Rosenstock, Michael Davitt, Liam Ó Muirthile, Gearóid Mac Lochlainn, and Celia de Fréine.

How to Submit Query by postal mail with 20 sample poems and a cover letter with brief bio and publication credits. Manuscripts are read by an editorial panel. No payment information provided.

$◎ CLOUD RIDGE PRESS

815 13th St., Boulder CO 80302. Established 1985. **Editor:** Elaine Kohler.

Book/Chapbook Needs Cloud Ridge Press is a ''literary small press for unique works in poetry and prose.'' Publishes letterpress and offset books in both paperback and hardcover editions. In poetry, publishes ''strong images of the numinous qualities in authentic experience grounded in a landscape and its people.'' The first book, published in 1985, was *Ondina: A Narrative Poem* by John Roberts. The book is 131 pages, digest-sized, handsomely printed on buff stock, cloth-bound in black with silver decoration and spine lettering; 800 copies were bound in Curtis Flannel and 200 copies bound in cloth over boards, numbered, and signed by the poet and artist. This letterpress edition, priced at $18/cloth and $12/paper, is not available in bookstores but only by mail from the press. The trade edition was photo-offset from the original, in both cloth and paper bindings, and is sold in bookstores. The press plans to publish 1-2 books/year.

How to Submit The press is not accepting unsolicited mss; writers should query first. Responds to queries in 2 weeks; to mss in one month. Accepts simultaneous submissions. Pays royalties of 10% plus a negotiable number of author's copies. A brochure is free on request; send #10 SASE.

$□ ◎ CLUBHOUSE JR. (Specialized: children, Christian)

8605 Explorer Dr., Colorado Springs CO 80920. Website: www.clubhousemagazine.org/club_jr/. Established 1988. **Associate Editor:** Suzanne Hadley.

• *Clubhouse Jr.* won the Evangelical Press Association Award for Youth Publication.

Magazine Needs *Clubhouse Jr.* is a monthly magazine published by Focus on the Family for 4- to 8-year-olds. Wants short poems—less than 100 words. "Poetry should have a strong message that supports traditional values. No cute-but-pointless work." *Clubhouse Jr.* is 16-20 pages, magazine-sized, web-printed on glossy paper, and saddle-stapled with 4-color paper cover, includes 4-color art. Has 96,000 subscribers. Single copy: $1.50; subscription: $15/year. Sample: $1.25 with 8×10 SASE. Make checks payable to Focus on the Family.

How to Submit Submit up to 5 poems at a time. Accepts simultaneous submissions; no previously published poems. Cover letter preferred. No fax or e-mail submissions. Time between acceptance and publication is up to one year. Seldom comments on rejected poems. Occasionally publishes theme issues (no theme list available). Guidelines available for SASE. Responds in up to 2 months. Pays $50-100. Acquires first rights.

◙ COAL CITY REVIEW

English Dept., University of Kansas, Lawrence KS 66045. E-mail: briandal@ku.edu. Established 1989. **Editor:** Brian Daldorph.

Magazine Needs Published in the fall, *Coal City Review* is an annual publication of poetry, short stories, reviews, and interviews—"the best material I can find." As for poetry, the editor quotes Pound: " 'Make it new.' " Does not want to see "experimental poetry, doggerel, 5-finger exercises, or beginner's verse." Has published poetry by Michael Gregg Michaud, Phil Miller, Walt McDonald, Thomas Zri Wilson, Virgil Suárez, and Denise Low. *Coal City Review* is 100 pages, digest-sized, professionally printed on recycled paper, perfect-bound, with light, colored card cover. Accepts about 5% of material received. Press run is 200 for 50 subscribers of which 5 are libraries. Subscription: $10. Sample: $6.

How to Submit Submit 6 poems at a time with name and address on each page. Accepts previously published poems occasionally; prefers not to receive simultaneous submissions. No submissions by e-mail. "Please do not send list of prior publications." Seldom comments on rejected poems. Guidelines available for SASE. Responds in up to 3 months. Pays one contributor's copy. Reviews books of poetry in 300-1,000 words, mostly single book format. Send materials for review consideration.

Book/Chapbook Needs & How to Submit *Coal City Review* also publishes occasional chapbooks and books as issues of the magazine, but does not accept unsolicited chapbook submissions. Most recent book is *Notes to the Man Who Shot Me: Vietnam War Poems* by John Musgrave.

Advice "Care more (much more) about writing than publication. If you're good enough, you'll publish."

◙ COFFEE HOUSE PRESS

27 N. Fourth St., Suite 400, Minneapolis MN 55401. (612)338-0125. Established 1984. **Senior Editor:** Christopher Fischbach.

• Coffee House Press books have won numerous honors and awards. As an example, *The*

Book of Medicines by Linda Hogan won the Colorado Book Award for Poetry and the Lannan Foundation Literary Fellowship.

Book Needs Publishes 12 books/year, 4-5 of which are poetry. Wants poetry that is "challenging and lively; influenced by the Beats, the NY School, LANGUAGE and post-LANGUAGE, or Black Mountain." Has published poetry collections by Victor Hernandez Cruz, Anne Waldman, Eleni Sikelianos, and Paul Metcalf.

How to Submit Submit 8-12 poems at a time. Accepts previously published poems. Cover letter and bio required. "Please include a SASE for our reply and/or the return of your manuscript." Seldom comments on rejected poems. Responds to queries in one month; to mss in up to 8 months. Always sends prepublication galleys. Send SASE for catalog. Absolutely no phone, fax, or e-mail queries.

☑ COLD MOUNTAIN REVIEW

English Dept., Appalachian State University, Boone NC 28608. (828)262-3098. Fax: (828)262-2133. E-mail: coldmountain@appstate.edu. Website: www.coldmountain.appstate.edu.

Magazine Needs *Cold Mountain Review* is published twice/year by the English Department at Appalachian State University and features poetry, interviews with poets, book reviews, and b&w line drawings and photographs. "We're open to diverse perspectives and styles." Has published poetry by Sarah Kennedy, Robert Morgan, Susan Ludvigson, Aleida Rodríguez, R.T. Smith, and Virgil Suárez. *Cold Mountain Review* is about 72 pages, digest-sized, neatly printed with one poem/page (or 2-page spread), perfect-bound, with light card stock cover. Publishes about 3% of the submissions received. For sample, send SASE or make donation to ASU Cold Mountain Review.

How to Submit Submit 3-5 poems at a time. No simultaneous submissions or previously published poems. Accepts submissions by postal mail only. "Please include name, address, phone number, and (if available) e-mail address on each poem." Cover letter with short bio required. Reads submissions year round, "though response is slower in summer." Guidelines available fo SASE. Responds in up to 3 months. Pays 2 contributor's copies.

$☑ COLORADO REVIEW; COLORADO PRIZE FOR POETRY

Dept. of English, Colorado State University, Ft. Collins CO 80523. (970)491-5449. E-mail: creview@colostate.edu. Website: www.coloradoreview.com. Established 1955 as *Colorado State Review*, resurrected 1967 under "New Series" rubric, renamed *Colorado Review* 1985. **Editor:** Stephanie G'Schwind. **Poetry Editors:** Jorie Graham and Donald Revell.

- Poetry published in *Colorado Review* has been frequently included in volumes of *The Best American Poetry*.

Magazine Needs *Colorado Review* is a journal of contemporary literature that appears 3 times/year combining short fiction, poetry, and personal essays. Has published poetry by Robert Creeley, Rebecca Wolff, Robert Haas, Mark Strand, Lucie Brock-Broido, Jane Miller, and Fanny Howe. *Colorado Review* is about 224 pages, digest-sized, professionally printed, notch-bound, with glossy card cover. Press run is 1,500 for 1,000 subscribers of which 100 are libraries. Receives about 10,000 submissions/year, accepts about 2%. Subscription: $24/year. Sample: $10.

How to Submit Submit about 5 poems at a time. No previously published poems. Simultaneous submissions OK, "but you must notify *CR* immediately if accepted elsewhere." No e-mail submissions. SASE required for response. Reads submissions September 1 through May 1 only. Responds in 2 months. Pays $5/printed page for poetry. Acquires first North American serial rights. Reviews books of poetry and fiction, both single and multi-book format. Send materials for review consideration.

Contest/Award Offerings Also sponsors the annual Colorado Prize for Poetry, established in 1995, offering an honorarium of $1,500 and publication. Book as a whole must be unpublished, though individual poems may have been published elsewhere. Submit a book-length ms on any subject in any form. Guidelines available for SASE. **Entry fee:** $25 (includes subscription). **Deadline:** January 15. Most recent award winner was G.C. Waldrep (2003). Judge was Donald Revell. Winner announced in May.

🖉 COLUMBIA: A JOURNAL OF LITERATURE AND ART

415 Dodge Hall, Columbia University, New York NY 10027. (212)864-4216. Fax: (212)854-7704. E-mail: columbiajournal@columbia.edu. Website: www.columbia.edu/cu/arts/journal/. Established 1977. **Editor:** S.K. Beringer. **Poetry Editors:** Idra Rosenberg and Kristen Henley.

Magazine Needs *Columbia* appears semiannually and "will consider any poem that is eclectic and spans from traditional to experimental genre." Has published poetry by Jane Hirschfield, Christina Pugh, Richard Howard, Eamon Grennan, Mary Jo Salter, Matthew Rohrer, and Mark Doty. *Columbia* is 180 pages, digest-sized, offset printed with notch binding, glossy cover, includes art and ads. Receives about 2,000 poems/year, accepts about 2%. Press run is 2,000 for 90 subscribers of which 30 are libraries. Subscription: $15/year, $25/2 years. Sample: $8; back issue: $10. Make checks payable to *Columbia Journal*.

How to Submit Submit up to 4 poems at a time. Accepts simultaneous submissions, when noted; no previously published poems. Cover letter preferred. Reads submissions year round. Poems are circulated to an editorial board. Seldom comments on rejected poems. "Solicits theme section for each issue." Upcoming themes available on website. Recent themes include Film and Writing; Reinventing Fairy Tales, Myth and Legends; and Beyond Sportswriting: Spectatorship, Exhaustion, Competition. Guidelines available for SASE, by fax, by e-mail, or on website. Responds in 4 months. Pays 2 contributor's copies. Acquires first North American serial rights.

Contest/Award Offerings Sponsors annual contest with an award of $500. **Entry fee:** $10. See website for submission deadline. Submit no more than 4 poems/entry. All entrants receive a copy of the issue publishing the winners.

🖉 COMMON GROUND REVIEW; COMMON GROUND POETRY CONTEST

21 Primrose St., West Springfield MA 01089. Website: http://members.cox.net/cgreview/. Established 1999. **Editor:** Larry O'Brien.

Magazine Needs *Common Ground Review* appears biannually, publishing poetry and original artwork. Wants poetry with strong imagery; well-written free or traditional forms. No greeting card verse, overly sentimental, or political poetry. Has published poetry by James Doyle, Martin Galvin, Lyn Lifshin, Virgil Suárez, and Rennie McQuilken. *Common Ground Review* is 40-58 pages, digest-sized, high-quality photocopied, saddle-stapled, with card cover, includes 4-6 pages of original artwork. Receives about 1,000 poems/year, accepts less than 10%. Publishes about 35 poems/issue. Press run is 125-150. Single copy: $6.50. Make checks payable to *Common Ground Review*.

How to Submit Submit 1-5 poems at a time. Line length for poetry is 40 maximum. No previously published poems or simultaneous submissions. No fax, e-mail, or disk submissions. Cover letter is required. "Poems should be single-spaced; include name, address, phone, e-mail address, brief biography, and SASE (submissions without SASE will be discarded)." Reads submissions all year. Submit seasonal poems 6 months in advance. Time between acceptance and publication is 4-6 months. Poems are circulated to an editorial board. "Editor reads and culls submissions. Final decisions made by editorial board." Seldom comments on rejected poems. Guidelines available in magazine or on website. Responds in 2 months. Pays one contributor's copy. Acquires one-time rights.

Contest/Award Offerings Annual contest. 1st Prize: $100; 2nd Prize: $50; 3rd Prize: $25. **Entry fee:** $10 for 1-3 unpublished poems. **Deadline:** February 28.

Advice "Read journal before submitting. Beginning poets need to read what's out there, get into workshops, and work on revising. Attend writers' conferences. Listen and learn."

☐ ◉ **COMMON THREADS; OHIO HIGH SCHOOL POETRY CONTESTS (Specialized: membership, students)**
3520 State Route 56, Mechanicsburg OH 43044. (937)834-2666. Website: www.geocities.com/theoh iopoetryassociation/. Established 1928. **Editor:** Amy Jo Zook. Ohio Poetry Association is a state poetry society open to members from outside the state, an affiliate of the National Federation of State Poetry Societies. (See separate listing for Ohio Poetry Association in the Organizations section.)

Magazine Needs *Common Threads* is the Ohio Poetry Association's biannual poetry magazine, appearing in April and October. Only members of OPA may submit poems. Does not want to see poetry which is highly sentimental, overly morbid, religiously coercive, or pornograpic—and nothing over 40 lines. ''We use beginners' poetry, but would like it to be good, tight, revised. In short, not first drafts. Too much is sentimental or prosy when it could be passionate or lyric. We'd like poems to make us think as well as feel something.'' Accepts poetry written by children ''if members or high school contest winners.'' Has published poetry by David Shevin, Cathryn Essinger, Timothy Russell, Yvonne Hardenbrook, Henry B. Stobbs, and Dalene Stull. *Common Threads* is 52 pages, digest-sized, computer-typeset, with matte card cover. ''*Common Threads* is a forum for our members, and we do use reprints so new members can get a look at what is going well in more general magazines.'' Annual dues, including 2 issues of *Common Threads*: $15. Senior (over 65): $12. Single copies: $2.

How to Submit Accepts previously published poems, if ''author is upfront about them. All rights revert to poet after publication.'' Accepts submissions by postal mail only. Frequently publishes seasonal poems. Guidelines available for SASE or on website.

Contest/Award Offerings Ohio Poetry Association sponsors an annual contest for unpublished poems written by high school students in Ohio, with categories for traditional and modern, plus several other categories. March deadline, with 3 money awards in each category. For contest information, write Ohio Poetry Association, % Elouise Postle, 4761 Willow Lane, Lebanon OH 45036. ''We publish student winners in a book of winning poems before reprinting their work in *Common Threads*. Also, we have a quarterly contest open to all poets: entry fee, 2 money awards, and publication. Write to Janeen Lepp, 1798 Sawgrass Dr., Reynoldsburg OH 43068 (#10 SASE) or e-mail janeenlepp@juno.com for dates and themes.''

◙ **THE COMSTOCK REVIEW; COMSTOCK WRITERS' GROUP, INC.; MURIEL CRAFT BAILEY MEMORIAL AWARD; JESSE BRYCE NILES MEMORIAL CHAPBOOK AWARD**
4956 St. John Dr., Syracuse NY 13215. (315)488-8077. E-mail: poetry@comstockreview.org. Website: www.comstockreview.org. Established 1987 as *Poetpourri*, published by the Comstock Writers' Group, Inc. **Managing Editor:** Peggy Sperber Flanders.

Magazine Needs *The Comstock Review* appears biannually: Volume I in summer, Volume II in winter. Wants ''well-written free and traditional verse. Metaphor and fresh, vivid imagery encouraged. Poems over 40 lines discouraged. No obscene, obscure, patently religious, or greeting card verse. Few Haiku.'' Has published poetry by Elinor Benedict, Jim Daniels, Keith Flynn, Alison Luterman, Marilyn Bates, Lois McKee, and Susan Terris. *The Comstock Review* is about 100 pages, digest-sized, professionally printed, perfect-bound. Press run is 600. Single copy: $9; subscription: $16/year; $28/2 years. Samples through year 2002: $6.

How to Submit Submit 3-6 poems at a time with name, address, and phone number or e-mail address on each page. No previously published poems. Simultaneous submissions discouraged. No e-mail submissions. Cover letter with short bio is preferred. Reads submissions January 1 through March 15 only (at present; check website). Acceptances mailed out 4-6 weeks after close of reading period. ''Rejections may receive editorial commentary and may take slightly longer.'' Guidelines available in magazine, for SASE, or on website. Pays one contributor's copy. Acquires first North American serial rights.

Contest/Award Offerings 1) The annual **Muriel Craft Bailey Memorial Award** offers 1st Prize: $1,000; 2nd Prize: $250; 3rd Prize: $100; Honorable Mentions; publication of all finalists. **Entry fee:** $3/poem. Limit of 40 lines/poem. No previously published poems (includes both print and electronic publications) or simultaneous submissions. **Postmark deadline:** July 1. May offer discounted awards edition to entrants. Before submitting, send SASE or check website for current rules. 2004 judge: Molly Peacock. 2) The **Jesse Bryce Niles Memorial Chapbook Award** offers $1,000 plus publication and 50 author's copies, with copy to each entrant. Offered every other year. "Submission deadlines vary; usually late summer." Query with SASE or check website for complete rules, which must be followed.

☑ CONCHO RIVER REVIEW; FORT CONCHO MUSEUM PRESS

P.O. Box 10894, Angelo State University, San Angelo TX 76909. (915)942-2273. Fax: (915)942-2155. E-mail: bradleyjw@hal.lamar.edu. Website: www.angelo.edu/dept/english/concho_river_re view.htm. Established 1984. **Editor:** James A. Moore. **Poetry Editor:** Jerry Bradley.

Magazine Needs *Concho River Review* is a literary journal published twice/year. "Prefer shorter poems, few long poems accepted; particularly looking for poems with distinctive imagery and imaginative forms and rhythms. The first test of a poem will be its imagery." Short reviews of new volumes of poetry are also published. Has published poetry by Walt McDonald, Robert Cooperman, Mary Winters, William Wenthe, and William Jolliff. *Concho River Review* is 120-138 pages, digest-sized, professionally printed, flat-spined, with matte card cover. Accepts 35-40 of 600-800 poems received/year. Press run is 300 for about 200 subscribers of which 10 are libraries. Subscription: $14. Sample: $5.

How to Submit "Please submit 3-5 poems at a time. Use regular legal-sized envelopes—no big brown envelopes; no replies without SASE. Type must be letter-perfect, sharp enough to be computer scanned." Accepts submissions by e-mail (as attachment). Responds in 2 months. Pays one contributor's copy. Acquires first rights.

Advice "We're always looking for good, strong work—from both well-known poets and those who have never been published before."

☐ CONCRETE WOLF

P. O. Box 730, Amherst NH 03031-0730. E-mail: editors@concretewolf.com. Website: http://concre tewolf.com. Established 2001. **Editors:** Brent Allard, Lana Ayers, and Martha D. Hall. Member: CLMP.

Magazine Needs *Concrete Wolf* appears biannually. "We like to see fresh perspectives on common human experiences, with careful attention to words. No specifications as to form, subject matter, or style. Poems that give the impression the poet is in the room." Does not want "poetry that is all head, or preaches rather than speaks." Has published poetry by Martha Miller, Brian Moreau, Jeanne Kent, Frank Bogan, Gertrude F. Bantle, and Nancy Brady Cunningham. *Concrete Wolf* is 85 pages, magazine-sized, duplex-printed, perfect-bound, with matte card stock cover with b&w art. Receives about 200 poems/month, accepts about 15%. Publishes about 70 poems/issue. Press run is 1,000 for 75 subscribers of which 10 are libraries, 30% shelf sales; 10% are distributed free to writing organizations. Single copy: $10; subscription: $20 (includes annual chapbook winner). Sample: $7. Make checks payable to *Concrete Wolf*.

How to Submit Submit up to 5 poems at a time. Line length for poetry is 300 maximum. Accepts previously published poems and simultaneous submissions. Accepts submissions by postal mail only. Reads submissions June through September 1. Time between acceptance and publication is up to one year. "Poetry is individually reviewed by 3 editors and then discussed. Poems agreed upon by all editors are accepted." Often comments on rejected poems. Guidelines available in magazine, for SASE, or on website. Responds in up to one year. Pays 2 contributor's copies. Acquires one-time rights.

Contest/Award Offerings Holds annual chapbook contest; write for details.

Also Offers Website will occasionally post writing exercises. Future plans include a supplementary CD of poets reading their work.

Advice "Poetry exists for everyone, not just the academic. Remember that poetry is work that requires crafting."

$⬛ CONFRONTATION MAGAZINE

English Dept., C.W. Post Campus of Long Island University, Brookville NY 11548-1300. (516)299-2720. Fax: (516)299-2735. E-mail: mtucker@liu.edu. Established 1968. **Editor-in-Chief:** Martin Tucker. **Poetry Editor:** Michael Hartnett.

Magazine Needs *Confrontation Magazine* is "a semiannual literary journal with interest in all forms. Our only criterion is high literary merit. We think of our audience as an educated, lay group of intelligent readers. We prefer lyric poems. Length generally should be kept to 2 pages. No sentimental verse." Has published poetry by David Ray, T. Alan Broughton, David Ignatow, Philip Appleman, Jane Mayhall, and Joseph Brodsky. *Confrontation* is about 300 pages, digest-sized, professionally printed, flat-spined, with a circulation of 2,000. Receives about 1,200 submissions/year, accepts about 150, has a 6- to 12-month backlog. Subscription: $10/year. Sample: $3.

How to Submit Submit no more than 10 pages, clear copy. No previously published poems. Accepts queries by e-mail, but not submissions. Do not submit mss June through August. "Prefer single submissions." Publishes theme issues. Upcoming themes available for SASE. Responds in 2 months. Sometimes sends prepublication galleys. Pays $5-50 and one contributor's copy with discount available on additional copies. Staff reviews books of poetry. Send materials for review consideration.

Also Offers Basically a magazine, they do on occasion publish "book" issues or "anthologies." Their most recent "occasional book" is *Clown at Wall*, stories and drawings by Ken Bernard.

Advice "We want serious poetry, which may be humorous and light-hearted on the surface."

$⬛ THE CONNECTICUT POETRY REVIEW

P.O. Box 818, Stonington CT 06378. Established 1981. **Poetry Editors:** J. Claire White and Harley More.

Magazine Needs *The Connecticut Poetry Review* is a "small press annual magazine. We look for poetry of quality which is both genuine and original in content. No specifications except length: 10-40 lines." Has published poetry by John Updike, Robert Peters, Diane Wakoski, and Marge Piercy. *The Connecticut Poetry Review* is 45-60 pages, flat-spined, digest-sized, "printed letterpress by hand on a Hacker Hand Press from Monotype Bembo." Receives over 2,500 submissions/year, accepts about 20, has a 3-month backlog. Press run is 400 for 80 subscribers of which 35 are libraries. Sample: $3.50.

How to Submit Reads submissions April through June and September through December only. Responds in 3 months. Pays $5/poem plus one contributor's copy.

Advice "Study traditional and modern styles. Study poets of the past. Attend poetry readings and write. Practice on your own."

⬛ CONNECTICUT REVIEW

Southern Connecticut State University, 501 Crescent St., New Haven CT 06515. (203)392-6737. Fax: (203)392-5748. E-mail: ctreview@southernct.edu. Website: www.southernct.edu/projects/ctreview. Established 1968. **Editor:** Vivian Shipley.

● Poetry published in this review has been included in *The Best American Poetry* and *The Pushcart Prize* anthologies; has received special recognition for Literary Excellence from Public Radio's series *The Poet and the Poem*; and has won the Phoenix Award for Significant Editorial Achievement from the Council of Editors of Learned Journals (CELJ).

Magazine Needs *Connecticut Review*, published biannually, contains essays, poetry, articles, fiction, b&w photographs, and color artwork. Has published poetry by Jack Bedell, Maria Gillan, Colette Inez, Maxine Kumin, Tony Fusco, Faith Vicinanza, Dana Gioia, and Marilyn Nelson. *Connecticut Review* is 208 pages, digest-sized, offset-printed, perfect-bound, with glossy 4-color cover and 8-color interior art. Receives about 2,500 poems/year, accepts about 5%. Press run is 3,000 for subscriptions of which 400 are libraries, with 1,000 distributed free to Connecticut State libraries and high schools. Sample: $8. Make checks payable to Connecticut State University.

How to Submit Submit 3-5 typed poems at a time with name, address, and phone number in the upper left corner, with SASE for reply only. Accepts submissions by postal mail only. Guidelines available for SASE. Pays 2 contributor's copies. Acquires first or one-time rights.

⊘ COPPER CANYON PRESS; HAYDEN CARRUTH AWARD

P.O. Box 271, Port Townsend WA 98368. (877)501-1393. Fax: (360)385-4985. E-mail: poetry@coppercanyonpress.org. Website: www.coppercanyonpress.org. Established 1972. **Editor:** Sam Hamill.

Book/Chapbook Needs Copper Canyon publishes books of poetry. Has published collections by Lucille Clifton, Hayden Carruth, Carolyn Kizer, Olga Broumas, Ruth Stone, and Jim Harrison.

How to Submit Currently accepts no unsolicited poetry. E-mail queries and submissions will go unanswered.

Contest/Award Offerings Copper Canyon Press publishes one volume of poetry each year by a new or emerging poet through its Hayden Carruth Award. "For the purpose of this award, an emerging poet is defined as a poet who has published not more than 2 books." Winner receives $1,000 advance, book publication with Copper Canyon Press, and a one-month residency at the Vermont Studio Center. Each unbound ms submitted should be a minimum of 46 typed pages on white paper, paginated consecutively with a table of contents. Author's name or address must not appear anywhere on ms (this includes both title and acknowledgments pages). Please do not staple or paper-clip ms. Include $25 handling fee (check payable to Copper Canyon Press), submission form (available on website), and SASE for notification (mss will be recycled, not returned). **Deadline:** postmarked between November 1 and November 30, 2004. No entries by e-mail or fax. Winner announced February 21, 2005. Past winners include Sascha Feinstein's *Misterioso*, Rebecca Wee's *Uncertain Grace*, Jenny Factor's *Unraveling at the Name*, Peter Pereira's *Saying the World*, and Ben Lerner's *Lichtenberg Figures*. Past judges include Jane Miller (2000), Marilyn Hacker (2001), and Gregory Orr (2002). Further guidelines available for SASE and on website.

◖ THE CORTLAND REVIEW

2061 NE 73rd St., Seattle WA 98115. E-mail: tcr@cortlandreview.com. Website: www.cortlandreview.com. Established 1997. **Editor-in-Chief:** Guy Shahar. **Contact:** Poetry Submission Reader.

Magazine Needs *The Cortland Review* is an online literary magazine (no print version) "publishing in text and audio, and it's free. We publish poetry, essays, interviews, fiction, book reviews, etc." Has published poetry by W.S. Merwin, Charles Simic, Yehuda Amichai, Dick Allen, Linda Pastan, Billy Collins, David Lehman, Marge Piercy, and R.T. Smith.

How to Submit Submit 3-5 poems at a time. No previously published poems or simultaneous submissions. *The Cortland Review* "prefers online submissions through our online submission form. Please visit website for full submission guidelines. Snail mail is also acceptable." Cover letter required. Time between acceptance and publication is up to one year, sometimes longer. Seldom comments on rejected poems. Always sends prepublication galleys. Acquires first rights. Staff reviews books and chapbooks of poetry and other magazines in 100 words, multi-book format. Send materials for review consideration.

$◖ CRAB ORCHARD REVIEW; CRAB ORCHARD AWARD SERIES IN POETRY; THE RICHARD PETERSON POETRY PRIZE

Dept. of English, Southern Illinois University, Carbondale IL 62901-4503. Website: www.siu.edu/

~crborchd. Established 1995. **Poetry Editor:** Allison Joseph. **Managing Editor:** Jon C. Tribble.

● *Crab Orchard Review* received a 2002 Literary Award and a 2003 Operating Grant from the Illinois Arts Council. Poetry from *Crab Orchard Review* has also appeared in *The Best American Poetry* and *Beacon Best of 1999* and *2000*.

Magazine Needs *Crab Orchard Review* appears biannually in January and July. "We are a general interest literary journal publishing poetry, fiction, creative nonfiction, interviews, book reviews, and novel excerpts." Wants all styles and forms from traditional to experimental. No greeting card verse; literary poetry only. Has published poetry by Chad Davidson, Deborah Cummins, Rohan Preston, Orlando Richard Menes, Chi-Wai Au, and John Guzlowski. *Crab Orchard Review* is 280-300 pages, digest-sized, professionally printed, perfect-bound, with (usually) glossy card cover with color photos. Receives about 10,000 poems/year, accepts about 1%. Publishes about 40-50 poems/issue. Press run is 2,500 for 2,000 subscribers of which 400 are libraries; 100 exchanged with other journals; remainder in shelf sales. Subscription: $15. Sample: $8.

How to Submit Submit up to 5 poems at a time. Accepts simultaneous submissions with notification; no previously published poems. No fax or e-mail submissions. Cover letter preferred. "Indicate stanza breaks on poems of more than one page." Reads submissions April to November for our Summer/Fall special issue, December to April for regular, non-thematic Winter/Spring issue. Time between acceptance and publication is 6-12 months. Poems are circulated to an editorial board. "Poems that are under serious consideration are discussed and decided on by the managing editor and poetry editor." Seldom comments on rejected poems. Publishes theme issues. Upcoming themes and guidelines available in magazine, for SASE, or on website. Responds in up to 9 months. Pays $15/page, $100 minimum, plus 2 contributor's copies and one year's subscription. Acquires first North American serial rights. Staff reviews books of poetry in 500-700 words, single book format. Send materials for review consideration to Managing Editor Jon C. Tribble.

Contest/Award Offerings 1) **Crab Orchard Award Series in Poetry** offers annual award of 1st Prize: $3,500 and publication of a book-length ms; and 2nd Prize: $1,500 and publication of a book-length ms. Cash prize totals reflect a $1,500 honorarium for each winner for a reading at Southern Illinois University Carbondale. Publication contract is with Southern Illinois University Press. Entrants must be U.S. citizens or permanent residents. Individual poems may have been previously published, but collection as a whole must be unpublished, written in English. May be under consideration elsewhere, but series editor must be informed immediately upon acceptance. Manuscripts should be typewritten or computer generated (letter quality only, no dot matrix), single-spaced; clean photocopy is recommended as mss are not returned. See guidelines for complete formatting instructions. Guidelines available for SASE or on website. **Entry fee:** $25/submission (includes subscription to *Crab Orchard Review*). Make checks payable to Crab Orchard Award Series. **2003 deadline:** was October 1-November 1. 2003 winners were Jon Pineda (1st Prize, *Birthmark*) and Lee Ann Roripaugh (2nd Prize, *Year of the Snake*). Also sponsors first book competition. **2003 Deadline:** was May 15-July 1. 2003 winner was Amy Fluery (*Beautiful Trouble*). See website for details or contact the series editor. 2) **The Richard Peterson Poetry Prize** offers annual award of $1,500 plus publication in Winter/Spring issue of *Crab Orchard Review*. Submissions must be unpublished original work not under consideration elsewhere, written in English by a U.S. citizen or permanent resident. Name, address, telephone number, and/or e-mail address should appear only on the title page of ms; author's name should not appear on any subsequent pages. Mark "poetry" on outside of envelope. Include #10 SASE for notification of winners. Guidelines available for SASE or on website. **Entry fee:** $15/entry (one poem equals one entry; poet may submit up to 3 separate entries if not entering the fiction or nonfiction categories of the literary contest). Make checks payable to *Crab Orchard Review*. Each fee entitles entrant to a one-year subscription, extension, or gift subscription; indicate choice and include complete address. **2004 deadline:** was February 1-March 15.

Publishers of Poetry

Advice "Include SASE with all submissions and all queries. We don't respond to submissions via e-mail, so please continue to send SASE (#10 size minimum) with submissions."

CRAZYHORSE; CRAZYHORSE FICTION AND POETRY AWARDS

Dept. of English, College of Charleston, 66 George St., Charleston SC 29424. (843)953-7740. E-mail: crazyhorse@cofc.edu. Established 1960. **Poetry Editors:** Paul Allen and Carol Ann Davis.

● Richard Jackson's *This* won a 2004 Pushcart Award for *Crazyhorse*; Dinty Moore's *Son of Mr. Green Jeans* will be reprinted in *Harper's* magazine.

Magazine Needs *Crazyhorse* appears biannually and publishes fine fiction, poetry, and essays. "Send your best words our way. We like to print a mix of writing regardless of its form, genre, school, or politics. We're especially on the lookout for writing that doesn't fit the categories." Does not want "writing with nothing at stake. Before sending, ask 'What's reckoned with that's important for other people to read?' " Has published poetry by David Wojahn, Mary Ruefle, Nance Van Winkle, Andrew Hudgins, James Grinwis, and Lola Haskins. *Crazyhorse* is 150-200 pages, $8^{3}/_{4} \times 8^{1}/_{2}$, perfect-bound, with 4-color glossy cover. Receives about 8,000 poems/year. Publishes about 40 poems/issue. Press run is 1,500. Single copy: $8.50; subscription: $15/year, $25/2 years, $40/3 years. Sample: $5. Make checks payable to *Crazyhorse*.

How to Submit Submit 3-5 poems at a time. Accepts simultaneous submissions; no previously published poems. No fax, e-mail, or disk submissions. Cover letter is preferred. Reads submissions year round. "We read slower in summer." Time between acceptance and publication is 6 months. Seldom comments on rejected poems. Guidelines available in magazine, for SASE, or by e-mail. Responds in 3 months. Sometimes sends prepublication galleys. Pays 2 contributor's copies plus one-year subscription (2 issues). Acquires first rights.

Contest/Award Offerings The Crazyhorse Fiction and Poetry Awards: $1,000 and publication in *Crazyhorse*. Send SASE for details.

Advice "Feel strongly; then write."

THE CREAM CITY REVIEW

P.O. Box 413, Dept. of English, University of Wisconsin at Milwaukee, Milwaukee WI 53201. (414)229-4708. E-mail: creamcity@uwm.edu. Website: www.uwm.edu/Dept/English/ccr/index.html. **Editor:** Erica Wiest. **Poetry Editors:** Beth Bretl and Jennifer Dworshack-Kinter.

● Poetry published in this review has been included in past volumes of *The Best American Poetry*.

Magazine Needs *The Cream City Review* is a nationally distributed literary magazine published twice/year by the university's Creative Writing Program. "We seek to publish all forms of writing, from traditional to experimental. We strive to produce issues which are challenging, diverse, and of lasting quality. We are not interested in sexist, homophobic, racist, or formulaic writings." Has published poetry by William Harrold, Maxine Chernoff, Kate Braverman, Billy Collins, Bob Hicok, and Allison Joseph. They do not include sample lines of poetry; "Best to buy a copy—we publish the best from new and established writers. We like an energetic mix." *The Cream City Review* is about 200 pages, digest-sized, perfect-bound, with full-color cover on 70 lb. paper. Press run is 1,000 for 450 subscribers of which 40 are libraries. Single copy: $8; subscription: $15/year, $28/2 years; institutional subscription: $25/year. Sample: $5.

How to Submit "Include SASE when submitting, and please submit no more than 5 poems at a time." Accepts simultaneous submissions when notified. "Please include a few lines about your publication history and other information you think of interest." Accepts submissions by postal mail only. Reads submissions September 1 through April 1 only. Editors sometimes comment on rejected poems. Guidelines available for SASE. Responds in up to 6 months. Payment includes one-year subscription. Acquires first rights. Reviews books of poetry in 1-2 pages. Send materials for review consideration to the poetry editors.

Contest/Award Offerings Sponsors an annual poetry contest. Submit 3 poems/entry. **Deadline:** November 1. **Entry fee:** $10. Awards $100 plus publication; all entries considered for publication.

◪ CREOSOTE

Dept. of English, Mohave Community College, 1977 W. Acoma Blvd., Lake Havasu City AZ 86403. Established 2000. **Editor:** Ken Raines.

Magazine Needs *Creosote* is an annual publication of poetry, fiction, and literary nonfiction appearing in May. Has "a bias favoring more traditional forms, but interested in any and all quality poems." Has "a bias against confessional and beat-influenced poetry, but will consider everything." Has published poetry by William Wilborn, Ruth Moose, and Star Coulbrooke. *Creosote* is 48 pages, digest-sized, saddle-stapled, with card cover. Receives about 500 poems/year, accepts about 5%. Publishes about 25 poems/issue. Press run is 500 for 30 subscribers of which 5 are libraries, 200 shelf sales; 100+ are distributed free to contributors and others. Single copy: $4. Sample: $2. Make checks payable to Mohave Community College.

How to Submit Submit up to 5 poems at a time. Line length for poetry is open. Accepts simultaneous submissions, "but please notify us ASAP if accepted elsewhere"; no previously published poems. Accepts disk submissions; no e-mail submissions. Cover letter is preferred. "Disk submissions must be accompanied by a hard copy." Reads submissions September 1 through February 28. Time between acceptance and publication is 2-3 months. Poems are circulated to an editorial board. "All work which passes initial screening is considered by at least 2 (usually more) readers." Seldom comments on rejected poems. Guidelines available for SASE. Responds in 6 months "at most, usually sooner." Pays 3 contributor's copies. Acquires one-time rights.

Advice "Love words. Resist the urge to pontificate. Beware a self-congratulatory tone. Shun sloppy expression."

▦ ◪ ◎ CRESCENT MOON PUBLISHING; PASSION (Specialized: anthology, gay/lesbian, love/romance, erotica, occult, religious, spirituality, women/feminism)

P.O. Box 393, Maidstone, Kent ME14 5XU United Kingdom. Phone: 01144-1622-729593. E-mail: jr@crescentmoon.org.uk. Website: www.crescentmoon.org.uk. Established 1988. **Editor:** Jeremy Robinson.

Magazine Needs "We publish a quarterly magazine, *Passion* ($4 each, $17 subscription). It features poetry, fiction, reviews, and essays on feminism, art, philosophy, and the media. Many American poets are featured, as well as British poets such as Jeremy Reed, Penelope Shuttle, Alan Bold, D.J. Enright, and Peter Redgrove. Contributions welcome."

Book/Chapbook Needs Crescent Moon publishes about 25 books and chapbooks/year on arrangements **subsidized by the poet.** Wants "poetry that is passionate and authentic. Any form or length." Not "the trivial, insincere or derivative. We are also publishing 2 anthologies of new American poetry each year entitled *Pagan America*." Has also published studies of Rimbaud, Rilke, Cavafy, Shakespeare, Beckett, German Romantic poetry, and D.H. Lawrence. Books are usually about 76 pages, flat-spined, digest-sized. Anthologies now available ($8.95 or $17 for 2 issues of *Pagan America*) include: *Pagan America: An Anthology of New American Poetry*; *Love in America: An Anthology of Women's Love Poetry*; *Mythic America: An Anthology of New American Poetry*; and *Religious America: An Anthology of New American Poetry*.

How to Submit Submit 5-10 poems at a time. Cover letter with brief bio and publishing credits required ("and please print your address in capitals"). Send SASE (or SAE and IRCs) for upcoming anthology themes. Responds to queries in one month, to mss in 2 months. Sometimes sends prepublication galleys.

Advice "Generally, we prefer free verse to rhymed poetry."

$ ◎ CRICKET; SPIDER, THE MAGAZINE FOR CHILDREN; LADYBUG, THE MAGAZINE FOR YOUNG CHILDREN; BABYBUG, THE LISTENING AND LOOKING MAGAZINE FOR INFANTS AND TODDLERS (Specialized: children); CICADA (Specialized: teens)
P.O. Box 300, Peru IL 61354-0300. Website: www.cricketmag.com. *Cricket* established 1973. *Ladybug* established 1990. *Spider* established 1994. *Babybug* established 1995. *Cicada* established 1998. **Editor-in-Chief:** Marianne Carus.

Magazine Needs *Cricket* (for ages 9-14) is a monthly, circulation 73,000, using "serious, humorous, nonsense rhymes" for children and young adults. Does not want "forced or trite rhyming or imagery that doesn't hang together to create a unified whole." Sometimes uses previously published work. *Cricket* is 64 pages, 8×10, saddle-stapled, with color cover and full-color illustrations inside. *Ladybug*, also monthly, circulation 131,000, is similar in format and requirements but is aimed at younger children (ages 2-6). *Spider*, also monthly, circulation 78,000, is for children ages 6-9. Format and requirements similar to *Cricket* and *Ladybug*. *Cicada*, appearing bimonthly, circulation 16,000, is a magazine for ages 14 and up, publishing "short stories, poems, and first-person essays written for teens and young adults." Wants "serious or humorous poetry; rhymed or free verse." *Cicada* is 128 pages, digest-sized, perfect-bound, with full-color cover, includes b&w illustrations. *Babybug*, published 10 times/year, circulation 48,000, is a read-aloud magazine for ages 6 months to 2 years. *Babybug* is 24 pages, 6¼×7, printed on cardstock with nontoxic glued spine and full-color illustrations. The magazines receive over 1,200 submissions/month, use 25-30, and have up to a 2-year backlog. Sample of *Cricket*, *Ladybug*, *Spider*, or *Babybug*: $5; sample of *Cicada*: $8.50.

How to Submit Do not query. Submit no more than 5 poems—up to 50 lines (2 pages max.) for *Cricket*; up to 20 lines for *Spider* and *Ladybug*; up to 25 lines for *Cicada*; up to 8 lines for *Babybug*. No restrictions on form. Guidelines available for SASE or on website. Responds in 4 months. Payment for all is up to $3/line and 6 contributor's copies. "All submissions are automatically considered for all 5 magazines."

Also Offers *Cricket* and *Spider* hold a poetry, story, or art contest each month. *Cricket* accepts entries from readers of all ages; *Spider* from readers ages 10 and under. Current contest themes and rules appear in each issue.

✪ ◢ ◎ CROSS-CULTURAL COMMUNICATIONS; CROSS-CULTURAL REVIEW OF WORLD LITERATURE AND ART IN SOUND, PRINT, AND MOTION; CROSS-CULTURAL MONTHLY; CROSS-CULTURAL REVIEW CHAPBOOK ANTHOLOGY; INTERNATIONAL WRITERS SERIES (Specialized: bilingual, translations)
239 Wynsum Ave., Merrick NY 11566-4725. (516)868-5635. Fax: (516)379-1901. E-mail: cccpoetry @aol.com. Website: www.cross-culturalcommunications.com. Established 1971. **Contact:** Stanley H. and Bebe Barkan.

   • Cross-Cultural Communications won the 1996 Poor Richard's Award "for a quarter-century of high-quality publishing," presented by The Small Press Center in New York.

Magazine Needs & How to Submit *Cross-Cultural Monthly* focuses on bilingual poetry and (some) prose. Subscription (12 issues/editions): $100. Sample: $10 postpaid. Pays one contributor's copy.

Book/Chapbook Needs & How to Submit *Cross-Cultural Review* began as a series of chapbooks (6-12/year) of collections of poetry translated from various languages, and continues as the Holocaust, Women Writers, Latin American Writers, African Heritage, Italian Heritage, International Artists, Art & Poetry, Jewish, Israeli, Yiddish, Hebrew, American, Bengali, Bulgarian, Cajun, Catalan, Chicano, Chinese, Dutch, Estonian, Finnish, Gypsy (Roma), Korean, Macedonian, Polish, Russian, Serbian, Sicilian, Swedish, Scandinavian, Turkish, Ukrainian, Welsh, and Long Island and Brooklyn Writers Chapbook Series (with a number of other permutations in the offing)—issued simultaneously in palm-sized and regular paperback and cloth-binding editions, and boxed and canned editions, as well as audiocassette, CD, and videocassette. The Cross-Cultural International Writers Series, focusing on leading poets from various countries, includes titles by Leo Vroman (Holland)

and Pablo Neruda (Chile). The Holocaust series is for survivors. In addition to publications in these series, Cross-Cultural Communications has published anthologies and postcard and broadside portfolio collections by dozens of poets from many countries, a number in special biligual limited editions, including such poets and translators as Joan Alcover, Bohdan Boychuk, Stanley Kunitz, Vinicius de Moraes, Gregory Rabassa, Rainer Maria Rilke, Louis Simpson, William Stafford, Daniel Weissbort, with complementary artwork by various international artists such as Eduardo Arranz-Bravo (Catalonia), Nicolò D'Alessandro (Sicily), Picasso (Spain), Tchouki (Bulgaria), and Alfred Van Loen (Holland/USA). Sample chapbook: $10 postpaid. Guidelines available for SASE. Pays 10% of print run.

Also Offers Cross-Cultural Communications continues to produce the International Poets and Writers Literary Arts Week in New York.

☑ CRUCIBLE; SAM RAGAN PRIZE

Barton College, College Station, Wilson NC 27893. (252)399-6456. E-mail: tgrimes@barton.edu. Established 1964. **Editor:** Terrence L. Grimes.

Magazine Needs *Crucible* is an annual, published in November, using "poetry that demonstrates originality and integrity of craftsmanship as well as thought. Traditional metrical and rhyming poems are difficult to bring off in modern poetry. The best poetry is written out of deeply felt experience which has been crafted into pleasing form. No very long narratives." Has published poetry by Robert Grey, R.T. Smith, and Anthony S. Abbott. *Crucible* is 100 pages, digest-sized, professionally printed on high-quality paper, with matte card cover. Press run is 500 for 300 subscribers of which 100 are libraries, 200 shelf sales. Sample: $7.

How to Submit Submit 5 poems at a time between Christmas and mid-April only. No previously published poems or simultaneous submissions. Responds in up to 4 months. "We require 3 unsigned copies of the manuscript and a short biography including a list of publications, in case we decide to publish the work." Pays contributor's copies.

Contest/Award Offerings The Sam Ragan Prize ($150), in honor of the former Poet Laureate of North Carolina, and other contests (prizes of $150 and $100). Send SASE for guidelines.

Advice Editor leans toward free verse with attention paid particularly to image, line, stanza, and voice. However, he does not want to see poetry that is "forced."

☑ CURBSIDE REVIEW

P.O. Box 667189, Houston TX 77266-7189. (713)529-0198. E-mail: curbsidereview@yahoo.com. Website: www.curbsidereview.org. Established 2000. **Co-Editors/Publishers:** Carolyn Adams and R.T. Castleberry.

Magazine Needs *Curbside Review* appears monthly. "Our motto on the masthead is from W.B. Yeats: 'Our words must seem to be inevitable.' " Wants mature, crafted poetry in all styles and forms, "though we prefer modern free verse and prose poetry. We like intensity, dark humor, and wit." Has published poetry by Simon Perchik, B.Z. Niditch, Carol Frith, Radames Ortiz, and Dennis Saleh. *Curbside Review* is 4 pages, magazine-sized, copier-printed, folded. Receives about 1,200 poems/year, accepts about 20%. Publishes about 10 poems/issue. Press run is 400; all distributed free to local poetry groups and events, local independent bookstores. Single copy: free with #10 SASE.

How to Submit Submit 2 copies of 5 poems at a time. Line length for poetry is 50 maximum. Accepts simultaneous submissions; no previously published poems. No fax, e-mail, or disk submissions. Cover letter is preferred. "We have a strict 'don't ask, don't tell' policy on previously published/ simultaneous submissions. We read continuously throughout the year." Submit seasonal poems 4 months in advance. Time between acceptance and publication varies. Poems are circulated to an editorial board. "We often take more than one poem from writers, so publication is ongoing. Rather than reject, we often ask for revisions on promising poems." Never comments on rejected poems.

Guidelines available in magazine, for SASE, or by e-mail. Responds in 3 months. Pays 2 contributor's copies. Acquires one-time rights.

Advice "We publish *poetry* only. Since a sample copy is free, please take advantage of that to read it for a sense of our style."

▣ ◪ CURRENT ACCOUNTS; BANK STREET WRITERS; BANK STREET WRITERS COMPETITION

16-18 Mill Lane, Horwich, Bolton, Lancashire BL6 6AT England. Phone/fax: (01204)669858. E-mail: bswscribe@aol.com. Website: http://hometown.aol.co.uk/bswscribe/myhomepage/newsletter.html. Established 1994. **Editor:** Rod Riesco.

Magazine Needs *Current Accounts* is a biannual, publishing poetry, fiction, and nonfiction by members of Bank Street Writers, and other contributors. Open to all types of poetry; maximum 100 lines. "No requirements, although some space is reserved for members." Has published poetry by Pat Winslow, M.R. Peacocke, and Gerald England. *Current Accounts* is 52 pages, A5, photocopied, saddle-stapled, with card cover with b&w or color photo or artwork. Receives about 300 poems/year, accepts about 5%. Press run is 80 for 6 subscribers, 40 shelf sales; 8 distributed free to competition winners. Subscription: UK £4. Sample: UK £2. Make checks payable to Bank Street Writers (sterling checks only).

How to Submit Submit up to 6 poems at a time. Unpublished poems preferred; no simultaneous submissions. Accepts e-mail submissions (pasted into body of message). Cover letter required, and SAE or IRC essential for postal submissions. Guidelines available for SASE, by fax, by e-mail, or on website. Time between acceptance and publication is 6 months. Seldom comments on rejected poems. Responds in 2 months. Pays one contributor's copy. Acquires first rights.

Contest/Award Offerings Sponsors the annual Bank Street Writers Poetry and Short Story Competition. Submit poems up to 40 lines, any subject or style. **Deadline:** January 31. **Entry fee:** £3/poem. Entry form available for SAE and IRC (or download from website).

Also Offers Bank Street Writers meets once a month and offers workshops, guest speakers, and other activities. Write for details.

Advice "We like originality of ideas, images, and use of language. No inspirational or religious verse unless it's also good in poetic terms."

◻ CURRICULUM VITAE; SIMPSON PUBLICATIONS; CV POETRY POSTCARD PROJECT

P.O. Box 1082, Franklin PA 16323. E-mail: simpub@hotmail.com. Established 1995. **Managing Editor:** Amy Dittman.

Magazine Needs *Curriculum Vitae* appears biannually in January and July and is "a zine where quality work is always welcome. We'd like to see more metrical work, especially more translations, and well-crafted narrative free verse is always welcome. We're also interested in expanding our list of innovative side projects, books, graphic novels, chapbooks like *The Iowa Monster*, and the CV Poetry Postcard Project. Query with full manuscripts or well-thought-out plans with clips. We do not want to see rambling Bukowski-esque free verse or poetry that overly relies on sentimentality." *Curriculum Vitae* is 40 pages, digest-sized, photocopied, saddle-stapled, with 2-color card stock cover. Receives about 500 poems/year, accepts about 75. Press run is 1,000 for 300 subscribers of which 7 are libraries, 200 shelf sales. Subscription: $6 (4 issues). Sample: $4.

How to Submit Submit 3 poems at a time. "Submissions without a SASE cannot be acknowledged due to postage costs." Accepts previously published poems and simultaneous submissions. Cover letter "to give us an idea of who you are" preferred. Time between acceptance and publication is 8 months. Poetry is circulated among 3 board members. Often comments on rejected poems. Publishes theme issues. Guidelines available for SASE or by e-mail. Responds within one month. Pays 2 contributor's copies plus one-year subscription.

Book/Chapbook Needs & How to Submit Simpson Publications also publishes about 5 chapbooks/ year. Interested poets should query with full mss.

Also Offers "We are currently looking for poets who would like to be part of our Poetry Postcard series." Interested writers should query to The *CV* Poetry Postcard Project at the above address for more information.

◢ CUTBANK

English Dept., University of Montana, Missoula MT 59812. (406)243-6156. E-mail: cutbank@selway .umt.edu. Website: www.umt.edu/cutbank. Established 1973. **Contact:** Poetry Editor.

Magazine Needs *CutBank* is a biannual literary magazine which publishes regional, national, and international poetry, fiction, interviews, and artwork. Has published poetry by Richard Hugo, Dara Wier, Sandra Alcosser, and Jane Hirshfield. Publishes 25 pages of poetry out of about 100 pages/ issue. Press run is 500 for 250 subscribers of which 30% are libraries. Single copy: $6.95; subscription: $12/2 issues. Sample: $4.

How to Submit Submit 3-5 poems at a time, single-spaced with SASE. Simultaneous submissions discouraged but accepted with notification. "We accept submissions from August 15 through March 15 only. Deadlines: Fall issue, November 15; Spring issue, March 15." Guidelines are available for SASE or by e-mail. Responds in up to 3 months. Pays 2 contributor's copies. All rights return to author upon publication.

⊡ ⊡ ◢ DALHOUSIE REVIEW

Dalhousie University, Halifax NS B3H 4R2 Canada. (902)494-2541. Fax: (902)494-3561. E-mail: dalhousie.review@dal.ca. Website: www.dal.ca/~dalrev/. Established 1921. **Editor:** Dr. Ronald Huebert.

Magazine Needs *Dalhousie Review* appears 3 times/year. Has published poetry by Martin Bennett, Ogaga Ifowodo, Kanina Dawson, Jacqueline Karp, and David Rachel. *Dalhousie Review* is 144 pages, digest-sized. Accepts about 10% of poems received. Press run is 600 for 450 subscribers. Single copy: $15; subscription: $22.50 (Canadian); 28 (US). Sample: $15. Make checks payable to *Dalhousie Review*.

How to Submit No previously published poems. "Submissions should be typed on plain white paper, double-spaced throughout. Spelling preferences are those of *The Canadian Oxford Dictionary*: catalogue, colour, program, travelling, theatre, and so on. Beyond this, writers of fiction and poetry are encouraged to follow whatever canons of usage might govern the particular story or poem in question, and to be inventive with language, ideas, and form. Poems should, in general, not exceed 40 lines, but there will of course be valid exceptions to these rules. Initial submissions are by means of hard copy only." Accepts e-mail submissions from outside North America only. "Please enclose a SASE (or SAE and IRC) for response." Reads submissions year round. Seldom comments on rejected poems. Occasionally publishes theme issues. Upcoming themes and guidelines available for SAE and IRC. Pays 2 contributor's copies and 10 off-prints.

$◢ DANA LITERARY SOCIETY ONLINE JOURNAL

P.O. Box 3362, Dana Point CA 92629-8362. Website: www.danaliterary.org. Established 2000. **Editor:** Ronald D. Hardcastle.

Magazine Needs *Dana Literary Society Online Journal* appears monthly. Contains poetry, fiction, nonfiction, and editorials. "All styles are welcome—rhyming/metrical, free verse, and classic—but they must be well-crafted and throught-provoking. We want no pornography. Neither do we want works that consist of pointless flows of words with no apparent significance." Has published poetry by A.B. Jacobs, C. David Hay, Raymond HV Gallucci, and Earl Jay Perel. *Dana Literary Society Online Journal* is equivalent to approximately 50 printed pages. Receives about 600 poems/year, accepts about 10%. Publishes about 5 poems/issue.

How to Submit Submit up to 3 poems at a time. Line length for poetry is 120 maximum. Accepts previously published poems and simultaneous submissions. Accepts submissions by postal mail only. Time between acceptance and publication is 3 months. Poems are selected by Society director and *Online Journal* editor. Often comments on rejected poems. Guidelines available on website. Responds in 2 weeks. Pays $25 for each poem accepted. Acquires right to display in *Online Journal* for one month.

Advice "View the poetry on our website. We favor works that are well-crafted and thought-provoking."

🌐 ◯ ◎ DANDELION ARTS MAGAZINE; FERN PUBLICATIONS (Specialized: membership/subscription)

24 Frosty Hollow, East Hunsbury, Northants NN4 OSY England. Phone/Fax: 01604-701730. Established 1978. **Editor/Publisher:** Mrs. Jacqueline Gonzalez-Marina, M.A.

● Fern Publications subsidizes costs for their books, paying no royalties.

Magazine Needs *Dandelion Arts Magazine*, published biannually, is "a platform for new and established poets and prose writers to be read throughout the world." Wants poetry "not longer than 35-40 lines. Modern but not wild." Does not want "bad language poetry, religious or political, nor offensive to any group of people in the world." Has published poetry by Andrew Duncan, Donald Ward, Andrew Pye, John Brander, and Gerald Denley. *Dandelion Arts* is about 25 pages, A4, with thermal binding, b&w and color illustrations, original cover design, some ads. Receives about 200-300 poems/year, accepts about 40%. Press run is up to 1,000 for about 100 subscribers of which 10% are universities and libraries, some distributed free to chosen organizations. Subscription: £14 (UK), £20 (Europe), £25 (US), £25 (ROW). Sample: half price of subscription. Make checks payable to J. Gonzalez-Marina.

How to Submit Poets must become member-subscribers of *Dandelion Arts Magazine* and poetry club in order to be published. Submit 4-6 poems at a time. Accepts simultaneous submissions; no previously published poems. Accepts fax submissions. Cover letter required. "Poems must be typed out clearly and ready for publication, if possible, accompanied by a SAE or postal order to cover the cost of postage for the reply." Reads submissions any time of the year. Time between acceptance and publication is 2-6 months. "The poems are read by the editor when they arrive, and a decision is taken straight away." Some constructive comments on rejected poems. Guidelines available for SASE (or SAE and IRC), by fax, or by e-mail. Responds within 3 weeks. Reviews books of poetry. Send materials for review consideration.

Also Offers *Dandelion Arts* includes information on poetry competitions and art events.

Book/Chapbook Needs & How to Submit Fern Publications is a subsidy press of artistic, poetic, and historical books and publishes 2 paperbacks/year. Books are usually 50-80 pages, A5 or A4, "thermal bound" or hand-finished. Query first with 6-10 poems. **Requires authors to subscribe to *Dandelion Arts Magazine*.** Responds to queries and mss in 3 weeks. "All publications are published at a cost agreed beforehand and paid in advance."

Advice "Consider a theme from all angles and explore all the possibilities, never forgetting the grammar! Stay away from religious, political, or offensive issues. Become a subscriber and get a better idea about the magazine. Submit material for publication and hope to have your work accepted."

$ ◪ JOHN DANIEL AND COMPANY, PUBLISHER; FITHIAN PRESS

Daniel & Daniel Publishers, Inc., P.O. Box 2790, McKinleyville CA 95519. (707)839-3495. Fax: (707)839-3242. E-mail: dandd@danielpublishing.com. Website: www.danielpublishing.com. Established 1980. Reestablished 1985.

Book/Chapbook Needs John Daniel, a general small press publisher, specializes in literature, both prose and poetry. "Book-length manuscripts of any form or subject matter will be considered, but we do not want to see pornographic, libelous, illegal, or sloppily written poetry." Has published *The Light of Invisible Bodies* by Jeanne Lohmann, *Travel Among Stars* by Margareta Horiba, and *Photo/Bomb/Red Chair* by Barbara Lefcowitz. Publishes about 6 flat-spined poetry paperbacks, averaging 80 pages, each year. Press runs average between 500-1,000. No longer issues a print catalog, but all books are shown and described on website.

How to Submit Send 12 sample poems and bio. Responds to queries in 2 weeks, to mss in 2 months. Accepts simultaneous submissions. No fax or e-mail submissions. Always sends prepublication galleys. Pays 10% royalties of net receipts. Acquires English-language book rights. Returns rights upon termination of contract.

Also Offers Fithian Press books are subsidized, the author paying production costs and receiving royalties of 60% of net receipts. Books and rights are the property of the author, but publisher agrees to warehouse and distribute for one year if desired.

Advice "We receive over 5,000 unsolicited manuscripts and query letters a year. We publish only a few books a year, of which fewer than half are received unsolicited. Obviously the odds are not with you. For this reason we encourage you to send out multiple submissions, and we do not expect you to tie up your chances while waiting for our response. Also, poetry does not make money, alas. It is a labor of love for both publisher and writer. But if the love is there, the rewards are great."

DARENGO; SESHAT: CROSS-CULTURAL PERSPECTIVES IN POETRY AND PHILOSOPHY (Specialized: translations)

P.O. Box 9313, London E17 8XL United Kingdom. Phone/fax: (44)181-679-4150. Darengo established 1989. *Seshat* established 1997. **Editor/Proprietor:** Terence DuQuesne. **Editor:** Mark Angelo de Brito.

Magazine Needs *Seshat*, published biannually, "provides a focus for poetry enthusiasts by publishing high-quality poems in English and in translation. It also prints prose articles which highlight connections between the poetic, the philosophical, and the spiritual. *Seshat* is committed to the view that poetry and other art forms are vitalizing and raise consciousness and thus should not be regarded as minority interests. Poetry is not merely an aesthetic matter: it can and should help to break down the barriers of class, race, gender, age, and sexual preference. *Seshat* is named for the Egyptian goddess of sacred writing and measurement." Has published poetry by Sappho, Anthony James, Martina Evans, Ellen Zaks, and Dwina Murphy-Gibb. *Seshat* is 80 pages, offset-printed with stitched binding, laminated paper cover, includes graphics. Press run is 200. Single copy: £10 (payable in sterling only plus £5 postage outside UK); subscription: £20.

How to Submit Submit up to 5 poems at a time. Accepts previously published poems; no simultaneous submissions. Accepts disk submissions. Cover letter required. Time between acceptance and publication is 3 months. Often comments on rejected poems. Guidelines available for SASE (or SAE and IRC). Responds in 2 weeks. Always sends prepublication galleys. Pays one contributor's copy, more on request. Poets retain copyright. Reviews books and chapbooks of poetry and other magazines in 1,000 words. Send materials for review consideration.

Book/Chapbook Needs & How to Submit Darengo currently does not accept unsolicited mss.

DEAD END: CITY LIMITS (Specialized: dark subjects; failure of religion, society, romance; horror; fallen/dark angels)

The Good Intentions Paving Co., 1875 Century Park East, Suite H-2554, Los Angeles CA 90067. (310)712-7060. E-mail: goodintentionspaving@hotmail.com. Website: www.goodintentionspaving .com. Established 2003. **Publisher/Editor:** R.T. St. Claire.

Magazine Needs "We are a website created primarily to promote our various creative projects such as *No Sleep* (TV show), *CandyAppleBlack* (film and comic book), and our web-based dark poetry page, *Dead End: City Limits*." All styles/forms of poetry welcome, "but it needs to speak to the darkness in our souls. No up-with-people, hey, let's build a teen center, Happy Scrappy Hero Pup, paint a smiley face on a sun-bleached skull, hearts-and-flowers crap. This world is rotten to its core, and we aren't getting any divine help from anyone any time soon, so let's wake up and call a spade a spade. Hope is nothing more than a mean trick used to keep us submissive. If you don't understand what that means, don't submit your work to us." *Dead End: City Limits* is published online only. Receives about 25 poems/year, accepts about 3. Publishes about 3 poems/issue.

How to Submit Submit 3 poems at a time. Line length for poetry is 30 maximum. Accepts previously published poems and simultaneous submission. Accepts e-mail submissions (only in body of e-mail, no attachments); no disk submissions. Reads submissions "all the time." Time between acceptance and publication is "unknown. There is no actual [editorial] 'board.' You mail us 3 poems; if we like them, we will e-mail you back about featuring your work on the poetry page of our site. If we do not plan on using your work, we will let you know, but rejection e-mails will take awhile for us to get to." Never comments on rejected poems. Guidelines available on website. Response time is "unknown. If we like what you send, you'll hear from us." No payment. Acquires one-time rights.

Advice "Pretty simple. We are The Good Intentions Paving Co. We maintain a poetry page dedicated to dark poets on our website. Go to the site. You'll understand very quickly if we are for you. If what you see fits what you write, submit some of your work to us. If we like it, we'll contact you and let you know that we'd like to post it on our poetry page for a month or so. If we don't like it, you may not hear back from us for a very, very long time, if ever."

⊘ ◎ DEAD FUN (Specialized: gothic/horror)

P.O. Box 752, Royal Oak MI 48068-0752. E-mail: horror@deadfun.com. Website: www.deadfun.com. **Editoress:** Kelli. **Co-Editor:** Jaysin.

- *Dead Fun* **"remains but is currently on an indefinite hiatus, therefore NOT accepting submissions at this time."**

⊘ DEBUT REVIEW

P.O. Box 266461, Kansas City MO 64126-6461. E-mail: miklorenzo@aol.com. Established 1999. **Editor:** Michael Lorenzo.

Magazine Needs *Debut Review* appears annually to "showcase the work of established and emerging poets." *Debut Review* is not a specialized market. "What I am looking for is well-written work— nothing unpolished or vulgar." While the magazine is open to all poetic forms, the editor prefers "coherent, concise pieces, peppered lightly with literary devices like personification, simile, metaphor, etc." *Debut Review* is about 35-50 pages, digest-sized, professionally printed, perfect-bound. Currently does not offer subscriptions.

How to Submit Submit 3-5 poems by e-mail only (as attachment) between June 1 and October 31 of each year. "The e-mail should contain a brief bio about the poet to help keep the format of the magazine consistent. Poets will be notified of the acceptance of their work by e-mail within 30 days." Sometimes comments on rejections. **While there is no payment for poems or fee required for publication, poets must send $5 to receive a copy of the edition in which their work appears.**

$⊘ ◎ DECOMPOSITIONS (Specialized: horror)

4209 33rd Ave., Cincinnati OH 45209. (513)924-1512. E-mail: brosenberger@earthlink.net. Website: http://home.earthlink.net/~brosenberger/decompositions.html. Established 2001. **Minister of Decay:** Brian Rosenberger.

Magazine Needs *Decompositions* is a monthly e-zine devoted to dark poetry with a focus on horror, psychological or graphic. "It just has to be dark. A sense of humor is also welcomed." Has published poetry by Karl Koweski, Kurt Newton, Michael Arnzen, Christina Sng, Gary West, and Charlee

Jacob. *Decompositions* is published online only, includes art/graphics. Receives about 200 poems/year, accepts about 40. Publishes about 10 poems/issue.

How to Submit Submit 5 poems at a time. No line length for poetry, but prefers shorter poems. Accepts previously published poems and simultaneous submissions. "Reprints are OK, but I would like to know where they first appeared." Also accepts art. Prefers e-mail submissions; no fax or disk submissions. Cover letter is preferred. Reads submissions year round. Submit seasonal poems 3 months in advance. Time between acceptance and publication is 2-4 months. "Either it fits what I am looking for or it doesn't. I do try to comment on all work submitted. It would be in your best interest to check out an issue before you submit." Guidelines available for SASE, by e-mail, or on website. Responds in up to 3 weeks. "Payment is $2 U.S. upon acceptance." Acquires one-time rights.

⊠ ☑ DELMAR: A LITERARY ANNUAL

215 Reedway, St. Louis MO 63122-2614. E-mail: editorial@delmarmag.org. Website: www.delmar mag.org. Established 1989. **Executive Editor:** Jeff Hamilton.

Magazine Needs *Delmar: A Literary Annual* is "a St. Louis literary magazine with a national reputation for excellence and careful presentation of the highest quality work. We publish literary fiction, poetry that fits the categories reductively named experimental and mainstream, and literary work that fits none of these descriptions. We are committed to a local scene but are always looking for ways to extend beyond it." Wants poetry in categories "that include, but are not limited to, avant-garde, free verse, light verse, and traditional. *Delmar 11* will be a thematically planned issue on nonfiction; poetry, story, drama, criticism, expository prose apply." Does not want "work in which it's clear the author lacks faith." Has published poetry by Matthea Harvey, Carl Phillips, Jennifer Atkinson, Eric Pankey, and Jason Sommer. *Delmar* is 80-100 pages, digest-sized, offset-printed (lithography), perfect-bound, with coated coverstock with color art, includes line art or grayscale images. Receives about 200 poems/year. Publishes about 20 poems/issue. Press run is 800. Single copy: $8; subscription: $8. Make checks payable to Delmar, Inc.

How to Submit Submit any number of poems at a time. No previously published poems or simultaneous submissions. No e-mail or disk submissions. Cover letter is preferred. "Cover letters should include *brief* bio and selected list of previous publications. Send either SASE (or IRC) for return of the manuscript, OR a disposable copy of the manuscript with a #10 SASE for reply only." Reads submissions year round; deadline for *Delmar 11* is October 2004. Time between acceptance and publication is between 6 months and one year. "Poems are first read by executive editor and guest editor, then distributed to other members of editorial board for review and selection." Always comments on rejected poems. Guidelines available on website. Responds in up to 4 months. Pays 2 contributor's copies. Acquires first rights, electronic rights, and reprint rights. Reviews books and chapbooks of poetry; word count varies. Send materials for review consideration to Jeff Hamilton, Executive Editor.

Advice "Read the dictionary; read books about words; read poetry."

⊠ $☑ ◎ DESCANT (Specialized: themes and miscellanies)

Box 314, Station P, Toronto ON M5S 2S8 Canada. (416)593-2557. E-mail: descant@web.net. Website: www.descant.on.ca. Established 1970. **Editor-in-Chief:** Karen Mulhallen.

Magazine Needs *Descant* is "Canada's pre-eminent literary magazine. We publish an assortment of national and international material, which has previously included writers such as Lorna Crozier, P.K. Page, Patrick Friesen, and Leon Rooke." *Descant* is 120-300 pages, over-sized digest format, elegantly printed and illustrated on heavy paper, flat-spined with colored, glossy cover. Receives 1,200 unsolicited submissions/year, accepts less than 100. Press run is 1,200. Sample: $8.50 plus postage.

How to Submit Submit typed ms of no more than 10 poems, name and address on first page, and last name on each subsequent page. Include e-mail address or SASE with Canadian stamps, or SAE and IRCs. No previously published poems or simultaneous submissions. Guidelines and upcoming themes available for SASE (or SAE and IRC) or on website. Responds within 9 months. Pays "approximately $100." Acquires first rights.

Advice "The best advice is to know the magazine you are submitting to. Please read the magazine before submitting."

◖ DESCANT: FORT WORTH'S JOURNAL OF POETRY AND FICTION

English Dept., Box 297270, Texas Christian University, Fort Worth TX 76129. Fax: (817)257-6239. E-mail: descant@tcu.edu. Website: www.eng.tcu.edu/journals/descant/index.html. Established 1956. **Editor:** Dave Kuhne.

Magazine Needs *descant* appears annually during the summer. Wants "well-crafted poems of interest. No restrictions as to subject matter or form. We usually accept poems 60 lines or fewer but sometimes longer poems." *descant* is 100+ pages, digest-sized, professionally printed and bound with matte card cover. "We publish 30-40 pages of poetry per year. We receive probably 3,000 poems annually." Press run is 500 for 350 subscribers. Single issue: $12, $18 outside US. Sample: $6.

How to Submit No simultaneous submissions. No fax or e-mail submissions. Reads submissions September through April only. Responds in 6 weeks. Pays 2 contributor's copies.

Contest/Award Offerings The Betsy Colquitt Award for poetry, $500 prize awarded annually to the best poem or series of poems by a single author in an issue. *descant* also offers a $250 award for an outstanding poem in an issue. Complete contest rules and guidelines available for SASE or by e-mail.

ℕ ◯ ◎ DESERT VOICES (Specialized: Desert Southwest)

Palo Verde College, One College Dr., Blythe CA 92225. (760)921-5500 or -5449 (Minyard). Fax: (760)922-0230. E-mail: aminyard@paloverde.edu. **Co-Editors:** Applewhite Minyard and Joe Jondrea.

Magazine Needs *Desert Voices* is a biannual literary magazine of poetry, art, and short stories especially for the Desert Southwest. Wants poems generally one page or less; especially interested in the Desert Southwest. Does not want "pornography or excessive sexual imagery (erotica OK; profanity in context)." *Desert Voices* is 36 pages, digest-sized, offset-printed, stapled. Receives about 100 poems/year, accepts about 20. Publishes about 10 poems/issue. Press run is 1,000 for subscribers of which 10 are libraries; a number are distributed free to students. Single copy: $1. Make checks payable to Palo Verde College.

How to Submit Submit maximum of 3 poems at a time. Accepts simultaneous submissions; no previously published poems. Accepts e-mail (attachment in MS Word or plain text) and disk (MS Word) submissions; no fax submissions. Cover letter is preferred. Include SASE for return or reply. Reads submissions September through June. Time between acceptance and publication is 2-3 months. Poems are circulated to an editorial board. "Three readers plus editors read and rate submissions. We publish once per semester, and student submissions are considered first." Seldom comments on rejected poems. Occasionally publishes theme issues. Guidelines available for SASE or by e-mail. Responds in 2 months. Pays 2 contributor's copies. Acquires one-time rights.

Advice "Poetry should be real; that is, it should resonate with deeply felt issues that reveal something about the poet."

$◖ ◎ DEVO'ZINE (Specialized: Christian; youth; themes)

1908 Grand Ave., P.O. Box 340004, Nashville TN 37203-0004. E-mail: devozine@upperroom.org. Website: www.devozine.org. **Editor:** Sandi Miller.

Magazine Needs & How to Submit *Devo'Zine* is a bimonthly devotional magazine for youth ages

13-18. Offers meditations, scripture, prayers, poems, stories, songs, and feature articles to "aid youth in their prayer life, introduce them to spiritual disciplines, help them shape their concept of God, and encourage them in the life of discipleship." Ordinarily 20-line limit on poetry. List of upcoming themes and guidelines available for SASE or on website. Pays $25.

◖ ◎ DIAL BOOKS FOR YOUNG READERS (Specialized: children)

345 Hudson St., New York NY 10014. Website: www.penguinputnam.com. **Contact:** Submissions.
Book/Chapbook Needs & How to Submit Publishes some illustrated books of poetry for children. Has published poetry by J. Patrick Lewis and Nikki Grimes. Do not submit unsolicited mss. Query first with sample poems and cover letter with brief bio and publication credits. SASE required with all correspondence. Accepts simultaneous submissions; no previously published poems. Send queries Attn: Submissions. Responds to queries in up to 4 months. Payment varies.

◖ ◎ JAMES DICKEY NEWSLETTER (Specialized: membership/subscription, nature/rural/ecology)

1620 College St., Dept. of English, University of South Carolina, Columbia SC 29208. Fax: (803)777-9064. E-mail: thesingw@gwm.sc.edu. Website: www.jamesdickey.org. Established 1984. **Editor:** William B. Thesing.
Magazine Needs *James Dickey Newsletter* is a biannual newsletter, published in the spring and fall, devoted to critical articles/studies of James Dickey's works/biography and bibliography. "Publishes a few poems of high quality. No poems lacking form, meter, or grammatical correctness." Has published poetry by Linda Roth, Paula Goff, and John Van Peenen. *James Dickey Newsletter* is 50 pages, 8½ × 5½, neatly offset (back and front), with a card back-cover, saddlestiched. Subscription: $12/year for individuals (includes membership in the James Dickey Society), $14 for institutions in the US, $15.50 for institutions outside the US. Sample: $8.
How to Submit Contributors should follow MLA style and standard ms form, sending one copy, double-spaced. Cover letter required. Accepts e-mail (pasted into body of message) and fax submissions. "However, if a poet wants written comments/suggestions line by line, then mail manuscript with SASE." Pays 2 contributor's copies. Acquires first rights. Reviews "only works on Dickey or that include Dickey."
Advice "We accept only grammatically correct, full sentences (except rarely a telling fragment). No first-person narratives."

◖ DINER; POETRY OASIS INC.; DINER ANNUAL POETRY CONTEST

P.O. Box 60676, Greendale Station, Worcester MA 01606-2378. (508)853-4143. E-mail: eve@spoken word.to. Website: www.spokenword.to/diner. Established 2000. **Editors:** Eve Rifkah and Abby Millager.
Magazine Needs *Diner* appears biannually in May and November. Each issue publishes 2 feature poets. "Our taste is eclectic, ranging from traditional forms through all possibilities of style. We want to see poems that take risks, play/push language with an ear to sound." Accepts translations. Has published poetry by Gray Jacobik, Rosmarie Waldrop, Judith Hemschemeyer, and John Hodgen. *Diner* is 104 pages, digest-sized, perfect-bound, with glossy card cover with photo, includes b&w graphics. Publishes about 50 poems/issue. Press run is 500. Single copy: $10; subscription: $18. Sample: $8. Make checks payable to Poetry Oasis.
How to Submit Submit no more than 5 poems. Accepts simultaneous submissions; no previously published poems. Accepts e-mail submissions (as attachments) from abroad only. Cover letter and SASE required. Guidelines available by e-mail or on website. Responds in up to 6 months. Pays one contributor's copy. Reviews books.
Contest/Award Offerings The *Diner* Annual Poetry Contest. Send entries to the contest % Christine Cassidy, 51 Park St., Mansfield MA 02048. 1st Prize: $500; 2nd Prize: $100; 3rd Prize: $50; plus 3

honorable mentions. All winning poems published in Fall/Winter edition of *Diner*. "Do not list your name on submitted poems. Send a cover letter with name, address, e-mail, and titles of poems." **Entry fee:** $10 for 3 poems or $22 to include a one-year subscription. **Deadline:** January 31. Past judges include X.J. Kennedy and Mary Ruefle.

◐ DMQ REVIEW

E-mail: editors@dmqreview.com. Website: www.dmqreview.com. **Editor-in-Chief:** Sally Ashton.
Magazine Needs *DMQ Review* appears quarterly as "a quality online magazine of poetry presented with visual art. We are interested in finely crafted poetry that needs to be read." Has published poetry by Bob Hickock, Ilya Kaminsky, Jane Hirshfield, William Logan, John Kennedy, and Sidney Wade. *DMQ Review* is published online; art/photography appears with the poetry. Receives about 3,000-5,000 poems/year, accepts about 1%. Publishes about 10-20 poems/issue.
How to Submit Submit 3 poems at a time. Accepts simultaneous submissions (with notifications only); no previously published poems. E-mail submissions only. "Paste poems in the body of an e-mail only; No attachments will be read. Please read and follow complete submission guidelines on our website." Reads submissions year round. Time between acceptance and publication is 1-3 months. Poems are circulated to an editorial board. Never comments on rejected poems. Responds within 2 months. Acquires first rights.
Also Offers Nominates for the Pushcart Prize. "We also consider submissions of visual art, which we publish with the poems in the magazine with links to the artists' websites."
Advice "Read recent issues of *DMQ Review* before submitting, and send your best work."

✪ ◐ ◎ DOLPHIN-MOON PRESS; SIGNATURES (Specialized: regional)

P.O. Box 22262, Baltimore MD 21203. Established 1973. **President:** James Taylor.
Book/Chapbook Needs Dolphin-Moon is "a limited-edition (500-1,000 copies) press which emphasizes quality work (regardless of style), often published in unusual/'radical' format." The writer is usually allowed a strong voice in the look/feel of the final piece. "We've published magazines, anthologies, chapbooks, pamphlets, perfect-bound paperbacks, records, audio cassettes, and comic books. All styles are read and considered, but the work should show a strong spirit and voice. Although we like the feel of 'well-crafted' work, craft for its own sake won't meet our standards either." Has published work by Teller, Michael Weaver, John Strausbaugh, Josephine Jacobsen, and William Burroughs. Send SASE for catalog and purchase samples, or send $15 for their "sampler" (which they guarantee to be up to $25 worth of their publications).
How to Submit First, send sample of 6-10 pages of poetry and a brief cover letter. No fax or e-mail submissions. Responds to queries, or to submission of whole work (if invited), in up to one month. Always sends prepublication galleys. Pays in author's copies, negotiable, though usually 10% of the run. Acquires first edition rights.
Advice "Our future plans are to continue as we have since 1973, publishing the best work we can by local, up-and-coming, and nationally recognized writers—in a quality package."

◐ DOUBLE ROOM: A JOURNAL OF PROSE POETRY AND FLASH FICTION

E-mail: double_room@hotmail.com. Website: www.webdelsol.com/Double_Room. Established 2002. **Co-Editors:** Mark Tursi and Peter Conners. Web Designer and Associate Editor: Cactus May. Publisher: Michael Neff, Web del Sol.
Magazine Needs *Double Room* is a biannual online literary journal devoted entirely to the publication and discussion of prose poetry and flash fiction. Each issue also features contemporary artwork, reviews, and special features. Has published poetry by Cole Swensen, Rosmarie Waldrop, Ray Gonzalez, Sean Thomas Dougherty, Holly Iglesias, and Christopher Kennedy. *Double Room* is published online only, with art/graphics solicited by the editors. Publishes about 50 poems/issue.
How to Submit Guidelines available on website. Acquires first North American serial rights. Re-

views books and chapbooks of prose poetry and flash fiction. "See our website for review guidelines."

Advice "In addition to publishing the pp/ff forms, *Double Room* seeks to push them to the forefront of literary consideration by offering a Discussion On The Forms section in which contributors are asked to comment on a question related to the genre. For this reason we are looking for writers who, in addition to writing these forms, are interested in briefly discussing various aspects of them."

$⊚ DOVETAIL: A JOURNAL BY AND FOR JEWISH/CHRISTIAN FAMILIES (Specialized: interfaith marriage)

45 Lilac Ave., Hamden CT 06517. (203)865-6327. E-mail: DebiT4RLS@aol.com. Website: www.dov etailinstitute.org. Established 1991. **Editor:** Debi Tenner.

Magazine Needs *Dovetail*, published bimonthly, provides "strategies and resources for interfaith couples, their families and friends." Wants poetry related to Jewish/Christian marriage issues. No general religious themes. Has published work by Janet Landman, Donald R. Stoltz, and Eric Wolk Fried. *Dovetail* is 12-16 pages, magazine-sized, stapled, includes 1-5 ads. Receives about 10 poems/year, accepts about 1%. Press run is 1,000 for 700 subscribers. Single copy: $5; subscription: $29.95. Make checks payable to DI-IFR.

How to Submit Submit one poem at a time. Accepts previously published poems and simultaneous submissions. Accepts e-mail (pasted into body of message) submissions. Time between acceptance and publication is up to one year. Poems are circulated to an editorial board. "Clergy and other interfaith professionals review draft issues." Seldom comments on rejected poems. Publishes theme issues. Guidelines and upcoming themes available for SASE, by e-mail, or by fax. Responds in one month. Pays $10-20 plus contributor's copies. Acquires first North American serial rights. Reviews other magazines in 500 words, single and multi-book format.

Advice "We get 20 inappropriately denomination-oriented poems for every one that actually relates to interfaith marriage. Don't waste your time or ours with general Christian or 'inspirational' themes."

◻ DOWN IN THE DIRT; SCARS PUBLICATIONS

829 Brian Court, Gurnee IL 60031. E-mail: alexrand@scars.tv. Website: http://scars.tv (*Down in the Dirt* mag button). Established 1993. **Editor:** Alexandria Rand.

Magazine Needs & How to Submit *Down in the Dirt* appears "as often as work is submitted to us to guarantee a good-length issue." Does not want smut, rhyming poetry, or poetry already accepted for *Children, Churches and Daddies* (see separate listing in this section). Has published work by I.B. Rad, Jennifer Rowan, Cheryl A. Townsend, Tom Racine, David-Matthew Barnes, and Michael Estabrook. *Down in the Dirt* is published electronically, either on the Web or in e-book form (PDF file). Accepts previously published poems. Prefers e-mail submissions; accepts disk submissions formatted for Macintosh. Guidelines and sample issues available for SASE, by e-mail, or on website.

Also Offers Scars Publications sometimes sponsors a book contest. Write or e-mail (Editor@scars. tv) for information. "The website is a more comprehensive view of what *Down in the Dirt* does. All the information is there." Also able to publish chapbooks. Write for more information.

✪ ⊕ ◻ DRAGONHEART PRESS; LIVING POETS online poetry journal; DRAGONHEART PRESS POETRY COMPETITION

11 Menin Rd., Allestree, Derby, Derbyshire DE22 2NL England. E-mail: livingpoets@seanwoodwar d.com. Website: http://welcome.to/livingpoets. Established 1995. **Executive Editor:** Mr. S. Woodward.

Magazine Needs *Living Poets* is an online showcase for poetry. Wants "crafted poetry with strong imagery. No constrained rhyming structures." Receives about 400 poems/year, accepts about 20%. Sample (printed): $10. Make checks payable to S. Woodward.

How to Submit Submit 3 poems at a time. Accepts previously published poems and simultaneous submissions. Cover letter with bio and publication credits preferred. Time between acceptance and publication is 1-2 months. Often comments on rejected poems. Publishes theme issues. Guidelines available for SASE, by e-mail, or on website. Responds in one month. Pays one contributor's copy. Reviews books and chapbooks of poetry or other magazines in single book format. Send materials for review consideration to Review Editor, Dragonheart Press.

Contest/Award Offerings Sponsors Dragonheart Press Poetry Competition. Send SASE (or SAE and IRC) for details.

DREAM HORSE PRESS; DREAM HORSE PRESS NATIONAL POETRY CHAPBOOK PRIZE; THE ORPHIC PRIZE FOR POETRY

P.O. Box 640746, San Jose CA 95164-0746. E-mail: dreamhorsepress@yahoo.com. Website: www.dreamhorsepress.com. Established 1999.

- **"The press currently reads submissions that are entered in its contests ONLY (see below). Please see website for details and instructions. Do not submit outside of contests; unsolicited submissions will be recycled unread."**

Contest/Award Offerings 1) **Dream Horse Press National Poetry Chapbook Prize** offers annual award of a cash prize and multiple copies of a handsomely printed chapbook (amounts change yearly, check website for current information). 2003 prize was $300 and 20 copies. Submissions may be previously published in magazines/journals but not in books or chapbooks. May be entered in other contests with notification. "Submit 16-24 paginated pages of poetry in a readable font with acknowledgments, bio, SASE for results, and entry fee." Multiple submissions acceptable (with separate fee for each entry). Poet's name should not appear anywhere on ms. All mss will be recycled. **Entry fee:** changes annually; check website (2003 fee was $12). Fees accepted by check or money order. **Deadline:** check website. All entries will be considered for publication. Recent winners include Ryan G. Van Cleave for *The Florida Letters*, Rob Carney for *New Fables, Old Songs*, and Jason Gray for *Adam & Eve Go to the Zoo*. 2) **The Orphic Prize for Poetry** offers annual award of $500, publication of a book-length ms, and 20 author's copies. Submissions may be entered in other contests, "but if your manuscript is accepted for publication elsewhere you must notify Dream Horse Press immediately." Entry fees are non-refundable. Submit 48-80 paginated pages of poetry, table of contents, acknowledgments, bio, and SASE for results (mss will be recycled after judging). Writers' names should not appear anywhere on the ms. Include name and biographical information in separate cover letter, and include e-mail address when available. All entries will be considered for publication. Both free and formal verse styles are welcome. Guidelines available on website. **Entry fee:** $20/ms entered. **Deadline:** was May 1 for 2004; check website for deadlines and details for subsequent years. "Judging will be anonymous."

DREXEL ONLINE JOURNAL

Pennoni Honors College, Drexel University, 3210 Cherry St., Philadelphia PA 19104. (215)895-6469. Fax: (215)895-6288. E-mail: doj@drexel.edu. Website: www.drexel.edu/doj. Established 2001. **Poetry Editors:** Valerie Fox and Lynn Levin.

Magazine Needs *Drexel Online Journal* is "a general interest magazine." No limitations as to form. Translations welcome. Has published poetry by Gerald Stern, Barbara Crooker, Elton Glaser, Marilyn Chin, Betsy Sholl, Lewis Warsh, Lydia Cortes, and Michael McGoolaghan. *Drexel Online Journal* is published online. Accepts about 5% of poems received. Publishes about 5 poems/issue. Sample available free on website.

How to Submit Submit up to 5 poems at a time. No previously published poems. "Submit by postal mail with SASE or via e-mail with 'Poetry Submission' in subject field." Time between acceptance and publication is 3 months. Poems are circulated to an editorial board. "We currently have 3 readers who go by consensus." Occasionally comments on rejected poems. Guidelines available on website. Responds in 2 months. Pay varies. Acquires first rights.

Advice "Our tastes are diverse."

◐ ◎ THE DRIFTWOOD REVIEW (Specialized: regional, Michigan)

P.O. Box 2042, Bay City MI 48707. Established 1996. **Poetry Editor:** Jeff Vande Zande.

Magazine Needs "An annual publication, *The Driftwood Review* strives to publish the best poetry and fiction being written by Michigan writers—known and unknown. We consider any style, but are particularly fond of poetry that conveys meaning through image. Rhyming poetry stands a poor chance." Has published poetry by Daniel James Sundahl, Danny Rendleman, Anca Vlasopolos, Terry Blackhawk, and Linda Nemec Foster. *The Driftwood Review* is 100-125 pages, digest-sized, professionally-printed, perfect-bound, with glossy card cover with b&w artwork. Receives about 500 poems/year, accepts about 5-7%. Press run is 200 for 75 subscribers. Subscription: $6.

How to Submit Submit 3-5 poems at a time. No previously published poems or simultaneous submissions. Cover letter preferred. "Cover letter should include a brief bio suitable for contributor's notes. No SASE? No reply." Reads submissions January 1 through September 15 only. Time between acceptance and publication is 9 months. Seldom comments on rejected poems. "Will comment on work that's almost there." Responds in 3 months. Pays one contributor's copy and provides the opportunity to advertise a book. Acquires first North American serial rights. Staff reviews chapbooks of poetry by Michigan writers only in 500 words, single book format. Send chapbooks for review consideration.

Advice "Strive to express what you have to say with image."

⊠ $□ ◎ DSAME; TRACE OF THE HAND: THE ALL-5-SENSES ZINE EXPERIENCE; BNB (Specialized: membership; social issues; women's issues)

Website: www.geocities.com/loveandunity2020.

Magazine Needs "Two things will cause your submission to be immediately discarded faster than anything else: Numerous misspelled words (except in handwritten diary format poems) and any submission from nonmembers. It is important to realize that in our desire to give voice to the social issues in ignored areas of the world, we are currently open to easy submissions which are basically 'a diary style format of poetry writing.' We are also very interested in other experimental forms of poetry. Examples are poetry written in a comic strip, through surreal paintings, poetry photojournals, etc.; the possibilities are limitless." Wants "all topics and tones of poetry from members, no matter how juvenile or serious, including, but not limited to, non-violent activism and civil disobedience poetry. Also, authors who are fluent in Spanish have the option of submitting a Spanish version of their English material provided that the English material accompanies it. No translations of author's work. Nothing that promotes, rationalizes, and/or justifies violence (including violent activism), ageism, ableism (which includes the physically and mentally disabled/challenged), classism, racism, sexism, or any form of discrimination against any person's sexual orientation, religion, or lack of religion." *Trace of the Hand: The All-5-Senses Zine Experience* is magazine-sized, "typically photocopied but sometimes offset-printed, using 100% post-consumer recycled paper. The content and texture of the cover greatly varies." Includes b&w or color artwork of all mediums "including photographs, cartoons, collages, rubberstamping, hand-punched patterns, individually hand-imprinted paintings on the back covers, etc." Press run greatly varies. Between 10-100 are distributed free to large zine libraries and zine review publications worldwide. See website for purchase and subscription options and payment methods.

How to Submit No previously published poems or simultaneous submissions; "we accept only new material." No e-mail or disk submissions. Reads submissions year round "from members only." Time between acceptance and publication varies. Never comments on rejected poems. **Free mem-**

bership required. Guidelines available on website (link #9). "It is our desire that our infobook guidelines will be available to female authors of all social classes in the U.S.A. and Canada, even those who don't use computers. Thus, a public librarian can easily go to either of our websites, click on link #7 (for a short infobook) or link #7a (for a long infobook) and print it out for anyone." Response time varies. See website for complete details about payment and Free-Op Circulation for BNB members. "Poet retains ownership of all poems submitted." Reviews chapbooks of poetry and other zines/journals. "Prints 3-D Zine Reviews and 3-D Zine and Chapbook Profiles of non-members only after poets have been specifically invited to do so by the editor. We do not print 3-D Zine reviews of current or former members."

Book/Chapbook Needs & How to Submit Manuscripts are selected through open submission "from members only. Furthermore, each BNB member, throughout the U.S.A. and Canada, will decide individually if they want to circulate another BNB author's publication once accepted." Zines and chapbooks are typically a maximum of 56 pages, "photocopied but sometimes offset-printed. Members individually make that choice." Includes artwork of all mediums. Manuscripts may not include previously published poems. "Please keep in mind that most of the chapbooks we accept are printed 90% 'as is,' all topics and tones including, but not limited to, social issues and non-violent activism that society would rather ignore. We must boldly state that strikingly beautiful layout and astonishingly elegant page design is far more important than content because we want to print poetry that will be treasured, given as gifts, and circulated rather than discarded. Some of the most important issues in the world have been ignored due to poor presentation." **Must be a member.** "Currently, membership is open only to women age 18 and over in 42 U.S. states, all U.S. territories, and all of Canada." Response time varies. Pays author one copy and $25. "If any of your material is selected for a future anthology, your permission will be sought and further payment will be made." Order sample books by sending $10 U.S., $19 Canada, $30 World, "which includes secure, delivery confirmation shipping where available. (Please print out current subscription prices and order forms found in the infobooks on our website.)"

Also Offers "Link #9 on our website is a printable webpage which gives further detailed information about more benefits of BNB membership."

Advice "We believe poetry should be fresh, alive, and perhaps even spontaneously written from your sincere feelings, rather than limited to the rehearsed and reconstructed confines of rhythm, meter, and the traditional styles of ancient celebrities who established so-called 'rules' of writing poetry. The poetry may express pain, happiness, humor, but it is most important that the emotions are sincere. In this way poetry can act as a vehicle giving voice to the unheard.''

$ ÉCRITS DES FORGES (Specialized: foreign language, French)

1497 Laviolette, Trois-Rivières QC G9A 5G4 Canada. (819)379-9813. Fax: (819)376-0774. E-mail: ecrits.desforges@tr.cgocable.ca. Website: www.ecritsdesforges.com. Established 1971. **Président:** Gaston Bellemare. **Directrice Générale:** Maryse Baribeau.

Book/Chapbook Needs & How to Submit Écrits des Forges publishes poetry only—45-50 paperback books of poetry/year—and wants poetry that is "authentic and original as a signature. We have published poetry from more than 1,000 poets coming from most of the francophone countries: André Romus (Belgium), Amadou Lamine Sall (Sénégal), Nicole Brossard, Bernard Pozier, Blaude Beausoleil, Jean-Marc Desgent, and Jean-Paul Daoust (Québec).'' Books are usually 80-88 pages, digest-sized, perfect-bound, with 2-color cover with art. Query first with a few sample poems and cover letter with brief bio and publication credits. Responds to queries in up to 6 months. Pays royalties of 10-20%, advance of 50% maximum, and 25 author's copies. Order sample books by writing or faxing.

Also Offers Sponsors the International Poetry Festival/Festival international de la poésie. "One hundred fifty poets from 30 countries based on the 5 continents read their poems over a 10-day period in

70 different cafés, bars, restaurants, etc.; 30,000 persons attend. All in French." For more information, see website: www.fiptr.com.

⬤ EDGZ

Edge Publications, P.O. Box 799, Ocean Park WA 98640. Established 2000. **Publisher/Editor:** Blaine R. Hammond.

Magazine Needs *Edgz* appears semiannually in (or around) March and September and publishes "poetry of all sorts of styles and schools. Our purpose is to present poetry with transpersonal intentions or applications, and to put poets on a page next to other poets they are not used to appearing next to." Wants "a broad variety of styles with a transpersonal intent. *Edgz* has 2 main reasons for existence: My weariness with the attitude that whatever kind of poetry someone likes is the only legitimate poetry; and my desire to present poetry addressing large issues of life: meaning, oppression, exaltation, and whatever else you can think of. Must be engaged; intensity helps." Does not want "anything with a solely personal purpose; dense language poetry; poetry that does not take care with the basics of language, or displays an ignorance of modern poetry. No clichés, gushing, sentimentalism, or lists of emotions. Nothing vague or abstract. No light verse, but humor is fine." Accepts poetry by children, "but not childish poetry; they compete with adult poets on an equal basis." Has published poetry by Joan Payne Kincaid, Jesse Freeman, Bob Cooperman, R. Yurman, Carolyn Maddux, and Alan Catlin. *Edgz* is digest-sized, laser-printed, saddle-stapled, with 94 lb. card stock cover with art/graphics (not comix); printed on paper "made of no virgin wood fibers." Single copy: $7; subscription: $13 (2 issues). Sample: $4. Make checks payable to Edge Publications.

How to Submit Submit 3-5 poems at a time; "a longer poem may be submitted by itself." No limits on line length. Accepts simultaneous submissions; no previously published poems. Accepts submissions by postal mail only. "I don't mind more than one poem to a page or well-traveled submissions; these are ecologically sound practices. I like recycled paper. Submissions without SASE will be gratefully used as note paper. No postcards in place of SASE. Please do not fold poems separately. Handwritten OK if poor or incarcerated." Reads submissions year round. **Deadlines:** February 1 and August 1. Time between acceptance and publication is 1-6 months. Often comments on rejected poems "as I feel like it. I don't provide criticism services." Guidelines available for SASE. Responds in up to 6 months. Pays one contributor's copy/published poem, with discounts on additional copies. Acquires first rights plus anthology rights ("just in case").

Advice "It is one thing to require subscriptions in order to be published. It is something else to charge reading fees. In a world that considers poetry valueless, reading fees say it is less than valueless—editors should be compensated for being exposed to it. I beg such editors to cease the practice. I advise everyone else not to submit to them, or the practice will spread. My most common rejection note is 'too personal for my thematic focus.' "

$⬤ ◎ THE EIGHTH MOUNTAIN PRESS (Specialized: women writers)

624 SE 29th Ave., Portland OR 97214. E-mail: eighthmt@pacifier.com. Established 1985. **Editor:** Ruth Gundle.

Book/Chapbook Needs Eighth Mountain is a "small press publisher of literary works by women." Has published poetry by Lucinda Roy, Maureen Seaton, Irena Klepfisz, Almitra David, Judith Barrington, and Elizabeth Woody. Publishes one book of poetry averaging 128 pages every few years. "Our books are handsomely designed and printed on acid-free paper in both quality trade paperbacks and library editions." Initial press run is 2,500.

How to Submit "We expect to receive a query letter along with a few poems. A résumé of published work, if any, should be included. Work should be typed, double-spaced, and include your name on each page. If you want to know if your work has been received, enclose a separate, stamped postcard." Accepts submissions by postal mail and by e-mail (pasted into body of message). Responds within 6 weeks. SASE (#10 envelope) must be included for response. ''Full postage must be included if return of the work submitted is desired.'' Pays 7-8% royalties. Acquires all rights. Returns rights if book goes out of print.

88: A JOURNAL OF CONTEMPORARY AMERICAN POETRY

% Hollyridge Press, P. O. Box 2872, Venice CA 90294. (310)712-1238. Fax: (310)828-4860. E-mail: T88AJournal@aol.com. Website: www.hollyridgepress.com. Established 1999. **Managing Editor:** Ian Wilson. Member: PMA.

• Poetry published here was included in the 2003 volume of *The Best American Poetry*.

Magazine Needs *88: A Journal of Contemporary American Poetry* appears annually publishing essays on poetry and poetics, also reviews. Wants mainstream, experimental, lyric, lyric narrative, and prose poems. ''Will consider work that incorporates elements of humor, elements of surrealism. No light verse, limericks, children's poetry.'' Has published poetry by Tony Hoagland, Thomas Lux, Rosmarie Waldrup, and Matthea Harvey. *88* is 176 pages, digest-sized, printed on-demand, perfect-bound, with 4-color soft cover, includes very limited art/graphics, ads. Publishes about 80 poems/issue. Single copy: $13.95.

How to Submit Submit 5 poems at a time. No previously published poems or simultaneous submissions. No fax, e-mail, or disk submissions. Cover letter is required. Poems should be typed, single-spaced on one side of paper; indicate stanza breaks if poem is longer than one page. Name and address should appear on every page. ''Unsolicited submissions accompanied by a proof-of-purchase coupon clipped from the back of the journal are read year round. Without proof-of-purchase, unsolicited submissions are considered March 1 through May 31 only. Unsolicited submissions received outside these guidelines will be returned unread. Submissions sent without SASE will be discarded.'' Time between acceptance and publication is up to 9 months. ''Managing editor has the final decision of inclusion, but every poem is considered by an editorial board consisting of contributing editors whose suggestions weigh heavily in the process.'' Guidelines available in magazine, on website, and for SASE. Responds in up to 6 months. Sometimes sends prepublication galleys. Pays one contributor's copy. Acquires one-time rights. Reviews books of poetry in 500-1,000 words, single and multi-book format. Send materials for review consideration to Ian Wilson, managing editor. Also accepts essays on poetics and contemporary American poetry and poets, 5,000 words maximum.

Advice ''We believe it's important for poets to support the journals to which they submit. Because of print-on-demand, *88* is always available. We recommend becoming familiar with the journal before submitting.''

EKPHRASIS (Specialized: ekphrastic verse); THE EKPHRASIS PRIZE; FRITH PRESS

P.O. Box 161236, Sacramento CA 95816-1236. E-mail: frithpress@aol.com. Website: www.hometo wn.aol.com/ekphrasis1. *Ekphrasis* established 1997, Frith Press 1995. **Editors:** Laverne Frith and Carol Frith.

• The Frith Press Open Poetry Chapbook Competition is on hiatus. 2003 winner was Jim Willis for *The Darwin Point*. Until further notice, Frith Press will publish occasional chapbooks by invitation only. Poems from *Ekphrasis* have been featured on *Poetry Daily*.

Magazine Needs *Ekphrasis*, appearing in March and September, is a biannual ''outlet for the growing body of poetry focusing on individual works from any artistic genre.'' Wants ''poetry whose main content is based on individual works from any artistic genre. Poetry should transcend mere description. Form open. No poetry without ekphrastic focus. No poorly crafted work. No archaic language.'' Nominates for Pushcart Prize. Has published poetry by Jeffrey Levine, Peter Meinke, David Hamilton, Barbara Lefcowitz, Molly McQuade, and Annie Finch. *Ekphrasis* is 40-50 pages, digest-sized, photocopied and saddle-stapled. Subscription: $12/year. Sample: $6. Make checks payable, in US funds, to Laverne Frith.

How to Submit Submit 3-7 poems at a time with SASE. Accepts previously published poems "infrequently, must be credited"; no simultaneous submissions. Accepts submissions by postal mail only. Cover letter required including short bio with representative credits and phone number. Time between acceptance and publication is up to one year. Seldom comments on rejected poems. Guidelines available for SASE or on website. Responds in 4 months. Pays one contributor's copy. Acquires first North American serial or one-time rights.

Contest/Award Offerings The Ekphrasis Prize, $300 and publication for a single poem, is sponsored and judged by the editors of *Ekphrasis*. Guidelines available for SASE or on website.

Advice "With the focus on ekphrastic verse, we are bringing attention to the interconnections between various artistic genres and dramatizing the importance and universality of language. Study in the humanities is essential background preparation for the understanding of these interrelations."

$⬛ ELLIPSIS MAGAZINE

Westminster College of Salt Lake City, 1840 S. 1300 East, Salt Lake City UT 84105. (801)832-2321. E-mail: Ellipsis@westminstercollege.edu. Website: www.westminstercollege.edu/ellipsis. Established 1967. **Faculty Advisor:** Natasha Sajé. **Contact:** Poetry Editor (rotating editors).

Magazine Needs *Ellipsis* is an annual appearing in April. Needs "good literary poetry, fiction, essays, plays, and visual art." Has published work by Allison Joseph, Molly McQuade, Virgil Suárez, Maurice Kilwein-Guevara, Richard Cecil, and Ron Carlson. *Ellipsis* is 120 pages, digest-sized, perfect-bound, with color cover. Press run is 2,000 with most copies distributed free through college. Sample: $7.50.

How to Submit Submit 3-5 poems at a time. No previously published poems. Accepts simultaneous submissions if notified of acceptance elsewhere. No fax or e-mail submissions. Include SASE and brief bio. Reads submissions August 1 to November 1. Responds in up to 5 months. Pays $10/poem, plus one contributor's copy.

Contest/Award Offerings "All accepted poems are eligible for the *Ellipsis* Award, which includes a $100 prize. Past judges include Jorie Graham, Sandra Cisneros, Phillip Levine, and Stanley Plumly."

Also Offers Westminster College hosts Writers@Work, an annual literary conference, which sponsors a fellowship competition and features distinguished faculty. (See separate listing for Writers@Work in the Conferences & Workshops section.)

⬛ ⬛ EMPLOI PLUS; DGR PUBLICATION

1256 Principale N. St. #203, L'Annonciation QC J0T 1T0 Canada. Phone/fax: (819)275-3293. Established 1988 (DGR Publication), 1990 (*Emploi Plus*). **Publisher:** Daniel G. Reid.

Magazine Needs *Emploi Plus* is published irregularly. ("Next issue of *Emploi Plus* to be published 2005 latest.") Features poems and articles in French or English. Has published poetry by Robert Ott. Has published *Alexiville, Planet Earth* by D.G. Reid. *Emploi Plus* is 12 pages, $7 \times 8\frac{1}{2}$, photocopied, stapled, with b&w drawings and pictures, no ads. Press run is 500, distributed free. Sample: free.

How to Submit *Does not accept unsolicited submissions.*

$⬛ EMRYS JOURNAL

P.O. Box 8813, Greenville SC 29604. E-mail: ldishman@charter.net. Website: www.emrys.org. Established 1982. **Editor:** L.B. Dishman. **Contact:** Poetry Editor.

Magazine Needs *Emrys Journal* is an annual appearing in April. Wants "literary or narrative poetry less than 36 lines. Rhyming needs to be oustanding to be considered." Has published poetry by Kristin Berkey-Abbott, Adriano Scopino, John Popielaski, J. Morris, and Terri McCord. *Emrys Journal* is up to 120 pages, digest-sized, handsomely printed, flat-spined. Press run is 400 for 250

Revision

Finding the heart of the poem

My first memory of revision was being asked to recopy a book report in fourth grade. Shocked that my first attempt had not been perfect, I responded with a temper tantrum and a flood of tears. Since then, my parents have never stopped expressing surprise that I've chosen a career so heavily involved with revision. In truth, that fourth grader still cries out every time I open a collection of poems in desperate need of *something*.

Anyone who has ever returned to an old draft knows that moment of quiet sadness when you realize your piece is not, after all, the Poem of the Century. You might also recognize the mental silence that occurs when you try to decide how to "fix" the poem. At any given bookstore there's a wide variety of books about the art and craft of poetry; look for books on the art of revision, however, and you have a long search ahead of you.

Yet, in many ways, revision is where the true craft and technique of poetry take place. While the original concept or inspiration is important, it is the revision process that draws out and accentuates the heart of the poem.

The art of revision is the art of establishing a good critical distance from the poem so you can see everything it's doing at once. In her book of essays, *Nine Gates*, Jane Hirsch-field writes, "Every good poem begins in language awake to its own connections—language that hears itself and what is around it [and] sees itself and what is around it." In a good poem, every word, every line break, every silence works together to create a unified expression.

When we read others' poems, it's often easier to see what is working and what isn't; when it comes to our own poems, we're blinded by what we had set out to do. In order to understand the connections in your own poems, you have to be able to make an important and difficult divorce: you have to forget what you *want* the poem to say in order to be able to hear what the poem *actually says*. Although we want to believe the divine muse of inspiration has fused those two things, it's very rare in early drafts. That kind of unity is the job of revision.

Give It Time

Time away from your work is the easiest way to create distance. I've often heard it said that the best "cure" for a poem is to let it sit untouched in a drawer for a year. Quite often something miraculous happens when we review the draft of a poem we haven't read in a long time; suddenly we can spot exactly what the poem needs.

Even more miraculous is when we realize the poem is strong and doesn't actually need much revision. Time brings inherent distance because the emotions and experiences that originally motivated the piece have faded. At this point it's easier to ask yourself, "What will this poem make other people see, hear, smell, taste, think, and feel?"

Sometimes you won't be able to wait a year to work on a poem again. But even a week can change your perspective on the piece. I've also heard of poets taking more creative measures to establish distance, such as trying to imagine they just found the poem on the sidewalk, or that it was e-mailed to them anonymously. I even know one person who mails his poems back to himself so he can look at them in a fresh and different way.

Focus on the Specifics

Another way to force some distance between you and your poem is to focus on specific craft elements. At this stage of the writing process, it's helpful to think of the poem as a puzzle and of revision as a rearrangement of the puzzle pieces. I make a list of elements to consider, such as images, similes, metaphors, line breaks, meter, rhyme, stanza arrangement, title, and so on; then I consider each particular word and think about its connotations. Can each word support its own weight in the poem?

You can also ask yourself questions like:

- How do the first lines set the tone for the rest of the poem? Are they vital to the work or do they just function as an introduction?
- Are the images sharp? Do they enact the five senses?
- Are my line breaks interesting and effective?
- What do my similes and metaphors imply about the subject?
- Can I change the syntax by adding questions, direct thoughts, or fragments?
- Where do the last lines leave the audience?
- Could this poem benefit from a more/less formal structure?

On a broader scale, you could be more drastic and cut a stanza, a line, or an image in order to find out what that part was contributing most to the rest of the poem. In any case, when you focus on specifics, you should be examining the way the small details support the larger emotional picture of the poem.

Get Feedback

Working on poems alone can be isolating and frustrating. Often you will need to rely on others to tell you if your poem is communicating effectively; or at the very least, to tell you what they hear the poem saying.

In his poem "On Revision" in *The Art of Writing*, Wen Fu says, "Even with the right reason, words / sometimes clang; sometimes language flows, / though the ideas themselves remain trivial. / Know one from the other / and the writing will be clearer; / confuse the two, and everything will suffer." Understanding the difference between these two things often requires the help of another reader; finding perspective about your poems is a process that can take years of practice and conversation with others who are enmeshed in the same struggles.

If you don't know others who write, there are a number of ways to search them out. Many poets find writing communities through local readings and workshops, online or correspondence classes, or college courses. Fair warning, however: A lot of feedback can be a mixed blessing unless you remember not to take the responses personally.

It's common to be confronted with contradictory feedback about a poem as well. How should you respond when two people love the first two lines, two people hate them, and one person thinks they should move to the end of the poem? Of course, there is no simple answer. The best thing you can do is consider those lines carefully. When a number of people focus on a specific element in a poem (whether word, line, or image), it means there's energy there. It's up to you to decide whether it's good or bad energy. No group of people will ever agree about everything in a poem, but the patterns in feedback can be very informative.

Be Adventurous

When all else fails, just start making changes. As long as you have an original draft, you can always return to it. Adventurous revision is a great learning tool in its own right as it gives us a chance to see the effects of a variety of different changes. Experiment with the suggestions you receive from other readers and see how they transform the poem. The best results can come from letting go of the reins and simply playing with words.

Know When to Stop

In his poem "Introduction to Poetry," Billy Collins suggests we "take a poem / and hold it up to the light/ like a color slide / or press an ear against its hive." Later he laments, "all they want to do / is tie the poem to a chair with a rope / and torture a confession out of it." When you are particularly energized by a poem (or, to be honest, if you're particularly neurotic about your work), it's all too easy to revise a poem until the emotion and movement are gone. A good friend of mine often tells me, "Put it away. Quit strangling your poems." Remember that revision doesn't guarantee a better poem—it's possible for it to become less clear and less powerful. Sometimes the best way to help a poem is to love it, work with it, then let it rest.

—*Amy Ratto*

Amy Ratto's poems have been widely published, and she's the author of a prize-winning chapbook, *Bread and Water Body*. She was an editor with *Writer's Digest*, *Fiction Writer Magazine*, and *Personal Journaling* and is former editor-in-chief of *CutBank*. She lives in Missoula, Montana, with her husband and daughter.

---

subscribers of which 10 are libraries. "About 10 poems are selected for inclusion." Single copy: $15. Sample: $15 with SASE (7×10) and 4 first-class stamps.

How to Submit Submit up to 5 poems, no more than 25 pages total. Include SASE. No previously published poems. Accepts e-mail submissions (as attachment). Reads submissions August 15 through December 1 only. Time between acceptance and publication is up to 8 months. Guidelines available for SASE or on website. Responds "by the end of the reading period." Pays $25/published poem and 5 contributor's copies.

ENGLISH JOURNAL

College of Education, Columbus State University, Columbus GA 31907-5645. (706)565-3682. Fax: (796)569-3134. E-mail: brewpoem@hotmail.com Website: www.englishjournal.colostate.edu. **Poetry Editor:** James Brewbaker.

Magazine Needs The *English Journal* is looking for the best poems under 40 lines, particularly with teaching or learning as the subject matter. "We are an education journal open to all topics except erotica, etc. that are not appropriate for teacher/student audiences. Because of space limitations, we accept fewer than 10% of submissions."

How to Submit Submit 2 copies of up to 5 poems, in any style, of any topic. "Generally, poems should be no longer than 40 lines." No previously published poems or simultaneous submissions. No fax or e-mail submissions. Cover letter required; include phone number, e-mail address, and brief biographical information. "Include your name, address, and e-mail address on each poem. Notification regarding receipt of your poems, acceptances, and rejections is by e-mail. If you want materials returned, enclose a SASE." Pays 2 contributor's copies.

⊕ ⊘ ENITHARMON PRESS

26B Caversham Rd., London NW5 2DU United Kingdom. Phone: (20)7482 5967. Fax: (20)7284 1787. E-mail: books@enitharmon.co.uk. Established 1967. **Poetry Editor:** Stephen Stuart-Smith.

Book/Chapbook Needs Enitharmon is a publisher of fine editions of poetry and literary criticism in paperback, and some hardback, editions. "We publish about 15 volumes/year averaging 100 pages each." Has published books of poetry by John Heath-Stubbs, Ted Hughes, David Gascoyne, Thom Gunn, Ruth Pitter, and Anthony Thwaite.

How to Submit "Substantial backlog of titles to produce, so no submissions possible before 2006."

$⊘ EOTU EZINE OF FICTION, ART & POETRY; CLAM CITY PUBLICATIONS

2102 Hartman, Boise ID 83704. (208)322-3408. E-mail: editor@clamcity.com (inquiries); submissions@clamcity.com (submissions). Website: www.clamcity.com/eotu.html. Established 2000 online; started as print zine in late 1980s. **Contact:** Larry Dennis.

Magazine Needs *EOTU Ezine* appears bimonthly online, specializing in fiction, art, and poetry. "All fiction, art, and poetry needs to be published to have meaning. We do what we can to make that happen. We are open to all genres, though we tend toward literary and speculative work, science fiction, fantasy, and horror, because that's where the editor's tastes lie. Since we are not funded by advertising or subscription sales, we aren't really audience-driven. Each issue is a reflection of what the editor is into at the time. We are more an artistic endeavor than a business." Has published poetry by Bruce Boston, Charles Saplak, Mike Allen, and Ann Schwader. "Present circulation is about 30,000 page views per issue."

How to Submit Line length for poetry is 30 maximum. Accepts previously published poems; no simultaneous submissions. Accepts e-mail submissions; "Send in body of e-mail message with no formatting; put title of work, 'poem,' or 'poetry submission' in subject line. Include brief bio." Seldom comments on rejected poems. Occasionally publishes theme issues. "We have been known to do theme issues, but they aren't usually decided upon until 2-4 months before publication. Writers should check our guidelines page on the website for current themes." Responds in up to 3 months. Pays $5/poem. Acquires one-time online rights; "When a poem is published in an issue, it will remain in the current issue for 2 months and then be archived."

Advice "As far as we have been able to tell through our years of zine publishing, there are only 2 tips a beginning writer must follow to succeed: 1) Read a few issues of any magazine you are thinking of sending work to; and 2) read and follow submission guidelines. If you do only these two things, you will go far."

⊘ EPICENTER

P.O. Box 367, Riverside CA 92502. E-mail: poetry@epicentermagazine.org. Website: www.epicentermagazine.org. Established 1994. **Contact:** Rowena Silver.

Magazine Needs *Epicenter* is a biannual poetry and short story forum open to all styles. "*Epicenter* is looking for ground-breaking poetry, essays, and short stories from new and established writers. No angst-ridden, sentimental, or earthquake poetry. We are not adverse to graphic images if the work is well presented and contains literary merit." Has published poetry by Doug Shy, Virgil Suárez, Lon Risley, Max Berkovitz, Stan Nemeth, and Vicki Solheid. *Epicenter* is 44 pages, digest-sized, saddle-stapled, with semi-glossy paper cover, includes b&w graphics. Receives about 1,000 submissions/year, accepts about 5%. Press run is 400 for 250 shelf sales. Single copy: $5. Sample: $5.75. Make checks payable to Rowena Silver.

How to Submit Submit up to 5 poems. Include SASE with sufficient postage for return of materials. Accepts previously published poems and simultaneous submissions. Accepts e-mail submissions (pasted into body of message/as attachment). Seldom comments on rejected poems. Guidelines available in magazine, for SASE, by e-mail, or on website. Pays one contributor's copy. Acquires one-time and electronic rights.

$☑ EPOCH

251 Goldwin Smith, Cornell University, Ithaca NY 14853. (607)255-3385. Website: www.arts.cornell.edu/english/epoch.html. Established 1947. **Editor:** Michael Koch. **Poetry Editor:** Nancy Vieira Couto.

Magazine Needs *Epoch* appears 3 times/year and has a distinguished and long record of publishing exceptionally fine poetry and fiction. Has published work by such poets as John Bensko, Jim Daniels, Allison Joseph, Maxine Kumin, Heather McHugh, and Kevin Prufer. *Epoch* is 128 pages, digest-sized, professionally printed, flat-spined, with glossy color cover. Accepts less than 1% of the many submissions received each year. *Epoch* goes to 1,000 subscribers. Sample: $5. Subscription: $11/year domestic, $15/year foreign.

How to Submit No simultaneous submissions. Reads submissions between September 15 and April 21. Responds in up to 10 weeks. Occasionally provides criticism on mss. Pays 3 contributor's copies and $5-10/page. "We pay more when we have more!" Acquires first serial rights.

Advice "Read the magazine."

🌐 ☻ ◎ EUROPEAN JUDAISM (Specialized: ethnic, religious)

Kent House, Rutland Gardens, London SW7 1BX England. Established 1966. **Poetry Editor:** Ruth Fainlight.

Magazine Needs *European Judaism* is a glossy, elegant "twice-yearly magazine with emphasis on European Jewish theology/philosophy/literature/history, with some poetry in every issue. It should preferably be short and have some relevance to matters of Jewish interest." Has published poetry by Linda Pastan, Elaine Feinstein, Daniel Weissbort, and Dannie Abse. *European Judaism* is 110 pages, digest-sized, flat-spined, rarely includes art or graphics. Has a press run of 950, about half of which go to subscribers (few libraries). Subscription: $27.

How to Submit Submit 3-4 poems at a time. "No material is read or returned if not accompanied by SASE (or SAE with IRCs). We cannot use American stamps. Also, I prefer unpublished poems, but poems from published books are acceptable." Cover letter required. Pays one contributor's copy.

$☑ ◎ EVANGEL; LIGHT AND LIFE COMMUNICATIONS (Specialized: religious, Christian)

P.O. Box 535002, Indianapolis IN 46253-5002. Established 1897. **Editor:** J. Innes.

Magazine Needs *Evangel* is a weekly adult Sunday school paper. "Devotional in nature, it lifts up Christ as the source of salvation and hope. The mission of *Evangel* is to increase the reader's understanding of the nature and character of God and the nature of a life lived for Christ. Material that fits this mission and isn't longer than one page will be considered." No rhyming work. *Evangel* is 8 pages, digest-sized (2 8½×11 sheets folded), printed in 4-color, unbound, includes photos and graphics. Accepts about 5% of poetry received. Press run is about 15,000. Subscription: $2.25/quarter (13 weeks). Sample: free for #10 SASE.

How to Submit Submit no more than 5 poems at a time. Accepts simultaneous submissions. Cover letter preferred. "Poetry must be typed on 8½×11 white paper. In the upper left-hand corner of each page, include your name, address, phone number, and social security number. In the upper right-hand corner of cover page, specify what rights you are offering. One-eighth of the way down the page, give the title. All subsequent material must be double-spaced, with one-inch margins." Submit seasonal poems one year in advance. Seldom comments on rejected poems. Guidelines available for #10 SASE; "write 'guidelines request' on your envelope so we can sort it from the submissions." Responds in up to 2 months. Pays $10 plus 2 contributor's copies. Acquires one-time rights.

Advice "Poetry is used primarily as filler. Send for sample and guidelines to better understand what and who the audience is."

☑ THE EVANSVILLE REVIEW; THE WILLIS BARNSTONE TRANSLATION PRIZE

1800 Lincoln Ave., Evansville IN 47722. Phone/fax: (812)488-1042. Established 1989. **Editor:** Carolina Cuervo.

- Poetry published in *The Evansville Review* has been included in *Best American Poetry* and the *Pushcart Prize* anthology.

Magazine Needs *The Evansville Review* appears annually in April and publishes "prose, poems, and drama of literary merit." Wants "anything of quality." No excessively experimental work, or erotica. Has published poetry by Joseph Brodsky, J.L. Borges, John Updike, Willis Barnstone, Rita Dove, and Vivian Shipley. *The Evansville Review* is 140-200 pages, digest-sized, perfect-bound, includes art on cover only. Receives about 1,000 poems/year, accepts about 2%. Publishes 45 poems/issue. Press run is 1,500. Sample: $5.

How to Submit Submit 3-5 poems at a time. Considers previously published poems and simultaneous submissions. Cover letter with brief bio required. Include SASE. Reads submissions September 1 through December 10 only. Time between acceptance and publication is 3 months. Poems are circulated to an editorial board. Seldom comments on rejected poems. Guidelines available for SASE. Responds within 3 months of the deadline. Pays 2 contributor's copies. Rights remain with poet.

Contest/Award Offerings The Willis Barnstone Translation Prize offers annual award of $1,000 and publication in *The Evansville Review*. Submissions must be unpublished and may be entered in other contests. Submit 1-10 poems; line limit is 200 lines. Guidelines available for SASE or on website. **Entry fee:** $5 for the first poem; $3 for each subsequent poem. Does not accept entry fees in foreign currencies. **Deadline:** December 1. Competition receives 400 entries/year. 2003 winners were Marilyn Hacker and Ralph Angel. Final judge for the 2004 contest is Willis Barnstone. Winner will be announced in April in *The Evansville Review* and through entrants' SASEs.

▨ $☑ EVENT

Douglas College, P.O. Box 2503, New Westminster BC V3L 5B2 Canada. (604)527-5293. Fax: (604)527-5095. E-mail: event@douglas.bc.ca. Website: http://event.douglas.bc.ca. Established 1971. **Poetry Editor:** Gillian Harding-Russell.

Magazine Needs *Event* appears 3 times/year and is "a literary magazine publishing high-quality contemporary poetry, short stories, creative nonfiction, and reviews. In poetry, we tend to appreciate the narrative and (sometimes) the confessional modes. In any case, we are eclectic and always open to content that invites involvement. We publish mostly Canadian writers." Has published poetry by Tom Wayman, Lorna Crozier, Russell Thornton, Don McKay, A.F. Moritz, Marlene Cookshaw, and Tim Bowling. *Event* is 136 pages, digest-sized, finely printed, flat-spined, with glossy cover. Press run is 1,300 for 700 subscribers of which 50 are libraries. Subscription: $22/year, $35/2 years. Sample back issue: $5.35; current issue: $8.49. Prices include GST. US subscribers please pay in US funds. Overseas and institutions: $32/year, $48/2 years. Sample: $9.

How to Submit Submit 5 poems at a time. No previously published poems. No fax or e-mail submissions. Brief cover letter with publication credits required. Include SASE (Canadian postage only) or SAE and IRCs. "Tell us if you'd prefer your manuscript to be recycled rather than returned." Time between acceptance and publication is within one year. Sometimes comments on rejected poems. Responds in up to 6 months. Pays honorarium. Acquires first North American print rights.

◎ EXIT 13 (Specialized: geography/travel)

% Tom Plante, P.O. Box 423, Fanwood NJ 07023-1162. (908)889-5298. E-mail: exit13magazine@yahoo.com. Established 1987. **Editor:** Tom Plante.

Magazine Needs *Exit 13* is a "contemporary poetry annual" using poetry that is "short, to the point, with a sense of geography." Has published poetry by Errol Miller, Adele Kenny, Charles Plymell, Ruth Moon Kempher, D.E. Steward, and Ruth Holzer. *Exit 13*, #11, was 76 pages. Press run is 300. Sample: $7.

How to Submit Accepts simultaneous submissions and previously published poems. Accepts submissions by postal mail and by e-mail (no attachments). Guidelines available in magazine or for SASE. Responds in 4 months. Pays one contributor's copy. Acquires one-time and possible anthology rights.

Advice *"Exit 13* looks for adventure, a living record of places we've experienced. Every state, region, country, and ecosystem is welcome. Write about what you know and have seen. Send a snapshot of an 'Exit 13' road sign and receive a free copy of the issue in which it appears.''

failbetter.com

63 Eighth Ave., Suite #3A, Brooklyn NY 11217. E-mail: submissions@failbetter.com. Website: www .failbetter.com. Established 2000. **Editor:** Thom Didato. Member: CLMP.

- *failbetter.com is the only online literary journal to receive honorable mention in the 2003 Pushcart Prize.*

Magazine Needs *failbetter.com* is an online literary journal "in the spirit of a traditional print journal, dedicated to publishing literary fiction, poetry, and artwork. We place a high degree of importance on originality, believing that even in this age of trends it is still possible.'' Publishes translations and interviews. Has published poetry by Jen Benka, Monica de la Torre, Stephen Oliver, and David Starkey. *failbetter.com* is published exclusively online with art/graphics. Receives about 800 poetry submissions/year, accepts about 9-12. Publishes 3-4 poets/issue.

How to Submit Submit 4-6 poems at a time. Line length for poetry is open. "We are not concerned with length: One good sentence may find a home here; as the bulk of mediocrity will not.'' Accepts simultaneous submissions; no previously published poems. Encourages e-mail submissions. "All e-mail submissions should include title in header. All poetry submissions must be included in the body of your e-mail. Please do not send attached files. If for whatever reason you wish to submit a MS Word attachment, please query first.'' Submissions also accepted by postal mail. "Please note, however, any materials accepted for publication must ultimately be submitted in electronic format in order to appear on our site.'' Cover letter is preferred. Reads submissions year round. Time between acceptance and publication ranges from up to 4 months. Poems are circulated to an editorial board. Often comments on rejected poems. "It is not unusual to ask poets to re-submit, and their subsequent submissions have been accepted.'' Guidelines available on website. Responds in up to 2 months to e-mail submissions; up to 4 months by postal mail. "We will not respond to any e-mail inquiry regarding receipt confirmation or status of any work under consideration.'' No payment. Acquires exclusive first-time Internet rights; works will also be archived online. All other rights, including opportunity to publish in traditional print form, revert to the artist. Nominates work for *Pushcart Prize* consideration.

Advice "With a readership of 30,000, *failbetter* simply offers to expose poets' works to a much broader world-wide audience than the typical print journal. For both established and emerging poets our advice remains the same: We strongly recommend that you not only read the previous issue, but also sign up on our e-mail list (subscribe@failbetter.com) to be notified of future publications. Most importantly, know that what you are saying could only come from you. When you are sure of this, please feel free to submit.''

THE FAIRFIELD REVIEW

544 Silver Spring Rd., Fairfield CT 06430-1947. (203)256-1960. E-mail: fairfieldreview@hpmd.com. Website: www.farifieldreview.org. Established 1997. **Editors:** Janet and Edward Granger-Happ.

Magazine Needs *The Fairfield Review* appears 2 times/year as an e-zine featuring poetry and short stories from new and established authors. "We prefer free style poems, approachable on first reading, but with the promise of a rich vein of meaning coursing along under the consonants and vowels.'' Does not want "something better suited for a Hallmark card.'' Accepts poetry written by children; requires parents' permission/release for children under 18. Has published poetry by Taylor Graham, Kelley Jean White, and Michael Zack. *The Fairfield Review* is 20-30 pages published online (HTML). Receives about 450 poems/year, accepts about 8%. Publishes up to 20 poems/issue.

How to Submit Submit 3 poems at a time. Line length for poetry is 75 maximum. Accepts previously published poems with permission; no simultaneous submissions. Accepts e-mail and disk submissions. Cover letter is preferred. "We strongly prefer submissions via e-mail or e-mail attachment. Notifications are sent exclusively via e-mail. An e-mail address is required with all submissions. Reads submissions continually. Time between acceptance and publication is "usually less than 2 months." Poems are circulated to an editorial board. Often comments on rejected poems, if requested and submitted via e-mail. Guidelines available on website. Responds in up to one year. Always sends prepublication galleys (online only). Acquires first rights, right to retain publication in online archive issues, and the right to use in "Best of *The Fairfield Review*" anthologies. Ocassionally reviews books of poetry. "We consider reviews of books from authors we have published or who are referred to us."

Contest/Award Offerings "We select poems from each issue for 'Editor's Choice' awards, plus 'Reader's Choice' awards based on readership frequency."

Advice "Read our article 'Writing Qualities to Keep in Mind.' "

FAT TUESDAY

560 Manada Gap Rd., Grantville PA 17028. (717)469-7159. E-mail: lionelstevroid@yahoo.com. Website: www.egroups.com/group/FatTuesday. Established 1981. **Editor-in-Chief:** F.M. Cotolo. **Editor:** Lionel Stevroid.

Magazine Needs *Fat Tuesday* is published irregularly as "a Mardi Gras of literary, visual, and audio treats featuring voices, singing, shouting, sighing, and shining, expressing the relevant to irreverent." Wants "prose poems, poems of irreverence, gems from the gut. Particularly interested in hard-hitting 'autofiction.' " Has published poetry by Chuck Taylor, Charles Bukowski, Mark Cramer, and Cotolo Patrick Kelly. *Fat Tuesday* is up to 60 pages, typeset (large type, heavy paper), saddle-stapled, with card cover, usually chapbook style (sometimes magazine-sized, unbound), includes cartoons, black line art, and ads. Press run is 1,000/year with poetry on 80% of the pages. Receives hundreds of submissions/year, accepts about 3-5%; has a 3- to 5-month backlog, "but usually try to respond with personal, not form, letters." All editions are $5, postage paid. "Contact us about our new purchase-and-publish plan."

How to Submit Submit any number of poems at a time. No previously published poems or simultaneous submissions. Accepts e-mail submissions (pasted into body of message). "Cover letters are fine, the more amusing the better." Publishes theme issues. Guidelines and upcoming themes available for SASE or by e-mail. Responds in up to 3 months. Pays 2 contributor's copies if audio. Rights revert to author after publication.

Also Offers "In 1998, *Fat Tuesday* was presented in a different format with the production of a stereo audio cassette edition. *Fat Tuesday's Cool Noise* features readings, music, collage, and songs, all in the spirit of *Fat*'s printed versions. Other *Cool Noise* editions will follow. *Fat Tuesday* solicits artists who wish to have their material produced professionally in audio form. Call the editors about terms and prices or how you can release a stereo audio cassette entirely of your own material. *Fat Tuesday* has released *Seven Squared*, by Frank Cotolo, and is looking for other audio projects. In-print magazines will still be produced as planned. You can hear Cotolo music and purchase CDs on our website."

Advice "Support the magazine that publishes your work!"

FAULTLINE

Dept. of English & Comparative Literature, University of California—Irvine, Irvine CA 92697-2650. (949)824-1573. E-mail: faultline@uci.edu. Website: www.humanities.uci.edu/faultline. Established 1991. **Editor:** A.J. Collins. **Contact:** Poetry Editor.

• Poetry published by this journal has also been selected for inclusion in a *Pushcart Prize* anthology.

Magazine Needs On shelves in June, *Faultline* is an annual journal of art and literature occasionally edited by guest editors and published at the University of California, Irvine. Wants "well-made poems that intellectually and emotionally surprise the reader and writer." Has published poetry by Larissa Szporluk, Jennifer Clarvoe, Lee Upton, and Sam Hamill. *Faultline* is about 150 pages, digest-sized, professionally printed on 60 lb. paper, perfect-bound, with 80 lb. coverstock, includes color and b&w art and photos. Receives about 1,500 poems/year, accepts about 5%. Press run is 1,000. Single copy: $10. Sample: $5.

How to Submit Submit up to 5 poems at a time. Accepts simultaneous submissions, "but please note in cover letter that the manuscript is being considered elsewhere." No fax or e-mail submissions. Cover letter preferred. Do not include name and address on ms, to assist anonymous judging. Reads submissions September 1 through March 1 only. Poems are selected by a board of up to 6 readers. Seldom comments on rejected poems. Guidelines available for SASE or on website. Responds in 3 months. Pays 2 contributor's copies. Acquires first or one-time serial rights.

FEATHER BOOKS; THE POETRY CHURCH MAGAZINE; CHRISTIAN HYMNS & SONGS (Specialized: membership/subscription; religious, Christian)

P.O. Box 438, Shrewsbury SY3 0WN United Kingdom. Phone/fax: (01743)872177. E-mail: john@waddysweb.freeuk.com. Website: www.waddysweb.freeuk.com. Feather Books established 1982. *The Poetry Church Magazine* established 1996. **Contact:** Rev. John Waddington-Feather, editor.

Magazine Needs *The Poetry Church Magazine* appears quarterly and contains Christian poetry and prayers. Wants "Christian or good religious poetry—usually around 20 lines, but will accept longer." Does not want "unreadable blasphemy." Accepts poetry written by children over age 10. Has published poetry by Laurie Bates, Joan Smith, Idris Caffrey, Walter Nash, and Susan Glyn. "Publishes subscribers' work only." *The Poetry Church Magazine* is 40 pages, digest-sized, photocopied, saddle-stapled, with laminated cover with b&w art. Receives about 1,000 poems/year, accepts about 500. Press run is 1,000 for 400 subscribers of which 10 are libraries. Single copy free; subscription (4 magazines): £8 ($15 US). Sample: £3 ($5.50 US). Make checks payable in sterling to Feather Books. Payment can also be made through website.

How to Submit *The Poetry Church Magazine* "publishes only subscribers' poems as they keep us solvent." Submit 2 typed poems at a time. Accepts previously published poems and simultaneous submissions. Accepts e-mail submissions (as attachment). Cover letter preferred with information about the poet. All work must be submitted by postal mail with SASE (or SAE and IRC). Time between acceptance and publication is 4 months. "The editor does a preliminary reading, then seeks then the advice of colleagues about uncertain poems." Responds within one week. Pays one contributor's copy. Poets retain copyright.

Book/Chapbook Needs & How to Submit Feather Books publishes the Feather Books Poetry Series, books of Christian poetry and prayers. Has recently published poetry collections by the Glyn family, Walter Nash, David Grieve, and Rosie Morgan Barry. "We have now published 181 poetry collections by individual Christian poets." Books are usually photocopied and saddle-stapled with laminated covers. "Poets' works are selected for publication in collections of around 20 poems in our Feather Books Poetry Series. We do not insist, but most poets pay for small run-offs of their work, e.g., around 50-100 copies for which we charge $270 per 50. If they can't afford it, but are good poets, we stand the cost. We expect poets to read our *Poetry Church Magazine* to get some idea of our standards."

Also Offers Feather Books also publishes *Christian Hymns & Songs*, a quarterly supplement by Grundy and Feather. And, each winter and summer, selected poems appear in *The Poetry Church Anthology*, the leading Christian poetry anthology used in churches and schools. Began a new chapbook collection, the Christianity and Literature Series, which focuses on academic work. "The first, just published, is a paper by Dr. William Ruleman, of Wesley College, Tennessee, entitled *W.H. Auden's Search for Faith*. Other titles include *Six Contemporary Women Christian Poets* by Dr. Patricia Batstone; *In a Quiet Place: J.B. Priestley & Religion* by Michael Nelson; 'The Dream of the Rood,' 'The Wanderer,' 'The Seafarer': Three Old English Early Christian Poems of the 8th Century*, newly translated by Reverend John Waddington-Feather, with an introduction by Professor Walter Nash; and *Women Hymn-Writers of the 19th Century* by Dr. E.L. Edmonds.''

Advice ''We find it better for poets to master rhyme and rhythm before trying free verse. Many poets seem to think that if they write 'down' a page they're writing poetry, when all they're doing is writing prose in a different format.''

☑ FEELINGS OF THE HEART

1704 21st Ave. #61, Gulfport MS 39502-1022. Phone/fax: (228)863-7026 (call to ensure line is free before faxing). E-mail: aharnischfitchie1@juno.com. Website: www.feelingsoftheheart.net. Established 1999. **Editor/Publisher/Founder:** Alice M. Harnisch-Fitchie.

Magazine Needs *Feelings of the Heart* appears biannually as Winter/Spring and Summer/Fall issues. Wants ''*good* poetry from the heart.'' Has published poetry by Geneva Jo Anthony, Victoria DeLaVergne, Richard Sponaugle, Chris Crittenden, and George R. Beck. *Feelings of the Heart* is 50 pages, magazine-sized, computer-printed, stapled, with artist cover, includes ads from other publications. Receives about 100 poems/year, accepts about 95%. Publishes 20+ poems/issue. Press run is 100. Single copy: $6; subscription: $18/year, $36/2 years (2-year subscribers receive free gift with order). Sample: $6. Make checks payable to Alice M. Fitchie.

How to Submit Submit 5 poems at a time with ''name and address on every poem submitted.'' Line length for poetry is 20-40. Accepts previously published poems and simultaneous submissions. Accepts e-mail (pasted into body of message) and disk submissions. ''Send up to 5 poems per e-mail but only 3 e-mails per day.'' Cover letter is required. ''Please enclose SASE or IRC with all correspondence.'' Submit seasonal poems 2 months in advance. Time between acceptance and publication is 2 weeks. Poems ''are read by me, the editor, and decided by the poetic intent of poetry submitted.'' Often comments on rejected poems. Guidelines available for SASE, by e-mail, or on website. Responds in 2 weeks with SASE. Sometimes sends prepublication galleys. Acquires first rights. Reviews books and chapbooks of poetry and other magazines in 200 words or less, single book format. Send materials for review consideration.

Also Offers Also prints poetry chapbooks for those interested in being self-published. Write for details.

Advice ''*Write* poetry for yourself; *publish* for everyone else!''

☑ ◎ FEMINIST STUDIES (Specialized: women/feminism)

0103 Taliaferro Hall, University of Maryland, College Park MD 20742. (301)405-7415. Fax: (301)405-8395. E-mail: femstud@umail.umd.edu or info@feministstudies.org Website: www.feministstudies.org. Established 1969. **Contact:** Creative Writing Editor.

Magazine Needs *Feminist Studies* appears 3 times/year and ''welcomes a variety of work that focuses on women's experience, on gender as a category of analysis, and that furthers feminist theory and consciousness.'' Has published poetry by Janice Mirikitani, Paula Gunn Allen, Cherrie Moraga, Audre Lorde, Valerie Fox, and Diane Glancy. *Feminist Studies* is 250 pages, elegantly printed, flat-spined, paperback. Press run is 8,000 for 7,000 subscribers, of which 1,500 are libraries. There are 4-10 pages of poetry in each issue. Sample: $15.

How to Submit ''All subscribers should send one copy (no SASE) to the above address. Work will not be returned.'' No simultaneous submissions; will only consider previously published poems under special circumstances. No fax or e-mail submissions. Manuscripts are reviewed twice a year, in May and December. **Deadlines:** May 1 and December 1. Authors will receive notice of the board's decision by July 10 and February 10. Guidelines available on website. Always sends prepublication galleys. Pays 2 contributor's copies. Commissions reviews of books of poetry. Send materials for review consideration to Claire G. Moses.

$⬚ FIELD: CONTEMPORARY POETRY AND POETICS; FIELD TRANSLATION SERIES; FIELD POETRY SERIES; FIELD POETRY PRIZE; OBERLIN COLLEGE PRESS

10 N. Professor St., Oberlin College, Oberlin OH 44074. (440)775-8408. E-mail: oc.press@oberlin. edu (inquiries only). Website: www.oberlin.edu/ocpress. Established 1969. **Poetry Editors:** David Young and Martha Collins.

- Work published in *FIELD* has been frequently included in volumes of *The Best American Poetry.*

Magazine Needs *FIELD* is a biannual literary journal appearing in October and April, with "emphasis on poetry, translations, and essays by poets." Wants the "best possible" poetry. Has published poetry by Marianne Boruch, Miroslav Holub, Charles Wright, Billy Collins, Jon Loomis, Charles Simic, and Sandra McPherson. *FIELD* is 100 pages, digest-sized, printed on rag stock, flat-spined, with glossy card color cover. Subscription: $14/year, $24/2 years. Sample: $7 postpaid.

How to Submit Submit up to 5 poems at a time. Include cover letter and SASE. Reads submissions year round. No previously published poems or simultaneous submissions. No e-mail submissions. Seldom comments on rejected poems. Guidelines available for SASE, by e-mail, or on website. Responds in one month. Always sends prepublication galleys. Pays $15/page plus 2 contributor's copies. Staff reviews books of poetry. Send materials for review consideration.

Book/Chapbook Needs & How to Submit Publishes books of translations in the *FIELD* Translation Series, flat-spined, hardcover editions averaging 150 pages. Query regarding translations. Also publishes books of poetry in the *FIELD* Poetry Series, by invitation only. Write for catalog or visit website to buy sample books.

Contest/Award Offerings Sponsors the annual *FIELD* Poetry Prize for a book-length collection of poems, awarding $1,000 and publication in the *FIELD* Poetry Series. Submit non-returnable mss of 50-80 pages. **Postmark deadline:** during May only. **Entry fee:** $22 (includes one-year subscription to *FIELD*). Make checks payable to Oberlin College Press. 2003 winner was Jonah Winter. Complete guidelines available for SASE or on website.

⬚ FINISHING LINE PRESS; MM REVIEW; NEW WOMEN'S VOICES CHAPBOOK SERIES; FINISHING LINE PRESS OPEN CHAPBOOK COMPETITION

P.O. Box 1016, Cincinnati OH 45201-1016. E-mail: FinishingBooks@aol.com. Website: www.homet own.aol.com/FinishingL/. Established 1998. **Editor:** C.J. Morrison (and occasionally guest editors). **Contact:** Poetry Editor.

Magazine Needs & How to Submit "We are currently publishing chapbooks only and have suspended publishing of *MM Review* for the next 2 years to focus on chapbook publication."

Book/Chapbook Needs & How to Submit Finishing Line Press seeks to "discover new talent" and hopes to publish chapbooks by both men and women poets who have not previously published a book or chapbook of poetry. Has published *Looking to the East with Western Eyes* by Leah Maines, *Like the Air* by Joyce Sidman, *Startling Art* by Dorothy Sutton, *Foreign Correspondence* by Timothy Riordan, and *Man Overboard* by Steven Barza. Publishes 20-30 poetry chapbooks/year. Chapbooks are usually 25-30 pages, digest-sized, laser-printed, saddle-stapled, with card covers with textured matte wrappers, include b&w photos. Submit ms of 16-24 pages with cover letter, bio, acknowledgments, and **$12 reading fee.** Responds to queries and to mss in up to one month. Pay varies; pays in author's copies. "Sales profits, if any, go to publish the next new poet." Order sample chapbooks by sending $6 to Finishing Line Press.

Contest/Award Offerings 1) New Women's Voices Chapbook Competition. **Entry fee:** $12. **Dead-**

line: December 31. 2) Finishing Line Press Open Chapbook Competition. Open to all poets regardless of past publications. **Deadline:** January 15.

Advice "We are very open to new talent. If the poetry is great, we will consider it for a chapbook."

⊕ ◔ FIRE

Field Cottage, Old Whitehill, Tackley, Kidlington, Oxfordshire OX5 3AB United Kingdom. Website: www.poetical.org. Established 1994. **Editor:** Jeremy Hilton.

Magazine Needs *Fire* appears 3 times/year "to publish little-known, unfashionable, or new writers alongside better-known ones." Wants "experimental, unfashionable, demotic work; longer work encouraged. Use of rhyme schemes and other strict forms *not* favored." Has published poetry by Philip Levine, Marilyn Hacker, Adrian C. Louis, Tom Pickard, Allen Fisher, Gael Turnbull, and David Hart. *Fire* is up to 180 pages, A5. Receives about 400 poems/year, accepts about 35%. Press run is 300 for 230 subscribers of which 20 are libraries. Single copy: £4, add £1 postage Europe, £2 postage overseas. Subscription (3 issues): £7, add £2 postage Europe, £4 postage overseas.

How to Submit Accepts previously published poems; no simultaneous submissions. Cover letter preferred. Time between acceptance and publication "varies enormously." Often comments on rejected poems. Guidelines available for SASE or on website. Responds in 2 months. Sometimes sends prepublication galleys, "but rarely to overseas contributors." Pays one contributor's copy.

Advice "Read a copy first. Don't try to tailor your work to any particular style, format, or formula. Free expression, strongly imaginative work preferred."

◔ FIRST CLASS; FOUR-SEP PUBLICATIONS

P.O. Box 86, Friendship IN 47021. E-mail: christopherm@four-sep.com. Website: www.four-sep.com. Established 1994. **Editor:** Christopher M.

Magazine Needs *First Class* appears in May and November and "publishes excellent/odd writing for intelligent/creative readers." Wants "short postmodern poems, also short fiction." No traditional work. Has published poetry by Bennett, Locklin, Roden, Splake, Catlin, and Huffstickler. *First Class* is 60 pages, 4¼×11, printed, saddle-stapled, with colored cover. Receives about 1,500 poems/year, accepts about 30. Press run is 300-400. Sample (including guidelines): $6, or mini version $1. Make checks payable to Christopher M.

How to Submit Submit 5 poems at a time. Accepts previously published poems and simultaneous submissions. Does not accept fax or e-mail submissions. Cover letter preferred. Time between acceptance and publication is 2-4 months. Often comments on rejected poems. Guidelines available in magazine, for SASE, or on website. Responds in 3 weeks. Pays one contributor's copy. Acquires one-time rights. Reviews books of poetry and fiction. Send materials for review consideration.

Also Offers Chapbook production available.

Advice "Belt out a good, short, thought-provoking, graphic, uncommon piece."

⊞ ⊕ ◎ FIRST OFFENSE (Specialized: form/style)

Syringa, Stodmarsh, Canterbury, Kent CT3 4BA England. E-mail: Tim@firstoffense.co.uk. Website: www.firstoffense.co.uk. Established 1985. **Contact:** Tim Fletcher.

Magazine Needs *First Offense* is published 1-2 times/year. "The magazine is for contemporary poetry and is not traditional, but is received by most ground-breaking poets." Wants "contemporary, language, and experimental poetry and articles. No traditional work." *First Offense* is photocopied, "so we need well typed manuscripts, word processed." Press run is 300. Subscription: £2.50 plus 75¢ p&h. Make checks payable to Tim Fletcher.

How to Submit No previously published poems. "No reply without SASE or SAE and IRC." Reviews books and chapbooks of poetry and other magazines.

Advice "Always buy a copy before submitting for research so as not to waste everyone's time."

✖ ◖ FIRST STEP PRESS; STEPPING STONES MAGAZINE: A LITERARY MAGAZINE FOR THE INNOVATIVE ARTS; CRIMSON RIVERS MAGAZINE

P.O. Box 902, Norristown PA 19404-0902. E-mail: First_Step_Press@hotmail.com. Established 1996 originally, then discontinued publication; re-debuted in 2004. **Editor:** Trinae Angelique Ross.

Magazine Needs *Stepping Stones Magazine: ALMIA* appears 4 times/year and wants "poems written from within the writer's soul. I look at the piece to see if it says something out of the ordinary. Roses are not always red, nor violets blue . . . if you're going to use a cliché, freshen it up a bit and make me think I haven't heard it elsewhere. I want to publish pieces I *want* to share with others. Save the highbrow, stuffy pieces for the academics; this magazine is for those of us still struggling to find our voices. Though free verse is preferred, I will consider rhymed verse if written well." Does not want "short fiction disguised as poetry, poems that say 'I am a poem about . . .', or crazily-formatted poems." Has published poetry by Patrick McKinnon, Michael Hathaway, and Maggie Pierce Secara. *Stepping Stones Magazine: ALMIA* is 60 pages, magazine-sized, and published electronically on disk in PDF format. Receives about 600 poems/year, accepts about 10-15%. Publishes about 20-25 poems/issue. Single copy: free.

Magazine Needs *Crimson Rivers Magazine* is published irregularly but released in October in the year of its creation and explores the darkest regions of the human condition. "Poetry appearing in *Crimson Rivers* should not be afraid to push the envelope. Visceral writing is a plus. Keep in mind, however, that *Crimson Rivers* will not publish anything dealing with the exploitation of minors or the degradation of any group based on race, religion, gender, or sexual preference. When it comes to *Crimson Rivers*, the goals are simple: **scare the reader**. Do whatever it takes to make the reader afraid to continue reading, and we all will have done our jobs for yet another year." Created similarly to *Stepping Stones Magazine* in PDF format.

How to Submit Submit 5 poems at a time for *Stepping Stones*; no more than 4 poems at a time for *Crimson Rivers*. Line length for poetry is 100 maximum for both publications. Accepts previously published poems (note where and when ms originally appeared) and simultaneous submissions (with notification of acceptance elsewhere). Accepts e-mail (pasted into body of message) and disk submissions. "Format electronically as a Microsoft Word document (.doc) or Rich Text File (.rtf); use Times New Roman (12 point) or Courier New (10 point) fonts only." Cover letter is required. Reads submissions year round. Submit seasonal poems 6 months in advance. Time between acceptance and publication is 3-6 months. Often comments on rejected poems. Guidelines available for SASE or by e-mail. Responds in one month. Sometimes sends prepublication galleys. Pays one contributor's copy. Acquires one-time rights. "First Step Press reserves the right to reprint previously published material for future anthologies or a future 'Best of' issue." Reviews chapbooks of poetry and other magazines/journals in 500 words.

Also Offers "Free advertising space is available for those wishing to promote their website, book, or other literary venture. The continuing goal of First Step Press is to provide sanctuary for new and established writers, to hone their skills and commune with one another within the comfort of both publications' electronic pages."

Advice "*Stepping Stones Magazine* is created with the intent to instruct, inform, and entertain. Though it is a literal testing ground for writers experimenting with their craft, I still approach publishing as a profession and expect writers to act accordingly. Above all, believe in your worth as a writer. If you do not feel confident about the work you're submitting to the magazine, you cannot honestly expect me to feel confident about my selecting or publishing the piece."

▦ ◖ FIRST TIME; INTERNATIONAL HASTINGS POETRY COMPETITION

The Snoring Cat, 16 Marianne Park, Dudley Rd., Hastings, East Sussex TN35 5PU England. Phone/fax: 01424 428855. E-mail: firsttime@carefree.net. Established 1981. **Editor:** Josephine Austin.

Magazine Needs *First Time*, published biannually in April and October, is open to "all kinds of poetry—our magazine goes right across the board—which is why it is one of the most popular in

Great Britain.'' *First Time* is 80-100 pages, digest-sized, saddle-stapled, contains several poems on each page, in a variety of small type styles, on lightweight stock, with glossy one-color card cover. Subscription: $13. Sample: $2 plus postage. ''Please send dollars.''

How to Submit Submit 6 poems with name and address of poet on each. Poems submitted must not exceed 30 lines. No previously published poems. No e-mail submissions. Cover letter and SAE required. Time between acceptance and publication is up to 2 months. ''Although we can no longer offer a free copy as payment, we can offer one at a discounted price of $3 plus postage.''

Contest/Award Offerings The annual International Hastings Poetry Competition for poets 18 and older offers awards of £150, £75, and £50. **Entry fee:** £2/poem.

Advice ''Keep on 'pushing your poetry.' If one editor rejects you, then study the market and decide which is the correct one for you. Try to type your own manuscripts as longhand is difficult to read and doesn't give a professional impression. Always date your poetry — ©[year] and sign it. Follow your way of writing, don't be a pale imitation of someone else; sooner or later styles change, and you will either catch up or be ahead.''

☑ 5 AM

P.O. Box 205, Spring Church PA 15686. Established 1987. **Editors:** Ed Ochester and Judith Vollmer.

Magazine Needs *5 AM* is a poetry publication that appears twice/year. Open in regard to form, length, subject matter, and style. However, they do not want poetry that is ''religious,'' or ''naive rhymers.'' Has published poetry by Virgil Suárez, Nin Andrews, Alicia Ostriker, Edward Field, Billy Collins, and Denise Duhamel. *5 AM* is a 24-page, offset tabloid. Receives about 5,000 poems/year, accepts about 2%. Press run is 1,200 for 650 subscribers of which 25 are libraries, about 300 shelf sales. Subscription: $15/4 issues. Sample: $5.

How to Submit No previously published poems or simultaneous submissions. Seldom comments on rejected poems. Responds within 6 weeks. Pays 2 contributor's copies plus subscription. Acquires first rights.

⭐ ☑ 580 SPLIT

P.O. Box 9982, Mills College, Oakland CA 94613-0982. (510)430-2217. Fax: (510)430-3398. E-mail: five80split@yahoo.com. Website: www.mills.edu/580Split. Established 1999. **Contact:** Poetry Editor. Member: CLMP.

Magazine Needs *580 Split* appears annually in May. Publishes ''high-quality, innovative poetry and fiction. Open to style and form. Rhyming poetry must be stellar. Open to experimental, visual, language, and concrete poetry.'' Has published poetry by Lisa Jarnot, Lyn Hejinian, Clark Coolidge, D.A. Powell, Liz Waldner, and Wenceslau Maldonado. *580 Split* is 120 pages, digest-sized, professionally printed, perfect-bound, with cardstock cover with b&w photo, includes b&w art/graphics. Receives about 2,000 poems/year, accepts 1-5%. Publishes about 25 pages of poetry/issue. Press run is 650 for 20 subscribers of which 15 are libraries, 500 shelf sales. Single copy: $7.50; subscription: $7.50. Sample: $5. Make checks payable to *580 Split*.

How to Submit Submit up to 5 poems at a time. No previously published poems or simultaneous submissions. No e-mail or disk submissions. Cover letter is preferred. ''Poems not accompanied by SASE are recycled immediately.'' Reads submissions July 1 through November 1. Time between acceptance and publication is 4 months. Poems are circulated to an editorial board and voted on. Seldom comments on rejected poems. Guidelines available in magazine, for SASE, by e-mail, or on website. Responds in up to 6 months. Sometimes sends prepublication galleys. Pays 2 contributor's copies. Acquires first North American serial rights.

Advice ''Familiarize yourself with our magazine and editorial vision to find out if we're the best place for your work.''

✳ ☑ FIVE FINGERS REVIEW

P.O. Box 4, San Leandro CA 94577. Phone/fax: (510)632-5769. E-mail: jrobles@aaahawk.com. Website: www.fivefingersreview.org. Established 1987. **Editor:** Jaime Robles.

Magazine Needs *Five Fingers Review* is published annually in May and is "interested in quality work from a wide spectrum of ideas and styles. Committed to publishing innovative work by emerging and established writers." Wants "all styles and forms, must be excellent and original work in the chosen form." Has published poetry by Gillian Conoley, Jackson Mac Low, Carl Phillips, Brenda Hillman, Elizabeth Robinson, and Peter Gizzi. *Five Fingers Review* is digest-sized, offset-printed, perfect-bound, with 4-color cover (usually work by contributing artist), includes art/graphics and ads. Publishes about 125 poems/issue. Press run is 1,000. Single copy: $13; subscription: $16/2 issues. Make checks payable to *Five Fingers Review*.

How to Submit Submit 3-5 poems at a time. Line length for poetry is open. Accepts simultaneous submissions; no previously published poems. No fax, e-mail, or disk submissions. Cover letter is preferred. "Don't forget the SASE." Time between acceptance and publication "depends." "Most poems are solicited by contributing editors. At least 2 people read unsolicited submissions." Seldom comments on rejected poems. Regularly publishes theme issues. List of upcoming themes and guidelines available for SASE or on website. Responds in up to 6 months. Always sends prepublication galleys. Pays 2 contributor's copies plus discount on additional copies. Acquires one-time rights. Reviews books and chapbooks of poetry and other magazines/journals. Send materials for review consideration to J. Robles.

Contest/Award Offerings Offers contest in poetry and fiction. **Deadline:** June 1, 2005. Guidelines available on website.

Also Offers Runs local reading series in San Francisco Bay area.

$ ☑ ◎ FLESH AND BLOOD: QUIET TALES OF DARK FANTASY & HORROR (Specialized: horror, dark fantasy, off-beat, supernatural)

121 Joseph St., Bayville NJ 08721. E-mail: HorrorJackF@aol.com. Website: www.fleshandbloodpress.com. Established 1997. **Editor-in-Chief:** Jack Fisher. **Senior Editor:** Robert Swartwood.

Magazine Needs Appearing 4 times/year, *Flesh and Blood* publishes work of dark fantasy and the supernatural. Wants surreal, bizarre, and avant-garde poetry. No "rhyming or love poems." Has published poetry by Charles Jacob, Mark McLaughlin, Kurt Newton, Wendy Rathbone, and J.W. Donnelly. *Flesh and Blood* is 52-60 pages, full-sized, saddle-stapled, with glossy full-color cover, includes art/graphics and ads. Receives about 200 poems/year, accepts about 10%. Publishes 4-6 poems/issue. Press run is 700 for 400 subscribers, 100 shelf sales; 50 distributed free to reviewers. Subscription: $16. Sample: $6. Make checks payable to Jack Fisher.

How to Submit Submit up to 5 poems at a time. Line length for poetry is 3 minimum, 30 maximum. No previously published poems or simultaneous submissions. Accepts e-mail submissions (pasted into body of message). Cover letter is preferred. "Poems should be on separate pages, each with the author's address. Cover letter should include background writing credits." Time between acceptance and publication is up to 10 months. Guidelines available for SASE or on website. Responds in 2 months. Pays $10-20/poem and one contributor's copy.

Advice "Be patient, professional, and courteous."

Ⓝ ◯ ◎ FLESH FROM ASHES PUBLICATIONS; FLESH FROM ASHES MAGAZINE (Specialized: political and social issues; experimental forms)

601½ N. Main St., Findlay OH 45840. (419)420-9086. E-mail: anakatora@fleshfromashes.net. Website: www.fleshfromashes.net. Established 2002. **Publisher/Editor:** Robin Coe.

Magazine Needs *flesh from ashes* appears quarterly "using the power of art to subvert political and corporate propaganda. Rise from the ashes of your social disillusion and take a creative stand against the political and corporate propaganda that perpetuates spiritual, psychological, and physical death.'' Wants ''political/social, experimental, gay/lesbian, animal rights, environmental, human rights, postmodern [poetry]. We do not publish poetry that doesn't have a political or social theme, except in the case of where the format is pushing the current ideas of the art form.'' Has published poetry by Thomas Paul (WORDWULF) SternerHowe. *flesh from ashes* is 48 pages, digest-sized, self-printed, stapled, with colored glossy-paper cover, includes drawings/paintings and ads. Receives about 10-20 poems/year, accepts about 90%. Publishes about 6-10 poems/issue. Press run is 1,000 for 1,000 subscribers. Single copy: $4; subscription: $12. Make checks payable to flesh from ashes publications.

How to Submit Submit any number of poems at a time. Accepts simultaneous submissions; no previously published poems. Accepts e-mail (pasted into body of message) and disk submissions. Cover letter is preferred. Include SASE. Reads submissions year round. Submit seasonal poems 4 months in advance. Time between acceptance and publication is 3 months. Poems are circulated to an editorial board. Always comments on rejected poems. Occasionally publishes theme issues. List of upcoming themes and guidelines available on website. Responds in one month. Pays one contributor's copy. Acquires one-time rights; returns rights to poets. Reviews books and chapbooks of poetry and other magazines/journals in 300 words, single book format. Send materials for review consideration to Robin Coe.

Book/Chapbook Needs & How to Submit flesh from ashes publications features poetry that focuses on political and social issues. ''We also publish poetry that pushes the boundaries of current styles, including experimental poetry.'' Publishes 5 chapbooks/year. Manuscripts are selected through open submission. Chapbooks are 20-48 pages, printed in-house, stapled, with glossy covers, include paintings/drawings. Query first, with a few sample poems and a cover letter with brief bio and publication credits. Chapbook mss may include previously published poems. Responds to queries in 2 months. Pays royalties of 40-60%.

Also Offers ''flesh from ashes is a new organization. The magazine comes out 4 times per year. The company will be expanding to publish novels and is currently looking for submissions.''

Advice ''Write about what you feel the most passion for.''

FLOATING BRIDGE PRESS (Specialized: regional/Washington State)

% Richard Hugo House, 1634 11th Ave., Seattle WA 98122. E-mail: floatingbridgepress@yahoo.com. Website: www.scn.org/arts/floatingbridge. Established 1994. **Contact:** Editor.

Book/Chapbook Needs Floating Bridge Press is ''supported by the Seattle Arts Commission, King County Arts Commission, Washington State Arts Commission, and the Allen Foundation for the Arts.'' The press publishes chapbooks and anthologies by Washington State poets, selected through an annual contest (see guidelines below). Has published *Geography* by Kellie Russell Agodon, *The End of Forgiveness* by Joseph Green, *X: a poem* by Chris Forhan, and *Blue Willow* by Molly Tenenbaum. In 1997, the press began publishing *Pontoon*, an annual anthology featuring the work of Washington State poets. *Pontoon* is 96 pages, digest-sized, offset-printed, perfect-bound, with matte cardstock cover. For a sample chapbook or anthology, send $8 postpaid.

Contest/Award Offerings For consideration, Washington poets (only) should submit a chapbook ms of 20-24 pages of poetry. **Entry fee:** $12. Include SASE for results only. **Deadline:** usual reading period is November 1 to February 15. Accepts previously published individual poems and simultaneous submissions. Author's name must not appear on the ms; include a separate page with title, name, address, phone number, and acknowledgments of any previous publications. Manuscripts are judged anonymously and will not be returned. In addition to publication, the winner receives $500, 15 author's copies, and a reading in the Seattle area. All entrants receive a copy of the winning chapbook and will be considered for inclusion in *Pontoon*.

☑ FLUME PRESS

California State University at Chico, 400 W. First St., Chico CA 95929-0830. (530)898-5983. E-mail: flumepress@csuchico.edu. Website: www.csuchico.edu/engl/flumepress. Established 1984. **Poetry Editor:** Casey Huff.

Book/Chapbook Needs Flume Press publishes poetry chapbooks. "We have few biases about form, although we appreciate control and crafting, and we tend to favor a concise, understated style, with emphasis on metaphor rather than editorial commentary." Has published chapbooks by Tina Barr, Luis Omar Salinas, Pamela Uschuk, Martha M. Vertreace, John Brehm, and David Graham.

Contest/Award Offerings Chapbooks are chosen from a biennial competition. **Entry fee:** $20 (each entrant receives a copy of the winning chapbook). Submit 24-32 pages, including title, contents, and acknowledgments. Considers simultaneous submissions. Sometimes sends prepublication galleys. Winner receives $500 and 25 author's copies. Sample: $8. **Postmark deadline:** December 1, 2006. Guidelines available on website.

☑ FLYWAY, A LITERARY REVIEW

206 Ross Hall, Iowa State University, Ames IA 50011-1201. Fax: (515)294-6814. E-mail: flyway@iastate.edu. Website: www.flyway.org. Established 1961. **Editor-in-Chief:** Stephen Pett.

Magazine Needs Appearing 3 times/year, *Flyway* "is one of the best literary magazines for the money; it is packed with some of the most readable poems being published today—all styles, forms, lengths, and subjects." The editor shuns elite-sounding free verse with obscure meanings, and pretty-sounding formal verse with obvious meanings. *Flyway* is 112 pages, digest-sized, professionally printed, perfect-bound, with matte card cover with color. Press run is 600 for 400 subscribers of which 100 are libraries. Subscription: $18. Sample: $7.

How to Submit Submit 4-6 poems at a time. Cover letter is preferred. "We do not read manuscripts between the end of May and the end of August." May be contacted by fax. Publishes theme issues (Native American, Latino, Arab American). Responds in 6 weeks (often sooner). Pays 2 contributor's copies. Acquires first rights.

Contest/Award Offerings Sponsors an annual award for poetry, fiction, and nonfiction. Details available for SASE or on website.

✦ ☑ FOLIO, A Literary Journal at American University

Dept. of Literature, American University, Washington DC 20016. (202)885-2990. Fax: (202)885-2938. E-mail: folio_editors@yahoo.com. Website: www.american.edu/cas/lit/folio. Established 1984. **Editor-in-Chief:** Sandra Beasley.

Magazine Needs *Folio* appears 2 times/year. Wants work "that ignites and endures, is artful and natural, daring and elegant. Will accept formal and free verse." Does not want work of a sexually graphic or discriminatory nature. Has published poetry by Allison Joseph, Henry Taylor, Denise Duhamel, Nathalie Handal, Patrick Rosal, and Kathleen Kirk. *Folio* is 80 pages, digest-sized, with matte cover with graphic art. Receives about 1,000 poems/year, accepts about 25. Publishes about 12 poems/issue. Press run is 350 for 30 subscribers of which 5 are libraries, 50 shelf sales; 50-60 are distributed free to the American University community and contributors. Single copy: $6; subscription: $12/year. Make checks payable to *Folio*.

How to Submit Submit 4-6 poems at a time. Considers simultaneous submissions "with notice." No fax, e-mail, or disk submissions. Cover letter is preferred. "SASE required for notification only; manuscripts are not returned." Reads submissions September 1 through March 1. Time between acceptance and publication is 2 months. Poems are circulated to an editorial board; "Reviewed by editorial staff and senior editors." Seldom comments on rejected poems. Occasionally publishes theme issues. Guidelines available in magazine. Pays 2 contributor's copies. Acquires first North American serial rights.

☐ ◎ **FOR CRYING OUT LOUD, INC. (Specialized: women survivors of sexual abuse)**
46 Pleasant St., Cambridge MA 02139. E-mail: fcol_snlc@hotmail.com. Established 1985. **Contact:** Survivors Newsletter Collective.

Magazine Needs *For Crying Out Loud* appears quarterly "to provide a forum for the voices of women survivors of childhood sexual abuse. Each issue focuses on a theme. Recent themes include Trust; Justice; Memory; and Incest, Politics, and Power. We publish poetry by women abuse survivors, often (though not always) on topics related to abuse and healing from abuse, any form or style." Does not want poetry that is anti-survivor or anti-woman. *For Crying Out Loud* is 12 pages, magazine-sized, offset-printed in b&w, side-stapled, with paper cover, occasional line drawings and clip art. Receives about 160 poems/year, accepts about 25%. Publishes 8-10 poems/issue. Press run is 400 for 200 subscribers of which 10 are libraries, 20 shelf sales; 50 are distributed free to Cambridge, MA Women's Center. Single copy: $3; subscription: $10/4 issues, $18/8 issues, $25/ 12 issues. Sample: $3. Make checks payable to Survivors Newsletter Collective.

How to Submit Submit 3-6 poems at a time. Accepts previously published poems and simultaneous submissions. No fax, e-mail, or disk submissions. Cover letter is preferred. Reads submissions year round. Submit seasonal poems 3 months in advance. Time between acceptance and publication is 3 months. "The newsletter is edited by an editorial collective which votes on all submissions." Never comments on rejected poems. Regularly publishes theme issues. List of upcoming themes and guidelines available for SASE. Responds in 3 months; **does not return submitted work.** Pays one contributor's copy plus a year's subscription. Acquires one-time rights. Reviews books and chapbooks of poetry and other magazines/journals in 500 words, single book format. "We often review books and other resources that we feel will be of interest to our readers." Send materials for review consideration to Survivors Newsletter Collective.

Advice "Our mission is to break the silence around childhood sexual abuse and to empower survivors of abuse. We are interested in poetry (and prose of up to 500 words) that is related to this mission. We especially like to see work that is related to the theme of a particular issue."

☑ ◎ **THE FORMALIST; HOWARD NEMEROV SONNET AWARD (Specialized: form, metrical)**
320 Hunter Dr., Evansville IN 47711. Website: www2.evansville.edu/theformalist/. Established 1990. **Editor:** William Baer.

Magazine Needs *The Formalist*, appearing biannually in spring/summer and fall/winter, is "dedicated to contemporary *metrical* poetry written in the great tradition of English-language verse. We're looking for well-crafted poetry in a contemporary idiom which uses meter and the full range of traditional poetic conventions in vigorous and interesting ways. We're especially interested in sonnets, couplets, tercets, ballads, the French forms, etc. We're not, however, interested in haiku (or syllabic verse of any kind) or sestinas. Only rarely do we accept a poem over 2 pages, and we have no interest in any type of erotica, blasphemy, vulgarity, or racism. Finally, we suggest that those wishing to submit to *The Formalist* become familiar with the journal beforehand. We are also interested in metrical translations of the poetry of major, formalist, non-English poets—from the ancient Greeks to the present." Has published poetry by Derek Walcott, Richard Wilbur, John Updike, Maxine Kumin, X.J. Kennedy, and W.D. Snodgrass. *The Formalist* is 128 pages, digest-sized, offset-printed on bond paper, perfect-bound, with colored card cover. Subscription: $14/ year, $26/2 years (add $8/year for foreign subscription). Sample: $7.50.

How to Submit Submit 3-5 poems at a time. No simultaneous submissions, previously published poems, or disk submissions. A brief cover letter is recommended, and a SASE is necessary for a reply and return of ms. Responds within 2 months. Guidelines available for SASE or on website. Pays 2 contributor's copies. Acquires first North American serial rights.

Contest/Award Offerings The Howard Nemerov Sonnet Award offers $1,000 and publication in

The Formalist for the best unpublished sonnet. The final judge for 2003 was Dana Gioia. **Entry fee:** $3/sonnet. **Postmark deadline:** June 15. Guidelines available for SASE.

FORPOETRY.COM

E-mail: submissions@forpoetry.com. Website: www.forpoetry.com. Established March 1999. **Editor:** Jackie Marcus.

Magazine Needs *ForPoetry.Com* is a web magazine with daily updates. "We wish to promote new and emerging poets, with or without MFAs. We will be publishing established poets, but our primary interest is in publishing excellent poetry, prose, and reviews. We are interested in lyric poetry, vivid imagery, open form, natural landscape, philosophical themes, but not at the expense of honesty and passion: model examples: Robert Hass, James Wright, Charles Wright's *The Other Side of the River*, Montale, Neruda, Levertov, and Louise Glück. No city punk, corny sentimental fluff, or academic workshop imitations." Has published poetry by Sherod Santos, John Koethe, Jane Hirshfield, Erin Believ, and Kathy Fagan. "We receive lots of submissions and are very selective about acceptances, but we will always try to send a note back on rejections."

How to Submit Submit no more than 2 poems at a time. Accepts simultaneous submissions; no previously published poems. E-mail submissions only; include text in body of message, no attachments. Cover letter is preferred. Reads submissions September through May only. Time between acceptance and publication is 2-3 weeks. Poems are circulated to an editorial board. "We'll read all submissions and then decide together on the poems we'll publish." Comments on rejected poems "as often as possible." Guidelines available on website. Responds in 2 weeks. Reviews books and chapbooks of poetry and other magazines in 800 words.

Advice "As my friend Kevin Hull said, 'Get used to solitude and rejection.' Sit on your poems for several months or more. Time is your best critic."

4*9*1 NEO-NAIVE IMAGINATION (Specialized: style/neo-naive)

P.O. Box 24306, Lakeland FL 33802. E-mail: stompdncr@aol.com. Website: www.491.20m.com. Established 1997. **Editor:** Donald Ryburn. **Assistant Editor:** Juan Beauregard-Montez.

Magazine Needs *4*9*1 Neo-Naive Imagination* appears continuously as an online publication featuring poetry, art, photography, essays, and interviews. Wants "poetry of neo-naive genre. No academic poetry, limited and fallacious language." Has published poetry by Duane Locke and Jesus Morales-Montez.

How to Submit Submit 3-6 poems at a time. Accepts previously published poems and simultaneous submissions. Prefers fax, e-mail (pasted into body of message, "submission" in subject box; no attachments accepted or opened), disk, or CD-ROM submissions. "Would like to hear the poet's own words, not some standard format." Cover letter with picture and SASE preferred. Time between acceptance and publication varies. Response time varies. Payment varies. Acquires first or one-time rights. Reviews books and chapbooks of poetry and other magazines. Send materials for review consideration.

Also Offers Sponsors a series of creative projects. Write or visit the website for details.

FOUR WAY BOOKS; INTRO PRIZE IN POETRY; LEVIS POETRY PRIZE

Box 535, Village Station, New York NY 10014. (212)334-5430. Fax: (212)334-5435. E-mail: four_way _editors@yahoo.com. Website: www.fourwaybooks.com. Established 1993. **Director:** Martha Rhodes.

• Four Way Books has received grants from the Greenwall Fund of The Academy of American Poets and from the Carnegie Foundation.

Book/Chapbook Needs & How to Submit Four Way Books publishes poetry and short fiction. Wants full-length (book length: 48-100 pages) poetry mss. Does not want individual poems or poetry intended for children/young readers. Has published poetry by D. Nurkse, Noelle Kocot,

Susan Wheeler, Nancy Mitchell, Henry Israeli, and Paul Jenkins, among others. Publishes 8 poetry books and one anthology/year. Manuscripts are selected through open submission and through competition. Books are about 70 pages, offset-printed digitally, perfect-bound, with paperback binding, art/graphics on covers. Book mss may include previously published poems. See website for complete submission guidelines. Responds to queries in 4 months. Payment varies. Order sample books from Four Way Books online or through bookstores.

Contest/Award Offerings 1) **The Intro Prize in Poetry** is a biennial contest with prizes including book publication, honorarium ($1,000), and a reading at one or more participating series. Open to U.S. poets who have not yet published a book. "Submit one manuscript, 48-100 pages suggested. You may submit via e-mail or regular mail by the deadline. For complete information, you must refer to our guidelines on our website." **Entry fee:** $25. **Postmark deadline:** was March 31 for 2004. 2) **The Levis Poetry Prize** is a biennial contest with prizes including book publication, honorarium ($1,000), and a reading at one or more participating series. Open to any U.S. poet. "Submit one manuscript, 48-100 pages suggested. More than one manuscript may be submitted, but each must be entered separately. Your name should appear on the entry form and the title page of the manuscript and nowhere else. Include SASE if you would like notification of the winner." Entry form and guidelines available for SASE or on website. **Entry fee:** $25. **Postmark deadline:** March 31, 2005. Receives about 1,000 entries/year. 2003 winner was Pimone Triplett. "Winner announced by mail and on our website." Copies of winning books available through Four Way Books online and at bookstores (to the trade through University Press of New England).

Advice "Four Way Books is a not-for-profit organization dedicated to encouraging, supporting, and promoting the craft of writing and identifying and publishing writers at decisive stages in their careers."

FOURTEEN HILLS: THE SFSU REVIEW

Creative Writing Dept., San Francisco State University, 1600 Holloway Ave., San Francisco CA 94132. (415)338-3083. Fax: (415)338-7030. E-mail: hills@sfsu.edu. Website: http://userwww.sfsu. edu/~hills/. Established 1994. **Contact:** Poetry Editor.

Magazine Needs *Fourteen Hills* is a semiannual appearing in December and May. "We are seeking high-quality, innovative work." Has published poetry by Alice Notley, C.D. Wright, Sherman Alexie, and Virgil Suárez. *Fourteen Hills* is 170 pages, digest-sized, professionally printed, perfect-bound, with glossy card cover. Receives about 900 poems/year, accepts approximately 5-10%. Press run is 600 for 125 subscribers of which 25 are libraries. Single copy: $7; subscription: $12/year, $21/2 years. Sample: $5.

How to Submit Submit 5 poems at a time. Accepts simultaneous submissions, "but please indicate if this is the case"; no previously published poems. Cover letter is preferred. Reads submissions August-September for the Fall issue; January-February for the Spring issue. "The editorial staff is composed entirely of graduate students from the Creative Writing Program at SFSU." Seldom comments on rejected poems. Guidelines available in magazine or on website. Responds in 6 months. Always sends prepublication galleys. Pays 2 contributor's copies.

Advice "Please read an issue of *Fourteen Hills* before submitting."

FREE LUNCH

P.O. Box 717, Glenview IL 60025-0717. Website: www.poetsfreelunch.org. Established 1988. **Editor:** Ron Offen.

Magazine Needs *Free Lunch* is a "poetry journal interested in publishing the whole spectrum of what is currently being produced by American poets. Features a 'Mentor Series,' in which an established poet introduces a new, unestablished poet. Mentor poets are selected by the editor. Mentors have included Maxine Kumin, Billy Collins, Lucille Clifton, Donald Hall, Carolyn Forché, Wanda Coleman, Lyn Lifshin, and Stephen Dunn. Especially interested in experimental work and work by unestablished poets. Hope to provide all serious poets living in the U.S. with a free subscription. For details on free subscription send SASE. Regarding the kind of poetry we find worthwhile, we like metaphors, similes, arresting images, and a sensitive and original use of language. We are interested in all genres—experimental poetry, protest poetry, formal poetry, etc. No restriction on form, length, subject matter, style, purpose. No aversion to form, rhyme.'' Has published poetry by Thomas Carper, Jared Carter, Billy Collins, David Wagoner, Donald Hall, D. Nurkse, James Reiss, and Cathy Song. *Free Lunch*, published 2 times/year, is 32-40 pages, digest-sized, attractively printed and designed, saddle-stapled. Press run is 1,200 for 1,000 free subscriptions and 200 paid of which 15 are libraries. Subscription: $12 ($15 foreign). Sample: $5 ($6 foreign).

How to Submit ''Submissions must be limited to 3 poems and are considered only between September 1 and May 31. Submissions sent at other times will be returned unread. Although a cover letter is not mandatory, I like them. I especially want to know if a poet is previously unpublished, as I like to work with new poets.'' Accepts simultaneous submissions; no previously published poems. Editor comments on rejected poems and tries to return submissions within 3 months. Guidelines available for SASE. Pays one contributor's copy plus subscription.

Contest/Award Offerings The Rosine Offen Memorial Award, a prize of $200, is awarded to one poem in each issue of *Free Lunch*. Winners are selected solely by the Board of Directors of Free Lunch Arts Alliance, and are announced in the following issue.

Advice ''Archibald MacLeish said, 'A poem should not mean/ But be.' I have become increasingly leery of the ego-centered lyric that revels in some past wrong, good-old-boy nostalgia, or unfocused ecstatic experience. Not receptive to poems about writing poems, other poems, poetry reading, etc. Poetry is concerned primarily with language, rhythm, and sound; fashions and trends are transitory and to be eschewed; perfecting one's work is often more important than publishing it.''

☑ FREEFALL

Undead Poets Press, 15735 Kerstyn St., Taylor MI 48180. (313)941-8123. E-mail: mauruspoet@yahoo.com. Established 1999. **Editor/Publishers:** Marc Maurus and T. Anders Carson.

Magazine Needs *freefall* appears 3 times/year in April, July, and October. *freefall* publishes the quality work of beginners as well as established poets. ''Free verse or formal poetry is okay, and our acceptance policy is broad. No concrete, shape, or greeting card verse. No gratuitous language or sex. No fuzzy animals or syrupy nature poems.'' Has published poetry by B.Z. Niditch, Lyn Lifshin, David Lawrence, Michael Estabrook, and Joe Speer. *freefall* is 40 pages, digest-sized, laser-printed, saddle-stapled, with card stock cover. Receives about 200 poems/year, accepts about 50%. Publishes about 30-40 poems/issue. Press run is 250 for 50 subscribers of which 10 are libraries, 25 shelf sales; 25 are distributed free to small press reviewers. Single copy: $5; subscription: $10. Sample: $5. Make checks payable to Marc Maurus.

How to Submit Submit 5-10 poems at a time. Line length for poetry is 3 minimum, 80 maximum. Accepts previously published poems with notification; no simultaneous submissions. Accepts e-mail submissions; no fax or disk submissions. Cover letter is preferred. ''Snail mail preferred, please send SASE. E-mail submissions in body, not attached.'' Reads submissions all year. Submit seasonal poems 6 months in advance. Time between acceptance and publication is 6 months. Poems are circulated to an editorial board. ''If a poem is high quality, I accept it right away; poor work is rejected immediately, and those on the fence are circulated to as many as 3 other guest editors.'' Often comments on rejected poems. ***Poems may be sent for critique only for $2 each plus SASE.*** Guidelines available for SASE. Responds in 2 weeks. Pays one contributor's copy. Acquires first rights; rights always revert to author on publication. Reviews chapbooks of poetry and other magazines/journals in 500 words, single book format. Send materials for review consideration to Marc Maurus.

Advice ''We prefer to see crafted work, not unedited one-offs. We welcome as much formal verse as we can because we feel there is a place for it.''

⬛ $◐ FREEFALL MAGAZINE

Alexandra Writers' Centre Society, 922 Ninth Ave. SE, Calgary AB T2G 0S4 Canada. Phone/fax: (403)264-4730. E-mail: awcs@telusplanet.net. Website: www.alexandrawriters.org. Established 1990. **Editor:** Sharon Drummond. **Managing Editor:** Ellen Kelly. Member: AMPA.

Magazine Needs Published in March and October, *"FreeFall's* mandate is to encourage the voices of new, emerging, and experienced writers and provide an outlet for their work. Contains: fiction, nonfiction, poetry, interviews related to writers/writing; artwork and photographs suitable for b&w reproduction." Wants "poems in a variety of forms with a strong voice, effective language, and fresh images." Has published poetry by Anne Burke, Lyle Weiss, Myrna Garanis, Liz Rees, Bob Stamp, and Judith Robb. *FreeFall* is 40-44 pages, magazine-sized, "xerox digital" printed, saddle-stapled, with 60 lb. paper cover, includes art/graphics. Receives about 50-60 poems/year, accepts about 20%. Publishes 12-18 poems/issue. Press run is 350 for 270 subscribers of which 20 are libraries, 80 shelf sales; 30 distributed free to contributors, promotion. Single copy: $8.50 US, $7.50 Canadian; subscription: $14 US, $12 Canadian. Sample: $6.50 US, $5.50 Canadian.

How to Submit Submit 2-5 poems at a time. Line length for poetry is 60 maximum. No previously published poems or simultaneous submissions. Accepts disk submissions (ASCII, text format) with hard copy, but no fax or e-mail submissions. Cover letter with 2-line bio and SASE required. Reads submissions March through April and October through November only. Time between acceptance and publication is 6 months. Poems are circulated to an editorial board. "All submissions are read by 4 editors." Seldom comments on rejected poems. Occasionally publishes theme issues. Guidelines and upcoming themes available for SAE and IRC, by e-mail, in magazine, or on website. Responds in 3 months. Pays $5 Canadian/page and one contributor's copy. Acquires first North American serial rights.

Also Offers See website for information about the Alexandra Writers' Centre Society activities and services and for additional information about *FreeFall* magazine. Hosts an annual fiction and poetry contest. **Deadline:** October 1.

🌐 ◐ FREEXPRESSION

P.O. Box 4, West Hoxton NSW 2171 Australia. Phone: (02)9607 5559. Fax: (02)9826 6612. E-mail: freexpression@bigpond.com.au. Established 1993. **Managing Editor:** Peter F. Pike.

Magazine Needs *FreeXpresSion* is a monthly publication containing "creative writing, how-to articles, short stories, and poetry including cinquain, haiku, etc., and bush verse." Open to all forms. "Christian themes OK. Humorous material welcome. No gratuitous sex; bad language OK. We don't want to see anything degrading." Has published poetry by Ron Stevens, John Ryan, and Ken Dean. *FreeXpresSion* is 28 pages, magazine-sized, offset-printed, saddle-stapled, with paper cover, includes b&w graphics. Receives about 1,500 poems/year, accepts about 50%. Press run is 500 for 300 subscribers of which 20 are libraries. Single copy: $3.50 AUS; subscription: $35 AUS ($55 overseas airmail). For sample, send large SAE with $1 stamp.

How to Submit Submit 3-4 poems at a time. "Very long poems are not desired but would be considered." Accepts previously published poems and simultaneous submissions. Accepts submissions on disk, by fax, by postal mail, and by e-mail (include in body of message). Cover letter is preferred. Time between acceptance and publication is 2 months. Seldom comments on rejected poems. Publishes theme issues. List of upcoming themes available by e-mail and in magazine. Guidelines available in magazine, for SAE and IRC, by fax, or by e-mail. Responds in 2 months. Sometimes sends prepublication galleys. Pays one contributor's copy, additional copies available at half price. Acquires first Australian rights only. Reviews books of poetry in 500 words. Send materials for review consideration.

Contest/Award Offerings Sponsors annual contest with 2 categories for poetry: blank verse (up to 40 lines); traditional verse (up to 80 lines). 1st Prize in blank verse: $200; 2nd Prize: $100; 1st Prize in traditional rhyming poetry: $250; 2nd Prize: $150; 3rd Prize: $100.

Also Offers *FreeXpresSion* also publishes books up to 200 pages through subsidy arrangements with authors.
Advice "Keep it short and simple."

☐ ◎ FRODO'S NOTEBOOK (Specialized: poetry by teens)

23 N. Pine St., Jacobus PA 17407. E-mail: editors@frodosnotebook.com. Website: www.frodosnote book.com. Established 1998. **Redactor in Chief:** Daniel Klotz. **Senior Poetry Editor:** Tina Dischinger. Member: the Words Work Network (WoW Net at www.wow-schools.net).
Magazine Needs *Frodo's Notebook* is an online international quarterly of poetry, fiction, and essays by teens. Wants all styles, particularly narrative and personal poems. Does not want unfinished work or work by writers over 19 years of age. *Frodo's Notebook* is published online only. Receives about 1,000 poems/year, accepts about 70. Publishes about 15 poems/issue. All issues available online at no cost.
How to Submit No previously published poems or simultaneous submissions. Accepts e-mail submissions; no fax or disk submissions. Cover letter is required. "Carefully read submission guidelines available on the website." Reads submissions year round. Time between acceptance and publication is 2-3 months. Poems are circulated to an editorial board. "Senior poetry editor makes final selection from a pool of submissions which has been narrowed down by other editors." Often comments on rejected poems. Responds in up to 6 weeks. Acquires first rights. Reviews books of poetry and other magazines/journals in 1,500 words, single book format. Send materials for review consideration to Daniel Klotz.
Advice "Your chances of acceptance skyrocket if you take the time to revise and edit very carefully, being sure to eliminate clichés."

⊕ ◔ FROGMORE PAPERS; FROGMORE POETRY PRIZE

18 Nevill Rd., Lewes, East Sussex BN7 1PF England. Website: www.frogmorepress.co.uk. Established 1983. **Poetry Editor:** Jeremy Page.
Magazine Needs *Frogmore Papers* is a biannual literary magazine with emphasis on new poetry and short stories. "Quality is generally the only criterion, although pressure of space means very long work (over 100 lines) is unlikely to be published." Has published "Other Lilies" by Marita Over and "A Plutonian Monologue" by Brian Aldiss, as well as poetry by Carole Satyamurti, John Mole, Linda France, Elizabeth Garrett, John Harvey, and John Latham. *Frogmore Papers* is 42 pages, photocopied in photoreduced typescript, saddle-stapled, with matte card cover. Accepts 3% of poetry received. Press run is 300 for 120 subscribers. Subscription: £7 ($20). Sample: £2 ($5). (US payments should be made in cash, not check.)
How to Submit Submit 5-6 poems at a time. Considers simultaneous submissions. Editor rarely comments on rejected poems. Responds in 6 months. Pays one contributor's copy. Staff reviews books of poetry in 2-3 sentences, single book format. Send materials for review consideration to Catherine Smith, 24 South Way, Lewes, East Sussex BN7 1LU England.
Contest/Award Offerings Sponsors the annual Frogmore Poetry Prize. Write for information.
Advice "My advice to people starting to write poetry is: Read as many recognized modern poets as you can, and don't be afraid to experiment."

$◎ FROGPOND: JOURNAL OF THE HAIKU SOCIETY OF AMERICA; HAIKU SOCIETY OF AMERICA AWARDS/CONTESTS (Specialized: form/style, haiku and related forms; translations)

P.O. Box 122, Nassau NY 12123. E-mail: ithacan@earthlink.net. Website: www.hsa-haiku.org. Established 1978. **Editor:** John Stevenson.
Magazine Needs *Frogpond* is the international journal of the Haiku Society of America and is published triannually (February, June, October). Wants "contemporary English-language haiku,

ranging from 1-4 lines or in a visual arrangement, focusing on a moment keenly perceived and crisply conveyed, using clear images and non-poetic language.'' Also accepts ''related forms: senryu, sequences, linked poems, and haibun. We welcome translations of any of these forms.'' Has published work by Cor van den Heuvel, George Swede, Peggy Willis Lyles, and Michael McClintock. *Frogpond* is 96 pages, digest-sized, perfect-bound. Receives about 20,000 submissions/year, accepts about 500. Publishes about 60 pages of poetry in each issue. *Frogpond* goes to 800 subscribers, of which 15 are libraries, as well as to over a dozen foreign countries. Sample back issues: $7 US, $9 ROW. Make checks payable to Haiku Society of America.

How to Submit Submit 5-10 poems, with 5 poems per $8\frac{1}{2} \times 11$ sheet, with SASE to the editor. No simultaneous submissions. Accepts submissions by e-mail (as attachment or pasted into body of message), on disk, or by postal mail. Information on the HSA and submission guidelines available for SASE. Responds ''usually'' in 3 weeks or less. Pays $1/accepted item. Poetry reviews usually 1,000 words or less. ''Authors are urged to send their books for review consideration.''

Contest/Award Offerings A ''best of issue'' prize is awarded for each issue of *Frogpond* through a gift from the Museum of Haiku Literature, located in Tokyo. The Society also sponsors The Harold G. Henderson Haiku Award Contest, the Gerald Brady Senryu Award Contest, the Bernard Lionel Einbond Memorial Renku Contest, the Nicholas A. Virgilio Memorial Haiku Competition for High School Students, and the Merit Book Awards for outstanding books in the haiku field.

Also Offers *HSA Newsletter*, edited by Pamela Miller Ness, appears 4 times/year and contains reports of the HSA quarterly meetings, regional activities, news of upcoming events, results of contests, publications activities, and other information.

Advice ''Submissions to *Frogpond* are accepted from both members and nonmembers, although familiarity with the journal will aid writers in discovering what it publishes.''

▓ $◻ FUGUE

Brink Hall, Room 200, University of Idaho, Moscow ID 83844-1102. E-mail: Fugue@uidaho.edu. Website: www.class.uidaho.edu/english/Fugue. Established 1989. **Poetry Editor:** Monica Mankin.

Magazine Needs *Fugue* is a biannual literary magazine of the University of Idaho, published in summer and winter. ''There are no limits on type of poetry; however, we are not interested in trite or quaint verse.'' Has published poetry by Sonia Sanchez, Simon Perchik, and Denise Duhamel. *Fugue* is up to 150 pages, perfect-bound. Receives about 400 poems/semester, accepts only 5-12 poems/issue. Press run is 250 plus an online version. Sample: $8.

How to Submit No previously published poems or simultaneous submissions. No e-mail submissions. SASE is required; ''Submissions without a #10 SASE will not be considered.'' Reads submissions September 1 through May 1 only. Time between acceptance and publication is up to one year. ''Submissions are reviewed by staff members and chosen with consensus by the editorial board. No major changes are made to a manuscript without authorial approval.'' Publishes theme issues. List of upcoming themes and guidelines available for SASE or on website. Responds in up to 5 months. Pays at least one contributor's copy and honorarium. Acquires first North American serial rights.

Contest/Award Offerings ''For information regarding our spring poetry contests, please review our website.''

Advice ''We are looking for poetry that takes risks while demonstrating powerful voice and careful attention to language and craft. Proper manuscript format and submission etiquette are expected; submissions without proper SASE will not be read or held on file.''

Ⓝ ◻ FULCRUM: an annual of poetry and aesthetics

334 Harvard St., Suite D-2, Cambridge MA 02139. (617)864-7874. E-mail: editor@fulcrumpoetry.com. Website: www.fulcrumpoetry.com. Established 2002. **Editors:** Philip Nikolayev, Katia Kapovich. Member: CLMP.

FULCRUM

an annual of poetry and aesthetics

Philosophies of Poetry

Number Two
2003

A detail of Mstislav Dobuzhinsky's "Summer Gardens in Winter" graces the cover of Issue Two, which included several of the artist's lithographs and a biographical essay.

• Received 2003 Award for Excellence in Print from the NPR-member program, "The Poet and the Poem."

Magazine Needs *Fulcrum: an annual of poetry and aesthetics*, appearing annually in February, is "an exquisite international journal of poetry and criticism with a philosophical bent." Wants "poetry that exhibits a strong aesthetic compulsion. All forms and styles; no 'schools.'" Does not want "'metapoetry' (pensive poems about poems) or 'based-on' poetry." Recently published poetry by Charles Bernstein, Billy Collins, W.N. Herbert, August Kleinzahler, Louis Simpson, and John Tranter. *Fulcrum* is 300 pages, digest-sized, professionally printed, flat-spined, glossy cover with b&w art, includes some b&w art in every issue and ads for literary magazines. Accepts about 2% of poems submitted. Publishes hundreds of poems/issue. Press run is 1,000. Single copy: $12 for individuals, $20 for libraries. Make checks payable to Fulcrum Annual.

How to Submit No e-mail or disk submissions. Cover letter is preferred. Include SASE (SAE with IRCs for international submissions). Reads submissions June-August only. Time between acceptance and publication is 6-8 months. "All poems and essays are accepted or rejected by the editors. Read *Fulcrum* before submitting!" Seldom comments on rejected poems. Regularly publishes theme issues. List of upcoming themes and guidelines available on website. Responds in 1-6 months. Sometimes sends prepublication galleys. Pays one contributor's copy. Acquires first rights.

Advice "There are no 'schools'—life is a vacation!"

◻ ◎ FURROW—THE UNDERGRADUATE LITERARY AND ART REVIEW (Specialized: undergraduates only); THE ORCHARD PRIZE FOR POETRY

UWM Union Box 194, University of Wisconsin-Milwaukee, P.O. Box 413, Milwaukee WI 53201. (414)229-3405. E-mail: furrow@csd.uwm.edu. Established 1999. **Poetry Editor:** Emily Hall. **Executive Editor:** Rachel Vander Weit.

Magazine Needs *Furrow—The Undergraduate Literary and Art Review* appears 2 times/year. "We simply want to see poetry that does not take for granted any of the prescribed aesthetic functions of a poem. A poem should have a certain felicity of expression and originality but also be sort of dangerous and fun. We want wild associations, pungent images, and layered meanings. For the most part, we are not interested in poetry that reinforces traditional styles or what is fashionable in poetry." Has published poetry by Erika Mueller, Sarah Schuetze, Mike Krull, Daniel John Frostman, Russ Bickerstaff, and Donald V. Kingsbury. *Furrow* is 45-70 pages, digest-sized, perfect-bound, with card stock cover. Receives about 400 poems/year, accepts about 10%. Publishes about 15 poems/issue. Press run is 400 for 25 subscribers of which 5 are libraries, 300 shelf sales; one distributed free to each contributor. Sample: free.

How to Submit Submit 3-5 poems at a time. Accepts simultaneous submissions; no previously published poems. Accepts e-mail and disk submissions. "Please include SASE and cover letter stating school, year in school, brief bio note (no more than 5 sentences), and contact information (address, phone, e-mail)." Reads submissions year round. Submit seasonal poems 2 months in advance. Time between acceptance and publication is 1-2 months. "Submissions are read by a single editor, acceptances notified upon approval of undergraduate status." Seldom comments on rejected poems. Guidelines available for SASE. Responds in 2 months. Pays one contributor's copy/ accepted piece. Acquires one-time rights. Reviews books and chapbooks of poetry and other magazines in 3,000 words maximum, single book format. Send materials for review consideration to Rachel Vander Weit.

Advice "We would like to think that our poets at least have the decency to want to change poetry and make it their own."

$☐ FUTURES MYSTERIOUS ANTHOLOGY MAGAZINE

902 W. Fifth St., Winona MN 55987-5120. (612)724-4023. E-mail: babs@fmam.biz. Website: www.f mam.biz. Established 1997. **Poetry Editor:** R.C. Hildebrandt.

Magazine Needs *Futures Mysterious Anthology Magazine* is a quarterly magazine containing short stories, poetry, artwork, and "inspiration for artists of all kinds. We want creative people with the fire to fly!" Does not want to receive gratuitous profanity or pornography. Has published poetry by Dr. Shuvendu Sen, Fredrick Zydec, Terry Barbieri, and Simon Perchik. *FMAM* is 130 pages, magazine-sized, with 2-color semigloss cover, includes art and ads. Receives about 250 poems/ year, accepts about 10%. Publishes 5-10 poems/issue. Press run is 4,500. Single copy: $9.95; subscription: $52. Sample (including guidelines): $8.

How to Submit Submit up to 5 poems at a time. Maximum length per poem is 1½ pages. Rarely accepts previously published poems. Accepts submissions by e-mail (pasted into body of message) and by postal mail. Cover letter with complete contact info and bio is required. "Capitalize the first letter of each word in the title; no underline, brackets, or unnecessary quotation marks. One poem per page; author's name (only) beneath each poem." Time between acceptance and publication is up to 6 months (notifies within 30 days prior to publication). "Works and bios may be edited for length and clarity." Often comments on rejected poems. "If you want to assure a critique of your work, you may inquire for rates, enclose a SASE." Occasionally publishes theme issues. Guidelines available on website. Responds in 6 weeks. Pays up to $50 "for best of the year." Once accepted, poems are kept on file for up to 2 years. All rights revert to author following one-time publication.

Contest/Award Offerings There are 2 Publisher's Choice Awards per issue (not necessarily for poetry). Winners receive $25 plus an award certificate and "their caricature done by our cartoonist, James Oddie. We suggest that you read an issue and get a feel for what we're all about before you submit." Annual Poetic Mayhem Contest pays several prizes (1st Prize: $100). Details on website and in magazine.

Advice "If it is flat on the page, it is not a poem. You have to make an impact in few words. In poetry the line is really all—like a commercial—you have to make an emotional statement in a flash."

⊞ ♡ ◎ GALAXY PRESS (Specialized: gay/lesbian/bisexual, love/romance, horror/ gothic)

71 Recreation St., Tweed Heads N.S.W., 2485 Australia. Phone: (07)5536-1997. Established 1978. **Editor:** Lance Banbury.

Book/Chapbook Needs Galaxy Press publishes "original avant-garde poetry and critical accounts exclusively of the acknowledged great poets, novelists, and dramatists. Latest imprint (November 2003) is a summary of the critical opinions of Lady Hope Hewitt (former lecturer, ANU, Canberra) on Shakespeare's *A Midsummer Night's Dream*." Books are usually 16-20 pages, 15×21cm, offset/ lithograph printed, with glossy color card covers, include art. Press run is 100. Obtain sample books or chapbooks by "written request."

How to Submit Accepts previously published poems and simultaneous submissions. Accepts submissions by postal mail only. Cover letter is preferred. Often comments on rejected poems. Responds to queries in 2 weeks. Pays 5 contributor's copies.

Advice "Interests tend toward the Romantic and Neuromantic styles; a warm, Keatsian approach to imagery and emotions always welcome, but not to the point of being naive."

◐ GARGOYLE MAGAZINE; PAYCOCK PRESS

P.O. Box 6216, Arlington VA 22206-0216. (202)234-3287. E-mail: atticus@atticusbooks.com. Website: www.atticusbooks.com. Established 1976. **Co-Editors:** Richard Peabody and Lucinda Ebersole.

Magazine Needs *Gargoyle Magazine* appears annually "to publish the best literary magazine we can. We generally run short one-page poems. We like wit, imagery, killer lines. Not big on rhymed verse or language school." Has published poetry by Kim Addonizio, Nin Andrews, Kenneth Carroll, Bruce A. Jacobs, Priscilla Lee, and Eileen Tabios. *Gargoyle* is 175 pages, digest-sized, offset-printed, perfect-bound, with color cover, includes photos, artwork, and ads. Accepts about 10% of the poems received each year. Press run is 2,000. Subscription: $20 for 2; $25 to institutions. Sample: $10. Make checks payable to Atticus Books.

How to Submit Submit 5 poems at a time. Accepts simultaneous submissions. Prefers e-mail submissions in Microsoft Word or WordPerfect format. Accepts submissions by postal mail also. Reads submissions Memorial Day through Labor Day only. Time between acceptance and publication is 5 months. Poems are circulated to an editorial board. "The 2 editors make some concessions but generally concur." Often comments on rejected poems. Responds in 2 months. Always sends prepublication galleys. Pays one contributor's copy and ½ off additional copies. Acquires first rights.

Book/Chapbook Needs & How to Submit Paycock Press has published 9-10 books since 1976 and is not currently seeking mss.

⊘ GECKO

P.O. Box 6492, Destin FL 32550. E-mail: geckogalpoet@hotmail.com. Established 1998. **Editor:** Rebecca Lu Kiernan.

Magazine Needs & How to Submit "Due to the overwhelming response of *Poet's Market* readers and personal projects of the editor, we are currenly closed to unsolicited manuscripts. We hope to change this in the future when an assistant will assume some of the editor's duties."

⊘ ◎ GENERATOR; GENERATOR PRESS (Specialized: visual poetry)

3503 Virginia Ave., Cleveland OH 44109. (216)351-9406. E-mail: generatorpress@msn.com. Website: www.generatorpress.com. Established 1987. **Editor:** John Byrum.

Magazine Needs *Generator* is an annual magazine "devoted to the presentation of all types of experimental poetry, focusing on language poetry and 'concrete' or visual poetic modes."

Book/Chapbook Needs Generator Press also publishes the Generator Press chapbook series; approximately one new title/year.

How to Submit Currently not accepting unsolicited mss for either the magazine or chapbook publication.

⊞ ◖ GENTLE READER

8 Heol Pen-y-Bryn, Penyrheol, Caerphilly, Mid Glam, South Wales CF83 2JX United Kingdom. Phone: (029)20 886369. E-mail: lynneejones@tiscali.co.uk. Established 1994. **Editor:** Lynne E. Jones.

Magazine Needs Published quarterly, *Gentle Reader* is "a short story magazine to encourage mostly new and unpublished writers worldwide. Poems provide food for thought and sometimes light relief." Wants "general easy to read verse, not too long, that appeals to a wide audience. Nothing obscure, odd, or esoteric.'' Accepts haiku. *Gentle Reader* is 48 pages, A5, desktop-published, stapled, with paper cover, includes clip art and scanned photos, reciprocal ads from other small presses. Receives about 50 poems/year, accepts up to 80%. Press run is 80 for 65 subscribers of which 5 are libraries. Single copy: £2.50, overseas £3.50; subscription: £8.50, overseas £12. Sample: £2. Make checks payable (in sterling) to L.E. Jones.

How to Submit Submit 2-3 poems at a time. Line length for poetry is 12 minimum, 30 maximum. Accepts previously published poems and simultaneous submissions. Accepts submissions by postal mail and by e-mail (as attachment or pasted into body of message; use slashes to indicate line breaks). ''Include IRCs, please, for reply and return of work.'' Cover letter is preferred. Time between acceptance and publication is up to one year. Guidelines available for SAE and IRC or by e-mail. Responds in 2 months. Acquires first British serial rights. Staff reviews other magazines in 50 words, single book format. Send materials for review consideration.

Advice ''Keep it simple.''

$☑ THE GEORGIA REVIEW

The University of Georgia, Athens GA 30602-9009. (706)542-3481. Website: www.uga.edu/garev. Established 1947. **Editor:** T.R. Hummer. **Contact:** The Editors.

Magazine Needs *The Georgia Review* appears quarterly. ''We seek the very best work we can find, whether by Nobel laureates and Pulitzer Prize-winners or by little-known (or even previously unpublished) writers. All manuscripts receive serious, careful attention.'' Has published poetry by Andrea Hollander Budy, Stephen Dunn, John Kinsella, and Pattiann Rogers. ''We have featured first-ever publications by many new voices over the years, but encourage all potential contributors to become familiar with past offerings before submitting.'' *The Georgia Review* is 208 pages, 7×10, professionally printed, flat-spined, with glossy card cover. Publishes 60-70 poems/year, less than .5% of those received. Press run is 5,500. Subscription: $24/year. Sample: $7.

How to Submit Submit 3-5 poems at a time. No simultaneous submissions. No submissions accepted from May 15 through August 15. Guidelines available for SASE or on website. Responds in 4 months. Always sends prepublication galleys. Pays $3/line, one-year subscription, and one contributor's copy. Acquires first North American serial rights. Reviews books of poetry. ''Our poetry reviews range from 500-word 'Book Briefs' on single volumes to 5,000-word essay reviews on multiple volumes.''

Advice ''Needless to say, competition is extremely tough. All styles and forms are welcome, but response times can be slow during peak periods in the fall and late spring.''

☐ GERONIMO REVIEW; MAOMAO PRESS

E-mail: geronimoreview@att.net. Website: http://home.att.net/∼geronimoreview. Established 1998. **Editor:** g. bassetti.

Magazine Needs At this time, *geronimo review* appears randomly as a zine. ''Submit whatever strikes your fancy. Literally. Anything. *geronimo review* will publish on its website virtually everything submitted. Overt pornography, hate speech, etc. taken under editorial advisement.'' Has 2 submission categories—Open (these submissions are graded ''mercilessly'' by both editors and readers) and Amateur (''graded on an appropriate scale''). Wants ''politics and political satire. *Anything* of unusual excellence, especially the short lyric.'' Has published poetry by Mark C. Peery, dada rambass, zeninubasho, geronimo bassetti, and Élan B. Yergmoul.

How to Submit Submit 3 poems at a time. Line length for poetry is 100 maximum (or the length demanded by the poem). Accepts simultaneous submissions; no previously published poems. Accepts submissions by e-mail only (as Word attachment or pasted into body of message). Reads submissions all year. Time between acceptance and publication is 2 weeks. Guidelines available on website. Responds in 3 weeks. Acquires all rights; returns to poet ''on request.'' Send materials for review consideration to *geronimo review*.

Book/Chapbook Needs & How to Submit MaoMao Press will publish essays on and reviews of poetry in the future. "Not presently accepting book submissions—watch our website."

Also Offers Plans anthology of *geronimo review* material. Also publishing essays on Shakespearean sonnets which address the question of authorship.

Advice "Don't be Susan Wheeler. Be in the tradition of Yeats, Frost, Carroll, Stevens, and be really original and inspire strong reactions."

▦ $▨ THE GETTYSBURG REVIEW

Gettysburg College, Gettysburg PA 17325. (717)337-6770. Fax: (717)337-6775. E-mail: mdrew@gett ysburg.edu. Website: www.gettysburgreview.com. Established 1988. **Editor:** Peter Stitt.

● Work appearing in *The Gettysburg Review* has been frequently included in *The Best American Poetry* and *Pushcart Prize* anthologies. As for the editor, Peter Stitt won the first PEN/ Nora Magid Award for Editorial Excellence.

Magazine Needs *The Gettysburg Review* is a multidisciplinary literary quarterly considering "well-written poems of all kinds." Has published poetry by Rita Dove, Beckian Fritz Goldberg, Charles Wright, Michelle Boisseau, Pattiann Rogers, Mark Doty, and Charles Simic. Accepts 1-2% of submissions received. Press run is 4,500 for 2,700 subscriptions. Subscription: $24/year. Sample: $7.

How to Submit Submit 3-5 poems at a time, with SASE. No previously published poems; simultaneous submissions OK. Cover letter is preferred. Reads submissions September through May only. Occasionally publishes theme issues. Response times can be slow during heavy submission periods, especially in the late fall. Pays $2.50/line, one-year subscription, and one contributor's copy. Essay-reviews are featured in most issues. Send materials for review consideration.

ℕ ▨ THE GIHON RIVER REVIEW

Johnson State College, 337 College Hill, Johnson VT 05656. Established 2001. **Contact:** Poetry Editor for submissions; Editor-in-Chief for inquiries (editors are students; contact names change on a yearly basis).

Magazine Needs *The Gihon River Review* is a biannual review of poetry, fiction, and creative nonfiction with a small compliment of art, usually photographs. Has published poetry by Stuart Friebert, Mark Borax, John David Christensen, Julia Shipley, Thomas Dorsett, and William Doreski. *The Gihon River Review* is 80 pages, digest-sized, offset-printed, perfect-bound, with 2-color cover on glossy coverstock, includes b&w photographs and prints. Receives about 1,000 poems/year, accepts about 3%. Publishes about 10-12 poems/issue. Press run is 650 for 10 subscribers of which 2 are libraries; 400 are distributed free to US colleges and universities with writing programs. Single copy: $5; subscription: $8 (2 issues). Make checks payable to *The Gihon River Review.*

How to Submit Submit 5 poems at a time. No previously published poems or simultaneous submissions. No disk submissions. Cover letter is required ("*brief* cover letter, with SASE"). Reads submissions all year except summer months; submissions received in late spring are read in fall. Time between acceptance and publication is one month. Poems are circulated to an editorial board. "All *GRR* staff read poetry. Editorial process is a group effort." Never comments on rejected poems. Occasionally publishes theme issues. List of upcoming themes available for SASE. Guidelines available in magazine. Pays 2 contributor's copies plus one year's subscription (2 issues). Acquires one-time rights.

▨ GIN BENDER POETRY REVIEW

P.O. Box 150932, Lufkin TX 75915. E-mail: ginbender@yahoo.com (inquiries); submissions@ginbe nder.com (submissions). Website: www.ginbender.com. Established 2002. **Founder/Chief Editor:** T.A. Thompson.

Magazine Needs *Gin Bender Poetry Review* is a literary webzine appearing 3 times/year, featuring both experienced and new writers. Wants poetry "from traditional to experimental." Does not want rhyme, sad love stories, greeting card verse. Has published poetry by Janet Buck, Lyn Lifshin, Cheryl Snell, Louie Crew, and John Grey. *Gin Bender Poetry Review* is published online only. Receives about 400 poems/year, accepts about 10%. Publishes about 20 poems/issue. Sample: free online.

How to Submit Submit 3-5 poems at a time. No previously published poems or simultaneous submissions. Accepts e-mail submissions; no fax or disk submissions. Cover letter is preferred. "We prefer e-mail submissions but also accept snail mail submissions with SASE." Reads submissions year round. Time between acceptance and publication is 4 months. Poems are circulated to an editorial board. "Submissions are read by an editorial staff of 3 people." Seldom comments on rejected poems. Guidelines available on website. Responds in up to 6 weeks. Acquires first rights.

Advice "Send us something that will grasp our soul with vehemence."

🌐 $⬚ GINNINDERRA PRESS

P.O. Box 53, Charnwood ACT 2615 Australia. E-mail: smgp@cyberone.com.au. Website: www.ginninderrapress.com.au. Established 1996. **Publisher:** Stephen Matthews.

Book/Chapbook Needs Ginninderra Press works "to give publishing opportunities to new writers." Has published poetry by Alan Gould and Geoff Page. Books are usually up to 72 pages, A5, laser-printed, saddle-stapled or thermal-bound, with board cover, sometimes includes art/graphics.

How to Submit Query first, with a few sample poems and cover letter with brief bio and publication credits. Accepts previously published poems; no simultaneous submissions. No fax or e-mail submissions. Time between acceptance and publication is 2 months. Seldom comments on rejected poems. Responds to queries in one week; to mss in 2 months. Pays royalties of 12.5%.

◪ GLASS TESSERACT

E-mail: editor@glasstesseract.com. Website: www.glasstesseract.com. Established 2001. **Editor:** Michael Chester.

Magazine Needs *Glass Tesseract* appears once or twice/year online and in hard copy and publishes poems and short stories. "Our purpose is to help bring works of art into the world. Our interests are eclectic." Wants poetry that is "rich in imagery, emotion, ideas, or the sound of language. We are open to all forms from rhyming sonnets to unrhymed, open-ended anything—so long as we feel that the poem is a work of art. We don't want sentimental, moralizing, devotional, cute, coy, or happy face poems." The hard copy of *Glass Tesseract* is 40-60 pages, digest-sized, laser-printed on linen paper, spiral-comb-bound, with color frontispiece, and art on cover. Publishes about 15-20 poems/issue. "Each issue is provided on the website as a read-only pdf file, free to all readers to download to their computers for viewing, printing, or copying to CD. Furthermore, a special rotating selections menu displays poems selected from past, present, and future issues." Hard copy: $12. Order by e-mail. Hard copy circulation is limited, largely consisting of contributor's copies and complimentary copies. The online magazine readership is about 600 over 6 months, and the selections menu receives 1,500 visitors/year.

How to Submit Submit up to 10 poems at a time. Accepts simultaneous submissions and, occasionally, reprints. Accepts e-mail submissions only (pasted into body of message; no attachments). Cover letter is optional. Reads submissions year round. Time between acceptance and publication is up to 15 months, except for online publication on rotating selections menu (not guaranteed to all), which can be at any time—sometimes immediately upon acceptance. Sometimes comments on rejected poems. Guidelines available in magazine, by e-mail, or on website. Responds in up to 4 months. Sometimes provides URL to online prepublication galleys. Pays one contributor's copy. Acquires one-time rights, which revert to author upon publication.

◪ ⊘ DAVID R. GODINE, PUBLISHER

9 Hamilton Place, Boston MA 02108. E-mail: info@godine.com. Website: www.godine.com. "**We do not accept any unsolicited materials.** Please visit our website for information about our submission policies."

⬛ GOOD FOOT

P.O. Box 681, Murray Hill Station, Dept. PM, New York NY 10156. E-mail: submissions@goodfootm agazine.com. Website: www.goodfootmagazine.com. Established 2000. **Editors:** Amanda Lea Johnson, Katherine Sarkis, Carmine Simmons, Matthew Thorburn.

Magazine Needs *Good Foot* appears biannually and "seeks vibrant, active poetry that is compelling and utterly readable. We invite a wide cross-section of work without restriction in form, style, or subject." Has published poetry by Rachel Hadas, Matthea Harvey, David Lehman, David Trinidad, Paul Violi, Susan Wheeler, Tony Tost, and Melanie Kenny. *Good Foot* is about 120 pages, 7×8.5, professionally offset-printed, perfect-bound, with color matte card cover, includes b&w photos/ artwork and back page ads. Receives about 1,000 poems/year, accepts about 10%. Press run is 1,000. Single copy: $8; subscription: $14. Sample: $8. Make checks payable to *Good Foot Magazine*.

How to Submit Submit no more than 3 poems at a time. Accepts simultaneous submissions ("with timely notice of acceptance elsewhere"); *absolutely* no previously published poems. Accepts submissions by e-mail (pasted into body of message; no attachments), on disk, and by postal mail. Cover letter is preferred. "Include brief bio in cover letter. Include SASE." Reads submissions February 1 through October 31. Submissions received during November, December, and January will be returned unread. Time between acceptance and publication is 6 months. "All submissions are read by all 4 editors." Seldom comments on rejected poems. Responds in up to 4 months. Pays one contributor's copy. Acquires first North American serial rights.

⬛ ⬛ ◉ GOOSE LANE EDITIONS (Specialized: regional, Canada)

469 King St., Fredericton NB E3B 1E5 Canada. (506)450-4251. Fax: (506)459-4991. Website: www.g ooselane.com. Established 1954. **Editorial Director:** Laurel Boone. **Poetry Editor:** Ross Leckie.

Book/Chapbook Needs Goose Lane is a small literary press publishing Canadian fiction, poetry, and nonfiction. Writers should be advised that Goose Lane considers mss by Canadian poets only. Receives about 400 mss/year, publishes 10-15 books/year, 4 of which are poetry collections. Has published *Karenin Sings the Blues* by Sharon McCartney and *Skaldance* by Gary Geddes.

How to Submit "Call to inquire whether we are reading submissions." Guidelines available for SASE. Always sends prepublication galleys. Authors may receive royalty of up to 10% of retail sale price on all copies sold. Copies available to author at 40% discount.

Advice "Many of the poems in a manuscript accepted for publication will have been previously published in literary journals such as *The Fiddlehead, The Dalhousie Review, The Malahat Review*, and the like."

⬛ $⬛ GRAIN; SHORT GRAIN CONTEST

P.O. Box 67, Saskatoon SK S7K 3K1 Canada. (306)244-2828. Fax: (306)244-0255. E-mail: grainmag @sasktel.net. Website: www.grainmagazine.ca. Established 1973. **Editor:** Kent Bruyneel. **Poetry Editor:** Gerry Hill.

● Grain was voted Saskatchewan Magazine of the Year, Western Magazine Awards 2001.

Magazine Needs "*Grain*, a literary quarterly, strives for artistic excellence and seeks poetry that is well-crafted, imaginatively stimulating, distinctly original." Has published poetry by Lorna Crozier, Don Domanski, Cornelia Haeussler, Partrick Lane, Karen Solie, and Monty Reid. *Grain* is 128-144 pages, digest-sized, professionally printed. Press run is 1,800 for 1,600 subscribers of which 100 are libraries. Receives about 1,200 submissions of poetry/year, accepts 80-140 poems. Subscription: $26.95/year, $39.95/2 years. Sample: $9.95. (Prices do not include GST; see website for US and foreign postage fees.)

How to Submit Submit up to 8 poems, typed single-spaced on 8½×11 paper, one side only. No previously published poems or simultaneous submissions. Accepts submission by postal mail only; no e-mail submissions. Cover letter is required. "Indicate the number of poems submitted, and include your address (with postal or zip code), phone number, and SASE (or SAE and IRC) or e-mail address for response (if you do not need your submission returned, provide an e-mail address and we will respond electronically and recycle your manuscript).'' Reads submissions September through May only. ''Manuscripts postmarked and/or received between June 1 and September 1 will be automatically returned to writers, unread.'' Guidelines available in magazine, for SASE (or SAE and IRC), by fax, by e-mail, or on website. Responds in up to 4 months. Pays $40/page—up to 5 pages or a maximum of $175—and 2 contributor's copies. Acquires first Canadian serial rights only. Copyright remains with the author.

Contest/Award Offerings The annual Short Grain Contest, which includes 4 categories: Prose Poems (a lyric poem written as a prose paragraph, or paragraphs, in 500 words or less); Dramatic Monologues (500 words or less); Postcard Stories (narrative fiction, 500 words or less); Long Grain of Truth (creative nonfiction, 5,000 words or less). Three $500 prizes in each category. **Entry fee:** $25 for 2 entries in the same category (includes a one-year subscription); $5 for up to 3 additional entries. ''U.S. and international entrants, pay in U.S. funds and add $4 postage for a total of $29 for the basic entry fee.'' **Postmark deadline:** usually between September 1 and January 31. See website for current guidelines. Also sponsors the Anne Szumigalski Editor's Prize: an annual award of $500 for the best poem or group of poems published each year in *Grain*.

Advice ''Only work of the highest literary quality is accepted. Read several back issues.''

✪ ☑ GRAND STREET

214 Sullivan St., 6C, New York NY 10012. (212)533-2944. Fax: (212)533-2737. E-mail: info@grandstreet.com. Website: www.grandstreet.com. **Poetry Editor:** James Lasdun.

- Work published in *Grand Street* has been included in *The Best American Poetry* and other anthologies.

How to Submit Submit up to 5 poems at a time. Accepts simultaneous submissions with notification; no previously published poems. Accepts submissions by postal mail only; no fax or e-mail submissions. Cover letter is required. ''Unused poems are recycled.'' Regularly publishes theme issues. Guidelines and upcoming themes available on website.

☑ GRAYWOLF PRESS

2402 University Ave., Suite 203, Saint Paul MN 55114. E-mail: wolves@graywolfpress.org (for book catalog requests only). Website: www.graywolfpress.org. Established 1974. **Contact:** Editorial Department.

- Poetry published by Graywolf Press has been included in the *Pushcart Prize* anthology.

Book/Chapbook Needs Graywolf Press does not read unsolicited mss. Considers mss *only* by poets widely published in journals of merit. Has published poetry by Jane Kenyon, David Rivard, Vijay Seshadri, John Haines, Eamon Grennan, Tess Gallagher, Tony Hoagland, William Stafford, Linda Gregg, Carl Phillips, and Dana Gioia. Sometimes sends prepublication galleys. No e-mail submissions or queries.

☑ GREEN HILLS LITERARY LANTERN

Truman State University, Division of Language & Literature, Kirksville MO 63501. (660)785-4513. E-mail: jksmith@grm.net or jbeneven@truman.edu. Website: http://ll.truman.edu/ghllweb/. **Poetry Editor:** Joe Benevento.

Magazine Needs *Green Hills Literary Lantern*, an annual journal of Truman State University appearing in summer or early fall, is open to short fiction and poetry of ''exceptional quality.'' Wants ''the best poetry, in any style, preferably understandable. There are no restrictions on subject matter, though pornography and gratuitous violence will not be accepted. Obscurity for its own sake is also frowned upon. Both free and formal verse forms are fine, though we publish more free verse overall. No haiku, limericks, or anything over 2 pages.'' Has published poetry by Jim Thomas, Phillip Dacey, Susan Terris, Louis Philips, Francine Tolf, and Julie Lechevsky. *Green Hills Literary*

Lantern is 200-300 pages, digest-sized, professionally printed, perfect-bound, with glossy 4-color cover. Receives submissions from more than 200 poets/year and publishes about 10% of the poets submitting—less than 10% of all poetry received. Press run is 500. Sample: $7.

How to Submit Submit 3-7 poems at a time, typed, one poem/page. Accepts simultaneous submissions, but not preferred; no previously published poems. No fax or e-mail submissions. Cover letter with list of publication credits is preferred. Often comments on rejected poems. Guidelines available for SASE or by e-mail. Responds within 4 months. Always sends prepublication galleys. Pays 2 contributor's copies. Acquires one-time rights.

Advice "Read the best poetry and be willing to learn from what you encounter. A genuine attempt is made to publish the best poems available, no matter who the writer. First time poets, well-established poets, and those in-between, all can and have found a place in the *Green Hills Literary Lantern*. We try to supply feedback, particularly to those we seek to encourage."

✣ ✓ GREEN'S MAGAZINE

P.O. Box 3236, Regina SK S4P 3H1 Canada. Established 1972. **Editor:** David Green.

Magazine Needs *Green's Magazine* is a literary quarterly "with a balanced diet of short fiction and poetry." Publishes "free/blank verse examining emotions or situations." Does not want greeting card jingles or pale imitations of the masters. Has published poetry by Robert L. Tener, B.Z. Niditch, Nannette Swift Melcher, Ruth Moon Kempher, and Giovanni Malito. *Green's Magazine* is 96 pages, digest-sized, typeset on buff stock, saddle-stapled, with matte card cover, includes line drawings. Press run is 300. Subscription: $15. Sample: $5.

How to Submit Submit 4-6 poems at a time. Prefers typescript, complete originals. No simultaneous submissions. "If © symbol used, poet must give permission to publish and state clearly that the work is previously unpublished." Time between acceptance and publication is usually 6 months. Usually comments on rejected mss. Guidelines available for SAE and IRC. Responds in 2 months. Pays one contributor's copy. Acquires first North American serial rights. Occasionally reviews books of poetry in up to 150-200 words.

Advice "Would-be contributors are urged to study the magazine first."

✓ THE GREENSBORO REVIEW; GREENSBORO REVIEW LITERARY AWARDS

English Dept., Room 134, McIver Bldg., University of North Carolina at Greensboro, P.O. Box 26170, Greensboro NC 27402. (336)334-5459. E-mail: jlclark@uncg.edu. Website: www.uncg.edu/eng/mfa. Established 1966. **Editor:** Jim Clark. **Contact:** Poetry Editor.

- ● Work published in this review has been consistently anthologized or cited in *Best American Short Stories*, *New Stories from the South*, *Pushcart Prize*, and *Prize Stories: The O. Henry Award*.

Magazine Needs *The Greensboro Review* appears twice/year and showcases well-made verse in all styles and forms, though shorter poems (under 50 lines) are preferred. Has published poetry by Stephen Dobyns, Thomas Lux, Stanley Plumly, Alan Shapiro, and Steve Orlen. *The Greensboro Review* is 128 pages, digest-sized, professionally printed, flat-spined, with colored matte cover. Uses about 25 pages of poetry in each issue, about 1.5% of the 2,000 submissions received for each issue. Subscription: $10/year, $25/3 years. Sample: $5.

How to Submit "Submissions (no more than 5 poems) must arrive by September 15 to be considered for the Spring issue (acceptances in December), or February 15 to be considered for the Fall issue (acceptances in May). Manuscripts arriving after those dates will be held for consideration for the next issue." No previously published poems or simultaneous submissions. No fax or e-mail submissions. Cover letter not required but helpful. Include number of poems submitted. Guidelines available in magazine, for SASE, or on website. Responds in 4 months. Always sends prepublication galleys. Pays 3 contributor's copies. Acquires first North American serial rights.

Contest/Award Offerings Sponsors an open competition for *The Greensboro Review* Literary

Awards, $500 for both poetry and fiction each year. **Deadline:** September 15. Guidelines available in magazine, for SASE, or on website.

Advice "We want to see the best being written regardless of theme, subject, or style."

⬇ ◎ GUERNICA EDITIONS INC.; ESSENTIAL POET SERIES, PROSE SERIES, DRAMA SERIES; INTERNATIONAL WRITERS (Specialized: bilingual/foreign language, ethnic/ nationality, translations)

P.O. Box 117, Toronto ON M5S 2S6 Canada. (416)658-9888. Fax: (416)657-8885. E-mail: guernicaed itions@cs.com. Website: www.guernicaeditions.com. Established 1978. **Poetry Editor:** Antonio D'Alfonso.

Book/Chapbook Needs "We wish to bring together the different and often divergent voices that exist in Canada and the U.S. We are interested in translations. We are mostly interested in poetry and essays on pluriculturalism." Has published work by Eugénio de Andrade (Portugal), Eugenio Cirese (Italy), Antonio Porta (Italy), Pasquale Verdicchio (Canada), Robert Flanagan (Canada), and Brian Day (Canada).

How to Submit Query with 1-2 pages of sample poems. Send SASE (Canadian stamps only) or SAE and IRCs for catalog.

Advice "We are interested in promoting a pluricultural view of literature by bridging languages and cultures. We specialize in international translation."

◔ GULF STREAM MAGAZINE

English Dept., Florida International University, 3000 NE 151 St., North Miami Campus, North Miami FL 33181. (305)919-5599. E-mail: Gulfstrm@fiu.edu. Website: w3.fiu.edu/gulfstrm. Established 1989. **Editor:** John Dufresne. **Associate Editor:** Diane Mooney.

Magazine Needs *Gulf Stream* is the biannual literary magazine associated with the creative writing program at FIU. Wants "poetry of any style and subject matter as long as it is of high literary quality." Has published poetry by Gerald Costanzo, Naomi Shihab Nye, Jill Bialosky, and Catherine Bowman. *Gulf Stream* is 96 pages, digest-sized, flat-spined, printed on quality stock, with matte card cover. Accepts less than 10% of poetry received. Press run is 1,000. Subscription: $15. Sample: $5.

How to Submit Submit no more than 5 poems at a time. Accepts simultaneous submissions with notification. Accepts submissions by postal mail, but prefers e-mail submissions. Cover letter is required. Reads submissions September 15 through February 1 only. Publishes theme issues. Guidelines available in magazine or on website. Responds in 3 months. Pays 2 contributor's copies and 2 subscriptions. Acquires first North American serial rights.

$⬜ ◎ HADROSAUR TALES (Specialized: science fiction/fantasy)

P.O. Box 2194, Mesilla Park NM 88047-2194. (505)527-4163. E-mail: hadrosaur.productions@veriz on.net. Website: http://hadrosaur.com. Established 1995. **Editor:** David L. Summers.

Magazine Needs "*Hadrosaur Tales* is a literary journal that appears 3 times/year and publishes well-written, thought-provoking science fiction and fantasy." Wants science fiction and fantasy themes. "We like to see strong visual imagery; strong emotion from a sense of fun to more melancholy is good. We do not want to see poetry that strays too far from the science fiction/fantasy genre." Has published poetry by Christina Sng, Gary Every, Sarah Guidry, and K.S. Hardy. *Hadrosaur Tales* is about 100 pages, digest-sized, printed on 60 lb. white paper, perfect-bound, with black drawing on card stock cover, uses cover art only, includes minimal ads. Receives about 100 poems/year, accepts up to 25%. Press run is 200 for 40 subscribers. Single copy: $6.95; subscription: $10/year. Sample: $6.95. Make checks payable to Hadrosaur Productions.

How to Submit Submit 1-5 poems at a time. Accepts previously published poems. No simultaneous submissions. Accepts e-mail submissions, pasted into body of message or as attachment (RTF format only). "For electronic mail submissions, please place the word 'Hadrosaur' in the subject line. Submissions that do not include this are subject to being destroyed unread. Poetry will not be returned unless sufficient postage is provided." Cover letter is preferred. Time between acceptance and publication is one year. Often comments on rejected poems. Guidelines available for SASE, by e-mail, or on website. Responds in one month. Sends prepublication galleys on request. Pays $2/poem plus 2 contributor's copies. Acquires one-time rights.

Advice "I select poems that compliment the short stories that appear in a given issue. A rejection does not necessarily mean that I disliked your poem, only that the given poem wasn't right for the issue. Keep writing and submitting your poetry."

☑ HAIGHT ASHBURY LITERARY JOURNAL

558 Joost Ave., San Francisco CA 94127. Established 1979-1980. **Editors:** Indigo Hotchkiss, Alice Rogoff, and Conyus.

Magazine Needs *Haight Ashbury* is a newsprint tabloid that appears 1-3 times/year. Uses "all forms including haiku. Subject matter sometimes political, but open to all subjects. Poems of background—prison, minority experience—often published, as well as poems of protest. Few rhymes." Has published poetry by Molly Fisk, Laura del Fuego, Dancing Bear, Lee Herrick, Janice King, and Laura Beausoleil. *Haight Ashbury Literary Journal* is 16 pages with graphics and ads. Press run is 2,500. Subscription: $12/4 issues; $35 for a lifetime subscription, which includes 3 back issues. Sample: $3.

How to Submit Submit up to 6 poems. "Please type one poem to a page, put name and address on every page, and include SASE. No bios." Each issue changes its theme and emphasis. Guidelines and upcoming themes available for SASE. Responds in 4 months. Pays 3 contributor's copies, small amount to featured writers. Rights revert to author. An anthology of past issues, *This Far Together*, is available for $15.

☑ ◎ HAIKU HEADLINES: A MONTHLY NEWSLETTER OF HAIKU AND SENRYU (Specialized: haiku and senryu; membership/subscription; nature)

1347 W. 71st St., Los Angeles CA 90044-2505. (323)971-3225. Established 1988. **Editor/Publisher:** Rengé/David Priebe.

Magazine Needs *Haiku Headlines* is "America's oldest monthly publication dedicated to the genres of haiku and senryu only." Prefers the 5/7/5 syllabic discipline, but accepts irregular haiku and senryu which display pivotal imagery and contrast. Has published haiku by Dorothy McLaughlin, Jean Calkins, Emily Romano, Dion O'Donnol, Edward J. Rielly, and Mark Arvid White. *Haiku Headlines* is 8 pages, $8\frac{1}{2} \times 11$, corner-stapled and punched for a 3-ring binder. "Each issue has a different color graphic front page. The back page showcases a Featured Haiku Poet with a photoportrait, biography, philosophy, and 6 of the poet's own favorite haiku." *Haiku Headlines* publishes 100 haiku/senryu per month. Has 175 subscribers. Single copy: $2 US, $2.25 Canada, $2.50 overseas; subscription: $24 US, $27 Canada, $30 overseas.

How to Submit Haiku/senryu may be submitted with 9 maximum/single page. Unpublished submissions from subscribers will be considered first. Nonsubscriber submissions will be accepted only if space permits and SASE is included. Guidelines available for SASE or in magazine. Responds in 2 months. Pays subscribers half-price rebates for issues containing their work; credits applicable to subscription. Nonsubscribers are encouraged to prepay for issues containing their work.

Contest/Award Offerings Monthly Readers' Choice Awards of $25, $15, and $10 are shared by the "Top Three Favorites." The "First Timer" with the most votes receives an Award of Special Recognition ($5).

⊕ ☑ ◎ HANDSHAKE; THE EIGHT HAND GANG (Specialized: science fiction/fantasy, horror)

5 Cross Farm, Station Rd. N., Fearnhead, Warrington, Cheshire WA2 0QG United Kingdom. Established 1992. **Contact:** J.F. Haines.

Magazine Needs *Handshake*, published irregularly, "is a newsletter for science fiction poets." Wants "science fiction/fantasy poetry of all styles. Prefer short poems." Does not want "epics or foul language." Has published poetry by L.A. Hood, Steve Sneyd, Andrew Darington, Geoff Stevens, and Bruce Boston. *Handshake* is one sheet of A4 paper, photocopied, includes ads. "It has evolved into being one side of news and information and one side of poetry." Receives about 50 poems/year, accepts up to 50%. Press run is 60 for 30 subscribers of which 5 are libraries. Subscription: SAE with IRC. Sample: SAE with IRC.

How to Submit Submit 2-3 poems, typed and camera-ready. No previously published poems or simultaneous submissions. Cover letter is preferred. Time between acceptance and publication varies. Editor selects "whatever takes my fancy and is of suitable length." Seldom comments on rejected poems. Publishes theme issues. Responds ASAP. Pays one contributor's copy. Acquires first rights. Staff reviews books or chapbooks of poetry or other magazines of very short length. Send materials for review consideration.

Also Offers *Handshake* is also the newsletter for The Eight Hand Gang, an organization for British science fiction poets, established in 1991. They currently have 60 members. Information about the organization can be found in the newsletter.

$ ☑ HANGING LOOSE PRESS; HANGING LOOSE

231 Wyckoff St., Brooklyn NY 11217. Website: www.hangingloosepress.com. Established 1966. **Poetry Editors:** Robert Hershon, Dick Lourie, Mark Pawlak, and Ron Schreiber.

Magazine Needs *Hanging Loose* appears in April and October and "concentrates on the work of new writers." Has published poetry by Sherman Alexie, Paul Violi, Donna Brook, Kimiko Hahn, Ron Overton, Jack Anderson, and Ha Jin. *Hanging Loose* is 120 pages, flat-spined, offset-printed on heavy stock, with a 4-color glossy card cover. One section contains poems by high-school-age poets. Sample: $9.

How to Submit Submit 4-6 "excellent, energetic" poems. No simultaneous submissions. "Would-be contributors should read the magazine first." Responds in 3 months. Pays small fee and 2 contributor's copies.

Book/Chapbook Needs & How to Submit Hanging Loose Press does not accept unsolicited book mss or artwork.

Advice "*Read* the magazine first."

$ ☑ HANOVER PRESS; THE UNDERWOOD REVIEW; THE UNDERWOOD REVIEW ANNUAL POETRY COMPETITION

P.O. Box 596, Newtown CT 06470-0596. E-mail: HanoverPress@faithvicinanza.com. Website: www.faithvicinanza.com/hanoverpress.htm. Established 1994. **Editor:** Faith Vicinanza.

Magazine Needs *The Underwood Review* appears annually and publishes poetry, short stories, essays, and b&w artwork including photographs. Wants "cutting-edge fiction, poetry, and art. We are not afraid of hard issues, love humor, prefer personal experience over nature poetry. We want poetry that is strong, gutsy, vivid images, erotica accepted. No religious poems; no 'Hallmark' verse." Accepts poetry written by young poets, high school and above. Has published poetry by Elizabeth Thomas, Sandra Bishop Ebner, Leo Connellan, Richard Cambridge, Michael Brown, and Vivian Shipley. *The Underwood Review* is 120-144 pages, digest-sized, offset-printed, perfect-bound, with card cover with computer graphics, photos, etc. Receives about 2,000 poems/year, accepts up to 3%. Press run is 1,000. Subscription: $13. Sample: $13. Make checks payable to Hanover Press/Faith Vicinanza.

How to Submit Submit up to 3 poems at a time. Accepts simultaneous submissions; no previously published poems. Accepts disk submissions. Cover letter with short bio (up to 60 words) preferred. Time between acceptance and publication is up to 8 months. Guidelines available in magazine or for SASE. Responds in 5 months. Pays 2 contributor's copies. Acquires one-time rights.

Contest/Award Offerings *The Underwood Review* Annual Poetry Competition offers 1st Prize: $500 and publication in *The Underwood Review*; 20 finalists published in the magazine, with winner and finalists invited to read at release party. Pays winners from other countries by bank check or money order in U.S. dollars. Submissions must be unpublished and may be entered in other contests. Submit 1-3 poems, no line limit, on any subject, in any style. No name on ms; include a cover letter with name, address, e-mail, and titles and first lines of poems entered. Guidelines available on website. **Entry fee:** $10/entry of up to 3 poems; accepts multiple submissions, each sent separately and accompanied by entry fee. Does not accept entry fees in foreign currencies; U.S. dollars only. **Deadline:** sbumissions accepted September 1 through November 1. Competition receives about 500 entries/year. Winners notified in February. "Long poems don't do well in competition. Too much can go wrong in a long poem."

Book/Chapbook Needs & How to Submit Hanover Press seeks "to provide talented writers with the opportunity to get published and readers with the opportunity to experience extraordinary poetry." Has published *Crazy Quilt* by Vivian Shipley; *Short Poems/City Poems* by Leo Connellan; *We Are What We Love* by Jim Scrimgeour; *What Learning Leaves* by Taylor Mali; *Dangerous Men* by David Martin; and *The Space Between* by Sandra Bishop Ebner. Publishes 5 paperbacks/year. Books are usually digest-sized, offset-printed, perfect-bound, with various covers, include art/graphics. Query first with a few sample poems and cover letter with brief bio and publication credits. Responds to queries in 4 months; to mss in 6 months. Pays 10% author's copies (100 out of a press run of 1,000 typically). Order sample books by sending $11.

Advice "Poets so often just mass submit their work without being familiar with the literary journal and its preferences. Please don't waste an editor's time or your postage."

☐ ◎ HARD ROW TO HOE; POTATO EYES FOUNDATION (Specialized: rural America)

P.O. Box 541-I, Healdsburg CA 95448. (707)433-9786. **Editor:** Joe E. Armstrong.

Magazine Needs *Hard Row to Hoe,* taken over from Seven Buffaloes Press in 1987, appears 3 times/year and is a "book review newsletter of literature from rural America, with a section reserved for short stories (about 2,000 words) and poetry featuring unpublished authors. The subject matter must apply to rural America, including nature and environmental subjects. Poems of 30 lines or less given preference, but no arbitrary limit. No style limits. Do not want any subject matter not related to rural subjects." Has published poetry by James Fowler, Robert Cooperman, John Perrault, Jennifer Rudsit, Ruth Daniels, and Kelly Jean White. *Hard Row to Hoe* is 12 pages, magazine-sized, side-stapled; 3 pages reserved for short stories and poetry. Press run is 300. Subscription: $8/year. Sample: $3.

How to Submit Submit 3-4 poems at a time. Accepts previously published poems only if published in local or university papers; no simultaneous submissions. Guidelines available for SASE. Editor comments on rejected poems "if I think the quality warrants." Pays 2 contributor's copies. Acquires one-time rights. Reviews books of poetry in 600-700 words. Send materials for review consideration.

☑ HARP-STRINGS POETRY JOURNAL; EDNA ST. VINCENT MILLAY "BALLAD OF THE HARP WEAVER" AWARD; VERDURE PUBLICATIONS

P.O. Box 640387, Beverly Hills FL 34464-0387. Fax: (352)746-7817. E-mail: verdure@digitalusa.net. Established 1989. **Editor:** Madelyn Eastlund.

Magazine Needs *Harp-Strings* appears quarterly. Wants "narratives, lyrics, prose poems, haibun, ballads, sestinas, and other traditional forms. Nothing 'dashed off' or trite; no broken prose masquerading as poetry." Has published poetry by Ruth Harrison, Nancy A. Henry, Robert Cooperman, and Barry Ballard. *Harp-Strings* is 16-20 pages, digest-sized, saddle-stapled, professionally printed on quality colored matte stock, with matte card cover. Accepts about 1% of poems received. Publishes about 12-16 poems/issue. Press run is 200 for 105 subscribers. Subscription: $12. Sample: $3.50.

How to Submit Submit 3-5 poems at a time. Line length for poetry is 14 minimum, 80 maximum ("more often find 40- to 60-line poems have best chance"). Accepts previously published poems **by invitation only**. No simultaneous submissions. Accepts e-mail submissions (pasted into body of message or as Word attachment only); no fax or disk submissions. Cover letter is "not necessary, but if enclosed should contain information on poet or poems. *Harp-Strings* does use brief contributor notes. Always include a SASE—lately poets seem to forget." Reads submissions only in February, May, August, and November. Responds at the end of each reading period. Accepted poems will apear in the next issue being planned following each reading period. Seldom comments on rejected poems. "A poem might not be right for us, but right for another publication. Rejection does not necessarily imply poem needs revisions." Pays one contributor's copy. Acquires one-time rights.

Contest/Award Offerings Sponsors the Edna St. Vincent Millay "Ballad of the Harp Weaver" Award ($50 and publication for a narrative poem, 40-100 lines). **Annual deadline:** August 15. **Entry fee:** $5 for 1-3 poems. Make checks payable to Madelyn Eastlund. "We may sponsor a special contest during each quarter." Contest guidelines available for SASE.

Advice "Some things I've noticed in the past year or 2 are the number of submissions with *no SASE*, submissions stuffed into very small envelopes, failure to put the poet's name on each poem submitted . . . And, evidently, attention not paid to what the magazine lists as 'needs,' because we get haiku, tanka, and other short verse. We also get 8-12 poems submitted with a note that 'this is from my book,' or worse—we get entire manuscripts, especially by e-mail, which we must return because we are not a press. It looks like many poets 'gun shot' their submissions."

⬛ HARPUR PALATE; MILTON KESSLER MEMORIAL PRIZE FOR POETRY
Dept. of English, Binghamton University, P.O. Box 6000, Binghamton NY 13902-6000. E-mail: hppoetry@hotmail.com (query only, no submissions). Website: http://harpurpalate.binghamton.edu. Established 2000. **Poetry Editors:** Anne Rashid and Thomas Rechtin.

Magazine Needs *Harpur Palate* appears biannually. "We're dedicated to publishing the best poetry and prose, regardless of style, form, and genre." Has published poetry by Virgil Suárez, Ryan G. Van Cleave, B.H. Fairchild, Tony Medina, Allison Joseph, and Ruth Stone. *Harpur Palate* is 100-120 pages, digest-sized, offset-printed, perfect-bound, with matte or glossy cover. Receives about 700 poems/year, accepts about 35. Publishes about 10-15 poems/issue. Press run is 500. Single copy: $8; subscription: $16/year (2 issues). Sample: $5. Make checks payable to *Harpur Palate*.

How to Submit Submit 3-5 poems at a time. "No

This cover, featuring a photograph by Mike Hovancsek, was the last one chosen by founding editor Toiya Kristen Finley, whose vision "embraced all genres of fiction and poetry."

Publishers of Poetry

line restrictions; entire submission must be 10 pages or less." Accepts simultaneous submissions, "but we must be notified immediately if the piece is taken somewhere else"; no previously published poems. No e-mail submissions. Cover letter is required. Accepts submissions all year. Time between acceptance and publication is 2 months. Poems are circulated to an editorial board. Seldom comments on rejected poems. Guidelines available for SASE, on website, or in magazine. Responds in up to 6 months. Pays 2 contributor's copies. Acquires first North American serial rights.

Contest/Award Offerings The Milton Kessler Memorial Prize for Poetry, $500 and publication in the Winter issue of *Harpur Palate*. "Contest opens on August 1." **Postmark deadline:** October 1. "Poems in any style, form, or genre are welcome. No more than 10 pages total for entry. Must be previously unpublished." **Entry fee:** $10/5 poems. "You may send as many poems as you wish, but no more than 5 poems per entry. Please send checks drawn on a U.S. bank, or money orders, made out to *Harpur Palate*. IMPORTANT: Checks *must* be made out to *Harpur Palate*." Complete guidelines available for SASE or on website. "We publish a Writing By Degrees supplement featuring fiction and poetry in the Winter issue. Writing By Degrees is a creative writing conference run by graduate students in Binghamton's Creative Writing Program."

Advice "We have no restrictions on subject matter or form. Quite simply, send us your highest-quality fiction and poetry. Read through all of our submission instructions very carefully before sending out your work (manuscripts that are not properly submitted will be discarded unread). Almost every literary magazine already says this, but it bears repeating: look at a copy of our publication (and other publications as well) to get an idea of the kind of writing published. Do an honest (perhaps even ruthless) assessment of your work to see if it's indeed ready to be submitted."

⊘ HARTWORKS; D.C. CREATIVE WRITING WORKSHOP

601 Mississippi Ave. SE, Washington DC 20032-3899. (202)297-1957. E-mail: info@dccww.org. Website: www.dccww.org. Established 2000. **Executive Director:** Nancy Schwalb, D.C. Creative Writing Workshop.

- Although this journal doesn't accept submissions from the general public, it's included here as an outstanding example of what a literary journal can be (for anyone of any age).

Magazine Needs *hArtworks* appears 3 times/year. "We publish the poetry of Hart Middle School students (as far as we know, Hart may be the only public middle school in the U.S. with its own poetry magazine) and the writing of guest writers such as Nikki Giovanni, Alan Cheuse, Arnost Lustig, Henry Taylor, Mark Craver, and Cornelius Eady, along with interviews between the kids and the grown-up pros. We also publish work by our writers-in-residence who teach workshops at Hart, and provide trips to readings, slams, museums, and plays." Wants "vivid, precise, imaginative language that communicates from the heart as well as the head." Does not want "poetry that only 'sounds' good; it also needs to say something meaningful." Has published poetry by Deandre Britten, Andre Harper, Dayna and Joseph Hudson, Shaquiel Jenkins, Jawara Johnson, and Brittany Love. *hArtworks* is 60 pages, magazine-sized, professionally printed, saddle-stapled, with card cover, includes photography. Receives about 1,000 poems/year, accepts about 20%. Publishes about 60 poems/issue. Press run is 500 for 75 subscribers of which 2 are libraries, 100 shelf sales; 100 distributed free to writers, teachers. Single copy: $5; subscription: $15. Sample: $5. Make checks payable to D.C. Creative Writing Workshop.

How to Submit "Writers-in-residence solicit most submissions from their classes, and then a committee of student editors makes the final selections. Each year, our second issue is devoted to responses to the Holocaust."

Advice "Read a lot; know something about how other writers approach their craft. Write a lot; build an understanding of yourself as a writer. Don't be so stubborn you settle into the same old poem you perfected in the past. Writing is not some static machine, but a kind of experience, a kind of growing."

✒ HAWAI'I PACIFIC REVIEW

1060 Bishop St., Honolulu HI 96813. (808)544-1108. Fax: (808)544-0862. E-mail: pwilson@hpu.e
du. Website: www.hpu.edu. Established 1986. **Editor:** Patrice Wilson.

Magazine Needs Published by Hawai'i Pacific University, *Hawai'i Pacific Review* is an annual
literary journal appearing in August or September. Wants "quality poetry, short fiction, and personal essays from writers worldwide. Our journal seeks to promote a world view that celebrates a
variety of cultural themes, beliefs, values, and viewpoints. We wish to further the growth of artistic
vision and talent by encouraging sophisticated and innovative poetic and narrative techniques."
Has published poetry by Wendy Bishop, B.Z. Niditch, Rick Bursky, Virgil Suárez, and Linda Bierds.
Hawai'i Pacific Review is 80-120 pages, digest-sized, professionally printed on quality paper, perfect-
bound, with coated card cover, includes original artwork. Receives 800-1,000 poems/year, accepts
up to 30-40. Press run is approximately 500 for 100 shelf sales. Single copy: $8.95. Sample: $5.

How to Submit Submit up to 5 poems, maximum 100 lines each. One submission/issue. "No
handwritten manuscripts." Accepts simultaneous submissions with notification; no previously published poems. No fax or e-mail submissions. Cover letter with 5-line professional bio including
prior publications is required. "Our reading period is September 1 through December 31 each year."
Seldom comments on rejected poems. Guidelines available for SASE or by e-mail. Responds within
3 months. Pays 2 contributor's copies. Acquires first North American serial rights.

Advice "We'd like to receive more experimental verse. Good poetry is eye-opening; it investigates
the unfamiliar or reveals the spectacular in the ordinary. Good poetry does more than simply
express the poet's feelings; it provides both insight and unexpected beauty. Send us your best
work!"

✒ HAZMAT REVIEW; CLEVIS HOOK PRESS

P.O. Box 30507, Rochester NY 14603-0507. Website: www.hazmatlitreview.org. Established 1996.
Contact: Editor.

Magazine Needs *HazMat Review* is a biannual literary review, "about 70% poetry; 25% short story;
5% misc. (essays, reviews, etc.). *HazMat* stands for 'hazardous material,' which we believe poetry
most definitely may be!" Wants "your best material; take chances; political pieces welcome; also
experimental and/or alternative; especially welcome pieces that show things are not what they
appear to be. We think poetry/fiction of the highest quality always has a chance. New Age, witches,
ghosts and goblins, vampires—probably not." Has published poetry by Eileen Myles, Marc Olm-
stead, Steve Hirsch, Jim Cohn, bobby johnson, Thom Ward, Lawrence Ferlinghetti, and Anne
Waldman. *HazMat Review* is 96 pages, digest-sized, professionally printed, perfect-bound, with
glossy color or b&w cover, sometimes includes photographs or original art. Receives about 700
poems/year, accepts up to 20%. Press run is 500 for 60 subscribers of which 5 are libraries, 100
shelf sales; 100 distributed free to coffeehouses for publicity. Single copy: $14; subscription: $25/
year. Sample: $7.

How to Submit Submit 3 poems at a time. Accepts previously published poems; no simultaneous
submissions. Accepts disk submissions. Cover letter is preferred. SASE requested. Time between
acceptance and publication is up to 2 years. Poems are circulated to an editorial board. "Editors
pass promising material to staff readers for second opinion and suggestions, then back to editors
for final decision." Often comments on rejected poems. Guidelines available on website. Responds
in 3 months. Pays 1-2 contributor's copies. Acquires one-time rights. Staff reviews chapbooks of
poetry.

Advice "We are encouraged by the renewed interest in poetry in recent years. If at all possible,
read the magazine first before submitting to get a feel for the publication."

✒ HELIKON PRESS

120 W. 71st St., New York NY 10023. Established 1972. **Poetry Editors:** Robin Prising and William
Leo Coakley. "We try to publish the best contemporary poetry in the tradition of English verse.

We read (and listen to) poetry and ask poets to build a collection around particular poems. We print fine editions illustrated by good artists. Unfortunately, we cannot encourage submissions.''

✎ HIDDEN OAK

P.O. Box 2275, Philadelphia PA 19103. E-mail: hidoak@att.net. Established 1999. **Editor:** Louise Larkins.

Magazine Needs *Hidden Oak* appears 3 times/year. Wants ''well-crafted poems which make imaginative use of imagery to reach levels deeper than the immediate and personal. Both traditional forms and free verse are accepted. Especially welcome are poems which include time-honored poetic devices and reveal an ear for the music of language.'' *Hidden Oak* is 60-68 pages, digest-sized, photocopied, stapled, with original art/photograph on cover, includes several b&w drawings. Receives about 500 poems/year, accepts up to 40%. Publishes about 50-60 poems/issue, usually one/page. Press run is 80-100. Single copy: $4; subscription: $11. Sample: $3. Make checks payable to Louise Larkins.

How to Submit Submit 3-6 poems at a time. Line length for poetry is 30 maximum. Accepts previously published poems; no simultaneous submissions. Accepts e-mail submissions; no disk submissions. Cover letter is preferred. Include SASE. Also accepts small b&w drawings, whether or not they are poem-related. Submit seasonal poems 2-3 months in advance. Time between acceptance and publication is up to 3 months. Seldom comments on rejected poems. Might publish theme issues in the future. Guidelines available for SASE or by e-mail. Responds in one week. Pays one contributor's copy. Does not review books or chapbooks.

$✎ ◎ HIGH PLAINS PRESS (Specialized: regional, American West)

P.O. Box 123, Glendo WY 82213. (307)735-4370. Fax: (307)735-4590. Website: www.highplainspress.com. Established 1985. **Poetry Editor:** Nancy Curtis.

Book/Chapbook Needs High Plains Press considers books of poetry ''specifically relating to Wyoming and the American West, particularly poetry based on historical people/events or nature. We mainly publish historical nonfiction, but do publish one book of poetry every year.'' Has published *Close at Hand* by Mary Lou Sanelli and *Bitter Creek Junction* by Linda Hasselstrom.

How to Submit Query first with 3 sample poems (from a 50-poem ms). Accepts fax submissions. Responds in 2 months. Time between acceptance and publication is up to 2 years. Always sends prepublication galleys. Pays 10% of sales. Acquires first rights. Catalog available on request; sample books: $5.

Advice ''Look at our previous titles.''

✎ ◎ HIGHLIGHTS FOR CHILDREN (Specialized: children)

803 Church St., Honesdale PA 18431. (570)253-1080. E-mail: editorial@highlights-corp.com. Website: www.highlights.com. Established 1946. **Contact:** Manuscript Submissions.

Magazine Needs *Highlights* appears every month using poetry for children ages 2-12. Wants ''meaningful and/or fun poems accessible to children of all ages. Welcome light, humorous verse. Rarely publish a poem longer than 16 lines, most are shorter. No poetry that is unintelligible to children, poems containing sex, violence, or unmitigated pessimism.'' Accepts poetry written by children and teens (pays only if 16 years or older). Has published poetry by Ruskin Bond, Aileen Fisher, Eileen Spinelli, and Carl Sandburg. *Highlights* is generally 42 pages, magazine-sized, full-color throughout. Receives about 300 submissions/year, accepts up to 30. Press run is 2.5 million for approximately 2.2 million subscribers. Subscription: $29.64/year (reduced rates for multiple years).

How to Submit ''Submit typed manuscript with very brief cover letter. Please indicate if simultaneous submission.'' No e-mail submissions. Editor comments on submissions ''occasionally, if manuscript has merit or author seems to have potential for our market.'' Guidelines available for SASE.

Responds "generally within one month." Always sends prepublication galleys. Payment: "money varies" plus 2 contributor's copies. Acquires all rights.

Advice "We are always open to submissions of poetry not previously published. However, we purchase a very limited amount of such material. We may use the verse as 'filler,' or illustrate the verse with a full-page piece of art. Please note that we do not buy material from anyone under 16 years old."

⬛ 🌐 ◎ HILLTOP PRESS (Specialized: science fiction)

4 Nowell Place, Almondbury, Huddersfield, West Yorkshire HD5 8PB England. Website (online catalog): www.bbr-online.com/catalogue. Established 1966. **Editor:** Steve Sneyd.

Book/Chapbook Needs Hilltop Press publishes "mainly science fiction poetry nowadays." Publications include a series of books on poetry in US and UK SFanzines as well as collections, new and reprint, by individual science fiction poets including Andrew Darlington, Peter Layton, Gavin Salisbury, J.P.V. Stewart, and Lee Ballentine. "New anthology of SF poetry from Oxford reading includes Brian Aldiss, etc." Orders from the US can be placed through the website of BBR Solutions Ltd. (see above).

How to Submit Does not accept unsolicited mss. Query (with SAE/IRC) with proposals for relevant projects.

Advice "My advice for beginning poets is a) persist—don't let any one editor discourage you. 'In poetry's house are many mansions,' what one publication hates another may love; b) be prepared for long delays between acceptance and appearance of work—the small press is mostly self-financed and part-time, so don't expect it to be more efficient than commercial publishers; c) *always* keep a copy of everything you send out; put your name and address on *everything* you send, and *always* include adequately stamped SAE."

🌐 $◪ ◎ HIPPOPOTAMUS PRESS (Specialized: form/style, Modernism); OUTPOSTS POETRY QUARTERLY; OUTPOSTS ANNUAL POETRY COMPETITION

22 Whitewell Rd., Frome, Somerset BA11 4EL England. Phone/fax: 01373-466653. *Outposts* established 1943, Hippopotamus Press established 1974. **Poetry Editor:** Roland John.

Magazine Needs "*Outposts* is a general poetry magazine that welcomes all work either from the recognized or the unknown poet." Wants "fairly mainstream poetry. No concrete poems or very free verse." Has published poetry by Jared Carter, John Heath-Stubbs, Lotte Kramer, and Peter Russell. *Outposts* is 60-120 pages, A5, litho-printed, perfect-bound, with laminated card cover, includes occasional art and ads. Receives about 46,000 poems/year, accepts approximately 1%. Press run is 1,600 for 1,200 subscribers of which 400 are libraries, 400 shelf sales. Single copy: $8; subscription: $26. Sample (including guidelines): $6. Make checks payable to Hippopotamus Press. "We prefer credit cards because of bank charges."

How to Submit Submit 5 poems at a time. "IRCs must accompany U.S. submissions." Accepts simultaneous submissions; no previously published poems. Accepts fax submissions. Cover letter is required. Time between acceptance and publications is 9 months. Comments on rejected poems "only if asked." Occasionally publishes theme issues. Upcoming themes available for SASE (or SAE and IRC). Responds in 2 weeks "plus post time." Sometimes sends prepublication galleys. Pays £8/poem plus one contributor's copy. Copyright remains with author. Staff reviews books of poetry in 200 words for "Books Received" page. Also uses full essays up to 4,000 words. Send materials for review consideration, attn. M. Pargitter.

Book/Chapbook Needs & How to Submit Hippopotamus Press publishes 6 books/year. "The Hippopotamus Press is specialized, with an affinity with Modernism. No Typewriter, Concrete, Surrealism." For book publication, query with sample poems. Accepts simultaneous submissions and previously published poems. Responds in 6 weeks. Pays 7½-10% royalties plus author's copies. Send for book catalog to buy samples.

Contest/Award Offerings The magazine also holds an annual poetry competition.

☑ HIRAM POETRY REVIEW

P.O. Box 162, Hiram OH 44234. (330)569-7512. Fax: (330)569-5166. E-mail: greenwoodwp@hiram. edu. Established 1966. **Poetry Editor:** Willard Greenwood.

Magazine Needs *Hiram Poetry Review* is an annual publication appearing in spring. "Since 1966, *Hiram Poetry Review* has published distinctive, beautiful, and heroic poetry. We're looking for works of high and low art. We tend to favor poems that are pockets of resistance in the undeclared war against 'plain speech,' but we are interested in any work of high quality." Circulation is 400 for 300 subscribers of which 150 are libraries. Although most poems appearing here tend to be lyric and narrative free verse under 50 lines, exceptions occur (a few longer, sequence, or formal works can be found in each issue). Subscription: $9/year; $23/3 years.

How to Submit Query or send 3–5 poems and a brief bio. Accepts simultaneous submissions. Does not accept e-mail submissions or poems over 3 single-spaced pages in length. Reads submissions year round. Responds in up to 6 months. Pays 2 contributor's copies. Acquires first North American serial rights; returns rights upon publication. Reviews books of poetry in single or multi-book format, no set length. Send materials for review consideration.

⊡ ☑ ◎ HOLIDAY HOUSE, INC. (Specialized: children)

425 Madison Ave., New York NY 10017. Established 1936. **Editor-in-Chief:** Regina Griffin. A trade children's book house. Has published hardcover books for children by John Updike and Walter Dean Myers. Publishes one poetry book/year averaging 32 pages. "The acceptance of complete book manuscripts of high-quality children's poetry is limited." Send a query with SASE before submitting.

$☑ THE HOLLINS CRITIC

P.O. Box 9538, Hollins University, Roanoke VA 24020-1538. (540)362-6275. Website: www.hollins. edu/grad/eng_writing/critic/critic.htm. Established 1964. **Editor:** R.H.W. Dillard. **Poetry Editor:** Cathryn Hankla.

Magazine Needs *The Hollins Critic* appears 5 times/year and publishes critical essays, poetry, and book reviews. Uses a few short poems in each issue, interesting in form, content, or both. Has published poetry by William Miller, R.T. Smith, David Huddle, Margaret Gibson, and Julia Johnson. *The Hollins Critic* is 24 pages, magazine-sized. Press run is 500. Subscription: $6/year ($7.50 outside US). Sample: $1.50.

How to Submit Submit up to 5 poems. Must be typewritten, with SASE. Reads submissions September 1 through December 15. Submissions received at other times will be returned unread. Responds in 6 weeks. Pays $25/poem plus 5 contributor's copies.

☑ HOME PLANET NEWS

Box 415, Stuyvesant Station, New York NY 10009. Established 1979. **Co-Editor:** Donald Lev.

Magazine Needs *Home Planet News* appears 3 times/year. "Our purpose is to publish lively and eclectic poetry, from a wide range of sensibilities, and to provide news of the small press and poetry scenes, thereby fostering a sense of community among contributors and readers." Wants "honest, well-crafted poems, open or closed form, on any subject. Poems under 30 lines stand a better chance. We do not want any work which seems to us to be racist, sexist, agist, anti-Semitic, or imposes limitations on the human spirit." Has published poetry by Layle Silbert, Robert Peters, Lyn Lifshin, and Gerald Locklin. *Home Planet News* is a 24-page tabloid, web offset-printed, includes b&w drawings, photos, cartoons, and ads. Receives about 1,000 poems/year, accepts up to 3%.

Press run is 1,000 for 300 subscribers. Subscription: $10/4 issues, $18/8 issues. Sample: $3.
How to Submit Submit 3-6 poems at a time. No limit on length, "but shorter poems stand a better chance." No previously published poems or simultaneous submissions. Cover letter is preferred. "SASEs are a must." Time between acceptance and publication is one year. Seldom comments on rejected poems. Occasionally publishes theme issues; "We announce these in magazine." Guidelines available for SASE, "however, it is usually best to simply send work." Responds in 4 months. Pays one-year gift subscription plus 3 contributor's copies. Acquires first rights. All rights revert to author on publication. Reviews books and chapbooks of poetry and other magazines in 1,200 words, single and multi-book format. Send materials for review consideration to Donald Lev. "Note: we do have guidelines for book reviewers; please write for them. Magazines are reviewed by a staff member."
Advice "Read many publications, attend readings, feel yourself part of a writing community, learn from others."

ℕ $◨ HOTEL AMERIKA

360 Ellis Hall, Ohio University, Athens OH 45701. (740)597-1360. E-mail: editors@hotelamerika.net. Website: www.hotelamerika.net. Established 2002. **Editor:** David Lazar. **Managing Editor:** Jean Cunningham.
• Work published in *Hotel Amerika* by Mark Irwin was included in the 2003 *Pushcart Prize* anthology, poems by John Hollander and Nathaniel Mackey were included in *The Best American Poetry*, 2004, and poets Cathleen Calbert and Colette Inez had work featured on *Poetry Daily*.
Magazine Needs *Hotel Amerika* is a biannual literary journal open to all genres and schools of writing, "from the most formalistic to the most avant-garde." Has published poetry by John Ashbery, Charles Bernstein, Charles Wright, Jean Valentine, Nathaniel Mackey, and Eleanor Wilner. *Hotel Amerika* is about 160 pages, magazine-sized, offset-printed, perfect-bound, with cardstock cover with artwork, sometimes includes art, occasionally prints ads. Receives about 1,500 poems/year, accepts about 100. Publishes about 50 poems/issue. Press run is 2,000 for 100 subscribers of which 10 are libraries, about 800 shelf sales. Single copy: $9; subscription: $18. Make checks payable to *Hotel Amerika*.
How to Submit Submit 3-6 poems at a time. No previously published poems or simultaneous submissions. No e-mail or disk submissions. Cover letter is preferred. "Please include titles of poems in the cover letter, and include a SASE for our response." Reads submissions September 1 through May 1. "The assistant editor and a consulting editor read the poetry submissions and pass their recommendations on to David Lazar, who makes all final decisions." Seldom comments on rejected poems. Guidelines available for SASE or on website. Responds in up to 3 months. Pays "a small honorarium when funds allow" and/or 1-2 contributor's copies. Acquires first North American serial rights; returns rights to poets.

▦ ◨ HQ POETRY MAGAZINE (THE HAIKU QUARTERLY); THE DAY DREAM PRESS

39 Exmouth St., Kingshill, Swindon, Wiltshire SN1 3PU England. Phone: 01793-523927. Website: www.noggs.dial.pipex.com/HQ.htm. Established 1990. **Editor:** Kevin Bailey.
Magazine Needs *HQ Poetry Magazine* is "a platform from which new and established poets can speak and have the opportunity to experiment with new forms and ideas." Wants "any poetry of good quality." Has published poetry by Al Alvarez, D.M. Thomas, James Kirkup, Cid Corman, Brian Patten, and Penelope Shuttle. *HQ Poetry Magazine* is 48-64 pages, A5, perfect-bound, includes art, ads, and reviews. Accepts about 5% of poetry received. Press run is 500-600 for 500 subscribers of which 30 are libraries. Subscription: £10 UK, £13 foreign. Sample: £2.80.
How to Submit No previously published poems or simultaneous submissions. Cover letter and SASE (or SAE and IRCs) required. Time between acceptance and publication is 3-6 months. Often comments on rejected poems. Responds "as time allows." Pays one contributor's copy. Reviews

books of poetry in about 1,000 words, single book format. Send materials for review consideration.
Also Offers Sponsors "Piccadilly Poets" in London, and "Live Poet's Society" based in Bath, Somerset, England. Also acts as "advisor to *Poetry on the Lake* Annual Poetry Festival in Orta, Italy."

◐ HUBBUB; VI GALE AWARD; ADRIENNE LEE AWARD; STOUT AWARD; ELISABETH FRANKLIN AWARD

5344 SE 38th Ave., Portland OR 97202. Established 1983. **Editors:** L. Steinman and J. Shugrue.
Magazine Needs Appearing once/year (usually in November/December), *Hubbub* is designed "to feature a multitude of voices from interesting contemporary American poets. We look for poems that are well-crafted, with something to say. We have no single style, subject, or length requirement and, in particular, will consider long poems. No light verse." Has published poetry by Madeline DeFrees, Cecil Giscombe, Carolyn Kizer, Primus St. John, Shara McCallum, and Alice Fulton. *Hubbub* is 50-70 pages, digest-sized, offset-printed, perfect-bound, with cover art only, usually no ads. Receives about 1,200 submissions/year, accepts up to 2%. Press run is 350 for 100 subscribers of which 12 are libraries, about 150 shelf sales. Subscription: $5/year. Sample: $3.35 (back issues), $5 (current issue).
How to Submit Submit 3-6 typed poems (no more than 6) with SASE. No previously published poems or simultaneous submissions. Guidelines available for SASE. Responds in 4 months. Pays 2 contributor's copies. Acquires first North American serial rights. "We review 2-4 poetry books/year in short (3-page) reviews; all reviews are solicited. We do, however, list books received/recommended." Send materials for review consideration.
Contest/Award Offerings Outside judges choose poems from each volume for 4 awards: Vi Gale Award ($100), Adrienne Lee Award ($50), Stout Award ($25), and Elisabeth Franklin Award ($25). There are no special submission procedures or entry fees involved.

✪ $◨ THE HUDSON REVIEW

684 Park Ave., New York NY 10021. Website: www.hudsonreview.com. **Editor:** Paula Deitz. **Contact:** Shannon Bond.
   ● Work published in *The Hudson Review* has been included in *The Best American Poetry*.
Magazine Needs *The Hudson Review* is a high-quality, flat-spined quarterly of 176 pages, considered one of the most prestigious and influential journals in the nation. Editors welcome all styles and forms. However, competition is extraordinarily keen, especially since poems compete with prose. Has published poetry by Marilyn Nelson, Hayden Carruth, Louis Simpson, and Dana Gioia. Subscription: $32 ($36 foreign)/year, institutions $38 ($42 foreign)/year. Sample: $9.
How to Submit Do not submit more than 10 poems at a time. No previously published or simultaneous submissions. Nonsubscribers may submit poems between April 1 and June 30 only. "Manuscripts submitted by subscribers who so identify themselves will be read throughout the year." Guidelines available in magazine, for SASE, or on website. Responds in 3 months. Always sends prepublication galleys. Pays 50¢/line and 2 contributor's copies.
Advice "Read the magazine to ascertain our style/sensibility."

◨ ◎ HUNGER MAGAZINE; HUNGER PRESS (Specialized: form, language-image experimentation)

1305 Old Route 28, Phoenicia NY 12464. (845)688-2332. E-mail: hunger@hvc.rr.com. Website: www.hungermagazine.com. Established 1997. **Publisher/Editor:** J.J. Blickstein.
Magazine Needs *Hunger Magazine* is an international zine based in the Hudson Valley and appears 2 times/year. "*Hunger* publishes mostly poetry but will accept some microfiction, essays, translations, cover art, interviews, and book reviews. Although there are no school/stylistic limitations, our main focus is on language-image experimentation with an edge. We publish no names for prestige, and most of our issues are dedicated to emerging talent. Well-known poets do grace our

pages to illuminate possibilities. No dead kitty elegies; Beat impersonators; Hallmark cards; 'I'm not sure if I can write poems'. All rhymers better be very, very good. We have published poetry by Amiri Baraka, Paul Celan, Robert Kelly, Anne Waldman, Janine Pommy Vega, Antonin Artaud, and Clayton Eshleman.'' *Hunger* is 75-100 pages, magazine-sized, saddle-stapled, with glossy full-color card cover, includes original artworks and drawings. Accepts about 10% of submissions. Press run is 250-500. Single issue: $8 plus $1 p&h ($11 foreign); subscription: $16 ($21 foreign). Back issue: $8. Chapbooks: $5. Make checks payable to Hunger Magazine & Press.

How to Submit "Send 3-10 pages and SASE." Accepts simultaneous submissions, if notified; no previously published poems. Accepts e-mail submissions and queries; include text in body of message "unless otherwise requested." Brief cover letter with bio and SASE required. "Manuscripts without SASEs will be recycled. Please proof your work and clearly indicate stanza breaks." Time between acceptance and publication is up to one year. Guidelines available in magazine, for SASE, by e-mail, or on website. Responds in up to 6 months, depending on backlog. Sends prepublication galleys upon request. Pays 1-3 contributor's copies depending on amount of work published. "If invited to be a featured poet, we pay a small honorarium and copies." Acquires first North American serial rights.

Advice "Please follow submission guidelines! Please be familiar with magazine content. The brief descriptions found in *Poet's Market* can only give one a general account of what a journal publishes. Do your research! Young poets, spend as much time reading as you do writing. Please, no unsolicited book-length manuscripts."

IBBETSON ST. PRESS

25 School St., Somerville MA 02143-1721. (617)628-2313. E-mail: dougholder@post.harvard.edu. Website: http://homepage.mac.com/rconte. Established 1999. **Editor:** Doug Holder. **Co-Editors:** Dianne Robitaille, Richard Wilhelm, Linda H. Conte, Marc Widershien, Robert K. Johnson, Erin Gumble, Lynne Sticklor.

Magazine Needs Appearing biannually in June and November, *Ibbetson St. Press* is "a poetry magazine that wants 'down to earth' poetry that is well-written; has clean, crisp images; with a sense of irony and humor. We want mostly free verse, but are open to rhyme. No maudlin, trite, overly political, vulgar for vulgar's sake, poetry that tells but doesn't show." Has published poetry by Robert K. Johnson, Don Divecchio, Timothy Gager, Brian Morrissey, Marc Godlfinger, Jennifer Matthews, and Deb Priestly. *Ibbetson St. Press* is 30 pages, magazine-sized, desktop-published, with plastic binding and cream coverstock cover, includes b&w prints and classified ads. Receives about 300 poems/year, accepts up to 40%. Press run is 200 for 30 subscribers. Also archived at Harvard, Brown, University of Wisconsin, and Buffalo University Libraries. Single copy: $5; subscription: $7. Sample: $2. Make checks payable to Ibbetson St. Press.

How to Submit Submit 3-5 poems at a time. Accepts previously published poems and simultaneous submissions. Accepts submissions by postal mail only. Cover letter is required. Time between acceptance and publication is up to 5 months. Poems are circulated to an editorial board. "Three editors comment on submissions." Guidelines available for SASE. Responds in 2 weeks. Pays one contributor's copy. Acquires one-time rights. Reviews books and chapbooks of poetry and other magazines in 250-500 words. Send materials for review consideration.

Book/Chapbook Needs & How to Submit "We also publish chapbooks by newer, little exposed poets of promise. In some cases we pay for all expenses, in others the poet covers publishing expenses." Has published *From the Same Corner of the Bar* by Tim Gager, *Relationships* by Marc Goldfinger, *In the Bar Apocalypse Now* by Gary Duehr, *Fairy Tales and Misdemeanors* by Jennifer Matthews, *Slow as a Poem* by Linda Haviland Conte, and *Inaccessibility of the Creator* by Jack Powers. Chapbooks are usually 20-30 pages, magazine-sized, photocopied, with plastic binding and white coverstock covers, include b&w prints. "Send complete manuscript for consideration, at least 20-30 poems with or without artwork." Responds to queries in one month. Pays 50 author's copies (out of a press run of 100). Order sample chapbooks by sending $5.

Advice "Please buy a copy of the magazine you submit to—support the small press. In your work, be honest. Don't affect."

$◨ THE ICONOCLAST

1675 Amazon Rd., Mohegan Lake NY 10547-1804. Established 1992. **Editor/Publisher:** Phil Wagner. Member: CLMP.

Magazine Needs *The Iconoclast* is a general interest literary publication appearing 6 times/year. Wants "poems that have something to say—the more levels the better. Nothing sentimental, obscure, or self-absorbed. Try for originality; if not in thought, then expression. No greeting card verse or noble religious sentiments. Look for the unusual in the usual, parallels in opposites, the capturing of what is unique or often unnoticed in an ordinary, or extraordinary, moment; what makes us human—and the resultant glories and agonies. Our poetry is accessible to a thoughtful reading public." Has published poetry by Luis C. Berriozabal, Carol Hamilton, and Newton Miner. *The Iconoclast* is 40-64 pages, journal-sized, photo offset on #45 white wove paper, with b&w art, graphics, photos, and ads. Receives about 2,000 poems/year, accepts up to 3%. Press run is 500-2,000 for 335 subscribers. Subscription: $15 for 8 issues. Sample: $2.50.

How to Submit Submit 3-4 poems at a time. Time between acceptance and publication is 4 months to one year. Sometimes comments on rejected poems. Guidelines available for SASE. Responds in one month. Pays one contributor's copy/published page or poem, 40% discount on extras, and $2-5/poem for first North American rights on publication. Reviews books of poetry in 250 words, single book format.

⬙ ⊕ ◔ IDIOM 23; BAUHINIA LITERARY AWARDS

Regional Centre of the Arts, Central Queensland University, Rockhampton 4702 Australia. Website: www.cqu.edu.au/idiom/. Established 1988. **Administrator/Coordinator:** Leonie Healey.

Magazine Needs "Named for the Tropic of Capricorn, *Idiom 23* is dedicated to developing the literary arts throughout the Central Queensland region. Submissions of original short stories, poems, and articles, b&w drawings and photographs are welcomed by the editorial collective. *Idiom 23* is not limited to a particular viewpoint but, on the contrary, hopes to encourage and publish a broad spectrum of writing. The collective seeks out creative work from community groups with as varied backgrounds as possible. The magazine hopes to reflect and contest idiomatic fictional representations of marginalized or non-privileged positions and values." Accepts poetry written by children 10 years of age and older. *Idiom 23*, published annually, is about 140 pages, $7^3/_4 \times 10$, professionally printed, perfect-bound, with 4-color cover, includes photos and line drawings, ads appear on last few pages. Single copy: $10.

How to Submit Accepts previously published poems. Accepts e-mail submissions. Cover letter is required. Poems are circulated to an editorial board. Reviews books of poetry in single book format. Send materials for review consideration to Leonie Healey at l.healey@cqu.edu.au.

Contest/Award Offerings Sponsors the Bauhinia Literary Awards for short stories and poetry. For poetry, offers the Open Award, Regional Award, and Student Award. Submit up to 3 poems, 50 lines maximum each. **Entry fee:** $5. **Postmark deadline:** June 30. Winning entries will be announced at the CQ Multicultural Fair and CQU Open Day in August. Outstanding entries will be published in *The Morning Bulletin* (Australian newspaper). Send SAE and IRC for complete details.

◨ ILLUMINATIONS, AN INTERNATIONAL MAGAZINE OF CONTEMPORARY WRITING

% Dept. of English, College of Charleston, 66 George St., Charleston SC 29424-0001. (843)953-1920. Fax: (843)953-3180. E-mail: lewiss@cofc.edu. Website: www.cofc.edu/Illuminations. Established 1982. **Editor:** Simon Lewis.

Publishers of Poetry

Magazine Needs *Illuminations* is published annually "to provide a forum for new writers alongside already established ones." Open as to form and style, and to translation. Does not want to see anything "bland or formally clunky." Has published poetry by Peter Porter, Michael Hamburger, Geri Doran, and Anne Born. *Illuminations* is 64-88 pages, digest-sized, offset-printed, perfect-bound, with 2-color card cover, includes photos and engravings. Receives about 1,500 poems/year, accepts up to 5%. Press run is 400. Subscription: $15/2 issues. Sample: $10.

How to Submit Submit up to 6 poems at a time. No previously published poems or simultaneous submissions. Accepts e-mail and fax submissions. Brief cover letter is preferred. Time between acceptance and publication "depends on when received. Can be up to a year." Publishes theme issues occasionally; "Issue 16 [2000] was a Vietnamese special; Issue 17 [2001] focused on Cuban and Latin American writing." Guidelines available by e-mail. Responds within 2 months. Pays 2 contributor's copies plus one subsequent issue. Acquires all rights. Returns rights on request.

ILLYA'S HONEY; DALLAS POETS COMMUNITY OPEN POETRY COMPETITION

% Dallas Poets Community, P.O. Box 700865, Dallas TX 75370. Website: www.dallaspoets.org. Established 1994, acquired by Dallas Poets Community in January 1998. **Managing Editor:** Ann Howells. **Contact:** Editor.

Magazine Needs *Illya's Honey* is a quarterly journal of poetry and micro fiction. "All subjects and styles are welcome, but we admit a fondness for free verse. Poems may be of any length but should be accessible, thought-provoking, fresh, and should exhibit technical skill. Every poem is read by at least 3 members of our editorial staff, all of whom are poets. No didactic or overly religious verse, please." Has published poetry by Lyn Lifshin, Joe Ahern, Seamus Murphy, Robert Eastwood, and Brandon Brown. *Illya's Honey* is 40 pages, digest-sized, saddle-stapled, with glossy card cover with b&w photograph. Receives about 2,000 poems/year, accepts about 5-10%. Press run is 250 for 80 subscribers, 50 shelf sales. Subscription: $18. Current issue: $6. Sample: $4.

How to Submit Submit 3-5 poems at a time. No previously published poems or simultaneous submissions. Cover letter is preferred. Include short biography. Occasionally comments on rejected poems. Guidelines available for SASE. Responds in up to 5 months. Pays one contributor's copy.

Contest/Award Offerings Annual Dallas Poets Community Open Poetry Competition. Submit mss to above address between May 1 and July 15. Format: one poem/page, any subject, any length to 3 pages; include cover sheet with contact information and name(s) of poems. **Entry fee:** $5/poem. Offers awards of 1st prize: $300; 2nd prize: $200; 3rd prize: $100. Winners are published in *Illya's Honey*.

$ IMAGE: A JOURNAL OF ARTS & RELIGION (Specialized: religion)

3307 3rd Ave. W., Seattle WA 98119. E-mail: image@imagejournal.org. Website: www.imagejournal.org. Established 1989. **Publisher:** Gregory Wolfe.

Magazine Needs *Image*, published quarterly, "explores and illustrates the relationship between faith and art through world-class fiction, poetry, essays, visual art, and other arts." Wants "poems that grapple with religious faith, usually Judeo-Christian." Has published poetry by Philip Levine, Scott Cairns, Annie Dillard, Mary Oliver, Mark Jarman, and Kathleen Norris. *Image* is 136 pages, 10×7, printed on acid-free paper, perfect-bound, with glossy 4-color cover, averages 10 pages of 4-color art/issue (including cover), includes ads. Receives about 800 poems/year, accepts up to 2%. Has 4,000 subscribers of which 100 are libraries. Subscription: $36. Sample: $12.

How to Submit Submit up to 4 poems at a time. No previously published poems. No e-mail submissions. Cover letter is preferred. Time between acceptance and publication is one year. Guidelines available on website. Responds in 3 months. Always sends prepublication galleys. Pays 4 contributor's copies plus $2/line ($150 maximum). Acquires first North American serial rights. Reviews books of poetry in 2,000 words, single or multi-book format. Send materials for review consideration.

Publishers of Poetry

⚃ ☑ IN POSSE REVIEW; IN POSSE REVIEW MULTI-ETHNIC ANTHOLOGY

E-mail: in_posse_review@yahoo.com. Website: www.webdelsol.com/InPosse. Established 1998. **Poetry Editor:** Ilya Kaminsky. Member: Web del Sol.

• Poetry from *In Posse Review* has been selected regularly for publication at www.versedaily.com, www.mobylives.com, and others.

Magazine Needs *In Posse Review* appears quarterly, published by Web del Sol. "We publish poetry, fiction, nonfiction, book reviews, and special issues. Many authors we published for the first time later went on to achieve national recognition and awards, such as the Lannan Foundation Fellowship, the Wilson Foundation Fellowship, the Ruth Lilly Fellowship, the Barnes & Noble 'Discover New Writers' Award, and others. We have published the work of poet laureates and high school students. The only criteria for publication is excellence of work submitted." Open to all styles and forms. "We are very, very selective and accept only about 5-10% of submissions." Has published poetry by Mary Rakow, Katherine Towler, Garth Greenwell, Ray Gonzalez, C.J. Sage, C.G. Waldrep, Mark Yakich, and Rachel Galvin. Receives about 5,000 poems/year, accepts about 10. Publishes about 15-20 poems/issue. *In Posse Review* is published on the Internet only.

How to Submit Submit 2-4 poems at a time. Accepts previously published poems; no simultaneous submissions. Accepts e-mail submissions ONLY (pasted into body of message). Acquires one-time rights. Reviews books and chapbooks of poetry. "Write us a letter before submitting your review and ask for specific guidelines."

Also Offers *In Posse Review Multi-Ethnic Anthology*, an ongoing project published along with *In Posse Review*; there is no deadline.

Advice "Read our publication and the editor's own books before submitting. If you are serious about writing and want your work to be considered seriously, you should show it by considering seriously the work we produce and publish."

⚃ ◎ IN THE GROVE (Specialized: regional, California)

P.O. Box 16195, Fresno CA 93755. (559)442-4600, ext. 8105. Fax: (559)265-5756. E-mail: inthegrove @rocketmail.com. Website: http://leeherrick.tripod.com/itg. Established 1996. **Publisher/Editor:** Lee Herrick. **Poetry Editor:** Zay Guffy-Bill.

Magazine Needs *In the Grove* appears 2 times/year and publishes "short fiction, essays, and poetry by new and established writers born or currently living in the Central Valley and throughout California." Wants "poetry of all forms and subject matter. We seek the originality, distinct voice, and craft of a poem. No greeting card verse or forced rhyme. Be fresh. Take a risk." Has published poetry by Ruth Schwartz, Corrine Hales, Ryan G. Van Cleave, Timothy Liu, Amy Uyematsu, and Renny Christopher. *In The Grove* is 80-100 pages, digest-sized, photocopied, perfect-bound, with heavy card stock cover. Receives about 500 poems/year, accepts up to 10%. Press run is 200 for 50 subscribers, 100 shelf sales; 50 distributed free to contributors, colleagues. Subscription: $12. Sample: $6.

How to Submit Submit 3-5 poems at a time. Accepts previously published poems "on occasion" and simultaneous submissions "with notice." Cover letter is preferred. Time between acceptance and publication is up to 6 months. "Poetry editor reads all submissions and makes recommendations to editor, who makes final decisions." Seldom comments on rejected poems. Guidelines available for SASE or on website. Responds in 3 months. Pays 2 contributor's copies. Acquires first or one-time rights. Rights return to poets upon publication.

◯ IN THE SPIRIT OF THE BUFFALO

Opportunity Assistance, 5141 O. St. 151, Lincoln NE 68510. (402)464-5223. E-mail: webmaster@op portunityassistance.com. Website: www.inthespiritofthebuffalo.com. Established 1996. **Publisher/ Editor:** Keith P. Stiencke.

Magazine Needs *In the Spirit of the Buffalo* is published 7 or 8 times/year as an e-mail newsletter to "provide a forum for poets and authors of all experience levels to be a positive influence for social awareness and change through creative personal expression." Wants "poetry that awakens social consciousness while still being positive in tone. Motivational, inspirational, and spiritual writing is highly acceptable. No poetry that promotes racism; no hate poetry; pornographic content is not acceptable."

How to Submit Submit up to 3 poems at a time. Accepts previously published poems; no simultaneous submissions. Accepts submissions on disk, by e-mail (pasted into body of message), by fax, or by postal mail; E-mail preferred. Cover letter is preferred; "we would appreciate being able to publish your contact information, however, it is not a requirement for publication." Time between acceptance and publication is 3-6 months. Seldom comments on rejected poems. Responds in up to 4 months. Acquires one-time rights. Send materials for review consideration.

✏ INDEFINITE SPACE (Specialized: experimental)

P.O. Box 40101, Pasadena CA 91114. Established 1992. **Editor:** Marcia Arrieta.

Magazine Needs *Indefinite Space* appears annually. Wants experimental, visual, minimalistic poetry. Does not want rhyming poetry. Has published poetry by Lisa Fishman, Dan Campion, Jeffrey Little, Crag Hill, W.B. Keckler, and Rob Cook. *Indefinite Space* is 36 pages, digest-sized, with b&w art. Single copy: $6; subscription: $10/2 issues. Make checks payable to Marcia Arrieta.

How to Submit Accepts simultaneous submissions; no previously published poems. No disk submissions. Seldom comments on rejected poems. Guidelines available for SASE. Responds in up to 3 months. Copyright retained by poets.

Ⓝ ✏ ◎ THE INDENTED PILLOW (Specialized: Tantra, sacred sexuality)

P.O. Box 3502, Camarillo CA 93011. E-mail: rjones@mymailstation.com. Established 2003. **Editor/ Publisher:** Ronald K. Jones.

Magazine Needs *The Indented Pillow* appears annually in January and publishes poems relating to the Tantric Experience in a single-to-multiple-sheet format. Wants poems "reflecting sexuality and sex practices of the Eastern philosophical tenets of Tantra, i.e., sex and spirit as one." *The Indented Pillow* is one or more pages, $8\frac{1}{2} \times 11$ single sheets, photocopied, folded, with 67 lb. cover, includes b&w ink drawings. Receives about 20 poems/year, accepts about 50%. Publishes about 8-10 poems/issue. Press run is 200 for 30 subscribers; 170 are distributed free to bookstores and relevant organizations. "Since *The Indented Pillow* is a free publication, circulation is often more than stated." Single copy: one first-class stamp; subscription: one first-class stamp.

How to Submit Submit 6 poems at a time. Line length for poetry is 20 maximum. Accepts previously published poems and simultaneous submissions. Accepts e-mail submissions (pasted into body of message). Reads submissions all year. Time between acceptance and publication is one year. Often comments on rejected poems. Guidelines available for SASE. Responds in one month. Pays 2 contributor's copies. Acquires one-time rights.

Advice "If you've had a spiritual experience in a sexual encounter, then you already know the meaning of Tantra."

✏ ◎ INDIAN HERITAGE PUBLISHING; INDIAN HERITAGE COUNCIL QUARTERLY; NATIVE AMERICAN POETRY ANTHOLOGY (Specialized: ethnic/nationality, Native American; nature/ecology; spirituality/inspirational; religious)

P.O. Box 2302, Morristown TN 37816. (423)277-1103. Established 1986. **CEO:** Louis Hooban.

- *Indian Heritage Council Quarterly* received the Evergreen Award from the Consortium of International Environmental Groups.

Magazine Needs *Indian Heritage Council Quarterly* devotes one issue to poetry with a Native American theme. Wants "any type of poetry relating to Native Americans, their beliefs, or Mother Earth." Does not want "doggerel." Has published poetry by Running Buffalo and Angela Evening Star

Dempsey. *Indian Heritage Council Quarterly* is 6 pages, digest-sized ($8\frac{1}{2} \times 11$ folded sheet with $5\frac{1}{2} \times 8\frac{1}{2}$ insert), photocopied. Receives about 300 poems/year, accepts up to 30%. Press run and number of subscribers vary; 50 distributed free to Indian reservations. Subscription: $10. Sample: "negotiable." Make checks payable to Indian Heritage Council.

How to Submit Submit up to 3 poems at a time. Accepts previously published poems (author must own rights only) and simultaneous submissions. Cover letter is required. Time between acceptance and publication is 3 months to one year. Poems are circulated to an editorial board. "Our editorial board decides on all publications." Seldom comments on rejected poems. Charges criticism fees "depending on negotiations." Publishes theme issues. List of upcoming themes and guidelines available for SASE. Responds within 3 weeks. Pay is negotiable. Acquires one-time rights. Staff reviews books or chapbooks of poetry or other magazines. Send materials for review consideration.

Book/Chapbook Needs & How to Submit Indian Heritage Publishing publishes chapbooks of Native American themes and/or Native American poets. Has published *Crazy Horse's Philosophy of Riding Rainbows*, *Native American Predictions*, and *The Vision: An Anthology of Native American Poetry*. Format of chapbooks varies. Query first, with a few sample poems and cover letter with brief bio and publication credits. Responds to queries within 3 weeks, varies for mss. Pays 33-50% royalties. **Offers subsidy arrangements that vary by negotiations, number of poems, etc.** For sample chapbooks, write to the above address.

Contest/Award Offerings Sponsors a contest for their anthology, "if approved by our editorial board. Submissions are on an individual basis—always provide a SASE."

Advice "Write from the heart and spirit, and write so the reader can understand or grasp the meaning. We seek poets/writers who have strong writing abilities in Native literature."

$✉ INDIANA REVIEW

Ballantine Hall 465, 1020 E. Kirkwood Ave., Bloomington IN 47405-7103. (812)855-3439. E-mail: inreview@indiana.edu. Website: www.indiana.edu/~inreview. Established 1976. **Contact:** Esther Lee.

- Poetry published in *Indiana Review* has been included in *The Best American Poetry* and *Pushcart Prize* anthologies.

Magazine Needs *Indiana Review* is a biannual of prose, poetry, creative nonfiction, book reviews, and visual art. "We look for an intelligent sense of form and language, and admire poems of risk, ambition, and scope. We'll consider all types of poems—free verse, traditional, experimental. Reading a sample issue is the best way to determine if *Indiana Review* is a potential home for your work. Any subject matter is acceptable if it is written well." Has published poetry by Philip Levine, Sherman Alexie, Lucia Perillo, Campbell McGrath, Charles Simic, Marilyn Chin, Alice Friman, Robert Perchan, Richard Siken, Elton Glaser, Cornelius Eady, Stuart Dybek, Timothy Liu, Julianna Baggott, and Alberto Rios. *Indiana Review* is 160 pages, digest-sized, professionally printed, flat-spined, with color matte cover. Receives about 7,000 submissions/year, accepts up to 60. Publishes about 40-60 pages of poetry/issue. Has 1,000 subscribers. Sample: $8.

How to Submit Submit 4-6 poems at a time; do not send more than 10 pages of poetry per submission. No electronic submissions. Pays $5/page ($10 minimum/poem), plus 2 contributor's copies and remainder of year's subscription. Acquires first North American serial rights only. "We try to respond to manuscripts in 3-4 months. Reading time is often slower during summer and holiday months." Brief book reviews are also featured. Send materials for review consideration.

Contest/Award Offerings Holds yearly poetry and prose-poem contests. Guidelines available for SASE.

Ⓝ $✉ INK POT; LIT POT; LIT POT PRESS, INC.

3909 Reche Rd., Suite #132, Fallbrook CA 92028. Phone/fax: (760)731-3111. E-mail: litpot@veryfast .biz. Website: www.literarypotpourri.com; www.litpotpress.com. Established 2001. **Editor-in-Chief:** Beverly A. Jackson. Member: CLMP.

- Winner of numerous website awards, including Five Star Award, Web 1000 Award, and Best of the Web award.

Magazine Needs *Ink Pot* is a "quarterly print literary journal" featuring contemporary poetry, fiction, and essays. Much of the material published in *Ink Pot* is reprinted online in the corresponding e-zine, *Lit Pot*. Wants "free verse and experimental forms; classic forms and fresh ideas." Does not want rhymed, children's, or religious poetry. Has published poetry by Terri Brown-Davidson, Richard Jackson, Tom Sheehan, Michael Spring, Kate Fetherston, and Roger Weingarten. *Ink Pot* is about 200 pages, digest-sized, print-on-demand, perfect-bound, with color cover. Receives about 200 poems/year, accepts about 35. Publishes about 2-40 poems/issue. Press run is 150 for 50 subscribers, 50 shelf sales; 50 are distributed free to writers/artists. Single copy: $12; subscription: $30. Make checks payable to Lit Pot Press, Inc.

How to Submit Submit up to 5 poems at a time. Line length for poetry is 3 minimum, 200 maximum; prefers shorter poems in free verse. No previously published poems. Accepts submissions by fax, e-mail (pasted into body of message/as attachment in .rtf, .txt, or .doc format), and postal mail (discouraged); no disk submissions. Prefers e-mail submissions with "the type of submission, your full name, the title of your work, and number of words" in the subject line. "All submissions must include name, address, brief third-person bio, and choice of payment (cash or contributor's copies of *Ink Pot*)." Submit seasonal poems 7 months in advance. Time between acceptance and publication is 6-8 months. "Poems are read by editor-in-chief, and possibly one other editor, before acceptance/rejection." Seldom comments on rejected poems. Guidelines available on website. Responds "in a few days." Always sends prepublication galleys (as electronic proofs). Pays $5, $10, or $15 (editor's discretion), **or** 2 contributor's copies. Acquires first North American serial rights; retains archival rights. Reviews books of poetry in 500-2,000 words, single book format.

Book/Chapbook Needs & How to Submit Lit Pot Press, Inc. publishes 4 poetry collections/year. "Poetry manuscripts are solicited at this time." Books are various lengths, printed on 60# paper, perfect-bound, with OPP-coated b&w covers. Chapbooks are 25 pages, offset-printed, print-on-demand, with cardstock covers. Query first, with a few sample poems and a cover letter with brief bio and publication credits. Book/chapbook mss may include previously published poems. "**Chapbooks are author-subsidy efforts right now.** Lit Pot Press has to approve collaborative chapbooks." Responds to queries in one week. Pays royalties of 100%. **Approximately 1% of books are author-subsidy-published each year.** Order sample books/chapbooks on website.

Advice "Read the e-zine to get an idea of our style and tastes. Read guidelines and contract on website before submitting."

THE INTERFACE; BUTTERMILK ART WORKS

% GlassFull Productions, P.O. Box 57129, Philadelphia PA 19111-7129. E-mail: madlove3000@excite.com. Website: www.baworks.com/Interface. Established 1997. **Publisher:** Earl Weeks.

Magazine Needs *The INTERFACE* is published quarterly online and covers wrestling, comic books, trading cards, science fiction, and politics. Wants "all kinds of work—romantic, political, social commentary. We want poetry that comes from your heart, that makes tears come to the eye or forces one to want to mobilize the troops. No poems of hate or discrimination." Has published poetry by Mike Emrys, Sheron Regular, Cassandra Norris, Emoni Brisbon, Darren Gilbert, and Monique Frederick. Receives about 20 poems/year, accepts up to 35%. Publishes 15 poems/issue.

How to Submit Submit 7 poems at a time. Accepts previously published poems and simultaneous submissions. Accepts submissions by e-mail, through online submission form, and by postal mail. Cover letter is preferred. Send all submissions % Earl Weeks. "We will consider accompanying illustration." Submit seasonal poems 6 months in advance. Time between acceptance and publication is 9 months. Poems are circulated to an editorial board. Occasionally publishes theme issues. Guidelines and upcoming themes available on website. Does not respond to submissions. Acquires two-time rights. "We also have a sister magazine, *The Maelan News*, available only on newsstands in Philly. If you wish not to be printed in the print mag, let us know."

Contest/Award Offerings Interface Positive Poetry Contest; check website for details.

Also Offers "We publish poetry, essays, videogame reviews, book reviews, fashion, science fiction, art, recipes, and more. We are very interested in reviewing your music and passing out any promo materials you have. We are trying to make *The INTERFACE* a meeting place for idea exchanges. We need your opinions and views, so submit them to us."

☐ ◎ INTERNATIONAL BLACK WRITERS; BLACK WRITER MAGAZINE (Specialized: ethnic)

535 Logan Dr. #903, Hammond IN 46320. (312)458-5745. Established 1970. **President/CEO:** Mable Terrell.

Magazine Needs & How to Submit *Black Writer* is a "quarterly literary magazine to showcase new writers and poets and provide educational information for writers. Open to all types of poetry." *Black Writer* is 30 pages, magazine-sized, offset-printed, with glossy cover. Press run is 1,000 for 200 subscribers. Subscription: $19/year. Sample: $1.50. Responds in 10 days, has one-quarter backlog. Pays 10 contributor's copies.

Book/Chapbook Needs & How to Submit For chapbook publication (40 pages), submit 2 sample poems and cover letter with short bio. Accepts simultaneous submissions. Pays in author's copies. For sample chapbook, send SASE with book rate postage.

Contest/Award Offerings Offers awards of $100, $50, and $25 for the best poems published in the magazine, and presents them to winners at annual awards banquet. International Black Writers is open to all writers.

◙ ◎ INTERNATIONAL POETRY REVIEW (Specialized: translations)

Dept. of Romance Languages, UNC-Greensboro, Greensboro NC 27402-6170. (336)334-5655. Fax: (336)334-5358. E-mail: k_mather@uncg.edu or kathleenkoestler@gbronline.com. Website: www. uncg.edu/rom/ipr.htm. Established 1975. **Editor:** Kathleen Koestler.

Magazine Needs *International Poetry Review* is a biannual, primarily publishing translations of contemporary poetry with corresponding originals (published on facing pages) as well as original poetry in English. Has published work by Richard Exner, René Char, Alvaro Mutis, and Tony Barnstone. *International Poetry Review* is 100 pages, digest-sized, professionally printed, perfect-bound, with 2- to 3-color cover. "We accept 5% of original poetry in English and about 30% of translations submitted." Press run is 500 for 200 subscribers. Subscription: $12/$20/$30 (for one, 2, and 3 years, respectively) for individuals, $20/$35/$50 for institutions. Sample: $5. Make checks payable to *International Poetry Review*.

How to Submit Submit no more than 6 pages of poetry. Accepts simultaneous submissions; no previously published poems. Reads submissions between September 1 and April 30. Seldom comments on rejected poems. Guidelines and upcoming themes available for SASE. Responds in up to 6 months. Pays one contributor's copy. All rights revert to authors and translators. Occasionally reviews books of poetry. Send materials for review consideration.

Advice "We strongly encourage contributors to subscribe. We prefer poetry in English to have an international or cross-cultural theme."

⊕ ◙ INTERPRETER'S HOUSE; BEDFORD OPEN POETRY COMPETITION

10 Farrell Rd., Wootton, Bedfordshire MK43 9DU United Kingdom. Established 1996. **Contact:** Merryn Williams.

Magazine Needs *Interpreter's House* appears 3 times/year (February, June, October) and publishes short stories and poetry. Wants "good poetry, not too long. No Christmas-card verse or incomprehensible poetry." Has published poetry by Dannie Abse, Tony Curtis, Pauline Stainer, Alan Brown-

Publishers of Poetry

john, Peter Redgrove, and R.S. Thomas. *Interpreter's House* is 74 pages, A5, with attractive cover design. Receives about 1,000 poems/year, accepts up to 5%. Press run is 300 for 200 subscribers. Subscription: £10. Sample: £3 plus 44p postage.

How to Submit Submit 5 poems at a time. No previously published poems or simultaneous submissions. Cover letter is preferred. Time between acceptance and publication is 2 weeks to 8 months. Often comments on rejected poems. Guidelines available for SASE (or SAE and IRC). Responds "fast." Pays one contributor's copy.

Contest/Award Offerings Sponsors the Bedford Open Poetry Competition. Send SAE and IRC for details.

⬛ ◎ INTRO (Specialized: students)

AWP, MS 1E3, George Mason University, Fairfax VA 22030. Website: http://awpwriter.org. Established 1970. **Publications Manager:** Supriya Bhatnagar.

- See separate listing for The Association of Writers & Writing Programs in the Organizations section.

Magazine Needs & How to Submit Students in college writing programs belonging to AWP may submit to this consortium of magazines publishing student poetry, fiction, and creative nonfiction. Open as to the type of poetry submitted, except they do not want "non-literary, haiku, etc. In our history, we've introduced Dara Wier, Carolyn Forché, Greg Pope, Norman Dubie, and others." All work must be submitted by the writing program. Programs nominate *Intro* works in the fall. Ask your AWP director for more information.

Contest/Award Offerings Donald Hall Prize for Poetry (see separate listing in Contests & Awards section).

◨ ◎ INVERTED-A, INC. (Specialized: form/style, traditional); INVERTED-A HORN

900 Monarch Way, Northport AL 35473-2663. E-mail: amnfn@well.com. Established 1977. **Editors:** Nets Katz and Aya Katz.

Magazine Needs *Inverted-A Horn* is an irregular periodical. Wants traditional poetry with meter and rhyme, and welcomes political topics, science fiction, and social issues. Does not want to see anything "modern, formless, existentialist." *Inverted-A Horn* is usually 9 pages, magazine-sized, offset-printed. Press run is 300. Samples: SASE with postage for 2 ounces (subject to availability).

How to Submit Accepts simultaneous submissions. Accepts submissions by postal mail and as ASCII file. Responds to queries in one month, to mss in 4 months. Pays one contributor's copy plus a 40% discount on additional copies.

Book/Chapbook Needs & How to Submit Inverted-A, Inc. is a very small press that evolved from publishing technical manuals for other products. "Our interests center on freedom, justice, and honor." Publishes one chapbook/year.

Advice "I strongly recommend that would-be contributors avail themselves of this opportunity to explore what we are looking for. Most of the submissions we receive do not come close."

🌐 ◨ IOTA; RAGGED RAVEN PRESS

1 Lodge Farm, Snitterfield, Warwicks CV37 0LR United Kingdom. Phone: 01789 730358. Fax: 01789 730320. E-mail: iotapoetry@aol.com. Website: www.iotapoetry.co.uk. Established 1988. **Editors:** Janet Murch and Bob Mee.

Magazine Needs *Iota* is a quarterly wanting "any style and subject; no specific limitations as to length." Has published poetry by Don Winter, John Robinson, Tony Petch, Donna Pucciani, Brian Daldorph, and Michael Kriesel. *Iota* is 60 pages, professionally printed, perfect-bound, with b&w laminated photograph litho cover. Publishes about 300 of 6,000 poems received. Press run is 300 for 150 subscribers of which 8 are libraries. Subscription: $24 (£12). Sample: $6 (£3).

How to Submit Submit 4-6 poems at a time. Prefers name and address on each poem, typed. No simultaneous submissions or previously published poems. Accepts e-mail submissions (pasted into body of message); no fax submissions. Responds in 3 weeks (unless production of the next issue takes precedence). "No SAE, no reply." Pays one contributor's copy. Reviews books of poetry. Send materials for review consideration.

Also Offers "The editors also run Ragged Raven Press, which publishes poetry collections, nonfiction, and an annual anthology of poetry linked to an international competition." Website: www.raggedraven.co.uk.

Advice "Read poetry, particularly contemporary poetry. Edit your own poems to tighten and polish."

$☑ THE IOWA REVIEW; THE TIM McGINNIS AWARD; THE IOWA AWARD

308 EPB, University of Iowa, Iowa City IA 52242. (319)335-0462. E-mail: iowa-review@uiowa.edu. Website: www.uiowa.edu/~iareview. Established 1970. **Editor:** David Hamilton.

• Poetry published in *The Iowa Review* has been frequently included in *The Best American Poetry* and the *Pushcart Prize* anthologies.

Magazine Needs *The Iowa Review* appears 3 times/year and publishes fiction, poetry, essays, reviews, and, occasionally, interviews. "We simply look for poems that at the time we read and choose, we find we admire. No specifications as to form, length, style, subject matter, or purpose. There are about 40 pages of poetry in each issue. Though we print work from established writers, we're always delighted when we discover new talent." *The Iowa Review* is 192 pages, professionally printed, flat-spined. Receives about 5,000 submissions/year, accepts up to 100. Press run is 2,900 for 1,000 subscribers of which about half are libraries; 1,500 distributed to stores. Subscription: $20. Sample: $7.

How to Submit Submit 3-6 poems at a time. No e-mail submissions. Cover letter (with title of work and genre) is encouraged; SASE required. Reads submissions "only during the Fall semester, September through November, and then contest entries in the Spring." Time between acceptance and publication is "around a year." Occasionally comments on rejected poems or offers suggestions on accepted poems. Responds in up to 4 months. Pays $25/page for the first page and $15 for each subsequent page, 2 contributor's copies, and a one-year subscription. Acquires first North American serial rights, non-exclusive anthology rights, and non-exclusive electronic rights.

Contest/Award Offerings Sponsors the Tim McGinnis Award. "The award, in the amount of $500, is given irregularly to authors of work with a light or humorous touch. We have no separate category of submissions to be considered alone for this award. Instead, any essay, story, or poem we publish will automatically be under consideration for the McGinnis Award. In 2003, we also instituted an Iowa Award in Poetry, Fiction, and Essay." **Entry Fee:** $15. **Postmark Deadline:** February 1. "Submit in January." Outside judges for finalists. Winners will receive $1,000 and publication. Several runners up will also be published. "Around 100 pages of each December issue are set aside for award winners and finalists."

◎ ITALIAN AMERICANA; JOHN CIARDI AWARD (Specialized: ethnic, Italian)

URI/CCE, 80 Washington St., Providence RI 02903-1803. (401)277-5306. Fax: (401)277-5100. E-mail: bonomoal@ital.uri.edu. Website: www.uri.edu/prov/italian/. Established 1974. **Editor:** Carol Bonomo Albright. **Poetry Editor:** Michael Palma.

Magazine Needs *Italian Americana* appears twice/year using 16-20 poems of "no more than 3 pages. No trite nostalgia about grandparents." Has published poetry by Mary Jo Salter and Jay Parini. *Italian Americana* is 150-200 pages, digest-sized, professionally printed, flat-spined, with glossy card cover. Press run is 1,000 for 900 subscribers of which 175 are libraries, 175 shelf sales. Singly copy: $10; subscription: $20/year, $35/2 years. Sample: $6.

How to Submit Submit 3 poems at a time. No previously published poems or simultaneous submissions. Cover letter is not required "but helpful." Name on first page of ms only. Do not submit poetry in July, August, or September. Occasionally comments on rejected poems. Responds in 6 weeks. Acquires first rights. Reviews books of poetry in 600 words, multi-book format. Send materials for review consideration to Prof. John Paul Russo, English Dept., University of Miami, Coral Gables FL 33124.

Contest/Award Offerings Along with the National Italian American Foundation, *Italian Americana* co-sponsors the annual $1,000 John Ciardi Award for Lifetime Contribution to Poetry. *Italian Americana* also presents $250 fiction or memoir award annually; and $1,500 in history prizes.

Advice "Single copies of poems for submissions are sufficient."

🌓 ◎ JACK MACKEREL MAGAZINE (Specialized: surrealism); ROWHOUSE PRESS

P.O. Box 23134, Seattle WA 98102-0434. Established 1992. **Editor:** Greg Bachar.

Magazine Needs *Jack Mackerel*, published quarterly, features poetry, fiction, and art. Has published poetry by Bell Knott, John Rose, and William D. Waltz. *Jack Mackerel* is 40-60 pages, digest-sized, printed on bond paper, with glossy card coverstock, includes b&w illustrations. Press run is 1,000. Subscription: $12. Sample: $5. Make checks payable to Greg Bachar.

How to Submit No previously published poems or simultaneous submissions. Cover letter is preferred. Seldom comments on rejected poems. Responds in one month. Pays 2 contributor's copies.

⚡ ◐ JAHBONE PRESS

1201 Larrabee St., #207, Los Angeles CA 90069. (714)997-6609. Website: www.chapman.edu/comm/english/jahbone/index.html. Established 1991. **Publisher:** Martin Nakell.

Book/Chapbook Needs & How to Submit Jahbone Press publishes experimental fiction and poetry. Wants to see innovative poetry, not traditional poetry. Has published poetry by Pascuale Verdicchio, Leland Hickman, and William Crandall. Publishes a variable number of titles/year. Books usually have a variable number of pages, are offset-printed, perfect-bound paperback with graphics. Query first, with a few sample poems and cover letter with brief bio and publication credits. Accepts simultaneous submissions. No e-mail or disk submissions. Responds to queries and mss in 2 months. Pays 20 author's copies (out of a press run of 1,000). Order sample books "through Small Press Distributors."

◐ ALICE JAMES BOOKS; NEW ENGLAND/NEW YORK AWARD; BEATRICE HAWLEY AWARD

University of Maine at Farmington, 238 Main St., Farmington ME 04938. Phone/fax: (207)778-7071. E-mail: ajb@umf.maine.edu. Website: www.alicejamesbooks.org. Established 1973. **Contest Coordinator:** Aimee Beal.

Book/Chapbook Needs "The mission of Alice James Books, a cooperative poetry press, is to seek out and publish the best contemporary poetry by both established and beginning poets, with particular emphasis on involving poets in the publishing process." Has published poetry by Jane Kenyon, Jean Valentine, B.H. Fairchild, and Matthea Harvey. Publishes flat-spined paperbacks of high quality, both in production and contents; no children's poetry or light verse. Publishes 6 paperback books/year, 80 pages each, in editions of 1,500.

How to Submit "Manuscripts are selected through 2 annual competitions—the Beatrice Hawley Award, a national award for poets living anywhere in the U.S., with no cooperative commitment, and the New England/New York Award, where winners become members of the cooperative with a 3-year commitment to the editorial board. The winners in both competitions receive a cash award of $2,000. Competition deadlines are in early fall and winter. Send SASE or check website for guidelines." No phone queries. Send 2 copies of the ms, SASE for notification, and submission fee. Accepts simultaneous submissions, but "we would like to know immediately when a manuscript is accepted elsewhere." Responds in 4 months.

☑ ◎ **JEWISH CURRENTS (Specialized: themes, politics; history; religious; ethnic/ nationality)**

22 E. 17th St., Suite 601, New York NY 10003-1919. (212)924-5740. Fax: (212)414-2227. E-mail: jewish.currents@verizon.net. Website: www.jewishcurrents.org. Established 1946. **Editor:** Lawrence Bush.

Magazine Needs *Jewish Currents* is a magazine appearing 6 times/year that publishes articles, reviews, fiction, and poetry pertaining to Jewish subjects or presenting a Jewish point of view on an issue of interest, including translations from the Yiddish and Hebrew (original texts should be submitted with translations). *Jewish Currents* is 40 pages, magazine-sized, offset-printed, saddle-stapled. Press run is 2,500 for 2,100 subscribers of which about 10% are libraries. Subscription: $30/year. Sample: $5.

How to Submit Submit one poem at a time, typed, double-spaced, with SASE. Include brief bio with author's publishing history. No previously published poems or simultaneous submissions. Does not accept fax submissions. Cover letter is required. Time between acceptance and publication is up to 2 years. Often comments on rejected poems. Responds within 3 months. Always sends prepublication galleys. Pays 6 contributor's copies. Reviews books of poetry.

Advice "Be intelligent, original, unexpected, comprehensible."

$ ☑ ◎ **JEWISH WOMEN'S LITERARY ANNUAL (Specialized: poetry/fiction by Jewish women)**

820 Second Ave., New York NY 10017. (212)751-9223. Established 1994. **Editor:** Dr. Henny Wenkart.

Magazine Needs *Jewish Women's Literary Annual* appears annually in April and publishes poetry and fiction by Jewish women. Wants "poems by Jewish women on any topic, but of the highest literary quality." Has published poetry by Alicia Ostriker, Savina Teubal, Grace Herman, Enid Dame, Marge Piercy, and Lesléa Newman. *Jewish Women's Literary Annual* is 160 pages, digest-sized, perfect-bound, with a laminated card cover, includes b&w art and photos. Receives about 1,500 poems/year, accepts about 10%. Press run is 1,500 for 650 subscribers. Subscription: $18/3 issues. Sample: $7.50.

How to Submit No previously published poems. No fax submissions. Poems are circulated to an editorial board. Often comments on rejected poems. Guidelines available for SASE. Responds in up to 5 months. Pays 3 contributor's copies plus a small honorarium. Rights remain with the poet.

Advice "Send only your very best. We are looking for humor, as well as other things, but nothing cutesy or smart-aleck. We do *no* politics; prefer topics *other than* 'Holocaust'."

☑ ◎ **JOEL'S HOUSE PUBLICATIONS; WILLIAM DEWITT ROMIG POETRY CONTEST (Specialized: religious/Christian; spirituality; recovery)**

P.O. Box 328, Beach Lake PA 18405-0328. (570)729-8709. Fax: (570)729-7246. E-mail: newbeginmin@ezaccess.net. Website: http://newbeginningmin.org. Established 1997. **Editor:** Kevin T. Coughlin.

Magazine Needs *Joel's House Publications* appears annually in December. Produced by New Beginning Ministry, Inc., a nonprofit corporation, *Joel's House Publications* is a newsletter featuring poetry, articles, and original art. Wants poetry that is related to recovery, spirituality; also Christian poetry. Will consider any length, positive topic, and structure. No poetry which is inappropriately sexually graphic or discriminatory in nature. Has published poetry by Cynthia Brackett-Vincent, John Waddington-Feather, Wendy Apgar, K.F. Homer, Melanie Schurr, and William DeWitt Romig. *Joel's House Publications* is 10-20 pages, digest-sized, offset-printed, saddle-stapled, with card stock cover, includes original and clip art. Receives about 25-50 poems/year, accepts about 25%. Publishes about 25-50 poems/issue. Press run is 1,000 for 100 subscribers; 200 distributed free to mailing list. Subscription: $5/year (one issue). Sample: $2 plus p&h. Make checks payable to New Beginning Ministry, Inc.

How to Submit Submit 3-5 poems at a time. No previously published poems or simultaneous submissions. Accepts submissions by fax, e-mail, postal mail, and on disk. Cover letter is preferred. "Always send a SASE, typed manuscript with name and address on each poem." Reads submissions all year. Time between acceptance and publication is up to one year. Seldom comments on rejected poems. Guidelines available for SASE. Responds in up to 6 weeks. Always sends prepublication galleys. Pays 2 contributor's copies. Acquires first rights.

Contest/Award Offerings Poetry contest (send SASE for details). "Poetry contest will be held every December. The William DeWitt Romig Poetry Award will be given to the poet who best demonstrates life through the art of poetry."

Also Offers Writing retreats (check website for details).

Advice "Keep writing—revise, revise, revise! If you write poetry, you are a poet. Be true to your craft."

☑ THE JOHNS HOPKINS UNIVERSITY PRESS

2715 N. Charles St., Baltimore MD 21218. Website: www.press.jhu.edu. Established 1878. "One of the largest American university presses, Johns Hopkins publishes primarily scholarly books and journals. We do, however, publish short fiction and poetry in the series Johns Hopkins: Poetry and Fiction, edited by John Irwin. Unsolicited submissions are not considered."

🌐 ☑ THE DAVID JONES JOURNAL; THE DAVID JONES SOCIETY

48 Sylvan Way, Sketty, Swansea, W. Glam SA2 9JB Wales. Phone: (01792)206144. Fax: (01792)205305. E-mail: anne.price-owen@sihe.ac.uk. Established 1997. **Editor:** Anne Price-Owen.

Magazine Needs *The David Jones Journal* annually publishes "material related to David Jones, the Great War, mythology, and the visual arts." Wants "poetry which evokes or recalls themes and/or images related to the painter/poet David Jones (1895-1974)." Has published poetry by John Mole, R.S. Thomas, Seamus Heaney, and John Montague. The journal is about 160 pages, digest-sized, camera-ready-printed, perfect-bound, with full-color card cover, includes b&w illustrations. Receives about 12 poems/year, accepts about 8%. Press run is 400 for 300 subscribers. Single copy: $12; subscription: $35. Sample: $10. Make checks payable to The David Jones Society.

How to Submit Submit one poem at a time. Accepts simultaneous submissions; no previously published poems. Accepts e-mail and disk submissions. Cover letter is preferred. Time between acceptance and publication is 6 months. Poems are circulated to an editorial board. "Two editors agree on publication." Occasionally publishes theme issues. Guidelines available by e-mail. Responds in 6 weeks. Sometimes sends prepublication galleys. Pays 2 contributor's copies. Acquires first rights. Reviews books and chapbooks of poetry and other magazines in 750 words, single book format. Open to unsolicited reviews. Send materials for review consideration.

$☑ THE JOURNAL

Dept. of English, Ohio State University, 164 W. 17th Ave., Columbus OH 43210. (614)292-4076. Fax: (614)292-7816. E-mail: thejournal@osu.edu. Website: www.english.ohio-state.edu/journals/the_journal/. Established 1972. **Co-Editors:** Kathy Fagan and Michelle Herman.

Magazine Needs *The Journal* appears twice yearly with reviews, quality fiction and nonfiction, and poetry. "We're open to all forms; we tend to favor work that gives evidence of a mature and sophisticated sense of the language." Has published poetry by Beckian Fritz Goldberg, Terrance Hayes, Bob Hicok, and Linda Bierds. *The Journal* is digest-sized, professionally printed on heavy stock, 128-144 pages, of which about 60 in each issue are devoted to poetry. Receives about 4,000 submissions/year, accepts about 200; has a 12-month backlog. Press run is 1,900. Subscription: $12. Sample: $7.

How to Submit No fax submissions. Occasionally comments on rejected poems. Occasionally publishes theme issues. Responds in up to 3 months. Pays 2 contributor's copies and an honorarium of $25-50 when funds are available. Acquires all rights. Returns rights on publication. Reviews books of poetry.

Advice "However else poets train or educate themselves, they must do what they can to know our language. Too much of the writing we see indicates poets do not, in many cases, develop a feel for the possibilities of language, and do not pay attention to craft. Poets should not be in a rush to publish—until they are ready."

☑ ◎ JOURNAL OF NEW JERSEY POETS (Specialized: regional, New Jersey)

English Dept., County College of Morris, 214 Center Grove Rd., Randolph NJ 07869-2086. (973)328-5471. Fax: (973)328-5425. E-mail: szulauf@ccm.edu. Website: www.ccm.edu/humanities/journal. htm. Established 1976. **Editor:** Sander Zulauf. **Associate Editors:** North Peterson, Gretna Wilkinson, Sara Pfaffenroth, and Debra DeMattio.

Magazine Needs Published annually, *Journal of New Jersey Poets* is "not necessarily about New Jersey—but of, by, and for poets from New Jersey." Wants "serious work that is regional in origin but universal in scope." Has published poetry by Amiri Baraka, X.J. Kennedy, Tina Kelley, Gerald Stern, Renée and Ted Weiss, and J. Chester Johnson. *Journal of New Jersey Poets* is about 72 pages, digest-sized, offset-printed. Press run is 900. Single copy: $10; subscription: $16/2 issues; institutions: $16/issue. Sample: $5.

How to Submit Submit up to 3 poems at a time; SASE with sufficient postage required for return of mss. Accepts e-mail and fax submissions, "but they will not be acknowledged or returned." **Annual deadline:** September 1. Responds in up to one year. Time between acceptance and publication is within one year. Pays 5 contributor's copies and one-year subscription. Acquires first North American serial rights. Only using solicited reviews. Send materials for review consideration.

Advice "Read the *Journal* before submitting. Realize we vote on everything submitted, and rejection is more an indication of the quantity of submissions received and the enormous number of poets submitting quality work."

☑ ◎ JOURNAL OF THE AMERICAN MEDICAL ASSOCIATION (JAMA) (Specialized: health concerns, themes)

515 N. State, Chicago IL 60610. Fax: (312)464-5824. E-mail: charlene_breedlove@ama-assn.org. Website: www.jama.com. Established 1883. **Associate Editor:** Charlene Breedlove.

Magazine Needs *JAMA*, a weekly journal, has a poetry and medicine column and publishes poetry "in some way related to a medical experience, whether from the point-of-view of a health care worker or patient, or simply an observer. No unskilled poetry." Has published poetry by Aimée Grunberger, Floyd Skloot, and Walt McDonald. *JAMA* is magazine-sized, flat-spined, with glossy paper cover. Accepts about 7% of 750 poems received/year. Has 360,000 subscribers of which 369 are libraries. Subscription: $66. Sample: free. "No SASE needed."

How to Submit Accepts simultaneous submissions, if identified; no previously published poems. "I always appreciate inclusion of a brief cover letter with, at minimum, the author's name and address clearly printed. Mention of other publications and special biographical notes are always of interest." Accepts fax submissions (include in body of message with postal address). "Poems sent via fax will be responded to by postal service." Accepts e-mail submissions (pasted into body of message). Publishes theme issues. Themes include AIDS, violence/human rights, tobacco, medical education, access to care, and end-of-life care. "However, we would rather that poems relate obliquely to the theme." List of upcoming themes available on website. Pays one contributor's copy, more by request. "We ask for a signed copyright release, but publication elsewhere is always granted free of charge."

⬡ 🌐 ⬤ K.T. PUBLICATIONS; THE THIRD HALF; KITE BOOKS; KITE MODERN POETS; KITE MODERN WRITERS

16 Fane Close, Stamford, Lincolnshire PE9 1HG England. Established 1989. **Editor:** Kevin Troop.

Magazine Needs *The Third Half* is a literary magazine published regularly. It contains "free-flowing and free-thinking material on most subjects. Open to all ideas and suggestions. No badly written or obscene scribbling." Has published Hannah Welfare, Michael Bangerter, Will Daunt, Tom Kelly, John Light, and Julie Ashpool. *The Third Half* is neatly printed, perfect-bound, with glossy cover, includes line drawings. Showcases 2 poets/issue. "Each poet has 24 pages with illustrations." Press run is 100-500. Single copy: £5.50 in UK. Sample: £10 overseas. Make checks payable to K.T. Publications.

How to Submit Submit 6 poems at a time. No previously published poems. Cover letter is preferred. Time between acceptance and publication "depends on the work and circumstances." **There is a £5 reading fee to cover costs.** Seldom comments on rejected poems. Occasionally publishes theme issues ("as themes present themselves"). Responds in 2 days. Always sends prepublication galleys. Pays 1-6 contributor's copies. "Copyright belongs to the poets/authors throughout."

Book/Chapbook Needs & How to Submit K.T. Publications and Kite Books publish "as much as possible each year" of poetry, short stories, and books for children—"at as high a standard as humanly possible." Books are usually 50-60 pages, A5, perfect-bound, with glossy covers, include art ("always looking for more.") Query first, with up to 6 sample poems and a cover letter with brief bio and publication credits. "Also include suitable SAE—so that I do not end up paying return postage every time."

Also Offers Offers a "reading and friendly help service to writers. Costs are reasonable." Write for details.

Advice "Be patient and undersanding, and try to realize that independent publishers can no longer *afford* to pay for everything *and* make any kind of living. It is not fair to expect."

⬤ ◎ KAIMANA: LITERARY ARTS HAWAII; HAWAII LITERARY ARTS COUNCIL (Specialized: regional)

P.O. Box 11213, Honolulu HI 96828. Website: www.hawaii.edu/hlac. Established 1974. **Editor:** Tony Quagliano.

- Poets published in *Kaimana* have received the Pushcart Prize, the Hawaii Award for Literature, the Stefan Baciu Award, the Cades Award, and the John Unterecker Award.

Magazine Needs *Kaimana*, an annual, is the magazine of the Hawaii Literary Arts Council. Poems with "some Pacific reference are preferred—Asia, Polynesia, Hawaii—but not exclusively." Has published poetry by Howard Nemerov, John Yau, Reuel Denney, Haunani-Kay Trask, Anne Waldman, Joe Balaz, Susan Schultz, and Paul Nelson. *Kaimana* is 64-76 pages, $7\frac{1}{2} \times 10$, saddle-stapled, with high-quality printing. Press run is 1,000 for 600 subscribers of which 200 are libraries. Subscription: $15, includes membership in HLAC. Sample: $10.

How to Submit Cover letter is preferred. Sometimes comments on rejected poems. Responds in "reasonable dispatch." Guidelines available in magazine. Pays 2 contributor's copies.

Advice "Hawaii gets a lot of 'travelling regionalists,' visiting writers with inevitably superficial observations. We also get superb visiting observers who are careful craftsmen anywhere. *Kaimana* is interested in the latter, to complement our own best Hawaii writers."

$◎ KALEIDOSCOPE: EXPLORING THE EXPERIENCE OF DISABILITY THROUGH LITERATURE AND FINE ARTS (Specialized: disability themes)

701 S. Main St., Akron OH 44311-1019. (330)762-9755. Fax: (330)762-0912. E-mail: mshiplett@uds akron.org. Website: www.udsakron.org. Established 1979. **Editor-in-Chief:** Gail Willmott.

Magazine Needs Published in January and July, *Kaleidoscope* is based at United Disability Services, a nonprofit agency. Poetry should deal with the experience of disability, but is not limited to that when the writer has a disability. *"Kaleidoscope* is interested in high-quality poetry with vivid, believable images, and evocative language. Works should not use stereotyping, patronizing, or offending language about disability." Has published poetry by Sandra J. Lindow, Gerald R. Wheeler, Desire Vail, and Sheryl L. Nelms. *Kaleidoscope* is 64 pages, magazine-sized, professionally printed, saddle-stapled, with 4-color semigloss card cover, includes b&w art. Press run is 1,500 for libraries, social service agencies, health-care professionals, universities, and individual subscribers. Single copy: $6; subscription: $10 individual, $15 agency. Sample: $6.

How to Submit Submit up to 6 poems at a time. Send photocopies with SASE for return of work. Accepts previously published poems and simultaneous submissions, "as long as we are notified in both instances." Accepts fax and e-mail submissions. Cover letter is required. All submissions must be accompanied by an autobiographical sketch and "should be double-spaced, with pages numbered, and with author's name on each page." **Deadlines:** March 1 and August 1. Publishes theme issues. Themes for 2005 include Mental Illness (January) and Parents and Children (July). Upcoming themes and guidelines available for SASE, by fax, by e-mail, and on website. Upcoming themes also announced in magazine. Responds in 3 weeks; acceptance or rejection may take 6 months. Pays $10-25 plus 2 contributor's copies. Rights return to author upon publication. Staff reviews books of poetry. Send materials for review consideration to Gail Willmott, editor-in-chief.

$⊘ ◎ KALLIOPE, A JOURNAL OF WOMEN'S LITERATURE & ART (Specialized: women writers & artists); SUE SANIEL ELKIND POETRY CONTEST

South Campus, 11901 Beach Blvd., Jacksonville FL 32246. (904)646-2081. Website: www.fccj.edu/kalliope. Established 1978. **Editor:** Mary Sue Koeppel.

Magazine Needs Appearing in fall and spring, *Kalliope* is a literary/visual arts journal published by Florida Community College at Jacksonville; the emphasis is on women writers and artists. "We like the idea of poetry as a sort of artesian well—there's one meaning that's clear on the surface and another deeper meaning that comes welling up from underneath. We'd like to see more poetry from Black, Hispanic, and Native American women. Nothing sexist, racist, or conventionally sentimental." Has published poetry by Marge Piercy, Ruth Stone, Jill Bialosky, Eleanor Wilner, Maxine Kumin, and Tess Gallagher. *Kalliope* calls itself "a journal of women's literature and art" and publishes fiction, interviews, and visual art in addition to poetry. *Kalliope* is about 120 pages, $7^1/4 \times 8^1/4$, flat-spined, handsomely printed on white stock, with glossy card cover, includes b&w photographs of works of art. Press run is 1,600 for 400-500 subscribers of which 100 are libraries, 800 shelf sales. Subscription: $16/year or $27/2 years. Sample: $9.

How to Submit Submit poems in batches of 3-5 with brief bio note, phone number, and address. No previously published poems. Accepts submissions by postal mail only. SASE required. Reads submissions September through April only. Because all submissions are read by several members of the editing staff, response time is usually up to 6 months. Publication will be within 6 months after acceptance. Criticism is provided "when time permits and the author has requested it." Publishes theme issues. Guidelines and upcoming themes available for SASE or on website. Pays $10 if grant money available, subscription if not, plus 2 contributor's copies. Acquires first publication rights. Reviews books of poetry, "but we prefer groups of books in one review." Send materials for review consideration.

Contest/Award Offerings Sponsors the Sue Saniel Elkind Poetry Contest. 1st Prize: $1,000; runners up published in *Kalliope*. **Deadline:** November 1. Details available for SASE or on website.

Advice *"Kalliope* is a carefully stitched patchwork of how women feel, what they experience, and what they have come to know and understand about their lives . . . a collection of visions from or about women all over the world. Send for a sample copy, to see what appeals to us, or better yet, subscribe!"

◪ KARAMU

Dept. of English, Eastern Illinois University, Charleston IL 61920. Established 1966. **Editor:** Olga Abella.

- *Karamu* has received grants from the Illinois Arts Council, and has won recognition and money awards in the IAC Literary Awards competition.

Magazine Needs *Karamu* is an annual, usually appearing in May, whose "goal is to provide a forum for the best contemporary poetry and fiction that comes our way. We especially like to print the works of new writers. We like to see poetry that shows a good sense of what's being done with poetry currently. We like poetry that builds around real experiences, real images, and real characters, and that avoids abstraction, overt philosophizing, and fuzzy pontifications. In terms of form, we prefer well-structured free verse, poetry with an inner, sub-surface structure as opposed to, let's say, the surface structure of rhymed quatrains. We have definite preferences in terms of style and form, but no such preferences in terms of length or subject matter. Purpose, however, is another thing. We don't have much interest in the openly didactic poem. We don't want poems that preach against or for some political or religious viewpoint. The poem should first be a poem." Has published poetry by Robyn Art, Stephanie Dickinson, James Doyle, Taylor Graham, Naton Leslie, and Simon Perchik. *Karamu* is 120 pages, digest-sized, handsomely printed (narrow margins), with matte cover, includes attractive b&w art. Receives submissions from about 700 poets each year, accepts 40-50 poems. Press run is 500 for 300 subscribers of which 15 are libraries. Single copy: $7.50. Sample: $6/2 back issues.

How to Submit Poems—in batches of no more than 5—may be submitted to Olga Abella. "We don't much like, but do accept, simultaneous submissions. We read September 1 through March 1 only; for fastest decision, submit January through March. Poets should not bother to query. We critique a few of the better poems. We want the poet to consider our comments and then submit new work." Time between acceptance and publication is up to one year. Occasionally publishes theme issues. Upcoming themes and guidelines available for SASE. Pays one contributor's copy. Acquires first serial rights.

Advice "Follow the standard advice: Know your market. Read contemporary poetry and the magazines you want to be published in. Be patient."

◪ KATYDID BOOKS

1 Balsa Rd., Santa Fe NM 87508. Website: http://katydidbooks.com. Established 1973. **Editors/ Publishers:** Karen Hargreaves-Fitzsimmons and Thomas Fitzsimmons.

Book/Chapbook Needs & How to Submit Katydid Books publishes 2 paperbacks and 2 hardbacks/ year. "We publish 2 series of poetry: Asian Poetry in Translation (distributed by University of Hawaii Press) and American Poets." Currently not accepting submissions.

◻ ◎ KELSEY REVIEW (Specialized: regional, Mercer County)

Mercer County Community College, P.O. Box B, Trenton NJ 08690. (609)586-4800, ext. 3326. Fax: (609)586-2318. E-mail: kelsey.review@mccc.edu. Website: www.mccc.edu. Established 1988. **Editor-in-Chief:** Robin Schore.

Magazine Needs *Kelsey Review* is an annual published in September by Mercer County Community College. It serves as "an outlet for literary talent of people living and working in Mercer County, New Jersey only." Has no specifications as to form, length, subject matter, or style, but does not want to see poetry about "kittens and puppies." Has published poetry by Linda Arntzenius, Vida Chu, Helen Gorenstein, Betty Lies, James Richardson, and John Timpane. *Kelsey Review* is about 80 glossy pages, 7×11, with paper cover, includes line drawings, no ads. Receives about 60 submissions/year, accepts 6-10. Press run is 2,000. All distributed free to contributors, area libraries, bookstores, and schools.

How to Submit Submit up to 6 poems at a time, typed. No previously published poems or simultaneous submissions. No fax or e-mail submissions. **Deadline:** May 1. Always comments on rejected poems. Guidelines available by e-mail. Responds in June of each year. Pays 5 contributor's copies. All rights revert to authors.

☑ KENNESAW REVIEW; DON RUSS POETRY PRIZE

Dept. of English, Building 27, Kennesaw State University, 1000 Chastain Rd., Kennesaw GA 30144-5591. E-mail: kr@kennesaw.edu. Website: www.kennesaw.edu/kr. Established 1987 as print journal; 2002 online. **Managing Editors:** Amy Whitney and Maren Blake.

Magazine Needs *Kennesaw Review* is an online literary journal appearing 2 times/year, publishing poetry, short fiction, essays, and reviews. Wants exceptional poetry, short fiction, and essays. "Our goal is to publish the best we can find, whether by experienced or emerging writers. We are open to both formal poems and free verse." Has published poetry by Kathryn Kirkpatrick, Luivette Resto, and Matthew W. Schmeer. *Kennesaw Review* is published online. Publishes about 15 poems/issue.

How to Submit Submit up to 5 poems at a time. Accepts simultaneous submissions if noted in cover letter; no previously published poems. No e-mail or disk submissions. Cover letter is preferred. "Submissions are by hard copy. Include your name, address, telephone number, e-mail address, and SASE for our response. Manuscripts must be typed, no smaller than 12 point. Do not send disks or e-mail attachments. Submissions will not be returned and will be recycled; therefore, do not send us your only copy." Reads submissions year round. Time between acceptance and publication is 3-6 months. Poems are circulated to an editorial board. "Poems are read and discussed in weekly editorial meetings." Seldom comments on rejected poems. Occasionally publishes theme issues. List of upcoming themes and guidelines available on website. Responds in 2 months. "The *Kennesaw Review* reserves rights for first online publication and for possible publication as a compiled annual edition in CD or print format, or both. Copyright remains with author." Reviews books and chapbooks of poetry and other magazines/journals in 500 words, single book format. Send materials for review consideration to Jeff Cebulski, review editor.

Contest/Award Offerings Annual Don Russ Poetry Prize. Awards $500 and publication for the best poem submitted to the competition. Submit 3-5 unpublished poems. **Entry fee:** $15. **Deadline:** January 30. For complete guidelines, see website.

Also Offers Possible print or CD annual.

Advice "Review the poetry on our site before submitting your work for our consideration."

$☑ THE KENYON REVIEW; THE WRITERS WORKSHOP

Kenyon College, Gambier OH 43022. (740)427-5208. Fax: (740)427-5417. E-mail: kenyonreview@kenyon.edu. Website: www.KenyonReview.org. Established 1939. **Editor:** David Lynn.

Magazine Needs *Kenyon Review* is a quarterly review containing poetry, fiction, essays, criticism, reviews, and memoirs. It features all styles, forms, lengths, and subject matters, but this market is more closed than others because of the volume of submissions typically received during each reading cycle. Has published poetry by Billy Collins, Diane Ackerman, John Kinsella, Carol Muske-Dukes, Diane di Prima, and Seamus Heaney. *Kenyon Review* is 180 pages, digest-sized, flat-spined. Receives about 4,000 submissions/year, has a one-year backlog. Publishes 50 pages of poetry/issue. Press run is 5,000 for both subscribers and newsstand sales. Sample: $10 (includes postage).

How to Submit Writers may contact by phone, fax, or e-mail, but may submit mss by postal mail only. Typical reading period is September 1 through March 31. Responds in 3 months. Pays $15/page plus 2 contributor's copies. Acquires first North American serial rights. Reviews books of poetry in 2,500-7,000 words, single or multi-book format. "Reviews are primarily solicited—potential reviewers should inquire first."

Also Offers Also sponsors The Writers Workshop, an annual 8-day event in June. Location: the campus of Kenyon College. Average attendance is 12 per class. Open to writers of fiction, nonfiction, and poetry. Conference is designed to provide intensive conversation, exercises, and detailed readings of participants' work. Past instructors have included Linda Gregerson, Jonet McAdams, Allison Joseph, P.F. Kluge, Rebecca McClanahan, Margot Livesey, Erin McGrow, Claire Messud, Nancy Zafris, and David Baker. College and non-degree graduate credit is offered. Application available for SASE and on website. Early application is encouraged as the workshops are limited.

Advice "Editor recommends reading recent issues to become familiar with the type and quality of writing being published before submitting your work."

☑ ◎ THE KERF (Specialized: animals, nature/ecology)

College of the Redwoods, 883 W. Washington Blvd., Crescent City CA 95531. Established 1995. **Editor:** Ken Letko.

Magazine Needs *The Kerf*, annually published in May, features "poetry that speaks to the environment and humanity." Wants "poetry that exhibits an environmental consciousness." Has published poetry by Ruth Daigon, Meg Files, James Grabill, and George Keithley. *The Kerf* is 40 pages, digest-sized, printed via Docutech, saddle-stapled, with CS2 coverstock. Receives about 2,000 poems/year, accepts up to 3%. Press run is 400, 150 shelf sales; 100 distributed free to contributors and writing centers. Sample: $5. Make checks payable to College of the Redwoods.

How to Submit Submit up to 5 poems (up to 7 pages) at a time. No previously published poems or simultaneous submissions. Reads submissions January 15 through March 31 only. Time between acceptance and publication is 3 months. Poems are circulated to an editorial board. "Our editors debate (argue for or against) the inclusion of each manuscript." Seldom comments on rejected poems. Guidelines available for SASE. Responds in 2 months. Sometimes sends prepublication galleys. Pays one contributor's copy. Acquires first North American serial rights.

☑ KING LOG

E-mail: davidcase@earthlink.net. Website: www.angelfire.com/il/kinglog. Established 1997. **Editors:** David Starkey, Carolie Parker-Lopez, David Case.

Magazine Needs *King Log* appears quarterly. Wants "accomplished poetry by American and Anglophone writers, whether experimental, confessional, or formalist. We are especially interested in poetry that captures the confusion of work/writing, romantic attachments, popular and high culture, history, and political and philosophical idealism and disillusion—comedy, irony, and passion." Does not want gushy, sentimental, macho, or precious work. Has published poetry by Jim Daniels, Barry Spacks, Katherine Swiggart, Walt McDonald, Evelyn Perry, and Paul Willis. *King Log* is 30 pages, published online with illustrations from *Aesop's Fables*. Receives about 400 poems/year, accepts about 60. Publishes about 20 poems/issue.

How to Submit Submit 3-5 poems at a time. No previously published poems or simultaneous submissions. Accepts e-mail submissions; no disk submissions. Cover letter is required. Reads submissions all year. Time between acceptance and publication is 3 months. Poems are circulated to an editorial board. "Development of consensus among 3 editors who, broadly, share a sensibility and do not often disagree." Seldom comments on rejected poems. Guidelines available on website. Responds in 3 weeks. No payment. Acquires one-time rights.

$☑ THE KIT-CAT REVIEW; GAVIN FLETCHER MEMORIAL PRIZE FOR POETRY

244 Halstead Ave., Harrison NY 10528-3611. (914)835-4833. Established 1998. **Editor:** Claudia Fletcher.

Magazine Needs *The Kit-Cat Review* appears quarterly and is "named after the 18th century Kit-Cat Club whose members included Addison, Steele, Congreve, Vanbrugh, Garth, etc. Its purpose is to promote/discover excellence and originality." Wants quality work—traditional, modern, experimental. Has published poetry by Coral Hull, Virgil Suárez, Margret J. Hoehn, Louis Phillips, Chayym Zeldis, and Romania's Nobel Prize nominee, Marin Sorescu. *The Kit-Cat Review* is 75 pages, digest-sized, laser-printed/photocopied, saddle-stapled, with colored card cover, includes b&w illustrations. Receives about 1,000 poems/year. Press run is 500 for 200 subscribers. Subscription: $25. Sample: $7. Make checks payable to Claudia Fletcher.

How to Submit Submit any number of poems at a time. Accepts previously published poems and simultaneous submissions. "Cover letter should contain any relevant bio." Time between acceptance and publication is 2 months. Responds within 2 months. Pays up to $100/poem and 2 contributor's copies. Acquires first or one-time rights.

Contest/Award Offerings Sponsors the annual Gavin Fletcher Memorial Prize for Poetry, an award of $1,000. **Deadline:** June 31 for publication in autumn issue.

KNOPF

1745 Broadway, New York NY 10019. Website: www.randomhouse.com/knopf. **Contact:** The Editors. Over the years Knopf has been one of the most important and distinguished publishers of poetry in the United States. Has published poetry by Cynthia Zarin, John Hollander, Kevin Young, Marge Piercy, and Edward Hirsch.

KOTAPRESS; KOTAPRESS POETRY JOURNAL

(206)251-6706. E-mail: editor@kotapress.com. Website: www.kotapress.com. Established 1999. **Editor:** Kara L.C. Jones.

Magazine Needs *KotaPress Poetry Journal* is a monthly online e-zine "seeking to publish new as well as seasoned poets. We seek to publish the best poetry that comes to us, and then to support the poet in whatever ways he or she may need. While form is sometimes important, we are more interested in content. We want to know what you have to say. We are interested in the honesty and conviction of your poems. Give us accessibility over form any day. Seeing tankas, for instance, in 5-7-5-7-7 form can be interesting and accessible, but do not send us words that you have stuffed into a form just to say you could write in form." Has published poetry by Charles Fishman, Ruth Daigon, Claudia Mauro, Patricia Wellingham-Jones, and John Fox.

How to Submit Submit 4 poems at a time. Accepts previously published poems; no simultaneous submissions. Accepts e-mail submissions *only* (pasted into body of message; no attachments). Cover letter is required. "Previously published poems must include credit to prior publication. Please include bio info in e-mail message. Be sure to give us contact info so we can get back to you." Accepts submissions year round on a rolling basis. Time between acceptance and publication is up to 2 months. Guidelines available on website. Responds in 2 months. Acquires one-time electronic rights and archive rights. "We do not remove works from our archives."

Contest/Award Offerings "We offer an annual contest that results in print books, so please see Poetry section of website for guidelines.

Also Offers Because we are an Internet magazine, we are able to provide writers with resources and support through links, articles, and services—as well as producing a high-quality poetry journal. Please see our website to find out more about us and about what we offer. We look forward to hearing from you and reading your poetry."

Advice "If you want to be a published writer, you must submit your work again and again and again to anywhere and everywhere. For every 100 rejections, you will quite possibly get one or 2 acceptances, but you won't get rejected or accepted if you don't submit in the first place!"

KRAX (Specialized: humor)

63 Dixon Lane, Leeds, Yorkshire LS12 4RR England. Established 1971. **Editor:** Andy Robson.

Magazine Needs *Krax* appears twice/year and publishes contemporary poetry from Britain and America. Wants "poetry that is light-hearted and witty; original ideas; 2,000 words maximum. Undesired: haiku, religious, or topical politics." All forms and styles considered. Has published poetry by Julia Darling, Mike Hoy, Gaia Holmes, and Rupert Mallin. *Krax* is 64 pages, digest-sized, offset-printed, saddle-stapled, includes b&w cartoons and graphics. Receives up to 1,000 submissions/year, accepts about 6%, has a 2- to 3-year backlog. Publishes 30 pages of poetry/issue. Single copy: £3.50 ($7); subscription: £10 ($20). Sample: $1 (75p).

How to Submit "Submit maximum of 6 pieces. Writer's name on same sheet as poem. Sorry, we cannot accept material on disk. SASE or SAE with IRC encouraged but not vital." No previously published poems or simultaneous submissions. Brief cover letter is preferred. Responds in 2 months. Pays one contributor's copy. Reviews books of poetry (brief, individual comments; no outside reviews). Send materials for review consideration.

Advice "Don't try to format a short idea; either write a short poem or find another topic."

KWIL KIDS PUBLISHING; MR. MARQUIS' MUSELETTER (Specialized: children/teen/young adult)

Box 29556, Maple Ridge BC V2X 2V0 Canada. E-mail: kmarquis@sd42.ca. Established 1996. **Editor:** Kwil or Mr. Marquis.

Magazine Needs *Mr. Marquis' Museletter* is a quarterly newsletter "publishing stories/poems to encourage and celebrate writers, readers, and researchers." Wants poetry that is "gentle; with compassionate truth and beauty; peace; humor; for children, by children, about children. No profane, hurtful, violent, political, or satirical work. Has published poetry by Matthew Stasinski Schnitzler, Annunziata Militano, Raanan Burd, Pamela Bond, Bryan Wilson, and Cathy Porter. *Mr. Marquis' Museletter* is 10 pages, includes b&w graphics. Receives about 400 poems/year, accepts about 80%. Publish 8 poems/issue. Press run is 200 for 150 subscribers. Subscription: $20, includes newsletter, newspaper, and greeting card publishing opportunities; a free subscription to Kwil's e-mail poetry list; reading, writing, and publishing tips; and encouragement galore. Sample: SASE (or SAE and IRC) and $2. Make checks payable to Mr. Marquis.

How to Submit Submit 5 poems at a time. Include SASE and parent's signature. Cover letter is preferred. Accepts e-mail submissions (pasted into body of message; no attachments). Submit seasonal poems 3 months in advance. Time between acceptance and publication is up to 3 months. Always comments on rejected poems. "Kwil always provides encouragement and personalized response with SASE (or SAE and IRC)." Occasionally publishes theme issues. Guidelines available for SASE (Canadian-stamped envelope, or IRC, or $1 for Canadian postage) or by e-mail. Responds in April, August, and December. Pays one contributor's copy. Acquires one-time rights.

Advice "Submit best and submit often; provide Canadian-stamped envelope; sign permission card; have fun writing."

LA PETITE ZINE

E-mail: lapetitezine@yahoo.com. Website: www.lapetitezine.org. **Co-Editors:** Jeffrey Salane and Danielle Pafunda. Member: CLMP.

• "Heidi Peppermint's 'Real Toads,' published in Issue #13, will appear in *The Best American Poetry 2004*, edited by Lyn Hejinian and series editor David Lehman."

Magazine Needs *La Petite Zine* is an online journal appearing about 3 times/year and featuring "new and established voices in poetry, fiction, creative nonfiction, and cross-genre work. While we do not offer parameters for content, form, or style, we ask that writers submit high-quality, well-crafted work. If it's not your best, don't send it." Does not want "writing that employs cliché in place of exploration of language, demonstrates an ignorance of contemporary poetry/literature or (especially) our publication, and/or relies on the sentimentality of its readers." Has published poetry by Joshua Beckman, Tina Celona, Arielle Greenberg, David Lehman, Joyelle McSweeney, and Jonah Winter. *La Petite Zine*'s home page "indexes all authors for each specific issue and offers links to past issues, as well as information about the journal, its interests and editors, and links to other sites. Art and graphics are supplied by Web del Sol. Additionally, we publish graphic poems, excerpts from graphic novels, and the like." Receives about 2,000 poems/year, accepts about 150 (approximately 8%). Publishes about 50 poems/issue. Free online; "there is no subscription, but readers are invited to sign up for e-mail notification of new issues at the submission address."

How to Submit Submit 3-5 poems at a time ("please adhere to this guideline"). Accepts simultaneous submissions, "but please notify us immediately if poems are accepted elsewhere"; no previously published poems. Accepts e-mail submissions (pasted into body of message or as attachment, Word document (preferred) or Rich Text Format); no disk submissions. Cover letter is required, with brief bio listing previous publications. "If submitting poems as an attachment, please include all poems in the same document. If we do not accept your work, please wait at least 6 months before resubmitting." Reads submissions all year. Time between acceptance and publication is up to 6 months. "The 2 co-editors make all decisions by consensus." Seldom comments on rejected poems. Occasionally publishes theme issues. List of upcoming themes available on website, when applicable. Guidelines available on website. Responds in up to 2 months "ideally." Always sends electronic prepublication galleys. No payment. Acquires first rights. Reviews books and chapbooks of poetry in 500 words, single and multi-book format. Send materials for review consideration to Danielle Pafunda, Park Hall, Room 254, English Dept., University of Georgia, Athens GA 30602.

Advice "No matter what sort of writer you are, you should read constantly and always become familiar with publications to which you are submitting: Who are the editors? Who have they published in the past? Is there a discernible aesthetic? Do they take chances on new voices? Always send your best, finished work, accompanied by a brief cover letter, including a short bio with any past publications (for those editors who encourage cover letters). Above all, do not let rejections discourage you. If they include comments, decide whether or not those comments are useful to your poetry, but don't let rejection dictate your work. Find those readers who can help you evolve as a writer and refine your voice."

Each cover, such as this one designed by Chris Majerik, features a lake-related image. The photo by Matt Stevenson "impressed us with the way the hard-edged lines of the pier play against the imprecise but dramatic sky".

☑ LAKE EFFECT

School of Humanities & Social Sciences, Penn State Erie, Station Rd., Erie PA 16563-1501. (814)898-6281. Fax: (814)898-6032. E-mail: gol1 @psu.edu. Established 1978 as *Tempus*; renamed *Lake Effect* in 2001. **Editor-in-Chief:** George Looney. Member: CLMP.

Magazine Needs *Lake Effect* is published annually in March/April "to provide an aesthetic venue for writing that uses language precisely to forge a genuine and rewarding experience for our readers. *Lake Effect* wishes to publish writing that rewards more than one reading, and to present side-by-side the voices of established and emerging writers." Wants "poetry aware of, and wise about, issues of craft in forming language that is capable of generating a rich and rewarding reading experience." Does not want "sentimental verse reliant on clichés." Has published poetry by Virgil Suárez, Eric Pankey, Fleda Brown, Dionisio D. Martinez, and Al Maginnes. *Lake Effect* is 150 pages, digest-sized, offset-printed, perfect-bound, with gloss by-flat film lamination cover. Receives about 1,500 poems/year, accepts about 3%. Publishes about 25-30 poems/issue. Press run is 800 for 300 shelf sales; 300 distributed free to contributors and writing programs. Single copy: $6; subscription: $6. Make checks payable to The Pennsylvania State University.

How to Submit Submit 3-5 poems at a time. No previously published poems; accepts simultaneous submissions. No fax, e-mail, or disk submissions. Cover letter is required. Reads submissions year round. Time between acceptance and publication is up to 4 months. Poems are circulated to an editorial board. "The poetry staff reads the poems, meets and discusses them to come to a consensus. Poetry editor, along with editor-in-chief, makes final decisions." Seldom comments on rejected poems. Guidelines available in magazine. Responds in up to 4 months. Pays 2 contributor's copies. Acquires first North American serial rights.

Advice "*Lake Effect* strives to provide an attractive venue for the good work of both established and emerging writers. We care about the integrity of poetry, and care for the poems we accept."

$ LANDFALL: NEW ZEALAND ARTS AND LETTERS (Specialized: regional)

University of Otago Press, P.O. Box 56, Dunedin, New Zealand. Phone: 0064 3 479 8807. Fax: 0064 3 479 8385. E-mail: landfall@otago.ac.nz. Established 1947. Originally published by Caxton Press, then by Oxford University Press, now published by University of Otago Press. **Editor:** Justin Paton.

Magazine Needs *Landfall* appears twice/year (in May and November). "Apart from occasional commissioned features on aspects of international literature, *Landfall* focuses primarily on New Zealand literature and arts. It publishes new fiction, poetry, commentary, and interviews with New Zealand artists and writers, and reviews of New Zealand books." Single issue: NZ $24.95; subscription: NZ $45 for 2 issues for New Zealand subscribers, A $30 for Australian subscribers, US $30 for other overseas subscribers.

How to Submit Submissions must be typed and include SASE. "Once accepted, contributions should, if possible, also be submitted on disk." No fax or e-mail submissions. Publishes theme issues. Guidelines and upcoming themes available for SASE. New Zealand poets should write for further information.

LANGUAGE AND CULTURE.NET (Specialized: bilingual/foreign language translations)

4000 Pimlico Dr., Suite 114-192, Pleasanton CA 94588. E-mail: review@languageandculture.net. Website: www.languageandculture.net. Established 2001. **Editor:** Liz Fortini.

Magazine Needs *Language and Culture.net* is a quarterly, "exclusively online publication of contemporary poetry." Also includes translations: Spanish, French, German, Portuguese, Italian, and Russian. Other languages under review. Translated poems will be published side by side with the English. No restrictions on form. Has published poetry by Susan Wilson and Sophie Bousset. Receives a varied number of poems/year. Publishes about 5-20 poems/issue.

How to Submit Submit 3 poems at a time. Line length for poetry is 70 maximum. Accepts previously published poems and simultaneous submissions. Accepts e-mail submissions (pasted into body of message; no attachments); no fax or disk submissions. "Return e-mail address must be included." Cover letter is optional. Reads submissions "yearly." Time between acceptance and publication is up to 3 months. Poems are circulated to an editorial board. Sometimes comments on rejected poems. Guidelines available on website. No payment. Acquires one-time rights.

Contest/Award Offerings *Language and Culture.net* Annual Poetry Contest. Awards $50. Submit up to 3 poems, maximum 40 lines each. May be dual-language; include English translation. Guidelines available on website. **Entry fee:** $5 for up to 3 poems. **Postmark deadline:** March 15, 2005.

Advice "Enrich your lives with different perspectives and poetry styles."

LAPWING PUBLICATIONS (Specialized: ethnic/nationality, Ireland); HA'PENNY PRESS; HA'PENNY PRIZE

1 Ballysillan Dr., Belfast BT14 8HQ United Kingdom. Phone/fax: 028 90 295 800. E-mail: catherine.g

retg1@NTLWorld.com. Website: www.irishreader.com/Pubs/Lapwing.htm. Established 1989. **Editor:** Dennis Greig.

Book/Chapbook Needs Lapwing publishes "emerging Irish poets and poets domiciled in Ireland, plus the new work of a suitable size by established Irish writers." Publishes 6-10 chapbooks/year. Wants poetry of all kinds. But, "no crass political, racist, sexist propaganda, even of a positive or 'pc' tenor." Has published Mary O'Donnell (*September Elegies*), Niall McGrath (*Parity*), John Stevenson (*Cherry Tree*), Mary M. Geoghegan (*Bright Unknown*), Philip Quaite (*Life of Zagoba*), and Zlatko Tomicic (*Croatia My Love*). Chapbooks are usually 44-52 pages, A5, Docutech-printed, saddle-stapled, with colored card covers, include occasional line art.

How to Submit "Submit 6 poems in the first instance; depending on these, an invitation to submit more may follow." Accepts simultaneous submissions; no previously published poems. Accepts e-mail submissions (pasted into body of message). Cover letter is required. Poems are circulated to an editorial board. "All submissions receive a first reading. If these poems have minor errors or faults, the writer is advised. If poor quality, the poems are returned. Those 'passing' first reading are retained, and a letter of conditional offer is sent." Often comments on rejected poems. Responds to queries in one month; to mss in 2 months. Pays 25 author's copies (out of a press run of 250).

Also Offers Sponsors the new imprint Ha'Penny Press and Prize. Send SASE for details. "Irishreader. com provides listing and info pages."

Advice "Clean; check spelling, grammar, punctuation, layout (i.e., will it fit a book page?); clear text. Due to limited resources, material will be processed well in advance of any estimated publishing date. All accepted material is strictly conditional on resources available, no favoritism. The Irish domestic market is small, the culture is hierarchical, poet/personality culture predominates, literary democracy is limited."

$☐ ◎ LEADING EDGE (Specialized: science fiction/fantasy)

3146 JKHB, Provo UT 84602. E-mail: tle@byu.edu Website: http://tle.clubs.byu.edu. **Editor:** Kristina Kugler.

Magazine Needs *Leading Edge* is a magazine appearing 2 times/year. Wants "high-quality poetry reflecting both literary value and popular appeal, and dealing with science fiction and fantasy. We accept traditional science fiction and fantasy poetry, but we like innovative stuff. No graphic sex, violence, or profanity." Has published poetry by Michael Collings, Tracy Ray, Susan Spilecki, and Bob Cook. *Leading Edge* is 170 pages, digest-sized, includes art. Accepts about 4 out of 60 poems received/year. Press run is 500 for 100 subscribers, 10 of which are libraries, 400 shelf sales. Single copy: $4.95; subscription: $12.50 (3 issues). Sample: $4.95.

How to Submit Submit one or more poems with name and address at the top of each page. "Please include SASE with every submission." No simultaneous submissions or previously published poems. No e-mail submissions. Cover letter is preferred; include name, address, phone number, length of poem, title, and type of poem. Guidelines available for SASE. Responds in one month. Always sends prepublication galleys. Pays $10 for the first 4 typeset pages, $1.50 for each additional page, plus 2 contributor's copies. Acquires first North American serial rights.

Advice "Poetry is given equal standing with fiction; it is not treated as filler, but as art."

◎ LIFTOUTS MAGAZINE; PRELUDIUM PUBLISHERS

520 SE Fifth St., Suite 4, Minneapolis MN 55414-1628. Fax: (612)305-0655. E-mail: barcass@mr.net. Established 1971. **Poetry Editor:** Barry Casselman. *Liftouts* appears irregularly as a "publisher of experimental literary work and work of new writers in translation from other languages." Currently not accepting unsolicited material.

◎ LIGHT

Box 7500, Chicago IL 60680. Website: www.lightquarterly.com. Established 1992. **Editor:** John Mella.

Magazine Needs *Light* is a quarterly of "light and occasional verse, satire, wordplay, puzzles, cartoons, and line art." Does not want "greeting card verse, cloying or sentimental verse." *Light* is 64 pages, perfect-bound, includes art and graphics. Single copy: $6; subscription: $20. Sample: $5 (back issues) with an additional $2 for first-class postage.

How to Submit Submit one poem/page, with name, address, poem title, and page number on each page. No previously published poems or simultaneous submissions. Seldom comments on rejected poems. Guidelines available for #10 SASE. Responds in 3 months or less. Always sends prepublication galleys. Pays 2 contributor's copies to domestic contributors, one to foreign contributors. Send materials for review consideration.

✒ ◎ LILLIPUT REVIEW (Specialized: form, 10 lines or less)

282 Main St., Pittsburgh PA 15201-2807. Website: http://donw714.tripod.com/lillieindex.html. Established 1989. **Editor:** Don Wentworth.

Magazine Needs *Lilliput* is a tiny (4½×3.6 or 3½×4¼), 12- to 16-page magazine, appearing irregularly and using poems in any style or form no longer than 10 lines. Has published *The Future Tense of Ash* by Miriam Sagan and *No Choice* by Cid Corman, as well as poetry by Pamela Miller Ness, Albert Huffstickler, Ed Baker, and Jen Besemer. *Lilliput Review* is laser-printed on colored paper and stapled. Press run is 350. Sample: $1 or SASE. Make checks payable to Don Wentworth.

How to Submit Submit up to 3 poems at a time. "Currently, every fourth issue is a broadside featuring the work of one particular poet." Editor comments on submissions "occasionally—always try to establish human contact." Guidelines available for SASE. Responds within 3 months. Pays 2 contributor's copies/poem. Acquires first rights.

Book/Chapbook Needs & How to Submit The Modest Proposal Chapbook Series began in 1994, publishing one chapbook/year, 18-24 pages in length. Chapbook submissions are by invitation only. Query with standard SASE. Sample chapbook: $3. Chapbook publications include *Half Emptied Out* by Lonnie Sherman.

Advice "A note above my desk reads 'Clarity & resonance, not necessarily in that order.' The perfect poem for *Lilliput Review* is simple in style and language, and elusive/allusive in meaning and philosophy. *Lilliput Review* is open to all short poems in approach and theme, including any of the short Eastern forms, traditional or otherwise."

✒ LIMITED EDITIONS PRESS; ART: MAG

P.O. Box 70896, Las Vegas NV 89170. (702)734-8121. E-mail: magman@iopener.net. Established 1982. **Editor:** Peter Magliocco.

Magazine Needs *ART:MAG* has "become, due to economic and other factors, more limited to a select audience of poets as well as readers. We seek to expel the superficiality of our factitious culture, in all its drive-thru, junk-food-brain, commercial-ridden extravagance—and stylize a magazine of hard-line aesthetics, where truth and beauty meet on a vector not shallowly drawn. Conforming to this outlook is an operational policy of seeking poetry from solicited poets primarily, though unsolicited submissions will be read, considered, and perhaps used infrequently. Sought from the chosen is a creative use of poetic styles, systems, and emotional morphologies other than banally constricting." Has published poetry by Seth McMillan, Shari O'Brien, Tom Page, Michael Daniel, Marjorie Roberts, and Luis C. Berriozabal. *ART: MAG*, appearing in 1-2 large issues of 100 copies/year, is limited to a few poets. Subscription: $8 (2 issues). Sample: $3 or more. Make checks payable to Peter Magliocco.

How to Submit Submit 5 poems at a time with SASE. "Submissions should be neat and use consistent style format (except experimental work). Cover letters are optional." Accepts simultaneous submissions; sometimes previously published poems. No fax or e-mail submissions. Sometimes comments on rejected poems. Publishes theme issues. Guidelines and upcoming themes available for SASE. Responds within 3 months. Pays one contributor's copy. Acquires first rights. Staff occasionally reviews books of poetry. Send materials for review consideration.

Book/Chapbook Needs & How to Submit "Recently published (in cooperation with Trafford Publishing) the novel *Nu-Evermore* by Peter Magliocco. For any other press chapbook possibilities, query the editor before submitting any manuscript."

Advice "The mag is seeking a futuristic aestheticism where the barriers of fact and fiction meet, where inner- and outer-space converge in the realm of poetic consciousness in order to create a more productively viable relationship to the coming *Nu-Evermore* of the 21st century."

☑ LINTEL

24 Blake Lane, Middletown NY 10940. (845)342-5224. Established 1977.

Book/Chapbook Needs "We publish poetry and innovative fiction of types ignored by commercial presses. We consider any poetry except conventional, traditional, cliché, greeting card types; i.e., we consider any artistic poetry." Has published poetry by Sue Saniel Elkind, Samuel Exler, Adrienne Wolfert, Edmund Pennant, and Nathan Teitel. "Typical of our work" is Teitel's book, *In Time of Tide*, 64 pages, digest-sized, professionally printed in bold type, flat-spined, with hard cover stamped in gold, jacket with art and author's photo on back.

How to Submit Not currently accepting unsolicited mss.

☑ LIPS

7002 Blvd. East, #2-26G, Guttenberg NJ 07093. (201)662-1303. Fax: (201)861-2888. E-mail: LBOSS79270@aol.com. Established 1981. **Poetry Editor:** Laura Boss.

Magazine Needs *Lips* "is a quality poetry magazine that is published twice/year and takes pleasure in publishing previously unpublished poets as well as the most established voices in contemporary poetry. We look for quality work: the strongest work of a poet; work that moves the reader; poems that take risks that work. We prefer clarity in the work rather than the abstract. Poems longer than 6 pages present a space problem." Has published poetry by Allen Ginsberg, Gregory Corso, Michael Benedikt, Maria Gillan, Stanley Barkan, Lyn Lifshin, Marge Piercy, Warren Woessner, David Ignatow, and Ishmael Reed. *Lips* is about 150 pages, digest-sized, flat-spined. Receives about 8,000 submissions/year, accepts about 1%, has a 6-month backlog. Circulation is 1,000 for 200 subscribers, of which about 100 are libraries. Sample: $10 plus $2 for postage.

How to Submit Poems should be submitted between September and March only; 6 pages maximum, typed; no query necessary. Responds in one month but has gotten backlogged at times. Sometimes sends prepublication galleys. Pays one contributor's copy. Acquires first rights. Send SASE for guidelines.

Advice "Remember the 2 T's: Talent *and* Tenacity."

☑ THE LISTENING EYE

Kent State Geauga Campus, 14111 Claridon-Troy Rd., Burton OH 44021. (440)286-3840. E-mail: grace_butcher@msn.com. Website: www.geocities.com/Athens/3716. Established 1970 for student work, 1990 as national publication. **Editor:** Grace Butcher. **Assistant Editors:** Jim Wohlken and Joanne Speidel.

Magazine Needs *The Listening Eye* is an annual publication, appearing in early fall, of poetry, short fiction, creative nonfiction, and art that welcomes both new and established poets and writers. Wants "high literary quality poetry. Prefer shorter poems (less than 2 pages) but will consider longer if space allows. Any subject, any style. No trite images or predictable rhyme." Accepts poetry written by children if high literary quality. Has published poetry by Alberta Turner, Virgil Suárez, Walter McDonald, and Simon Perchik. *The Listening Eye* is 52-60 pages, digest-sized, professionally printed, saddle-stapled, with card stock cover with b&w art. Receives about 200 poems/

year, accepts about 5%. Press run is 300. Single copy: $4. Sample: $4. Make checks payable to Kent State University.

How to Submit Submit up to 4 poems at a time, typed, single-spaced, one poem/page—name, address, phone number, and e-mail address in upper left-hand corner of each page—with SASE for return of work. Previously published poems occasionally accepted; no simultaneous submissions. No e-mail submissions. Cover letter is required. Reads submissions January 1 through April 15 only. Time between acceptance and publication is up to 6 months. Poems are circulated to the editor and 2 assistant editors who read and evaluate work separately, then meet for final decisions. Occasionally comments on rejected poems. Guidelines available in magazine or for SASE. Responds in one month. Pays 2 contributor's copies. Acquires first or one-time rights.

Contest/Award Offerings Awards $30 to the best sports poem in each issue.

Advice ''I look for tight lines that don't sound like prose, unexpected images, or juxtapositions; the unusual use of language, noticeable relationships of sounds; a twist in viewpoint, an ordinary idea in extraordinary language, an amazing and complex idea simply stated, play on words and with words, an obvious love of language. Poets need to read the 'Big 3'—cummings, Thomas, Hopkins—to see the limits to which language can be taken. Then read the 'Big 2'—Dickinson to see how simultaneously tight, terse, and universal a poem can be, and Whitman to see how sprawling, cosmic, and personal. Then read everything you can find that's being published in literary magazines today, and see how your work compares to all of the above.''

ℕ ◲ ◎ LITERARY MAMA (Specialized: writing by mothers about mothering)

E-mail: poetry@literarymama.com. Website: www.literarymama.com. Established 2003. **Poetry Editor:** Rachel Iverson (poetry@literarymama.com for submissions). Managing Editor: Amy Hudock (info@literarymama.com for inquiries).

Magazine Needs *Literary Mama*, a monthly online literary journal, publishes fiction, poetry, and creative nonfiction by writers of all ages who are mothers. ''We also publish literary criticism, book reviews, and profiles about mother writers. *Literary Mama* is doing something for mama-centric literature that no one else is doing. The poetry, fiction, and creative nonfiction that may be too long, too complex, too ambiguous, too deep, too raw, too irreverent, too ironic, too body conscious, and too full of long words for the general reader will find a home with us. While there are plenty of online literary magazines that publish writing like this, none devote themselves exclusively to writing about motherhood.'' Wants poems of any form that are ''extraordinary for their vision, craftsmanship, integrity, and originality; centered around parenting; written by writers who are also self-identified mothers: biological, non-biological, step, transgendered, adoptive.'' *Literary Mama* is published online only. Receives about 70 poems/month. Publishes about 6-10 poems/issue (about 10-15% of poems received).

How to Submit Submit a maximum of 4 poems at a time. Line length for poetry is open. Accepts previously published poems and simultaneous submissions. Accepts e-mail submissions (pasted into body of message); no disk submissions. Cover letter is required. ''Please include name, brief bio, and contact information.'' Reads submissions year round except for December and June. Time between acceptance and publication is 2-4 weeks. ''The final decision about all poetry submissions is made by the poetry editor.'' Sometimes comments on rejected poems. Guidelines available on website. Responds in up to 6 weeks. No payment. Acquires first rights for previously unpublished work, non-exclusive one-time rights for reprints. Reviews books and chapbooks of poetry. E-mail poetry@literarymama.com to query prior to sending materials for review consideration.

◲ THE LITERARY REVIEW: AN INTERNATIONAL JOURNAL OF CONTEMPORARY WRITING

Fairleigh Dickinson University, 285 Madison Ave., Madison NJ 07940. (973)443-8564. Fax:

(973)443-8364. E-mail: tlr@fdu.edu. Website: www.theliteraryreview.org. Established 1957. **Editor-in-Chief:** René Steinke. **Contact:** William Zander.

Magazine Needs *The Literary Review*, a quarterly, seeks "work by new and established poets which reflects a sensitivity to literary standards and the poetic form." No specifications as to form, length, style, subject matter, or purpose. Has published poetry by David Citino, Rick Mulkey, Virgil Suárez, Gary Fincke, and Dale M. Kushner. *The Literary Review* is 200 pages, digest-sized, professionally printed, flat-spined, with glossy color cover. Receives about 1,200 submissions/year, accepts 100-150, has a 12- to 16-month backlog. Publishes 50-75 pages of poetry/issue. Press run is 2,500 for 900 subscribers, of which one-third are overseas. Sample: $5 domestic, $6 outside US; request a "general issue."

How to Submit Submit up to 5 typed poems at a time. Accepts simultaneous submissions. No fax or e-mail submissions. Do not submit during the summer months of June, July, and August. At times the editor comments on rejected poems. Publishes theme issues. Responds in 3 months. Always sends prepublication galleys. Pays 2 contributor's copies. Acquires first rights. Reviews books of poetry in 500 words, single book format. Send materials for review consideration.

Also Offers Website features original work. Has published poetry by Renée Ashley and Catherine Kasper. Website contact is Louise Stahl.

Advice "Read a general issue of the magazine carefully before submitting."

★ 🌐 ◎ LITHUANIAN PAPERS (Specialized: nationality)

P.O. Box 777, Sandy Bay, Tasmania 7006 Australia. Phone: (+3)62252505. E-mail: A.Taskunas@utas.edu.au. Established 1987. **Editor:** Al Taskunas.

Magazine Needs *Lithuanian Papers* is "an annual English-language journal aimed at fostering research into all aspects of Lithuania and its people." Wants "high-standard poetry dealing with Lithuanian topics or any topics by Lithuanian poets (in English)." Nothing unethical or offensive. Has published poetry by Bruce Dawe, J. Reilly, J. Degutyté/transl. G. Slavenas, and Julius Keleras/Vyt Bakaitis. *Lithuanian Papers* is 80 pages, digest-sized, offset-printed, saddle-stapled, with light card cover, includes b&w photos and art, ads. Receives about 25 poems/year, accepts about 10%. Press run is 2,000 for 1,500 subscribers of which 100 are libraries, 100 shelf sales; 400 distributed free to members, students, etc. Sample: $8 (US) if available. Make checks payable to Lithuanian Studies Society (LSS).

How to Submit Submit 2-3 poems at a time. "If translation, the originals are also required." Line length for poetry is 4 minimum, 20 maximum. No previously published poems or simultaneous submissions. Accepts e-mail (pasted into body of message) and disk submissions. "Must be Mac-compatible." Cover letter is required. "The cover letter must contain a concise c.v. and be accompanied by 2 letters of recommendation." Reads submissions December 1 through June 30 only. Time between acceptance and publication is up to 6 months. Poems are circulated to an editorial board. "Short list read by at least 2 referees—more if in disagreement." Pays 2 contributor's copies "or more by special arrangement." Acquires all rights. Rights returned by negotiation.

Advice "The Chinese say that even the longest journey starts with a single step. We are open to that step—or any advanced strides along the way."

◙ LONE STARS MAGAZINE; "SONGBOOK" POETRY CONTEST

4219 Flint Hill St., San Antonio TX 78230-1619. Established 1992. **Editor/Publisher:** Milo Rosebud.

Magazine Needs *Lone Stars*, published 3 times/year, features "contemporary poetry." Wants poetry that holds a continuous line of thought. No profanity. Has published poetry by Sheila Roark, Tom Hendrix, and Patricia Rourke. *Lone Stars* is 25 pages, magazine-sized, photocopied, with some hand-written poems, saddle-stapled, bound with tape, includes clip art. Press run is 200 for 100 subscribers of which 3 are libraries. Single copy: $5; subscription: $15. Sample: $4.50.

How to Submit Submit 3-5 poems at a time with "the form typed the way you want it in print."

Charges reading fee of $1 per poem. Accepts previously published poems and simultaneous submissions. Cover letter is preferred. Time between acceptance and publication is 2 months. Publishes theme issues. List of upcoming themes and guidelines available for SASE. Responds within 3 months. Acquires one-time rights.

Contest/Award Offerings Sponsors annual "Songbook" (song-lyric poems) Poetry Contest. Details available for SASE.

⬠ ◎ LOONFEATHER ANNUAL; LOONFEATHER PRESS (Specialized: regional)

P.O. Box 1212, Bemidji MN 56619-1212. (218)444-4869. E-mail: brossi@paulbunyan.net. Established 1979. **Poetry Editors:** Betty Rossi and Gail Rixen.

Magazine Needs & How to Submit The literary magazine *Loonfeather* appears annually, "primarily but not exclusively for Minnesota writers." Prefers short poems of 42 lines or less. Accepts some traditional forms if well done; no generalizations on worn-out topics. *Loonfeather* is 98 pages, digest-sized, professionally printed in small type, with matte card cover, includes b&w art and ads. Subscription: $10/year. Query with 2-3 sample poems, cover letter, and list of previous publications. Reads submissions October, November, and December only. Pays 2 contributor's copies.

Book/Chapbook Needs & How to Submit Loonfeather Press publishes a limited number of quality poetry books. Has published *Green Journey Red Bird* by Mary Kay Rummel, *Dark Lake* by Kathryn Kysar, and *Outside After Dark: New and Selected Poems* by Susan Carol Hauser. "Currently have a backlog of accepted material for publication." Query with up to 10 sample poems, cover letter, and list of previous publications. Responds to queries in 6 months. Time between acceptance and publication is up to 2 years. Pays 10% royalties.

◗ LOS

150 N. Catalina St., No. 2, Los Angeles CA 90004. E-mail: lospoesy@earthlink.net. Website: http://home.earthlink.net/ ~ lospoesy. Established 1991. **Contact:** the Editors.

Magazine Needs *Los*, published 4 times/year, features poetry. Has published poetry by Jonathan Levant, Peter Layton, Steven Ray Smith, Ed Orr, Marty Walsh, and Jean Esteve. *Los* is digest-sized and saddle-stapled. Press run is 100.

How to Submit Accepts submissions by e-mail (pasted into body of message/as attachment) and by postal mail. Time between acceptance and publication is up to one month. Guidelines available on website. Responds in 3 months. Pays one contributor's copy.

Ⓝ ◎ LOTUS BLOOMS JOURNAL

P.O. Box 145, Farmington MI 48332. E-mail: lbjsubmissions@aol.com. Website: http://lotusblooms journal.com. Established 2001. **Contact:** Ulysses S. Parker, managing editor. Publisher: LaTonya M. Baldwin.

Magazine Needs *Lotus Blooms Journal* is a monthly online poetry journal. "A signature feature is our carefully selected or created art to compliment the poet's work." Wants "all forms and styles [of poetry]. Works selected for *Lotus* clearly suggest the poet is knowledgeable of form and structure. We look for creativity as well as technical mastery. We publish the novice to seasoned poet. We look for works that demonstrate a commitment to craft." Does not want forced rhyme. Has published poetry by Sarah Wilson, Robert Curtis. C. E. Laine, Dorothy M. Mienko, and Tara Betts. *Lotus Blooms* is published online; a special print version is published biannually. Receives about 850 poems/year, accepts about 10%. Publishes about 12-20 poems/issue.

How to Submit Accepts previously published poems and simultaneous submissions. Accepts e-mail submissions (pasted into body of message); no disk submissions. Cover letter is preferred. Reads submissions year round. Submit seasonal material one month in advance. Time between acceptance and publication is 2 months. Poems are circulated to an editorial board. "All submissions are read independently by two editors. Each editor selects an ideal group. The editors then compare lists. Any poem selected by both editors is accepted, and the remaining poem slots are filled in based on issue theme and the ability [of remaining poems] to express subtlety of the current theme that may not appear in the core group of poems." Seldom comments on rejected poems. Regularly publishes theme issues. List of upcoming themes and guidelines available on website. Responds in 3 weeks. Sometimes sends prepublication galleys. No payment. Acquires one-time rights.

Contest/Award Offerings "We conduct monthly poetry contests and award prizes (books or cash) for top finishers. We also conduct prose competitions with prizes (books or cash) awarded.

Also Offers *Lotus* operates a small private online poetry forum dedicated to helping our members write their best poetry. We also publish a biannual print *Lotus Blooms Journal*. *Lotus Blooms Journal* also sponsors Books for Kids, a national reading program for school children, kindergarten through high school (see http://lotusbloomsjournal.com/booksforkids.html)."

Advice "This is a great time to be a poet. There are many outlets to showcase your work. There are many places to learn the craft of writing poetry. For those who are novices focused on improving their craft, we suggest you read a great number of established poets and discover social groups online and in your community that support poetry. With a little effort, you will find a place or places that fit your sensibilities and temperament. Always have fun! Read, learn, write, enjoy poetry!"

☑ ◎ LOUISIANA LITERATURE; LOUISIANA LITERATURE PRIZE FOR POETRY (Specialized: regional)

SLU-792, Southeastern Louisiana University, Hammond LA 70402. (504)549-5022. E-mail: lalit@selu.edu. Website: www.selu.edu/orgs/lalit. **Editor:** Jack Bedell.

Magazine Needs *Louisiana Literature* appears twice/year. "We consider creative work from anyone, though we strive to showcase our state's talent. We appreciate poetry that shows firm control and craft, is sophisticated yet accessible to a broad readership. We don't use highly experimental work." Has published poetry by Claire Bateman, Elton Glaser, Gray Jacobik, Vivian Shipley, D.C. Berry, and Judy Longley. *Louisiana Literature* is 150 pages, 6³/₄×9³/₄, flat-spined, handsomely printed on heavy matte stock, with matte card cover. Single copies: $8 for individuals; subscription: $12 for individuals, $12.50 for institutions.

How to Submit Submit up to 5 poems at a time. No simultaneous submissions. No fax or e-mail submissions. "Send cover letter, including bio to use in the event of acceptance. Enclose SASE and specify whether work is to be returned or discarded." Reads submissions year round, "although we work more slowly in summer." Publishes theme issues. Guidelines and upcoming themes available for SASE or on website. Sometimes sends prepublication galleys. Pays 2 contributor's copies. Send materials for review consideration; include cover letter.

Contest/Award Offerings The Louisiana Literature Prize for Poetry offers a $400 award. Guidelines available for SASE.

Advice "It's important to us that the poets we publish be in control of their creations. Too much of what we see seems arbitrary."

☑ ◎ THE LOUISIANA REVIEW (Specialized: regional)

% Division of Liberal Arts, Louisiana State University at Eunice, P.O. Box 1129, Eunice LA 70535. (337)550-1315. E-mail: bfonteno@lsue.edu. Website: www.lsue.edu/LA-Review/. Established 1999. **Editors:** Dr. Jason Ambrosiano and Dr. Billy Fontenot.

Magazine Needs *The Louisiana Review* appears annually in the fall semester. "We wish to offer Louisiana poets, writers, and artists a place to showcase their most beautiful pieces. Others may submit Louisiana-related poetry, stories, interviews with Louisiana writers, and art. We want to publish the highest-quality poetry, fiction, art, and drama. For poetry, we like strong imagery, metaphor, and evidence of craft, but we do not wish to have sing-song rhymes, abstract, religious, or overly sentimental work." Has published poetry by Gary Snyder, Antler, David Cope, and Catfish McDaris. *The Louisiana Review* is 100-225 pages, magazine-sized, professionally printed, perfect-bound, includes photographs/artwork. Receives up to 2,000 poems/year, accepts 40-50. Press run is 300-600. Single copy: $8.

How to Submit Submit up to 5 poems at a time. No previously published poems. No fax or e-mail submissions. "Include cover letter indicating your association with Louisiana. Name and address should appear on each page." Reads submissions January 15 through March 31 only. Time between acceptance and publication is up to 2 years. Pays one contributor's copy. Poets retain all rights.

Advice "Be true to your own voice and style."

LOUISIANA STATE UNIVERSITY PRESS

P.O. Box 25053, Baton Rouge LA 70894-5053. (225)578-6618. Fax: (225)578-6461. Website: www.lsu.edu/lsupress. Established 1935. **Editor-in-Chief:** Sylvia Frank Rodrigue. A highly respected publisher of collections by poets such as Lisel Mueller, Margaret Gibson, Fred Chappell, Marilyn Nelson, and Henry Taylor. Publisher of the Southern Messenger Poets series edited by Dave Smith. **Currently not accepting poetry submissions; "fully committed through 2007."**

THE LOUISVILLE REVIEW

Spalding University, 851 S. Fourth St., Louisville KY 40203. (502)585-9911, ext. 2777. E-mail: louisvillereview@spalding.edu. Website: www.louisvillereview.org. Established 1976. **Contact:** Kathleen Driskell, associate editor.

Magazine Needs *The Louisville Review* appears twice/year. Uses any kind of poetry. Has a section devoted to children's poetry (grades K-12) called The Children's Corner. Has published poetry by Wendy Bishop, Gary Fincke, Michael Burkard, and Sandra Kohler. *The Louisville Review* is 100 pages, digest-sized, flat-spined. Receives about 700 submissions/year, accepts about 10%. Single copy: $8; subscription: $14. Sample: $4.

How to Submit Include SASE; no electronic submissions. Reads submissions year round. Time between acceptance and publication is up to 3 months. Submissions are read by 3 readers. "Poetry by children must include permission of parent to publish if accepted." Guidelines available on website. Pays 2 contributor's copies.

Advice "We look for the striking metaphor, unusual imagery, and fresh language."

LOW-TECH PRESS

30-73 47th St., Long Island City NY 11103. Established 1981. **Editor:** Ron Kolm. Has published *Bad Luck* by Mike Topp and *Goodbye Beautiful Mother* Tsaurah Litzky. **"We only publish solicited mss."**

LSR

P.O. Box 440195, Miami FL 33144. Established 1990. **Editor/Publisher:** Nilda Cepero.

Magazine Needs Appearing 2 times/year, *LSR* publishes poetry, book reviews, interviews, and line artwork. "Style, subject matter, and content of poetry open; we prefer contemporary with meaning and message. No surrealism, porn, or religious poetry. Reprints are accepted." Has published poetry by Catfish McDaris, Mike Catalano, Janine Pommey-Vega, Margarita Engle, and Evangeline Blanco. *LSR* is 20 pages, magazine-sized, offset-printed, saddle-stapled, with 60 lb. cover, includes line work, very few ads. Receives about 300 poems/year, accepts about 30%. Publishes 40-50 poems/issue. Press run is 3,000 for more than 100 subscribers of which 20 are libraries; the rest distributed free to selected bookstores in the US, Europe, and Latin America. Single copy: $4; subscription: $6. Sample: $5, including postage.

How to Submit Submit 4 poems at a time. Line length for poetry is 5 minimum, 45 maximum. Accepts previously published poems; no simultaneous submissions. Accepts disk submissions "only when accompanied by print-out." Cover letter is required. Include SASE and bio. Time between acceptance and publication is one year. Poems are circulated to an editorial board. "Three rounds by different editors. Editor/publisher acts on recommendations." Guidelines available for SASE. Responds in 9 months. Acquires one-time rights. Reviews books. "We will not write reviews; however, will consider those written by others, up to 750 words."

Also Offers *Poética*, a Spanish-language magazine published by *LSR*. (See separate listing in this section.)

Advice "Read as many current poetry magazines as you can."

LUCID MOON REVIEW POETRY WEBSITE AND NEWSLETTER

67 Norma Rd., Hampton NJ 08827. (908)735-4447. E-mail: ralphylucidmoon@yahoo.com. Website: www.lucidmoonpoetry.com. Established 1999 (website) and 2003 (newsletter). **Editor:** Ralph Haselmann, Jr.

Magazine Needs Online journal updated quarterly. *Lucid Moon Review Poetry Website and Newsletter* wants "underground Beat poetry and heartfelt, romantic love poetry, humor, moon-themed poetry, and poems with references to pop culture." Does not want "indeciperable, experimental poetry or annoying religious poetry." Has published poetry by Antler, Charles Bukowski, Ana Christy, Allen Ginsberg, Doug Holder, and Charles Plymell. "*Lucid Moon* is published on the home page, and there is a new issue each quarter. Old issues are archived elsewhere on the website. All poetry columns have been converted to guestbook-like areas, and you can type in or copy and paste one poem or column per week." Room for 8 pages of poetry in each newsletter.

How to Submit Accepts previously published poems and simultaneous submissions. Accepts submissions for the newsletter by e-mail only (as attachment in Microsoft Word or rich-text document). "I do not accept submissions in the body of the e-mail because the lines get broken up. Please do not send snail mail submissions or submissions on disk." Include cover letter (with name, date, address, and e-mail) and a 3-sentence bio. "Please write poem title in 12 Arial Bold font, black, then skip a line and write poem in 12 unbolded Arial black font. Skip a line between each poem." Time between submissions and acceptance is 6 months. "In the meantime, type in your poems in my guestbook poetry columns."

Advice "Read other poems posted on the website to get a feel for what I'm looking for. Cursing and sexual situations are okay, as long as they are not gratuitous. Let your poetry pen sing, dance, and soar! Check out my website every few months for the new newsletter, and please sign my guestbook."

$ ◻ ◎ LULLABY HEARSE (Specialized: experimental poetry with an edge)

26 Fifth St., Bangor ME 04401. (207)990-5839. E-mail: editor@lullabyhearse.com. Website: www.lullabyhearse.com. Established 2002. **Editor:** Sarah Ruth Jacobs.

Magazine Needs *Lullaby Hearse* appears quarterly and publishes writing, art, poetry, and vintage movie reviews, with emphasis on work with an edge. Wants "vivid, pained poetry within the genres of horror, experimental, urban, rural, erotic, and personal verse. We read for talent, solidity of voice, and loyalty to vision over fancy." Does not want "poems about writing, bland odes to nature, clumsy/heavy-handed rhyme, self-pitying lyrics, or far-out fantasy. Shocking poetry is fine, when it isn't created from a place of self-imposed ignorance. We prefer crudity over bombast." *Lullaby Hearse* is 50 pages, magazine-sized, photocopied, saddle-stapled, with color card cover with art. Receives about 650 poetry submissions/year, accepts about 30. Press run is 200 for 70 subscribers of which 10 are libraries, 100 shelf sales. Single copy: $5; subscription: $20. Make checks payable to Sarah Ruth Jacobs.

How to Submit Submit 3-10 poems at a time. Accepts simultaneous submissions; no previously published poems. Accepts e-mail submissions. Cover letter is preferred. "Include a SASE with all hard-copy submissions." Reads submissions year round. Time between acceptance and publication is up to 3 months. "I seldom postpone poems for the second upcoming issue. Instead I may delay in replying until all or a substantial amount of submissions have been received." Seldom comments on rejected poems. Guidelines available for SASE or on website. Responds in 6 weeks. Pays $5/poem and one contributor's copy. Acquires one-time rights. Reviews books and chapbooks of poetry and other magazines/journals in 1,000 words. Send materials for review consideration to Sarah Ruth Jacobs.

◪ LULLWATER REVIEW; LULLWATER PRIZE FOR POETRY

Emory University, P.O. Box 22036, Atlanta GA 30322. (404)727-6184. E-mail: LullwaterReview@yahoo.com. Established 1990. **Poetry Editors:** Gwyneth Driskill and Laurel DeCou.

Magazine Needs "Appearing in May and December, the *Lullwater Review* is Emory University's nationally distributed literary magazine, publishing poetry, short fiction, and artwork." Seeks poetry of any genre with strong imagery, original voice, on any subject. No profanity or pornographic material. Has published poetry by Amy Greenfield, Peter Serchuk, Katherine McCord, Virgil Suárez, and Ha Jin. *Lullwater Review* is 104-120 pages, magazine-sized, with full-color cover, includes b&w pictures. Press run is 2,500. Subscription: $12. Sample: $5.

How to Submit "Limit the number of submissions to 6 poems or fewer." Prefers poems single-spaced with name and contact info on each page. "Poems longer than one page should include page numbers." Accepts simultaneous submissions; no previously published poems. Accepts submissions by postal mail only. Cover letter is preferred. "We must have a SASE with which to reply. Poems may not be returned." Reads submissions September 1 through May 15 only. Time between acceptance and publication is up to 6 months. Poems are circulated to an editorial board. "A poetry editor selects approximately 16 poems per week to be reviewed by editors, who then discuss and decide on the status of each poem." Seldom comments on rejected poems. Guidelines and upcoming themes available for SASE. Responds in 5 months maximum. Pays 3 contributor's copies. Acquires first North American serial rights.

Contest/Award Offerings Sponsors the annual Lullwater Prize for Poetry. Award is $500 and publication. **Deadline:** November 1. **Entry fee:** $8. Guidelines available for SASE.

Advice "Keep writing, find your voice, don't get frustrated. Please be patient with us regarding response time. We are an academic institution."

◪ ◎ LUNA BISONTE PRODS; LOST AND FOUND TIMES (Specialized: style, experimental/avant-garde)

137 Leland Ave., Columbus OH 43214-7505. Website: www.johnmbennett.net. Established 1967. **Poetry Editor:** John M. Bennett.

Magazine Needs *Lost and Found Times* publishes experimental and avant-garde writing. Wants "unusual poetry, naive poetry, surrealism, experimental, visual poetry, collaborations—no poetry workshop or academic pabulum." Has published poetry by J. Leftwich, Sheila Murphy, J.S. Murnet, Peter Ganick, I. Argüelles, and A. Ackerman. *Lost and Found Times* is 60 pages, digest-sized, printed in photo-reduced typescript with wild graphics, with matte card cover with graphics. Press run is 350 for 75 subscribers of which 30 are libraries. Subscription: $30 for 5 numbers. Sample: $7.

How to Submit Submit anytime—preferably camera-ready (but this is not required). Responds in 2 days. Pays one contributor's copy. All rights revert to authors upon publication. Staff reviews books of poetry. Send materials for review consideration.

Book/Chapbook Needs & How to Submit Luna Bisonte Prods considers book submissions: query with samples and cover letter (but "keep it brief"). Chapbook publishing usually depends on grants or other subsidies, and is usually by solicitation. Will also consider subsidy arrangements on negotiable terms. A sampling of various Luna Bisonte Prods products—from posters and audio cassettes to pamphlets and chapbooks—available for $10.

Advice "Be blank."

☑ LUNGFULL! MAGAZINE

316 23rd St., Brooklyn NY 11215. E-mail: lungfull@rcn.com. Website: http://lungfull.org/index.ht ml. Established 1994. **Editor/Publisher:** Brendan Lorber.

- *LUNGFULL!* was the recipient of a multi-year grant from the New York State Council for the Arts.

Magazine Needs *LUNGFULL!*, published annually, prints "the rough draft of each poem, in addition to the final, so that the reader can see the creative process from start to finish." Wants "any style as long as it's urgent, immediate, playful, probing, showing great thought while remaining vivid and grounded. Poems should be as interesting as conversation." Does not want "empty poetic abstractions." Has published poetry by Alice Notley, Allen Ginsberg, Lorenzo Thomas, Tracie Morris, Hal Sirowitz, Sparrow, Eileen Myles, and Bill Berkson. *LUNGFULL!* is 200 pages, $8\frac{1}{2} \times 7$, offset-printed, desktop-published, perfect-bound, with glossy 2–color cover, includes lots of illustrations and photos, and a few small press ads. Receives about 1,000 poems/year, accepts 5%. Press run is 1,000 for 150 subscribers, 750 shelf sales; 100 distributed free to contributors. Single copy: $7.95; subscription: $31.80/4 issues, $15.90/2 issues. Sample: $9.50. Make checks payable to Brendan Lorber.

How to Submit "We recommend you get a copy before submitting." Submit up to 6 poems at a time. Accepts previously published poems and simultaneous submissions (with notification). "However, other material will be considered first and stands a much greater chance of publication." Accepts e-mail submissions. "We prefer hard copy by USPS—but e-submissions can be made in the body of the e-mail itself or in a file saved as text." Cover letter is preferred. Time between acceptance and publication is up to 8 months. "The editor looks at each piece for its own merit and for how well it will fit into the specific issue being planned based on other accepted work." Guidelines available by e-mail. Responds in 6 months. Pays 2 contributor's copies.

Also Offers "Each copy of *LUNGFULL! Magazine* now contains a short poem, usually from a series of 6, printed on a sticker—they can be removed from the magazine and placed on any flat surface to make it a little less flat. Innovatively designed and printed in black & white, previous stickers have included work by Sparrow, Rumi, Julie Reid, Donna Cartelli, Joe Maynard, and Jeremy Sharpe, among others."

Advice "Failure demands a certain dedication. Practice makes imperfection and imperfection makes room for the amazing. Only outside the bounds of acceptable conclusions can the astounding transpire, can writing contain anything beyond twittering snack food logic and the utilitarian pistons of mundane engineering."

☑ ◎ THE LUTHERAN DIGEST (Specialized: humor, nature/rural/ecology, religious/Christian, inspirational)

P.O. Box 4250, Hopkins MN 55343. (952)933-2820. Fax: (952)933-5708. E-mail: tldi@lutherandigest .com. Website: www.lutherandigest.com. Established 1953. **Editor:** David Tank.

Magazine Needs *The Lutheran Digest* appears quarterly "to entertain and encourage believers and to subtly persuade non-believers to embrace the Christian faith. We publish short poems (25 lines or less) that will fit in a single column of the magazine. Most are inspirational, but that doesn't necessarily mean religious. No avant-garde poetry or work longer than 25 lines." Has published poetry by Kathleen A. Cain, William Beyer, Margaret Peterson, Florence Berg, and Erma Boetkher. *The Lutheran Digest* is 64 pages, digest-sized, offset-printed, saddle-stapled, with 4-color paper cover, includes b&w photos and illustrations, local ads to cover cost of distribution. Receives about 200 poems/year, accepts 20%. Press run is 110,000; 105,000 distributed free to Lutheran churches. Subscription: $14/year, $22/2 years. Sample: $3.50.

How to Submit Submit 3 poems at a time. Line length for poetry is 25 maximum. Accepts previously published poems and simultaneous submissions. Accepts submissions by fax, by e-mail (as attachment), and by postal mail. Cover letter is preferred. "Include SASE if return is desired." Time between acceptance and publication is up to 9 months. Poems are circulated to an editorial board; "Selected by editor and reviewed by publication panel." Guidelines available for SASE or on website. Responds in 3 months. Pays credit and one contributor's copy. Acquires one-time rights.

Advice "Poems should be short and appeal to senior citizens. We also look for poems that can be sung to traditional Lutheran hymns."

◙ THE LYRIC; LESLIE MELLICHAMP AWARD

P.O. Box 110, Jericho Corners VT 05465. Phone/fax: (802)899-3993. E-mail: Lyric@sover.net. Established 1921 ("the oldest magazine in North America in continuous publication devoted to the publication of traditional poetry"). **Editor:** Jean Mellichamp-Milliken.

Magazine Needs *The Lyric* publishes about 55 poems each quarterly issue. "We use rhymed verse in traditional forms, for the most part, with an occasional piece of blank or free verse. Forty lines or so is usually our limit. Our themes are varied, ranging from religious ecstasy to humor to raw grief, but we feel no compulsion to shock, embitter, or confound our readers. We also avoid poems about contemporary political or social problems—grief but not grievances, as Frost put it. Frost is helpful in other ways: If yours is more than a lover's quarrel with life, we are not your best market. And most of our poems are accessible on first or second reading. Frost again: Don't hide too far away." Has published poetry by Rhina P. Espaillat, Maureen Cannon, Alfred Dorn, Margaret Menamin, Ruth Harrison, Glenna Holloway, and Lionel Willis. *The Lyric* is 32 pages, digest-sized, professionally printed with varied typography, with matte card cover. Press run is 750 for 600 subscribers of which 40 are libraries. Receives about 3,000 submissions/year, accepts 5%. Subscription: $15 US, $17 Canada and other countries (in US funds only). Sample: $4.

How to Submit Submit up to 6 poems at a time. "Will read, but do not prefer, simultaneous submissions; no previously published poems or translations. Cover letters often helpful, but not required." Guidelines available for SASE or by e-mail. Responds in 3 months (average); "inquire after 6 months." Pays one contributor's copy, and all contributors are eligible for quarterly and annual prizes totaling $750. "Subscription will not affect publication of submitted poetry."

Contest/Award Offerings "Among the yearly prizes awarded, we have recently added the Leslie Mellichamp Award of $100."

Advice "Our raison d'être has been the encouragement of form, music, rhyme, and accessibility in poetry. As we witness the growing tide of appreciation for traditional/lyric poetry, we are proud to have stayed the course for 83 years, helping keep the roots of poetry alive."

◙ LYRIC POETRY REVIEW

P.O. Box 980814, Houston TX 77098. (713)523-4193. E-mail: lyric@lyricreview.org. Website: www. lyricreview.org. Established 2001. **Editor:** Mira Rosenthal. **Managing Editor:** Heather Bigley. Member: Council of Literary Magazines and Presses (CLMP).

• *Lyric Poetry Review* was a Pushcart Prize winner for 2003.

Magazine Needs *Lyric Poetry Review* appears biannually and presents poetry by Americans, and translations of both little-known and celebrated poets from around the world. Also publishes literary essays. Wants "poems with singing power, poems with fresh energy to delight and awaken deep feeling. Lyric essays that use poetic logic and relate a mosaic of ideas." Does not want reviews or poems of more than 500 words. Has published poetry by Fanny Howe, Marilyn Hacker, Tony Hoagland, Tomaz Salamun, Czeslaw Milosz, and Jean Valentine. *Lyric Poetry Review* is 64 pages, digest-sized, offset-printed, perfect-bound, with full-color cover with original artwork. Receives about 500 poems/year, accepts about 5%. Publishes about 40 poems/issue. Press run is 1,000. Single copy: $8; subscription: $14/year (subscribers outside US add $5 postage). Make checks payable to *Lyric Poetry Review*.

How to Submit Submit 3-6 poems at a time. Accepts simultaneous submissions if notified; no previously published poems. No fax, e-mail, or disk submissions. Cover letter is required. Reads submissions year round. Time between acceptance and publication is up to 6 months. Poems are circulated to an editorial board. "Editorial decisions are made collectively by all associated editors. We strongly advise that those submitting work read a recent issue first." Seldom comments on rejected poems. Occasionally publishes theme issues. List of upcoming themes available by e-mail. Guidelines available in magazine, for SASE, or on website. Responds in up to 3 months. Always sends prepublication galleys. Pays 3 contributor's copies. Acquires first rights.

◎ M.I.P. COMPANY (Specialized: Russian erotica)

P.O. Box 27484, Minneapolis MN 55427. (763)544-5915. Fax: (612)871-5733. E-mail: mp@mipco.com. Website: www.mipco.com. Established in 1984. **Contact:** Michael Peltsman.

Book/Chapbook Needs & How to Submit M.I.P. Company publishes 3 paperbacks/year. Publishes only Russian erotic poetry, and prose written in Russian. Has published poetry collections by Mikhail Armalinsky and Aleksey Shelvakh. Accepts simultaneous submissions; no previously published poems. Responds to queries in one month. Seldom comments on rejected poems.

✪ ☑ THE MACGUFFIN; NATIONAL POET HUNT

Schoolcraft College, 18600 Haggerty Rd., Livonia MI 48152-2696. (734)462-4400, ext. 5327. Fax: (734)462-4679. E-mail: macguffin@schoolcraft.edu. Website: www.schoolcraft.cc.mi.us/macguffin/default.htm. Established 1984. **Editor:** Steven A. Dolgin.

Magazine Needs "*The MacGuffin* is a literary magazine which appears 2 times each year, in July and November. We publish the best poetry, fiction, nonfiction, and artwork we find. We have no thematic or stylistic biases. We look for well-crafted poetry. Long poems should not exceed 300 lines. Avoid pornography, trite, and sloppy poetry. We do not publish haiku, concrete, or light verse." Has published poetry by Linda Nemec Foster, Virgil Suárez, and Susan Terris. *The MacGuffin* is 164+ pages, digest-sized, professionally printed on heavy buff stock, flat-spined, with matte card cover, includes b&w illustrations and photos. Press run is 600 for 400 subscribers; the rest are local newsstand sales, contributor copies, and distribution to college offices. Single copy: $10; subscription: $18. Sample: $8.

How to Submit "The editorial staff is grateful to consider unsolicited manuscripts and graphics." Submit up to 5 poems at a time. Line length for poetry is 300 maximum. Poems should be typewritten. "We discourage simultaneous submissions." Accepts submissions by fax, on disk, by e-mail (as attachment), and through postal mail. When submitting by e-mail, "submit each work as a separate document attachment. Submissions made in the body of an e-mail will not be considered." Publishes theme issues. Upcoming themes available by fax, by e-mail, and for SASE. Guidelines available for SASE, by fax, by e-mail, or on website. Responds in 3 months; publication backlog is 6 months to 2 years. Pays 2 contributor's copies, "occasional money or prizes."

Contest/Award Offerings Also sponsors the National Poet Hunt, established in 1996, offering 1st Prize: $500; 2nd Prize: $250; 3rd Prize: $100; up to 3 honorable mentions; and publication. Submissions may be entered in other contests. Submit 5 typed poems on any subject in any form. Put name and address on *separate* 3×5 index card only. Upcoming themes available by fax, by e-mail, and for SASE. Guidelines available by fax, by e-mail, for SASE, and on website. **Entry fee:** $15/5 poems. **Deadline:** May 31. Judge for 2003 contest was Lucia Cordell-Getsi. Winners will be announced in August, and in *Poets and Writers* in the fall.

Advice "We will always comment on 'near misses.' Writing is a search, and it is a journey. Don't become sidetracked. Don't become discouraged. Keep looking. Keep traveling. Keep writing."

☑ MAD POETS REVIEW; MAD POETS REVIEW POETRY COMPETITION; MAD POETS SOCIETY

P.O. Box 1248, Media PA 19063-8248. E-mail: madpoets@comcast.net. Website: www.madpoetssociety.com. Established 1987. **Editor:** Eileen M. D'Angelo. **Associate Editor:** Camelia Nocella.

Magazine Needs *Mad Poets Review* is published annually in October/November. "Our primary purpose is to promote thought-provoking, moving poetry, and encourage beginning poets. We don't care if you have a 'name' or a publishing history, if your poetry is well-crafted. We are anxious for work with 'joie de vivre' that startles and inspires." No restrictions on subject, form, or style. "Just because our name is *Mad Poets Review* doesn't mean we want mad ramblings masquerading under the guise of poetry." No obsenities simply for shock value. Has published poetry by Gerald Stern, Naomi Shihab Nye, Greg Djanikian, Harry Humes, Maria Mazziotti Gillan, and Nathalie Anderson. *Mad Poets Review* is about 140 pages, digest-sized, attractively printed, perfect-bound, with textured card cover. Receives about 2,000 poems/year, accepts 100. Press run is 300. Single copy: $10. Sample: $12. Make checks payable to either Mad Poets Society or *Mad Poets Review*.

How to Submit Submit 6 poems at a time. "We accept first-class mail or e-mail submissions (no certified or Registered Mail). For e-mail, attach a Microsoft Word document (format is Times New Roman, 12 pt.). We will need a mailing address to send out a proof of the poem prior to publication, as well as a 3- to 4-line bio. Poems without a SASE with adequate postage will not be returned or acknowledged." Accepts previously published poems and simultaneous submissions. Cover letter is not necessary, but "include 3-4 sentences about yourself suitable for our Bio Notes section. Mark envelope 'contest' or 'magazine.'" Reads submissions January 1 through June 1 only. Time between acceptance and publication is 8 months. Often comments on rejected poems. Responds in 3 months. Pays one contributor's copy. Acquires one-time rights.

Contest/Award Offerings Sponsors the annual *Mad Poets Review* Poetry Competition. Complete contest guidelines available for SASE. **Entry fee:** $10 for up to 6 poems. Cash prizes awarded. Winners published in *Mad Poets Review*.

Also Offers "The Mad Poets Society is an active organization in Pennsylvania. We run several poetry series; have monthly meetings for members for critique and club business; coordinate a children's contest through Del. Co. School system; run an annual poetry festival the first Sunday in October; sponsor Mad Poets Bonfires for local poets and musicians; publish an annual literary calendar and newsletters that offer the most comprehensive listing available anywhere in the tri-state area. We send quarterly newsletters to members, as well as PA Poetry Society news covering state and national events."

Advice "It is advised that if someone is going to submit they see what kind of poetry we publish."

☑ THE MADISON REVIEW; PHYLLIS SMART YOUNG PRIZE IN POETRY

University of Wisconsin, Dept. of English, Helen C. White Hall, 600 N. Park St., Madison WI 53706. (608)263-2566. E-mail: madreview@mail.student.org.wisc.edu. Website: www.themadisonreview.org. Established 1978. **Contact:** Poetry Editor.

Magazine Needs *The Madison Review*, published in May and December, wants poems that are "smart and tight, that fulfill their own propositions. Spare us: religious or patriotic dogma and light verse." Has published poetry by Simon Perchik, Amy Quan Barry, Mitch Raney, Erica Meitner, and Henry B. Stobbs. Selects 15-20 poems from a pool of 750. Sample: $5.

How to Submit Submit up to 6 poems at a time. No simultaneous submissions. No e-mail submissions. Guidelines available in magazine, for SASE, by e-mail, or on website. Usually responds in 9 months. Pays 2 contributor's copies.

Contest/Award Offerings Phyllis Smart Young Prize in Poetry offers annual prize of $500 and publication in *The Madison Review* for "the best group of 3 unpublished poems submitted by a single author, any form." All entries will be considered as submissions to *The Madison Review*. Submissions must be unpublished. Submit 3 poems, any form, with SASE. Guidelines available for SASE, on website, and in announcement in *AWP* or *Poets & Writers* magazines. **Entry fee:** $5. Make checks or money orders payable to *The Madison Review*. **Deadline:** submissions accepted September 1-30 only. No mss returned; allow 9 months for response. Competition receives about 300 entries/year.

Advice "Contributors: Know your market! Read before, during, and after writing. Treat your poems *better* than job applications!"

◢ MAELSTROM

HC #1 Box 1624, Blakeslee PA 18610. E-mail: Imaelstrom@aol.com. Website: www.geocities.com/~readmaelstrom. Established 1997. **Editor:** Christine L. Reed. **Art Editor:** Jennifer Fennell.

Magazine Needs *Maelstrom*, a quarterly, "tries to be a volatile storm of talents throwing together art, poetry, short fiction, comedy, and tragedy." Wants any kind of poetry, "humor appreciated. No pornography." Has published poetry by Grace Cavalieri, Mekeel McBride, Daniela Gioseffi, and B.Z. Niditch. *Maelstrom* is 40-50 pages, 7 × 8½, saddle-stapled, with color cover, includes b&w art. Receives about 2,000 poems/year, accepts about 3%. Press run is 500 for 100 subscribers. Single copy: $5; subscription: $20. Sample: $4.

How to Submit Submit up to 4 poems at a time. Accepts previously published poems and simultaneous submissions. Accepts e-mail submissions "in the body of the e-mail message. Please do not send attached files." Cover letter is preferred. "Include name and address on every page. Send sufficient SASE for return of work." Time between acceptance and publication is up to 3 months. Seldom comments on rejected poems. Guidelines available by e-mail or on website. Responds in up to 6 months. Pays one contributor's copy. Acquires first North American serial or one-time rights. Staff reviews chapbooks of poetry and other magazines. Send materials for review consideration. "Material cannot be returned."

◢ THE MAGAZINE OF FANTASY & SCIENCE FICTION

P.O. Box 3447, Hoboken NJ 07030. E-mail: FandSF@aol.com. Website: www.fsfmag.com. Established 1949. **Editor:** Gordon Van Gelder.

- *The Magazine of Fantasy & Science Fiction* is a past winner of the Hugo Award and World Fantasy Award.

Magazine Needs *The Magazine of Fantasy & Science Fiction* appears monthly, 11 times/year. "One of the longest-running magazines devoted to the literature of the fantastic." Wants only poetry that deals with the fantastic or the science-fictional. Has published poetry by Rebecca Kavaler, Elizabeth Bear, and Robert Frazier. *The Magazine of Fantasy & Science Fiction* is 160 pages, digest-sized, offset-printed, perfect-bound, with glossy cover, includes ads. Receives about 20-40 poems/year, accepts about ½-1%. Publishes about 1-2 poems/year. Press run is 35,000 for 20,000 subscribers. Single copy: $3.95; subscription: $32.97. Sample: $5. Make checks payable to *The Magazine of Fantasy & Science Fiction*.

How to Submit Submit 1-3 poems at a time. No previously published poems or simultaneous submissions. No fax, e-mail, or disk submissions. Time between acceptance and publication is up to 9 months. "I buy poems very infrequently—just when one hits me right." Seldom comments on rejected poems. Guidelines available for SASE or on website. Responds in up to one month. Always sends prepublication galleys. Pays 2 contributor's copies. Acquires first North American serial rights.

$◢ ◎ THE MAGAZINE OF SPECULATIVE POETRY (Specialized: horror, fantasy, science fiction, science)

P.O. Box 564, Beloit WI 53512. Established 1984. **Editor:** Roger Dutcher.

Magazine Needs *The Magazine of Speculative Poetry* is a biannual magazine that features "the best new speculative poetry. We are especially interested in narrative form, but open to any form, any length (within reason); interested in a variety of styles. We're looking for the best of the new poetry utilizing the ideas, imagery, and approaches developed by speculative fiction, and will welcome experimental techniques as well as the fresh employment of traditional forms." Has published poetry by Mark Rudolph, Bruce Boston, Mario Milosevic, Sandra Lindow, and Laurel Winter. *The*

Magazine of Speculative Poetry is 24-28 pages, digest-sized, offset-printed, saddle-stapled, with matte card cover. Accepts less than 5% of some 500 poems received/year. Press run is 150-200, for nearly 100 subscribers. Subscription: $19/4. Sample: $5.

How to Submit Submit 3-5 poems at a time, double-spaced with a "regular old font. We are a small magazine, we can't print epics. Some poems run 2 or 3 pages, but rarely anything longer." No previously published poems or simultaneous submissions. "We like cover letters, but they aren't necessary. We like to see where you heard of us; the names of the poems submitted; a statement if the poetry manuscript is disposable; a big enough SASE; and if you've been published, some recent places." Editor comments on rejected poems "on occasion." Guidelines available for SASE. Responds in up to 2 months. Pays 3¢/word, minimum $5, maximum $25, plus one contributor's copy. Acquires first North American serial rights. "All rights revert to author upon publication, except for permission to reprint in any 'Best of' or compilation volume. Payment will be made for such publication." Reviews books of speculative poetry. Query on unsolicited reviews. Send materials for review consideration.

⬛ 🌐 ◪ MAGPIE'S NEST

176 Stoney Lane, Sparkhill, Birmingham B12 8AN United Kingdom. E-mail: magpies-nest@tiscali.co.uk. Established 1979. **Editor:** Mr. Bal Saini.

Magazine Needs *Magpie's Nest* appears quarterly and publishes "cutting-edge, modern poetry and fiction which deals with the human condition. No love poetry or self-obsessed work." *Magpie's Nest* receives about 200 poems/year, accepts about 25%. Press run is 200 for 150 subscribers, 50 shelf sales. Single copy: $2.50; subscription: $12.50. Sample: $3.

How to Submit Submit 4 poems at a time. Line length for poetry is 10 minimum, 40 maximum. Accepts previously published poems and simultaneous submissions. Accepts e-mail submission (pasted into body of message or as attachment). Cover letter is preferred. "Keep copies of poems submitted as poems which are not used are binned." Reads submissions September 1 through June 30 only. Time between acceptance and publication is 3 months. Seldom comments on rejected poems. Occasionally publishes theme issues. Responds in 3 months. Pays one contributor's copy. Reviews books of poetry and other magazines in 200 words, single book format. Send materials for review consideration.

Advice "Read past issues of magazine to assess the editor's taste/preference from the contents of the magazine."

◪ MAIN STREET RAG

4416 Shea Ln., Charlotte NC 28227. (704)573-2516. E-mail: editor@mainstreetrag.com. Website: www.MainStreetRag.com. Established 1996. **Publisher/Editor:** M. Scott Douglass.

Magazine Needs *Main Street Rag* is a quarterly that publishes "poetry, short fiction, essays, interviews, reviews, photos, art, cartoons, (political, satirical), and poetry collections as well as books—we are now a full service bindery with an online bookstore. We like publishing good material from people who are interested in more than notching another publishing credit, people who support small independent publishers like ourselves." *Main Street Rag* "will consider almost anything but prefer writing with an edge—either gritty or bitingly humorous." Has recently published work by Anthony S. Abbott, Nathan Graziano, Karla Huston, John Repp, David Slavitt, and Linda K. Sieniewicz. *Main Street Rag* is about 96 pages, digest-sized, perfect-bound, with 100 lb. laminated color cover. Publishes 30-40 poems and one short story per issue out of 2,500 submissions/year. Press run is about 1,000 for 300 subscribers of which 15 are libraries. "Sold nationally in bookstores." Single copy: $7; subscription: $20/year, $35/2 years. Sample: $7.

How to Submit Submit 6 pages of poetry at a time. No previously published poems or simultaneous submissions. No e-mail submissions. Cover letter is preferred with a brief bio "about the poet, not their credits." Has backlog of up to one year. Guidelines available for SASE or by e-mail. Responds within 6 weeks. Pays one copy and contributor's discount for the issue in which work appears. Acquires one-time rights.

Contest/Award Offerings Book-length poetry contest (48-80 pages). **Deadline:** January 31. **Entry fee:** $20. 1st Prize: $1,000 and 50 copies. Also offers chapbook contest. **Deadline:** May 31. **Entry fee:** $15. 1st Prize: $500 and 100 copies. Previous winners: David Chorlton, Alan Catlin, Dede Wilson, Nancy Kenney Connolly, Karla Huston, Pam Bernard, and Matt Morris.

Advice "Small press independents exist by and for writers. Without their support (and the support of readers) we have no reason to exist. Sampling first is always appreciated."

⬚ $⬚ THE MALAHAT REVIEW; LONG POEM PRIZE

P.O. Box 1700, STN CSC, University of Victoria, Victoria BC V8W 2Y2 Canada. (250)721-8524. E-mail: malahat@uvic.ca (inquiries only). Website: http://web.uvic.ca/malahat/. Established 1967. **Editor:** John Barton.

Magazine Needs: *The Malahat Review* is "a high-quality, visually appealing literary quarterly which has earned the praise of notable literary figures throughout North America. Its purpose is to publish and promote poetry and fiction of a very high standard, both Canadian and international. We are interested in various styles, lengths, and themes. The criterion is excellence." Has published poetry by Karen Solie and Don McKay. Receives about 2,000 poems/year, accepts about 100. Publishes 50 pages of poetry/issue. Has 1,000 subscribers of which 300 are libraries. Subscription: $40 Canadian (or US equivalent). Sample: $8 US.

How to Submit Submit 5-10 poems, addressed to editor. Include SASE with Canadian stamps or IRC with each submission. Guidelines available for SASE (or SAE and IRC). Responds within 3 months. Pays $30/anticipated magazine page plus 2 contributor's copies and one year's subscription. Acquires first world serial rights. Reviews Canadian books of poetry.

Contest/Award Offerings Sponsors the Long Poem Prize, 2 awards of $400 plus publication and payment at their usual rates, for a long poem or cycle 5-15 pages (flexible minimum and maximum). **Deadline:** March 1 of alternate years (2005, 2007, etc.). **Entry fee:** $40 Canadian or US equivalent (one-year subscription). Include name and address on a separate page.

$⬚ MAMMOTH BOOKS; MAMMOTH PRESS INC.

7 Juniata St., DuBois PA 15801. E-mail: info@mammothpressinc.org. Website: www.mammothpressinc.org. Established 1997. **Publisher:** Antonio Vallone.

Book/Chapbook Needs MAMMOTH books, an imprint of MAMMOTH press inc., publishes 2-4 paperbacks/year of creative nonfiction, fiction, and poetry through annual competitions. "We are open to all types of literary poetry." Has published *The House of Sages* by Philip Terman, *The Never Wife* by Cynthia Hogue, *These Happy Eyes* by Liz Rosenberg, and *Subjects for Other Conversations* by John Stigall. Books are usually 5×7 or 6×9, digitally-printed, perfect-bound; covers vary (1- to 4-color); include art.

Contest/Award Offerings Send mss to contest. **Not currently reading outside of contests.** For poetry mss, submit a collection of poems or a single long poem. Translations are accepted. "Manuscripts as a whole must not have been previously published. Some or all of each manuscript may have appeared in periodicals, chapbooks, anthologies, or other venues; these must be identified. Authors are responsible for securing permissions." Accepts simultaneous submissions. No e-mail submissions. Submit mss by postal mail, UPS, or FedEx only. Poetry mss should be single-spaced, no more than one poem/page. Reads submissions September 1 through February 28/29. **Entry fee:** $20. Make checks payable to MAMMOTH books. Time between acceptance and publication is up to 3 years. Poems are circulated to an editorial board. "Finalists will be chosen by the staff of MAMMOTH books in consultation with an outside editorial board and/or guest editor. Manuscripts will be selected based on merit only." Seldom comments on rejected mss. "Pays royalties: 10% of books printed." Other finalist mss may be selected for publication and offered a standard royalty contract and publication of at least 500 trade paperback copies. Finalists will be announced within 2 years from the end of each submission period. MAMMOTH press inc. reserves the right not to award a prize if no entries are deemed suitable. Complete rules are available for SASE or by e-mail. Order sample books by sending for information to their mailing address or e-mail.

Advice ''Read big. Write big. Publish small. Join the herd.''

☐ MANDRAKE POETRY REVIEW; THE MANDRAKE PRESS

Box 792, Larkspur CA 94977-0792. E-mail: mandrake@a4.pl. Website: www.mandrake.a4.pl/. Established 1993 in New York. **Editors:** Leo Yankevich and David Castleman.

Magazine Needs *Mandrake Poetry Review* appears at least twice/year. Seeks poetry in translation as well as content concerning ethnicity/nationality, politics, and social issues. Has published poetry by Michael Daugherty, George Held, Hugh Fox, Errol Miller, Simon Perchik, and Joan Peternel. *Mandrake Poetry Review* is 76-150 pages, A5, offset-printed, flat-spined, with glossy white card cover. Accepts about 10% of the poetry received. Press run is 500 for 100 subscribers from 3 continents. Single copy: $5 (by airmail); subscription: $20/2 years. Make checks payable to David Castleman.

How to Submit Submit up to 7 poems at a time. ''Send only copies of your poems, as we do not return poems with our reply.'' Accepts previously published poems and simultaneous submissions. Accepts e-mail submissions (pasted into body of message). Cover letter is preferred. Guidelines available for SASE. Responds in 2 months. Pays 2 contributor's copies, ''sometimes more.'' All rights revert to author. ''Poets are encouraged to send their books for review consideration to David Castleman. All editors and publishers whose books/chapbooks are selected for review will receive one copy of the issue in which the review appears. We publish 50-100 reviews yearly.''

☒ $☐ MANIFOLD PRESS; MANIFOLD CHAPBOOK; MANIFOLD MONTHLY

102 Bridge St., Plattsburgh NY 12901. (518)561-1565. E-mail: editormanifoldpress@msn.com. Website: www.manifoldpress.com. Established 2003. **Editor/Publisher:** Carol Frome. Member: PMA, CLMP, LPA.

Book/Chapbook Needs Manifold Press publishes collections of poetry. Wants ''good poetry that contains metaphor, imagery, fresh language, and vision.'' Does not want ''haiku, mindless rhyme, lines of verse without metaphor.'' Has published poetry by Charles Fishman, Linda Young, and Sarah Patton (through *Manifold Chapbook* online; first print collection to be released in 2004). Publishes 4 books/year, 8-12 chapbooks/year (chapbooks published electronically at this time). Manuscripts are selected through open submission. Books are usually 50-80 pages, offset-printed, Smyth-sewn with flat spines, quality 4-color process covers (''we work with authors to choose cover art'').

How to Submit No electronic submissions. Book/chapbook mss may include previously published poems. **We do not consider manuscripts or samples of poetry that are not accompanied by the reading fee ($20 per manuscript).** We do not even consider partial manuscripts without the reading fee. Doing so is unfair to all those who do send the fee.'' Responds to mss in 3 months. Pays royalties of 7%, $500 advance, and 10 author's copies (out of a press run of 1,000). Order sample books and view electronic chapbooks by visiting www.manifoldpress.com.

Also Offers ''*Manifold Chapbook* is an electronic monthly publication of the work of worthy poets. A free public service. Publication in *Manifold Chapbook* does not mean we will publish your book. *Manifold Monthly* is an informative electronic newsletter. *Critiques & Comments* is our website page devoted to reviews and commentaries on poetry and the poetry scene.''

Advice ''Do you read contemporary poetry? If not, you might not be doing a very good job writing it, either, no matter what your friends and relatives tell you. Read the website before submitting your work; try not to ask questions that are clearly answered there. Doing so makes us wonder how serious you are. Manifold Press is a serious poetry press and recognizes when individuals have plied their craft for a while. This does not mean a given poet needs to be widely recognized; we sincerely hope to balance our book list with the work of both known and little-known poets. The reading fee offsets the cost of publishing and marketing books. We are not running a contest and are under no obligation to choose 'a winner' or to publish manuscripts we deem to be unsuitable or to publish more manuscripts than we can afford to. After the first year, we're hoping to publish at least four books a year. To that end, we want to work with authors who will help us to sell their books by doing engaging readings, placing their books in all kinds of shops—we don't think that poetry should be confined to the halls of academe—and otherwise approaching the business of selling books in a creative fashion. Every book that earns back its costs means we can turn that money around and publish another poet's book.''

☑ MANKATO POETRY REVIEW

English Dept., 230 Armstrong Hall, Minnesota State University, Mankato MN 56001. (507)389-5511. E-mail: roger.sheffer@mankato.msus.edu. Website: www.english.mnsu.edu/publications/masthead.html. Established 1984. **Editor:** Roger Sheffer.

Magazine Needs *Mankato Poetry Review* is a semiannual magazine that is "open to all forms and themes, though we seldom print 'concrete poetry,' religious, or sentimental verse. We frequently publish first-time poets." Has published poetry by Edward Micus, Gary Fincke, Judith Skillman, and Walter Griffin. *Mankato Poetry Review* is 30 pages, digest-sized, typeset on 60 lb. paper, saddle-stapled, with buff matte card cover printed in one color. It appears usually in May and December and has a press run of 200. Subscription: $5/year. Sample: $2.50.

How to Submit Submit up to 6 poems at a time. Line length for poetry is 60 maximum. No previously published poems or simultaneous submissions. Cover letter is required. "Please include biographical note on separate sheet. Poems not accompanied by SASE will not be returned." **Deadlines:** April 15 (May issue) and November 15 (December issue). Do not submit mss in summer (May through August). Guidelines available for SASE. Responds in about 2 months; "We accept only what we can publish in next issue." Pays 2 contributor's copies.

Advice "We're interested in looking at longer poems—up to 60 lines, with great depth of detail relating to place (landscape, townscape).''

$☑ MĀNOA: A PACIFIC JOURNAL OF INTERNATIONAL WRITING

1733 Donaghho Rd., Honolulu HI 96822. Fax: (808)956-3083. E-mail: mjournal-l@hawaii.edu. Website: http://manoajournal.hawaii.edu. Established 1989. **Poetry Editor:** Frank Stewart.

● Poetry published in *Mānoa* has also appeared in volumes of *The Best American Poetry*.

Magazine Needs *Mānoa* appears twice/year. "We are a general interest literary magazine and consider work in many forms and styles, regardless of the authors' publishing history. However, we are not for the beginning writer. It is best to look at a sample copy of the journal before submitting." Has published poetry by Arthur Sze, Ai, Linda Gregg, Jane Hirshfield, and Ha Jin. *Mānoa* is 240 pages, 7×10, offset-printed, flat-spined, includes art and graphics. Receives about 1,000 poems/year, accepts 2%. Press run is over 2,500 for several hundred subscribers of which 100 are libraries, 400 shelf sales. "In addition, *Mānoa* is available through Project Muse to about 600 institutional subscribers throughout the world." Subscription: $22/year. Sample: $10.

How to Submit Query by mail or e-mail. Submit 3-5 poems at a time. Seldom comments on rejected poems. Guidelines available on website. Responds in 6 weeks. Always sends prepublication galleys. Pays "competitive" amount plus 2 contributor's copies. Reviews current books and chapbooks of poetry. Send materials for for review consideration to reviews editor.

Advice "We are not a regional journal, but each issue features a particular part of Asia or the Pacific; these features, which include poetry, are assembled by guest editors. The rest of each issue features work by poets from the U.S. and elsewhere. We welcome the opportunity to read poetry from throughout the country, but we are not interested in genre or formalist writing for its own sake, or in casual impressions of the Asia-Pacific region.''

✍ MARGIE/THE AMERICAN JOURNAL OF POETRY; THE MARJORIE J. WILSON AWARD FOR EXCELLENCE IN POETRY; "STRONG MEDICINE" AWARD; INTUIT HOUSE POETRY BOOK AWARD CONTEST

P.O. Box 250, Chesterfield MO 63006-0250. Fax: (636)532-0539. E-Mail: margiereview@aol.com. Website: www.margiereview.com. Established 2001. **Editor-in-Chief:** Robert Nazarene.

Magazine Needs *MARGIE/The American Journal of Poetry* appears annually in September. ''*MARGIE* publishes superlative poetry. No limits to school, form, subject matter. Imaginative, risk-taking poetry which disturbs and/or consoles is of paramount interest. A distinctive voice is prized.'' Has published poetry by Stephen Dunn, Emmylou Harris, Jane Hirshfield, Ted Kooser, Maxine Kumin, and Sherod Santos. ''*MARGIE* is about 350-400+ pages, digest-sized, professionally printed, perfect-bound, with glossy cover with art/graphics, includes ads. Receives about 25,000 poems/year, accepts less than 1%. Publishes about 150-200 poems/issue. Press run is 2,000 (circulation). Available by subscription only. Single copy (one-year subscription): $13.95 for individuals, $18.95 for institutions & foreign (prices include shipping & handling). Make checks payable to *MARGIE*.

How to Submit Submit 3-5 poems at a time. Line length for poetry is 90 maximum. Accepts simultaneous submissions (notify in cover letter); no previously published poems. No fax, e-mail, or disk submissions. Cover letter is required. ''A short bio is useful, but not required.'' Open reading: June 1 through October 15. ''Subscribers *only* may submit year round. Identify yourself as 'subscriber' on outside of submission envelope.'' Time between acceptance and publication is up to one year. Editor makes final decision. *Sometimes* comments on rejected poems. Guidelines available in magazine, for SASE, or on website. Responds in about 3 weeks. Sometimes sends prepublication galleys. Pays one contributor's copy. Acquires first rights. All rights revert to poet upon publication.

Contest/Award Offerings ''The Marjorie J. Wilson Award for Excellence in Poetry'' (spring); ''Strong Medicine'' Award (autumn); IntuiT House Poetry Book Award Contest (winter). Guidelines available for SASE or on website.

Advice ''Read, read, read. Then, read some more. Invest 90% of your literary life reading; 10% writing. Be audacious, innovative, distinctive.''

✍ ◎ MARGIN: EXPLORING MODERN MAGICAL REALISM (Specialized: magical realism)

321 High School Rd. NE, PMB #204, Bainbridge Island WA 98110. E-mail: smike10@qwest.net. Website: www.magical-realism.com. Established 2000. **Poetry Editor:** Kelli Russell Agodon.

Magazine Needs *Margin: Exploring Modern Magical Realism* is the world's only continuous survey of contemporary literary magical realism. We want accessible poetry where metamorphoses are authentic, and where the magical and mundane coexist. Metaphor alone does not qualify as magical realism. No light verse, forced rhyme, or language poetry, and *no* New Age, surrealism, Wiccan, or science fiction.'' *Margin* is published online (''as we find good poetry—no schedule''). Receives ''thousands'' of poems/year, accepts about 2%. Circulation is about 5,000 pageviews/month. Single copy: free; subscription: free, automated, private. Sample: visit website or send $2 for a copy of *Periphery*, our print zine sample.

How to Submit Submit up to 6 poems at a time. ''No preferred line length, but our bias runs to shorter rather than longer.'' Accepts previously published poems and simultaneous submissions (if notified). Accepts e-mail submissions (*no* attachments). ''Poems submitted without SASE will not be read or returned.'' See website for submission periods and contests deadlines. Accepts translations if matched with English-language originals at time of submission. Time between acceptance and publication is usually 6 months. Poems are circulated to an editorial board. ''Editors live in separate cities in the U.S. and Canada.'' Seldom comments on rejected poems (''Only when they are good poems but not magical realism. We send reading list of top 10 favorite magical realist poets or authors, plus bio and short definition of 'magical realism.' "). All work is considered for publication in both *Margin* and its print zine sample, *Periphery*. Occasionally publishes theme issues. Guidelines and upcoming themes available on website. "Spring 2005 theme: 'Quixotic Journeys: Magical Realism from Spain and Portugal.' " Responds in 6 months. Usually sends prepublication galleys as URL form. May offer small payment. Nominates for literary prizes. Rights acquired are negotiable. Reviews books and chapbooks of poetry in under 500 words ("but we are flexible"), single book and multi-book format. Send materials for review consideration to poetry editor ("Nothing academic!"). Also interested in articles, essays on poetry as magical realism, interviews of magical realist poets, and critical discussions of magical realist work by poets from around the world.

Also Offers "Broad global exposure has benefited many of our published writers."

Advice "*Understand* what magical realism is *before* submitting. See website for guidelines."

MARSH HAWK PRESS

P.O. Box 206, East Rockaway NY 11518. E-mail: MarshHawkPress@cs.com. Website: www.Marsh HawkPress.org. Established 2001.

Book/Chapbook Needs & How to Submit Marsh Hawk Press publishes books of "quality poetry of any lineage—post-Imagist-Objectivist, New York School, surrealist, experimental, language, concrete, etc." Has published poetry by Eileen Tabios, Sandy McIntosh, Ed Foster, Harriet Zinnes, Sharon Dolin, and Basil King. Publishes 6 poetry books/year. Manuscripts are selected through open submission. Books are 48-152 pages, photo offset-printed, perfect-bound, with 4-color covers. **Marsh Hawk Press currently accepts submissions only through its annual competition, the Marsh Hawk Press Prize.** "The press is a collective whose author-members agree to work with the press on all aspects of book production, including editing, design, distribution, sales, advertising, publicity, and fund raising."

Advice "See our website for our manifesto and contest information."

MARYMARK PRESS (Specialized: experimental/avant-garde)

45-08 Old Millstone Dr., East Windsor NJ 08520. (609)443-0646. Website: www.experimentalpoet.c om. Established 1994. **Editor/Publisher:** Mark Sonnenfeld.

Book/Chapbook Needs Marymark Press's goal is "to feature and promote experimental writers. I will most likely be publishing broadsides, give-out sheets, and chapbooks this year. I want to see experimental writing of the outer fringe. Make up words, sounds, whatever, but say something you thought never could be explained. Disregard rules if need be." No traditional, rhyming, or spiritual verse; no predictable styles. Has published poetry by Axel Monte, John Crouse, Jennifer Esrailian, Michelle Perez, and Marc De Hay.

How to Submit Submit 3 poems at a time. Accepts previously published poems and simultaneous submissions. Cover letter is preferred. "Copies should be clean, crisp, and camera-ready. I do not have the means to accept electronic submissions. A SASE should accompany all submissions, and a telephone number if at all possible." Upcoming themes and guidelines available for SASE. Time between acceptance and publication is one month. Seldom comments on rejected poems. Responds to queries and mss in up to 2 weeks. Pays at least 10 author's copies (out of a press run of 200-300). May offer subsidy arrangements. "It all depends upon my financial situation at the time. Yes, I might ask the author to subsidize the cost. It could be worth their while. I have good connections in the international small press." Order sample publications by sending a 6×9 SAE. "There is no charge for samples."

Advice "Experiment with thought, language, the printed word."

$⬚ THE MASSACHUSETTS REVIEW

South College, University of Massachusetts, Amherst MA 01003. (413)545-2689. E-mail: massrev@e xternal.umass.edu. Website: www.massreview.org. Established 1959. **Poetry Editors:** Paul Jenkins and Anne Halley.

- Work published in this review has been frequently included in volumes of *The Best American Poetry*.

Magazine Needs Appearing quarterly, *The Massachusetts Review* publishes "fiction, essays, artwork, and excellent poetry of all forms and styles." Has published poetry by Marilyn Hacker, Virgil Suárez, and Miller Williams. *The Massachusetts Review* is digest-sized, offset-printed on bond paper, perfect-bound, with color card cover, occasionally includes art and photography sections. Receives about 2,500 poems/year, accepts about 50. Press run is 1,600 for 1,100-1,200 subscribers of which 1,000 are libraries, the rest for shelf sales. Subscription: $22/year (US), $30 outside US, $30 for libraries. Sample: $8 (US), $11 outside US.

How to Submit No simultaneous submissions or previously published poems. Reads submissions October 1 through June 1 only. Guidelines available for SASE or on website. Responds in 6 weeks. Pays minimum of $10, or 35¢/line, plus 2 contributor's copies.

$⬚ ◎ MATURE YEARS (Specialized: senior citizen/aging; Christian)

P.O. Box 801, 201 Eighth Ave. S., Nashville TN 37202. (615)749-6292. Fax: (615)749-6512. E-mail: matureyears@umpublishing.org. Established 1954. **Editor:** Marvin W. Cropsey.

Magazine Needs *Mature Years* is a quarterly. "The magazine's purpose is to help persons understand and use the resources of Christian faith in dealing with specific opportunities and problems related to aging. Poems are usually limited to 16 lines and may, or may not, be overtly religious. Poems should not poke fun at older adults, but may take a humorous look at them. Avoid sentimentality and saccharine. If using rhymes and meter, make sure they are accurate." *Mature Years* is 112 pages, magazine-sized, perfect-bound, with full-color glossy paper cover. Press run is 55,000. Sample: $5.

How to Submit Line length for poetry is 16 lines of up to 50 characters maximum. Accepts fax submissions; prefers e-mail submissions. Submit seasonal and nature poems for spring during December through February; for summer, March through May; for fall, June through August; and for winter, September through November. Guidelines available for SASE or by e-mail. Responds in 2 months; sometimes a year's delay before publication. Pays $1/line upon acceptance.

$⬚ ◎ MEADOWBROOK PRESS (Specialized: anthologies; children; humor)

5451 Smetana Dr., Minnetonka MN 55343. Website: www.meadowbrookpress.com. Established 1975. **Contact:** Read 'Em, Rate 'Em Editor.

Book/Chapbook Needs Meadowbrook Press "is currently seeking poems to be posted on website and to be considered for future funny poetry book anthologies for children." Wants humorous poems aimed at children ages 6-12. "Poems should be fun, punchy, and refreshing. We're looking for new, hilarious, contemporary voices in children's poetry that kids can relate to." Accepts poetry written by children "only for website contests—not for publication in books. Grades 1-12." Has published poetry by Shel Silverstein, Jack Prelutsky, Jeff Moss, Kenn Nesbitt, and Bruce Lansky. Anthologies include *Kids Pick the Funniest Poems*, *A Bad Case of the Giggles*, and *Miles of Smiles*.

How to Submit "Please take time to read our guidelines, and send your best work." Submit up to 10 poems; one poem to a page with name and address on each. Line length for poetry is 15 maximum. Include SASE with submission. Accepts simultaneous submissions. Time between acceptance and publication is 1-2 years. Poems are tested in front of grade school students before being published. Guidelines available for SASE or on website. Pays $50-100/poem plus one contributor's copy.

◪ MEDICINAL PURPOSES LITERARY REVIEW; MARILYN K. PRESCOTT MEMORIAL POETRY CONTEST; POET TO POET, INC.

75-05 210th St., #6N, Bayside NY 11364. (718)776-8853. E-mail: dunnmiracle@juno.com. Established 1994. **Executive Editor:** Robert Dunn. **Associate Editor/Poetry Editor:** Leigh Harrison.

Magazine Needs *Medicinal Purposes* appears biannually and wants "virtually any sort of quality poetry. Please, no pornography, gratuitous violence, or hate mongering." Accepts poetry written by children for the Young Writers' column. Has published poetry by X.J. Kennedy, Rhina P. Espaillat, Maureen Holm, Ellen Peckham, and Kam Holifield. *Medicinal Purposes* is 32 pages, magazine-sized, professionally printed, perfect-bound, with card stock cover with b&w illustration, includes b&w illustrations. Receives 1,200 poems/year, accepts about 10%. Press run is 1,000 for 270 subscribers of which 6 are libraries, 30% shelf sales. Single copy: $9; subscription: $16/year. Sample: $6. Make checks payable to Poet to Poet.

How to Submit Submit 3 poems at a time. Line length for poetry is 60 maximum. No previously published poems or simultaneous submissions. Accepts e-mail submissions (pasted into body of message; no attachments). Cover letter is preferred. Include SASE. Time between acceptance and publication is up to 16 months. Often comments on rejected poems. Guidelines available for SASE or by e-mail. Responds in 3 months. Sends prepublication galleys to US contributors. Pays 2 contributor's copies. Acquires first rights.

Contest/Award Offerings Sponsors an annual poetry contest, 1st Prize: $50. Submit 3 poems of 6-16 lines each. **Entry fee:** $5. **Deadline:** June 15. Winners will be published in the year's end issue. Also administers the Marilyn K. Prescott Memorial Poetry Contest. Details available for SASE.

Advice "Poetry cannot be created out of a vacuum. Read the work of others, listen to performances, learn the difference between the universal and the generic, and most important—Get A Life! Do Things! If you get struck by lightning, then share the light. Only then do you stand a chance of finding your own voice."

◪ MELLEN POETRY PRESS

P.O. Box 450, Lewiston NY 14092-0450. (716)754-2266. Fax: (716)754-4056. E-mail: mellen@wzrd. com. Website: www.mellenpress.com. Established 1973. **Poetry Editor:** Patricia Schultz.

Book/Chapbook Needs "Mellen Poetry Press is a division of The Edwin Mellen Press, a scholarly press. We do not have access to large chain bookstores for distribution, but depend on direct sales and independent bookstores." Pays 5 author's copies, royalties "after 500 copies are sold for 5 years. We require no author subsidies. However, we encourage our authors to seek grants from Councils for the Arts and other foundations because these add to the reputation of the volume." Wants "original integrated work—living unity of poems, preferably unpublished, encompassable in one reading." Has published poetry by Andrew Oerke and James Sutton. Books are up to 128 pages, digest-sized, with hardcover binding; no graphics. Price: $39.95.

How to Submit Submit 70-120 sample poems with cover letter including bio and publication credits. "We do not print until we receive at least 50 prepaid orders. Successful marketing of poetry books depends on the author's active involvement. We send out free review copies to journals or newspapers when requested. An author may, but is not required to, purchase books that count toward the needed pre-publication sales."

Advice "We seek to publish volumes unified in mood, tone, theme."

$◙ THE MENNONITE (Specialized: Christian)

P.O. Box 347, Newton KS 67114-0347. (316)283-5100. Fax: (316)283-0454. E-mail: gordonh@theme nnonite.org. Website: www.themennonite.org. Established 1885. **Associate Editor:** Gordon Houser.

Magazine Needs *The Mennonite* is published twice/month and wants "Christian poetry—usually free verse, not too long, with multiple layers of meaning. No sing-song rhymes or poems that merely

describe or try to teach a lesson." Has published poetry by Jean Janzen and Julia Kasdorf. *The Mennonite* is 32 pages, magazine-sized, with full color cover, includes art and ads. Receives about 200 poems/year, accepts about 5%. Press run is 14,000 for 13,500 subscribers. Single copy: $2; subscription: $38.75. Sample: $1.
How to Submit Submit up to 4 poems at a time. Accepts previously published poems and simultaneous submissions. Prefers e-mail submissions. Cover letter is preferred. Time between acceptance and publication is up to 6 months. Seldom comments on rejected poems. Occasionally publishes theme issues. List of upcoming themes and guidelines available for SASE. Responds in 2 weeks. Pays $50-75 plus one contributor's copy. Acquires first or one-time rights.

$☑ MERIDIAN

University of Virginia, P.O. Box 400145, Charlottesville VA 22904-4145. (434)989-5793. E-mail: meridian@virginia.edu. Website: www.engl.virginia.edu/meridian. Established 1998. **Contact:** Poetry Editor.
Magazine Needs *Meridian* appears biannually, publishing poetry, fiction, interviews, and reviews. Has published poetry by David Kirby, Charles Wright, and Joelle Biele. *Meridian* is 190 pages, digest-sized, offset-printed, perfect-bound, with color cover, includes art. Receives about 2,500 poems/year, accepts about 30 (less than 1%). Publishes about 15 poems/issue. Press run is 1,000 for 750 subscribers of which 15 are libraries, 200 shelf sales; 150 are distributed free to writing programs. Single copy: $7; subscription: $10/year. Make checks payable to *Meridian*.
How to Submit Submit 1-5 poems at a time. Accepts simultaneous submissions; no previously published poems. No fax, e-mail, or disk submissions. Cover letter is preferred. Reads submissions September through May primarily. Time between acceptance and publication is 1-2 months. Seldom comments on rejected poems. Guidelines available on website. Responds in up to 2 months. Sometimes sends prepublication galleys. Pays $15/page ($250 maximum, as long as funding is available) and 2 contributor's copies (additional copies available at discount). Reviews books of poetry.

☐ ◎ MERIDIAN ANTHOLOGY OF CONTEMPORARY POETRY

P.O. Box 970309, Boca Raton FL 33497. E-mail: LetarP@aol.com. Website: www.Meridianantholog y.com. Established 2002. **Editor/Publisher:** Phyliss L. Geller. **Literary Editor:** Marilyn Krepf.
Magazine Needs *Meridian Anthology of Contemporary Poetry* appears annually in April and wants "poetry that is contemporary, insightful, and illuminating, that touches the nerves. It should have color, content, and be deciphering of existence." Does not want vulgarity, clichés. Has published poetry by June Owens, John Grey, Richard St. John, Gerald Zipper, and Brenda Serotte. *Meridian Anthology* is 96-120 pages, digest-sized, offset-printed, perfect-bound, with soft cover. Publishes about 90-110 poems/issue. Press run is 500-1,000. Single copy: $12 for soft cover. Make checks payable to *Meridian Anthology*.
How to Submit Submit 1-5 poems at a time. Line length for poetry is 39-78. Accepts simultaneous submissions and previously published poems. No fax, e-mail, or disk submissions. Cover letter is preferred. Must include SASE. Reads submissions from March to December. Submit seasonal poems 6 months in advance. Time between acceptance and publication is up to one year. Seldom comments on rejected poems. Guidelines available for SASE or on website. Responds in "3 weeks to 3 months, depending on backlog." Pays one contributor's copy. Acquires one-time rights.
Advice "A poem must have a reason for existence, some universal tendril."

$☑ MICHIGAN QUARTERLY REVIEW; LAURENCE GOLDSTEIN POETRY AWARD

Dept. PM, 3574 Rackham Bldg., University of Michigan, 915 E. Washington St., Ann Arbor MI 48109. (734)764-9265. E-mail: mqr@umich.edu. Website: www.umich.edu/~mqr. Established 1962. **Editor-in-Chief:** Laurence Goldstein.

Marie Jordan

Exploring poetry's magic side

> . . . A smile drips from the face of the sky
> like runny old people food—it forms
> a wet ribbon that is dawn
> and looks like oatmeal   The sky
> is full of oatmeal today . . .

—excerpt from "Starting Over"
from *Slow Dance on Stilts* (La Jolla Poets Press, 2001)

The introduction to this contemplative poem exemplifies the woman behind it: passionate, tender, thoughtful, yearning to experience all that life has to offer; a woman who possesses a healthy dose of humor and powerful observation skills. Poet, author, and teacher Marie Jordan (Giordano) calls it like she sees it, but with an artist's flair for shining light on the smallest detail.

When talking about writing, Jordan's eloquence makes it hard to distinguish her prose from her poetry. "Poetry is, for me, the magic link to entering the invisible, the intangible, and the shadow side of life," she explains. "Poetry unhinges taboos and restraints and gives permission to enter the private rooms in one's life and experience.

"Poetry forces the writer to plunge deeper into language," Jordan continues, "to examine and explore and find insight and meaning in tight spaces. Poetry squeezes the poet for meaning; it is an art that forces poet and reader alike into a place of breathtaking discovery. I am continually stunned by the magic of poetry."

And for this reason, when Jordan teaches college classes, she starts with modern poetry. "I want to challenge the mindset that poetry is rhymed sing-song pretty stuff in archaic language that you need *CliffsNotes*™ to decipher," she says.

Jordan has published nonfiction, children's books, and poetry under the names Marie Chapian, Marie Jordan, and now Marie Giordano. Why three names? The reasons range from personal to business.

"My married name was Chapian, and I wrote some 30 books under that name," Jordan explains. "Then, after my divorce, I took my maiden name back and began writing as Marie Jordan. When the first book of my Italian immigrant novel trilogy, *I Love You Like a Tomato*, came out, the publisher wanted me to use my ancestral family name, Giordano."

Jordan resisted this suggestion until her mother convinced her to use the name that was changed at Ellis Island. On her website (www.mariejordan.com), Jordan writes "it wasn't my idea to use the old family name, but now it's attached to me, I'm beginning to get used to it. It's a sort of return to the roots, I guess you might say. But on the other hand, it's being three identities."

Creating a pen name is not something Jordan recommends for all writers as a way to explore a deeper part of one's psyche. "I don't think a name changes a person. But many writers use different names for the different genres they write in. It's common to use other names in the mystery and romance genres, for example."

Like many writers, Jordan started very young. As early as first grade, her poems won contests. She recalls one prize-winning humorous poem about taking a bath and another about not liking soup. "These experiences reinforce what I teach my writing students— all of life is fodder for the page," Jordan says. She admits she has always taken poetry seriously, even the bad poems.

Seeing herself as a poet, however, took the publication of her first book, *City Psalms*, which "won some awards," Jordan says. Her most recent poetry collection, *Slow Dance on Stilts*, won the Award of Excellence from the San Diego Book Awards Association in 2001. Living in southern California with frequent sojourns to Italy, Jordan writes constantly and teaches creative writing and poetry at Mira Costa College.

Her first novel, *I Love You Like a Tomato* (Forge, 2003), has received critical and popular praise for its combination of poignancy with humor. In fact, most people cite her unusual and eclectic use of language as the book's power center.

Fusing poetry and fiction is a way of life for Jordan. "For me, poetry is to fiction writing what ballet is to the serious dancer," she says. "It's foundational."

An avid reader and advocate of reading, Jordan wrote her MFA thesis on the cross-genre writer, and after 50 some pages she felt she "had barely tapped the topic. Poetry focuses the writer in on the most minute detail, like filmmaking, in a way."

Walking across a room, for example—Jordan points out that even this banal action can become a monumental event in a poet's or filmmaker's hands. "When you give that action to a fictional character in a scene where there is conflict and a certain tension, you'll have a great time getting it on the page because you've learned to experience the action for more than the action itself."

Looking at common events in artistic terms came to a head with the September 11, 2001 attacks. "I've done a lot more thinking about the poet's role in society," says Jordan, who believes that role has changed. "[Robert Pinsky] was a fabulous laureate and did so much for poetry by listening to the public and giving them a voice. I think I used to see us as fringe folk, you know, out there reading our poems in coffeehouses and libraries to audiences of other poets."

During a 1998 Vermont Studio Center residency, Jordan doubted poetry's attraction and appeal to a general audience when a huge snowstorm struck the night of a scheduled reading. "The snow was deep, the winds fierce, the temperature plummeting downward," Jordan recalls in her Writing Life column on her website, "but the reading, which was to be held in a cold and drafty old building on the main street of town, was not canceled. I fully expected no one to show up. Who would go out on such a stormy night for a poetry reading?

"I was stunned that night when the people began arriving. Soon the place packed out and there wasn't an empty seat in the place. While the storm raged on outside, we were inside reading our poems to an appreciative and attentive audience. It was an amazing experience for me."

Poetry can draw people out into a blizzard, yet a perfectly balmy, sun-filled evening might find a public reading empty: This confirms the unexpected and fluid nature of poetry itself. You just never know when people need poetry.

"September 11 showed us a little of the power of poems," Jordan says. "When tragedy struck, we didn't quote from novels or memoirs, we didn't run out and look for certain paintings or sculptures, we turned to poetry to speak for us."

And yet, "The poetry section in bookstores has always been the smallest section, and so many great new books of poems aren't available in bookstores." The fact that so many poets are going unheard was the reason Jordan started an online poetry journal, *Roadspoetry.com*. "I know many wonderful poets whose work was not being read. I have produced poetry performances with my writing students and have also published student anthologies, but I wanted to publish a professional, quality poetry journal to reach a broader audience. The Internet was an ideal place for me."

Roadspoetry.com features some of today's best poets, known and unknown; people like Sydney Lea, Scott Cairns, Mark Jarman, Li-Young Lee, and others. "It's a lot of work, but the feedback we receive from readers makes it very gratifying," Jordan says. "I learned a lot from Sam Hamill, who founded Copper Canyon Press and tirelessly worked for years for no salary. When you are doing what you love, you can't do too much or work too hard."

—Amanda Lynch

Amanda Lynch has been a full-time freelance writer since 1996 and edits her own e-zine, *The Freedom Chronicles* (see www.amandawriter.com and www.freedomchronicles.com).

● Poetry published in *Michigan Quarterly Review* is frequently included in volumes of *The Best American Poetry* and was selected for the 2002 *Pushcart Prize* anthology.

Magazine Needs *Michigan Quarterly Review* is "an interdisciplinary, general interest academic journal that publishes mainly essays and reviews on subjects of cultural and literary interest." Uses all kinds of poetry except light verse. No specifications as to form, length, style, subject matter, or purpose. Has published poetry by Susan Hahn, Carl Phillips, Mary Oliver, and Yusef Komunyakaa. *Michigan Quarterly Review* is 160 pages, digest-sized, flat-spined, professionally printed, with glossy card cover, includes b&w photos and art. Receives about 1,400 submissions/year, accepts about 30, has a one-year backlog. Press run is 2,000 for 1,200 subscribers of which half are libraries. Single copy: $7; subscription: $25. Sample: $5 plus 2 first-class stamps.

How to Submit Prefers typed mss. No previously published poems or simultaneous submissions. No fax or e-mail submissions. Cover letter is preferred; "it puts a human face on the manuscript. A few sentences of biography is all I want, nothing lengthy or defensive." Publishes theme issues. Theme for autumn 2004 is "Vietnam: Beyond the Frame." Responds in 6 weeks. Always sends prepublication galleys. Pays $8-12/page. Acquires first rights only. Reviews books of poetry. "All reviews are commissioned."

Contest/Award Offerings The Laurence Goldstein Poetry Award, an annual cash prize of $1,000 given to the author of the best poem to appear in *Michigan Quarterly* during the calendar year. "Established in 2002, the prize is sponsored by the Office of the President of the University of Michigan."

Advice "There is no substitute for omnivorous reading and careful study of poets past and present, as well as reading in new and old areas of knowledge. Attention to technique, especially to rhythm and patterns of imagery, is vital."

$□ ◎ THE MID-AMERICA PRESS, INC.; THE MID-AMERICA POETRY REVIEW (Specialized: regional)

P.O. Box 575, Warrensburg MO 64093-0575. (660)747-4602. Press established 1976. **Editor:** Robert C. Jones.

Magazine Needs *The Mid-America Poetry Review* appears 3 times/year and publishes "well-crafted poetry primarily from—but not limited to—poets living in Missouri, Illinois, Arkansas, Oklahoma, Kansas, Nebraska, and Iowa. We are open to all styles and forms; what we look for is poetry by writers who know both what they are doing and why." Has published poetry by Brian Daldorph, Rhina P. Espaillat, Louis D. Brodsky, David Baker, Jim Thomas, and Barbara Van Noord. *The Mid-America Poetry Review* is 60-75 pages, digest-sized, offset-printed, perfect-bound, with matte paper cover. Receives about 1,000-2,000 poems/year, accepts about 15%. Press run is 750. Single copy: $6; subscription: $30/2 years. Make checks payable to The Mid-America Press, Inc.

How to Submit Submit 1-3 poems at a time. No previously published poems or simultaneous submissions. Cover letter is useful. "Type submissions, single- or double-spaced, on 8½×11 white paper; include name, address, and telephone number in top left or right corner. Enclose SASE for notification/guidelines. Do not send the only copy of your manuscript—unused submissions are recycled. One-page cover letter (if included) should list items to be considered; contain brief paragraphs of information about author and previous publications." Time between acceptance and publication may be up to one year. Sometimes comments on submissions. Guidelines available for SASE. Responds within 2 months. Sends prepublication galleys. Pays $5/poem and 2 contributor's copies on publication. Acquires first North American serial rights. Staff occasionally reviews books of poetry. Send materials for review consideration.

Book/Chapbook Needs & How to Submit The Mid-America Press, Inc. publishes 1-5 book-length poetry collections/year. "At present, the Press is not reading unsolicited book-length poetry manuscripts. The Mid-America Press Writing Award Competition has been discontinued until further notice." Mid-America Press, Inc. award-winning publications include *From Ink and Sandalwood* (1998) by Cecile M. Franking (winner of the 1999 Thorpe Menn Award for Writing Excellence); *Red Silk* (1999) by Maryfrances Wagner (winner of the 2000 Thorpe Menn Award for Writing Excellence); *Living Off the Land, a Gathering of Writing from The Warrensburg Writers Circle* (1999) edited by Robert C. Jones (First Place in The 2000 Walter Williams Major Work Award, from the Missouri Writers' Guild). Other publications include *Uncurling* (2000) by Jeanie Wilson, *Light and Chance* (2001) by Ardyth Bradley, *Dreaming the Bronze Girl* (2002) by Serina Allison Hearn, and *The Graveyard Picnic* (2002) by William Ford. Obtain sample books by sending $13.95/book.

⬛ MIDMARCH ARTS PRESS

300 Riverside Dr., New York NY 10025.

Book/Chapbook Needs & How to Submit Midmarch Arts Press publishes 4-6 paperbacks/year (only one poetry paperback/year). Query before submission. Has recently published *Mirror Mirror*, edited by Isabel Duke; *Split Verse*, edited by Meg Campbell and William Buke; *Solo Crossing* by Meg Campbell; *Sight Lines* by Charlotte Mandel; and *Whirling Round the Sun* by Suzanne Noguerre.

◕ MIDNIGHT MIND MAGAZINE

P.O. Box 146912, Chicago IL 60614. (312)545-6129. E-mail: submissions@midnightmind.com. Website: www.midnightmind.com. Established 2000. **Editor:** Brett Van Emst.

Magazine Needs *Midnight Mind Magazine*, a cultural review, appears biannually. Wants poetry of any style, any form. Does not want "poems about flowers (unless they are strange flowers)" or seasonal poems. Has published poetry by David Ray, Suzanne Burns, Jim Harrison, Dan Gerber, Phillip Corwin, Audrianne Hill, Tim Kahl, and Tom Short. *Midnight Mind Magazine* is 180 pages, magazine-sized, offset-printed, perfect-bound, with cardstock cover with photography, includes ads. Receives about 600 poems/year, accepts about 5%. Publishes about 10 poems/issue. Press run is 2,000 for 300 subscribers, 1,300 shelf sales; 100 are distributed free to the press, advertisers, and bookstores. Single copy: $10 (includes postage); subscription: $12/year, $20/2 years. Make checks payable to 3 A.M. Publishing.

How to Submit Submit any number of poems at a time. Line length is open. Accepts simultaneous submissions; no previously published poems. Accepts submissions by e-mail only. Cover letter with brief bio is required. "No crazy fonts!" Reads submissions year round. Time between acceptance and publication is up to 6 months. Poems are circulated to an editorial board. "There is a poetry editor, general editor, and advisory board—ALL are involved." Seldom comments on rejected poems. Regularly publishes theme issues. List of upcoming themes available by e-mail or on website. Guidelines available in magazine, for SASE, by e-mail, or on website. Responds in up to 6 months. Always sends prepublication galleys. Pays 2 contributor's copies. Acquires first North American serial rights. Reviews books and chapbooks of poetry and other magazines/journals in 500 words, single book format. Send materials for review consideration to Brett Van Emst.

Advice "Just write and send it out."

❏ THE MIDWEST QUARTERLY

Pittsburg State University, Pittsburg KS 66762. (620)235-4689. Fax: (620)235-4686. E-mail: smeats @pittstate.edu. Website: www.pittstate.edu/engl/midwest.html. Established 1959. **Poetry Editor:** Stephen Meats.

Magazine Needs *The Midwest Quarterly* "publishes articles on any subject of contemporary interest, particularly literary criticism, political science, philosophy, education, biography, and sociology. Each issue contains a section of poetry usually 12 poems in length. I am interested in well-crafted, though not necessarily traditional, poems that explore the inter-relationship of the human and natural worlds in bold, surrealistic images of a writer's imaginative, mystical experience. Sixty lines or less (occasionally longer if exceptional)." Has published poetry by David Baker, Fleda Brown, Jim Daniels, Naomi Shihab Nye, Greg Kuzma, Walt McDonald, Jeanne Murray Walker, and Peter Cooley. *The Midwest Quarterly* is 130 pages, digest-sized, professionally printed, flat-spined, with matte cover. Press run is 650 for 600 subscribers of which 500 are libraries. Receives about 4,000 poems/year, accepts about 60. Subscription: $15. Sample: $5.

How to Submit Submit no more than 10 poems at a time. Accepts simultaneous submissions; no previously published poems. No fax or e-mail submissions. Manuscripts should be typed with poet's name on each page. Editor comments on rejected poems "if the poet or poems seem particularly promising." Occasionally publishes theme issues. Guidelines and upcoming themes available for SASE, by fax, or by e-mail. Responds in 2 months, usually sooner. "Submissions without SASE cannot be acknowledged." Pays 2 contributor's copies. Acquires first serial rights. Reviews books of poetry by *Midwest Quarterly*-published poets only.

Advice "Keep writing; read as much contemporary poetry as you can lay your hands on; don't let the discouragement of rejection keep you from sending your work out to editors."

❏ ◎ MIDWEST VILLAGES & VOICES (Specialized: regional/Midwestern)

P.O. Box 40214, St. Paul MN 55104. (612)822-6878. Established 1979.

Book/Chapbook Needs & How to Submit Midwest Villages & Voices is a cultural organization and small press publisher of Midwestern poetry and prose. "We encourage and support Midwestern writers and artists. However, at this time submissions are accepted by invitation only. Unsolicited submissions are not accepted."

◎ MIDWIFERY TODAY (Specialized: childbirth)

P.O. Box 2672, Eugene OR 97402-0223. (541)344-7438. Fax: (541)344-1422. E-mail: editorial@mid wiferytoday.com. Website: www.midwiferytoday.com. Established 1986. **Editor-in-Chief:** Jan Tritten. **Editor:** Jessica Cagle.

Magazine Needs *Midwifery Today* is a quarterly that "provides a voice for midwives and childbirth educators. We are a midwifery magazine. Subject must be birth or birth profession related." Does not want poetry that is "off subject or puts down the subject." *Midwifery Today* is 75 pages, magazine-sized, offset-printed, saddle-stapled, with glossy card cover with b&w photos and b&w

artwork photos, includes ads. Uses about one poem/issue. Press run is 5,000 for 3,000 subscribers, 1,000 shelf sales. Subscription: $50. Sample: $10.

How to Submit No previously published poems. Accepts e-mail submissions (pasted into body of message/as attachment). Cover letter is required. Time between acceptance and publication is 1-2 years. Seldom comments on rejected poems. Publishes theme issues. Upcoming themes and deadlines available on website. Guidelines available for SASE or on website. Responds in 6 months. Pays 2 contributor's copies. Acquires first rights.

Advice "With our publication *please* stay on the subject."

◙ MILKWEED EDITIONS

1011 Washington Ave. S., Suite 300, Minneapolis MN 55415-1246. (612)332-3192. Fax: (612)215-2550. E-mail: editor@milkweed.org. Website: www.milkweed.org. Established 1984. **Contact:** Poetry Reader.

Book/Chapbook Needs Milkweed Editions is "looking for poetry manuscripts of high quality that embody humane values and contribute to cultural understanding." Not limited in subject matter. Open to writers with previously published books of poetry or a minimum of 6 poems published in nationally distributed commercials or literary journals. Accepts translations and bilingual mss. Published books of poetry include *Good Heart* by Deborah Keenan, *Turning Over the Earth* by Ralph Black, *Song of the World Becoming* by Pattiann Rogers, and *The Porcelain Apes of Moses Mendelssohn* by Jean Nordhaus.

How to Submit Submit 60 pages or more, typed on good quality white paper. Do not send originals. No submissions by fax or e-mail. Include SASE for reply. Unsolicited mss read in January and June *only*. "Milkweed can no longer return manuscripts in stamped book mailers. In the event that manuscripts are not accepted for publication, we prefer to recycle them. If you need your work returned, *please enclose a check for $5* rather than a stamped mailer." Guidelines available for SASE. Responds in up to 6 months. Catalog available on request, with $1.50 in postage.

$◙ MILLER'S POND; LOELLA CADY LAMPHIER PRIZE FOR POETRY; H&H PRESS

RR 2, Box 239, Middlebury Center PA 16935. (570)376-3361. Fax: (570)376-2674. E-mail: publisher @millerspondpoetry.com. Website: http://millerspondpoetry.com. Established 1987. **Publisher:** C.J. Houghtaling. **Editor:** David Cazden. **Web Editor:** Julie Damerell.

Magazine Needs Published in January, *miller's pond* is an annual magazine featuring contemporary poetry, interviews, reviews, and markets. "We want contemporary poetry that is fresh, accessible, energetic, vivid, and flows with language and rhythm. No religious, horror, pornographic, vulgar, rhymed, preachy, lofty, trite, or overly sentimental work." Has published poetry by Vivian Shipley, Barbara Crooker, Philip Memmer, and Shoshauna Shy. *miller's pond* is 48 pages, digest-sized, offset-printed, saddle-stapled, with cardstock cover. Receives about 200 poems/year, accepts 25-30 poems/issue. Press run is 200. Single copy: $10 plus $3.50 p&h. Sample (back issue) including guidelines: $8. Make checks payable to H&H Press.

How to Submit Submit 3-5 poems at a time. Line length for poetry is 40 maximum. Accepts previously published poems and simultaneous submissions. Accepts submissions by postal mail and through online submission form. Cover letter is preferred. "No returns without SASE." Reads submissions February 1 through October 1 only. Submissions received outside of the reading period may be held for the next reading period. Seldom comments on rejected poems. Guidelines available in magazine, for SASE, or on website. Responds in up to 11 months; "although we try to respond sooner, we are not always able to." Sometimes sends prepublication galleys. Pays $2/poem and one contributor's copy for work that appears in hard-copy version. Acquires one-time rights. Pays $5 for poetry book reviews, $10 for interviews with poets. See submission guidelines on website.

Contest/Award Offerings H&H Press sponsors the Loella Lamphier Prize for Poetry. 1st Prize: $100; 2nd Prize: $50; 3rd Prize: $25. Guidelines available on website. Send SASE. Also, website features original content not found in magazine. Accepts submissions through an online submission form only. Contact Julie Damerell, web editor.

Book/Chapbook Needs & How to Submit "H&H Press is a micro-publisher of poetry chapbooks and how-to-write books, with plans to expand into nonfiction and specialty books." Publishes one chapbook/year. Books are usually 24-36 pages, magazine-sized, offset-printed, saddle-stapled, with cardstock covers. Does NOT accept art. "Books published by invitation only; do not query. My requirements are simple—the poem/poetry must speak to me on more than one level and stay with me for more than just those few brief moments I'm reading it." Responds in 4 months. Pays royalties of 7% minimum, 12% maximum, and 25 author's copies (out of a press run of 200). Books are available for sale via website, phone, or fax.

Advice "Believe in yourself. Perseverance is a writer's best 'tool.' Study the contemporary masters: Vivian Shipley, Billy Collins, Maxine Kumin, Colette Inez, Hayden Carruth. Please check our website before submitting."

☐ ◎ MINDPRINTS, A LITERARY JOURNAL (Specialized: writers & artists with disabilities)

Learning Assistance Program, Allan Hancock College, 800 South College Dr., Santa Maria CA 93454-6399. (805)922-6966, ext. 3274. Fax: (805)922-3556. E-mail: pafahey@hancock.cc.ca.us. Website: www.hancockcollege.edu (click on Student Services, then Learning Assistance Program, then Mindprints). Established 2000. **Editor:** Paul Fahey.

● *Mindprints* was named one of the Top 30 Short Story Markets by *Writer's Digest* (June 2002).

Magazine Needs "*Mindprints, A Literary Journal* is a national annual publication of flash fiction, flash memoir, poetry, and black-and-white artwork. The journal is created as a forum for writers and artists with disabilities, but we also invite those who work in the field or have an interest in the population to submit their work. *Mindprints* takes great pride in showcasing new artists and giving voice to new writers. We also welcome and encourage established writers and artists." Wants all kinds of poetry. "We love anything short: haiku, haibun, cinquain; prose and rhyming poetry with unusual imagery." Has published poetry by Barbara Crooker, LaVonne Schoneman, Margaret Davidson, Marganit Alverez, Denize Lavoie Cain, and Joan C. Fingon. *Mindprints* is digest-sized, perfect-bound, with gloss laminated cover, includes b&w and digital artwork and photography. Receives about 150 poems/year, publishes about 22/issue. Press run is 600. "We sell copies at book fairs and to the community out of our office." Single copy: $6 plus $2 first-class postage. Make checks payable to Allan Hancock College.

How to Submit Submit up to 3 poems per reading period. Line length for poetry is 34 maximum. Accepts previously published poems and simultaneous submissions. Accepts e-mail submissions **only if poet resides outside the US**; accepts disk submissions only once the poems are accepted; no fax submissions. Cover letter is required. "Please send cover letter and SASE. In cover letter, tell us something about yourself, previous publications, if applicable, and tell us why you are submitting to *Mindprints*." Accepts submissions year round and begins reading collected submissions April 1; contributors are notified in late May. Time between acceptance and publication is 3-4 months. Poems are circulated to an editorial board. "We have a poetry editor who is an established poet and instructor at the college who reads the poetry and ranks it. (All identifying information has been removed.)" Seldom comments on rejected poems. Guidelines available in magazine, for SASE, or on website. Pays one contributor's copy. Acquires one-time rights.

Advice "We are one of the few national community college journals devoted to celebrating the work of artists and writers with disabilities. We look for a strong voice, unusual point of view, and rich imagery and description."

Ⓝ ☑ THE MINER'S CAT; LONELY MUNDI PRESS

P.O. Box 31624, Tucson AZ 85751. E-mail: theminerscatlitmag@msn.com. Established 2004. **Editor:** Linda Palmero.

Magazine Needs *The Miner's Cat* is a quarterly international journal of poetry, flash fiction, b&w art, and brief creative nonfiction. "Open to almost any style. Prefer free verse to forms, but will read all submissions with an open mind." Does not want greeting card verse. Has published poetry by Laraine Herring, Joseph Hutchison, Miriam Sagan, J.P. Dancing Bear, and Richard Garcia. *The Miner's Cat* is 48-60 pages, digest-sized, saddle-stapled, with cardstock cover with b&w art, includes decorative endpapers, integral bookmark, ads. Receives about 2,000 poems/year, accepts about 10%. Publishes about 50 poems/issue. Single copy: $6 US; subscription: $15 US. Make checks payable to Linda Palmero.

How to Submit Submit 3-7 poems at a time. Line length for poetry is open. No previously published poems or simultaneous submissions. Accepts e-mail submissions from international contributors only (pasted into body of message); "U.S. contributors must submit via snail mail"; no disk submissions. Cover letter is required. "Must include SASE for contact. Manuscripts recycled. Never send your only copy." Reads submissions all year. Submit seasonal poems 6-9 months in advance. Time between acceptance and publication is 6-9 months. "Poems may be read by a guest editor or editorial assistants, but I have the final say on publication." Often comments on rejected poems. "It's a good idea to have read at least one copy of a journal you plan to submit to." Guidelines available in magazine, for SASE, or by e-mail. Responds in up to 3 months. Sometimes sends prepublication galleys. Pays one or more contributor's copies. Acquires first North American serial rights. Reviews books and chapbooks of poetry and other magazines/journals in up to 500 words, single book format. Send materials for review consideration to Linda Palmero, editor.

Book/Chapbook Needs & How to Submit Lonely Mundi Press publishes one or more poetry chapbooks/year. Manuscripts are selected through open submission and through competition. "Please send SASE for specific guidelines as these may vary." Chapbooks are 16-24 pages, saddle-stapled, with heavy cardstock covers, include decorative endpapers, integral bookmarks, and b&w art/graphics. Query first, with a few sample poems and a cover letter with brief bio and publication credits. Book/chapbook mss may NOT include previously published poems. Responds to queries in 2 months; to mss in up to 6 months. Order sample chapbooks by sending $7 (includes postage) to Linda Palmero.

Advice "Turn off the censor. Write from the right brain first. Let the poems and pre-writing ferment for several months. Revise mercilessly. Read your poems aloud, and listen to other people read your poems. If you like what you hear, send your poems into the world."

◨ ◎ THE MINNESOTA REVIEW: A JOURNAL OF COMMITTED WRITING (Specialized: political, social issues)

English Dept., University of Missouri-Columbia, 110 Tate Hall, Columbia MO 65211. Fax: (573)882-5785. E-mail: editors@theminnesotareview.org. Established 1960. **Editor:** Jeffrey Williams.

Magazine Needs *The Minnesota Review* is a biannual literary magazine wanting "poetry which explores some aspect of social or political issues and/or the nature of relationships. No nature poems, and no lyric poetry without the above focus." Has published poetry by Hollander and Fuentes Lemus. *The Minnesota Review* is about 200 pages, digest-sized, flat-spined, with b&w glossy card cover, includes art. Press run is 1,500 for 800 subscribers. Subscription: $30/2 years to individuals; $45/year to institutions. Sample: $15.

How to Submit Address submissions to "Poetry Editor" (not to a specific editor). No fax or e-mail submissions. Cover letter including "brief intro with address" is preferred. SASE with sufficient postage required for return of mss. Publishes theme issues. Upcoming themes available for SASE. Responds in up to 4 months. Pays 2 contributor's copies. Acquires all rights. Returns rights upon request.

✪ ◻ ◎ MINORITY LITERARY EXPO (Specialized: membership, minorities)

216 Avenue T. Pratt City, Birmingham AL 35214. (205)798-9083. E-mail: kervinfondren@yahoo.com. Established 1990. **Editor:** Kervin Fondren.

Magazine Needs & How to Submit *Minority Literary Expo* is an annual literary professional publication featuring minority poets, writers, and professionals. "Organization membership open to all minority poets nationally. I want poems from minority poets that are holistic and wholesome, less than 24 lines each, any style, any form, any subject matter; no vulgar or hate poetry accepted. Poetry that expresses holistic views and philosophies is very acceptable. Literary value is emphasized. Selected poets receive financial awards, certificates, honorable mentions, critiques, and special poetic honors." Accepts poetry concerning ethnic minorities, homosexuals/bisexuals, students, women/feminism. No fee is charged for inclusion. Single copy: $25. Submit 1-2 poems at a time. Accepts disk submissions; no e-mail submissions. Guidelines and upcoming themes available for SASE or by e-mail. Pays one contributor's copy.

Contest/Award Offerings Annual poetry contributor's contest. Awards $150. **Deadline:** July annually.

Advice "We're interested in poetry, articles, and literary submissions that can be published in a professional journal."

$⊚ THE MIRACULOUS MEDAL (Specialized: religious, Catholic)

475 E. Chelten Ave., Philadelphia PA 19144-5785. (215)848-1010. Established 1928. **Editor:** Rev. James O. Kiernan, C.M.

Magazine Needs *Miraculous Medal* is a religious quarterly. "Poetry should reflect solid Catholic doctrine and experience. Any subject matter is acceptable, provided it does not contradict the teachings of the Roman Catholic Church. Poetry must have a religious theme, preferably about the Blessed Virgin Mary." Has published poetry by Gladys McKee. *Miraculous Medal* is 32 pages, digest-sized, saddle-stapled, with 2-color inside and cover, no ads. *Miraculous Medal* is used as a promotional piece and is sent to all clients of the Central Association of the Miraculous Medal. Circulation is 250,000.

How to Submit Sample and guidelines free for postage. Line length for poetry is 20 maximum, double-spaced. No simultaneous submissions or previously published poems. Responds in up to 3 years. Pays 50¢ and up/line, on acceptance. Acquires first North American rights.

☑ MISSISSIPPI REVIEW

University of Southern Mississippi, Box 5144, Hattiesburg MS 39406-5144. (601)266-4321. Fax: (601)266-5757. E-mail: fbx@comcast.net. Website: www.mississippireview.com. **Editor:** Frederick Barthelme. **Managing Editor:** Rie Fortenberry.

Magazine Needs & How to Submit *Mississippi Review* is a literary publication for those interested in contemporary literature. Publishes 2 issues annually; one, edited by a guest editor, uses only solicited material, while the other publishes contest finalists. "The guest editors for upcoming issues will always be listed on the website. If you can find no editor and issue listed there, then the magazine is not reading new work for the moment." Submissions accepted by e-mail (either as Word or RTF attachment or pasted into body of message). Guidelines available on website.

Contest/Award Offerings The Mississippi Review Prize. Contest open to all US writers except current or former students and employees of USM. Submit up to 3 poems (10 pages maximum). Does not accept previously published material. "Entrants should put 'MR Prize,' name, address, phone number, e-mail address, and title on page one of entry." No limit to number of entries. Reads submissions April 1 to October 1. **Entry fee:** $15. **Postmark Deadline:** October 1. Prize: publication and $1,000. Finalists published in prize issue. Each entrant receives a copy of prize issue. No mss returned. Winners announced in late January and published in April.

$☑ MISSOURI REVIEW; TOM MCAFEE DISCOVERY FEATURE; LARRY LEVIS EDITORS' PRIZE IN POETRY

1507 Hillcrest Hall, University of Missouri, Columbia MO 65211. (573)882-4474. E-mail: bern@mor eview.org. Website: www.morereview.org. Established 1978. **Poetry Editor:** Bern Mulvey.

Magazine Needs *Missouri Review* appears 3 times/year, publishing poetry features only—6-14 pages for each of 3-5 poets/issue. "By devoting more editorial space to each poet, *Missouri Review* provides a fuller look at the work of some of the best writers composing today." Has published poetry by Ellen Bass, Anna Meek, Timothy Liu, Bob Hicok, George Bilgere, and Camille Dungy. Subscription: $22. Sample: $8.

How to Submit Submit 6-12 poems at a time. No previously published poems. Include SASE. Reads submissions year round. Responds in up to 3 months. Sometimes sends prepublication galleys. Pays 3 contributor's copies and $25/page, $200 maximum. Acquires all rights. Returns rights "after publication, without charge, at the request of the authors." Staff reviews books of poetry.

Contest/Award Offerings Offers the Tom McAfee Discovery Feature at least once/year to showcase an outstanding young poet who has not yet published a book; poets are selected from regular submissions at the discretion of the editors. Also offers the Larry Levis Editors' Prize in Poetry. 1st Prize: $2,000 and publication. Three finalists receive a minimum of $100, or consideration for publication at regular rates. Enter any number of poems up to 10 pages. Guidelines available for SASE or on website. **Entry fee:** $15.

Advice "We remain dedicated to publishing at least one younger or emerging poet in every issue."

$☑ ◎ MODERN HAIKU; MODERN HAIKU HIGH SCHOOL SENIOR SCHOLARSHIPS (Specialized: translations; haiku/senryu/haibun)

P.O. Box 68, Lincoln IL 62656. Website: www.modernhaiku.org. Established 1969. **Editor:** Lee Gurga.

Magazine Needs *Modern Haiku* appears 3 times/year, in February, June, and October, and "is the foremost international journal of English-language haiku and criticism. We are devoted to publishing only the very best haiku being written; also publish articles on haiku and have the most complete review section of haiku books." Wants "contemporary haiku in English (including translations into English) that incorporate the traditional aesthetics of the haiku genre, but which may be innovative as to subject matter, mode of approach or angle of perception, and form of expression. Haiku, senryu, and haibun only. No tanka or other forms." Has published haiku by Billy Collins, Lawrence Ferlinghetti, Sharon Olds, Cor van den Heuvel, and Ellen Compton. *Modern Haiku* is 90 pages average, digest-sized, printed on heavy quality stock, with full-color cover illustrations. Receives about 12,000-14,000 submissions/year, accepts about 500. Publishes over 150 poems/issue. Press run is 800. Subscription: $22. Sample: $8.

How to Submit Submit on "8½ × 11 sheets, any number of haiku per sheet; put name and address on each sheet." Include SASE. No previously published haiku or simultaneous submissions. Guidelines available for SASE. Responds in 2 weeks. Pays $1/haiku (but no contributor's copy). Acquires first North American serial rights. Staff reviews books of haiku in 350-1,000 words, single book format. Send materials for review consideration with complete ordering information.

Contest/Award Offerings Offers 3 annual scholarships for the best haiku by high school seniors. Scholarships range from $200-500 (total $1,000). **Deadline:** mid-March. Rules available for SASE. Also offers $200 Best of Issue Awards.

Advice "Study what haiku really are. We do not want sentimentality, pretty-pretty, or pseudo-Japanese themes. Juxtaposition of seemingly disparate entities that nonetheless create harmony is very desirable."

◓ MOJO RISIN'; JOSH SAMUELS ANNUAL POETRY COMPETITION

P.O. Box 268451, Chicago IL 60626-8451. Established 1995. **Editor:** Ms. Josh Samuels.

Magazine Needs *mojo risin'*, published biannually in February and August, features "poetry, prose, short stories, articles, and black & white artwork in each issue." Wants "any form or style." Does not want "incest, racism, blatant sex, or anything written for shock value." Has published poetry by Steve DeFrance, John Grey, Harl Ristau, Lyn Lifshin, Joan Payne Kincaid, and Normal. *mojo risin'* is 36 pages, magazine-sized, photocopied, saddle-stapled, with colored cardstock cover, includes b&w artwork. Receives about 500 poems/year, accepts 30%. Press run is 300 for 200 subscribers. Subscription: $20/year; $30/2 years. Sample: $7.

How to Submit Subscription not required for acceptance. Submit 3-5 poems (2 pages maximum) at a time. No previously published poems or simultaneous submissions. Cover letter is preferred. Time between acceptance and publication is up to 6 months. The editor is solely responsible for all aspects of editing and publishing. Guidelines available for SASE. Responds within 10 days. Manuscripts not returned. Acquires first North American serial rights.

Contest/Award Offerings Sponsors the Josh Samuels Annual Poetry Competition. 1st Prize: $100; 2nd Prize: $75; 3rd Prize $50. **Entry fee:** $10/5 poems maximum. Any form, style, or subject. No previously published poems or simultaneous submissions. Manuscripts not returned. **Deadline:** November 30. Submissions read March through November only. Winners published and paid in February. Guidelines available for SASE.

Advice "Writers should never use form letters or preprinted cover letters with their submissions. I am offended by them and will likely reject the work. Also, always re-type previously rejected work from other editors. I don't want to know that I'm receiving work that no one else wants because I will usually follow suit."

▢ MONKEY'S FIST; PATHFINDER PRESS

P.O. Box 316, Madison ME 04950-0316. Established 2001. **Co-Editors:** Robin Merrill and Heidi Parker.

Magazine Needs *Monkey's Fist* appears sporadically. Wants "edgy, sassy, accessible poetry that lives in the real world. Have something to say and say it well." NOTE: "Our journal has nothing to do with monkeys, and we have two female editors. Keep these things in mind." Has published poetry by Nancy A. Henry, Louis McKee, Jennifer Stanley, and Karl Koweski. *Monkey's Fist* is 60 pages, digest-sized, photocopied, saddle-stapled, with cardstock cover with b&w art. Receives hundreds of poems/year, accepts about 5%. Publishes about 15-20 poems/issue. Press run is 100 for 50 subscribers. Single copy: $3; subscription: $6. Make checks payable to Robin Merrill.

How to Submit Submit 3 poems at a time. Accepts previously published poems and simultaneous submissions. No disk submissions. Cover letter is "absolutely mandatory. Have some manners. In your letter, name your favorite small press publication." Poems should be submitted one/page on plain white 8½×11 paper, name and address on each page. "Send in white #10 envelope and include SASE. We like creases and dislike big brown envelopes and wasted stamps." Reads submissions January 1 through February 28 **only**. Time between acceptance and publication is up to one year. "Poems are read by 2 editors who duke it out." Often comments on rejected poems. Occasionally publishes theme issues. List of upcoming themes and guidelines available in magazine. "Do not send for guidelines. Just be courteous and professional and follow the guidelines here." Responds in up to 2 months. Sometimes sends prepublication galleys. Pays one contributor's copy. Acquires one-time rights. Reviews chapbooks of poetry. Send materials for review consideration to Robin Merrill.

Book/Chapbook Needs & How to Submit Pathfinder Press publishes occasional chapbooks by poets published in *Monkey's Fist*. Chapbooks are photocopied, saddle-stapled, with b&w cardstock covers. Query first, with a few sample poems and a cover letter with brief bio. Chapbook mss may include previously published poems. "Our chaps are generally solicited, but if you have something that's going to take our heads off, we want to see it." Pays 20 author's copies (out of a press run of 50). Order sample chapbooks by sending $3 to Robin Merrill.

Contest/Award Offerings Prizes awarded to winner of the "Reader's Choice Award" of each issue.

Advice "Submit to *Monkey's Fist*. We don't care if we've never heard of you."

☐ MOTHER EARTH INTERNATIONAL JOURNAL; NATIONAL POETRY ASSOCIATION; POETRY FILM FESTIVAL

% National Poetry Association, 934 Brannan St., 2nd Floor, San Francisco CA 94103. (415)552-9261. Fax: (415)552-9271. Website: www.nationalpoetry.org. *Mother Earth International Journal* established 1991, National Poetry Association in 1976. **Editor/Publisher:** Herman Berlandt.

Magazine Needs *"Mother Earth International Journal* is the only on-going anthology of contemporary poetry in English translation from all regions of the world. *Mother Earth International Journal* provides a forum for poets to comment in poetic form on political, economic, and ecological issues." Wants "bold and compassionate poetry that has universal relevance with an emphasis on the world's current political and ecological crisis. No self-indulgent or prosaic stuff that lacks imagination." Has published poetry by Lawrence Ferlinghetti (USA), Tanure Ojaide (Nigeria), Marianne Larsen (Denmark), Ping Hsin (China), Simon Ortiz (USA), and Takashi Arima (Japan). *Mother Earth International Journal* is 60 pages, tabloid-sized, offset-printed, includes graphics and photographs. Receives about 4,000 poems/year, accepts 15%. Press run is 2,000 for 1,200 subscribers of which 280 are libraries. Subscription: $12/year. Sample: $3.75. Make checks payable to Uniting the World Through Poetry. "We encourage the purchase of a copy or a year's subscription."

How to Submit Submit 4 poems at a time. Accepts previously published poems and simultaneous submissions. No fax or e-mail submissions. Cover letter is preferred. Time between acceptance and publication is 4 months. Occasionally publishes theme issues. List of upcoming themes and guidelines available for SASE. Responds in 3 months. Sometimes sends prepublication galleys. Pays 2 contributor's copies. All rights revert to the author.

Contest/Award Offerings Sponsors a $50 prize for the best of "Your Two Best Lines," a benefit collage poem which will list all entries as a collective poem. As an **entry fee**, "a $5 check should be enclosed with submission."

Also Offers Also offers the National Poetry Association, currently working to establish an International Poetry Museum in San Francisco. For more information, check out www.internationalpoetry museum.org.

Advice *"Mother Earth International Journal* is an ongoing anthology of world contemporary poetry. For subscribers, we reduced the subscription from $18 to $12 per year. While all future issues will include an American section, we hope that all who send in entries will subscribe to *Mother Earth International Journal* to get a truly world perspective of universal concerns."

☑ MOUNT OLIVE COLLEGE PRESS; MOUNT OLIVE REVIEW; LEE WITTE POETRY CONTEST

634 Henderson St., Mount Olive NC 28365. (919)658-2502. Established 1987 (*Mount Olive Review*), 1990 (Mount Olive College Press). **Editor:** Dr. Pepper Worthington.

Magazine Needs *Mount Olive Review* features "literary criticism, poetry, short stories, essays, and book reviews." Wants "modern poetry." *Mount Olive Review* is magazine-sized. Receives about 2,000 poems/year, accepts 8%. Press run is 1,000. Single copy: $25. Make checks payable to Mount Olive College Press.

How to Submit Submit 6 poems at a time. No previously published poems or simultaneous submissions. Cover letter is preferred. Time between acceptance and publication varies. Poems are circulated to an editorial board. Seldom comments on rejected poems. Publishes theme issues. List of upcoming themes and guidelines available for SASE. Responds in 3 months. Sometimes sends prepublication galleys. Acquires first rights. Reviews books and chapbooks of poetry and other magazines. Send materials for review consideration.

Book/Chapbook Needs & How to Submit Mount Olive Press publishes 2 books/year and sponsors the Lee Witte Poetry Contest. Guidelines available for SASE. Books are usually digest-sized. Submit 12 sample poems. Responds to queries and mss in 3 months. Obtain sample books by writing to the above address.

⚅ ◌ MUDFISH; BOX TURTLE PRESS; MUDFISH POETRY PRIZE AWARD

184 Franklin St., New York NY 10013. (212)219-9278. E-Mail: mudfishmag@aol.com. Established 1983. **Editor:** Jill Hoffman.

Magazine Needs *Mudfish*, published by Box Turtle Press, is an annual journal of poetry and art. Wants free verse with "energy, intensity, and originality of voice, mastery of style, the presence of passion." Has published poetry by Charles Simic, Jennifer Belle, Stephanie Dickinson, Ronald Wardall, Doug Dorph, and John Ashberry. Press run is 1,200. Single copy: $10 plus $2.50 shipping and handling; subscription: $20 (2 years, including shipping).

How to Submit Submit 4-6 poems at a time. No previously published poems or simultaneous submissions. Responds from "immediately to 3 months." Sends prepublication galleys. Pays one contributor's copy.

Contest/Award Offerings Sponsors the Mudfish Poetry Prize Award: $1,000. **Entry fee:** $15 for up to 3 poems, $2 for each additional poem. **Deadline:** varies. Guidelines available for SASE.

◐ MUDLARK: AN ELECTRONIC JOURNAL OF POETRY & POETICS

Dept. of English, University of North Florida, Jacksonville FL 32224-2645. (904)620-2273. Fax: (904)620-3940. E-mail: mudlark@unf.edu. Website: www.unf.edu/mudlark. Established 1995. **Editor:** William Slaughter.

Magazine Needs *Mudlark* appears "irregularly, but frequently. *Mudlark* has averaged, from 1995-2004, 3 issues and 6 posters per year. *Mudlark* publishes in 3 formats: issues of *Mudlark* are the electronic equivalent of print chapbooks; posters are the electronic equivalent of print broadsides; and flash poems are poems that have news in them, poems that feel like current events. The poem is the thing at *Mudlark*, and the essay about it. As our full name suggests, we will consider accomplished work that locates itself anywhere on the spectrum of contemporary practice. We want poems, of course, but we want essays, too, that make us read poems (and write them?) differently somehow. Although we are not innocent, we do imagine ourselves capable of surprise. The work of hobbyists is not for *Mudlark*." Has published poetry by Sheila E. Murphy, John Kinsella, Chris Semansky, Diane Wald, Ian Randall Wilson, and Jeffrey Little. *Mudlark* is archived and permanently on view at www.unf.edu.

How to Submit Submit any number of poems at a time. "Because of our short turn-around time, we'd rather not receive simultaneous submissions. Previously published poems: Inasmuch as issues of *Mudlark* are the electronic equivalent of print chapbooks, some of the individual poems in them might, or might not, have been previously published; if they have been, that previous publication must be acknowledged. Only poems that have not been previously published will be considered for *Mudlark* posters, the electronic equivalent of print broadsides, or for *Mudlark* flash poems." Accepts both e-mail and air-mail submissions. Cover letter is optional. Time between acceptance and publication is up to 3 months. Seldom comments on rejected poems. Guidelines available for SASE, by e-mail, or on website. Responds in "one day to one month, depending . . ." Always sends prepublication galleys, "in the form of inviting the author to proof the work on a private website that *Mudlark* maintains for that purpose." Does not pay. However, "one of the things we can do at *Mudlark* to 'pay' our authors for their work is point to it here and there. We can tell our readers how to find it, how to subscribe to it, and how to buy it . . . if it is for sale. Toward that end, we maintain A-Notes (on the authors) we publish. We call attention to their work." Acquires one-time rights.

Advice "*Mudlark* has been reviewed well and often. At this early point in its history, *Mudlark* has established itself, arguably, as one of the few serious rivals in the first generation of the electronic medium, to print versions of its kind. Look at *Mudlark*, visit the website, spend some time there. Then make your decision: to submit or not to submit."

ⓃⒶ NAKED KNUCKLE

211 Rowland Ave., Modesto CA 95354. (209)571-8506. E-mail: gregwords@excite.com. Established 2003. **Editor:** Greg Edwards.

Magazine Needs *Naked Knuckle* appears 2-3 times/year. Wants "gravel-tongued, side-splittingly funny, gut-wrenching, well-crafted poetry that has something to say." Does not want "predictable rhyme, Hallmark-style junk, or nature poetry that never leaves the forest." Has published poetry by Paul Benton, Sam Pierstorff, Don Winter, Joseph Shields, Gordon Durham, and Taylor Graham. *Naked Knuckle* is 24 pages, digest-sized, photocopied, side-stapled, with cardstock cover with b&w line drawings or computer-generated graphics. Receives about 300 poems/year, accepts about 20%. Publishes about 20 poems/issue. Press run is 100. Single copy: $3; subscription: $8/3 issues. Make checks payable to Greg Edwards.

How to Submit Submit 3 poems at a time. No previously published poems or simultaneous submissions. No e-mail or disk submissions. Cover letter is preferred. "Tell me a little bit about who you are in your cover letter. Such as what you do for a living, where you go to school, stuff like that. Submissions sent without a SASE will not be read." Reads submissions year round. Time between acceptance and publication is 4-6 weeks. Responds in up to 4 months. Pays one contributor's copy. Acquires one-time rights.

Advice "*Naked Knuckle* aims to publish 'poetry that'll bust your mind's eye wide open.' So when submitting, don't be afraid to throw down your gloves and come out swinging raw-fisted. We love a good literary beating."

Ⓐ NANNY FANNY; FELICITY PRESS

2524 Stockbridge Dr. #15, Indianapolis IN 46268-2670. E-mail: nightpoet@prodigy.net. Established 1998. **Editor:** Lou Hertz.

Magazine Needs *Nanny Fanny* appears 3 times/year and "publishes accessible, high-quality poetry. Some artwork wanted (b&w 5″ square for cover)." Wants "external, extroverted observations and character studies. Most poems published are free verse. Formal poetry discouraged, except for light verse. Prefer 30 lines or less. No internalized, self-pitying poetry. Nothing under 8 lines or over 30 unless exceptional. No pornography, extremes of violence or language. No political or overly religious poems." Has published poetry by B.Z. Niditch, Patricia Wellingham-Jones, Ellaraine Lockie, and John Grey. *Nanny Fanny* is 40 pages, digest-sized, laser-printed, side-stapled, with colored 67 lb. illustrated cover. Receives about 1,000 poems/year, accepts about 8%. Press run is 150 for 40 subscribers, 2 of which are libraries; 50 distributed free to contributors, etc. Subscription: $10/3 issues. Sample: $4. Make checks payable to Lou Hertz.

How to Submit Submit 3-8 poems at a time, one poem/page with name and address on each. Accepts previously published poems ("if writer gives credit for previous appearance"); "query first about simultaneous submissions." No e-mail submissions. Accepts disk submissions. Cover letter with brief bio is preferred. "SASE is required." Time between acceptance and publication is up to 6 months. Usually comments on rejected poems. Guidelines available for SASE or by e-mail. Responds in up to 2 months. Sends prepublication galleys on request. Pays one contributor's copy. Acquires one-time rights. "Query first about reviews."

Book/Chapbook Needs Felicity Press is not currently open for submissions.

Advice "I want good quality poetry that the average person will be able to understand and enjoy. Let's use poetic imagery to draw them in, not scare them away."

✖Ⓐ NASSAU REVIEW

English Dept., Nassau Community College, Garden City NY 11530-6793. Established 1964. **Contact:** Editorial Board.

Magazine Needs *Nassau Review* is an annual "creative and research vehicle for Nassau College faculty and the faculty of other colleges." Wants "serious, intellectual poetry of any form or style.

No light verse or satiric verse." Submissions from adults only. "No college students; graduate students acceptable. Want only poems of high quality." Has published poetry by Patti Tana, Dick Allen, David Heyen, Joan Sevick, and Mario Susko. *Nassau Review* is about 190 pages, digest-sized, flat-spined. Receives up to 1,700 poems/year, accepts about 20-25. Press run is 1,200 for about 1,200 subscribers of which 200 are libraries. Sample: free.

How to Submit Submit *only* 3 poems per yearly issue. No previously published poems or simultaneous submissions. SASE required for return of ms. Reads submissions November 1 through March 1 only. Guidelines available for SASE. Responds in up to 4 months. Pays 2 contributor's copies.

Contest/Award Offerings Sponsors a yearly poetry contest with $200 award. **Deadline:** March 31.

Advice "We want professional-level, high-quality work!"

$🖂 THE NATION; "DISCOVERY"/THE NATION POETRY CONTEST

33 Irving Place, New York NY 10003. Established 1865. **Poetry Editor:** Grace Schulman.

• Poetry published by *The Nation* has been included in *The Best American Poetry*.

Magazine Needs & How to Submit *The Nation*'s only requirement for poetry is "excellence," which can be inferred from the list of poets they have published: Marianne Moore, Robert Lowell, W.S. Merwin, Maxine Kumin, Donald Justice, James Merrill, Richard Howard, May Swenson, Amy Clampitt, Edward Hirsch, and Charles Simic. Pays $1/line, not to exceed 35 lines, plus one contributor's copy. Accepts submissions by postal mail only. SASE required.

Contest/Award Offerings The magazine co-sponsors the Lenore Marshall Prize for Poetry, an annual award of $10,000 for an outstanding book of poems published in the US. For details, write to the Academy of American Poets, 584 Broadway, #1208, New York NY 10012 (also see separate listing in the Contests & Awards section). Also co-sponsors the "Discovery"/*The Nation* Poetry Contest ($300 each plus a reading at The Unterberg Poetry Center, 1395 Lexington Ave., New York NY 10128). **Deadline:** mid-February. Guidelines available for SASE, at www.92ndsty.org, or by calling (212)415-5759. (See separate listing for Unterberg Poetry Center in the Organizations section.)

🖂 THE NATIONAL POETRY REVIEW; THE ANNIE FINCH PRIZE FOR POETRY

P.O. Box 640625, San Jose CA 95164-0625. Website: www.nationalpoetryreview.com. Established 2003. **Editor:** C.J. Sage.

Magazine Needs "*The National Poetry Review* is a selective journal of contemporary verse appearing twice/year. It is open to well-crafted poetry in both formal and free verse modes but is especially fond of rich sound, image, extended metaphor, play *within* form, and unique diction and syntax. Does not want "confessional poetry, simple autobiography, narratives without musicality, prose poems, or vulgarity." Has published poetry by A.E. Stallings, R.T. Smith, Margot Schilpp, Molly Peacock, Rhina Espaillat, Diane Thiel, S.D. Lishan, and Kate Light. *The National Poetry Review* is about 50 pages, digest-sized, with full-color cover. Accepts less than 1% of submissions. Publishes about 30-40 poems/issue. Single copy: $6; subscription: $10/year. Make checks payable to C.J. Sage.

How to Submit Submit 3-5 poems at a time. Accepts simultaneous submissions with notification ONLY; no previously published poems. No fax, e-mail, or disk submissions. Cover letter is preferred. "Submit poems with brief bio, contact information including e-mail address if you have one (e-mail addresses will be kept confidential), and SASE. Please write *your own* address in the return address area of your SASE as well as in the addressee area." Reads submissions all year. Time between acceptance and publication is no more than 6 months. "The editor makes all publishing decisions." Seldom comments on rejected poems. Guidelines available in magazine or on website. Responds in up to 6 weeks. Pays one contributor's copy. Acquires first rights.

Contest/Award Offerings Offers a cash prize for the best poem published in *The National Poetry Review* each year. Also sponsors The Annie Finch Prize for Poetry, which offers annual award of

$300-500 (check website for current prize information) and publication in *The National Poetry Review*. Pays winners from other countries in U.S. dollars. Submissions must be unpublished and may be entered in other contests. Submit 3 poems on any subject, in any form, no length limit. No name or identifying information on poems. Include a separate cover letter with name, address, e-mail address, SASE for results, and brief bio. Guidelines available on website. **Entry fee:** $10 for up to 3 poems. Does not accept entry fees in foreign currencies; accepts U.S. dollars or check. **Deadline:** May 1 (date changes; check website for yearly deadline). 2004 contest judge was Annie Finch. Winner will be announced by mail (include SASE with entry for results) and on website. "Since all entries are considered for publication regardless of winning entry, reading a few issues of the magazine might be helpful."

Advice "Read an issue or two before submitting. Send only your very best work."

✅ THE NEOVICTORIAN/COCHLEA

P.O. Box 55164, Madison WI 53705. E-mail: eacam@execpc.com. Website: www.pointandcircumfe rence.com. Established 1995. **Editor:** Esther Cameron.

Magazine Needs *The Neovictorian/Cochlea* appears biannually and "seeks to promote poetry of introspection, dialogue, and social concern." Wants "poetry of beauty and integrity with emotional and intellectual depth, commitment to subject matter as well as language, and the courage to ignore fashion. Welcome: well-crafted formal verse, social comment (including satire), love poems, philosophical/religious poems, poems reflecting dialogue with other writers (in particular: responses to the work of Paul Celan)." Very rarely accepts poetry by children. Has published poetry by Ida Fasel, Carolyn Stoloff, Joseph Salemi, Richard Moore, Constance Rowell Mastores, and Michael Burch. *The Neovictorian/Cochlea* is 28-32 pages, magazine-sized, photocopied, saddle-stapled, with cardstock cover, inlcudes occasional graphics, no ads. Press run is 275 for 60 subscribers. Single copy: $6; subscription: $10.

How to Submit Submit 3-5 poems at a time. Accepts simultaneous submissions and, "on rare occasions, a previously published poem." Accepts e-mail submissions (pasted into body of message), but prefers postal mail. "First-time submissions by surface mail only." Cover letter is "not necessary. Poets whose work is accepted will be asked for titles of books available, to be published in the magazine." Time between acceptance and publication is up to one year. Often comments on rejected poems. Does not offer guidelines because "the tradition is the only 'guideline.' We do encourage contributors to write for a sample." Responds in up to 4 months. Pays 2 contributor's copies. Acquires first rights. *The Neovictorian/Cochlea* publishes the addresses of poets who would welcome correspondence. "Poets can also submit longer selections of work for publication on the 'Point and Circumference' website."

Advice "Like all our social functioning, poetry today suffers from a loss of community, which translates into a lack of real intimacy with the reader. Poets can work against this trend by remaining in touch with the poetry of past generations and by forming relationships in which poetry can be employed as the language of friendship. Publication should be an afterthought."

✅ NERVE COWBOY; LIQUID PAPER PRESS; NERVE COWBOY CHAPBOOK CONTEST

P.O. Box 4973, Austin TX 78765. Website: www.onr.com/user/jwhagins/nervecowboy.html. Established 1995. **Co-Editors:** Joseph Shields and Jerry Hagins.

Magazine Needs *Nerve Cowboy* is a biannual literary journal featuring contemporary poetry, short fiction, and b&w drawings. "Open to all forms, styles, and subject matter, preferring writing that speaks directly and minimizes literary devices. We want to see poetry of experience and passion which can find that raw nerve and ride it. We are always looking for that rare writer who inherently knows what word comes next." Has published poetry by Mark Weber, Robert Plath, Heather Abner, Joan Jobe Smith, Karl Koweski, Julie Lechevsky, and Fred Voss. *Nerve Cowboy* is 64 pages, 7 × 8½, attractively printed, saddle-stapled, with matte card cover with b&w art. Currently accepts about

5% of the submissions received. Press run is 300 for 175 subscribers. Subscription: $16/4 issues. Sample: $5.

How to Submit Submit 3-7 poems at a time, with name on each page. Accepts previously published poems with notification; no simultaneous submissions. Informal cover letter with bio and credits is preferred. Seldom comments on rejected poems. Guidelines available for SASE or on website. Responds in 2 months. Pays one contributor's copy. Acquires first or one-time rights.

Contest/Award Offerings Liquid Paper Press publishes 2-3 chapbooks/year but will not be accepting unsolicited chapbook mss in the foreseeable future. Only chapbook contest winners and solicited mss will be published in the next couple of years. For information on *Nerve Cowboy*'s annual chapbook contest, please send a SASE. **Entry fee:** $10. **Deadline:** January 31 of each year. Cash prizes and publication for 1st and 2nd place finishers. Chapbooks are 24-40 pages, digest-sized, photocopied, include some b&w artwork. Recent winners include James Edward O'Brien, Robert Plath, Lori Jakiela, Ralph Dranow, Christopher Jones, and Belinda Subraman. Publications include *When Patti Would Fall Asleep* by Michael Estabrook, *Hoeing Cotton in High Heels* by Wilma Elizabeth McDaniel, *Nothing But Candy* by Jennifer Jackson, *Everyone, Exquisite* by Bob Pajich, *The Back East Poems* by Gerald Locklin, and *Learning to Lie* by Albert Huffstickler. Send SASE for a complete list of available titles.

⊠ $⊘ THE NEW CRITERION

The Foundation for Cultural Review, Inc., 900 Broadway, Suite 602, New York NY 10003. Website: www.newcriterion.com. **Poetry Editor:** Robert Richman.

Magazine Needs *New Criterion* is a monthly (except July and August) review of ideas and the arts, which uses poetry of high literary quality. Has published poetry by Donald Justice, Andrew Hudgins, Elizabeth Spires, and Herbert Morris. It is 90 pages, 7×10, flat-spined. Poems here truly are open, with structured free verse and formal works. Sample: $4.75.

How to Submit Cover letter required with submissions. Responds in 3 months. Pays $2.50/line ($75 minimum).

Advice "To have an idea of who we are or what we stand for, poets should consult back issues."

$⊘ NEW ENGLAND REVIEW

Middlebury College, Middlebury VT 05753. (802)443-5075. Fax: (802)443-2088. E-mail: nereview@middlebury.edu. Website: www.middlebury.edu/~nereview/. Established 1978. **Editor:** Stephen Donadio.

• Work published in this review is frequently included in volumes of *The Best American Poetry*.

Magazine Needs *New England Review* is a prestigious, nationally distributed literary quarterly, 180 pages, 7×10, flat-spined, with elegant make-up and printing on heavy stock, and glossy cover with art. Receives 3,000-4,000 poetry submissions/year, accepts about 70-80 poems/year; has a 3- to 6-month backlog between time of acceptance and publication. The editors urge poets to read a few copies of the magazine before submitting work. Has published poetry by Nick Flynn, Henri Cole, Debora Greger, and Pimone Triplett. Subscription: $25. Sample: $8.

How to Submit Submit up to 6 poems at a time. Address submissions to Poetry Editor. No previously published poems. "Brief cover letters are useful." All submissions by postal mail; accepts *questions* by e-mail. Reads submissions postmarked September 1 through May 31 only. Response time is up to 3 months. Always sends prepublication galleys. Pays $10/page, $20 minimum, plus 2 contributor's copies. Also features essay-reviews. Send materials for review consideration.

⊘ NEW ISSUES PRESS; NEW ISSUES PRESS POETRY SERIES; NEW ISSUES PRESS FIRST BOOK POETRY PRIZE; THE GREEN ROSE PRIZE IN POETRY FOR ESTABLISHED POETS

Dept. of English, Western Michigan University, Kalamazoo MI 49008-5331. (269)387-8185. Fax:

(269)387-2562. E-mail: herbert.scott@wmich.edu. Website: www.wmich.edu/newissues. Established 1996. **Editor:** Herbert Scott.

Book/Chapbook Needs New Issues Press First Book Prize publishes 3-6 first books of poetry/year, one through its annual New Issues Poetry Prize. Additional mss will be selected from those submitted to the competition for publication in the series. "A national judge selects the prize winner and recommends other manuscripts. The editors decide on the other books considering the judge's recommendation, but are not bound by it." Past judges include Philip Levine, C.D. Wright, C.K. Williams, Campbell McGrath, Brenda Hillman, and Marianne Boruch. Books are published on acid free paper in editions of 1,500.

How to Submit Open to "poets writing in English who have not previously published a full-length collection of poems in an edition of 500 or more copies." Submit 48- to 72-page ms with one-paragraph bio, publication credits (if any), and $15 **entry fee**. No e-mail or fax submissions. Reads submissions June 1 through November 30 only. Complete guidelines available for SASE. Winner will be notified the following April. Winner receives $2,000 plus publication of manuscript.

Contest/Award Offerings New Issues Press also sponsors the Green Rose Prize in Poetry. Award is $2,000 and publication for a book of poems by an established poet who has published one or more full-length collections of poetry. **Entry fee:** $20/ms. Manuscripts accepted May 1 through September 30. Winner announced in January. Winners include Ruth Ellen Kocher, Christopher Bursk, Gretchen Mattox, Christine Hume, and Hugh Seidman. Other Green Rose poets include Michael Burkard, Maurice Kilwein Guevara, Mary Ann Samyn, Jim Daniels. Guidelines available for SASE, by fax, by e-mail, or on website.

Advice "Our belief is that there are more good poets writing than ever before. Our mission is to give some of the best of these a forum. Also, our books have been reviewed in *Publishers Weekly*, *Booklist*, and the *Library Journal* as well as being featured in the *Washington Post Book World* and the *New York Times Book Review* during 2000 and 2001. New Issues books are advertised in *Poets & Writers*, *APR*, *American Poet*, *The Bloomsbury Review*, etc. We publish 8-12 books of poems per year. New Issues Press is profiled in the May/June 2000 issue of *Poets & Writers*."

$⌨ NEW LETTERS; NEW LETTERS LITERARY AWARD

University of Missouri-Kansas City, Kansas City MO 64110. (816)235-1168. Fax: (816)235-2611. E-mail: newletters@umkc.edu. Website: www.newletters.org. Established 1934 as *University Review*, became *New Letters* in 1971. **Editor:** Robert Stewart.

Magazine Needs *New Letters*, a quarterly, "is dedicated to publishing the best short fiction, best contemporary poetry, literary articles, photography, and artwork by both established writers and new talents." Wants "contemporary writing of all types—free verse poetry preferred, short works are more likely to be accepted than very long ones." Has published poetry by Naomi Shihab Nye, Albert Goldbarth, Quincy Troupe, Ellen Bass, Nance Van Winckel, Walt McDonald, Joseph Millar, and Mia Leonin. *New Letters* is 120 pages, digest-sized, flat-spined, professionally printed, with glossy 4-color cover with art. Press run is 3,000 for 2,200 subscriptions of which about 40% are libraries. Receives about 7,000 submissions/year, accepts less than 1%, has a 6-month backlog. Publishes about 40-45 pages of poetry/issue. Poems appear in a variety of styles exhibiting a high degree of craft and universality of theme (rare in many journals). Subscription: $17. Sample: $7.

How to Submit Send no more than 6 poems at a time. No previously published poems or simultaneous submissions. Short cover letter is preferred. "We strongly prefer original typescripts, and we don't read between May 1 and October 1. No query needed." Upcoming themes and guidelines available for SASE, by e-mail, or on website. Responds in up to 10 weeks. Pays a small fee plus 2 contributor's copies.

Contest/Award Offerings The New Letters Literary Award is given annually for a group of 3-6 poems. Entry guidelines available for SASE. **Deadline:** May 19.

Advice "Write with originality and freshness in language, content, and style. Avoid clichés in imagery and subject."

◰ ◉ NEW NATIVE PRESS (Specialized: translations; marginalized and endangered languages)

P.O. Box 661, Cullowhee NC 28723. (828)293-9237. E-mail: newnativepress@hotmail.com. Established 1979. **Publisher:** Thomas Rain Crowe.

Book/Chapbook Needs New Native Press has "selectively narrowed its range of contemporary 20th century literature to become an exclusive publisher of writers in marginalized and endangered languages. All books published are bilingual translations from original languages into English." Publishes about 2 paperbacks/year. Has published *Kenneth Patchen: Rebel Poet in America* by Larry Smith; Gaelic, Welsh, Breton, Cornish, and Manx poets in an all-Celtic-language anthology of contemporary poets from Scotland, Ireland, Wales, Brittany, Cornwall, and Isle of Man, entitled *Writing The Wind: A Celtic Resurgence (The New Celtic Poetry)*; and *Kusumagraj* by Marathi (poet from Bombay, India). Books are sold by distributors in 4 foreign countries and in the US by library vendors and Small Press Distribution. Books are typically 80 pages, offset-printed on glossy 120 lb. stock, perfect-bound, with professionally-designed color cover.

How to Submit Not currently accepting submissions. For specialized translations only—authors should query first with 10 sample poems and cover letter with bio and publication credits. Accepts previously published poems and simultaneous submissions. Time between acceptance and publication is up to one year. Always comments on rejected poems. Responds in 2 weeks. Pays author's copies, "amount varies with author and title."

Advice "We are still looking for work indicative of rare and uniqe talent—and original voices using language experimentally and symbolically, if not subversively."

✪ ◰ ◉ NEW ORLEANS POETRY FORUM; GRIS-GRIS PRESS; DESIRE STREET (Specialized: membership)

257 Bonnabel Blvd., Metairie LA 70005-3738. Fax: (504)835-2005. E-mail: neworleanspoetryforum @yahoo.com. Poetry forum established 1971, press and magazine established 1994. **President:** Andrea S. Gereighty. **Editor:** Barbara Sahm Benjamin.

Magazine Needs *Desire Street* is the quarterly electronic magazine of the New Orleans Poetry Forum. "The Forum, a non-profit entity, has as its chief purpose the development of poets and contemporary poetry in the New Orleans area. To this end, it conducts a weekly workshop in which original poems are presented and critiqued according to an established protocol which assures a non-judgmental and non-argumentative atmosphere. A second aim of the New Orleans Poetry Forum is to foster awareness and support for poetry in the New Orleans area through readings, publicity, and community activities. Promotion is emphasized in order to increase acceptance and support for contemporary poetry." Wants "modern poetry on any topic—one page only. No rhyming verse; no porn, obscenity, or child molestation themes." Accepts poetry written by children over 8 years old. Has published poetry by Pinkie Gordon Lane, Ray Murphy, John Gery, Richard Katrovas, and Kalamu Ya Salaam. *Desire Street* is 8-10 pages, desktop-published, downloaded, photocopied and distributed, includes clip art. Receives about 550 poems/year, accepts 10%. Press run is 200 hard copies for 200 subscribers. Single copy: $3; subscription: $12/year. Sample (including guidelines): $5. Make checks payable to New Orleans Poetry Forum.

How to Submit Submit 2 poems at a time, 10-poem limit/year. Line length for poetry is one 8½×11 page only. Accepts previously published poems; no simultaneous submissions. Accepts submissions by fax, by e-mail, and on disk (in ASCII or MS Dos text). Cover letter is required. **Membership in the New Orleans Poetry Forum is required before submitting work.** Annual fee: $25, includes 4 issues of *Desire Street*, 52 3-hour workshops, and one year's free critique of up to 10 poems. Time between acceptance and publication is up to one year. Poems are circulated to an editorial board.

"First, poems are read by Andrea Gereighty. Then, poems are read by a board of 5 poets." Comments on rejected poems. Occasionally publishes theme issues. Upcoming themes and guidelines available for SASE, by fax, and in magazine. Responds in one year. Pays 10 contributor's copies. Acquires one-time rights.

Also Offers The Forum conducts weekly workshops on Wednesday nights at 257 Bonnabel Blvd. Also conducts workshops at schools and in prisons. Details available for SASE.

Advice "Read *Desire Street* first. Take your work seriously. Send 2 one-page original poems and bio. Be patient; we are all volunteers."

⊘ NEW ORLEANS POETRY JOURNAL PRESS

2131 General Pershing St., New Orleans LA 70115. (504)891-3458. Established 1956. **Publisher/Editor:** Maxine Cassin. **Co-Editor:** Charles de Gravelles.

Book/Chapbook Needs "We prefer to publish relatively new and/or little-known poets of unusual promise or those inexplicably neglected." Does not want to see "cliché or doggerel, anything incomprehensible or too derivative, or workshop exercises. First-rate lyric poetry preferred (not necessarily in traditional forms)." Has published books by Vassar Miller, Everette Maddox, Charles Black, Malaika Favorite, Raeburn Miller, Martha McFerren, Ralph Adamo, and Charles de Gravelles.

How to Submit This market is currently closed to all submissions.

Advice "1) Read as much as possible! 2) Write only when you must, and 3) Don't rush into print! No poetry should be sent without querying first! Publishers are concerned about expenses unnecessarily incurred in mailing manuscripts. *Telephoning is not encouraged.*"

$⊘ NEW ORLEANS REVIEW

Box 195, Loyola University, New Orleans LA 70118. (504)865-2295. Fax: (504)865-2294. Website: www.loyno.edu/~noreview. Established 1968. **Editor:** Christopher Chambers. **Poetry Editor:** Sophia Stone. **Book Review Editor:** Mary McCay.

Magazine Needs *New Orleans Review* publishes "poetry, fiction, and essays. We're looking for dynamic writing that demonstrates attention to the language and a sense of the medium; writing that engages, surprises, moves us. We suscribe to the belief that in order to truly write well, one must first master the rudiments: grammar and syntax, punctuation, the sentence, the paragraph, the line, the stanza." Has published poetry by Chrisopher Howell, Martha Zweig, Lee Upton, Jeffrey Levine, Carlie Rosemurgy, and D.C. Berry. *New Orleans Review* is 120-200 pages, elegantly printed, perfect-bound, with glossy card cover. Receives about 3,000 mss/year. Press run is 1,500. Single copy: $7. Sample: $5.

How to Submit Submit 3-6 poems at a time. No previously published poems. Accepts simultaneous submissions "if we're notified immediately upon acceptance elsewhere." Does not accept e-mail or fax submissions. Brief cover letter is preferred. Guidelines available on website. Responds in up to 4 months. Pays 2 contributor's copies and honorarium. Acquires first North American serial rights.

✂ ⊘ NEW ORPHIC REVIEW; NEW ORPHIC PUBLISHERS

706 Mill St., Nelson BC V1L 4S5 Canada. (250)354-0494. Fax: (250)352-0743. Established New Orphic Publishers (1995), New Orphic Review (1998). **Editor-in-Chief:** Ernest Hekkanen.

Magazine Needs "Appearing 2 times/year, *New Orphic Review* is run by an opinionated visionary who is beholden to no one, least of all government agencies like the Canada Council or institutions of higher learning. He feels Canadian literature is stagnant, lacks daring, and is terribly incestuous." *New Orphic Review* publishes poetry, novel excerpts, mainstream and experimental short stories, and articles on a wide range of subjects. Each issue also contains a *Featured Poet* section. "*New Orphic Review* publishes authors from around the world as long as the pieces are written in English and are accompanied by a SASE with proper Canadian postage and/or U.S. dollars to offset the cost of postage." Prefers "tight, well-wrought poetry over leggy, prosaic poetry. No 'fuck you' poetry; no rambling pseudo Beat poetry." Has published poetry by Catherine Owen, Steven Michael Berzensky (aka Mick Burrs), Robert Wayne Stedingh, John Pass, and Susan McCaslin. *New Orphic Review* is 120-140 pages, magazine-sized, laser-printed, perfect-bound, with color cover, includes art/graphics and ads. Receives about 400 poems/year, accepts about 10%. Press run is 500 for 250 subscribers of which 20 are libraries. Subscription: $25 (individuals), $30 (institutions). Sample: $15.

How to Submit Submit 6 poems at a time. Line length for poetry is 5 minimum, 30 maximum. Accepts simultaneous submissions; no previously published poems. Cover letter is preferred. "Make sure a SASE (or SAE and IRC) is included." Time between acceptance and publication is up to 8 months. Poems are circulated to an editorial board. The managing editor and associate editor refer work to the editor-in-chief. Seldom comments on rejected poems. Occasionally publishes theme issues. Guidelines available for SASE (or SAE and IRC). Responds in 2 months. Pays one contributor's copy. Acquires first North American serial rights.

Also Offers New Orphic Publishers publishes 4 paperbacks/year. However, all material is solicited.

$☑ THE NEW RENAISSANCE

26 Heath Rd. #11, Arlington MA 02474-3645. E-mail: MarcCreate@aol.com. Established 1968. **Editor-in-Chief:** Louise T. Reynolds. **Poetry Edit11.or:** Frank Finale.

Mallory Lake's "Bevagna, Umbria" (1999) "reflects several features in the spring issue, as well as the season." The pastel (courtesy of Pucker Gallery, Boston) was photographed by Max Coniglio, with cover design by Damian Bennett (logo by Arnold Skolnick).

Magazine Needs *the new renaissance* is "intended for the 'renaissance' person—the generalist, not the specialist. Publishes the best new writing and translations and offers a forum for articles on political, sociological topics; features established as well as emerging visual artists and writers, highlights reviews of small press, and offers essays on a variety of topics from visual arts and literature to science. Open to a variety of styles, including traditional." Has published poetry by Anita Susan Brenner, Ann Struther, Miguel Torga (trans. Alexis Levetin), Stephen Todd Booker, Rabindranath Togore (trans. Wendy Barker and S. Togore). *the new renaissance* is 144-182 pages, digest-sized, flat-spined, professionally printed on heavy stock, with glossy color cover. Receives about 650 poetry submissions/year, accepts about 40; has about a 1½- to 2-year backlog. Publishes about 24-40 pages of poetry/issue. Usual press run is 1,500 for 760 subscribers of which 132 are libraries. Single copy: $11.50 (recent), $12.50 (current), $7.50 (back issue). Subscriptions: $30/3 issues US, $35 Canada, $38 all others. All checks in US $. "A 3-issue subscription covers 18-22 months."

How to Submit Submit 3-6 poems at a time, "unless a long poem—then one." Accepts simultaneous submissions, if notified; no previously published poems "unless magazine's circulation was under 250." Always include SASE or IRC. Accepts submissions by postal mail only; "when accepted, we ask if a disk is available, and we prefer accepted translations to be available in the original language on disk. All poetry submissions are tied to our Awards Program for poetry published in a 3-issue volume; judged by independent judges. **Entry fee:** $16.50 for nonsubscribers, $11.50 for subscribers, for which they receive 2 back issues or a recent issue or an extension of their subscription. Submissions without entry fee are *returned unread.''* In 2003, reading period was January 2 through June 30. Guidelines available for SASE. Responds in 5 months. Pays $21-40, more for the occasional longer poem, plus one contributor's copy/poem. Acquires all rights but returns rights provided *the new renaissance* retains rights for any *the new renaissance* collection. Reviews books of poetry.

Contest/Award Offerings The Awards Program gives 3 awards of $250, $125, and $60, with 3 Honorable Mentions of $25 each.

Advice ''Read, read, read! And support the literary magazines that support serious writers and poets.'' *tnr* adds that ''in 2002, more than 350 separate submissions came in, all without the required fee. Since our *tnr* Poetry Awards Program has been in effect since 1995, and since we've notified all markets about our guidelines and entry fee, this just shows an indifferent, careless reading of our magazine's requirements.''

☐ NEW RIVERS PRESS; MINNESOTA VOICES PROJECT; HEADWATERS LITERARY COMPETITION

MSU Moorhead, 1104 Seventh Ave. S., Moorhead MN 56563. E-mail: nrp@mnstate.edu. Website: www.newriverspress.com Established 1968. **Editor:** Alan Davis.

Book/Chapbook Needs New Rivers Press publishes collections of poetry, novels or novellas, translations of contemporary literature, and collections of short fiction. ''We will continue to publish books regularly by new and emerging writers, especially those with a connection to Minnesota or to New York City, but we also welcome the opportunity to read work of every character and to publish the best literature available in America (the Many Americas Project, the American Fiction Project) and abroad (the New Rivers Abroad Project). Each October and November, through the MVP competition, we choose 3 books, one of them national (genre will vary by year) and 2 regional.'' Has published *The Pact* by Walter Roers, *Nice Girls* by Cezarija Abartis, *Mozart's Carriage* by Dan Bachhuber, *The Volunteer* by Candace Black, *The Hunger Bone* by Deb Marquart, and *Landing Zones* by Ed Micus.

How to Submit Book-length mss of poetry, short fiction, novellas, or creative nonfiction are all accepted. No fax or e-mail submissions. Guidelines and catalog available on website.

Contest/Award Offerings The Minnesota Voices Project (MVP). Awards $1,000 and publication of ms by New Rivers Press. Every third year, the poetry competition is national; other years, competition open only to residents of Minnesota or New York City who have not had a book published by a commercial or major university press nor have had more than 2 books published by small presses (excludes chapbooks). Entrants may only submit one ms to the MVP competition annually. Send 2 copies of complete ms (between 40 and 80 pages if poetry), placed in either a binder or a plain manila folder. Name and address should appear on outside and on title page; pages must be numbered. All previously published poems must be acknowledged. No co-authored mss. ''Simultaneous submissions are okay if noted as such. If your manuscript is accepted elsewhere during the judging, you must notify New Rivers Press immediately. If you do not give such notification and your manuscript is selected, your signature on the entry form gives New Rivers Press permission to go ahead with publication.'' Entry form and guidelines available on website. **Deadline:** postmarked between October 1 and November 30.

⊕ ☑ ◎ NEW WELSH REVIEW (Specialized: ethnic)

P.O. Box 170, Aberystwyth, Ceredigion SY23 1WZ Wales, United Kingdom. Phone: (0)1970-626230. E-mail: nwr@welshnet.co.uk. Established 1988. **Editor:** Francesca Rhydderch.

Magazine Needs *New Welsh Review* is a literary quarterly publishing articles, short stories, and poems. *New Welsh Review* is about 104 pages, printed on glossy paper in 3 colors, with laminated cover, includes photographs, graphics, and ads. Press run is 1,000. Subscription: £20 (£28.50 overseas airmail via cheque, Visa, or MasterCard). Sample: £7.50.

How to Submit Submit poems double-spaced. No simultaneous submissions or previously published poems. Accepts submissions by postal mail only. Responds in 3 months. Publication within 7 months. Reviews books of poetry.

🌐 $⬚ THE NEW WRITER; THE NEW WRITER PROSE AND POETRY PRIZES

P.O. Box 60, Cranbrook TN17 2ZR England. Phone: 01580 212626. Fax: 01580 212041. E-mail: admin@thenewwriter.com. Website: www.thenewwriter.com. Established 1996. **Poetry Editor:** Abi Hughes-Edwards.

Magazine Needs Published 6 times/year, "*The New Writer* is the magazine you've been hoping to find. It's *different* and it's aimed at writers with a serious intent; who want to develop their writing to meet the high expectations of today's editors. The team at *The New Writer* are committed to working with their readers to increase the chances of publication. That's why masses of useful information and plenty of feedback is provided. More than that, we let you know about the current state of the market with the best in contemporary fiction and cutting-edge poetry backed up by searching articles and in-depth features in every issue. We are interested in short fiction—2,000 words maximum, subscribers' only; short and long unpublished poems, provided they are original and undeniably brilliant; articles that demonstrate a grasp of contemporary writing and current editorial/publishing policies; news of writers' circles, new publications, competitions, courses, workshops, etc." No "problems with length/form, but anything over 2 pages (150 lines) needs to be brilliant. Cutting edge shouldn't mean inaccessible. No recent disasters—they date. No my baby/doggie poems; no God poems that sound like hymns, dum-dum rhymes, or comic rhymes (best left at the pub)." *The New Writer* is 56 pages, A4, professionally printed, saddle-stapled, with paper cover, includes clipart and b&w photos. Press run is 1,500 for 1,350 subscribers; 50 distributed free to publishers, agents. Single copy: £3.95; subscription: £33 in US. Sample: £3.95 or equivalent in IRCs. "A secure server for subscriptions and entry into the annual Prose & Poetry Prizes on the website. Monthly e-mail newsletter now included free of charge in the subscription package."

How to Submit Submit up to 6 poems at a time. Accepts previously published poems. Accepts e-mail submissions (pasted into body of message). Time between acceptance and publication is up to 6 months. Often comments on rejected poems. Offers criticism service: £12/6 poems. Guidelines available for SASE (or SAE with IRC) or on website. Pays £3 voucher plus one contributor's copy. Acquires first British serial rights. Reviews books and chapbooks of poetry and other magazines. Send materials for review consideration.

Contest/Award Offerings Sponsors the New Writer Prose & Poetry Prizes. An annual prize, "open to all poets writing in the English language, who are invited to submit an original, previously unpublished poem or collection of 6 to 10 poems. Up to 25 prizes will be presented, as well as publication for the prize-winning poets in an anthology, plus the chance for a further 10 shortlisted poets to see their work published in *The New Writer* during the year." Rules available by e-mail.

◑ NEW ZOO POETRY REVIEW; SUNKEN MEADOWS PRESS

P.O. Box 36760, Richmond VA 23235. Website: http://members.aol.com/newzoopoet. Established 1997. **Editor:** Angela Vogel.

Magazine Needs *New Zoo Poetry Review* is published annually in January and "tends to publish free verse in well-crafted lyric and narrative forms. Our goal is to publish established poets alongside lesser-known poets of great promise. *New Zoo Poetry Review* wants serious, intellectual poetry of any form, length, or style. Rhyming poetry only if exceptional. No light verse, song lyrics, or greeting card copy. If you are not reading the best of contemporary poetry, then *New Zoo Poetry Review* is not for you." Has published poetry by Heather McHugh, Diane Glancy, D.C. Berry, Natasha Sajé, and Martha Collins. *New Zoo Poetry Review* is 40 pages, digest-sized, photocopied, saddle-stapled, with glossy card cover with b&w photography. Receives about 1,000 poems/year, accepts approximately 4%. Press run is 200. Single copy: $5.

How to Submit Submit 3-5 poems at a time. Accepts simultaneous submissions; no previously published poems. Cover letter with brief bio is required. Seldom comments on rejected poems. Responds in 2 months. Pays one contributor's copy. Acquires first North American serial rights. "Poets are discouraged from submitting more than once in a 12-month period. Please do not write to us for these submission guidelines. We understand and encourage simultaneous submissions and think threatening to 'blacklist' poets who do so responsibly is unfortunate. *NZPR* responds to submissions in an appropriate timeframe and thereby gathers the best work out there."

☐ ◎ NEWSLETTER INAGO (Specialized: free-verse)

P.O. Box 26244, Tucson AZ 85726-6244. Established 1979. **Poetry Editor:** Del Reitz.

Magazine Needs *Newsletter Inago* is a monthly newsletter-format poetry journal. "Free verse and short narrative poetry preferred. Rhymed poetry must be truly exceptional (nonforced) for consideration. Due to format, 'epic' and monothematic poetry will not be considered. Cause-specific, political, or religious poetry stands little chance of consideration. A wide range of short poetry, showing the poet's preferably eclectic perspective is best for *Newsletter Inago*. No haiku, please." Has published poetry by Dana Thu, Kate Fuller-Niles, Jack Coulehan, Padma Jared-Thornlyre, Corina K. Cook, and Tom Rich. *Newsletter Inago* is 4-5 pages, corner-stapled. Press run is about 200 for subscriptions. No price is given for the newsletter, but the editor suggests a donation of $3.50/issue or $18.50 annually ($3.50 and $21 Canada, £8 and £21 UK). Make checks payable to Del Reitz.

How to Submit Submit 10-15 poems at a time. "Poetry should be submitted in the format in which the poet wants it to appear, and cover letters are always a good idea." Accepts simultaneous submissions and previously published poems. Sometimes comments on rejected poems. Guidelines available for SASE. Responds ASAP (usually within 2 weeks). Pays in contributor's copies. Copyright is retained by authors.

✖ ◎ NEWTOWN WRITERS; OFF THE ROCKS; SWELL (Specialized: gay/lesbian/bisexual/transgendered)

7501 North Sheridan, Suite D, Chicago IL 60626. E-mail: newtownwriters@aol.com. Website: www.newtownwriters.org. Established 1980. **Editor:** Jonathan Dixon.

Magazine Needs *Off The Rocks* is a biannual anthology of fiction, poetry, essays, and artwork by GLBT or GLBT-friendly writers/artists. Wants poetry with GLBT themes or a GLBT sensibility. Does not want political or socialist poetry. Has published "many poets over 20 years." *Off The Rocks* is 100 pages, digest-sized, professionally printed, perfect-bound, with color cover, includes some b&w art/graphics. Accepts about 20% of work submitted. Publishes about 10-12 poems/issue. Press run is 300-500. Single copy: $10. Make checks payable to NewTown Writers.

How to Submit Submit "as many poems as you want to send in." Line length for poetry is 30 maximum. Accepts simultaneous submissions; no previously published poems. Accepts e-mail submissions (pasted into body of message). Cover letter is preferred. Reads submissions continuously. Time between acceptance and publication can be months. Poems are circulated to an editorial board. Never comments on rejected poems. Guidelines available on website. Responds in months. No payment. Acquires one-time rights.

Also Offers "We also publish an online 'zine, *Swell*, that is posted several times a year on our website and accepts the same kind of work as *Off The Rocks*."

◙ NIMROD: INTERNATIONAL JOURNAL OF POETRY AND PROSE; NIMROD/HARDMAN AWARD: PABLO NERUDA PRIZE FOR POETRY

University of Tulsa, 600 S. College, Tulsa OK 74104-3189. (918)631-3080. Fax: (918)631-3033. E-mail: nimrod@utulsa.edu. Website: www.utulsa.edu/nimrod/. Established 1956. **Editor-in-Chief:** Francine Ringold. **Poetry Editor:** Manly Johnson.

● Poetry published in *Nimrod* has been included in *The Best American Poetry*.

Magazine Needs *Nimrod* "is an active 'little magazine,' part of the movement in American letters which has been essential to the development of modern literature." *Nimrod* publishes 2 issues/year: an awards issue in the fall, featuring the prize winners of their national competition, and a thematic issue each spring. "Poems in non-award issues range from formal to freestyle with several translations." Wants "vigorous writing that is neither wholly of the academy nor the streets; typed manuscripts." Has published poetry by Diane Glancy, Judith Strasser, Steve Lautermilch, Reeves Kegworth, and Robin Chopman. *Nimrod* is 200 pages, digest-sized, professionally printed on coated stock, flat-spined, with full-color glossy cover, includes b&w photos and art. Receives about 2,000 submissions/year, accepts 1%; has a 3- to 6-month backlog. Publishes 50-90 pages of poetry/issue. Press run is 3,500 for subscribers of which 200 are public and university libraries. Subscription: $17.50/year inside USA, $19 outside. Sample: $10. Specific back issues available.

How to Submit Submit 5-10 poems at a time. No fax or e-mail submissions. Publishes theme issues. Guidelines and upcoming themes available for SASE, by e-mail, or on website. Responds in up to 3 months. Pays 2 contributor's copies plus reduced cost on additional copies. "Poets should be aware that during the months that the Ruth Hardman Awards Competition is being conducted, reporting time on non-contest manuscripts will be longer."

Contest/Award Offerings Send business-sized SASE for rules for the Ruth G. Hardman Award: Pablo Neruda Prize for Poetry ($2,000 and $1,000 prizes). Entries accepted January 1 through April 30 each year. **Entry fee:** $20, includes 2 issues.

Also Offers Also sponsors the Nimrod/Hardman Awards Workshop, a one-day workshop held annually in October. Cost is about $50. Send SASE for brochure and registration form.

☑ 96 INC MAGAZINE

P.O. Box 15559, Boston MA 02215. (617)267-0543. Fax: (617)262-3568. Website: www.96inc.com. Established 1992. **Editors:** Julie Anderson, Vera Gold, and Nancy Mehegan.

Magazine Needs *96 Inc* is an annual literary magazine appearing in July that focuses on new voices, "connecting the beginner to the established, a training center for the process of publication." Wants all forms and styles of poetry, though "shorter is better." Has published poetry by Jennifer Barber, Peter Desmond, Dana Elder, Andrew Glaze, Judy Katz-Levine, and Patricia Li. *96 Inc* is 60-69 pages, magazine-sized, saddle-stapled, with coated card cover, includes b&w photos and graphics. Receives about 2,000 submissions/year, accepts about 5%. Press run is 3,000 for 500 subscribers of which 50 are libraries, 1,500 shelf sales. Single copy: $5; subscription: $15. Sample: $7.50.

How to Submit Accepts simultaneous submissions; no previously published poems. Time between acceptance and publication is one year or longer. Poems are circulated to an editorial board. Guidelines available for SASE. Responds in up to one year. Pays 4 contributor's copies plus subscription. Copyright reverts to author 2 months after publication. Occasionally, staff reviews books of poetry. Send materials for review consideration to Andrew Dawson.

Advice "*96 Inc* is an artists' collaborative and a local resource. It often provides venues and hosts readings in addition to publishing a magazine."

⭐ ☑ NITE-WRITER'S INTERNATIONAL LITERARY ARTS JOURNAL

137 Pointview Rd. #300, Pittsburgh PA 15227-3131. (412)885-3798. Established 1993. **Executive Editor/Publisher:** John A. Thompson Sr. **Associate Editor:** Bree Ann Orner.

Magazine Needs A quarterly open to beginners as well as professionals, *Nite-Writer's* is " 'dedicated to the emotional intellectual' with a creative perception of life." Wants strong imagery and accepts free verse, avant-garde poetry, haiku, and senryu. Open to length and subject matter. No porn or violence. Has published poetry by Lyn Lifshin, Rose Marie Hunold, Peter Vetrano, Carol Frances

Brown, and Richard King Perkins II. *Nite-Writer*'s is 30-50 pages, magazine-sized, laser-printed, with stock cover with sleeve, includes some graphics and artwork. Receives about 1,000 poems/ year, accepts about 10-15%. Press run is about 100 for more than 60 subscribers of which 10 are libraries. Single copy: $6; subscription: $20. Sample (when available): $4.

How to Submit Accepts previously published poems and simultaneous submissions. Cover letter is preferred. "Give brief bio, state where you heard of us, state if material has been previously published and where. Always enclose SASE if you seek reply and return of your material." Time between acceptance and publication is within one year. Always comments on rejected poems. Guidelines available for SASE. Responds in one month.

Advice "Don't be afraid to submit your material. Take rejection as advice—study your market. Create your own style and voice, then be heard. 'I am a creator, a name beneath words' (from my poem, 'unidentified-Identified')."

☑ NO EXIT

P.O. Box 454, South Bend IN 46624-0454. Established 1994. **Editor:** Mike Amato.

Magazine Needs *No Exit* is a quarterly forum "for the experimental as well as traditional excellence." Wants "poetry that takes chances in form or content. Form, length, subject matter, and style are open. No poetry that's unsure of why it was written. Particularly interested in long (not long-winded) poems." Has published poetry by David Lawrence, Gregory Fiorini, and Ron Offen. *No Exit* is 32 pages, saddle-stapled, digest-sized, with card cover with art. Accepts 10-15% of the submissions received. Press run is less than 500. Single copy: $5; subscription: $15 ($25 foreign). Sample: $4.

How to Submit Submit up to 5 poems ("send more if compelled, but I will stop reading after the fifth"). "No handwritten work, misspellings, colored paper, multiple type faces, typos, or long-winded cover letters and lists of publication credits." Accepts simultaneous submissions; no previously published poems. Time between acceptance and publication can vary from one month to one year. "No themes, but spring issues are devoted to a single poet. Interested writers should submit 24 pages of work. Don't bother unless of highest caliber. There are no other guidelines for single-author issues." Guidelines available for SASE. Responds in up to 3 months. Pays one contributor's copy plus one-year subscription. Acquires first North American serial rights plus right to reprint once in an anthology. "Also looking for articles, critical in nature, on poetry/poets."

Advice "Presentation means something; namely, that you care about what you do. Don't take criticism, when offered, personally. I'll work with you if I see something solid to focus on."

☑ NOMAD'S CHOIR

% Meander, 30-15 Hobart St. F4H, Woodside NY 11377. Established 1989. **Editor:** Joshua Meander.

Magazine Needs *Nomad's Choir* is a quarterly. Wants "love poems, protest poems, mystical poems, nature poems, poems of humanity, poems with solutions to world problems and inner conflict, poems with hope. Simple words, careful phrasing. Free verse, rhymed poems, sonnets, half-page parables, myths and legends, song lyrics. No curse words in poems, little or no name-dropping, no naming of consumer products, no 2-page poems, no humor, no bias writing, no poems untitled." Has published poetry by Mark Goldberg, Eman Rimawi, Robert McKenna, and K.J. Asad. *Nomad's Choir* is 12 pages, magazine-sized, typeset, saddle-stapled, with 3 poems/page. Receives about 150 poems/year, accepts 50. Press run is 400; all distributed free. Subscription: $5. Sample: $1.50. Make checks payable to Joshua Meander.

How to Submit Guidelines available for SASE. Line length for poetry is 9 minimum, 30 maximum. Responds in 2 months. Pays one contributor's copy.

Advice "Mail 4 poems, each on a different topic. Social commentary with beauty and hope gets first consideration."

✴ $◎ NORTH CAROLINA LITERARY REVIEW (Specialized: regional)

Dept. of English, East Carolina University, Greenville NC 27858-4353. (252)328-1537. E-mail: bauer m@mail.ecu.edu. Website: www.ecu.edu/nclr. Established 1992. **Editor:** Margaret Bauer.

- ● *North Carolina Literary Review* received the CELJ Best Journal Design Award in 1999 and Best New Journal Award in 1994.

Magazine Needs *North Carolina Literary Review* is an annual publication appearing in October that "contains articles and other works about North Carolina topics or by North Carolina authors." Wants "poetry by writers currently living in North Carolina, those who have lived in North Carolina, or those using North Carolina for subject matter." Has published poetry by Betty Adcock, James Applewhite, and A.R. Ammons. *North Carolina Literary Review* is 200 pages, magazine-sized. Receives about 250 submissions/year, accepts about 20%. Press run is 1,000 for 750 subscribers of which 100 are libraries; 100 shelf sales; 50 distributed free to contributors. Subscription: $20/2 years, $36/4 years. Sample: $15.

How to Submit Submit 3-5 poems at a time. No e-mail submissions. Cover letter is required. "Submit 2 copies and include SASE or e-mail address for response." Reads submissions August 1 through April 30 only. Time between acceptance and publication is up to one year. Often comments on rejected poems. Guidelines available for SASE, by e-mail, or on website. Responds in 2 months within reading period. Sometimes sends prepublication galleys. Pays with 2-year subscription plus 1-2 contributor's copies. Acquires first or one-time rights. Reviews books of poetry by North Carolina poets in up to 2,000 words, multi-book format. Poets from North Carolina may send books for review consideration.

✴ ◗ NORTHEAST; JUNIPER PRESS; JUNIPER BOOKS; THE WILLIAM N. JUDSON SERIES OF CONTEMPORARY AMERICAN POETRY; CHICKADEE; INLAND SEA SERIES; GIFTS OF THE PRESS

P.O. Box 8037, St. Paul MN 55108-8037. Website: www.ddgbooks.com. Established 1962. **Contact:** Editors.

- ● "Poets we have published won the Pulitzer Prize, the Posner Poetry Prize, and the Midwest Book Award."

Magazine Needs & How to Submit *Northeast* is an annual literary magazine appearing in January. Has published Lisel Muller, Alan Bronghton, and Bruce Cutler. *Northeast* is digest-sized and saddle-stapled. Subscription: $33/year ($38 for institutions), "which brings you one issue of the magazine and the Juniper Books, Chickadees, the William N. Judson Series of Contemporary American Poetry Books, and some gifts of the press, a total of about 3-5 items. See our website or send SASE for catalog to order individual items; orders can be placed by calling the Order Dept. at (207)778-3454." Sample: $3. No submissions by fax or e-mail. Responds in up to 2 months. Pays 2 contributor's copies.

Book/Chapbook Needs & How to Submit Juniper Press does not accept unsolicited book/chapbook mss.

Advice "Please read us before sending manuscripts. It will aid in your selection of materials to send. If you don't like what we do, please don't submit."

◗ NORTHEAST ARTS MAGAZINE

P.O. Box 4363, Portland ME 04101. Established 1990. **Publisher/Editor:** Mr. Leigh Donaldson.

Magazine Needs *Northeast Arts Magazine* is a biannual using poetry, short fiction, essays, reviews, art, and photography that is "honest, clear, with a love of expression through simple language, under 30 lines. We maintain a special interest in work that reflects cultural diversity in New England and throughout the world." Has published poetry by Steve Lutrell, Eliot Richman, Elizabeth R. Curry, Bob Begieburg, and Alisa Aran. *Northeast Arts Magazine* is 32 or more pages, digest-sized, professionally printed, with 1-color coated card cover. Accepts 10-20% of submissions. Press run is 500-1,000 for 150 subscribers of which half are libraries, 50 to arts organizations. An updated arts information section and feature articles are included. Subscription: $10. Sample: $4.50.

How to Submit Reads submissions November 1 through February 1 only. "A short bio is helpful." Guidelines available for SASE. Responds in 3 months. Pays 2 contributor's copies. Acquires first North American serial rights.

⬜ NORTHERN STARS MAGAZINE; NORTH STAR PUBLISHING

N17285 Co. Rd. 400, Powers MI 49874. Website: http://members.aol.com/WriterNet/NorthStar.ht ml. Established 1997. **Editor:** Beverly Kleikamp.

Magazine Needs *Northern Stars* is published bimonthly and "welcomes submissions of fiction, nonfiction, and poetry on any subject or style. The main requirement is good clean family reading material. Nothing you can't read to your child or your mother. No smut or filth." Has published poetry by Terri Warden, Gary Edwards, Paul Truttman, and Sarah Jensen. Has published poetry chapbooks as well, including *Curved Paths* by Nancy M. Ryan and *A Child's World* by Holly Swick. *Northern Stars Magazine* is 32 pages, magazine-sized, photocopied, saddle-stapled, with cardstock cover, may include b&w line drawings and photographs. "Send SASE for subscription information." Single copy: $5; subscription: $21. Make checks payable to Beverly Kleikamp or *Northern Stars Magazine*.

How to Submit Submit up to 5 poems at a time, no more than 25 lines each. Accepts previously published poems and simultaneous submissions. Cover letter is preferred. "Manuscripts must be typed—please do not submit handwritten material." Often comments on rejected poems. Occasionally publishes theme issues. Guidelines available for SASE. "No payment, but nonsubscribers are notified of publication." No fee for regular subscribers. All rights return to authors on publication.

Contest/Award Offerings Sponsors monthly alternating issues contest for poetry and fiction/nonfiction (i.e., poetry contest in March-April issue, fiction/nonfiction in May-June). **Entry fee:** $2.50/poem for non-subscribers, $1/poem for subscribers. **Deadline:** 20th of month preceding publication. Guidelines available for SASE. Publishes an annual chapbook of contest winners and honorable mentions. "I also publish many chapbooks for others now for an 'affordable' price to the writer." Chapbook prices and information, including new chapbook contest guidelines, available for SASE.

Also Offers Also has a regular column, "Somewhere In Michigan," featuring people/places/events, etc., tied in with Michigan.

Advice "Send good clean family reading material."

⬜ NORTHWEST REVIEW

369 PLC, University of Oregon, Eugene OR 97403. (541)346-3957. Fax: (541)346-1509. E-mail: jwitte@oregon.uoregon.edu. Website: http://darkwing.uoregon.edu/engl/deptinfo/NWR.html. Established 1957. **Poetry Editor:** John Witte.

● Poetry published by *Northwest Review* has been included in *The Best American Poetry*.

Magazine Needs *Northwest Review* "is a triannual publication appearing in May, September, and January. The only criterion for acceptance of material for publication is that of excellence. There are no restrictions on length, style, or subject matter. But we smile on originality." Has published poetry by Alan Dugan, Charles Bukowski, Ted Hughes, Olga Broumas, Gary Snyder, and William Stafford. *Northwest Review* is digest-sized, flat-spined. Receives about 3,500 submissions/year, accepts about 4%; has up to a 4-month backlog. Publishes 25-40 pages of poetry/issue. Press run is 1,300 for 1,200 subscribers of which half are libraries. Sample: $4. Single copy: $8; subscription: $22 (3 issues).

How to Submit Submit 6-8 poems clearly reproduced. No simultaneous submissions. Accepts submissions by postal mail only. Guidelines available on website. Responds within 3 months. Pays 3 contributor's copies.

Advice "Persist."

$⬛ NORTHWOODS PRESS, THE POET'S PRESS; NORTHWOODS JOURNAL, A MAGAZINE FOR WRITERS; C.A.L. (CONSERVATORY OF AMERICAN LETTERS)

P.O. Box 298, Thomaston ME 04861-0298. (207)354-0998. Fax: (207)354-8953. E-mail: cal@americ anletters.org. Website: www.americanletters.org. Northwoods Press established 1972, *Northwoods Journal, a magazine for writers* 1993. **Editor:** Robert Olmsted.

Magazine Needs & How to Submit *Northwoods Journal, a magazine for writers* is a quarterly literary magazine that publishes fiction, essays, reviews, nonfiction, and poetry. "The journal is interested in all writers who feel they have something to say and who work to say it well. We have no interest in closet writers, or credit seekers. All writers seeking an audience, working to improve their craft, and determined to 'get it right' are welcome here." *Northwoods Journal* is about 40 pages, digest-sized. Subscription: $18/year. Membership to C.A.L. ($25/year) includes subscription. Sample: $6.50 with 6×9 SASE ($1.06 postage). **Reading fee:** $1/2 poems for C.A.L. members, $1/poem for nonmembers. Make reading fee checks payable to C.A.L. "C.A.L. offers one free read (up to 5 poems) per year if poetry is submitted simultaneously with membership or renewal." No simultaneous submissions or previously published poems. No e-mail submissions; accepts postal mail submissions only. Guidelines available for SASE or on website; "see guidelines before submitting anything." Pays 10¢/line on average; "We do not provide free issues."

Book Needs & How to Submit "We consider books by *working* poets only. No subsidy permitted. No closet poets or credit seekers. All accepted books offer opportunity to include CD of author (or others) reading the book, or selections from the book. Original CD to be produced by author as we have no recording studio. No reading fee for book-length works. We would like to publish up to 12 books per year, but never receive enough quality manuscripts." Also publishes books through the Annual Poetry Contest. Offers $100 and a publishing contract to the 3 best mss. "No more than 10% of the manuscript (by line count) may have been previously published. Manuscript must be complete, with color cover (or design), all front matter including dedication, copyright page, title page, contents, or whatever you envision. Blank pages should also be included where desired."

Entry fee: $10 for nonmembers, $8 for members. **Deadline:** December 31, annually. "If your manuscript is one of the best 3, we will hold it until it is beaten. Once beaten, it will be returned with a sincere thank you." Previous winners include *The Mushroom Papers* by Anne Harding Woodworth, *What Rough Beast* by S.M. Hall III, and *Adventures through Time and Space, The Northwest Corner of the North American Continent and Other Matters, With the Help of My Favorite White Goddess Aphrodite* by Erik Peterson. "Ultimately, manuscript must be on disk, but do not submit on disk."

Also Offers *The Northwoods Anthology*. The Spring 2005 will be the second annual edition. Accepts poetry, fiction, and photography. **Deadline:** October 31, 2004. Guidelines available for #10 SASE or on website. Pays cash on acceptance.

Advice "Reading fees hold submissions down to a level that someone with 'yes' authority can actually read. They limit competition in a big way. We never get enough of anything. Reading this blurb does not equal 'knowing your market.' Read a few issues. Anyone who submits to a magazine or anthology they've never seen deserves whatever happens to them."

N ⬛ ⬛ Nthposition

London UK. E-mail: todd@toddswift.com. Website: www.nthposition.com. Established 2002. **Poetry Editor:** Todd Swift.

• Readers' poll winner in the 2004 Utne Independent Press Awards.

Magazine Needs *Nthposition.com* is an eclectic, London-based monthly online journal dedicated to poetry, fiction, and nonfiction "with a weird or innovative edge. *Nthposition* is open to all kinds of poetry—from spoken word to new formalist to linguistically innovative. We also publish political poetry." Does not want poetry from never-before-published authors. Has published poetry by Paul Hoover, Charles Bernstein, Mimi Khalvati, Ruth Fainlight, Bob Holman, and Stephanie Bolster. Receives about 4,000 poems/year, accepts about 10%. Publishes about 40 poems/issue.

How to Submit Submit 4 poems at a time. Line length for poetry is open. No previously published poems or simultaneous submissions. Accepts e-mail submissions (pasted into body of message); no disk submissions. Cover letter is required. "A brief author's bio is appreciated." Reads submissions throughout the year. Time between acceptance and publication is one month. "Poems are read and selected by the poetry editor, who uses his own sense of what makes a poem work online to select." Never comments on rejected poems. Occasionally publishes theme issues. List of upcoming themes available on website. Guidelines available by e-mail or on website. Responds in one week. No pay. Does not request rights.

Also Offers Special theme e-books from time to time, such as *100 Poets Against the War*.

Advice "Never give up; keep writing. Poetry is a life's work." •

☐ ◎ NUTHOUSE; TWIN RIVERS PRESS (Specialized: humor)

P.O. Box 119, Ellenton FL 34222. Website: http://hometown.aol.com/Nuthous499/index2.html. Press established 1989, magazine established 1993. **Editor:** Ludwig Von Quirk.

Magazine Needs *Nuthouse*, "your place for humor therapy," appears every 2 months using humor of all kinds, including homespun and political. Wants "humorous verse; virtually all genres considered." Has published poetry by Holly Day, Daveed Garstenstein-Ross, and Don Webb. *Nuthouse* is 12 pages, digest-sized, photocopied from desktop-published originals. Receives about 500 poems/year, accepts about 100. Press run is 100 for 50 subscribers. Subscription: $5/4 issues. Sample: $1.25. Make checks payable to Twin Rivers Press.

How to Submit Accepts previously published poems and simultaneous submissions. Time between acceptance and publication is 6 months to one year. Often comments on rejected poems. Responds within one month. Pays one contributor's copy/poem. Acquires one-time rights.

☐ ◎ THE OAK; THE GRAY SQUIRREL (Specialized: senior citizens); THE ACORN (Specialized: children); THE SHEPHERD (Specialized: religious; inspirational)

1530 Seventh St., Rock Island IL 61201. (309)788-3980. **Poetry Editor:** Betty Mowery.

Magazine Needs & How to Submit *The Oak*, established in 1990, is a "publication for writers, featuring poetry and fiction." Wants poetry of "no more than 35 lines and fiction of no more than 500 words. No restrictions as to types and style, but no pornography or love poetry." *The Oak* appears quarterly. Established in 1991, *The Gray Squirrel* is now included in *The Oak* and accepts poetry of no more than 35 lines and fiction up to 500 words from poets 60 years of age and up. Uses more than half of about 100 poems received each year. Press run is 250, with 10 going to libraries. Subscription: $10. Sample: $3. Make all checks payable to *The Oak*. Submit 5 poems at a time. Include a SASE or mss will not be returned. Accepts simultaneous submissions and previously published poems. Responds in one week. "*The Oak* does not pay in dollars or copies, but you need not purchase to be published." Acquires first or second rights. *The Oak* holds several contests. Guidelines available for SASE.

Magazine Needs & How to Submit *The Acorn*, established in 1988, is a "newsletter for young authors, and teachers or anyone else interested in our young authors." Accepts mss from kids in grades K-12; poetry of no more than 35 lines; fiction of no more than 500 words. *The Acorn* appears 4 times/year and accepts well over half of submitted mss. Press run is 100, with 6 going to libraries. Subscription: $10. Sample: $3. Make all checks payable to *The Oak*. Submit 5 poems at a time. Accepts simultaneous submissions and previously published poems. Responds in one week. "*The Acorn* does not pay in dollars or copies, but you need not purchase to be published." Acquires first or second rights. Young authors submitting to *The Acorn* should put either age or grade on mss.

The Shepherd, established in 1996, is a quarterly publishing inspirational poetry from all ages. Poems may be up to 35 lines, and fiction up to 500 words. "We want something with a message but not preachy." Subscription: $10 (4 issues). Sample: $3. Make checks payable to *The Oak*. Include SASE with all submissions.

Contest/Award Offerings Sponsors numerous contests. Guidelines available for SASE.

Advice "Write tight poems with a message; don't write about lost loves or crushes. Study the markets for word limit and subject. Always include SASE, or rejected manuscripts will not be returned. Please make checks for *all* publications payable to *The Oak*."

$ ☑ ◎ OCEAN VIEW BOOKS (Specialized: form/style, surrealism)

P.O. Box 9249, Denver CO 80209. Established 1981. **Editor:** Lee Ballentine.

Book/Chapbook Needs Ocean View Books publishes "books of poetry by poets influenced by surrealism." Publishes 2 paperbacks and 2 hardbacks/year. No "confessional/predictable, self-referential poems." Has published poetry by Anselm Hollo, Janet Hamill, and Tom Disch. Books are usually 100 pages, digest-sized, offset-printed, perfect-bound, with 4-color card covers, include art. "Our books are distinctive in style and format. Interested poets should order a sample book for $8 (in the US) for an idea of our focus before submitting."

How to Submit Submit a book project query including 5 poems. Accepts previously published poems and simultaneous submissions. Cover letter is preferred. Time between acceptance and publication is up to 2 years. "If our editors recommend publication, we may circulate manuscripts to distinguished outside readers for an additional opinion. The volume of submissions is such that we can respond to queries only if we are interested in the project. If we're interested we will contact you within 4 months." Pays $100 honorarium and a number of author's copies (out of a press run of 500). "Terms vary per project."

Advice "In 15 years, we have published about 50 books—most consisted of previously published poems from good journals. A poet's 'career' must be well-established before undertaking a book."

☐ OFFERINGS

P.O. Box 1667, Lebanon MO 65536-1667. Established 1994. **Editor:** Velvet Fackeldey.

Magazine Needs *Offerings* is a poetry quarterly. "We accept traditional and free verse from established and new poets, as well as students. Prefer poems of less than 30 lines. No erotica." Currently overstocked with nature themes. Has published poetry by Rochelle Hope Mehr, Jocelyne Kamerer, Robert Donald Spector, and Charles Portolano. *Offerings* is 50-60 pages, digest-sized, neatly printed, saddle-stapled, with paper cover. Receives about 500 poems/year, accepts about 25%. Press run is 100 for 75 subscribers, 25 shelf sales. Single copy: $5; subscription: $16. Sample: $3.

How to Submit Submit typed poems with name and address on each page. Students should also include grade level. SASE required. No simultaneous submissions. Seldom comments on rejected poems. Guidelines available for SASE. Responds in up to one month. All rights revert to author after publication.

Advice "We are unable to offer payment at this time (not even copies). We welcome beginning poets."

☑ OPEN HAND PUBLISHING INC.

P.O. Box 20207, Greensboro NC 27420. (336)292-8585. Fax: (336)292-8588. E-mail: info@openhan d.com. Website: www.openhand.com. Established 1981. **Publisher:** Richard Koritz. Open Hand is a "literary/political book publisher bringing out flat-spined paperbacks as well as cloth cover editions about African-American and multicultural issues." Has published *Where Are the Love Poems for Dictators?* by E. Ethelbert Miller, *Old Woman of Irish Blood* by Pat Andrus, and *Stone on Stone: Poetry by Women of Diverse Heritages* edited by Zoë Anglesey. Does not consider unsolicited mss.

⊠ ☑ OPEN SPACES

6327 C SW Capitol Hwy., Suite 134, Portland OR 97239. (503)227-5764. Fax: (503)227-3401. E-mail: info@open-spaces.com. Website: www.open-spaces.com. Established 1997. **Poetry Editor:** Susan Juve-Hu Bucharest.

Magazine Needs *"Open Spaces* is a quarterly which gives voice to the Northwest on issues that are regional, national, and international in scope. Our readership is thoughtful, intelligent, widely read, and appreciative of ideas and writing of the highest quality. With that in mind, we seek thoughtful, well-researched articles and insightful fiction, reviews, and poetry on a variety of subjects from a number of different viewpoints. Although we take ourselves seriously, we appreciate humor as well." *Open Spaces* is 64 pages, magazine-sized, sheet-fed-printed, with cover art, includes graphics and original art throughout. "We have received many submissions and hope to use 3-4 per issue." Press run is 5,000-10,000. Subscription: $25/year. Sample: $10. Make checks payable to Open Spaces Publications, Inc.

How to Submit Submit 3-5 poems at a time. Accepts simultaneous submissions. Accepts submissions by postal mail only; no fax or e-mail submissions. Cover letter is required. Time between acceptance and publication is 2-3 months. Poems are circulated to an editorial board. Seldom comments on rejected poems. Guidelines available on website. Responds in up to 4 months. Payment varies. Reviews books and chapbooks of poetry.

Advice "Poets we have published include Vern Rutsala, Pattiann Rogers, Lou Masson, and William Jolliff. Poetry is presented with care and respect."

☐ ◎ OPENED EYES POETRY & PROSE MAGAZINE (Specialized: membership/ subscription; senior citizens; students; African-American, Caribbean); KENYA BLUE POETRY AWARD CONTEST

P.O. Box 21708, Brooklyn NY 11202-1708. (718)703-4008. E-mail: kenyablue@excite.com. Website: http://kenyablue.tripod.com. Established 1998. **Editor-in-Chief:** Kenya Blue.

Magazine Needs Appearing 3 times/year, *Opened Eyes* is a "venue for seniors, known poets, novice poets, and minority poets; offering a supportive environment and challenging environment." Wants "free verse, traditional forms; prose—all styles; all subject matter; short, poetic stories. No hate or sexually explicit/graphic poetry." Has published poetry by Frank Attanasia, McGuffy Ann Morris, Carol D. Meeks, and Bonnie Mitchell Phelps. *Opened Eyes* is magazine-sized, photocopied, either strip-bound or comb-bound, with cardstock cover, includes art/graphics and ads. Receives about 70 poems/year, accepts about 95%. Publishes up to 30 poems/issue. Press run is 100 for 50 subscribers, 24 shelf sales. Subscription: $18/year. Sample: $7. Make checks payable to K. Blue.

How to Submit Submit 1-3 poems at a time with **$4 reading fee if nonsubscriber**. Line length for poetry is 30 maximum. Accepts previously published poems and simultaneous submissions. Accepts e-mail submissions (pasted into body of message). "Type name, address, and e-mail address in upper left-hand corner. Submit typed poem in desired format for magazine, and editor will try to accommodate." Time between acceptance and publication is up to 2 months. "Poems are circulated to editor and poetry consultant." Occasionally publishes theme issues. List of upcoming themes available for SASE. Guidelines available in magazine, for SASE, or by e-mail. Responds in 3 weeks. Acquires one-time rights.

Contest/Award Offerings Sponsors the Kenya Blue Poetry Award contest. Winner paid in copies of magazine. Kenya Blue Award topics change yearly.

Advice "Be creative via poetry—let the poet in you emerge from a caterpillar into a beautiful butterfly."

⊞ $☐ ORBIS: AN INTERNATIONAL QUARTERLY OF POETRY AND PROSE

17 Greenhow Ave., W. Kirby, Wirral CH48 5EL United Kingdom. E-mail: carolebaldock@hotmail.c om. Established 1968. **Editor:** Carole Baldock.

Magazine Needs *Orbis*, appearing quarterly, is supported by Arts Council England, North West. "We are looking for more work from young people (this includes 20-somethings) and women writers." Features "news, reviews, views, letters, prose, and quite a lot of poetry." *Orbis* is 80 pages, digest-sized, flat-spined, professionally printed, with glossy card cover. Receives "thousands" of submissions/year. Single copy: £4 (£5 overseas, €9, $9); subscription: £15/4 issues (£20 overseas, €32, $32).

How to Submit Submit up to 4 poems by postal mail (one poem/page); enclose SASE (or SAE and 2 IRCs) with *all* correspondence. Accepts e-mail submissions from outside UK only; send no more than 2 poems, pasted into body of message (no attachments). Responds in up to one month. Reviews books and other magazines. Send books for review consideration to Rupert Loydeil, 11 Sylvan Rd., Exeter, Devon EX4 6EW United Kingdom. Send magazines for review consideration to Matt Bryden, 28A Tadcaster Rd., Dringhouses, York YO24 1LQ United Kingdom.

Contest/Award Offerings Prizes in each issue: £50 for featured writer (3-4 poems); £50 Readers' Award for piece receiving the most votes; £50 split among 4 (or more) runners-up.

OSIRIS, AN INTERNATIONAL POETRY JOURNAL/UNE REVUE INTERNATIONALE (Specialized: bilingual; translations)

P.O. Box 297, Deerfield MA 01342-0297. E-mail: amoorhead@deerfield.edu. Established 1972. **Poetry Editor:** Andrea Moorhead.

Magazine Needs *Osiris* is a semiannual that publishes contemporary poetry in English, French, and Italian without translation, and in other languages with translation, including Polish, Danish, and German. Wants poetry that is "lyrical, non-narrative, multi-temporal, post-modern, well-crafted. Also looking for translations from non-IndoEuropean languages." Has published poetry by Yves Broussard (France), George Moore (USA), Flavio Ermini (Italy), Louise Warren (Quebec), Carlos de Oliveira (Portugal), and Ingrid Swanberg (USA). *Osiris* is 40-48 pages, digest-sized, perfect-bound, includes graphics and photos. There are 15-20 pages of poetry in English/issue of this publication. Press run is 500 with 50 subscription copies sent to college and university libraries, including foreign libraries. Receives 200-300 submissions/year, accepts about 12. Single copy: $7.50; subscription: $15. Sample: $3.

How to Submit Submit 4-6 poems at a time. "Poems should be sent by postal mail." Include short bio and SASE with submission. "Translators should include a letter of permission from the poet or publisher as well as copies of the original text." Responds in one month. Sometimes sends prepublication galleys. Pays 5 contributor's copies.

Advice "It is always best to look at a sample copy of a journal before submitting work, and when you do submit work, do it often and do not get discouraged. Try to read poetry and support other writers."

OTHER VOICES

Garneau P.O. Box 52059, 8210-109 St., Edmonton AB T6G 2T5 Canada. E-mail: vzenari@shaw.ca. Website: www.othervoices.ab.ca. Established 1988. **Contact:** Poetry Editors.

Magazine Needs *Other Voices* appears 2 times/year in the summer and winter. "We are devoted to the publication of quality literary writing—poetry, fiction, nonfiction; also reviews and artwork. We encourage submissions by new and established writers. Our only desire for poetry is that it is good! We encourage submissions by women and members of minorities, but we will consider everyone's. We never publish popular/sentimental greeting-card-type poetry or anything sexist, racist, or homophobic." Has published poetry by Bert Almon, Heidi Greco, Robin S. Chapman, Zoë Landale, and Erina Harris. *Other Voices* is 100-120 pages, 21½×14cm, professionally printed, perfect-bound, with color cover, includes art and ads. Receives about 800 poems/year, accepts 4%. Press run is 500 for 330 subscribers of which 7 are libraries, 60 shelf sales. Subscription: $18/year in Canada, $23 US, $28 overseas. Sample: $8.

How to Submit Submit 2-6 poems at a time. Include SAE with IRC. "Please limit your submissions to a maximum of 6 pages of poetry, and send only one submission every 6 months." No previously published poems or simultaneous submissions. Cover letter is preferred. "Please include short bio. Phone numbers, fax numbers, and e-mail addresses are helpful." **Spring submission deadline:** March 1; **fall deadline:** September 1 (received, not postmarked, by). Time between acceptance and publication is one month. Poems are circulated to an editorial board. "Poems are read and assessed independently by 3 poetry editors. After the deadline, we gather and 'haggle' over which poems to accept." Seldom comments on rejected poems. Guidelines available for SASE (or SAE with IRC) or on website. Responds in up to 6 months. Pays 2 contributor's copies and one-year subscription, or 4 contributor's copies. Acquires first North American serial rights. Reviews books of poetry in 1,000 words, single or double-book format. Send materials for review consideration to Editorial Collective.

Contest/Award Offerings "We typically hold one contest per year, but the time, fees, and theme vary. Check our website for details."

Advice "Please take note of our September and March deadlines. If you just miss a deadline, it could take up to 6 months for a reply."

☺ OVER THE TRANSOM

825 Bush St. #203, San Francisco CA 94108. (415)928-3965. E-mail: jsh619@earthlink.net. Established 1997. **Editor:** Jonathan Hayes.

Magazine Needs *Over The Transom*, a free publication of art and literature, appears 2 times/year. Open to all styles of poetry. Has published poetry by Candy Smith, Justin Barrett, W.B. Keckler, John Grey, Alan Catlin, and Donna Kuhn. *Over The Transom* is 32 pages, magazine-sized, saddle-stapled, with cardstock cover, includes b&w art. Receives about 1,000 poems/year, accepts about 20%. Publishes about 25 poems/issue. Press run is 700 for 100 subscribers; 500 distributed free to cafes, bookstores, and bars. Single copy: free. Sample: $3. Make checks payable to Jonathan Hayes.

How to Submit Submit 5 poems at a time. Accepts previously published poems and simultaneous submissions. Accepts e-mail submissions; no fax or disk submissions. Cover letter is required. Must include a SASE. Reads submissions all year. Time between acceptance and publication is 2-6 months. Poems are circulated to an editorial board. "We look for the highest quality poetry that best fits the issue." Never comments on rejected poems. Occasionally publishes theme issues. Guidelines available for SASE or by e-mail. Responds in 2 months. Sometimes sends prepublication galleys. Pays one contributor's copy. Acquires first rights.

Advice "Editors have differing tastes, so don't be upset by rejection. Always send a SASE for response."

☺ P.D.Q. (POETRY DEPTH QUARTERLY)

5836 North Haven Dr., North Highlands CA 95660. (916)331-3512. E-mail: poetdpth@aol.com Website: www.poetrydepthquarterly.com. Established 1995. **Contact:** G. Elton Warrick, publisher.

• "Joyce Odam, our poetry editor, submits nominations for the Pushcart Prize."

Magazine Needs Published quarterly, *P.D.Q.* wants "original poetry that clearly demonstrates an understanding of craft. All styles accepted." Does not want "poetry which is overtly religious, erotic, inflammatory, or demeans the human spirit." Has published poetry by Jane Blue, Taylor Graham, James Mackie, Carol Hamilton, B.Z. Niditch, and Cleo Griffith. *P.D.Q.* is 35-60 pages, digest-sized, coated and saddle-stapled, with glossy color cover, includes original art. Receives 1,800-2,000 poems/year, accepts about 10%. Press run is 200 of which 5 subscribers are libraries. Single copy: $5.50; subscription: $20/year, $38/2 years, $56/3 years (add $12/year for foreign subscriptions). Make checks payable to G. Elton Warrick.

How to Submit Submit 3-5 poems of any length, "typewritten and presented exactly as you would

$ 5.50

POETRY DEPTH QUARTERLY

JULY - AUGUST – SEPTEMBER – 2003

"I thought it would be fun to have a *Poetry Depth Quarterly* wizard reading on the cover," says publisher G. Elton Warrick. He created the Harry Potter-themed look using one of his own images and the Photo Fantasy computer program.

like them to appear," maximum 52 characters/line (including spaces), with name and address on every page. All submissions require SASE (or SAE with IRC) and cover letter with short 3- to 10-line bio. "Manuscripts without SASE or sufficient postage will not be read or returned." No previously published poems or simultaneous submissions. "No download submissions." Accepts e-mail submissions when sent to the publisher, *not to the editor*; include legal name and postal address with each page of poetry. Guidelines available for SASE, by e-mail, or on website. Responds in 3 months. Pays one contributor's copy. **Advice** "Read the contemporary poetry publications. Read, read, read. Spell-check before submission. Always offer your best work."

PARADOXISM; XIQUAN PUBLISHING HOUSE; PARADOXISM ASSOCIATION (Specialized: avant-garde, experimental)

University of New Mexico, Gallup NM 87301. E-mail: smarand@unm.edu. Website: www.gallup.unm.edu/ ~ smarandache/a/paradoxism.htm. Established 1990. **Editor:** Florentin Smarandache. **Magazine Needs** *Paradoxism* is an annual journal of "avant-garde poetry, experiments, poems without verses, literature beyond the words, anti-language, non-literature and its literature, as well as the sense of the non-sense; revolutionary forms of poetry. Paradoxism is based on excessive use of antitheses, antinomies, contradictions, paradoxes in creation. It was set up in the 1980s by the editor as an anti-totalitarian protest." Wants "avant-garde poetry, 1-2 pages, any subject, any style (lyrical experiments). No classical, fixed forms." Has published poetry by Paul Georgelin, Titu Popescu, Ion Rotaru, Michéle de LaPlante, and Claude LeRoy. *Paradoxism* is 52 pages, digest-sized, offset-printed, with soft cover. Press run is 500. "It is distributed to its collaborators, U.S. and Canadian university libraries, and the Library of Congress as well as European, Chinese, Indian, and Japanese libraries."

How to Submit No previously published poems or simultaneous submissions. Do not submit mss in the summer. "We do not return published or unpublished poems or notify the author of date of publication." Responds in up to 3 weeks. Pays one contributor's copy.

Book/Chapbook Needs & How to Submit Xiquan Publishing House also publishes 2 paperbacks and 1-2 chapbooks/year, including translations. The poems must be unpublished and must meet the requirements of the Paradoxism Association. Responds to queries in 2 months, to mss in up to 3 weeks. Pays 50 author's copies. Sample e-books available on website at www.gallup.unm.edu/ ~ smarandache/ebooksliterature.htm.

Advice "We mostly receive traditional or modern verse, but not avant-garde (very different from any previously published verse). We want anti-literature and its literature, style of the non-style, poems without poems, non-words and non-sentence poems, very upset free verse, intelligible unintelligible language, impersonal texts personalized, transformation of the abnormal to the normal. Make literature from everything; make literature from nothing!"

☑ PARNASSUS LITERARY JOURNAL

P.O. Box 1384, Forest Park GA 30298-1384. (404)366-3177. Established 1975. **Editor:** Denver Stull.
Magazine Needs "Our sole purpose is to promote poetry and to offer an outlet where poets may be heard. We welcome well-constructed poetry, but ask that you keep it uplifting, and free of language that might be offensive to one of our readers. We are open to all poets and all forms of poetry, including Oriental, 24-line limit, maximum 3 poems." No erotica or translations. Has published poetry by Najwa Salam Brax, Brian McCurrie, Tom Noyes, Gerald Zipper, and Louis T. Canton. *Parnassus Literary Journal*, published 3 times/year, is photocopied from typescript, saddled-stapled, with colored card cover, includes an occasional drawing. Receives about 1,500 submissions/year, accepts 350. Press run is 300 for 200 subscribers of which 5 are libraries. Circulation includes Japan, England, Greece, India, Korea, Germany, and Netherlands. Single copy: $7 US and Canada, $9.50 overseas; subscription: $18 US and Canada, $25 overseas. Sample: $3. Offers 20% discount to schools, libraries, and for orders of 5 copies or more. Make checks or money orders payable to Denver Stull.
How to Submit Submit up to 3 poems, up to 24 lines each, with #10 SASE. "Submissions received with postage due will be returned unread. Only one poem per page (haiku excepted)." Include name and address on each page of ms. "I am dismayed at the haphazard manner in which work is often submitted. I have a number of poems in my file containing no name and/or address. Simply placing your name and address on your envelope is not enough." Accepts previously published poems and simultaneous submissions. Cover letter including something about the writer is preferred. "Definitely" comments on rejected poems. "We do not respond to submissions or queries not accompanied by SASE." Guidelines available for SASE or in magazine. Responds within one week. "We regret that the ever-rising costs of publishing forces us to ask that contributors either subscribe to the magazine or purchase a copy of the issue in which their work appears." Pays one contributor's copy. All rights remain with the author. Readers vote on best of each issue.
Advice "Write about what you know. Read your work aloud. Does it make sense? Rewrite, rewrite, rewrite."

$ ☑ ◎ PASSEGGIATA PRESS (Specialized: ethnic, regional, translations, women/feminism)

420 W. 14th St., Pueblo CO 81003. (719)544-1038. Fax: (719)544-7911. E-mail: passegpress@cs.com. Established 1973. **Publisher:** Donald E. Herdeck. **Editor:** Judith F. Fodor.
Book/Chapbook Needs "Published poets only welcomed, and only non-European and non-American poets . . . We publish literature by creative writers from the non-Western world (Africa, the Middle East, the Caribbean, and Asia/Pacific)—poetry only by non-Western writers, or good translations of such poetry if original language is Arabic, French, African vernacular, etc." Has published *An Ocean of Dreams* by Mona Saudi, *Sky-Break* by Lyubomir Levchev, *The Right to Err* by Nina Iskreuko, and *The Journey of Barbarus* by Ottó Orbán. Also publishes anthologies and criticisms focused on relevant themes.
How to Submit Query with 4-5 samples, bio, and publication credits. Responds to queries in one month, to submissions (if invited) in 1-2 weeks. Always sends prepublication galleys. Offers 7.5% royalty contract (5% for translator). Acquires worldwide English rights. Send SASE for catalog to buy samples.

✴ ◻ ◎ PATH PRESS, INC. (Specialized: ethnic)

P.O. Box 2925, Chicago IL 60690. (847)424-1620. Fax: (847)424-1623. E-mail: pathpressinc@aol.com. Established 1969. **President:** Bennett J. Johnson.
Book/Chapbook Needs & How to Submit Path Press is a small publisher of books and poetry primarily "by, for, and about African-American and Third World people." The press is open to all types of poetic forms; emphasis is on high quality. Submissions should be typewritten in ms format;

submissions by e-mail (as attachment) accepted. Writers should send sample poems, credits, and bio. The books are "hardback and quality paperbacks."

⊘ PAVEMENT SAW; PAVEMENT SAW PRESS; PAVEMENT SAW PRESS CHAPBOOK AWARD; TRANSCONTINENTAL POETRY AWARD

P.O. Box 6291, Columbus OH 43206-0291. E-mail: info@pavementsaw.org. Website: www.pavementsaw.org. Established 1992. **Editor:** David Baratier.

Magazine Needs *Pavement Saw*, which appears annually in August, wants "letters and short fiction, and poetry on any subject, especially work. Length: 1-2 pages. No poems that tell, no work by a deceased writer, and no translations." Dedicates 10-15 pages of each issue to a featured writer. Has published poetry by Simon Perchik, Dana Curtis, Sofia Starres, Alan Catlin, Tony Gloeggler, Sean Killian, and Tracy Philpot. *Pavement Saw* is 88 pages, digest-sized, perfect-bound. Receives about 14,500 poems/year, accepts less than 1%. Press run is 550 for about 300 subscribers, about 250 shelf sales. Single copy: $6; subscription: $12. Sample: $5. Make checks payable to Pavement Saw Press.

How to Submit Submit 5 poems at a time. "No fancy typefaces." Accepts simultaneous submissions, "as long as poet has not published a book with a press run of 1,000 or more"; no previously published poems. No e-mail submissions. Cover letter is required. Seldom comments on rejected poems. Guidelines available for SASE. Responds in 4 months. Sometimes sends prepublication galleys. Pays 2 contributor's copies. Acquires first rights.

Book/Chapbook Needs & How to Submit The press also publishes books of poetry. "Most are by authors who have been published in the journal." Published "7 titles in 2000 and 9 titles in 2001; 8 are full-length books ranging from 72 to 612 pages."

Contest/Award Offerings Sponsors the Transcontinental Poetry Award. "Each year, Pavement Saw Press will seek to publish at least one book of poetry and/or prose poems from manuscripts received during this competition. Competition is open to anyone who has not previously published a volume of poetry or prose. Writers who have had volumes of poetry and/or prose under 40 pages printed, or printed in limited editions of no more than 500 copies, are eligible. **Submissions are accepted during June and July only.**" **Entry fee:** $15. Awards publication, $1,000, and a percentage of the press run. Include stamped postcard and SASE for ms receipt acknowledgement and results notification. Guidelines available for SASE. Also sponsors the Pavement Saw Press Chapbook Award. Submit up to 32 pages of poetry with a cover letter. **Entry fee:** $10. Awards publication, $500, and 10% of print run. "All entrants will receive 2 chapbooks. No need for SASE." **Deadline:** December 31. Guidelines available for SASE.

⊞ ◻ ◎ PEACE & FREEDOM; EASTERN RAINBOW; PEACE & FREEDOM PRESS (Specialized: subscribers)

17 Farrow Rd., Whaplode Drove, Spalding, Lincs PE12 OTS England. E-mail: p_rance@yahoo.co.uk. Website: http://uk.geocities.com/p_rance/pandf.htm. Established 1985. **Editor:** Paul Rance.

Magazine Needs *Peace & Freedom* is a magazine appearing 2 times/year. "We are looking for poems up to 32 lines. Those new to poetry are welcome. The poetry we publish is pro-animal rights/welfare, anti-war, environmental; poems reflecting love; erotic, but not obscene poetry; humorous verse and spiritual, humanitarian poetry. With or without rhyme/meter." Has published poetry by Dorothy Bell-Hall, Freda Moffatt, Bernard Shough, Mona Miller, and Andrew Savage. *Peace & Freedom*'s format varies but publishes at least 30 poems in each issue. Subscription: US $20, UK £10/6 issues. Sample: US $5, UK £1.75. "Sample copies can only be purchased from the above address. Advisable to buy a sample copy first. Banks charge the equivalent of $5 to cash foreign checks in the U.K., so please only send bills, preferably by registered post."

How to Submit No simultaneous submissions or previously published poems. "E-mail submissions are now welcome, but no more than 3 poems, please, and no attachments." No fax submissions.

Poets are requested to send bios. Reads submissions all year. Publishes theme issues. Upcoming themes available for SAE with IRC, by e-mail, on website, and in magazine. Usually responds to submissions in less than a month, with IRC/SAE. "Work without correct postage will not be responded to or returned until proper postage is sent." Pays one contributor's copy. Reviews books of poetry.

Contest/Award Offerings "*Peace & Freedom* now holds regular poetry contests as does one of our other publications, *Eastern Rainbow*, which is a magazine concerning 20th century popular culture using poetry up to 32 lines. Subscription: US $20, UK £10/6 issues. Further details of competitions and publications available for SAE and IRC."

Also Offers Also publishes anthologies. Details on upcoming anthologies and guidelines are available for SAE with IRC, by e-mail, on website, and in magazine.

Advice "Too many writers have lost the personal touch that editors generally appreciate. It can make a difference when selecting work of equal merit."

☑ PEARL; PEARL POETRY PRIZE; PEARL EDITIONS

3030 E. Second St., Long Beach CA 90803-5163. (562)434-4523 or (714)968-7530. E-mail: pearlmag @aol.com. Website: www.pearlmag.com. Established 1974. **Poetry Editors:** Joan Jobe Smith, Marilyn Johnson, and Barbara Hauk.

Magazine Needs *Pearl* is a literary magazine appearing 2 times/year in April and November. "We are interested in accessible, humanistic poetry that communicates and is related to real life. Humor and wit are welcome, along with the ironic and serious. No taboos, stylistically or subject-wise. We don't want to see sentimental, obscure, predictable, abstract, or cliché-ridden poetry. Our purpose is to provide a forum for lively, readable poetry that reflects a wide variety of contemporary voices, viewpoints, and experiences—that speaks to real people about real life in direct, living language, profane, or sublime. Our Fall/Winter issue is devoted exclusively to poetry, with a 12- to 15-page section featuring the work of a single poet." Has published poetry by Fred Voss, David Hernandez, Denise Duhamel, Kim Addonizio, Charles Harper Webb, and Lisa Glatt. *Pearl* is 96-121 pages, digest-sized, perfect-bound, offset-printed, with glossy cover. Press run is 700 for 150 subscribers of which 7 are libraries. Subscription: $18/year, includes a copy of the winning book of the Pearl Poetry Prize. Sample: $7.

How to Submit Submit 3-5 poems at a time. No previously published poems. "Simultaneous submissions must be acknowledged as such." Prefers poems no longer than 40 lines, each line no more than 10-12 words, to accommodate page size and format. "Handwritten submissions and unreadable printouts are not acceptable." No e-mail submissions. "Cover letters are appreciated." Reads submissions September through May only. Time between acceptance and publication is up to one year. Guidelines available for SASE or on website. Responds in 2 months. Sometimes sends prepublication galleys. Pays one contributor's copy. Acquires first serial rights.

Book/Chapbook Needs Pearl Editions "only publishes the winner of the Pearl Poetry Prize. All other books and chapbooks are *by invitation only*."

Contest/Award Offerings "We sponsor the Pearl Poetry Prize, an annual book-length contest, judged by one of our more well-known contributors." Winner receives publication, $1,000, and 25 author's copies. **Entries accepted May 1 to July 15. Entry fee:** $20, includes a copy of the winning book. Complete rules and guidelines are available for SASE or on website. Recent books include *How JFK Killed My Father* by Richard M. Berlin, *Traveler in Paradise* by Donna Hilbert, *Trigger Finger* by Micki Myer, and *Bus Ride to a Blue Movie* by Anne-Marie Levine.

Advice "Advice for beginning poets? Just write from your own experience, using images that are as concrete and sensory as possible. Keep these images fresh and objective. Always listen to the music."

ℕ ☑ PEBBLE LAKE REVIEW; PEBBLE LAKE REVIEW FICTION & POETRY CONTEST

15318 Pebble Lake Dr., Houston TX 77095. E-mail: submissions@pebblelakereview.com. Website: http://pebblelakereview.com. Established 2003. **Editor:** Amanda Auchter. **Assistant Editor:** Jeffrey A. Wood.

Magazine Needs *Pebble Lake Review* is a quarterly online and print literary magazine featuring high-quality poetry and fiction "from contributors around the world." Wants "high-quality, image-rich poetry that demonstrates attention to language, form, and craft." Does not want "cliché subjects or language, Hallmark-style writing, anything too abstract, racist or erotic material." Has published poetry by Ace Boggess, Jessica McMichael, Jim Adams, Julia Lisella, Scott Wiggerman, and Judy Kronenfeld. *Pebble Lake Review* (print version) is 60 pages, digest-sized, laser-printed, saddle-stapled, with cardstock cover with color artwork/photography, includes internal b&w photography and artwork. Receives about 300 poems/year, accepts about 25%. Publishes about 20 poems/issue. Press run is 100 for 30 subscribers of which 40 are shelf sales; 25 are distributed free to contributors. Single copy: $8; subscription: $24. Make checks payable to Amanda Auchter.

How to Submit Submit 5 poems at a time. Line length for poetry is 40 maximum. Accepts previously published poems and simultaneous submissions. Accepts e-mail submissions (pasted into body of message; attachments accepted if Word documents); no disk submissions. Cover letter is required. "List publication credits, if any. Always include a SASE with postal mail submissions." Reads submissions year round. Time between acceptance and publication is 3 months. "Poems are circulated between the editors, and the decision is finalized by the editor-in-chief." Seldom comments on rejected poems. Guidelines available in magazine, for SASE, by e-mail, or on website. Responds in one month. Sometimes sends prepublication galleys. Pays one contributor's copy. Acquires one-time rights; rights are returned to author upon publication. Reviews books and chapbooks of poetry in 350-500 words, single book format. Send materials for review consideration to Amanda Auchter.

Contest/Award Offerings *Pebble Lake* Annual Fiction & Poetry Contest. "Top prizewinner in each category receives $100 plus 5 contributor's copies of the Award Issue and feature in special online version. Submit up to 5 poems or one short story of up to 5,000 words. Include cover letter and SASE for notification." **Entry fee:** $10. "All entrants receive copy of winning issue. Top 3 winners in each category are published in the Award Issue, and all entries will be considered for publication in other issues." **Deadline:** May 31.

☑ PEGASUS

P.O. Box 61324, Boulder City NV 89006. Established 1986. **Editor:** M.E. Hildebrand.

Magazine Needs *Pegasus* is a poetry quarterly "for serious poets who have something to say and know how to say it using sensory imagery." Avoid "religious, political, and pornographic themes." Has published poetry by John Grey, Elizabeth Perry, Diana K. Rubin, Lyn Lifshin, Robert K. Johnson, and Nikolas Macioci. *Pegasus* is 32 pages, digest-sized, desktop-published, saddle-stapled, with colored paper cover. Publishes 10-15% of the poetry received. Circulation is 200. Subscription: $20. Sample: $6.

How to Submit Submit 3-5 poems, 3-40 lines each. Accepts previously published poems, provided poet retains rights; no simultaneous submissions. Guidelines available for SASE. Responds in 2 weeks. Publication is payment. Acquires first or one-time rights.

☑ ◎ THE PEGASUS REVIEW (Specialized: themes)

P.O. Box 88, Henderson MD 21640-0088. (410)482-6736. Established 1980. **Editor:** Art Bounds.

Magazine Needs "*The Pegasus Review* is a bimonthly, in a calligraphic format, and each issue is based on a specific theme. Since themes might be changed, it is suggested to inquire as to current themes. With a magazine in this format, strictly adhere to guidelines—brevity is the key. Poetry—not more than 24 lines (the shorter the better); fiction (short short—about 2½ pages would be ideal); essays and cartoons. All material must pertain to indicated themes only. Poetry may be in any style (rhyming, free verse, haiku)." Has published poetry by Marcy Winter, C. David Hay, Michael Keshigian, and Terry Thomas. Press run is 120 for 100 subscribers, of which 2 are libraries. Subscription: $12. Sample: $2.50.

How to Submit Submit 3-5 poems with name and address on each page. Accepts previously published poems, if there is no conflict or violation of rights agreement, and simultaneous submissions, but author must notify proper parties once specific material is accepted. Brief cover letter with specifics as they relate to one's writing background welcome. Upcoming themes and guidelines available for SASE. Responds within one month, often with a personal response. Pays 2 contributor's copies.

Contest/Award Offerings Offers occasional book awards throughout the year.

Advice "Although the publishing marketplace is changing, continue to improve your work as well as market it. It needs to be shared."

$⬛ ✉ ◎ PELICAN PUBLISHING COMPANY (Specialized: children; regional)

Box 3110, Gretna LA 70054-3110. E-mail: editorial@pelicanpub.com. Website: www.pelicanpub.com. Established 1926. **Editor-in-Chief:** Nina Kooij.

Book/Chapbook Needs Pelican is a "moderate-sized publisher of cookbooks, travel guides, regional books, and inspirational/motivational books," which accepts poetry for "hardcover children's books only, preferably with a regional focus. However, our needs for this are very limited; we do 12 juvenile titles per year, and most of these are prose, not poetry." Has published *Nurse's Night Before Christmas* by David Davis. Books are 32 pages, large-format (magazine-sized), include illustrations. Two of their popular series are prose books about Gaston the Green-Nosed Alligator by James Rice and Clovis Crawfish by Mary Alice Fontenot. Has a variety of books based on "The Night Before Christmas," adapted to regional settings such as Cajun, prairie, and Texas. Typically Pelican books sell for $15.95. Write for catalog or go to website to buy samples.

How to Submit *Currently not accepting unsolicited mss.* Query first with cover letter including "work and writing backgrounds and promotional connections." No previously published poems or simultaneous submissions. Guidelines available for SASE or on website. Responds to queries in one month; to mss (if invited) in 3 months. Always sends prepublication galleys. Pays royalties. Acquires all rights. Returns rights upon termination of contract.

Advice "We try to avoid rhyme altogether, especially predictable rhyme. Monotonous rhythm can also be a problem."

⬛ $⬛ ✉ PEN & INC PRESS; REACTIONS; PRETEXT

School of English & American Studies, University of East Anglia, Norwich, Norfolk NR4 7TJ United Kingdom. Phone: (01603)592 783. Fax: (01603)507 728. E-mail: info@penandinc.co.uk. Website: www.penandinc.co.uk. Established 1999. **Contact** (*Reactions*): The Editor. **Managing Editor** (*Pretext*): Katri Skala.

Book/Chapbook Needs & How to Submit "Pen & Inc Press is a small pocket of resistance and a statement of independence as part of the new wave of community-based publications which offer a fresh perspective on the writers and writing that are important at the start of the 21st century. Pen & Inc Press aims to publish good writing, whether it be poetry, short fiction, essays, or criticism." Publishes 3 perfect-bound paperbacks/year, selected through both open submission and commission. Books are usually 150-200 pages, glue-bound, with full-color or b&w gloss card covers with original image or photograph (color/b&w). Send a maximum of 10 poems and cover letter with brief bio and publication credits. Responds to queries in 4 months. Order books/publications by sending "cover price to Pen & Inc Press address above. UK Sterling only accepted. Transactions by debit/credit card fine also."

Magazine Needs & How to Submit *Reactions* is "a round-up of the best new poets from around the UK and abroad. Selected from open submission, *Reactions* features the work of poets who are at a first collection stage or working towards it, and contains work by 30 UK and international poets. The emphasis is on emerging writers.'' Has published poetry by Liz Almond, Carrie Etter, Helen Ivory, Anne Berkeley, Roy Blackman, Frank Dullaghan, Margaret Gillio, Stephanie Norgate, Andrea Holland, and Robert Seatter. ''Submissions are invited from writers who have had a first collection or pamphlet published (but not a single), and from those who have not yet reached that stage. If you are interested in submitting work, please send to The Editor. Must be accompanied by a cover letter which lists the titles of your poems, plus a short biography of no more than 70 words. Single copy: £9.99 (USA/ROW), £8.99 (Europe), and £7.99 (UK), all including postage and packing. Submit a maximum of 10 poems at a time. Accepts original, unpublished poems. Accepts postal submissions only. ''Poems must be your own original work and must not be accepted for publication by any other magazine or anthology. Enclose an SAE.'' Reads submissions on an ongoing basis. Time between acceptance and publication is dependent on publication date of book. Guidelines available in magazine, by e-mail, on website, or for SAE. Responds in 4 months. Pays fee of £50 and one contributor's copy.

Magazine Needs & How to Submit *Pretext*, appearing biannually in May and November, is ''the international literary magazine from the acclaimed University of East Anglia. With over 200 pages of new poetry, short fiction, essays, criticism, and novel extracts from new and established writers, it provides a cutting-edge platform for creative writing from Great Britain and beyond. There are no editorial restrictions on subject or style, just an insistence on quality and perspective that the work strongly asserts where it's coming from and is well realized on the page.'' Has published poetry by Margaret Atwood, Romesh Gunesekera, Hilary Davies, Alan Jenkins, Graham Mort, and Egon Schiele. *Pretext* is a 200-page, book-sized magazine, litho-printed, glue-bound, with full-color gloss cover, 3-5 photographs/images (b&w) within the book to illustrate text, includes ads. Receives about 500 poems/year, accepts about 25%. Publishes about 5 poems/issue. Print run is 1,000 for 100 subscribers of which 10 are libraries, 500 shelf sales; 100 distributed free to contributors/reviewers. Single copy: £9.99 (USA/ROW), £8.99 (Europe), £7.99 (UK), all including postage and packing; subscription: £18 (USA/ROW), £8.99 (Europe), £14 (UK), all including postage and packing. Make checks payable to The University of East Anglia. Guidelines available in magazine, by e-mail, on website, or for SAE. Responds in 4 months. Always sends pre-publication galleys. Pays £50 fee and one contributor's copy. UK and international copyright remains with author at all times. See submission details above for *Reactions*. ''Poems are received and passed to the editorial board for relevant publication. Consultation process involving editors and contributing editors occurs. Poems are accepted or rejected, or passed back to poet for rewriting if deemed necessary.''

Advice ''Write well and good and do not despair. Try and try again. If you write well, you will be recognized one day.''

🌐 📠 PENNINE INK

⁒ Mid Pennine Arts, The Gallery, Yorke St., Burnley BB11 1HD Great Britain. Phone: (01282)703657. E-mail: sheridans@casanostra.p3online.net. Established 1983. **Editor:** Laura Sheridan.

Magazine Needs *Pennine Ink* appears annually in January using poems and short prose items. Wants ''poetry up to 40 lines maximum. Consider all kinds.'' *Pennine Ink* is 48 pages, A5, with b&w illustrated cover, includes small local ads and 3 or 4 b&w graphics. Receives about 400 poems/year, accepts about 40. Press run is 500. ''Contributors wishing to purchase a copy of *Pennine Ink* should enclose £3 ($6 US) per copy.''

How to Submit Submit up to 6 poems at a time. Accepts previously published poems and simultaneous submissions. Accepts submissions by e-mail. Seldom comments on rejected poems. Responds in 3 months. Pays one contributor's copy.

Advice ''Prose and poetry should be accompanied by a suitable stamped, addressed envelope (SASE or SAE with IRCs) for return of work.''

⊞ ⊡ PENNINE PLATFORM

Frizingley Hall, Frizinghall Rd., Bradford, West Yorkshire BD9 4LD United Kingdom. Established 1973. **Poetry Editor:** Nicholas Bielby.

Magazine Needs *Pennine Platform* appears 2 times/year, in spring and fall. Wants any kind of poetry but concrete. "Poems must appeal to the mind's ear." No specifications of length, but poems of fewer than 40 lines have a better chance. "All styles—effort is to find things good of their kind. Preference for religious or sociopolitical awareness of an acute, not conventional, kind." Has published poetry by Gerard Benson, Joolz, Gaia Holmes, Milner Place, Seán Body, and Ian Parks. *Pennine Platform* is 60 pages, A5, digitally printed, stapled, with matte card cover with graphics. Receives about 500 submissions/year, accepts about 90, has a 6-month backlog. Circulation is 300 including libraries and universities. Subscription: £8.50 UK, £10 rest of Europe, £12 ROW (all payable in sterling only). Sample: £4.50 UK, £5 ROW.

How to Submit Submit up to 6 poems, typed. Editor comments on all poems (*if SAE provided*). Responds in up to 6 months. Pays one contributor's copy. Acquires first serial rights. Reviews books of poetry, multi-book format. Send materials for review consideration.

Advice "Write well in meter on serious (not solemn) themes, so a voice may appeal to the mind's ear."

⊡ PENNSYLVANIA ENGLISH

Penn State DuBois, DuBois PA 15801-3199. (814)375-4814. E-mail: ajv2@psu.edu. Established 1988 (first issue in March 1989). **Editor:** Antonio Vallone.

Magazine Needs *Pennsylvania English*, appearing annually, is "a journal sponsored by the Pennsylvania College English Association." Wants poetry of "any length, any style." Has published poetry by Liz Rosenberg, Walt MacDonald, Amy Pence, Jennifer Richter, and Jeff Schiff. *Pennsylvania English* is up to 200 pages, digest-sized, perfect-bound, with full-color cover. Press run is 500. Subscription: $10/year.

How to Submit Submit 3 or more typed poems at a time. Include SASE. Considers simultaneous submissions but not previously published poems. Guidelines available for SASE. Responds in 6 months. Pays 3 contributor's copies.

Advice "Poetry does not express emotions; it evokes emotions. Therefore, it should rely less on statements and more on images."

⊡ ◎ THE PENWOOD REVIEW (Specialized: spirituality)

P.O. Box 862, Los Alamitos CA 90720-0862. E-mail: penwoodreview@charter.net. Website: http://webpages.charter.net/penwoodreview/penwood.htm. Established 1997. **Editor:** Lori M. Cameron.

Magazine Needs *The Penwood Review*, published biannually, "seeks to explore the spiritual and sacred aspects of our existence and our relationship to God." Wants "disciplined, high-quality, well-crafted poetry on any subject. Prefer poems be less than 2 pages. Rhyming poetry must be written in traditional forms (sonnets, tercets, villanelles, sestinas, etc.)" Does not want "light verse, doggerel, or greeting card-style poetry. Also, nothing racist, sexist, pornographic, or blasphemous." Has published poetry by Kathleen Spivack, Anne Babson, Hugh Fox, Anselm Brocki, Nina Tassi, and Gary Guinn. *The Penwood Review* is about 40 pages, magazine-sized, saddle-stapled, with heavy card cover. Press run is 50-100. Single copy: $6; subscription: $12.

How to Submit Submit 3-5 poems, one/page with the author's full name, address, and phone number in the upper right hand corner. No previously published poems or simultaneous submissions. Accepts e-mail submissions (pasted into body of message). Cover letter is preferred. Time between acceptance and publication is up to 1½ years. "Submissions are circulated among an editorial staff for evaluations." Seldom comments on rejected poems. Responds in up to 4 months. For payment, offers subscription discount of $10 and, with subscription, one additional contributor's copy. Acquires one-time rights.

$⬙ THE PEOPLE'S PRESS

4810 Norwood Ave., Baltimore MD 21207-6839. Phone/fax: (410)448-0254. Press established 1997, firm established 1989. **Contact:** Submissions Editor.

Book/Chapbook Needs "The goal of the types of material we publish is simply to move people to think and perhaps act to make the world better than when we inherited it." Wants "meaningful poetry that is mindful of human rights/dignity." Has published *Late* by Kelley Jean White, MD; *Hard Hooved Hussy* by Mary Alice Ramsey, *Sweet Somethings* by Garrett Flagg and Marvin Pirila, *Braids* by Rasheed Adero Merritt, *60 Pieces of My Heart* by Jennifer Closs, and *2000 Here's to Humanity* by various artists. Accepts poetry written by children; parental consent is mandatory for publication. Books are at least 50 pages, digest-sized, photocopied, perfect-bound, saddle-stapled, with soft cover, includes art/graphics.

How to Submit Query first with 1-5 sample poems and a cover letter with brief bio and publication credits. SASE required for return of work and/or response. No submissions by fax. Time between acceptance and publication is 6 months to one year. Seldom comments on rejected poems. Publishes theme issues. Guidelines available for SASE. Responds to queries within 6 weeks; to mss in within 3 months. Pays royalties of 5-20% and 30 author's copies (out of a press run of 500). Order sample books by sending $8.

Contest/Award Offerings The People's Press sponsors an annual Poetry Month Contest in April. "Prizes and/or publication possibilities vary from contest to contest." Details available for SASE.

Advice "Expound on something that moves you within the realm of human rights/dignity, and hopefully we will be moved also."

⬙ ⬙ PERIHELION; DEL SOL PRESS

E-mail: perihelion@webdelsol.com. Website: http://webdelsol.com/Perihelion. Established 1996. **Editor-in-Chief:** Joan Houlihan. Member: CLMP.

Magazine Needs *Perihelion* is an online poetry journal that appears 3 times/year. "Along with poetry, we publish reviews, translations, interviews, and features related to poetry." Wants "the best possible." Has published poetry by Robin Behn, Franz Wright, Cal Bedient, Martha Zweig, Larissa Szporluk, and Quan Barry.

How to Submit Submit 4-5 poems at a time. Accepts simultaneous submissions; no previously published poems. Accepts e-mail submissions (pasted into body of message or as attachment); no disk submissions. Cover letter is preferred. Reads submissions year round. Time between acceptance and publication is 2-6 months. "Poetry editor and editor make selections." Seldom comments on rejected poems. Guidelines available on website. Responds in up to 6 months. Sometimes sends prepublication galleys (online). Reviews books and chapbooks of poetry.

Book/Chapbook Needs & How to Submit Del Sol Press publishes poetry, fiction, and nonfiction. Publishes 2-3 poetry books and one anthology/year. Manuscripts are selected through open submission as well as through competition. Publishes one poetry book through the annual Del Sol Poetry Prize contest. (See separate listing in Contests & Awards section.) Books are 60-100 pages, print-on-demand, perfect-bound, with cloth covers, include varied art/graphics. Query first, with a few sample poems and a cover letter with brief bio and publication credits. Book mss may include previously published poems. Responds to queries in 2 weeks; to mss in up to 6 months. Order sample books through Del Sol Press website at http://webdelsol.com/DelSolPress.

⬙ ⬙ PERMAFROST: A LITERARY JOURNAL; MIDNIGHT SUN POETRY CHAPBOOK CONTEST

% English Dept., P.O. Box 755720, University of Alaska Fairbanks, Fairbanks AK 99775. E-mail: ftjag@uaf.edu. Website: www.uaf.edu/english/permafrost. Established 1977. **Contact:** Poetry Editor.

Magazine Needs An annual published in August, *Permafrost* contains poems, short stories, creative nonfiction, and b&w drawings, photographs, and prints. "We survive on both new and established writers, and hope and expect to see your best work. We publish any style of poetry provided it is conceived, written, and revised with care. While we encourage submissions about Alaska and by Alaskans, we also encourage and welcome poems about anywhere and from anywhere. We have published work by E. Ethelbert Miller, W. Loran Smith, Peter Orlovsky, Jim Wayne Miller, Allen Ginsberg, Jean Genet, and Andy Warhol." *Permafrost* is about 200 pages, digest-sized, professionally printed, flat-spined, includes b&w graphics and photos. Subscription: $10. Sample: $6.

How to Submit Submit 3-6 poems, typed, single or double-spaced, and formatted as they should appear. Considers simultaneous submissions. **Deadline:** March 15. Does not accept submissions between March 15 and September 1. Editors comment only on mss that have made the final round. Guidelines available for SASE, on website, or by e-mail. Responds in 3 months. Pays 2 contributor's copies; reduced contributor rate on additional copies.

Contest/Award Offerings *Permafrost* also sponsors the Midnight Sun Poetry Chapbook Contest. Guidelines available for SASE or on website. **Entry fee:** $10, includes a subscription to the journal. **Deadline:** March 15.

☑ ◎ PERSPECTIVES (Specialized: Christian)

Dept. of English, Hope College, Holland MI 49422-9000. Established 1986. **Poetry Editor:** Francis Fike.

Magazine Needs *Perspectives* appears 10 times/year. The journal's purpose is "to express the Reformed faith theologically; to engage in issues that Reformed Christians meet in personal, ecclesiastical, and societal life, and thus to contribute to the mission of the church of Jesus Christ." Wants "both traditional and free verse of high quality. Prefer traditional form. Publish 1-2 poems every other issue, alternating with a Poetry Page on great traditional poems from the past." Has published poetry by Rhoda Janzen, David Middleton, and Frederik Zydek. *Perspectives* is 24 pages, magazine-sized, web-offset, saddle-stapled, with paper cover containing b&w illustration. Receives about 50 poems/year, accepts 6-10. Press run is 3,300 for 3,000 subscribers of which 200 are libraries. Subscription: $30. Sample: $3.50.

How to Submit No previously published poems or simultaneous submissions. No e-mail submissions. Cover letter is preferred. Include SASE. "Submissions without SASE will not be returned." Time between acceptance and publication is 6 months or less. Occasionally comments on rejected poems. Responds in up to 3 months. Pays 5 contributor's copies. Acquires first rights.

☑ ◎ PERUGIA PRESS (Specialized: women)

P.O. Box 60364, Florence MA 01062. E-mail: info@perugiapress.com. Website: www.perugiapress.com. Established 1997. **Director:** Susan Kan.

Book/Chapbook Needs "Perugia Press publishes one collection of poetry each year, by a woman at the beginning of her publishing career (first or second books only). Our books appeal to people who have been reading poetry for decades, as well as those who might be picking up a book of poetry for the first time. Slight preference for narrative poetry." Has published *Seamless* by Linda Tomol Pennisi, *Red* by Melanie Braverman, *The Work of Hands* by Catherine Anderson, *Finding the Bear* by Gail Thomas, *Impulse to Fly* by Almitra David, *A Wound on Stone* by Faye Gore, and *Reach* by Janet E. Aalfs. Books are an average of 88 pages, offset-printed, perfect-bound. Print run is 500-1,200.

How to Submit Perugia Press is now accepting mss through annual contest only. Send 48-72 pages on white paper, "with legible typeface, pagination, and fastened with a removable clip. Include *two* cover pages: one with title of manuscript, name, address, telephone number, and e-mail address, and one with just manuscript title. Include table of contents and acknowledgments page." Cover letter and bio not required. Individual poems may be previously published. Accepts simultaneous submissions if notified of acceptance elsewhere. No e-mail submissions. No translations or self-published books. "Poet must be a living U.S. resident." **Entry fee:** $20/ms. Make checks payable to Perugia Press. **Postmark deadline:** between August 1 and November 15; "No FedEx or UPS." SASE for April 1 notification only; mss will be recycled. Judges: panel of Perugia authors, booksellers, scholars, etc. Prize: $1,000 and publication. Guidelines available on website. Order sample books by sending $14.

☑ PHI KAPPA PHI FORUM

129 Quad Center, Mell St., Auburn University AL 36849-5306. (334)844-5200. Fax: (334)844-5994. E-mail: kaetzjp@auburn.edu. Website: www.auburn.edu/natforum. Established 1915. **Editor:** James P. Kaetz. **Contact:** Poetry Editors.

Magazine Needs *Phi Kappa Phi Forum* is the quarterly publication of Phi Kappa Phi using quality poetry. *Phi Kappa Phi Forum* is 48 pages, magazine-sized, professionally printed, saddle-stapled, with full-color paper cover and interior. Receives about 300 poems/year, accepts about 20. Press run is 110,000 for 108,000 subscribers of which 300 are libraries. Subscription: $25.

How to Submit Submit 3-5 short (one page or less in length) poems at a time, including a biographical sketch with recent publications. Accepts e-mail submissions. Reads submissions about every 3 months. Responds in about 4 months. Pays 10 contributor's copies.

✪ ☑ PHOEBE; GREG GRUMMER POETRY AWARD

MSN 206, George Mason University, 4400 University Dr., Fairfax VA 22030. (703)993-2915. E-mail: phoebe@gmu.edu. Website: www.gmu.edu/pubs/phoebe. Established 1970. **Editor:** Lisa Ampleman. **Poetry Editor:** Tracy Zeman.

Magazine Needs *Phoebe* is a literary biannual, appearing in September and February, "looking for imagery that will make your thumbs sweat when you touch it." Has published poetry by C.D. Wright, Russell Edson, Yusef Komunyakaa, Rosemarie Waldrop, and Leslie Scalapino. Press run is 3,000, with 35-40 pages of poetry in each issue. *Phoebe* receives 4,000 submissions/year. Single copy: $6; subscription: $12/year.

How to Submit Submit up to 5 poems at a time; submissions should be accompanied by a SASE and a short bio. No simultaneous submissions. Does not accept e-mail submissions. Guidelines available for SASE or on website. Responds in up to 6 months. Pays 2 contributor's copies or one-year subscription.

Contest/Award Offerings Sponsors the Greg Grummer Poetry Award. Awards $1,000 and publication for winner, possible publication for finalists, and a copy of awards issue to all entrants. Submit up to 4 poems, any subject, any form, with name on cover page only. No previously published submissions. **Entry fee:** $12/entry. **Deadline:** December 1. Contest receives 300-400 submissions. Back copy of awards issue: $6. Guidelines available for SASE or on website.

☑ PIKEVILLE REVIEW

Humanities Dept., Pikeville College, Pikeville KY 41501. (606)218-5002. Fax: (606)218-5225. E-mail: eward@pc.edu. Website: www.pc.edu. Established 1987. **Editor:** Elgin M. Ward.

Magazine Needs "There's no editorial bias though we recognize and appreciate style and control in each piece. No emotional gushing." *Pikeville Review* appears annually in July, accepting about 10% of poetry received. *Pikeville Review* is 94 pages, digest-sized, professionally printed, perfect-bound, with glossy card cover with b&w illustration. Press run is 500. Sample: $4.

How to Submit No simultaneous submissions or previously published poems. Editor sometimes comments on rejected poems. Guidelines available for SASE or on website. Pays 5 contributor's copies.

$ ☑ ◎ PINE ISLAND JOURNAL OF NEW ENGLAND POETRY (Specialized: regional, New England)

P.O. Box 317, West Springfield MA 01090-0317. Established 1998. **Editor:** Linda Porter.

Magazine Needs *Pine Island* appears 2 times/year "to encourage and support New England poets and the continued expression of New England themes." Wants poems of "up to 30 lines; haiku and other forms welcome; especially interested in New England subjects or themes. No horror, no erotica." Has published poetry by Larry Kimmel, Carol Purington, and Wanda D. Cook. *Pine Island* is 50 pages, digest-sized, desktop-published, saddle-stapled, with cardstock cover with art. Press run is 200 for 80 subscribers. Subscription: $10. Sample: $5. Library rate available. Make checks payable to Pine Island Journal.

How to Submit "Writers must be currently residenced in New England." Submit 5 poems at a time. Line length for poetry is 30 maximum. No previously published poems or simultaneous submissions. Cover letter with brief bio is preferred. Include SASE. Time between acceptance and publication is 6 months. Seldom comments on rejected poems. Responds in up to 2 months. Pays $1/poem and one contributor's copy. Acquires first rights. Accepts poetry book/chapbook submissions for books received and books reviewed pages. "Book/chapbook should be less than one year old to be considered, and cannot be returned. Author or editor must currently reside in New England and will receive a copy of the issue in which their listing or review appears."

☐ THE PINK CHAMELEON—ONLINE

E-mail: dpfreda@juno.com. Website: www.geocities.com/thepinkchameleon/index.html. Established 1985 (former print version), 1999 (online version). **Editor:** Dorothy P. Freda.

Magazine Needs *Pink Chameleon—Online* wants "family-oriented, upbeat poetry, any genre in good taste that gives hope for the future. For example, poems about nature, loved ones, rare moments in time. No pornography, no cursing, no swearing, nothing evoking despair." *The Pink Chameleon* is published online. Receives about 50 poems/year, accepts about 50%. Publishes about 25 poems/issue.

How to Submit Submit 1-4 poems at a time. Line length for poetry is 6 minimum, 24 maximum. Accepts previously published poems; no simultaneous submissions. "Only e-mail submissions considered. Please, *no attachments*. Include work in the body of the e-mail itself. Use plain text. Include a brief bio." Reads submissions all year. Time between acceptance and publication is 2 months. "As editor, I reserve the right to edit for grammar, spelling, sentence structure, flow; omit redundancy and any words or material I consider in bad taste. No pornography, no violence for the sake of violence, no curse words. Remember, this is a family-oriented electronic magazine." Often comments on rejected poems. Guidelines available by e-mail or on website. Responds in one month. No payment. Acquires one-time, one-year publication rights. All rights revert to poet one year after publication online.

Advice "Always keep a typed hard copy or a back-up disk of your work for your files. Mail can go astray. And I'm human, I can accidentally delete or lose the submission."

☐ ◎ THE PIPE SMOKER'S EPHEMERIS (Specialized: pipes and pipe smoking)

20-37 120th St., College Point NY 11356-2128. Established 1964. **Editor/Publisher:** Tom Dunn.

Magazine Needs "The *Ephemeris* is a limited-edition, irregular quarterly for pipe smokers and collectors and anyone else who is interested in its varied contents. Publication costs are absorbed by the editor/publisher, assisted by any contributions—financial or otherwise—that readers might wish to make." Wants poetry with themes related to pipes and pipe smoking. Issues are 116 pages, magazine-sized, offset, saddle-stapled, with coated stock covers and illustrations. Has also published collections covering the first and second 15 years of the *Ephemeris*, and issues a triennial "Collector's Dictionary."

How to Submit Accepts submissions on disk. Cover letter is required with submissions; include any credits. Pays 1-2 contributor's copies. Staff reviews books of poetry. Send materials for review consideration.

Nikki Giovanni

An interview

Photo by Jan Cobb

N ikki Giovanni was the first living, breathing poet I ever saw. Looking back after all these years, this sounds simple-minded to say—but until I saw her, I hadn't realized that being a poet was something someone *did*. As a high school student sitting in a crowded auditorium in Cincinnati, I remember Giovanni reading poems that held me in rapt attention. She and her big smile moved all over the stage, and her energy shook all of us. I wish I could remember what she said. But I do remember the revolution that took place in my mind when I realized that all poets were not dead white men, and that all of them did not use words like "thou," "canst," and "betoketh."

Little did I know that Giovanni had made a career of writing to foster support for black American arts, history, and culture. Originally known for her aggressive, revolutionary poems of the 1960s, she has grown and changed throughout her 30-plus years of writing and publishing. Her newest volume, *The Collected Poetry of Nikki Giovanni* (William Morrow, 2003), is a testament to a woman who has devoted her life to an unswerving focus on racial politics and understanding in the United States. Throughout her career, Giovanni has been named Woman of the Year by numerous magazines and organizations; has had awards and honors named after her; has been given the keys to numerous cities including New York, Dallas, and Los Angeles; and has received over 20 honorary degrees. Most recently, she received her third NAACP Image Award for *Blues: For All the Changes*, received a Virginia Governor's Award for the Arts, was a poetry judge for The National Book Awards, and was the first to receive the Rosa Parks Women of Courage Award. She is currently University Distinguished Professor at Virginia Tech University in Blacksburg, Virginia.

You recently released your *Collected Poems* with work spanning over 30 years. Congratulations.
Well, it's not as large a book as some other people would do. I tend to write books thematically. My early books all fold into each other, but I never did just try to write everything at one time. I just tried to write some decent poems that I hope expressed a feeling.

As I look through this collection, I notice the feeling of the poems has changed significantly. How do you see the emotions shifting?
If you're going to stay around, you have to try to make adjustments. You can't have solutions when you write, you have to have the questions. You keep asking these questions, and you have feelings about what is right and wrong. But those feelings change with maturity, and I think that my writing reflects that. Also, poets talk about life; and as you keep

watching, things make you upset because you wish that things could be better. After 9/11 when the World Trade Towers went down, people turned to poetry. The Internet just lit up with poetry. People were writing poems because writing allows us to have emotions and ask questions and helps us to make adjustments.

Would you do anything differently?
Not significantly. What really surprises me about my own work is that I was fearless! I just went forth into the woods. Somebody said, ''There's bears in the woods,'' and I said, ''Yeah. Okay, well, those bears aren't mad at me!''

Tell me about the change in your style. Even if someone just flipped through this book and looked at the physical forms of the poems, they would see a change from tight revolutionary bursts of poetry to long prose-style pieces full of ellipses toward the end.
I have a new understanding of why James Joyce wrote *Ulysses*! Someone who reviewed [my new poems] said [they were] like a ticker tape of my mind. And I really liked that, because there had been an urgency from the war and from America's relationship with race. I wanted to get the details in these poems. I wasn't trying to say ''I'm right,'' I was just trying to say ''these are the things informing my opinion.''

You have talked about empathy in terms of poetry and in terms of just being human. In your poems I see a combination of empathy and anger. Do you see yourself balancing those things throughout your career?
I think I balance them a lot. People and things still make you angry, and you still have to put yourself in someone else's shoes. For example, I think it's fair to say that Saddam Hussein is not a nice guy, but you had to empathize when they showed the video of the soldier putting his hands in his mouth. It was humiliating and it reminded me of slavery, so even though there is nothing about him to like, I felt sorry for him.

In one of your essays, you wrote that the most we can bring to the page is honesty. But don't we always filter ourselves as writers? Can't we always choose what to be honest about?
Well, I don't know that I would agree with you. We don't choose what we're honest about. We choose what we're interested in. You have to be honest, and if you can't be honest then you should leave it alone. There are always things that you don't know enough or care enough about. But what you take on, you have to own honestly. The readers don't have to agree, but they have to be able to at least say, ''Well, hell, she at least is honest!''

But can't one make an argument that every person's vision, even racist or colonial vision, is honest?
The Klan says they are being honest in their vision, but hatred is not an honest vision. Hatred is a lack of vision. Colonialism and racism are lacks of vision.

In an interview for *Essence* magazine, you said you didn't want to be a role model. Why is that?
Because it's such a copout. All change in the world has happened because someone did something that hadn't been done before. I know you're not supposed to be, but I'm a big

fan of Christopher Columbus. I like old Chris because he just said, "I'm gonna go around the world." Somebody said, "The world is flat," and he said, "Well. Okay, I'm gonna go anyway." They said, "You'll fall off the edge of the world," and he said, "Then, dammit, I'll fall off the edge of the world, but I am not going to stay in this place." People don't need someone to follow—most of the time they just need people to get out of their way! I'm not saying everyone is a self-starter, but I am not going to hold myself up as an image of what someone can become. Whatever it is, I am doing the best that I can do—whether it's writing a poem in 1968, 1998, or 2004, I am writing the best poem I know how to write. So if that's a role model, then, I guess the message is to simply do the best you can do.

—Amy Ratto

Amy Ratto's poems have been widely published, and she's the author of a prize-winning chapbook, *Bread and Water Body*. She was an editor with *Writer's Digest*, *Fiction Writer Magazine*, and *Personal Journaling* and is former editor-in-chief of *CutBank*. She lives in Missoula, Montana, with her husband and daughter.

☑ PITCHFORK; PITCHFORK PRESS

2002 A Guadalupe St. #461, Austin TX 78705. Established 1998. **Editor:** Christopher Gibson.
Magazine Needs *Pitchfork* is a biannual publishing "freaky goodness." Wants post-beat and surreal poetry—"erotic, psychotic, and surreal poetry. No hack work." Has published poetry by Gerald Nicosia, Ira Cohen, Lawrence Welsh, Steve Dalachinsky, and Robert L. Penick. *Pitchfork* is 60-80 pages, digest-sized, photocopied, saddle-stapled, with colored paper cover. Press run varies. Single copy: $4; subscription: $10 (includes 2 issues and a chapbook of choice). Sample: $3. Make checks payable to Christopher Gibson.
How to Submit Submit 3-7 poems at a time. Accepts previously published poems and simultaneous submissions, "but let us know." Cover letter is preferred. "Include name and address on each page; always include SASE." Time between acceptance and publication is 6 months. Seldom comments on rejected poems. Response time varies. Pays one contributor's copy. Acquires all rights. Returns rights.
Book/Chapbook Needs & How to Submit Pitchfork Press publishes 2 chapbooks/year. Has published *Factory Stiff* by William Hart and *Unoccupied Zone* by Doug Draime. Chapbooks are usually 40-60 pages, digest-sized, photocopied, side-stapled. However, they are not accepting unsolicited mss at this time.

☑ PITT POETRY SERIES; UNIVERSITY OF PITTSBURGH PRESS; AGNES LYNCH STARRETT POETRY PRIZE

3400 Forbes Ave., Pittsburgh PA 15260. (412)383-2466. Website: www.pitt.edu/~press. Established 1968. **Poetry Editor:** Ed Ochester.
Book/Chapbook Needs University of Pittsburgh Press, through the Pitt Poetry Series, publishes at least 4 books/year by established poets, and one by a new poet—the winner of the Starrett Poetry Prize competition. Wants "poetry of the highest quality; otherwise, no restrictions—book manuscripts should be a minimum of 48 pages." Has published books of poetry by Lynn Emanuel, Larry Levis, Billy Collins, and Alicia Ostriker. Their booklist also features such poets as Etheridge Knight, Sharon Olds, Ronald Wallace, David Wojahn, and Toi Derricotte.
How to Submit Unpublished poets or poets "who have published chapbooks or limited editions of less than 750 copies" must submit through the Agnes Lynch Starrett Poetry Prize (see below). Poets who have previously published books should query. For poetry series, submit "entire manuscripts only." Accepts simultaneous submissions. Cover letter is preferred. Reads submissions from

established poets in September and October only. Seldom comments on rejected poems. Always sends prepublication galleys.

Contest/Award Offerings Sponsors the Agnes Lynch Starrett Poetry Prize. "Poets who have not previously published a book should send SASE for rules of the Starrett competition, the only vehicle through which we publish first books of poetry." The Starrett Prize awards $5,000 and book publication. **Entry fee:** $20. **Postmark deadline:** between March 1 and April 30. Competition receives 1,000 entries.

PLAINSONGS

Dept. of English, Hastings College, Hastings NE 68902-0269. (402)461-7352. Fax: (402)461-7756. E-mail: dm84342@alltel.net. Established 1980. **Editor:** Dwight C. Marsh.

Magazine Needs *Plainsongs* is a poetry magazine that "accepts manuscripts from anyone, considering poems on any subject in any style, but free verse predominates. Plains region poems encouraged." Has published poetry by Steve Benson, Ace Boggess, Gaylord Brewer, Ed Chalberck, Blaine Hammond, Lisa Miller, Harry Oliver, and Lisa Roullard. *Plainsongs* is 40 pages, digest-sized, set on laser, printed on thin paper, saddle-stapled, with one-color matte card cover with generic black logo. "Published by the English department of Hastings College, the magazine is partially financed by subscriptions. Although editors respond to as many submissions with personal attention as they have time for, the editor offers specific observations to all contributors who also subscribe." The name suggests not only its location on the Great Plains, but its preference for the living language, whether in free or formal verse. *Plainsongs* is committed to poems only, to make space without visual graphics, bio, reviews, or critical positions. Subscription: $12/3 issues. Sample: $4.

How to Submit Submit up to 6 poems at a time with name and address on each page. **Deadlines:** August 15 for fall issue; November 15 for winter; March 15 for spring. Notification is mailed 5-6 weeks after deadlines. Pays 2 contributor's copies and one-year subscription, with 3 award poems in each issue receiving $25. "A short essay in appreciation accompanies each award poem." Acquires first rights.

Advice "We like to hear tension in the lines, with nothing flaccid."

$ PLANET: THE WELSH INTERNATIONALIST

P.O. Box 44, Aberystwyth, Ceredigion SY23 3ZZ, Wales. Phone: 01970-611255. Fax: 01970-611197. E-mail: planet.enquiries@planetmagazine.org.uk. Website: http://planetmagazine.org.uk. Established 1970. **Editor:** John Barnie.

Magazine Needs *Planet* is a bimonthly cultural magazine, "centered on Wales, but with broader interests in arts, sociology, politics, history, and science." Wants "good poetry in a wide variety of styles. No limitations as to subject matter; length can be a problem." Has published poetry by Nigel Jenkins, Anne Stevenson, and Mertyl Morris. *Planet* is 128 pages, A5, professionally printed, perfect-bound, with glossy color card cover. Receives about 500 submissions/year, accepts about 5%. Press run is 1,550 for 1,500 subscribers of which about 10% are libraries, 200 shelf sales. Single copy: £3.25; subscription: £15 (overseas: £16). Sample: £4.

How to Submit No previously published poems or simultaneous submissions. Accepts submissions on disk, as e-mail attachment, and by postal mail. SASE or SAE with IRCs essential for reply. Time between acceptance and publication is 6-10 months. Seldom comments on rejected poems. Send SASE (or SAE and IRCs if outside UK) for guidelines. Responds within a month or so. Pays £25 minimum. Acquires first serial rights only. Reviews books of poetry in 700 words, single or multibook format.

THE PLAZA (Specialized: bilingual)

U-Kan, Inc., Yoyogi 2-32-1, Shibuya-ku, Tokyo 151-0053, Japan. Phone: 81-3-3379-3881. Fax: 81-3-3379-3882. E-mail: plaza@u-kan.co.jp. Website: http://u-kan.co.jp. Established 1985. **Contact:** The Editor.

Magazine Needs *The Plaza* is an annual, currently published only online, which "represents a borderless forum for contemporary writers and artists" and includes poetry, fiction, and essays published simultaneously in English and Japanese. Wants "highly artistic poetry dealing with being human and interculturally related. Nothing stressing political, national, religious, or racial differences. *The Plaza* is edited with a global view of mankind." Has published poetry by Al Beck, Antler, Charles Helzer, Richard Alan Bunch, Morgan Gibson, and Kikuzou Hidari. *The Plaza* is 50 full-color pages. Available free to all readers on the Internet. Receives about 600 poems/year, accepts 2%.

How to Submit Accepts simultaneous submissions; no previously published poems. Accepts e-mail and fax submissions. "No e-mail attachments. Cover letter is required. Please include telephone and fax numbers or e-mail address with submissions. As *The Plaza* is a bilingual publication in English and Japanese, it is sometimes necessary, for translation purposes, to contact authors. Japanese translations are prepared by the editorial staff." Seldom comments on rejected poems. Responds within 2 months. Proofs of accepted poems are sent to the authors one month before online publication. Reviews books of poetry, usually in less than 500 words. Send materials for review consideration.

Advice "*The Plaza* focuses not on human beings but humans being human in the borderless world."

$☑ PLEIADES; LENA-MILES WEVER TODD POETRY SERIES; PLEIADES PRESS

Dept. of English and Philosophy, Central Missouri State University, Warrensburg MO 64093. (660)543-8106. E-mail: kdp8106@cmsu2.cmsu.edu. Website: www.cmsu.edu/englphil/pleiades.html. Established in 1990. **Editor:** Kevin Prufer.

Magazine Needs *Pleiades* is a biannual journal, appearing in April and October, publishing poetry, fiction, literary criticism, belles lettres (occasionally), and reviews. It is open to all writers. Wants "avant-garde, free verse, and traditional poetry, and some quality light verse. Nothing pretentious, didactic, or overly sentimental." Has published poetry by James Tate, Joyce Carol Oates, Brenda Hillman, Dara Wier, Rafael Campo, and David Lehman. *Pleiades* is 160 pages, digest-sized, perfect-bound, with a heavy coated cover and color cover art. Receives about 3,000 poems/year, accepts 1-3%. Press run is 2,500-3,000, about 200 distributed free to educational institutions and libraries across the country, several hundred shelf sales. Single copy: $6; subscription: $12. Sample: $5. Make checks payable to Pleiades Press.

How to Submit Submit 3-5 poems at a time. Accepts simultaneous submissions with notification; no previously published poems. Cover letter with brief bio is preferred. Time between acceptance and publication can be up to one year. Each poem published must be accepted by 2 readers and approved by the poetry editor. Seldom comments on rejected poems. Guidelines available for SASE or on website. Responds in up to 3 months. Payment varies. Acquires first and second serial rights.

Contest/Award Offerings Sponsors the Lena-Miles Wever Todd Poetry Series. "We will select one book of poems in open competition and publish it in our Pleiades Press Series. Louisiana State University Press will distribute the collection." Has published *The Green Girls* by John Blair, *A Sacrificial Zinc* by Matthew Cooperman, and *The Light in Our Houses* by Al Maginnes. **Entry fee:** $15. **Postmark deadline:** September 30 annually. Complete guidelines available for SASE or on website.

$☑ PLOUGHSHARES

Emerson College, 120 Boylston St., Boston MA 02116. (617)824-8753. Website: www.pshares.org. Established 1971.

- Work published in *Ploughshares* is frequently selected for inclusion in volumes of *The Best American Poetry*.

Magazine Needs *Ploughshares* is "a journal of new writing guest-edited by prominent poets and writers to reflect different and contrasting points of view." Editors have included Carolyn Forché,

Gerald Stern, Rita Dove, Chase Twichell, and Marilyn Hacker. Has published poetry by Donald Hall, Li-Young Lee, Robert Pinsky, Brenda Hillman, and Thylias Moss. The triquarterly is 250 pages, digest-sized. Receives about 2,500 poetry submissions/year. Press run is 6,000. Subscription: $24 domestic, $36 foreign. Sample: $10.95 current issue, $8.50 back issue.

How to Submit "We suggest you read a few issues before submitting." Accepts simultaneous submissions. Do not submit mss from April 1 to July 31. Responds in up to 5 months. Always sends prepublication galleys. Pays $25/printed page per poem ($50 min, $250 max), plus 2 contributor's copies and a subscription.

$ THE PLOWMAN

The Plowman Ministries—A Mission for Christ, Box 414, Whitby ON L1N 5S4 Canada. (905)668-7803. Established 1988. **Editor:** Tony Scavetta.

Magazine Needs *The Plowman* appears annually in July or August using "didactic, eclectic poetry; all forms. We will also take most religious poetry except satanic and evil. We are interested in work that deals with the important issues in our society. Social and environmental issues are of great importance." *The Plowman* is 20 pages, magazine-sized, photocopied, unbound, includes clip art and market listings. Accepts 70% of the poetry received. Press run is 15,000 for 1,200 subscribers of which 500 are libraries. Single copy: $5; subscription: $10. Sample free.

How to Submit Submit up to 5 poems (preferably 38 lines or less). Accepts previously published poems and simultaneous submissions. Cover letter is required. No SASE necessary. Always comments on rejected poems. Guidelines available for SASE. Responds in up to 2 weeks. Always sends prepublication galleys. Pays one contributor's copy. Reviews books of poetry.

Book/Chapbook Needs & How to Submit Also publishes 125 chapbooks/year. Responds to queries and mss in one month. **Reading fee:** $25/book. Pays 20% royalties. Has published *Poems of Joy* by Eva Marie Ippolitio, *Now Playing La Vida* by C.E. Larsen, *A Journey Back to the Light* by Scott J. Miller, and *Go On, Be Happy* by Kaye Byrne.

Contest/Award Offerings Offers monthly poetry contests. **Entry fee:** $2/poem. 1st Prize: 50% of the proceeds; 2nd Prize: 25%; 3rd Prize: 10%. The top poems are published. "Balance of the poems will be used for anthologies."

PLUM RUBY REVIEW

P.O. Box 71, Belmont MA 02478. E-mail: submissions@plumrubyreview.com. Website: www.plum rubyreview.com. Established 2003. **Contact:** Crystal King (at Belmont address); G.S. McCormick (P.O. Box 81, Station Place du Parc, Montreal QC H2X 4A3 Canada).

Magazine Needs "The *Plum Ruby Review* is a bimonthly online showcase for unpublished fiction, poetry, nonfiction (memoir, essay, travel pieces), and art (photography as well as traditional and contemporary art forms). We are delighted by works that are vivid, imaginative, fresh, and accessible. We seek unpublished, evocative, polished poems from established, emerging, and unknown writers. Carefully read the submission guidelines available on our website. We are open to all genres and forms if the execution is masterful. Translations are also welcome." Does not want poetry that is "full of clichés and/or lacks emotion. On the same token, anything overly melodramatic (rhyming love poetry often falls into this category) will most likely end up being returned/rejected. We have nothing against rhyme, metered, or form poetry; but as it is difficult to write well, this is frequently the kind we reject. If you write dense prose poems, the same advice applies. We're not interested in religious/inspirational poetry, sappy love poems, or greeting card verse." Has published poetry by Rane Arroyo, Harding Stedler, Duane Locke, Gordon Moyer, and Paul Kloppenborg. Receives about 500-700 poems/year, accepts about 20%. Publishes about 20 poems/issue.

How to Submit Submit 6 poems at a time. Line length for poetry is open at this time, "but we tend to prefer shorter pieces." No previously published poems or simultaneous submissions. Accepts e-mail (pasted into body of message) and disk submissions. "If e-mail won't show the proper formatting of the poem you'd like to submit, please query us first." Cover letter is preferred. Reads submissions year round. Submit seasonal poems 3 months in advance. Time between acceptance and publication is 2 weeks to 2 months. "Each poem is read by 2 initial readers, then passed on or rejected. Those passed are read 2-3 more times, then narrowed down to final pieces selected for publication." Seldom comments on rejected poems. Guidelines available on website. Responds in up to 2 months. Acquires first rights. Reviews 4-6 poetry books or chapbooks/year. Send materials for review consideration to either Crystal King or G.S. McCormick at the appropriate addresses above.

Advice "We believe you need to READ poetry (and a lot of it) in order to write great poetry yourself. Become voracious, devour the poetic form of others, and you will see your own writing transform."

◻ ◎ POCKETS (Specialized: Christian; children)

1908 Grand Ave., P.O. Box 340004, Nashville TN 37203-0004. E-mail:pockets@upperroom.org. Website:www.pockets.org. **Contact:** Lynn W. Gilliam, associate editor.

Magazine Needs & How to Submit *Pockets* is an interdenominational magazine for children ages 6-12, published monthly except in February. "Each issue is built around a specific theme with material (including poetry) that can be used by children in a variety of ways. Submissions do not need to be overly religious; they should help children experience a Christian lifestyle that is not always a neatly wrapped moral package but is open to the continuing revelation of God's will." Line length for poetry is 22 lines maximum (short poems preferred). Accepts one-time previously published poems. No e-mail submissions. Submissions should be typed, double-spaced, on $8\frac{1}{2} \times 11$ paper, accompanied by SASE for return. "Writers who wish to save postage and are concerned about paper conservation may send a SASP for notification of accepted manuscripts; we will recycle the paper the submission is printed on. Please list the name of the submission(s) on the card." Reads submissions year round. Always publishes theme issues ("themes are set each year in December"). List of upcoming themes and guidelines available on website (under "For Adults/Writer's Corner"). Pays $25. Pays on acceptance; may place mss on long-term hold for specific issues. Acquires newspaper, periodical, and electronic rights.

◪ POEM; HUNTSVILLE LITERARY ASSOCIATION

P.O. Box 2006, Huntsville AL 35804. Established 1967. **Editor:** Rebecca Harbor.

Magazine Needs *Poem* appears twice/year, in May and November, consisting entirely of poetry. "We publish both traditional forms and free verse. We want poems characterized by compression, rich vocabulary, significant content, and evidence of 'a tuned ear and practiced pen.' We equally welcome submissions from established poets as well as from less-known and beginning poets." Has published poetry by Kathryn Kirkpatrick, R.T. Smith, and Ronald Wallace. *Poem* is a flat-spined, digest-sized, 90-page journal that contains more than 60 poems, generally featured one to a page, printed on good stock paper, with a clean design and a matte cover. Press run is 400 (all subscriptions, including libraries). Subscription: $20. Sample: $7.

How to Submit "We do not accept translations, previously published poems, or simultaneous submissions. Best to submit December through March and June through September. We prefer to see a sample of 3-5 poems per submission, with SASE. We generally respond within 6 weeks. We are a nonprofit organization and can pay only in contributor's copies." Pays 2 contributor's copies. Acquires first serial rights.

◪ POEMS & PLAYS; THE TENNESSEE CHAPBOOK PRIZE

English Dept., Middle Tennessee State University, Murfreesboro TN 37132. (615)898-2712. Established 1993. **Editor:** Gaylord Brewer.

Magazine Needs *Poems & Plays* is an annual "eclectic publication for poems and short plays," published in the spring. No restrictions on style or content of poetry. Has published poetry by Naomi Wallace, Kate Gale, Richard Newman, Ron Koertge, and Moira Egan. *Poems & Plays* is 88 pages, digest-sized, professionally printed, perfect-bound, with coated color card cover, includes art. "We receive 1,500 poems per issue, typically publish 30-35." Press run is 800. Subscription: $10/2 issues. Sample: $6.

How to Submit No previously published poems or simultaneous submissions (except for chapbook submissions). Reads submissions October 1 through December 31 only. "Work is circulated among advisory editors for comments and preferences. All accepted material is published in the following issue." Usually comments on rejected poems. Responds in 2 months. Pays one contributor's copy. Acquires first publication rights only.

Contest/Award Offerings "We accept chapbook manuscripts (of poems or short plays) of 20-24 pages for The Tennessee Chapbook Prize. Any combination of poems or plays, or a single play, is eligible. The winning chapbook is printed as an interior chapbook in *Poems & Plays*, and the author receives 50 copies of the issue. **SASE and $10 (for reading fee and one copy of the issue) required. Dates for contest entry are the same as for the magazine (October 1 through December 31).** Past winners include Julie Lechevsky, David Kirby, Angela Kelly, and Rob Griffith. The chapbook competition annually receives over 150 manuscripts from the U.S. and around the world."

⬛ POESY MAGAZINE

P.O. Box 7823, Santa Cruz CA 95061. (831)460-1048. E-mail: info@poesy.org. Website: www.poesy .org. Established 1991. **Editor/Publisher:** Brian Morrisey.

Magazine Needs *POESY Magazine* appears quarterly as "an anthology of American poetry. *POESY*'s main concentrations are Boston, Massachusetts and Santa Cruz, California, 2 thriving homesteads for poets, beats, and artists of nature. Our goal is to unite the 2 scenes, updating poets on what's happening across the country. We like to see original poems that express observational impacts with clear and concise imagery. Acceptence is based on creativity, composition, and relation to the format of *POESY*. Please do not send poetry with excessive profanity. We would like to endorse creativity beyond the likes of everyday babble." Has published poetry by Lawrence Ferlinghetti, Jack Hirschman, Edward Sanders, Herschel Silverman, Linda Lerner, Simon Perchik, and Corey Mesler. *POESY* is 16 pages, magazine-sized, newsprint, glued/folded, includes computer-generated and quarter-page ads. Receives about 1,000 poems/year, accepts about 10%. Publishes about 26 poems/issue. Press run is 1,000, most distributed free to local venues. Single copy: $1; subscription: $12/year. Sample: $2. Make checks payable to Brian Morrisey.

How to Submit Submit 4-6 poems at a time. Line length for poetry is 32 maximum. No previously published poems or simultaneous submissions. Accepts e-mail and disk submissions; no fax submissions. "Snail mail submissions are preferred with a SASE." Cover letter is preferred. Reads submissions year round. Time between acceptance and publication is one month. "Poems are accepted by the Santa Cruz editor/publisher based on how well the poem stimulates our format." Sometimes comments on rejected poems. Guidelines available in magazine, for SASE, or by e-mail. Responds in one month. Sometimes sends prepublication galleys. Pays 3 contributor's copies. Acquires one-time rights. Reviews books and chapbooks of poetry and other magazines/journals in 1,000 words, single book format. Send materials for review consideration to *POESY*, % Brian Morrisey.

Advice "Branch away from typical notions of love and romance. Become one with your surroundings and discover a true sense of natural perspective."

⬛ POET LORE

The Writer's Center, 4508 Walsh St., Bethesda MD 20815. (301)654-8664. Fax: (301)654-8667. E-mail: postmaster@writer.org. Website: www.writer.org. Established 1889. **Editors:** Rick Cannon, E. Ethelbert Miller, and Jody Bolz. **Contact:** DeeDee Clendenning.

Magazine Needs *Poet Lore* is a biannual dedicated "to the best in American and world poetry and timely reviews and commentary. We look for fresh uses of traditional forms and devices, but any kind of excellence is welcome." Has published poetry by Adrian Blevins, Fleda Brown, David Wagoner, Martin Galvin, Carrie Etter, and Maria Terrone. *Poet Lore* is 140 pages, digest-sized, professionally printed, perfect-bound, with glossy card cover. Receives about 4,200 poems/year, accepts 125. Circulation includes 600 subscriptions of which 200 are libraries. Single copy: $9; subscription: $18. "Add $1/single copy for shipping; add $5 postage for subscriptions outside U.S."
How to Submit "Submit typed poems, with author's name and address on each page; SASE required. No electronic submissions. Simultaneous submissions OK with notification in cover letter." Guidelines available for SASE or on website. Responds in 3 months. Pays 2 contributor's copies. Reviews books of poetry. Send materials for review consideration.

⊕ ◻ ◎ POETCRIT (Specialized: membership)

Maranda, H.P. 176 102 India. Phone: 01894-238277. E-mail: dcchambrial@indiatimes.com. Established 1988. **Editor:** Dr. D.C. Chambial.
Magazine Needs *Poetcrit* appears each January and July "to promote poetry and international understanding through poetry. Purely critical articles on various genres of literature are also published." Wants poems of every kind. Has published poetry by Ruth Wilder Schuller (US), Danae G. Papastratau (Greece), Shiv K. Kumar (India), Joy B. Cripps (Australia), and O.P. Bhatnagar (India). *Poetcrit* is 100 pages, magazine-sized, offset-printed, with simple paper cover, includes ads. Receives about 1,000 poems/year, accepts 20%. Press run is 1,000 for 500 subscribers of which 100 are libraries, 200 shelf sales; 400 distributed free to new members. Single copy: $9; subscription: $15. Sample: $10. Make checks payable to Dr. D.C. Chambial.
How to Submit "Membership required for consideration." Submit 3 poems at a time. Line length for poetry is 25 maximum. Accepts simultaneous submissions; no previously published poems. Cover letter is required. Reads submissions September 1 through 20 and March 1 through 20. Poems are circulated to an editorial board. "All poems reviewed by various editors and selected for publication." Occasionally publishes theme issues. List of upcoming themes and guidelines available for SASE (or SAE with IRC). Responds in about one month. Pays one contributor's copy. Acquires one-time rights. Reviews books and chapbooks of poetry and other magazines in 1,000 words, single book format.
Advice "Beginners should meditate well on their themes before writing."

⊕ ◻ POETIC HOURS

43 Willow Rd., Carlton, Nolts NG4 3BH England. E-mail: erranpublishing@hotmail.com. Website: www.poetichours.homestead.com. Established 1993. **Editor:** Nicholas Clark.
Magazine Needs *Poetic Hours* is published biannually "to encourage and publish new poets, i.e., as a forum where good but little known poets can appear in print, and to raise money for Third World charities. The magazine features articles and poetry by subscribers and others." Wants "any subject, rhyme preferred but not essential; suitable for wide ranging readership, 30 lines maximum." Does not want "gothic, horror, extremist, political, self-interested." *Poetic Hours* is 36 pages, A4, printed, saddle-stapled, and illustrated throughout with Victorian woodcuts. Receives about 500 poems/year, accepts about 40%. Press run is 400 of which 12 are for libraries, 300 shelf sales. Subscription: £7 sterling, overseas payments in sterling (Europe and EC) or US dollars ($20 from USA or Canada). Subscribe online from our website or send bankers checks (UK only) or cash. Sample: £3.75. Make checks payable to Erran Publishing.
How to Submit "Poets are encouraged to subscribe or buy a single copy, though not required." Submit up to 5 nonreturnable poems at a time, via e-mail from website where possible. Accepts previously published poems; no simultaneous submissions. Prefers e-mail submissions in attachments; accepts disk submissions. Cover letter is required. Time between acceptance and publication

is 3 months. "Poems are read by editors and, if found suitable, are used." Always comments on rejected poems. Responds "immediately, whenever possible." Acquires one-time rights.

Also Offers "Poetic Hours Online" at www.poetichours.homestead.com features original content by invitation of editor only.

Advice "We welcome newcomers and invite those just starting out to have the courage to submit work. The art of poetry has moved from the hands of book publishers down the ladder to the new magazines. This is where all the best poetry is found." *Poetic Hours* is non-profit-making; all proceeds go to various charities, particularly well-building and children's charities. A page of each issue is set aside for reporting how money is spent.

⦿ POETIC MATRIX PRESS; POETIC MATRIX, A PERIODIC LETTER; POETIC MATRIX SLIM VOLUME SERIES

P.O. Box 1223, Madera CA 93639. (559)673-9402. E-mail: poeticmatrix@yahoo.com. Website: www.poeticmatrix.com. Established 1997 in Yosemite. **Editor/Publisher:** John Peterson.

Magazine Needs *Poetic Matrix, a periodic letteR* appears 2-3 times/year. Wants poetry that "creates a 'place in which we can live' rather than telling us about the place. Poetry that draws from the imaginal mind and is rich in the poetic experience—hence the poetic matrix." Does not want poetry that talks about the experience. Has published poetry by Jeff Mann, Grace Marie Grafton, Tony White, Kathryn Kruger, James Downs, Joan Michelson, and Brandon Cesmat. *Poetic Matrix, a periodic letteR* is 4-12 pages, newsletter format, includes b&w art. Publishes about 10-20 poems/issue. Press run is 500 for 250 subscribers; 150 distributed free to interested parties, etc. Subscription: $12/4 issues. Make checks payable to *Poetic Matrix*.

How to Submit "Poems for *letteR* are generally, but not always, drawn from the call for manuscripts for the *Poetic Matrix* Slim Volume Series." Guidelines available for SASE or by e-mail. Pays in contributor's copies. Acquires one-time rights. Reviews books and chapbooks of poetry and other magazines/journals in 500-1,000 words, single and multi-book format. Send materials for review consideration to John Peterson, editor.

Book/Chapbook Needs & How to Submit Poetic Matrix Press publishes books (60-90 pages), slim volumes (44-55 pages, perfect-bound), and chapbooks (20-30 pages). "Poetic Matrix Press hosts a new Slim Volume Series call for submissions of manuscripts 45-55 pages. The manuscript selected will be published with full-color cover, perfect binding, and ISBN. The selected poet will receive 100 copies of the completed book and a $200 honorarium." Full guidelines and submission dates available for SASE or by e-mail. Charges reading fee for yearly slim volume series submissions only. For chapbook and book information, contact the publisher. Order sample copies from Poetic Matrix Press.

Advice "If poets and lovers of poetry don't write, publish, read, purchase poetry books, etc., then we will have no say in the quality of our contemporary culture and no excuses for the abuses of language, ideas, truth, beauty, and love in our cultural life."

ⓃⓏⓄ POÉTICA (Specialized: Spanish language only)

P.O. Box 925, Isabela PR 00662. Established 2004. **Editor:** Alberto Martínez-Márquez (address submissions to Mr. Martínez-Márquez only). Publisher: Nilda Cepero.

Magazine Needs *Poética*, which appears 2 times/year, is a Spanish-language literary magazine published by *LSR* (see separate listing in this section). "We publish original poetry and book reviews in the Spanish language only. Style, subject matter, and content of poetry are open; however, porn, religious, or political poetry are not welcome." *Poética* is 20 pages, digest-sized, offset-printed, saddle-stapled, with 60 lb. cover, includes "very few" ads. Press run is 500. Single copy: $2 (US), $3 (foreign); subscription: $4/year. Sample: $3, including postage.

How to Submit Submit 4 or 5 poems at a time. Line length for poetry is 5 minimum, 45 maximum. Accepts disk submissions only when accompanied by print-out. Cover letter is required. "Include

SASE with bio and e-mail address.'' Guidelines available in magazine or for SASE. Responds in 9 months. Acquires one-time rights. Open to unsolicited book/chapbook/magazine reviews.
Advice "Read as many current poetry magazines as you can."

◻ POETREE MAGAZINE

E-mail: poetree@nycap.rr.com. Website: www.poetreemagazine.org/. Established 2002. **Editor:** Jennifer R. McIntosh.

Magazine Needs *Poetree Magazine* appears quarterly online. Open to poets of all ages and skills. Wants "all styles and forms about interesting topics. Looking for creativity." Does not want "porn or obscenity; overly religious work; puppy love poems you'd be embarrassed by 10 years from now." Accepts poetry written by young writers. "Please include age or grade with submission." Has published poetry by Hamida Owusu. *Poetree Magazine* is published online only. Publishes about 6 poems/issue.

How to Submit Accepts previously published poems and simultaneous submissions. Accepts e-mail (pasted into body of message) submissions; no disk submissions. Cover letter is preferred. "Must include name and contact method (either valid e-mail address or phone number). Only original work." Reads submissions continuously. Time between acceptance and publication is 2 weeks. "I am the sole editor. If a poem moves me, I publish it." Guidelines available on website. Responds in 2 months ("depends on how busy I am"). Poets retain rights after publication.

Book/Chapbook Needs & How to Submit *Poetree Magazine* publishes e-chapbooks, "online collections of poems by one author." Publishes 4 chapbooks/year. Manuscripts are selected through open submission. Chapbooks are published online with clip art illustrations. May include previously published poems. Responds to queries in weeks.

Advice "Don't give up! Keep writing. Use your local library to find great resources on writing and publishing."

$◻ POETRY; THE POETRY FOUNDATION; BESS HOKIN PRIZE; LEVINSON PRIZE; FREDERICK BOCK PRIZE; J. HOWARD AND BARBARA M.J. WOOD PRIZE; RUTH LILLY POETRY PRIZE; RUTH LILLY POETRY FELLOWSHIP; JOHN FREDERICK NIMS MEMORIAL PRIZE; FRIENDS OF LITERATURE PRIZE; UNION LEAGUE CIVIL AND ARTS POETRY PRIZE

1030 N. Clark St., Chicago IL 60610. E-mail: poetry@poetrymagazine.org (send Letters to the Editor to editors@poetrymagazine.org). Website: www.poetrymagazine.org. Established 1912. **Editor:** Christine Wiman.

- Work published in *Poetry* is frequently selected for inclusion in *The Best American Poetry* and *The Pushcart Prize: Best of the Small Presses*.

Magazine Needs *Poetry* "is the oldest and most distinguished monthly magazine devoted entirely to verse. Established in Chicago in 1912, it immediately became the international showcase for new poetry, publishing in its earliest years, and often for the first time, such giants as Ezra Pound, Robert Frost, T.S. Eliot, Marianne Moore, and Wallace Stevens. *Poetry* has continued to print the major voices of our time and to discover new talent, establishing an unprecedented record. There is virtually no important contemporary poet in the English language who has not, at a crucial stage in his or her career, depended on *Poetry* to find a public: John Ashbery, Dylan Thomas, Edna St. Vincent Millay, James Merrill, Anne Sexton, Sylvia Plath, James Dickey, Thom Gunn, David Wagoner, et al. *Poetry* publishes, without affiliation with any movements or schools, what August Kleinzahler has called 'the most interesting and influential journal for and about poetry in America right now.'" *Poetry* is an elegantly printed, flat-spined, $5\frac{1}{2} \times 9$ magazine. Receives over 9,000 submissions/year, accepts about 300-350; has a backlog of up to 9 months. Press run is 14,258 for 10,000 subscribers of which 33% are libraries. Single copy: $3.75; subscription: $35, $38 for institutions. Sample: $5.50.

How to Submit Submit up to 4 poems at a time with SASE. No simultaneous submissions. No e-mail submissions. Guidelines available for SASE. Responds in 4 months. Pays $6/line for poetry, $150/page of prose. Acquires all rights. Returns rights upon written request. Reviews books of poetry in multi-book formats of varying lengths. Send books for review consideration to the editors.

Contest/Award Offerings Six prizes (named in heading) ranging from $300 to $5,000 are awarded annually to poets whose work has appeared in the magazine that year. Only verse already published in *Poetry* is eligible for consideration, and no formal application is necessary. *Poetry* also sponsors the Ruth Lilly Poetry Prize, an annual award of $100,000, and the Ruth Lilly Poetry Fellowship, 2 annual awards of $15,000 to young poets to support their further studies in poetry and creative writing.

Also Offers For information on Poetry Day and other reading/lecutre series, visit www.poetrymagazine.org.

POETRY INTERNATIONAL

Dept. of English, San Diego State University, San Diego CA 92182-8140. (619)594-1523. Fax: (619)594-4998. E-mail: fmoramar@mail.sdsu.edu. Website: http://poetryinternational.sdsu.edu. Established 1996. **Editor:** Fred Moramarco.

Magazine Needs *Poetry International*, published annually in November, is "an eclectic poetry magazine intended to reflect a wide range of poetry being written today." Wants "a wide range of styles and subject matter. We're particularly interested in translations." Does not want "cliché-ridden, derivative, obscure poetry." Has published poetry by Adrienne Rich, Robert Bly, Hayden Carruth, Kim Addonizio, Maxine Kumin, Billy Collins, and Gary Soto. *Poetry International* is 200 pages, perfect-bound, with coated card stock cover. Press run is 1,000. Single copy: $12; subscription: $24/2 years.

How to Submit Submit up to 5 poems at a time. Accepts simultaneous submissions "but prefer not to"; no previously published poems. No fax or e-mail submissions. Reads submissions September 1 through December 30 only. Time between acceptance and publication is 8 months. Poems are circulated to an editorial board. Seldom comments on rejected poems. Responds in up to 4 months. Pays 2 contributor's copies. Acquires all rights. Returns rights "50/50," meaning they split with the author any payment for reprinting the poem elsewhere. "We review anthologies regularly."

Advice "We're interested in new work by poets who are devoted to their art. We want poems that matter—that make a difference in people's lives. We're especially seeking good translations and prose by poets about poetry."

$ POETRY IRELAND REVIEW; POETRY IRELAND

120 St. Stephen's Green, Dublin 2, Ireland. Phone: (353)(1)4789974. Fax: (353)(1)4780205. E-mail: poetry@iol.ie. Website: www.poetryireland.ie. Established 1979. **Director:** Joseph Woods.

Magazine Needs *Poetry Ireland Review*, the magazine of Ireland's national poetry organization, "provides an outlet for Irish poets; submissions from abroad also considered. No specific style or subject matter is prescribed. We strongly dislike sexism and racism." Has published poetry by Seamus Heaney, Michael Longley, Denise Levertov, Medbh McGuckian, and Charles Wright. Occasionally publishes special issues. *Poetry Ireland Review* appears quarterly. Receives up to 8,000 submissions/year, accepts about 3%; has a 2-month backlog. Publishes 60 pages of poetry/issue. Press run is 1,200 for 800 subscriptions. Single copy: IR£7.99; subscription: IR£30.50 Ireland and UK, IR£40.50 overseas (surface). Sample: $10.

How to Submit Submit up to 6 poems at a time. Include SASE (or SAE and IRC). "Submissions not accompanied by SAEs will not be returned." No previously published poems or simultaneous submissions. No e-mail submissions. Time between acceptance and publication is up to 3 months. Seldom comments on rejected poems. Guidelines available for SASE (or SAE and IRC). Responds in 2 months. Pays IR£32/poem or one-year subscription. Reviews books of poetry in 500-1,000 words.

Also Offers *Poetry Ireland Review* is published by Poetry Ireland, an organization established to "promote poets and poetry throughout Ireland." Poetry Ireland offers readings, an information service, an education service, library and administrative center, and a bimonthly newsletter giving news, details of readings, competitions, etc. for IR£8/year. Also sponsors an annual poetry competition. Details available for SASE (or SAE and IRC).

Advice "Keep submitting: Good work will get through."

⊞ ☑ POETRY KANTO

Kanto Gakuin University, Kamariya-cho 3-22-1, Kanazawa-Ku, Yokohama 236-8502, Japan. Established 1984. **Editor:** William I. Elliott.

Magazine Needs *Poetry Kanto* appears annually in August and is published by the Kanto Poetry Center. The magazine publishes well-crafted original poems in English and in Japanese. Wants "anything except pornography; English haiku and tanka; poems under 30 lines." Has published work by Vi Gale, A.D. Hope, Peter Robinson, Naomi Shihab Nye, Nuala Ni Dhomhnaill, and Christopher Middleton. *Poetry Kanto* is 60-80 pages, digest-sized, nicely printed (the English poems occupy the first half of the issue, the Japanese poems the second), saddle-stapled, with matte card cover. Press run is 700, of which 400 are distributed free to schools, poets, and presses; it is also distributed at poetry seminars. The magazine is unpriced. For sample, send SAE with IRCs.

How to Submit Interested poets should query from February through March with SAE and IRCs before submitting. No previously published poems or simultaneous submissions. Often comments on rejected poems. Responds to mss in 2 weeks. Pays 3-5 contributor's copies.

Advice "Start reading or re-reading English-language poets since the 11th centry in order to study what one's predecessors have done!"

☑ POETRY MIDWEST

(843)661-1503. E-mail: submit@poetrymidwest.org (submissions); editors@poetrymidwest.org (queries). Website: www.poetrymidwest.org. Established 2000. **Editor/Publisher:** Matthew W. Schmeer.

Magazine Needs *Poetry Midwest* appears 3 times/year (winter, spring/summer, fall) and features poetry, nongenre microfiction, and brief creative nonfiction from new and established writers. Wants free verse, traditional Western forms, traditional Asian forms other than haiku and senryu, prose poems, long poems, nongenre microfiction (up to 300 words), and brief creative nonfiction (up to 300 words). Does not want science fiction, fantasy, inspirational, religious, or children's verse or fiction; anything of an overtly political or religious nature; or spoken word poetry. Has published poetry by A.D. Winans, Ryan G. Van Cleave, Robin Reagler, Suzanne Burns, Joseph Somoza, and Richard Garcia. *Poetry Midwest* is 20-100 pages, published online as a (free) downloadable Adobe Acrobat PDF file. Receives about 1,500 poems/year, accepts about 7%. Publishes about 25-40 poems/issue ("varies per quality of submissions").

How to Submit Submit 3 poems at a time. Line length for poetry is 3 minimum, 10 pages maximum. Accepts simultaneous submissions; no previously published poems. "Submit via e-mail *only*. Submissions should be pasted into the body of an e-mail message with 'Poetry Midwest Submission' in subject line (omit quotation marks). Absolutely no e-mail file attachments. E-mail messages containing attachments will be deleted upon receipt. Do not send submissions via postal mail; they will be returned unread." Reads submissions year round. Submit seasonal poems 3-6 months in advance. Time between acceptance and publication is 3 months to one year. "I read submissions as they are received, deciding whether or not to use a piece based on its own literary merits and whether it fits in with other poems selected for an issue in progress." Seldom comments on rejected poems. Guidelines available by e-mail or on website. Responds in up to 6 months. Acquires first rights or first North American serial rights as well as First Electronic Rights, Reprint Rights, and Electronic Archival Rights.

Advice "Since *Poetry Midwest* is freely available online, there is no excuse for not reading an issue to sample the type of work the journal tends to feature. Poets should do their research before submitting to any journal; otherwise, they may be wasting not only their time, but the editor's time, too. Online journals are deluged with submissions, and following the posted guidelines will let the editor know you want your submission seriously considered."

◻ POETRY MOTEL; POETRY MOTEL WALLPAPER BROADSIDE SERIES

P.O. Box 202, Kailua-Kona HI 96745. Established 1984. **Editors:** Patrick McKinnon, Bud Backen, and Linda Erickson.

Magazine Needs *Poetry Motel* appears "every 260 days" as a poetry magazine with some fiction and memoire. Wants poetry of "any style, any length." Has published poetry by Adrian C. Louis, Ron Androla, Todd Moore, Albert Huffsticker, Antler, and Serena Fusek. *Poetry Motel* is 52 pages, digest-sized, offset-printed, stapled, with wallpaper cover, includes collages. Receives about 1,000 poems/year, accepts about 5% Publishes about 50 poems/issue. Press run is 1,000 for 400 subscribers of which 10 are libraries. Single copy: $9.95; subscription: $17.95/2 issues, $199/forever. Make checks payable to P. McKinnon.

How to Submit Submit 3-6 pages at a time. Accepts previously published poems and simultaneous submissions. No fax, e-mail, or disk submissions. "Include SASE or brief bio." Reads submissions all year. Time between acceptance and publication varies. Never comments on rejected poems. Guidelines available in magazine and for SASE. Responds in "one week to never." Pays 1-5 contributor's copies. Acquires no rights. Reviews books and chapbooks of poetry and other magazines/journals in varied lengths. Send materials for review consideration to Linda Erickson.

Advice "All work submitted is considered for both the magazine and the broadside series."

⊕ ◪ POETRY NOTTINGHAM; NOTTINGHAM OPEN POETRY COMPETITION; NOTTINGHAM POETRY SOCIETY

11, Orkney Close, Stenson Fields, Derbyshire DE24 3LW United Kingdom. Website: http://nottinghampoetrysociety.co.uk. Established 1946. **Editor:** Adrian Buckner.

Magazine Needs *Poetry Nottingham* is the quarterly magazine of the Nottingham Poetry Society, which meets monthly for readings, talks, etc. Open for submissions from anyone; features articles, letters, news, and reviews in addition to poetry. *Poetry Nottingham* is 6×8, professionally printed. Receives about 1,500 submissions/year, accepts approximately 120; usually has a one- to 3-month backlog. Publishes 56 pages of poetry/issue. Press run is 300 for 200 subscribers. Single copy: £2.75 ($9.75 US); subscriptions: £17 sterling or $34 US.

How to Submit Submit up to 6 poems at any time, or articles up to 500 words on current issues in poetry. No previously published poems. Accepts submissions by postal mail only. "Send SAE and 3 IRCs for stamps. No need to query, but cover letter is required." Responds in 2 months. Pays one contributor's copy. Staff reviews books of poetry. Send materials for review consideration.

Book/Chapbook Needs & How to Submit Poetry Nottingham Publications occasionally publishes collections by individual poets. Query or see website for details.

Contest/Award Offerings The Nottingham Open Poetry Competition offers cash prizes, annual subscriptions, and publication in *Poetry Nottingham*. Open to all. Check website for address and details. Contact for Nottingham Poetry Society and website is Jeremy Duffield, 71 Saxton Ave., Heanor, Derbyshire DE75 7PZ United Kingdom.

Advice "The new editor favors quality of imagery and language, in preference to the anecdotal."

◻ POETRY OF THE PEOPLE

3341 SE 19th Ave., Gainesville FL 32641. (352)375-0244. E-mail: poetryforaquarter@yahoo.com. Website: www.angelfire.com/fl/poetryofthepeople. Established 1986. **Poetry Editor:** Paul Cohen.

Magazine Needs *Poetry of the People* is a leaflet that appears monthly. "We take all forms of poetry, but we like humorous poetry, love poetry, nature poetry, and fantasy. No racist or highly ethnocentric poetry will be accepted. I do not like poetry that lacks images or is too personal or contains rhyme to the point that the poem has been destroyed. All submitted poetry will be considered for posting on website, which will be updated every month." Also accepts poetry written in French and Spanish. Has published poetry by Laura Stamps, Dan Matthews, Jenica Deer, Shannon Dixon, Kristi Castro, and Peggy C. Hall. *Poetry of the People* is 4 pages, magazine-sized, sometimes printed on colored paper. Issues are usually theme oriented. Samples: $4 for 11 pamphlets. "New format is being devised."

How to Submit Submit "as many poems as you want." Include SASE. Accepts submissions on disk, by e-mail, and by postal mail. Cover letter with biographical information is required. "I feel autobiographical information is important in understanding the poetry." Poems are returned within 6 months. Editor comments on rejected poems "often." Upcoming themes available for SASE. Guidelines available by e-mail or on website. Pays 10 contributor's copies. Acquires first rights.

Advice "You should appeal to as broad an audience as possible. Nature makes people happy."

⍟ ◻ ◎ POETS AT WORK (Specialized: subscription)

P.O. Box 232, Lyndora PA 16045. Established 1985. **Editor/Publisher:** Jessee Poet.

Magazine Needs All contributors are expected to subscribe. "Every poet who writes within the dictates of good taste and within my 20-line limit will be published. I accept all forms and themes of poetry, including seasonal and holiday, but no porn, profanity, horror, bilingual/foreign language, translations, or feminism." Accepts poetry written by children if they are subscribers; "I have a lot of student subscribers." Has published poetry by Dr. Karen Springer, William Middleton, Ann Gasser, Warren Jones, and Ralph Hammond. *Poets at Work*, a bimonthly, is generally 36-40 pages, magazine-sized, saddle-stapled, photocopied from typescript, with colored paper cover. Subscription: $23. Sample: $4.

How to Submit If a subscriber, submit 5-10 poems at a time. Line length for poetry is 20 maximum. Accepts simultaneous submissions and previously published poems. Guidelines available for SASE. Responds within 2 weeks. Pays nothing, not even a copy. "Because I publish hundreds of poets, I cannot afford to pay or give free issues. Every subscriber, of course, gets an issue."

Contest/Award Offerings Subscribers have many opportunities to regain their subscription money in the numerous contests offered in each issue. Send SASE for flyer for separate monthly and special contests.

Advice "Read others' poetry and then write, revise, and submit."

⍟ $◻ THE POET'S CANVAS

P.O. Box 334, McKinney TX 75070. E-mail: editor@poetscanvas.org. Website: www.poetscanvas.org. Established 1999. **Managing Editor:** L.A. Schuler. Publisher: Bill Stevenson.

Magazine Needs *The Poet's Canvas* is a quarterly e-zine that "seeks to publish the creative work of talented, critically thinking minds and welcomes quality contemporary and formal poetry in a variety of themes. Submissions of original poetry and prose, artwork, as well as opinions and articles on the craft of writing are welcome year round." Wants contemporary and experimental verse and welcomes a variety of traditional forms (Elizabethan and contemporary sonnet, villanelle, heroic couplet, pastoral, and blank verse). "Well-crafted contemporary free verse or formal poetry by older teens is considered." Does not want "poems that represent only inward-turned writing or that never reach beyond the confines of personal space." Has published poetry by Larry Fontenot, Suzanne Frischkorn, Sharon Kourous, Walt McDonald, Michael Pollick, and Shoshauna Shy. *The Poet's Canvas* is published online, about 25-30 web pages/issue, includes "original artwork by various artists and of a variety of styles and themes used for the cover and for interior page enhancement." Receives about 3,500 poems/year, accepts about 3%. Publishes about 25 poems/issue.

How to Submit Submit 3-6 poems at a time. Priority is given to unpublished poetry. Accepts previously published poems only if they've appeared in a traditional print venue, and publishing credit must be included with submission; no simultaneous submissions. Accepts e-mail submissions (via e-mail address published within submission guidelines, pasted into body of message); no disk submissions. "As file attachments are not desired with initial submissions, submit poetry as plain text in an e-mail and use usual notations to indicate special formatting. Example: an underscore before and after an italicized word or phrase; a series of hyphens to indicate indentation, etc." Reads submissions year round. Time between acceptance and publication is 2-8 weeks. Poems are circulated to an editorial board. "Submissions are considered by all members of the editorial staff or, on occasion, a juried guest editor. Once a decision is reached, a letter of rejection or acceptance is sent by e-mail. Poets with meritorious work published in a given year are nominated for the annual Pushcart Prize." Seldom comments on rejected poems. Guidelines available on website. Responds in up to 2 months. Always sends prepublication galleys. "Compensation for accepted work is made in 3 ways: 1) A single poem by a beginning poet may receive the Editor's Choice Award consisting of publication in *Poet's Canvas*; 2) Payment for all other poetry accepted for publication is $10 per unpublished poem; 3) Four to 10 selections of a single poet's body of work may receive a Featured Poet run with compensation of $10 per unpublished poem. Featured Poet selection is by invitation only and is always awarded to a previous contributor." Acquires one-time rights.

Advice "Read at least 2 of the most recent issues and consider the submission guidelines carefully prior to submitting poetry. A poem is evaluated for its rich and fresh use of language, uncommon turn of phrase, content that moves a reader emotionally in some way, and attention to craft. In the case of formal poetry, form should be reasonably adhered to as to be recognizable; ability and experience with formal poetry is undoubtedly a must."

⊠ ◻ THE POET'S HAVEN; THE POET'S HAVEN DIGEST

Website: www.PoetsHaven.com. Established 1997. **Publisher:** Vertigo Xi'an Xavier.

Magazine Needs *The Poet's Haven* is a website featuring poetry, artwork, stories, reviews, essays, and much more. "Work should be emotional, personal, and intimate with the author or subject. Topics can cover just about anything. Material that is obscene, excessively vulgar, pornographic, racist, or religious will not be accepted." Has published poetry by Warren Gillespie, Terri A. Hateley, Elizabeth Hendricks, Alex Lupa, and Elisha Porat. Work published on the website is left on the site permanently. Receives about 4,000 poems/year, accepts about 75%.

How to Submit Accepts previously published poems and simultaneous submissions. Accepts online submissions ONLY. Time between acceptance and publication is 2 weeks to one year. Never comments on rejected poems. Guidelines available on website. No payment. Acquires rights to publish on the website and/or in the print magazine. Poet retains rights to have poems published elsewhere.

Also Offers Also publishes *The Poet's Haven Digest*, a print magazine with some line art and ads. See website for current production schedule. Pays one contributor's copy for publication in *The Poet's Haven Digest* only. Message forums, chat room, e-mail newsletter, an online store, website hosting for authors and artists, and a music compilation CD are also available.

⊘ POETS ON THE LINE

P.O. Box 20292, Brooklyn NY 11202-0007. E-mail: llerner@mindspring.com. Website: www.echonyc.com/~poets. Established 1995 (founded by Andrew Gettler and Linda Lerner). **Editor:** Linda Lerner. Currently not accepting unsolicited work.

⊠ ◻ POETS' PODIUM

2-3265 Front Rd., E. Hawksbury ON K6A 2R2 Canada. E-mail: kennyel@hotmail.com. Website: http://geocities.com/poetspodium/. Established 1993. **Associate Editors:** Ken Elliott, Catherine Heaney Barrowcliffe, Robert Piquette, and Ron Barrowcliffe.

Magazine Needs *Poets' Podium* is a quarterly newsletter published "to promote the reading and writing of the poetic form, especially among those being published for the first time." Poetry specifications are open. However, does not want poetry that is gothic, erotic/sexual, gory, bloody, or that depicts violence. Publishes 25 poems/issue. Subscription: $10 (US). Sample: $3 (US). "Priority is given to valued subscribers. Nevertheless, when there is room in an issue we will publish nonsubscribers."

How to Submit Submit 3 poems at a time. Line length for poetry is 4 minimum, 25 maximum. Accepts previously published poems and simultaneous submissions. Cover letter is required. Include SASE (or SAE and IRC), name, address, and telephone number; e-mail address if applicable. Time between acceptance and publication varies. Guidelines available for SASE (or SAE and IRC), by fax, or by e-mail. Pays 3 contributor's copies. All rights remain with the author.

Advice "Poetry is a wonderful literary form. Try your hand at it. Send us the fruit of your labours."

⭐ 🌐 ◯ POLYGON

West Newington House, 10 Newington Rd., Edinburgh EH9 1QS Scotland. Phone: +44 (0) 131 668 4371. Fax: +44 (0) 131 668 4466. E-mal: neville@birlinn.co.uk. Website: www.birlinn.co.uk. Established 1969. **Editor:** Neville Moir.

Book/Chapbook Needs & How to Submit Polygon publishes new poets, first-time collections, young voices, and Gaelic/English translations. Has published poetry by Kenneth White, Liz Lochhead, and Ian Hamilton Finlay. Accepts submissions by postal mail and on disk. Query or see website for details.

⭐ 🌐 🔘 ◎ POLYPHONIES (Specialized: French translations)

8, rue des Imbergères, 92330 Sceaux, France. Established 1985. **Editor:** Pascal Culerrier. **Editorial Committee:** Pascal Boulanger, Laurence Breysse, François Comba, Emmanuelle Dagnaud, Jean-Yves Masson, and Alexis Pelletier.

Magazine Needs *Polyphonies* appears twice/year. "Every case is a special one. We want to discover the new important voices of the world to open French literature to the major international productions. For example, we published Brodsky in French when he was not known in our country and had not yet won the Nobel Prize. No vocal poetry, no typographic effects." Has published poetry by Mario Luzi (Italy), Jeremy Reed (Great Britain), Octavio Paz (Mexico), and Claude Michel Cluny (France). *Polyphonies* is about 110 pages, 6½×9½, flat-spined, with glossy card cover, printed completely in French. Press run is 850 for 300 subscribers.

How to Submit Uses translations of previously published poems. Pays 2 contributor's copies.

Advice "Our review is still at the beginning. We are in touch with many French editors. Our purpose is to publish together, side-by-side, poets of today and of yesterday."

🔘 PORCUPINE LITERARY ARTS MAGAZINE

P.O. Box 259, Cedarburg WI 53012. E-mail: ppine259@aol.com. Website: http://members.aol.com/ppine259. Established 1996. **Managing Editor:** W.A. Reed.

Magazine Needs *Porcupine*, published biannually, contains featured artists, poetry, short fiction, and visual art work. "There are no restrictions as to theme or style. Poetry should be accessible and highly selective. If a submission is not timely for one issue, it will be considered for another." Has published poetry by Carol Hamilton, James Grabill, and George Wallace. *Porcupine* is 100-150 pages, digest-sized, offset, perfect-bound, with full-color glossy cover, includes b&w photos and art (occasionally use color inside, depending on artwork). Receives about 500 poems/year, accepts 10%. Press run is 1,500 for 500 subscribers of which 50 are libraries, 500 shelf sales; 100 distributed free. Single copy: $8.95; subscription: $15.95. Sample: $5.

How to Submit Submit up to 3 poems, one/page with name and address on each. Include SASE. "The outside of the envelope should state: 'Poetry.' " No previously published poems or simultaneous submissions. Accepts e-mail submissions (pasted into body of message). Time between acceptance and publication is 6 months. "Poems are selected by editors and then submitted to managing editor for final approval." Seldom comments on rejected poems. Guidelines available for SASE or on website. Responds in 3 months. Pays one contributor's copy. Acquires one-time rights.

◯ POTLUCK CHILDREN'S LITERARY MAGAZINE (Specialized: children/teens)

P.O. Box 546, Deerfield IL 60015-0546. (847)948-1139. Fax: (847)317-9492. E-mail: susan@potluck magazine.org. Website: http://potluckmagazine.org. Established 1997. **Editor:** Susan Napoli Picchietti.

Magazine Needs *Potluck* is a not-for-profit magazine published quarterly "to provide a forum which encourages young writers to share their voice and to learn their craft. Open to all styles, forms, and subjects—we just want well-crafted poems that speak to the reader. No poems so abstract they only have meaning to the writer. Violent, profane, or sexually explicit poems will not be accepted." *Potluck* is 48 pages, digest-sized, photocopied, saddle-stapled, with 60 lb. glossy paper cover with original artwork. Receives about 350 poems/quarter. Publishes 15-20 poems/issue. Press run is over 1,110 for 150 subscribers, 800 shelf sales. Single copy: $5.80 US ($7.80 Canada); subscription: $21.99 US ($31.99 Canada). Sample (including guidelines): $4.25.

How to Submit Submit up to 3 poems at a time. Line length for poetry is 30 maximum. No previously published poems or simultaneous submissions. Accepts submissions by fax, by e-mail (pasted into body of message), and by postal mail. Cover letter is optional. "Submissions without a SASE or an e-mail address will not be considered." Poems are circulated to an editorial board. "We each review every poem, make our remarks on them, then discuss our view of each—the best works make the issue." Always comments on rejected poems. Guidelines available in magazine, for SASE, by fax, by e-mail, or on website. Responds 6 weeks after deadline. Pays one contributor's copy. Acquires first rights. Reviews chapbooks of poetry.

Advice "Be present; write what you see, hear, taste, smell, observe, and what you feel/experience. Be honest, clear, and choose your words with great care. Enjoy."

◼ ◯ THE POTOMAC

2020 Pennsylvania Ave. NW, Suite 443, Washington DC 20006. E-mail: the_potomac@cox.net. Website: www.webdelsol.com/The_Potomac. Established 2004. **Editor:** Blake Walmsley. Member: Web del Sol.

Magazine Needs *The Potomac* is a quarterly online literary magazine featuring political commentary, cutting-edge poetry, flash fiction, and reviews. Open to all forms of poetry by new and established writers. Has published poetry by Jim Daniels, Elaine Equi, Maurice Oliver, Holly Iglesias, and Ilya Kaminsky. Receives a "variable" number of poems/year, accepts about 50-60. Publishes about 12-15 poems/issue. Free online.

How to Submit Submit any number of poems at a time. Line length for poetry is open. No previously published poems or simultaneous submissions. Accepts e-mail submissions (as attachment); no disk submissions. Cover letter is preferred. Reads submissions year round. Time between acceptance and publication is 3 months. Often comments on rejected poems. Guidelines available on website. Responds in 2 months. Sometimes sends prepublication galleys. No payment. Acquires one-time rights. Reviews books and chapbooks of poetry and other magazines/journals in up to 2,000 words, single and multi-book format. Send materials for review consideration.

Advice "We welcome the opportunity to read work from new writers."

◼ $◯ ◎ POTTERSFIELD PORTFOLIO; POTTERSFIELD PORTFOLIO SHORT POEM COMPETITION (Specialized: regional, Canada)

9879 Kempt Head Rd., Ross Ferry NS B1X 1N3 Canada. Website: www.magomania.com. Established 1979. **Editor:** Douglas A. Brown. **Contact:** Kathy Mac.

Magazine Needs Appearing in June and December, *Pottersfield Portfolio* is a "literary magazine publishing fiction, poetry, essays, and reviews by authors from Canada. No restrictions on subject matter or style. However, we will not use religious, inspirational, or children's poetry. No doggerel or song lyrics." Has published poetry by David Zieroth, Don Domanski, Jean McNeil, and Alden Nowlan. *Pottersfield* is 90 pages, magazine-sized, professionally printed, perfect-bound, with b&w cover, includes photos and ads. Receives about 3,000 poems/year, accepts 5%. Press run is 1,500 for 350 subscribers of which 25 are libraries, 750 shelf sales. Single copy: $9; subscription: $26. Sample: $9. "Subscribers from outside Canada please remit in U.S. dollars."

How to Submit Canadian poets should submit 6 poems at a time. No previously published poems. Include SAE and IRCs. Cover letter is strongly preferred. "Submissions should be on white paper of standard dimensions ($8^{1}/_{2} \times 11$). Only one poem per page." Time between acceptance and publication is 3 months. Guidelines available in magazine or on website. Responds in 5 months. Pays $10/printed page to a maximum of $50 plus one contributor's copy. Acquires first Canadian serial rights.

Contest/Award Offerings Sponsors the *Pottersfield Portfolio* Short Poem Competition. **Deadline:** May 1 each year. **Entry fee:** $20 for 3 poems, each of which must be no more than 20 lines in length. Fee includes subscription. Write for details or consult website.

Advice "Only submit your work in a form you would want to read yourself. Subscribe to some literary journals. Read lots of poetry."

$ THE PRAIRIE JOURNAL; PRAIRIE JOURNAL PRESS (Specialized: regional, prairie; themes)

P.O. Box 61203, Brentwood Post Office, 217-3630 Brentwood Rd. NW, Calgary AB T2L 2K6 Canada. E-mail: prairiejournal@yahoo.com. Website: www.geocities.com/prairiejournal. Established 1983. **Editor:** A. Burke.

Magazine Needs *The Prairie Journal* appears twice/year. Wants poetry of "any length, free verse, contemporary themes (feminist, nature, urban, non-political), aesthetic value, a poet's poetry." Does not want to see "most rhymed verse, sentimentality, egotistical ravings. No cowboys or sage brush." Has published poetry by Liliane Welch, Cornelia Hoogland, Sheila Hyland, Zoe Lendale, and Chad Norman. *Prairie Journal* is 40-60 pages, $7 \times 8^{1}/_{2}$, offset, saddle-stapled, with card cover, includes b&w drawings and ads. Receives about 1,000 poems/year, accepts 10%. Press run is 600 for 200 subscribers of which 50% are libraries, the rest are distributed on the newsstand. Subscription: $8 for individuals, $15 for libraries. Sample: $8 ("Use postal money order").

How to Submit No simultaneous submissions or previously published poems. Does not accept e-mail submissions. Guidelines available for postage (but "no U.S. stamps, please"—get IRCs from the Post Office) or on website. "We will not be reading submissions until such time as an issue is in preparation (twice yearly), so be patient and we will acknowledge, accept for publication, or return work at that time." Sometimes sends prepublication galleys. Pays $10-50 plus one contributor's copy. Acquires first North American serial rights. Reviews books of poetry, "but must be assigned by editor. Query first."

Book/Chapbook Needs & How to Submit For chapbook publication, Canadian poets only (preferably from the region) should query with 5 samples, bio, and publication credits. Responds to queries in 2 months, to mss in 6 months. Payment in modest honoraria. Has published *Voices From Earth*, selected poems by Ronald Kurt and Mark McCawley, and *In the Presence of Grace* by McCandless Callaghan. "We also publish anthologies on themes when material is available."

Also Offers Publishes "Poems of the Month" online. Submit up to 4 poems for $1 reading fee.

Advice "Read recent poets! Experiment with line length, images, metaphors. Innovate."

▦ ◯ ◎ PRAKALPANA LITERATURE; KOBISENA (Specialized: bilingual; form)

P-40 Nandana Park, Kolkata 700034, West Bengal, India. Phone: (91)(033)2403-0347. E-mail: prakal pana@rediffmail.com. Website: http://prakalpana.tripod.com. *Kobisena* established 1972; *Prakalpana Literature* press 1974, magazine 1977. **Editor:** Vattacharja Chandan.

Magazine Needs "We are a small press which publishes only Prakalpana (a mixed form of prose, poetry, graphics, and art), experimental Sarbangin (whole) poetry, experimental, b&w art and photographs, essays on the Prakalpana movement and the Sarbangin poetry movement, letters, literary news, and very few books on Prakalpana and Sarbangin literature. Purpose and form: for advancement of poetry in the super-space age, the poetry must be really experimental, using mathematical signs and symbols and visualizing the pictures inherent in the alphabet (within typography) with sonorous effect accessible to people. That is Sarbangin poetry. Length: within 30 lines (up to 4 poems). Prakalpana is a mixed form of prose, poetry, essay, novel, story, play with visual effect, and it is not at all short story as it is often misunderstood. Better send 6 IRCs to read *Prakalpana Literature* first and then submit. Length: within 16 pages (up to 2 prakalpanas) at a time. Subject matter: society, nature, cosmos, humanity, love, peace, etc. Style: own. We do not want to see traditional, conventional, academic, religious, mainstream, and poetry of prevailing norms and forms." Has published Sarbangin poetry by Dilip Gupta, Margarita Engle, Satya Ranjan Biswas, Jim DeWitt, Utpal, and Nikhil Bhowmick. Has published Prakalpana by Derek White, Vattacharja Chandan, and Boudhayan Nukhopadhyay. *Prakalpana Literature*, an annual, is 128 pages, 7×4½, saddle-stapled, printed on thin stock, with matte card cover. *Kobisena*, which also appears once/year, is 16 pages, digest-sized, newsletter format, has no cover. Both magazines use both English and Bengali. Receive about 400 poems/year, accept about 10%. Press run is 1,000 for each, and each has about 500 subscribers of which 50 are libraries. Samples: 40 rupees for *Prakalpana*, 4 rupees for *Kobisena*; overseas: 6 IRCs and 3 IRCs, respectively, or exchange of avant-garde magazines.

How to Submit Submit 4 poems at a time. Accepts submissions by e-mail (as attachment or pasted into body of message), on disk, and by postal mail. Cover letter with short bio and small photo/sketch of poet/writer/artist is required; camera-ready copy (4×6½) preferred. Time between acceptance and publication is within one year. After being published in the magazines, poets may be included in future anthologies with translations into Bengali/English if and when necessary. "Joining with us is welcome but not a pre-condition." Editor comments on rejected poems "if wanted." Guidelines available for SAE with IRC. Pays one contributor's copy. Reviews books of poetry, fiction, and art, "but preferably experimental books." Poets, writers, and artists may send materials for review consideration.

Advice "We believe that only through poetry, fiction, and art, the deepest feelings of humanity as well as nature and the cosmos can be best expressed and conveyed to the peoples of the ages to come. And only poetry can fill up the gap in the peaceless hearts of dispirited peoples, resulting from the retreat of god and religion with the advancement of hi-tech. So, in an attempt, since the inception of the Prakalpana Movement in 1969, to reach that goal in the experimental way, we stand for Sarbangin poetry. And to poets and all concerned with poetry, we wave the white handkerchief saying (in the words of Vattacharja Chandan), 'We want them who want us.' "

◯ PREMIERE GENERATION INK

P.O. Box 2056, Madison WI 53701-2056. E-mail: poetry@premieregeneration.com. Website: www.premieregeneration.com. Established 1998. **Contact:** Poetry Editor.

Magazine Needs *Premiere Generation Ink* appears twice/year and publishes "high-quality, honest poetry in a print journal as well as multimedia online. We also want art, photos, and live audio or video poetry for the website. Mail experimental video poetry as VHS cassette. We want poetry less concerned with being poetry than with being honest and true. Any length, format, style, or subject matter, but, please, no pretentious or contrived poetry." Has published poetry by Ruth Stone, Liz

Rosenberg, Martín Espada, Alix Olson, and Virgil Suárez. *Premiere Generation Ink* is 30-40 pages, digest-sized, b&w or color, saddle-stapled, with cardstock cover in color or b&w, includes art/graphics. Single copy: $5; subscription: $18. Sample: $5.

How to Submit Submit up to 5 poems at a time. Rarely accepts previously published poems; simultaneous submissions OK but not encouraged. No e-mail submissions. Cover letter is preferred ("casual and personal; need not be formal"). Purchase sample or visit website prior to submitting. Time between acceptance and publication is up to 8 months. "Editorial board reviews all submissions: collective decision." Often comments on rejected poems "if author has read the journal or visited the website." Tries to comment on first submissions. Requests that author buy a sample before resubmitting. Guidelines available for SASE, by e-mail, or on website. Responds within 6 months. Pays 2-5 contributor's copies. Acquires first or reprint rights.

Also Offers *Premiere Generation Ink* publishes books "in cooperation with authors in order to promote their art to a larger audience via the Web and the journal. Any net profit after covering production costs will be split equally between the author and *PGI*. Our main goal is to distribute quality art to a larger audience. We expect to work closely with the author on the format and layout of the book." Order sample books by mail or online. **Prior to submitting for chapbook publication, purchase a sample copy (required). Donations accepted.** "*Premiere Generation Ink* actively seeks help with distribution of books, journals, and promotional material as well as help with website, multimedia, and print production."

🔲 $🖂 THE PRESBYTERIAN RECORD (Specialized: inspirational, Christian)

50 Wynford Dr., North York ON M3C 1J7 Canada. (416)441-1111. Fax: (416)441-2825. E-mail: tdickey@presbyterian.ca. Established 1876. **Poetry Editor:** Tom Dickey.

Magazine Needs *The Presbyterian Record* is "the national magazine that serves the membership of The Presbyterian Church in Canada (and many who are not Canadian Presbyterians). We seek to stimulate, inform, inspire; to provide an 'apologetic' and a critique of our church and the world (not necessarily in that order!)." Wants poetry that is "inspirational, Christian, thoughtful, even satiric but not maudlin. No 'sympathy card' type verse à la Edgar Guest or Francis Gay. It would take a very exceptional poem of epic length for us to use it. Shorter poems, 10-30 lines, preferred. Blank verse OK (if it's not just rearranged prose). 'Found' poems. Subject matter should have some Christian import (however subtle)." Has published poetry by Margaret Avison, Wendy Turner Swanson, Fredrick Zydek, John Grey, T.M. Dickey, and Carol Hamilton. *The Presbyterian Record* appears 11 times/year. Press run is 47,000. Subscription: $18.

How to Submit Submit 3-6 poems at a time; seasonal work 6 weeks before month of publication. Accepts simultaneous submissions; rarely accepts previously published poems. Poems should be typed, double-spaced. Accepts fax and e-mail submissions, "but will not necessarily reply to unsolicited faxes or e-mails." Pays $30-50/poem. Acquires one-time rights.

🔲 🔲 🖂 PRESENCE (Specialized: form, Oriental)

12 Grovehall Ave., Leeds LS11 7EX United Kingdom. E-mail: martin.lucas@talk21.com. Website: http://freespace.virgin.net/haiku.presence. Established 1995. **Contact:** Dr. Martin Lucas.

Magazine Needs *Presence*, published 3 times/year, features haiku, senryu, renga, tanka, etc. Wants "haiku or haiku-related/haiku-influenced work. Maximum length: 16 lines (including title and spaces)." Does not want "anything longer than 16 lines (except renga)." Has published poetry by Owen Bullock, Gary Hotham, Cicely Hill, and Carrie Etter. *Presence* is 52-60 pages, A5, photocopied, perfect-bound, with brushdrawn art on card cover, includes illustrations. Receives about 2,000 poems/year, accepts about 10%. Press run is 200 for 150 subscribers of which 5 are libraries, 10 shelf sales. Single copy: £3.50 ($7 US) by air mail; subscription: £10 ($20 US) for 3 issues by air mail. Sample: £3.50 ($7 US). Please pay in US bills (no checks).

How to Submit Submit 4-12 poems at a time. "Please ensure that separate poems can be identified, and not mistaken for a sequence.'' No previously published poems or simultaneous submissions. Accepts e-mail submissions (pasted into body of message). Cover letter is preferred. Time between acceptance and publication is 4 months. Comments on rejected poems if requested. Guidelines available for SASE (or SAE with IRC) or on website. Responds within one month. Pays one contributor's copy. Copyright remains with author. Staff reviews books or chapbooks of poetry or other magazines in 100-1,500 words, single book format. Send materials for review consideration.

Advice ''The more you read the better you'll write.''

PRESS HERE (Specialized: form, haiku and tanka)

22230 NE 28th Place, Sammamish WA 98074-6408. E-mail: WelchM@aol.com. Established 1989. **Editor/Publisher:** Michael Dylan Welch.

- Press Here publications have won the first-place Merit Book Award and other awards from the Haiku Society of America.

Book/Chapbook Needs Press Here publishes award-winning books of haiku, tanka, and related poetry by the leading poets of these genres, as well as essays, criticism, and interviews about these genres. ''We publish work only by those poets who are already frequently published in the leading haiku and tanka journals.'' Does not want any poetry other than haiku, tanka, and related genres. Has published poetry by Lee Gurga, paul m., Paul O. Williams, Pat Shelley, Cor van den Heuvel, and William J. Higginson. Publishes 2-3 poetry books/year, plus occasional books of essays or interviews. Manuscripts are selected through open submission. Books are 32-112 pages, offset-printed, perfect-bound and saddle-stapled, with glossy paperback covers, include photographs.

How to Submit Query first, with a few sample poems and a cover letter with brief bio and publication credits. Book mss may include previously published poems (''previous publication strongly preferred''). ''All proposals must be by well-established haiku or tanka poets, and must be for haiku or tanka poetry, or criticism/discussion of these genres. If the editor does not already know your work well from leading haiku and tanka publications, then he is not likely to be interested in your manuscript.'' Responds to queries in up to one month; to mss in up to 2 months. Pays a negotiated percentage of author's copies (out of a press run of 200-1,000). Catalog available for #10 SASE.

Advice ''Press Here publishes only 2-3 titles per year by leading haiku and tanka poets. For Press Here to publish your book, you will likely already know other Press Here books and the work of their authors, and the editor would most likely already know you and your work. If not, then establish yourself in these genres first by publishing extensively in the leading haiku or tanka journals.''

THE PRESS OF THE THIRD MIND (Specialized: erotica; occult; Dadaism; surrealism)

1301 North Dearborn #1007, Chicago IL 60610. (312)337-3122. E-mail: bradleylastname@eudoram ail.com. Established 1985. **Poetry Editor:** Bradley Bongblaster.

Book/Chapbook Needs The Press of the Third Mind is a small press publisher of artist books, poetry, and fiction. ''We are especially interested in found poems, Dada, surrealism, written table-scraps left on the floors of lunatic asylums by incurable psychotics, etc.'' Has published *Blest This Poet Crest on My Chest* by Robert Pomehrn and *The Intrusive Ache of Morning* by Patrick Porter. Press run is 1,000, with books often going into a second or third printing.

How to Submit Submit up to 20 sample poems. ''No anthologized manuscripts where every poem has already appeared somewhere else.'' Accepts simultaneous submissions if noted. No e-mail submissions. ''Cover letter is good, but we don't need to know everything you've published since age 9 in single-spaced detail.'' Authors are paid ''as the publication transcends the break-even benchmark.'' The press has released an 80-page anthology entitled *Empty Calories*, and published a deconstructivist novel about the repetition compulsion: *The Squeaky Fromme Gets the Grease.* Order sample books by sending $1.43 postage.

Advice "We are the press, of the third mind, an eye for an eye, till the hole whirled is blind."

★ ◙ ◎ PRIMAVERA (Specialized: women)

P.O. Box #37-7547, Chicago IL 60637. Established 1975. **Contact:** Board of Editors.

Although the magazine addresses women's experiences, "we rarely feature women's images on the cover." However, the photography by Allison Veltman "struck us as arresting—for any magazine." Cover design by Lisa Grayson.

Magazine Needs *Primavera* is "an irregularly published but approximately annual magazine of poetry and fiction reflecting the experiences of women. We look for strong, original voice and imagery; generally prefer free verse, fairly short length; related, even tangentially, to women's experience." Has published poetry by Diane Seuss, Yvonne Zipter, Paula Sergi, Gail Martin, and Jack Bartley. *Primavera* is elegantly printed, flat-spined, generously illustrated with photos and graphics. Receives over 1,000 submissions of poetry/year, accepts about 25. Publishes 25-30 pages of poetry/issue. Press run is 1,000. Single copy: $10. Sample: $5.

How to Submit Submit up to 6 poems at any time; no queries. No simultaneous submissions. Editors comment on rejected poems "when requested or inspired." Guidelines available for SASE. Responds in up to 6 months. Pays 2 contributor's copies. Acquires first-time rights.

$◙ PROVINCETOWN ARTS; PROVINCETOWN ARTS PRESS

650 Commercial St., Provincetown MA 02657-1725. (508)487-3167. E-mail: cbusa@mediaone.net. Established 1985. **Editor:** Christopher Busa.

Magazine Needs An elegant annual using quality poetry, "*Provincetown Arts* focuses broadly on the artists and writers who inhabit or visit the tip of Cape Cod, and seeks to stimulate creative activity and enhance public awareness of the cultural life of the nation's oldest continuous art colony. Drawing upon a century-long tradition rich in visual art, literature, and theater, *Provincetown Arts* publishes material with a view towards demonstrating that the artists' colony, functioning outside the urban centers, is a utopian dream with an ongoing vitality." Has published poetry by Bruce Smith, Franz Wright, Sandra McPherson, and Cyrus Cassells. *Provincetown Arts* is about 170 pages, magazine-sized, perfect-bound, with full-color glossy cover. Press run is 10,000 for 500 subscribers of which 20 are libraries, 6,000 shelf sales. Sample: $10.

How to Submit Submit up to 3 typed poems at a time. All queries and submissions should be via postal mail. Reads submissions October through February. Guidelines available for SASE. Responds in 3 months. Usually sends prepublication galleys. Pays $25-100/poem plus 2 contributor's copies. Acquires first rights. Reviews books of poetry in 500-3,000 words, single or multi-book format. Send materials for review consideration.

Book/Chapbook Needs & How to Submit The Provincetown Arts Press has published 8 volumes of poetry. The Provincetown Poets Series includes *At the Gate* by Martha Rhodes, *Euphorbia* by

Anne-Marie Levine, a finalist in the 1995 Paterson Poetry Prize, and *1990* by Michael Klein, co-winner of the 1993 Lambda Literary Award.

☐ THE PUCKERBRUSH PRESS; THE PUCKERBRUSH REVIEW

76 Main St., Orono ME 04473-1430. Press established 1971; *Review* established 1978. **Poetry Editor:** Constance Hunting.

Magazine Needs & How to Submit *The Puckerbrush Review* is a literary magazine published twice/year. Looks for freshness and simplicity, but does not want to see "confessional, religious, sentimental, dull, feminist, incompetent, derivative" poetry. Has published poetry by Wolly Swist and Muska Nagel. Submit 5 poems at a time. Guidelines available for SASE. Pays 2 contributor's copies.

Book/Chapbook Needs & How to Submit The Puckerbrush Press is a small press publisher of flat-spined paperbacks of literary quality. Has published *Revelation* by Robert Taylor, *At Fifteen* by May Sarton (early journal), and *Catching Beauty* by May Sarton. For book publication, query with 10 sample poems. Prefers no simultaneous submissions. Offers criticism for a fee: $100 is usual. Pays 10% royalties plus 10 author's copies.

Advice "Just write the best and freshest poetry you can."

☑ ◎ PUDDING HOUSE PUBLICATIONS; PUDDING MAGAZINE: THE INTERNATIONAL JOURNAL OF APPLIED POETRY; PUDDING HOUSE CHAPBOOK COMPETITIONS; PUDDING HOUSE INNOVATIVE WRITERS PROGRAMS (Specialized: political, social issues, popular culture reflected in poetry arts)

81 Shadymere Lane, Columbus OH 43213. (614)986-1881. E-mail: info@puddinghouse.com. Website: www.puddinghouse.com. Established 1979. **Editor:** Jennifer Bosveld.

Magazine Needs Pudding House Publications provides "a sociological looking glass through poems that speak to the pop culture, struggle in a consumer and guardian society, and more—through 'felt experience.' Speaks for the difficulties and the solutions. Additionally a forum for poems and articles by people who take poetry arts into the schools and the human services." Publishes *Pudding* every several months, also chapbooks, anthologies, broadsides. "Wants what hasn't been said before. Speak the unspeakable. Don't want preachments or sentimentality. Don't want obvious traditional forms without fresh approach. Long poems OK as long as they aren't windy. Interested in receiving poetry on popular culture, rich brief narratives, i.e. 'virtual journalism' (see website)." Has published poetry by Knute Skinner, David Chorlton, Mary Winters, and Robert Collins. Publishes up to 60 pages of poetry/issue—digest-sized, 70 pages, offset-composed on Microsoft Word PC. Press run is 1,500 for 1,100 subscribers. Subscription: $29.95/4 issues. Sample: $8.95.

How to Submit Submit 3-10 poems at a time with SASE. "Submissions without SASEs will be discarded." No postcards. No simultaneous submissions. Previously published submissions respected, "but include credits." Likes cover letters and "cultivates great relationships with writers." Sometimes publishes theme issues. Guidelines available on website only. Responds on same day (unless traveling). Pays one contributor's copy; $10 and 4 contributor's copies to featured poets. Returns rights "with *Pudding* permitted to reprint." Send materials for review consideration or listing as recommended. "See our website for vast calls for poems for magazine, chapbooks, and anthologies; for poetry and word games; and essays and workshop announcements."

Book/Chapbook Needs & How to Submit Has recently published *The Allegories* by Dan Sicoli, *Barb Quill Down* by Bill Griffin, *Sonnets to Hamlet* by David Rigsbee, *Mischief* by Charlene Fix, and over 120 others last year. Chapbooks considered outside of competitions, no query. **Reading fee:** $10. Send complete ms and cover letter with publication credits and bio. Editor sometimes comments, will critique on request for $4/page of poetry or $85/hour in person.

Contest/Award Offerings Pudding House is the publisher of the nationwide project POETS' GREATEST HITS—an invitational. They have nearly 500 chapbooks and books in print. Pudding House offers an annual chapbook competition. **Entry fee:** $10. **Deadline:** September 30. Guidelines and details available on website.

Also Offers "Our website is one of the greatest poetry websites in the country—calls, workshops, publication list/history, online essays, games, guest pages, calendars, poem of the month, poet of the week, much more." The website also links to the site for The Unitarian Universalist Poets Cooperative and American Poets Opposed to Executions, both national organizations.

Advice "Editors have pet peeves. I won't respond to postcards. I require SASEs. I don't like cover letters that state the obvious, poems with trite concepts, or meaning dictated by rhyme. Thoroughly review our website; it will give you a good idea about our publication history and editorial tastes."

◖◎ THE PUDDIN'HEAD PRESS (Specialized: regional/Chicago)

P.O. Box 477889, Chicago IL 60647. (708)656-4900. E-mail: phbooks@compuserve.com. Established 1985. **Editor-in-Chief:** David Gecic.

Book/Chapbook Needs The Puddin'head Press is interested in "well-rounded poets who can support their work with readings and appearances. Most of our poets are drawn from the performance poetry community." Wants "quality poetry by active poets. We occasionally publish chapbook-style anthologies and let poets on our mailing lists know what type of work we're interested in for a particular project." Does not want experimental, overly political poetry, or poetry with overt sexual content; no shock or novelty poems. Has published poetry by John Dickson, Nina Corwin, JJ Jameson, and Jeff Helgeson.

How to Submit Puddin'head Press publishes one book and one chapbook/year. Books/chapbooks are 30-100 pages, perfect-bound or side-stapled ("we use various formats"). Responds to queries in one month; to mss in 3 months. Poets must include SASE with submission. Pays various royalty rates "depending on the publication. We usually have a press run of 500 books." **About 25% of books are author-subsidy published.** Terms vary. Order sample books/chapbooks by sending $10 (price plus postage) to The Puddin'head Press (also available through Amazon).

Also Offers "We prefer to work closely with poets in the Chicago area. There are numerous readings and events that we sponsor. We do our own distribution, primarily in the Midwest, and also do distribution for other small presses. Please send a SASE for a list of our current publications and publication/distribution guidelines."

Advice "It is difficult to find a quality publisher. Poets must have patience and find a press that will work with them. The most important part of publication is the relationship between poet and publisher. Many good books will never be seen because the poet/publisher relationship is not healthy. If a poet is involved in the literary world, he will find a publisher, or a publisher will find him."

◖ PUERTO DEL SOL

Box MSC3, New Mexico State University, Las Cruces NM 88003-8001. (505)646-2345. Fax: (505)646-7725. E-mail: puerto@nmsu.edu. Website: www.nmsu.edu/~puerto/welcome.html. Established 1972 (in present format). **Poetry Editor:** Kathleene West. **Editor-in-Chief:** Kevin McIlvoy.

Magazine Needs "We publish a literary magazine twice per year. Interested in poems, fiction, essays, photos, and translations, usually from the Spanish. Also (generally solicited) reviews and interviews with writers. We want top-quality poetry, any style, from anywhere. Excellent poetry of any kind, any form." Has published poetry by Richard Blanco, Maria Ercilla, Pamela Gemin, John Repp, and Lee Ann Roripaugh. *Puerto del Sol* is 150 pages, digest-sized, professionally printed, flat-spined, with matte card cover with art. Receives about 900 poetry submissions/year, accepts about 50. Publishes 40-50 pages of poetry/issue. Press run is 1,250 for 300 subscribers of which 25-30 are libraries. Subscription: $10/2 issues. Sample: $8.

How to Submit Submit 3-6 poems at a time, one poem/page. Accepts simultaneous submissions. No e-mail submissions. Brief cover letter is welcome. "Do not send publication vitae." Reads mss

September 1 to February 1 only. Offers editorial comments on most mss. Tries to respond within 6 months. Sometimes sends prepublication galleys. Pays 2 contributor's copies.

Advice "Read the magazine before submitting work."

🌐 ⬙ PULSAR POETRY MAGAZINE; LIGDEN PUBLISHERS

34 Lineacre, Grange Park, Swindon, Wiltshire SN5 6DA United Kingdom. Phone: (01793)875941. E-mail: pulsar.ed@btopenworld.com. Website: www.pulsarpoetry.com. Established 1992. **Editor:** David Pike. **Editorial Assistant:** Jill Meredith.

Magazine Needs *Pulsar*, published quarterly, "encourages the writing of poetry from all walks of life. Contains poems, reviews, and editorial comments." Wants "hard-hitting, thought-provoking work; interesting and stimulating poetry." Does not want "racist material. Not keen on religious poetry." Has published poetry by Merryn Williams, Liz Atkin, Li Min Hua, Virgil Suárez, and Michael Newman. *Pulsar* is 36 pages, A5, professionally printed, saddle-stapled, with glossy full-color cover, includes photos and ads. Press run is 300 for 100 subscribers of which 40 are libraries; several distributed free to newspapers, etc. Subscription: $30 (£12 UK). Sample: $7. Make checks payable to Ligden Publishers.

How to Submit Submit 3 poems at a time, "preferably typed." No previously published poems or simultaneous submissions. "Send no more than 2 poems via e-mail; file attachments will not be read." Cover letter is preferred; include SAE with IRCs. "Poems can be published in next edition if it is what we are looking for. The editor and assistant read all poems." Time between acceptance and publication is about one month. Seldom comments on rejected poems. Guidelines available for SASE (or SAE and IRC) or on website. Responds within 3 weeks. Pays one contributor's copy. "Originators retain copyright of their poems." Acquires first rights. Staff reviews poetry books and poetry audio tapes (mainstream); word count varies. Send materials for review consideration.

Advice "Give explanatory notes if poems are open to interpretation. Be patient and enjoy what you are doing. Check grammar, spelling, etc. (should be obvious). Note: we are a non-profit-making society."

🌐 ⬙ PURPLE PATCH; THE FIRING SQUAD

25 Griffiths Rd., West Bromwich B7I 2EH England. E-mail: ppatch66@hotmail.com. Website: www.poetrywednesbury.co.uk. Established 1975. **Editor:** Geoff Stevens.

Magazine Needs *Purple Patch* is a quarterly poetry and short prose magazine with reviews, comments, and illustrations. "All good examples of poetry considered, but prefer 40 lines maximum. Do not want poor rhyming verse, non-contributory swear words or obscenities, hackneyed themes." Has published poetry by Raymond K. Avery, Bryn Fortey, Bob Mee, B.Z. Niditch, and Steve Sneyd. *Purple Patch* is 24 pages, digest-sized, photocopied, side-stapled, with cover on the same stock with b&w drawing. Receives about 2,500 poems/year, accepts about 8%. Publishes 40 poems/issue. Circulation "varies." Subscription: £5 UK/3 issues; $20 US (send dollars). Make checks (sterling only) payable to G. Stevens.

How to Submit "Send 2 or more poems with return postage paid." Accepts submissions by postal mail only. Cover letter with short self-introduction is preferred. Reads submissions year round. Time between acceptance and publication is 4 months. Comments on rejected poems. Occasionally publishes theme issues. List of upcoming themes available for SASE (or SAE and IRCs). Guidelines available in magazine or on website. Response time is one month to Great Britain; can be longer to US. Pays one contributor's copy "to European writers only; overseas contributors must purchase a copy to see their work in print." Acquires first British serial rights. Staff reviews poetry chapbooks, short stories, and tapes in 30-300 words. Send materials for review consideration.

Also Offers *The Firing Squad* is a broadsheet of short poetry of a protest or complaint nature, published at irregular intervals. "All inquiries, submissions of work, etc., must include SASE or SAE and IRCs, or $1 U.S./Canadian for return/reply."

Advice "Don't just send *one* poem. Send *at least* two, and I'll try to like them."

$☑ QED PRESS; CYPRESS HOUSE

155 Cypress St., Fort Bragg CA 95437. (707)964-9520. Fax: (707)964-7531. E-mail: qedpress@mcn.o rg. Website: www.cypresshouse.com. Established 1985. **Editor:** Joe Shaw.

Book/Chapbook Needs "QED Press seeks clear, clean, intelligent, and moving work." Publishes 1-2 paperbacks/year. Wants "concrete, personal, and spare writing. No florid rhymed verse." Has published poetry by Victoria Greenleaf, Luke Breit, Paula Tennant (Adams), and Cynthia Frank. Books are usually about 100 pages, digest-sized, offset-printed, perfect-bound, with full-color CS1 10 pt. covers.

How to Submit "We prefer to see all the poems (about 100 pages or 75-80 poems) to be bound in a book." Accepts previously published poems and simultaneous submissions. Cover letter is required. "Poets must have prior credits in recognized journals, and a minimum of 50% new material." Time between acceptance and publication is up to one year. Poems are circulated to an editorial board. "We publish only 1-2 poetry books each year—by consensus." Seldom comments on rejected poems. Responds to queries and mss in 3 months. Pays royalties of 7½-12% and 25 author's copies (out of a press run of 500-1,000). Order sample books by sending SASE for catalog.

Also Offers Through the imprint Cypress House, offers subsidy arrangements and "we provide typesetting, design, marketing, and promotion services for independent presses and self-publishers. We are not a vanity press." **Fifty percent of books are author-subsidy-published each year.**

⊞ $◻ QUANTUM LEAP; Q.Q. PRESS

York House, 15 Argyle Terrace, Rothesay, Isle of Bute PA20 0BD Scotland, United Kingdom. Established 1997. **Editor:** Alan Carter.

Magazine Needs *Quantum Leap* is a quarterly poetry magazine. Wants "all kinds of poetry—free verse, rhyming, whatever—as long as it's well written and preferably well punctuated, too. We rarely use haiku." Has published poetry by Pamela Constantine, Ray Stebbing, Leigh Eduardo, Sam Smith, Sky Higgins, Norman Bissett, and Gordon Scapens. *Quantum Leap* is 40 pages, digest-sized, desktop-published, saddle-stapled, with card cover, includes clip art and ads for other magazines. Receives about 2,000 poems/year, accepts about 15%. Press run is 200 for 180 subscribers. Single copy: $10; subscription: $34. Sample: $9. Make checks payable to Alan Carter. "All things being equal in terms of a poem's quality, I will sometimes favor that of a subscriber (or someone who has at least bought an issue) over a nonsubscriber, as it is they who keep us solvent."

How to Submit Submit 6 poems at a time. Line length for poetry is 36 ("normally"). Accepts previously published poems (indicate magazine and date of first publication) and simultaneous submissions. Cover letter is required. "Within the UK, send a SASE; outside it, send IRCs to the value of what has been submitted." Time between acceptance and publication is usually 3 months "but can be longer now, due to magazine's increasing popularity." Sometimes comments on rejected poems. Guidelines available for SASE (or SAE and IRC). Responds in 3 weeks. Pays £2 sterling. Acquires first or second British serial rights.

Book/Chapbook Needs Under the imprint "Collections," Q.Q. Press offers subsidy arrangements "to provide a cheap alternative to the 'vanity presses'—poetry only." Charges £140 sterling for 50 32-page books (A4), US $260 plus postage. Please write for details. Order sample books by sending $12 (postage included). Make checks payable to Alan Carter.

Contest/Award Offerings Sponsors open poetry competitions and competitions for subscribers only. Send SAE and IRC for details.

Advice "Submit well-thought-out, well-presented poetry, preferably well punctuated, too. If rhyming poetry, make it flow and don't strain to rhyme. I don't bite, and I appreciate a short cover letter, but not a long, long list of where you've been published before! Please do not add U.S. stamps to IRCs. They have no validity here. If you want to increase the value, just send extra IRCs.''

⚡ $✉ QUARTERLY WEST

255 S. Central Campus Dr., Dept. of English/LNCO3500, University of Utah, Salt Lake City UT 84112-9109. (801)581-3938. E-mail: dhawk@earthlink.net. Website: www.utah.edu/quarterlyw est/. Established 1976. **Editor:** David Hawkins. **Poetry Editors:** Nicole Walker and Mike White.

• Poetry published in *Quarterly West* has appeared in *The Best American Poetry* and in numerous *Pushcart Prize* anthologies.

Magazine Needs *Quarterly West* is a semiannual literary magazine that seeks ''original and accomplished literary verse—free or formal. No greeting card or sentimental poetry.'' Also publishes translations. Has published poetry by Robert Pinsky, Eavan Boland, Albert Goldbarth, William Matthews, Agha Shahid Ali, and Heather McHugh. *Quarterly West* is 200 pages, digest-sized, offset-printed, with 4-color cover art. Receives 2,500 submissions/year, accepts less than 1%. Press run is 1,900 for 500 subscribers of which 300-400 are libraries. Subscription: $14/year, $25/2 years. Sample: $7.50.

How to Submit Submit 3-5 poems at a time; if translations, include originals. Accepts simultaneous submissions, with notification; no previously published poems. Reads submissions from September 1 to May 1. Seldom comments on rejected poems. Guidelines available for SASE or on website. Responds in up to 6 months. Pays $15-100 plus 2 contributor's copies. Acquires first North American serial rights. Returns rights with acknowledgment and right to reprint. Reviews books of poetry in 1,000-3,000 words.

⚡ ✉ ◎ QUEEN OF ALL HEARTS (Specialized: inspirational, Christian)

26 S. Saxon Ave., Bay Shore NY 11706. (631)665-0726. Fax: (631)665-4349. E-mail: pretre@worldne t.att.net. Established 1950. **Poetry Editor:** Joseph Tusiani.

Magazine Needs *Queen of All Hearts* is a bimonthly that uses poetry ''dealing with Mary, the Mother of Jesus—inspirational poetry. Not too long.'' Has published poetry by Fernando Sembiante and Alberta Schumacher. *Queen of All Hearts* is 48 pages, magazine-sized, professionally printed on heavy stock with various colors of ink and paper, includes graphics and photos. Receives 40-50 submissions/year, accepts 1-2/issue. Has approximately 2,000 subscriptions. Single copy: $3.50; subscription: $22/year. Sample: $4.

How to Submit Submit double-spaced mss. Accepts fax submissions; no e-mail submissions. Editor sometimes comments on rejected poems. Responds within one month. Pays 6 contributor's copies (sometimes more) and complimentary subscription.

Advice ''Try and try again! Inspiration is not automatic!''

$□ ◎ ELLERY QUEEN'S MYSTERY MAGAZINE (Specialized: mystery/suspense)

475 Park Ave. S., 11th Floor, New York NY 10016. E-mail: elleryqueen@dellmagazines.com. Website: www.themysteryplace.com. Established 1941. **Contact:** Janet Hutchings.

Magazine Needs *Ellery Queen's Mystery Magazine*, appearing 10 times/year, uses primarily short stories of mystery, crime, or suspense. *Ellery Queen's Mystery Magazine* is 144 pages (double-issue, published twice/year, is 240 pages), digest-sized, professionally printed on newsprint, flat-spined, with glossy paper cover. Subscription: $43.90. Sample: $3.99 (available on newsstands).

How to Submit Accepts simultaneous submissions; no previously published poems. Accepts submissions by postal mail only. Include SASE with submissions. Guidelines available for SASE or on website. Responds in 3 months. Pays $15-65 plus 3 contributor's copies.

◼ ◪ QUERCUS REVIEW; QUERCUS REVIEW PRESS ANNUAL POETRY BOOK AWARD

435 College Ave., Modesto CA 95350. (209)575-6183. E-mail: poetree@juno.com. Website: www.q uercusreview.com. Established 1999. **Editor:** Sam Pierstorff.

Magazine Needs *Quercus Review* is an annual journal of literature and art, appearing in May and publishing "numerous nationally recognized and award-winning poets from across the nation." Wants high-quality poetry, short fiction, and b&w art. Seeks "writing that reflects a unique voice. No rhyme, religious, or cliché writing." Has published poetry by X.J. Kennedy, Gerald Locklin, Naomi Shihab Nye, Amiri Baraka, Charles Harper Webb, and Dorianne Laux. *Quercus Review* is 95 pages, digest-sized, professionally printed, perfect-bound, with full-color cover. Receives about 500 poems/year, accepts about 10-15%. Publishes about 50 poems/issue. Press run is 500 for 50 subscribers of which 10 are libraries, 350 shelf sales; 100 are distributed free to contributors and local bookstores. Single copy: $7; subscription: $10/2 years. Make checks payable to MJC (QR).

How to Submit Submit 3-5 poems at a time. No previously published poems or simultaneous submissions. No e-mail or disk submissions. Cover letter is required. Include SASE and brief bio. Reads submissions year round, but always responds in March/April. Time between acceptance and publication is usually 3-6 months. "Poems are selected by 5-person staff of editors, which rotates annually." Guidelines available on website. Sometimes sends prepublication galleys. Pays one contributor's copy, plus ½ price discount on additional copies. Acquires first rights.

Contest/Award Offerings Quercus Review Press sponsors an annual poetry book award. Publishes one poetry book/year, selected through competition only (46-80 pages in ms format). **Entry fee:** $20. **Deadline:** submissions accepted May 1 through August 1. Books are 50-80 pages, professionally printed, perfect-bound, with full-color covers. Book mss may include previously published poems. Submission guidelines available on website.

Advice "Avoid overusing the world 'soul,' but feel free to drown us in fresh imagery and bold language. We like poems with a pulse. Make us laugh or cry, but don't bore or try too hard to impress us."

◪ ◎ RADIX MAGAZINE (Specialized: poetry that expresses a Christian world-view)

P.O. Box 4307, Berkeley CA 94704. E-mail: radixmag@aol.com. Website: www.radixmagazine.c om. Established 1969. **Editor:** Sharon Gallagher. **Poetry Editor:** Luci Shaw.

Magazine Needs *Radix* wants poems "that reflect a Christian world-view, but aren't preachy." Has published poetry by John Leax, Walter McDonald, Evangeline Paterson, and Luci Shaw. *Radix* is 32 pages, magazine-sized, offset-printed, saddle-stapled, with 60 lb. self cover. Receives about 50 poems/year, accepts about 20%. Publishes about 2-3 poems/issue. Press run varies. Sample: $5. Make checks payable to *Radix Magazine*.

How to Submit Submit 1-4 poems at a time. No previously published poems or simultaneous submissions. Accepts e-mail submissions only. Submit seasonal poems 6 months in advance. Time between acceptance and publication is 3 months to 3 years. "We have a serious backlog. The poetry editor accepts or rejects poems and sends the accepted poems to the editor. The editor then publishes poems in appropriate issues. If more than one poem is accepted from any poet, there will probably be a long wait before another is published, because of our backlog of accepted poems." Seldom comments on rejected poems. "Familiarity with the magazine is helpful, but not required." Occasionally publishes theme issues. Responds in 2 months. Pays 2 contributor's copies. Acquires first rights. Returns rights upon request. Reviews books of poetry.

Advice "*Radix* has a distinctive voice and often receives submissions that are completely inappropriate. Familiarity with the magazine is recommended before sending any submissions."

◫ ◪ RAINBOW CURVE

P.O. Box 93206, Las Vegas NV 89193-3206. E-mail: rainbowcurve@sbcglobal.net. Website: www.ra inbowcurve.com. Established 2001. **Poetry Editor**: Julianne Bonnet.

Publishers of Poetry

Magazine Needs *Rainbow Curve* is a biannual forum for short fiction and poetry. Wants "well-crafted poetry that works both on the surface *and* beneath it." Does not want rhyme, traditional forms, Hallmark greeting card sentiment. Has published poetry by Virgil Suárez and Terry Ehret. *Rainbow Curve* is 100 pages, digest-sized, offset-printed, perfect-bound, with 4-color glossy 10 pt. CIS cover. Receives about 3,500 poems/year, accepts about 2%. Publishes about 10 poems/issue. Press run is 250. Single copy: $8; subscription: $16. Sample: $6. Make checks payable to *Rainbow Curve*.

How to Submit Submit 3 poems at a time. Accepts simultaneous submissions; no previously published poems. Accepts e-mail submissions (as attachment, must be MS Word 6.0 or higher format only). Cover letter is preferred. "Include SASE with sufficient postage for reply and return of manuscript. If return of manuscript is not desired, we will respond via e-mail, if requested." Reads submissions year round. Time between acceptance and publication is 6 months. Seldom comments on rejected poems. Purchase of sample copy is suggested. Guidelines available in magazine, for SASE, or on website. Responds in 3 months. Always sends prepublication galleys. Pays one contributor's copy. Acquires first North American serial rights.

Advice "It is always a good idea to read a magazine before submitting to it—that way you have a good idea if your writing style fits with the editorial slant of the publication."

◙ THE RAINTOWN REVIEW

P.O. Box 40851, Indianapolis IN 46240. Website: http://members.iquest.net/~pkanouse. Established 1996. **Editor:** Patrick Kanouse.

Magazine Needs *The Raintown Review* is published twice/year and contains only poetry. Wants well-crafted poems—metered, syllabic, or free-verse. "While attention is paid to formal verse, *The Raintown Review* does publish all kinds of poetry. The one criterion: quality." Has published poetry by William Baer, Jared Carter, Annie Finch, and Len Roberts. *The Raintown Review* is about 60 pages, chapbook-sized, desktop-published, saddle-stapled, with card cover. Receives about 900 poems/year, accepts 10-15%. Press run is about 100 with most going to subscribers and contributors. Subscription: $24/year. Sample: $7.

How to Submit Submit up to 4 poems at a time. No length restrictions. Accepts previously published poems (with acknowledgement of previous publication) and simultaneous submissions. No e-mail submissions. Cover letter is preferred. "We prefer contributors write for guidelines before submitting work." Guidelines available for SASE or on website. Tries to respond in up to 3 months. Pays one contributor's copy and 2-issue subscription. Acquires one-time rights.

✪ ⊘ ◎ RARACH PRESS (Specialized: bilingual/foreign language; ethnic/nationality; nature/ecology; spirituality; philosophy)

1005 Oakland Dr., Kalamazoo MI 49008. (616)388-5631. Established 1981. **Owner:** Ladislav Hanka. Books are handmade with original art and range in price from $100 to $3,500. Not open to unsolicited mss.

Advice "Start your own press and self-publish."

$⊘ RATTAPALLAX; RATTAPALLAX PRESS

532 La Guardia Place, Suite 353, New York NY 10012. (212)560-7459. E-mail: info@rattapallax.com. Website: www.rattapallax.com. Established 1998. **Editor-in-Chief:** Martin Mitchell.

Magazine Needs "A biannual journal of contemporary literature, *Rattapallax* is Wallace Steven's word for the sound of thunder." Wants "extraordinary poetry—words that are well crafted and sing, words that recapture the music of the language, words that bump into each other in extraordinary ways and leave the reader touched and haunted by the experience. We do not want ordinary words about ordinary things." Has published poetry by Anthony Hecht, Sharon Olds, Lou Reed, Marilyn Hacker, Billy Collins, and Glyn Maxwell. *Rattapallax* is 128 pages, magazine-sized, offset-printed, perfect-bound, with 12 pt. CS1 cover, includes photos, drawings, and CD with poets. Receives about 5,000 poems/year, accepts 2%. Press run is 2,000 for 100 subscribers of which 50 are libraries, 1,200 shelf sales; 200 distributed free to contributors, reviews, and promos. Single copy: $7.95; subscription: $14/year. Sample (including guidelines): $7.95. Make checks payable to *Rattapallax*.

How to Submit Submit 3-5 poems at a time. Accepts simultaneous submissions; no previously published poems. Accepts e-mail submissions from outside the US and Canada; all other submissions must be sent via postal mail. "SASE is required, and e-mailed submissions should be sent as simple text." Cover letter is preferred. Reads submissions all year; issue deadlines are June 1 and December 1. Time between acceptance and publication is 6 months. Poems are circulated to an editorial board. "The editor-in-chief, senior editor, and associate editor review all the submissions and then decide on which to accept every week. Near publication time, all accepted work is narrowed, and unused work is kept for the next issue." Often comments on rejected poems. Guidelines available by e-mail or on website. Responds in 2 months. Always sends prepublication galleys. Pays 2 contributor's copies. Acquires first rights.

Book/Chapbook Needs & How to Submit Rattapallax Press publishes "contemporary poets and writers with unique, powerful voices." Publishes 5 paperbacks and 3 chapbooks/year. Books are usually 64 pages, digest-sized, offset-printed, perfect-bound, with 12 pt. CS1 covers, include drawings and photos. Query first with a few sample poems, cover letter with brief bio and publication credits, and SASE. Requires authors to first be published in *Rattapallax*. Responds to queries in one month; to mss in 2 months. Pays royalties of 10-25%. Order sample books by sending SASE and $7.

◪ RATTLE

12411 Ventura Blvd., Studio City CA 91604. (818)986-3274. E-mail: stellasueL@aol.com. Website: www.rattle.com. Established 1994. **Editor:** Alan Fox. **Poetry Editor:** Stellasue Lee. Address submissions to Stellasue Lee.

Magazine Needs *RATTLE* is a biannual poetry publication (appearing in June and December) that also includes interviews with poets, essays, and reviews. Wants "high-quality poetry of any form, 3 pages maximum. Nothing unintelligible." Accepts some poetry written by children ages 10 to 18. Has published poetry by Lucille Clifton, Charles Simic, Mark Doty, Sharon Olds, Billy Collins, and Stephen Dunn. *RATTLE* is 196 pages, digest-sized, neatly printed, perfect-bound, with 4-color coated card cover. Receives about 8,000 submissions/year, accepts 250. Press run is 4,000. Subscription: $28/2 years. Sample: $8. Make checks payable to *RATTLE*.

How to Submit Submit up to 5 poems at a time with name, address, and phone number on each page in upper right hand corner. Include SASE. No previously published poems or simultaneous submissions. Accepts e-mail (pasted into body of message) and fax submissions. Cover letter and e-mail address, if possible, is required as well as a bio. Guidelines available in magazine, by e-mail, or on website. Reads submissions all year. Seldom comments on rejected poems unless asked by the author. Responds in up to 2 months. Pays 2 contributor's copies. Rights revert to authors upon publication. Welcomes essays up to 2,000 words on the writing process, and book reviews on poetry up to 250 words. Send materials for review consideration.

▢ ◙ RAW DOG PRESS; POST POEMS (Specialized: poetry under 7 lines)

151 S. West St., Doylestown PA 18901-4134. Website: www.freeyellow.com/members/rawdog. Established 1977. **Poetry Editor:** R. Gerry Fabian.

Magazine Needs "Publishes Post Poems annual—a postcard series. We want short poetry (3-7 lines) on any subject. The positive poem or the poem of understated humor always has an inside track. No taboos, however. All styles considered. Anything with rhyme had better be immortal."

Has published poetry by Don Ryan, John Grey, and the editor, R. Gerry Fabian. Send SASE for catalog to buy samples.

How to Submit Submit 3-5 poems at a time. Prefers shorter poetry. Always comments on rejected poems. Guidelines available on website. Pays contributor's copies. Acquires all rights. Returns rights on mention of first publication. Sometimes reviews books of poetry.

Book/Chapbook Needs & How to Submit Raw Dog Press welcomes new poets and detests second-rate poems from 'name' poets. "We exist because we are dumb like a fox, but even a fox takes care of its own." Send SASE for catalog to buy samples.

Also Offers Offers criticism for a fee; "if someone is desperate to publish and is willing to pay, we will use our vast knowledge to help steer the manuscript in the right direction. We will advise against it, but as P.T. Barnum said. . . ."

Advice "I get poems that do not fit my needs. At least one quarter of all poets waste their postage because they do not read the requirements. Also, there are too many submissions without a SASE and they go directly into the trash!"

☑ RB'S POETS' VIEWPOINT

Box 940, Eunice NM 88231. Established 1989. **Editor:** Robert Bennett.

Magazine Needs *RB's Poets' Viewpoint*, published bimonthly, features poetry and cartoons. Wants "general and religious poetry, sonnets, and sijo with a 21-line limit." Does not want "vulgar language." Has published poetry by Robert D. Spector, Ruth Ditmer Ream, Ruth Halbrooks, and Delphine Ledoux. *RB's Poets' Viewpoint* is 34 pages, digest-sized, photocopied, saddle-stapled, includes drawings and cartoons. Receives about 400 poems/year, accepts about 90%. Press run is 60. Subscription: $8. Sample: $2. Make checks payable to Robert Bennett.

How to Submit Submit 3 poems, typed single-spaced. **Reading fee:** $1.50/poem. Accepts previously published poems and simultaneous submissions. Reads submissions February, April, June, August, October, and December only. Time between acceptance and publication is one month. "Poems are selected by one editor." Often comments on rejected poems. Guidelines available for SASE. Responds in one month. Pays one contributor's copy. Acquires one-time rights.

Contest/Award Offerings Sponsors contests for general poetry, religious poetry, sonnets, and sijo with 1st Prizes of $20, $6, and $5, respectively, plus publication in *RB's Poets' Viewpoint*. **Entry fee:** 50¢/poem (sijo), $1.50/poem (all others). Guidelines available for SASE.

◗ REARVIEW QUARTERLY

E-mail: rearviewquarterly@yahoo.com. Website: http://rearview.domynoes.net. Established 2002. **Editors:** Erica Mayyasi, Laura Arellano-Weddleton.

Magazine Needs *Rearview Quarterly* publishes poetry, short prose, and b&w artwork and photography. Wants all poetry, especially narrative poetry. Does not want erotica or overly religious poetry. Has published poetry by Helen Losse, Janet Buck, and Gwendolyn Joyce Mintz. *Rearview Quarterly* is 32 pages, digest-sized, photocopied, hand-bound, with cardstock cover with illustration, includes b&w art/graphics. Receives about 500 poems/year, accepts less than 10%. Publishes about 12 poems/issue. Press run is 50 for 10 subscribers, 25 shelf sales; 15 are distributed free to contributors. Single copy: $2.50; subscription: $10. Sample: $2. Make checks payable to *Rearview Quarterly*.

How to Submit Submit up to 7 poems at a time. Accepts previously published poems and simultaneous submissions. Accepts e-mail submissions **only**; no fax or disk submissions. Cover letter is preferred. Reads submissions year round. Submit seasonal poems 3 months in advance. Time between acceptance and publication is less than 3 months. Poems are circulated to an editorial board. "Poems are read individually by both editors. If we both like the poem, it is 'first-cut.' The first-cut poems are then looked at as a group, and the final decision is made based on how the poems read together." Seldom comments on rejected poems. Guidelines available for SASE, by e-mail, or on website. Responds in up to 6 weeks. Pays one contributor's copy. Acquires first North American serial rights.

Advice "Take chances and tell it like it is. We want to read about life—real life, not something sugar-coated."

▣ ◪ ◎ THE RED CANDLE PRESS; CANDELABRUM POETRY MAGAZINE (Specialized: form/style, metrical and rhymed)

Rose Cottage, Threeholes Bridge, Wisbech PE14 9JR England. E-mail: rcp@poetry7.fsnet.co.uk. Website: www.members.tripod.com/redcandlepress. Established 1970. **Editor:** M.L. McCarthy, M.A.

Magazine Needs Red Candle Press "is a formalist press, specially interested in metrical and rhymed poetry, though free verse is not excluded. We're more interested in poems than poets: that is, we're interested in what sort of poems an author produces, not in his or her personality." Publishes the magazine, *Candelabrum*, twice/year (April and October). Wants "good-quality metrical verse, with rhymed verse specially wanted. Elegantly cadenced free verse is acceptable. Accepts 5-7-5 haiku. No weak stuff (moons and Junes, loves and doves, etc.) No chopped-up prose pretending to be free verse. Any length up to about 40 lines for *Candelabrum*, any subject, including eroticism (but not porn)—satire, love poems, nature lyrics, philosophical—any subject, but nothing racist, ageist, or sexist." Has published poetry by Pam Russell, Ryan Underwood, David Britton, Alice Evans, Jack Harvey, Nick Spargo. *Candelabrum* is digest-sized, staple-spined, with small type, exemplifies their intent to "pack in as much as possible, wasting no space, and try to keep a neat appearance with the minimum expense." Uses about 40 pages (some 70 poems) in each issue. Receives about 2,000 submissions/year, of which 10% is accepted, usually holds over poems for the next year. Press run is 900 for 700 subscribers of which 22 are libraries. Sample: $6 in bills only; non-sterling checks not accepted.

How to Submit "Submit anytime. Enclose one IRC for reply only; 3 IRCs if you wish manuscript returned. If you'd prefer a reply by e-mail, without return of unwanted manuscript, please enclose one British first-class stamp, IRC, or U.S. dollar bill to pay for the call. Each poem on a separate sheet please, neat typescripts or neat legible manuscripts. Please, no dark, oily photostats, no colored ink (only black or blue). Author's name and address on each sheet, please." No simultaneous submissions. No e-mail submissions. Guidelines available on website. Responds in about 2 months. Pays one contributor's copy.

Advice "Traditional-type poetry is much more popular here in Britain, and we think also in the United States, now than it was in 1970, when we established *Candelabrum*. We always welcome new poets, especially traditionalists, and we like to hear from the U.S.A. as well as from here at home. General tip: Study the various outlets at the library, or buy a copy of *Candelabrum*, or borrow a copy from a subscriber, before you go to the expense of submitting your work. The Red Candle Press regrets that, because of bank charges, it is unable to accept dollar cheques. However, it is always happy to accept U.S. dollar bills."

◪ RED DRAGON PRESS

P.O. Box 19425, Alexandria VA 22320-0425. Website: www.reddragonpress.com. Established 1993. **Editor/Publisher:** Laura Qa.

Book/Chapbook Needs Red Dragon Press publishes 3-4 chapbooks/year. Wants "innovative, progressive, and experimental poetry and prose using literary symbolism, and aspiring to the creation of meaningful new ideas, forms, and methods. We are proponents of works that represent the nature of man as androgynous, as in the fusing of male and female symbolism, and we support works that deal with psychological and parapsychological topics." Has published *Spectator Turns Witness* by George Karos and *The Crown of Affinity* by Laura Qa. Chapbooks are usually 64 pages, digest-sized, offset-printed on trade paper, perfect-bound, with 1-10 illustrations.

How to Submit Submit up to 5 poems at a time with SASE. Accepts previously published poems and simultaneous submissions. Cover letter with brief bio is preferred. **Reading fee:** $5 for poetry and short fiction, $10 for novels; check or money order payable to Red Dragon Press. Time between acceptance and publication is 8 months. Poems are circulated to an editorial board. "Poems are selected for consideration by the publisher, then circulated to senior editor and/or poets previously published for comment. Poems are returned to the publisher for further action, i.e., rejection or acceptance for publication in an anthology or book by a single author. Frequently, submission of additional works is required before final offer is made, especially in the process for a book by a single author." Often comments on rejected poems. Charges criticism fee of $10/page on request. Responds to queries in 10 weeks, to mss in one year. Purchase sample books at book stores, or mail-order direct from Red Dragon Press at the above address.

$ ☑ ◎ RED MOON PRESS; THE RED MOON ANTHOLOGY; CONTEMPORARY HAIBUN (Specialized: haiku and related forms)
P.O. Box 2461, Winchester VA 22604-1661. (540)722-2156. Fax: (708)810-8992. E-mail: redmoon@shentel.net. Website: www.haikuworld.org/books/redmoon. Red Moon Press established 1994, *Contemporary Haibun* established 1999 as *American Haibun & Haiga*. **Editor/Publisher:** Jim Kacian.

Magazine Needs *Contemporary Haibun*, published annually in April, is the first Western journal dedicated to haibun and haiga. Has published poetry by William J. Higginson, Tom Clausen, A.C. Missias, Steve Sanfield, Bruce Ross, and Stephen Addiss. The magazine is 128 pages, digest-sized, offset-printed on quality paper, with heavy stock 4-color cover. Receives several hundred submissions/year, accepts about 5%. Print run is 1,000 for subscribers and commercial distribution. Subscription: $16.95 plus $3 p&h. Sample available for SASE or by e-mail.

How to Submit Submit up to 3 haibun or haiga at a time with SASE. Considers previously published poems. Accepts submissions by fax, on disk, by e-mail (pasted into body of message or as attachment), and by postal mail. Time between acceptance and publication varies according to time of submission. Poems will be read by editorial board. "Only haibun and haiga will be considered. If you are unfamiliar with the form, consult *Journey to the Interior*, edited by Bruce Ross, or previous issues of *Contemporary Haibun*, for samples and some discussion." Guidelines available in magazine, for SASE, or by e-mail. Pays $1/page. Acquires first North American serial rights.

Book/Chapbook Needs Red Moon Press "is the largest and most prestigious publisher of English-language haiku and related work in the world." Publishes *The Red Moon Anthology*, an annual volume of the finest English-language haiku and related work published anywhere in the world. *The Red Moon Anthology* is offset-printed, perfect-bound, with glossy 4-color heavy-stock cover. Inclusion is by nomination of the editorial board only. The press also publishes 6-8 volumes/year, usually 3-5 individual collections of English-language haiku, as well as 1-3 books of essays, translations, or criticism of haiku. Under other imprints, the press also publishes chapbooks of various sizes and formats.

How to Submit Query with book theme and information, and 30-40 poems, or draft of first chapter. Responds to queries in 2 weeks, to mss (if invited) in 3 months. "Each contract separately negotiated."

Advice "Haiku is a burgeoning and truly international form. It is nothing like what your fourth-grade teacher taught you years ago, and so it is best if you familiarize yourself with what is happening in the form (and its close relatives) today before submitting. We strive to give all the work we publish plenty of space in which to resonate, and to provide a forum where the best of today's practitioners can be published with dignity and prestige. All our books have either won awards or are awaiting notification. We intend to work hard to keep it that way."

✪ ◪ RED OWL MAGAZINE

35 Hampshire Rd., Portsmouth NH 03801-4815. (603)431-2691. E-mail: RedOwlMag@juno.com. Established 1995. **Editor:** Edward O. Knowlton.

Magazine Needs *Red Owl* is a biannual magazine of poetry and b&w art published in the spring and fall. "Ideally, poetry here might stress a harmony between nature and industry; add a pinch of humor for spice. Nothing introspective or downtrodden. Sometimes long poems are OK, yet poems which are 10 to 20 lines seem to fit best." Also open to poems on the subjects of animals, gay/lesbian issues, horror, psychic/occult, nature/ecology, science fiction/fantasy, and women/feminism. Has published poetry by Irene Carlson, Rod Farmer, Giovanni Malito, Robert Donald Spector, Gerald R. Wheeler, and Gerald Zipper. *Red Owl* is about 70 pages, magazine-sized, neatly photocopied in a variety of type styles, spiral-bound, with heavy stock cover, includes b&w art. "Out of a few hundred poems received, roughly one third are considered." Single copy: $10; subscription: $20. Sample (including brief guidelines): $10, includes shipping and handling. Make checks payable to Edward O. Knowlton.

How to Submit Submit 4 poems at a time. No previously published poems or simultaneous submissions. Accepts e-mail submissions. "Submit in the spring for the fall issue—and vice versa." Cover letter is preferred. "Relay cover letter and each poem separately. I mostly use the 'Net to answer questions; this isn't the best home for 'noetics' or 'noetry.' I'd prefer to receive the submissions I get via the U.S.P.S. since I feel it's more formal—and I'm not in that big of a hurry, nor do I feel that this world has reached a conclusion. . . ." Seldom comments on rejected poems. Guidelines available in magazine. Responds in up to 3 months. Pays one contributor's copy.

Advice "Try and be bright; hold your head up. Yes, there are hard times in the land of plenty, yet we might try to overshadow them. . . ."

◪ RED WHEELBARROW

De Anza College, 21250 Stevens Creek Blvd., Cupertino CA 95014. (408)864-8600. E-mail: SplitterRa ndolph@fhda.edu. Website: www.deanza.edu/redwheelbarrow. Established 1976 (as *Bottomfish Magazine*). **Editor:** Randolph Splitter.

● "Note: We are not affiliated with Red Wheelbarrow Press or any similarly named publication."

Magazine Needs *Red Wheelbarrow* is an annual college-produced magazine appearing in spring or summer. Wants "diverse voices." Has published poetry by Mark Brazaitis, Taylor Graham, John Wickersham, Virgil Suárez, Mario Susko, and Morton Marcus. *Red Wheelbarrow* is 140-220 pages, book-sized, well-printed on heavy stock with b&w graphics, perfect-bound. Press run is on demand. Single copy: $7.50.

How to Submit Submit 3-5 poems at a time. "Before submitting, writers are strongly urged to purchase a sample copy or visit our website." Accepts e-mail submissions. Best submission times: September through January. Annual deadline: January 31. Include SASE or (preferably) e-mail address for reply. Responds in up to 6 months, depending on backlog. Pays 2 contributor's copies.

✪ ◪ REDIVIDER (formerly *Beacon Street Review*)

Dept. of Writing, Literature, and Publishing, Emerson College, 120 Boylston St., Boston MA 02118. E-mail: redivider_editor@yahoo.com. Established (as *Beacon Street Review*) in 1990. **Poetry Editor:** Chris Tonelli. Member: CLMP.

Magazine Needs *Redivider* appears biannually, publishing high-quality poetry, fiction, and creative nonfiction, as well as interviews and book reviews. "All styles of poetry are welcome. Most of all, we look for language that seems fresh and alive on the page, that tries to do something new. Read a sample copy for a good idea. We do not publish greeting card verse or inspirational verse." Has published poetry by Kate Clanchy, William Virgil Davis, Dorianne Laux, David Lawrence, Valerie Nieman, and Jennifer Perrine. *Redivider* is 100 pages, digest-sized, offset-printed, perfect-bound, with 4-color artwork on cover stock. Receives about 1,000 poems/year, accepts about 30%. Publishes about 15 poems/issue. Press run is 2,000. Single copy: $6; subscription: $10. Make checks payable to *Redivider* at Emerson College.

How to Submit Submit 3-6 poems at a time. Accepts simultaneous submissions ("please notify us *immediately* if your work is taken elsewhere"); no previously published poems. No e-mail or disk submissions. Cover letter is required. Reads submissions year round. Time between acceptance and publication is 6 months. "Poems are read first by poetry editors, then by a board of readers. Final decisions are made by the board." Seldom comments on rejected poems. Guidelines available in magazine, for SASE, or by e-mail. Responds in 5 months. Pays 2 contributor's copies. Acquires first North American serial rights. Reviews books of poetry in 500-2,000 words, single-book format. Send materials for review consideration Attn: Review Copies.

Advice "Consider subscribing and supporting your fellow writers!"

THE REDNECK REVIEW, an online poetry journal (Specialized: regional/Southern literary tradition)
PMB 177, 931 Monroe Dr. NE, Suite 102, Atlanta GA 30308-1778. E-mail: editor@redneckreview.com. Website: www.redneckreview.com. Established 2000. **Editor:** Penya Sandor.

Magazine Needs *The Redneck Review* is a biannual online poetry journal "born out of the rich literary tradition of the South. We are looking for writing that is interesting, has energy, and doesn't feel like homework." Has published poetry by Denise Duhamel, Marie Howe, Walt McDonald, Hal Sirowitz, Ben Satterfield, and Jean Trounstine. *The Redneck Review* is published online. Publishes about 15-20 poems/issue.

How to Submit Submit no more than 5 poems at a time. Accepts previously published poems and simultaneous submissions. Accepts e-mail and disk submissions; no fax submissions. Cover letter is preferred. "If sending submissions by postal mail, include SASE unless you have an e-mail address. Poems won't be returned." Time between acceptance and publication "depends. *I* read the poems." Often comments on rejected poems. Guidelines available on website. Response time varies. Sometimes sends prepublication galleys. No payment. "Authors retain rights, but we ask that they mention our journal if they publish the poem again." Send materials for review consideration to *The Redneck Review*.

Advice "There are many respectable literary journals that publish well-written but dull writing. We would prefer to read literature that is electric, not just technically well crafted."

REFLECTIONS LITERARY JOURNAL
P.O. Box 1197, Roxboro NC 27573. (336)599-1181 ext. 231. E-mail: reflect@piedmont.cc.nc.us. Established 1999. **Editor:** Ernest Avery.

Magazine Needs *Reflections Literary Journal* appears annually in June, publishing poetry, short fiction, and creative nonfiction. Wants any styles and forms of poetry, including translations, of any length. Does not want material using obscenities or culturally insensitive material ("these tend to be rejected by our editorial panel"). Has published poetry by J.E. Bennett, Fred Chappell, Sara Claytor, Betsy Humphreys, Sheri Narin, and Lynn Veach Sadler. *Reflections Literary Journal* is 140-170 pages, digest-sized. Receives about 200 poems/year, accepts about 10%. Publishes about 20 poems/issue. Press run is 250 for 20 subscribers of which 4 are libraries, 150 shelf sales; 75 are distributed free to contributors, editors, advisors, local schools, and cultural sites. Single copy: $7; subscription: $7. Sample: $5 for back issue. Make checks payable to *Reflections Literary Journal*.

How to Submit Submit up to 5 poems at a time. Accepts previously published poems and simultaneous submissions (if notified). Accepts e-mail submissions (as MS Word attachments); no fax submissions. Cover letter is optional. "Include a 50-word brief bio with submission. Include one copy with name and address and one copy without. Single-space poetry submissions. Affix adequate postage to SAE for return of manuscript if desired, or use first-class stamps on SAE for notification." Reads submissions September 1 through December 31. Time between acceptance and publication is 10 weeks. Poems are ready by an editorial board. "Our 8- to 12-member editorial board ranks submissions through 'blind' readings. Every board member reads and ranks every submission; board members refrain from ranking their own submissions." Seldom comments on rejected poems. Guidelines available in magazine, for SASE, or by e-mail. Responds in up to 9 months (in March or April). Pays one contributor's copy. Acquires first North American serial rights (if poem is unpublished) or one-time rights (if poem is previously published).

✪ ☑ RENAISSANCE ONLINE MAGAZINE

P.O. Box 3246, Pawtucket RI 02861. E-mail: submit@renaissancemag.com. Website: www.renaissancemag.com. Established 1996. **Editor:** Kevin Ridolfi. E-mail submissions only.

Magazine Needs "Updated monthly, *Renaissance Online* strives to bring diversity and thought-provoking writing to an audience that usually settles for so much less. Poetry should reveal a strong emotion and be able to elicit a response from the reader. No nursery rhymes or profane works." Accepts poetry written by teenagers, "but they must meet the same standard as adults." Has published poetry by Kevin Larimer, Josh May, and Gary Meadows. Receives about 60 poems/year, accepts about 50%.

How to Submit Submit 3 poems at a time. No previously published poems or simultaneous submissions. Accepts e-mail submissions only (pasted into body of message). Cover letter is preferred. *Renaissance Online Magazine* is published online only and likes to see potential writers read previous works before submitting. Time between acceptance and publication is 3 months. Poems are circulated to an editorial board. "Poems are read by the editor; when difficult acceptance decisions need to be reached, the editorial staff is asked for comments." Often comments on rejected poems. Occasionally publishes theme issues. Guidelines available for SASE or on website. Responds in 2 months. Acquires all online publishing rights. Reviews books of poetry.

◎ REVISTA/REVIEW INTERAMERICANA (Specialized: ethnic; regional)

Inter-American University of Puerto Rico, Box 5100, San Germán PR 00683. Phone: (787)264-1912, ext. 7229 or 7230. Fax: (787)892-6350. E-mail: reinter@sg.inter.edu. Website: www.sg.inter.edu/revista-ciscla/revista/. **Editor:** Mario R. Cancel.

Magazine Needs Published online and in hard copy. *Revista/Review* is a bilingual scholarly journal oriented to Puerto Rican, Caribbean, and Hispanic American and inter-American subjects, poetry, short stories, and reviews.

How to Submit See website for details.

☑ RHINO

P.O. Box 591, Evanston IL 60204. Website: www.rhinopoetry.org. Established 1976. **Editors:** Deborah Rosen, Alice George, Kathleen Kirk, and Helen Degen Cohen.

• "*RHINO* has won 7 Illinois Arts Council Literary Awards over the last 3 years."

Magazine Needs *RHINO* "is an annual poetry journal, appearing in March, which also includes short-shorts and occasional essays on poetry. Translations welcome. The editors delight in work which reflects the author's passion, originality, and artistic conviction. We also welcome experiments with poetic form, sophisticated wit, and a love affair with language. Prefer poems under 100 lines." Has published poetry by Maureen Seaton, James McManus, Floyd Skoot, Lucia Getsi, and Richard Jones. *RHINO* is 150 pages, digest-sized, printed on high-quality paper, with card cover with art. Receives 1,500 submissions/year, accepts 60-80. Press run is 1,000. Single copy: $10. Sample: $8.

How to Submit Submit 3-5 poems with SASE. Accepts simultaneous submissions with notification; no previously published poems. Submissions are accepted April 1 through October 1. Guidelines available for SASE or on website. Responds in up to 6 months. Pays 2 contributor's copies. Acquires first rights only.

N ◪ RHAPSOIDIA

P.O. Box 76, Redlands CA 92373. E-mail: mkarman@esri.com. Website: http://rhapsoidia.com. Established 2002. **Poetry Editor:** Michael Karman.

Magazine Needs *Rhapsoidia*, published quarterly, caters to experimental writing. Wants "metapoetry, experimental, fresh, innovative. Generally, we want poetry that emphasizes language over narrative. That is, we're more interested in the shaping than the thing shaped. So poems about personal experience will be considered, but only if they're cunningly written." Has published poetry by Judy Kronenfeld, Christopher Mulrooney, and Paul Kloppenborg. *Rhapsoidia* is 40-56 pages, digest-sized, saddle-stapled, with glossy cover, includes illustrations and photos. Receives about 360 poems/year, accepts about 10%. Publishes about 6 poems/issue. Press run is 350. Single copy: $4.45 ($2.95 plus $1.50 s&h). Make checks payable to Mark Manalang.

How to Submit Submit 3-5 poems at a time. No previously published poems or simultaneous submissions. Accepts e-mail submissions (pasted into body of message); no disk submissions. Cover letter is preferred. "Because formatting is often essential to poetry and e-mail tends to de-format, you may send a snail mail submission to Poetry Editor Michael Karman at the address above, but please include your e-mail address so we can respond to you." Reads submissions year round. Time between acceptance and publication is 3 months. Seldom comments on rejected poems. Guidelines available in magazine or on website. Pays one contributor's copy. Responds in 3 months. Acquires first North American serial rights.

◪ RIO GRANDE REVIEW

P.M. Box 671, 500 W. University Ave., El Paso TX 79968-0622. E-mail: rgr@utep.edu. Website: www.utep.edu/rgr. **Contact:** Poetry Editor.

Magazine Needs *Rio Grande Review*, an annual student publication from the University of Texas at El Paso appearing in March, contains poetry; flash, short, and nonfiction; short drama; photography and line art. *Rio Grande Review* is 168 pages, digest-sized, professionally printed, perfect-bound, with card cover with line art. Subscription: $8/year, $15/2 years.

How to Submit Submit no more than 5 poems at a time. No simultaneous submissions. Accepts e-mail submissions (pasted into body of message). Include bio information with submission. "Submissions are recycled regardless of acceptance or rejection." SASE for reply only. Guidelines available for SASE, by e-mail, or on website. Pays 2 contributor's copies. "Permission to reprint material remains the decision of the author. However, *Rio Grande Review* does request it be given mention."

◪ RIVER CITY

English Dept., University of Memphis, Memphis TN 38152. (901)678-4591. Fax: (901)678-2226. E-mail: rivercity@memphis.edu. Website: www.people.memphis.edu/~rivercity. Established 1980. **Editor:** Dr. Mary Leader.

Magazine Needs *River City* appears biannually (winter and summer) and publishes fiction, poetry, interviews, and essays. Has published poetry by Marvin Bell, Maxine Kumin, Jane Hirshfield, Terrance Hayes, Paisley Rekaal, S. Beth Bishop, and Virgil Suárez. *River City* is 160 pages, 7×10, perfect-bound, professionally printed, with 4-color glossy cover. Publishes 40-50 pages of poetry/issue. Subscription: $12. Sample: $7. Press run is 2,000.

How to Submit Submit no more than 5 poems at a time with SASE. Accepts submissions by e-mail (as attachment). Include SASE. Does not read mss June through August. *River City* no longer publishes theme issues. Guidelines available for SASE or by e-mail. Responds in up to 3 months. Pays 2 contributor's copies.

$ ◪ RIVER CITY PUBLISHING

1719 Mulberry St., Montgomery AL 36106. E-mail: agordon@rivercitypublishing.com. Website: www.rivercitypublishing.com. Established 1989. **Editor:** Ashley Gordon. **Contact:** Staff Editor.

Book/Chapbook Needs "We publish serious or academic poetry; no religious, romantic, or novelty material. Collections from previously published poets only." Publishes 1-2 poetry hardbacks/year. Has recently published *Either/Ur* by Shawn Sturgeon, *The Soft Blare* by Nick Norwood, and *Ready to Eat the Sky* by Kevin Pilkington, all selected by Andrew Hudgins.

How to Submit "Experienced poets should submit high-quality collections of at least 40 poems, including information about previous publications in literary journals or chapbooks." Most mss selected by nationally known poet, others by staff. Responds in up to 9 months. "E-mail queries are accepted. Submissions should be hard copy only." Guidelines available for SASE, by fax, by e-mail, or on website. Pays industry-standard royalties and author's copies.

☑ RIVER KING POETRY SUPPLEMENT

P.O. Box 122, Freeburg IL 62243. (618)234-5082. Fax: (618)355-9298. E-mail: riverkng@icss.net. Established 1995. **Editors:** Wayne Lanter, Donna Biffar, Phil Miller, Emily Lambeth-Climaco.

Magazine Needs *River King Poetry Supplement*, published biannually in August and February, features "all poetry with commentary about poetry." Wants "serious poetry." Does not want inspirational or prose poetry; no prose cut into short lines. Has published poetry by Alan Catlin, R.G. Bishop, Phil Dacey, John Knoepfle, P.F. Allen, David Ray, and Lyn Lifshin. *River King* is 8-12 pages, tabloid-sized, press-printed, folded, includes line art. Receives about 6,000 poems/year, accepts about 2%. Press run is 5,000 of which 600 are for libraries.

How to Submit Submit 3-6 poems at a time. No simultaneous submissions or previously published poems. Accepts fax and e-mail submissions. Time between acceptance and publication is up to 6 months. Responds in up to 6 months. Pays 10 contributor's copies.

☑ RIVER OAK REVIEW

Elmhurst College, 190 Prospect Ave., Elmhurst IL 60126. (630)617-6483. Established 1993. **Poetry Editor:** Ann Frank Wake.

Magazine Needs *River Oak Review* is an annual literary magazine (will become biannual in 2006) publishing high-quality poetry, short fiction, and creative nonfiction. "We've historically encouraged writers with Midwestern connections, but are dedicated to finding the best established and new talent anywhere." Has published poetry by Billy Collins, Maureen Seaton, Constance Vogel, and Margaret Gibson. *River Oak Review* is at least 128 pages, digest-sized, neatly printed, perfect-bound, with glossy color cover with art. Receives over 1,500 poems/year, publishes about 1-2%. Press run is 1,000, distributed mostly through subscriptions. Single copy: $12; subscription: $12/year, $20/2 years. Sample: $5. Make checks payable to *River Oak Review*.

How to Submit Submit 4-6 poems at a time. Accepts simultaneous submissions if notified; no previously published poems. Poems circulated to 2 readers, then the poetry editor. Sometimes comments on rejections. Guidelines available for SASE. Responds in 3 months. Pays 2 contributor's copies.

Contest/Award Offerings Annual poetry contest offers $500 and publication in *River Oak Review*. Submit up to 4 poems at a time, typed, with name, address, phone number on cover letter only. Entries not returned. Send SASE for contest guidelines and notification of winner. **Entry fee:** $15. Make checks payable to *River Oak Review*. **Deadline:** September 1.

Advice "Put in the time. Read and study, pay careful attention to craft, and send only excellent work. We agree in principle with Stanley Kunitz, who told his poetry students to 'End on an image and don't explain it!' While we don't mean this literally, we do think that a 'less is more' philosophy usually results in better poems."

$☑ RIVER STYX MAGAZINE; BIG RIVER ASSOCIATION

634 N. Grand Ave., 12th Floor, St. Louis MO 63103. Website: www.riverstyx.org. Established 1975. **Editor:** Richard Newman. **Managing Editor:** Joanne Drew.

• Poetry published in *River Styx* has been selected for inclusion in past volumes of *The Best American Poetry*, *Beacon Best*, and *Pushcart Prize* anthologies.

Magazine Needs *River Styx*, published 3 times/year (April, August, December), is "an international, multicultural journal publishing both award-winning and previously undiscovered writers. We feature poetry, short fiction, essays, interviews, fine art, and photography." Wants "excellent poetry—original, energetic, musical, and accessible. Please don't send us chopped prose or opaque poetry that isn't about anything." Has published poetry by Louis Simpson, Molly Peacock, Marilyn Hacker, Yusef Komunyakaa, Andrew Hudgins, and Catie Rosemurgy. *River Styx* is 100 pages, digest-sized, professionally printed on coated stock, perfect-bound, with color cover, includes b&w art, photographs, and ads. Receives about 8,000 poems/year, accepts 60-75. Press run is 2,500 for 1,000 subscribers of which 80 are libraries. Sample: $7. Subscription: $20/year, $35/2 years.

How to Submit Submit 3-5 poems at a time, "legible copies with name and address on each page." Reads submissions May 1 through November 30 only. Time between acceptance and publication is within one year. Editor sometimes comments on rejected poems. Publishes one theme issue/year. Guidelines available for SASE or on website. Responds in up to 5 months. Pays 2 contributor's copies plus one-year subscription, and $15/page if funds available. Acquires one-time rights.

Contest/Award Offerings Sponsors annual poetry contest. Past judges include Miller Williams, Ellen Bryant Voigt, Marilyn Hacker, Philip Levine, Mark Doty, Naomi Shihab Nye, Billy Collins, and Molly Peacock. **Deadline:** May 31. Guidelines available for SASE.

RIVERSTONE, A PRESS FOR POETRY; RIVERSTONE POETRY CHAPBOOK AWARD

P.O. Box 1421, Carefree AZ 85377. Established 1992. **Editor:** Margaret Holley.

Book/Chapbook Needs Riverstone publishes one chapbook/year through an annual contest. Recent chapbooks includ *Reading the Night Sky* by Margo Stever, *A Record* by Anita Barrows, *Dragon Lady: Tsukimi* by Martha Modena Vertreace, *Everything Speaking Chinese* by G. Timothy Gordon, *Balancing on Light* by Margaret Hoen, and *Into Grace* by Lisa Rhoades. The 2003 winner, Julie Lechevsky's *I'm a Serious Something*, is 40 pages, digest-sized, attractively printed on 70 lb. paper, hand-sewn, with gray endleaves and a brick-red card stock cover.

Contest/Award Offerings To be considered for the contest, submit chapbook ms of 24-36 pages, "including poems in their proposed arrangement, title page, contents, and acknowledgments. All styles welcome." Accepts previously published poems, multiple entries, and simultaneous submissions. Include 6×9 SASE or larger for notification and copy of last year's chapbook. Guidelines available for SASE. **Entry fee:** $8. **Postmark deadline:** June 30. Winner receives publication, 50 author's copies, and a cash prize of $100. Sample: $5.

ROANOKE REVIEW

English Dept., Roanoke College, 221 College Lane, Salem VA 24153. Website: www.roanoke.edu/roanokereview/. Established 1967. **Poetry Editor:** Paul Hanstedt.

Magazine Needs *Roanoke Review* is an annual literary review appearing in June which uses poetry that is "grounded in strong images and unpretentious language." Has published poetry by David Citino, Jeff Daniel Marion, and Charles Wright. *Roanoke Review* is 200 pages, digest-sized, professionally printed, with matte card cover with full-color art. Receives 400-500 submissions of poetry/year, accepts 40-60. Publishes 25-30 pages of poetry/issue. Press run is 250-300 for 150 subscribers of which 50 are libraries. Subscription: $13/2 years. Sample: $2.

How to Submit Submit original typed mss, no photocopies. Guidelines available on website. Responds in 3 months. Pays 2 contributor's copies.

Advice "Be real. Know rhythm. Concentrate on strong images."

◫ $⧄ ◎ ROCKY MOUNTAIN RIDER MAGAZINE (Specialized: horses; cowboys; regional)

P.O. Box 1011, Hamilton MT 59840-1011. (406)363-4085. Fax: (406)363-1056. Website: www.rocky mountainrider.com. Established 1993. **Editor:** Natalie Riehl.

Magazine Needs *Rocky Mountain Rider Magazine* is a regional, monthly, all-breed horse magazine. Wants "cowboy poetry; western or horse-themed poetry. Please keep length to no more than 5 verses." *Rocky Mountain Rider Magazine* is 64+ pages, magazine-sized, web offset on newsprint, stapled. Publishes 1-2 poems/issue.

How to Submit Submit 1-10 poems at a time. Accepts previously published poems and simultaneous submissions. Cover letter is preferred. Seldom comments on rejected poems. Occasionally publishes theme issues. List of upcoming themes and guidelines available for SASE. Pays $10/poem. Acquires one-time rights. Reviews books of poetry. Send materials for review consideration.

◫ ◲ $◐ ◎ RONSDALE PRESS (Specialized: regional/Canada)

3350 W. 21st Ave., Vancouver BC V6S 1G7 Canada. (604)738-4688. Fax: (604)731-4598. E-mail: ronhatch@pinc.com. Website: www.ronsdalepress.com. Established 1988. **Director:** Ronald B. Hatch.

Book Needs Publishes 3 flat-spined paperbacks of poetry/year—by Canadian poets only—classical to experimental. "Ronsdale looks for poetry manuscripts which show that the writer reads and is familiar with the work of some of the major contemporary poets. It is also essential that you have published some poems in literary magazines. We have never published a book of poetry when the author has not already published a goodly number in magazines." Has published *Taking the Breath Away* by Harold Rhenisch, *Two Shores/Deux rives* by Thuong Vuong-Riddick, *Cobalt 3* by Kevin Roberts, *Ghost Children* by Lillian Boraks-Nemetz, *Poems for a New World* by Connie Fife, *Steveston* by Daphne Marlatt, and *After Ted & Sylvia* by Chrystal Hurdle.

How to Submit Query first, with sample poems and cover letter with brief bio and publication credits. Accepts previously published poems and simultaneous submissions. Often comments on rejected poems. Responds to queries in 2 weeks, to mss in 2 months. Pays 10% royalties and 10 author's copies. Write for catalog to purchase sample books.

Advice "Ronsdale looks for poetry with echoes from previous poets. To our mind, the contemporary poet must be well-read."

$◻ ◎ ROOK PUBLISHING (Specialized: rhyming poetry/sonnet)

1805 Calloway Dr., Clarksville TN 37042. (931)648-6225. Established 1996. **Publisher:** E.A. Lawson.

Book/Chapbook Needs & How to Submit Rook Publishing's goal is "to secure and to re-introduce meaningful sonnet/rhyming poetry in published paperback books of 100-150 pages." Wants "rhyming poetry/sonnet on any subject. We would love poems for children; 10-50 lines seem to work well, open to any style. No profanity, religion-bashing, gay/lesbian subject matter, vampires, gore, aliens, pornography, haiku, free verse, or poems in poor taste." Has published poetry by Mary Louise Westbrook, Stephen Scaer, and Byron Von Rosenberg. Rook Publishing publishes 2 paperbacks/year. Books are usually 100-120 pages, 5×7, photocopied, perfect-bound, with 4-color covers, include original/in-house art. Accepts submissions by postal mail only. "No query letter will be necessary; published poems are fine with us." Responds to queries in 10 weeks. Pays royalties of 15-25%, $100, and 3 author's copies (out of a press run of 300-500); or 5 author's copies (out of a press run of 500). Order sample books by sending $8.50 to Rook Publishing.

Advice "Due to the high volume, limit single poems to 3. We still accept manuscripts along listed themes. Send only your best efforts."

☑ ROSE ALLEY PRESS

4203 Brooklyn Ave. NE #103A, Seattle WA 98105. (206)633-2725. E-mail: rosealleypress@juno.com. Website: www.rosealleypress.com. Established 1995. **Publisher/Editor:** David D. Horowitz. "We presently do not read unsolicited manuscripts."

☑ ROSEBUD

N3310 Asje Rd., Cambridge WI 53523. Website: www.rsbd.net. Established 1993. **Poetry Editor:** Ron Ellis **(send poems to P.O. Box 671236, Chugiuk AK 99567)**.

Magazine Needs *Rosebud* "is now the second-highest circulated literary quarterly in America. It has published many of the most prominent voices in the nation and has been listed as among the very best markets for writers. We have published *Star Trek*'s Leonard Nimoy, Ursula K. Le Guin, Robert Pinsky, Philip Levine, Seamus Heaney, Gary Snyder, and the list goes on. Annually, we nominate poets whose work has appeared in *Rosebud* for The Pushcart Prizes." *Rosebud* is "elegantly printed in full glossy color. Press run is 10,000. *Rosebud* is sold in over 1,700 bookstores in the U.S., Canada, and UK." Also uses artwork and fiction.

How to Submit Submit no more than 5 poems at a time to poetry editor (see special address above). "We rarely publish poems longer than one page in length." Include SASE and a brief cover letter with bio. Responds in 3 months.

Advice "Let the poems speak for themselves; don't tell the reader what to think or expect in your cover letter. Make your poems accessible to a wide audience—what interests you may not interest others. Avoid rhyming poetry and poems that try to be too deep (heavy allusions to mythological, biblical, and philosophical references). Great writing is often simply told, using the language of the everyday. A mentor once told me not to waste postage sending out my poetry. He was wrong! Keep trying, but learn from the effort."

☑ ROSEWATER PUBLICATIONS; THROUGH SPIDER'S EYES

223 Chapel St., Leicester MA 01524-1115. E-mail: rosewaterbooks@yahoo.com. Website: www.rosewaterpublications.com. Established 1997. **Editor:** April M. Ardito.

Magazine Needs *Through Spider's Eyes*, appearing annually, is "a showcase of the best of what RoseWater Publications receives. The best art is about art or has a strong message. We prefer coffeehouse and slam style poems, work that is just as powerful spoken as written. Multi-layered work always appreciated. Prefer modern and experimental work. Rhymed poetry must be exceptional; biased against 'God is great' and 'See the pretty trees and flowers' poetry." Has published poetry by Timothy McCoy, Gwen Ellen Rider, Ed Fuqua, Jay Walker, Craig Nelson, and Alex Stolis. *Through Spider's Eyes* is 20-36 pages, digest-sized, photocopied b&w. Receives and accepts varied number of poems/year. Publishes about 10-40 poems/issue. Press run is 50. Single copy: $4.50. Make checks payable to April M. Ardito. Accepts personal checks, money orders, or PayPal for all samples (no longer offers subscriptions).

How to Submit "No minimum/maximum number of poems to submit. Prefer that poets submit a full chapbook-length manuscript." Line length for poetry is 3 minimum, 250 maximum. Accepts previously published poems; no simultaneous submissions. Accepts e-mail submissions, either as attachment (.txt or .doc format) or pasted into body of message. Cover letter is preferred. Likes "disposable manuscripts and casual, personal cover letters; SASE required." Reads submissions year round. Does not publish seasonal poems. Time between acceptance and publication is up to one year. "Editor always attempts to read all submissions personally, but has a few people who help out when submissions get overwhelming." Seldom comments on rejected poems. Responds in up to 6 months. Pays one contributor's copy per accepted poem. Acquires one-time rights and reprint rights (possible inclusion in an anthology at a later date). Reviews books and chapbooks of poetry and other magazines/journals in less than one page, single book format. Send materials for review consideration to April M. Ardito.

Book/Chapbook Needs & How to Submit RoseWater Publications "wants to create an aesthically pleasing product for poets who spend as much time on the stage as with the page." Hopes to publish full-length anthologies in the future. Publishes 5-10 chapbooks/year. Chapbooks are usually 20-64 pages, photocopied b&w, stapled, with colored paper, cardstock, or business stock cover with original cover design. "Please send full manuscript (16-60 pages). We do not wish to see queries. We would prefer to see a poet's full vision." Responds to mss in up to 6 months. Pays 50% of copies (out of a press run of 50-100). Order sample books/chapbooks by sending $4.50 to April M. Ardito.

Also Offers Also publishes poetry for vending machines. Send full ms (up to 120 lines), titled. Press run of 40, author receives 20 copies. Format is $8\frac{1}{2} \times 11$ sheet folded in eighths.

Advice "Spend a lot of time reading and re-reading, writing and re-writing. Always try to keep one finger on the pulse of contemporary poetry, as much to know what isn't working as what is. Stay true to yourself and your vision. Use your words to lure others into your experiences."

☐ ◎ RUAH; POWER OF POETRY (Specialized: spirituality)

Dominican School of Philosophy/Theology, 2401 Ridge Rd., Berkeley CA 94709. Fax: (510)596-1860. E-mail: cjrenzop@yahoo.com. Website: www.popruah.org. Established 1990. **General Editor:** C.J. Renz, O.P. **Editors:** Ann Applegarth and Daniel Richards.

Magazine Needs *Ruah*, an annual journal published in June, "provides a 'non-combative forum' for poets who have had few or no opportunities to publish their work. Theme: spiritual poetry. The journal has 3 sections: general poems, featured poet, and chapbook contest winners." Wants "poetry which is of a 'spiritual nature,' i.e., describes an experience of the transcendent. No religious affiliation preferences; no style/format limitations. No 'satanic verse'; no individual poems longer than 4 typed pages." Has published poetry by Jean Valentine, Alberto Rios, Luci Shaw, and Wendell Berry. *Ruah* is 60-80 pages, digest-sized, photocopied, perfect-bound, with glossy card stock cover with color photo, includes occasional b&w sketches of original artwork. Receives about 350 poems/year, accepts 10-20%. Press run is 250 for about 100 subscribers of which 7 are libraries, 10 shelf sales; 50 distributed free to authors, reviewers, and inquiries. Subscription: donated cost of $10 plus $1.75 p&h. Sample: $5 plus $1.75 p&h. Make checks payable to Power of Poetry/DSPT.

How to Submit Submit 3-5 poems/year. Accepts simultaneous submissions; no previously published poems. Accepts submissions by e-mail (as MS Word 97 file attachments or pasted into body of message), by fax, on disk, and by postal mail. Chapbooks, however, cannot be submitted by e-mail. "Do not mail submissions to publisher's address. Contact general editor via e-mail for current address, or send written inquiries to Dominican School." Reads submissions December through March only. Time between acceptance and publication is up to 6 months. Poems are circulated to an editorial board. "Poems are reviewed by writers and/or scholars in field of creative writing/literature." Guidelines available for SASE or by e-mail. Responds in 2 weeks. Pays one contributor's copy/poem. Acquires first rights.

Contest/Award Offerings Power of Poetry publishes one chapbook of spiritual poetry/year through their annual competition. Chapbooks are usually 24 pages, and are included as part of *Ruah*. "Poets should e-mail general editor for contest guidelines and submission address, or write to Dominican School." **Entry fee:** $10. **Deadline:** December 30. Responds to queries in up to 6 weeks; to mss in up to 6 months. Winner receives $100 plus publication in a volume of *Ruah* and 25 author's copies (out of a press run of 250).

Advice "*Ruah* is a gathering place in which new poets can come to let their voices be heard alongside of and in the context of 'more established' poets. The journal hopes to provide some breakthrough experiences of the Divine at work in our world."

☑ RUNES, A REVIEW OF POETRY

Arctos Press, P.O. Box 401, Sausalito CA 94966-0401. (415)331-2503. Fax: (415)331-3092. E-mail: RunesRev@aol.com. Website: http://members.aol.com/Runes. Established 2000. **Editors:** Susan Terris and CB Follett. Member: SPAN, BAIPA.

Magazine Needs *RUNES, A Review Of Poetry* appears annually. ''Our taste is eclectic, but we are looking for excellence in craft.'' Wants ''poems that have passion, originality, and conviction. We are looking for narrative and lyric poetry that is well-crafted and has something surprising to say. No greeting card verse.'' Has published poetry by Lucille Clifton, Norman Dubie, Jane Hirshfield, Shirley Kaufman, Li-Young Lee, and David St. John. *RUNES* is 160 pages, digest-sized, professionally-printed, flat-spined, with full-color cover, includes art/graphics. Receives about 6,000 poems/ year, accepts 100. Press run is 1,500 for 900 subscribers of which 35 are libraries. Single copy: $12; subscription: $12. Sample: $10. Make checks payable to Arctos Press.

How to Submit Submit no more than 5 poems at a time. Prefers poems under 100 lines. Accepts simultaneous submissions if notified; no previously published poems. No e-mail or disk submissions. SASE required. Reads submissions April 1 through May 31 (postmark) only. Time between acceptance and publication is 6 months. Seldom comments on rejected poems. Regularly publishes theme issues. Themes will be ''Signals'' in 2005, ''Hearth'' in 2006. Guidelines and themes available for SASE, by e-mail, in magazine, or on website. Responds in 4 months. Sometimes sends prepublication galleys. Pays one contributor's copy. Acquires first North American rights.

Contest/Award Offerings Poetry competition for 2005 will have same theme as magazine—''Signals.'' 2005 judge will be Lucille Clifton. **Entry fee:** $15/3 poems, $3 for each additional poem. ''The entry fee covers a one-year subscription. For publication in *Runes*, it is *not* necessary to enter competition. All submitted poems will be read.'' Make checks payable to Arctos Press. (See separate listing for Arctos Press in this section.)

Advice ''No one can write in a vacuum. If you want to write good poetry, you must read good poetry—classic as well as modern work.''

🌐 ☑ S.W.A.G., THE MAGAZINE OF SWANSEA'S WRITERS AND ARTISTS; S.W.A.G. NEWSLETTER

Dan-y-Bryn, 74 CWM Level Rd., Brynhyfryd, Swansea SA5 9DY Wales, United Kingdom. Established 1992. **Chairman/Editor:** Peter Thabit Jones.

Magazine Needs *S.W.A.G.* appears biannually and publishes poetry, prose, articles, and illustrations. ''Our purpose is to publish good literature.'' Wants ''first-class poetry—up to 40 lines, any style.'' Has published poetry by Adrian Mitchell, Alan Llwyd, Mike Jenkins, and Dafydd Rowlands. *S.W.A.G.* is 48 pages, A4, professionally printed on coated paper and saddle-stapled with glossy paper cover, photos and illustrations. Publishes 12-20 poems/issue. Press run is 500 for 120 subscribers of which 50 are libraries. Subscription: £5. Sample (including guidelines): £2.50 plus postage.

How to Submit ''Interested poets should obtain sample beforehand (to see what we offer).'' Submit 6 poems, typed. No previously published poems or simultaneous submissions. Cover letter is required. Time between acceptance and publication is 4-6 months. Poems are circulated to an editorial board. ''Editor chooses/discusses choices with board.'' Guidelines available for SASE (or SAE with IRCs). Responds ASAP. Pays 2 contributor's copies plus a copy of S.W.A.G.'s newsletter. Staff reviews books or poetry (half page to full). Send materials for review consideration.

Also Offers The Swansea Writers and Artists Group (S.W.A.G.) also publishes a newsletter containing information on the group's events. Send SASE for details on the organization. ''We also publish Welsh language poetry.''

$☑ ◎ SACHEM PRESS (Specialized: bilingual, translations)

P.O. Box 9, Old Chatham NY 12136-0009. Established 1980. **Editor:** Louis Hammer.

Book/Chapbook Needs Sachem is a small press publisher of poetry and fiction, both hardcover and flat-spined paperbacks. Wants to see "strong, compelling, even visionary work, English-language or translations." Has published poetry by Cesar Vallejo, Yannis Ritsos, 24 leading poets of Spain (in an anthology), Miltos Sahtouris, and Louis Hammer. The paperbacks are about 120 pages and cost $6.95 or $9.95. The anthology of Spanish poetry contains 340 pages and costs $24; each poem is printed in both English and Spanish, and there are biographical notes about the authors.

How to Submit No new submissions, only statements of projects, until January 2005. Submit mss January through April only. Royalties are 10% maximum, after expenses are recovered, plus 50 author's copies. Rights are negotiable. Book catalog is free "when available," and poets can purchase books from Sachem "by writing to us, 33⅓% discount."

⊘ ◎ SACRED JOURNEY: THE JOURNAL OF FELLOWSHIP IN PRAYER (Specialized: multifaith spirituality)

291 Witherspoon St., Princeton NJ 08542. (609)924-6863. Fax: (609)924-6910. E-mail: editorial@sacredjourney.org. Website: www.sacredjourney.org. Established 1950. **Contact:** Editor.

Magazine Needs *Sacred Journey* is an interfaith bimonthly "concerned with prayer, meditation, spiritual life, and service to others," using short poetry "with deep religious (or spiritual) feeling." *Sacred Journey* is 48 pages, digest-sized, professionally printed, saddle-stapled, with glossy card cover. Accepts about 10% of submissions received. Press run is 10,000. Subscription: $18. Sample free.

How to Submit Submit 1-5 poems at a time, double-spaced. Accepts simultaneous submissions and "sometimes" previously published poems if reprint permission is readily available. Accepts e-mail submissions (pasted into body of message). Cover letter with contact information is required. Responds in 2 months. Pays 5 contributor's copies.

$⬜ ◎ ST. ANTHONY MESSENGER (Specialized: religious, spirituality/inspirational)

28 W. Liberty St., Cincinnati OH 45202-6498. Fax: (513)241-0399. Website: www.americancatholic. org. **Poetry Editor:** Christopher Heffron.

- *St. Anthony Messenger* poetry occasionally receives awards from the Catholic Press Association Annual Competition.

Magazine Needs *St. Anthony Messenger* is a monthly 56-page magazine, with a press run of 340,000, for Catholic families, mostly with children in grade school, high school, or college. Some issues feature a poetry page that uses poems appropriate for their readership. Poetry submissions are always welcome despite limited need. Accepts poetry by young writers, ages 14 and up.

How to Submit "Submit seasonal poetry (Christmas/Easter/nature poems) several months in advance. Submit a few poems at a time; do not send us your entire collection of poetry. We seek to publish accessible poetry of high quality. Poems must be original, under 25 lines; spiritual/inspirational in nature a plus, but not required. We do not publish poems that have already been published—must be first run. Please include your social security number with your submission." Accepts submissions by fax, e-mail, and postal mail. Guidelines available on website, by fax, or for standard SASE; free sample for 9×12 SASE. Pays $2/line on acceptance plus 2 contributor's copies. Acquires first worldwide serial rights.

$⊘ ◎ ST. JOSEPH MESSENGER & ADVOCATE OF THE BLIND (Specialized: religious)

537 Pavonia Ave., P.O. Box 288, Jersey City NJ 07303. Established 1898. **Poetry Editor:** Sister Mary Kuiken, C.S.J.P.

Magazine Needs *St. Joseph Messenger* is semiannual and publishes "brief but thought-filled poetry; do not want lengthy and issue-filled." Most of the poets they have used are previously unpublished. Receives 400-500 submissions/year, accepts about 50. *St. Joseph Messenger* is 16 pages, magazine-sized, and prints about 2 pages of poetry/issue. Press run 14,000. Subscription: $5.

How to Submit Currently oversupplied; not accepting submissions. Sometimes comments on rejected poems. Publishes theme issues. Guidelines, a free sample, and upcoming themes available for SASE. Responds within one month. Pays $5-20/poem plus 2 contributor's copies.

▨ ◯ ◎ ST. LINUS REVIEW (Specialized: religious/orthodox Catholicism)

5239 S. Sandusky Ave., Tulsa OK 74135. E-mail: editor@stlinusreview.com. Website: www.stlinusr eview.com. Established 2003. **Editor:** William Ferguson.

Magazine Needs *St. Linus Review* is a biannual journal of poetry and prose written by and for orthodox Catholics. Wants "poetry and prose of diverse subject matter (does not have to be religious) in diverse styles. Prefer quality rhyming verse and structured styles but will accept free verse and other." Does not want "profanity, graphic portrayals of violence or sex, erotica, or works which openly or in general tendency detract from the teachings of the Catholic Church." Has published poetry by Pavel Chichikov, Kate Watkins Furman, Dennis Schenkel, and Sarah DeCorla-Souza. *St. Linus Review* is about 40 pages, digest-sized. Receives about 100 poems/year, accepts about 50%. Publishes about 25 poems/issue. Press run is 70 for 25 subscribers. Single copy: $6; subscription: $12/year. Make checks payable to William Ferguson.

How to Submit Submit up to 5 poems at a time. No previously published poems or simultaneous submissions. Prefers e-mail submissions (as attachment in MS Word); no disk submissions. "We'll accept manuscripts mailed to our physical address; however, manuscripts will not be returned. Name, city/state, and e-mail address on each submission." Reads submissions year round. Time between acceptance and publication is 4-6 months. "Poems are read by the editor and 2 associate editors who select poems to be used in the review." Never comments on rejected poems. "Writers are requested to help support the review by subscribing. However, there is no requirement to subscribe." Guidelines available on website. Pays one contributor's copy. Acquires first rights.

Contest/Award Offerings Offers "Best of Review" award in poetry and prose categories, presented annually. Small cash prize.

Advice "Bright, bold orthodoxy in structured verse with strong, engaging words will win our hearts."

◪ SALT HILL; SALT HILL POETRY PRIZE

English Dept., Syracuse University, Syracuse NY 13244-1170. (315)443-1984. E-mail: salthill@cas.s yr.edu. Website: http://students.syr.edu/salthill/. Established 1994. **Editor:** Ellen Litman. **Contact:** Poetry Editor.

Magazine Needs *Salt Hill*, published biannually, features "high-quality contemporary writing including poetry, fiction, essays, book reviews, and artwork." Also seeks hypertext submissions for online issues. E-mail URL to letthewordsout@aol.com. or visit website for more information. "*Salt Hill* has an open aesthetic and a revolving editorialship. Imagination, technical innovation, and a sense of humor are all appreciated, but we publish good poems of all varieties." Has published poetry by Campbell McGrath, Dean Young, Kim Addonizio, and James Tate. *Salt Hill* is 120-150 pages, digest-sized, perfect-bound, includes art, photography, and ads. Receives about 3,000 poems/year, accepts about 2%. Press run is 1,000. Subscription: $15. Sample: $8.

How to Submit Submit 5 poems at a time. Accepts simultaneous submissions; no previously published poems. Cover letter preferred with a brief bio. Time between acceptance and publication is up to 8 months. Seldom comments on rejected poems. Guidelines available for SASE. Responds in up to 6 months. Pays 2 contributor's copies. Acquires one-time rights. Reviews books or chapbooks of poetry or other magazines in 900-3,000 words and/or essay reviews of single/multi-book format. Send materials for review consideration to Book Review Editor at the above address.

Contest/Award Offerings Sponsors annual *Salt Hill* Poetry Prize. 1st Prize: $500 and publication; 2nd Prize: $250 and publication; 3rd Prize: $100 and publication. Submit unpublished poems with name, address, and phone number on each. **Entry fee:** $5 for up to 150 lines (1-3 poems); $3 extra for every additional 100 lines. Include SASE. **Postmark deadline:** January 15.

⬚ ◯ THE SAME

P.O. Box 16415, Kansas City MO 64131. E-mail: editor@tsmag.itgo.com. Website: http://tsmag.itgo .com. Established 2000. **Co-Editors:** Carl Calvert Bettis and Philip Miller.

Magazine Needs *The Same*, a publication of poetry, fiction, essays, and literary criticism, appears 2 times/year in May and November. Wants "eclectic to formal to free verse, traditional to experimental, all subject matter." Does not want misogyny, homophobia, racism, or inspirational. Has published poetry by David Ray, Judy Ray, Gary Lechliter, Phyllis Becker, Stephen Clay Dearborn, and John Mark Eberhart. *The Same* is 24-32 pages, magazine-sized, desktop-published/photocopied, saddle-stapled, with cardstock cover with b&w artwork, includes line art. Receives about 400 poems/year, accepts about 25%. Publishes about 25-50 poems/issue. Press run is 150 for 125 shelf sales; 25 are distributed free to contributors. Single copy: $5; subscription: $10/2 issues, $20/4 issues. Make checks payable to Carl Calvert Bettis.

How to Submit Submit 1-7 poems at a time. Line length for poetry is 120 maximum. No previously published poems or simultaneous submissions. Accepts e-mail submissions (pasted into body of message); no disk submissions. "Include SASE if you want a response. If you don't want your manuscript returned, you may omit the SASE if we can respond via e-mail." Reads submissions year round. Submit seasonal poems 6 months in advance. Time between acceptance and publication is up to 6 months. "Co-editors take turns as primary editor for each issue. Primary editor generally makes all decisions for his issue." Seldom comments on rejected poems. Guidelines available for SASE, by e-mail, or on website. Responds in 6 weeks. Pays one contributor's copy. Acquires first North American serial rights and online rights for up to 6 months; returns rights to poet.

Book/Chapbook Needs & How to Submit Publishes 0-3 chapbooks/year. **Solicited mss only.** Chapbooks are 24-32 pages, desktop-published/photocopied, saddle-stapled, with cardstock covers, include line art. Pays 25-50 author's copies (out of a press run of 50-100). Order sample chapbooks by sending $5 to *The Same*.

Advice "Our motto is 'Everyone else is different, but we're the same!' We try to be eclectic and non-doctrinaire."

$⬚ SARABANDE BOOKS, INC.; THE KATHRYN A. MORTON PRIZE IN POETRY

2234 Dundee Rd., Suite 200, Louisville KY 40205. (502)458-4028. Fax: (502)458-4065. E-mail: online contact form. Website: www.SarabandeBooks.org. Established 1994. **Editor-in-Chief:** Sarah Gorham.

Book/Chapbook Needs Sarabande Books publishes books of poetry of 48 pages minimum. Wants "poetry that offers originality of voice and subject matter, uniqueness of vision, and a language that startles because of the careful attention paid to it—language that goes beyond the merely competent or functional." Has published poetry by Eleanor Lerman, Frank Bidart, Ralph Angel, Baron Wormser, and Afaa Michael Weaver.

How to Submit Query with 10 sample poems **during the month of September only** (open submission season). Accepts previously published poems if acknowledged as such, and simultaneous submissions "if notified immediately of acceptance elsewhere." No fax or e-mail submissions. SASE must always be enclosed. Seldom comments on rejected poems. Guidelines available for SASE or on website. Responds to queries in 3 months; to mss (if invited) in 6 months. Pays 10% royalties plus author's copies.

Contest/Award Offerings The Kathryn A. Morton Prize in Poetry, Sarabande Books, Inc. P.O. Box 4456, Louisville KY 40204. Awarded to a book-length ms (at least 48 pages). Entry form required. Guidelines available in November for SASE or on website. Winner receives $2,000 cash, publication, and a standard royalty contract. All finalists are considered for publication. "At least half of our list is drawn from contest submissions." **Entry fee:** $20. **Deadline:** reads entries January 1 through February 15 only. Competition receives 1,200 entries. 2002 contest winner was Carrie St. George Comer for *The Unrequited*. Judge was Stephen Dunn.

Advice "We recommend that you request our catalog and familiarize yourself with our books. Our complete list shows a variety of style and subject matter."

⬇ ☑ SCRIVENER

Poetry Dept., McGill University, 853 Sherbrooke St. W., Montreal QC H3A 2T6 Canada. (514)398-6588. E-mail: scrivenermag@hotmail.com. Established 1980. **Contact:** Addy Liftin and Dan Huffaker.

Magazine Needs *Scrivener* is an annual review of contemporary literature and art published in April by students at McGill University. With a circulation throughout North America, *Scrivener* publishes the best of new Canadian and international poetry, short fiction, criticism, essays, reviews, and interviews. "*Scrivener* is committed to publishing the work of new and unpublished writers." Has published poetry by Nicola Little, Shane Neilson, Giovanni Malito, and Sharon Desmarais. *Scrivener* is 120 pages, $8\frac{1}{2} \times 7$, printed on coated paper, perfect-bound, includes 25 pages of b&w photography. Text and graphics are printed in b&w duotone cover. Subscription: $9.50 Canadian in Canada, $12 Canadian in US, $14 Canadian anywhere else. Prices include postage.

How to Submit Contributors are encouraged to submit in early fall. **Deadline:** January 15. Send 5-10 poems, one poem/page; be sure that each poem is identified separately, with titles, numbers, etc. Accepts e-mail submissions (attachments or pasted into body of message). Submissions require SASE for return. Comments or questions regarding back issues or submissions may be sent by e-mail. *Scrivener* only operates fully between September and April. Responds in 6 months. Pays one contributor's copy (multiple copies available upon request).

◯ SEAWEED SIDESHOW CIRCUS

P.O. Box 234, Jackson WI 53037. (414)791-1109. Fax: (262)677-0896. E-mail: sscircus@aol.com. Website: http://hometown.aol.com/SSCircus/sscweb.html. Established 1994. **Editor:** Andrew Wright Milam.

Book/Chapbook Needs & How to Submit Seaweed Sideshow Circus is "a place for young or new poets to publish a chapbook." Has published *Main Street* by Steven Paul Lansky and *The Moon Incident* by Amy McDonald. Publishes one chapbook/year. Chapbooks are usually 30 pages, digest-sized, photocopied, saddle-stapled, with cardstock covers. Send 5-10 sample poems and cover letter with bio and credits. Responds to queries in 3 weeks; to mss in 3 months. Pays royalties of 10 author's copies (out of a press run of 100). Order sample chapbooks by sending $6.

⊕ ☑ SECOND AEON PUBLICATIONS

19 Southminster Rd., Roath, Cardiff CF23 SAT Wales. Phone/fax: (02920)493093. E-mail: peter@peterfinch.co.uk. Website: www.peterfinch.co.uk. Established 1966. **Poetry Editor:** Peter Finch. Does not accept unsolicited mss.

☑ SEEMS

P.O. Box 359, Lakeland College, Sheboygan WI 53082-0359. (920)565-1276 or (920)565-3871. Fax: (920)565-1206. E-mail: kelder@excel.net. Website: www1.lakeland.edu/seems/. Established 1971. **Editor:** Karl Elder.

Magazine Needs *SEEMS* is published irregularly. Handsomely printed, nearly square ($7 \times 8\frac{1}{4}$) magazine, saddle-stapled, generous with white space on heavy paper. Two of the issues are considered chapbooks, and the editor suggests sampling *SEEMS #14, What Is The Future Of Poetry?* for $5, consisting of essays by 22 contemporary poets, and "If you don't like it, return it, and we'll return your $5." *Explain That You Live: Mark Strand with Karl Elder* (#29) is available for $3. There are usually about 20 pages of poetry/issue. Has published poetry by Kim Bridgford, Rob Cook, Doug Flaherty, John Grey, Andrew Krewer, and Joanne Lowery. Print run is 500 for over 250 subscribers of which 20 are libraries. Single copy: $4; subscription: $16/4 issues.

How to Submit There is a 1- to 2-year backlog. "People may call or fax with virtually any question, understanding that the editor may have no answer." No simultaneous submissions. No fax or e-mail submissions. Guidelines available on website. Responds in up to 3 months (slower in summer). Pays one contributor's copy. Acquires first North American serial rights and permission to publish online. Returns rights upon publication.

Advice "Visit the new *SEEMS* website."

✪ ☑ SENECA REVIEW

Hobart and William Smith Colleges, Geneva NY 14456-3397. (315)781-3392. Fax: (315)781-3348. E-mail: senecareview@hws.edu. Website: www.hws.edu/senecareview/. Established 1970. **Editor:** Deborah Tall. **Associate Editor:** John D'Agata.

● Poetry published in *Seneca Review* has been included in *The Best American Poetry* and *The Pushcart Prize* anthology.

Magazine Needs *Seneca Review* is a biannual. Wants "serious poetry of any form, including translations. No light verse. Also essays on contemporary poetry and lyrical nonfiction." Has published poetry by Seamus Heaney, Rita Dove, Denise Levertov, Stephen Dunn, and Hayden Carruth. *Seneca Review* is 100 pages, digest-sized, professionally printed on quality stock, perfect-bound, with matte card cover. "You'll find plenty of free verse here—some accessible and some leaning toward experimental—with the emphasis on voice, image, and diction. All in all, poems and translations complement each other and create a distinct editorial mood each issue." Receives 3,000-4,000 poems/year, accepts about 100. Press run is 1,000 for 500 subscribers of which half are libraries, about 250 shelf sales. Subscription: $11/year, $20/2 years, $28/3 years. Sample: $5.

How to Submit Submit 3-5 poems at a time. No simultaneous submissions or previously published poems. Reads submissions September 1 through May 1 only. Responds in up to 3 months. Pays 2 contributor's copies and a 2-year subscription.

$☑ THE SEWANEE REVIEW

University of the South, Sewanee TN 37383-1000. (931)598-1246. E-mail: rjones@sewanee.edu. Website: www.sewanee.edu/sreview/home.html. Established 1892, thus being our nation's oldest continuously published literary quarterly. **Editor:** George Core.

Magazine Needs "Fiction, criticism, and poetry are invariably of the highest establishment standards. Many of our major poets appear here from time to time." *The Sewanee Review* has published poetry by Wendell Berry, George Bilgere, Catherine Savage Brosman, David Mason, Leslie Norris, and Christian Wiman. Each issue is a hefty paperback of nearly 200 pages, conservatively bound in matte paper, always of the same typography. Open to all styles and forms: formal sequences, metered verse, structured free verse, sonnets, and lyric and narrative forms—all accessible and intelligent. Press run is 3,100. Sample: $8.50 (US), $9.50 (foreign). Subscription: $24/year, $30/year (institutions).

How to Submit Submit up to 6 poems at a time. Line length for poetry is 40 maximum. No simultaneous submissions. No electronic submissions. "Unsolicited works should not be submitted between June 1 and August 31. A response to any submission received during that period will be greatly delayed." Guidelines available for SASE, by e-mail, or on website. Responds in 6 weeks. Pays 60¢/line, plus 2 contributor's copies (and reduced price for additional copies). Also includes brief, standard, and essay-reviews.

Contest/Award Offerings Presents the Aiken Taylor Award for Modern American Poetry to established poets. Poets *cannot* apply for this prize.

Advice "Please keep in mind that for each poem published in *The Sewanee Review*, approximately 250 poems are considered."

◻ ◎ SHEMOM (Specialized: motherhood)

2486 Montgomery Ave., Cardiff CA 92007. E-mail: pdfrench@cox.net. Established 1997. **Editor:** Peggy French.

Magazine Needs "Appearing 2-4 times/year, *Shemom* celebrates motherhood and the joys and struggles that present themselves in that journey. It includes poetry, essays, book and CD reviews, recipes, art, and children's poetry. Open to any style, prefer free verse. We celebrate motherhood and related issues. Haiku and native writing also enjoyed. Love to hear from children." *Shemom* is a 10- to 20-page zine. Receives about 70 poems/year, accepts 50%. Press run is 50 for 30 subscribers. Single copy: $3; subscription: $12/4 issues. Sample: $3.50. Make checks payable to Peggy French.

How to Submit Submit 3 poems at a time. Accepts previously published poems and simultaneous submissions. Accepts e-mail submissions (as attachment or pasted into body of message). "Prefer e-mail submission, but not required; if material is to be returned, please include a SASE." Guidelines available for SASE or by e-mail. Time between acceptance and publication is 3 months. Responds in 2 months. Pays one contributor's copy. Acquires one-time rights.

$◻ SHENANDOAH; THE JAMES BOATWRIGHT III PRIZE FOR POETRY

Mattingly House, 2 Lee Ave., Washington and Lee University, Lexington VA 24450-0303. (540)458-8765. E-mail: lleech@wlu.edu. Website: http://shenandoah.wlu.edu. Established 1950. **Editor:** R.T. Smith.

- Poetry published in *Shenandoah* has been included in *The Best American Poetry*.

Magazine Needs Published at Washington and Lee University, *Shenandoah* is a triannual literary magazine. Has published poetry by Mary Oliver, Andrew Hudgins, W.S. Merwin, and Rita Dove. *Shenandoah* is 224 pages, digest-sized, perfect-bound, professionally printed, with full-color cover. Generally, it is open to all styles and forms. Press run is 2,000. Subscription: $22/year; $40/2 years; $54/3 years. Sample: $8.

How to Submit All submissions should be typed on one side of the paper only. Your name and address must be clearly written on the upper right corner of the ms. No simultaneous submissions. No e-mail submissions. Include SASE. Reads submissions September 1 through May 30 only. Responds in 3 months. Pays $2.50/line, one-year subscription, and one contributor's copy. Acquires first publication rights. Staff reviews books of poetry in 7-10 pages, multi-book format. Send materials for review consideration. Most reviews are solicited.

Contest/Award Offerings Sponsors the James Boatwright III Prize For Poetry, a $1,000 prize awarded annually to the author of the best poem published in *Shenandoah* during a volume year.

◻ SHIP OF FOOLS; SHIP OF FOOLS PRESS

Box 1028, University of Rio Grande, Rio Grande OH 45674-9989. (740)992-3333. Website: http://meadhall.homestead.com. Established 1983. **Editor:** Jack Hart. **Assistant Editor:** Catherine Grosvenor. **Review Editor:** James Doubleday.

Magazine Needs *Ship of Fools* is "more or less quarterly." Wants "coherent, well-written, traditional or modern, myth, archetype, love—most types. No concrete, incoherent, or greeting card poetry." Has published poetry by Rhina Espaillat, Paula Tatarunis, Simon Perchik, and Lyn Lifshin. *Ship of Fools* is digest-sized, saddle-stapled, offset printed, includes cover art and graphics. Press run is 183 for 45 subscribers of which 5 are libraries. Subscription: $8/4 issues. Sample: $2.

How to Submit No previously published poems or simultaneous submissions. Cover letter is preferred. Often comments on rejected poems. Guidelines available for SASE. Responds in one month. "If longer than 6 weeks, write and ask why." Pays 1-2 contributor's copies. Reviews books of poetry.

Book/Chapbook Needs & How to Submit "We have no plans to publish chapbooks in the next year due to time constraints."
Advice "Forget yourself; it is not you that matters, but the words."

◎ SHIRIM, A JEWISH POETRY JOURNAL (Specialized: ethnic)

259 St. Joseph Ave., Long Beach CA 90803. (310)476-2861. Established 1982. **Editor:** Marc Dworkin.
Magazine Needs *Shirim* appears biannually and publishes "poetry that reflects Jewish living without limiting to specific symbols, images, or contents." Has published poetry by Robert Mezcy, Karl Shapiro, and Grace Schulmon. *Shirim* is 40 pages, 4×5, desktop-published, saddle-stapled, with card stock cover. Press run is 200. Subscription: $7. Sample: $4.
How to Submit Submit 4 poems at a time. No previously published poems or simultaneous submissions. Cover letter is preferred. Seldom comments on rejected poems. Regularly publishes theme issues. Responds in 3 months. Acquires first rights.

$◙ sidereality: a journal of speculative & experimental poetry

Columbia SC. E-mail: managingeditor@sidereality.com. Website: www.sidereality.com. Established 2002. **Managing Editor:** Clayton A. Couch.
Magazine Needs *sidereality: a journal of speculative & experimental poetry* appears quarterly as an Internet-only e-journal. "We consider a broad range of styles and forms, but we are looking specifically for poems which challenge reader expectations and imbue the English language with vitality and 'newness.' " Does not want clichéd, non-specific, or vague poetry. Has published poetry by Joel Chace, W.B. Keckler, Nick Piombino, MTC Cronin, Bruce Boston, Michael Arnzen, Eileen Tabios, Charles Fishman, Susan Terris, Vernon Frazer, and John Amen. *sidereality* is 80-100 pages, published online, with a web page cover with digital art. Receives about 800-900 poems/year, accepts about 15%. Publishes 60-70 poems/issue.
How to Submit Submit 1-10 poems at a time. No previously published poems or simultaneous submissions. Accepts e-mail submissions; no disk submissions. Cover letter is preferred. "*sidereality* accepts only e-mail submissions. Send to poetryeditor@sidereality.com with poems in the body of the message or in an attached file (.doc or .rtf format)." Reads submissions all year. Time between acceptance and publication is 2-5 months. Often comments on rejected poems. Guidelines available on website. Responds in up to one month. Sometimes sends prepublication galleys. Pays $2/poem. "We purchase first printing world exclusive rights for 3 months, after which time you may republish your work elsewhere, so long as *sidereality* is noted as the original publisher. We hope that you will allow *sidereality* to maintain your work in its archives indefinitely, but should you decide to remove it, contact Clayton A. Couch with the request." Reviews books and chapbooks of poetry and other magazines/journals. Send materials for review consideration to Steven J. Stewart, Reviews Editor, stevenj1@hotmail.com.
Advice "Read, read as much as you can. Take risks with your writing, and most importantly, allow your poems room to grow."

✪ ◙ SIERRA NEVADA COLLEGE REVIEW

999 Tahoe Blvd., Incline Village NV 89451. Established 1990. **Editor:** June Sylvester Saraceno.
Magazine Needs *Sierra Nevada College Review* is an annual literary magazine published in May, featuring poetry and short fiction by new writers. "We want image-oriented poems with a distinct, genuine voice. Although we don't tend to publish 'light verse,' we do appreciate, and often publish, poems that make us laugh. We try to steer clear of sentimental, clichéd, or obscure poetry. No limit on length, style, etc." Has published poetry by Virgil Suárez, Carol Frith, and Alan Britt. *Sierra Nevada College Review* is about 75 pages, with cover art only. "We receive approximately 500 poems/year and accept approximately 50." Press run is 500. Subscription: $10/year. Sample: $5.
How to Submit Submit 5 poems at a time. Accepts simultaneous submissions; no previously pub-

lished poems. Reads submissions September 1 through March 1 only. Sometimes comments on rejected poems. Responds in about 3 months. Pays 2 contributor's copies.

Advice "We're looking for poetry that shows subtlety and skill."

$⧉ SILVERFISH REVIEW PRESS; GERALD CABLE BOOK AWARD

P.O. Box 3541, Eugene OR 97403. (541)344-5060. E-mail: sfrpress@earthlink.net. Established 1979. **Editor:** Rodger Moody.

Contest/Award Offerings Silverfish Review Press sponsors the Gerald Cable Poetry Contest. A $1,000 cash award and publication is awarded annually to the best book-length ms *or* original poetry by an author who has not yet published a full-length collection. No restrictions on the kind of poetry or subject matter; translations not acceptable. Has published *Why They Grow Wings* by Nin Andrews, *Odd Botany* by Thorpe Moeckel, *Bodies that Hum* by Beth Gylys, and *Inventing Difficulty* by Jessica Greenbaum. Books are $12 plus $3.50 p&h. A **$20 entry fee** must accompany the ms; make checks payable to Silverfish Review Press. Guidelines available for SASE or by e-mail. Pays 10% of press run (out of 1,000).

"We look for a single arresting image that is thought provoking, potentially unforgettable," says advisory editor June Sylvester Saraceno. Ignacio Delgado's "Near Sky Smile" was taken in Tibet near Mount Everest.

⧉ SIMPLYWORDS

605 Collins Ave. #23, Centerville GA 31028. Phone/fax: (478)953-9482 (between 10 a.m. and 5 p.m. only). E-mail: simplywordspoetry@yahoo.com. Website: http://geocities.com/simplywordsp oetry. Established 1991. **Editor:** Ruth Niehaus.

Magazine Needs *SimplyWords* is a quarterly magazine open to all types, forms, and subjects. "No foul language or overtly sexual works." Accepts poetry written by children ages 8 and up; "there are no reading fees for children." Has published poetry by Cheryl Dempsey, Barbara Cagle Ray, Sheila B. Roark, Donald Harmande, and Daniel Green. *SimplyWords* is 34-38 pages, magazine-sized, deskjet-printed and spiral-bound, with photo on cover, includes clip art. Receives about 500 poems/year, accepts about 90%. Press run is 60-100 "depending on subscriptions and single-issue orders in-house." Single copy: $7.50; subscription: $23.50/4 issues.

How to Submit "Send SASE for guidelines *before* submitting; write 'GUIDELINES' in big block letters on left-hand corner of envelope." Line length for poetry is 28 maximum. No e-mail submissions. Cover letter and SASE are required. "Name, address, phone number, e-mail address (if available), and line count must be on each page submitted." **Reading fee:** $1/poem for non-subscribers, 50¢ for subscribers. Time between acceptance and publication "depends on what issue your work is accepted for." Guidelines available for SASE or by e-mail.

Also Offers An online poetry club at http://groups.yahoo.com/group/simplywordspoetry.

Advice "Send for guidelines!"

Publishers of Poetry

⊕ ☑ SKALD

2 Greenfield Terrace, Menai Bridge, Anglesey LL59 5AY Wales, United Kingdom. Phone: 1248-716343. E-mail: submissions@skald.co.uk. Website: www.skald.co.uk. Established 1994. **Contact:** Zoë Skoulding and Ian Davidson.

Magazine Needs *Skald* appears 2 times/year and publishes "poetry and prose in Welsh and English. It aims to publish a broad range of writing, including the innovative and experimental, and it is interested in the connections and differences between the local and the international, the visual and the verbal." Features reviews and artwork. *Skald* is 30-40 pages, A5, professionally printed, saddle-stapled, with textured card cover, includes b&w artwork. Receives about 300 poems/year, accepts about 25%. Press run is 300 for 20 subscribers, 250 shelf sales; 20 distributed free to other magazines, art boards. Single copy: £3; subscription: £6/year (payments in sterling only).

How to Submit Submit 6 poems at a time. No previously published poems or simultaneous submissions. Brief cover letter is preferred. Time between acceptance and publication is 4 months. Often comments on rejected poems. Responds in one month. Pays one contributor's copy.

☻ SKIDROW PENTHOUSE

44 Four Corners Rd., Blairstown NJ 07825. (908)362-6808 or (212)286-2600. Established 1998. **Co-Editors:** Rob Cook and Stephanie Dickinson.

Magazine Needs *Skidrow Penthouse* is published "to give emerging and idiosyncratic writers a new forum in which to publish their work. We are looking for deeply felt authentic voices, whether surreal, confessional, New York School, formal, or free verse. Work should be well crafted: attention to line-break and diction. We want poets who sound like themselves, not workshop professionals. We don't want gutless posturing, technical precision with no subject matter, explicit sex and violence without craft, or abstract intellectualizing. We are not impressed by previous awards and publications." Has published poetry by Lisa Jarnot, Christopher Edgar, Aase Berg, Karl Tierney, James Grinwis, and Robyn Art. *Skidrow Penthouse* is 280 pages, 6×9, professionally printed, perfect-bound, with 4-color cover, includes original art and photographs. Receives about 500 poems/year, accepts 3%. Publishes 35-40 poems/issue. Press run is 300 for 50 subscribers; 10% distributed free to journals for review consideration. Single copy: $12.50; subscription: $20. Make checks payable to Rob Cook or Stephanie Dickinson.

How to Submit Submit 3-5 poems at a time. Accepts previously published poems and simultaneous submissions. "Include a legal sized SASE; also name and address on every page of your submission. No handwritten submissions will be considered." Time between acceptance and publication is one year. Seldom comments on rejected poems. Responds in 2 months. Pays one contributor's copy. Acquires one-time rights. Reviews books and chapbooks of poetry and other magazines in 1,500 words, single book format. Send materials for review consideration.

Also Offers "We're trying to showcase a poet in each issue by publishing up-to-60-page collections within the magazine." Send query with SASE.

Advice "We get way too many anecdotal fragments posing as poetry; too much of what we receive feels like this morning's inspiration mailed this afternoon. The majority of those who submit do not seem to have put in the sweat a good poem demands. Also, the ratio of submissions to sample copy purchases is 50:1. Just because our name is *Skidrow Penthouse* does not mean we are a repository for genre work or 'eat, shit, shower, and shave' poetry."

◘ ◎ SKIPPING STONES: A MULTICULTURAL CHILDREN'S MAGAZINE; ANNUAL YOUTH HONOR AWARDS (Specialized: bilingual; children/teens; ethnic/nationality; nature/ecology; social issues)

P.O. Box 3939, Eugene OR 97403. (541)342-4956. E-mail: editor@skippingstones.org. Website: www.skippingstones.org. Established 1988. **Editor:** Arun Toké.

• Now in its 16th year, *Skipping Stones* is the recipient of EdPress, NAME, and Parent's Choice Awards, among others.

Magazine Needs *Skipping Stones* is an award-winning "nonprofit magazine published bimonthly during the school year (5 issues) that encourages cooperation, creativity, and celebration of cultural and ecological richness." Wants poetry by young writers under 18; 30 lines maximum on "nature, multicultural and social issues, family, freedom . . . uplifting." No work by adults. *Skipping Stones* is magazine-sized, saddle-stapled, printed on recycled paper. Receives about 500-1,000 poems/year, accepts 10%. Press run is 2,500 for 1,700 subscribers. Subscription: $25. Sample: $5.

How to Submit Submit up to 3 poems at a time. Accepts simultaneous submissions; no previously published poems. Accepts e-mail submissions included in body of message. Cover letter is preferred. "Include your cultural background, experiences, and the inspiration behind your creation." Time between acceptance and publication is up to 9 months. Poems are circulated to a 3-member editorial board. "Generally a piece is chosen for publication when all the editorial staff feel good about it." Seldom comments on rejected poems. Publishes theme issues. Guidelines and upcoming themes available for SASE. Responds in up to 4 months. Pays one contributor's copy, offers 25% discount for more. Acquires first serial rights and non-exclusive reprint rights.

Contest/Award Offerings Sponsors Annual Youth Honor Awards for 7- to 17-year-olds. Theme for Annual Youth Honor Awards is "Multicultural and Nature Awareness." **Deadline:** June 20 each year. **Entry fee:** $3 (includes a free issue featuring winners). Details available for SASE.

☑ SLANT: A JOURNAL OF POETRY

Box 5063, University of Central Arkansas, 201 Donaghey Ave., Conway AR 72035-5000. (501)450-5107. Website: www.uca.edu/divisions/academic/english/Slant/HOMPAGE.html. Established 1987. **Editor:** James Fowler.

Magazine Needs *Slant* is an annual using *only* poetry. Wants "traditional and 'modern' poetry, even experimental, moderate length, any subject on approval of Board of Readers; purpose is to publish a journal of fine poetry from all regions of the United States and beyond. No haiku, no translations." Accepts poetry written by children ("although we're not a children's journal.") Has published poetry by Michael Borich, Linda Casebeer, William Greenway, Pearl Karrer, Peter Swanson, and Alexandra Van de Kamp. *Slant* is 120 pages, professionally printed on quality stock, flat-spined, with matte card cover. Receives about 1,500 poems/year, accepts 70-80. Press run is 200 for 70-100 subscribers. Sample: $10.

How to Submit Submit up to 5 poems of moderate length with SASE between September and mid-November. "Put name, address (including e-mail if available), and phone number on the top of each page." No simultaneous submissions or previously published poems. Editor comments on rejected poems "on occasion." Allow 3-4 months from November 15 deadline for response. Pays one contributor's copy.

Advice "I would like to see more formal and narrative verse."

☐ SLAPERING HOL PRESS; SLAPERING HOL PRESS CHAPBOOK COMPETITION

300 Riverside Dr., Sleepy Hollow NY 10591-1414. (914)332-5953. Fax: (914)332-4825. E-mail: info @writerscenter.org. Website: www.writerscenter.org/slaperinghol.html. Established 1990. **Contact:** Margo Stever.

Book/Chapbook Needs "Slapering Hol Press is the small press imprint of The Hudson Valley Writers' Center. It was created in 1990 to provide publishing opportunities for emerging poets who have not yet published a book or chapbook, and to publish occasional anthologies. One chapbook is selected for publication on the basis of an annual competition [see below]." Has published *The Last Campaign* by Rachel Loden, *The Landscape of Mind* by Jianqing Zheng, *Scottish Café* by Susan Case, and *Water Stories* by Brighde Mullins. Slapering Hol Press publishes one or 2 chapbooks/

year. Chapbooks are usually less than 40 pages, offset-printed, hand-sewn, with 80 lb. cover weight covers.

Contest/Award Offerings Slapering Hol Press Chapbook Competition offers annual award of $1,000, publication, 10 author's copies, and a reading at The Hudson Valley Writers' Center. Pays winners from other countries with check in U.S. currency. Open only to poets who have not previously published a book or chapbook. Submit 16-20 pages of poetry, collection or one long poem, any form or style. **Entry fee:** $10. Make checks payable to The Hudson Valley Writers' Center. "Manuscript should be anonymous with separate cover sheet containing name, address, phone number, e-mail address, a bio, and acknowledgments." Manuscripts will not be returned. Include SASE for results only. Guidelines available for SASE, by fax, e-mail, or on website. **Deadline:** May 15. Competition receives 200-300 entries. 2003 contest winner was David Tucker (*Days When Nothing Happens*). Winner will be announced in September. Copies of winning books available through website.

▢ ◎ SLATE & STYLE (Specialized: blind writers)

Dept. PM, 2704 Beach Dr., Merrick NY 11566. (516)868-8718. Fax: (516)868-9076. E-mail: LoriStay @aol.com. **Editor:** Loraine Stayer.

Magazine Needs *Slate & Style* is a quarterly for blind writers, available on cassette, in large print, Braille, and by e-mail, "including articles of interest to blind writers, resources for blind writers. Membership/subscription is $10 per year, all formats. Division of the National Federation of the Blind." Poems may be "5-36 lines. Prefer contributors to be blind writers, or at least writers by profession or inclination. New writers welcome. No obscenities. Will consider all forms of poetry including haiku. Interested in new talent." Accepts poetry by young writers, but please specify age. Has published poetry by Mary Brunoli, Kerry Elizabeth Thompson, John Gordon Jr., Katherine Barr, and Nancy Scott. The print version of *Slate & Style* is 28-32 pages, magazine-sized, stapled, with a fiction and poetry section. Press run is 200 for 160 subscribers of which 4-5 are libraries. Subscription: $10/year. Sample: $2.50.

How to Submit Submit 3 poems once or twice/year. No simultaneous submissions or previously published poems. Accepts submissions by e-mail (pasted into body of message). Cover letter is preferred. "On occasion we receive poems in Braille. I prefer print, since Braille slows me down. Typed is best." Do not submit mss in July. Editor comments on rejected poems "if requested." Guidelines available in magazine, for SASE, by e-mail, or on website. Responds in "2 weeks if I like it." Pays one contributor's copy. Reviews books of poetry. Send materials for review consideration.

Contest/Award Offerings Offers an annual poetry contest. **Entry fee:** none. "We will pay $5/poem published as a result of the contest." **Deadline:** June 1. Write for details. Also holds a contest for blind children; write for details.

Advice "Before you send us a poem, read it aloud. Does it sound good to you? We put our poetry into tape format, so we want it to sound and look good."

$▢ SLOPE; SLOPE EDITIONS

% Ethan Paquin, Editor, Medaille College, 18 Agassiz Circle, Buffalo NY 14214. E-mail: ethan@slop e.org (for magazine) or info@slope.org (for press). Website: www.slope.org (for magazine) or www.slopeeditions.org (for press). Established 1999. **Editor-in-Chief:** Ethan Paquin. **Senior Editor:** Christopher Janke. **Managing Editors:** Molly Dorozenski and Jon Link. Member: CLMP.

• Poetry featured in *Slope* has been included in *The Best American Poetry*.

Magazine Needs *Slope* "is a quarterly, online journal of poetry featuring work that is challenging, dynamic, and innovative. We encourage new writers while continuing to publish award-winning and established poets from around the world." Wants "no particular style. Interested in poetry in translation." Has published poetry by Forrest Gander, Paul Hoover, Eleni Sikelianos, James Tate, Bruce Beasley, and Charles Bernstein.

Publishers of Poetry

How to Submit Submit 3-6 poems at a time. No previously published poems or simultaneous submissions. Accepts submissions by e-mail only (as attachments). "Submit poems via e-mail to the address on the website." Reads submissions year round. Time between acceptance and publication is 3-6 months. Seldom comments on rejected poems. Guidelines available by e-mail or on website. Responds in 3 months. Acquires one-time rights. Reviews books and chapbooks of poetry in 400 words, single book format. Send materials for review consideration; "query first."

Book/Chapbook Needs "Slope Editions publishes books of innovative poetry." Wants "writing of superior quality, of no particular style. As an offshoot of the online journal *Slope*, Slope Editions believes in actively promoting and supporting its authors, especially via the Web." Has published (first books) *The Body* by Jenny Boully, *Bivouac* by Laura Solomon, *Maine* by Jonah Winter, *Unfathoms* by Kirsten Kaschock, and *Zoo Music* by William Waltz. Manuscripts are selected through competition (see below). Books are professionally-printed paperbacks, perfect-bound, 60-120 pages.

Contest/Award Offerings Slope Editions Book Prize, an annual contest whose past judges include David Lehman, Dean Young, and Donald Revell. Winner receives $1,000 and publication. See website for complete guidelines.

◢ SMARTISH PACE; ERSKINE J. POETRY PRIZE

P.O. Box 22161, Baltimore MD 21203. Website: www.smartishpace.com. Established 1999. **Editor:** Stephen Reichert.

Magazine Needs *Smartish Pace*, published in April and October, contains poetry and translations. "*Smartish Pace* is an independent poetry journal and is not affiliated with any institution." No restrictions on style or content of poetry. Has published poetry by Campbell McGrath, Carl Dennis, Paul Muldoon, Maxine Kumin, Alicia Ostriker, and Stephen Dunn. *Smartish Pace* is about 140 pages, digest-sized, professionally printed, perfect-bound, with color, heavy stock cover. Receives about 3,000 poems/year, accepts 4%; publishes 100 poems/issue. Press run is 500 for 300 subscribers. Subscription: $20. Sample: $6.

How to Submit Submit no more than 6 poems at a time. Accepts simultaneous submissions; no previously published poems. "Please provide prompt notice when poems have been accepted elsewhere. Cover letter with bio and SASE is required." Submit seasonal poems 8 months in advance. Time between acceptance and publication is up to one year. Guidelines available for SASE or on website. Responds in up to 8 months. Pays one contributor's copy. Acquires first rights. Encourages unsolicited reviews, essays, and interviews. Send materials for review consideration. All books received will also be listed in the Books Received section of each issue and on the website along with ordering information and a link to the publisher's website.

Contest/Award Offerings "*Smartish Pace* hosts the annual Erskine J. Poetry Prize. Submit 3 poems with $5 entry fee in either check or money order made payable to *Smartish Pace*. Additional poems may be submitted for $1 per poem. No more than 8 poems may be submitted (8 poems = $5 + $5 = $10). Winners receive cash prizes and publication. Recent winners include Dina Hardy, Christine Stewart, and Jacqueline Kolosov. See website for complete information."

Also Offers Also available on website: Poets Q&A, where you can ask questions of poets and read their responses. Recent participants include Robert Pinsky, Jorie Graham, Stephen Dunn, Carl Dennis, Eavan Boland, Campbell McGrath, and Robert Hass.

Advice "Visit our website. Read a few issues."

⊕ ◢ SMOKE

First Floor, Liver House, 96 Bold St., Liverpool L1 4HY England. Phone: (0151)709-3688. Website: www.windowsproject.demon.co.uk. Established 1974. **Editor:** Dave Ward.

Magazine Needs *Smoke* is a biannual publication of poetry and graphics. Wants "short, contemporary poetry, expressing new ideas through new forms." Has published poetry by Carol Ann Duffy,

Roger McGough, Jackie Kay, and Henry Normal. *Smoke* is 24 pages, A5, offset-litho-printed, stapled, with paper cover, includes art. Receives about 3,000 poems/year, accepts about 40. Press run is 750 for 350 subscribers of which 18 are libraries, 100 shelf sales; 100 distributed free to contributors/ other mags. Subscription: $5 (cash). Sample: $1. Make checks payable to Windows Project (cash preferred/exchanges rate on cheques not viable).

How to Submit Submit 6 poems at a time. Accepts previously published poems and simultaneous submissions. Cover letter preferred. Time between acceptance and publication is 6 months. Seldom comments on rejected poems. Responds in 2 weeks. Pays one contributor's copy.

$☑ ◎ SNOWY EGRET (Specialized: animals, nature)

P.O. Box 29, Terre Haute IN 47808. Established 1922 by Humphrey A. Olsen. **Contact:** Editors.

Magazine Needs Appearing in spring and autumn, *Snowy Egret* specializes in work that is "nature-oriented: poetry that celebrates the abundance and beauty of nature or explores the interconnections between nature and the human psyche." Has published poetry by Conrad Hilberry, Lyn Lifshin, Gayle Eleanor, James Armstrong, and Patricia Hooper. *Snowy Egret* is 60 pages, magazine-sized, offset, saddle-stapled, includes original graphics. Receives about 500 poems/year, accepts about 30. Press run is 800 for 500 subscribers of which 50 are libraries. Sample: $8; subscription: $15/year, $25/2 years.

How to Submit Guidelines available for #10 SASE. Responds in one month. Always sends prepublication galleys. Pays $4/poem or $4/page plus 2 contributor's copies. Acquires first North American and one-time reprint rights.

Advice "First-hand, detailed observation gives poetry authenticity and immediacy."

☐ SO YOUNG!; ANTI-AGING PRESS, INC.

P.O. Box 142174, Coral Gables FL 33114. (305)662-3928. Fax: (305)661-4123. E-mail: julia2@gate.n et. Established 1992 press, 1996 newsletter. **Editor:** Julia Busch.

Magazine Needs *So Young!* is a bimonthly newsletter publishing "anti-aging/holistic health/humorous/philosophical topics geared to a youthful body, attitude, and spirit." Wants "short, upbeat, fresh, positive poetry. The newsletter is dedicated to a youthful body, face, mind, and spirit. Work can be humorous, philosophical fillers. No off-color, suggestive poems, or anything relative to first night, or unrequited love affairs." *So Young!* is 12 pages, magazine-sized (8×11 sheets, 3-hole-punched, stapled), unbound. Receives several hundred poems/year, accepts 6-12. Press run is 700 for 500 subscribers. Subscription: $35. Sample: $6.

How to Submit Submit up to 10 poems at a time. Accepts previously published poems and simultaneous submissions. Prefers e-mail submissions (pasted into body of message). Cover letter is preferred. Time between acceptance and publication "depends on poem subject matter—usually 6-8 months." Guidelines available for SASE. Responds in 2 months. Pays 10 contributor's copies. Acquires one-time rights.

☑ THE SOCIETY OF AMERICAN POETS (SOAP); IN HIS STEPS PUBLISHING COMPANY; THE POET'S PEN; PRESIDENT'S AWARD FOR EXCELLENCE

P.O. Box 3563, Macon GA 31205-3563. (478)788-1848. Fax: (478)788-0925. E-mail: DrRev@cox.net. Established 1984. **Editor:** Dr. Charles E. Cravey.

Magazine Needs *The Poet's Pen* is a literary quarterly of poetry and short stories. "Open to all styles of poetry and prose—both religious and secular. No gross or 'X-rated' poetry without taste or character." Has published poetry by Najwa Salam Brax, Henry Goldman, Henry W. Gurley, William Heffner, Linda Metcalf, and Charles Russ. *The Poet's Pen* uses poetry primarily by members and subscribers, but outside submissions are also welcomed. Sample copy: $10. Membership: $30/ year; $25/students.

How to Submit Submit 3 poems per quarter, include name and address on each page. "Submissions or inquiries will not be responded to without a #10 business-sized SASE. We do stress originality and have each new poet and/or subscriber sign a waiver form verifying originality.'' Accepts simultaneous submissions and previously published poems, if permission from previous publisher is included. Publishes seasonal/theme issues. Upcoming themes and guidelines available for SASE, by fax, in publication, or by e-mail. Sometimes sends prepublication galleys. Editor ''most certainly'' comments on rejected poems.

Book/Chapbook Needs & How to Submit In His Steps publishes religious and other books. Also publishes music for the commercial record market. Query for book publication.

Contest/Award Offerings Sponsors several contests each quarter which total $100-250 in cash awards. Editor's Choice Awards each quarter. President's Award for Excellence has a prize of $50; **deadline:** November 1. Also publishes a quarterly anthology that has poetry competitions in several categories with prizes of $25-100.

Advice ''Be honest with yourself above all else. Read the greats over and again and study styles, grammar, and what makes each unique. Meter, rhythm, and rhyme are still the guidelines that are most acceptable today.''

$ ▨ ◎ SOJOURNERS (Specialized: religious; political)

2401 15th St. NW, Washington DC 20009. (202)328-8842. Website: www.sojo.com. Established 1975. **Poetry Editor:** Rose Marie Berger.

Magazine Needs *Sojourners* appears 6 times/year. ''We focus on faith, politics, and culture from a radical Christian perspective. We publish one poem/month depending on length. We look for seasoned, well-crafted poetry that reflects the issues and perspectives covered in our magazine. Poetry using non-inclusive language (any racist, sexist, or homophobic poetry) will not be accepted.'' *Sojourners* is about 48 pages, magazine-sized, offset-printed, saddle-stapled, with 4-color paper cover, includes photos and illustrations throughout. Receives about 400 poems/year, accepts approximately 10-12. Press run is 50,000 for 40,000 subscribers of which 500 are libraries, 2,000 shelf sales. Single copy: $4.95; subscription: $30. Sample free.

How to Submit Submit up to 3 poems at a time. Line length for poetry is 30 maximum. ''All poems must be original and unpublished.'' Accepts submissions by postal mail only (no electronic or faxed submissions). Cover letter with brief (3 sentences) bio is required. Editor occasionally comments on submissions. Guidelines available on website. Pays $25/poem plus 5 contributor's copies. ''We assume permission to grant reprints unless the author requests otherwise.''

Advice ''Read the magazine first to familiarize yourself with our perspective.''

Ⓝ ▨ ◎ SONG OF THE SAN JOAQUIN (Specialized: regional/San Joaquin Valley); POETS OF THE SAN JOAQUIN

P.O. Box 1161, Modesto CA 95353-1161. E-mail: SSJQ03psj@yahoo.com. Website: www.Chaparral Poets.org/html. Established 2003. **Contact:** Editor.

Magazine Needs *Song of the San Joaquin* appears quarterly and features ''subjects about or pertinent to the San Joaquin Valley of Central California. This is defined geographically as the region from Fresno to Stockton, and from the foothills on the west to those on the east.'' Wants all forms and styles of poetry. ''Keep subject in mind.'' Does not want pornographic, demeaning, vague, or trite approaches. Has published poetry by Susan Wooldridge, debee loyd, Gordon Durham, Marnelle White, Tom Myers, and Nancy Haskett. *Song of the San Joaquin* is 44 pages, digest-sized, directcopied, saddle-stapled, with cardstock cover with glossy color photo. Publishes about 40 poems/issue. Press run is 200, ''subscriber base still to be determined,'' 25 copies to libraries; 40 are distributed free to contributors.

How to Submit Submit up to 5 poems at a time. Line length is open, ''however, poems under 40 lines have the best chance.'' Accepts previously published poems; no simultaneous submissions. No e-mail or disk submissions. Cover letter is preferred. ''SASE required. All submissions must be typed on one side of the page only. Proofread submissions carefully. Name, address, phone number, e-mail address on all pages. Cover letter should include any awards, honors, and previous publications for each poem, and a biographical sketch of 75 words or less." Reads submissions "periodically throughout the year." Submit seasonal poems at least 3 months in advance. Time between acceptance and publication is 3-6 months. "Poems are circulated to an editorial board of 5 who then decide on the final selections." Seldom comments on rejected poems. Occasionally publishes theme issues. List of upcoming themes available for SASE, by e-mail, or on website. Guidelines available in magazine, for SASE, by e-mail, or on website. Responds in up to 3 months. Pays one contributor's copy. Acquires one-time rights.

Contest/Award Offerings "Poets of the San Joaquin, which sponsors this publication, is a chapter of California Federation of Chaparral Poets, Inc. PSJ holds an annual local young poets' contest as well as regular poetry contests, and publishes an annual anthology of members' works. Information available for SASE or by e-mail."

Advice "Know the area about which you write. Poems do not need to be agricultural or nature-oriented but should reflect the lifestyles of the California Central Valley."

✪ ☑ SOUNDINGS EAST

Salem State College, Salem MA 01970. (978)542-6205. Website: www.salemstate.edu/soundingse ast/. Established 1978. **Advisory Editor:** J.D. Scrimgeour.

Magazine Needs "*Soundings East* is published once/year in May by Salem State College. We accept short fiction, creative nonfiction, short reviews, and contemporary poetry. We publish both established and previously unpublished writers and artists. All forms of poetry welcome." Has published poetry by Allison Joseph, Virgil Suárez, and Bill Tremblay. *Soundings East* is 64 pages, digest-sized, flat-spined, with glossy card cover with b&w photo, includes b&w drawings and photos. Receives about 500 submissions/year, accepts about 40-50. Press run is 2,000 for 120 subscribers of which 35 are libraries. Subscription: $10/year. Sample: $5.

How to Submit Submit 3-8 poems at a time. Accepts simultaneous submissions with notification. Be prompt when notifying *Soundings East* that work was accepted elsewhere. Reads submissions September 1 through April 20 only. Fall deadline: November 20; spring: April 20. Guidelines available in magazine or on website. Responds within 4 months. Pays 3 contributor's copies. Rights revert to author upon publication.

✪ ☑ SOUTH CAROLINA REVIEW

Center for Electronic & Digital Publishing, 611 Strode Tower, Clemson University, Box 340522, Clemson SC 29634-0522. (864)656-3151 or 656-5399. Fax: (864)656-1345. Website: www.clemson. edu/caah/cedp/scrintio.htm. Established 1968. **Editor:** Wayne Chapman.

Magazine Needs *South Carolina Review* is a biannual literary magazine "recognized by the *New York Quarterly* as one of the top 20 of this type." Will consider "any kind of poetry as long as it's good. No stale metaphors, uncertain rhythms, or lack of line integrity. Interested in seeing more traditional forms. Format should be according to new MLA Stylesheet." Has published poetry by Stephen Cushman, Alberto Ríos, and Richard Rodriguez. *South Carolina Review* is 200 pages, digest-sized, professionally printed, flat-spined, and uses about 25-40 pages of poetry in each issue. Reviews of recent issues back up editorial claims that all styles and forms are welcome; moreover, poems were accessible and well-executed. Press run is 600 for 400 subscribers of which 250 are libraries. Receives about 1,000 submissions of poetry/year, accepts about 60; has a one-year backlog. Sample: $12.

How to Submit Submit 3-10 poems at a time in an "8×10 manila envelope so poems aren't creased." No previously published poems or simultaneous submissions. No e-mail submissions. "Editor prefers a chatty, personal cover letter plus a list of publishing credits." Do not submit during June, July, August, or December. Publishes theme issues. Responds in 2 months. Pays in contributor's copies. Staff reviews books of poetry.

✅ ◎ THE SOUTHERN CALIFORNIA ANTHOLOGY (Specialized: anthology); ANN STANFORD POETRY PRIZES

c/o Master of Professional Writing Program, WPH 404, University of Southern California, Los Angeles CA 90089-4034. (213)740-3252. Established 1983.

Magazine Needs *The Southern California Anthology* is an "annual literary review of serious contemporary poetry and fiction. Very open to all subject matters except pornography. Any form, style OK." Has published poetry by Robert Bly, Donald Hall, Allen Ginsberg, Lisel Mueller, James Ragan, Nikki Giovanni, W.S. Merwin, and John Updike. *The Southern California Anthology* is 144 pages, digest-sized, perfect-bound, with a semi-glossy color cover featuring one art piece. Press run is 1,500, with 50% going to subscribers of which 50% are libraries, 30% are for shelf sales. Sample: $5.95.

How to Submit Submit 3-5 poems between September 1 and January 1 only. No simultaneous submissions or previously published poems. All decisions made by mid-February. Guidelines available for SASE. Responds in 4 months. Pays 2 contributor's copies. Acquires all rights.

Contest/Award Offerings The Ann Stanford Poetry Prizes ($1,000, $200, and $100) for unpublished poems. **Entry fee:** $10 (5 poem limit). **Deadline:** April 15. Include cover sheet with name, address, and titles, as well as SASE for contest results. All entries are considered for publication, and all entrants receive a copy of *The Southern California Anthology*.

$ ☑ THE SOUTHERN REVIEW

43 Allen Hall, Louisiana State University, Baton Rouge LA 70803-5005. (225)578-5108. Fax: (225)578-5098. E-mail: bmacon@lsu.edu. Website: www.lsu.edu/thesouthernreview. Established 1935 (original series), 1965 (new series). **Editor:** James Olney. **Associate Editor:** John Easterly.

• Work published in this review has been frequently included in *The Best American Poetry* and appeared in *The Beacon's Best of 1999*.

Magazine Needs *The Southern Review* "is a literary quarterly that publishes fiction, poetry, critical essays, and book reviews, with emphasis on contemporary literature in the U.S. and abroad, and with special interest in Southern culture and history. Selections are made with careful attention to craftsmanship and technique and to the seriousness of the subject matter. We are interested in any variety of poetry that is well crafted, though we cannot normally accommodate excessively long poems (i.e., 10 pages and over)." All styles and forms welcome, although accessible lyric and narrative free verse appear most often in recent issues. Has published poetry by Mary Oliver, Sharon Olds, Reynolds Price, and Ellen Bryant Voigt. *The Southern Review* is 240 pages, digest-sized, flat-spined, with matte card cover. Receives about 6,000 submissions of poetry/year. Press run is 2,500 for 2,100 subscribers of which 70% are libraries. Subscription: $25. Sample: $8.

How to Submit "We do not require a cover letter, but we prefer one giving information about the author and previous publications." Prefers submissions of up to 6 pages. No fax or e-mail submissions. Guidelines available for SASE or on website. Responds in one month. Pays $20/printed page plus 2 contributor's copies. Acquires first North American serial rights. Staff reviews books of poetry in 3,000 words, multi-book format. Send materials for review consideration.

$ ☑ SOUTHWEST REVIEW; ELIZABETH MATCHETT STOVER MEMORIAL AWARD; MORTON MARR POETRY PRIZE

307 Fondren Library West, P.O. Box 750374, Southern Methodist University, Dallas TX 75275-0374. (214)768-1037. Fax: (214)768-1408. E-mail: swr@mail.smu.edu. Website: www.southwestreview. org. Established 1915. **Editor:** Willard Spiegelman.

• Poetry published in *Southwest Review* has been included in *The Best American Poetry* and the *Pushcart Prize* anthology.

Magazine Needs *Southwest Review* is a literary quarterly that publishes fiction, essays, poetry, and interviews. "It is hard to describe our preference for poetry in a few words. We always suggest that potential contributors read several issues of the magazine to see for themselves what we like. But some things may be said: We demand very high quality in our poems; we accept both traditional and experimental writing, but avoid unnecessary obscurity and private symbolism; we place no arbitrary limits on length but find shorter poems easier to fit into our format than longer ones. We have no specific limitations as to theme." Has published poetry by Albert Goldbarth, John Hollander, Mary Jo Salter, James Hoggard, Dorothea Tanning, and Michael Rosen. *Southwest Review* is 144 pages, digest-sized, perfect-bound, professionally printed, with matte text stock cover. Receives about 1,000 submissions of poetry/year, accepts about 32. Poems tend to be lyric and narrative free verse combining a strong voice with powerful topics or situations. Diction is accessible and content often conveys a strong sense of place. Circulation is 1,500 for 1,000 subscribers of which 600 are libraries. Subscription: $24. Sample: $6.

How to Submit No simultaneous submissions or previously published poems. Guidelines available for SASE or on website. Responds within one month. Always sends prepublication galleys. Pays cash plus contributor's copies.

Contest/Award Offerings The $250 Elizabeth Matchett Stover Memorial Award is awarded annually for the best poems, chosen by editors, published in the preceding year. The $1,000 Morton Marr Poetry Prize gives an annual award to a poem by a writer who has not yet published a first book; poems submitted should be in a "traditional" form. Details available on website.

☑ THE SOW'S EAR POETRY REVIEW

355 Mount Lebanon Rd., Donalds SC 29638-9115. (864)379-8061. E-mail: errol@kitenet.net. Established 1988. **Editor:** Kristin Camitta Zimet. **Contact:** Errol Hess, managing editor.

Magazine Needs *The Sow's Ear* is a quarterly. "We are open to many forms and styles, and have no limitations on length. We try to be interesting visually, and we use graphics to complement the poems. Though we publish some work from our local community of poets, we are interested in poems from all over. We publish a few by previously unpublished poets." Has recently published poetry by Andrea Carter Brown, Corrine Clegg Hales, Jerry McGuire, Virgil Suárez, Susan Terris, and Franz Wright. *The Sow's Ear Poetry Review* is 32 pages, magazine-sized, professionally printed, saddle-stapled, with matte card cover. Receives about 2,000 poems/year, accepts about 100. Press run is 600 for 500 subscribers of which 15 are libraries, 20-40 shelf sales. Subscription: $10. Sample: $5.

How to Submit Submit up to 5 poems at a time with SASE. Accepts simultaneous submissions if you tell them promptly when work is accepted elsewhere; no previously published poems. Enclose brief bio. No e-mail submissions. Guidelines available for SASE or by e-mail. Responds in up to 6 months. Pays 2 contributor's copies. Acquires first publication rights. Most prose (reviews, interviews, features) is commissioned.

Contest/Award Offerings Offers an annual contest for unpublished poems. **Entry fee:** $2/poem. 1st Prize: $1,000; publication for 15-20 finalists. For contest, submit poems in September/October, with name and address on a separate sheet. Submissions of 5 poems/$10 receive a subscription. Include SASE for notification. 2001 Judge: Dabney Stuart. Also sponsors a chapbook contest in March/April. **Entry fee:** $10. 1st Prize: $1,000, publication, 25 author's copies, and distribution to subscribers. Send SASE or e-mail for chapbook contest guidelines.

Advice "Four criteria help us judge the quality of submissions: Does the poem make the strange familiar or the familiar strange or both? Is the form of the poem vital to its meaning? Do the sounds of the poem make sense in relation to the theme? Does the little story of the poem open a window on the Big Story of the human situation?"

N ☑ SP QUILL QUARTERLY MAGAZINE

Shadow Poetry, P.O. Box 125, Excelsior Springs MO 64024. Fax: (208)977-9114. E-mail: spquill@sh adowpoetry.com. Website: www.shadowpoetry.com/magazine/spquill.html. Established 2000 (Shadow Poetry website); 2003 (*SP Quill*). **Contact:** Marie Summers, chief editor. Poetry Editor: Andrea Dietrich.

Magazine Needs *"SP Quill Quarterly Magazine* is a chapbook-style magazine for poets, writers, and poetry lovers, filled with poetry, short stories, book reviews, contests, interviews, profiles, and more." Wants high quality poetry, short stories, and artwork. Does not want "anything in poor taste." Accepts poetry, stories, quotes, and artwork from ages 13 and up. *SP Quill Quarterly Magazine* is 52 pages, digest-sized, saddle-stapled, with cardstock cover with b&w artwork (cover design remains the same from issue to issue), includes ads related to poetry, writing, and publishing. Receives about 300 poems/quarter, accepts about 50/issue. Single copy: $7.95 US, $8.95 Canada, $9.95 international; subscription: $20/year U.S., $24/year Canada, $28/year international. Make checks payable to Shadow Poetry.

How to Submit Submit one poem at a time. Line length for poetry is 3 minimum, 30 maximum. Accepts simultaneous submissions; no previously published poems. Accepts fax, e-mail (pasted into body of message), and disk submissions as well as submissions through online form. Cover letter is preferred. "Name of author, street address, and e-mail address must accompany all submissions, no exceptions. A small author bio may accompany poetry. If work is accepted, participants will be contacted by mail or e-mail within 3 weeks of magazine release date. Rejection letters are not sent." Submission deadlines are November 20 (Winter issue), February 28 (Spring issue), May 31 (Summer issue), and August 31 (Fall issue). Time between acceptance and publication is 3 weeks. "Poems are decided upon and edited by the poetry editor and chief editor. Final drafts will be e-mailed or mailed to the accepted poet." Never comments on rejected poems. Welcomes seasonal poems for the appropriate issue. Guidelines available in magazine or on website. Acquires first rights. Reviews books and chapbooks of poetry.

Contact/Award Offerings Shadow Poetry sponsors The Little Bitty Poetry Competition, Rhyme Time Poetry Contest, Shadow Poetry Seasonal Poetry Competition, Shadow Poetry's Bi-Annual Chapbook Competition, and Zen Garden Haiku Contest. (See separate listings in the Contests & Awards section.)

☑ SPILLWAY

P.O. Box 7887, Huntington Beach CA 92615-7887. (714)968-0905. Website: www.tebotbach.org. Established 1991. **Editors:** Mifanwy Kaiser and J.D. Lloyd.

Magazine Needs *Spillway* is an annual journal, published in November, "celebrating writing's diversity and power to affect our lives. Open to all voices, schools, and tendencies. We publish poetry, translations, reviews, essays, and b&w photography." Has published poetry by John Balaban, Sam Hamill, Robin Chapman, Richard Jones, and Eleanor Wilner. *Spillway* is about 176 pages, digest-sized, attractively printed, perfect-bound, with 2-color or 4-color card cover. Press run is 2,000. Single copy: $9; subscription: $16/2 issues, $28/4 issues. Sample (including guidelines): $10. Make checks payable to *Spillway*.

How to Submit Submit 3-6 poems at a time, 10 pages total. Accepts previously published work ("say when and where") and simultaneous submissions ("say where also submitted"). Accepts e-mail (as a Word attachment or pasted into body of message) or disk submissions. Cover letter with brief bio and SASE required. Reads submissions year round. "No cute bios." Responds in up to 6 months. Pays one contributor's copy. Acquires one-time rights. Reviews books of poetry in 500-2,500 words maximum. Send materials for review consideration.

Advice "We have no problem with simultaneous or previously published submissions. Poems are murky creatures—they shift and change in time and context. It's exciting to pick up a volume, read a poem in the context of all the other pieces, and then find the same poem in another time and place. And, we don't think a poet should have to wait until death to see work in more than one volume. What joy to find out that more than one editor values one's work. Our responsibility as editors, collectively, is to promote the work of poets as much as possible—how can we do this if we say to a writer, 'you may only have a piece published in one volume and only one time'? "

◘ SPINDRIFT

Shoreline Community College, 16101 Greenwood Ave. N., Seattle WA 98133. (206)546-5864. E-mail: spindrift@shore.ctc.edu. Established 1962. Faculty Advisor: Gary Parks. **Contact:** Poetry Editor.

Magazine Needs *Spindrift*, published annually, is open to all varieties of poetry except greeting card style. Has published poetry by Lyn Lifshin, Mary Lou Sanelli, James Bertolino, Edward Harkness, and Richard West. *Spindrift* is 125 pages, handsomely printed, 8″ square, flat-spined, includes visual art as well as literature. Press run is 500. Single copy: $8. Sample: $2.

How to Submit "Submit 2 copies of each poem, 6 lines maximum. The author's name should not appear on the submitted work. Include SASE and cover letter with 2-3 lines of biographical information including name, address, phone number, e-mail address, and a list of all materials sent. We accept submissions postmarked between September and January; editorial responses are mailed by March 15." Guidelines available for SASE. Pays one contributor's copy. All rights revert to author upon publication.

Advice "Read the magazine. Be distinctive, love language, work from the heart, but avoid sentimentality."

◘ SPINNING JENNY

Black Dress Press, P.O. Box 1373, New York NY 10276. Website: www.blackdresspress.com. Established 1994. **Editor:** C.E. Harrison.

Magazine Needs *Spinning Jenny* appears once/year in April. Has published poetry by Tina Cane, Sara Fox, Matthew Lippman, and Ian Randall Wilson. *Spinning Jenny* is 112 pages, digest-sized, perfect-bound, with heavy card cover. "We accept less than 5% of unsolicited submissions." Press run is 1,000. Single copy: $8; subscription: $15/2 issues. Sample: $8.

How to Submit No previously published poems or simultaneous submissions. Accepts e-mail submissions (include in body of message). Seldom comments on rejected poems. Guidelines available for SASE or on website. Responds within 3 months. Pays 5 contributor's copies. Authors retain rights.

◘ ◙ SPITBALL: THE LITERARY BASEBALL MAGAZINE; CASEY AWARD (Specialized: baseball)

5560 Fox Rd., Cincinnati OH 45239. Website: www.angelfire.com/oh5/spitball, Established 1981. **Editor-in-Chief:** Mike Shannon.

Magazine Needs *Spitball* is "a unique biannual magazine devoted to poetry, fiction, and book reviews exclusively about baseball. Newcomers are very welcome, but remember that you have to know the subject; we do, and our readers do. Perhaps a good place to start for beginners is one's personal reactions to the game, a game, a player, etc., and take it from there." *Spitball* is 96-pages, digest-sized, computer typeset, perfect-bound. Receives about 1,000 submissions/year, accepts about 40. "Many times we are able to publish accepted work almost immediately." Circulation is 1,000 for 750 subscribers of which 25 are libraries. Subscription: $12. Sample: $6. "**We now require all first-time submitters to purchase a sample copy for $6.** This is a one-time-only fee, which we regret, but economic reality dictates that we insist those who wish to be published in *Spitball* help support it, at least at this minimum level."

How to Submit "We are not very concerned with the technical details of submitting, but we do prefer a cover letter with some bio info. We also like batches of poems and prefer to use several of same poet in an issue rather than a single poem." Pays 2 contributor's copies.

Contest/Award Offerings "We sponsor the Casey Award (for best baseball book of the year) and hold the Casey Awards Banquet in late February or early March. Any chapbook of baseball poetry should be sent to us for consideration for the 'Casey' plaque that we award to the winner each year."

Advice "Take the subject seriously. We do. In other words, get a clue (if you don't already have one) about the subject and about the poetry that has alreadyd been done and published about baseball. Learn from it . . . think about what you can add to the canon that is original and fresh . . . and don't assume that just anybody with the feeblest of efforts can write a baseball poem worthy of publication. And most importantly, stick with it. Genius seldom happens on the first try."

ℕ ◪ THE SPLINTER REVIEW

P.O. Box 471303, San Francisco CA 94147. E-mail: submissions@thesplinterreview.com. Website: www.thesplinterreview.com. Established 2003. **Editor:** Madeleine Shephard. **Contributing Editor:** Kevin McKelvey.

Magazine Needs *The Splinter Review* is published biannually and features poetry, fiction, nonfiction, and book reviews. Wants "tangible poetry to capture slivers of human experience." Does not want religious, inspirational, violent, or pornographic verse. Has published poetry by Michael Scott Cain, Rhonda Janzen, and Tucker Burton. *The Splinter Review* is 30-40 pages, magazine-sized, professionally-printed, saddle-stapled, with glossy cover with b&w photography or artwork. Receives about 800 poems/year, accepts about 3%. Publishes about 12 poems/issue. Press run is 200 for 175 subscribers; 20 are distributed free to contributing writers. Single copy: $6; subscription: $12. Make checks payable to *The Splinter Review*.

How to Submit Submit 3-5 poems at a time. Line length for poetry is 5 minimum, 50 maximum. Accepts simultaneous submissions; no previously published poems. No e-mail or disk submissions. Cover letter is required. "Avoid folding submissions. Cover letters should state whether poems have been simultaneously submitted. A brief biography including previously published work is preferred. Submissions without SASE will not be considered." Reads submissions year round. Submit seasonal poems 6 months in advance. Time between acceptance and publication varies. Poems are read by at least 2 contributing editors. Often comments on rejected poems. Occasionally publishes theme issues. List of upcoming themes available for SASE or on website. Guidelines available in magazine, for SASE, or on website. Responds in 3 months. Pays one contributor's copy. Acquires one-time rights.

⊞ ◯ SPLIZZ

4 St. Marys Rise, Burry Port, Carms SA16 OSH Wales. E-mail: a_jmorgan@yahoo.co.uk. Website: www.stmarys4.freeserve.co.uk/Splizz.htm. Established 1993. **Editor:** Amanda Morgan.

Magazine Needs *Splizz*, published quarterly, features poetry, prose, reviews of contemporary music, and background to poets. Wants "any kind of poetry. We have no restrictions regarding style, length, subjects." Does not want "anything racist or homophobic." Has published Colin Cross (UK), Anders Carson (Canada), Paul Truttman (U.S.), Jan Hansen (Portugal), and Gregory Arena (Italy). *Splizz* is 40-44 pages, A5, saddle-stapled, includes art and ads. Receives about 200-300 poems/year, accepts about 90%. Press run is 150 for 35 subscribers. Single copy: £1.50 UK, 5 IRCs elsewhere; subscription: £6 UK, £10 elsewhere. Sample: £1.50 UK, 5 IRCs elsewhere. Make checks payable to Amanda Morgan (British checks only).

How to Submit Submit 5 poems, typed submissions preferred. Name and address must be included on each page of submitted work. Include SAE with IRCs. No previously published poems or simultaneous submissions. Accepts e-mail submissions (as attachments). Cover letter with short bio is required. Time between acceptance and publication is 4 months. Often comments on rejected poems. Charges criticism fee: "Just enclose SAE/IRC for response, and allow 1-2 months for delivery. For those sending IRCs, please ensure that they have been correctly stamped by your post office." Guidelines available in magazine, for SASE (or SAE and IRC), or by e-mail. Responds in 2 months. Sometimes sends prepublication galleys. Reviews books or chapbooks of poetry or other magazines in 50-300 words. Send materials for review consideration. E-mail for further enquiries. **Advice** "Beginners seeking to have their work published, send your work to *Splizz*, as we specialize in giving new poets a chance."

THE SPOON RIVER POETRY REVIEW; SPOON RIVER EDITORS' PRIZE CONTEST

4240/English Dept., Illinois State University, Normal IL 61790-4240. Website: www.litline.org/spoon. Established 1976. **Editor:** Lucia Getsi.

Magazine Needs *Spoon River Poetry Review* is a biannual "poetry magazine that features newer and well-known poets from around the country and world." Also features one Illinois poet/issue at length for the magazine's Illinois Poet Series. "We want interesting and compelling poetry that operates beyond the ho-hum, so-what level, in any form or style about anything; language that is fresh, energetic, committed; a poetics aware of itself and of context." Also uses translations of poetry. Has published poetry by Stuart Dybek, Robin Behn, Dave Smith, Beth Ann Fennelly, Dorothea Grünzweig, and Alicia Ostriker. *Spoon River Poetry Review* is 128 pages, digest-sized, laser-set, with card cover, includes photos and ads. Receives about 3,000 poems/month, accepts 1%. Press run is 1,500 for 800 subscribers, of which 100 are libraries. Subscription: $16. Sample (including guidelines): $10.

How to Submit "No simultaneous submissions unless we are notified immediately if a submission is accepted elsewhere. Include name and address on every poem." Do not submit mss April 15 through September 15. Editor comments on rejected poems "many times, if a poet is promising." Guidelines available in magazine or on website. Responds in 3 months. Pays a year's subscription. Acquires first North American serial rights. Reviews books of poetry. Send materials for review consideration.

Contest/Award Offerings Sponsors the Editor's Prize Contest for previously unpublished work. One poem will be awarded $1,000 and published in the fall issue of *Spoon River Poetry Review*, and two runners-up will receive $100 each and publication in the fall issue. Entries must be previously unpublished. **Entry fee:** $16, includes one-year subscription. **Deadline:** April 15. Write for details. Past winners include Aleida Rodríguez and Susette Bishop.

Advice "Read. Workshop with poets who are better than you. Subscribe to at least 5 literary magazines a year, especially those you'd like to be published in."

SPOUT MAGAZINE

P.O. Box 581067, Minneapolis MN 55458-1067. Website: www.spoutpress.com. Established 1989. **Editors:** John Colburn and Michelle Filkins.

Magazine Needs *Spout* appears approximately 3 times/year providing "a paper community of unique expression." Wants "poetry of the imagination, poetry that surprises. We enjoy the surreal, the forceful, the political, the expression of confusion." No light verse, archaic forms or language. Has published poetry by Gillian McCain, Larissa Szporluk, Matt Hart, Sarah Manguso, and Richard Siken. *Spout* is 40-60 pages, saddle-stapled, with card stock or glossy cover (different color each issue). Receives about 400-450 poems/year, accepts about 10%. Press run is 200-250 for 35-40 subscribers, 100-150 shelf sales. Single copy: $4; subscription: $15. Sample: $4.

How to Submit Submit up to 6 poems at a time. Accepts previously published poems and simultaneous submissions. Cover letter preferred. Time between acceptance and publication is 2-3 months. Poems are circulated to an editorial board. "Poems are reviewed by 2 of 3 editors, those selected for final review are read again by all 3." Seldom comments on rejected poems. Guidelines available for SASE or on website. Responds in 4 months. Pays one contributor's copy.

Advice "Read a copy of the magazine to understand our editorial biases."

☑ ◎ SPRING: THE JOURNAL OF THE E.E. CUMMINGS SOCIETY (Specialized: membership/subscription)

33-54 164th St., Flushing NY 11358-1442. (718)353-3631 or (718)461-9022. Fax: (718)353-4778. E-mail: EECSPRINGNF@aol.com. Website: www.gvsu.edu/english/Cummings/Index.html. **Editor:** Norman Friedman.

Magazine Needs *Spring* is an annual publication, usually appearing in fall, designed "to maintain and broaden the audience for Cummings and to explore various facets of his life and art." Wants poems in the spirit of Cummings, primarily poems of one page or less. Nothing "amateurish." Has published poetry by John Tagliabue, Jacqueline Vaught Brogan, and Gerald Locklin. *Spring* is about 180 pages, digest-sized, offset-printed, perfect-bound, with light card stock cover. Press run is 500 for 200 subscribers of which 15 are libraries, 300 shelf sales. Subscription or sample: $17.50.

How to Submit No previously published poems or simultaneous submissions. Accepts submissions by fax and by e-mail (as attachment). Cover letter is required. Reads submissions January through March only. Seldom comments on rejected poems. Guidelines available for SASE. Responds in 6 months. Pays one contributor's copy.

Advice "Contributors are required to subscribe."

🔀 ◻ ◎ SPRING TIDES (Specialized: children)

Savannah Country Day School, 824 Stillwood Dr., Savannah GA 31419-2643. (912)925-8800. Fax: (912)920-7800. E-mail: Houston@savcds.org. Website: www.savcds.org. Established 1989. **Contact:** Connie Houston.

Magazine Needs Appearing in December, *Spring Tides* is an annual literary magazine by children 5-12 years of age. "Children from ages 5 through 12 may submit material. Please limit poems to 20 lines. All material must be original and created by the person submitting it. A statement signed by the child's parent or teacher attesting to the originality must accompany all work." *Spring Tides* is 28 pages, digest-sized, attractively printed, saddle-stapled, with glossy card cover, includes b&w and 4-color art. Press run is 500; given to students at Savannah Country Day School and sold to others. Single copy: $5.

How to Submit Accepts simultaneous submissions. Accepts submissions by postal mail only. SASE required. "Poems with or without illustrations may be submitted." Reads submissions January through August only. Poems are circulated to an editorial board. Always comments on rejected poems. Guidelines available in magazine or for SASE. Responds in 4 months. Pays one contributor's copy.

☑ SPUNK

Box 55336, Hayward CA 94545. (415)974-8980. Established 1996. **Editor:** Violet Jones.

Magazine Needs Appearing 2 times/year, *Spunk: The Journal of Unrealized Potential* contains "writings and artwork of every nature. We are an outlet for spontaneous expressions only. Save the self-satisfied, over-crafted stuff for *Paris Review*, please." *Spunk* is up to 70 pages, silkscreened, photocopied, hand-bound. Receives about 800-1,000 poems/year, accepts less than 5%. Press run is 500; all distributed free to anyone who really, really wants them. Sample: $1. No checks.

How to Submit Submit any number of poems at a time. No previously published poems or simultaneous submissions. Cover letter is preferred. "Just make us happy we opened the envelope—how you do this is up to you." Time between acceptance and publication is up to one year. Often comments on rejected poems. Occasionally publishes theme issues. Guidelines and upcoming themes available for SASE. Responds in up to one year. Pays one contributor's copy. Acquires first

North American serial rights. Staff occasionally reviews books and chapbooks of poetry and other magazines in 100-500 words, single book format. Send materials for review consideration. "Our review section has expanded; we run reviews every issue now."

✪ ⊕ $◪ STAND MAGAZINE

School of English, University of Leeds, Leeds LS2 9JT England. Phone: +44 (0)113 233 4794. Fax: +44 (0)113 233 4791. E-mail: stand@leeds.ac.uk. Website: www.people.vcu.edu/~dlatane/stand.html. **Contact:** Jon Glover, Matthew Welton, John Whale. **US Editor:** David Latané, Dept. of English, Virginia Commonwealth University, Richmond VA 23284-2005. E-mail: dlatane@vcu.edu.

Magazine Needs *Stand*, established by Jon Silkin in 1952, is a highly esteemed literary quarterly. *Stand* seeks more subscriptions from U.S. readers and also hopes that the magazine will be seriously treated as an alternative platform to American literary journals. *Library Journal* calls *Stand* "one of England's best, liveliest, and truly imaginative little magazines." Among better-known American poets whose work has appeared here are John Ashbery, Mary Jo Bang, Brian Henry, and Michael Mott. Poet Donald Hall says of it, "among essential magazines, there is Jon Silkin's *Stand*, politically left, with reviews, poems, and much translation from continental literature." *Stand* is about 64 pages, A5 (landscape), professionally printed on smooth stock, flat-spined, with matte color cover, includes ads. Press run is 2,000 for 1,000+ subscribers of which 600 are libraries. Subscription: $49.50. Sample: $13.

How to Submit No fax or e-mail submissions. Cover letter is required with submissions, "assuring us that work is not also being offered elsewhere." Publishes theme issues. Always sends prepublication galleys. Pays £25/poem (unless under 6 lines) and one contributor's copy. Acquires first world serial rights for 3 months after publication. If work appears elsewhere, *Stand* must be credited. Reviews books of poetry in 3,000-4,000 words, multi-book format. Send materials for review consideration.

⊕ $◪ STAPLE

Padley Rise, Nether Padley, Grindleford, Hope Valley, Derbys S32 2HE United Kingdom or 35 Carr Rd., Walkley, Sheffield S6 2WY United Kingdom. Established 1982 (redesigned 2001). **Co-Editors:** Ann Atkinson and Elizabeth Barrett.

Magazine Needs *Staple* appears 3 times/year and "accepts poetry, short fiction, and articles about the writing process." *Staple* is 100 pages, perfect-bound. Press run is 500 for 350 subscribers. Single copy: £5; subscription: £20/year. Sample: £3.50.

How to Submit Submit 6 poems at a time. No simultaneous submissions or previously published poems. Cover letter is preferred. Include SAE and 2 IRCs. Submission deadlines are end of March, July, and November. Editors sometimes comment on rejected poems. Responds in up to 3 months. Pays £5/poem.

Ⓝ ◪ STEEL TOE BOOKS; STEEL TOE BOOKS POETRY PRIZE

Dept. of English, 20C Cherry Hall, Western Kentucky University, 1 Big Red Way, Bowling Green KY 42101-3576. (270)745-5769. E-mail: tom.hunley@wku.edu. Established 2003. **Editor/Publisher:** Dr. Tom C. Hunley.

• "We currently do not read manuscripts outside of our annual contest." (See below.)

Book/Chapbook Needs & How to Submit Steel Toe Books publishes "full-length, single-author poetry collections. Our books are professionally-designed and -printed. We look for workmanship (economical use of language, high-energy verbs, precise literal descriptions, original figurative language, poems carefully arranged as a book); a unique style and/or a distinctive voice; clarity; emotional impact; humor (word plays, hyperbole, comic timing); performability (a Steel Toe poet is at home on the stage as well as on the page)." Does not want "dry verse, purposely obscure language, poetry by people who are so wary of being called 'sentimental' they steer away from any recognizable human emotions, poetry that takes itself so seriously that it's unintentionally funny.'' Has published poetry by James Doyle. Publishes one poetry book/year. Manuscripts are selected through competition. "During odd-numbered years (such as 2005), the contest is open to all poets. During even-numbered years (such as 2006), it is a first book contest. Poems are circulated to an editorial board and the winner is chosen by a well-known guest editor.'' Guest editors have included Charles Harper Webb (2004) and David Kirby (2003). Books are 48-64 pages, perfect-bound, full-color cover with art/graphics. Book mss may include previously published poems. Responds to mss in 3 months. Pays $500 and 26 author's copies (out of a press run of 500). Order sample books by sending $10 to Steel Toe Books.

Contest/Award Offerings Steel Toe Books Poetry Prize offers annual award of $500 plus 25 copies of a professionally-designed, full-length poetry collection. Submissions may be entered in other contests, and mss may include previously published poems. Submit 48-64 pages, any style of poetry ("would like to see more poetry in forms"). Include 2 title pages: one with contact information, one without. **Entry fee:** $20/book ms. **Deadline:** May 1. Competition receives about 70 mss/year. 2003 winner was James Doyle for *Einstein Considers a Sand Dune*, chosen by judge David Kirby. Winner will be announced by mail. Copies of winning books available from the publisher or through Amazon.com. "All entrants receive a copy." "When entering any contest, expect to get something in return for your entry fee. Everyone who enters our contest receives a) a copy of the winning book; b) personal comments on each manuscript submitted; and c) a reasonable chance of winning.''

$☐ STICKMAN REVIEW: AN ONLINE LITERARY JOURNAL

2890 N. Fairview Dr., Flagstaff AZ 86004. (386)254-8306. E-mail: editors@stickmanreview.com. Website: www.stickmanreview.com. Established 2001.

Magazine Needs *Stickman Review* is a biannual online literary journal dedicated to publishing great poetry, fiction, nonfiction, and artwork. Wants poetry "that is literary in intent, no restrictions on form, subject matter, or style. We would prefer not to see rhyming poetry." Publishes about 15 poems/issue.

How to Submit Submit 5 poems at a time. Accepts simultaneous submissions; no previously published poems. Accepts e-mail submissions *only*; no fax or disk submissions. Cover letter is preferred. Reads submissions year round. Time between acceptance and publication is 2 months. "Currently, the editors-in-chief review all submissions." Sometimes comments on rejected poems. Guidelines available on website. Responds in up to 4 months. Pays $10/poem, up to $20 per author. Acquires first rights.

Advice "Keep writing and submitting. A rejection is not necessarily a reflection upon the quality of your work. Be persistent, trust your instincts, and sooner or later, good things will come."

$☐ ⊚ STONE SOUP, THE MAGAZINE BY YOUNG WRITERS AND ARTISTS; THE CHILDREN'S ART FOUNDATION (Specialized: children)

P.O. Box 83, Santa Cruz CA 95063. (831)426-5557. Fax: (831)426-1161. E-mail: editor@stonesoup.com. Website: www.stonesoup.com. Established 1973. **Editor:** Ms. Gerry Mandel.

• *Stone Soup* has received both Parents' Choice and Edpress Golden Lamp Honor Awards.

Magazine Needs *Stone Soup* publishes writing and art by children through age 13; wants free verse poetry but no rhyming poetry, haiku, or cinquain. *Stone Soup*, published 6 times/year, is magazine-sized, professionally printed on heavy stock, with 10-12 full-color art reproductions inside and a full-color illustration on the coated cover, saddle-stapled. Receives 5,000 poetry submissions/year, accepts about 12. Publishes 2-4 pages of poetry/issue. Press run is 20,000 for 14,000 subscribers, 5,000 to bookstores, 1,000 other. Sample: $5. A membership in the Children's Art Foundation at $33/year includes a subscription to the magazine.

How to Submit Submissions can be any number of pages, any format. Include name, age, home address, and phone number. Don't include SASE; responds only to those submissions under consideration and cannot return mss. Do not send original artwork. No simultaneous submissions. No e-mail submissions. Guidelines available for SASE, by e-mail, or on website. Responds in up to 6 weeks. Pays $40, a certificate, and 2 contributor's copies plus discounts. Acquires all rights. Returns rights upon request. Open to reviews by children.

☑ STORY LINE PRESS; NICHOLAS ROERICH POETRY PRIZE

Three Oaks Farm, P.O. Box 1240, Ashland OR 97520-0055. (541)512-8792. Fax: (541)512-8793. E-mail: mail@storylinepress.com. Website: www.storylinepress.com. Established 1985. **Executive Director:** Robert McDowell.

- Books published by Story Line Press have received such prestigious awards as the Lenore Marshall Prize, the Whiting Award, and the Harold Morton Landon Prize.

Contest/Award Offerings Story Line Press publishes annually the winner of the Nicholas Roerich Poetry Prize for a first full-length collection of poetry. Offers $1,000 advance, publication, and a book launch/reading at the Roerich Museum in New York. Enter a ms of original poetry in English, at least 48 pages in length. Complete guidelines available for SASE or on website. **Entry fee:** $20 for reading and processing. **Deadline:** October 31.

Also Offers Story Line Press annually publishes 10-15 books of poetry, literary criticism, memoir, fiction, and books in translation. Has published collections by such poets as Alfred Corn, Annie Finch, Donald Justice, Mark Jarman, and David Mason. Query first.

☐ THE STORYTELLER

2441 Washington Rd., Maynard AR 72444. (870)647-2137. E-mail: storyteller1@cox-internet.com. Website: www.freewebz.com/fossilcreek. Established 1996. **Editor:** Regina Williams.

Magazine Needs *The Storyteller*, a quarterly magazine, "is geared to, but not limited to new writers and poets." Wants "any form up to 40 lines, any matter, any style, but must have a meaning. Do not throw words together and call it a poem. Nothing in way of explicit sex, violence, horror, or explicit language. I would like it to be understood that I have young readers, ages 9-18." Has published poetry by W.C. Jameson, Bryan Byrd, and Sol Rubin. *Storyteller* is 72 pages, magazine-sized, desktop-published, with slick cover with original pen & ink drawings, includes ads. Receives about 300 poems/year, accepts about 40%. Press run is 600 for over 500 subscribers. Single copy: $6 US, $8 Canada and foreign; subscription: $20; $24 Canada & foreign. Sample (if available): $6 US, $8 Canada and foreign.

How to Submit Submit 3 poems at a time, typed and double-spaced. Accepts previously published poems and simultaneous submissions, "but must state where and when poetry first appeared." Send submissions by postal mail only. Cover letter is preferred. **Reading fee:** $1/poem. Time between acceptance and publication is 9 months. Poems are circulated to an editorial board. "Poems are read and discussed by staff." Sometimes comments on rejected poems. Occasionally publishes theme issues. Upcoming themes and guidelines available for SASE; guidelines also available on website. Responds in up to 5 weeks. Acquires first or one-time rights. Reviews books and chapbooks of poetry by subscribers only. Send materials for review consideration to Ruthan Riney, associate editor.

Contest/Award Offerings Sponsors a quarterly contest. "Readers vote on their favorite poems. Winners receive copy of magazine and certificate suitable for framing. We also nominate for the Pushcart Prize." For yearly contest announcements and winners, go to http://expage.com/fossilcreekpub.

Advice "Be professional. Do not send 4 or 5 poems on one page. Send us poetry written from the heart."

☑ STRAY DOG; PRILLY & TRU PUBLICATIONS, INC.

P.O. Box 713, Amawalk NY 10501. E-mail: straydog@bestweb.net. Website: www.prillyandtru.com. Established 2000. **Editor/Publisher:** j.v. morrissey.

Magazine Needs *Stray Dog* appears annually in June or July and seeks "to publish the best, most powerful work we can find," including contemporary poetry, short-shorts, and art. "We print high-quality poetry, short-shorts, and b&w art in any form or style. We're looking for work that is evocative and incisive, work that will leave skid marks on the reader's emotional highway. Prior publication credits admired but not required." Does not want to see anything "preachy, whiny, obscure, pornographic, gratuitously violent, or trite." Has published poetry by A.D. Winans, Virgil Suárez, Richard Kostelanetz, Stephanie Dickinson, Joan P. Kincaid, t. kilgore spake, and Marco North. *Stray Dog* is 64 pages, digest-sized, Docutech-printed, saddle-stitched, with glossy card cover, includes b&w art. Receives about 1,500 poems/year, accepts 3%. Publishes about 40-45 poems/issue. Press run is 250. Single copy: $6; subscription: $6/year. Sample: $5. Make checks payable to Stray Dog.

How to Submit Submit 3-5 poems at a time. Line length for poetry is 2 pages maximum. Accepts simultaneous submissions; no previously published poems. No e-mail or disk submissions. Cover letter is preferred. "All submissions and correspondence must be accompanied by SASE for response and return of work; name/address/phone number on each page. No handwritten work. Include 2- to 3-line bio." Reads submissions year round. Time between acceptance and publication is within one year. Sometimes comments on rejected poems. Guidelines available for SASE, by fax, e-mail, or on website. Responds in up to 5 months. Pays 2 contributor's copies. Acquires first North American serial rights.

Book/Chapbook Needs & How to Submit Prilly & Tru Publications, Inc. is "not publishing books or chapbooks at this time, but plans to in the future."

Advice "Surprise me! Blow me away! Knock the neon-striped toe socks off my feet! Think 'indie' film, not network TV."

⊕ ◱ STRIDE PUBLICATIONS

11 Sylvan Rd., Exeter, Devon EX4 6EW England. E-mail: editor@stridebooks.co.uk. Website: www.stridebooks.co.uk and www.stridemagazine.co.uk. Established 1982. **Managing Editor:** Rupert Loydell.

Book/Chapbook Needs Stride Publications publishes poetry, poetry sequences, and an online magazine. Wants to see any poetry that is "new, inventive, nothing self-oriented, emotional, no narrative or fantasy, rhyming doggerel, light verse, or the merely-confessional." Has published work by Peter Redgrove, William Everson, Sheila E. Murphy, Peter Finch, and Charles Wright. Stride Publications publishes paperbacks (80-200 pages) of poetry, plus a few anthologies.

How to Submit Unsolicited submissions for book publication are accepted. "All submissions must be typewritten/word-processed and have an SAE included" with IRCs. Authors should read the submission guidelines on the website first. Cover letter required with bio, summary, and review quotes. Queries will be answered in 6 weeks and mss reported on in 3 months or more. Pays author's copies. Reviews of books and music for magazine welcome. E-mail for review guidelines. Send materials for review consideration.

⊕ ◱ ◎ STUDIO, A JOURNAL OF CHRISTIANS WRITING (Specialized: Christian, spirituality)

727 Peel St., Albury, New South Wales 2640 Australia. Phone/fax: 61 2 6021 1135. E-mail: pgrover@bigpond.com. Established 1980. **Publisher:** Paul Grover.

Magazine Needs *Studio* is a quarterly journal publishing "poetry and prose of literary merit, offering a venue for previously published, new, and aspiring writers, and seeking to create a sense of community among Christians writing." The journal also publishes occasional articles as well as news and reviews of writing, writers, and events of interest to members. In poetry, the editors want "shorter pieces but with no specification as to form or length (necessarily less than 200 lines), subject matter, style, or purpose. People who send material should be comfortable being published under this banner: *Studio, A Journal of Christians Writing.''* Has published poetry by John Foulcher, Les Murray, and other Australian poets. *Studio* is 36 pages, digest-sized, professionally printed on high-quality recycled paper, saddle-stapled, with matte card cover, includes graphics and line drawings. Press run is 300, all subscriptions. Subscription: $60 (Aud) for overseas members. Sample available (airmail to US) for $10 (Aud).

How to Submit Submissions must be typed and double-spaced on one side of A4 white paper. Accepts simultaneous submissions. Name and address must appear on the reverse side of each page submitted. Cover letter is required; include brief details of previous publishing history, if any. SAE with IRC required. Response time is 2 months; time between acceptance and publication is 9 months. Pays one contributor's copy. Acquires first Australian rights. Reviews books of poetry in 250 words, single book format. Send materials for review consideration.

Contest/Award Offerings The magazine conducts a biannual poetry and short story contest.

Advice ''The trend in Australia is for imagist poetry and poetry exploring the land and the self. Reading the magazine gives the best indication of style and standard, so send for a sample copy before sending your poetry. Keep writing, and we look forward to hearing from you.''

☑ STUDIO ONE

Haehn Campus Center, College of St. Benedict, St. Joseph MN 56374. E-mail: studio1@csbsju.edu. Established 1976. Editor changes yearly.

Magazine Needs *Studio One*, an annual literary and visual arts magazine appearing in May, is designed as a forum for local, regional, and national poets/writers. No specifications regarding form, subject matter, or style of poetry submitted. However, poetry no more than 2 pages stands a better chance of publication. Has published poetry by Bill Meissner, Eva Hooker, and Larry Schug. *Studio One* is 50-80 pages, typeset, with soft cover. Includes 1-3 short stories, 22-30 poems, and 10-13 visual art representations. Receives 600-800 submissions/year. No subscriptions, but a sample copy can be obtained by sending a self-addressed stamped manilla envelope and $6 for p&h. Make checks payable to *Studio One*.

How to Submit Accepts simultaneous submissions, no more than 5 per person. No previously published poems. Accepts e-mail submissions (pasted into body of message); clearly show page breaks and indentations. **Deadline:** January 1 for spring publication. Seldom comments on rejected poems. Send SASE for results.

☾ SULPHUR RIVER LITERARY REVIEW

P.O. Box 19228, Austin TX 78760-9228. (512)292-9456. Established 1978, reestablished 1987. **Editor/Publisher:** James Michael Robbins.

Magazine Needs Appearing in March and September, *Sulphur River* is a biannual of poetry, prose, and artwork. ''No restrictions except quality.'' Does not want poetry that is ''trite or religious, or verse that does not incite thought.'' Has published poetry by Marie C. Jones, E.G. Burrows, Ken Fontenot, Virgil Suárez, Marilyn E. Johnston, and Simon Perchik. *Sulphur River* is digest-sized, perfect-bound, with glossy cover. Receives about 2,000 poems/year, accepts 4%. Press run is 350 for 200 subscribers, 100 shelf sales. Subscription: $12. Sample: $7.

How to Submit No previously published poems or simultaneous submissions. Often comments on rejected poems, ''although a dramatic increase in submissions has made this increasingly difficult.'' Guidelines available for SASE. Responds in one month. Always sends prepublication galleys. Pays 2 contributor's copies.

Also Offers ''*Sulphur River* also publishes full-length volumes of poetry; latest book: *The Alchemy of Loss* by Nola Perez.''

Advice ''Read everything.''

⚡ $◨ THE SUN

107 N. Roberson St., Chapel Hill NC 27516. Website: www.thesunmagazine.org. Established 1974. **Editor:** Sy Safransky.

Magazine Needs *The Sun* is "noted for honest, personal work that's not too obscure or academic. We avoid traditional, rhyming poetry, as well as limericks and haiku. We're open to almost anything else: free verse, prose poems, short and long poems." Has published poetry by John Hodgen, Stuart Kestenbaum, Ruth L. Schwartz, Richard Lehnert, and Lesléa Newman. *The Sun* is 48 pages, magazine-sized, offset-printed on 50 lb. paper, saddle-stapled, includes b&w photos and graphics. Circulation is 60,000 for 58,000 subscribers of which 500 are libraries. Receives 3,000 submissions of poetry/year, accepts about 30; has a 1- to 3-month backlog. Subscription: $34. Sample: $5.

How to Submit Submit up to 6 poems at a time. Poems should be typed and accompanied by a cover letter. Accepts previously published poems, but simultaneous submissions are discouraged. Guidelines available for SASE. Responds within 3 months. Pays $50-250 on publication plus contributor's copies and subscription. Acquires first serial or one-time rights.

◨ SUN POETIC TIMES

P.O. Box 790526, San Antonio TX 78279-0526. (210)325-8122. E-mail: sunpoets@hotmail.com. Established 1994. **Co-Editors:** Rod C. Stryker and Michelle M. Gallagher.

Magazine Needs *Sun Poetic Times*, a literary and visual arts magazine, appears 2-4 times/year to "publish all types of literary and visual art from all walks of life. We take all types. Our only specification is length—one page in length if typed, 2 pages if handwritten (legibly)." Has published poetry by Naomi Shihab Nye, Chris Crabtree, Trinidad Sanchez, Jr., and Garland Lee Thompson, Jr. *Sun Poetic Times* is 24-28 pages, magazine-sized, attractively printed, saddle-stapled, with card stock cover, includes b&w line drawings/halftones. Receives about 300 poems/year, accepts about 20%. Press run is 250, 100 shelf sales. Subscription: $10/2 issues, $20/1 year (4 issues). Sample: $5 and SASE. Make checks payable to Sun Poetic Times.

How to Submit Submit 3-5 poems at a time. Accepts simultaneous submissions; no previously published poems. Accepts e-mail submissions included in body of message (no attached files). Cover letter is preferred. "In cover letters, we like to hear about your publishing credits, reasons you've taken up the pen, and general B.S. like that (biographical info)." Time between acceptance and publication is up to one year. Seldom comments on rejected poems. Occasionally publishes theme issues. Guidelines and upcoming themes available for SASE or by e-mail. E-mail queries welcome. Responds in up to 9 months. Pays one contributor's copy. Rights revert back to author upon publication.

⚡ ◨ ◎ SUNDRY: A Journal of the Arts (Specialized: special attention to poets from OH, IN, MI, PA, WV, KY)

Sundry Publishing Company, 109 Jepson Ave., St. Clairsville OH 43950. (740)526-0215. E-mail: griesbeck@sundryjournal.com. Website: www.sundryjournal.com. Established 1993. **Poetry Editor**: Gretchen Riesbeck. Member: CLMP.

Magazine Needs *Sundry: A Journal of the Arts* is a small, monthly literary journal "publishing high quality, original short fiction, poetry, essays, artwork and photography from artists nationally. Our geographic market includes Ohio, Indiana, Michigan, Pennsylvania, West Virginia, and Kentucky, and we give special preference to writers from these states, though we publish and print artists from all over the United States. Our format is strictly black and white, open to all genres, and we cultivate a bookish, East Coast, semi-urban visual theme. We're eager to work with new artists, though we prefer to receive poetry submissions from poets who, while potentially never published, have been writing for some time and have developed a voice." Open to all forms, "even experimental, but please avoid undisciplined writing. We very rarely publish poetry that is traditionally cliché, tacky, overly sappy, or that generally appeals to audiences that prefer NASCAR and Reba McEntire.

Our readers are sophisticated, educated, and tend to be fairly well read." Accepts poetry written by children and teens. "*Sundry* publishes an annual (soon to be semi-annual) Young Writers issue, usually in the fall. The issue contains work by artists aged 12-17." *Sundry* is generally 40 pages, digest-sized, standard printing, saddle-stapled, 60# white cover with b&w logo and b&w cover photo of the month, includes b&w photography and graphics and various ads. Receives about 1,000 poems/year, accepts about 75. Publishes about 5-15 poems/issue. Press run is 500 for 100 subscribers of which 10 are libraries, 300 shelf sales; 25 are distributed free. Single copy: $3.50; subscription: $11.99 for 6 months. Make checks payable to The Sundry Publishing Co.

How to Submit Submit no more than 10 poems at a time. Line length for poetry is open. Accepts simultaneous submissions; no previously published poems. No e-mail or disk submissions. Cover letter is required. "No SASE, no response. Please avoid overly unconventional font sizes and types in your submissions." Reads submissions year round. Submit seasonal poems 3 months in advance. Time between acceptance and publication is 1-3 months. Poems are circulated to an editorial board. "Poetry is sent to poetry editor's attention; she reviews them and selects ones she wishes the board to consider. Board then deliberates and selects based on majority vote." Often comments on rejected poems ("we try to comment as much as possible"). Occasionally publishes theme issues. List of upcoming themes and guidelines available on website. Responds in up to 3 months. Pays 5-10 contributor's copies. Acquires first North American serial rights. Reviews books of poetry.

Book/Chapbook Needs & How to Submit The Sundry Publishing Company publishes annual chapbooks of *Best of Sundry: A Journal of the Arts* (2003, 2004, etc.). Publishes one anthology/year. Manuscripts are selected through competition ("best of published work from issues of *Sundry* in one year"). Anthologies are 100-250 pages, standard printing, glue-in binding, vellum cover, include "plenty" of art/graphics. Responds to queries in up to 3 weeks; to mss in up to 3 months. Pays royalties of 2½-5%.

Advice " Don't send us a first draft that was written last night at five a.m. Let your work sit with you a while, and invest the time and energy into polishing it. Sometimes your work won't need any polishing, but other times it will."

☑ ◎ SUPERIOR POETRY NEWS (Specialized: translations; regional, Rocky Mountain West); SUPERIOR POETRY PRESS

P.O. Box 424, Superior MT 59872. Established 1995. **Editors:** Ed and Guna Chaberek.

Magazine Needs *Superior Poetry News* appears quarterly and "publishes the best and most interesting of new poets, as well as established poets, we can find. Also, we encourage lively translation into English from any language." Wants "general, rural, Western, or humorous poetry; translations; 40 lines or less. Nothing graphically sexual; containing profanity." Accepts poetry by young writers; the only restriction is quality, not age. Has published poetry by Simon Perchik, Bob Kimm, Lyn Lifshin, John Grey, makyo, and John Raven. *Superior Poetry News* is 12-24 pages, digest-sized, photocopied. Receives about 2,000 poems/year, accepts 10-20%. Press run is 75-100 for 50 subscribers; 3-5 distributed free to libraries. Single copy: 75¢; subscription: $2.75/4 issues.

How to Submit Submit 3-5 poems at a time. No previously published poems or simultaneous submissions (unless stated). Cover letter with short bio is preferred. Time between acceptance and publication is 3 months. Seldom comments on rejected poems. Guidelines available for SASE. Responds in one week. Pays one contributor's copy. Acquires first rights. Staff reviews books and chapbooks of poetry and other magazines in 50 words, single book format. Send materials for review consideration with return postage (overseas contributors please include 2 IRCs).

Also Offers "*Superior Poetry News* is now repositoried at the University of Wisconsin (Madison) Memorial Library."

Advice "Original—be original."

◻ ◙ SUZERAIN ENTERPRISES; LOVE'S CHANCE MAGAZINE (Specialized: love/ romance; erotica); FIGHTING CHANCE MAGAZINE (Specialized: horror; mystery; science fiction/fantasy)

P.O. Box 60336, Worcester MA 01606. Established 1994. **Editor/Publisher:** Milton Kerr.

Magazine Needs *Love's Chance Magazine* and *Fighting Chance Magazine* are each published 3 times/year to "give unpublished writers a chance to be published and to be paid for their efforts." *Love's Chance* deals with romance; *Fighting Chance* deals with dark fiction, horror, and science fiction. "No porn, ageism, sexism, racism, children in sexual situations." Has published poetry by Gary McGhee, T.R. Barnes, Dan Buck, Mark Sonnenfeld, Robert Donald Spector, Cecil Boyce, and Ellaraine Lockie. Both magazines are 15-30 pages, magazine-sized, photocopied, side-stapled, with computer-designed paper cover. Both receive about 500 poems/year, accept about 10%. Press runs are 100 for 70-80 subscribers. Subscription: $12/year for each. Samples: $4 each. Make checks payable to Suzerain Enterprises.

How to Submit For both magazines, submit 3 poems at a time. Line length for poetry is 20 maximum. Accepts previously published poems and simultaneous submissions. Cover letter is preferred. "Proofread for spelling errors, neatness; must be typewritten in standard manuscript form. No handwritten manuscripts." Time between acceptance and publication is 3 months. Often comments on rejected poems. Guidelines available for SASE or in magazine. Responds in 6 weeks. Acquires first or one-time rights.

Advice "Proofread your work. Edit carefully. Use spell check. Send correct postage and always include a SASE. Don't let rejection slips get you down. Don't be afraid to write something different. Keep submitting and don't give up."

⊠ $◻ SWAN SCYTHE PRESS

2052 Calaveras Ave., Davis CA 95616-3021. E-mail: sandyjmc@mindspring.com. Website: www.s wanscythe.com. Established 1999. **Editor/Publisher:** Sandra McPherson.

- Has been awarded a California Arts Council Multicultural Entry Grant and a Fideicomiso para la Cultura Mexico-EUA/US-Mexico Fund for Culture Grant.

Book/Chapbook Needs Swan Scythe Press publishes "poetry chapbooks, a few full-sized poetry collections, and one anthology. A multi-ethnic press primarily publishing emerging writers, we have also published established poets such as Ted Joans and Jordan Smith." Books should be thematically unified with fresh subject matter. "Every kind of poem from formal to prose poem is welcome." Has published poetry by Emmy Perez, Maria Melendez, John Olivares Espinoza, Karen An-hwei Lee, Pos Moua, and Walter Pavlich. Publishes one poetry book/year, 3 chapbooks/year, and one anthology/year. Manuscripts are selected through competition. "In 2003 we did not have our usual annual contest ($15 reading fee per 36-page manuscript) but instead selected books only through solicitation. We hope we will be able to return to the contest in a future year." Check website for latest information. Books/chapbooks are 36-85 pages, commercially-printed, perfect-bound, with full-color paper covers, include internal illustrations, occasionally in color, of fine art and folk art.

How to Submit Book/chapbook mss may include previously published poems. Responds to queries in one week; to mss in 10 weeks. Pays advance of $200 and 50 author's copies (out of a press run of 500). Order sample books/chapbooks by sending $11 to Swan Scythe Press (also available through website).

☑ SWEET ANNIE & SWEET PEA REVIEW

7750 Highway F-24 W, Baxter IA 50028. (641)417-0020. E-mail: sweetann@pcpartner.net. Established 1995. **Editor/Publisher:** Beverly A. Clark.

Magazine Needs *Sweet Annie & Sweet Pea Review*, published quarterly, features short stories and poetry. Wants "poems of outdoors, plants, land, heritage, women, relationships, olden times—

simpler times." Does not want "obscene, violent, explicit sexual material, obscure, long-winded materials, overly religious materials." Has published poetry by Anne Carol Betterton, Mary Ann Wehler, Ellaraine Lockie, Celeste Bowman, Dick Reynolds, and Susanne Olson. *Sweet Annie & Sweet Pea Review* is 30 pages, digest-sized, offset-printed, on bond paper with onion skin page before title page, saddle-stapled, with medium card cover with art. Receives about 200 poems/year, accepts 25-33%. Press run is 40. Subscription: $24. Sample: $7. Make checks payable to Sweet Annie Press.

How to Submit Submit 6-12 poems at a time. **Reading fee:** $5/author submitting. "Strongly recommend ordering a sample issue prior to submitting; preference is given to poets and writers following this procedure and submitting in accordance with the layout used consistently by this press." Accepts simultaneous submissions; no previously published poems. No e-mail submissions. Cover letter is preferred; "include phone number and personal comments about yourself." Time between acceptance and publication is 9 months. Often comments on rejected poems. Occasionally publishes theme issues. "We select for theme first, content second; narrow selections through editors." Pays one contributor's copy. Acquires all rights. Returns rights with acknowledgment in future publications. Will review chapbooks of poetry or other magazines of short length, reviews 500 words or less. Send materials for review consideration.

N $ SWINK

5042 Wilshire Blvd. #628, Los Angeles CA 90036. (310)281-7694. Fax: (310)861-5996. E-mail: editor s@swinkmag.com. Website: www.swinkmag.com. Established 2003. **Poetry Editor:** David Hernandez. Member: CLMP.

Magazine Needs *Swink* is a "bi-coastal, biannual print magazine dedicated to identifying and promoting literary talent in both established and emerging writers. We're interested in writing that pushes the boundaries of the traditional—writing that is new in concept, form, or execution; that reflects a diversity of thought, experience, or perspective; that provokes or entertains. We seek to publish quality work by established poets and emerging talents. We want to see poems that are original in content, evocative in imagery, with a strong command of the language." Does not want obscure, derivative, or sentimental poetry. Has published poetry by Lucia Perillo, Bob Hicok, Beckian Fritz Goldberg, and D. Nurkse. *Swink* is 224 pages, approximately 7×9, perfect-bound, with full-color cover, includes ads. Accepts about 1% of poems submitted. Publishes about 20 poems/issue. Press run is 3,000. Single copy: $10; subscription: $16. Make checks payble to Swink, Inc.

How to Submit Submit 3-5 poems at a time. Accepts simultaneous submissions; no previously published poems. No fax, e-mail, or disk submissions. Cover letter is preferred. Reads submissions year round. Time between acceptance and publication is 2 months to a year. Poems are circulated to an editorial board. Seldom comments on rejected poems. Occasionally publishes theme issues. Guidelines available on website. Responds in up to 3 months. Always sends prepublication galleys. Pays $25 and 2 contributor's copies. Acquires first North American serial rights as well as one-time anthology rights and serial online rights.

Contest/Award Offerings "Annual poetry competitions for emerging and established writers are held at various times throughout the year. Please see our website for details."

SYCAMORE REVIEW

Dept. of English, Purdue University, 500 Oval Dr., West Lafayette IN 47907-2038. (765)494-3783. Fax: (765)494-3780. E-mail: sycamore@purdue.edu. Website: www.sla.purdue.edu/sycamore/. Established 1988 (first issue May 1989). **Contact:** Poetry Editor.

• Poetry published by *Sycamore Review* has appeared in the *Pushcart Prize* anthology.

Magazine Needs *Sycamore Review* is published biannually in January and June. "We accept personal essays, short fiction, drama, translations, and quality poetry in any form. We aim to publish many diverse styles of poetry from formalist to prose poems, narrative, and lyric." Has published poetry by Denise Levertov, Mark Halperin, Amy Gerstler, Mark Halliday, Dean Young, and Ed Hirsch. *Sycamore Review* is 160 pages, digest-sized, flat-spined, professionally printed, with matte color cover. Press run is 1,000 for 200 subscribers of which 50 are libraries. Subscription: $12; $14 outside US. Sample: $7. Make checks payable to Purdue University (Indiana residents add 5% sales tax.)

How to Submit Submit 3-6 poems at a time. Name and address on each page. Accepts simultaneous submissions, if notified immediately of acceptance elsewhere; no previously published poems except translations. No fax or e-mail submissions. Cover letters not required but invited; include phone number, short bio, and previous publications, if any. "We read August 1 through March 1 only." Guidelines available for SASE. Responds in 4 months. Pays 2 contributor's copies. Acquires first North American rights. After publication, all rights revert to author. Staff reviews books of poetry. Send materials for review consideration to editor-in-chief.

Advice "Poets who do not include a SASE do not receive a response."

$☐ SYNERGEBOOKS

1235 Flat Shoals Rd., King NC 27021. (336)994-2405. Fax: (336)994-8403. E-mail: inquiries@synerg ebooks.com. Website: www.synergebooks.com. Established 1999. **Acquisitions Editor:** Deb Staples. Member: EPPRO, SPAN, EPC, PMA.

Book/Chapbook Needs SynergEbooks specializes in quality works by talented new writers in every available digital format, including CD-ROMs and paperback. "Poetry must have a very unique twist or theme and must be edited. We are looking specifically for poetry with religious overtones." Does not accept unedited work. Has published poetry by Theresa Jodray, Brenda Roberts, Vanyell Delacroix, Joel L. Young, and Minerva Bloom. SynergEbooks publishes up to 40 titles/year, 2-5 of them poetry. Books are usually 45-150 pages, print-on-demand, with paperback binding.

How to Submit Query by e-mail, with a few sample poems and cover letter with brief bio and publication credits. "We prefer no simultaneous submissions, but inform us if this is the case." Accepts submissions on disk or by e-mail (as attachment) *only*. "Please do not send poetry via postal mail. Valid, working e-mail address is required." Responds to queries in one month; to mss in up to 5 months. Pays royalties of 35-40%.

Advice "We are inundated with more poetry than prose every month; but we will accept the occasional anthology with a unique twist that is original and high quality. New poets welcome."

🌐 ⊘ TAK TAK TAK

BCM Tak, London WC1N 3XX England. Website: www.taktaktak.com. Established 1986. **Editors:** Andrew and Tim Brown. *Tak Tak Tak* appears occasionally in print and on cassettes. "However, we are currently not accepting submissions."

♻ ☐ ◎ TALE SPINNERS; MIDNIGHT STAR PUBLICATIONS (Specialized: country living, being 'one with nature')

R.R. #1, Ponoka AB T4J 1R1 Canada. (403)783-2521. Established 1996. **Editor/Publisher:** Nellie Gritchen Scott.

Magazine Needs *Tale Spinners* is a quarterly " 'little literary magazine with a country flavor,' for writers who love country and all it stands for." Wants poetry, fiction, anecdotes, personal experiences, etc., "pertaining to country life. Children's poetry welcome." No "scatological, prurient, sexually explicit, or political content." Accepts poetry written by children ages 6 and up. Has published poetry by Pamela Bond, Karen-Jean Matsko-Hood, Dudley Laufman, Thomas Sampson, Kenneth Leonhardt, and Ruth Latta. *Tale Spinners* is 48 pages, digest-sized, photocopied, saddle-stapled, with light cardstock cover, includes clip art or freehand graphics. Receives about 100 poems/year, accepts about 80%. Press run is 75 for 50 subscribers. Subscription: $20. Sample: $5 plus $1 p&h.

How to Submit Submit up to 6 poems at a time. "Short poems preferred, but will use narrative poems on occasion." Accepts previously published poems. Cover letter ensures a reply. Include a SAE and IRC. Submit seasonal poems at least 2 months in advance. Time between acceptance and publication is 3 months. Often comments on rejected poems. Guidelines available for SASE. Responds in 2 weeks. Pays one contributor's copy.

Book/Chapbook Needs & How to Submit "Midnight Star Publications is not accepting chapbook manuscripts at present."

Advice "Read the magazine and/or send for guidelines."

Ⓝ $□ TALENT MAGAZINE; TALENT MAGAZINE'S POETRY CONTEST

"I See Lightning!" P.O. Box 577, Martins Ferry OH 43935. E-mail: info@talentmagazinegroup.com. Website: http://talentmagazinegroup.com. Established 2004. **Poetry Editor:** Tammy Kunik.

Magazine Needs *Talent* is a monthly magazine covering "all aspects of creative writing, including advice from professionals, networking, job markets, etc." Wants haiku, traditional dramatic, and traditional narrative poetry. *Talent Magazine* is magazine-sized, desktop-published, with 50 lb. coated stock cover with color artwork, includes 2- and 4-color and b&w art and photos, also ads. Publishes about 3 poems/issue. Subscription: $6/year online, $24/year print. Sample: free online. Make checks payable to *Talent Magazine*.

How to Submit Submit 5 poems at a time. Line length for poetry is 5 minimum, 55 maximum. Accepts previously published poems (for regular submissions, not contests) and simultaneous submissions. No e-mail or disk submissions. No cover letter; "we prefer you use our Form 500, located under 'submission guidelines' on website." Reads submissions year round. Submit seasonal poems 3-6 months in advance. Time between acceptance and publication is "normally" 3 months. "Our poetry editor recommends to the managing editor and editor. Together, we review." Always comments on rejected poems. Responds in 3 months. Pays $10-25. Acquires one-time rights and one-time electronic rights.

Contest/Award Offerings Sponsors contest to celebrate April as National Poetry Month. "Poem style is at the discretion of the poet, but please try to limit to 55 lines or thereabout." Poem must be previously unpublished. No SASE required; no poems will be returned. 1st Prize: $100, half-page photo profile and publication in April issue, one-year membership in the National Writers' Association, a reading by a published poet as well as an active poets' group, *Talent*'s poetry trophy, press releases in all participating newspapers in winner's state and in *Talent Merchandise*, the monthly newsletter of the NWA, plus a one-year online subscription to *Talent*. 2nd/3rd Prize: $75/ $50, quarter-page photo profile and publication in April issue, a reading by a published poet and an active poets' group, *Talent*'s 2nd/3rd Prize Award, press releases in all participating newspapers in winner's state and in *Talent Merchandise*, plus a one-year online subscription to *Talent*. 4th/5th Prize: $35/$25, eighth-page photo profile and publication in April issue, a reading by a published poet as well as an active poets' group, *Talent*'s 4th/5th Prize Award, press releases in all participating newspapers in winner's state and in *Talent Merchandise*, plus a one-year online subscription to *Talent*. 6th through 20th Prize: Honorable Mention in the April issue of *Talent*. **Entry fee:** $5/ group of 3 poems, unlimited entries. (For outside U.S., send IRC equivalent.) **Postmark deadline:** December 1, 2004-February 28, 2005. Entry form and guidelines available on website.

Advice "We love poems that are themed. Not to *our* themes. Example: poem about raising kids, poem about cats, poem about writing a novel, etc.; not just airy, thoughtless, meaningless poems."

⊕ ☑ TALVIPÄIVÄNSEISAUS SPECIALS

Oritie 4C24, FIN-01200 Vantaa, Finland. E-mail: tpsprod@hotmail.com. Established 1987. **Editor:** Timo Palonen.

Magazine Needs *Talvipäivänseisaus Specials* appear annually now that the editor has retired *Muuna Takeena*. Does not want to see experimental poems. *Talvipäivänseisaus Specials* are about 30 pages, magazine-sized, photocopied, stapled, with cover with photo/drawing, includes photos/drawings inside. Receives about 50 poems/year, accepts 90%. Press run is 300. Sample: $3 or €4. "No checks."

How to Submit Submit 3 poems at a time. Accepts simultaneous submissions; no previously published poems. Accepts e-mail submissions (pasted into body of message). Cover letter is required. Time between acceptance and publication is 6 months. Pays one contributor's copy.

Advice "I read; if I like, it could be printed. If I do not like, I send forward to other zine makers."

⊘ ◎ TAMEME (Specialized: bilingual; regional)

199 First St., #335, Los Altos CA 94022. Website: www.tameme.org. Established 1999. **Contact:** Poetry Editor.

• *Tameme* was awarded a grant from the US-Mexico Fund for Culture.

Magazine Needs "*Tameme* is an annual literary magazine dedicated to publishing new writing from North America in side-by-side English-Spanish format. *Tameme*'s goals are to play an instrumental role in introducing important new writing from Canada and the United States to Mexico, and vice versa, and to provide a forum for the art of literary translation. By 'new writing' we mean the best work of serious literary value that has been written recently. By 'writing from North America' we mean writing by citizens or residents of Mexico, the United States, and Canada." Has published poetry by Alberto Blanco, Jaime Sabines, Colette Inez, Juana Goergen, and Ray González. *Tameme* is 225 pages, digest-sized. Receives about 200 poems/year, accepts 1%. Press run is 2,000. Subscription: $14.95. Sample: $14.95. Make checks payable to Tameme, Inc.

How to Submit *Tameme* is currently closed to unsolicited mss.

◻ ◎ TAPESTRIES (Specialized: senior citizens; anthology)

MWCC Life Program, 444 Green St., Gardner MA 01440. (978)630-9176. Fax: (978)632-6155. E-mail: alanahb@earthlink.net or lwickman@mwcc.mass.edu. Established 2001. **Editor:** Patricia B. Cosentino, Life Program, Mount Wachusett Community College.

Magazine Needs *Tapestries* appears annually in October as "an anthology for senior citizens of poetry, short stories, features on family, heritage, tradition, and folklore. Our anthology is subsidized by Mount Wachusett Community College through a grant from Massachusetts Cultural Council for senior citizen writers and poets." Wants any style poetry; no restrictions on form, "but must be no longer than 24 lines." Does not want "political, propaganda, pornographic, or sexually explicit material as this is a 'family' magazine. We do not exclude religious poems, but they must have non-sectarian universality." Has published poetry by Maxine Kumin, Victor Howes, Diana Der-Hovanessian, John Tagliabue, bg Thurston, and Robert D. Wetmore. *Tapestries* is 100 pages, magazine-sized, offset-printed, tape-bound, with card stock/offset cover. Receives about 500 poems/year, accepts about 10%. Publishes about 25-30 poems/issue. Press run is 500. Single copy: $5 plus $3 postage. Make checks payable to MWCC Life Program.

How to Submit Submit 3-5 poems at a time. Line length for poetry is 24 maximum. Accepts previously published poems and simultaneous submissions. Accepts e-mail and disk submissions; no fax submissions. Cover letter is preferred (only if work is previously published). "Prefer hard copy submissions. Send SASE to MWCC Life Program for guidelines." **Deadline:** March 31. Time between acceptance and publication is 4 months. Poems are circulated to an editorial board of 3-4 judges. Occasionally publishes theme issues. List of upcoming themes available for SASE, by e-mail, or on website. Guidelines available for SASE, by fax, e-mail, or on website. Responds in 3 months. No payment. Acquires first North American serial rights.

Advice "As an anthology we accept original and/or previously published material, but prefer original. Our authors range in age from 50-92 in our most recent issue. We want humor and wisdom in our writings.''

⬤ TAR RIVER POETRY

English Dept., East Carolina University, Greenville NC 27858-4353. (252)328-6046. Website: www.e cu.edu/english/journals. Established 1978. **Editor:** Peter Makuck.

Magazine Needs ''We are not interested in sentimental, flat-statement poetry. What we would like to see is skillful use of figurative language, poems that appeal to the senses.'' *Tar River* appears twice/year as an ''all-poetry'' magazine that accepts dozens of poems in each issue, providing the talented beginner and experienced writer with a forum that features all styles and forms of verse. Has published poetry by Betty Adcock, Henry Taylor, Gray Jacobik, Natasha Sajé, Fred Chappell, and James Harms. *Tar River* is 60 pages, digest-sized, professionally printed on salmon stock, with matte card cover with photo, includes some decorative line drawings. Receives 6,000-8,000 submissions/year, accepts 150-200. Press run is 900 for 500 subscribers of which 125 are libraries. Subscription: $12. Sample: $6.50.

How to Submit Submit 3-6 poems at a time. ''We do not consider previously published poems or simultaneous submissions. Double or single-spaced OK. Name and address on each page. We do not consider manuscripts during summer months.'' Reads submissions September 1 through April 15 only. Editors will comment ''if slight revision will do the trick.'' Guidelines available for SASE or on website. Responds in 6 weeks. Pays 2 contributor's copies. Acquires first rights. Reviews books of poetry in 4,000 words maximum, single or multi-book format. Send materials for review consideration.

Advice ''Poets are first readers. Read and study traditional and contemporary poetry.''

⬤ TARPAULIN SKY

22259 Christanna Highway, Lawrenceville VA 23868. E-mail: info@tarpaulinsky.com (inquiries) or poetry@tarpaulinsky.com (submissions). Website: www.tarpaulinsky.com. Established 2002. **Poetry Editors:** Christian Peet, Lizzie Harris, and Jonathan Livingston.

Magazine Needs *Tarpaulin Sky* is a quarterly online literary journal ''publishing highest-quality poetry, prose, art, photography, interviews, and reviews. We are open to all styles and forms, providing the forms appear inevitable and/or inextricable from the poems. We are especially fond of inventive/experimental and trans-genre work. The best indication of our aesthetic is found in the journal we produce: Please read it before submitting your work. Also, hard copy submissions are received by different editors at different times: Again, check guidelines before submitting.'' Has published poetry by Barry Gifford, Louis Jenkins, Joan Larkin, Gordon Wassman, Mark Turpin, and Thomas Swiss. *Tarpaulin Sky* is published online only. Receives about 3,000 poems/year. Publishes about 20-30 poems/issue.

How to Submit Submit 3 or more poems at a time. Accepts simultaneous submissions; no previously published poems. Accepts e-mail submissions; no fax or disk submissions. Cover letter is preferred. ''E-mail submissions are best received as attachments in .rtf or .pdf formats.'' Reads submissions year round. Time between acceptance and publication is one month. ''All poems are read by 3 poetry editors. We aim for consensus.'' Often comments on rejected poems. Guidelines available for SASE, by e-mail, or on website. Responds in up to 2 months. Always sends prepublication galleys (electronic). Acquires first rights. Reviews books and chapbooks of poetry.

✪ ⬤ ◎ TATTOO HIGHWAY (Specialized: theme-based)

E-mail: smcaulay@csuhayward.edu. Website: www.tattoohighway.org. Established 1998. **Editor:** Sara McAulay.

Magazine Needs *Tattoo Highway* is a ''graphics-heavy biannual online journal of poetry, literary prose, new media, and art. We're open to most styles, including New Media; we like formal poems if well handled. Mainly we want language that is fresh, vivid, and original; writing that is smart and a little edgy, that engages with the world beyond the writer's own psyche." Does not want "self-pity, navel-contemplation, clichés, workshop hackery." Has published poetry by MTC Cronin, John Gilgun, Walt McDonald, Ian McBryde, Margaret Szumowski, and Kelley White. *Tattoo Highway* is published online only with original jpeg art/graphics. Receives about 800 poems/year, accepts about 50. Publishes about 25 poems/issue.

How to Submit Accepts previously published poems ("see guidelines on website") and simultaneous submissions. Accepts e-mail submissions (pasted into body of message); no disk submissions. "For hypertext or New Media (Flash, etc.) submissions, please provide a URL where we may view the work." Reading periods vary. "Typically last three moths; see guidelines." Poems are circulated to an editorial board. "Blind readings by editorial board. Several rounds of 'triage' during the reading period, usually handled by e-mail. Face-to-face editorial meeting shortly after submission deadline, where final selections are made. Editor and poetry editor have final say." Sometimes comments on rejected poems. "If a poem has its moments, though it doesn't quite work, we try to acknowledge that. We encourage near-misses to try us again." Regularly publishes theme issues. List of upcoming themes and guidelines available on website. Responds in up to 3 months ("within one week of deadline"). Always sends prepublication galleys. No payment. Acquires first electronic rights; rights revert to author 90 days after online publication date.

Contest/Award Offerings "Picture Worth 500 Words" contest for poetry/prose. No entry fee, small prizes. See guidelines on website.

Advice "Read some past issues before submitting."

⊞ ☑ TEARS IN THE FENCE

38 Hodview, Stourpaine, Nr. Blandford Forum, Dorset DT11 8TN England. Phone: 0044 1258-456803. Fax: 0044 1258-454026. E-mail: westrow@cooperw.fsnet.co.uk. Website: www.wandering dog.co.uk. Established 1984. **General Editor:** David Caddy.

Magazine Needs *Tears in the Fence* appears 3 times/year and is a "small press magazine of poetry, fiction, interviews, articles, reviews, and graphics. We are open to a wide variety of poetic styles. Work that is unusual, perceptive, risk-taking as well as imagistic, lived, and visionary will be close to our purpose. However, we like to publish a variety of work." Has published poetry by John Kinsella, Peter Robinson, Ed Ochester, Joan Poulson, Donna Hilbert, Ketaki Kushari Dyson, Jeremy Reed, and Michelle Noteboom. *Tears in the Fence* is 128 pages, A5, docutech-printed on 110 gms. paper, perfect-bound, with matte card cover, includes b&w art and graphics. Press run is 800, of which 512 go to subscribers. Subscription: $20/4 issues. Sample: $7.

How to Submit Submit 6 typed poems with IRCs. Accepts submissions by e-mail (pasted into body of message), on disk, or by postal mail. Cover letter with brief bio is required. Publishes theme issues. List of upcoming themes available for SASE. Responds in 3 months. Time between acceptance and publication is 10 months "but can be much less." Pays one contributor's copy. Reviews books of poetry in 2,000-3,000 words, single or multi-book format. Send materials for review consideration.

Also Offers The magazine runs a regular series of readings in London and an annual international literary festival. Also publishes books. Titles include *Hanging Windchimes In a Vacuum* by Gregory Warren Wilson, *Heart Thread* by Joan Jobe Smith, and *The Hong Kong/Macao Trip* by Gerald Locklin.

Advice "I think it helps to subscribe to several magazines in order to study the market and develop an understanding of what type of poetry is published. Use the review sections and send off to magazines that are new to you."

☑ TEBOT BACH

P.O. Box 7887, Huntington Beach CA 92615-7887. (714)968-0905. E-mail: info@tebotbach.org. Website: www.tebotbach.org. **Editor/Publisher:** Mifanwy Kaiser

Book/Chapbook Needs & How to Submit Tebot Bach (Welsh for "little teapot") publishes books of poetry. Titles include *Cantatas* by Jeanette Clough, *48 Questions* by Richard Jones, *The Way In* by Robin Chapman, and *Written in Rain: New and Selected Poems 1985-2000* by M.L. Liebler. Query first with sample poems and cover letter with brief bio and publication credits. Include SASE. Responds to queries and mss, if invited, in one month. Time between acceptance and publication is up to 2 years. Write to order sample books.

Also Offers An anthology of California poets, published annually in April. Must be current or former resident of California in order to submit, but no focus or theme required for poetry. Deadline for submission is in August, annually. Submit up to 6 poems with "California Anthology" written on lower left corner of envelope. Accepts submissions by e-mail (pasted into body of message or as attachment in Word).

$⬛ TEMPORARY VANDALISM RECORDINGS; THE SILT READER

P.O. Box 6184, Orange CA 92863-6184. E-mail: tvrec@yahoo.com. Website: http://home.surewest. net/aphasiapress/. Established 1991 (Temporary Vandalism Recordings), 1999 (*The Silt Reader*). **Editors:** Robert Roden and Barton M. Saunders.

Magazine Needs *The Silt Reader* is published biannually in January and August. "Form, length, style and subject matter can vary. It's difficult to say what will appeal to our eclectic tastes." Does not want "strictly rants, overly didactic poetry." Has published poetry by M. Jaime-Becerra, Gerald Locklin, Simon Perchik, Margaret Garcia, and Don Winter. *The Silt Reader* is 32 pages, $4^{1}/_{4} \times 5^{1}/_{2}$, saddle-stapled, photocopied, with colored card cover, includes some ads. Accepts less than 10% of poems received. Press run is 500. Sample: $2. Make checks payable to Robert Roden.

How to Submit Submit 5 neatly typed poems at a time. Accepts previously published poems and simultaneous submissions. No e-mail submissions. Cover letter is preferred. Time between acceptance and publication is 6 months. "Two editors' votes required for inclusion." Seldom comments on rejected poems. Responds in up to 6 months. Guidelines available for SASE or on website. Pays 2 contributor's copies. Acquires one-time rights.

Book/Chapbook Needs & How to Submit Temporary Vandalism Recordings publishes 2 chapbooks/year. Chapbooks are usually 40 pages, photocopied, saddle-stapled, with an initial press run of 100 (reprint option if needed). Submit 10 sample poems, with SASE for response. "Publication in some magazines is important, but extensive publishing is not required." Responds in 6 months. Pays 50% royalty (after costs recouped) and 5 author's copies (out of a press run of 100). For sample chapbooks send $5 to the above address.

⬛ ⬛ 10TH MUSE

33 Hartington Rd., Southampton, Hants SO14 0EW England. E-mail: andyj@noplace.screaming.net. Established 1990. **Editor:** Andrew Jordan.

Magazine Needs *10th Muse* "includes poetry and reviews, as well as short prose (usually no more than 2,000 words) and graphics. I prefer poetry with a strong 'lyric' aspect. I enjoy experimental work that corresponds with aspects of the pastoral tradition. I have a particular interest in the cultural construction of landscape." Has published poetry by Peter Riley, Andrew Duncan, Richard Caddel, Ian Robinson, John Welch, and Jeremy Hooker. *10th Muse* is 48-72 pages, A5, photocopied, saddle-stapled, with card cover, no ads. Press run is 200. "U.S. subscribers—send $10 in bills for single copy (including postage)."

How to Submit Submit up to 6 poems. Include SASE (or SAE with IRCs). Accepts submissions by postal mail and e-mail (pasted into body of message). Often comments on rejected poems. Responds in 3 months. Pays one contributor's copy. Staff reviews books of poetry. Send materials for review consideration.

Advice "Poets should read a copy of the magazine first."

$☑ ◎ THEMA (Specialized: themes)

Thema Literary Society, P.O. Box 8747, Metairie LA 70011-8747. E-mail: thema@cox.net. Website: http://members.cox.net/thema. Established 1988. **Editor:** Virginia Howard. **Poetry Editor:** Gail Howard. Address poetry submissions to Gail Howard.

- *THEMA* is supported by a grant from the Louisiana Division of the Arts, Office of Cultural Development, Department of Culture, Recreation and Tourism, in cooperation with the Louisiana State Arts Council as administered by Art Council of New Orleans.

Magazine Needs *THEMA* is a triannual literary magazine using poetry related to specific themes. "Each issue is based on an unusual premise. Please, please send SASE for guidelines before submitting poetry to find out the upcoming themes." Upcoming themes (and submission deadlines) include: *Bookstore Cowboy* (November 1, 2004), *Umbrellas in the Snow* (March 1, 2005), *The Renaissance Child* (July 1, 2005). "No scatologic language, alternate life-style, explicit love poetry." Poems will be judged with all others submitted. Has published poetry by Barry Ballard, John Grey, L.G. Mason, and Jill Williams. *THEMA* is 150 pages, digest-sized, professionally printed, with matte card cover. Receives about 400 poems/year, accepts about 8%. Press run is 500 for 270 subscribers of which 30 are libraries. Subscription: $16. Sample: $8.

How to Submit Submit up to 3 poems at a time with SASE. All submissions should be typewritten and on standard 8½×11 paper. Submissions are accepted all year, but evaluated after specified deadlines. Guidelines and upcoming themes available for SASE, on website, by e-mail, and in magazine. Editor comments on submissions. Pays $10/poem plus one contributor's copy. Acquires one-time rights.

Advice "Do *not* submit to *THEMA unless* you have one of *THEMA's* upcoming themes in mind. And be sure to specify which one!"

✴ ☑ THIN AIR MAGAZINE: A JOURNAL OF THE LITERARY ARTS

Graduate Creative Writing Association of Northern Arizona University, P.O. Box 23549, Flagstaff AZ 86002. (520)523-6743. Fax: (520)523-7074. Website: www.nau.edu/english/thinair/. Established 1995. **Contact:** Poetry Editor.

Magazine Needs *Thin Air* is a biannual literary magazine of poetry, fiction, nonfiction, and essays. "The aesthetic we use in selecting work for our magazine is a simple one: Does it catch our eyes and our minds? Is it something we want not only to read, but to re-read? If this describes your writing, then we would love to see a submission." Has published poetry by Vivian Shipley, Nancy Johnson, and Charles H. Webb. *Thin Air* is 50 pages, digest-sized, attractively printed, permabound, with coated color cover, includes art. Receives about 300 poems/year, accepts 10%. Press run is 300-500 for 70 subscribers of which 5 are libraries, 225-425 shelf sales. Single copy: $4.95; subscription: $9. Sample: $4.

How to Submit Submit up to 10 poems at a time. Accepts simultaneous submissions with notification; no previously published poems. Cover letter preferred. Reads submissions August through April only. Time between acceptance and publication is 2 months. Seldom comments on rejected poems. Guidelines available for SASE. Responds in one month. Pays 2 contributor's copies. Acquires all rights and extends republishing rights to the author subject to acknowledgement of original publication in *Thin Air*. Reviews books and chapbooks of poetry and other magazines in 700-1,200 words, single book format. Send materials for review consideration.

Contest/Award Offerings Sponsors annual contest for poetry. **Deadline:** January 31. Rules available for SASE.

☑ THIRD COAST

Dept. of English, Western Michigan University, Kalamazoo MI 49008-5092. (616)387-2675. Fax: (616)387-2562. Website: www.wmich.edu/thirdcoast. Established 1995. **Editors:** Cody Todd and Amanda Warner. **Contact:** Poetry Editors.

Magazine Needs Appearing in March and September, *Third Coast* is a biannual national literary magazine of poetry, prose, creative nonfiction, and translation. Wants "excellence of craft and originality of thought. Nothing trite." Has published poetry by Billy Collins, Ted Kooser, Alan Shapiro, Margo Schlipp, Mark Halliday, and Philip Levine. *Third Coast* is 160 pages, digest-sized, professionally printed, perfect-bound, with 4-color cover with art. Receives about 2,000 poems/year, accepts approximately 3-5%. Press run is 1,200 for 650 subscribers of which 50 are libraries, 350 shelf sales. Single copy: $6; subscription: $14/year, $25/2 years, $35/3 years.

How to Submit Submit up to 5 poems at a time. No previously published poems or simultaneous submissions. No electronic submissions. Cover letter with bio is preferred. "Poems should be typed single-spaced, with the author's name on each page. Stanza breaks should be double-spaced." Poems are circulated to assistant poetry editors and poetry editors; poetry editors make final decisions. Seldom comments on rejected poems. Guidelines available for SASE or on website. Responds in 4 months. Pays 2 contributor's copies plus one-year subscription. Acquires first rights.

Contest/Award Offerings 2005 Poetry Award. 1st Prize: $1,000 and publication; 4 finalists receive notification in prize-winning issue (Fall 2005), and possible publication. Final judge: Sydney Lea. **Postmark deadline:** November 15, 2004. See website for rules.

✅ ◎ THOUGHTS FOR ALL SEASONS: THE MAGAZINE OF EPIGRAMS (Specialized: epigrams; humor; themes)

% Prof. Em. Michel Paul Richard, editor, 86 Leland Rd., Box 34, Becket MA 01223. Established 1976. **Contact:** Editor.

Magazine Needs *Thoughts for All Seasons* "is an irregular serial: designed to preserve the epigram as a literary form; satirical. All issues are commemorative. Volume 6 marks the centennial of *Devil's Dictionary* by Ambrose Bierce (circa 1904)." Rhyming poetry and nonsense verse (e.g., original limericks) with good imagery will be considered although most modern epigrams are prose—no haiku. *Thoughts for All Seasons* is 80 pages, offset from typescript, saddle-stapled, with card cover, includes full-page illustrations. Accepts about 20% of material submitted. Press run is 500-1,000. There are several library subscriptions, but most distribution is through direct mail or local bookstores and newsstand sales. Single copy: $6 (includes p&h).

How to Submit "Submit at least one or two pages of your work, 10-12 epigrams, or 2-4 poems." Include SASE and one-paragraph bio. Accepts simultaneous submissions; no previously published epigrams "unless a thought is appended which alters it." Editor comments on rejected poems. Themes for Volume 6 include Satirical Tips for Good Health and New Lyrics for Old Songs. Guidelines available in magazine or for SASE. Responds in one month. Pays one contributor's copy, additional discounted copies.

Advice "Study a current or back issue of *TFAS*."

✅ THREE CANDLES

E-mail: editor@threecandles.org. Website: www.threecandles.org. Established 1999. **Editor:** Steve Mueske.

Magazine Needs *Three Candles* is published online and posts updates "when qualified poetry is available, generally once or twice a week. Though I am not particular about publishing specific forms of poetry, I prefer to be surprised by the content of the poems themselves. I believe that poetry should have some substance and touch, at least tangentially, on human experience." Does not want poems that are "overtly religious, sexist, racist, or unartful." Has published poetry by Jeffrey Levine, Deborah Keenan, Joyce Sutphen, Ray Gonzalez, and Paul Perry. *Three Candles* is a "high-quality online journal, professionally designed and maintained." Receives about 5,000 poems/year. Publishes "approximately 4-6 poets/month, about 10 poems. Many poems I publish are solicited directly from poets." Receives 40,000 hits/month.

How to Submit Submit 3-5 poems at a time. No simultaneous submissions or previously published poems. Accepts e-mail submissions *only*. Send poems "as the body of the text or, if special formatting is used, as attachments in Word or rich text format. In the body of the e-mail, I want a short bio, a list of previous publications, the certification statement that appears on the 'information' page on the website, and a brief note about what writing poetry means to you as an artist." Accepts submissions year round. Time between acceptance and publication is about 6 weeks. "Reading the journal is important to get an idea of the level of craft expected." Guidelines available on website. Responds within 2 months. Does not send prepublication galleys but "allows author to make any necessary changes before a formal announcement is e-mailed to the mailing list." No payment "at this time." Acquires first rights. Copyright reverts to author after publication.

Advice "The online poetry community is vital and thriving. Take some time and get to know the journals that you are submitting to. Don't send work that is like what is published. Send work that is as good but different in a way that is uniquely your own."

3 cup morning

13865 Dillabough Rd., R.R. #1, Chesterville ON K0C 1H0 Canada. Fax: (613)448-1478. E-mail: threecupmorning@aol.com. Website: http://3cupmorning.topcities.com. Established 1999. **Editor:** Gen O'Neil.

Magazine Needs Published bimonthly online and in print as a 4-page (double-sided) newsletter, *3 cup morning* is "a platform for beginning and novice poets to showcase their work. We firmly believe that seeing your work in print is the single greatest encouragement needed to continue. Every poet should have the opportunity to see their work in print—at least once anyway." Accepts all types of poetry—haiku, traditional, experimental, free form, etc. No graphic violence, hate, profanity, or graphic sex. Has published poetry by Robert Hogg, Valerie Poynter, J. Kevin Wolfe, Mary-Ann Hazen, and Ruth Witter. Subscription: $20 Canadian, $25 US, $30 all others. Sample: $20. Make checks (Canada and US only) or International Money Orders payable to Gen O'Neil.

How to Submit Submit 5 poems at a time. Line length for poetry is 3 minimum, 40 maximum. Accepts previously published poems and simultaneous submissions. Prefers e-mail submissions but accepts "anything that is neatly typed or printed." Electronic submissions can be sent in html or plain text (pasted into body of message; no attachments). "All 'snail mail' work must be neatly typed on white paper with your name and address on every page. We do not return work, so please don't send the only copy you have." Submit seasonal poems well in advance. Time between acceptance and publication is 2 months. Poems are circulated to an editorial board. Guidelines available on website. "We guarantee that at least one poem from each submission will be printed in our publication. If you would like to be published on the web, please say so in your cover letter. All work appears in the print copy first, and 2 weeks later online. Each person who submits poetry receives a copy of the newsletter."

Advice "We look for poetry that is visible. Poetry you can see and touch and feel."

$ THE THREEPENNY REVIEW

P.O. Box 9131, Berkeley CA 94709. (510)849-4545. Website: www.threepennyreview.com. Established 1980. **Poetry Editor:** Wendy Lesser.

- Work published in this review has also been included in *The Best American Poetry* and *Pushcart Prize* anthologies.

Magazine Needs *Threepenny Review* "is a quarterly review of literature, performing and visual arts, and social articles aimed at the intelligent, well-read, but not necessarily academic, reader. Nationwide circulation. Want: formal, narrative, short poems (and others). Prefer under 100 lines. No bias against formal poetry, in fact a slight bias in favor of it." Has published poetry by Thom Gunn, Frank Bidart, Seamus Heaney, Czeslaw Milosz, and Louise Glück. Features about 10 poems in each 36-page tabloid issue. Receives about 4,500 submissions of poetry/year, accepts about 12. Press run is 10,000 for 8,000 subscribers of which 150 are libraries. Subscription: $25. Sample: $12.

How to Submit Submit up to 5 poems at a time. Do not submit mss June through August. Guidelines available for SASE or on website. Responds in up to 2 months. Pays $100/poem plus one-year subscription. Acquires first serial rights. "Send for review guidelines (SASE required)."

☒ $☑ TICKLED BY THUNDER, HELPING WRITERS GET PUBLISHED SINCE 1990

14076-86A Ave., Surrey BC V3W 0V9 Canada. E-mail: info@tickledbythunder.com. Website: www. tickledbythunder.com. Established 1990. **Publisher/Editor:** Larry Lindner.

Magazine Needs *Tickled by Thunder* appears up to 4 times/year, using poems about "fantasy particularly, about writing or whatever. Require original images and thoughts. Keep them short (up to 40 lines)—not interested in long, long poems. Nothing pornographic, childish, unimaginative. Welcome humor and creative inspirational verse." Has published poetry by Laleh Dadpour Jackson and Helen Michiko Singh. *Tickled by Thunder* is 24 pages, digest-sized, published on Macintosh. Has 1,000 readers/subscribers. Subscription: $12/4 issues. Sample: $2.50.

How to Submit Include 3-5 samples of writing with queries. No e-mail submissions. Cover letter is required with submissions; include "a few facts about yourself and brief list of publishing credits." Editor comments on rejected poems "80% of the time." Guidelines available for SASE or on website. Responds in up to 6 months. Pays 2¢/line, $2 maximum. Acquires first rights. Reviews books of poetry in up to 300 words. Open to unsolicited reviews. Send materials for review consideration.

Contest/Award Offerings Offers a poetry contest 4 times/year. **Deadlines:** the 15th of February, May, August, and October. **Entry fee:** $5 for one poem; free for subscribers. Prize: cash, publication, and subscription.

Also Offers Publishes author-subsidized chapbooks. "We are interested in student poetry and publish it in our center spread: *Expressions*." Send SASE (or SAE and IRC) for details.

☒ ☑ TIGER'S EYE PRESS; TIGER'S EYE: A JOURNAL OF POETRY

P.O. Box 214582, Sacramento CA 95821-9998. E-mail: tigerseyepoet@hotmail.com. Website: www. tigerseyejournal.com. Established 2001. **Editors:** Colette Jonopulos, JoAn Osborne.

Magazine Needs *Tiger's Eye: A Journal of Poetry* is a biannual journal featuring both established and unknown poets. "Besides publishing the work of several poets in each issue, we feature 3 poets in interviews, giving the reader insight into their lives and writing habits." Wants "both free verse and traditional forms, no restrictions on subject or length. Poems with distinct imagery and viewpoint are preferred." Does not want overly erotic, violent, or sentimental poetry. Accepts poetry "from young people age 14 and up; please notify editors if under 18." Has published poetry by Taylor Graham, Alan Catlin, Robert Schuler, Virgil Suárez, Lin Lifshin, and Joyce Odam. *Tiger's Eye* is digest-sized, saddle-stapled, with 80 lb. cardstock cover with color photo. Receives about 300 poems/year, accepts about 100. Publishes about 50 poems/issue. Press run is 200; 30 are distributed free to poets and advertisers. Single copy: $5; subscription: $10/2 issues. Make checks payable to Tiger's Eye Press.

How to Submit Submit up to 5 poems at a time. Accepts simultaneous submissions ("please indicate"); no previously published poems. No e-mail or disk submissions. Cover letter is required. "We respond only if a SASE is included with submission." Reads submissions year round; deadlines are approximately February 28 and August 31. Submit seasonal poems 6 months in advance. Time between acceptance and publication is 3 months. "All poems are read by the editors, divided into acceptances, rejections, or maybes. Our 3 featured poets are chosen, then letters and e-mails are sent out." Seldom comments on rejected poems. Guidelines available in magazine, for SASE, by e-mail, or on website. Responds in 6 months. Always sends prepublication galleys. Pays one contributor's copy to each poet, 2 to featured poets and contest winners. Acquires one-time rights.

Contest/Award Offerings Offers biannual poetry contest with prizes of $100, $50, and $25. Submit 3 poems, 2 copies of each, plus bio, cover letter, and SASE. **Entry fee:** $10. Each entrant receives one copy of *Tiger's Eye*. **Deadline:** February 28 and August 31 (same as for journal). Judged by independent judge. **Send contest entries only** to P.O. Box 2935, Eugene OR 97402.

Advice "We accept poems from new poets with as much enthusiasm as from established poets. Poems with clean images, unique subjects, and strong voices have a good chance of being published in *Tiger's Eye*."

◙ TIMBER CREEK REVIEW

8969 UNCG Station, Greensboro NC 27413. E-mail: timber_creek_review@hoopsmail.com. Established 1994. **Editor:** John M. Freiermuth. **Associate Editor:** Roslyn Willett.

Magazine Needs *Timber Creek Review* appears quarterly, publishing short stories, literary nonfiction, and poetry. Wants all types of poetry. Does not want religious or pornographic poetry. Has published poetry by Robert Parham, Helen Jones, Pete Lee, Mitchell Metz, Lisz H. Rashley, and Marcel Gauthier. *Timber Creek Review* is 80-92 pages, digest-sized, laser-printed, stapled, with colored paper cover, minimum graphics. Receives about 800 poems/year, accepts about 5%. Publishes about 11-18 poems/issue. Press run is 150 for 120 subscribers of which 2 are libraries, 30 shelf sales. Single copy: $4.50; subscription: $16. Sample: $4.50. Make checks payable to J.M. Freiermuth.

How to Submit Submit 3-4 poems at a time. Line length for poetry is 3 minimum. Accepts simultaneous submissions; no previously published poems. No fax, e-mail, or disk submissions. Cover letter is required. Reads submissions year round. Submit seasonal poems 10 months in advance. Time between acceptance and publication is 1-3 months. Never comments on rejected poems. Occasionally publishes theme issues. Guidelines available for SASE or by e-mail. Responds in up to 6 months. Pays one contributor's copy. Acquires first North American serial rights.

◙ ◎ TIME OF SINGING, A MAGAZINE OF CHRISTIAN POETRY (Specialized: literary religious)

P.O. Box 149, Conneaut Lake PA 16316. E-mail: timesing1@earthlink.net. Website: www.timeofsinging.bizland.com. Established 1958-1965, revived 1980. **Editor:** Lora H. Zill.

Magazine Needs *Time of Singing* appears 4 times/year. "Collections of uneven lines, series of phrases, preachy statements, unstructured 'prayers,' and trite sing-song rhymes usually get returned. I look for poems that 'show' rather than 'tell.' The viewpoint is unblushingly Christian—but in its widest and most inclusive meaning." Wants free verse and well-crafted rhyme; would like to see more forms. Has published poetry by John Grey, Luci Shaw, Bob Hostetler, Frances P. Reid, Barbara Crooker, and Charles Waugaman. *Time of Singing* is 44 pages, digest-sized, offset from typescript, with decorative line drawings scattered throughout. Receives over 800 submissions/year, accepts about 175. Press run is 300 for 150 subscribers. Subscription: $17 US, $21 (US) for Canada, and $30 (US) for overseas. Sample: $4, or 2 for $6 postage paid.

How to Submit Submit up to 5 poems at a time, single-spaced. "I prefer poems under 40 lines, but will publish up to 60 lines if exceptional." Accepts previously published poems (say when/where appeared) and simultaneous submissions. Accepts e-mail submissions (pasted into body of message). Time between acceptance and publication is up to one year. Editor comments with suggestions for improvement if close to publication. Guidelines and contest rules available for SASE, by e-mail, or on website. Responds in 2 months. Pays one contributor's copy.

Contest/Award Offerings Sponsors theme contests for specific issues.

Advice "Study the craft. Be open to critique. A poet is often too close to his/her work and needs a critical, honest eye. *Time of Singing* publishes more literary-style verse, not greeting card style."

◙ TITAN PRESS; MASTERS AWARDS

Box 17897, Encino CA 91416. E-mail: ucla654@yahoo.com. Website: www.titanpress.info. Established 1980. **Publisher:** Stephanie Wilson.

Book/Chapbook Needs & How to Submit Titan Press is "a small press presently publishing 6-7 works per year including poetry, photojournals, calendars, novels, etc. We look for quality, freshness, and that touch of genius.'' In poetry, ''we want to see verve, natural rhythms, discipline, impact, etc. We are flexible but verbosity, triteness, and saccharine make us cringe. *We now read and publish only manuscripts accepted from the Masters Award.*'' Has published books by Bebe Oberon, Walter Calder, Exene Vida, Carlos Castenada, and Sandra Gilbert. Their tastes are for poets such as Adrienne Rich, Li-Young Lee, Charles Bukowski, and Czeslaw Milosz. ''We have strong liaisons with the entertainment industry and like to see material that is media-oriented and au courant.''

Contest/Award Offerings ''We sponsor the Masters Awards, established in 1981, including a $1,000 grand prize annually, plus each winner (and the 5 runners-up in poetry) will be published on website or in a clothbound edition and distributed to selected university and public libraries, news mediums, etc. There is a one-time-only **$15 administration and reading fee** per entrant. Submit a maximum of 5 poems or song lyric pages (no tapes) totaling no more than 150 lines. Any poetic style or genre is acceptable, but a clear and fresh voice, discipline, natural rhythm, and a certain individuality should be evident. Further application and details available with a #10 SASE.''

Advice ''Please study what we publish before you consider submitting.''

✖ ☯ ◎ TOUCHSTONE LITERARY JOURNAL (Specialized: bilingual/foreign language, form/style, translations); PANTHER CREEK PRESS

P.O. Box 130233, The Woodlands TX 77393-0233. E-mail: panthercreek3@hotmail.com. Website: www.panthercreekpress.com. Established 1975. **Poetry Editor:** William Laufer. **Managing Editor:** Guida Jackson. (Mail for book projects should be sent to Panther Creek Press, P.O. Box 130233, Panther Creek Station, Spring TX 77393-0233, attn: Guida Jackson.)

Magazine Needs *Touchstone Literary Journal* is an annual appearing in December that publishes ''experimental or well-crafted traditional forms, including sonnets, and translations. No light verse or doggerel.'' Has published poetry by Paul Christensen, Walter McDonald, Paul Ramsey, Omar Pound, and Christopher Woods. *Touchstone* is 100 pages, digest-sized, flat-spined, professionally printed in small, dark type, with glossy card cover. Subscription: $9.

How to Submit Submit 5 poems at a time. ''Cover letter telling something about the poet piques our interest and makes the submission seem less like a mass mailing.'' Sometimes sends prepublication galleys. Pays 2 contributor's copies. Reviews books of poetry. Send materials for review consideration to review editor.

Book/Chapbook Needs & How to Submit Panther Creek Press also publishes an occasional chapbook. Send SASE for chapbook submission guidelines. Recent titles include *Living on the Hurricane Coast* by Robb Jackson, *The Mottled Air* by Paul Christensen, *Leopards, Oracles, and Long Horns: Three West African Epic Cycles* by chichi layor, *Watching the Worlds Go By, Selected Poems* by Omar Pound, and *Under a Riverbed Sky* by Christopher Woods. ''Query first, with SASE. Absolutely no mail is answered without SASE or e-mail address.''

☯ TRAINED MONKEY PRESS; TRAINED MONKEY BROADSIDES

701 Isabella #1, Newport KY 41071. E-mail: trainedmonkeypress@hotmail.com. Established 2000. **Editor:** Vic Grunkenmeyer.

Magazine Needs Trained Monkey Broadsides appear monthly and include poetry, album reviews, short fiction, and photos. They are given away free at distribution points, and by mail for $1. Trained Monkey Broadsides are 10 pages, digest-sized, saddle-stapled, with paper covers, include art/graphics and business-card-size and flyer-size ads. Receives about 100 poems/year, accepts about 20%. Publishes about 4 poems/issue. Press run is 200 for 20 subscribers; 150 are distributed free to bars, businesses, and music stores. Single copy: $1; subscription: $10/year. Sample: $1.

How to Submit Submit 3-6 poems at a time. Line length for poetry is 1 minimum, 50 maximum. No previously published poems or simultaneous submissions. Accepts e-mail submissions; no fax

Publishers of Poetry

or disk submissions. Cover letter is preferred. "Always send SASEs when submitting." Reads submissions year round. Time between acceptance and publication is 2 months. Submissions may be circulated within the editorial board. Seldom comments on rejected poems. Guidelines available in magazine or by e-mail. Responds in one month. Pays one contributor's copy. Acquires one-time rights. Reviews books and chapbooks of poetry and other magazines/journals in 200 words, single book format. Send materials for review consideration to Trained Monkey Press.

Book/Chapbook Needs & How to Submit The goal of Trained Monkey Press publications is "to get people to pick them up and read. We look for strong words; good poetry in any form that is about something. Satire is encouraged." Does not want "didactic, preachy, wishy-washy whining." Has published poetry by Joey Shannanagins, Tom Case, David Garza, Cliff Spisak, Julie Judge, and Mr. Spoons. Trained Monkey Press publishes 5-7 chapbooks/year. Chapbooks are usually 30 pages, saddle-stapled, with stock covers, include art/graphics. Query first, with a few sample poems and a cover letter with brief bio and publication credits. Responds to queries in one month; to mss in 2 months. Pays 5 author's copies (out of a press run of 100). Order sample chapbooks by sending $5 to Trained Monkey Press.

Advice "Get it out . . . submit to the monkey."

☐ ◎ TRANSCENDENT VISIONS (Specialized: people living with mental illness)

251 S. Olds Blvd., 84-E, Fairless Hills PA 19030-3426. (215)547-7159. Established 1992. **Editor:** David A. Kime.

Magazine Needs *Transcendent Visions* appears 1-2 times/year "to provide a creative outlet for psychiatric survivors/ex-mental patients." Wants "experimental, confessional poems; strong poems dealing with issues we face. Any length or subject matter is OK, but shorter poems are more likely to be published. No rhyming poetry." Has published poetry by Jennifer A. Fulco, Chriss-Spike Quatrone, Richard Arnold, and Susan Weicksel Mull. *Transcendent Visions* is 24 pages, magazine-sized, photocopied, corner-stapled, with paper cover, includes b&w line drawings. Receives about 100 poems/year, accepts 20%. Press run is 200 for 50 subscribers. Subscription: $6. Sample: $3. Make checks payable to David Kime.

How to Submit Submit 5 poems at a time. Accepts previously published poems and simultaneous submissions. Cover letter is preferred. "Please tell me something unique about you, but I do not care about all the places you have been published." Time between acceptance and publication is 6 months. Guidelines available for SASE. Responds in 4 months. Pays one contributor's copy. Acquires first or one-time rights. Staff reviews books and chapbooks of poetry and other magazines in 20 words. Send materials for review consideration.

Also Offers "I also publish a political zine called *Crazed Nation*, featuring essays concerning mental illness."

Advice "Find your own voice."

✪ ◪ TRESTLE CREEK REVIEW

English Dept., LKH 204-G, North Idaho College, 1000 W. Garden Ave., Coeur d'Alene ID 83814-2199. (208)769-7877. Fax: (208)769-3431. E-mail: lawallin@nic.edu. Established 1982-83. **Editor:** Lori Wallin.

Magazine Needs *Trestle Creek Review* is a "2-year college creative writing program production. Purposes: 1) expand the range of publishing/editing experience for our small band of writers; 2) expose them to editing experience; 3) create another outlet for serious, beginning writers. We're fairly eclectic and accept poetry, fiction, and creative nonfiction. We favor poetry strong on image and sound, character-drive fiction, and nonfiction that addresses the universals of the human condition; spare us the romantic, the formulaic, and the clichéd." Has published poetry by Sean Brendan-Brown, E.G. Burrows, Ron McFarland, and Mary Winters. *Trestle Creek Review* is a 57-page annual, digest-sized, professionally printed on heavy buff stock, perfect-bound, with matte cover with art.

Receives 100 submissions/year, accepts about 30. Press run is 300-600. Sample: $5.

How to Submit No previously published poems or simultaneous submissions. Accepts e-mail submissions (as attachment in Word or .rtf format); no fax submissions. **Deadline:** March 1 (for May publication). Responds by May 30. Pays 2 contributor's copies.

Advice "Be neat; be precise; don't romanticize or cry in your beer; strike the surprising, universal note. Know the names of things."

☑ TULANE REVIEW

122 Norman Mayer, New Orleans LA 70118. (504)865-5160. Fax: (504)862-8958. E-mail: litsoc@tulane.edu. Website: www.tulane.edu/~litsoc. Established 1988. **Editor:** Leslie White.

• *Tulane Review* is the recipient of an AWP Literary Magazine Design Award.

Magazine Needs *Tulane Review* is a national biannual literary journal seeking quality submissions of prose, poetry, and art. "We consider all types of poetry, but prefer poems between 1-2 pages. We favor imaginative poems with bold, inventive images." Has published poetry by Virgil Suárez, Tom Chandler, Gaylord Brewer, and Ryan Van Cleave. *Tulane Review* is 80 pages, 7×9, perfect-bound, with 100# cover with full-color artwork, includes 10-12 pieces of internal art and ads for literary journals. Receives about 600 poems/year, accepts about 30. Publishes about 15 poems/issue. Single copy: $5; subscription: $10. Make checks payable to *Tulane Review*.

How to Submit Submit up to 6 poems at a time. Accepts simultaneous submissions; no previously published poems. No fax, e-mail, or disk submissions. Cover letter is required. "Include brief biography." Reads submissions year round. Time between acceptance and publication is 2 months. Poems are circulated to an editorial board. "Poems are reviewed anonymously by a review board under a poetry editor's supervision. Recommendations are given to the editor, who makes final publication decisions." Often comments on rejected poems. Guidelines available in magazine, for SASE, by e-mail, or on website. Responds in 2 months. Pays 3 contributor's copies. Acquires first North American serial rights.

Also Offers "We have contests periodically that present cash awards to poets, writers, and artists."

✪ ☑ ◎ TUNDRA: THE JOURNAL OF THE SHORT POEM (Specialized: form/poetry of 13 or fewer lines, including haiku and tanka)

22230 NE 28th Place, Sammamish WA 98074-6408. E-mail: WelchM@aol.com. Established 1999. **Editor/Publisher:** Michael Dylan Welch.

Magazine Needs *Tundra: The Journal of the Short Poem* is a biannual journal showcasing all short poetry, including haiku, tanka, and other genres. Wants "short poetry of 13 or fewer lines rooted in immediate and objective imagery, including haiku and tanka." Does not want religious, topical, or confessional poetry. Has published poetry by Dana Gioia, X.J. Kennedy, Jane Hirshfield, Peter Pereira, Robert Bly, and Madeleine DeFrees. *Tundra* is 128 pages, digest-sized, offset-printed, perfect-bound, with glossy cover, includes photography. Receives about 14,000 poems/year, accepts about .05%. Publishes about 150-200 poems/issue. Press run is 1,200 for 700 subscribers of which 10 are libraries, 50 shelf sales; 10 are distributed free to places such as poetry centers. Single copy: $9; subscription: $21/3issues. Make checks payable to Michael D. Welch.

How to Submit Submit 3-5 poems at a time ("up to 10 is okay if as short as haiku"). No previously published poems or simultaneous submissions. Accepts e-mail submissions (pasted into body of message); no disk submissions. "Please include a #10 SASE with sufficient postage for return of the manuscript or for a response. Cover letters are optional—okay the first time you submit, but unnecessary thereafter unless you say something you know the editor needs to know. *Tundra* does not publish bios, so there's no need to include them except for the editor's information. For e-mail submissions, no attached files, please! Please always include your full postal address with each e-mail submission." Reads submissions year round. Time between acceptance and publication "varies, but sometimes up to a year. The editor makes the sole decision, and may occasionally offer suggestions on poems whether accepted or returned. The editor will clearly indicate if he wants to see a revision." Sometimes comments on rejected poems. "I recommend seeing an issue before submitting, but no purchase or subscription is required." Guidelines available for SASE or by e-mail. Responds in up to one month. Sometimes sends prepublication galleys. Pays one contributor's copy. Acquires first rights. "Rights revert to author after publication, but we in future want to include selected poems on a website." Reviews books and chapbooks of poetry in 500-2,000 words, single and multi-book format. Send materials for review consideration to Michael Dylan Welch.

Advice "If your work centers on immediate and objective imagery, *Tundra* is interested. All submissions must be 13 or fewer lines, with only very rare exceptions (where each line is very short). If you think that a haiku is merely 5-7-5 syllables, then I do not want to see your work (see 'Becoming a Haiku Poet' online at www.haikuworld.org/begin/mdwelch.apr2003.html for reasons why). Due to the excessive volume of inappropriate submissions for *Tundra* in the past, I now encourage only well-established poets to submit."

⊘ TURKEY PRESS

6746 Sueno Rd., Isla Vista CA 93117-4904. Established 1974. **Poetry Editors:** Harry Reese and Sandra Reese. "We do not encourage solicitations of any kind to the press. We seek out and develop projects on our own."

$⊘ turnrow

English Dept., The University of Louisiana at Monroe, Monroe LA 71209. (318)342-1520. Fax: (318)342-1491. E-mail: ryan@ulm.edu or heflin@ulm.edu. Website: http://turnrow.ulm.edu. Established 2000. **Editors:** Jack Heflin and William Ryan.

Magazine Needs *turnrow* appears biannually and seeks submissions of nonfiction of a general interest, short fiction, poetry, translations, interviews, art, and photography. Has published poetry by CD Wright, Mary Ruefle, Christopher Howell, Gonzalo Rojas, Robert Kelly, and Brooks Haxton. *turnrow* is 200 pages, digest-sized, offset-printed, perfect-bound, with full-color cover, includes art, graphics, photography. Receives about 5,000 poems/year, accepts about .01%. Publishes about 6-10 poems/issue. Press run is 1,000 for 200 subscribers of which 15 are libraries, 400 shelf sales. Single copy: $7; subscription: $12/year, $20/2 years. Sample: $7. Make checks payable to *turnrow*.

How to Submit Submit 3 poems at a time. Line length for poetry is open. No previously published poems or simultaneous submissions. No fax, e-mail, or disk submissions. Cover letter is preferred. Reads submissions September 15 through May 15. Time between acceptance and publication is 6 months. Seldom comments on rejected poems. Occasionally publishes theme issues. List of upcoming themes and guidelines available for SASE or on website. Responds in 2 months. Sometimes sends prepublication galleys. Pays $50 and 2 contributor's copies. Acquires first rights.

⊘ 24.7; RE-PRESST

30 Forest St., Providence RI 02906. (401)521-4728. Established 1994. **Poetry Editor:** David Church. **Currently not accepting submissions**.

⊘ TWILIGHT ENDING

21 Ludlow Dr., Milford CT 06460-6822. (203)877-3473. Established 1995. **Editor/Publisher:** Emma J. Blanch.

Magazine Needs *Twilight Ending* appears 3 times/year, publishing "poetry and short fiction of the highest caliber, in English, with universal appeal." Has featured the work of poets from the US, Canada, Europe, Middle East, Japan, and New Zealand. Wants "poems with originality in thought and in style, reflecting the latest trend in writing, moving from the usual set-up to a vertical approach. We prefer unrhymed poetry; however, we accept rhymed verse if rhymes are perfect. We look for the unusual approach in content and style with clarity. No haiku. No poems forming a design. No foul words. No translations. No bio. No porn." Prefers seasonal/nature poems. *Twilight Ending* is digest-sized, "elegantly printed on white linen paper, with one poem with title per page (12-30 lines)." Receives about 1,500 poems/year, accepts 10%. Press run is 120 for 50 subscribers of which 25 are libraries. Sample: $6 US, $6.50 Canada, $7 Europe, $8 Middle East, Japan, and New Zealand. Make checks payable to Emma J. Blanch.

How to Submit Submit only 3-4 poems at a time. "Use standard $8\frac{1}{2} \times 11$ white paper. Type each poem, single-spaced, one poem per page. Each poem must have a title. No abbreviation. Type name, address, and zip code on top right hand corner of each page." No previously published poems or simultaneous submissions, nor poems submitted to contests while in consideration for *Twilight Ending*. Include white stamped business envelop for reply (overseas contributors should include 2 IRCs). No fax or e-mail submissions. "When accepted, poems will not be returned, so keep copies." **Submission deadlines:** mid-December for winter issue, mid-April for spring/summer issue, mid-September for fall issue. No backlog, "all poems are destroyed after publication." Often comments on rejected poems. Guidelines available for SASE. Responds in one week. Pays nothing—not even a copy. Acquires first rights.

Advice "If editing is needed, suggestions will be made for the writer to rework and resubmit a corrected version. The author always decides; remember that you deal with experts."

◙ TWO RIVERS REVIEW

P.O. Box 158, Clinton NY 13323. E-mail: tworiversreview@juno.com. Website: http://trrpoetry.trip od.com. Established 1998. **Editor:** Philip Memmer.

Magazine Needs *Two Rivers Review* appears biannually and "seeks to print the best of contemporary poetry. All styles of work are welcome, so long as submitted poems display excellence." Has published poetry by Billy Collins, Gary Young, Michael Waters, Meg Kearney, and Reginald Shepherd. *Two Rivers Review* is 44 pages, digest-sized, professionally printed on cream-colored paper, with card cover. Subscription: $10. Sample (current issue): $5. "Poets wishing to submit work may obtain a sample copy for the reduced price of $4."

How to Submit Submit no more than 4 poems at a time with cover letter (optional) and SASE (required). Simultaneous submissions are considered with notification. No e-mail submissions. Guidelines available for SASE, by e-mail, or on website. Responds to most submissions within one month. Acquires first rights.

Contest/Award Offerings Sponsors the annual *Two Rivers Review* Poetry Prize with May deadline. In 2002, *Two Rivers Review* began publishing chapbooks through the *Two Rivers Review* Poetry Chapbook Prize. Two chapbooks are published each year, selected through an annual competition with a December deadline. Poets published through this series include Kip Zegers and Harry Humes. Guidelines available for SASE or on website.

◪ ◎ U.S. 1 WORKSHEETS; U.S. 1 POETS' COOPERATIVE (Specialized: regional/New Jersey and area surrounding U.S. 1 corridor)

P.O. Box 127, Kingston NJ 08528-0127. Website: www.geocities.com/princetonpoets2001/index.ht ml. Established 1973. **Contact:** E.A. Socolow, consulting editor.

Magazine Needs *U.S. 1 Worksheets* is a literary annual (February/March double-issue) that uses high-quality poetry and fiction. "We prefer complex, well-written work." Has published poetry by Alicia Ostriker, James Richardson, Frederick Tibbetts, Lois Marie Harrod, James Haba, Charlotte Mandel, and David Keller. *U.S. 1 Worksheets* is 72 pages, digest-sized, saddle-stapled, with b&w cover art. "We read a lot but take very few." Subscription: $7, $12/2 years. "Requests for back issues, sample copies, and subscriptions should be addressed to Jane Rawlings, circulation manager (address above)."

How to Submit Submit 5 poems at a time. Rarely accepts previously published poems; no simultaneous submissions. "Send 3 copies of each poem submitted. Include name, address, and phone number in upper right hand corner of one copy; title only on 2 copies. We use a rotating board of editors; we read in May and June, and can no longer return manuscripts. A self-addressed, stamped postcard will get our decision on submissions." Guidelines available for SASE. Pays one contributor's copy.

Advice "Look at past issues; consult the website."

✪ ⊕ ☑ UNDERSTANDING MAGAZINE; DIONYSIA PRESS LTD.

20 A Montgomery St., Edinburgh, Lothian EH7 5JS Great Britain. Phone/fax: (0131)4780680. Established 1989. **Contact:** Denise Smith.

Magazine Needs *Understanding Magazine*, published once/year, features "poetry, short stories, parts of plays, reviews, and articles." Wants "original poetry." Has published poetry by Susanna Roxman, D. Zervanou, and Thom Nairn. *Understanding* is A5 and perfect-bound. Receives 2,000 poems/year. Press run is 1,000 for 500 subscribers. Single copy: £4.50; subscription: £9. Sample: £3. Make checks payable to Dionysia Press.

How to Submit Submit 5 poems at a time. Accepts simultaneous submissions; no previously published poems. Accepts fax submissions. Time between acceptance and publication is 6-10 months. Poems are circulated to an editorial board. Often comments on rejected poems. Responds in 6 months or more. Always sends prepublication galleys. Pays one contributor's copy. Acquires all rights. Returns rights after publication. Staff reviews books or chapbooks of poetry or other magazines. Send materials for review consideration.

Book/Chapbook Needs & How to Submit Dionysia Press Ltd. publishes 14 paperbacks and chapbooks of poetry/year. "Sometimes we select from submissions or competitions." Has published *Let Me Sing My Song* by Paul Hullah; *Poems* by Klitos Kyrou, translated by Thom Nairn and D. Zervanou; *Sailing the Sands* by James Andrew; and *The Feeble Lies of Orestes Chalkiopoulos* by Andreas Mitsou. Books are usually A5, perfect-bound, with hard covers with art. Query first, with a few sample poems and cover letter with brief bio and publication credits. Responds to queries in 2-6 months. Pays author's copies. "We usually get arts council grants, or poets get grants for themselves." For sample books or chapbooks, write to the above address.

Contest/Award Offerings Sponsors poetry competitions with cash prizes. Guidelines available for SASE.

◫ $☑ UNIVERSITY OF ALBERTA PRESS

Ring House 2, Edmonton AB T6G 2E1 Canada. (780)492-3662. Fax: (780)492-0719. E-mail: uap@ual berta.ca. Website: www.uap.ualberta.ca. Established 1969. **Contact:** Michael Luski, acquisitions editor.

Book/Chapbook Needs "The University of Alberta Press is a scholarly press, generally publishing

U.S. 1 WORKSHEETS
U.S. 1 POETS' COOPERATIVE
PRINCETON, NEW JERSEY

30th ANNIVERSARY ISSUE

This 30th anniversary cover copies the original 1972 cover. Says Elizabeth Anne Socolow, consulting editor, "Our group named itself after the old Boston Post Road, our region's 'spine,' along which members lived." Original photographer was Wes Townsend; graphic design/art direction by Mary Szilagyi Durkee.

nonfiction plus some literary titles.'' Publishes 1-2 paperback poetry titles/year. Looking for ''mature, thoughtful work—nothing too avant-garde. No juvenile or 'Hallmark verse.' '' Has published *An Ark of Koans* by E.D. Blodgett, *Bloody Jack* by Dennis Cooley, and *The Hornbooks of Rita K* by Robert Kroetsch.

How to Submit Query first, with 10-12 sample poems and cover letter with brief bio and publication credits. ''Do not send complete manuscript on first approach.'' Accepts previously published poems. Accepts e-mail and disk submissions. Time between acceptance and publication is 6-10 months. Poems are circulated to an editorial board. ''The process is: acquiring editor to editorial group meeting to 2 external reviewers to press committee to acceptance.'' Seldom comments on rejected poems. Responds to queries in 3 months. Pays royalties of 10% of net plus 10 author's copies. See website to order sample books.

☑ UNIVERSITY OF GEORGIA PRESS; CONTEMPORARY POETRY SERIES

330 Research Dr., Suite B100, University of Georgia, Athens GA 30602-4901. Website: www.ugapress.com. Press established 1938, series established 1980. **Series Editor:** Bin Ramke. **Poetry Competition Coordinator:** Andrew Berzanskis.

- Poetry published by University of Georgia Press has been included in the *Pushcart Prize* anthology.

Contest/Award Offerings Through its annual competition, the press publishes 4 paperback collections of poetry/year, 2 of which are by poets who have not had a book published. Recent winners include *The Book of Motion* by Tung-Hui Hun, *What Animal* by Oni Buchanan, *Vertical Elegies 5* by Sam Truitt, and *The Blaze of the Pui* by Mark McMorris.

How to Submit ''Writers should query first for guidelines and submission periods. Please enclose SASE.'' There are no restrictions on the type of poetry submitted, but ''familiarity with our previously published books in the series may be helpful.'' No fax or e-mail submissions. **Entry fee:** $20. Make checks payable to University of Georgia Press. Manuscripts are *not* returned after the judging is completed. Guidelines available for SASE or on website.

☑ THE UNIVERSITY OF MASSACHUSETTS PRESS; THE JUNIPER PRIZE

P.O. Box 429, Amherst MA 01004-0429. (413)545-2217. Fax: (413)545-1226. E-mail: info@umpress.umass.edu. Website: www.umass.edu/umpress. Established 1964. **Contact:** Alice I. Maldonado, assistant editor and web manager.

Contest/Award Offerings The press offers an annual competition for the Juniper Prize, in alternate years to first and subsequent books. In even-numbered years (2004, 2006, etc.), only ''subsequent'' books will be considered: mss whose authors have had at least one full-length book or chapbook of poetry published or accepted for publication. Such chapbooks must be at least 30 pages, and self-published work is not considered to lie within this ''books and chapbooks'' category. In odd-numbered years (2003, 2005, etc.), only ''first books'' will be considered: mss by writers whose poems may have appeared in literary journals and/or anthologies but have not been published, or been accepted for publication, in book form. Has published *The Double Task* by Gray Jacobik, *Song of the Cicadas* by Môllg-Lan, *Heartwall* by Richard Jackson, *At the Site of Inside Out* by Anna Rabinowitz, *Cities and Towns: Poems* by Arthur Vogelsang, and *Fugitive Red* by Karen Donovan. ''Poetry books are approximately $14 for paperback editions and $24 for cloth.'' Submissions must not exceed 70 pages in typescript. Include paginated contents page; provide the title, publisher, and year of publication for previously published volumes. A list of poems published or slated for publication in literary journals and/or anthologies must also accompany the ms. Such poems may be included in the ms and must be identified. ''Manuscripts by more than one author, entries of more than one manuscript simultaneously or within the same year, and translations are not eligible.'' **Entry fee:** $25 plus SASE for notification; mss will not be returned. **Postmark deadline:** September 30. The award is announced in April/May and publication is scheduled for the following spring. The amount of the prize is $1,000 and is in lieu of royalties on the first print run. Poet also receives 12 copies in one edition or 6 copies each if published in both hardcover and paperbound editions. Fax, call, or send SASE to the above address for guidelines and/or further information. Entries are to be mailed to Juniper Prize, University of Massachusetts, Amherst MA 01003.

◙ UNIVERSITY OF WISCONSIN PRESS; BRITTINGHAM PRIZE IN POETRY; FELIX POLLAK PRIZE IN POETRY

Dept. of English, 600 N. Park St., University of Wisconsin, Madison WI 53706. Website: www.wisc.edu/wisconsinpress/index.html. Brittingham Prize inaugurated in 1985. **Poetry Editor:** Ronald Wallace.

Contest/Award Offerings The University of Wisconsin Press publishes primarily scholarly works, but they offer the annual Brittingham Prize and the Felix Pollak Prize, both $1,000 plus publication. These prizes are the only way in which this press publishes poetry. Rules available for SASE or on website. Qualified readers will screen all mss. Winners will be selected by "a distinguished poet who will remain anonymous until the winners are announced in mid-February." Past judges include Rita Dove, Alicia Ostriker, Mark Doty, Ed Hirsch, Kelly Cherry, and Robert Bly. Winners include Tony Hoagland, Stephanie Strickland, Derick Burleson, Cathy Colman, Greg Rappleye, Roy Jacobstein, and Anna Meek. For both prizes, **submit between September 1 and September 30**, unbound ms volume of 50-80 pages, with name, address, and telephone number on title page. No translations. Poems must be previously unpublished in book form. Poems published in journals, chapbooks, and anthologies may be included but must be acknowledged. There is a non-refundable **$25 entry fee** which must accompany the ms. (Checks to University of Wisconsin Press.) Mss will not be returned. Contest results available for SASE. "Previous winners of the prizes may submit subsequent book manuscripts between November 1 and November 30."
Advice "Each submission is considered for both prizes (one entry fee only)."

◻ THE UNKNOWN WRITER

P.O. Box 698, Ramsey NJ 07446. E-mail: unknown_writer_2000@yahoo.com. Website: www.fyreflyjar.net/uw.html. Established 1995. **Poetry Editor:** Amy Van Orden.

Magazine Needs "We are a print magazine publishing poetry and fiction by up-and-coming writers who have small-press credits. We also delight in giving quality writers a start with their first publication. Send us strong, rich poetry with attention to imagery, emotion, and detail. We enjoy the traditional and structured forms like sonnet and haiku as much as experimental and modern free verse. Any subject matter is acceptable as long as the poem makes a direct connection with the reader. Keep the work fresh, intelligent, and mindful." Does not want forced rhyme, limericks, or vulgar work. No profane or sexually explicit material and no graphic violence. Accepts poetry from young adults (16 or older). *The Unknown Writer* is usually 40 pages, digest-sized, saddle-stapled, with cardstock cover, includes b&w line art and photos (when possible). Publishes up to 7 poems/issue. Single copy: $4, subscription: $15 (2 issues).

How to Submit Submit 3-5 poems at a time. Line length for poetry is 2 minimum, 100 maximum. Accepts simultaneous submissions; no previously published poems. "Please be respectful and tell us if a poem is accepted elsewhere." Accepts e-mail (as attachment but prefers pasted into body of message) and disk submissions. Cover letter is preferred. "Through postal mail, include a SASE, full address, and e-mail address. With e-mail submissions, include full contact information and introduce yourself in a short note; don't just send poems. Tell us if the submission is simultaneous." Reads submissions all year. Time between acceptance and publication is up to 9 months. Guidelines available for SASE, by e-mail, or on website. "Please check website for recent news and information, as we may change our guidelines." Responds in up to 6 months. Pays one contributor's copy. Acquires first worldwide rights.

Advice "We want to discover new, talented writers who need their first break or have a handful of previous acceptances, but new does not mean clichéd or careless. Write about your passion with rich language. Read your poems to others and get feedback. Support and participate in local poetry readings. Then revise and proofread. Writing is a practice and a craft. If we reject your first submission but tell you to submit again, we mean it. Keep trying.''

🌐 ☑ ◎ URTHONA MAGAZINE (Specialized: Buddhism)

9A Auckland Rd., Cambridge CB5 8DW United Kingdom. Phone: (01223) 309470. E-mail: urthona. mag@virgin.net. Website: www.urthona.com. Established 1992. **Contact:** Poetry Editor.

Magazine Needs *Urthona*, published biannually, explores the arts and Western culture from a Buddhist perspective. Wants ''poetry rousing the imagination.'' Does not want ''undigested autobiography, political, or New-Agey poems.'' Has published poetry by Peter Abbs, Robert Bly, and Peter Redgrove. *Urthona* is 60 pages, A4, offset-printed, saddle-stapled, with 4-color glossy cover, includes b&w photos, art, and ads. Receives about 300 poems/year, accepts about 40. Press run is 1,200 for 200 subscribers plus shelf sales in Australia and America. ''See website for current subscription rates.'' Sample (including guidelines): $7.99 US, $8.99 Canadian.

How to Submit Submit 6 poems at a time. No previously published poems or simultaneous submissions. Accepts submissions by e-mail (as attachment). Cover letter is preferred. Time between acceptance and publication is up to 8 months. Poems are circulated to an editorial board and read and selected by poetry editor. Other editors have right of veto. Responds within 6 months. Pays one contributor's copy. Acquires one-time rights. Reviews books or chapbooks of poetry or other magazines in 600 words. Send materials for review consideration.

☑ UTAH STATE UNIVERSITY PRESS; MAY SWENSON POETRY AWARD

Logan UT 84322-7800. (435)797-1362. Fax: (435)797-0313. E-mail: michael.spooner@usu.edu. Website: www.usu.edu/usupress. Established 1972. **Poetry Editor:** Michael Spooner. Publishes poetry only through the May Swenson Poetry Award competition annually. Has published *Dear Elizabeth* and *May Out West* by May Swenson, *Plato's Breath* by Randall Freisinger, *The Owl Question* by Faith Shearin, *Borgo of the Holy Ghost* by Stephen McLeod, and *She Took Off Her Wings and Shoes* by Suzette Marie Bishop. See website for details.

N ☑ VAL VERDE PRESS

30163 Lexington Dr., Castaic CA 91384. E-mail: woeltjen@thevine.net. Established 2003. **Publisher/Editor:** Lance Woeltjen. ''We publish perfect-bound, quality paperback titles. We do not accept unsolicited submissions at this time.''

☑ VALPARAISO POETRY REVIEW

Dept. of English, Valparaiso University, Valparaiso IN 46383-6493. (219)464-5278. Fax: (219)464-5511. E-mail: vpr@valpo.edu. Website: www.valpo.edu/english/vpr/. Established 1999. **Editor:** Edward Byrne.

Magazine Needs *Valparaiso Poetry Review: Contemporary Poetry and Poetics* is ''a biannual online poetry journal accepting submissions of unpublished or previously published poetry, book reviews, author interviews, and essays on poetry or poetics that have not yet appeared online and for which the rights belong to the author. Query for anything else.'' Wants poetry of any length or style, free verse or traditional forms. Has published poetry by Charles Wright, Jonathan Holden, Reginald Gibbons, Janet McCann, Laurence Lieberman, Beth Simon, and Margot Schilpp. *Valparaiso Poetry Review* is published online only. Receives about 500 poems/year, accepts about 7%. Publishes about 17 poems/issue.

How to Submit Submit 3-5 poems at a time (no more than 5). Accepts previously published poems (''original publication must be identified to ensure proper credit'') and simultaneous submissions. Accepts e-mail submissions (but prefers postal mail; for e-mail, paste into body of message, no attachments); no fax or disk submissions. Cover letter is preferred. Include SASE. Reads submissions year round. Time between acceptance and publication is 6-12 months. Seldom comments on rejected poems. Guidelines available on website. Responds in up to 6 weeks. Acquires one-time rights. "All rights remain with author." Reviews books of poetry in single book and multi-book format. Send materials for review consideration to Edward Byrne, editor.

⌶ ⊕ ⦸ VAN GOGH'S EAR: WORLD POETRY FOR THE NEW MILLENNIUM

French Connection Press, 12 rue Lamartine, Paris 75009 France. Phone: (+33)1 40 16 11 47. Fax: (+33)1 40 16 07 01. E-mail: frenchcxpress@noos.fr. Website: www.frenchcx.com. Established 2002. **Founder/Editor:** Ian Ayres.

• Poetry published in *VAN GOGH'S EAR* has been included in *The Best American Poetry 2004*.

Magazine Needs *VAN GOGH'S EAR* is an annual anthology, appearing in December, "devoted to publishing excellent poetry in English by major voices and innovative new talent from around the globe. Without affiliation with specific movements or schools of poetry, we seek only to publish the best poetry being written. The anthology welcomes all work, from traditional to experimental, daring, thought-provoking poetry of unusual forms and language genius." Has published poetry by Yoko Ono, John Ashbery, Alice Notley, Norman Mailer, Joyce Carol Oates, and John Rechy. *VAN GOGH'S EAR* is 220 pages, digest-sized, digitally-printed, perfect-bound, with 4-color matte cover with commissioned artwork, includes b&w photos/drawings and b&w ads. Receives about 1,000 poems/year, accepts about 10%. Publishes about 96 poems/issue. Press run is 2,000 for 10 subscribers, 1,870 shelf sales; 120 are distributed free to contributors and reviewers. Single copy: $17; subscription: $30/2 years. Make checks payable to Committee on Poetry-VGE, P.O. Box 582, Stuyvesant Station, New York NY 10009.

How to Submit Submit 5 poems at a time. Line length for poetry is 165 maximum. Accepts previously published poems; no simultaneous submissions. Accepts disk submissions; no fax or e-mail submissions. Cover letter is preferred. "Please include SASE or e-mail address and a brief biography." Reads submissions January 1 through July 4. **Charges $5 (US) reading fee for non-subscribers.** Time between acceptance and publication is one year. "Each and every poem is closely read by all members of the editorial board. The members initial each poem and mark an 'E' for excellent, 'G' for good, or an 'OK.' The 'excellent' and 'good' poems are read again with diversity in mind. Another vote is made upon which poems will make the upcoming issue the best one yet." Seldom comments on rejected poems. "Our continued existence, and continued ability to read your work, depends mainly on subscriptions/donations. Therefore, we must ask that you at least purchase a sample copy before submitting work." Guidelines available in magazine or on website. Responds in 9 months. Always sends prepublication galleys. Pays one contributor's copy. Acquires one-time rights.

Also Offers Runs an international reading series year round. "Venues have included City Lights Bookstore in San Francisco, CBGB's in New York City, Shakespeare & Co. Bookshop in Paris, and Calder Bookshop in London. More recent venues have included Prague, Portland, Los Angeles, and Iowa City."

Advice "We equally embrace work that shows mastery of versification alongside wild work inspired by Rimbaud's 'derangement of all the senses.' We not only encourage the exploration of every possible approach to poetry but going beyond anything yet imagined. And we are very open to poets who haven't been published before. Being published isn't as important as the poetry itself."

◎ VEGETARIAN JOURNAL (Specialized: children/teens; vegetarianism); THE VEGETARIAN RESOURCE GROUP

P.O. Box 1463, Baltimore MD 21203. Website: www.vrg.org. Established 1982.

Magazine Needs The Vegetarian Resource Group is a publisher of nonfiction. *Vegetarian Journal* is a quarterly, 36 pages, magazine-sized, professionally printed, saddle-stapled, with glossy card cover. Press run is 20,000. Sample: $3.

How to Submit "Please, no submissions of poetry from adults; 18 and under only."

Contest/Award Offerings The Vegetarian Resource Group offers an annual contest for ages 18 and under: $50 savings bond in 3 age categories for the best contribution on any aspect of vegetarianism. "Most entries are essay, but we would accept poetry with enthusiasm." **Postmark deadline:** May 1. Details available for SASE.

🍁 🌀 ◎ VEHICULE PRESS; SIGNAL EDITIONS (Specialized: regional/Canada)

P.O. Box 125 Station Place du Parc, Montreal QC H2X 4A3 Canada. (514)844-6073. Fax: (514)844-7543. E-mail: vp@vehiculepress.com. Website: www.vehiculepress.com. **Poetry Editor:** Carmine Starnino. **Publisher:** Simon Dardick.

Book/Chapbook Needs Vehicle Press is a "literary press with a poetry series, Signal Editions, publishing the work of Canadian poets only." Publishes flat-spined paperbacks and hardbacks. Has published *White Stone: The Alice Poems* by Stephanie Bolster (winner of the 1998 Governor-General's Award for Poetry), *Araby* by Eric Ormsby, and *Fielder's Choice* by Elise Partridge. Publishes Canadian poetry that is "first-rate, original, content-conscious."

How to Submit Query before submitting.

🌐 ◖ VERANDAH

c/o Faculty of Arts, Deakin University, 221 Burwood Hwy., Burwood, Victoria, Australia 3125. Phone: 61.3.9251.7134. E-mail: verandah@deakin.edu.au. Website: www.deakin.edu.au/verandah/. Established 1986. **Contact:** Poetry Editor.

Magazine Needs *Verandah* appears annually in September and is "a high-quality literary journal edited by professional writing students. It aims to give voice to new and innovative writers and artists." Has published poetry by Christos Tsiolka, Dorothy Porter, Seamus Heaney, Les Murray, Ed Burger, and Joh Muk Muk Burke. *Verandah* is 120 pages, professionally printed on glossy stock, flat-spined, with full-color glossy card cover. Sample: AU$15.

How to Submit Accepts submissions by postal mail *only*. **Annual deadline:** May 31. **Reading fee:** AU$5 (or AU$10 for 3 poems); Deakin University students exempted ("please provide student number!"). Pays one contributor's copy "with prizes awarded accordingly." Acquires first Australian publishing rights.

◖ VERSE

Dept. of English, University of Georgia, Athens GA 30602. Website: www.versemag.org. Established 1984. **Editors:** Brian Henry and Andrew Zawacki.

• Poetry published in *Verse* has also appeared in *The Best American Poetry* and the *Pushcart Prize* anthology.

Magazine Needs *Verse* appears 3 times/year and is "an international poetry journal which also publishes interviews with poets, essays on poetry, and book reviews." Wants "no specific kind; we look for high-quality, innovative poetry. Our focus is not only on American poetry, but on all poetry written in English, as well as translations." Has published poetry by James Tate, Christine Hume, Dean Young, John Ashbery, Dara Wier, and Mark Strand. *Verse* is 128-416 pages, digest-sized, professionally printed, perfect-bound, with card cover. Receives about 5,000 poems/year, accepts 1%. Press run is 1,000 for 600 subscribers of which 200 are libraries, 200 shelf sales. Subscription: $18 for individuals, $36 for institutions. Current issue $10. Sample: $6.

How to Submit Submit up to 5 poems at a time, no more than twice/year. Accepts simultaneous submissions; no previously published poems. Cover letter is required. Time between acceptance and publication is up to 18 months. Often comments on rejected poems. "The magazine often publishes special features—recent features include younger American poets, Mexican poetry, Scottish poetry, Latino poets, prose poetry, women Irish poets, and Australian poetry—but does not publish 'theme' issues.'' Guidelines available on website. Responds in up to 4 months. Always sends prepublication galleys. Pays 2 contributor's copies plus a one-year subscription. Send materials for review consideration.

Advice ''Read widely and deeply. Avoid inundating a magazine with submissions; constant exposure will not increase your chances of getting accepted.''

$☑ THE VIRGINIA QUARTERLY REVIEW; EMILY CLARK BALCH PRIZE

1 West Range, P.O. Box 400223, Charlottesville VA 22904-4223. (434)924-3124. Fax: (434)924-1397. Website: www.virginia.edu/vqr. Established 1925. **Poetry Board:** David Lee Rubin (chairman), Angie Hogan, and Karen Kevorkian.

Magazine Needs *The Virginia Quarterly Review* uses about 20 pages of poetry in each issue. No length or subject restrictions. Issues have largely included lyric and narrative free verse, most of which features a strong message or powerful voice. *The Virginia Quarterly Review* is 200-300 pages, digest-sized, flat-spined. Press run is 4,000.

How to Submit Submit up to 5 poems and include SASE. ''You will *not* be notified otherwise.'' No simultaneous submissions. Responds in 3 months or longer ''due to the large number of poems we receive.'' Guidelines and upcoming themes available for SASE, by e-mail, or on website; do not request by fax. Pays $5/line.

Contest/Award Offerings Also sponsors the Emily Clark Balch Prize, an annual prize of $1,000 given to the best poem published in the review during the year. 2003 winner was Charles Harper Webb.

▣ $◩ ◎ VOICEWORKS MAGAZINE (Specialized: youth culture)

42 Courtney St., North Melbourne, VIC 3051 Australia. Phone: (03)9326 8367. Fax: (03)9326 8076. E-mail: vworks@vicnet.net.au. Website: www.expressmedia.org.au. Established 1985. **Editor:** Kelly Chander.

Magazine Needs *Voiceworks* appears 4 times/year to publish ''young,'' ''new,'' ''emerging'' writers under 25 years of age. ''We have no specifications for poetry, except the poets must be under 25 years of age. No racist, stolen, or libelous work.'' *Voiceworks* is 80 pages, magazine-sized, perfect-bound, includes art/graphics and ads. Receives about 400 poems/year, accepts 14%. Publishes 14 poems/issue. Press run is 1,000. Single copy: $7; subscription: $25.50/year. Sample: $4. Make checks payable to Express Media/*Voiceworks Magazine*.

How to Submit Submit no more than 8 poems at a time. Accepts simultaneous submissions; no previously published poems. Accepts e-mail and disk submissions. Cover letter is required. ''We need a short bio and SASE (or SAE and IRC). If giving a disk or submitting by e-mail, save the file as a Rich Text format.'' Reads submissions January 4 through 11, April 4 through 11, July 4 through 11, and October 4 through 11 only. Time between acceptance and publication is 2 months. Poems are circulated to an editorial board. ''We all read the submissions, make comments, and decide what to publish.'' Often comments on rejected poems. Publishes theme issues. Guidelines and upcoming themes available for SASE (or SAE with IRCs), by fax, or by e-mail. Responds in 2 months. Pays $50. Poets retain rights. Staff reviews books and chapbooks of poetry and other magazines. Send materials for review consideration.

◩ VOICINGS FROM THE HIGH COUNTRY; HIGH COUNTRY WORD CRAFTERS

4920 S. Oak St., Casper WY 82601. Established 2000. **Editor:** Ella J. Cvancara.

Magazine Needs *Voicings from the High Country* appears annually in the spring. Wants ''poetry with substance, not just pretty words; understandable, rather than obscure; poetry that goes beyond the self. Biased toward free verse that is worldly rather than introspective, tells a story, and uses many/most/all of the 5 senses.'' Also accepts haiku for a haiku page. No ''rhyming, pornography,

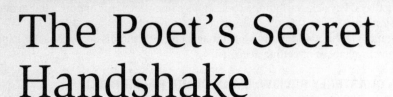
The Poet's Secret Handshake

Publishers of Poetry

When developing poets ask how to get their work published, I'm always tempted to tell the truth: write something good. In most cases, though, the truth is too brutal and won't serve. These poets are looking for the secret handshake. I offer here a handful of quotes and 28 "secrets" for writing well and getting published:

Motivation and Inspiration

Every time I look out the window, I see a poem passing.
  —Gwendolyn Brooks

Poets put their poems on one word at a time like everybody else.
  —Mariana G. Warner

Poems have to be about something, but they're usually not about what they're about.
  —Nancy Williams

- To a poet, no experience is complete until you've written about it.
- If you don't return calls from your Muse, after awhile she'll stop calling.
- Wiggle the words this way and that. Dance your way toward what you mean to say.
- If you aren't in the mood to write, writing can change your mood.
- To paraphrase Mark Twain, the man or woman who doesn't write holds no advantage over the one who can't.
- One of the best reasons for writing is that you can't *not* write.
- Do not be alarmed if your angel in the attic becomes a beast in the basement; they're the same Muse.
- The poet's gift is the exercise of other people's imaginations.

Craft and Technique

Poets are allowed to use the word beautiful three times in their lives. I still have two coming.
  —Robert Frost, in his eighties

There are no approximate words in a poem.
  —Emily Dickinson

The muse does not bother with rewriting, so I had to do that myself.
  —Howard Weinburg

- We first learn to write poetry by reading. It pretty much stays that way over the course of a lifetime.
- Write less poetry of the mirror and more poetry of the window.
- Write every poem as if it were the only poem of yours the reader will experience.
- For a multiple-choice exam, your first thought is likely to be your best bet. But not in writing a poem.
- If you really love a passage you've written, almost always it does not belong.
- The poet, like the fiction writer, may choose to write in a variety of narrative voices. Be someone else for awhile.
- With each rewrite, you will glean something of use in the final draft, or at least eliminate a lot of lousy approximations.
- If you continue to school yourself, you will learn technique, layer by layer, until you are sagging with the stuff. Then one day you will break free of it and start writing naturally.
- Voice will likely not ring true until you have accepted yourself as a poet.

Publication and Marketing

I have never had writer's block, but I have definitely had publisher's block.
    —Lee Smith

Writing is the only profession where no one considers you ridiculous if you earn no money.
    —Jules Renard

- When you write a poem, you are really writing as many poems as there are readers of that poem.
- The first step toward publication is moving from submitting your work for praise to submitting your work for critique.
- The tough question you must ask yourself in writing poetry is "Who cares?"
- Never submit a poem still damp with inspiration.
- Before you submit a poem for publication, set it aside for a day or two, then re-create it from memory (no peeking). You'll keep the essentials, leave out the clutter and writerly stuff.
- Every issue of a magazine or journal tells you exactly what the editor is looking for.
- Every experienced editor knows her readers. That's how she got to be experienced.
- When an editor takes the time to comment on your poems, send a thank-you note, whether the poems are accepted for publication or not.
- For a well-written poem, a rejection slip may represent nothing more than an error in marketing.
- Publication doesn't make you a poet; writing does. The real reward is not in having your work published but in having written well.
- The difference between writing and publishing is rewriting.

—Paul Raymond Martin

Paul Raymond Martin has published more than 300 poems, stories, and nonfiction pieces. His three-volume set of *The Writer's Little Instruction Books* will be published by Writer's Digest Books in Spring 2005.

Publishers of Poetry

violent language, 'Hallmark' verse, political poems, or overtly religious poetry. No poetry that's unsure of why it was written, is demeaning to the human spirit, or untitled.'' Has published poetry by Todd Balazic, Skylar H. Burris, and Linda Ruhle. *Voicings from the High Country* is 35-40 pages, digest-sized, computer-generated, stapled, with 110 lb. cardstock cover, includes in-house artistic photography. Receives about 200 poems/year, accepts about 15%. Publishes about 35 poems/issue. Press run is 75 for 45 shelf sales; 30 distributed free to contributors. Single copy: $5. Make checks payable to Ella J. Cvancara.

How to Submit Submit 3 poems at a time. Accepts previously published poems; no simultaneous submissions. No fax, e-mail, or disk submissions. Cover letter is required with a 3- to 5-line bio. ''Submit each poem on a separate page with name and address in upper right corner; typed or computer-generated; 35 lines or less; include SASE for response.'' Reads submissions July 1 through February 1 *only*. Time between acceptance and publication is 3 months. ''Poems are circulated to a 3-member editorial board with the names of the poets removed. They are ranked according to a ranking system.'' Seldom comments on rejected poems. Guidelines available for SASE. Responds in 6 months. Pays one contributor's copy. Acquires one-time rights.

Advice ''Beginners often write about themselves. Reach beyond yourself, avoid clichés, search for fresh language. Use metaphor and simile. Strike a spark with words. Nothing is off limits to the poet.''

VQONLINE (Specialized: volcanoes and volcanology)

8009 18th Lane SE, Lacey WA 98503. (360)455-4607. E-mail: jmtanaka@webtv.net. Website: http://community.webtv.net/JMTanaka/VQ. Established 1992. **Editor:** Janet M. Cullen Tanaka.

Magazine Needs *VQOnline* is an ''interest'' publication for professional and amateur volcanologists and volcano buffs. Wants ''any kind of poetry as long as it is about volcanoes and/or the people who work on them.'' Does not want ''over-emotive, flowery stuff or anything not directly pertaining to volcanoes.'' Has published poetry by Dane Picard and C. Martinez. Free on the Internet, no subscription costs.

How to Submit Submit any number of poems. Accepts previously published poems, with permission of the original copyright holder, and simultaneous submissions. Accepts disk (ASCII compatible) and e-mail (pasted into body of message; no attachments) submissions. Time between acceptance and publication is 6 months. Always comments on rejected poems. ''I try not to outright reject, preferring to ask for a rewrite.'' Guidelines available for SASE, by e-mail, or on website. Responds in one month. Pays up to 5 contributor's copies. ''Contributors may copyright in the usual fashion. But there is as yet no mechanism on the Internet to keep users honest. We also need written permission to publish on the Internet.'' Reviews books or chapbooks of poetry or other magazines by guest reviewers. Send materials for review consideration if subject is volcanoes.

Advice ''I want to concentrate on the positive aspects of volcanoes—gifts from God, 'partners' in creation, resources, beauty, awe, etc.''

WAKE UP HEAVY (WUH); WAKE UP HEAVY PRESS

P.O. Box 4668, Fresno CA 93744-4668. E-mail: wuheavy@yahoo.com. Established 1998. **Editor/Publisher:** Mark Begley.

Magazine Needs *Wake Up Heavy* is not currently publishing magazine issues, nor accepting submissions for the magazine. The first 4 issues of *Wake Up Heavy* included poetry/prose by Laura Chester, Wanda Coleman, Fielding Dawson, Edward Field, Michael Lally, and Diane Wakoski. ''These out-of-print issues are available through the Web at www.abebooks.com. Many of the poems published have been reprinted in major collections by these authors; most notably, 3 poems by Wanda Coleman that originally appeared in the premier issue of the magazine and were later reprinted in her National Book Award-nominated collection *Mercurochrome* (Black Sparrow Press, 2001). Any other questions about future magazine publications should be sent to the above e-mail address.''

How to Submit *Wake Up Heavy* is not currently accepting submissions of any kind, and the magazine has been halted indefinitely.

Book/Chapbook Needs & How to Submit "Chapbooks and broadsides by single authors have become our main focus. Wake Up Heavy Press has published chapbooks/pamphlets of single poems (Michael Lally's long, prose poem *¿Que Pasa Baby?*; Diane Wakoski's *Trying to Convince Robert* and *Inviting John & Barbara*), groups of poems, stories (Wanda Coleman's *Crabs for Breakfast*; Fielding Dawson's *The Dirty Blue Car* and *Backtalk*), memoirs (Wanda Coleman's Pushcart Prize-nominated *Love-ins with Nietzsche*), and chapters from novels (Laura Chester's *Kingdom Come*)." Wake Up Heavy Press publishes 2-3 chapbooks/pamphlets per year. Chapbooks/pamphlets are usually copied/offset-printed, saddle-stapled, with heavy coverstock, some contain drawings or photos, and most include a signed/numbered edition. "Again, these titles are available via the Web at www.abebooks.com. Also, you can e-mail about upcoming publications/the availability of past ones. Chapbooks, pamphlets, and broadsides are *strictly from solicitations. Please do not send mss for these publications.*" Wake Up Heavy Press pays authors in copies, 50% of the press run, which is usually between 130-200 copies. Inquire about samples at the above e-mail address.

☑ WASHINGTON SQUARE, A JOURNAL OF THE ARTS

19 University Place, Room 219, New York University Graduate Creative Writing Program, New York NY 10003. E-mail: washington.square.journal@nyu.edu. Website: www.nyu.edu/gsas/program/cwp/wsr.htm. Established 1994 as *Washington Square* (originally established in 1979 as *Ark/Angel*). **Editors:** T.M. Jongbloedt and Andrea Luttrell. **Contact:** Adam Day.

Magazine Needs Published in December and May, *Washington Square* is "a non-profit literary journal publishing fiction, poetry, and essays by new and established writers. It's edited and produced by the students of the NYU Creative Writing Program." Wants "all poetry of serious literary intent." Has published poetry by Billy Collins, Rick Moody, A.E. Stalling, Dana Levin, Timothy Lin, and Arthur Sze. *Washington Square* is about 150 pages. Press run is 2,000. Subscription: $12. Sample: $6.

How to Submit Submit up to 6 poems at a time; name and contact information should appear on every page. Accepts simultaneous submissions if noted. Accepts submissions by postal mail only. Cover letter with short bio is required. Reads submissions September through April only. Time between acceptance and publication is up to 6 months. Poems are circulated to an editorial board. "The poetry editors and editorial staff read all submissions, discuss, and decide which poems to include in the journal." Sometimes comments on rejected poems. Guidelines available for SASE or by e-mail. Responds in up to 4 months. Pays 2 contributor's copies and a one-year subscription. Acquires first North American serial rights. Sometimes reviews books and chapbooks of poetry and other magazines in 300 words. Send materials for review consideration.

Advice "Keep in mind that the staff changes each academic year."

☑ WATER MARK PRESS

138 Duane St., New York NY 10013. Established 1978. **Editor:** Coco Gordon. Currently does not accept any unsolicited poetry.

- Note: Please do not confuse Water Mark Press with the imprint Watermark Press, used by other businesses.

☐ ◎ WATERWAYS: POETRY IN THE MAINSTREAM (Specialized: themes); TEN PENNY PLAYERS (Specialized: children/teen/young adult); BARD PRESS

393 St. Paul's Ave., Staten Island NY 10304-2127. (718)442-7429. E-mail: tenpennyplayers@SI.RR.com. Website: www.tenpennyplayers.org. Established 1977. **Poetry Editors:** Barbara Fisher and Richard Spiegel.

Magazine Needs Ten Penny Players "publishes poetry by adult poets in *Waterways*, a magazine that is published 11 times/year. We do theme issues and are trying to increase an audience for poetry and the printed and performed word. The project produces performance readings in public spaces and is in residence year round at the New York public library with workshops and readings. We publish the magazine *Waterways*, anthologies, and chapbooks. We are not fond of haiku or rhyming poetry; never use material of an explicit sexual nature. We are open to reading material from people we have never published, writing in traditional and experimental poetry forms. While we do 'themes,' sometimes an idea for a future magazine is inspired by a submission, so we try to remain open to poets' inspirations. Poets should be guided, however, by the fact that we are children's and animal rights advocates and are a NYC press." Has published poetry by Ida Fasel, Albert Huffstickler, Joy Hewitt Mann, and Will Inman. *Waterways* is 40 pages, $4\frac{1}{4} \times 7$, photocopied from various type styles, saddle-stapled, with matte card cover, includes b&w drawings. Accepts 60% of poems submitted. Press run is 150 for 58 subscribers of which 12 are libraries. Subscription: $25. Sample: $2.60.

How to Submit Submit less than 10 poems for first submission. Accepts simultaneous submissions. Accepts e-mail submissions (pasted into body of message). Guidelines for upcoming themes available for SASE. "Since we've taken the time to be very specific in our response, writers should take seriously our comments and not waste their emotional energy and our time sending material that isn't within our area of interest. Sending for our theme sheet and a sample issue and then objectively thinking about the writer's own work is practical and wise. Manuscripts that arrive without a return envelope are not sent back." Editors sometimes comment on rejected poems. Responds in less than one month. Pays one contributor's copy. Acquires one-time publication rights.

Book/Chapbook Needs & How to Submit Chapbooks published by Ten Penny Players are "by children and young adults only—*not by submission*; they come through our workshops in the library and schools. Adult poets are published through our Bard Press imprint, *by invitation only*. Books evolve from the relationship we develop with writers we publish in *Waterways* and whom we would like to give more exposure."

Advice "We suggest that poets attend book fairs and check our website. It's a fast way to find out what we are publishing. Without meaning to sound 'precious' or unfriendly, the writer should understand that small press publishers doing limited editions and all production work inhouse are working from their personal artistic vision and know exactly what notes will harmonize, effectively counterpoint, and meld. Many excellent poems are sent back to the writers by *Waterways* because they don't relate to what we are trying to create in a given month."

⬛ WAVELENGTH: POEMS IN PROSE AND VERSE

1753 Fisher Ridge Rd., Horse Cave KY 42749-9706. Established 1999. **Editor/Publisher:** David P. Rogers.

Magazine Needs *Wavelength: Poems in Prose and Verse* appears 3 times/year. "We want poems that use lively images, intriguing metaphor, and original language. Long poems OK; would like to see more prose poems. Rhyme is almost always a liability. All subjects and styles considered as long as the poem is thought-provoking or uses language in an innovative way." Does not want "rhymed, very religious—anything that sacrifices creativity for convention." Has published poetry by Robert Cooperman, Lyn Lifshin, Francis Blessington, Ann Taylor, Albert Haley, and Virgil Suárez. *Wavelength* is 35 pages, digest-sized, laser-printed, perfect-bound, with heavy cardstock cover with illustration. Receives about 450 poems/year, accepts 5-10%. Publishes about 30 poems/issue. Press run is 150 for 25 subscribers, 20-25 shelf sales; 100 distributed free to the public. Single copy: $6; subscription: $15. Sample: $6. Make checks payable to Dr. David P. Rogers.

How to Submit Submit 1-10 poems at a time. Line length for poetry is 30 maximum. Accepts previously published poems and simultaneous submissions, "but please do *not* withdraw the poem after we've accepted it." No e-mail or disk submissions. Cover letter is preferred. "SASE or no response. Brief bio preferred. Poet's name and address must appear on every page. Poets who want poems returned should include sufficient postage.'' Submit seasonal poems 3 months in advance. Time between acceptance and publication is up to one year. Seldom comments on rejected poems. ''Please do *not* write for guidelines. Just send a courteous submission following the guidelines in the *Poet's Market* entry.'' Responds in 4 months. Pays one contributor's copy. Acquires one-time rights. Reviews books and chapbooks of poetry in 100-150 words, single book format. Send materials for review consideration to David P. Rogers.

Advice ''Read and write every day. If a poem still seems good a year after you wrote it, send it out. Be original. Say something clever, and ask what will the *reader* get out of it? Editor has a weakness for synesthesia.''

☑ WAYNE LITERARY REVIEW

% Dept. of English, Wayne State University, Detroit MI 48202. Established 1960. **Editor:** Richard Brixton.

Magazine Needs *Wayne Literary Review* appears biannually. ''Our philosophy is to encourage a diversity of writing styles. Send your favorites. If you like them, others probably will, too.'' Does not want ''lack of craft, gratuitous sex and violence.'' *Wayne Literary Review* is 75 pages, digest-sized. Receives about 1,000 poems/year, accepts about 5%. Publishes about 25 poems/issue. Press run is 1,000 for free distribution to the public.

How to Submit Submit 3 poems at a time. No previously published poems or simultaneous submissions. No fax, e-mail, or disk submissions. Cover letter is preferred. ''Send SASE with proper postage.'' Reads submissions anytime. Submit seasonal poems 6 months in advance. Time between acceptance and publication is 6 months. Poems are circulated to an editorial board. Seldom comments on rejected poems. Guidelines available for SASE. Responds in 3 months. Pays 2 contributor's copies. Acquires first North American serial rights.

☑ WEST ANGLIA PUBLICATIONS

P.O. Box 2683, La Jolla CA 92038. **Editor:** Wilma Lusk.

Book Needs West Anglia Publications wants only the best poetry and publishes one paperback/ year. Wants ''contemporary poems, well wrought by poets whose work has already been accepted in various fine poetry publications. This is not a press for beginners.'' Has published poetry by Gary Morgan, Kathleen Iddings, and John Theobald. Books are usually 75-100 pages, digest-sized, perfect-bound. Sample book: $10 plus $1.50 p&h.

How to Submit Query with 6 poems, cover letter, professional bio, and SASE. ''Don't send entire manuscript unless requested by Editor.'' Pays 100 author's copies.

⊕ $☑ WESTERLY; PATRICIA HACKETT PRIZE

English, Communication, and Cultural Studies, University of Western Australia, Crawley, Western Australia 6009. Phone: (08)9380-2101. Fax: (08) 9380-1030. E-mail: westerly@cyllene.uwa.edu.au. Website: http://westerly.uwa.edu.au. Established 1956. **Editors:** Dennis Haskell and Delys Bird. **Poetry Editor:** Mark Reid.

Magazine Needs *Westerly* is a literary and cultural annual, appearing in November, which publishes quality short fiction, poetry, literary critical, socio-historical articles, and book reviews with special attention given to Australia, Asia, and the Indian Ocean region. ''We don't dictate to writers on rhyme, style, experimentation, or anything else. We are willing to publish short or long poems. We do assume a reasonably well-read, intelligent audience. Past issues of *Westerly* provide the best guides. Not consciously an academic magazine.'' *Westerly* is about 200 pages, digest-sized, ''electronically printed.'' Press run is 1,200. Subscription: $16 (US), $23.95 (AUS).

How to Submit Submit up to 6 poems at a time. Accepts fax and e-mail (in an attached file, Word 6 format; if submission is short, include in body of e-mail) submissions. ''Please do not send simultaneous submissions. Cover letters should be brief and non-confessional.'' **Deadline:** June

30. Time between acceptance and publication "can be up to one year depending on when work is submitted." Responds in 3 months. Pays minimum of AU$50 plus one contributor's copy. Acquires first publication rights; requests acknowledgment on reprints. Reviews books of poetry in multibook format in an annual review essay. Send materials for review consideration.

Contest/Award Offerings The Patricia Hackett Prize (value approx. AU$750) is awarded annually for the best contribution published in the previous year's issue of *Westerly*.

Advice "Be sensible. Write what matters for you, but think about the reader. Don't spell out the meanings of the poems and the attitudes to be taken to the subject matter—i.e., trust the reader. Don't be swayed by literary fashion. Read the magazine if possible before sending submissions."

$🖉 WESTERN HUMANITIES REVIEW

University of Utah, 255 S. Central Campus Dr., Room 3500, Salt Lake City UT 84112-0494. (801)581-6070. Fax: (801)585-5167. E-mail: whr@mail.hum.utah.edu. Website: www.hum.utah.edu/whr. Established 1947. **Managing Editor:** Paul Ketzle.

• Poetry published in this review has been selected for *The Best American Poetry* as well as the 2002 and 2003 *Pushcart Prize* anthologies.

Magazine Needs Appearing in April and October, *Western Humanities Review* is a semiannual publication of poetry, fiction, and a small selection of nonfiction. Wants "quality poetry of any form, including translations." Has published poetry by Scott Cairns, Philip Levine, Bin Ramke, Lucie Brock-Broido, Timothy Liu, John Hollander, and Barbara Hamby. *Western Humanities Review* is 112-144 pages, digest-sized, professionally printed on quality stock, perfect-bound, with coated card cover. Receives about 900 submissions/year, accepts less than 10%, publishes approximately 60 poets. Press run is 1,100 for 1,000 subscribers of which 900 are libraries. Subscription: $16 to individuals in the US. Sample: $10.

How to Submit "We do not publish writer's guidelines because we think the magazine itself conveys an accurate picture of our requirements." Accepts simultaneous submissions; no previously published poems. No fax or e-mail submissions. Reads submissions October 1 through May 31 only. Time between acceptance and publication is 1-4 issues. Managing editor makes an initial cut, then the poetry editor makes the final selections. Seldom comments on rejected poems. Occasionally publishes special issues. Responds in up to 6 months. Pays $5/published page and 2 contributor's copies. Acquires first serial rights.

Contest/Award Offerings Also offers an annual contest for Utah poets.

🖉 WESTVIEW: A JOURNAL OF WESTERN OKLAHOMA

100 Campus Dr., SWOSU, Weatherford OK 73096. (580)774-3168. Established 1981. **Editor:** Fred Alsberg.

Magazine Needs *Westview* is a semiannual publication that is "particularly interested in writers from the Southwest; however, we are open to work of quality by poets from elsewhere. We publish free verse, prose poems, and formal poetry." Has published poetry by Carolynne Wright, Miller Williams, Walter McDonald, Robert Cooperman, Alicia Ostriker, and James Whitehead. *Westview* is 64 pages, magazine-sized, perfect-bound, with full-color glossy card cover. Receives about 500 poems/year, accepts 7%. Press run is 700 for 300 subscribers of which about 25 are libraries. Subscription: $10/2 years. Sample: $5.

How to Submit Submit 5 poems at a time. Cover letter including biographical data for contributor's note is requested with submissions. "Poems on 3.5 computer disk are welcome so long as they are accompanied by the hard copy and the SASE has the appropriate postage." Editor comments on submissions "when close." Manuscripts are circulated to an editorial board; "we usually respond within 2-3 months." Pays one contributor's copy.

◙ WHITE HERON; WHITE HERON PRESS

P.O. Box 251, Paradise CA 95967. E-mail: whEditor@hotmail.com or editor@whiteheron-press.com. Website: www.whiteheron-press.com. Established 1997. **Editor:** Kevin Hull.

Magazine Needs *White Heron* is published annually in August. "We are interested in lyric poetry, vivid imagery, open form, natural landscape, philosophical themes, but not at the expense of honesty and passion; model examples: Wendell Berry, Gabriela Mistral, and Issa." Has published poetry by Bill Witherup, Corrinne Lee, Georgette Perry, Ken Meisel, and Michael Hannon. *White Heron Review* is 24-32 pages, digest-sized, professionally printed, saddle-stapled, with card stock cover, sometimes includes art. Also publishes some poems on the website. Single copy: $7; subscription: $10. Make checks payable to Kevin Hull.

How to Submit Submit up to 3 poems at a time. "Long poems, because of space, are rarely taken." Accepts previously published poems "by request only" and simultaneous submissions. Accepts submissions by e-mail (pasted into body of message), on disk, and by postal mail. Reads submissions February through May. Time between acceptance and publication is up to 6 months. Guidelines available by e-mail or on website. Pays one contributor's copy.

Book/Chapbook Needs & How to Submit White Heron Press also considers chapbook publication (year round). "Each manuscript considered on its own merits, regardless of name recognition. Basic production costs variable. Query or send manuscript and I'll respond."

Advice "Do the work. Get used to solitude and rejection."

◙ WHITE PELICAN REVIEW

P.O. Box 7833, Lakeland FL 33813. Established 1999. **Editor:** Nancy J. Wiegel.

Magazine Needs *White Pelican Review* is a biannual literary journal, appearing in April and October, dedicated to publishing poetry of the highest quality. "Although a relatively new publication, *White Pelican Review* seeks to attract writing that goes beyond competency to truly masterful acts of imagination." Has published poetry by Trent Busch, Barbara Lefcowitz, Virgil Suárez, and Peter Meinke. *White Pelican Review* is about 48 pages, digest-sized, photocopied from typescript, saddle-stapled, with matte cardstock cover. Receives about 3,000 poems/year, accepts 3%. Press run is 250 for 100 subscribers of which 10 are libraries. Single copy: $4; subscription: $8/year for individuals, $10/year for institutions. Make checks payable to *White Pelican Review*.

How to Submit Submit 3-5 poems at a time. Line length for poetry is 60 maximum. No previously published poems or simultaneous submissions. Cover letter and SASE are required. "Please include name, address, telephone number, and (if available) e-mail address on each page. No handwritten poems." Reads submissions year round. Time between acceptance and publication is 3 months. Poems are circulated to an editorial board. Seldom comments on rejected poems. Guidelines available for SASE. Responds in 6 months. Pays one contributor's copy. Acquires one-time rights.

Contest/Award Offerings "The Lake Hollingsworth Prize of $100 is offered to the most distinguished poem in each issue."

WHITE PINE PRESS; THE WHITE PINE PRESS POETRY PRIZE

P.O. Box 236, Buffalo NY 14201. E-mail: wpine@whitepine.org. Website: www.whitepine.org. Established 1973. **Editor:** Dennis Maloney. **Managing Director:** Elaine LaMattina.

Contest/Award Offerings White Pine Press publishes poetry, fiction, literature in translation, and essays in perfect-bound paperbacks. "**We accept unsolicited work by U.S. poets *only* for our annual competition—the White Pine Poetry Prize.** We are always open to submissions of poetry in translation." Competition awards $1,000 plus publication to a book-length collection of poems by a US author. **Entry fee:** $20. **Deadline:** November 30. Guidelines available for SASE or on website. No e-mail submissions. Has published *The Burning Point* by Frances Richey (winner of the White Pine Poetry Prize), *In What Disappears* by John Brandi, and *At the Threshold of Memory: New and Selected Poems* by Marjorie Agosín.

☑ ◎ TAHANA WHITECROW FOUNDATION; CIRCLE OF REFLECTIONS (Specialized: Native American, animals, nature, spirituality/inspirational)

2350 Wallace Rd. NW, Salem OR 97304. (503)585-0564. Fax: (503)585-3302. E-mail: tahana@open. org. Website: www.open.org/tahana. Established 1987. **Executive Director:** Melanie Smith.

Contest/Award Offerings The Whitecrow Foundation conducts one spring/summer poetry contest on Native American themes in poems up to 30 lines in length. **Deadline:** May 31. No haiku, Seiku, erotic, or porno poems. **Reading fee:** $3/poem, $10/4poems. Winners, honorable mentions, and selected other entries are published in a periodic anthology, *Circle of Reflections*. Winners receive free copies (at least 2) and are encouraged to purchase others for $6.95 plus $2 handling in order to "help ensure the continuity of our contests." No fax or e-mail submissions. Guidelines available for SASE.

Advice "We seek unpublished Native American writers. Poetic expressions of full-bloods, mixed bloods, and empathetic non-Indians need to be heard. Future goals include chapbooks. Advice to new writers: Practice, practice, practice to tap into your own rhythm and to hone and sharpen material; don't give up."

Ⓝ ☑ WILD PLUM

P.O. Box 49019, Austin TX 78765-9019. Website: www.wildplumpoetry.com. Established 2003. **Founding Editor/Publisher:** Constance Campbell.

Magazine Needs WILD PLUM is published annually in June and is "dedicated to bringing readers an array of voices and styles, embracing the best of the new while still honoring tradition and form. We seek to publish poets from the U.S. and abroad." Wants "all styles and voices. We are very open to well-crafted rhyming poems, as well as haiku. Stay away from greeting card verse/sentiments. No pornography. No self-aggrandizing." Has published poetry by Lyn Lifshin, Alvin Pang, Cyril Wong, Simon Perchik, and Scott Wiggerman. WILD PLUM is 48-60 pages, digest-sized, saddle-stapled, with cover featuring artwork. Receives about 800-1,000 poems/year, accepts about 5%. Publishes about 35-50 poems/issue. Press run is about 300; about 40 are distributed free to literary reviewers "and poets we admire." Single copy: $8.50; subscription: pre-publication price is $6.50. Make checks payable to Constance Campbell.

How to Submit Submit 3-5 poems at a time. Line length for poetry is 3 minimum, 70 maximum. No previously published poems or simultaneous submissions. No e-mail or disk submissions. Cover letter is required. "Please visit our website before making any submissions. Our current guidelines will be available there. Please include specific publishing credits in bio in cover letter, if applicable." Time between acceptance and publication "depends on how close to publication you submitted. The editor reads all submissions carefully and then passes on the ones that seem best to the members of the editorial advisory board. They are then re-read and discussed before we arrive at our final decision." Comments on rejected poems "as often as possible." Guidelines available on website. Responds in "2 weeks or 6 months, depending on how close we are to our publication date when your submission is received." Pays one contributor's copy. Acquires first rights. "We may publish your poem on the website and, if so, archive it there as well. Also, we acquire the right to reprint in future anthologies."

Contest/Award Offerings "We plan to offer an annual contest with cash prizes. Winners will always be announced *and* published on our website, in addition to the print journal. The editors will nominate *PLUM* poems to the Pushcart Prize committee."

☑ WILD VIOLET

P.O. Box 39706, Philadelphia PA 19106-9706. E-mail: wildvioletmagazine@yahoo.com. Website: www.wildviolet.net. Established 2001. **Editor:** Alyce Wilson.

Magazine Needs *Wild Violet* appears quarterly online. "Our goal is to democratize the arts: to make the arts more accessible and to serve as a creative forum for writers and artists." Wants "poetry that is well crafted, that engages thought, that challenges or uplifts the reader. We have published free verse, haiku, and blank verse. If the form suits the poem, we will consider any form." Does not want "abstract, self-involved poetry; poorly managed form; excessive rhyming; self-referential poems that do not show why the speaker is sad, happy, or in love." Has published poetry by Erik Kestler, Jules St. John, Sam Vaknin, Leanne Kelly, John Haag, Jim DeWitt, and Rich Furman. *Wild Violet* is published online with photos, artwork, and graphics. Accepts about 20% of work submitted. Publishes about 10-15 poems/issue.

How to Submit Submit 3-5 poems at a time. Accepts simultaneous submissions; no previously published poems. Accepts e-mail submissions; no fax or disk submissions. Cover letter is preferred. "Include poem(s) in body of e-mail or send as a text or Microsoft Word attachment." Reads submissions year round. Submit seasonal poems 3 months in advance. Time between acceptance and publication is 3 months. "Decisions on acceptance or rejection are made by the editor. Contests are judged by an independent panel." Seldom comments on rejected poems, unless requested. Occasionally publishes theme issues. List of upcoming themes and guidelines available by e-mail. Responds in up to 6 weeks. Pays by providing a bio and link on contributor's page. All rights retained by author. Reviews books and chapbooks of poetry in 250 words, single book format. Send materials for review consideration to Alyce Wilson, editor.

Contest/Award Offerings Holds an annual poetry contest. 1st Prize: $100 and publication in *Wild Violet*. **Entry fee:** $5. Guidelines available by e-mail or on website.

Advice "Read voraciously; experience life and share what you've learned. Write what is hardest to say; don't take any easy outs."

WILLARD & MAPLE

163 S. Willard St., Freeman 302, Box 34, Burlington VT 05401. E-mail: willardandmaple@champlain.edu. Established 1996. **Contact:** Poetry Editor.

Magazine Needs *Willard & Maple* appears annually in April and is "a student-run literary magazine from Champlain College's Professional Writing Program that publishes a wide array of poems, short stories, creative essays, short plays, pen & ink drawings, photos, and computer graphics." Wants "creative work of the highest quality." Does not want any submissions over 5 typed pages in length; all submissions must be in English. Has published poetry by P-R Smith, Robert James Berry, Cheryl Burghdurf, Bill Everts, and David Trame. *Willard & Maple* is 125 pages, digest-sized, digitally printed, perfect-bound, includes internal art/graphics. Receives about 500 poems/year, accepts about 20%. Publishes about 50 poems/issue. Press run is 600 for 80 subscribers of which 4 are libraries; 200 are distributed free to the Champlain College writing community. Single copy: $8.50. Make checks payable to Champlain College.

How to Submit Submit up to 5 poems at a time. Line length for poetry is 100 maximum. Accepts simultaneous submissions; no previously published poems. Accepts e-mail and disk submissions; no fax submissions. Cover letter is required. "Please provide current contact information including an e-mail address. Single-space submissions, one poem/page." Reads submissions September 1 through April 30. Time between acceptance and publication is less than one year. Poems are circulated to an editorial board. "All editors receive a blind copy to review. They meet weekly throughout the academic year. These meetings consist of the submissions being read aloud, discussed, and voted upon." Seldom comments on rejected poems. Occasionally publishes theme issues. List of upcoming themes available by e-mail. Responds in 2 months. Pays 2 contributor's copies. Acquires one-time rights. Reviews books and chapbooks of poetry and other magazines/journals in 1,200 words. Send materials for review consideration to the poetry editor.

Advice "Work hard, be good, never surrender!"

THE WILLIAM AND MARY REVIEW

Campus Center, College of William and Mary, P.O. Box 8795, Williamsburg VA 23187-8795. (757)221-3290. E-mail: review@wm.edu. Established 1962. **Contact:** Poetry Editors.

Magazine Needs *The William and Mary Review* is an annual, appearing in May, "dedicated to publishing new work by established poets as well as work by new and vital voices." Has published poetry by Cornelius Eady, Minnie Bruce Pratt, Edward Field, Dan Bellm, Forrest Gander, and Walter Holland. *The William and Mary Review* is about 120 pages, digest-sized, professionally printed on coated paper, perfect-bound, with 4-color card cover, includes 4-color artwork and photos. Receives about 5,000 poems/year, accepts 12-15. Press run is 3,500. Has 250 library subscriptions, about 500 shelf sales. Sample: $5.50.

How to Submit Submit one poem/page, batches of up to 6 poems addressed to poetry editors. Cover letter is required; include address, phone number, e-mail address (if available), past publishing history, and brief bio note. Reads submissions September 1 through February 15 *only*. Responds in up to 4 months. Pays 5 contributor's copies.

Advice "If you lie in your cover letter, we usually figure it out. Submit considered, crafted poetry, or don't bother. No guidelines, just send poems."

WILLOW REVIEW; COLLEGE OF LAKE COUNTY READING SERIES

College of Lake County, 19351 W. Washington St., Grayslake IL 60030-1198. (847)223-6601, ext. 2956. Fax: (847)543-3956. E-mail: mlatza@clcillinois.edu. Established 1969. **Editor:** Michael F. Latza.

● The *Willow Review* is partially supported by a grant from the Illinois Arts Council, a state agency.

Magazine Needs "We are interested in poetry and fiction of high quality with no preferences as to form, style, or subject." Has published poetry by Lisel Mueller, Lucien Stryk, David Ray, Louis Rodriguez, John Dickson, and Garrett Hongo; interviews with Gregory Orr, Diane Ackerman, and Li-Young Lee. *Willow Review* is an 88- to 96-page, flat-spined annual, digest-sized, professionally printed, with a 4-color cover featuring work by an Illinois artist. Editors are open to all styles, free verse to form, as long as each poem stands on its own as art and communicates ideas. Press run is 1,000, with distribution to bookstores nationwide. Subscription: $15/3 issues, $25/5 issues. Sample back issue: $4.

How to Submit Submit up to 5 poems. Accepts submissions on disk and by postal mail. Reads submissions from September to May. Sometimes sends prepublication galleys. Pays 2 contributor's copies. Acquires first North American serial rights. Prizes totaling $400 are awarded to the best poetry and short fiction/creative nonfiction in each issue.

Also Offers The College of Lake County Reading Series: 4-7 readings/academic year; has included Angela Jackson, Thomas Lux, Charles Simic, Isabel Allende, Donald Justice, Gloria Naylor, David Mura, Galway Kinnell, Lisel Mueller, Amiri Baraka, Stephen Dobyns, Heather McHugh, Linda Pastan, Tobias Wolff, William Stafford, and others. One reading is for contributors to *Willow Review*. Readings are usually held on Thursday evenings, for audiences of about 150 students and faculty of the College of Lake County and other area colleges, and residents of local communities. They are widely publicized in Chicago and suburban newspapers.

$ WINDSTORM CREATIVE

P.O. Box 28, Port Orchard WA 98366. E-mail: wsc@windstormcreative.com (queries only). Website: www.windstormcreative.com. Established 1989. **Senior Editor:** Ms. Cris DiMarco.

Book/Chapbook Needs Windstorm Creative Ltd. publishes "thoughtful, quality work; must have some depth." Publishes 12 paperbacks/year. Wants "a minimum of 100 publishable, quality poems; book length. You must be familiar with our published poetry before you submit work." Has published poetry by Jack Rickard, Vacirca Vaughn, Rudy Kikel, Alden Reimonenq, Lesléa Newman, and Michael Hattersley.

How to Submit Current guidelines on website. "All submissions must include mailing label and submission form found on website." If invited, send entire mss, 100 poems minimum. Accepts previously published poems and simultaneous submissions. No e-mail submissions. "A bio with publishing history, a page about the collection's focus, theme, etc., will help in the selection process." Time between acceptance and publication is 18 months. Poems are circulated to an editorial board. "Senior editor reviews all work initially. If appropriate for our press, work is given to board for review." Seldom comments on rejected poems. Responds to queries and to mss in 6 months. Pays 15% royalties.

WORCESTER REVIEW; WORCESTER COUNTY POETRY ASSOCIATION, INC. (Specialized: regional)

6 Chatham St., Worcester MA 01609. (508)797-4770. Website: www.geocities.com/Paris/LeftBank/6433. Established 1973. **Managing Editor:** Rodger Martin.

Magazine Needs *Worcester Review* appears annually "with emphasis on poetry. New England writers are encouraged to submit, though work by other poets is used also." Wants "work that is crafted, intuitively honest and empathetic, not work that shows the poet little respects his work or his readers." Has published poetry by May Swenson, Robert Pinsky, and Walter McDonald. *Worcester Review* is 160 pages, digest-sized, professionally printed in dark type on quality stock, flat-spined, with glossy card cover. Press run is 1,000 for 300 subscribers of which 50 are libraries, 300 shelf sales. Subscription: $25 (includes membership in WCPA). Sample: $6.

How to Submit Submit up to 5 poems at a time. "I recommend 3 or less for most favorable readings." Accepts simultaneous submissions "if indicated"; previously published poems "only on special occasions." Editor comments on rejected poems "if manuscript warrants a response." Publishes theme issues. List of upcoming themes and guidelines available for SASE. Responds in up to 9 months. Pays 2 contributor's copies. Acquires first rights.

Contest/Award Offerings Has an annual contest for poets who live, work, or in some way (past/present) have a Worcester County connection or are WCPA members.

Advice "Read some. Listen a lot."

WORD SALAD

721 Holloway St., Durham NC 27707. (910)815-0982. E-mail: bruce@wordsalad.net. Website: http://wordsalad.net. Established 1995. **Publisher:** Bruce Whealton. **Editors:** Bruce Whealton, Jr. and Jean Jones.

Magazine Needs Published quarterly online, *Word Salad* "continuously accepts original poetry. Although we do not restrict ourselves to one subject area or style, the Web allows us to receive a large number of poems and select the highest quality, and we offer worldwide exposure. We are open to any form, style, or subject matter; length should be no more than 2 typed pages. We accept poetry in Spanish to reflect the international nature of the Internet. No greeting card verse or forced rhyme; avoid love poems unless you have something original to say. We accept gay/lesbian/bisexual poetry and have an interest in dark/horror poetry as well as poetry dealing with homelessness and mental illness." Has published poetry by Scott Urban, John Marshall, and Martin Kirby. Receives about 1,200 poems/year, accepts about 10%.

How to Submit Submit 3 poems at a time. No previously published poems or simultaneous submissions. Accepts submissions by e-mail, via online submission form, and by postal mail. "**Read the submission guidelines first.**" Cover letter is preferred. Indicate whether submission is for publication, or contest (see below). "We receive 200-300 poems per quarter and publish 20-30. Most of the submissions are received via e-mail. We ask that poets read the submission guidelines on the Web." Time between acceptance and publication is about 3 months. Seldom comments on rejected poems. Occasionally Publishes theme issues. List of upcoming themes and guidelines available on website. Responds in about 3 months. Sometimes sends prepublication galleys. Open to unsolicited reviews.

Contest/Award Offerings Sponsors an annual contest to raise funds for Poets Against Poverty.

"The contest runs through June, and the winners are announced July 4. There is an entry fee, and awards will be paid to the first-, second-, and third-place winners. See http://poetsagainstpoverty.wordsalad.net for links and details regarding this contest and this cause."

Also Offers Offers an online writers' resource area with forums, chat rooms, links, and more at http://wordsalad.net/resources.

⬚ THE WORD WORKS; THE WASHINGTON PRIZE

P.O. Box 42164, Washington DC 20015. Fax: (703)527-9384. E-mail: editor@wordworksdc.com. Website: www.wordworksdc.com. Established 1974. **Editor-in-Chief:** Hilary Tham.

Book/Chapbook Needs Word Works "is a nonprofit literary organization publishing contemporary poetry in single author editions, usually in collaboration with a visual artist. We sponsor an ongoing poetry reading series, educational programs, the Capital Collection—publishing mostly metropolitan Washington, D.C. poets, and the Washington Prize—an award of $1,500 for a book-length manuscript by a living American poet." Previous winners include *Survivable World* by Ron Mohring, *Phoenix Suites* by Miles Waggoner, *One Hundred Children Waiting for a Train* by Michael Atkinson, *Last Heat* by Peter Blair, *Tipping Point* by Fred Marchant, and *Stalking the Florida Panther* by Enid Shomer. Submission open to any American writer except those connected with Word Works. Entries accepted between February 1 and March 1. **Postmark deadline:** March 1. Winners are announced at the end of June. Publishes perfect-bound paperbacks and occasional anthologies and wants "well-crafted poetry; open to most forms and styles (though not political themes particularly). Experimentation welcomed. We want more than a collection of poetry. We care about the individual poems—the craft, the emotional content, and the risks taken—but we want manuscripts where one poem leads to the next. We strongly recommend you read the books that have already won the Washington Prize. Buy them, if you can, or ask your libraries to purchase them. (Not a prerequisite.)" Most books are $10.

Contest/Award Offerings "Currently we are only reading unsolicited manuscripts for the Washington Prize (see above)." Accepts simultaneous submissions, if so stated. Accepts submissions by first-class postal mail only. Always sends prepublication galleys. Payment is 15% of run (usually of 1,000). Guidelines and catalog available for SASE or on website. Occasionally comments on rejected poems. "We do have a contest for D.C.-area high school students who compete to read in our Miller Cabin Series." Young poets should submit ms with cover letter (detailing contact info, high school and grade, expected graduation date, and list of submitted poem titles) and SASE from January 1 to March 31. Send to Attn: W. Perry Epes. Two winners will receive an honorarium and a chance to read work.

Advice "Get community support for your work, know your audience, and support contemporary literature by buying and reading the small press."

⬚ WORDS OF WISDOM

8969 UNCG Station, Greensboro NC 27413. E-mail: wowmail@hoopsmail.com. Established 1981. **Editor:** Mikhammad Abdel-Ishara.

Magazine Needs *Words of Wisdom* appears quarterly with short stories, essays, and poetry. Wants all types of poetry, except religious or pornographic. Has published poetry by David Sapp, Sid Miller, Simon Perchik, C.L. Bledsoe, Barbara Wiedmann, and Brenda K. Ledford. *Words of Wisdom* is 76-88 pages, digest-sized, laser-printed, saddle-stapled, with cover with art. Receives about 600 poems/year, accepts about 8-10%. Publishes about 12-18 poems/issue. Press run is 160 for 100 subscribers of which 2 are libraries, 50 shelf sales. Single copy: $4.50; subscription: $16. Sample: $4.50. Make checks payable to J.M. Freiermuth.

How to Submit Submit 3-5 poems at a time. Line length for poetry is 30 maximum. Accepts simultaneous submissions; *absolutely NO previously published poems.* No fax, e-mail, or disk submissions. Cover letter is required. Reads submissions all year. Submit seasonal poems 10 months in advance.

Time between acceptance and publication is 6-9 months. Seldom comments on rejected poems. Occasionally publishes theme issues. Guidelines available for SASE or by e-mail. Responds in up to 6 months. Pays one contributor's copy. Acquires first North American serial rights.

Advice "Turn off the Internet! Surf through a book of poetry."

$□ ◎ THE WRITE CLUB (Specialized: membership)

P.O. Box 1454, Conover NC 28613. (828)256-3821. E-mail: poetsnet@juno.com. Established 2001. **Club President/Editor:** Nettie C. Blackwelder.

Magazine Needs *The Write Club* appears quarterly. "We print *one* original poem from *each* of our members in *each* quarterly club booklet. These poems are voted on by all members. We pay $1 to each member for each vote his/her poem receives. Each booklet also contains 4 assignments for all members who want to do them (usually poetry assignments). Our poetry specifications are open as to form, subject matter, style, or purpose. Just send your best. We don't print anything indecent or offensive." Has published poetry by Carolyn Marie Baatz, Raymond Green, Lisa Beck, Doris Nance, and Daniel Lee Walker. *The Write Club* is 32 pages, 4¼×11, computer-printed, saddle-stapled, with color cardstock cover. Receives about 300 poems/year, accepts about 90%. Publishes about 60 poems/issue. Press run is 50 for 32 subscribers; 12 distributed free to anyone who requests information. Single copy: $2; subscription: $15 (membership). Sample: $1 (or 3 first-class stamps). Make checks payable to Nettie C. Blackwelder.

How to Submit Submit one poem at a time. Line length for poetry is 3 minimum, 30 maximum. Accepts previously published poems and simultaneous submissions. No e-mail, fax, or disk submissions. Cover letter is preferred. "Send SAE and 3 first-class stamps (or $1) for information and sample booklet before submitting poetry." Reads submissions all year. Submit seasonal poems 3 months in advance. Time between acceptance and publication is 3 months. "Poems are voted on by our members. Each vote is worth $1 to that poem's author." **Membership required** (all members receive subscription to club booklet). Guidelines available for SASE or by e-mail. Responds in 3 months. Pays $1 per vote, per poem. Acquires one-time rights.

Advice "Rhythm is the music of the soul and sets the pace of a poem. A clever arrangement of words means very little if they have no sense of 'stop' and 'go.' If you're not sure about the rhythm of a poem, reading it aloud a few times will quickly tell you which words don't belong or should be changed. My advice is rewrite, rewrite, rewrite until you love *every* word and phrase 'as is.' "

◎ WRITE ON!! POETRY MAGAZETTE

P.O. Box 901, Richfield UT 84701-0901. (435)896-6669. E-mail: jimnipoetry@yahoo.com. Website: www.fortunecity.com/victorian/stanmer/244/rpmagazette.html. Established 1998. **Editor:** Jim Garman.

Magazine Needs *Write On!! Poetry Magazette* appears monthly and features "poetry from poets around the world." Wants poetry of "any style; all submissions must be suitable for all ages to read. No adult or vulgar material." Has published poetry by Diane Ashley, Joan Danylak, Linda Woolven, Faith Selby, and Benita Glickman. *Write On!!* is 24 pages, digest-sized, photostat-copied, saddle-stapled, with color card cover. Receives about 500 poems/year, accepts about 50%. Publishes about 24 poems/issue. Press run is 50 for 10 subscribers of which one is a library, 10 shelf sales. Single copy: $4. Sample: $3. Make checks payable to Jim Garman.

How to Submit Submit 1-6 poems at a time. Line length for poetry is 6 minimum, 28 maximum. Accepts previously published poems and simultaneous submissions. Accepts e-mail submissions (pasted into body of message; no attachments); no fax or disk submissions. Reads submissions year round. Submit seasonal poems 2 months in advance. Time between acceptance and publication is one month. Never comments on rejected poems. Occasionally publishes theme issues. List of upcoming themes available by e-mail. Guidelines available on website. Responds in 3 weeks. Acquires first rights.

Advice "Send only your best material after it has been refined."

✪ ☑ WRITER'S BLOC

Dept. of Language & Literature, Texas A&M University-Kingsville, MSC 162, Kingsville TX 78363-8202. E-mail: c-downs@tamuk.edu. Website: www.tamuk.edu/langlit/writer's.htm. Established 1980. **Faculty Sponsor:** C. Downs.

Magazine Needs *Writer's Bloc* is an annual journal appearing in September, publishing poetry, fiction, creative nonfiction, and graphic art. About half of its pages are devoted to the works of Texas A&M University-Kingsville students and half to the works of writers and artists from all over the world. Wants quality poetry; no restrictions on content or form. *Writer's Bloc* is 80-96 pages, digest-sized. Press run is 300-500. Subscription: $5. Sample: $6.

How to Submit Submit no more than 3 pages of poetry (prose poems OK). Line length for poetry is 50 maximum. Accepts simultaneous submissions (encouraged); no previously published poems. Submissions should be typed, double-spaced; SASE required for reply. Reads submissions September through January only. "Manuscripts are published upon recommendation by a staff of students and faculty." Seldom comments on rejected poems. Guidelines available in magazine or for SASE. "Acceptance letters are sent out in September." Pays one contributor's copy.

$☑ WRITERS' JOURNAL

P.O. Box 394, Perham MN 56573-0394. (218)346-7921. Fax: (218)346-7924. E-mail: writersjournal@lakesplus.com. Website: www.writersjournal.com. Established 1980. **Poetry Editor:** Esther M. Leiper.

Magazine Needs *Writers' Journal* is a bimonthly magazine "for writers and poets that offers advice and guidance, motivation, and inspiration to the more serious and published writers and poets." Features 2 columns for poets: "Esther Comments," which specifically critiques poems sent in by readers, and "Every Day with Poetry," which discusses a wide range of poetry topics, often—but not always—including readers' work. Wants "a variety of poetry: free verse, strict forms, concrete, Oriental. But we take nothing vulgar, preachy, or sloppily written. Since we appeal to those of different skill levels, some poems are more sophisticated than others, but those accepted must move, intrigue, or otherwise positively capture me. 'Esther Comments' is never used as a negative force to put a poem or a poet down. Indeed, I focus on the best part of a given work and seek to suggest means of improvement on weaker aspects." Accepts poetry written by school-age children. Has published poetry by Lawrence Schug, Diana Sutliff, and Eugene E. Grollmes. *Writers' Journal* is 64 pages (including paper cover), magazine-sized, professionally printed. Receives about 900 submissions/year, accepts about 25 (including those used in columns). Publishes 4-5 pages of poetry/issue (including columns). Circulation is 26,000. Single copy: $4.99; subscription: $19.97/year (US), Canada/Mexico add $15, Europe add $30, all others add $35. Sample: $5.

How to Submit "Short is best: 25-line limit, we do not use longer. Three to four poems at a time is just right." No query. Accepts submissions by postal mail only. Responds in up to 5 months. Pays $5/poem plus one contributor's copy.

Contest/Award Offerings The magazine also has poetry contests for previously unpublished poetry. Submit poems on any subject or in any form, 25 lines maximum. "Submit in duplicate: one with name and address, one without." Send SASE for guidelines. **Deadlines:** April 30, August 30, and December 30. **Reading fee for each contest:** $3/poem. Competition receives 1,000 entries/year. Winners announced in *The Writers' Journal* and on website.

☑ ◎ WRITING FOR OUR LIVES; RUNNING DEER PRESS (Specialized: women, feminism)

647 N. Santa Cruz Ave., The Annex, Los Gatos CA 95030-4350. (408)354-8604. Established 1991. **Editor/Publisher:** Janet McEwan.

Magazine Needs *"Writing For Our Lives* serves as a vessel for poems, short fiction, stories, letters, autobiographies, and journal excerpts from the life stories, experiences, and spiritual journeys of women." Wants poetry that is "personal, life-saving, autobiographical, serious—but don't forget humorous, silence-breaking—many styles, many voices. Women writers only, please." Has published poetry by Sara V. Glover, Kennette Harrison, Sara Regina Mitcho, and Eileen Tabios. *Writing For Our Lives* is 80-92 pages, $5^{1}/_{4} \times 8^{1}/_{4}$, printed on recycled paper, perfect-bound, with matte card cover. Receives about 400 poems/year, accepts 5%. Press run is 500. Subscription: $15.50/2 issues (CA residents add 8.25% sales tax). Back issues and overseas rates available; send SASE for info. Sample: $8, $11 overseas.

How to Submit Submit up to 5 typed poems with name and phone number on each page. Accepts previously published poems ("sometimes") and simultaneous submissions. Include 2 SASEs; "at least one of them should be sufficient to return manuscripts if you want them returned." Closing date is August 15. Usually responds in 3 days, occasionally longer. "As we are now shaping 2-4 issues in advance, we may ask to hold certain poems for later consideration over a period of 18 to 24 months." Seldom comments on rejected poems. Guidelines available in magazine or for SASE. Pays 2 contributor's copies, discount on additional copies, and discount on 2-issue subscription. Acquires first world-wide English language serial (or one-time reprint) rights.

Advice "Our contributors and circulation are international. We welcome new writers, but cannot often comment or advise. We do not pre-announce themes. Subscribe or try a sample copy— gauge the fit of your writing with *Writing For Our Lives*—support our ability to serve women's life-sustaining writing."

★ ◐ YALE UNIVERSITY PRESS; THE YALE SERIES OF YOUNGER POETS COMPETITION

P.O. Box 209040, New Haven CT 06520-9040. E-mail: yyp@yalepress3.unipress.edu. Website: www.yale.edu/yup/subjects/poetry. Established 1919. **Contact:** Yale Series of Younger Poets Competition.

Contest/Award Offerings The Yale Series of Younger Poets Competition is open to poets under age 40 who have not had a book previously published. Poets are not disqualified by previous publication of limited editions of no more than 300 copies, or previously published poems in newspapers and periodicals, which may be used in the book ms if so identified. Submit ms of 48-64 pages from October 1 to November 15. No e-mail submissions. **Entry fee:** $15. Guidelines and rules are available for SASE or on website. Previous winners include Richard Kenney, Carolyn Forché, and Robert Hass.

◐ YALOBUSHA REVIEW

University of Mississippi, Dept. of English, Bondurant Hall, P.O. Box 1848, University MS 38677-1848. E-mail: yalobush@olemiss.edu. Website: www.olemiss.edu/depts/english/pubs/yalobusha_review.html. Established 1995. **Contact:** Poetry Editor.

Magazine Needs *Yalobusha Review* appears annually in April "to promote new writing and art, creative nonfiction, fiction, and poetry." Does not want anything over 10 pages. Has published poetry by Charles Wright, Tom Chandler, and Claude Wilkinson. *Yalobusha Review* is 126 pages, digest-sized, with glossy cover, includes b&w photos and drawings. Receives 300-400 poems/year, accepts about 15%. Publishes about 20 poems/issue. Press run is 500; 50 are distributed free to chosen writers/artists. Single copy: $10. Sample: $8. Make checks payable to *Yalobusha Review*.

How to Submit Submit 10 poems maximum at a time. Length for poetry is 1 page minimum, 10 pages maximum. No previously published poems. Accepts disk submissions; no e-mail submissions. Cover letter is required. Include SASE. Reads submissions July through November. Submit seasonal poems 4 months in advance. Time between acceptance and publication is 4 months. Poems are circulated to an editorial board: reader to specific editor (prose/poetry) to editor-in-chief to editorial board (including advisors). Never comments on rejected poems. Occasionally publishes theme issues. Guidelines available for SASE or on website. Responds in up to 4 months. Pays 2 contributor's copies. Acquires all rights. Returns full rights upon request.

Advice "It seems as though poetry has become so regional, leaving us to wonder, 'Where is the universal?' "

☐ YA'SOU! A CELEBRATION OF LIFE

P.O. Box 77463, Columbus OH 43207. Established 2000. **Editor:** David D. Bell. Website: http://yasouon line.tripod.com.

Magazine Needs *Ya'sou! A celebration of life* appears quarterly. "Our purpose is to celebrate life. We like thought-provoking and uplifting material in any style and subject matter. We would like to see poetry essays, short stories, articles, and b&w artwork." Does not want "sexually explicit, pornographic, or violent poetry. I'd like more poetry written by children; parental consent required." Receives about 200 poems/year, accepts about 75%. Publishes about 40-50 poems/issue. Single copy: $5; subscription: $16/year. Make checks payable to David D. Bell.

How to Submit Submit 5 poems at a time. Line length for poetry is 30 maximum. "Your name and complete address should be at the top left-hand corner of every poem." Accepts previously published poems and simultaneous submissions. Cover letter is preferred. **Reading fee:** $1.50/poem, "or design your own page (8½×11) with as many poems you wish for $5." Work submitted by postal mail should be camera-ready. SASE required. Reads submissions all year. Time between acceptance and publication varies. "All work is read and chosen by the editor." Pays one contributor's copy.

Advice "Let your own unique voice be heard. Remember, express your heart, live your soul, and celebrate life."

$☐ YELLOW BAT REVIEW; YELLOW BAT PRESS

1338 W. Maumee, Idlewilde Manor #136, Adrian MI 49221. E-mail: sernotti@yellowbat.com. Website: www.yellowbat.com. Established 2001. **Editor:** Craig Sernotti.

Magazine Needs *Yellow Bat Review* appears semiannually as "a pocket-sized journal of eclectic writing, publishing both poetry and prose. *Yellow Bat Review* hopes to be *the* home for all types of poetry from subtle to humorous to strange and anything in between." Open to all schools and genres. No restrictions on form or content. Likes offbeat, surreal, gritty work. Nothing sentimental, no weak lines, no teenage angst. Has published poetry by Brian Evenson, Lyn Lifshin, Duane Locke, Todd Moore, and Scott H. Urban. *Yellow Bat Review* is 30+ pages, 4¼×5½, photocopied, saddle-stapled, with glossy b&w card stock cover. Accepts less than 5% of submissions. Subscribers include academic libraries. Single copy: $2.50; subscription: $8 (4 issues). Sample: $2.50. Make checks payable to Richard Geyer.

How to Submit Submit up to 4 poems at a time. Line length for poetry is 20 maximum. Accepts previously published poems (rarely); no simultaneous submissions. No fax or disk submissions. Strongly prefers e-mail submissions (pasted into body of message). Cover letter is preferred. Time between acceptance and publication is 2-8 months. Often comments on rejected poems. Occasionally publishes theme issues. Guidelines available on website or by e-mail. Responds in up to 2 months. Always sends prepublication galleys. Pays $5/poem plus 2 contributor's copies. Acquires first North American serial rights.

Book/Chapbook Needs & How to Submit Yellow Bat Press occasionally publishes pocket-sized chapbooks of dark poetry. Chapbook submissions are by invitation only. Chapbooks are 10-32 pages, photocopied, saddle-stapled, with glossy b&w card stock covers. Order sample chapbooks by sending $3 to Richard Geyer.

Advice "To beginners, try us, try everything. Experience only comes if you try. To everyone, we hope *Yellow Bat Review* will be a breath of fresh air in a world of dry lit mags. We don't care about being 'safe.' If the work is fresh and lively it will be published, regardless of school or style. Whether the poet is an 'unknown' or a 'well-known' is meaningless; it's the poem that counts."

Ⓝ Ⓓ Ⓞ ZEEK (Specialized: Jewish writers/themes preferred)

P.O. Box 20491, Parkwest Finance Station, New York NY 10025. E-mail: zeek@zeek.net. Website: www.zeek.net. Established 2002. **Poetry Editor:** Matthue Roth. Chief Editor: Jay Michaelson.

Magazine Needs *Zeek Magazine* is a monthly Jewish journal of thought and culture. Wants poetry that is "poetically daring, with shades of the numinous as it manifests in moments non-poets would ignore." Does not want "cliched, 'inspirational,' or ethnocentric writing; something that could serve as a greeting card, political poster, etc.; cynicism." Has published poetry by Hal Sirowitz, Matthue Roth, Abraham Mezrich, David Goldstein, and Sara Seinberg. *Zeek* is published in both print and online versions. Print version is 96 pages, digest-sized, perfect-bound, includes photography. Receives about 500 poems/year, accepts about 5. Publishes about 2 poems/issue. Press run for print version is 1,000 for 200 subscribers; online version gets 2,000 hits/month. Single copy: $7; subscription: $14/year. Make checks payable to Metatronics Inc.

How to Submit Submit 3 poems at a time. Accepts simultaneous submissions; no previously published poems. Accepts e-mail (pasted into body of message) and disk submissions. **E-mail preferred.** "E-mail will be read much faster and is much more likely to be published." Cover letter is preferred. Reads submissions year round. Time between acceptance and publication varies. Poems are circulated to an editorial board. "Poetry editor has final approval but editorial board of four can propose or reject." Seldom comments on rejected poems. Occasionally publishes theme issues. List of upcoming themes and guidelines available on website. Responds in one month. Pays 5 contributor's copies (to poets published in print edition). Acquires one-time rights. Reviews books of poetry.

Advice "If someone else can say it, let them. If no one else can say it, say *that*."

Ⓓ ZILLAH: A POETRY JOURNAL

P.O. Box 202, Port Aransas TX 78373-0202. E-mail: lightningwhelk@msn.com. Established 2001. **Editor/Publisher:** Pamela M. Smith.

Magazine Needs Appearing quarterly, *Zillah* is " 'not your mother's poetry.' Simply put, in the year 3999 an archaeologist's dig produces a copy of *Zillah* in situ and, reading it, the treasure hunter knows what it was like to live during the second and third millennia." Does not want pornography, gratuitous violence, evil or devil worship, or anything that lacks quality. *Zillah* is 40-50 pages, $7 \times 8\frac{1}{2}$, stapled, with 80 lb. coverstock, includes b&w original art or graphics. Receives about 1,200 poems/year. Single copy: $4; subscription: $16. Make checks payable to Pamela M. Smith.

How to Submit Submit 5-6 poems at a time. Line length for poetry is 60 maximum. Accepts previously published poems and simultaneous submissions. Accepts e-mail submissions. "SASE essential, typed, double-spaced, one poem to a page." Reads submissions all year. Submit seasonal poems 6 months in advance. Time between acceptance and publication is up to one year. Never comments on rejected poems. Responds in 2 months. Pays one contributor's copy. Acquires first North American serial rights or second reprint rights; rights revert to author after publication.

Advice "Everyone should write, everyone should write poetry. Take a leap of faith. Think of writing as a natural state of being. Let go from a stream of consciousness, from the heart, from depth— edit and refine later."

$☑ ZOO PRESS; KENYON REVIEW PRIZE IN POETRY FOR A FIRST BOOK; PARIS REVIEW PRIZE IN POETRY

P.O. Box 22990, Lincoln NE 68542. (402)770-8104. Fax: (402)614-2026. E-mail: editors@zoopress.o rg. Website: www.zoopress.org. Established 2000.

Book/Chapbook Needs "Zoo Press aims to publish the best writers writing in the English language, and will endeavor to do it at the rate of at least 10 manuscripts of admirable quality a year (in print and electronic formats as they become available), providing we can find them. We're confident we can. By quality we mean originality, an awareness of tradition, formal integrity, rhetorical variety (i.e., invective, satire, argument, irony, etc.), an impressive level of difficulty, authenticity, and, above all, beauty." Wants high-quality poetry mss. Does not want mss written by those who do not regularly read poetry. Has published poetry by Rachel Hadas, Joseph Harrison, Eric Ormsby, and Jeff Tweedy. Zoo Press publishes 10 paperbacks/year through open submissions and competition. Books are usually 50-100 pages, perfect-bound, with 2- to 4-color matte covers. Books available from local bookstores, online vendors, or through website.

Contest/Award Offerings 1) **Kenyon Review Prize in Poetry for a First Book.** Offers annual award of $3,500 and publication. Entrants must never have published a full-length collection of poetry. Contestants should send one copy of a ms of between 48 and 100 pages, typed single-spaced, with no more than one poem/page. See guidelines for additional formatting information. Contestants who have published poems in magazines may include those in the ms submitted, along with a page of acknowledgments. Submissions may be entered in other contests. Guidelines available for SASE, by e-mail, or on website. **Entry fee:** $25/submission. Does not accept entry fees in foreign currencies; American dollars only. **2004 Deadline:** was March 15. Competition receives 500-1,000 entries/year. 2003 winner was Randall Mann (*Complaint in the Garden*). Advises, "David Baker, the prize's recurring judge, is an eclectic editor with an eye for quality. We define quality in poetry as an awareness of tradition, formal integrity, rhetorical variety (i.e., invective, satire, argument, irony, etc.), an impressive level of difficulty in the project undertaken, authenticity, and, above all, beauty. All poetry manuscripts should aspire to these ideals." 2) **Paris Review Prize in Poetry.** Offers annual award of $5,000, a reading in NYC, and publication by Zoo Press. Latest information and guidelines not available at press time; see website for updates. 2002 winner was Jennifer Anna Gosetti-Ferencei (*After the Palace Burns*). Advises, "Richard Howard, the prize's recurring judge, is one of the most eclectic editors of poetry in the United States, so it's difficult to qualify or quantify his aesthetic more than to say he will choose a high-quality manuscript." 3) Also sponsors The Parnassus Prize in Poetry Criticism (contact for details).

Advice "Please read our books, or magazines published by our partners, to get a feel for the quality and substance of poetry being published here."

☑ ZUZU'S PETALS QUARTERLY ONLINE

P.O. Box 4853, Ithaca NY 14852. (607)539-1141. E-mail: info@zuzu.com. Website: www.zuzu.c om. Established 1992. **Editor:** T. Dunn.

Magazine Needs "We publish high-quality fiction, essays, poetry, and reviews on our award-winning website, which was featured in *USA Today Online*, *Entertainment Weekly*, *Library Journal*, and *Newsday*. Becoming an Internet publication allows us to offer thousands of helpful resources and addresses for poets, writers, editors, and researchers, as well as to greatly expand our readership. Free verse, blank verse, experimental, visually sensual poetry, etc. are especially welcome here. We're looking for a freshness of language, new ideas, and original expression. No 'June, moon, and spoon' rhymed poetry. No light verse. I'm open to considering more feminist, ethnic, alternative poetry, as well as poetry of place." Has published poetry by Ruth Daigon, Robert Sward, Laurel Bogen, W.T. Pfefferle, and Kate Gale. *Zuzu's Petals* is 70-100 pages, includes full-color artwork, and is an electronic publication available free of charge on the Internet. "Many libraries, colleges, and coffeehouses offer access to the Internet for those without home Internet accounts."

Receives about 3,000 poems/year, accepts about 10%. Copies free online, printed sample: $5.

How to Submit Submit up to 4 poems at a time. Accepts previously published poems and simultaneous submissions. Submissions via e-mail (pasted into body of message) are welcome, as well as submissions in ASCII (DOS IBM) format on 3½" disks. "Cover letters are not necessary. The work should speak for itself." Seldom comments on rejected poems. Guidelines available in magazine, for SASE, by e-mail, or on website. Responds in up to 2 months. Acquires one-time electronic rights. Staff reviews books of poetry in approximately 200 words. Send materials for review consideration.

Also Offers Publishes digital poetry videos. "Please e-mail for details before sending."

Advice "Read as much poetry as you can. Go to poetry readings, read books and collections of verse. Eat poetry for breakfast, cultivate a love of language, then write!"

Contests & Awards

T his section contains a wide array of poetry competitions and literary awards. These range from state poetry society contests with a number of modest monetary prizes to prestigious honors bestowed by private foundations, elite publishers, and renowned university programs. Because these listings reflect such a variety of skill levels and degrees of competitiveness, it's important to read each carefully and note its unique requirements. *Never* enter a contest without consulting the guidelines and following directions to the letter (including manuscript formatting, number of lines or pages of poetry accepted, amount of entry fee, entry forms needed, and other details).

Important

Important note: As we gathered information for this edition of *Poet's Market*, we found that some competitions hadn't yet established their 2005 fees and deadlines. In such cases, we list the most recent information available as a general guide. Always consult current guidelines for updates before entering any competition.

WHERE TO ENTER?

While it's perfectly okay to "think big" and aim high, being realistic may improve your chances of winning a prize for your poetry. Many of the listings in the Contests & Awards section begin with symbols that reflect their level of difficulty:

Contests ideal for beginners and unpublished poets are coded with the (▢) symbol. That's not to say these contests won't be highly competitive—there may be a large number of entries. However, you may find these entries are more on a level with your own, increasing your chances of being "in the running" for a prize. Don't assume these contests reward low quality, though. If you submit less than your best work, you're wasting your time and money (in postage and entry fees).

Contests for poets with more experience are coded with the (◪) symbol. Beginner/ unpublished poets are usually still welcome to enter, but the competition is keener here. Your work may be judged against that of widely published, prize-winning poets, so consider carefully whether you're ready for this level of competition. (Of course, nothing ventured, nothing gained—but those entry fees *do* add up.)

Contests for accomplished poets are coded with the (◉) symbol. These may have stricter entry requirements, higher entry fees, and other conditions that signal these programs are not intended to be "wide open" to all poets.

Specialized contests are coded with the (◎) symbol. These may include regional contests; awards for poetry written in a certain form or in the style of a certain poet; contests for women, gay/lesbian, ethnic, or age-specific poets (for instance, children or older adults); contests for translated poetry only; and many others.

There are also symbols that give additional information about contests. The (🅽) symbol indicates the contest is newly established and new to *Poet's Market*; the (✖) symbol indicates this contest did not appear in the 2004 edition; the (✖) symbol identifies a Canadian contest or award and the (🌐) symbol an international listing. Sometimes Canadian and international contests require that entrants live in certain countries, so pay attention when you see these symbols.

ADDITIONAL CONTESTS & AWARDS
Many magazines and presses prefer to include their contests with their listings in the Publishers of Poetry section (under **Contest/Award Offerings**). Therefore, we provide a supplement at the end of this section as a cross reference to these opportunities. For details about a contest associated with a market in this list, go to that market's page number.

WHAT ABOUT ENTRY FEES?
Most contests charge entry fees, and these are usually quite legitimate. The funds are used to cover expenses such as paying the judges, putting up prize monies, printing prize editions of magazines and journals, and promoting the contest through mailings and ads. If you're concerned about a poetry contest or other publishing opportunity, see Are You Being Taken? on page 33 for advice on some of the more questionable practices in the poetry world.

OTHER RESOURCES
Widen your search for contests beyond those listed in *Poet's Market*. Many Internet writer's sites have late-breaking announcements about competitions old and new (see Additional Resources on page 475). Often these sites offer free electronic newsletter subscriptions, sending valuable information right to your e-mail inbox.

The writer's magazines at your local bookstore regularly include listings for upcoming contests, as well as deadlines for artist's grants at the state and national level. (See Additional Resources on page 475 for a few suggestions; also, Grants on page 435.) The Association of Writers & Writing Programs (AWP) is a valuable resource, including its publication, *Writer's Chronicle*. (See Organizations, page 460.) State poetry societies are listed throughout this book; they offer many contests, as well as helpful information for poets (and mutual support). To find a specific group, search the General Index for listings under your state's name or look under "society"; also consult the Geographical Index on page 510.

Don't overlook your local connections. City and community newspapers, radio and TV announcements, bookstore newsletters and bulletin boards, and your public library can be terrific resources for competition news, especially regional contests.

Finally, don't miss the Insider Report on page 410, featuring perspectives on contest judging from **Dr. James Barnes, screener for the T.S. Eliot Prize in Poetry**.

Contests & Awards

ℕ $◻ AGHA SHAHID ALI PRIZE IN POETRY

University of Utah Press, 1795 E. South Campus Dr., #101, Salt Lake City UT 84112. (801)581-6771. Fax: (801)581-3365. E-mail: info@upress.utah.edu. Website: www.upress.utah.edu/AghaShahidAli.html. Established 2003. University of Utah Press and the Univerrsity of Utah Department of English offer an annual award of $1,000 and publication of a book-length poetry ms. Pays winners from other countries by wire transfer. Submissions may be previously published and may be entered in other contests. "However, entrants must notify the Press immediately if the collection submitted is accepted for publication elsewhere during the competition." Submit 48-64 typed pages of poetry, with no names or other identifying information appearing on title page or within ms. Include cover sheet with complete contact information (name, address, telephone, e-mail address). Submissions must be in English. Mss will not be returned; include SASE for notification only. Guidelines available on website. **Entry fee:** $25/book submission (includes cost, plus postage, of one copy of the winning publication). Does not accept entry fees in foreign currencies. **Deadline:** submit March 1-March31, 2005. Competition receives about 500 mss/year. Most recent winner was Ann Lauinger (2003). Judge for the 2004 award was Christopher Merrill. Winner will be announced in September on the website and through press releases and the Press catalog. Copies of winning books are available from University of Utah Press.

✪ $◻ ◎ THE AMY AWARD (Specialized: women 30 or under in NYC metropolitan region; form/lyric)

Guild Hall of East Hampton, 158 Main St., East Hampton NY 11937. (631)329-1151. Fax: (631)329-1151*51. E-mail: info@guildhall.org. Website: www.guildhall.org. Established 1996. **Contact:** Paula Trachtman. Offers annual honorarium plus a reading with a well-known poet in the *Writers at Guild Hall* series. Submissions may be previously published and may be entered in other contests. Submit 3 lyric poems of no more than 50 lines each, with name, address, and phone on each page. Accepts entries by fax and regular mail. Enclose SASE and bio. Entrants must be women 30 years of age or under residing on Long Island or in the New York metropolitan region. Do *not* send for guidelines; all information is contained in advertisements. **Deadline:** September 1. Most recent winners were Wendy Wisner, Jessica Soffer, and Kerry Ann Minto. Judges have included Fran Caster, David Ignatow, Philip Appleman, Edward Butscher, Siv Cedering, and Simon Perchik. Winners will be announced 6-8 weeks in advance by phone and mail. Guild Hall is the East End of Long Island's leading cultural center. It hosts, besides major museum, theater, and musical events, the *Writers at Guild Hall* series. Readers have included Tom Wolfe, Kurt Vonnegut, Joseph Brodsky, Maxine Kumin, Allen Ginsberg, Sharon Olds, John Ashbery, E.L. Doctorow, Eileen Myles, Linda Gregg, and Molly Peacock. "Future competitions will be run by *Poet's & Writer's*. Contact person to be decided." Watch for details.

✪ $◻ THE APR/HONICKMAN FIRST BOOK PRIZE

The American Poetry Review, 117 S. 17th St., Suite 910, Philadelphia PA 19103. (215)496-0439. Fax: (215)569-0808. Website: www.aprweb.org. Established 1972. **Award Director:** Elizabeth Scanlon. Offers annual award of $3,000 and publication of a book length ms. Open to U.S. citizens writing in English and who have not yet published a book-length collection of poems. Submissions must be unpublished as a book-length work exceeding 25 pages, although "poems previously published in periodicals or limited-edition chapbooks may be included." Ms may be submitted elsewhere, "but please notify us immediately if it is accepted for publication." Submit a poetry ms of 48 pages or more, single-spaced, paginated, with a table of contents and acknowledgments (a good copy is acceptable). Include 2 title pages: 1) first shows name, address, phone number, and the book title; 2) second contains the ms title only. Name or other identifying information should not appear anywhere in the ms besides the first title page. Use a plain file folder for the ms. Mss will not be returned. Include SASE for notification of contest results as well as a SAS postcard for notification of receipt of ms. Guidelines available for SASE or on website. **Entry fee:** $25/book ms. Does not accept entry fees in foreign currencies; U.S. dollars only. **Deadline:** October 31. Use First Class Mail only to send mss. Competition receives about 1,000 mss/year. Recent winners include James McCorkle (2003), Kathleen Ossip (2002), and Ed Pavlic (2001). 2004 judge will be Yusef Komunya-kaa. Winner will be announced by January 31 by SASE and in the March/April issue of *The American Poetry Review*. Copies of winning books available from *APR* or most bookstores.

$ARIZONA LITERARY CONTEST & BOOK AWARDS

Arizona Authors Association, P.O. Box 87857, Phoenix AZ 85080-7857. (602)769-2066. Fax: (623)780-0468. E-mail: contest@azauthors.com. Website: www.azauthors.com. **Contact:** Vijaya Schartz, president. Arizona Authors Association sponsors annual literary contest in poetry, short story, essay, unpublished novels, and published books (fiction, nonfiction, and children's litera-ture). Awards publication in *Arizona Literary Magazine*, radio interview, publication of novel by 1st Books Library, and $100 1st Prize in each category. Pays winners from other countries by International Money Order. Does not accept entry fees in foreign currencies. Poetry submissions must be unpublished and may be entered in other contests. Submit any number of poems on any subject up to 42 lines. Entry form and guidelines available for SASE. **Entry fee:** $10/poem. **Submission period:** January 1 through July 1. Competition receives 1,000 entries/year. Recent poetry winners include Ellaraine Lockie, Lynn Veach Sadler, Don Struble, Ymasumac Maranon, and Betty Brownlow. Judges are Arizona authors, editors, reviewers, and readers. Winners will be announced at an award banquet in Phoenix by November 15.

$ARIZONA STATE POETRY SOCIETY ANNUAL CONTEST; THE SANDCUTTERS

12811 W. Beechwood Dr., Sun City West AZ 85375. Website www.azpoetry.org/. **ASPS President:** Dorothy Zahner. Offers a variety of cash prizes in several categories ranging from $10-125; 1st, 2nd, and 3rd place winners are published in *The Sandcutter*, ASPS's quarterly publication, which also lists names of Honorable Mention winners. See guidelines for detailed submission information (available for SASE or on website). **Entry fee:** varies according to category; see guidelines. **Postmark Deadline:** was September 15 for 2003. Competition receives over 1,000 entries/year. ''ASPS sponsors a variety of monthly contests for members. Membership is available to anyone anywhere.''

☐ ARKANSAS POETRY DAY CONTEST; POETS' ROUNDTABLE OF ARKANSAS

605 Higdon, Apt. 109, Hot Springs AR 71913. (501)321-4226. E-mail: vernaleeh@hotmail.com. **Contact:** Verna Lee Hinegardner. Over 25 categories, many open to all poets. Brochure available in June; deadline in September; awards given in October. Guidelines available for SASE.

$☐ ◎ ARTIST TRUST; ARTIST TRUST GAP GRANTS; ARTIST TRUST/WSAC FELLOWSHIPS (Specialized: regional/WA)

1835 12th Ave., Seattle WA 98122. (206)467-8734. Fax: (206)467-9633. E-mail: info@artisttrust.org. Website: www.artisttrust.org. **Director of Grant Programs:** Fionn Meade. Artist Trust is a nonprofit arts organization that provides grants to artists (including poets) who are residents of the state. Accepts inquiries by mail, fax, or e-mail. **Deadline:** varies each year. Each competition receives 400-750 entries/year. Most recent winners include Jennifer S. Davis, David Shields, and Gregory Spatz. Also publishes, 3 times/year, a journal of news about arts opportunities and cultural issues.

⋈ ⋈ $☑ ASSOCIATION OF ITALIAN CANADIAN WRITERS LITERARY CONTEST, The Association of Italian Canadian Writers

℅ Delia De Santis, Treasurer, 2961 Delia Crescent, Bright's Grove ON N0N 1C0, Canada. E-mail: deliadesantis@yahoo.com. Established 2002. **Award Directors:** Delia De Santis and Venera Fazio.

Offers annual award of 1st Prize: $100; 2nd Prize: Honorary Mention. "*ASCENTI Magazine* (www.acce nti.ca) will publish the 1st Prize winners. French- and Italian-language winners must provide English translations in order to be published." Pays winners from other countries by money order. Submissions must be unpublished and may not be submitted elsewhere. Submit up to 3 poems of up to 40 lines each. All forms are acceptable, and entries may be submitted in English, French, or Italian. Send triplicate copies of each poem, each page numbered, no name on mss; include cover letter listing poem titles, name, home and e-mail addresses, telephone number, and include statement that poems have not been previously published or submitted elsewhere. Guidelines available by e-mail from Venera Fazio (veneraf@ebtech). **Entry fee:** $10 Canadian for members of the AICW; $20 Canadian for non-members; $15 U.S. Accepts entry fees in foreign currencies. **Deadline:** April 3. Competition receives about 100 entries/year. 2003 winners were Gilda Morina Syverson (1st Prize, "One All Soul's Day") and Salvatore Amico M. Buttaci (Honorary Mention, "Acquaviva in the Morning"). Trilingual judges for 2003 were Caterina Soteriadis and Filippo Salvatore. Winners will be announced by August 15, by e-mail to each participant. "The Association of Italian Canadian Writers (AICW), established in 1986, supports the work and educational interests of Italian-Canadian writers, critics, dramatists, playwrights, musicians, academics, and visual and performance artists."

⚡ $⊘ AUTUMN HOUSE POETRY PRIZE; AUTUMN HOUSE PRESS

87 Westwood St., Pittsburgh PA 15211. (412)381-4261. E-mail: simms@duq.edu. Website: http:// autumnhouse.org. Established 1998. **Award Director:** Michael Simms. Offers annual award of $1,000 and book publication. Pays winners from other countries by International Money Order. Submissions may be previously published and may be entered in other contests. Submit 48-80 pages of poetry. Guidelines available for SASE, by e-mail, or on website. **Entry fee:** $20/ms. Does not accept fees in foreign currencies; accepts International Money Order or VISA/MasterCard. **Deadline:** June 30. Competition receives 500 entries/year. Most recent winner was Deborah Slicer for *The White Calf Kicks*. Judge for 2004 contest was Alicia Ostriker. Winner will be announced each fall through ads in *American Poetry Review*, *Poets & Writers*, and *Writer's Chronicle*. Copies of winning books available from Amazon.com, Barnes & Noble, Borders, Small Press Distribution, Baker & Taylor, and others. "Autumn House Press has 3 poetry programs: 1) Autumn House Poetry Series publishes books by major American poets such as Ed Ochester, Sue Ellen Thompson, and Jo McDougall. 2) Autumn House Poetry Prize is an open competition. 3) Autumn House Master Poets Series invites major poets to Pittsburgh for readings, workshops, and radio interviews." Entrants should "read and follow the guidelines."

$○ THE BACKWATERS PRIZE

The Backwaters Press, 3502 N. 52nd St., Omaha NE 68104-3506. (402)451-4052. E-mail: gkosm6273 5@aol.com. Website: www.thebackwaterspress.homestead.com. Established 1998. **Contest Director:** Greg Kosmicki. Offers annual prize of $1,000 plus publication, promotion, and distribution. "Submissions may be entered in other contests and this should be noted in cover letter. Backwaters Press must be notified if manuscripts are accepted for publication at other presses." Submit up to 80 pages on any subject, any form. "Poems must be written in English. No collaborative work accepted. Parts of the manuscript may be previously published in magazines or chapbooks, but entire manuscript may not have been previously published." Manuscript should be typed (or word processed) in standard poetry format—single-spaced, one poem per page, one side only. Guidelines available for SASE, by e-mail, or on website. **Entry fee:** $25. Does not accept entry fees in foreign currencies. Send postal money order or personal check in U.S. dollars. **Deadline:** postmarked by June 4. Competition receives 350-400 entries/year. Most recent contest winner was Michelle Gillett (2003 for *Blinding the Goldfinches*). 2003 judge was Hayden Carruth. Winner will be announced in AWP *Chronicle* ad, in *Poets & Writer's* "Recent Winners," and on Backwaters website. Copies of winning books available through The Backwaters Press or Amazon.com. "The Backwaters Press is a nonprofit press dedicated to publishing the best new literature we can find. Send your best work."

✪ 🌐 ◻ ◎ BBC WILDLIFE MAGAZINE POET OF THE YEAR AWARDS (Specialized: nature)

BBC Wildlife Magazine, Broadcasting House, Whiteladies Rd., Bristol BS8 2LR United Kingdom. Phone: +44(0)117 973 8402. Fax: +44(0)117 946 7075. E-mail: wildlife.magazine@bbc.co.uk. Established 1994. **Award Director:** Nina Epton. Offers annual prize of £500, publication in *BBC Wildlife Magazine*, plus the poem is read on BBC radio 4's "Poetry, Please" program. Runners-up receive cash prizes plus publication in *BBC Wildlife Magazine*. Pays winners from other countries by International Money Order. Submissions must be unpublished. Submit one poem on the natural world in any form, 50 lines maximum. Guidelines available for SASE (or SAE and IRC) or by fax or e-mail. "No entry fees. The entry form usually appears in our April issue, but it's best to check with our office first." **Deadline:** varies from year to year. Competition receives 1,500-2,000 entries/year. 2003 award winner was Mark Goodwin. 2003 judges included Simon Rae (poet), Philip Gross (poet), Sara Davies (producer of "Poetry, Please"), Roger Deakin (poet and author), Roger McGough (poet and broadcaster), Helen Dunmore (poet and novelist), and Rosamund Kidman Cox (editor of *BBC Wildlife Magazine*). Winner announced in October *BBC Wildlife Magazine*. "Contact us for information before sending a poem in."

$◪ GEORGE BENNETT FELLOWSHIP

Phillips Exeter Academy, 20 Main St., Exeter NH 03833-2460. Website: www.exeter.edu. Established 1968. **Selection Committee Coordinator:** Charles Pratt. Provides an annual $10,000 fellowship plus residency (room and board) to a writer with a ms in progress. The Fellow's only official duties are to be in residence while the academy is in session and to be available to students interested in writing. The committee favors writers who have not yet published a book-length work with a major publisher. Application materials and guidelines available for SASE or on website. **Entry fee:** $5. Does not accept entry fees in foreign currencies; accepts cash, money order, or check in U.S. dollars. **Deadline:** December 1. Competition receives 190 entries. Recent award winners were Anne Campisi (2001-2002), Maggie Dietz (2002-2003), and Nia Stephens (2003-2004). Winners will be announced by mail in March. "Please, no telephone calls or e-mail inquiries."

$◎ BEST OF OHIO WRITERS WRITING CONTEST (Specialized: regional/Ohio residents)

P.O. Box 91801, Cleveland OH 44101. (216)421-0403. E-mail: pwlgc@yahoo.com. Website: www.pwlgc.com/ohiowriter.html. Offers annual contest for poetry, fiction, creative nonfiction, and "Writers on Writing" (any genre). 1st Prize: $150, 2nd Prize: $50, plus publication for first-place winner of each category in a special edition of *Ohio Writer*. Submit up to 3 typed poems, no more than 2 pages each, unpublished mss only. Open only to Ohio residents. "Entries will be judged anonymously, so please do not put name or other identification on manuscript. Attach entry form (or facsimile) to submission. Manuscripts will not be returned." Include SASE for list of winners. Entry form and guidelines available for SASE or by e-mail. **Entry fee:** $15/first entry in each category (includes one-year subscription or renewal to *Ohio Writer*); $2 for each additional entry in same category (limit 3/category). **Deadline:** July 31. Judges have included Larry Smith, Richard Hague, Ron Antonucci, and Sheila Schwartz. Winners announced in the November/December issue of *Ohio Writer*.

$◎ BINGHAMTOM UNIVERSITY MILT KESSLER POETRY BOOK AWARD (Specialized: poets over 40)

Binghamton University Creative Writing Program, P.O. Box 6000, Binghamton NY 13865. (607)777-2713. Fax: (607)777-2408. E-mail: cwpro@binghamton.edu. Website: http://english.binghamton.edu/cwpro/. Established 2001. **Award Director:** Maria Mazziotti Gillan. Offers annual award of $1,000 and a reading at the university for a book of poetry judged best of those published that year by a poet over the age of 40. "Submit books published that year; do not submit manuscripts." Entry form and guidelines available for SASE, by e-mail, or on website. **Entry fee:** none; "just submit 3 copies of book." **Deadline:** March 1. Competition receives 500 books/year. Most recent winner was Quincy Troupe (2003). 2003 judge was Laura Boss. Winner will be announced in June in *Poets & Writers* and on website, or by SASE if provided. (NOTE: Not to be confused with the Milton Kessler Memorial Prize for Poetry; see listing for *Harpur Palate* in the Publishers of Poetry section.)

$☑ BLUESTEM PRESS AWARD

Emporia State University, English Dept., Box 4019, Emporia KS 66801-5087. (620)341-5216. Fax: (620)341-5547. Website: www.emporia.edu/bluestem/index.htm. Established 1989. **Director:** Philip Heldrich. Offers annual award of $1,000 and publication for an original book-length collection of poems. Submissions must be unpublished and may be entered in other contests (with notification). Submit a typed ms of at least 48 pages on any subject in any form with a #10 SASE for notification. Guidelines and information available for SASE. **Entry fee:** $20. Does not accept entry fees in foreign currencies; send U.S. check or money order. **Deadline:** March 1. Competition receives 500-700 entries/year. Most recent award winner was Patricia Hooper. Judge was B.H. Fairchild. Winner will be announced in 3-6 months by flier in SASE to participants, on website, and in the trade journals. Copies of winning poems or books available from the Bluestem Press at the above number or through website. "Enter early to avoid missing the deadline; manuscripts will *not* be accepted after the deadline and will not be returned. Also, looking at the different winners from past years would help."

◩ $◎ BP NICHOL CHAPBOOK AWARD (Specialized: regional/Canada)

316 Dupont St., Toronto ON M5R 1V9 Canada. (416)964-7919. Fax: (416)964-6941. Established 1985. Offers $1,000 (Canadian) prize for the best poetry chapbook (10-48 pages) in English published in Canada. Submit 3 copies (not returnable) and a brief curriculum vitae of the author. Accepts inquiries by fax. **Deadline:** March 31. Competition receives between 40-60 entries on average.

◩ ⊕ $◻ CATALPA WRITER'S PRIZE

Australian-Irish Heritage Association, P.O. Box 1583, Subiaco, West Australia 6904 Australia. Phone: 08 9287-2712. Fax: 08 9287 2713. E-mail: aiha@irishheritage.net. Website: www.irishherita ge.net. Established 1997. **Award Director:** Joe O'Sullivan. Offers annual awards. See website for current year's entry details.

$◎ CAVE CANEM POETRY PRIZE (Specialized: ethnic/African American); CAVE CANEM FOUNDATION, INC.

P.O. Box 4286, Charlottesville VA 22905. Fax: (434)977-8106. E-mail: cavecanempoets@aol.com. Website: www.cavecanempoets.org. Award established 1999; organization 1996. **Award Director:** Carolyn Micklem, Cave Canem director. Offers "annual first book award dedicated to presenting the work of African American poets who have not been published by a professional press. The winner will receive $500 cash, publication, and 50 copies of the book." **U.S. poets only.** "Send 2 copies of manuscript of 50-75 pages. The author's name should not appear on the manuscript. Two title pages should be attached to each copy. The first must include the poet's name, address, telephone, and the title of the manuscript; the second should list the title only. Number the pages. Manuscripts will not be returned, but a SASE postcard can be included for notice of manuscript receipt. Simultaneous submissions should be noted. If the manuscript is accepted for publication elsewhere during the judging, immediate notification is requested." Guidelines available for SASE or on website. There is no entry fee. **Deadline:** May 15 of each year. Received 120 entries in 2003.

Most recent award winners were Kyle Dargan (2003), Tracy K. Smith (2002), Lyrae Van Clief-Stefanan (2001), and Major Jackson (2000). Most recent judges were Harryette Mullen (2004), Quincy Troupe (2003), Kevin Young (2002), and Marilyn Nelson (2001). Winners will be announced by press release in October of year of contest. Copies of winning books are available from "any bookseller, because the publishers are Graywolf Press ('99 and '02), University of Georgia ('00 and '03), and University of Pittsburgh ('01 and '04). Cave Canem sponsors a week-long workshop/retreat each summer and regional workshops in New York City and Minnesota. (See Cave Canem listing in Conferences & Workshops section.) It sponsors readings in cities in various parts of the country. The winner of the Prize and the judge are featured in an annual reading." Recommends "since this is a highly competitive contest, you should be at a stage in your development where some of your poems have already been published in literary journals. Manuscripts not adhering to guidelines will not be forwarded to judge nor returned to applicant."

$▢ CNW/FFWA FLORIDA STATE WRITING COMPETITION

Florida Freelance Writers Association, P.O. Box A, North Stratford NH 03590-0167. (603)922-8338. E-mail: contest@writers-editors.com. Website: www.writers-editors.com. Established 1978. **Award Director:** Dana K. Cassell. Offers annual awards for nonfiction, fiction, children's literature, and poetry. Awards for each category are 1st Prize: $100 plus certificate; 2nd Prize: $75 plus certificate; 3rd Prize: $50 plus certificate; plus Honorable Mention certificates. Submissions must be unpublished. Submit any number of poems on any subject in traditional forms, free verse, or children's. Entry form and guidelines available for SASE or on website. Accepts inquiries by e-mail. **Entry fee:** $3/poem (members), $5/poem (nonmembers). **Deadline:** March 15. Competition receives 350-400 entries/year. Competition is judged by writers, librarians, and teachers. Winners will be announced on May 31 by mail and on website.

$▣ DANA AWARD IN POETRY

7207 Townsend Forest Ct., Browns Summit NC 27214. (336)656-7009. E-mail: danaawards@pipe line.com (for emergency questions only). Website: www.danaawards.com. Established 1996. **Award Chair:** Mary Elizabeth Parker. Offers annual award of $1,000 for the best group of 5 poems. Pays winners from other countries by check in U.S. dollars. Submissions must be unpublished and not under promise of publication when submitted; may be simultaneously submitted elsewhere. Submit 5 poems on any subject, in any form; no light verse. Entries by regular mail only. Include SASE for winners list. No mss will be returned. Include separate cover sheet with name, address, phone, e-mail address, and titles of poems. Guidelines available for SASE, by e-mail, or on website. **Entry fee:** $15/5 poems. Does not accept entry fees in foreign currencies; accepts bank draft, International Money Order, or check in U.S. dollars only, drawn on U.S. bank. No personal checks written on foreign banks. **Postmark deadline:** October 31. Competition receives 400-500 poetry entries. Recent judges were Enid Shomer and Michael White. Winner will be announced in early spring by phone, letter, and e-mail.

▨ $▣ THE DOROTHY DANIELS ANNUAL HONORARY WRITING AWARD

The National League of American Pen Women, Inc.—Simi Valley Branch, P.O. Box 1485, Simi Valley CA 93062. E-mail: cdoering@adelphia.net. Established 1980. **Award Director:** Carol Doering. Offers annual award of 1st Prize: $100 in each category: poetry, fiction, nonfiction. Pays winners from other countries by check in U.S. currency. Submissions must be unpublished. Submit any number of poems, 50 lines maximum each, on any subject, free verse or traditional. Manuscript must not include name and address. Include cover letter with name, address, phone, title, category of each entry, and line count for each poem. Poem must be titled and typed on $8\frac{1}{2} \times 11$ white paper, single- or double-spaced, one poem/page. Guidelines and winners list available by e-mail. **Entry fee:** $5/poem. Does not accept entry fees in foreign currencies; send "checks which consider the exchange rate, or U.S. cash money." **Deadline:** July 31. Competition receives 1,500 entries/year. Recent award winner was Linda Smith. Winners will be announced by mail in early November. "Request rules and follow them carefully—always include SASE." The National League of American Pen Women, a nonprofit organization headquartered in Washington, DC, was established in 1897 and has a membership of more than 7,000 professional writers, artists, and composers. The Simi Valley Branch, of which noted novelists Dorothy Daniels and Elizabeth Forsythe Hailey are Honorary Members, was established in 1977.

🅽 $🖉 DEL SOL PRESS ANNUAL POETRY PRIZE

E-mail: joanh@theworld.com. Website: http://webdelsol.com/DelSolPress/contest.htm. Established 2003. **Award Director:** Joan Houlihan. Offers annual award of a $1,500 honorarium and book publication. Submissions may include previously published poems and may be entered in other contests. "Poet should have some prior publications of individual poems." Guidelines available on website. **Entry fee:** $22 (includes copy of winning book if 8x10 SASE is sent with entry). Make checks payable to Web Del Sol. Does not accept entry fees in foreign currencies; U.S. dollars only. **Deadline:** January 15, 2005. 2003 judge was Lucie Brock-Broido. Winners will be announced on website. Copies of winning books available from Del Sol Press. "Web del Sol is the nation's largest online publisher of contemporary periodicals and hosts many poetry-related journals, including *Perihelion* (www.webdelsol.com/Perihelion), as well as columns and articles on poetry. It also hosts online publication-oriented poetry workshops (www.webdelsol.com/Algonkian/Poetry)." Advice: "Send only your best. Our standards are high. Check the poetry we publish on webdelsol.com." (See separate listing for *Perihelion* in the Publishers of Poetry section and for The Concord Table Publication Workshop in the Conferences & Workshops section.)

✪ $▢ MILTON DORFMAN NATIONAL POETRY PRIZE

% Rome Art & Community Center, 308 W. Bloomfield St., Rome NY 13440. (315)336-1040. Fax: (315)336-1090. E-mail: racc@borg.com. Website: www.borg.com/~racc. **Contact:** Chris Galin. Annual award for unpublished poetry. Prizes: $500, $250, and $150. **Entry fee:** $8/poem (American funds only; $10 returned check penalty). Make checks payable to Rome Art & Community Center. Poets must be 18 years of age to enter. Contest opens January 1. **Deadline:** April 30 for 2004. Include name, address, and phone number on each entry. Poems are published in center's newsletter. Award ceremony and poetry reading in June. Competition receives about 1,000 entries/year. Judge to be announced. Winners notified by May. Results available for SASE.

$🖉 T.S. ELIOT PRIZE FOR POETRY; TRUMAN STATE UNIVERSITY PRESS

100 E. Normal, Kirksville MO 63501-4221. (660)785-7199. Fax: (660)785-4480. E-mail: tsup@truman.edu. Website: http://tsup.truman.edu. Press established 1986. **Contact:** Nancy Rediger. Offers annual award of $2,000, publication, and 10 copies as first prize. Submit 60-100 pages, include 2 title pages, one with name, address, phone, and ms title; the other with only the title. Individual poems may have been previously published in periodicals or anthologies, but the collection must not have been published as a book. Include SASE if you wish acknowledgement of receipt of your ms. Manuscripts will not be returned. Guidelines available for SASE or on website. Accepts inquiries by fax and e-mail. **Entry fee:** $25. **Deadline:** October 31. Competition receives more than 500 entries/year. Recent contest winners were Barbara Campbell (2003), James Gurley (2002), and Christopher Bakken (2001).

🌐 $🖉 T.S. ELIOT PRIZE (Specialized: regional/UK, Ireland)

The Poetry Book Society, Book House, 45 East Hill, London SW18 20Z United Kingdom. Phone: (020)8874 6361. Fax: (020)8870 0865. E-mail: info@poetrybooks.co.uk. Website: www.poetrybooks.co.uk. Established 1993. **Award Director:** Chris Holifield. Offers annual award for the best poetry collection published in the UK/Republic of Ireland each year. Prize: £10,000 (donated by Mrs. Valerie Eliot). Pays winners from other countries through publisher. Submissions must be previously published and may be entered in other contests. **Book/ms must be submitted by publisher** and have been published (or scheduled to be published) the year of the contest. Entry form and guidelines available for SASE or by fax or e-mail. Accepts inquiries by fax and e-mail. **Deadline:** early August. Competition receives 100 entries/year. Most recent contest winner was Alice Oswald. Recent judges include George Szirtes, David Harsent, and Mimi Khalvati. Winner will be announced in January.

$☑ THE ROBERT FROST FOUNDATION ANNUAL POETRY AWARD

The Robert Frost Foundation, Heritage Place, 439 S. Union St., Lawrence MA 01843. (978)725-8828. E-mail: frostfoundation@comcast.net. Website: www.frostfoundation.org. Established 1997. Offers annual award of $1,000. Pays winners from other countries in U.S. dollars. Submissions may be entered in other contests. Submit up to 3 poems of not more than 3 pages each (2 copies of each poem, one with name, address, and phone number), written in the spirit of Robert Frost. Guidelines available for SASE and on website. **Entry fee:** $10/poem. Does not accept entry fees in foreign currencies. **Deadline:** September 1. Competition receives over 400 entries/year. 2003 winner was Ned Balbo. Winners will be announced at the annual Frost Festival and by SASE following the Festival (late October). Winning poem can be viewed on website.

⬛ $□ ◎ JOHN GLASSCO TRANSLATION PRIZE (Specialized: translation, regional/ Canadian)

Literary Translators' Association of Canada, Université Concordia, SB 335, 1455, boul. de Maisonneuve Ouest, Montreal QC H3G 1M8 Canada. (514)848-8702. Fax: (514)848-4514. E-mail: ltac@alco r.concordia.ca. Website: www.attlc-ltac.org. **Contact:** Kathleen Merken, membership secretary. $1,000 awarded annually for a translator's first book-length literary translation into French or English, published in Canada during the previous calendar year. The translator must be a Canadian citizen or landed immigrant. Eligible genres include fiction, creative nonfiction, poetry, published plays, and children's books. Write for application form. Accepts inquiries by e-mail. **Deadline:** June 30. Competition receives 15 entries/year. Most recent prize winner was Yoldanda Amzallag. Winner will be announced by e-mail to members and by press release after formal presentation of award on International Translation Day (September 30).

Ⓝ $☑ RHEA AND SEMOUR GORSLINE POETRY COMPETITION

Cloudbank Books, P.O. Box 610, Corvallis OR 97339. (541)752-0075. Website: www.cloudbankbooks.c om. Established 2003. **Award Director:** Michael Malan. Offers annual award of $500 plus book publication. Open to poets who have been residents of U.S. or Canada for at least 2 years. Submissions may be previously published individually but ms as a whole must be unpublished (publication credit for each poem should appear on the acknowledgments page). Manuscripts may be entered in other contests, but poet must notify contest if ms is accepted elsewhere. Submit up to 71 pages of poetry (in English); page count includes contents, acknowledgments, section openers, and pages used to present quotation or notes. Type one poem/page on one side of paper. Include 2 title pages: 1) First should include poet's name, address, telephone number, and title of ms. 2) Second should include ms title only. Poet's name and any other personal information should not appear on pages of ms except first title page. Mss will not be returned; enclose SASP for confirmation of delivery. Hard copy only, no disks. Guidelines available for SASE. **Entry fee:** $20/book ms. Does not accept entry fees in foreign currencies; accepts U.S. money order or cash. **Deadline:** August 15. Judge is Vern Rutsala. Winners will be announced by SASE in October and in the March issue of *Poets & Writers*. Copies of winning books are available from Cloudbank Books and Amazon.

⚄ $◻ THE GREAT BLUE BEACON POETRY CONTEST; THE GREAT BLUE BEACON

1425 Patriot Dr., Melbourne FL 32940. (321)253-5869. E-mail: ajircc@juno.com. Established 1997. **Award Director:** A.J. Byers. Offers prizes approximately 3 times/year, as announced, of 1st: $25; 2nd: $15; 3rd: $10. "Winning poem to be published in *The Great Blue Beacon* (amounts will be increased if sufficient entries are received.)" *The Great Blue Beacon* is a quarterly newsletter for all writers. Sample copy: $1 and 55¢ stamp (or IRC). Subscription: $10/year, students $8; outside the U.S. $14. Submissions must be unpublished and may be entered in other contests. Submit up to 3 poems maximum on any subject in any form. "Submit 3 typed copies of each entry, no more than 24 lines/poem. On one copy, place your name, address, and telephone number on the upper left-hand corner of the first page. No name or address on the second or third copies." Guidelines available for SASE or by e-mail. Accepts inquiries by e-mail. **Entry fee:** $3/poem ($2 for subscribers to *The Great Blue Beacon*). Does not accept entry fees in foreign currencies; U.S. dollars only. Make checks payable to Andy Byers. Competition receives 200-300 entries/year. Most recent contest winners were Anne-Marie Legan, Irene Foley, and Peggy C. Hall. Winners will be announced approximately 2 months after deadline date. "Contestants must send SASE or e-mail address with entry to receive notification of results. Follow guidelines, particularly line limits. Submit your best work."

⚄ $◪ GREAT LAKES COLLEGES ASSOCIATION NEW WRITERS AWARD

The Philadelphia Center, North American Building, 121 South Broad St., 7th Floor, Philadelphia PA 19107. (215)735-7300. Fax: (215)735-7373. E-mail: clark@philactr.edu. Website: www.glca.org/index.cfm. **Director:** Dr. Mark Andrews Clark. Offers annual award to the best first book of poetry and the best first book of fiction among those **submitted by publishers**. The winning authors tour several of the 12 GLCA-member colleges (as invited) reading, lecturing, visiting classes, doing workshops, and publicizing their books. Each writer receives an honorarium of at least $300 from each college visited, as well as travel expenses, hotel accommodations, and hospitality. Usually, one winner (fiction) tours in the fall, and the other winner (poetry) tours in the spring, following the competition. Submissions must be previously published. Publishers should submit 4 copies of galleys or the printed book plus a statement of the author's agreement to commit to the college tour. Guidelines available for SASE, by e-mail, or on website. Accepts inquiries by fax. **Deadline:** February 28 (submit as early as possible after January 1). Competition receives about 50 entries for poetry, 35 for fiction/year. 2003 winners were Beth Ann Fennelly for *Open House* (poetry) and Kellie Wells for *Compression Scars* (fiction). Winners will be announced in May.

ℕ $◪ THE DONALD HALL PRIZE FOR POETRY; AWP AWARD SERIES

AWP, MS 1E3, George Mason University, Fairfax VA 22030. E-mail: awp@gmu.edu. Website: http://awpwriter.org. Established 2003. The Association of Writers & Writing Programs (AWP) sponsors an annual competition for the publication of excellent new book-length works, the AWP Award Series, which includes The Donald Hall Prize for Poetry. Offers annual award of $4,000 and publication for the best book-length ms of poetry (book-length defined for this competition as 48 pages minimum of text). Open to published and unpublished poets alike. "Poems previously published in periodicals are eligible for inclusion in submissions, but manuscripts previously published in their entirety, including self-published, are not eligible. As the series is judged anonymously, no list of acknowledgements should accompany your manuscript. You may submit your manuscript to other publishers while it is under consideration by the Award Series, but you must notify AWP immediately in writing if your manuscript is accepted elsewhere. No e-mail or phone calls, please." Manuscripts must be typed and single-spaced on good quality paper, $8\frac{1}{2} \times 11$. Photocopies or copies from letter-quality printers acceptable, but no dot matrix. Manuscripts should not be bound or in a folder; binder-clip or rubber-band mss together. No mss will be returned. Include SASP for confirmation of receipt of ms; SASE for notification of winners. Guidelines, including important formatting information and eligibility requirements, available on website. **Entry fee:** handling fee of $10 (AWP members) or $20 (nonmembers). Does not accept entry fees in foreign currencies; check or money order in U.S. dollars, drawn on U.S. bank, payable to AWP. **2004 Deadline:** mss accepted January 1-February 28. 2005 judges TBA. AWP is a nonprofit organization of writers, teachers, colleges, and universities. (See separate listing for the Association of Writers & Writing Programs (AWP) in the Organizations section.)

$☑ ◎ J.C. AND RUTH HALLS AND DIANE MIDDLEBROOK FELLOWSHIPS IN POETRY (Specialized: MFA or equivalent degree in creative writing)

Wisconsin Institute for Creative Writing, English Dept., 600 North Park St., Madison WI 53706. Website: http://creativewriting.wisc.edu. Established 1986. **Director:** Jesse Lee Kercheval. Offers annual fellowships, will pay $25,000 for one academic year. Applicants will teach one creative writing class/semester at University of Wisconsin and give a public reading at the end of their stay. Submissions may be entered in other contests. Submit 10 poems maximum on any subject, in any form. *Applicants must have a MFA or equivalent degree in creative writing.* Applicants cannot have published a book (chapbooks will not disqualify an applicant). Guidelines available for SASE or on website. **Reading fee:** $20. Accepts reading fees in foreign currencies. **Deadline:** Applications must be received in the month of February. Competitions receive 200 entries/year. Judges are faculty of creative writing program. Results will be sent to applicants by May 1. "The fellowships are administered by the Program in Creative Writing at the University of Wisconsin-Madison. Funding is provided by the Jay C. and Ruth Halls Writing Fund and the Carl Djerassi and Diane Middlebrook Fund through the University of Wisconsin Foundation."

$☑ THE HODDER FELLOWSHIP

Council of the Humanities, Joseph Henry House, Princeton University, Princeton NJ 08544. E-mail: humcounc@princeton.edu. Website: www.princeton.edu/~humcounc. Awarded to humanists in the early stages of their careers. "Typically, Hodder Fellows have published one highly acclaimed book and are undertaking significant new work that might not be possible without the 'studious leisure' afforded by this fellowship." Preference is given to applicants outside academia. **Candidates for the Ph.D. are not eligible.** Hodder Fellows spend an academic year in residence in Princeton working on independent projects in the humanities. Stipend is approximately $54,000. Most recent Hodder Fellows were Anthony Doerr and Sarah Mangus. Submit a résumé, sample of previous work (10 pages maximum, not returnable), a project proposal of 2-3 pages, and SASE. Guidelines available for SASE or on website. Announcement of the Hodder Fellow is posted on the website in March. **Postmark deadline:** November 1.

ℕ $☑ TOM HOWARD/JOHN H. REID POETRY CONTEST

% Winning Writers, 351 Pleasant St., PMB 222, Northampton MA 01060-3961. E-mail: johnreid@mail.qango.com. Website: www.geocities.com/rastar330/poetry.htm. Established 2003. **Award Director:** John H. Reid. Offers annual award of 1st Prize: $1,000; 2nd Prize: $400; 3rd Prize: $200; and Highly Commended entries share a prize pool of $280. Winners and Highly Commended entries will be published in an anthology. Pays winners from other countries by bank draft in equivalent of U.S. dollars. Submissions may be previously published and may be entered in other contests. Submit any number of poems of any number of lines on any subject/theme, in any form. Guidelines available by e-mail or on website. **Entry fee:** $5 U.S. for each 25 lines (or part thereof). Accepts entry fees in foreign currencies, "but U.S. preferred. Bank charges may apply to foreign currency payments." **Deadline:** September 30. Competition received 500 entries in 2003, but "we expect more in 2004." 2003 winner was Jennie Herrera. 2004 contest judge: John H. Reid (Tom Howard). Winners will be announced "hopefully, by late November." Copies of winning anthologies available from Lulu Books (www.lulu.com/filmindex). Sponsored and organized by John Howard Reid,

B.A., "who has spent a lifetime in the publishing industry: author of 17 published novels (under the 'Tom Howard' pseudonym), numerous books of film criticism, *How to Win Writing Contests*, etc. Editor of prize-winning anthologies and himself an award-winning poet, playwright, and prose writer." Advice: "Read the guidelines carefully and study the poems selected for the first anthology, *End of Season.*"

⊠ $☑ HENRY HOYNS POE/FAULKNER FELLOWSHIPS

Creative Writing Program, 219 Bryan Hall, P.O. Box 400121, University of Virginia, Charlottesville VA 22904-4121. (434)924-6675. Fax: (434)924-1478. E-mail: LRS9E@virginia.edu. Website: www.e ngl.virginia.edu/cwp. **Program Director:** Lisa Russ Spaar. Annual fellowships in poetry and fiction of varying amounts for candidates for the M.F.A. in creative writing. Sample poems/prose required with application. Accepts inquiries by fax and e-mail. **Deadline:** January 1. Competition receives 300-400 entries.

$◎ JOSEPH HENRY JACKSON AWARD; JAMES D. PHELAN AWARD; MARY TANENBAUM AWARD FOR NONFICTION (Specialized: regional/CA, NV)

% Intersection for the Arts, 446 Valencia St., San Francisco CA 94103. (415)626-2787. Fax: (415)626-1636. E-mail: info@theintersection.org. Website: www.theintersection.org. **Contact:** Awards Coordinator. Offers the Jackson Award ($2,000), established in 1955, to the author of an unpublished work-in-progress of fiction (novel or short stories), nonfictional prose, or poetry. Applicants must be residents of northern California or Nevada for 3 consecutive years immediately prior to the January 31 deadline and must be between the ages of 20 and 35 as of the deadline. Offers the Phelan Award ($2,000), established in 1935, to the author of an unpublished work-in-progress of fiction (novel or short stories), nonfictional prose, poetry, or drama. Applicants must be California-born (although they may now reside outside of the state), and must be between the ages of 20 and 35 as of the January 31 deadline. Offers the Tanenbaum Award ($2,000), established in 1987, to the author of an unpublished work-in-progress of nonfiction. Applicants must be residents of northern California or Nevada for 3 consecutive years immediately prior to the January 31 deadline and must be between the ages of 20 and 35 as of the deadline. Manuscripts for all 3 awards must be accompanied by an application form. The award judge will use a name-blind process. Manuscripts should be copied on the front and back of each page and must include a separate cover page that gives the work's title and the applicant's name and address. The applicant's name should only be listed on the cover page; do not list names or addresses on the pages of the ms. Applicants may, however, use the ms title and page numbers on the pages of the ms. Manuscripts with inappropriate identifying information will be deemed ineligible. Three copies of the ms should be forwarded with one properly completed current year's official application form to the address listed above. Guidelines available on website. **Deadline:** entries accepted November 15 through January 31. Competitions receive 150-180 entries. Recent contest winners include Richard Dry, Matthew Iribarne, Julie Orringer, and Joelle Fraser.

$☑ ◎ JAPANESE LITERARY TRANSLATION PRIZE (Specialized: translation/Japanese into English)

Donald Keene Center of Japanese Culture, Columbia University, 507 Kent Hall, New York NY 10027. (212)854-5036. Fax: (212)854-4019. E-mail: donald-keene-center@columbia.edu. Website: www.columbia.edu/cu/ealac/dkc. **Associate Director:** Yurika Kurakata. Established 1981. The Donald Keen Center of Japanese Culture at Columbia University annually awards $5,000 in Japan-U.S. Friendship Commission Prizes for the Translation of Japanese Literature. A prize is given for the best translation of a modern work of literature or for the best classical literary translation, or the prize is divided between a classical and a modern work. Pays winners from other countries in U.S. dollars. "Special attention is given to new or unpublished translators, and citizens of all nationalities are eligible.'' Submissions may be previously published and entered in other contests. Translated works submitted for consideration in 2004 may include: a) unpublished mss; b) works in press; c) translations published during the 2 years prior to the prize year. Submit 7 copies of book-length ms or published book. Entry form and guidelines available for SASE, by fax, e-mail, or on website. **Deadline:** February 1 each year. Competition receives 20-25 entries/year. 2003 award winners were Shogo Oketani/Leza Lowitz and Charles S. Inouye. Winners will be announced through press releases and on website.

$☐ JOHN WOOD COMMUNITY COLLEGE ADULT CREATIVE WRITING CONTEST

John Wood Community College, 1301 S. 48th St., Quincy IL 62305. (217)641-4903. Fax: (217)228-9483. E-mail: ssparks@jwcc.edu. Website: www.jwcc.edu. Established 1990. **Contest Coordinator:** Sherry L. Sparks. Offers annual award for original, unpublished poetry, fiction, and nonfiction. Categories include haiku/limerick; light or humorous poetry; traditional rhyming poem; non-rhyming poem; and Lewis and Clark poem. Cash prizes based on dollar amount of entries. 1st, 2nd, and 3rd Prizes awarded in each category. Guidelines available for SASE, by fax, e-mail, or on website. **Entry fee:** $5/poem; $7/nonfiction or fiction piece. Does not accept entry fees in foreign currencies; accepts cash in U.S. dollars as well as Western Union and American Express checks. **Deadline:** entries accepted January 1 through April 1. Competition receives 150-175 entries. Contest is in coordination with the Mid Mississippi River Writers Conference.

$☐ ◎ HELEN VAUGHN JOHNSON MEMORIAL HAIKU AWARD (Specialized: forms/haiku); POETRY FOR PETS (Specialized: animals)

Women in the Arts, P.O. Box 2907, Decatur IL 62524. (217)872-0811. Established 2001. **Contact:** Award Director. Offers annual award for traditional haiku. 1st Prize: $25; 2nd Prize: $15; 3rd Prize: $10. Pays winners from other countries by money order. Submissions may be previously published and may be entered in other contests. Submit unlimited number of poems of 5 lines about nature in traditional 5-7-5 haiku format; must not refer to people; no title. Name, address, and phone number should appear in upper righthand corner of each page. Guidelines available for SASE. **Entry fee:** $1/haiku. Accepts entry fees in foreign currencies. **Deadline:** January 17 annually. Competition receives 100 entries. 2003 winners were Marilyn Voorhees, Earl Dean, and Lucy Rowan. ''Judge is a publishing, professional writer living outside the state of Illinois. New judge annually.'' Winners will be announced February 20 annually. ''Study traditional haiku; we do not accept anything but 5-7-5.'' Also offers Poetry for Pets, an annual prize of $25 each in 2 categories (rhymed and unrhymed poetry). Submissions may be previously published, must be your own work. Submit any number of poems, no more than 24 lines each (excluding title) on the subject of ''pets.'' Entries must be typed and titled, with poet's name and address on back of page. Include #10 SASE for list of winners. **Entry fee:** $2/poem, or 3 poems for $5. **Postmark Deadline:** June 1. ''Two winners will be published in a special flyer. After paying prizes and expenses of contest, the remainder of the entry fees will be donated to The Humane Society of the United States.'' Make all checks payable to *WITA*.

$✉ ◎ HAROLD MORTON LANDON TRANSLATION AWARD

The Academy of American Poets, 588 Broadway, Suite 604, New York NY 10012-3210. (212)274-0343. Fax: (212)274-9427. E-mail: academy@poets.org. Website: www.poets.org. Award established 1976. **Executive Director:** Tree Swenson. **Awards Coordinator:** Ryan Murphy. Offers one $1,000 award each year to a U.S. citizen for translation of a book-length poem, a collection of poems, or a verse-drama translated into English from any language. Guidelines available for SASE or on website. **Deadline:** December 31 of year in which book was published. 2003 winner was W.S. Merwin for *Sir Gawain and the Green Knight*, chosen by Robert Bly. (For further information about The Academy of American Poets, see separate listing in the Organizations section.)

Contests & Awards

$◙ THE JAMES LAUGHLIN AWARD

The Academy of American Poets, 588 Broadway, Suite 604, New York NY 10012-3210. (212)274-0343. Fax: (212)274-9427. E-mail: academy@poets.org. Website: www.poets.org. Offered since 1954. **Executive Director:** Tree Swenson. **Awards Coordinator:** Ryan Murphy. Offers $5,000 prize to recognize and support a poet's second book (ms must be under contract to a publisher). Submissions must be made by a publisher in ms form. The Academy of American Poets distributes copies of the Laughlin Award-winning book to its members. Poets must be American citizens. Entry form, signed by the publisher, required; entry form and guidelines available for SASE or on website. **Deadline:** submissions accepted between January 1 and May 15. Winners announced in August. 2003 winner was Vijay Shshadri for *The Long Meadow*, chosen by Mary Jo Bang, Thom Gunn, and Campbell McGrath. (For further information about The Academy of American Poets, see separate listing in the Organizations section.)

🕊 $◎ THE STEPHEN LEACOCK MEMORIAL MEDAL FOR HUMOUR (Specialized: humor; regional/Canada); THE NEWSPACKET

Stephen Leacock Associates, P.O. Box 854, Orillia ON L3V 3P4 Canada. (705)835-7061. Fax: (705)835-7062. E-mail: spruce@encode.com. Website: www.leacock.ca. **Contact:** Marilyn Rumball (corresponding secretary). **Award Chairman:** Judith Rapson. Annual prize presented for a book of humor in prose, verse, drama, or any book form—by a Canadian citizen. "Book must have been published in the current year and no part of it may have been previously published in book form." Submit 10 copies of book, 8×10 b&w photo, bio, and entry fee. **Entry fee:** $50 CAN. Prize: Silver Leacock Medal for Humour and Laurentian Bank of Canada cash award of $10,000. **Deadline:** December 31. Competition receives 40-50 entries. The 2003 winner was *With Axe and Flask—A History of Persephone Township from Pre-Cambrian Days to the Present* by Dan Needles. The committee also publishes *The Newspacket* 3 times/year.

$◻ THE LEAGUE OF MINNESOTA POETS CONTEST

P.O. Box 1173, Brainerd MN 56401-1173. E-mail: mlarkin@brainerd.net. **Contest Chair:** Mary Larkin. Annual contest offers 18 different categories, with 3 prizes in each category ranging from $10-125. See guidelines for poem lengths, forms, and subjects. Guidelines available for #10 SASE or by e-mail. **Nonmember fee:** $1/poem per category; $2/poem (limit 6) for Grand Prize category. **Members fee:** $5 for 17 categories; $1/poem (limit 6) for Grand Prize category. Make checks payable to LOMP Contest. **Deadline:** July 31. Nationally known, non-Minnesota judges. Winners will be announced at the October LOMP Conference and by mail.

$◎ LITERARY GIFT OF FREEDOM; A ROOM OF HER OWN (Specialized: U.S. women writers; women in arts)

P.O. Box 778, Placitas NM 87043. E-mail: info@aroomofherownfoundation.org. Website: www.aroomofherownfoundation.org. Established 2001. **Award Director:** Darlene Chandler Bassett. Offers biennial award of "up to $50,000 over 2 years, with a mentor for advice and dialogue and access to the Advisory Council for professional and business consultation." NOTE: Literary Award grants alternate with visual arts, but poetry rotates with other writing genres. Open to U.S. citizens only. Submissions may be previously published and may be entered in other contests. "The successful applicant will have a well articulated creative project concept and a clear plan for how it may be accomplished." Applicant must submit detailed application with attachments. Application form and guidelines available by e-mail or on website (application available November of each grant cycle). **Entry fee:** $25/application, U.S. dollars only. **Postmark deadline:** on or before February 1. Receives 420 applications/grant cycle. Most recent winner was Jennifer Tseng (2002). Judges for the 2002 award were Dorothy Allison, R.S. Gwynn, Ramona King, and Charles E. Little. A new panel is chosen for each grant cycle. Recipient is contacted personally by telephone. Award recipients and finalists plus excerpts are posted on website. "A Room Of Her Own provides innovative arts patronage for women writers and artists through Gift of Freedom Awards. A Room Of Her Own Foundation is a 501(c)(3) nonprofit organization, organized and operated to further the vision of Virginia Woolf and bridge the often fatal gap between a woman's economic reality and her artistic creation. Even in this millennium, many women artists lack the privacy and financial stability essential to artistic output." Advice: "Read our entire website, read application, instructions, and hints and follow instructions exactly."

🅽 $◨ LITERARY SASHIMI AWARD; GORSKY PRESS

P.O. Box 42024, Los Angeles CA 90042. E-mail: gorskypress@hotmail.com. Website: www.gorskyp ress.com. Established 2001. **Award Director:** Felizon Vidad. Offers annual award of $1,000 and publication of winning ms by Gorsky Press. Pays winners from other countries in U.S. funds. Submissions may be previously published and may be entered in other contests. Submit a complete 60-80 page ms. Poems may be single- or double-spaced. Exceptions may be made for mss slightly larger than 80 pages. Authors should not put their names anywhere within the ms. Include 2 title pages: one title page with the ms title, author's name, address, and phone number; second title page with only the ms title. Guidelines available by e-mail or on website. **Entry fee:** $15/entry. Does not accept entry fees in foreign currencies; U.S. funds only. **Deadline:** July 15. Competition receives 200-300 entries/year. 2003 winner was Bucky Sinister (*Whiskey and Robots*). 2003 judge was Felizon Vidad. Winner will be announced by post and on the website in September. Copies of winning books available from Gorsky Press. "Our purpose is to publish books that will expose readers to new, exciting ideas. We struggle to give a voice to writers who are willing to take risks, to move their writing beyond easy classifications, to take the reader out of his normal world, and to allow the reader to re-examine contemporary, day-to-day society. In short, we are looking for and publishing writers who are lively and socially conscious and would otherwise be ignored by larger publishers." Advice: "Be original."

$◻ THE LITTLE BITTY POETRY COMPETITION

Shadow Poetry, P.O. Box 125, Excelsior Springs MO 64024. Fax: (208)977-9114. E-mail: shadowpoet ry@shadowpoetry.com. Website: www.shadowpoetry.com. Established 2000. **Award Director:** James Summers. Offers quarterly award of 1st Prize: $40; 2nd Prize: $20; 3rd Prize: $10; plus the top 3 winners also receive a certificate, printed copy of their poem, and a ribbon. Pays winners from other countries in U.S. dollars only by International Money Order. Submissions may be previously published and may be entered in other contests. Submit unlimited number of poems of 3-12 lines on any subject, in any form. "Entry form must be present with mail-in entries; name, address, phone number, and e-mail address (when available) on upper left-hand corner of each poem submitted. Enclose SASE for winners list. Include an additional SASE for entry receipt (optional). If no SASE is included for receipt, Shadow Poetry will e-mail an entry confirmation to the contestant, if applicable." Entry form and guidelines available for SASE or on website. **Entry fee:** $1.50/poem. Make checks payable to Shadow Poetry. Does not accept entry fees in foreign currencies; accepts International Money Order, cash (U.S. dollars), or payments through PayPal for foreign entries. **Deadlines:** March 31, June 30, September 30, and December 31. Winners will be announced "15 days after each quarterly contest ends, by e-mail and to those who requested a winners list. Results will also be posted on the Shadow Poetry website."

$◨ ◎ MARIN ARTS COUNCIL INDIVIDUAL ARTIST GRANTS (Specialized: regional/ Marin Co. CA)

650 Las Gallinas Ave., San Rafael CA 94903. (415)499-8350. Fax: (415)499-8537. E-mail: grants@m arinarts.org. Website: www.marinarts.org. Established 1987. **Grants Program Director:** Lance Walker. Offers biennial grants starting at $4,000 to residents of Marin County, CA only. Submissions

must have been completed within last 3 years. Submit 10 pages on any subject, in any form. *Open to Marin County residents only*—"must have lived in Marin County for one year prior to application, be 18 or over and not in an arts degree program." Entry form and guidelines available for SASE or on website. Accepts inquiries by fax and e-mail. **Deadline:** January. Winners will be announced June of each year. "The Marin Arts Council offers grants in 13 different categories to individual artists living in Marin County. Deadlines and categories alternate each year. The next deadline for poetry is expected to be January 2005. Call for more information." Competition receives 50-100 entries.

$☑ THE LENORE MARSHALL POETRY PRIZE

The Academy of American Poets, 588 Broadway, Suite 604, New York NY 10012-3210. (212)274-0343. Fax: (212)274-9427. E-mail: academy@poets.org. Website: www.poets.org. Award established 1975. **Executive Director:** Tree Swenson. **Awards Coordinator:** Ryan Murphy. Offers $25,000 for the most outstanding book of poems published in the U.S. in the preceding year; administered in conjunction with *The Nation*. Contest is open to books by living American poets published in a standard edition (40 pages or more in length with 500 or more copies printed). **Self-published books are not eligible.** Publishers may enter as many books as they wish. Four copies of each book must be submitted and none will be returned. Guidelines, required entry form available for SASE or on website. **Entry fee:** $25/title. **Deadline:** entries must be submitted between April 1 and June 15. Finalists announced in October; winner announced in November. 2003 winner was Eamon Grennan for *Still Life with Waterfall* (Graywolf Press), chosen by Judith Ortiz Cofer, Andrew Hudgins, and Robert Wrigley. (For further information about The Academy of American Poets, see separate listing in the Organizations section.)

▦ $☐ ◎ MELBOURNE POETS UNION ANNUAL NATIONAL POETRY COMPETITION (Specialized: regional/Australian poets)

Melbourne Poets Union, P.O. Box 266, Flinders Lane, Victoria 8009 Australia. Established 1977. **Contact:** Leon Shann. Offers annual prizes of $1,250 plus book vouchers, book prizes. Pays winners from other countries "with a cheque in foreign currency, after negotiation with winner." Submissions must be unpublished. Submit unlimited number of poems on any subject, in any form, up to 30 lines. "Open to Australian residents living in Australia or overseas." Entry form and guidelines available for SASE (or SAE and IRC). **Entry fee:** AUS $5/poem; AUS $12/3 poems. Accepts entry fees in foreign currencies. **Deadline:** October 31. Competition receives over 500 entries/year. Recent winners include Kathryn Lomer, John West, and Susan Kruss. Winners will be announced on the last Friday of November by newsletter, mail, and phone. "The $1,250 prize money comes directly from entry money, the rest going to paying the judge and costs of running the competition."

✪ $☐ MISSISSIPPI VALLEY POETRY CONTEST

Midwest Writing Center, P.O. Box 3188, Rock Island IL 61204. (563)359-1057. **Chairman:** Max J. Molleston. Offers annual prizes of approximately $1,500 for unpublished poems in categories for students (elementary, junior, and senior high), adults, Mississippi Valley, senior citizens, jazz, religious, humorous, rhyming, haiku, ethnic, and history. Submissions must be unpublished. **Entry fee:** $8 for up to 5 poems; no limit to number of entries. **Fee for children:** $5 for up to 5 poems. Send check or U.S. dollars. Professional readers present winning poems to a reception at an award evening in May. **Deadline:** April 1. Competition receives 1,000+ entries.

$◎ MONEY FOR WOMEN (Specialized: women/feminism); GERTRUDE STEIN AWARD; FANNIE LOU HAMER AWARD

Barbara Deming Memorial Fund, Inc., P.O. Box 630125, Bronx NY 10463. **Executive Director:** Susan Pliner. Offers biannual small grants of up to $1,500 to feminists in the arts "whose work addresses women's concerns and/or speaks for peace and justice from a feminist perspective." Pays Canadian winners in U.S. dollars. Submissions may be previously published and entered in other contests. Application form available for SASE. **Entrants must use application form with correct deadline date.** Applicants must be citizens of U.S. or Canada. **Application fee:** $10. Accepts entry fees by postal money order or checks drawn on U.S. funds. **Deadline:** June 30. Competition receives 400 entries/year. Recent award winners were Kelle Groom, Danielle Montgomery, Lisa J. Parker, and Michele Thorsen. Winners will be announced in May and October. Also offers the Gertrude Stein Award for outstanding work by a lesbian, and the Fannie Lou Hamer Award for work which combats racism and celebrates women of color.

$🖉 JENNY McKEAN MOORE WRITER IN WASHINGTON

Dept. of English, George Washington University, Washington DC 20052. (202)994-6515. Fax: (202)994-7915. E-mail: dmca@gwu.edu. Website: www.gwu.edu/~english. Offers fellowship for a visiting lecturer in creative writing, about $50,000 for 2 semesters. Apply by November 15 with résumé and writing sample of 25 pages or less. Awarded to poets and fiction writers in alternating years.

$🖉 SAMUEL FRENCH MORSE POETRY PRIZE

English Dept., 406 Holmes, Northeastern University, Boston MA 02115. (617)373-4546. Fax: (617)373-2509. E-mail: g.rotella@neu.edu. Website: www.casdn.neu.edu/~english/pub/morse.h tm. **Editor:** Prof. Guy Rotella. Offers book publication (ms 50-70 pages) by Northeastern University Press and an annual award of $1,000. Open to U.S. poets who have published no more than one book of poetry. Entry must be unpublished in book form but may include poems published in journals and magazines. Guidelines available on website (under "Publications"). Accepts inquiries by e-mail. **Entry fee:** $15. **Deadline:** August 1 for inquiries; September 15 for single copy of ms. Manuscripts will not be returned. Competition receives approximately 400 entries/year. Recent award winners include Jennifer Atkinson, Ted Genoways, and Catherine Sasanov. Most recent judge was Rosanna Warren.

$◻ NASHVILLE NEWSLETTER POETRY CONTEST

P.O. Box 60535, Nashville TN 37206-0535. Established 1977. **Editor/Publisher:** Roger Dale Miller. Offers quarterly prizes of $50, $25, and $10 plus possible publication in newsletter (published poets receive 3 copies of *Newsletter* in which their work appears), and at least 50 Certificates of Merit. Pays winners from other countries with check in U.S. funds. Submit one unpublished poem to a page, any style or subject up to 40 lines, with name and address in upper left corner. Send large #10 SASE for more information and/or extra entry forms for future contests. **Entry fee:** $5 for up to 3 poems. Must be sent all at once for each contest. Does not accept entry fees in foreign currencies; accepts check/money order in U.S. funds. "All other nonwinning poems will be considered for possible publication in future issues." Competition receives over 700 entries/year. Most recent winners were Dennis R. Norville, Judith Lundin, John R. Roberts, Anne-Marie Legan, and Jeanne Park. Recent judges were Hazel Kirby and J. Craddock. Winners will be announced by mail. Sample: $3. Responds in up to 10 weeks.

$◻ NATIONAL WRITERS UNION ANNUAL NATIONAL POETRY COMPETITION

P.O. Box 2409, Aptos CA 95001. E-mail: bonnie.thomas@att.net. Website: www.mbay.net/~nwu. 2004 competition sponsored by Santa Cruz/Monterey Local 7 of the National Writers Union. 1st Prize: $500; 2nd Prize: $300; 3rd Prize: $200. Guidelines available for SASE or on website. **Entry fee:** $4/poem (maximum length 3 pages). **Postmark Deadline:** November 30. Competition receives about 1,000 entries/year. A prominent woman poet will again judge winners. Winners will be announced in February 2005.

From the Judge's Side of the Fence

The poetry contest circuit can be rewarding, confusing, and costly. *Caveat emptor* applies, but recognizing potential hazards can be difficult. *Poet's Market* sought advice from Dr. James Barnes, Distinguished Professor of English at Brigham Young University in Provo, Utah. Dr. Barnes serves as the poetry contest screener for the annual T. S. Eliot Prize in Poetry, offered by Truman State University, Kirkville, Missouri. For poets interested in both single-poem and book-length contests, Dr. Barnes offers a perspective from the judge's side of the fence.

Can you shed some light on the criteria a poet should consider when choosing a single-poem contest?
Entrants should be aware of how many poems the magazine sponsoring the contest normally prints in each issue. *The Missouri Review*, for example, runs relatively few pages of poetry in any one issue, compared to the space reserved for prose. Yet a prize for best poem or group of poems is given each year. It is important that anyone submitting for prizes, whether magazine publication or book publication, understand the odds of winning the big cigar.

A great number of literary magazines across the nation offer contests wherein, if the submission does not win a prize, it nonetheless may be chosen for publication, though this will never be guaranteed by the sponsoring magazine. Of course, it is good consolation to be chosen for publication and makes one feel better about not winning the contest prize.

In a handful of cases, payment of entry fee into annual or semi-annual magazines or anthologies will guarantee publication; however, no good poet would want his or her work to appear in any of those take-all publications.

Poets often are told their poems will be winners and will appear in an anthology with other winning poems *if* they buy a copy of the anthology. Do reputable contests urge or require an entrant to purchase an anthology to win a contest?
Absolutely not. One should not be made to subscribe to or purchase an item relating to the result of any contest. An entry fee itself is the only passport, beyond the obligatory manuscript, one should have to provide to the contest.

Could you offer potential entrants some insight into contests that judge a complete manuscript of poetry as opposed to single-poem contests?
Manuscript contests select complete works for the purpose of publication, so a reputable press is desired in all cases. Entrants should consider what press will be doing the actual

publishing of the winning manuscript. Entry fees may range from ten to twenty-five dollars, and for this fee you are entitled to answers to basic questions. One should consider what the rewards beyond publication are: how much the prize, how much the royalties, how many copies the print run. The entrant should be entitled to these answers before entering. Any entrant should know this, or he or she should not be entering the contest. The names of screeners and judges should be withheld; however, if no contact e-mail, phone number, or address is given freely, and no information allowed, then something stinks very badly like sour apples.

Most legitimate contests receive hundreds of entries, and many rely on contest screeners like you to cull the entries. Please describe a little of the process you employ when you first read submissions for the T. S. Eliot Prize in Poetry.

The T. S. Eliot Prize in Poetry is totally freelance and honestly screened and judged; but one must understand that no screener is going to read, word by word, 700 or more manuscripts. I will read carefully the first eight or ten pages of a manuscript. Any poet worth his ink will make sure his best poems in the manuscript will be in the front section, in the first few pages. If not, the poet is taking a real chance of washing out immediately. If I do not like the first eight or ten pages of a manuscript, I will not read on. Why should I? I'll not be responsible for passing on to any judge a manuscript that has bad poems in the first ten pages!

Also, I detest manuscripts that seem to think they need the crutch that an epigraph might lend. I see too many that have quotes from these poets especially: Eliot, Stevens, Bishop, Pound, Yeats, Rilke. All-time favorite epigraphs come from Rainer Maria Rilke and Wallace Stevens. Not my favorites, however! If the manuscript is strong, it needs no help from any dead (or living) poet of any persuasion.

The selection process for the Truman State University Press T. S. Eliot Prize dictates that we have an equitable balance between male and female entrants. If the ratio of male/female manuscripts runs, say, 400:300 (a total of 700 manuscripts), then I will try for a 40:30 ratio for the semi-finalists category. Judges vary on the number of semi-finalists they wish to read, but it is usually between 50 and 100, though more often on the low side. The judge for the Eliot Prize will usually pick four finalists, then rank them by his choices, one through four. Number one is the winner of the annual Eliot prize, which means an award of $2,000 and publication in a normal print run. Occasionally, others in the finalists' list are offered publication at a standard royalty rate.

How many times do you read through the entries before selecting those you pass on to the judges?

Before I pass on the 50 or so manuscripts to the final judge, I will have read them through three or sometimes four times.

Do similarities in style, mood, or tone exist in the manuscripts that stand out for you?

I look for similarity in tone among the poems of any one manuscript, but I do not wish for, nor read for, similarity of tone, mood, style, or anything else among the various manuscripts. I know what I do not like in poetry, but I do not yet know everything that I may like. Therefore, I must read.

Can you cite mistakes entrants make that guarantee their poem(s) will be cut immediately?

If one begins each or nearly each poem with "I" or "My" in the first ten words, then he does not stand much of a chance with me as screener or judge. If one does not know that poems have tone, form, and content, then she is wasting her time and mine. It always helps that the typeface chosen for the manuscript be pleasing to the eye. So, too, the presentation on the page. Too much bold typeface, too light a type, too small a type, too large a type—any of these can kill interest in reading.

What advice or suggestions would you like to share with potential poetry contest entrants?

Prepare your poem or manuscript carefully. Yours is one of many entries. You want it to stand out, but you must abide by the rules of the contest. If, for example, the rules say send it unbound, then you do not send it in a folder. Follow the specifications. When in doubt, contact the sponsor of the contest.

Is there one thing you wish more contestants knew before entering a contest?

Yes. Judges look for the highest quality possible in a manuscript. Beginning poets who do not know they are beginning poets are wasting their time and money by submitting. One should know whether his work is good enough to compete. Nearly all the manuscripts received for the Eliot Prize are competent, good enough to be in any contest. In conclusion, contestants should bear in mind that judges have different tastes. Whatever manuscript fails one year may indeed be a winner the next, but you can be sure that the winning manuscript will have won on its literary merits.

—Denise Meyers

Denise Meyers has published short stories and articles in *ByLine Magazine*, *The Sun*, *Novel Writing Magazine*, and *Novel & Short Story Writer's Market*. She's currently president of Pennwriters, Inc., a multi-genre writer's organization based in Pennsylvania.

$☐ NEW MILLENNIUM AWARD FOR POETRY; NEW MILLENNIUM WRITINGS

Room M2, P.O. Box 2463, Knoxville TN 37901. Website: www.mach2.com. **Editor:** Don Williams. Offers 2 annual awards of $1,000 each. Pays winners from other countries by money order. Submissions must be previously unpublished but may be entered in other contests. Submit up to 3 poems, 5 pages maximum. No restrictions on style or content. Include name, address, phone number, and a #10 SASE for notification. All contestants receive the next issue at no additional charge. Printable entry form on website. Manuscripts are not returned. Guidelines available for SASE or on website. Accepts inquiries by e-mail. **Entry fee:** $17. Make checks payable to New Millennium Writings. Does not accept entry fees in foreign currencies; send money order drawn on U.S. bank. **Deadlines:** June 17 and November 17. Competition receives 2,000 entries/year. "Two winners and selected finalists will be published." Most recent award winner was Charlotte Pence. "Contests are not the only avenues to publication. We also accept—at no cost, no entry fee—general submissions for publication during the months of October, November, and December only. These should be addressed to Poetry Editor. There are no restrictions as to style, form, or content. Submitters should enclose SASE for correspondence purposes."

$☑ NEW RIVER POETS QUARTERLY POETRY AWARDS

New River Poets, 5545 Meadowbrook St., Zephyrhills FL 33541-2715. Established 2000. **Awards**

Coordinator: June Owens. Offers 1st Prize: $65; 2nd Prize: $45; 3rd Prize: $35 for each quarterly contest, plus 5 Honorable Mentions. Pays winners from other countries by International Bank Money Order. Submissions may be previously published and may be entered in other contests. Submit 1-4 poems of up to 42 lines each on any subject, in any form. "Send 2 copies each poem on 8½×11 white paper; poet's identification on only one copy of each. If previously published, state where/when. At bottom of each poem, state 'Author owns all rights.' If in a traditional form, state form. Quarter for which work is submitted must appear upper right." Guidelines available for SASE. **Entry fee:** 1-4 poems for $5; $1 each additional; no limit. Prefers U.S. funds. **Deadline:** November 15, February 15, May 15, August 15. Competition receives 800 entries/year. Most recent award winners were Melissa Dereberry, Maureen Tolman Flannery, and Donna Jean Tennis. Most recent contest judges were Maureen Tolman Flannery, Virginia H. McKinnie, and Sophie Soil (Canada). (First Place winners are invited to judge a subsequent competition). Winners will be announced by mail within 45 days of deadline. "New River Poets is a chartered Chapter of Florida State Poets Association, Inc. and member of National Federation of State Poetry Societies (NFSPS). Its purpose is to acknowledge and reward outstanding poetic efforts. NRP's first issue of its anthology, *Watermarks: One*, appeared in Summer 2004; it includes the work of previous winners of NRP Poetry Awards. *Watermarks: Two* is scheduled for Spring 2007, but is not open to general submissions." Advises to "send your best. Always include SASE. Our 'rules' are quite wide open, but please adhere. Remember that competition is not only good for the cause of poetry but for the poetic soul, a win-win situation."

$☑ NEWBURYPORT ART ASSOCIATION ANNUAL SPRING POETRY CONTEST

12 Charron Dr., Newburyport MA 01950. E-mail: espmosk@juno.com. Website: www.newburyport art.org. Established 1990. **Contest Coordinator:** Rhina P. Espaillat. Offers annual awards of 1st Prize: $200, 2nd Prize: $150, 3rd Prize: $100, plus a number of Honorable Mentions and certificates. All winners, including Honorable Mention poets, are invited to read their own entries at the Awards Day Reading in May. Open to anyone over 16 years old. Pays all winners, including those from other countries, with NAA check. Submissions must be previously unpublished, may be entered in other contests. Submit any number of poems, each no more than 3 pages in length. Must be typed, single- or double-spaced, on white 8½×11 paper; each poem must have a title. Send 2 copies of each poem: one without identification, one bearing your name, address, e-mail, and telephone number. Include SASE for notification of contest results. Any number of poems accepted, but all must be mailed together in a single envelope with one check covering the total entry fee. Guidelines available for SASE, by e-mail, and on website. **Entry fee:** $3/poem. Does not accept entry fees in foreign currencies; send U.S. cash, check, or money order. Make checks payable to NAA Poetry Contest (one check for all entries). **Postmark deadline:** March 15. 2003 winners were Alfred Nicol, Michele Leavitt, and Len Krisak, plus 14 Honorable Mentions. 2003 judge was Charles Martin. Do not submit entries without first securing a copy of the guidelines, then follow them carefully.

$☐ ◎ NFSPS COLLEGE/UNIVERSITY LEVEL POETRY AWARDS (Specialized: student writing)

3444 South Dover Terrace, Inverness FL 34452-7116. (352)344-3456. Fax: (352)746-7817. E-mail: sybella@digitalusa.net. Website: www.nfsps.org. **Chairman:** Sybella Beyer-Snyder. Offers 2 annual awards of $500 each; one as the Edna Meudt Memorial Award, the second as the Florence Kahn Memorial Award. Award includes publication of winning mss with 75 copies awarded to the respective poet. Recipients will be invited to read at the annual NFSPS (National Federation of State Poetry Societies) convention; NFSPS will provide an additional travel stipend to be presented at the convention to recipients in attendance (winners are responsible for the balance of convention costs). Open to all freshmen, sophomores, juniors, and seniors of an accredited university or college.

Submit a ms of 10 original poems, one poem to each page, single-spaced, each poem titled. **Each poem must be no more than 46 lines (including spaces between stanzas) and have no more than 50 characters/line (including spaces between words and punctuation).** Manuscript must be titled and must include cover page with name, address, phone number in upper left-hand corner; ms title centered on page. May include dedication page. No other identification on any page other than cover page. **NOTE:** *A NFSPS official 2005 application, completed and duly notarized,* **must** *accompany ms at time of submission.* No e-mail submissions or special deliveries; First Class Mail only. Entry form and guidelines available for SASE or on website. **Entry fee:** none. **2004 Deadline:** notarized applications and mss received on or before February 1 (no entry mailed before January 1). For 2004 competition, winners selected on or before March 31 and announced after April 15; each recipient's state poetry society also notified. Copies of published award mss available on NFSPS website. (See separate listing for National Federation of State Poetry Societies in Organizations section and for NFSPS Competitions and Stevens Poetry Manuscript Contest in this section.)

$◻ NFSPS COMPETITIONS; ENCORE PRIZE POEM ANTHOLOGY

50-Category Annual Contest Chairman: Kathleen Pederzani, 121 Grande Blvd., Reading PA 19608-9680 (e-mail: pederzanik@aol.com). Website: www.nfsps.org. NFSPS sponsors a national contest with 50 different categories each year, including the NFSPS Founders Award of 1st Prize: $1,500; 2nd Prize: $500; 3rd Prize: $250. **Entry fees for members:** $1/poem or $8 total for 8 or more categories, plus $5/poem for NFSPS Founders Award (limit 4 entries in this category alone). All poems winning over $15 are published in the *ENCORE Prize Poem Anthology*. Rules for all contests are given in a brochure available from Madelyn Eastlund, editor of *Strophes* newsletter, at 310 South Adams St., Beverly Hills FL 34465 (e-mail: verdure@digitalusa.net); or from Kathleen Pederzani at the address above; or on the NFSPS website. You can also write for the address of your state poetry society. NFSPS also sponsors the annual Stevens Poetry Manuscript Competition and the NFSPS College/University Level Poetry Awards (see separate listings in this section; for further information about the National Federation of State Poetry Societies [NFSPS], see separate listing in the Organizations section.)

$◻ ◎ FRANK O'HARA AWARD CHAPBOOK COMPETITION; THORNGATE ROAD PRESS (Specialized: gay/lesbian/bisexual)

Dept. of English and Humanities, Pratt Institute, 200 Willoughby Ave., Brooklyn NY 11205. (718)636-3790. E-mail: jelledge@pratt.edu (inquiries only). Established 1996. **Award Director/Publisher:** Jim Elledge. Offers annual award of $500, publication, and 25 copies. Submissions may be a combination of previously published and unpublished work and may be entered in other contests. Submit 16 pages on any topic, in any form. Another 4 pages for front matter are permitted, making a maximum total of 20 pages. Poets must be gay, lesbian, or bisexual (any race, age, background, etc.). One poem/page. Guidelines available for SASE. Accepts inquiries by e-mail. **Entry fee:** $15/entry. Make checks payable to Thorngate Road Press. **Deadline:** February 1. Competition receives 200-300 entries. Most recent contest winner was Aaron Smith (*What's Required*). Judge is a nationally recognized gay, lesbian, or bisexual poet. Judge remains anonymous until the winner has been announced (by April 15). Copies of winning books may be ordered by sending $6 to the above address made out to Thorngate Road Press. "Thorngate Road publishes at least 2 chapbooks annually, and they are selected by one of 2 methods. The first is through the contest. The second, the Berdache Chapbook Series, is by invitation only. We published chapbooks by Kristy Nielsen, David Trinidad, Reginald Shepherd, Karen Lee Osborne, Timothy Liu, and Maureen Seaton in the Berdache series." Although the contest is only open to gay, lesbian, bisexual, and transgendered authors, the content of submissions does not necessarily have to be gay, lesbian, bisexual, or transgendered.

$☐ OHIO POETRY DAY CONTESTS

Ohio Poetry Day Association, 3520 St. Route 56, Mechanicsburg OH 43044. (937)834-2666. Established 1937. **Contact:** Contest Chairman. Offers annual slate of 30-40 contest categories. Prizes range from $75 on down; all money-award poems published in anthology (runs over 100 pages). Pays winners from other countries in cash. "The bank we use does not do *any* exchange at any price." Submissions must be unpublished. Submit one poem/category on topic and in form specified. Some contests open to everyone, but others open only to Ohio poets. "Each contest has its own specifications. Entry must be for a specified category, so entrants *need rules*." Entry form and guidelines available for SASE. **Entry fee:** $8 inclusive, unlimited number of categories. Does not accept entry fees in foreign currencies; cash or checks drawn on U.S. bank only. **Deadline:** usually end of May; see guidelines for each year's deadline. Competition receives up to 4,000 entries/year. Winners and judges for most recent contest listed in winners' book. Judges are never announced in advance. Winners list available in August for SASE (enclose with poem entries); prizes given in October. Copies of winning books available from Amy Jo Zook for $7-8 (prices can differ from year to year) plus $1.50 postage for one or 2 books. "Ohio Poetry Day is the umbrella. Individual contests are sponsored by poetry organizations and/or individuals across the state. OPD sponsors one, plus Poet of the Year and Student Poet of the Year; have 4 memorial funds." Join mailing list at any time by sending contact information by postcard or letter. Advice: "Revise, follow rules, look at individual categories for a good match."

★ $◎ NATALIE ORNISH POETRY AWARD (Specialized: regional/TX); SOEURETTE DIEHL FRASER TRANSLATION AWARD (Specialized: translations, regional/TX); TEXAS INSTITUTE OF LETTERS BEST BOOK OF POETRY AWARD

% Frances Vick, Texas Institute of Letters, 3700 Mockingbird Lane, Dallas TX 75205. (214)528-2655. Fax: (214)528-2460. E-mail: franvick@aol.com. Website: www.stedwards.edu/newc/marks/til. **Contact:** Frances Vick. Established 1947. The Texas Institute of Letters gives annual awards for books by Texas authors, including the Natalie Ornish Poetry Award, a $1,000 award for best first volume of poetry. Books must have been first published in the year in question, and entries may be made by authors or by their publishers. One copy of each entry must be mailed to each of 3 judges, with "information showing an author's Texas association . . . if it is not otherwise obvious." Poets must have lived in Texas for at least 2 consecutive years at some time or their work must reflect a notable concern with matters associated with the state. The Soeurette Diehl Fraser Translation Award ($1,000) is given for best translation of a book into English, and Best Book of Poetry Award offers a $5,000 prize. Write during the fall for complete guidelines. Accepts inquiries by fax or e-mail. **Deadlines:** see website. Competitions receive 30 entries/year.

★ $☐ PACIFIC NORTHWEST WRITERS ASSOCIATION (PNWA) LITERARY CONTEST

P.O. Box 2016, Edmonds WA 98020-9516. (425)673-2665. Fax: (425)771-9588. E-mail: pnwa@pnwa.org. Website: www.pnwa.org. Established 1956. **Award Director:** Dana Murphy-Love. Offers annual award of 1st Prize: Zola Award and pin, $600 cash, certificate, and reading by performers at a Zola in Performance event; 2nd Prize: $300 cash, certificate; 3rd Prize: $150 cash, certificate. Pays winners from other countries by check in U.S. currency. Submissions must be unpublished but may be entered in other contests. Submit 3 one-page poems, single-spaced within stanza, double-spaced between stanzas. Use 12 point font on computer or pica type on typewriter in Courier, Times Roman, or New Times Roman. Include title of collection of 3 poems on each page in upper right-hand corner. Send 3 copies of collection in large mailing envelope. Include SASE and entry fee with submission form (which can be downloaded from website). Entry form and guidelines available for SASE or on website. **Entry fee:** $35 for PNWA members, $45 for non-PNWA members for each 3-poem collection; only one submission allowed. Does not accept entry fees in foreign currencies; U.S. dollars only. **2005 Deadline:** February 21. Competition receives 75 entries/

year. Most recent winners were Julie Gerrard, Ronda Broatch, and Robert Singer. Judges are "all respected members of the literary community." Winners will be announced at Awards Banquet at annual PWNA Summer Writers Conference in Seattle, WA. "The Pacific Northwest Writers Association, a nonprofit organization, is dedicated to Northwest writers and the development of writing talent from pen to publication through education, accessibility to the publishing industry, and participation in an interactive vital writer community. In addition to the annual Literary Contest, PNWA hosts an annual conference each summer in the Seattle area. Members are given opportunities to read their unpublished work through events called The Word is Out." See website for further membership and conference details.

$⬙ PAUMANOK POETRY AWARD; THE VISITING WRITERS PROGRAM

English Dept., Knapp Hall, Farmingdale State University of New York, 2350 Broadhollow Rd., Farmingdale NY 11735. E-mail: brownml@farmingdale.edu. Website: www.farmingdale.edu/. Established 1990. **Director:** Dr. Margery Brown. Offers 1st Prize of $1,000 plus an all-expense-paid feature reading in their 2005-2006 series (*Please note:* travel expenses within the continental U.S. only). Also awards two 2nd Prizes of $500 plus expenses for a reading in the series. Pays winners from other countries in U.S. dollars. Submit cover letter, one-paragraph literary bio, and 3-5 poems (no more than 10 pages total), published or unpublished. Include cover page with name, address, and phone number. **Entry fee:** $25. Make checks payable to Farmingdale State University of New York, VWP. **Postmark deadline:** by September 15. Does not accept entry fees in foreign currencies. Send money order in U.S. dollars. Send SASE for results (to be mailed by late December); results also posted on website. Guidelines available for SASE or on website. Accepts inquiries by e-mail. Competition receives over 600 entries. 2003 contest winners were George Drew (1st Prize) and Richard Michelson and Gerry LaFemina (2nd Prizes).

$◎ PEN CENTER USA WEST LITERARY AWARD IN POETRY (Specialized: regional/ west of the Mississippi)

PEN Center USA West, 672 S. Lafayette Park Place, #42, Los Angeles CA 90057. (213)365-8500. Fax: (213)365-9616. E-mail: awards@penusa.org. Website: www.penusa.org. **Contact:** Awards Coordinator. Offers annual $1,000 cash award to a book of poetry published during the previous calendar year. Open to writers living west of the Mississippi. Submit 4 copies of the entry. Entry form and guidelines available for SASE, by fax, e-mail, or on website. **Entry fee:** $35. **Deadline:** December 17. Most recent award winner was Donald Revell. Judges were Michael Davidson, Andrew Maxwell, and Marjorie Perloff. Winner will be announced in a May 2005 press release and honored at a ceremony in Los Angeles.

$⬙ ◎ PENNSYLVANIA POETRY SOCIETY ANNUAL CONTEST

(610)374-5848. E-mail: aubade@bluetruck.net. Website: www.nfsps.com/pa/pps-contests.html. **Contest Chairman:** Steve Concert, 6 Kitchen Ave., Harvey's Lake PA 18618. Offers Annual Contest with grand prize awards of $100, $50, and $25; other categories offer $25, $15, and $10. May enter 3 poems for grand prize at $2 each for members and nonmembers alike. Also offers prizes in other categories of $25, $15, and $10 (one entry/category); only one poem accepted in each of remaining categories. A total of 17 categories open to all, 4 categories for members only. **Entry fee:** for members entering categories 2-21, $2.50 inclusive; for nonmembers entering categories 2-15 and 17-21, $1.50 each. Guidelines available for SASE or on website. **Deadline:** January 15. Also sponsors the Pegasus Contest **for PA students only**, grades 5-12. For information send SASE to Carol Clark Williams, Chairman, 445 North George St., York PA. **Deadline:** February 1. Carlisle Poets Contest open to all poets. **Deadline:** October 31. Guidelines available for SASE from Joy Campbell, Chairman, 10 Polecat Rd., Landisburg PA 17040. The Society publishes a quarterly newsletter with member poetry and challenges, plus an annual soft-cover book of prize poems from the Annual

Contest. Winning Pegasus Contest poems are published in a booklet sent to schools. PPS membership dues: $17/fiscal year. Make checks payable to PPS, Inc., mail to Richard R. Gasser, Treasurer, at 801 Spruce St., West Reading PA 19611-1448.

$☑ POETIC LICENSE CONTEST; MKASHEF ENTERPRISES

P.O. Box 688, Yucca Valley CA 92286-0688. E-mail: alayne@inetworld.net. Website: www.asidozin es.com. Established 1998. **Poetry Editor:** Alayne Gelfand. Offers a biannual poetry contest. 1st Prize: $500, 2nd Prize: $100, 3rd Prize: $40, plus publication in anthology and one copy. Pays winners from other countries in U.S. cash, by money order, or through PayPal. Five honorable mentions receive one copy; other poems of exceptional interest will also be included in the anthology. **Themes and deadlines available for SASE.** Submit any number of poems, any style, of up to 50 lines/poem (poems may have been previously published). Include name, address, and phone number on each poem. Enclose a SASE for notification of winners. Accepts submissions by regular mail, on disk, or by e-mail (attachment or pasted into body of message). "Judges prefer original, accessible, and unforced works." Guidelines available for SASE or by e-mail. **Entry fee:** $1/poem. "We're looking for fresh word usage and surprising imagery. Please keep in mind that our judges prefer non-rhyming poetry. Each contest seeks to explode established definitions of the theme being spotlighted. Be sure to send SASE or e-mail for current theme and deadline."

▨ $◻ POETRY IN PRINT CONTEST

P.O. Box 30981, Albuquerque NM 87190-0981. Phone/Fax: (505)888-3937. Established 1991. **Award Director:** Robert G. English. Offers annual award of 1st Prize: $1,000; 2nd and 3rd Prize and Honorable Mention awarded plaques with certificates. Pays winners from other countries with business check in U.S. dollars. Submissions may be previously published and may be entered in other contests. Submit unlimited number of poems, 60 lines total. Include name and telephone number on each page of submission. Include SASE for notification of winners. Guidelines available for SASE or by fax. **Entry fee:** $10. **Deadline:** August 1. Competition receives about 500 entries. Most recent winners were Ellen H. Calvert, Bettye Blankenship, Janice Meznarich, and Ann S. Lance. Judge is Robert G. English. Winners will be announced in August by telephone and through SASEs. "Think TRUTH. I like humanitarian although I accept any subject."

$POETRY SOCIETY OF AMERICA AWARDS

Poetry Society of America, 15 Gramercy Park, New York NY 10003. (212)254-9628. Website: www.p oetrysociety.org. Offers the following awards open to PSA members only: The Writer Magazine/ Emily Dickinson Award ($250, for a poem inspired by Dickinson though not necessarily in her style); Cecil Hemley Memorial Award ($500, for a lyric poem that addresses a philosophical or epistemological concern); Lyric Poetry Award ($500, for a lyric poem on any subject); Lucille Medwick Memorial Award ($500, for an original poem in any form on a humanitarian theme); Alice Fay Di Castagnola Award ($1,000 for a manuscript-in-progress of poetry or verse-drama). The following awards are open to both PSA members and nonmembers: Louise Louis/Emily F. Bourne Student Poetry Award ($250, for the best unpublished poem by a student in grades 9-12 from the U.S.); George Bogin Memorial Award ($500, for a selection of 4-5 poems that use language in an original way to reflect the encounter of the ordinary and the extraordinary and to take a stand against oppression in any of its forms); Robert H. Winner Memorial Award ($2,500, to acknowledge original work being done in mid-career by a poet who has not had substantial recognition, open to poets over 40 who have published no more than one book). Entries for the Norma Farber First Book Award ($500) and the William Carlos Williams Award (purchase prize between $500 and $1,000, for a book of poetry published by a small press, nonprofit, or university press) must be submitted directly by publishers. Complete submission guidelines for all awards are available on website. **Entry fee:** all of the above contests are free to PSA members; nonmembers pay $15 to enter any or all of contests 6-8; $5 for high school students to enter single entries in the student poetry competition; high school teachers/administrators may submit unlimited number of students' poems (one entry/student) to student poetry award for $20. **Deadline:** submissions must be postmarked between October 1 and December 21. Additional information available on website. (See separate listing for Poetry Society of American in the Organizations section and for the PSA Chapbook Fellowships in this section.)

◪ $□ ◎ THE POETRY SOCIETY OF VIRGINIA ANNUAL CONTESTS (Specialized: forms/sonnet, haiku, limerick; humor; students; themes)

P.O. Box 35160, Richmond VA 23235. E-mail: contest@poetrysocietyofvirginia.org. Website: www. PoetrySocietyOfVirginia.org. **Contact:** Contest Chair. Offers contests in various categories including the Bess Gresham Memorial (garden or gardeners); Brodie Herndon Memorial (the sea); Judah, Sarah, Grace, and Tom Memorial (inter-ethnic amity); Cenie H. Moon Prize (women); Karma Deane Ogden Memorial (PSV members only); and the Edgar Allan Poe Memorial. (All of the previous categories are open to any form, have limits of 32-48 lines, and some have specific subjects as noted.) The following group of contests require specific forms: the J. Franklin Dew Award (series of 3-4 haiku), Carleton Drewry Memorial (lyric or sonnet about mountains), Handy Andy Prize (limerick), Emma Gray Trigg Memorial (lyric, 64-line limit, PSV members only), Nancy Byrd Turner Memorial (sonnet), plus categories that change annually. Final groups of poems open to students only (no fees required): S-1, Grades 1-2; S-2, Grades 3-4; S-3, Grades 5-6; S-4, Grades 7-8; S-5, Grades 9-10; S-6, Grades 11-12; and S-7, Undergraduate. All poems are open to nonmembers except those noted above. Cash prizes range from $10-100. Pays winners from other countries with IRCs or through PayPal account. Contest information available for SASE or on website (guidelines *must* be followed). Does not accept submissions by e-mail. **Entry fee:** Adults, $2/poem; no fee for student entries. Send **all entries** to Contest Chair at the address above. **Deadline:** January 19 for all contests (Edgar Allan Poe's birthday). Each category averages about 80 entries/year. Winning entries will be published in a booklet unless author indicates otherwise. Also publishes the *Poetry Society of Virginia Newsletter*, which provides PSV members with information about upcoming meetings and local events. Includes some poetry by members, book reviews, and notices of publication/contest opportunities.

$☑ ◎ POETS' CLUB OF CHICAGO; HELEN SCHAIBLE SHAKESPEAREAN/PETRARCHAN SONNET CONTEST (Specialized: form/sonnet)

1212 S. Michigan Ave., Apt. 2702, Chicago IL 60605. **Chairperson:** Tom Roby. The annual Helen Schaible Shakespearean/Petrarchan Sonnet Contest is open to anyone. **For sonnets only!** Offers 1st Prize: $50; 2nd Prize: $35; 3rd Prize: $15; plus 3 non-cash Honorable Mentions. Submit only one entry (2 copies) of either a Shakespearean or a Petrarchan sonnet, which must be original and unpublished. Entry must be typed on 8½×11 paper, double-spaced. Name and address in the upper righthand corner on only one copy. *All necessary guidelines appear in this listing.* **Entry fee:** none. **Postmark deadline:** September 1. Competition receives 120 entries/year. Most recent contest winners were Catherine Moran, Emery L. Campbell, and Ellin G. Anderson. The judge is June Owens. Winners will be notified by mail by October 31. Include SASE with entry to receive winners' list. The Poets' Club of Chicago meets monthly at the Chicago Cultural Center to critique their original poetry, which the members read at various venues in the Chicago area and publish in diverse magazines and books. Members also conduct workshops at area schools and libraries by invitation.

$□ POETS' DINNER CONTEST

2214 Derby St., Berkeley CA 94705-1018. (510)841-1217. **Contact:** Dorothy V. Benson. **Contestant must be present to win.** Submit 3 anonymous typed copies of original, unpublished poems in not more than 3 of the 8 categories (Humor, Love, Nature, Beginnings & Endings, Spaces & Places, People, Theme (changed annually), and Poet's Choice). Winning poems (Grand Prize, 1st, 2nd, 3rd) are read at an awards banquet and Honorable Mentions are presented. Cash prizes awarded; Honorable Mention receives books. The event is nonprofit. Since 1927 there has been an annual awards banquet sponsored by the ad hoc Poets' Dinner Committee, currently at the Holiday Inn in Emaryville. Contest guidelines available for SASE. **Entry fee:** none. **2004 Deadline:** January 13. Competition receives about 300 entries. Recent contest winners include Stephen Sadler (Grand Prize and a 1st Prize), Carol Frith, Maggie Morley, Amy MacLennan, Frank Taber, and Amy Miller (1st Prizes). *Remembering*, an anthology of winning poems from the Poet's Dinner over the last 25 years, is available by mail for $10.42 from Dorothy V. Benson at the contest address.

ⓝ $⊘ ⓞ THE POETS ON PARNASSUS PRIZE (Specialized: illness and healing, medical writing); THE PHAROS MAGAZINE; POETS ON PARNASSUS

UCSF/*The Pharos Magazine*, P.O. Box 1142, Mill Valley CA 94941. (415)381-8641. E-mail: hdwatts @earthlink.net. Website: http://poetry-and-jazz.com. Established 2000. **Award Directors:** David Watts, MD; Joan Baranow. Offers annual award (although sometimes skips a year). 1st Prize: $500; top 3-5 poems entered published in *The Pharos*. Pays winners from other countries in U.S. dollars. Submissions must be unpublished; may be entered in other contests. Submit 5 pages of poetry on illness and healing, in any form. **Entry fee:** $7.50/entry. Does not accept entry fees in foreign currencies; U.S. dollars only. **Deadline:** May 15. Competition receives 120 submissions/contest. Recent judges were John Stone and Jack Coulehan. Winners will be announced in *The Pharos* ("we telephone the winners"). "Poets on Parnassus is a campus organization that brings readings, workshops, and special poetry events to a health sciences campus."

◪ $⊘ PORTLANDIA CHAPBOOK CONTEST; THE PORTLANDIA GROUP

PMB 225, 6663 SW Beaverton-Hillsdale Hwy., Portland OR 97225. Established 1999. **Award Director:** Karen Braucher. Offers annual prize of $200, publication of chapbook, and 30 copies. Submit 24 pages of poetry with 2 title pages (one with title and personal info, the other with title only), table of contents, acknowledgments, and bio. Include SASE for results; no mss will be returned. "See guidelines for the year you are submitting." Guidelines available for SASE. **Entry fee:** $12/ entry. Does not accept entry fees in foreign currencies; accepts check on U.S. bank or U.S. money order. **Deadline:** check annual guidelines (was March 1 for 2004). Competition receives about 200 entries/year. Past winners include David Biespel, Eliza A. Garza, John Surowiecki, and Judith Taylor. Copies of winning chapbooks ($6, includes shipping) are available from The Portlandia Group.

$⊘ THE PSA CHAPBOOK FELLOWSHIPS

Poetry Society of America, 15 Gramercy Park, New York NY 10003. (212)254-9628. Website: www.p oetrysociety.org. Established 2002. Offers the PSA National Chapbook Fellowships and the PSA New York Chapbook Fellowships, with 4 prizes (2 for each fellowship) of $1,000, publication of the chapbook ms with distribution by the PSA, and an invitation to read at The PSA Festival of New American Poets in April. National Chapbook Fellowships open to any U.S. resident who has not published a full-length poetry collection; New York Chapbook Fellowships open to any New York City resident (in the 5 boroughs) who is 30 or under and has not published a full-length poetry collection. *Poets may apply to one contest only.* Complete submission guidelines for both fellowships available on website. **Entry fee:** $12 for both PSA members and nonmembers. Accepts entry fees in U.S. dollars only, by check or money order to Poetry Society of American. **Deadline:** entries accepted between October 1 and December 21 (postmarked). Does not accept entries by fax or e-mail. Most recent winners were Dawn Lundy Martin, *The Morning Hour*, and Kerri Webster, *Rowing Through Fog* (PSA National Chapbook Fellows); and Paul Killebrew, *Forget Rita*, and Tess Taylor,

The Misremembered World (PSA New York Chapbook Fellows). Most recent judges were Robert Creeley and Mary Oliver (PSA National Chapbook Fellowships); and Henri Cole and Jean Valentine (PSA New York Chapbook Fellowships). Additional information available on website. (See separate listing for Poetry Society of America in the Organizations section and for the Poetry Society of America Awards in this section.)

⚡ $⊘ PULITZER PRIZE IN LETTERS

% The Pulitzer Prize Board, 709 Journalism, Columbia University, New York NY 10027. (212)854-3841. Fax: (212)854-3342. E-mail: pulitzer@www.pulitzer.org. Website: www.pulitzer.org. **Contact:** the Pulitzer Prize Board. Offers 5 prizes of $10,000 and certificate each year, including one in poetry, for books published in the calendar year preceding the award. Entry form and guidelines available for SASE, by fax, or on website. Accepts inquiries by fax and e-mail. Submit 4 copies of published books (or galley proofs if book is being published after November), photo, bio, entry form. **Entry fee:** $50. **Deadlines:** July 1 for books published between January 1 and June 30; November 1 for books published between July 1 and December 31. Competition receives 150 entries/year. Most recent award winner was *Moy Sand and Gravel* by Paul Muldoon, published by Farrar, Straus & Giroux. Judges were Helen Vendler, Robert Pinsky, and Stephen Yenser.

⚡ ⚡ $◎ QWF A.M. KLEIN PRIZE FOR POETRY; QUEBEC WRITERS' FEDERATION; QWRITE (Specialized: regional/Quebec; translations)

1200 Atwater Ave., Montreal QC H3Z 1X4 Canada. Phone/fax: (514)933-0878. E-mail: admin@qwf. org. Website: www.qwf.org. **Administrative Director:** Lori Schubert. Offers annual awards of $2,000 each for poetry, fiction, nonfiction, first book, and translation. Submissions must be previously published. Open to authors "who have lived in Quebec for at least 3 of the past 5 years." Submit 4 copies of a book of at least 48 pages. Write for entry form. Accepts inquiries by fax and e-mail. **Entry fee:** $10/submission. **Deadlines:** May 31 for books published between October 1 and May 15; August 15 for books published between May 15 and September 30 (bound proofs are acceptable; the finished book must be received by September 30). Competition receives approximately 50 entries. 2003 poetry winner was Susan Gillis for *Volta*. Past poetry judges have included NourBese Philip, Carolyn Souai, and John Steffler. Winners will be announced in November. "QWF was formed in 1988 to honor and promote literature written in English by Quebec authors." QWF also publishes *QWRITE*, "a newsletter offering information and articles of interest to membership and the broader community."

$◙ ◎ THE RAIZISS/DE PALCHI TRANSLATION AWARD (Specialized: Italian poetry translated into English)

The Academy of American Poets, 588 Broadway, Suite 604, New York NY 10012-3210. (212)274-0343. Fax: (212)274-9427. E-mail: academy@poets.org. Website: www.poets.org. Established 1934. **Executive Director:** Tree Swenson. **Awards Coordinator:** Ryan Murphy. Awarded for outstanding translations of modern Italian poetry into English. A $5,000 book prize and a $20,000 fellowship are awarded in alternate years. **Book Prize Deadline:** submissions accepted in odd-numbered years September 1 through November 1. **Fellowship Deadline:** submissions accepted in even-numbered years September 1 through November 1. Guidelines and entry form available for SASE or on website. 2003 winner was Andrew Frisardi for *The Selected Poems of Giuseppe Ungaretti* (Farrar, Straus & Giroux), chosen by Phillis Levin and Rosanna Warren. (For further information about The Academy of American Poets, see separate listing in the Organizations section.)

⚡ $☐ ◎ RHYME TIME POETRY CONTEST (Specialized: rhyming poetry)

Shadow Poetry, P.O. Box 125, Excelsior Springs MO 64024. Fax: (208)977-9114. E-mail: shadowpoetry@shadowpoetry.com. Website: www.shadowpoetry.com. Established 2000. **Award Director:**

James Summers. Offers quarterly awards of 1st Prize: $50; 2nd Prize: $25; 3rd Prize: $10; plus top 3 winners also receive a certificate, printed copy of winning poem, and a ribbon. Pays winners from other countries in U.S. dollars only by International Money Order. Submissions may be previously published and may be entered in other contests. Submit unlimited number of poems of 4-28 lines each, on any subject. **All poems must rhyme.** ''Entry form must be present with mail-in entries; name, address, phone number, and e-mail address (when available) on upper left-hand corner of each poem submitted. Enclose SASE for winner's list and an additional SASE for entry receipt (optional). If no SASE is included for receipt, Shadow Poetry will e-mail an entry confirmation to the contestant, if applicable.'' Entry form and guidelines available for SASE, by fax, or on website. **Entry fee:** $2/poem. Make checks payable to Shadow Poetry. Does not accept entry fees in foreign currencies; pay by International Money Order, cash (U.S. dollars), or payments through PayPal. **Quarterly deadlines:** March 31, June 30, September 30, and December 31. Competition receives about 150 entries/quarter. Winners will be announced 15 days after each quarterly contest ends by e-mail and to those who requested a winner's list with SASE. Results also will be posted on the Shadow Poetry website.

✵ ☑ MARY ROBERTS RINEHART AWARDS

Mail Stop Number 3E4, English Dept., George Mason University, Fairfax VA 22030-4444. (703)993-1180. E-mail: bgompert@gmu.edu. Website: www.gmu.edu/departments/writing. **Contact:** Barb Gomperts. Three annual grants of $2,000 each are awarded in spring for the best nominated ms in fiction, nonfiction, and poetry. ''Grants are made only for unpublished works by writers who have not yet published a book or whose writing is not regularly appearing in nationally circulated commercial or literary magazines. Writers may see a grant in only one category in any given year; an author not granted an award one year may apply in succeeding years, but once a writer receives an award, he or she may not apply for another, even in a different genre. Grant recipients must be U.S. citizens.'' **A writer's work must be nominated in writing by an established author, editor, or agent**. Nominations must be accompanied by a sample of the nominee's work (10 pages of individual or collected poems/30 pages of fiction or nonfiction). **Postmark deadline:** November 30. ''Grants will be announced early in the following March on the awards web page. Candidates who wish to receive a printed announcement should submit a #10 SASE.'' Competition receives over 300 entries. Guidelines available for SASE, by e-mail, or on website.

◎ ROANOKE-CHOWAN POETRY AWARD (Specialized: regional/NC); NORTH CAROLINA LITERARY AND HISTORICAL ASSOCIATION

4610 Mail Service Center, Raleigh NC 27699-4610. (919)807-7290. Fax: (919)733-8807. E-mail: michael. hill@ncmail.net. Website: www.ah.dcr.state.nc.us/affiliates/lit-hist/awards/awards.htm. **Awards Coordinator:** Michael Hill. Offers annual award for ''an original volume of poetry published during the 12 months ending June 30 of the year for which the award is given.'' Open to ''authors who have maintained legal or physical residence, or a combination of both, in North Carolina for the 3 years preceding the close of the contest period.'' Submit 3 copies of each entry. Guidelines available for SASE or by fax or e-mail. **Deadline:** July 15. Competition receives about 15 entries. Winner will be announced by mail October 15. 2003 winner was Michael Chitwood for *Gospel Road Going*.

$☑ ◎ SARASOTA POETRY THEATRE PRESS; SOULSPEAK; EDDA POETRY CHAPBOOK COMPETITION FOR WOMEN; ANIMALS IN POETRY (Specialized: women/feminism; animals/pets)

P.O. Box 48955, Sarasota FL 34230-6955. (941)366-6468. Fax: (941)954-2208. E-mail: soulspeak1@ comcast.net. Website: www.soulspeak.org. Established 1994-1998. **Award Director:** Scylla Liscombe. Offers 2 annual contests for poetry with prizes ranging from 1st Prize: $50 plus publication in an anthology to 1st Prize: $100 plus 50 published chapbooks. Honorable Mentions also awarded.

Pays winners from other countries in copies. Guidelines and details about theater available for SASE, by e-mail, or on website. Accepts queries by e-mail. **Entry fees:** range from $4/poem to $10/ms. **Postmark deadline:** Animals in Poetry, June 30 (winners notified in September); Edda Poetry Chapbook Competition for Women, February 28 (winners notified in May). Competitions receive an average of 600 entries/year. Judges for contests are the staff of the press and ranking state poets. Winners are notified by mail. "Sarasota Poetry Theatre Press is a division of SOULSPEAK/Sarasota Poetry Theatre, a nonprofit organization dedicated to encouraging poetry in all its forms through the Sarasota Poetry Theatre Press, Therapeutic SOULSPEAK for at-risk youth, and the SOULSPEAK Studio. We are looking for honest, not showy, poetry; use a good readable font. Do not send extraneous materials."

◎ SEASONAL POETRY COMPETITION (Specialized: themes/4 seasons and holidays)

P.O. Box 125, Excelsior Springs MO 64024. Fax: (208)977-9114. E-mail: shadowpoetry@shadowpoetry.com. Website: www.shadowpoetry.com. Established 2000. **Award Director:** James Summers. Offers biannual award of 1st Prize: $100; 2nd prize: $50; 3rd Prize: $25; plus the top 3 winners also receive a certificate, printed copy of winning poem, and a ribbon. Pays winners from other countries in U.S. dollars only by International Money Order. Submissions may be previously published and may be entered in other contests. Submit maximum of 10 poems/poet, 30 line limit/poem, must be written on the topics of the 4 seasons (winter, spring, summer, and/or fall) or the holidays (Christmas, Valentine's Day, Easter, etc.), in any form. "Entry form must be present with mail-in entries; name, address, phone number, e-mail address (when available) on upper left-hand corner of each poem submitted. Enclose SASE for winners list. Include an additional SASE for entry receipt (optional). If no SASE is included for receipt, Shadow Poetry will e-mail an entry confirmation to the contestant, if applicable." Entry form and guidelines available for SASE or on website. **Entry fee:** $3/poem. Does not accept entry fees in foreign currencies; accepts International Money Order, cash (U.S. dollars), or payments through PayPal for foreign entries. **Deadlines:** June 30 and December 31. Winners will be announced "15 days after each contest ends, by e-mail and to those who requested a winners list. Results will also be posted on the Shadow Poetry website."

$☐ SHADOW POETRY'S BI-ANNUAL CHAPBOOK COMPETITION

Shadows Ink Publications, P.O. Box 125, Excelsior Springs MO 64024. Fax: (208)977-9114. E-mail: shadowpoetry@shadowpoetry.com. Website: www.shadowpoetry.com. Established 2000. **Award Director:** James Summers. Offers biannual award of $100, 50 copies of published chapbook with ISBN, and 25% royalties paid on each copy sold through Shadow Poetry (retail only). Pays winners from other countries in U.S. dollars only by International Money Order. Submissions must be unpublished and may be entered in other contests. (Winning poet retains copyrights and may publish poems elsewhere later.) Submit ms of 16-40 pages, including poetry and acknowledgments, on any subject, in any form . "Cover letter required with name, address, phone, age, and e-mail address. Enclose cover letter, manuscript, and cover ideas/art, if applicable, in #90 (9×12) envelope. Include #10 SASE for winner notification." Guidelines available for SASE or on website. **Entry fee:** $10/ms. Make checks payable to Shadow Poetry. Does not accept entry fees in foreign currencies; accepts International Money Order, cash (U.S. dollars) for foreign entries. **Deadlines:** June 30 and December 31. "Notification of winners no later than 20 days after deadline by SASE." Copies of winning or sample chapbooks available from Shadow Poetry for $6.25 (see website for titles).

$☐ SHADOWS INK POETRY CONTEST

Shadows Ink Publications, P.O. Box 125, Excelsior Springs MO 64024. Fax: (208)977-9114. E-mail: shadowpoetry@shadowpoetry.com. Website: www.shadowpoetry.com. Established 2000. **Award Director:** James Summers. Offers annual award of 1st Prize: $100 and chapbook publication; 2nd

Prize: $75; 3rd Prize: $35; top 3 winners also receive a certificate, printed copy of their poem, and a ribbon. The top 40 placing poems will be published in a Shadows Ink Poetry Chapbook, and all poets appearing in this publication will receive one free copy (additional copies available for $5 each plus shipping). Pays winners from other countries in U.S. dollars only by International Money Order. Submissions must be unpublished and may be entered in other contests. (Winning poets retain copyrights and may publish poems elsewhere later.) Submit maximum of 10 poems, 24 line limit each, on any subject, in any form. "Entry form must be present with mail-in entries; name, address, phone number, and e-mail address (when available) on upper left-hand corner of each poem submitted. Enclose SASE for winners list. Include an additional SASE for entry receipt (optional). If no SASE is included for receipt, Shadow Poetry will e-mail an entry confirmation to the contestant, if applicable." Entry form and guidelines available for SASE or on website. **Entry fee:** $5/poem. Make checks payable to Shadow Poetry. Does not accept entry fees in foreign currencies; accepts International Money Order, cash (U.S. dollars), or payments through PayPal for foreign entries. **Deadline:** December 31. Competition receives 125 entries/year. "Winners will be announced February 1 by e-mail and to those who requested a winners list. Results will also be posted on the Shadow Poetry website."

$□ KAY SNOW WRITING AWARDS; WILLAMETTE WRITERS

9045 SW Barbur Blvd., Suite 5A, Portland OR 97219-4027. (503)452-1592. Fax: (503)452-0372. E-mail: wilwrite@teleport.com. Website: www.willamettewriters.com. Established 1986. **Award Director:** Marlene Howard. Offers annual awards of 1st Prize: $300, 2nd Prize: $150, 3rd Prize: $50. Pays winners from other countries by postal money order. Submissions must be unpublished. Submit up to 2 poems (one entry fee), maximum 5 pages total, on any subject, in any style or form, single-spaced, one side of paper only. Entry form and guidelines available for SASE or on website. Accepts inquiries by fax or e-mail. **Entry fee:** $10 for members of Willamette Writers; $15 for nonmembers. Does not accept entry fees in foreign currencies; only accepts a check drawn on a U.S. bank. **Deadline:** May 15. Competition receives 150 entries. Most recent winners were Nick Antosca, Sherry Mikkelson, Sheri Harper, Meredith Stewart, and Sari Weston. Winners will be announced July 31. "Write and send in your very best poem. Read it aloud. If it still sounds like the best poem you've ever heard, send it in."

✪ $⊘ RICHARD SNYDER PRIZE

Ashland Poetry Press, English Dept., Ashland University, Ashland OH 44805. (419)289-5979 or (419)289-5110. Website: www.ashland.edu/aupoetry. Established 1997. **Award Director:** Stephen Haven. Offers annual award of $1,000 plus book publication in a paper-only edition of 1,000 copies. Submissions must be unpublished in book form and may be entered in other contests. Submit 50-80 pages of poetry. **Reading fee:** $20. Does not accept entry fees in foreign currencies; U.S. dollars only. **Deadline:** June 30. Competition receives 350 entries/year. Most recent winners were Carol Barrett (2002), Corrinne Clegg Hales (2001), and Jan Lee Ande (2000). Judge for each year's competition is Robert Phillips. Winners will be announced in *Writer's Chronicle* and *Poets & Writers*. Copies of winning books available from Small Press Distribution and directly from the Ashland University Bookstore. The Ashland Poetry Press publishes 2-4 books of poetry/year.

✪ $⊘ SOUL-MAKING LITERARY COMPETITION

National League of American Pen Women, Nob Hill, San Francisco Bay Area Branch, 1544 Sweetwood Dr., Colma CA 94015-2029. Phone/fax: (650)756-5279. E-mail: PenNobHill@aol.com. Website: www.soulmakingcontest.us. Established 1993. **Award Director:** Eileen Malone. Offers annual award with cash prizes in each of several literary categories, including poetry and prose poem. 1st Prize: $100; 2nd Prize: $50; 3rd Prize: $25. Pays winners from other countries by check drawn on American bank. Submissions may be previously published. Submit 3 one-page poems on soul-making theme; any form for open poetry category. No names or other identifying information on mss; include 3×5 card with name, address, phone, fax, e-mail, title(s) of work, and category entered. Include SASE for contest results. No mss will be returned. Guidelines available on website. **Entry fee:** $5/entry. Does not accept entry fees in foreign currencies; U.S. dollars only. **Deadline:** November 30. Competition receives 300 entries/year. Names of winners and judges are posted on website. Winners will be announced in January by SASE and on website. Winners are invited to read at the Koret Auditorium, San Francisco. Event is televised. "National League of American Pen Women is a professional organization of writers, artists, and composers headquartered in Washington, D.C.; includes membership of 6,000. Pen Women are involved in a variety of community arts outreach programs. 'Some say the world is a vale of tears, I say it is a place of soul making.' Use this quote as inspiration."

ℕ $☐ SPANISH MOSS LITERARY COMPETITION

New Pike Press, P.O. Box 6620, Banks AL 36005. (334)244-8920. E-mail: poettennis@aol.com. Website: www.alabamapoets.org. Established 2002. **Award Director:** John Curbow. Offers annual award in categories of poetry, fiction, and nonfiction. 1st Prize: $100 and publication; 2nd Prize: $50 and publication; 3rd Prize: $25 and publication in each category. Pays winners from other countries with check drawn on U.S. bank. Submissions must be unpublished but may be entered in other contests. Submit up to 3 poems, 60 lines maximum, on any subject, in any form. "One copy of each entry. Type category and name in upper left corner; do NOT put ID on entries. Include one cover sheet with the author's name and address, the category entered, and the title of each poem." All entries must be titled and typed on 8½×11 bond paper only, no fancy typefaces, single-spaced (poetry only). No poems will be returned; send SASE for contest results. Guidelines available for SASE, by e-mail, or on website. For guidelines by SASE, send to Donna Jean Tennis, Editor, New Pike Press, P.O. Box 230787, Montgomery AL 36123. **Entry fee:** $10 for 1-3 poems. Make checks payable to New Pike Press. Does not accept entry fees in foreign currencies; U.S. dollars only. **Postmark Deadline:** submit October 1-31. Competition receives 200-400 poems/year. Judge for the 2003 contest was Lola Haskins. Winners will be announced early in the year following contest deadline by SASE and on website. Copies of winning anthologies available from New Pike Press. "New Pike Press sponsors several contests each year, including categories in poetry, fiction, and nonfiction. Read poetry for fun, proofread thoroughly, buy books on writing poetry and study them. Rule number one for winning poetry contests: ENTER."

ℕ $☐ SPIRE PRESS POETRY CONTEST; SPIRE MAGAZINE

532 LaGuardia Place, Suite 298, New York NY 10012. E-mail: editor@spirepress.org. Website: www.spirepress.org. Established 2002. **Award Director:** Shelly Reed. Offers annual award of publication with royalty contract and promotion; sometimes cash prizes (see guidelines for each year). Submissions must be unpublished and may be entered in other contests as long as Spire Press is informed. Submit a chapbook ms of 18-60 poems on any subject, in any form (shorter poems preferred). Ms should be typed on white paper **and** on a labeled 3.5" floppy disk. Include SASE. **Entry fee:** $10/ms. Does not accept entry fees in foreign currencies; U.S. dollars only. **Deadline:** December 31. Competition receives 200 entries/year. Most recent winner was Loren Kleinman for *Flamenco Sketches* (2003). Judge for 2005 contest to be determined. Winners will be announced on website one month after contest deadline. Copies of winning chapbooks available through website, Amazon, selected bookstores, and Spire Press. Spire Press also publishes *Spire*, "a biannual magazine of exceptional quality. *Spire* is magazine-sized, perfect-bound, with color cover and artwork. We receive 300 regular submissions per week. Submit 3-5 poems at a time. We pay one contributor's copy. Always check our website for updates. We prefer poetry to be accessible and appeal to the senses. Rhyming poetry is usually rejected."

⚔ $⌧ WALLACE E. STEGNER FELLOWSHIPS

Creative Writing Program, Stanford University, Stanford CA 94305-2087. (650)725-1208. Fax: (650)723-3679. E-mail: vfhess@stanford.edu. Website: www.stanford.edu/dept/english/cw/. **Program Administrator:** Virginia Hess. Offers 5 fellowships in poetry of $22,000 plus tuition of over $6,000/year for promising writers who can benefit from 2 years of instruction and criticism at the Writing Center. "We do not require a degree for admission. No school of writing is favored over any other. Chronological age is not a consideration." **Postmark deadline:** December 1. Accepts inquiries by fax and e-mail. Competition receives about 1,000 entries/year. 2003-2004 fellows in poetry include Amaud Johnson, Shara Lessley, Emily Rosko, Bruce Snider, and Brian Spears.

⌧ THE WALLACE STEVENS AWARD

The Academy of American Poets, 588 Broadway, Suite 604, New York NY 10012-3210. (212)274-0343. Fax: (212)274-9427. E-mail: academy@poets.org. Website: www.poets.org. Award established 1994. **Executive Director:** Tree Swenson. **Awards Coordinator:** Ryan Murphy. Awards $150,000 annually to recognize outstanding and proven mastery in the art of poetry. **No applications are accepted.** 2003 winner was Richard Wilbur, chosen by Alice Fulton, Glyn Maxwell, Heather McHugh, C.K. Williams, and Al Young. (For further information about The Academy of American Poets, see separate listing in the Organizations section.)

$⌻ STEVENS POETRY MANUSCRIPT CONTEST

1510 S. 7th St., Brainerd MN 56401. Website: www.nfsps.org. **Contact:** Doris Stengel. National Federation of State Poetry Societies (NFSPS) offers annual award of $1,000, publication of ms, and 50 author's copies. Individual poems may have been previously published in magazines, anthologies, or chapbooks, but not the entire ms as a collection; accepts simultaneous submissions. Submit 35-60 pages of poetry by a single author, typewritten, one poem or column of poetry to a page. Number pages, but no author identification throughout ms. Include 2 cover/title pages; one with no author identification, the other with name of poet, address, phone number, and state poetry society member affiliation, if applicable. No bulky folders or binders; plain manila folder and/or staples permitted. No illustrations. Include SASE for winner's list. No disk submissions; no certified or registered mail. Manuscripts will not be returned. Guidelines available for SASE or on website. **Entry fee:** $15 for NFSPS members; $20 for nonmembers. Make checks or money orders payable to NFSPS. **Postmark Deadline:** October 15. Winners will be announced in January following deadline; entrants who include a SASE will be notified of winner. Winning ms will be sold at annual NFSPS convention and winning poet (if present) will read from the ms. Copies of winning mss available through NFSPS website. (See separate listing for National Federation of State Poetry Societies in the Organizations section and for NFSPS Competitions and NFSPS College/University Level Poetry Awards in this section.)

⚔ ⚑ $⌧ ⊚ THE DAN SULLIVAN MEMORIAL POETRY CONTEST (Specialized: Canadian residents only); THE WORD WEAVER; THE WRITERS' CIRCLE OF DURHAM REGION

P.O. Box 323, Ajax ON L1S 3C5 Canada. (905)259-6520. E-mail: info@wcdr.org. Website: www.wcdr.org. Established 1995. **Award Director:** Nancy Del Col. Offers annual award in 3 categories. *Children:* 1st Prize: $75; 2nd Prize: $50; 3rd Prize: $25. *Youth:* 1st Prize: $150; 2nd Prize: $100; 3rd Prize: $75. *Adult:* 1st Prize: $300; 2nd Prize: $200; 3rd Prize: $100. Winners published in *The Word Weaver* and on WCDR website. Contest open to Canadian residents only. Submissions must be unpublished. "Poems may be of any subject matter, type, or style. Length of each entry must not exceed 30 written lines. This may be one poem, or up to 3 short poems whose cumulative total does not exceed 30 lines. There are no limits to the number of entries a person may submit, but each must be submitted separately with the appropriate entry fee." All entries must be typed, single-sided, on plain 8½ × 11 paper. Double-spacing not required. Number pages if poems continue past one page. Pages should not be stapled together. Title of each poem should appear at the top of the page. Send 2 copies of each poem, one with complete author information (name, address, e-mail where applicable) and one blind (no author information). Bios will be solicited from the winners. No submissions by e-mail or fax. Entries will not be returned. Guidelines available on website. **Entry fee:** $10 adult; $5 youth and children. Does not accept entry fees in foreign currencies; cheque only, made payable to WCDR. **Deadline:** February 15. Competition receives about 200-250 entries/year. 2003 winner was Irene Livingston. 2004 contest judges were Nik Beat, Lolette Kuby, Bernice Lever, Jenny Sacco, and Heather Whaley. Winners will be announced in June and winning entries posted on website. ''The Writers' Circle of Durham Region is a nonprofit umbrella organization dedicated to encouraging and promoting the art and skill of writing, fostering literacy, and providing moral support to writers through education and networking, both independently and in cooperation with existing organizations.'' Advice: ''Be original in your writing, but follow the rules when submitting.''

$◫ ◎ TOWSON UNIVERSITY PRIZE FOR LITERATURE (Specialized: regional/Maryland)

Towson University, College of Liberal Arts, Towson MD 21252. (410)704-2128. Fax: (410)704-6392. E-mail: charriss@towson.edu. Website: http://towson.edu. **Award Director:** Dean of the College of Liberal Arts (with the guidance of the English Department). Offers annual prize of $1,000 ''for a single book or book-length manuscript of fiction, poetry, drama, or imaginative nonfiction by a Maryland writer. The prize is granted on the basis of literary and aesthetic excellence as determined by a panel of distinguished judges appointed by the university. The first award, made in the fall of 1980, went to novelist Anne Tyler.'' Work must have been published within the 3 years prior to the year of nomination or must be scheduled for publication within the year in which nominated. Submit 5 copies of work in bound form or in typewritten, double-spaced ms form. Entry form and guidelines available for SASE. Accepts inquiries by e-mail. **Deadline:** June 15. Competition receives 8-10 entries. Most recent contest winners were Karren Alenier and Barbara Hurd (co-winners).

$◫ KATE TUFTS DISCOVERY AWARD; KINGSLEY TUFTS POETRY AWARD

Poetic Gallery for the Kingsley and Kate Tufts Poetry Awards, Claremont Graduate University, 160 E. 10th St., Harper East B7, Claremont CA 91711-6165. (909)621-8974. Website: www.cgu.edu/tufts/. Established 1992 (Kingsley Tufts Award) and 1993 (Kate Tufts Award). Kate Tufts Discovery Award offers $10,000 annually ''for a first book by a poet of genuine promise.'' Kingsley Tufts Poetry Award offers $100,000 annually ''for a work by an emerging poet, one who is past the very beginning but has not yet reached the acknowledged pinnacle of his/her career.'' Books for the 2005 prizes must have been published between September 15, 2003 and September 15, 2004. Entry form and guidelines available for SASE or on website. **Deadline:** September 15. Most recent award winners were Linda Gregerson (Kingsley Tufts, 2003) and Joanie Mackowski (Kate Tufts, 2003). Winners announced in February. Check website for updated deadlines and award information.

⊕ $◫ ◎ VER POETS OPEN COMPETITION; HIGH LIGHTS COMPETITION (Specialized: 15-19 years of age)

Ver Poets, Haycroft, 61/63 Chiswell Green Lane, St. Albans, Hertfordshire AL2 3AL United Kingdom. Phone: (01727)867005. E-mail: may.badman@virgin.net. Established 1974. **Organiser/Editor:** May Badman. Offers annual open competition with prizes totaling £1,000, plus a free copy of anthology, *Vision On* with winning and selected poems. Pays winners from other countries in sterling by cheque. Submissions must be unpublished. Submit any number of poems on any subject, ''open as to style, form, content. Sincere writing of high quality and skill gets the prizes. Poem must be no more than 30 lines excluding title, typed on white A4 sheets. Entry forms provided, pseudonyms to be used on poems.'' Two copies of poems required. No e-mail submissions. **Entry fee:** £3/poem. Entry form and guidelines available for SASE (or SAE and IRC) or by e-mail. Accepts entry fees in foreign currencies. **Deadline:** April 30. Competition receives about 1,000 entries/ year. 2004 adjudicator was Lawrence Sail. Winners announced at an ''Adjudication & Tea'' event in June each year and by post. Copies of winning anthologies available from May Badman at the contest address. Also offers the High Lights Competition for young poets (aged 15-19) with prizes of £500, £300, and 2 equal 3rd Prizes of £100 each (plus 36 runners-up). All winners included in *Vision On* anthology. **Entry fee:** £3/poem. Entry form and guidelines available for SASE (or SAE and IRC) or by e-mail. **Deadline:** March 31. 2004 adjudicator was Kit Wright. ''We have local and postal members, meet regularly in St. Albans, study poetry and the writing of it, try to guide members to reach a good standard, arrange 3 competitions per year with prizes and anthologies for members only. Plus the annual open competition. We do expect a high standard of art and skill. We make a gift to a charity each year.''

N $◎ WAR POETRY CONTEST (Specialized: war-themed poetry)

Winning Writers, 351 Pleasant St., PMB 222, Northampton MA 01060-3961. (866)946-9748. Fax: (413)280-0539. E-mail: warcontest@winningwriters.com. Website: www.winningwriters.com/ann ualcontest.htm. Established 2001. **Award Director:** Adam Cohen. Offers annual award of 1st Prize: $1,000; 2nd Prize: $500; 3rd Prize: $250; 10 Honorable Mentions. All prizewinners receive online publication at WinningWriters.com; selected finalists may also receive online publication. ''Non-U.S. winners will be paid in U.S. currency if a check is inconvenient.'' Submissions must be unpublished and may be entered in other contests. Submit 1-3 poems of up to 500 lines total on the theme of war, any form, style, or genre. No name on ms pages, typed or computer-printed on letter-size white paper, single-sided. Guidelines available for SASE or on website. **Entry fee:** $10 for group of 1-3 poems. Does not accept entry fees in foreign currencies; ''U.S. dollars only, payment accepted by credit card, check, money order, or (last resort) currency.'' **Deadline:** March 1-May 31. Competition receives about 700 entries/year. 2003 winner was Robert Randolph for ''Floating Girl.'' 2003 judge was Jendi Reiter. Winners announced on November 15 at WinningWriters.com. Entrants who provided valid e-mail addresses will also receive notification. (See separate listing for the Wergle Flomp Poetry Contest in this section and for Winning Writers in the Additional Resources section.)

N $◎ WERGLE FLOMP POETRY CONTEST (Specialized: humor/parody of vanity contest entries)

Winning Writers, 351 Pleasant St., PMB 222, Northampton MA 01060-3961. (866)946-9748. Fax: (413)280-0539. E-mail: flompcontest@winningwriters.com. Website: www.winningwriters.com/ contestflomp.htm. Established 2001. **Award Director:** Adam Cohen. Offers annual award of 1st Prize: $817.70; 2nd Prize: $132; 3rd Prize: $57.95; plus Honorable Mentions. All prizewinners receive online publication at WinningWriters.com. ''Non-U.S. winners will be paid in U.S. currency if a check is inconvenient.'' Submissions may be previously published and may be entered in other contests. Submit one poem of any length, in any form, but must be ''a humor poem that has been submitted to a 'vanity poetry contest' as a joke. See website for examples.'' Entries accepted **only** through website; no entries by regular mail. Guidelines available on website. **Entry fee:** none. **Deadline:** August 15-April 1. Competition receives about 700 entries/year. 2003 winner was Callaghan Howard for ''An Ode to Buns.'' 2003 judge was Jendi Reiter. Winners announced on August 15 at WinningWriters.com. Entrants who provided valid e-mail addresses will also receive notification. ''Please read the past winning entries and the judge's comments published at WinningWriters.com. Guidelines are a little unusual—please follow them closely.'' (See separate listing for the War Poetry Contest in this section and for Winning Writers in the Additional Resources section.)

▦ $◙ WESTERN AUSTRALIAN PREMIER'S BOOK AWARDS (Specialized: regional/ Western Australia)

State Library of Western Australia, Alexander Library Bldg., Perth Cultural Centre, Perth, Western Australia 6000 Australia. Phone: (61 8)9427 3330. Fax: (61 8)9427 3336. E-mail: jham@liswa.wa.go v.au. Website: www.liswa.wa.gov.au/pba.html. Established 1982. **Award Director:** Ms. Julie Ham. Offers annual poetry prize of AUS $7,500 for a published book of poetry. Winner also eligible for Premier's Prize of AUS $20,000. Submissions must be previously published. Open to poets born in Western Australia, current residents of Western Australia, or poets who have resided in Western Australia for at least 10 years at some stage. Entry form and guidelines available by mail or on website. Accepts inquiries by fax and e-mail. **Entry fee:** none. **Deadline:** January 6. Competition receives about 10-15 entries in poetry category/year (120 overall). Most recent winner was *Halfway Up the Mountain* by Dorothy Hewett. 2003 judges were Prof. Brian Dibble, Ms. Suzanne Wyche, Dr. Simon Adams, and Mr. Zolton Kovacs. Winners announced in June each year (i.e., June 2003 for 2002 awards) at a presentation dinner given by the Premier of Western Australia. "The contest is organized by the State Library of Western Australia, with money provided by the Western Australian State Government to support literature."

◙ WHITING WRITERS' AWARDS; MRS. GILES WHITING FOUNDATION

1133 Avenue of the Americas, 22nd Floor, New York NY 10036-6710. **Director:** Barbara K. Bristol. The Foundation makes awards of $35,000 each to up to 10 writers of fiction, nonfiction, poetry, and plays chosen by a selection committee drawn from a list of recognized writers, literary scholars, and editors. Recipients of the award are selected from nominations made by writers, educators, and editors from communities across the country whose experience and vocations bring them in contact with individuals of unusual talent. The nominators and selectors are appointed by the foundation and serve anonymously. **Direct applications and informal nominations are not accepted by the foundation.**

$◙ THE WALT WHITMAN AWARD

The Academy of American Poets, 588 Broadway, Suite 604, New York NY 10012-3210. (212)274-0343. Fax: (212)274-9427. E-mail: academy@poets.org. Website: www.poets.org. Award established 1975. **Executive Director:** Tree Swenson. **Awards Coordinator:** Ryan Murphy. Offers $5,000 plus publication of a poet's first book by Louisiana State University Press. The Academy of American Poets distributes copies of the Whitman Award-winning book to its members. Winner also receives a one-month residency at the Vermont Studio Center. Submit mss of 50-100 pages. Poets must be American citizens. Entry form required; entry form and guidelines available for SASE or on website. **Entry fee:** $25. **Deadline:** submit between September 15 and November 15. 2003 winner was Tony Tost for *Invisible Bride*, chosen by C.D. Wright. (For further information about The Academy of American Poets, see separate listing in the Organizations section.)

$◙ STAN AND TOM WICK POETRY PRIZE

Wick Poetry Program, Dept. of English, Kent State University, P.O. Box 5190, Kent OH 44242-0001. (330)672-2067. Fax: (330)672-2567. E-mail: wickpoet@kent.edu. Website: http://dept.kent.edu/ wick. Established 1994. **Program Coordinator:** Maggie Anderson. Offers annual award of $2,000 and publication by Kent State University Press. Submissions must be unpublished as a whole and may be entered in other contests as long as the Wick program receives notice upon acceptance elsewhere. Submit 48-68 pages of poetry. Open to poets writing in English who have not yet published a full-length collection. Entries must include cover sheet with poet's name, address, telephone number, and title of ms. Guidelines available for SASE or on website. **Entry fee:** $20. Does not accept entry fees in foreign currencies; send money order or U.S. check. **Deadline:** May 1.

Competition receives 700-800 entries. 2003 contest winner was Lee Peterson. 2003 judge was Jean Valentine.

$◎ THE RICHARD WILBUR AWARD (Specialized: American poets)

Dept. of English, University of Evansville, 1800 Lincoln Ave., Evansville IN 47722. (812)479-2963. Website: http://english.evansville.edu/english/WilburAwardGuidelines.htm. **Series Director:** William Baer. Offers a biennial award (even-numbered years) of $1,000 and book publication to "recognize a quality book-length manuscript of poetry." Submissions must be unpublished original poetry collections ("although individual poems may have had previous journal publications") and "public domain or permission-secured translations may comprise up to one-third of the manuscript." Submit ms of 50-100 typed pages, unbound, bound, or clipped. Open to all American poets. Manuscripts should be accompanied by 2 title pages: one with collection's title, author's name, address, and phone number; one with only the title. Include SASE for contest results. Submissions may be entered in other contests. Manuscripts are *not* returned. Guidelines available for SASE or on webiste. **Entry fee:** $25/ms. **Deadline:** was December 3 for 2004. Next competition will be in 2006. Competition receives 300-500 entries. Recent contest winner was Thomas Carper. Judge for last contest was Charles Martin. The winning ms is published and copyrighted by the University of Evansville Press.

$☑ ◎ WORLD ORDER OF NARRATIVE AND FORMALIST POETS (Specialized: subscription; form/metrical)

P.O. Box 580174, Station A, Flushing NY 11358-0174. Established 1980. **Contest Chairman:** Dr. Alfred Dorn. Sponsors contests in a number of categories for traditional and contemporary poetic forms, including the sonnet, blank verse, ballade, sapphics, villanelle, and new forms created by Alfred Dorn. Prizes total at least $5,000. **Entry fee:** None, but only subscribers to *The Formalist* are eligible for the competition. Complete contest guidelines available for SASE from Alfred Dorn. "Our focus is on metrical poetry characterized by striking diction and original metaphors. We do not want trite or commonplace language." **2005 Deadline:** November 19. Competition receives about 3,000 entries. Past contest winners include Rhina P. Espaillat, Len Krisak, Deborah Warren, and Roy Scheele. Recent judges include William Baer and Gail White. Winners' list will be mailed to contestants after poems have been judged. (For more information on *The Formalist*, see listing in the Publishers of Poetry section.)

◉ $□ THE WRITERS BUREAU POETRY AND SHORT STORY COMPETITION

The Writers Bureau, Sevendale House, 7 Dale St., Manchester M1 1JB England. Phone: +44 161 228 2362. Fax: +44 161 228 3533. E-mail: comp@writersbureau.com. Website: www.writersbureau.com/resources.htm. Established 1994. **Contact:** Head of Student Services. Offers annual prizes of 1st Place: £1,000, 2nd: £400, 3rd: £200, 4th: £100, six 5th Place prizes of £50, and publication in *Freelance Market News*. Submissions must be unpublished. "Any number of entries may be sent. There is no set theme or form. Entries must be typed, and no longer than 40 lines." Accepts entries by regular mail or by fax. Entry form available for SASE or on website. Accepts inquiries by fax or e-mail. **Entry fee:** £5/$8. **Deadline:** late July. 2003 winners included Brian Johnstone, Anthony Watts, Jean Watkins, and John Crick. 2004 judge was Alison Chisholm. Winner(s) will be announced in September. "The Writers Bureau is a distance learning college offering correspondence courses in Journalism, Creative Writing, and Poetry." (See listing for *Freelance Market News* in the Additional Resources section.)

$□ THE W.B. YEATS SOCIETY ANNUAL POETRY COMPETITION

W.B. Yeats Society of New Yc... National Arts Club, 15 Gramercy Park S, New York NY 10003. (212)780-0605. Website: www.YeatsSociety.org. Established 1994. **President:** Andrew McGowan.

Offers annual $250 cash prize for 1st Place, $100 cash prize for 2nd Place, and optional Honorable Mentions. Open to beginner as well as established poets. Winners are invited to read their winning entries at the Taste of the Yeats Summer School, held each April in New York; also inducted as Honorary Members of the Society (a 501(c)(3) charitable organization). Submissions may be entered in other contests. Submit any number of unpublished poems in any style or form, up to 60 lines each, typed on letter-size paper without poet's name. Guidelines available for SASE or on website; no entry form required. **Reading fee:** $8 for first poem, $7 per additional poem. Attach a 3×5 card to each entry containing the poem's title along with the poet's name, address, and phone/fax/e-mail. **Annual deadline:** February 15. Receives 200-300 entries/year. 2003 winners were J. Michael Parish (1st), Victoria Givotovsky (2nd), and Alice Friman and H.E. Wright (Honorable Mentions). 2004 judge was Grace Schulman. Winners selected by March 31 and announced in April. Winning entries and judge's report are posted on the Society's website. Printed report available for SASE. (See separate listing for W.B. Yeats Society of New York in the Organizations section.)

◎ ZEN GARDEN HAIKU CONTEST (Specialized: form/style, haiku)

Shadow Poetry, P.O. Box 125, Excelsior Springs MO 64024. Fax: (208)977-9114. E-mail: shadowpoetry@shadowpoetry.com. Website: www.shadowpoetry.com. Established 2000. **Award Director:** James Summers. Offers annual award of 1st Prize: $100; 2nd Prize: $50; 3rd Prize: $25, plus the top 3 winners also receive a certificate, a printed copy of their poem, and a ribbon. Pays winners from other countries in U.S. dollars only by International Money Order. Submissions may be previously published and may be entered in other contests. Submit any number of haiku on any subject. "Haiku entries must be typed on 8½×11 paper, submitted in duplicate. Poet's name, address, phone number, and e-mail address (if applicable) in the upper left-hand corner of one sheet. If submitting more than one haiku, each poem must be typed on separate sheets (3×5 index card entries welcome). Submit haiku entries in duplicate, neatly handwritten or typed, with poet information on the back of only one card. Repeat method for multiple submissions." Entry form and guidelines available for SASE or on website. **Entry fee:** $2/haiku. Make checks payable to Shadow Poetry. Does not accept entry fees in foreign currencies; accepts International Money Order, cash (U.S. dollars), or payments through PayPal for foreign entries. **Deadline:** December 31. Winners will be announced February 1 each year "by e-mail and to those who requested a winners list. Results will also be posted on the Shadow Poetry website."

ADDITIONAL CONTESTS & AWARDS

The following listings also contain information about contests and awards. Turn to the page numbers indicated for details about their offerings.

Contests & Awards

Grants

State & Provincial

Arts councils in the United States and Canada provide assistance to artists (including poets) in the form of fellowships or grants. These grants can be substantial and confer prestige upon recipients; however, **only state or province residents are eligible**. Because deadlines and available support vary annually, query first (with a SASE) or check websites for guidelines.

UNITED STATES ARTS AGENCIES

Alabama State Council on the Arts, 201 Monroe St., Montgomery AL 36130-1800. (334)242-4076. E-mail: staff@arts.state.al.us. Website: www.arts.state.al.us.

Alaska State Council on the Arts, 411 W. Fourth Ave., Suite 1-E, Anchorage AK 99501-2343. (907)269-6610 or (888)278-7424. E-mail: aksca_info@eed.state.ak.us. Website: www.educ.state.ak.us/aksca.

Arizona Commission on the Arts, 417 W. Roosevelt, Phoenix AZ 85003. (602)255-5882. E-mail: general@ArizonaArts.org. Website: www.ArizonaArts.org.

Arkansas Arts Council, 1500 Tower Bldg., 323 Center St., Little Rock AR 72201. (501)324-9766. E-mail: info@arkansasarts.com. Website: www.arkansasarts.com.

California Arts Council, 1300 I St., Suite 930, Sacramento CA 95814. (916)322-6555 or (800)201-6201. Website: www.cac.ca.gov.

Colorado Council on the Arts, 1380 Lawrence St., Suite 1200, Denver CO 80204-2059. (303)866-2723. E-mail: coloarts@state.co.us. Website: www.coloarts.state.co.us.

Connecticut Commission on the Arts, 1 Financial Plaza, 755 Main St., Hartford CT 06103. (860)566-4770 or (800)411-1312. E-mail: artsinfo@ctarts.org. Website: www.ctarts.org.

Delaware Division of the Arts, Carvel State Office Bldg., 820 N. French St., 4th Floor, Wilmington DE 19801. (302)577-8278 (New Castle Co.) or (302)739-5304 (Kent or Sussex Counties). E-mail: delarts@state.de.us. Website: www.artsdel.org.

District of Columbia Commission on the Arts & Humanities, 410 Eighth St. NW, 5th Floor, Washington DC 20004. (202)724-5613. E-mail: cah@dc.gov. Website: http://dcarts.dc.gov.

Florida Arts Council, Division of Cultural Affairs, Florida Dept. of State, 1001 DeSoto Park Dr., Tallahassee FL 32301. (850)245-6470. E-mail: info@florida-arts.org. Website: www.florida-arts.org.

Georgia Council for the Arts, 260 14th St., Suite 401, Atlanta GA 30318. (404)685-2787. E-mail: gaarts@gaarts.org. Website: www.gaarts.org.

Guam Council on the Arts & Humanities Agency, 703 E. Sunset Blvd., Tiyan GU. (671)475-2242. E-mail: kaha1@kuentos.guam.net. Website: www.guam.net/gov/kaha.

Hawaii State Foundation on Culture & the Arts, 250 S. Hotel St., 2nd Floor, Honolulu HI 96813. (808)586-0300. Website: www.state.hi.us/sfca.

Idaho Commission on the Arts, 2410 N. Old Penitentiary Rd., Boise ID 83712. (208)334-2119 or (800)278-3863. E-mail: info@ica.state.id.us. Website: www2.state.id.us/arts.

Illinois Arts Council, James R. Thompson Center, 100 W. Randolph, Suite 10-500, Chicago IL 60601. (312)814-6750. E-mail: info@arts.state.il.us. Website: www.state.il.us/agency/iac.

Indiana Arts Commission, 150 W. Market St., #618, Indianapolis IN 46204. (317)232-1268. E-mail: arts@iac.in.state.us. Website: www.in.gov/arts.

Iowa Arts Council, Capitol Complex, 600 E. Locust, Des Moines IA 50319-0290. (515)281-6412. Website: www.iowaartscouncil.org.

Kansas Arts Commission, 700 SW Jackson, Suite 1004, Topeka KS 66603-3761. (785)296-3335. E-mail: KAC@arts.state.ks.us. Website: http://arts.state.ks.us.

Kentucky Arts Council, Old Capitol Annex, 300 W. Broadway, Frankfort KY 40601-1980. (502)564-3757 or (888)833-2787. E-mail: kyarts@ky.gov. Website: www.kyarts.org.

Louisiana Division of the Arts, P.O. Box 44247, Baton Rouge LA 70804-4247. (225)342-8180. E-mail: arts@crt.state.la.us. Website: www.crt.state.la.us/arts.

Maine Arts Commission, 25 State House Station, 193 State St., Augusta ME 04333-0025. (207)287-2724. E-mail: MaineArts.info@maine.gov. Website: www.mainearts.com.

Maryland State Arts Council, 175 W. Ostend St., Suite E, Baltimore MD 21230. (410)767-6555. E-mail: msac@msac.org. Website: www.msac.org.

Massachusetts Cultural Council, 10 St. James Ave., 3rd Floor, Boston MA 02116-3803. (617)727-3668. E-mail: web@art.state.ma.us. Website: www.massculturalcouncil.org.

Michigan Council for Arts & Cultural Affairs, 702 W. Kalamazoo St., P.O. Box 30705, Lansing MI 48909-8205. (517)241-4011. E-mail: artsinfo@michigan.gov. Website: www.michigan.gov/hal/0,1607,7-160-17445_19272---,00.html.

Minnesota State Arts Board, Park Square Court, 400 Sibley St., Suite 200, St. Paul MN 55101-1928. (651)215-1600 or (800)866-2787. E-mail: msab@arts.state.mn.us. Website: www.arts.state.mn.us.

Mississippi Arts Commission, 239 N. Lamar St., Suite 207, Jackson MS 39201. (601)359-6030. Website: www.arts.state.ms.us.

Missouri Arts Council, Wainwright State Office Complex, 111 N. Seventh St., Suite 105, St. Louis MO 63101-2188. (314)340-6845 or (866)407-4752. E-mail: moarts@ded.mo.gov. Website: www.missouriartscouncil.org.

Montana Arts Council, P.O. Box 202201, Helena MT 59620-2201. (406)444-6430. E-mail: mac@state.mt.us. Website: www.art.state.mt.us.

National Assembly of State Arts Agencies, 1029 Vermont Ave. NW, 2nd Floor, Washington DC 20005. (202)347-6352. E-mail: nasaa@nasaa-arts.org. Website: www.nasaa-arts.org.

Nebraska Arts Council, Joslyn Castle Carriage House, 3838 Davenport St., Omaha NE 68131-2389. (402)595-2122 or (800)341-4067. Website: www.nebraskaartscouncil.org.

Nevada Arts Council, 716 N. Carson St., Suite A, Carson City NV 89701. (775)687-6680. Website: http://dmla.clan.lib.nv.us/docs/arts.

New Hampshire State Council on the Arts, $2\frac{1}{2}$ Beacon St., 2nd Floor, Concord NH 03301-4974. (603)271-2789. Website: www.nh.gov/nharts.

New Jersey State Council on the Arts, 225 W. State St., P.O. Box 306, Trenton NJ 08625. (609)292-6130. E-mail: njsca@arts.sos.state.nj.us. Website: www.njartscouncil.org.

New Mexico Arts, Dept. of Cultural Affairs, P.O. Box 1450, Santa Fe NM 87504-1450. (505)827-6490. Website: www.nmarts.org.

New York State Council on the Arts, 175 Varick St., New York NY 10014-4604. (212)627-4455. Website: www.nysca.org.

North Carolina Arts Council, Dept. of Cultural Resources, Raleigh NC 27699-4632. (919)733-2111. E-mail: ncarts@ncmail.net. Website: www.ncarts.org.

North Dakota Council on the Arts, 1600 E. Century Ave., Suite 6, Bismarck ND 58503. (701)328-7590. E-mail: comserv@state.nd.us. Website: www.state.nd.us/arts.

Ohio Arts Council, 727 E. Main St., Columbus OH 43205-1796. (614)466-2613 or (888)243-8622. Website: www.oac.state.oh.us.

Oklahoma Arts Council, P.O. Box 52001-2001, Oklahoma City OK 73152-2001. (405)521-2931. E-mail: okarts@arts.state.ok.us. Website: www.arts.state.ok.us.

Oregon Arts Commission, 775 Summer St. NE, Suite 200, Salem OR 97301-1284. (503)986-0082. E-mail: oregon.artscomm@state.or.us. Website: www.oregonartscommission.org.

Pennsylvania Council on the Arts, Room 216, Finance Bldg., Harrisburg PA 17120. (717)787-6883. Website: www.pacouncilonthearts.org.

Institute of Puerto Rican Culture, P.O. Box 9024184, San Juan PR 00902-4184. (787)724-0700. E-mail: www@icp.gobierno.pr. Website: www.icp.gobierno.pr.

Rhode Island State Council on the Arts, 83 Park St., 6th Floor, Providence RI 02903-1037. (401)222-3880. E-mail: info@arts.ri.gov. Website: www.arts.ri.gov.

South Carolina Arts Commission, 1800 Gervais St., Columbia SC 29201. (803)734-8696. E-mail: goldstsa@arts.state.sc.us. Website: www.state.sc.us/arts.

South Dakota Arts Council, 800 Governors Dr., Pierre SD 57501. (605)773-3131. E-mail: sdac@state.sd.us. Website: www.state.sd.us/deca/sdarts.

Tennessee Arts Commission, Citizens Plaza Bldg., 401 Charlotte Ave., Nashville TN 37243-0780. (615)741-1701. Website: www.arts.state.tn.us.

Texas Commission on the Arts, P.O. Box 13406, Austin TX 78711-3406. (512)463-5535. E-mail: front.desk@arts.state.tx.us. Website: www.arts.state.tx.us.

Utah Arts Council, 617 E. South Temple, Salt Lake City UT 84102. (801)236-7555. Website: http://arts.utah.gov.

Grants

Vermont Arts Council, 136 State St., Drawer 33, Montpelier VT 05633-6001. (802)828-3291. E-mail: info@vermontartscouncil.org. Website: www.vermontartscouncil.org.

Virgin Islands Council on the Arts, 41-42 Norre Gade, St. Thomas VI 00802. (340)774-5984. E-mail: adagio@islands.vi. Website: http://vicouncilonarts.org.

Virginia Commission for the Arts, Lewis House, 223 Governor St., 2nd Floor, Richmond VA 23219-2010. (804)225-3132. E-mail: arts@arts.virginia.gov. Website: www.arts.state. va.us.

Washington State Arts Commission, 234 Eighth Ave. SE, P.O. Box 42675, Olympia WA 98504-2675. (360)753-3860. Website: www.arts.wa.gov.

West Virginia Commission on the Arts, The Cultural Center, 1900 Kanawha Blvd. E., Charleston WV 25305-0300. (304)558-0220. Website: www.wvculture.org/arts.

Wisconsin Arts Board, 101 E. Wilson St., 1st Floor, Madison WI 53702. (608)266-0190. E-mail: artsboard@arts.state.wi.us. Website: www.arts.state.wi.us.

Wyoming Arts Council, 2320 Capitol Ave., Cheyenne WY 82002. (307)777-7742. Website: http://wyoarts.state.wy.us.

CANADIAN PROVINCES ARTS AGENCIES

Alberta Foundation for the Arts, 901 Standard Life Centre, 10405 Jasper Ave., Edmonton AB T5J 4R7. (780)427-9968. Website: www.cd.gov.ab.ca/all_about_us/commissions/arts.

British Columbia Arts Council, P.O. Box 9819, Stn. Prov. Govt., Victoria BC V8W 9W3. (250)356-1718. E-mail: BCArtsCouncil@gems2.gov.bc.ca. Website: www.bcartscouncil.ca.

The Canada Council for the Arts, 350 Albert St., P.O. Box 1047, Ottawa ON K1P 5V8. (613)566-4414. Website: www.canadacouncil.ca.

Manitoba Arts Council, 525-93 Lombard Ave., Winnipeg MB R3B 3B1. (204)945-2237. E-mail: info@artscouncil.mb.ca. Website: www.artscouncil.mb.ca.

New Brunswick Arts Board (NBAB), 634 Queen St., Suite 300, Fredericton NB E3B 1C2. (866)460-2787. Website: www.artsnb.ca.

Newfoundland & Labrador Arts Council, P.O. Box 98, St. John's NL A1C 5H5. (709)726-2212 or (866)726-2212. E-mail: nlacmail@nfld.net. Website: www.nlac.nf.ca.

Nova Scotia Arts Council. See Arm's Length Funding for the Arts (ALFA). E-mail: alfa1@chebucto.ns.ca. Website: http://alfa.chebucto.org.

Ontario Arts Council, 151 Bloor St. W., 5th Floor, Toronto ON M5S 1T6. (416)961-1660. E-mail: info@arts.on.ca. Website: www.arts.on.ca.

Prince Edward Island Council of the Arts, 115 Richmond St., Charlottetown PE C1A 7K7. (902)368-4410. E-mail: peiarts@peiartscouncil.com. Website: www.peiartscouncil.com.

Quebec Council for Arts & Literature, 79 boul. René-Lévesque Est, 3e étage, Quebec QC G1R 5N5. (418)643-1707. E-mail: info@calq.gouv.qc.ca. Website: www.calq.gouv.qc.ca.

The Saskatchewan Arts Board, 2135 Broad St., Regina SK S4P 3V7. (306)787-4056. E-mail: sab@artsboard.sk.ca. Website: www.artsboard.sk.ca.

Yukon Arts Section, Cultural Services Branch, Dept. of Tourism & Culture, Government of Yukon, Box 2703, Whitehorse YT Y1A 2C6. (867)667-8589. E-mail: arts@gov.yk.ca. Website: www.btc.gov.yk.ca/cultural/arts.

Grants

Conferences & Workshops

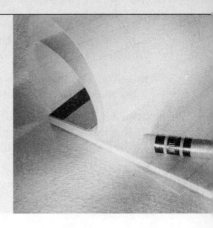

Important

T here are times when we want to immerse ourselves in learning. Or perhaps we crave a change of scenery, the creative stimulation of being around other artists, or the uninterrupted productivity of time alone to work.

That's what this section of *Poet's Market* is all about, providing a selection of writing conferences and workshops, artist colonies and retreats, poetry festivals, and even a few opportunities to go travelling with your muse. These listings give the basics: contact information, a brief description of the event, lists of past presenters, and offerings of special interest to poets. Contact an event that interests you for additional information, including up-to-date costs and housing details. **(Please note that most directors had not finalized their 2005 plans when we contacted them for this edition of *Poet's Market*. However, where possible, they provided us with their 2004 dates, costs, faculty names, or themes to give you a better idea of what each event has to offer.)**

Before you seriously consider a conference, workshop, or other event, determine what you hope to get out of the experience. Would a general conference with one or two poetry workshops among many other types of sessions be acceptable? Or are you looking for something exclusively focused on poetry? Do you want to hear poets speak about poetry writing, or are you looking for a more participatory experience, such as a one-on-one critiquing session or a group workshop? Do you mind being one of hundreds of attendees, or do you prefer a more intimate setting? Are you willing to invest in the expense of travelling to a conference, or would something local better suit your budget? Keep these questions and others in mind as you read these listings, view websites, and study conference brochures.

Some listings are coded with symbols to provide certain "information at a glance." The (🅽) symbol indicates a newly established conference/workshop new to *Poet's Market*; the (✖) symbol indicates this conference/workshop did not appear in the 2004 edition; the (🍁) symbol denotes a Canadian event and the (🌐) symbol one located outside the U.S. and Canada.

🖲 ANAM CARA WRITER'S AND ARTIST'S RETREAT

Eyeries, Beara, West Cork, Ireland. Phone: 353 (0)27 74441. Fax: 353 (0)27 74448. E-mail: anamcara retreat@eircom.net. Website: www.anamcararetreat.com. **Director:** Sue Booth-Forbes. Offers one-week to one-month individual retreats as well as workshops for writers and artists. Length of workshops varies with subject and leader/facilitator. Location: ''Beara is a rural and hauntingly beautiful part of Ireland that is kept temperate by the Gulf Stream. The retreat sits on a hill overlooking Coulagh Bay, the mountains of the Ring of Kerry, and the Slieve Mishkish Mountains of Beara. The village of Eyeries is a short walk away.'' Average attendance: 5 residents at the retreat when working individually; 12-18 workshop participants.

Purpose/Features ''Anam Cara is open to novice as well as professional writers and artists. Applicants are asked to provide a written description on the focus of their work while on retreat. Residencies are on a first-come, first-deposit-in basis.'' 2004 workshops included Poetry, Painting, and Proprioceptive Writing.

Costs/Accommodations 2004 individual retreat costs ranged from €570-670/week depending on room. Meals and other services, except phone and Internet use, included. Residency fee includes full room and board, laundry, sauna, Jacuzzi, 5 acres of gardens, meadows, riverbank and cascades, river island, swimming hole, and several spots, such as the ruin of a stone mill and a newly created beehive hut, in which to work. Overflow from workshops stay in nearby B&Bs, a short walk away. Transportation details available on website.

Additional Info Requests for specific information about rates and availability can be made through the website; also available by fax or e-mail. Brochure available on request.

✪ 🌐 ART WORKSHOPS IN GUATEMALA

4758 Lyndale Ave. S., Minneapolis MN 55409-2304. (612)825-0747. Fax: (612)825-6637. E-mail: info@artguat.org. Website: www.artguat.org. **Director:** Liza Fourré. Established 1995. Annual 10-day creative writing courses, held in February, March, July, and October. Location: workshops held in Antigua, the old colonial capital of Guatemala. Average attendance: limit 10 students.

Purpose/Features Art Workshops in Guatemala provides the perfect getaway for creative writers of all skill levels to study with experienced instructors while being inspired by Guatemala's incredibly beautiful landscapes and warm-hearted people. Offerings include ''Poetry/Snapshots in Words'' (was March 14-23, 2004) with Roseann Lloyd and ''Journey of the Soul'' with Sharon Doubiago. ''This workshop is designed for those desiring to write from their true voice through aesthetic exercises, self-exploration, memory retrieval, independent writing, and lively class discussions.''

Costs/Accommodations 2004 cost was $1,850; includes ''air transportation from U.S., tuition, lodging in a beautiful old colonial home, a hearty breakfast, and ground transport.''

Additional Info Individual poetry critiques included. Call, write, e-mail, fax, or check website.

ASPEN SUMMER WORDS WRITING RETREAT & LITERARY FESTIVAL; ASPEN WRITERS' FOUNDATION

110 E. Hallam St., Suite 116, Aspen CO 81611. (970)925-3122. Fax: (970)920-5700. E-mail: info@asp enwriters.org. Website: www.aspenwriters.org. Established 1976. Annual 5-day writing retreat and concurrent 5-day literary festival. 2004 dates: June 26-30. Location: The Given Institute and Paepke Auditorium in Aspen. Average attendance: 72 for the retreat, over 200 for the festival.

Purpose/Features Offers more than a dozen events for readers and writers. Retreat includes intensive workshops in poetry, fiction, creative nonfiction, advanced fiction, and magazine symposium. Offerings for poets include workshops, readings, publishing panels, and agent/editor meetings. 2004 poetry faculty included Jane Hirshfield. Festival speakers included Erica Jong, Anita Shreve, and the retreat and symposium faculty.

Costs/Accommodations 2004 tuition for 4-day workshop was $375; for 2-day symposium, $195.

2004 cost for the literary festival (5-day pass) was $150; $30 discount for registering for both the festival and retreat or symposium. Meals and other services charged separately, ''though we offer complimentary morning coffee and pastries for students and 2 wine and hors d'oeuvres receptions for ASW registrants.'' Information on overnight accommodations available on website.

Additional Info Writing sample required with application. Brochure and application available by phone, fax, e-mail (include regular mailing address with all e-mail inquiries), or on website.

BREAD LOAF WRITERS' CONFERENCE; BAKELESS LITERARY PUBLICATION PRIZES

Middlebury College, Middlebury VT 05753. (802)443-5286. Fax: (802)443-2087. E-mail: blwc@mid dlebury.edu. Website: www.middlebury.edu/~blwc. **Director:** Michael Collier. **Administrative Manager:** Noreen Cargill. Established 1926. Annual 11-day event usually held in mid-August. Location: mountain campus of Middlebury College. Average attendance: 230.

Purpose/Features Conference is designed to promote dialogue among writers and provide professional critiques for students. Conference usually covers fiction, nonfiction, and poetry.

Costs/Accommodations 2004 conference cost was $2,030 (contributor) or $1,945 (auditor), including tuition, room, and board. Fellowships and scholarships for the conference available. ''Candidates for fellowships must have a book published. Candidates for scholarships must have published in major literary periodicals or newspapers. Application and supporting materials due by March 1. See website for further details. Awards are announced in June for the conference in August.'' Taxis to and from the airport or bus station are available.

Additional Info Individual critiques also available. Sponsors the Bakeless Literary Publication Prizes, an annual book series competition for new authors of literary works in poetry, fiction, and creative nonfiction. Details, conference brochure, and application form available for SASE or on website. Accepts inquiries by fax and e-mail.

CATSKILL POETRY WORKSHOP

Hartwick College, Oneonta NY 13820. (607)431-4448. Fax: (607)431-4457. E-mail: frostc@hartwick .edu. Website: www.hartwick.edu/library/catskill/poetry.htm. **Director:** Carol Frost. Annual weeklong event. 2004 dates were June 19-26. Location: Hartwick College, a small, private college in the Catskill Mountain area. Average attendance: up to 40.

Purpose/Features Open to ''talented adult writers.'' Workshops cover poetry only. Offerings include ''traditional meters, free verse lineation and uses of metaphor; individual instruction.'' 2004 faculty were Ellen Voigt, Dave Smith, Stephen Dunn, Natasha Trethewey, C. Dale Young, Carol Frost, Michael Waters, Sydney Wade, Kurt Brown, and Sean Singer.

Costs/Accommodations 2004 cost was $1,050, including tuition, room and board. Housing available in on-site facilities. Cost for commuters was $650, tuition and lunch included. Deposit required of all attendees.

Additional Info Two individual ms conferences scheduled for each participant. Registration forms available for SASE and on website. Accepts inquiries by fax and e-mail.

CAVE CANEM

P. O. Box 4286, Charlottesville VA 22905-4286. E-mail: cavecanempoets@aol.com. Website: www.c avecanempoets.org/. **Contact:** Carolyn Micklem, foundation director. Established 1996. Annual weeklong workshop for African-American poets. Usually held last week in June. Location: University of Pittsburgh at Greensburg, PA. Average attendance: 50.

Purpose/Features Open to African-American poets. Participants selected based on a sample of 6-8 poems. Offerings include workshops by fellows and faculty, evening readings. Participants are assigned to groups of about 9 and remain together throughout session, with different faculty leading each workshop. 2004 faculty included Toi Derricotte, Cornelius Eady, Kwame Dawes, Erica Hunt, Patricia Smith, and Al Young, with guest poets Lucille Clifton and Kevin Young.

Costs/Accommodations 2004 cost was $495. Meals and other services included. For complete information, contact Cave Canem.

Additional Information Poets should submit 6-8 poems with cover letter. 2004 postmark deadline was March 15, with accepted poets notified by April 30. Cave Canem Foundation also sponsors the Cave Canem Poetry Prize (see separate listing in Contests & Awards section). Brochure and registration information available for SASE and on website. Accepts inquiries by e-mail.

CENTRUM'S PORT TOWNSEND WRITERS' CONFERENCE

% Centrum, P.O. Box 1158, Port Townsend WA 98368. (360)385-3102. Fax: (360)385-2470. E-mail: info@centrum.org. Website: www.centrum.org. **Program Manager:** Sam Hamill. **Assistant to the Director/Registrar:** Carla Vander Ven. Established 1974. Annual 10-day event held the second week in July. 2004 dates: July 15-24. Location: Fort Worden State Park, historic seaside entrance to Puget Sound. Average attendance: 150 (limit of 16/critiqued workshop).

Purpose/Features Open to all serious writers. Conference usually covers fiction (no genre fiction), poetry, and creative nonfiction. Offerings include limited-enrollment critiqued workshops with private conference or open enrollment workshops. Also included are open mic readings, faculty readings, and technique classes. 2004 faculty included poets Erin Belieu, Wanda Coleman, Martin Espada, Joseph Stroud, and Emily Warn.

Costs/Accommodations 2003 cost was $495 for critiqued workshop tuition, $395 open enrollment workshop tuition; $200-420 room and board. Information on overnight accommodations available.

Additional Info Members of critiqued workshops must submit writing samples. Brochure and registration form available for SASE or on website.

CHENANGO VALLEY WRITERS' CONFERENCE

Office of Summer Programs, Colgate University, 13 Oak Dr., Hamilton NY 13346. (315)228-7771. Fax: (315)228-7975. E-mail: info@cvwc.net. Website: www.cvwc.net. **Conference Director:** Matthew Leone. Established 1996. Annual weeklong event usually held in the middle of June. 2004 dates: June 20-26. Location: Colgate University; has "an expansive campus, with classrooms, dormitories, libraries, and recreational facilities all in close proximity to each other." Average attendance: 75.

Purpose/Features Open to "all serious writers or aspirants. Our purpose is to work on honing writing skills: fiction, poetry, and nonfiction prose are covered." 2004 poetry staff included Bruce Smith, Peter Balakian, and David Thoreen.

Costs/Accommodations 2004 cost was $995 for tuition, room, and board; $750 for day students; $895 and $695 before March 15; $875 and $625 for returnees. Discounts available through fellowships, typically $100-450. Room and board only (no workshops): $295. "Will pick up airport, bus, and train station arrivals with prior notification for $35/trip." Accommodations include air-conditioned residencies (single rooms available at no extra charge), shared bathrooms; board includes breakfast, lunch, and dinner.

Additional Info Each applicant must submit a ms with his/her application. Individual poetry critiques available. Submit poems in advance to Matthew Leone. Brochures and registration forms available for SASE or on website. Accepts inquiries by fax and e-mail.

COLORADO MOUNTAIN WRITERS' WORKSHOP

P.O. Box 85394, Tucson AZ 85754. (520)465-1520. Fax: (520)572-0620. E-mail: megfiles@cs.com. Website: www.sheilabender.com. **Director:** Meg Files. Established 1999. Annual 5-day event. 2004 dates were June 21-25. Location: Steamboat Springs, CO, on the mountaintop campus of Colorado Mountain College. Average attendance: 50.

Purpose/Features Open to all writers, beginning and experienced. "The workshop includes sessions on writing and publishing fiction, nonfiction, and poetry, as well as manuscript workshops and individual critiques and writing exercises." Faculty includes Sheila Bender, Jack Heffron, and Meg Files. Other special features include "a beautiful high-country site, extensive and intensive hands-on activities, individual attention, and a supportive atmosphere."

Costs/Accommodations 2004 cost was $400 for tuition; dorm rooms and meals available on site.

Additional Info Individual critiques available. Submit 5 poems in advance to Meg Files.

▨ THE CONCORD TABLE PUBLICATION WORKSHOP

Boston Comment, 242 Parker St., Acton MA 01720. (978)897-0712. E-mail: joan@bostoncomment.com. Website: www.bostoncomment.com. **Director:** Joan Houlihan. Established 2000. Usually held year round in 8-week sessions starting mid-January. 2004 dates: January 17-March 6, March 13-May 8, May 15-July 3, July 10-August 28, September 4-October 23, and October 30-December 18. Location: Emerson Umbrella, 40 Stow St., Concord MA. Average attendance: 6-8 poets/session (limited to 8).

Purpose/Features Open to all poets interested in publishing in journals and/or publishing chapbook and book-length mss. Offerings include 3 consecutively run, intensive workshops focused on the 3 phases of publication: Building a Portfolio, Moving Toward Publication, and Preparing a Book Manuscript. 2005 faculty will be "Joan Houlihan, workshop leader, author, and director of The Boston Comment series; also editor-in-chief of the nationally known online poetry journal, *Perihelion*, and poetry editor of Del Sol Press. See website for more information."

Costs/Accommodations 2005 workshop cost is $350/session.

Additional Information Brochure and registration form available by e-mail. Accepts inquiries by phone or e-mail. (See separate listing for *Perihelion* in the Publishers of Poetry section and for Del Sol Press Annual Poetry Prize in the Contests & Awards section.)

THE CONFERENCE ON TEACHING AND POETRY

Robert Frost Place, Franconia NH 03580. (603)823-5510. E-mail: donald.sheehan@dartmouth.edu. Executive Director: Donald Sheehan. **Co-Director of Teacher Conference:** Baron Wormser. Annual event held in late June. 2003 dates were June 23-27.

Purpose/Features Intended for high school and middle school classroom teachers. Daily sessions include talks on poetry and teaching, workshops on teaching poems, workshops for teachers who write poems, and teacher sharing sessions as well as talks by working teachers on poetry in the curriculum. 2003 guest faculty included Christopher Jane Corkery, Thomas Chandler, Kate Rushin, and Douglas Goetsch. Resident staff: Baron Wormser, David Capella, and Donald Sheehan.

Costs/Accommodations 2003 fee for 5-day program was $450 (NH teachers $350), plus $372 for 3 graduate credits from the University of New Hampshire College for Lifelong Learning. Room and board available locally.

Additional Info To apply, send letter describing current teaching situation and literary interests, along with $15 processing fee. (See separate listings for Frost Place Annual Festival of Poetry and Frost Place Seminar in this section.)

DJERASSI RESIDENT ARTISTS PROGRAM

Applications 2006, 2325 Bear Gulch Rd., Woodside CA 94062. (650)747-1250. Fax: (650)747-0105. E-mail: drap@djerassi.org. Website: www.djerassi.org. **Residency Coordinator:** Judy Freeland. Established 1979. Offers 4-week residencies, at no cost, for writers and other creative artists. Residencies available mid-March through mid-November. Location: In a spectacular rural setting in the Santa Cruz Mountains, one hour south of San Francisco. Average attendance: 60 artists each year.

Purpose/Features Residencies are awarded competitively to emerging and mid-career artists as well as artists with established national or international reputations. Purpose is "to support and enhance the creativity of artists by providing uninterrupted time for work, reflection, and collegial interaction."

Costs/Accommodations Artists selected are offered room, board, and studio space at no cost. "Three rooms in The Artists' House are set up to accommodate writers, each with a large desk, work space, and outdoor deck."

Additional Info Deadline for accepting applications is February 15 each year (i.e., 2005) for a residency in the following year (2006). Requires $25 application fee. Application materials available for SASE or on website.

✖ GERALDINE R. DODGE POETRY FESTIVAL

Geraldine R. Dodge Foundation, P.O. Box 1239, Morristown NJ 07962-1239. (973)540-8443 ext. 5. Website: www.dodgepoetryfestival.org. Established 1986. Biennial 4-day event usually held in early fall. 2004 dates: September 30-October 3. Location: Duke Farms, Hillsborough, NJ (near Somerville). Average attendance: 17,500 total for 2002 festival.

Purpose/Features Biennial celebration of poetry for poets, students, teachers, and the general public. Presents panels, talks, and workshops about a range of topics and issues related to poetry; and an ambitious schedule of poetry readings featuring the cream of contemporary poets. 2002 participants included Stanley Kunitz, Robert Pinsky, Rita Dove, Billy Collins, Robert Haas, Mark Doty, Brenda Hillman, Lucille Clifton, and the list goes on and on.

Costs/Accommodations Fee charged; check website for latest information. Passes can be purchased for multiple days. Participants responsible for own lodging and meals. Information on overnight accommodations in area hotels available on website.

Additional Information Brochure and registration form available on website; sign up online for mailing list for future brochures and announcements. Accepts inquiries by phone.

EASTERN KENTUCKY UNIVERSITY CREATIVE WRITING CONFERENCE

English Dept., Case Annex 467, Richmond KY 40475. (859)622-3091. E-mail: christine.delea@eku.edu. Website: www.english.eku.edu/conferences. **Conference Director:** Christine Delea. Established 1964. Annual 5-day event usually held Monday through Friday of the third week in June. Location: Eastern Kentucky University. Average attendance: 15.

Purpose/Features Open to poetry and fiction. Provides lectures, workshops, and private conferences with visiting writers to "help writers increase their skills in writing poetry and fiction." A ms of 4-8 poems (8 pages maximum) must be submitted by May 20 and accepted before enrollment in conference is allowed. Offerings include workshop discussions and individual conferences. 2003 poetry faculty included Harry Brown, Christine Delea, and James Baker Hall.

Costs/Accommodations 2003 costs were $122 undergraduate and $176 graduate (in-state fees), $335 undergraduate and $487 graduate (out-of-state fees; prices subject to change). Participants responsible for their own meals, available on campus. Cost for housing in on-site facilities was $15/night single occupancy, $10/night double occupancy. "Must bring your own sheets, pillow, blanket."

Additional Info Brochure available for SASE or request by e-mail. Additional information available on website.

FINE ARTS WORK CENTER

24 Pearl St., Provincetown MA 02657. (508)487-9960. Fax: (508)487-8873. E-mail: workshops@fawc.org. Website: www.fawc.org. Established 1968. The Fine Arts Work Center in Provincetown "is a nonprofit organization dedicated to providing emerging writers and visual artists with time and space in which to pursue independent work in a community of peers." Seven-month fellowships are awarded to poets and fiction writers in the emerging stages of their careers; professional juries make admissions decisions. 2004 Summer Program fees were $480 for each weeklong workshop and $235 for each weekend workshop. Accommodations for 6 nights cost $500. See website for details and an application form.

✦ FISHTRAP

P.O. Box 38, Enterprise OR 97828. (541)426-3623. E-mail: rich@fishtrap.org. Website: www.fishtra p.org. **Director:** Rich Wandschneider. Established 1988. Holds annual gatherings, summer workshops, and intensive residential craft workshops. 2004 dates were Winter Fishtrap—February 20-22; Summer Workshops—July 5-9; Summer Gathering—July 9-11. Location: "Winter site is a meeting room attached to a motel at Wallowa Lake, Oregon (off season); summer site is an old Methodist church camp." Average attendance: 50 for Winter Fishtrap ("always sold out"); 8 workshops (12 people/workshop) for Summer Workshop; 90 for Summer Gathering.

Purpose/Features Open to anyone. "Fishtrap's goal is to promote good writing and clear thinking in and about the West. Also to encourage and promote new writers. Offerings include a poetry workshop. There are always craft workshops on fiction, poetry, nonfiction; sometimes in children's writing, playwriting, songwriting, etc." Theme for 2004 Winter: "Forgiveness and the Unforgivable."

Costs/Accommodations 2004 Winter Fishtrap cost was $275-420 including meals (higher price includes lodging); Summer Workshop was $275, Gathering was $175, meals and lodging available at $32/day at camp. Lodging also available at nearby motels.

Additional Info Awards 5 fellowships annually. Receives 80-100 entries/year. "Award is room and board and workshop registration for Summer Fishtrap." Brochure and registration form available for SASE or request by e-mail. Each year the selected writings of workshop students and workshop instructors are published in an anthology.

FROST PLACE ANNUAL FESTIVAL OF POETRY

Robert Frost Place, Franconia NH 03580. (603)823-5510. E-mail: donald.sheehan@dartmouth.edu. Executive Director: Donald Sheehan. **Director of Festival Admissions:** David Keller. Established 1978. Annual weeklong event held late July and early August at Robert Frost's house and barn, made into a center for poetry and the arts. 2003 dates were July 27-August 1. Average attendance: 50-55.

Purpose/Features Open to poets only. 2004 guest faculty included Major Jackson, Thomas Lux, Toi Derricotte, Baron Wormser, Ellen Bryant Voight, and B.H. Fairchaild.

Costs/Accommodations 2003 cost was $725 (participant), plus a $25 reading fee. Auditor fee: $500. Room and board available locally; information sent upon acceptance to program.

Additional Info Application should be accompanied by 3 pages of your own poetry. Brochure and registration form available for SASE. (See separate listings for The Conference on Teaching and Poetry and The Frost Place Seminar in this section.)

FROST PLACE SEMINAR

Robert Frost Place, Franconia NH 03580. (603)823-5510. E-mail: donald.sheehan@dartmouth.edu. **Seminar Co-Directors:** Baron Wormser and Donald Sheehan. Held annually in early August following the Frost Place Annual Festival of Poetry (see separate listing in this section). 2003 dates were August 4-8. Average attendance: limited to 16 participants.

Purpose/Features Open to those who have participated in the Festival of Poetry at least once prior to the summer for which you are applying. Includes daily lecture/seminar on poetry of the past, workshops focusing on participant poems, evening readings. 2003 guest faculty: Margaret Rabb and Christopher Bursk.

Costs/Accommodations 2003 fee was $575 (including room), plus $75 for two meals daily and $25 reading fee.

Additional Info Admission competitive. To apply, send cover letter outlining goals for your participation and 3 pages of your own poetry. (See separate listings for Frost Place Annual Festival of Poetry and The Conference on Teaching and Poetry in this section.)

GREEN LAKE WRITERS CONFERENCE

Green Lake Conference Center, W2511 State Highway 23, Green Lake WI 54941-9599. (800)558-8898. E-mail: RussannHaddig@glcc.org. Website: www.glcc.org. **Contact:** Russann Haddig. Established 1946. Annual weeklong event. 2004 dates: August 14-20. Location: Green Lake at the national conference center for American Baptists. Average attendance: 65-80.

Purpose/Features "Our only requirement is a desire to learn and grow in your craft." Conference covers poetry, fiction, script, suspense, nonfiction/inspirational, and writing for children. 2004 poetry instructors included Ellen Kort.

Costs/Accommodations 2004 program fee was $110. Housing and meals extra. Housing Information Request form provided online.

Additional Info Scholarships available. Brochure available on website.

⚡ HEARTLAND WRITERS CONFERENCE; HEARTLAND WRITERS GUILD

P.O. Box 652, Kennett MO 63857-0652. (618)998-8360. E-mail: hwg@heartlandwriters.org. Website: www.heartlandwriters.org. **Conference Coordinator:** Harry Spiller. Established 1989. Biennial 3-day event. 2004 dates: June 3-5. Location: Coach House Inn, Sikeston MO. Average attendance: 150.

Purpose/Features Open to all writers of popular fiction, nonfiction, and poetry. Offerings include critique sessions. Speakers for next conference are 10 agents and editors from prominent New York-based publishing houses/agencies, as well as 12 published authors from the Midwest.

Costs/Accommodations Most recent conference cost was $200, including most meals. Information on overnight accommodations available. Accommodations include special rates at area hotels.

Additional Info Contest sponsored as part of conference. Judges are industry professionals. Send name and address to be included on conference mailing list. Accepts inquiries by e-mail.

HIGHLAND SUMMER WORKSHOP

P.O. Box 7014, Radford University, Radford VA 24142. (540)831-5366. Fax: (540)831-5951. E-mail: jasbury@radford.edu. **Director:** Grace Toney Edwards. Established 1977. Annual 2-week event held the first 2 weeks in June. Location: Radford University campus. Average attendance: 20-25.

Purpose/Features Open to everyone. "The conference, a lecture-seminar-workshop combination, is conducted by well-known guest writers and offers the opportunity to study and practice creative and expository writing within the context of regional culture." Topics covered vary from year to year. Poetry, fiction, and essays (prose) are generally covered each year. The last workshop was led by Robert Morgan, Richard Hague, Kathryn Stripling Byers, and Sharyn McCrumb.

Costs/Accommodations Costs range from $630-1,275 plus $16/day for meals. Individual meals may also be purchased. On-site housing costs range from $19-28/night. On-site accommodations available at Norwood Hall. Accommodations also available at local motels.

Additional Info Brochure and registration form available for SASE. Accepts inquiries by fax and e-mail.

HOFSTRA UNIVERSITY SUMMER WRITERS' CONFERENCE

University College for Continuing Education, 250 Hofstra University, Hempstead NY 11549. (516)463-7600. E-mail: uccelibarts@hofstra.edu. Website: www.hofstra.edu/Academics/UCCE/. **Director:** Marion Flomenhaft. Established 1972. Annual 10-day event. 2004 dates: July 12-23. Location: Hofstra University. Average attendance: 60-70.

Purpose/Features Open to all writers. "Each workshop includes both group and individual sessions and totals more than 25 contact hours between student and teacher." 2004 poetry presenters included Janet Kaplan.

Costs/Accommodations 2004 conference cost was $430. "Lodging in residence halls can be arranged for participants 19 years of age or older."

Additional Info Additional information available by phone, e-mail, or on website.

INDIANA UNIVERSITY WRITERS' CONFERENCE

Ballantine Hall 464, Indiana University, Bloomington IN 47405. (812)855-1877. Fax: (812)855-9535. E-mail: writecon@indiana.edu. Website: www.indiana.edu/~writecon. **Director:** Amy M. Locklin. Established 1940. Annual weeklong event usually held the last week in June at the university student union. Average attendance: 100.

Purpose/Features Open to all. Conference covers fiction and poetry. Offerings include workshops and classes. 2004 faculty in poetry included Terrance Hayes, Brigit Pegeen Kelly, Li-Young Lee, Maureen Seaton, and Karen Volkman.

Costs/Accommodations 2004 conference cost was $350 for conference and classes; $500 for conference, classes, and one workshop; plus $50 application fee. Information on overnight accommodations available. "Rooms available in the student union or in a dorm."

Additional Info Workshop applicants receive private consultation with workshop leader. Submit 10 pages of poetry in advance. Submit separate ms of 3-5 poems for scholarship consideration. "Scholarship manuscripts must be postmarked by May 1." Brochure and registration form available for SASE or on website (printable registration form available online). Accepts inquiries by fax or e-mail.

IOWA SUMMER WRITING FESTIVAL

University of Iowa, 100 Oakdale Campus, W310, Iowa City IA 52242-5000. (319)335-4160. Fax: (319)335-4039. E-mail: iswfestival@uiowa.edu. Website: www.uiowa.edu/~iswfest. **Director:** Amy Margolis. Established 1987. Annual event held each summer in June and July for six weeks. Includes one-week and weekend workshops at the University of Iowa campus. Average attendance: 150/week.

Purpose/Features Open to "all adults who have a desire to write." Conference offers courses in nearly all writing forms. 2003 offerings included 21 poetry classes for all levels (135 classes offered overall). Poetry faculty included Bruce Bond, Michael Dennis Browne, Lisa Chavez, Vince Gotera, Jim Heynen, and Richard Jackson.

Costs/Accommodations 2003 conference cost was $210 for a weekend course and $435-460 for a one-week course. Participants responsible for their own meals. Accommodations available at the Iowa House and the Sheraton. Housing in residence hall costs about $31/night.

Additional Info Participants in week-long workshops have private conference/critique with workshop leader. Send for brochure and registration form. Accepts inquiries by phone, fax, or e-mail.

THE IWWG SUMMER CONFERENCE

The International Women's Writing Guild, P.O. Box 810, Gracie Station, New York NY 10028. (212)737-7536. Fax: (212)737-9469. E-mail: iwwg@iwwg.org. Website: www.iwwg.com. **Executive Director:** Hannelore Hahn. Established 1978. 2004 dates were June 18-25. Location: Skidmore College in Saratoga Springs, NY. Average attendance: 500 maximum.

Purpose/Features Open to all women. Around 70 workshops offered each day. 2004 poetry presenters included Barbara Garro, Marj Hahne, D.H. Melhem, Myra Shapiro, and Susan Baugh.

Costs/Accommodations 2004 cost for the full 7-day conference was $900 (single), $790 (double) for IWWG members; $925 (single), $815 (double) for nonmembers. Includes program and room and board for 7 nights, 21 meals at Skidmore College. Shorter conference stays available.

Additional Info Post-conference retreat weekend also available. Additional information available for SASE, by e-mail, or on website.

⚡ JENTEL ARTIST RESIDENCY PROGRAM

Jentel Foundation, 130 Lower Piney Creek Rd., Banner WY 82832. (307)737-2311. Fax: (307)737-2305. E-mail: Jentel@jentelarts.org. Website: www.jentelarts.org. **Executive Director:** Mary Jane Edwards. Established 2000. Biannual one-month residency, always held the 15th of one month through the 13th of the following month. Application deadlines are September 15 and January 15 annually. Location: Banner, WY. Average attendance: 2 writers in any genre (also 4 visual artists in any media).

Purpose/Features Residency program for writers and visual artists who are U.S. citizens or from the international community currently residing in the U.S., are 25 years and older, and are not matriculated students. "Set in a rural ranch setting in the foothills of the Big Horn Mountains of North Central Wyoming, Jentel offers unfettered time and space to focus on the creative process, experience of the Wyoming landscape, and interact as desired with a small community of writers and artists." Special features include Jentel Presents, a monthly evening of slide presentations and readings by residents in one of the surrounding communities.

Costs/Accommodations Residents are responsible for travel expenses and personal items. "Jentel provides a private accommodation in a shared living space, a comfortable private studio, and a $400 stipend to help defray the cost of food and personal expenses. Staff takes residents grocery shopping weekly after the stipend is distributed. Staff will pick up and drop off residents at the airport and bus station in Sheridan, 20 miles from the ranch setting of Jentel." Accommodation provided in a large house with common living and dining areas; fully equipped kitchen; library with computer, printer, and Internet access; media room with television, video player, and CD player; special private bedroom; and private studio.

Additional Information Brochure and registration form available for self-addressed mailing label and 60 cents postage or on website. Accepts inquiries by phone, fax, or e-mail.

KEY WEST WRITERS' WORKSHOP

5901 College Rd., Key West FL 33040. (305)296-9081. Fax: (305)292-2392. E-mail: weinman_i@firn.edu. Website: www.fkcc.cc. **Director:** Irving Weinman. Established 1996. Five annual weekend sessions usually held from late January to early March. Location: the conference room of Key West's historic Old City Hall and locations in Old Town, Key West. Average attendance: limited to 10 for poetry weekends, 12 for fiction.

Purpose/Features "**Not for beginners**." Brings "the best writers into an intimate workshop setting with serious writers at all but beginning stages of their writing careers. Workshops are offered in poetry and fiction." 2004 poetry staff included Robert Creeley, Sharon Olds, and Martin Espada.

Costs/Accommodations 2004 conference cost was $300/weekend, tuition only. Participants responsible for their own meals. Information on overnight accommodations available.

Additional Info Brochure and registration form available for SASE, by e-mail, or on website. Accepts inquiries by fax and e-mail.

LIGONIER VALLEY WRITERS CONFERENCE; THE LOYALHANNA REVIEW

P.O. Box B, Ligonier PA 15658. (724)238-4747. E-mail: online contact form. Website: www.ligonierv alleywriters.org/conference.asp. Established 1986. Annual 2-day event. 2004 dates were July 9 & 10. Location: Ligonier, PA. Average attendance: 40-50.

Purpose/Features Open to anyone interested in writing. 2004 poetry presenters included Paolo Corso and Jim Daniels.

Costs/Accommodations 2003 cost was approximately $200. Participants responsible for their own dinner and lodging. Information on overnight accommodations available for registrants.

Additional Info Registration form and additional information available online. "We also publish *The Loyalhanna Review*, a literary journal, which is open to participants."

THE LITERARY FESTIVAL AT ST. MARY'S

St. Mary's College of Maryland, St. Mary's City MD 20686. E-mail: msglaser@smcm.edu. Website: www.smcm.edu/academics/litfest. **Contact:** Dr. Michael S. Glaser. Semiannual event held during the early summer in even years (i.e., 2004, 2006). Approximately 18 guest poets and artists participate in and lead workshops, seminars, and readings. Concurrent with the festival, St. Mary's College offers 2-week intensive writing workshops in poetry and fiction and a 10-day writer's community retreat.

Purpose/Features The poetry and fiction workshop engages the participants in structured writing experiences. Intended for anyone with a serious interest in writing. Offers 4 college credits or may be taken as non-credit courses. The retreat, designed for the serious writer, offers individual plans for writing alone or in conjunction with other participants.

Additional Info For application or more information on these workshops or the festival, write to Michael S. Glaser at the above address. Accepts inquiries by e-mail.

◩ MONTEREY COWBOY POETRY & MUSIC FESTIVAL

528 Abrego, PMB 153, Monterey CA 93940. (831)899-6758. E-mail: info@montereycowboy.com. Website: www.montereycowboy.com. **Contact:** J.P. "Mick" Vernon, President. Established 1998. Annual event held for 2 days, 3 nights the first weekend of December. 2004 dates: December 3, 4, 5. Location: Monterey Conference Center. Average attendance: 2,000.

Purpose/Features Open to the general public. Celebrates cowboy poetry and music. Offerings include 9 separate shows of varying theme, most featuring 2 poets and 2 musicians; a few feature strictly poets. Other special features include an open mic at noon on Saturday and Sunday, and a Western art and gear show.

Costs/Accommodations In 2003, individual shows cost either $10 or $30; an all-event pass was $160. Covers admission costs only; participants responsible for own housing and meals. Information on overnight accommodations available. Accommodations include special rates at area hotels.

Additional Information Brochure available on website. Accepts inquiries by phone or e-mail.

MOUNT HERMON CHRISTIAN WRITERS CONFERENCE

P.O. Box 413, Mount Hermon CA 95041. (831)335-4466. Fax: (831)335-9413. E-mail: rachelw@mhc amps.org. Website: www.mounthermon.org/writers. **Director of Adult Ministries:** David R. Talbott. Established 1970. Annual 5-day event held Friday through Tuesday over Palm Sunday weekend. 2005 dates: March 18-22. Location: Full hotel-service-style conference center in heart of California redwoods near San Jose. Average attendance: 425-475.

Purpose/Features Open to "anyone interested in the Christian writing market." Conference is very broad based. Always covers poetry, fiction, article writing, writing for children, plus an advanced track for published authors. Offerings have included several workshops, sessions on the greeting card industry, and individual one-hour workshops (including a workshop for scriptwriters in 2004). "We usually have 45-50 teaching faculty made up of publishing reps of leading Christian book and magazine publishers, plus 20-25 selected freelancers." Other special features have included an advance critique service (no extra fee); residential conference, with meals taken family-style with faculty; private appointments with faculty; and an autograph party. "High spiritual impact."

Costs/Accommodations 2004 conference cost was $970 deluxe; $800 standard; $650 economy; $575 student dormitory; including 13 meals, snacks, on-site housing, and $350 tuition fee. No-housing fee: $610. $25 airport, Greyhound, or Amtrack shuttle from San Jose, CA.

Additional Info Brochure and registration form available on request or on website. Accepts inquiries by fax or e-mail.

NAPA VALLEY WRITERS' CONFERENCE

Napa Valley College, 1088 College Ave., St. Helena CA 94574. (707)967-2900. E-mail: writecon@napavalley.edu. Website: www.napavalley.edu/writersconf/. **Poetry Director:** Nan Cohen. Established 1981. Annual week-long event usually held the last week in July or first week in August. 2004 dates were July 25-30. Location: Upper Valley Campus in the historic town of St. Helena, 30 minutes north of Napa in the heart of the valley's wine growing community. Average attendance: 48 in poetry and 48 in fiction.

Purpose/Features "The conference has maintained its emphases on process and craft, featuring a faculty as renowned for the quality of their teaching as for their work. It has also remained small and personal, fostering an unusual rapport between faculty writers and conference participants. The poetry session provides the opportunity to work both on generating new poems and on revising previously written ones. Daily workshops emphasize writing new poems—taking risks with new material and forms, pushing boundaries in the poetic process." The 2004 poetry faculty included Mary Jo Bang, Brenda Hillman, Harryette Mullen, and Arthur Sze. "Participants register for either the poetry or the fiction workshops, but panels and craft talks are open to all writers attending. Evenings feature readings by the faculty that are open to the public and hosted by Napa Valley wineries."

Costs/Accommodations 2004 cost was $650, not including meals or housing. A limited number of scholarships are available. Information on overnight accommodations available. "Through the generosity of Napa residents, limited accommodations in local homes are available on a first-come, first-served basis for a fee of $30 for the week."

Additional Info All applicants are asked to submit a qualifying ms with their registration (no more than 5 poems) as well as a brief description of their writing background. 2004 application deadline: May 28. Brochure and registration form available for SASE or on website.

NATIONAL COWBOY POETRY GATHERING; WESTERN FOLKLIFE CENTER

501 Railroad St., Elko NV 89801. (775)738-7508. Fax: (775)738-2900. E-mail: tbaer@westernfolklife.org. Website: www.westernfolklife.org. **Contact:** Gathering Manager. Usually held end of January. 2004 dates: January 24-31. Location: Western Folklife Center or the Elko Convention Center, plus other venues.

Purpose Features Early Gathering activities (first weekend and early in week) feature workshops, evening performances, and exhibits. The Gathering swings into full gear on Wednesday with concert and keynote address, followed by 3 days of poetry and music, exhibits, panel discussions, and videos/films. 2004 workshops included "Set Your Words Free" with Paul Zarzyski, as well as readings and poetry/music sessions.

Costs/Accommodations 2004 advance ticket cost: $35 for 3-day Guest Pass (including program book and guest pass pin); $15 for Single Day Pass (program book purchased separately). Ticket cost does not include handling charge or credit card fee; prices increase for non-advance tickets. Advance tickets go on sale in early September. Participants responsible for own meals and housing (there are many motels and casinos in Elko). Advance reservations recommended.

Additional Information The Western Folklife Center distributes books and tapes of cowboy poetry and songs as well as other cowboy memorabilia; also sponsors a variety of other community programs throughout the year. Additional information available about the Center and the Gathering on website.

PENNWRITERS ANNUAL CONFERENCE; PENNWRITERS, INC.; IN OTHER WORDS CONTEST; PENNWRITERS POETRY CONTEST

E-mail: PaulaJMatter@compuserve.com. Website: http://pennwriters.org. **Conference Coordinator:** Paula Matter. Established 1987. Annual 2½-day event. 2004 dates were May 14-16. Location: Grantville, PA; check website for 2005 location. Average attendance: 200.

Purpose/Features Open to all writers, novice to multi-published. Covers fiction, nonfiction, and poetry. Offers workshops/seminars, appointments with agents and editors, autograph party, contests—all multi-genre oriented. Theme for 2004 conference was "Get a Clue!"

Costs/Accommodations 2004 conference cost was $140 (members), $165 (nonmembers) for all days of conference, including some meals. Special meal events are additional. "Scholarship awards are presented to Pennwriters members who are winners in our annual writing contests." Information on overnight accommodations available.

Additional Info Pennwriters sponsors 2 contests open to poets: 1. In Other Words Contest, held during annual conference, open to conference attendees only. Divisions for poetry, fiction, and nonfiction. Complete rules on website. Awards prizes; judged by peers. 2. Sometimes offers the Pennwriters Poetry Contest, open to all; nonmembers pay slightly higher fee. Cash prizes of $50, $25, $10. Complete guidelines on website. Brochure and registration form available for SASE or on website. Accepts inquiries by fax and e-mail. "The Pennwriters Annual Conference is sponsored by Pennwriters, Inc., a nonprofit organization with goals to help writers get published."

PIMA WRITERS' WORKSHOP

Pima College, 2202 W. Anklam Rd., Tucson AZ 85709-0170. (520)206-6084. E-mail: mfiles@pima.edu. **Director:** Meg Files. Established 1987. Annual 3-day event. 2004 dates were May 21-23. Location: Pima College's Center for the Arts, "includes a proscenium theater, a black box theater, a recital hall, and conference rooms, as well as a courtyard with amphitheater." Average attendance: 250.

Purpose/Features Open to all writers, beginning and experienced. "The workshop includes sessions on all genres (nonfiction, fiction, poetry, writing for children and juveniles, screenwriting) and on editing and publishing, as well as manuscript critiques and writing exercises." Past faculty has included Robert Morgan, Sharman Apt Russell, Barbara Kingsolver, Larry McMurtry, Nancy Mairs, Peter Meinke, Steve Kowit, David Citino, and others. Other special features include "accessibility to writers, agents, and editors; and the workshop's atmosphere—friendly and supportive, practical and inspirational."

Costs/Accommodations 2004 conference cost was $70. Participants responsible for their own meals. Information on overnight accommodations available.

Additional Info Individual poetry critiques available. Submit 3 poems in advance to Meg Files. Brochure and registration form available for SASE or by fax or e-mail. Accepts inquiries by e-mail.

⚡ POETRY ALIVE! SUMMER RESIDENCY INSTITUTE FOR TEACHERS

20 Battery Park, Suite 505, Asheville NC 28801. (800)476-8172 or (828)255-7636. Fax: (828)232-1045. E-mail: poetry@poetryalive.com. Website: www.poetryalive.com. **Contact:** Bob Falls. Established 1990. Annual 7-day events. 2004 dates were June 20-26, July 11-17, July 18-24. Location: University of North Carolina at Asheville. Average attendance: 20/session.

Purpose/Features Open to anyone. Themes or panels for conference have included "creative writing (poetry), reader response techniques, poem performance techniques, and teaching." Speakers at past conferences have included Ken and Nadine Delano (performance poetry, writing) and Cheryl Bromley Jones (reader response, writing). Other special features include a trip to Connemara, the Carl Sandburg Home, and dinner out in downtown Asheville.

Costs/Accommodations 2004 conference cost was $800, including meals and housing in on-site facilities; shared dorm rooms with bed, desk, and shared bath. Private room available for additional cost. Discounts available to local commuters "who don't pay the cost of food and lodging." Transportation to and from the event not provided. "We provide transportation from the airport."

Additional Info Brochure and registration form available by fax, e-mail, or on website. Accepts inquiries by fax or e-mail. "This workshop is designed specifically for teachers or any poet interested in working with students in the schools or as an educational consultant."

(S.O.M.O.S.) SOCIETY OF THE MUSE OF THE SOUTHWEST; CHOKECHERRIES

P.O. Box 3225, Taos NM 87571. (505)758-0081. Fax: (505)758-4802. E-mail: somos@laplaza.com. Website: www.somostaos.org. **Executive Director:** Dori Vinella. Established 1983. "We offer readings, special events, and workshops at different times during the year, many during the summer." Length of workshops varies. Location: various sites in Taos. Average attendance: 10-50.

Purpose/Features Open to anyone. "We offer workshops in various genres—fiction, poetry, nature writing, etc." Past workshop speakers have included Denise Chavez, Alfred Depew, Marjorie Agosin, Judyth Hill, Robin Becker, and Robert Westbrook. Other special features include the 2-day Annual Taos Storytelling Festival in October, a Winter Writers Series (January-February), and Summer Writer's Series (July-August).

Costs/Accommodations Cost for workshops ranges from $30-175, excluding room and board. Information on overnight accommodations available.

Additional Info Additional information available by fax, e-mail, or on website. Accepts inquiries by fax and e-mail. "Taos has a wonderful community of dedicated and talented writers who make S.O.M.O.S. workshops rigorous, supportive, and exciting." Also publishes *Chokecherries*, an annual anthology.

SAGE HILL FALL POETRY COLLOQUIUM

P.O. Box 1731, Saskatoon SK S7K 3S1 Canada. Phone/fax: (306)652-7395. E-mail: sage.hill@sasktel .net. Website: www.sagehillwriting.ca/fall.html. **Executive Director:** Steven Ross Smith. Established 1995. Annual event. 2004 dates: November 16-30. Location: St. Michael's Retreat, Lumsden, Saskatchewan.

Purpose/Features Offers "an intensive 2-week working and critiquing retreat designed to assist poets with manuscripts-in-progress. Each writer will have a significant publishing record and will wish to develop his/her craft and tune a manuscript. There will be ample time for writing, one-on-one critiques, and group meetings to discuss recent thinking in poetics." Eight writers will be selected from applications. Writers from anywhere may apply. 2004 instructors include Gary Shikatani (facilitator) and Louise Bernice Halfe (guest poet).

Costs/Accommodations 2004 cost: $1,095, including tuition, accommodations, and meals. Van transportation from airport can be arranged for a fee. Participants encouraged to provide own transportation.

Additional Info Additional information available for SASE or on website. Most recent application deadline: August 31, 2004.

SAGE HILL WRITING SUMMER EXPERIENCE

P.O. Box 1731, Saskatoon SK S7K 3S1 Canada. Phone/fax: (306)652-7395. E-mail: sage.hill@sasktel .net. Website: www.sagehillwriting.ca/summer.html. **Executive Director:** Steven Ross Smith. Established in 1990. Annual 10-day adult program usually held the end of July through the beginning of August. 2004 dates were July 26-August 4. Location: St. Michael's Retreat, Lumsden, Saskatchewan. Average attendance: varies according to specific workshop (usually 6-11 participants).

Purpose/Features Open to writers, 19 years of age and older, who are working in English. No geographic restrictions. The retreat/workshops are designed to "offer a special working and learning opportunity to writers at different stages of development. Top quality instruction, a low instructor-writer ratio, and the rural Saskatchewan setting offers conditions ideal for the pursuit of excellence in the arts of fiction and poetry." Offerings include a poetry workshop and poetry colloquium. 2004 poetry faculty included George Elliott Clarke, Phil Hall, and Sue Goyette.

Costs/Accommodations 2004 conference cost was $795, including instruction, accommodations, and meals, and all facilities. Van transportation from airport can be arranged for a fee. On-site accommodations offer individual rooms with a writing desk and washroom.

Additional Info Individual critiques offered. Writing sample required with application. 2004 application deadline was April 23. Additional information available for SASE or on website.

SAN DIEGO STATE UNIVERSITY WRITERS' CONFERENCE

5250 Campanile Dr., San Diego CA 92182-1920. (619)594-2517. Fax: (619)594-8566. E-mail: kicarter @mail.sdsu.edu. Website: www.ces.sdsu.edu. **Coordinator of Noncredit Community Education:** Kevin Carter. Established 1984. Annual 3-day event. 2004 dates were January 23-25. Location: Doubletree Hotel (Mission Valley), 7450 Hazard Center Dr., San Diego. Average attendance: 400.

Purpose/Features Open to writers of fiction, nonfiction, children's books, poetry, and screenwriting. "We have participants from across North America." Offers numerous workshops in fiction, nonfiction, general interest, children's books, screenwriting, magazine writing, and poetry. Speakers at last conference included Abby Zidle (assistant editor, Bantam Dell Publishing Group) and screenwriter Madeline DiMaggio. Other special features include networking lunch, editor/agent appointments and consultations, and novel-writing workshops.

Costs/Accommodations 2004 cost was $310-430 (through January 2), including one meal. Transportation to and from the event provided by the Doubletree Hotel. Information on overnight accommodations available. Accommodations include special rates at the Doubletree Hotel.

Additional Info See website for details. "Editors and agents give awards for favorite submissions." Information and registration form available on website. Accepts inquiries by phone, fax, or e-mail.

SANTA BARBARA WRITERS' CONFERENCE

P.O. Box 304, Carpinteria CA 93014. (805)684-2250. Fax: (805)684-7003. E-mail: online e-mail form. Website: www.sbwc.org. **Conference Director:** Barnaby Conrad. Established 1973. Annual event held the last week in June. 2004 dates were June 25-July 1. Location: Westmont College in Montecito. Average attendance: 350.

Purpose/Features Open to everyone. Covers all genres of writing. Workshops in poetry offered. 2004 poetry staff included Alison Luterman, Perie J. Longo, and Bill Wilkins.

Costs/Accommodations 2004 conference cost (including all workshops and lectures, 2 dinners, and room and board in residence halls), was $1,325 single, $1,025 double occupancy; $400 day students.

Additional Info Individual poetry critiques available; submit one ms of no more than 3,000 words in advance with SASE. Competitions with awards sponsored as part of conference. Additional information available for SASE or on website.

SEWANEE WRITERS' CONFERENCE

310 St. Luke's Hall, 735 University Ave., Sewanee TN 37383-1000. (931)598-1141. E-mail: cpeters@ sewanee.edu. Website: www.sewaneewriters.org. **Creative Writing Programs Manager:** Cheri B. Peters. Established 1990. Annual 12-day event held the last 2 weeks in July. Location: the University of the South ("dormitories for housing, Women's Center for public events, classrooms for workshops, Sewanee Inn for dining, etc."). Attendance: about 105.

Purpose/Features Open to poets, fiction writers, and playwrights who submit their work for review in a competitive admissions process. "Participants belong to a workshop devoted to constructive critique of members' manuscripts; in addition, each participant has a manuscript conference with a faculty member. Readings, craft lectures, panels, and Q&A sessions round out the formal offerings; numerous social functions offer opportunities for informal exchange and networking. Genre, rather than thematic, workshops are offered in each of the 3 areas." 2004 faculty members included Andrew Hudgins, Margot Livesey, Tim O'Brien, Alan Shapiro, Dave Smith, and Mark Strand. Other speakers include editors, agents, and additional writers.

Costs/Accommodations 2004 conference cost was $1,325, including room and board. Each year scholarships and fellowships based on merit are available on a competitive basis. "We provide free bus transportation from the Nashville airport on the opening day of the conference and back to the airport on the closing day.''

Additional Info A ms should be sent in advance after admission to the conference. Write for brochure and application forms; no SASE necessary. Accepts inquiries by e-mail.

THE SOUTHAMPTON COLLEGE WRITERS CONFERENCE

239 Montauk Hwy., Southampton NY 11968. (631)287-8175. Fax: (631)287-8253. E-mail: writers@s outhampton.liu.edu. Website: www.southampton.liu.edu/summer. **Summer Director:** Carla Caglioti. Established 1976. Annual 10-day event. 2004 dates were July 14-25. Location: Southampton College of Long Island University ''in the heart of the Hamptons, one of the most beautiful and culturally rich resorts in the country.'' Average attendance: 12/workshop.

Purpose/Features Open to new and established writers, graduate students, and upper-level undergraduate students. Conference covers poetry, fiction, short story, playwriting, and nonfiction. Offerings include a poetry workshop. 2004 faculty included Billy Collins, Carol Muske-Dukes, Frank McCourt, Bharati Mukkherjee, Clark Blaise, and Roger Rosenblatt.

Costs/Accommodations 2004 conference cost was $2,150 for workshop, room and board; $1,750 tuition only. Accommodations include ''Writers Residence Hall, single sex suites, shared room and lavatory. Some small singles available at extra cost on first-come basis.''

Additional Info ''Evening events will feature regular faculty and award-winning visiting authors. Participants will also enjoy a rich schedule of formal and informal social gatherings—author receptions, open mic nights, and special literary events. Early registration is encouraged.'' Brochure and registration form available by e-mail or on website. Accepts inquiries by fax and e-mail.

SPLIT ROCK ARTS PROGRAM

University of Minnesota, 360 Coffey Hall, 1420 Eckles Ave., St. Paul MN 55108-6084. (612)625-8100. Fax: (612)624-6210. E-mail: srap@cce.umn.edu. Website: www.cce.umn.edu/splitrockarts/ . **Program Associate:** Sherry Quan Lee. Established 1983. Annual summer series of weeklong workshops in creative writing, visual art, design, and creativity enhancement. 2004 dates were July 4-August 14. Location: ''Workshops are held on the University's Twin Cities Campus in the heart of one of the most culturally alive metropolitan areas in the country.'' Average attendance: 550.

Purpose/Features Open to ''anyone over 18 years old who has an interest in the visual and literary arts. The program is a popular destination for an eclectic audience of lifelong learners through its promise of intensive study with outstanding artists and writers from around the world.'' Areas of concentration include poetry, stories, memoirs, novels, and personal essays. 2004 program instructors included Sharon Doubiago, Ray Gonzalez, James Harms, Dorianne Laux, Pablo Medina, Joseph Millar, Hilda Raz, and more.

Costs/Accommodations 2004 tuition was $550. ''Scholarships are available to help motivated, committed writers and artists attend Split Rock workshops.'' Air-conditioned on-campus private accommodations are available; 2004 cost was $300.

Additional Info Online and printed catalogs available in late February. Registration also open in late February. Accepts inquiries by phone or e-mail.

STEAMBOAT SPRINGS WRITERS CONFERENCE

P.O. Box 774284, Steamboat Springs CO 80477. (970)879-8079. E-mail: sswriters@cs.com. Website: www.steamboatwriters.com. **Director:** Harriet Freiberger. Established 1982. Annual one-day event usually held mid-July. 2004 conference was July 17. Location: a ''renovated train station, the Depot is home of the Steamboat Springs Arts Council—friendly, relaxed atmosphere.'' Average attendance: 35-40 (registration limited).

Purpose/Features Open to anyone. Conference is ''designed for writers who have limited time.

Instructors vary from year to year, offering maximum instruction during a weekend at a nominal cost." 2004 featured science fiction writer Connie Willis and poet David Mason.

Costs/Accommodations 2004 cost was $45, including luncheon and all seminars. "A variety of lodgings available."

Additional Info Brochure and registration form available for SASE, by e-mail, or on website. Optional: Friday evening dinner (cost not included in registration fee); readings by participants (no cost).

TAOS SUMMER WRITERS' CONFERENCE

University of New Mexico, Dept. of English Language and Literature, MSC03 2170, 1 University of New Mexico, Albuquerque NM 87131-0001. (505)277-6248. Fax: (505)277-5573. E-mail: taosconf@unm.edu. Website: www.unm.edu/~taosconf. **Director:** Sharon Oard Warner. Established 1999. Annual 5-day (weeklong) and 2-day (weekend) workshops usually held mid-July. Location: Sagebrush Inn in Taos. Average attendance: 180 total; 100 places available in weekend, 170 places available in weeklong workshops. Class size limited to 12/class, usually smaller.

Purpose/Features Open to everyone, beginners to experienced. Minimum age is 18. Friendly, relaxed atmosphere with supportive staff and instructors. Offers both weekend and weeklong workshops in such areas as fiction, creative nonfiction, memoir, travel narrative, screenwriting, playwrighting, and poetry. 2004 workshop presenters included Lisa Chavez, Cindy Chinelly, Laurie Kutchins, Robert McDowell, and Levi Romero. Special features include evening events, open mic sessions, tours of the D.H. Lawrence Ranch, and a museum crawl.

Costs/Accommodations 2004 conference cost was $250 for weekend, $525 for weeklong sessions, $725 combo. Includes workshop registration and special events. Nearest airport is Albuquerque Sunport. Taos is about 2½ hours north of Albuquerque. Information on overnight accommodations available. Sagebrush Inn and Comfort Suites offer special rates.

Additional Info Offers 4 merit-based scholarships (2 for poetry, 2 for fiction) providing tuition remission for individual workshops at the conference. Applicants must be registered to apply. Brochure and registration form available by e-mail or on website. "Taos is a unique experience of a lifetime. The setting and scenery are spectacular; historical and natural beauty abound. Our previous attendees say they have been inspired by the place and by the friendly, personal attention of our instructors."

🌐 TÝ NEWYDD WRITERS' CENTRE

Taliesin Trust, Llanystumdwy, Cricieth, Gwynedd LL52 0LW Wales, United Kingdom. Phone: 0441766 522811. Fax: 0441766 523095. E-mail: tynewydd@dial.pipex.com. Website: www.tynewydd.org. **Director:** Sally Baker. Established 1990. Holds 4½-day courses throughout the year, Monday evening through Saturday morning. Location: Tý Newydd, The National Writers' Centre for Wales. Average attendance: 16/course maximum.

Purpose/Features Open to anyone over 16 years of age. Courses are designed to "promote the writing and understanding of literature by providing creative writing courses at all levels for all ages. Courses at Tý Newydd provide the opportunity of working intimately and informally with 2 professional writers." Courses specifically for poets of all levels of experience and ability are offered throughout the year.

Costs/Accommodations 2004 cost for a 4½-day course was £345 (inclusive), shared room; some weekend courses available, cost was £140 (inclusive), shared room. Transportation to and from Centre available if arranged at least a week in advance. Participants stay at Tý Newydd House in shared bedrooms or single bedrooms.

Additional Info Brochure and registration form available for SASE. Accepts inquiries by fax and e-mail.

UND WRITERS CONFERENCE

University of North Dakota, Dept. of English, Grand Forks ND 58202-7209. (701)777-3321. Fax: (701)777-2373. E-mail: james_mckenzie@und.nodak.edu. Website: www.undwritersconference.org. **Director:** James McKenzie. Established 1970. Annual 4- to 5-day event. 2003 dates were March 25-29. Location: The "UND student Memorial Union, with occasional events at other campus sites, especially the large Chester Fritz Auditorium or the North Dakota Museum of Art." Average attendance: 3,000-5,000. "Some individual events have as few as 20, some over 1,000."

Purpose/Features All events are free and open to the public. "The conference is really more of a festival, though it has been called a conference since its inception, with a history of inviting writers from all genres. The conference's purpose is public education, as well as a kind of bonus curriculum at the University. It is the region's premier intellectual and cultural event." 2004 guests included Elmaz Abinader, Tony Buba, Annie Dawid, Louise Erdrich, Albert Goldbarth, Marilynne Robinson, Mark Turcotte, and Larry Wolwode. "They read, participate in panels, and otherwise make themselves available in public and academic venues." 2004 was the 35th Anniversary Conference. Other special features include open mic student/public readings every morning, informal meetings with writers, autograph sessions, dinners, and receptions.

Additional Info Brochure available for SASE. Accepts inquiries by e-mail.

UNIVERSITY OF WISCONSIN-MADISON'S SCHOOL OF THE ARTS AT RHINELANDER

715 Lowell Center, 610 Langdon St., Madison WI 53703. (608)263-3494. Fax: (608)262-1694. E-mail: kberigan@dcs.wisc.edu. Website: www.dcs.wisc.edu/lsa/writing/index.html. **Administrative Coordinator:** Kathy Berigan. Established 1964. Annual 5-day event. 2004 session held July 26-30. Location: local junior high school. Average attendance: 300.

Purpose/Features Open to all levels and ages. Offerings include poetry workshops and related workshops in creativity.

Costs/Accommodations 2004 workshop cost ranged from $139-329; credit fees are additional. Information on overnight accommodations available.

Additional Info Catalog available in mid-March. Additional information available by phone, e-mail, or on website.

◪ VICTORIA SCHOOL OF WRITING

Suite 306-620 View St., Victoria BC V8W 1J6 Canada. (250)595-3000. E-mail: vicwrite@islandnet.com. Website: www.victoriaschoolofwriting.org/. **Director:** John Gould. Established 1996. Annual 5-day event. 2004 dates were July 18-23. Location: "Residential school in natural, park-like setting. Easy parking, access to university, downtown." Average attendance: 100.

Purpose/Features "A 3- to 10-page manuscript is required as part of the registration process, which is open to all. The general purpose of the workshop is to give hands-on assistance with better writing, working closely with established writers/instructors. We have workshops in fiction, poetry, and nonfiction; plus 3 other workshops which vary." Offerings include intensive 5-day workshops (16 hours of instruction and one-on-one consultation). 2004 poetry faculty included Marlene Cookshaw and Jay Ruzesky.

Costs/Accommodations 2003 workshop cost was $575 Canadian, including opening reception, 5 lunches, and final-night banquet. Other meal/accommodation packages available; see website. "For people who register with payment in full before May 1, the cost is $525 Canadian (2003)."

Additional Info Contest sponsored as part of conference. Competition receives approximately 200 entries. Brochure and registration form available through online request form. Accepts inquiries by e-mail.

WESLEYAN WRITERS CONFERENCE

Wesleyan University, Middletown CT 06457. (860)685-3604. Fax: (860)685-2441. E-mail: agreene@wesleyan.edu. Website: www.wesleyan.edu/writers. **Director:** Anne Greene. Established 1956. Annual 5-day event usually held the third week in June. 2004 dates were June 20-25. Location: the campus of Wesleyan University "in the hills overlooking the Connecticut River, a brief drive from the Connecticut shore. Wesleyan's outstanding library, poetry reading room, and other university facilities are open to participants." Average attendance: 100.

Purpose/Features "The conference welcomes everyone interested in the writer's craft. Participants are a diverse, international group, including both experienced and new writers. You may attend any of the seminars, including poetry, the novel, short story, fiction techniques, literary journalism, and memoir." Recent special sessions included "New Fiction," "The Writer's Life," "The Poetry of Engagement," "Writing Memoirs," "Writing About Social Issues," and "Publishing." Offerings include ms consultations and daily seminars. 2004 faculty in poetry included Elizabeth Willis, Peter Gizzi, and Maggie Nelson.

Costs/Accommodations 2003 cost, including meals, was $725 (day rate); $850 (boarding rate). "Wesleyan has scholarships for journalists, fiction writers, nonfiction writers, and poets. Request brochure for application information." Information on overnight accommodations available. "Conference participants may stay in university dormitories or off campus in local hotels."

Additional Info Individual ms critiques available. Registration for critiques must be made before the conference. Accepts inquiries by phone, fax, or e-mail.

WRITERS@WORK

Conference Registration, P.O. Box 540370, North Salt Lake UT 84054-0370. (801)292-9285. E-mail: contact@writersatwork.org. Website: www.writersatwork.org/conference.html. **Contact:** Lisa Peterson. Established 1985. Annual event. 2004 dates were June 22-26. Location: the beautiful Westminster College campus in Salt Lake City. Average attendance: limited to 15/workshop.

Purpose/Features Open to writers of all levels. Schedule includes workshops where students get feedback on mss; in-class writing sessions and craft discussions; and Blank Page workshops "where students can learn to spark their creativity when facing that blank page of paper." Offerings include week-long workshop, readings by faculty and other featured poets, and daily afternoon panels providing insight to the process of writing and submitting work. 2004 poetry faculty included Gregory Orr.

Costs/Accommodations 2004 cost was $395 for workshop, afternoon sessions (excluding "The Blank Page"), and 30-minute ms consultation. Six-hour Blank Page workshop cost was $125. Roundtable Box Lunch discussion also available for $15 (for full workshop participants only). Limited number of Westminster residency suites available for $150/week (must be 18 years of age). (A 3% fee added to all costs for online registration.) Information on other overnight accommodations available.

Additional Information Also offers the Writers@Work Fellowship Competition for fiction, nonfiction, and poetry. See website for complete details.

THE WRITERS' CENTER AT CHAUTAUQUA

Box 408, Chautauqua NY 14722. (216)295-1824. E-mail: peninah49@aol.com. Website: www.ciweb.org/writers.html. **Director:** Patricia Averbach. Established 1988. Annual season of 9 separate weeklong workshops held late June to late August. Participants may attend one week or more. Location: Victorian lakeside village in western New York; most Writers' Center programs offered in the CLSC Alumni Hall. Average attendance: no more than 12/workshop.

Purpose/Features Provides "a lively community of writers at all levels of development who cultivate the courage, craft, and vision necessary to grow as artists" under the tutelage of a nationally recognized poet-in-residence. Poetry workshops meet 2 hours daily, 8:30-10:30 a.m. 2004 workshop topics included revising/re-envisioning your poems, approaches to narrative poetry, the sound of meaning, and an intense study of sensual imagery. 2004 poetry faculty included Richard Foerster, David Chin, William Heyen, Carol Frost, Wendy Mnookin, Terrance Hayes, George Looney, Jim

Daniels, and Jeffrey Harrison. Other features include free Sunday afternoon readings by writers-in-residence, Creative Writing Symposiums on Wednesday evenings, and Brown Bag lunches and lectures every Friday at noon.

Costs/Accommodations 2004 tuition was $95/weeklong workshop. Participants responsible for gate fees ($245/week), housing, and meals. See website for accommodations options, which range from the Atheneum Hotel to local rooming houses and condos. Access best by car or plane to Jamestown, NY.

Additional Info Most workshop leaders offer private half hour conferences. Fee: $25, payable directly to leader. Additional information available for SASE, by e-mail, or on website.

Organizations

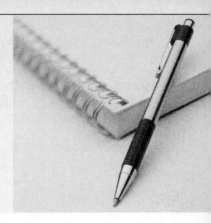

There are many organizations of value to poets. These groups may sponsor workshops and contests, stage readings, publish anthologies and chapbooks, or spread the word about publishing opportunities. A few provide economic assistance or legal advice. The best thing organizations offer, though, is a support system where poets can turn for a pep talk, a hard-nosed (but sympathetic) critique of a manuscript, or simply the comfort of talking and sharing with others who understand the challenges (and joys) of writing poetry.

Whether national, regional, or as local as your library or community center, each organization has something special to offer. The listings in this section reflect the membership opportunities available to poets with a variety of organizations. Some groups provide certain services to both members and nonmembers.

Certain symbols may appear at the beginning of some listings. The (▓) symbol indicates a newly established organization new to *Poet's Market*; the (▓) symbol indicates this organization did not appear in the 2004 edition; the (▓) symbol denotes a Canadian organization and the (▓) symbol one headquartered outside the U.S. and Canada.

Since some organizations are included in listings in the Publishers of Poetry, Contest & Awards, and Conferences & Workshops sections of this book, we've cross-referenced these listings under Additional Organizations at the end of this section. For further details about an organization associated with a market in this list, go to that market's page number.

To find out more about groups in your area (including those that may not be listed in *Poet's Market*), contact your YMCA, community center, local colleges and universities, public library, and bookstores (and don't forget newspapers and the Internet). If you can't find a group that suits your needs, consider starting one yourself. You might be surprised to find there are others in your locality who would welcome the encouragement, feedback, and moral support of a writer's group.

THE ACADEMY OF AMERICAN POETS; THE AMERICAN POET

588 Broadway, Suite 604, New York NY 10012-3210. (212)274-0343. Fax: (212)274-9427. E-mail: academy@poets.org. Website: www.poets.org. **Executive Director:** Tree Swenson. Established 1934. Robert Penn Warren wrote in *Introduction to Fifty Years of American Poetry*, an anthology published in 1984 containing one poem from each of the 126 Chancellors, Fellows, and Award Winners of the Academy: "What does the Academy do? According to its certificate of incorporation, its purpose is 'To encourage, stimulate and foster the production of American poetry. . . .' The responsibility for its activities lies with the Board of Directors and the Board of Chancellors, which has included, over the years, such figures as Louise Bogan, W.H. Auden, Witter Bynner, Randall Jarrell, Robert Lowell, Robinson Jeffers, Marianne Moore, James Merrill, Robert Fitzgerald, F.O. Matthiessen and Archibald MacLeish—certainly not members of the same poetic church." Awards The Walt Whitman Award; The James Laughlin Award; The Harold Morton Landon Translation Award; The Lenore Marshall Poetry Prize; The Raiziss/de Palchi Translation Award; and The Wallace Stevens Award. (For further details, see individual listings in the Contests & Awards section.) Also awards The Fellowship of the Academy of American Poets ($25,000 to honor distinguished poetic achievement, no applications accepted) and grants from the Greenwall Fund (to support the publication of first books of poetry by non-commercial presses). *American Poet* is an informative biannual periodical sent to those who contribute $35 or more/year. Membership: begins at $35/year "though those who join at higher levels receive complimentary copies of award books and other benefits. The Academy also sponsors National Poetry Month (April), an annual celebration of the richness and vitality of American poetry; the Online Poetry Classroom, an educational resource and online teaching community for high school teachers; and the Poetry Audio Archive, a collection of audio recordings of poetry readings. Additionally, the Academy maintains one of the liveliest and most comprehensive poetry sites on the Internet, at www.poets.org."

ADIRONDACK LAKES CENTER FOR THE ARTS

P.O. Box 205, Rte. 28, Blue Mountain Lake NY 12812. (518)352-7715. Fax: (518)352-7333. E-mail: alca@telenet.net. Website: www.adk-arts.org. **Program Director:** Darren Miller. Established in 1967 to promote "visual and performing arts through programs and services, to serve established professional and aspiring artists and the region through educational programs and activities of general interest." An independent, private, nonprofit educational organization open to everyone. Currently has 1,300 members. Levels of membership: individual, family, and business. Offerings include workshops for adults and children, reading performances, discussions, and lectures. Offers a "comfortable, cozy performance space—coffeehouse setting with tables, candles, etc." Computers available for members and artists. Publishes a triannual newsletter/schedule containing news, articles, photos, and a schedule of events. "All members are automatically sent the schedule and others may request a copy." Sponsors a few readings each year. "These are usually given by the instructor of our writing workshops. There is no set fee for membership, a gift of any size makes you a member." Members meet each July. Additional information available for SASE or on website.

THE AMERICAN POETS' CORNER

The Cathedral Church of St. John the Divine, Cathedral Heights, 1047 Amsterdam Ave., New York NY 10025. (212)316-7540. Website: www.stjohndivine.org/arts/ampoetscorn.html. Initiated in 1984 with memorials for Emily Dickinson, Walt Whitman, and Washington Irving. Similar in concept to the British Poets' Corner in Westminster Abbey, was established and dedicated to memorialize this country's greatest writers. A board of electors chooses one deceased author each year for inclusion in The American Poets' Corner; poets and novelists chosen in alternate years. The Cathedral is also home to the Muriel Rukeyser Poetry Wall, a public space for posting poems, which was dedicated in 1976 by Ms. Rukeyser and the Cathedral's Dean. Send poems for the Poetry Wall to the above address.

THE ASSOCIATION OF WRITERS AND WRITING PROGRAMS; THE WRITER'S CHRONICLE

Mailstop 1E3, George Mason University, Fairfax VA 22030. (703)993-4301. E-mail: awp@gmu.edu. Website: www.awpwriter.org. Established 1967. Offers a variety of services to the writing community, including information, job placement assistance (helps writers find jobs in teaching, editing, and other related fields), writing contests, literary arts advocacy, and forums. Annual individual membership: $59/year; $99/2 years; students who provide photocopy of valid student ID pay $37/year. Membership includes 6 issues of *The Writer's Chronicle* (containing information about grants and awards, publishing opportunities, fellowships, and writing programs) and 7 issues of *AWP Job List* (employment opportunity listings for writers). Other member benefits and opportunities available. *The Writer's Chronicle* is available by subscription only for $20/year (6 issues). Also sponsors the AWP Award Series for poetry, fiction, and creative nonfiction, which includes the Donald Hall Prize for Poetry (see separate listing in Contests & Awards section). Guidelines and additional information available on website.

⊠ AUTHORS LEAGUE FUND

31 E. 28th St., 10th Floor, New York NY 10016. **Administrator:** Sarah Heller. Makes interest-free loans to published authors and professional playwrights in need of temporary help because of illness or an emergency. No grants.

COLUMBINE STATE POETRY SOCIETY OF COLORADO

P.O. Box 6245, Westminster CO 80021. (303)431-6774. E-mail: anitajg5@aol.com. Website: http://members.aol.com/copoets. **Secretary/Treasurer:** Anita Jepson-Gilbert. Established in 1978 to promote the writing and appreciation of poetry throughout Colorado. Statewide organization open to anyone interested in poetry. Currently has 93 total members. Levels of membership: Members at Large, who do not participate in the local chapters but who belong to the National Federation of State Poetry Societies and to the Colorado Society; and local members, who belong to the national, state, and local chapters in Denver or Salida, Colorado. Offerings for the Denver Chapter include weekly workshops and monthly critiques. Sponsors contests, awards for students and adults. Sponsors the Annual Poets Fest where members and nationally known writers give readings and workshops that are open to the public. Membership dues: $12 state and national; $35 local, state, and national. Members meet weekly. Additional information available for SASE, by phone, e-mail, or on website.

GEORGIA POETRY SOCIETY; GEORGIA POETRY SOCIETY NEWSLETTER

P.O. Box 28337, Atlanta GA 30358. Website: www.georgiapoetrysociety.com. **President:** Rosemary Mauldin. Established 1979 to further the purposes of the National Federation of State Poetry Societies, Inc. (NFSPS) to secure fuller public recognition of the art of poetry, stimulate an appreciation of poetry, and enhance the writing and reading of poetry. Statewide organization open to any person who is in accord with the objectives listed above. Currently has over 300 total members. Levels of membership: Active, $20 ($35 family), fully eligible for all aspects of membership; Student, $10, does not vote or hold office, and must be full-time enrolled student through college level; Lifetime, same as Active but pays a one-time membership fee of $300, receives free anthologies each year, and pays no contest entry fees. Offerings include affiliation with NFSPS. At least one workshop is held annually. Contests are sponsored throughout the year, some for members only (complete guidelines available for SASE or on website). Accepts entry fees in U.S. dollars only. Publishes *Georgia Poetry Society Newsletter*, a quarterly, also available to nonmembers on request or on website. At each quarterly meeting (open to the public) members have an opportunity to read their own poems. Sponsors Poetry in the Schools project. Additional information available on website.

★ INTERNATIONAL WOMEN'S WRITING GUILD; NETWORK

P.O. Box 810, Gracie Station, New York NY 10028. (212)737-7536. Fax: (212)737-9469. E-mail: dirhahn@aol.com. Website: www.iwwg.com. **Founder/Executive Editor:** Hannelore Hahn. Established 1976 as "a network for the personal and professional empowerment of women through writing." The Guild publishes a bimonthly 32-page journal, *Network*, which includes members' achievements, contests, calendar, and publishing information. Other activities and benefits include annual national and regional events, such as the summer conference (see separate listing for The IWWG Summer Conference in the Conferences & Workshops section); "regional clusters" (independent regional groups); round robin ms exchanges; agent list; and group health insurance. Membership dues: $45/year (domestic and overseas). Additional information available by fax, e-mail, or on website.

◎ IOWA POETRY ASSOCIATION (Specialized: regional/Iowa residents); IPA NEWSLETTER; LYRICAL IOWA

2325 61st St., Des Moines IA 50322. (515)279-1106. **Editor:** Lucille Morgan Wilson. Established 1945 "to encourage and improve the quality of poetry written by Iowans of all ages." Statewide organization open to "anyone interested in poetry, with a residence or valid address in the state of Iowa." Currently has about 425 total members. Levels of membership: Regular and Patron ("same services, but patron members contribute to cost of running the association"). Offerings include "semiannual workshops to which a poem may be sent in advance for critique; annual contest—also open to nonmembers—with no entry fee; *IPA Newsletter*, published 5 or 6 times/year, including a quarterly national publication listing of contest opportunities; and an annual poetry anthology, *Lyrical Iowa*, containing prize-winning and high-ranking poems from contest entries, available for purchase at production cost plus postage. No requirement for purchase to ensure publication." Membership dues: $8/year (Regular); $15 or more/year (Patron). "Semiannual workshops are the only 'meetings' of the Association." Additional information (Iowa residents only) available for SASE.

THE KENTUCKY STATE POETRY SOCIETY; PEGASUS; KSPS NEWSLETTER

P.O. Box 157, West Paducah KY 42086. Website: http://windpub.com/ksps. **Contact:** Ellen Kelly, president. Established in 1966 to promote interest in writing poetry, improve skills in writing poetry, present poetry readings and poetry workshops, and publish poetry. Regional organization open to all. Currently has about 215 total members. Member of The National Federation of State Poetry Societies (NFSPS). Offerings include association with other poets, information on contests and poetry happenings across the state and nation; annual state and national contests; national and state annual conventions with workshops, selected speakers, and open poetry readings. Sponsors workshops, contests, awards. Membership includes the quarterly *KSPS Newsletter*. Also includes a quarterly newsletter, *Strophes*, of the NFSPS; and the KSPS journal, *Pegasus*, published 3 times yearly: a spring/summer and fall/winter issue which solicits good poetry for publication (need not be a member to submit), and a Prize Poems issue of 1st Place contest winners in over 40 categories. Members or nationally known writers give readings that are open to the public. Membership dues: students $5; adults $20; senior adults $15. Other categories: Life; Patron; Benefactor. Members meet annually. Membership information available for SASE and on website.

★ LIVING SKIES FESTIVAL OF WORDS; THE WORD

250 Thatcher Dr. E., Moose Jaw SK S6J 1L7 Canada. (306)691-0557. Fax: (306)693-2994. E-mail: word.festival@sasktel.net. Website: www.festivalofwords.com. **Operations Manager:** Lori Dean.

"Established in 1996, the purpose/philosophy of the organization is to celebrate the imaginative uses of languages. The Festival of Words is a registered nonprofit group of over 150 volunteers who present an enjoyable and stimulating celebration of the imaginative ways we use language. We operate year round bringing special events to Saskatchewan, holding open microphone coffeehouses for youth, and culminating in an annual summer festival in July which features activities centered around creative uses of language." National organization open to writers and readers. Currently has 285 total members. Offerings include "The Festival of Words programs with readings by poets, panel discussions, and workshops. In addition, poets attending get to share ideas, get acquainted, and conduct impromptu readings. The activities sponsored are held in the Moose Jaw Library/Art Museum complex, as well as in various venues around the city." Sponsors workshops as part of the Festival of Words. "We are also associated with *FreeLance* magazine, a publication of the Saskatchewan Writers' Guild. This publication features many useful articles dealing with poetry writing and writing in general." Also publishes *The Word*, a newsletter appearing approximately 6-7 times/year containing news of Festival events, fund-raising activities, profiles of members, reports from members. Available to nonmembers. First issue is free. Members and nationally known writers give readings that are open to the public. Sponsors open mic readings for members and for the public. Membership dues: $5, $15/3 years. Additional information available for SASE, by fax, e-mail, or on website.

MASSACHUSETTS STATE POETRY SOCIETY, INC.; BAY STATE ECHO; THE NATIONAL POETRY DAY CONTEST; THE GERTRUDE DOLE MEMORIAL CONTEST; AMBASSADOR OF POETRY AWARD; POET'S CHOICE CONTEST; THE NAOMI CHERKOFSKY MEMORIAL CONTEST; OF THEE I SING! CONTEST; ARTHUR (SKIP) POTTER MEMORIAL CONTEST

64 Harrison Ave., Lynn MA 01905. **President:** Jeanette C. Maes. Established 1959, dedicated to the writing and appreciation of poetry and promoting the art form. Statewide organization open to anyone with an interest in poetry. Currently has 200 total members. Offerings include critique groups. Sponsors workshops, contests including The National Poetry Day Contest, with prizes of $25, $15, and $10 (or higher) for each of 30 categories. Pays winners from other countries in U.S. currency. **Entry fee:** $8. **Deadline:** August 1. Competition receives about 2,000 entries/year. Also sponsors these contests: The Gertrude Dole Memorial Contest, with prizes of $25, $15, and $10. **Entry fee:** $3. **Deadline:** March 1. Ambassador of Poetry Award, with prizes of $50, $30, and $20. **Entry fee:** $3/poem. **Deadline:** April 15 annually. The Poet's Choice Contest, with prizes of $50, $25, and $15. **Entry fee:** $3/poem. **Deadline:** November 1. The Naomi Cherkofsky Memorial Contest, with prizes of $50, $30, and $20. **Entry fee:** $3/poem. **Deadline:** June 30. The "Of Thee I Sing!" Contest, with prizes of $50, $25, and $15. **Deadline:** January 15. Arthur (Skip) Potter Memorial Contest with prizes of $50, $30, and $20. **Entry fee:** $3. **Deadline:** December 15 annually. Does not accept entry fees in foreign currencies. Guidelines available for SASE. Publishes a yearly anthology of poetry and a yearly publication of student poetry contest winners. Also publishes *Bay State Echo*, a newsletter, 5 times/year. Members or nationally known writers give readings that are open to the public. Sponsors open mic readings for members and the public for National Poetry Day. Membership dues: $12/year. Members meet 5 times/year. Additional information available for SASE.

■ MOUNTAIN WRITERS SERIES; MOUNTAIN WRITERS SERIES NEWSLETTER

Mountain Writers Center, 3624 SE Milwaukie Ave., Portland OR 97202. (503)236-4854. Fax: (503)731-9735. E-mail: pdxmws@mountainwriters.org. Website: www.mountainwriters.org. **Associate Director:** Scott Bergler. Established 1973, "Mountain Writers Series is an independent nonprofit organization dedicated to supporting writers, audiences, and other sponsors by promoting literature and literacy through artistic and educational literary arts events in the Pacific Northwest." The Center is open to both members and nonmembers. Currently has about 150 total members.

Levels of membership: Contributing ($100), Supporting ($500), Patron ($1,000), Basic ($50), Student/Retired ($25), and Family ($75). "Members have access to our extensive poetry library, resource center, and space as well as discounts to most events. Members receive a triannual newsletter. Mountain Writers Series offers intensive one-day and 2-day workshops, weekend master classes, 5-week, 8-week, and 10-week courses about writing." Authors who have participated recently include David James Duncan, Linda Gregg, C.K. Williams, Li-Young Lee, Kim Addonizio, and David St. John. "The Mountain Writers Center is a 100-year-old Victorian house with plenty of comfortable gathering space, a reading room, visiting writers room, library, resource center, garden, and Mountain Writers Series offices." Sponsors conferences/workshops. Publishes the *Mountain Writers Center Newsletter*. Available to nonmembers for $12/year. Sponsors readings that are open to the public. Nationally and internationally known writers are sponsored by the Mountain Writers Series Northwest Regional Residencies Program (reading tours) and the campus readings program (Pulitzer Prize winners, Nobel Prize winners, MacArthur Fellows, etc.). Additional information available for SASE, by fax, e-mail, or on website.

NATIONAL FEDERATION OF STATE POETRY SOCIETIES, INC.; STROPHES

Website: www.nfsps.org. Established in 1959, "NFSPS is a nonprofit organization exclusively educational and literary. Its purpose is to recognize the importance of poetry with respect to national cultural heritage. It is dedicated solely to the furtherance of poetry on the national level and serves to unite poets in the bonds of fellowship and understanding." Currently has 7,000 total members. Any poetry group located in a state not already affiliated, but interested in affiliating, with NFSPS may contact the membership chairman. In a state where no valid group exists, help may also be obtained by individuals interested in organizing a poetry group for affiliation. **Membership Chair:** Sy Swann, 2736 Creekwood Lane, Ft. Worth TX 76123-1105. (817)292-8598 or (605)768-2127 (June and July). Fax: (817)531-6593. E-mail: JFS@flash.net. Most reputable state poetry societies are members of the National Federation and advertise their various poetry contests through the NFSPS quarterly newsletter, *Strophes*, sample copy available for SASE and $1, edited by Madelyn Eastlund, 310 South Adams St., Beverly Hills FL 34465 (e-mail: verdure@digitalusa.net). **Beware of organizations calling themselves state poetry societies (however named) that are not members of NFSPS,** as such labels are sometimes used by vanity schemes trying to sound respectable. NFSPS holds an annual 3-day convention in a different state each year with workshops, an awards banquet, and addresses by nationally known poets. Sponsors an annual 50-category national contest. (See separate listing for NFSPS College/University Level Poetry Awards, NFSPS Competitions, and the Stevens Manuscript Contest in the Contests & Awards section.) Additional information available by e-mail or on website.

NATIONAL WRITERS ASSOCIATION; AUTHORSHIP

3140 S. Peoria, #295, Aurora CO 80014. (303)841-0246. Fax: (303)841-2607. Website: www.nationalwriters.com. **Executive Director:** Sandy Whelchel. Established 1937. National organization with regional affiliations open to writers. Currently has 3,000 total members. Levels of membership: Professional, Regular, and Student. Hosts an annual Summer Conference where workshops, panels, etc., are available to all attendees, including poets. Also offers a yearly poetry writing contest with cash awards of $100, $50, and $25. Pays winners from other countries by US check. **Entry fee:** $10/poem. Accepts entry fees in foreign currencies. **Deadline:** October 1. Send SASE for judging sheet copies. Publishes *Authorship*, an annual magazine. Sample copy available for 9 × 12 envelope with $1.21 postage. Available to nonmembers for $18. Membership dues: Professional $85; others $65. Members meet monthly. Additional information available for SASE or by fax or e-mail. Contest forms available on website.

NEVADA POETRY SOCIETY

P.O. Box 7014, Reno NV 89510. (775)322-3619. **President:** Sam Wood. Established in 1976 to encourage the writing and critiquing of poetry. Statewide organization. Currently has 30 total members. Levels of membership: Active and Emeritus. Offerings include membership in the National Federation of State Poetry Societies (NFSPS), including their publication, *Strophes*; monthly challenges followed by critiquing of all new poems; lessons on types of poetry. Members of the society are occasionally called upon to read to organizations or in public meetings. Membership dues: $10 (includes membership in NFSPS). Members meet monthly. Additional information available for SASE. "We advise poets to enter their poems in contests before thinking about publication."

THE NORTH CAROLINA POETRY SOCIETY; BROCKMAN/CAMPBELL BOOK AWARD CONTEST

(Officers change annually; please contact us through our website at www.sleepycreek.net/poetry.) Established 1932 to "foster the writing of poetry; to bring together in meetings of mutual interest and fellowship the poets of North Carolina; to encourage the study, writing, and publication of poetry; and to develop a public taste for the reading and appreciation of poetry." Statewide and out-of-state organization open to "all interested persons." Currently has about 320 members. Levels of membership: Adult ($25/year) and Student ($10/year). NCPS conducts 6 general meetings and numerous statewide workshops each year, sponsors annual poetry contests with categories for adults and students (open to anyone, with small fee for nonmembers; December/January deadline; cash prizes), publishes the contest-winning poems in the annual book *Pinesong*; publishes a newsletter and supports other poetry activities. Also sponsors the annual Brockman/Campbell Book Award Contest for a book of poetry (over 20 pages) by a North Carolina poet (native-born or current resident for 3 years). Prize: $150 and a Revere-style bowl. **Entry fee:** $10 for nonmembers. **Deadline:** May 1. Competitions receive 300 entries/year. Most recent contest winners include Dannye Romine Powell, Betty Adcock, Robert Morgan, and Kathryn Byer. Nationally known writers give readings that are open to the public. Sponsors open mic readings that are open to the public. Additional information available on website.

OHIO POETRY ASSOCIATION; OHIO POETRY ASSOCIATION NEWSLETTER

Website: www.geocities.com/theohiopoetryassociation. **President:** Bob Casey, 129 Columbus Rd., Fredericktown OH 43019. (740)694-5013 or (740)398-0489 (cell). E-mail: bob@poeticaljourneys.com. Established in 1929 as Verse Writers' Guild of Ohio to promote the art of poetry and further the support of poets and others who support poetry. "We sponsor contests, seminars, readings, and publishing opportunities for poets of all ages and abilities throughout and beyond Ohio." Statewide membership with additional members in several other states, Japan, and England. Affiliated with the National Federation of State Poetry Societies (NFSPS). Organization open to "poets and writers of all ages and ability, as well as to nonwriting lovers of poetry in all its forms." Currently has about 215 total members. Levels of membership: Regular, Student (including college undergrads), Associate, Senior, Life, and Honorary. Member benefits include regular contests, meeting/workshop participation, assistance with writing projects, networking; twice-yearly magazine, *Common Threads*, 4 state newsletters, 4 NFSPS newsletters, membership in NFSPS, and contest information and lower entry fees for NFSPS contests. Members are automatically on the mailing list for Ohio Poetry Day contest guidelines. "We are cosponsors of Ohio Poetry Day. Individual chapters regularly host workshops and seminars. We publish *Common Threads*, a semiannual, saddle-bound anthology of poetry (open to submission from **members only**)." (See separate listing for *Common Threads* in the Publishers of Poetry section; for Ohio Poetry Day in the Contests & Awards section.) Publishes the *Ohio Poetry Association Newsletter*, a quarterly which includes general news, member accomplishments, publishing opportunities, contests, editorials, items of interest to poets and writers. Members and nationally known writers give readings that are open to the public (at quarterly meetings; public is invited). Sponsors open mic readings for members and the public ("though more likely at local levels"). Past readers have included Lisa Martinovic, David Shevin, Michael Bugeja, David Citino, and Danika Dinsmore. Membership dues: $12 senior; $15 regular; $5 associate and student. Members meet quarterly (September, December, March, May). Additional information available by e-mail or on website. "All poets need an organization to share info, critique, publish, sponsor contests, and just socialize. We do all that."

PITTSBURGH POETRY EXCHANGE

P.O. Box 4279, Pittsburgh PA 15203. (412)481-POEM. Website: http://trfn.clpgh.org/forpoems/. **Coordinator:** Michael Wurster. Established in 1974 as a community-based volunteer organization for local poets, it functions as a service organization and information exchange, conducting ongoing workshops, readings, forums, and other special events. No dues or fees. "Any monetary contributions are voluntary, often from outside sources. We've managed not to let our reach exceed our grasp." Currently has about 30 members. Reading programs are primarily committed to local and area poets, with honorariums of $25-85. Sponsors a minimum of 3 major events each year in addition to a monthly workshop; includes reading programs in conjunction with community arts festivals, such as the October South Side Poetry Smorgasbord—a series of readings throughout the evening at different shops (galleries, bookstores). Poets from out of town may contact the Exchange for assistance in setting up readings at bookstores to help sell their books. "We have been partnering with Autumn House Press in co-sponsoring events and bringing some of its authors to town." Members and nationally known poets give readings that are open to the public. Members meet on an ongoing basis, at least twice monthly. Additional information available for SASE or on website.

POETRY BOOK SOCIETY; THE PBS BULLETIN

Book House, 45 East Hill, London SW18 2QZ England. Phone: +44 (0)20 8870 8403. Fax: +44 (0)20 8870 0865. E-mail: info@poetrybooks.co.uk. Website: www.poetrybooks.co.uk. Established 1953 "to promote the best newly published contemporary poetry to as wide an audience as possible." A book club with several membership packages available. Full membership dues are £32 (UK) or £42 (overseas) and include 4 books of new poetry and *The PBS Bulletin*. The selectors also recommend other books of special merit, which are obtainable at a 25% discount. The Poetry Book Society is subsidized by the Arts Council of England. Please write, e-mail, or check website for details.

POETRY IN THE ARTS, INC.; ARDENT!; MOONCROSSED 33/33 (Specialized: zine for teens)

5801 Highland Pass, Austin TX 78731. (512)453-7920. E-mail: jljohns@poetryinarts.org. Website: www.poetryinarts.org. Established 1985. Publishes 2 online zines, *Ardent!* and *MoonCrossed 33/33* (a zine for teens), and an annual anthology, *MoonCrossed*. Sponsors a range of winner-take-all literary competitions and editor's choice awards. Pays a percentage of donor procedes. Additional information available on website.

POETRY SOCIETY OF AMERICA; CROSSROADS: THE JOURNAL OF THE POETRY SOCIETY OF AMERICA

15 Gramercy Park, New York NY 10003. (212)254-9628. Website: www.poetrysociety.org. **Executive Director:** Alice Quinn. Established 1910, the PSA is a national nonprofit organization for poets and lovers of poetry. Sponsors readings and lectures as well as programs such as Poetry in Motion; partners with The Favorite Poem Project. Levels of Membership: Student ($25), Member ($45), Supporter ($65), Sustainer ($100), Patron ($250), Benefactor ($500), and Angel ($1,000). All paid members receive *Crossroads: The Journal of the Poetry Society of American*; additional benefits available as membership levels increase. Free to join PSA mailing list for news of upcoming events.

PSA also sponsors a number of competitions for members and nonmembers (see separate listing for Poetry Society of America Awards in the Contests & Awards section).

POETS & WRITERS, INC.; POETS & WRITERS MAGAZINE; A DIRECTORY OF AMERICAN POETS AND FICTION WRITERS

72 Spring St., Suite 301, New York NY 10012. (212)226-3586. Website: www.pw.org. Poets & Writers, Inc., was established in 1970 to foster the development of poets and fiction writers and to promote communication through the literary community. The largest nonprofit literary organization in the nation, it offers information, support, publications, and exposure to writers at all stages in their careers. Sponsors programs such as the Writers Exchange Contest (emerging poets and fiction writers are introduced to literary communities outside their home states), Readings/Workshops, and publication in print and online of *A Directory of American Poets & Fiction Writers*. Publishes *Poets & Writers Magazine* (print), plus *Poets & Writers Online* offers topical information, the Speak-easy writers' message forum, links to over 1,000 websites of interest to writers, and a searchable database of over 4,800 listings from the *Directory*.

POETS' AND WRITERS' LEAGUE OF GREATER CLEVELAND; OHIO WRITER; POETRY: MIRROR OF THE ARTS; WRITERS AND THEIR FRIENDS

12200 Fairhill Rd., Townhouse 3-A, Cleveland OH 44120. (216)421-0403. E-mail: pwlgc@yahoo.com. Website: www.pwlgc.com. **Executive Director:** Darlene Montonaro. "Established in 1974 to foster a supportive community for poets and writers throughout Northern Ohio and to expand the audience for creative writing among the general public." Currently has 300 total members. The Literary Center offers classes, meeting space, and a retreat center for writers. PWLGC conducts a monthly workshop where poets can bring their work for discussion. Publishes a monthly calendar of literary events in NE Ohio; a bimonthly magazine, *Ohio Writer*, which includes articles on the writing life, news, markets, and an annual writing contest in all genres (see separate listing for Best of *Ohio Writer* Writing Contest in the Contests & Awards section); and 2 chapbooks/year featuring an anthology of work by area poets. "The PWLGC also sponsors a dramatic reading series, *Poetry: Mirror of the Arts*, which unites poetry and other art forms performed in cultural settings; and *Writers & Their Friends*, a biennial literary showcase of new writing (all genres), performed dramatically by area actors, media personalities, and performance poets." Membership dues: $25/year, includes subscription to *Ohio Writer Magazine* and discounts on services and facilities at the Literary Center. Additional information available for SASE, by e-mail, or on website.

✪ POETS THEATRE

20 Broadway, Hornell NY 14843. E-mail: larryandjoe@hotmail.com. Website: http://poetstheater.tripod.com. **Director:** Larry Arena. Established 1981. Sponsors reading series now in 23rd year. A featured poet, followed by open readings and refreshments. No admission; donations accepted. Meets 9 times/year. Additional information available by e-mail.

🌐 SCOTTISH POETRY LIBRARY; SCHOOL OF POETS; CRITICAL SERVICE; SCOTTISH POETRY INDEX

5 Crichton's Close, Edinburgh EH8 8DT Scotland. Phone: (0131)557-2876. Fax: (0131)557-8393. E-mail: inquiries@spl.org.uk. Website: www.spl.org.uk. **Director:** Robyn Marsack. **Librarian:** Iain Young. A reference information source and free lending library, also lends by post and has a travelling van service lending at schools, prisons, and community centres. Arranges poetry-writing workshops throughout Scotland, mainly for young people. The library has a web-based catalogue available at www.spl.org.uk allowing searches of all the library's resources, including books, magazines, and audio material, over 10,000 items of Scottish and international poetry. Need not be a member to borrow material; memberships available strictly to support the library's work. Levels

of membership: £20 individual, £10 concessionary, £30 organizational. Benefits include biannual newsletter, annual report, new publications listing, and use of members' room at the library. The School of Poets is open to anyone; "at meetings members divide into small groups in which each participant reads a poem which is then analyzed and discussed." Meetings normally take place at 7:30 p.m. on the second Tuesday of each month at the library. Also offers a Critical Service in which groups of up to 6 poems, not exceeding 200 lines in all, are given critical comment by members of the School: £15 for each critique (with SAE). Publishes the *Scottish Poetry Index*, a multi-volume indexing series, photocopied, spiral-bound, that indexes poetry and poetry-related material in selected Scottish literary magazines from 1952 to present; and an audio CD of contemporary Scottish poems, *The Jewel Box* (January 2000). Members and nationally known writers give readings that are open to the public. Additional information available by e-mail or on website.

SOUTH CAROLINA WRITERS WORKSHOP; THE QUILL

P.O. Box 7104, Columbia SC 29202. Website: www.scwriters.com. Established 1990 "to offer writers a wide range of opportunities to improve their writing, network with others, and gain practical 'how to' information about getting published." Statewide organization open to all writers. Currently has 280 total members. Offerings include "chapter meetings where members give readings and receive critiques; *The Quill*, SCWW's bimonthly newsletter which features writing competitions and publishing opportunities; an annual conference with registration discount for members; 2 free seminars each year; and an annual anthology featuring members' work." Chapters meet in libraries, bookstores, and public buildings. Sponsors 3-day annual conference at Myrtle Beach and literary competitions in poetry, fiction, and nonfiction. Members and nationally known writers give readings that are open to the public. Sponsors open mic reading for members and the public at the annual conference. Membership dues: $50/year Individual; $75/year Family. Chapters meet bimonthly or monthly. Additional information available on website.

UNIVERSITY OF ARIZONA POETRY CENTER

1600 East 1st St., Tucson AZ 85721. (520)626-3765. Fax: (520)621-5566. E-mail: poetry@u.arizona. edu. Website: www.poetrycenter.arizona.edu. **Executive Director:** Gail Browne. Established in 1960 "to maintain and cherish the spirit of poetry." Open to the public. The Center is a contemporary poetry archive and a nationally acclaimed poetry collection that includes over 50,000 items. Programs and services include a library with a noncirculating poetry collection and space for small classes; poetry-related meetings and activities; facilities, research support, and referral information about poetry and poets for local and national communities; the Visiting Poets and Writers Reading Series; educational outreach programs; a one-month summer residency offered each year to an emerging writer selected by jury; and poetry awards, readings, and special events for high school, undergraduate, and graduate students. Publishes a biannual newsletter. Additional information available for SASE, by fax, e-mail, or on website. "One can become a 'Friend of the Poetry Center' by making an annual contribution."

THE UNTERBERG POETRY CENTER OF THE 92ND STREET Y; "DISCOVERY"/THE NATION POETRY CONTEST

1395 Lexington Ave., New York NY 10128. (212)415-5759. E-mail: unterberg@92y.org. Website: www.92y.org. Offers annual series of readings by major literary figures (weekly readings late September through May), writing workshops, master classes in fiction and poetry, and lectures and literary seminars. Also co-sponsors the "Discovery"/*The Nation* Poetry Contest (see separate listing for *The Nation* in the Publishers of Poetry section). **Deadline:** January. Competition receives approximately 1,000 entries/year. Additional information available for SASE or on website.

✖ WEST VIRGINIA POETRY SOCIETY (WVPS); WV CROSSROADS; LAURELS

617 Boggs Run Rd., Bentwood WV 26031. (304)232-2512. E-mail: lebloomfield@webtv.net. Website: http://wvpoetrysociety.com. **President:** Larry Bloomfield. Established in 1950 to "encourage creative writing and an appreciation of poetry; to foster the establishment of active community chapters of WVPS." Has statewide, regional, and national membership; "not limited to WV residents." Affiliated with the National Federation of State Poetry Societies (NFSPS). Open to "all poets and lovers of poetry." Currently has about 225 total members. Levels of membership: local/community chapters of WVPS; state membership automatically includes membership in NFSPS (the National Society). Membership benefits include a quarterly newsletter (state and national); annual poetry contests; and state and national conventions "with outstanding presenters." Sponsors conferences/workshops and contests/awards. Publishes *WV Crossroads*, a quarterly newsletter which contains president's message; state, local, regional, and national news; and contest information. *WV Crossroads* editor is Betty Grugin (jbgrug@citynet.net). Members also receive *Laurels*, quarterly anthology, and the NFSPS newsletter, *Strophes*. Not available to nonmembers. Members and nationally known writers give readings that are open to the public. Sponsors open mic readings for members and the public. "Meetings and annual conventions may be attended by nonmembers. Many readings are in conjunction with special occasions such as National Poetry Month/Day." Membership dues: $15 annually. Local chapters of WVPS meet monthly and at the annual convention (state and national). "The West Virginia Poetry Society is an important link to the arts in WV. It maintains active involvement locally, regionally, and nationally in the realm of creative writing." Additional information available on website.

🌐 THE WORDSMITHS (CHRISTIAN POETRY GROUP); WORDSMITHS NEWSLETTER

493 Elgar Rd., Mont Albert North, Victoria 3129 Australia. Phone/fax: (03) 9890 5885. E-mail: pep@vicnet.net.au. Website: http://amani.org.au/poetica_christi. **Managing Editor:** Jean Sietzema-Dickson. Established 1987 to provide a meeting place where poets could share their work for critique and encouragement. "We have met monthly (except in January) since 1987 and began publishing in 1990. Our concern, as a group, has been to encourage the development of excellence in our writing and to speak out with a distinctive voice. **We do not accept unsolicited manuscripts for publication. Our brief is to publish *Australian* Christian poetry.**" Currently has 27 members, mostly from the greater Melbourne area. Offerings include monthly workshops, plus "we subscribe to several magazines, have occasional guest poets and a Quiet Day once a year when we meet from 10 a.m.-4 p.m. to spend some time together in directed silence and writing." Sponsors annual competition. Holds occasional public readings by invitation and open readings once a month. Through publishing arm, Poetica Christi Press, has published 4 group anthologies of the writing of the Wordsmiths and the works of 7 individual poets. Also sends out the *Wordsmiths Newsletter*, appearing quarterly and available to members for AUS $20/year as part of membership. Members meet monthly. Additional information and catalogues available for SASE, by fax, e-mail (to Janette Fernando at rogerfernando@aol.com), or on website.

THE WRITER'S CENTER; WRITER'S CAROUSEL

4508 Walsh St., Bethesda MD 20815. (301)654-8664. E-mail: postmaster@writer.org. Website: www.writer.org. **Director:** Karen Goodwin. Established 1976, "the Writer's Center is a literary crossroads designed to encourage the creation and distribution of contemporary literature. To support these goals we offer a host of interrelated programs and services including: workshops in all genres, a gallery of books and journals, readings and conferences, publications, desktop publishing center, meeting and workspace, and information and communication center. We welcome all genres and levels of skill as well as the other arts. These activities take place seven days a week in a 12,200 square foot facility, a former community center." Some 2,600 members support the center with annual donations. Publishes *Writer's Carousel*, a bimonthly magazine of articles and writing news.

Also publishes *Poet Lore*, America's oldest poetry journal. (See separate listing for *Poet Lore* in the Publishers of Poetry section). Membership dues: $40/year general, $25/year student, $50/year family. Additional information available by e-mail or on website.

WRITERS INFORMATION NETWORK; THE WIN-INFORMER

The Professional Association for Christian Writers, P.O. Box 11337, Bainbridge Island WA 98110. (206)842-9103. Fax: (206)842-0536. E-mail: WritersInfoNetwork@juno.com. Website: www.christi anwritersinfo.net. **Director:** Elaine Wright Colvin. Established in 1983 "to provide a much needed link between writers and editors/publishers of the religious publishing industry, to further professional development in writing and marketing skills of Christian writers, and to provide a meeting ground of encouragement and fellowship for persons engaged in writing and speaking." International organization open to anyone. Currently has 1,000 members. Offerings include market news, networking, editorial referrals, critiquing, and marketing/publishing assistance. Sponsors conferences and workshops around the country. Publishes a 32- to 36-page bimonthly magazine, *The Win-Informer* containing industry news and trends, writing advice, announcements, and book reviews. The magazine will also consider "writing-related poetry, up to 24 lines, with inspirational/ Christian thought or encouragement. We accept first rights only." Sample copy: $10. Membership dues: $40 U.S./one year, $75/2 years; $50/year in U.S. equivalent funds for Canada and foreign, $95/2 years. Additional information available for SASE.

THE WRITERS ROOM

740 Broadway, 12th Floor, New York NY 10003. (212)254-6995. Fax: (212)533-6059. E-mail: writers room@writersroom.org. Website: www.writersroom.org. Established in 1978 to provide a "home away from home" for any writer who needs a place to work. Open 24 hours a day, 7 days a week, for members only. Large loft provides desk space, Internet access, library, and storage. Supported by the National Endowment for the Arts, the New York State Council on the Arts, the New York City Department of Cultural Affairs, and private sector funding. Membership dues: vary from $300 to $500/half year, plus one-time initiation fee of $50. Call for application or download from website.

✪ ✇ THE WRITERS' UNION OF CANADA; THE WRITERS' UNION OF CANADA NEWSLETTER

40 Wellington St. E, 3rd Floor, Toronto ON M5E 1C7 Canada. (416)703-8982. Fax: (416)504-7656. E-mail: info@writersunion.ca. Website: www.writersunion.ca. Established 1973. Dedicated to advancing the status of Canadian writers by protecting the rights of published authors, defending the freedom to write and publish, and serving its members. National organization open to poets who have had a trade book published by a commercial or university press; must be a Canadian citizen or landed immigrant. Currently has over 1,400 total members. Offerings include contact with peers, contract advice/negotiation, grievance support, and electronic communication. Sponsors conferences/workshops. Sponsors Annual General Meeting, usually held in May, where members debate and determine Union policy, elect representatives, attend workshops, socialize, and renew friendships with their colleagues from across the country. Publishes *The Writers' Union of Canada Newsletter* 6 times/year. Membership dues: $180/year. Regional reps meet with members when possible. For writers not eligible for membership, the Union offers, for a fee, publications on publishing, contracts, and more; a Manuscript Evaluation Service for any level writer; Contract Services, including a Self-Help Package; and 3 annual writing competitions for developing writers. Additional information available for SASE (or SAE and IRC), by fax, e-mail, or on website.

W.B. YEATS SOCIETY OF NEW YORK; POET PASS BY!

National Arts Club, 15 Gramercy Park S, New York NY 10003. Website: www.YeatsSociety.org. **President:** Andrew McGowan. Established in 1990 "to promote the legacy of Irish poet and Nobel

Laureate William Butler Yeats through an annual program of lectures, readings, poetry competition, and special events.'' National organization open to anyone. Currently has 450 total members. Offerings include an annual poetry competition (see separate listing for W.B. Yeats Society Annual Poetry Competition in the Contests & Awards section) and *Poet Pass By!*, an annual ''slam'' of readings, songs, and music by poets, writers, entertainers. Also sponsors conferences/workshops. Each April, presents an all-day Saturday program, ''A Taste of the Yeats Summer School in Ireland.'' Nationally known writers give readings that are open to the public. Membership dues: $25/year; $15/year students. Members meet approximately monthly, September to June. Additional information available for SASE or on website; no inquiries by fax or e-mail.

ADDITIONAL ORGANIZATIONS

The following listings also contain information about organizations. Turn to the page numbers indicated for details about their offerings.

Resources

Additional Resources

This section lists publications and websites that focus on information about writing and publishing poetry. While there are few markets for your work, some of these resources do identify promising leads for your submission efforts. You'll also find advice on craft, poet interviews, reviews of books and chapbooks, events calendars, and other valuable material. For print publications, we provide contact information; however, you may also find these publications in your library or bookstore or be able to order them through your favorite online booksellers. (The ⊠ symbol at the beginning of a listing denotes a Canadian publication and the ⊕ symbol an international one.)

Internet resources for poetry continue to grow, and there are far too many to list here. However, among the following listings you'll find those key sites every poet should bookmark. Although we confirmed every address at press time, URLs can become outdated quickly; if a site comes up "not found," enter the name of the site in a search engine to check for a new address.

Some listings in the Publishers of Poetry, Contests & Awards, and Conferences & Workshops sections include references to informative print publications (such as handbooks and newsletters). We've cross-referenced these markets in the Additional Publications of Interest list at the end of this section. To find out more about a publication of interest associated with one of these markets, go to that market's page number.

THE ACADEMY OF AMERICAN POETS

Website: www.poets.org. One of the most comprehensive poetry websites on the Internet. (See separate listing for the Academy of American Poets in the Organizations section.)

ALIEN FLOWER

Website: www.alienflower.org. An interactive medium for poets to share ideas about poetry and its place in society; includes advice, articles, exercises, and offers a free e-mail newsletter.

ASK JEEVES

Website: www.ask.com. Internet search engine.

ASSOCIATION OF WRITERS AND WRITING PROGRAMS (AWP)

Website: www.awpwriter.org. Home site for AWP, offers membership information, AWP contest guidelines, articles and advice, and career links for writing and publishing. (See separate listing in the Organizations section.)

🌐 THE BBR DIRECTORY

P.O. Box 625, Sheffield S1 3GY United Kingdom. E-mail: directory@bbr-online.com. Website: www .bbr-online.com/directory. **Editor/Publisher:** Chris Reed. Established 1996. *The BBR Directory* "is a monthly e-mail newssheet for everyone involved with or interested in the small press. Providing accurate and up-to-date information about what's happening in independent publishing all over the world, *The BBR Directory* is the ideal starting point for exploring the small press and for keeping tabs on who exactly is publishing what, and when." For a free subscription, send a blank e-mail to directory-subs-on@bbr-online.com or sign up through website. Website includes resources for writers, message board, and archived back issues of *The BBR Directory*.

CANADIAN POSTAL SERVICE

Website: www.canadapost.ca. Provides all necessary information for mailing to, from, and within Canada. Includes downloadable *Canada Postal Guide©*.

CAVE CANEM

Website: www.cavecanempoets.org. Site for the Cave Canem group offers "A Home for Black Poetry" on the Internet, including information about Cave Canem programs, poems, and links. (See separate listings in the Contests & Awards, Conferences & Workshops, and Organizations sections.)

DOGPILE

Website: www.dogpile.com. Uses metasearch technology to "search the search engines" and return results from Google, Yahoo, AltaVista, Ask Jeeves, About, LookSmart, Overture, Teoma, FindWhat, and others.

DUSTBOOKS; INTERNATIONAL DIRECTORY OF LITTLE MAGAZINES & SMALL PRESSES; DIRECTORY OF POETRY PUBLISHERS; SMALL PRESS REVIEW

P.O. Box 100, Paradise CA 95967. (800)477-6110. Fax: (530)877-0222. E-mail: dustbooks@dcsi.net. Website www.dustbooks.com. Dustbooks publishes a number of books useful to writers. Send SASE for catalog or check website. Regular publications include *The International Directory of Little Magazines & Small Presses*, published annually with 900 pages of magazine and book publisher listings, plus subject and regional indexes. *Directory of Poetry Publishers* has similar information for over 2,000 poetry markets. *Small Press Review* is a bimonthly magazine carrying updates of listings in *The International Directory*, small press needs, news, announcements, and reviews.

ELECTRONIC POETRY CENTER
Website: http://epc.buffalo.edu. Resource offering links to magazines, poets, and sites of interest on the Internet, including indexes to blogs and sound poetry.

FAVORITE POEM PROJECT
Website: www.favoritepoem.org. Site for the project founded by Robert Pinsky to celebrate, document, and promote poetry's role in American lives.

FIRST DRAFT: THE JOURNAL OF THE ALABAMA WRITERS' FORUM; THE ALABAMA WRITERS' FORUM
Alabama State Council on the Arts, 201 Monroe St., Montgomery AL 36130-1800. (334)242-4076 ext. 233. Fax: (334)240-3269. E-mail: awfl@arts.state.al.us. Website: www.writersforum.org. **Editor:** Jay Lamar. Established 1992. Appears 2 times/year with news, features, book reviews, and interviews relating to Alabama writers. "We do not publish original poetry or fiction." *First Draft* lists markets for poetry, contests/awards, and workshops. Accepts advertising for publishers, conferences, workshops (request ad rates from awfl@arts.state.al.us). Sponsored by the Alabama Writers' Forum. Reviews books of poetry, fiction, and nonfiction by "Alabama writers or from Alabama presses." Subscription: $35/year, includes membership. Sample: $5.

GOOGLE
Website: www.google.com. Internet search engine.

HAIKU SOCIETY OF AMERICA
Website: www.hsa-haiku.org. Includes membership information, contest guidelines, announcements, links, and more.

INTERNAL REVENUE SERVICE (IRS)
Website: www.irs.ustreas.gov. Includes federal tax information, resources, publications, and forms for individuals and businesses.

THE LIBRARY OF CONGRESS
Website: http://lcweb.loc.gov. Put "poetry" in the site search engine and retrieve over 2,300 results of interest, including the site for the U.S. Poet Laureate and the Poetry 180 Project to promote poetry to high school students.

⊕ MILLENNIUM ARTS MAGAZINE
P.O. Box 21, Liverpool L19 3RX England. Phone: 0151 427 8297. Fax: 0151 291 6280. E-mail: mamuk@webspawner.com. Website: www.webspawner.com/users/mamuk/index.html. Established 1995. Primarily an art-associated News-'n'-Information website. Includes a literary arts section with readings, competitions, and other information.

NATIONAL FEDERATION OF STATE POETRY SOCIETIES (NFSPS)
Website: www.nfsps.org. Site for this national umbrella organization includes NFSPS contest information, contact information and links to affiliated state poetry societies, and an online version of the quarterly newsletter, *Strophes*. (See separate NFSPS listings in the Contests & Awards and Organizations sections.)

PARA PUBLISHING

Box 8206-240, Santa Barbara CA 93118-8206. (800)727-2782, Fax: (805)968-1379. E-mail: info@ParaPublishing.com. Website: www.parapublishing.com. Website offers hundreds of pages of valuable book writing, publishing, and promoting information. Author/publisher Dan Poynter's how-to titles on book publishing and self-publishing include *The Self-Publishing Manual: How to Write, Print and Sell Your Own Book* as well as *Canadian Book Publishing*. Also available are Special Reports on various aspects of book production, promotion, marketing, and distribution. Ordering information available on webiste.

PERSONAL POEMS

% F. Jean Hesse, 102 Rockford Dr., Athens GA 30605. (706)208-0420. F. Jean Hesse started a business in 1980 writing poems for individuals for a fee (for greetings, special occasions, etc.). Others started similar businesses after she began instructing them in the process, especially through a cassette tape training program and other materials. Send SASE for free brochure or $20 plus $5.50 p&h for training manual, *How to Make Your Poems Pay*. Has also published a 400-page paperback book, *For His Good Pleasure*, a one-year collection of poems for daily reading "to comfort and inspire." Available for $12.95 plus $3.50 p&h. Make checks payable to F. Jean Hesse.

POETIC VOICES

http://poeticvoices.com. Monthly online poetry journal includes poems, features, news, and advice.

POETRY DAILY

Website: www.poems.com. A new poem every day, plus news, reviews, and special features.

POETRY FLASH; BAY AREA BOOK REVIEWERS ASSOCIATION (BABRA)

1450 Fourth St. #4, Berkeley CA 94710. (510)525-5476. Fax: (510)525-6752. E-mail: info@poetryflash.org (NOTE: **does not respond by e-mail to poetry submissions**). Website: www.poetryflash.org. **Editor:** Joyce Jenkins. Established 1972. Appears 6 times/year. "*Poetry Flash*, a Poetry Review & Literary Calendar for the West, publishes reviews, interviews, essays, and information for writers. Poems, as well as announcements about submitting to other publications, appear in each issue." *Poetry Flash* focuses on poetry, but its comprehensive literary calendar also includes events celebrating all forms of creative writing, with a focus on the West Coast, particularly California. *Poetry Flash* also sponsors a weekly poetry reading series at Cody's Books in Berkeley and sponsors the Bay Area Book Reviewers Association Awards. Subscription $16/6 issues.

POETRY SOCIETY OF AMERICA

Website: www.poetrysociety.org. Includes membership and award information, poet resources, and more. (See separate listing in the Organizations section.)

POETRY TODAY ONLINE

Website: www.poetrytodayonline.com. Includes how-to and motivational articles, forums, links, and more.

POETS & WRITERS ONLINE

Website: www.pw.org. Includes searchable *A Directory of American Poets & Fiction Writers*, informational resources, and more. (See separate listing for Poets & Writers, Inc. in the Organizations section.)

THE POETS' CORNER
Website: www.theotherpages.org/poems. Text site that includes 6,700 works by 780 poets, plus poet bios and photos, indexes, and The Daily Poetry Break.

PUSHCART PRESS
Box 380, Wainscott NY 11975. (631)324-9300. Website: www.wwnorton.com/trade/affiliates.htm. **Editor:** Bill Henderson. The Pushcart Press, an affiliate publisher of W.W. Norton & Co., publishes the acclaimed annual *Pushcart Prize* anthology, Pushcart Editor's Book Award, and other quality literature, both fiction and nonfiction. "The most-honored literary series in America, *The Pushcart Prize* has been named a notable book of the year by the *New York Times* and hailed with Pushcart Press as 'among the most influential in the development of the American book business' over the past century." *The Pushcart Prize* is available for $35 (cloth) or $17 (paperback).

RAIN TAXI REVIEW OF BOOKS
P.O. Box 3840, Minneapolis MN 55403. E-mail: info@raintaxi.com. Website: www.raintaxi.com. Established 1996. *Rain Taxi Review of Books* is a quarterly publication produced in both print and online versions (the latter with completely different material). The print version is available by subscription and free in bookstores nationwide. "We publish reviews of books that are overlooked by mainstream media, and each issue includes several pages of poetry reviews, as well as author interviews and original essays." Poets and publishers may send books for review consideration. Subscription: $12 domestic, $24 international. Sample: $4. "We DO NOT publish original poetry. Please don't send poems."

TANKA SOCIETY OF AMERICA
Website: http://hometown.aol.com/tsapoetry/TankaSocietyofAmerica-index.html. Offers membership information, contest guidelines and winning poems, definitions and discussion of tanka.

U.S. COPYRIGHT OFFICE
Website: www.loc.gov/copyright. Offers copyright basics and FAQ, records search, directions for registering work for copyright, and other information.

U.S. POSTAL SERVICE
Website: www.usps.com. Extensive site includes postage rates, mail preparation and mailing directions, domestic and foreign shipping options, and much more.

WEB DEL SOL
Website: http://webdelsol.com. Must-see site for anyone interested in contemporary literary arts. "*Web del Sol* cannot be classified as a literary publication or an Internet portal in the traditional sense (though it contains both subsets), but rather as a literary arts new media complex which pushes the envelope of both definitions."

WINNING WRITERS.COM
Website: www.winningwriters.com. Resources for poets and writers, including *Poetry Contest Insider* (quarterly, published online, subscription required), links, manuscript tips, "bad contest" warning signs, Winning Writers contests, and free newsletter. (See separate listings in Contests & Awards section.)

WORD WORKS NETWORK (WoW)
Website: www.wow-schools.net. With its mission to "restore to prominence the art of writing in American high school," WoW's site offers resources, links, chat lounge, advice on starting high school literary journals, with links to exceptional journals.

WORDWRIGHTS CANADA

P.O. Box 456, Station O, Toronto ON M4A 2P1 Canada. E-mail: wordwrights@sympatico.ca. Website: www3.sympatico.ca/susanio/WWC.html. Established 1985. **Director:** Susan Ioannou. Publishes *A Magical Clockwork: The Art of Writing the Poem* (160 pages, $16.95). Also offers an online course in poetry writing.

WRITER BEWARE

Website: www.sfwa.org/beware. Science Fiction and Fantasy Writers of American, Inc. offers a page on their website devoted to scam alerts, common publishing practices that take advantage of writers, case studies, and a section on legal recourse for writers.

WRITER'S DIGEST BOOKS

4700 East Galbraith Rd., Cincinnati OH 45236. (800)448-0915. Website www.writersdigest.com. Writer's Digest Books publishes a remarkable array of books useful to all types of writers. In addition to *Poet's Market*, books for poets include *You Can Write Poetry* by Jeff Mock, *Creating Poetry* by John Drury, *The Art and Craft of Poetry* by Michael J. Bugeja, *The Writer's Digest Writing Clinic* (which includes a poetry segment), and *The Pocket Muse* by Monica Wood (stimulating inspiration for all writers, including poets). Call or write for a complete catalog or log on to www.writersdigest.com, which includes individual web pages for fiction, nonfiction, children's, poetry, personal writing, and scriptwriting, plus markets, tips, and special content. **PLEASE NOTE:** *Writer's Digest Books does not publish poetry.*

YAHOO

Website: www.yahoo.com. Internet search engine.

ADDITIONAL PUBLICATIONS

The following listings also contain information about instructive publications for poets. Turn to the page numbers indicated for details about their offerings.

Poets in Education

hether known as PITS (Poets in the Schools), WITS (Writers in the Schools), or similar names, programs exist nationwide that coordinate residencies, classroom visits, and other opportunities for experienced poets to teach students poetry writing. Many state arts agencies include such "arts in education" programs in their activities (see Grants on page 435 for contact information). Another good source is the National Assembly of State Arts Agencies (see below), which includes a directory of contact names and addresses for arts education programs state-by-state. The following list is a mere sampling of programs and organizations that link poets with schools. Contact them for information about their requirements (some may insist poets have a strong publication history, others may prefer classroom experience) or check their websites where available.

The Academy of American Poets, 588 Broadway, Suite 604, New York NY 10012-3210. (212)274-0343. E-mail: academy@poets.org. Website: www.poets.org (includes links to state arts in education programs).

Arkansas Writers in the Schools, WITS Director, 333 Kimpel Hall, University of Arkansas, Fayetteville AR 72701. (479)575-4301. E-mail: wits@cavern.uark.edu. Website: www.uark.edu/~wits.

California Poets in the Schools, 1333 Balboa St., Suite 3, San Francisco CA 94118. (415)221-4201. E-mail: info@cpits.org. Website: www.cpits.org.

e-poets.network, a collective online cultural center that promotes education through video-conferencing (i.e., "distance learning"); also includes the *Voces y Lugares* project. Website: http://learning.e-poets.net (includes online contact form).

Idaho Writers in the Schools, Log Cabin Literary Center, 801 S. Capitol Blvd., Suite 100, Boise ID 83702. (208)331-8000. Website: www.logcablit.org/wits.html.

Indiana Writers in the Schools, University of Evansville, Dept. of English, 1800 Lincoln Ave., Evansville IN 47722. Website: http://english.evansville.edu.

Michigan Creative Writers in the Schools, ArtServe Michigan, 17515 W. Nine Mile Rd., Suite 1025, Southfield MI 48075. (248)557-8288. E-mail: education@artservemichigan.org. Website: www.artservemichigan.org.

National Assembly of State Arts Agencies, 1029 Vermont Ave. NW, 2nd Floor, Washington DC 20005. (202)347-6352. E-mail: nasaa@nasaa-arts.org. Website: www.nasaa-arts.org.

PEN in the Classroom (PITC), Pen Center USA West, 672 S. Lafayette Park Place, #41, Los Angeles CA 90057. (213)365-8500. Website: www.penusa.org/pitc.html.

"Pick-a-Poet," The Humanities Project, Arlington Public Schools, 1426 N. Quincy St., Arlington VA 22207. (703)228-6299. Website: www.humanitiesproject.org.

Potato Hill Poetry, 6 Pleasant St. N. #2, Natick MA 01760. (508)652-9908 or (888)576-3879. E-mail: info@potatohill.com. Website: www.potatohill.com (includes online contact form).

Teachers & Writers Collaborative, 5 Union Square W., New York NY 10003-3306. (212)691-6590 or (888)266-5789. E-mail: info@twc.org. Website: www.twc.org.

Texas Writers in the Schools, 1523 W. Main, Houston TX 77006. (713)523-3877. E-mail: mail@writersintheschools.org. Website: www.writersintheschools.org.

Writers & Artists in the Schools, COMPAS, 304 Landmark Center, 75 W. Fifth St., St. Paul MN 55102. (651)292-3249. E-mail: dei@compas.org. Website: www.compas.org.

Glossary of Listing Terms

A3, A4, A5. Metric equivalents of $11^3/_4 \times 16^1/_2$, $8^1/_4 \times 11^3/_4$, and $5^7/_8 \times 8^1/_4$ respectively.

Anthology. A collection of selected writings by various authors.

Attachment. A computer file electronically "attached" to an e-mail message.

b&w. Black & white (photo or illustration).

Bio. A short biographical statement often requested with a submission.

Camera-ready. Poems ready for copy camera platemaking; camera-ready poems usually appear in print exactly as submitted.

Chapbook. A small book of about 24-50 pages.

Circulation. The number of subscribers to a magazine/journal.

CLMP. Council of Literary Magazines and Presses; service organization for independent publishers of fiction, poetry, and prose.

Contributor's copy. Copy of book or magazine containing a poet's work, sometimes given as payment.

Cover letter. Brief introductory letter accompanying a poetry submission.

Coverstock. Heavier paper used as the cover for a publication.

Digest-sized. About $5^1/_2 \times 8^1/_2$, the size of a folded sheet of conventional printer paper.

Download. To "copy" a file, such as a registration form, from a website.

Electronic magazine. See *online magazine*.

E-mail. Mail sent electronically using computer and modem or similar means.

Euro. Currency unit for the 11 member countries of the European Union; designated by EUR or the € symbol.

FAQ. Frequently Asked Questions.

Font. The style/design of type used in a publication; typeface.

Galleys. First typeset version of a poem, magazine, or book/chapbook.

GLBT. Gay/lesbian/bisexual/transgender (as in "GLBT themes").

Honorarium. A token payment for published work.

Internet. A worldwide network of computers offering access to a variety of electronic resources.

IRC. International Reply Coupon; a publisher can exchange IRCs for postage to return a manuscript to another country.

JPEG. Short for *Joint Photographic Experts Group*; an image compression format that allows digital images to be stored in relatively small files for electronic mailing and viewing on the Internet.

Magazine-sized. About $8^1/_2 \times 11$, the size of an unfolded sheet of conventional printer paper.

ms. Manuscript.

mss. Manuscripts.

Multi-book review. Several books by the same author or by several authors reviewed in one piece.

Offset-printed. Printing method in which ink is transferred from an image-bearing plate to a "blanket" and then from blanket to paper.

Online magazine. Publication circulated through the Internet or e-mail.

p&h. Postage & handling.

p&p. Postage & packing.

"Pays in copies." See *contributor's copy*.

PDF. Short for *Portable Document Format*, developed by Adobe Systems, that captures all elements of a printed document as an electronic image, allowing it to be sent by e-mail, viewed online, and printed in its original format.

Perfect-bound. Publication with glued, flat spine; also called "flat-spined."

POD. See *print-on-demand*.

Press run. The total number of copies of a publication printed at one time.

Previously published. Work that has appeared before in print, in any form, for public consumption.

Print-on-demand. Publishing method that allows copies of books to be published as they're requested, rather than all at once in a single press run.

Publishing credits. A poet's magazine publications and book/chapbook titles.

Query letter. Letter written to an editor to raise interest in a proposed project.

Reading fee. A monetary amount charged by an editor or publisher to consider a poetry submission without any obligation to accept the work.

Rights. A poet's legal property interest in his/her literary work; an editor or publisher may acquire certain rights from the poet to reproduce that work.

ROW. "Rest of world."

Royalties. A percentage of the retail price paid to the author for each copy of a book sold.

Saddle-stapled. A publication folded, then stapled along that fold; also called "saddle-stitched."

SAE. Self-addressed envelope.

SASE. Self-addressed, stamped envelope.

SASP. Self-addressed, stamped postcard.

Simultaneous submission. Submission of the same manuscript to more than one publisher at the same time.

Subsidy press. Publisher who requires the poet to pay all costs, including typesetting, production, and printing; sometimes called a "vanity publisher."

Tabloid-sized. 11×15 or larger, the size of an ordinary newspaper folded and turned sideways.

Text file. A file containing only textual characters (i.e., no graphics or special formats).

Unsolicited manuscript. A manuscript an editor did not ask specifically to receive.

Website. A specific address on the Internet that provides access to a set of documents (or "pages").

Glossary of Poetry Terms

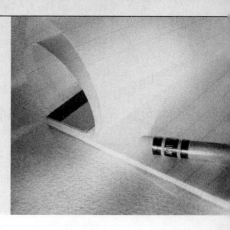

This glossary is provided as a quick-reference only, briefly covering poetic styles and terms that may turn up in articles and listings in *Poet's Market*. For a full understanding of the terms, forms, and styles listed here, as well as common literary terms not included, consult a solid textbook or handbook (ask your librarian or bookseller for recommendations).

Abstract poem: conveys emotion through sound, textures, and rhythm and rhyme rather than through the meanings of words.

Acrostic: initial letters of each line, read downward, form a word, phrase, or sentence.

Alliteration: close repetition of consonant sounds, especially initial consonant sounds. (Also known as *consonance*.)

Alphabet poem: arranges lines alphabetically according to initial letter.

American cinquain: derived from Japanese haiku and tanka by Adelaide Crapsey; counted syllabic poem of 5 lines of 2-4-6-8-2 syllables, frequently in iambic feet.

Anapest: foot consisting of 2 unstressed syllables followed by a stress (- - ′).

Assonance: close repetition of vowel sounds.

Avant-garde: work at the forefront—cutting edge, unconventional, risk-taking.

Ballad: narrative poem often in ballad stanza (4-line stanza with 4 stresses in lines 1 and 3, 3 stresses in lines 2 and 4, which also rhyme).

Ballade: 3 stanzas rhymed *ababbcbC* (*C* indicates a refrain) with envoi rhymed *bcbC*.

Beat poetry: anti-academic school of poetry born in '50s San Francisco; fast-paced free verse resembling jazz.

Blank verse: unrhymed iambic pentameter.

Caesura: a deliberate rhetorical, grammatical, or rhythmic pause, break, cut, turn, division, or pivot in poetry.

Chant: poem in which one or more lines are repeated over and over.

Cinquain: any 5-line poem or stanza; also called "quintain" or "quintet." (See also *American cinquain*.)

Concrete poetry: see *emblematic poem*.

Confessional poetry: work that uses personal and private details from the poet's own life.

Consonance: see *assonance*.

Couplet: stanza of 2 lines; pair of rhymed lines.

Dactyl: foot consisting of a stress followed by 2 unstressed syllables (′ - -).

Didactic poetry: poetry written with the intention to instruct.

Eclectic: open to a variety of poetic styles (as in "eclectic taste").

Ekphrastic poem: verbally presents something originally represented in visual art, though more than mere description.

Elegy: lament in verse for someone who has died, or a reflection on the tragic nature of life.

Emblematic poem: words or letters arranged to imitate a shape, often the subject of the poem.

Enjambment: continuation of sense and rhythmic movement from one line to the next; also called a "run-on" line.

Envoi: a brief ending (usually to a ballade or sestina) no more than 4 lines long; summary.

Epic poetry: long narrative poem telling a story central to a society, culture, or nation.

Epigram: short, witty, satirical poem or saying written to be remembered easily, like a punchline.

Epigraph: a short verse, note, or quotation that appears at the beginning of a poem or section; usually presents an idea or theme on which the poem elaborates, or contributes background information not reflected in the poem itself.

Epitaph: brief verse commemorating a person/group of people who died.

Experimental poetry: work that challenges conventional ideas of poetry by exploring new techniques, form, language, and visual presentation.

Foot: unit of measure in a metrical line of poetry.

Found poem: text lifted from a non-poetic source such as an ad and presented as a poem.

Free verse: unmetrical verse (lines not counted for accents, syllables, etc.).

Ghazal: Persian poetic form of 5-15 unconnected, independent couplets; associative jumps may be made from couplet to couplet.

Greeting card poetry: resembles verses in greeting cards; sing-song meter and rhyme.

Haibun: originally, a Japanese form in which elliptical, often autobiographical prose is interspersed with haiku.

Haikai no renga: see *renku.*

Haiku: originally, a Japanese form of a single vertical line with 17 sound symbols in a 5-7-5 pattern. In English, typically a 3-line poem with fewer than 17 syllables in no set pattern, but exhibiting a 2-part juxtapositional structure, seasonal reference, imagistic immediacy, and a moment of keen perception of nature or human nature. The term is both singular and plural.

Hokku: the starting verse of a renga or renku, in 5, 7, and then 5 sound symbols in Japanese; or in three lines, usually totaling fewer than 17 syllables, in English; the precursor for what is now called haiku. (See also *haiku*).

Iamb: foot consisting of an unstressed syllable followed by a stress (- ').

Iambic pentameter: consists of 5 iambic feet per line.

Imagist poetry: short, free verse lines that present images without comment or explanation; strongly influenced by haiku and other Oriental forms.

Kyrielle: French form; 4-line stanza with 8-syllable lines, the final line a refrain.

Language poetry: attempts to detach words from traditional meanings to produce something new and unprecedented.

Limerick: 5-line stanza rhyming *aabba*; pattern of stresses/line is traditionally 3-3-2-2-3; often bawdy or scatalogical.

Line: basic compositional unit of a poem; measured in feet if metrical.

Linked poetry: written through the collaboration of 2 or more poets creating a single poetic work.

Long poem: exceeds length and scope of short lyric or narrative poem; defined arbitrarily, often as more than 2 pages or 100 lines.

Lyric poetry: expresses personal emotion; music predominates over narrative or drama.

Metaphor: 2 different things are likened by identifying one as the other (A = B).

Meter: the rhythmic measure of a line.

Modernist poetry: work of the early 20th century literary movement that sought to break with the past, rejecting outmoded literary traditions, diction, and form while encouraging innovation and reinvention.

Narrative poetry: poem that tells a story.

New Formalism: contemporary literary movement to revive formal verse.

Nonsense verse: playful, with language and/or logic that defies ordinary understanding.

Octave: stanza of 8 lines.

Ode: a songlike, or lyric, poem; can be passionate, rhapsodic, and mystical, or a formal address to a person on a public or state occasion.

Pantoum: Malayan poetic form of any length; consists of 4-line stanzas, with lines 2 and 4 of one quatrain repeated as lines 1 and 3 of the next; final stanza reverses lines 1 and 3 of the previous quatrain and uses them as lines 2 and 4; traditionally each stanza rhymes *abab*.

Petrarchan sonnet: octave rhymes *abbaabba*; sestet may rhyme *cdcdcd, cdedce, ccdccd, cddcdd, edecde,* or *cddcee*.

Prose poem: brief prose work with intensity, condensed language, poetic devices, and other poetic elements.

Quatrain: stanza of 4 lines.

Refrain: a repeated line within a poem, similar to the chorus of a song.

Regional poetry: work set in a particular locale, imbued with the look, feel, and culture of that place.

Renga: originally, a Japanese collaborative form in which 2 or more poets alternate writing 3 lines, then 2 lines for a set number of verses (such as 12, 18, 36, 100, and 1,000). There are specific rules for seasonal progression, placement of moon and flower verses, and other requirements. (See also *linked poetry*.)

Rengay: an American collaborative 6-verse, thematic linked poetry form, with 3-line and 2-line verses in the following set pattern for 2 or 3 writers (letters represent poets, numbers indicate the lines in each verse): A3-B2-A3-B3-A2-B3 or A3-B2-C3-A2-B3-C2. All verses, unlike renga or renku, must develop at least one common theme.

Renku: the modern term for renga, and a more popular version of the traditionally more aristocratic renga. (See also *linked poetry*.)

Rhyme: words that sound alike, especially words that end in the same sound.

Rhythm: the beat and movement of language (rise and fall, repetition and variation, change of pitch, mix of syllables, melody of words).

Rondeau: French form of usually 15 lines in 3 parts, rhyming *aabba aabR aabbaR* (*R* indicates a refrain repeating the first word or phrase of the opening line).

Senryu: originally, a Japanese form, like haiku in form, but chiefly humorous, satirical, or ironic, and typically aimed at human foibles. (See also *haiku* and *zappai*.)

Sequence: a group or progression of poems, often numbered as a series.

Sestet: stanza of 6 lines.

Sestina: fixed form of 39 lines (6 unrhymed stanzas of 6 lines each, then an ending 3-line stanza), each stanza repeating the same 6 non-rhyming end-words in a different order; all 6 end-words appear in the final 3-line stanza.

Shakespearean sonnet: rhymes *abab cdcd efef gg*.

Sijo: originally a Korean narrative or thematic lyric form. The first line introduces a situation or problem that is countered or developed in line 2, and concluded with a twist in line 3. Lines average 14-16 syllables in length.

Simile: comparison that uses a linking word (*like, as, such as, how*) to clarify the similarities.

Sonnet: 14-line poem (traditionally an octave and sestet) rhymed in iambic pentameter;

often presents an argument but may also present a description, story, or meditation.

Spondee: foot consisting of 2 stressed syllables (′ ′).

Stanza: group of lines making up a single unit; like a paragraph in prose.

Strophe: often used to mean "stanza"; also a stanza of irregular line lengths.

Surrealistic poetry: of the artistic movement stressing the importance of dreams and the subconscious, nonrational thought, free associations, and startling imagery/juxtapositions.

Tanka: originally, a Japanese form in one or 2 vertical lines with 31 sound symbols in a 5-7-5-7-7 pattern. In English, typically a 5-line lyrical poem with fewer than 31 syllables in no set syllable pattern, but exhibiting a caesura, turn, or pivot, and often more emotional and conversational than haiku.

Tercet: stanza or poem of 3 lines.

Terza rima: series of 3-line stanzas with interwoven rhyme scheme (*aba, bcb, cdc* . . .).

Trochee: foot consisting of a stress followed by an unstressed syllable (′ -).

Villanelle: French form of 19 lines (5 tercets and a quatrain); line 1 serves as one refrain (repeated in lines 6, 12, 18), line 3 as a second refrain (repeated in lines 9, 15, 19); traditionally, refrains rhyme with each other and with the opening line of each stanza.

Visual poem: see *emblematic poem*.

Waka: literally, "Japanese poem", the precursor for what is now called tanka. (See also *tanka*.)

War poetry: poems written about warfare and military life; often written by past and current soldiers; may glorify war, recount exploits, or demonstrate the horrors of war.

Zappai: originally Japanese; an unliterary, often superficial witticism masquerading as haiku or senryu; formal term for joke haiku or other pseudo-haiko.

Zeugma: a figure of speech in which a single word (or, occasionally, a phrase) is related in one way to words that precede it, and in another way to words that follow it.

Chapbook Publishers

A poetry chapbook is a slim volume of 24-50 pages (although chapbook lengths can vary; some are even published as inserts in magazines). Many publishers and journals solicit chapbook manuscripts through competitions. Read listings carefully, check websites where available, and request guidelines before submitting. See Frequently Asked Questions on page 7 for further information about chapbooks and submission formats.

Special Indexes

Book Publishers Index

The following are magazines and publishers that consider full-length book manuscripts (over 50 pages, often much longer). See Frequently Asked Questions on page 7 for further information about book manuscript submission.

Special Indexes

Special Indexes

Openness to Submissions

In this section, all magazines, publishers, and contests/awards with primary listings in *Poet's Market* are categorized according to their openness to submissions (as indicated by the symbols that appear at the beginning of each listing). Note that some markets are listed in more than one category.

◯ WELCOMES SUBMISSIONS FROM BEGINNING POETS

ⓓ PREFERS SUBMISSIONS FROM EXPERIENCED POETS, WILL CONSIDER WORK FROM BEGINNING POETS

Special Indexes

Special Indexes

❤ PREFERS SUBMISSIONS FROM SKILLED, EXPERIENCED POETS, FEW BEGINNERS

⊚ MARKET WITH A SPECIALIZED FOCUS

Special Indexes

Geographical Index

This section offers a breakdown of U.S. publishers and conferences/workshops arranged alphabetically by state or territory, followed by listings for Canada, Australia, France, Ireland, Japan, the United Kingdom, and other countries—a real help when trying to locate publishers in your region as well as conferences and workshops convenient to your area.

Conferences & Workshops

COLORADO
Publishers of Poetry

Conferences & Workshops

CONNECTICUT
Publishers of Poetry

Special Indexes

Conferences & Workshops

NORTH CAROLINA
Publishers of Poetry

DISCOVER
A World of WRITING SUCCESS

Get **2 FREE ISSUES** of *Writer's Digest!*

Are you ready to be praised, published, and paid for your writing? It's time to invest in your future with *Writer's Digest*! Beginners and experienced writers alike have been relying on *Writer's Digest*, the world's leading magazine for writers, for more than 80 years — and it keeps getting better! Each issue is brimming with:

- Inspiration from writers who have been in your shoes
- Detailed info on the latest contests, conferences, markets, and opportunities in every genre
- Tools of the trade, including reviews of the latest writing software and hardware
- Writing prompts and exercises to overcome writer's block and rekindle your creative spark
- Expert tips, techniques, and advice to help you get published
- And so much more!

That's a lot to look forward to every month. Let *Writer's Digest* put you on the road to writing success!

NO RISK!
Send No Money Now!

☐ **Yes!** Please rush me my 2 FREE issues of *Writer's Digest* — the world's leading magazine for writers. If I like what I read, I'll get a full year's subscription (12 issues, including the 2 free issues) for only $19.96. That's 67% off the newsstand rate! If I'm not completely happy, I'll write "cancel" on your invoice, return it and owe nothing. The 2 FREE issues are mine to keep, no matter what!

Name _____

Address _____

City _____

State_____ZIP _____

Subscribers in Canada will be charged an additional US$10 (includes GST/HST) and invoiced. Outside the U.S. and Canada, add US$10 and remit payment in U.S. funds with this order. Annual newsstand rate: $59.88. Please allow 4–6 weeks for first-issue delivery.

Writer's Digest   www.writersdigest.com

J4FPMK

Get **2** FREE
TRIAL ISSUES of
Writer's Digest

Packed with creative inspiration, advice, and tips to guide you on the road to success, *Writer's Digest* offers everything you need to take your writing to the next level! You'll discover how to:

- Create dynamic characters and page-turning plots
- Submit query letters that publishers won't be able to refuse
- Find the right agent or editor
- Make it out of the slush-pile and into the hands of publishers
- Write award-winning contest entries
- And more!

See for yourself by ordering your 2 FREE trial issues today!

Special Indexes

Conferences & Workshops

VIRGIN ISLANDS
Publishers of Poetry

OTHER COUNTRIES
Publishers of Poetry

Conferences & Workshops

Special Indexes

Subject Index

This index focuses on markets indicating a specialized area of interest, whether regional, poetic style, or specific topic (these markets show a ◎ symbol at the beginning of their listings). It also includes markets we felt offered special opportunities in certain subject areas. Subject categories are listed alphabetically, with additional subcategories indicated under the "Specialized" heading (in parentheses behind the market's name). **Please note:** 1) This index only partially reflects the total markets in this book; many do not identify themselves as having specialized interests and so are not included here. 2) Many specialized markets have more than one area of interest and will be found under multiple categories. 3) When a market appears under a heading in this index, it does not necessarily mean it considers *only* poetry associated with that subject, poetry *only* from that region, etc. It's still best to read all listings carefully as part of a thorough marketing plan.

Bilingual/Foreign Language

Christian

Online Markets

Seems 321
Slope 328
Stickman Review 341
sidereality 324
Tarpaulin Sky 352
Tattoo Highway 352
Three Candles 356
3 cup morning 357
Valparaiso Poetry Review 368
VQOnline 374
White Heron 379
Wild Violet 380
Word Salad 383
Zeek 389
Zuzu's Petals 390

**Poetry By Children
(considers submissions)**
American Tanka 52
American Tolkien Society 52
Ascent (Canada) 59
Aurorean, The 60
Axe Factory Review 62
Barnwood Press 64
Bear Creek Haiku 67
Bibliophilos 72
Blind Man's Rainbow 75
Capper's 91
Chapultepec Press 95
Chiron Review 99
Common Threads 111
Confrontation Magazine 113
Cricket 118
Current Accounts 120
Decompositions 124
Diner 127
Edgz 133
Fairfield Review 142
Fat Tuesday 143
Feather Books 144
Feelings of the Heart 145
Fire 147
Five Fingers Review 150
4*9*1 Neo-Naive Imagination 154
Frogpond 158
Green's Magazine 168
hArtworks 174
Highlights for Children 176
HQ Poetry Magazine 179
Idiom 23 182

Indian Heritage Publishing 185
Jewish Currents 192
Joel's House Publications 192
Kelsey Review 197
Kerf, The 199
Kwil Kids Publishing 201
Listening Eye, The 206
Louisville Review 211
Lutheran Digest 214
Mandrake Poetry Review 221
Meadowbrook Press 225
Medicinal Purposes Literary Review 226
Mindprints 234
Mississippi Valley Poetry Contest 408
Modern Haiku 237
Nanny Fanny 241
Neovictorian/Cochlea, The 243
New Orleans Poetry Forum 246
Northern Stars Magazine 255
Northwoods Press 256
Oak, The 257
Offerings 258
Opened Eyes 259
Peace & Freedom 264
Pelican Publishing Company 267
People's Press, The 270
Pink Chameleon—Online, The 273
Poetree Magazine 284
Poetry of the People 287
Poetry Society of Virginia Contests 418
Poets at Work 288
Potluck Children's Literary Magazine 291
Quantum Leap 300
Quercus Review 302
Rattle 304
RB's Poets' Viewpoint 305
Red Moon Press 307
Redneck Review, The 309
Reflections Literary Journal 309
Riverstone 313
Same, The 320
Shemom 323
SimplyWords 325
Skipping Stones 326
Slant 327
Slate & Style 328
Society of American Poets, The 330
Song of the San Joaquin 331
Spring Tides 339
Spunk 339

Religious

Science Fiction

Senior Citizen/Aging

Social Issues

Specialized (misc.)

Special Indexes

Translations

General Index

Markets that appeared in the *2004 Poet's Market* but are not included in this edition are identified by two-letter codes explaining their absence. These codes are: **(DS) discontinued; (ED) editorial decision; (HA) on hiatus; (NP) no longer publishing poetry; (NR) no (or late) response to requested verification of information; (OB) out of business** (or, in the case of contests or conferences, cancelled); **(OS) overstocked; (RR) removed by request of the market** (no reason given); **(UF) uncertain future; (UC) unable to contact;** and **(RP) restructuring/purchased.**